Thomas Reid

The Works of Thomas Reid D. D.

Now fully collected, with selections from his unpublished letters

Thomas Reid

The Works of Thomas Reid D. D.
Now fully collected, with selections from his unpublished letters

ISBN/EAN: 9783742836854

Manufactured in Europe, USA, Canada, Australia, Japa

Cover: Foto ©Andreas Hilbeck / pixelio.de

Manufactured and distributed by brebook publishing software (www.brebook.com)

Thomas Reid

The Works of Thomas Reid D. D.

THE WORKS

OF

THOMAS REID, D.D.

NOW FULLY COLLECTED,

WITH SELECTIONS FROM HIS UNPUBLISHED LETTERS.

PREFACE,

NOTES AND SUPPLEMENTARY DISSERTATIONS,

BY

SIR WILLIAM HAMILTON, BART.,

ADVOCATE; A.M. (OXON.); ETC.; CORRESPONDING MEMBER OF THE INSTITUTE OF FRANCE; HONORARY MEMBER OF THE AMERICAN ACADEMY OF ARTS AND SCIENCES; OF THE LATIN SOCIETY OF JENA; ETC.; PROFESSOR OF LOGIC AND METAPHYSICS IN THE UNIVERSITY OF EDINBURGH.

PREFIXED,

STEWART'S ACCOUNT OF THE LIFE AND WRITINGS OF REID.

VOL. II.

SEVENTH EDITION.

EDINBURGH:

MACLACHLAN AND STEWART.

LONDON: LONGMAN, GREEN, LONGMAN, ROBERTS, AND GREEN.

MDCCCLXXII.

ON EARTH, THERE IS NOTHING GREAT BUT MAN;
IN MAN, THERE IS NOTHING GREAT BUT MIND.

ESSAYS

ON THE

ACTIVE POWERS OF MAN.

By THOMAS REID, D.D., F.R.S.E.,

PROFESSOR OF MORAL PHILOSOPHY IN THE UNIVERSITY OF GLASGOW.

"He hath shewed thee, O Man, what is good."—MICAH.

☞ The only authentic edition of the "Essays on the Active Powers" is that of 1788, in 4to; and from that edition the present is taken. The pages of the original impression are here also marked, and by them all *prospective* references made.—H.

INTRODUCTION.

THE division of the faculties of the human mind into *Understanding* and *Will** is very ancient, and has been very generally adopted; the former comprehending all our *Speculative*, the latter all our *Active* powers.†

It is evidently the intention of our Maker, that man should be an active and not merely a speculative being. For this purpose, certain active powers have been given him, limited indeed in many respects, but suited to his rank and place in the creation.

Our business is to manage these powers, by proposing to ourselves the best ends, planning the most proper system of conduct that is in our power, and executing it with industry and zeal. This is true wisdom; this is the very intention of our being.

Everything virtuous and praiseworthy must lie in the right use of our power; everything vicious and blameable in the abuse of it. What is not within the sphere of our power cannot be imputed to us either for blame or praise. These are self-evident truths, to which every unprejudiced mind yields an immediate and invincible assent. [2]

Knowledge derives its value from this, that it enlarges our power, and directs us in the application of it. For, in the right employment of our active power consists all the honour, dignity, and worth, of a man, and, in the abuse and perversion of it, all vice, corruption, and depravity.

We are distinguished from the brute animals, not less by our active than by our speculative powers.

The brutes are stimulated to various actions by their instincts, by their appetites, by their passions. But they seem to be necessarily determined by the strongest impulse, without any capacity of self-government. Therefore we do not blame them for what they do; nor have we any reason to think that they blame themselves. They may be trained up by discipline, but cannot be governed by law. There is no evidence that they have the conception of a law, or of its obligation.

Man is capable of acting from motives of a higher nature. He perceives a dignity and worth in one course of conduct, a demerit and turpitude in another, which brutes have not the capacity to discern.

He perceives it to be his duty to act the worthy and the honourable part, whether his appetites and passions incite him to it or to the contrary. When he sacrifices the gratification of the strongest appetites or passions to duty, this is so far from diminishing the merit of his conduct, that it greatly increases it, and affords, upon reflection, an inward satisfaction and triumph, of which brute-animals are not susceptible. When he acts a contrary part, he has a consciousness of demerit, to which they are no less strangers. [3]

Since, therefore, the active powers of man make so important a part of his constitution, and distinguish him so eminently from his fellow-animals, they deserve no less to be the subject of philosophical disquisition than his intellectual powers.

A just knowledge of our powers, whether intellectual or active, is so far of real importance to us, as it aids us in the exercise of them. And every man must acknowledge, that to act properly is much more valuable than to think justly or reason acutely. [4]

---

* See above, p. 242, a, note †.

The division of the powers into those of the *Understanding* and those of the *Will*, is very objectionable. It is, as I have before observed, taken from the Peripatetic distinction of these into *gnostic* or *cognitive*, and *orectic* or *appetent*; but the original division is far preferable to the borrowed; for, in the first place, the term *Understanding* usually and properly denotes only a part—the higher part—of the cognitive faculties, and is then exclusive of sense, imagination, memory, &c., which it is now intended to include. In the second place, the term *Will* is also usually and properly limited to our higher appetencies, or rational determinations, as opposed to our lower appetencies, or irrational desires, which last, however, it is here employed to comprehend. In the third place, both the original and borrowed divisions are improper, inasmuch as they either exclude or improperly include a third great class of mental phenomena—the phenomena of *Feeling*.—H.

† The distribution of our powers into *Speculative* and *Active*, is also very objectionable. Independently of the objection common to it with that into the powers of the understanding and the powers of the will—that the *Feelings* are excluded or improperly included—it is liable to objections peculiar to itself. In the first place, *Speculation*, or *Theory*, is a certain kind or certain application of knowledge; therefore, *Speculation* is not a proper term by which to denote the cognitive operations in general. In the second place, *speculation* and *knowledge* are not opposed to *action*, but to *practice* or *doing*, or, as it is best expressed in German, *das Handeln*. *Speculative* powers ought not, therefore, to have been opposed to *active*. In the third place, the distinction of *active* powers is in itself vicious, because it does not distinguish, or distinguishes wrongly. *Active* is opposed to *inactive*; but it is not here intended to be said, that the cognitive powers are inactive; but merely that the action of the powers of appetency is different in kind from the action of the powers of knowledge. The term *active* does not, therefore, express what was meant, or rather does express what was not meant. It is to be observed, however, that the English language is very defective in terms requisite to denote the distinctions in question.—H.

[1-4]

ESSAYS

ON THE

ACTIVE POWERS OF MAN.

ESSAY I.

OF ACTIVE POWER IN GENERAL.

CHAPTER I.

OF THE NOTION OF ACTIVE POWER.

To consider gravely what is meant by *Active Power*, may seem altogether unnecessary, and to be mere trifling. It is not a term of art, but a common word in our language, used every day in discourse, even by the vulgar. We find words of the same meaning in all other languages; and there is no reason to think that it is not perfectly understood by all men who understand the English language.

I believe all this is true, and that an attempt to explain a word so well understood, and to shew that it has a meaning, requires an apology.

The apology is, That this term, so well understood by the vulgar, has been darkened by philosophers, who, in this as in many other instances, have found great difficulties about a thing which, to the rest of mankind, seems perfectly clear.

This has been the more easily effected, because Power is a thing so much of its own kind, and so simple in its nature, as not to admit of a logical definition. [6]

It is well known that there are many things perfectly understood, and of which we have clear and distinct conceptions, which cannot be logically defined. No man ever attempted to define magnitude; yet there is no word whose meaning is more distinctly or more generally understood. We cannot give a logical definition of thought, of duration, of number, or of motion.

When men attempt to define such things, they give no light. They may give a synonymous word or phrase, but it will probably be a worse for a better. If they will define, the definition will either be grounded upon a hypothesis, or it will darken the subject rather than throw light upon it.

The Aristotelian definition of motion—that it is "*Actus entis in potentia, quatenus in potentia*," has been justly censured by modern philosophers;* yet I think it is matched by what a celebrated modern philosopher has given us, as the most accurate definition of belief—to wit, "That it is a lively idea related to or associated with a present impression." ("Treatise of Human Nature," vol i. p. 172.) "Memory," according to the same philosopher, "is the faculty by which we repeat our impressions, so as that they retain a considerable degree of their first vivacity, and are somewhat intermediate betwixt an idea and an impression."

Euclid, if his editors have not done him injustice, has attempted to define a right line, to define unity, ratio, and number. But these definitions are good for nothing. We may indeed suspect them not to be Euclid's; because they are never once quoted in the Elements, and are of no use.

I shall not therefore attempt to define Active Power, that I may not be liable to the same censure; but shall offer some observations that may lead us to attend to the conception we have of it in our own minds.

1. Power is not an object of any of our external senses, nor even an object of consciousness.† [7]

That it is not seen, nor heard, nor touched, nor tasted, nor smelt, needs no proof. That we are not conscious of it, in the proper sense of that word, will be no less evident, if we reflect, that consciousness is that power of the mind by which it has an immediate knowledge of its own operations. Power is not an operation of the mind, and therefore no object of consciousness. Indeed, every operation of the mind is the exertion of some power of the mind; but

---

* Whether *justly*, may be disputed.—H.

† Inasmuch as by consciousness, Reid means our immediate internal *experience*, he is right.—H.

we are conscious of the operation only—the* power lies behind the scene; and, though we may justly infer the power from the operation, it must be remembered, that inferring is not the province of consciousness, but of reason.

I acknowledge, therefore, that our having any conception or idea of power is repugnant to Mr Locke's theory, that all our simple ideas are got either by the external senses, or by consciousness. Both cannot be true. Mr Hume perceived this repugnancy, and consistently maintained, that we have no idea of power. Mr Locke did not perceive it. If he had, it might have led him to suspect his theory; for when theory is repugnant to fact, it is easy to see which ought to yield. I am conscious that I have a *conception* or *idea** of power; but, strictly speaking, I am not conscious that I have *power*.

I shall have occasion to shew, that we have very early, from our constitution, a conviction or belief of some degree of active power in ourselves. This belief, however, is not consciousness—for we may be deceived in it; but the testimony of consciousness can never deceive. Thus, a man who is struck with a palsy in the night, commonly knows not that he has lost the power of speech till he attempts to speak; he knows not whether he can move his hands and arms till he makes the trial; and if, without making trial, he consults his consciousness over so attentively, it will give him no information whether he has lost these powers, or still retains them. [8]

From this we must conclude, that the powers we have are not an object of consciousness, though it would be foolish to censure this way of speaking in popular discourse, which requires not accurate attention to the different provinces of our various faculties. The testimony of consciousness is always unerring, nor was it ever called in question by the greatest sceptics, ancient or modern.

2. A *second* observation is—That, as there are some things of which we have a *direct*, and others of which we have only a *relative*,† conception; Power belongs to the latter class.

As this distinction is overlooked by most writers in logic, I shall beg leave to illustrate it a little, and then shall apply it to the present subject.

Of some things, we know what they are in themselves; our conception of such things I call *direct*. Of other things, we know not what they are in themselves, but only that they have certain properties or attributes, or certain relations to other things; of these our conception is only *relative*.*

To illustrate this by some examples:—In the university library, I call for the book, press L, shelf 10, No. 10; the library-keeper must have such a conception of the book I want as to be able to distinguish it from ten thousand that are under his care. But what conception does he form of it from my words? They inform him neither of the author, nor the subject, nor the language, nor the size, nor the binding, but only of its mark and place. His conception of it is merely relative to these circumstances; yet this relative notion enables him to distinguish it from every other book in the library.

There are other relative notions that are not taken from accidental relations, as in the example just now mentioned, but from qualities or attributes essential to the thing. [9]

Of this kind are our notions both of body and mind. What is body? It is, say philosophers, that which is extended, solid, and divisible. Says the querist, I do not ask what the properties of body are, but what is the thing itself; let me first know directly what body is, and then consider its properties? To this demand, I am afraid the querist will meet with no satisfactory answer; because our notion of body is not direct but relative to its qualities. We know that it is something extended, solid, and divisible, and we know no more.

Again, if it should be asked, What is mind? It is that which thinks. I ask not what it does, or what its operations are, but what it is. To this I can find no answer; our notion of mind being not direct, but relative to its operations, as our notion of body is relative to its qualities.

There are even many of the qualities of body, of which we have only a relative conception. What is heat in a body? It is a quality which affects the sense of touch in a certain way. If you want to know, not how it affects the sense of touch, but what it is in itself—this, I confess, I know not. My conception of it is not direct, but relative to the effect it has upon bodies. The notions we have of all those qualities which Mr Locke calls secondary, and of those he calls powers of bodies—such as the power of the magnet to attract iron, or of fire to burn wood—are relative.

Having given examples of things of which our conception is only relative, it may be proper to mention some of which it is direct. Of this kind, are all the primary qualities of

---

* It would have been better if Reid had abstained from the term *idea* in this relation, or indeed altogether. The word *notion* would be here preferable.—H.

† The word *relative* is here again improperly used. Is not *all* our knowledge relative? It would be better to say *direct* and *indirect*, or *immediate* and *mediate*. See above, p. [illegible], note *.—H.

* See preceding note.—H.

body—figure, extension, solidity, hardness, fluidity, and the like. Of these we have a direct and immediate knowledge from our senses. To this class belong also all the operations of mind of which we are conscious. I know what thought is, what memory, what a purpose, what a promise. [10]

There are some things of which we can have both a direct and a relative conception. I can directly conceive ten thousand men, or ten thousand pounds, because both are objects of sense, and may be seen. But, whether I see such an object, or directly conceive it, my notion of it is indistinct; it is only that of a great multitude of men, or of a great heap of money; and a small addition or diminution makes no perceptible change in the notion I form in this way. But I can form a relative notion of the same number of men or of pounds, by attending to the relations which this number has to other numbers, greater or less. Then I perceive that the relative notion is distinct and scientific; for the addition of a single man, or a single pound, or even of a penny, is easily perceived.

In like manner, I can form a direct notion of a polygon of a thousand equal sides and equal angles. This direct notion cannot be more distinct, when conceived in the mind, than that which I get by sight, when the object is before me; and I find it so indistinct, that it has the same appearance to my eye, or to my direct conception, as a polygon of a thousand and one, or of nine hundred and ninety-nine sides. But, when I form a relative conception of it, by attending to the relation it bears to polygons of a greater or less number of sides, my notion of it becomes distinct and scientific, and I can demonstrate the properties by which it is distinguished from all other polygons.* From these instances, it appears that our relative conceptions of things are not always less distinct, nor less fit materials for accurate reasoning than those that are direct; and that the contrary may happen in a remarkable degree.

Our conception of power is relative to its exertions or effects. Power is one thing; its exertion is another thing. It is true, there can be no exertion without power; but there may be power that is not exerted. Thus, a man may have power to speak when he is silent; he may have power to rise and walk when he sits still. [11]

But, though it be one thing to speak, and another to have the power of speaking, I apprehend we conceive of the power as something which has a certain relation to the effect. And of every power we form our notion by the effect which it is able to produce.

3. It is evident that Power is a *quality*, and cannot exist without a subject to which it belongs.

That power may exist without any being or subject to which that power may be attributed, is an absurdity, shocking to every man of common understanding.

It is a quality which may be varied, not only in degree, but also in kind; and we distinguish both the kinds and degrees by the effects which they are able to produce.

Thus a power to fly, and a power to reason, are different kinds of power, their effects being different in kind. But a power to carry one hundred weight, and a power to carry two hundred, are different degrees of the same kind.

4. We cannot conclude the want of power from its not being exerted; nor from the exertion of a less degree of power, can we conclude that there is no greater degree in the subject. Thus, though a man on a particular occasion said nothing, we cannot conclude from that circumstance, that he had not the power of speech; nor from a man's carrying ten pound weight, can we conclude that he had not power to carry twenty.

5. There are some qualities that have a *contrary*, others that have not: Power is a quality of the latter kind.

Vice is contrary to virtue, misery to happiness, hatred to love, negation to affirmation; but there is no contrary to power. Weakness or impotence are defects or privations of power, but not contraries to it. [12]

If what has been said of power be easily understood, and readily assented to, by all who understand our language, as I believe it is, we may from this justly conclude, That we have a distinct notion of power, and may reason about it with understanding, though we can give no logical definition of it.

If power were a thing of which we have no idea, as some philosophers have taken much pains to prove—that is, if power were a word without any meaning—we could neither affirm nor deny anything concerning it with understanding. We should have equal reason to say that it is a substance, as that it is a quality; that it does not admit of degrees as that it does. If the understanding immediately assents to one of these assertions, and revolts from the contrary, we may conclude with certainty, that we put some meaning upon the word *power*—that is, that we have some idea of it. And it is chiefly for the sake of this conclusion, that I have enumerated so many obvious things concerning it.

The term *active power* is used, I conceive,

[10-12]

* This example of the Polygon is taken from Des Cartes or Arnauld.—H.

to distinguish it from *speculative powers*.* As all languages distinguish action from speculation, the same distinction is applied to the powers by which they are produced. The powers of seeing, hearing, remembering, distinguishing, judging, reasoning, are speculative powers; the power of executing any work of art or labour is active power.

There are many things related to power, in such a manner that we can have no notion of them if we have none of power. [13]

The exertion of active power we call *action*;† and, as every action produces some change, so every change must be caused by some exertion, or by the cessation of some exertion of power. That which produces a change by the exertion of its power we call the *cause* of that change; and the change produced, the *effect* of that cause.

When one being, by its active power, produces any change upon another, the last is said to be *passive*, or to be acted upon. Thus we see that action and passion, cause and effect, exertion and operation, have such a relation to active power, that, if it be understood, they are understood of consequence; but if power be a word without any meaning, all those words which are related to it, must be words without any meaning. They are, however, common words in our language; and equivalent words have always been common in all languages.

It would be very strange indeed, if mankind had always used these words so familiarly, without perceiving that they had no meaning; and that this discovery should have been first made by a philosopher of the present age.

With equal reason it might be maintained, that though there are words in all languages to express sight, and words to signify the various colours which are objects of sight; yet that all mankind, from the beginning of the world, had been blind, and never had an idea of sight or of colour. But there are no absurdities so gross as those which philosophers have advanced concerning ideas.

CHAPTER II.

THE SAME SUBJECT.

There are, I believe, no abstract notions, that are to be found more early, or more universally, in the minds of men, than those of *acting* and *being acted* upon. Every child that understands the distinction between striking and being struck, must have the conception of action and passion. [14]

We find accordingly, that there is no language so imperfect but that it has active and passive verbs and participles; the one signifying some kind of action; the other being acted upon. This distinction enters into the original contexture of all languages.

Active verbs have a form and construction proper to themselves; passive verbs a different form and a different construction. In all languages, the nominative to an active verb is the agent; the thing acted upon is put in an oblique case. In passive verbs, the thing acted upon is the nominative, and the agent, if expressed, must be in an oblique case; as in this example—*Raphael drew the Cartoons; the Cartoons were drawn by Raphael.*

Every distinction which we find in the structure of all languages, must have been familiar to those who framed the languages at first, and to all who speak them with understanding.

It may be objected to this argument, taken from the structure of language, in the use of active and passive verbs, that active verbs are not always used to denote an action, nor is the nominative before an active verb, conceived in all cases to be an agent, in the strict sense of that word; that there are many passive verbs which have an active signification, and active verbs which have a passive. From these facts, it may be thought a just conclusion, that, in contriving the different forms of active and passive verbs, and their different construction, men have not been governed by a regard to any distinction between action and passion, but by chance, or some accidental cause. [15]

In answer to this objection, the fact on which it is founded must be admitted; but I think the conclusion not justly drawn from it, for the following reasons:—

1. It seems contrary to reason to attribute to chance or accident what is subject to rules, even though there may be exceptions to the rule. The exceptions may, in such a case, be attributed to accident, but the rule cannot. There is perhaps hardly anything in language so general as not to admit of exceptions. It cannot be denied to be a general rule, that verbs and participles have an active and a passive voice; and, as this is a general rule, not in one language only, but in all the languages we are acquainted with, it shews evidently that men, in the earliest stages, and in all periods of society, have distinguished action from passion.

2. It is to be observed, that the forms of language are often applied to purposes different from those for which they were originally intended. The varieties of a lan-

* Not from *passive* Power. See above, p. 511, note †, and below, p. [illegible], note *.—H.

† Also *operation* and *energy* (ἐνέργεια, the being in work.) *Energy* is often ignorantly used in English for *force*. In Latin, *functio*, *functio muneris*, corresponds to operation or performance; with us *function* denotes something to be performed.—H.

guage, even the most perfect, can never be made equal to all the variety of human conceptions. The forms and modifications of language must be confined within certain limits, that they may not exceed the capacity of human memory. Therefore, in all languages, there must be a kind of frugality used, to make one form of expression serve many different purposes, like Sir Hudibras' dagger, which, though made to stab or break a head, was put to many other uses. Many examples might be produced of this frugality in language. Thus, the Latins and Greeks had five or six cases of nouns, to express the various relations that one thing could bear to another.* The genitive case must have been at first intended to express some one capital relation, such as that of possession or of property; but it would be very difficult to enumerate all the relations which, in the progress of language, it was used to express. The same observation may be applied to other cases of nouns. [16]

The slightest similitude or analogy is thought sufficient to justify the extension of a form of speech beyond its proper meaning, whenever the language does not afford a more proper form. In the moods of verbs, a few of those which occur most frequently are distinguished by different forms, and these are made to supply all the forms that are wanting. The same observation may be applied to what is called the *voices* of verbs. An active and a passive are the capital ones; some languages have more, but no language so many as to answer to all the variations of human thought. We cannot always coin new ones, and therefore must use some one or other of those that are to be found in the language, though at first intended for another purpose.

3. A third observation in answer to the objection is, that we can point out a cause of the frequent misapplication of active verbs, to things which have no proper activity—a cause which extends to the greater part of such misapplications, and which confirms the account I have given of the proper intention of active and passive verbs.

As there is no principle that appears to be more universally acknowledged by mankind, from the first dawn of reason, than that every change we observe in nature must have a cause; so this is no sooner perceived, than there arises in the human mind a strong desire to know the causes of those changes that fall within our observation. *Felix qui potuit rerum cognoscere causas*, is the voice of nature in all men. Nor is there anything that more early distinguishes the rational from the brute creation, than this avidity to know the causes of things, of which I see no sign in brute-animals. [17]

It must surely be admitted, that, in those periods wherein languages are formed, men are but poorly furnished for carrying on this investigation with success. We see that the experience of thousands of years is necessary to bring men into the right track in this investigation, if indeed they can yet be said to be brought into it. What innumerable errors rude ages must fall into with regard to causes, from impatience to judge, and inability to judge right, we may conjecture from reason, and may see from experience; from which I think it is evident, that, supposing active verbs to have been originally intended to express what is properly called action, and their nominatives to express the agent; yet, in the rude and barbarous state wherein languages are formed, there must be innumerable misapplications of such verbs and nominatives, and many things spoken of as active which have no real activity.

To this we may add, that it is a general prejudice of our early years, and of rude nations, when we perceive anything to be changed, and do not perceive any other thing which we can believe to be the cause of that change, to impute it to the thing itself, and conceive it to be active and animated, so far as to have the power of producing that change in itself. Hence, to a child, or to a savage, all nature seems to be animated; the sea, the earth, the air, the sun, moon, and stars, rivers, fountains and groves, are conceived to be active and animated beings. As this is a sentiment natural to man in his rude state, it has, on that account, even in polished nations, the verisimilitude that is required in poetical fiction and fable, and makes personification one of the most agreeable figures in poetry and eloquence.*

The origin of this prejudice probably is, that we judge of other things by ourselves, and therefore are disposed to ascribe to them that life and activity which we know to be in ourselves.

A little girl ascribes to her doll the passions and sentiments she feels in herself. Even brutes seem to have something of this nature. A young cat, when she sees any brisk motion in a feather or a straw, is prompted, by natural instinct, to hunt it as she would hunt a mouse. [18]

Whatever be the origin of this prejudice

* The Sanscrit, if I recollect, has ten. Thus, while in Latin the relations of *with*, *from*, *by*, &c., are confusedly denoted by one form of inflection, called the ablative; in Sanscrit, these different relations are distinctly pointed out by different cases.—H

* See Schiller's "Die Götter Griechenlands," and Wordsworth passim.—H.

[16-18]

in mankind, it has a powerful influence upon language, and leads men, in the structure of language, to ascribe action to many things that are merely passive; because, when such forms of speech were invented, those things were really believed to be active. Thus we say, the wind blows, the sea rages, the sun rises and sets, bodies gravitate and move.

When experience discovers that these things are altogether inactive, it is easy to correct our opinion about them; but it is not so easy to alter the established forms of language. The most perfect and the most polished languages are like old furniture, which is never perfectly suited to the present taste, but retains something of the fashion of the times when it was made.

Thus, though all men of knowledge believe that the succession of day and night is owing to the rotation of the earth round its axis, and not to any diurnal motion of the heavens, yet we find ourselves under a necessity of speaking in the old style, of the sun's rising and going down, and coming to the meridian. And this style is used, not only in conversing with the vulgar, but when men of knowledge converse with one another. And if we should suppose the vulgar to be at last so far enlightened as to have the same belief with the learned, of the cause of day and night, the same style would still be used.

From this instance we may learn, that the language of mankind may furnish good evidence of opinions which have been early and universally entertained, and that the forms contrived for expressing such opinions, may remain in use after the opinions which gave rise to them have been greatly changed. [19]

Active verbs appear plainly to have been first contrived to express action. They are still in general applied to this purpose. And though we find many instances of the application of active verbs to things which we now believe not to be active, this ought to be ascribed to men's having once had the belief that those things are active, and perhaps, in some cases, to this, that forms of expression are commonly extended, in course of time, beyond their original intention, either from analogy, or because more proper forms for the purpose are not found in language.

Even the misapplication of this notion of action and active power shews that there is such a notion in the human mind, and shews the necessity there is in philosophy of distinguishing the proper application of these words, from the vague and improper application of them, founded on common language or on popular prejudice.

Another argument to shew that all men have a notion or idea of active power is, that there are many operations of mind common to all men who have reason, and necessary in the ordinary conduct of life, which imply a belief of active power in ourselves and in others.

All our volitions and efforts to act, all our deliberations, our purposes and promises, imply a belief of active power in ourselves; our counsels, exhortations, and commands, imply a belief of active power in those to whom they are addressed.

If a man should make an effort to fly to the moon—if he should even deliberate about it, or resolve to do it—we should conclude him to be a lunatic; and even lunacy would not account for his conduct, unless it made him believe the thing to be in his power.

If a man promises to pay me a sum of money to-morrow, without believing that it will then be in his power, he is not an honest man; and, if I did not believe that it will then be in his power, I should have no dependence on his promise. [20]

All our power is, without doubt, derived from the Author of our being, and, as he gave it freely, he may take it away when he will. No man can be certain of the continuance of any of his powers of body or mind for a moment; and, therefore, in every promise, there is a condition understood—to wit, if we live, if we retain that health of body and soundness of mind which is necessary to the performance, and if nothing happen, in the providence of God, which puts it out of our power. The rudest savages are taught by nature to admit these conditions in all promises, whether they be expressed or not; and no man is charged with breach of promise, when he fails through the failure of these conditions.

It is evident, therefore, that, without the belief of some active power, no honest man would make a promise, no wise man would trust to a promise; and it is no less evident that the belief of active power, in ourselves or in others, implies an idea or notion of active power.

The same reasoning may be applied to every instance wherein we give counsel to others, wherein we persuade or command. As long, therefore, as mankind are beings who can deliberate and resolve and will, as long as they can give counsel, and exhort, and command, they must believe the existence of active power in themselves and in others, and, therefore, must have a notion or idea of active power.

It might farther be observed, that power is the proper and immediate object of ambition, one of the most universal passions of the human mind, and that which makes the greatest figure in the history of all ages. Whether Mr Hume, in defence of his system, would maintain that there is no such passion in mankind as ambition, or that ambition is not a vehement desire of power, or that men may have a vehement desire of power, without having any idea of power, I will not pretend to divine. [21]

I cannot help repeating my apology for insisting so long in the refutation of so great an absurdity. It is a capital doctrine in a late celebrated system of human nature, that we have no idea of power, not even in the Deity; that we are not able to discover a single instance of it, either in body or spirit, either in superior or inferior natures; and that we deceive ourselves when we imagine that we are possessed of any idea of this kind.

To support this important doctrine, and the outworks that are raised in its defence, a great part of the first volume of the "Treatise of Human Nature" is employed. That system abounds with conclusions the most absurd that ever were advanced by any philosopher, deduced with great acuteness and ingenuity from principles commonly received by philosophers. To reject such conclusions as unworthy of a hearing, would be disrespectful to the ingenious author; and to refute them is difficult, and appears ridiculous.

It is difficult, because we can hardly find principles to reason from more evident than those we wish to prove; and it appears ridiculous, because, as this author justly observes, next to the ridicule of denying an evident truth, is that of taking much pains to prove it.

Protestants complain, with justice, of the hardship put upon them by Roman Catholics, in requiring them to prove that bread and wine is not flesh and blood.* They have, however, submitted to this hardship for the sake of truth. I think it is no less hard to be put to prove that men have an idea of power.

What convinces myself that I have an idea of power is, that I am conscious that I know what I mean by that word, and, while I have this consciousness, I disdain equally to hear arguments for or against my having such an idea. But, if we would convince those, who, being led away by prejudice or by authority, deny that they have any such idea, we must condescend to use such arguments as the subject will afford, and such as we should use with a man who should deny that mankind have any idea of magnitude or of equality. [22]

The arguments I have adduced are taken from these five topics:—1. That there are many things that we can affirm or deny concerning power, with understanding. 2. That there are, in all languages, words signifying, not only power, but signifying many other things that imply power, such as action and passion, cause and effect, energy, operation, and others. 3. That, in the structure of all languages, there is an active and passive form in verbs and participles, and a different construction adapted to these forms, of which diversity no account can be given, but that it has been intended to distinguish action from passion. 4. That there are many operations of the human mind familiar to every man come to the use of reason, and necessary in the ordinary conduct of life, which imply a conviction of some degree of power in ourselves and in others. 5. That the desire of power is one of the strongest passions of human nature.

* The Catholics require nothing of the kind. They admit that *physically* the bread and wine are bread and wine; and only contend that, *hyperphysically*, in a spiritual, mysterious, and inconceivable sense, they are really flesh and blood. Those, therefore, who think of disproving the doctrine of transubstantiation, by proving that in the eucharist bread and wine remain physically bread and wine, are guilty of the idle sophism called *mutatio elenchi*.—H.

CHAPTER III.

OF MR LOCKE'S ACCOUNT OF OUR IDEA OF POWER.

This author, having refuted the Cartesian doctrine of innate ideas, took up, perhaps too rashly, an opinion that all our simple ideas are got, either by Sensation or by Reflection—that is, by our external senses, or by consciousness of the operations of our own minds.

Throughout the whole of his "Essay," he shews a fatherly affection to this opinion, and often strains very hard to reduce our simple ideas to one of those sources, or both. Of this several instances might be given, in his account of our idea of *substance*, of *duration*, of *personal identity*. Omitting these as foreign to the present subject, I shall only take notice of the account he gives of our idea of *power*. [23]

The sum of it is, that observing, by our senses, various changes in objects, we collect the possibility in one object to be changed, and in another a possibility of making that change, and so come by that idea which we call power.

Thus we say the fire has a power to melt gold, and gold has power to be melted; the first he calls active, the second passive power.

He thinks, however, that we have the most distinct notion of active power, by attending to the power which we ourselves exert, in giving motion to our bodies when at rest, or in directing our thoughts to this or the other object as we will. And this way of forming the idea of power he attributes to reflection, as he refers the former to sensation.

On this account of the origin of our idea

of power, I would beg leave to make two remarks, with the respect that is most justly due to so great a philosopher and so good a man.

1. Whereas he distinguishes power into *active* and *passive*, I conceive passive power is no power at all. He means by it, the possibility of being changed. To call this *power*, seems to be a misapplication of the word. I do not remember to have met with the phrase *passive power* in any other good author. Mr Locke seems to have been unlucky in inventing it; and it deserves not to be retained in our language.* [24]

Perhaps he was unwarily led into it, as an opposite to active power. But I conceive we call certain powers *active*, to distinguish them from other powers that are called *speculative*.† As all mankind distinguish action from speculation, it is very proper to distinguish the powers by which those different operations are performed into active and speculative. Mr Locke, indeed, acknowledges that active power is more properly called power; but I see no propriety at all in passive power; it is a powerless power, and a contradiction in terms.

2. I would observe, that Mr Locke seems to have imposed upon himself, in attempting to reconcile this account of the idea of power to his favourite doctrine, that all our simple ideas are ideas of sensation, or of reflection.

There are two steps, according to his account, which the mind takes in forming this idea of power: *first*, It observes changes in things; and, *secondly*, From these changes it infers a cause of them, and a power to produce them.

If both these steps are operations of the external senses, or of consciousness, then the idea of power may be called an idea of sensation, or of reflection. But, if either of those steps requires the co-operation of other powers of the mind, it will follow, that the idea of power cannot be got by sensation, nor by reflection, nor by both together.* Let us, therefore, consider each of these steps by itself.

First, We observe various changes in things. And Mr Locke takes it for granted, that changes in external things are observed by our senses, and that changes in our thoughts are observed by consciousness.

I grant that it may be said, that changes in things are observed by our senses, when we do not mean to exclude every other faculty from a share in this operation. And it would be ridiculous to censure the phrase, when it is so used in popular discourse. [25]

But it is necessary to Mr Locke's purpose, that changes in external things should be observed by the senses alone, excluding every other faculty; because every faculty that is necessary in order to observe the change, will claim a share in the origin of the idea of power.

Now, it is evident, that memory is no less necessary than the senses, in order to our observing changes in external things, and therefore the idea of power, derived from the changes observed, may as justly be ascribed to memory as to the senses.

Every change supposes two states of the thing changed. Both these states may be past; one of them at least must be past; and one only can be present. By our senses we may observe the present state of the thing; but memory must supply us with the past; and, unless we remember the past state, we can perceive no change.

The same observation may be applied to consciousness. The truth, therefore, is, that, by the senses alone, without memory, or by consciousness alone, without memory, no change can be observed. Every idea, therefore, that is derived from observing changes in things, must have its origin, partly from memory, and not from the senses alone, nor from consciousness alone, nor from both together.†

The *second* step made by the mind in forming this idea of power is this:—From the changes observed we collect a cause of those changes, and a power to produce them.

Here one might ask Mr Locke, whether it is by our senses that we draw this conclusion, or is it by consciousness? Is reasoning the province of the senses, or is it

---

* This paragraph is erroneous in almost all its statements. Locke did not invent the phrase *passive power*. The distinction of *δύναμις τοῦ ποιεῖν* (δ. ποιητική) *potentia activa*, and *δύναμις τοῦ πάσχειν* (δ. παθητική) *potentia passiva*, was established, if not invented, by Aristotle; and, subsequently to him, it became one not only common but classical. So far, therefore, is the phrase *passive power* from being not to be met with in any other good author, it is to be found in almost *every* metaphysical system whatever before Locke. Reid understands by *Power* merely *Active Power*, *Efficacy*, *Force*, *Vis*; and in this exclusive sense, *Passive Power* is certainly "a contradiction in terms." But this is not the meaning attached to it by philosophers in general. The Greek language, I may observe, affords a fine illustration of the contrast and correlation of *power active* and *power passive* in its adjectives ending in τικος and τος. It has also others to express power in action, and power that must of necessity be exerted. —H.

† See last note, and note *, at p. 515.—H.

* Locke does not exclude the co-operation of other faculties. Sensation and Reflection are, in his philosophy, the exclusive *sources*, and not the exclusive *elaborators* of our notions. The only question is, do all our notions *spring* from experience? H.

† Mr Locke did not, like Reid, contradistinguish consciousness and memory, as two separate and special faculties; but memory he properly regarded as a mere modification of consciousness. The same may be said in regard to our reasoning power in what follows.—H.

[24, 25]

the province of consciousness? If the senses can draw one conclusion from premises, they may draw five hundred, and demonstrate the whole elements of Euclid. [26]

Thus, I think, it appears, that the account which Mr Locke himself gives of the origin of our idea of power, cannot be reconciled to his favourite doctrine—That all our simple ideas have their origin from sensation or reflection; and that, in attempting to derive the idea of power from these two sources only, he unawares brings in our memory, and our reasoning power, for a share in its origin.

CHAPTER IV.

OF MR HUME'S OPINION OF THE IDEA OF POWER.

This very ingenious author adopts the principle of Mr Locke before mentioned—That all our simple ideas are derived either from sensation or reflection. This he seems to understand even in a stricter sense than Mr Locke did. For he will have all our simple ideas to be copies of preceding impressions, either of our external senses or of consciousness. "After the most accurate examination," says he, "of which I am capable, I venture to affirm, that the rule here holds without any exception, and that every simple idea has a simple impression which resembles it, and every simple impression a correspondent idea. Every one may satisfy himself in this point, by running over as many as he pleases."

I observe here, by the way, that this conclusion is formed by the author rashly and unphilosophically. For it is a conclusion that admits of no proof but by induction; and it is upon this ground that he himself founds it. The induction cannot be perfect till every simple idea that can enter into the human mind be examined, and be shewn to be copied from a resembling impression of sense or of consciousness. No man can pretend to have made this examination of all our simple ideas without exception; and, therefore, no man can, consistently with the rules of philosophising, assure us, that this conclusion holds without any exception. [27]

The author professes, in his title page, to introduce into moral subjects, the experimental method of reasoning. This was a very laudable attempt; but he ought to have known that it is a rule in the experimental method of reasoning—That conclusions established by induction ought never to exclude exceptions, if any such should afterwards appear from observation or experiment. Sir Isaac Newton, speaking of such conclusions, says, "Et si quando in experiundo postea reperiatur aliquid, quod a parte contraria faciat; tum demum, non sine istis exceptionibus affirmetur conclusio opportebit." "But," says our author, "I will venture to affirm that the rule here holds without any exception."

Accordingly, throughout the whole treatise, this general rule is considered as of sufficient authority, in itself, to exclude, even from a hearing, everything that appears to be an exception to it. This is contrary to the fundamental principles of the experimental method of reasoning, and, therefore, may be called rash and unphilosophical.

Having thus established this general principle, the author does great execution by it among our ideas. He finds, that we have no idea of *substance*, material or spiritual; that body and mind are only certain trains of related impressions and ideas; that we have no idea of *space* or *duration*, and no idea of *power*, active or intellectual. [28]

Mr Locke used his principle of sensation and reflection with greater moderation and mercy. Being unwilling to thrust the ideas we have mentioned into the *limbo* of non-existence, he stretches sensation and reflection to the very utmost, in order to receive these ideas within the pale; and draws them into it, as it were, by violence.

But this author, instead of shewing them any favour, seems fond to get rid of them.

Of the ideas mentioned, it is only that of *power* that concerns our present subject. And, with regard to this, the author boldly affirms, "That we never have any idea of Power; that we deceive ourselves when we imagine we are possessed of any idea of this kind."

He begins with observing, "That the terms *efficacy*, *agency*, *power*, *force*, *energy*, are all nearly synonymous; and, therefore, it is an absurdity to employ any of them in defining the rest. By this observation," says he, "we reject at once all the vulgar definitions which philosophers have given of *power* and *efficacy*."

Surely this author was not ignorant that there are many things of which we have a clear and distinct conception, which are so simple in their nature, that they cannot be defined any other way than by synonymous words. It is true that this is not a logical definition; but that there is, as he affirms, an absurdity in using it, when no better can be had, I cannot perceive.

He might here have applied to *power* and *efficacy*, what he says, in another place, of *pride* and *humility*. "The passions of *pride* and *humility*," he says, "being simple and uniform impressions, it is impossible we can ever give a just definition of them. As the words are of general use, and the things they represent the most common of any, every one, of himself, will be able to form a just notion of them without danger of mistake." [29]

He mentions Mr Locke's account of the idea of Power—that, observing various changes in things, we conclude that there must be somewhere a power capable of producing them, and so arrive at last, by this reasoning, at the idea of Power and Efficacy.

"But," says he, "to be satisfied that this explication is more popular than philosophical, we need but reflect on two very obvious principles: first, *That Reason alone can never give rise to any original idea*;* and, secondly, *That Reason, as distinguished from Experience, can never make us conclude that a cause, or productive quality, is absolutely requisite to every beginning of existence*."†

Before we consider the two principles which our author opposes to the popular opinion of Mr Locke, I observe—

First, That there are some *popular* opinions, which, on that very account, deserve more regard from philosophers than this author is willing to bestow.

That things cannot begin to exist, nor undergo any change, without a cause that hath power to produce that change, is indeed so popular an opinion that, I believe, this author is the first of mankind that ever called it in question. It is so popular that there is not a man of common prudence who does not act from this opinion, and rely upon it every day of his life. And any man who should conduct himself by the contrary opinion, would soon be confined as insane, and continue in that state till a sufficient cause was found for his enlargement. [30]

Such a popular opinion as this stands upon a higher authority than that of philosophy; and philosophy must strike sail to it, if she would not render herself contemptible to every man of common understanding.

For though, in matters of deep speculation, the multitude must be guided by philosophers, yet, in things that are within the reach of every man's understanding, and upon which the whole conduct of human life turns, the philosopher must follow the multitude, or make himself perfectly ridiculous.

Secondly, I observe, that whether this popular opinion be true or false, it follows, from men's having this opinion, that they have an idea of power. A false opinion about power, no less than a true, implies an idea of power; for how can men have any opinion, true or false, about a thing of which they have no idea?

The *first* of the very obvious principles which the author opposes to Mr Locke's account of the idea of power, is—*that Reason alone can never give rise to any original idea*.

This appears to me so far from being a very obvious principle, that the contrary is very obvious.

Is it not our reasoning faculty that gives rise to the idea of reasoning itself?* As our idea of sight takes its rise from our being endowed with that faculty, so does our idea of reasoning. Do not the ideas of demonstration, of probability, our ideas of a syllogism, of major, minor and conclusion, of an enthymeme, dilemma, sorites, and all the various modes of reasoning, take their rise from the faculty of reason? Or is it possible that a being, not endowed with the faculty of reasoning, should have these ideas? This principle, therefore, is so far from being obviously true, that it appears to be obviously false. [31]

The *second* obvious principle is, *That Reason, as distinguished from Experience, can never make us conclude, that a cause, or productive quality, is absolutely requisite to every beginning of existence*.

In some "Essays on the Intellectual Powers of Man," I had occasion to treat of this principle,—That every change in nature must have a cause; and, to prevent repetition, I beg leave to refer the reader to what is said upon this subject, Essay vi, Chap. 6. I endeavoured to shew that it is a first principle, evident to all men come to years of understanding. Besides its having been universally received, without the least doubt, from the beginning of the world, it has this sure mark of a first principle, that the belief of it is absolutely necessary in the ordinary affairs of life, and, without it, no man could act with common prudence, or avoid the imputation of insanity. Yet a philosopher, who acted upon the firm belief of it every day of his life, thinks fit, in his closet, to call it in question.

He insinuates here that we may know it from *experience*. [?] I endeavoured to shew, that we do not learn it from experience, for two reasons.

First—Because it is a necessary truth, and has always been received as a necessary truth. Experience gives no information of what is necessary, or of what must be.†

We may know from experience, what is,

* In other words—there are no *native* or *a priori* notions in the intellect; all are immediate or mediate educts from experience.—H.

† In other words, that we cannot, on the *Principle of Contradiction*, shew, that for everything which begins to be, a cause must have been.—H.

* Mr Hume says, "reason *alone*."—H.

† See above, pp. 321, a; 455, b; 460, a; and notes. See also note T.—H.

[29–31]

or what was, and from that may probably conclude what shall be in like circumstances; but, with regard to what must necessarily be, experience is perfectly silent.

Thus we know, by unvaried experience, from the beginning of the world, that the sun and stars rise in the east and set in the west. But no man believes, that it could not possibly have been otherwise, or that it did not depend upon the will and power of Him who made the world, whether the earth should revolve to the east or to the west. [32]

In like manner, if we had experience, ever so constant, that every change in nature we have observed, actually had a cause, this might afford ground to believe, that, for the future, it shall be so; but no ground at all to believe that it must be so, and cannot be otherwise.

Another reason to shew that this principle is not learned from experience is—*That experience does not shew us a cause of one in a hundred of those changes which we observe, and therefore can never teach us that there must be a cause of all.*

Of all the paradoxes this author has advanced, there is not one more shocking to the human understanding than this, That things may begin to exist without a cause.* This would put an end to all speculation, as well as to all the business of life. The employment of speculative men, since the beginning of the world, has been to investigate the causes of things. What pity is it, they never thought of putting the previous question, Whether things have a cause or not? This question has at last been started; and what is there so ridiculous as not to be maintained by some philosopher?

Enough has been said upon it, and more, I think, than it deserves. But, being about to treat of the active powers of the human mind, I thought it improper to take no notice of what has been said by so celebrated a Philosopher, to shew that there is not, in the human mind, any idea of power.† [33]

CHAPTER V.

WHETHER BEINGS THAT HAVE NO WILL NOR UNDERSTANDING MAY HAVE ACTIVE POWER.

That active power is an attribute, which cannot exist but in some being possessed of that power, and the subject of that attribute, I take for granted as a self-evident truth. Whether there can be active power in a subject which has no thought, no understanding, no will, is not so evident.

The ambiguity of the words *power*, *cause*, *agent*, and of all the words related to these, tends to perplex this question. The weakness of human understanding, which gives us only an indirect and relative conception of power, contributes to darken our reasoning, and should make us cautious and modest in our determinations.

We can derive little light in this matter from the events which we observe in the course of nature. We perceive changes innumerable in things without us. We know that those changes must be produced by the active power of some agent; but we neither perceive the agent nor the power, but the change only. Whether the things be active, or merely passive, is not easily discovered. And though it may be an object of curiosity to the speculative few, it does not greatly concern the many.

To know the event and the circumstances that attended it, and to know in what circumstances like events may be expected, may be of consequence in the conduct of life; but to know the real efficient, whether it be matter or mind, whether of a superior or inferior order, concerns us little. [34]

Thus it is with regard to all the effects we ascribe to nature.

Nature is the name we give to the efficient cause of innumerable effects which fall daily under our observation. But, if it be asked what nature is—whether the first universal cause or a subordinate one, whether one or many, whether intelligent or unintelligent—upon these points we find various conjectures and theories, but no solid ground upon which we can rest. And I apprehend the wisest men are they who are sensible that they know nothing of the matter.

From the course of events in the natural world, we have sufficient reason to conclude the existence of an eternal intelligent First Cause. But whether He acts immediately in the production of those events, or by subordinate intelligent agents, or by instruments that are unintelligent, and what the number, the nature, and the different offices, of those agents or instruments may be—these I apprehend to be mysteries placed beyond the limits of human knowledge. We see an established order in the succession of natural events, but we see not the bond that connects them together.

Since we derive so little light, with regard to efficient causes and their active power, from attention to the natural world, let us next attend to the moral, I mean to human actions and conduct.

Mr Locke observes very justly, "That, from the observation of the operation of

* This is not Hume's assertion; but that, on the psychological doctrine generally admitted, we have no valid assurance that they may not.—H.

† On Brown's criticism of Reid, see Note Q.—H.

bodies by our senses, we have but a very imperfect obscure idea of active power, since they afford us not any idea in themselves of the power to begin any action, either of motion or thought." He adds, "That we find in ourselves a power to begin or forbear, continue or end, several actions of our minds and motions of our bodies, barely by a thought or preference of the mind, ordering, or, as it were, commanding the doing or not doing such a particular action. This power which the mind has thus to order the consideration of any idea, or the forbearing to consider it, or to prefer the motion of any part of the body to its rest, and *vice versa*, in any particular instance, is that which we call *the will*. The actual exercise of that power, by directing any particular action, or its forbearance, is that which we call *volition* or *willing*." [35]

According to Mr Locke, therefore, the only clear notion or idea we have of active power, is taken from the power which we find in ourselves to give certain motions to our bodies, or a certain direction to our thoughts; and this power in ourselves can be brought into action only by willing or volition.

From this, I think, it follows, that, if we had not will, and that degree of understanding which will necessarily implies, we could exert no active power, and, consequently, could have none; for power that cannot be exerted is no power. It follows, also, that the active power, of which only we can have any distinct conception, can be only in beings that have understanding and will.

Power to produce any effect, implies power not to produce it. We can conceive no way in which power may be determined to one of these rather than the other, in a being that has no will.

Whatever is the effect of active power, must be something that is contingent. Contingent existence is that which depended upon the power and will of its cause. Opposed to this, is necessary existence, which we ascribe to the Supreme Being, because his existence is not owing to the power of any being. The same distinction there is between contingent and necessary truth. [36]

That the planets of our system go round the sun from west to east, is a contingent truth; because it depended upon the power and will of Him who made the planetary system, and gave motion to it. That a circle and a right line can cut one another only in two points, is a truth which depends upon no power nor will, and, therefore, is called necessary and immutable. Contingency, therefore, has a relation to active power, as all active power is exerted in contingent events, and as such events can have no existence but by the exertion of active power.

[35–37]

When I observe a plant growing from its seed to maturity, I know that there must be a cause that has power to produce this effect. But I see neither the cause nor the manner of its operation.

But, in certain motions of my Body and directions of my thought, I know not only that there must be a cause that has power to produce these effects, but that I am that cause; and I am conscious of what I do in order to the production of them.

From the consciousness of our own activity, seems to be derived not only the clearest, but the only conception we can form of activity, or the exertion of active power.*

As I am unable to form a notion of any intellectual power different in kind from those I possess, the same holds with respect to active power. If all men had been blind, we should have had no conception of the power of seeing, nor any name for it in language. If man had not the powers of abstraction and reasoning, we could not have had any conception of these operations. In like manner, if he had not some degree of active power, and if he were not conscious of the exertion of it in his voluntary actions, it is probable he could have no conception of activity, or of active power. [37]

A train of events following one another ever so regularly, could never lead us to the notion of a cause, if we had not, from our constitution, a conviction of the necessity of a cause to every event.

And of the manner in which a cause may exert its active power, we can have no conception, but from consciousness of the manner in which our own active power is exerted.

With regard to the operations of nature, it is sufficient for us to know, that, whatever the agents may be, whatever the manner of their operation or the extent of their power, they depend upon the First Cause, and are under his control; and this indeed is all that we know; beyond this we are left in darkness. But, in what regards human actions, we have a more immediate concern.

It is of the highest importance to us, as moral and accountable creatures, to know what actions are in our own power, because it is for these only that we can be accountable to our Maker, or to our fellow-men in society; by these only we can merit praise or blame; in these only all our prudence, wisdom, and virtue must be employed; and, therefore, with regard to them, the wise Author of nature has not left us in the dark.

* From this consciousness, many philosophers have, after Locke, endeavoured to deduce our whole notion of *Causality*. The ablest development of this theory is that of M. Maine de Biran; the ablest refutation of it that of his friend and editor, M. Cousin.—H

Every man is led by nature to attribute to himself the free determinations of his own will, and to believe those events to be in his power which depend upon his will. On the other hand, it is self-evident, that nothing is in our power that is not subject to our will.

We grow from childhood to manhood, we digest our food, our blood circulates, our heart and arteries beat, we are sometimes sick and sometimes in health; all these things must be done by the power of some agent; but they are not done by our power. How do we know this? Because they are not subject to our will. This is the infallible criterion by which we distinguish what is our doing from what is not; what is in our power from what is not. [38]

Human power, therefore, can only be exerted by will, and we are unable to conceive any active power to be exerted without will. Every man knows infallibly that what is done by his conscious will and intention, is to be imputed to him, as the agent or cause; and that whatever is done without his will and intention, cannot be imputed to him with truth.

We judge of the actions and conduct of other men by the same rule as we judge of our own. In morals, it is self-evident that no man can be the object either of approbation or of blame for what he did not. But how shall we know whether it is his doing or not? If the action depended upon his will, and if he intended and willed it, it is his action in the judgment of all mankind. But if it was done without his knowledge, or without his will and intention, it is as certain that he did it not, and that it ought not to be imputed to him as the agent.

When there is any doubt to whom a particular action ought to be imputed, the doubt arises only from our ignorance of facts; when the facts relating to it are known, no man of understanding has any doubt to whom the action ought to be imputed.

The general rules of imputation are self-evident. They have been the same in all ages, and among all civilized nations. No man blames another for being black or fair, for having a fever or the falling sickness; because these things are believed not to be in his power; and they are believed not to be in his power, because they depend not upon his will. We can never conceive that a man's duty goes beyond his power, or that his power goes beyond what depends upon his will. [39]

Reason leads us to ascribe unlimited power to the Supreme Being. But what do we mean by unlimited power? It is power to do whatsoever he wills. To suppose him to do what he does not will to do, is absurd.

The only distinct conception I can form of active power is, that it is an attribute in a being by which he can do certain things if he wills. This, after all, is only a relative conception. It is relative to the effect, and to the will of producing it. Take away these, and the conception vanishes. They are the handles by which the mind takes hold of it. When they are taken away, our hold is gone. The same is the case with regard to other relative conceptions. Thus velocity is a real state of a body, about which philosophers reason with the force of demonstration; but our conception of it is relative to space and time. What is velocity in a body? It is a state in which it passes through a certain space in a certain time. Space and time are very different from velocity; but we cannot conceive it but by its relation to them. The effect produced, and the will to produce it, are things different from active power, but we can have no conception of it, but by its relation to them.

Whether the conception of an efficient cause, and of real activity, could ever have entered into the mind of man, if we had not had the experience of activity in ourselves, I am not able to determine with certainty. The origin of many of our conceptions, and even of many of our judgments, is not so easily traced as philosophers have generally conceived. No man can recollect the time when he first got the conception of an efficient cause, or the time when he first got the belief that an efficient cause is necessary to every change in nature. [40] The conception of an efficient cause may very probably be derived from the experience we have had in very early life of our own power to produce certain effects. But the belief, that no event can happen without an efficient cause, cannot be derived from experience. We may learn from experience what *is*, or what *was*, but no experience can teach us what *necessarily must be*.*

In like manner, we probably derive the conception of pain from the experience we have had of it in ourselves; but our belief that pain can only exist in a being that hath life, cannot be got by experience, because it is a necessary truth; and no necessary truth can have its attestation from experience.

If it be so that the conception of an efficient cause enters into the mind, only from the early conviction we have that we are the efficients of our own voluntary actions, (which I think is most probable,) the notion of efficiency will be reduced to this, That it is a relation between the cause and the effect, similar to that which is between us and our voluntary actions. This is surely

* See above, pp. 373, a; 455, b; 470, a; 501, b; and notes. See also Note I—II.

the most distinct notion, and, I think, the only notion we can form of real efficiency.

Now it is evident, that, to constitute the relation between me and my action, my conception of the action, and will to do it, are essential. For what I never conceived nor willed, I never did.

If any man, therefore, affirms, that a being may be the efficient cause of an action, and have power to produce it, which that being can neither conceive nor will, he speaks a language which I do not understand. If he has a meaning, his notion of power and efficiency must be essentially different from mine; and, until he conveys his notion of efficiency to my understanding, I can no more assent to his opinion than if he should affirm that a being without life may feel pain. [41]

It seems, therefore, to me most probable, that such beings only as have some degree of understanding and will, can possess active power: and that inanimate beings must be merely passive, and have no real activity. Nothing we perceive without us affords any good ground for ascribing active power to any inanimate being; and everything we can discover in our own constitution, leads us to think that active power cannot be exerted without will and intelligence.

CHAPTER VI.

OF THE EFFICIENT CAUSES OF THE PHÆNOMENA OF NATURE.

If active power, in its proper meaning, requires a subject endowed with will and intelligence, what shall we say of those active powers which philosophers teach us to ascribe to matter—the powers of corpuscular attraction, magnetism, electricity, gravitation, and others? Is it not universally allowed, that heavy bodies descend to the earth by the power of gravity; that, by the same power, the moon, and all the planets and comets, are retained in their orbits? Have the most eminent natural philosophers been imposing upon us, and giving us words instead of real causes?

In answer to this, I apprehend, that the principles of natural philosophy have, in modern times, been built upon a foundation that cannot be shaken, and that they can be called in question only by those who do not understand the evidence on which they stand. But the ambiguity of the words *cause*, *agency*, *active power*, and the other words related to these, has led many to understand them, when used in natural philosophy, in a wrong sense, and in a sense which is neither necessary for establishing the true principles of natural philosophy, nor was ever meant by the most enlightened in that science. [42]

To be convinced of this, we may observe that those very philosophers who attribute to matter the power of gravitation, and other active powers, teach us, at the same time, that matter is a substance altogether inert, and merely passive; that gravitation, and the other attractive or repulsive powers which they ascribe to it, are not inherent in its nature, but impressed upon it by some external cause, which they do not pretend to know or to explain. Now, when we find wise men ascribing action and active power to a substance which they expressly teach us to consider as merely passive and acted upon by some unknown cause, we must conclude that the action and active power ascribed to it are not to be understood strictly, but in some popular sense.

It ought likewise to be observed, that although philosophers, for the sake of being understood, must speak the language of the vulgar—as when they say, the sun rises and sets, and goes through all the signs of the zodiac—yet they often think differently from the vulgar. Let us hear what the greatest of natural philosophers says, in the eighth definition prefixed to his "*Principia*;"—"Voces autem attractionis, impulsus, vel propensionis cujuscunque in centrum, indifferenter et pro se mutuo promiscue usurpo; has voces non physice sed mathematice considerando. Unde caveat lector, ne per hujus modi voces cogitet me speciem vel modum actionis, causamve aut rationem physicam, alicubi definire; vel centris (quæ sunt puncta mathematica) vires vere et physice tribuere, si forte centra trahere, aut vires centrorum esse, dixero."

In all languages, action is attributed to many things which all men of common understanding believe to be merely passive. Thus, we say the wind blows, the rivers flow, the sea rages, the fire burns, bodies move, and impel other bodies. [43]

Every object which undergoes any change must be either active or passive in that change. This is self-evident to all men from the first dawn of reason; and, therefore, the change is always expressed in language, either by an active or a passive verb. Nor do I know any verb, expressive of a change, which does not imply either action or passion. The thing either changes, or it is changed. But it is remarkable in language, that when an external cause of the change is not obvious, the change is always imputed to the thing changed, as if it were animated, and had active power to produce the change in itself. So we say, the moon changes, the sun rises and goes down.

Thus active verbs are very often applied, and active power imputed to things, which a little advance in knowledge and experience teaches us to be merely passive. This property, common to all languages, I endeavoured to account for in the second chapter of this Essay, to which the reader is referred.

A like irregularity may be observed in the use of the word signifying *cause*, in all languages, and of the words related to it.

Our knowledge of causes is very scanty in the most advanced state of society, much more is it so in that early period in which language is formed. A strong desire to know the causes of things, is common to all men in every state; but the experience of all ages shews, that this keen appetite, rather than go empty, will feed upon the husks of real knowledge where the fruit cannot be found.

While we are very much in the dark with regard to the real agents or causes which produce the phænomena of nature, and have, at the same time, an avidity to know them, ingenious men frame conjectures, which those of weaker understanding take for truth. The fare is coarse, but appetite makes it go down. [44]

Thus, in a very ancient system, love and strife were made the causes of things.* Plato made the causes of things to be matter, ideas, and an efficient architect; Aristotle, matter, form, and privation; Des Cartes thought matter, and a certain quantity of motion given it by the Almighty at first, to be all that is necessary to make the material world; Leibnitz conceived the whole universe, even the material part of it, to be made up of *monades*, each of which is active and intelligent, and produces in itself, by its own active power, all the changes it undergoes from the beginning of its existence to eternity.

In common language, we give the name of a *cause* to a reason, a motive, an end, to any circumstance which is connected with the effect, and goes before it.

Aristotle, and the schoolmen after him, distinguished four kinds of causes—the Efficient, the Material, the Formal, and the Final. This, like many of Aristotle's distinctions, is only a distinction of the various meanings of an ambiguous word; for the Efficient, the Matter, the Form, and the End, have nothing common in their nature, by which they may be accounted species of the same *genus*;† but the Greek word which we translate *cause*, had these four different meanings in Aristotle's days, and we have added other meanings.‡ We do not indeed call the matter or the form of a thing its cause; but we have final causes, instrumental causes, occasional causes, and I know not how many others.

Thus the word *cause* has been so hackneyed, and made to have so many different meanings in the writings of philosophers, and in the discourse of the vulgar, that its original and proper meaning is lost in the crowd. [45]

With regard to the phænomena of nature, the important end of knowing their causes, besides gratifying our curiosity, is, that we may know when to expect them, or how to bring them about. This is very often of real importance in life; and this purpose is served by knowing what, by the course of nature, goes before them and is connected with them; and this, therefore, we call the *cause* of such a phænomenon.

If a magnet be brought near to a mariner's compass, the needle, which was before at rest, immediately begins to move, and bends its course towards the magnet, or perhaps the contrary way. If an unlearned sailor is asked the cause of this motion of the needle, he is at no loss for an answer. He tells you it is the magnet; and the proof is clear; for, remove the magnet, and the effect ceases; bring it near, and the effect is again produced. It is, therefore, evident to sense, that the magnet is the cause of this effect.

A Cartesian philosopher enters deeper into the cause of this phænomenon. He observes, that the magnet does not touch the needle, and therefore can give it no impulse. He pities the ignorance of the sailor. The effect is produced, says he, by magnetic effluvia, or subtile matter, which passes from the magnet to the needle, and forces it from its place. He can even shew you, in a figure, where these magnetic effluvia issue from the magnet, what round they take, and what way they return home again. And thus he thinks he comprehends perfectly how, and by what cause, the motion of the needle is produced.

A Newtonian philosopher inquires what proof can be offered for the existence of magnetic effluvia, and can find none. He therefore holds it as a fiction, a hypothesis; and he has learned that hypotheses ought to have no place in the philosophy of nature. He confesses his ignorance of the real cause of this motion, and thinks that his business, as a philosopher, is only to find from experiment the laws by which it is regulated in all cases. [46]

These three persons differ much in their sentiments with regard to the real cause of this phænomenon; and the man who knows most is he who is sensible that he knows nothing of the matter. Yet all the three speak the same language, and acknowledge that the cause of this motion is the attractive or repulsive power of the magnet.

* The system of Empedocles.—H.

† They all have this in common—that each is an antecedent, which not being, the consequent, called the effect, would not be.—H.

‡ See above, p. 75; below, Essay IV. cc. 2, 3.—H.

What has been said of this, may be applied to every phænomenon that falls within the compass of natural philosophy. We deceive ourselves if we conceive that we can point out the real efficient cause of any one of them.

The grandest discovery ever made in natural philosophy, was that of the law of gravitation, which opens such a view of our planetary system that it looks like something divine. But the author of this discovery was perfectly aware, that he discovered no real cause, but only the law or rule, according to which the unknown cause operates.

Natural philosophers, who think accurately, have a precise meaning to the terms they use in the science; and, when they pretend to shew the cause of any phænomenon of nature, they mean by the cause, a law of nature of which that phænomenon is a necessary consequence.

The whole object of natural philosophy, as Newton expressly teaches, is reducible to these two heads: first, by just induction from experiment and observation, to discover the laws of nature; and then, to apply those laws to the solution of the phænomena of nature. This was all that this great philosopher attempted, and all that he thought attainable. And this indeed he attained in a great measure, with regard to the motions of our planetary system, and with regard to the rays of light. [47]

But supposing that all the phænomena that fall within the reach of our senses, were accounted for from general laws of nature, justly deduced from experience—that is, supposing natural philosophy brought to its utmost perfection—it does not discover the efficient cause of any one phænomenon in nature.

The laws of nature are the rules according to which the effects are produced; but there must be a cause which operates according to these rules. The rules of navigation never navigated a ship; the rules of architecture never built a house.

Natural philosophers, by great attention to the course of nature, have discovered many of her laws, and have very happily applied them to account for many phænomena; but they have never discovered the efficient cause of any one phænomenon; nor do those who have distinct notions of the principles of the science make any such pretence.

Upon the theatre of nature we see innumerable effects, which require an agent endowed with active power; but the agent is behind the scene. Whether it be the Supreme Cause alone, or a subordinate cause or causes; and if subordinate causes be employed by the Almighty, what their nature, their number, and their different offices may be—are things hid, for wise reasons without doubt, from the human eye.

It is only in human actions, that may be imputed for praise or blame, that it is necessary for us to know who is the agent; and in this, nature has given us all the light that is necessary for our conduct. [48]

CHAPTER VII.

OF THE EXTENT OF HUMAN POWER.

Every thing laudable and praiseworthy in man, must consist in the proper exercise of that power which is given him by his Maker. This is the talent which he is required to occupy, and of which he must give an account to Him who committed it to his trust.

To some persons more power is given than to others; and to the same person, more at one time and less at another. Its existence, its extent, and its continuance, depend solely upon the pleasure of the Almighty; but every man that is accountable must have more or less of it. For, to call a person to account, to approve or disapprove of his conduct, who had no power to do good or ill, is absurd. No axiom of Euclid appears more evident than this.

As power is a valuable gift, to underrate it is ingratitude to the giver; to overrate it, begets pride and presumption, and leads to unsuccessful attempts. It is therefore, in every man, a point of wisdom to make a just estimate of his own power. *Quid ferre recusent, quid valeant humeri.*

We can only speak of the power of man in general; and as our notion of power is relative to its effects, we can estimate its extent only by the effects which it is able to produce.

It would be wrong to estimate the extent of human power by the effects which it has actually produced. For every man had power to do many things which he did not, and not to do many things which he did; otherwise he could not be an object either of approbation or of disapprobation to any rational being. [49]

The effects of human power are either immediate, or they are more remote.

The immediate effects, I think, are reducible to two heads. We can give certain motions to our own bodies; and we can give a certain direction to our own thoughts.

Whatever we can do beyond this, must be done by one of these means, or both.

We can produce no motion in any body in the universe, but by moving first our own body as an instrument. Nor can we produce thought in any other person, but by thought and motion in ourselves.

Our power to move our own body, is not only limited in its extent, but in its nature is subject to mechanical laws. It may be compared to a spring endowed with the power of contracting or expanding itself, but which cannot contract without drawing equally at both ends, nor expand without pushing equally at both ends; so that every action of the spring is always accompanied with an equal reaction in a contrary direction.

We can conceive a man to have power to move his whole body in any direction, without the aid of any other body, or a power to move one part of his body without the aid of any other part. But philosophy teaches us that man has no such power.

If he carries his whole body in any direction with a certain quantity of motion, this he can do only by pushing the earth, or some other body, with an equal quantity of motion in the contrary direction. If he but stretch out his arm in one direction, the rest of his body is pushed with an equal quantity of motion in the contrary direction. [50]

This is the case with regard to all animal and voluntary motions, which come within the reach of our senses. They are performed by the contraction of certain muscles; and a muscle, when it is contracted, draws equally at both ends. As to the motions antecedent to the contraction of the muscle, and consequent upon the volition of the animal, we know nothing, and can say nothing about them.

We know not even how those immediate effects of our power are produced by our willing them. We perceive not any necessary connection between the volition and exertion on our part, and the motion of our body that follows them.

Anatomists inform us, that every voluntary motion of the body is performed by the contraction of certain muscles, and that the muscles are contracted by some influence derived from the nerves. But, without thinking in the least, either of muscles or nerves, we will only the external effect, and the internal machinery, without our call, immediately produces that effect.

This is one of the wonders of our frame, which we have reason to admire; but to account for it, is beyond the reach of our understanding.

That there is an established harmony between our willing certain motions of our bodies, and the operation of the nerves and muscles which produces those motions, is a fact known by experience. This volition is an act of the mind. But whether this act of the mind have any physical effect upon the nerves and muscles; or whether it be only an occasion of their being acted upon by some other efficient, according to the established laws of nature, is hid from us. So dark is our conception of our own power when we trace it to its origin. [51]

We have good reason to believe, that matter had its origin from mind, as well as all its motions; but how, or in what manner, it is moved by mind, we know as little as how it was created.

It is possible, therefore, for any thing we know, that what we call the immediate effects of our power, may not be so in the strictest sense. Between the will to produce the effect, and the production of it, there may be agents or instruments of which we are ignorant.

This may leave some doubt, whether we be, in the strictest sense, the efficient cause of the voluntary motions of our own body. But it can produce no doubt with regard to the moral estimation of our actions.

The man who knows that such an event depends upon his will, and who deliberately wills to produce it, is, in the strictest moral sense, the cause of the event; and it is justly imputed to him, whatever physical causes may have concurred in its production.

Thus, he who maliciously intends to shoot his neighbour dead, and voluntarily does it, is undoubtedly the cause of his death, though he did no more to occasion it than draw the trigger of the gun. He neither gave to the ball its velocity, nor to the powder its expansive force, nor to the flint and steel the power to strike fire; but he knew that what he did must be followed by the man's death, and did it with that intention; and therefore he is justly chargeable with the murder. [52]

Philosophers may therefore dispute innocently, whether we be the proper efficient causes of the voluntary motions of our own body; or whether we be only, as Malebranche thinks, the occasional causes. The determination of this question, if it can be determined, can have no effect on human conduct.

The other branch of what is immediately in our power, is to give a certain direction to our own thoughts. This, as well as the first branch, is limited in various ways. It is greater in some persons than in others, and in the same person is very different, according to the health of his body and the state of his mind. But that men, when free from disease of body and of mind, have a considerable degree of power of this kind, and that it may be greatly increased by practice and habit, is sufficiently evident from experience, and from the natural conviction of all mankind.

Were we to examine minutely into the connection between our volitions, and the direction of our thoughts which obeys these volitions—were we to consider how we are able to give attention to an object for a certain time, and turn our attention to another when we choose, we might perhaps find it difficult to determine whether the mind itself be the sole efficient cause of the voluntary changes in the direction of our thoughts, or whether it requires the aid of other efficient causes.

I see no good reason why the dispute about efficient and occasional causes, may not be applied to the power of directing our thoughts, as well as to the power of moving our bodies. In both cases, I apprehend, the dispute is endless, and, if it could be brought to an issue, would be fruitless.

Nothing appears more evident to our reason, than that there must be an efficient cause of every change that happens in nature. But when I attempt to comprehend the manner in which an efficient cause operates, either upon body or upon mind, there is a darkness which my faculties are not able to penetrate. [53]

However small the immediate effects of human power seem to be, its more remote effects are very considerable.

In this respect, the power of man may be compared to the Nile, the Ganges, and other great rivers, which make a figure upon the globe of the earth, and, traversing vast regions, bring sometimes great benefit, at other times great mischief, to many nations: yet, when we trace those rivers to their source, we find them to rise from inconsiderable fountains and rills.

The command of a mighty prince, what is it but the sound of his breath, modified by his organs of speech? But it may have great consequences: it may raise armies, equip fleets, and spread war and desolation over a great part of the earth.

The meanest of mankind has considerable power to do good, and more to hurt himself and others.

From this I think we may conclude, that, although the degeneracy of mankind be great, and justly to be lamented, yet men, in general, are more disposed to employ their power in doing good, than in doing hurt, to their fellow-men. The last is much more in their power than the first; and, if they were as much disposed to it, human society could not subsist, and the species must soon perish from the earth.

We may first consider the effects which may be produced by human power upon the material system.

It is confined indeed to the planet which we inhabit; we cannot remove to another: nor can we produce any change in the annual or diurnal motions of our own. [54]

But, by human power, great changes may be made upon the face of the earth; and those treasures of metals and minerals that are stored up in its bowels, may be discovered and brought forth.

The Supreme Being could, no doubt, have made the earth to supply the wants of man, without any cultivation by human labour. Many inferior animals, who neither plant, nor sow, nor spin, are provided for by the bounty of Heaven. But this is not the case with man.

He has active powers and ingenuity given him, by which he can do much for supplying his wants; and his labour is made necessary for that purpose.

His wants are more than those of any other animal that inhabits this globe; and his resources are proportioned to them, and put within the sphere of his power.

The earth is left by nature in such a state as to require cultivation for the accommodation of man.

It is capable of cultivation, in most places, to such a degree, that, by human labour, it may afford subsistence to an hundred times the number of men it could in its natural state.

Every tribe of men, in every climate, must labour for their subsistence and accommodation; and their supply is more or less comfortable, in proportion to the labour properly employed for that purpose.

It is evidently the intention of Nature, that man should be laborious, and that he should exert his powers of body and mind for his own, and for the common, good. And, by his power properly applied, he may make great improvement upon the fertility of the earth, and a great addition to his own accommodation and comfortable state. [55]

By clearing, tilling, and manuring the ground, by planting and sowing, by building cities and harbours, draining marshes and lakes, making rivers navigable, and joining them by canals, by manufacturing the rude materials which the earth, duly cultivated, produces in abundance, by the mutual exchange of commodities and of labour, he may make the barren wilderness the habitation of rich and populous states.

If we compare the city of Venice, the province of Holland, the empire of China, with those places of the earth which never felt the hand of industry, we may form some conception of the extent of human power upon the material system, in changing the face of the earth, and furnishing the accommodations of human life.

But, in order to produce those happy changes, man himself must be improved.

His animal faculties are sufficient for the preservation of the species; they grow up of themselves, like the trees of the forest, which require only the force of nature and the influences of Heaven.

His rational and moral faculties, like the earth itself, are rude and barren by nature, but capable of a high degree of culture; and this culture he must receive from parents, from instructors, from those with whom he lives in society, joined with his own industry.

If we consider the changes that may be produced by man upon his own mind, and upon the minds of others, they appear to be great. [56]

Upon his own mind he may make great improvement, in acquiring the treasures of useful knowledge, the habits of skill in arts, the habits of wisdom, prudence, self-command, and every other virtue. It is the constitution of nature, that such qualities as exalt and dignify human nature are to be acquired by proper exertions; and, by a contrary conduct, such qualities as debase it below the condition of brutes.

Even upon the minds of others, great effects may be produced by means within the compass of human power; by means of good education, of proper instruction, of persuasion, of good example, and by the discipline of laws and government.

That these have often had great and good effects on the civilization and improvement of individuals and of nations, cannot be doubted. But what happy effects they might have, if applied universally with the skill and address that is within the reach of human wisdom and power, is not easily conceived, or to what pitch the happiness of human society, and the improvement of the species, might be carried.

What a noble, what a divine employment of human power is here assigned us! How ought it to rouse the ambition of parents, of instructors, of lawgivers, of magistrates, of every man in his station, to contribute his part towards the accomplishment of so glorious an end!

The power of man over his own and other minds, when we trace it to its origin, is involved in darkness, no less than his power to move his own and other bodies.

How far we are properly efficient causes, how far occasional causes, I cannot pretend to determine. [57]

We know that habit produces great changes in the mind; but how it does so, we know not. We know that example has a powerful, and, in the early period of life, almost an irresistible effect; but we know not how it produces this effect. The communication of thought, sentiment, and passion, from one mind to another, has something in it as mysterious as the communication of motion from one body to another.

We perceive one event to follow another, according to established laws of nature, and we are accustomed to call the first the cause, and the last the effect, without knowing what is the bond that unites them. In order to produce a certain event, we use means which, by laws of nature, are connected with that event; and we call ourselves the cause of that event, though other efficient causes may have had the chief hand in its production.

Upon the whole, human power, in its existence, in its extent, and in its exertions is entirely dependent upon God, and upon the laws of nature which he has established. This ought to banish pride and arrogance from the most mighty of the sons of men. At the same time, that degree of power which we have received from the bounty of Heaven, is one of the noblest gifts of God to man; of which we ought not to be insensible, that we may not be ungrateful, and that we may be excited to make the proper use of it.

The extent of human power is perfectly suited to the state of man, as a state of improvement and discipline. It is sufficient to animate us to the noblest exertions. By the proper exercise of this gift of God, human nature, in individuals and in societies, may be exalted to a high degree of dignity and felicity, and the earth become a paradise. On the contrary, its perversion and abuse is the cause of most of the evils that afflict human life. [59]

ESSAY II.

OF THE WILL.

CHAPTER I.

OBSERVATIONS CONCERNING THE WILL.

EVERY man is conscious of a power to determine, in things which he conceives to depend upon his determination. To this power we give the name of *Will*; and, as it is usual, in the operations of the mind, to give the same name to the power and to the act of that power, the term *will* is often put to signify the act of determining, which more properly is called *volition*.

Volition, therefore, signifies the act of

willing and determining, and Will is put indifferently to signify either the power of willing or the act.

But the term *will* has very often, especially in the writings of philosophers, a more extensive meaning, which we must carefully distinguish from that which we have now given.

In the general division of our faculties into Understanding and Will, our passions, appetites, and affections are comprehended under the will; and so it is made to signify, not only our determination to act or not to act, but every motive and incitement to action. [60]

It is this, probably, that has led some philosophers to represent desire, aversion, hope, fear, joy, sorrow, all our appetites, passions, and affections, as different modifications of the will,* which, I think, tends to confound things which are very different in their nature.

The advice given to a man, and his determination consequent to that advice, are things so different in their nature, that it would be improper to call them modifications of one and the same thing. In like manner, the motives to action, and the determination to act or not to act, are things that have no common nature, and, therefore, ought not to be confounded under one name, or represented as different modifications of the same thing.

For this reason, in speaking of the will in this Essay, I do not comprehend under that term any of the incitements or motives which may have an influence upon our determinations, but solely the determination itself, and the power to determine.

Mr Locke has considered this operation of the mind more attentively, and distinguished it more accurately, than some very ingenious authors who wrote after him.

He defines volition to be, "An act of the mind knowingly exerting that dominion it takes itself to have over any part of the man, by employing it in, or withholding it from any particular action."

It may more briefly be defined—The determination of the mind to do, or not to do, something which we conceive to be in our power. [61]

If this were given as a strictly logical definition, it would be liable to this objection, that the determination of the mind is only another term for volition. But it ought to be observed, that the most simple acts of the mind do not admit of a logical definition. The way to form a clear notion of them is, to reflect attentively upon them as we feel them in ourselves. Without this reflection, no definition can give us a distinct conception of them.

For this reason, rather than sift any definition of the will, I shall make some observations upon it, which may lead us to reflect upon it, and to distinguish it from other acts of mind, which, from the ambiguity of words, are apt to be confounded with it.

First, Every act of will must have an object. He that wills must will something; and that which he wills is called the object of his volition. As a man cannot think without thinking of something, nor remember without remembering something, so neither can he will without willing something. Every act of will, therefore, must have an object; and the person who wills must have some conception, more or less distinct, of what he wills.

By this, things done voluntarily are distinguished from things done merely from instinct, or merely from habit.

A healthy child, some hours after its birth, feels the sensation of hunger, and, if applied to the breast, sucks and swallows its food very perfectly. We have no reason to think, that, before it ever sucked, it has any conception of that complex operation, or how it is performed. It cannot, therefore, with propriety, be said that it wills to suck. [62]

Numberless instances might be given of things done by animals without any previous conception of what they are to do, without the intention of doing it. They act by some inward blind impulse, of which the efficient cause is hid from us; and, though there is an end evidently intended by the action, this intention is not in the animal, but in its Maker.

Other things are done by habit, which cannot properly be called voluntary. We shut our eyes several times every minute while we are awake; no man is conscious of willing this every time he does it.

A *second* observation is, That the immediate object of will must be some action of our own.

By this, will is distinguished from two acts of the mind, which sometimes takes its name, and thereby are apt to be confounded with it. These are desire and command.

The distinction between will and desire, has been well explained by Mr Locke; yet many later writers have overlooked it, and have represented desire as a modification of will.*

Desire and will agree in this, that both must have an object, of which we must have some conception; and, therefore, both must be accompanied with some degree of understanding. But they differ in several things.

* See following note.—H.

* Rather—*Will* as a modification of *Desire*. This has been done, since Reid, (to say nothing of others,) also by Dr Thomas Brown, in whose scheme there is thus virtually abolished all rational freedom, all responsible agency, all moral distinctions.—H.

The object of desire may be anything which appetite, passion, or affection leads us to pursue; it may be any event which we think good for us, or for those to whom we are well affected. I may desire meat, or drink, or ease from pain; but, to say that I will meat, or will drink, or will ease from pain, is not English. There is, therefore, a distinction in common language between desire and will. And the distinction is, That what we will must be an action, and our own action; what we desire may not be our own action; it may be no action at all. [63]

A man desires that his children may be happy, and that they may behave well. Their being happy is no action at all; their behaving well is not his action but theirs.

With regard to our own actions, we may desire what we do not will, and will what we do not desire; nay, what we have a great aversion to.

A man a-thirst has a strong desire to drink, but, for some particular reason, he determines not to gratify his desire. A judge, from a regard to justice, and to the duty of his office, dooms a criminal to die, while, from humanity or particular affection, he desires that he should live. A man, for health, may take a nauseous draught, for which he has no desire, but a great aversion. Desire, therefore, even when its object is some action of our own, is only an incitement to will, but it is not volition. The determination of the mind may be, not to do what we desire to do. But, as desire is often accompanied by will, we are apt to overlook the distinction between them.

The command of a person is sometimes called his will, sometimes his desire; but, when these words are used properly, they signify three different acts of the mind.

The immediate object of will is some action of our own; the object of a command is some action of another person over whom we claim authority; the object of desire may be no action at all.

In giving a command, all these acts concur; and, as they go together, it is not uncommon in language to give to one the name which properly belongs to another.

A command being a voluntary action, there must be a will to give the command. Some desire is commonly the motive to that act of will, and the command is the effect of it. [64]

Perhaps it may be thought that a command is only a desire expressed by language, that the thing commanded should be done. But it is not so. For a desire may be expressed by language when there is no command; and there may possibly be a command, without any desire that the thing commanded should be done. There have been instances of tyrants who have laid grievous commands upon their subjects, in order to reap the penalty of their disobedience, or to furnish a pretence for their punishment.

We might farther observe, that a command is a social act of the mind. It can have no existence but by a communication of thought to some intelligent being; and therefore implies a belief that there is such a being, and that we can communicate our thoughts to him.

Desire and will are solitary acts, which do not imply any such communication or belief.

The immediate object of volition, therefore, must be some action, and our own action.

A *third* observation is, That the object of our volition must be something which we believe to be in our power, and to depend upon our will.

A man may desire to make a visit to the moon, or to the planet Jupiter, but he cannot will or determine to do it; because he knows it is not in his power. If an insane person should make an attempt, his insanity must first make him believe it to be in his power. [65]

A man in his sleep may be struck with a palsy, which deprives him of the power of speech; when he awakes, he attempts to speak, not knowing that he has lost the power. But when he knows by experience that the power is gone, he ceases to make the effort.

The same man, knowing that some persons have recovered the power of speech after they had lost it by a paralytical stroke, may now and then make an effort. In this effort, however, there is not properly a will to speak, but a will to try whether he can speak or not.

In like manner, a man may exert his strength to raise a weight which is too heavy for him. But he always does this, either from the belief that he can raise the weight, or for a trial whether he can or not. It is evident, therefore, that what we will must be believed to be in our power, and to depend upon our will.

The *next* observation is, That when we will to do a thing immediately, the volition is accompanied with an effort to execute that which we willed.

If a man wills to raise a great weight from the ground by the strength of his arm, he makes an effort for that purpose proportioned to the weight he determines to raise. A great weight requires a great effort; a small weight a less effort. We say, indeed, that to raise a very small body requires no effort at all. But this, I apprehend, must be understood either as a figurative way of speaking, by which things very small are accounted as nothing; or it is owing to our giving no attention to very small efforts, and therefore having no name for them. [66]

Great efforts, whether of body or mind, are attended with difficulty, and, when long continued, produce lassitude, which requires that they should be intermitted. This leads us to reflect upon them, and to give them a name. The name *effort* is commonly appropriated to them; and those that are made with ease, and leave no sensible effect, pass without observation and without a name, though they be of the same kind, and differ only in degree from those to which the name is given.

This effort we are conscious of, if we will but give attention to it; and there is nothing in which we are in a more strict sense active.

The *last* observation is, That in all determinations of the mind that are of any importance, there must be something in the preceding state of the mind that disposes or inclines us to that determination.

If the mind were always in a state of perfect indifference, without any incitement, motive, or reason, to act, or not to act, to act one way rather than another, our active power, having no end to pursue, no rule to direct its exertions, would be given in vain. We should either be altogether inactive, and never will to do anything, or our volitions would be perfectly unmeaning and futile, being neither wise nor foolish, virtuous nor vicious.

We have reason therefore to think, that, to every being to whom God hath given any degree of active power, he hath also given some principles of action, for the direction of that power to the end for which it was intended.

It is evident that, in the constitution of man, there are various principles of action suited to our state and situation. A particular consideration of these is the subject of the next essay; in this we are only to consider them in general, with a view to examine the relation they bear to volition, and how it is influenced by them. [67]

CHAPTER II.

OF THE INFLUENCE OF INCITEMENTS AND MOTIVES UPON THE WILL.

We come into the world ignorant of every thing, yet we must do many things in order to our subsistence and well-being. A new-born child may be carried in arms, and kept warm by his nurse; but he must suck and swallow his food for himself. And this must be done before he has any conception of sucking or swallowing, or of the manner in which they are to be performed. He is led by nature to do these actions without knowing for what end, or what he is about. This we call *instinct*.

In many cases there is no time for voluntary determination. The motions must go on so rapidly that the conception and volition of every movement cannot keep pace with them. In some cases of this kind, instinct, in others habit, comes in to our aid.

When a man stumbles and loses his balance, the motion necessary to prevent his fall would come too late, if it were the consequence of thinking what is fit to be done, and making a voluntary effort for that purpose. He does this instinctively.

When a man beats a drum or plays a tune, he has not time to direct every particular beat or stop by a voluntary determination; but the habit which may be acquired by exercise answers the purpose as well.

By instinct, therefore, and by habit, we do many things without any exercise either of judgment or will.

In other actions the will is exerted, but without judgment. [68]

Suppose a man to know that, in order to live, he must eat. What shall he eat? How much? And how often? His reason can answer none of these questions; and therefore can give no direction how he should determine. Here, again, nature, as an indulgent parent, supplies the defects of his reason; giving him appetite, which shews him when he is to eat, how often, and how much; and taste, which informs him what he is and what he is not to eat. And by these principles he is much better directed than he could be without them, by all the knowledge he can acquire.

As the Author of nature has given us some principles of action to supply the defects of our knowledge, he has given others to supply the defects of our wisdom and virtue.

The natural desires, affections, and passions, which are common to the wise and to the foolish, to the virtuous and to the vicious, and even to the more sagacious brutes, serve very often to direct the course of human actions. By these principles men may perform the most laborious duties of life, without any regard to duty; and do what is proper to be done, without regard to propriety; like a vessel that is carried on in her proper course by a prosperous gale, without the skill or judgment of those that are aboard.

Appetite, affection, or passion, give an impulse to a certain action. In this impulse there is no judgment implied. It may be weak or strong; we can even conceive it irresistible. In the case of madness it is so. Madmen have their appetites and passions; but they want the power of self-government; and therefore we do not impute their actions to the man, but to the disease.

In actions that proceed from appetite or passion, we are passive in part, and only in part active. They are therefore partly imputed to the passion; and if it is supposed to be irresistible, we do not impute them to the man at all. [69]

Even an American savage judges in this manner: When in a fit of drunkenness he kills his friend—as soon as he comes to himself, be is very sorry for what he has done; but pleads that drink, and not he, was the cause.

We conceive brute animals to have no superior principle to control their appetites and passions. On this account, their actions are not subject to law. Men are in a like state in infancy, in madness, and in the delirium of a fever. They have appetites and passions, but they want that which makes them moral agents, accountable for their conduct, and objects of moral approbation or of blame.

In some cases, a stronger impulse of appetite or passion may oppose a weaker. Here also there may be determination and action without judgment.

Suppose a soldier ordered to mount a breach, and certain of present death if he retreats, this man needs not courage to go on—fear is sufficient. The certainty of present death if he retreats, is an overbalance to the probability of being killed if he goes on. The man is pushed by contrary forces, and it requires neither judgment nor exertion to yield to the strongest.

A hungry dog acts by the same principle, if meat is set before him with a threatening to beat him if he touch it. Hunger pushes him forward, fear pushes him back with more force, and the strongest force prevails.

Thus we see, that, in many even of our voluntary actions, we may act from the impulse of appetite, affection, or passion, without any exercise of judgment, and much in the same manner as brute animals seem to act. [70]

Sometimes, however, there is a calm in the mind from the gales of passion or appetite, and the man is left to work his way, in the voyage of life, without those impulses which they give. Then he calmly weighs goods and evils, which are at too great a distance to excite any passion. He judges what is best upon the whole, without feeling any bias drawing him to one side. He judges for himself as he would do for another in his situation; and the determination is wholly imputable to the man, and not in any degree to his passion.

Every man come to years of understanding, who has given any attention to his own conduct, and to that of others, has, in his mind, a scale or measure of goods and evils, more or less exact. He makes an estimate of the value of health, of reputation, of riches, of pleasure, of virtue, of self-approbation, and of the approbation of his Maker. These things, and their contraries, have a comparative importance in his cool and deliberate judgment.

When a man considers whether health ought to be preferred to bodily strength, fame to riches; whether a good conscience and the approbation of his Maker, to everything that can come in competition with it; this appears to me to be an exercise of judgment, and not any impulse of passion or appetite.

Everything worthy of pursuit, must be so, either intrinsically, and upon its own account, or as the means of procuring something that is intrinsically valuable. That it is by judgment that we discern the fitness of means for attaining an end, is self-evident; and in this, I think, all philosophers agree. But that it is the office of judgment to appreciate the value of an end, or the preference due to one end above another, is not granted by some philosophers. [71]

In determining what is good or ill, and, of different goods, which is best, they think we must be guided, not by judgment, but by some natural or acquired taste, which makes us relish one thing and dislike another.

Thus, if one man prefers cheese to lobsters, another lobsters to cheese, it is vain, say they, to apply judgment to determine which is right. In like manner, if one man prefers pleasure to virtue, another virtue to pleasure, this is a matter of taste, judgment has nothing to do in it. This seems to be the opinion of some philosophers.

I cannot help being of a contrary opinion. I think we may form a judgment, both in the question about cheese and lobsters, and in the more important question about pleasure and virtue.

When one man feels a more agreeable relish in cheese, another in lobsters, this, I grant, requires no judgment; it depends only upon the constitution of the palate. But, if we would determine which of the two has the best taste, I think the question must be determined by judgment; and that, with a small share of this faculty, we may give a very certain determination—to wit, that the two tastes are equally good, and that both of the parties do equally well, in preferring what suits their palate and their stomach.

Nay, I apprehend, that the two persons who differ in their tastes will, notwithstanding that difference, agree perfectly in their judgment, that both tastes are upon a footing of equality, and that neither has a just claim to preference. [72]

Thus it appears, that, in this instance, the office of taste is very different from that of judgment; and that men, who differ most in taste, may agree perfectly in their judgment, even with respect to the tastes wherein they differ.

To make the other case parallel with this, it must be supposed that the man of pleasure and the man of virtue agree in their judgment, and that neither sees any reason to prefer the one course of life to the other.

If this be supposed, I shall grant that neither of these persons has reason to condemn the other. Each chooses according to his taste, in matters which his best judgment determines to be perfectly indifferent.

But it is to be observed, that this supposition cannot have place, when we speak of men, or indeed of moral agents. The man who is incapable of perceiving the obligation of virtue when he uses his best judgment, is a man in name, but not in reality. He is incapable either of virtue or vice, and is not a moral agent.

Even the man of pleasure, when his judgment is unbiassed, sees that there are certain things which a man ought not to do, though he should have a taste for them. If a thief breaks into his house and carries off his goods, he is perfectly convinced that he did wrong, and deserves punishment, although he had as strong a relish for the goods as he himself has for the pleasures he pursues.

It is evident that mankind, in all ages, have conceived two parts in the human constitution that may have influence upon our voluntary actions. These we call by the general names of *passion* and *reason*; and we shall find, in all languages, names that are equivalent. [73]

Under the former, we comprehend various principles of action, similar to those we o serve in brute-animals, and in men who have not the use of reason. *Appetites*, *affections*, *passions*, are the names by which they are denominated; and these names are not so accurately distinguished in common language, but that they are used somewhat promiscuously. This, however, is common to them all, that they draw a man toward a certain object, without any farther view, by a kind of violence; a violence which, indeed, may be resisted, if the man is master of himself, but cannot be resisted without a struggle.

Cicero's phrase for expressing their influence is—"Hominem huc et illuc rapiunt." Dr Hutcheson uses a similar phrase—"Quibus agitatur mens et bruto quodam impetu fertur." There is no exercise of reason or judgment necessary in order to feel their influence.

With regard to this part of the human constitution, I see no difference between the vulgar and philosophers.

As to the other part of our constitution, which is commonly called *reason*, as opposed to passion, there have been very subtile disputes among modern philosophers, whether it ought to be called reason, or be not rather some internal sense or taste.

Whether it ought to be called reason, or by what other name, I do not here inquire, but what kind of influence it has upon our voluntary actions.

As to this point, I think all men must allow that this is the manly part of our constitution, the other the brute part. This operates in a calm and dispassionate manner; a manner so like to judgment or reason, that even those who do not allow it to be called by that name, endeavour to account for its having always had the name; because, in the manner of its operation, it has a similitude to reason. [74]

As the similitude between this principle and reason has led mankind to give it that name, so the dissimilitude between it and passion has led them to set the two in opposition. They have considered this cool principle as having an influence upon our actions so different from passion, that what a man does coolly and deliberately, without passion, is imputed solely to the man, whether it have merit or demerit; whereas, what he does from passion is imputed in part to the passion. If the passion be conceived to be irresistible, the action is imputed solely to it, and not at all to the man. If he had power to resist, and ought to have resisted, we blame him for not doing his duty; but, in proportion to the violence of the passion, the fault is alleviated.

By this cool principle, we judge what ends are most worthy to be pursued, how far every appetite and passion may be indulged, and when it ought to be resisted.

It directs us, not only to resist the impulse of passion when it would lead us wrong, but to avoid the occasions of inflaming it; like Cyrus, who refused to see the beautiful captive princess. In this he acted the part both of a wise and a good man; firm in the love of virtue, and, at the same time, conscious of the weakness of human nature, and unwilling to put it to too severe a trial. In this case, the youth of Cyrus, the incomparable beauty of his captive, and every circumstance which tended to inflame his desire, exalts the merit of his conduct in resisting it.

It is in such actions that the superiority of human nature appears, and the specific difference between it and that of brutes. In them we may observe one passion combating another, and the strongest prevailing; but we perceive no calm principle in their constitution, that is superior to every passion, and able to give law to it. [75]

The difference between these two parts of our constitution, may be farther illustrated by an instance or two wherein passion prevails.

If a man, upon great provocation, strike another, when he ought to keep the peace, he blames himself for what he did, and acknowledges that he ought not to have yielded to his passion. Every other person agrees with his sober judgment. They think he did wrong in yielding to his passion, when he might and ought to have resisted its impulse. If they thought it impossible to bear the provocation, they would not blame him at all; but, believing that it was in his power, and was his duty, they impute to him some degree of blame, acknowledging, at the same time, that it is alleviated in proportion to the provocation; so that the trespass is imputed partly to the man and partly to the passion. But, if a man deliberately conceives a design of mischief against his neighbour, contrives the means, and executes it, the action admits of no alleviation, it is perfectly voluntary, and he bears the whole guilt of the evil intended and done.

If a man, by the agony of the rack, is made to disclose a secret of importance with which he is entrusted, we pity him more than we blame him. We consider, that such is the weakness of human nature, that the resolution, even of a good man, might be overcome by such a trial. But, if he have strength of mind, which even the agony of the rack could not subdue, we admire his fortitude as truly heroical. [76]

Thus, I think, it appears that the common sense of men (which, in matters of common life, ought to have great authority) has led them to distinguish two parts in the human constitution, which have influence upon our voluntary determinations. There is an irrational part, common to us with brute animals, consisting of appetites, affections, and passions; and there is a cool and rational part. The first, in many cases, gives a strong impulse, but without judgment and without authority. The second is always accompanied with authority. All wisdom and virtue consist in following its dictates; all vice and folly in disobeying them. We may resist the impulses of appetite and passion, not only without regret, but with self-applause and triumph; but the calls of reason and duty can never be resisted without remorse and self-condemnation.

The ancient philosophers agreed with the vulgar, in making this distinction of the principles of action. The irrational part, the Greeks called ὁρμὴ. Cicero calls it *appetitus*, taking that word in an extensive sense, so as to include every propensity to action which is not grounded on judgment.

The other principle the Greeks called νοῦς [and λόγον]; Plato calls it the ἡγεμονικόν, or leading principle. "*Duplex enim est vis animorum atque naturæ*," says Cicero, "*una pars in appetitu posita est, quæ est ὁρμὴ Græce, quæ hominem huc et illuc rapit; altera in ratione, quæ docet, et explanat, quid faciendum fugiendumve sit; ita fit, ut ratio præsit, appetitus obtemperet.*"—[De Off. L. 1. c. 28.]

The reason of explaining this distinction here is, that these two principles influence the will in different ways. Their influence differs, not in degree only, but in kind. This difference we feel, though it may be difficult to find words to express it. We may, perhaps, more easily form a notion of it by a similitude. [77]

It is one thing to push a man from one part of the room to another; it is a thing of a very different nature to use arguments to persuade him to leave his place and go to another. He may yield to the force which pushes him, without any exercise of his rational faculties; nay, he must yield to it, if he do not oppose an equal or a greater force. His liberty is impaired in some degree; and, if he has not power sufficient to oppose, his liberty is quite taken away, and the motion cannot be imputed to him at all. The influence of appetite or passion seems to me to be very like to this. If the passion be supposed irresistible, we impute the action to it solely, and not to the man. If he had power to resist, but yields after a struggle, we impute the action partly to the man, and partly to the passion.

If we attend to the other case, when the man is only urged by arguments to leave his place, this resembles the operation of the cool or rational principle. It is evident that, whether he yields to the arguments or not, the determination is wholly his own act, and is entirely to be imputed to him. Arguments, whatever be the degree of their strength, diminish not a man's liberty; they may produce a cool conviction of what we ought to do, and they can do no more. But appetite and passion give an impulse to act, and impair liberty, in proportion to their strength.

With most men, the impulse of passion is more effectual than bare conviction; and, on this account, orators, who would persuade, find it necessary to address the passions, as well as to convince the understanding; and, in all systems of rhetoric, these two have been considered as different intentions of the orator, and to be accomplished by different means. [78]

CHAPTER III.

OF OPERATIONS OF MIND WHICH MAY BE CALLED VOLUNTARY.

The faculties of *Understanding* and *Will*, are easily distinguished in thought, but very rarely, if ever, disjoined in operation.

In most, perhaps in all the operations of mind for which we have names in language, both faculties are employed, and we are both intellective and active.

Whether it be possible that intelligence may exist without some degree of activity, or impossible, is, perhaps, beyond the reach of our faculties to determine; but, I apprehend, that, in fact, they are always conjoined in the operations of our minds.

It is probable, I think, that there is some degree of activity in those operations which we refer to the understanding; accordingly, they have always, and in all languages, been expressed by active verbs; as, *I see*, *I hear*, *I remember*, *I apprehend*, *I judge*, *I reason*. And it is certain that every act of will must be accompanied by some operation of the understanding; for he that wills must apprehend what he wills, and apprehension belongs to the understanding.

The operations I am to consider in this chapter, I think, have commonly been referred to the understanding; but we shall find that the will has so great a share in them, that they may, with propriety, be called *voluntary*. They are these three, *Attention*, *Deliberation*, and *Fixed Purpose*, or *Resolution*. [79]

1. *Attention* may be given to any object, either of sense or of intellect, in order to form a distinct notion of it, or to discover its nature, its attributes, or its relations. And so great is the effect of attention, that, without it, it is impossible to acquire or retain a distinct notion of any object of thought.

If a man hear a discourse without attention, what does he carry away with him? If he see St Peter's or the Vatican without attention, what account can he give of it? While two persons are engaged in interesting discourse, the clock strikes within their hearing, to which they give no attention—what is the consequence? The next minute they know not whether the clock struck or not. Yet their ears were not shut. The usual impression was made upon the organ of hearing, and upon the auditory nerve and brain; but from inattention the sound either was not perceived, or passed in the twinkling of an eye, without leaving the least vestige in the memory.

A man sees not what is before his eyes when his mind is occupied about another object. In the tumult of a battle a man may be shot through the body without knowing anything of the matter, till he discover it by the loss of blood or of strength.

The most acute sensation of pain may be deadened, if the attention can be vigorously directed to another object. A gentleman of my acquaintance, in the agony of a fit of the gout, used to call for the chess-board.

As he was fond of that game, he acknowledged that, as the game advanced and drew his attention, the sense of pain abated, and the time seemed much shorter.

Archimedes, it is said, being intent upon a mathematical proposition, when Syracuse was taken by the Romans, knew not the calamity of the city, till a Roman soldier broke in upon his retirement, and gave him a deadly wound; on which he lamented only that he had lost a fine demonstration. [80]

It is needless to multiply instances to shew, that when one faculty of the mind is intensely engaged about any object, the other faculties are laid, as it were, fast asleep.

It may be farther observed, that, if there be anything that can be called *genius* in matters of mere judgment and reasoning, it seems to consist chiefly in being able to give that attention to the subject which keeps it steady in the mind, till we can survey it accurately on all sides.

There is a talent of imagination, which bounds from earth to heaven, and from heaven to earth in a moment. This may be favourable to wit and imagery; but the powers of judging and reasoning depend chiefly upon keeping the mind to a clear and steady view of the subject.

Sir Isaac Newton, to one who complimented him upon the force of genius which had made such improvements in mathematics and natural philosophy, is said to have made this reply, which was both modest and judicious, That if he had made any improvements in those sciences, it was owing more to patient attention than to any other talent.

Whatever be the effects which attention may produce, (and I apprehend they are far beyond what is commonly believed,) it is for the most part in our power.

Every man knows that he can turn his attention to this subject or to that, for a longer or a shorter time, and with more or less intenseness, as he pleases. It is a voluntary act, and depends upon his will. [81]

But what was before observed of the will in general, is applicable to this particular exertion of it, That the mind is rarely in a state of indifference, left to turn its attention to the object which to reason appears most deserving of it. There is, for the most part, a bias to some particular object, more than to any other; and this not from any judgment of its deserving our attention more, but from some impulse or propensity, grounded on nature or habit.

It is well known that things new and uncommon, things grand, and things that are beautiful, draw our attention, not in proportion to the interest we have, or think we have in them, but in a much greater proportion.

Whatever moves our passions or affections, draws our attention, very often, more than we wish.

You desire a man not to think of an unfortunate event which torments him. It admits of no remedy. The thought of it answers no purpose but to keep the wound bleeding. He is perfectly convinced of all you say. He knows that he would not feel the affliction, if he could only not think of it; yet he hardly thinks of anything else. Strange! when happiness and misery stand before him, and depend upon his choice, he chooses misery, and rejects happiness with his eyes open!

Yet he wishes to be happy, as all men do. How shall we reconcile this contradiction between his judgment and his conduct?

The account of it seems to me to be this: The afflicting event draws his attention so strongly, by a natural and blind force, that he either hath not the power, or hath not the vigour of mind to resist its impulse, though he knows that to yield to it is misery, without any good to balance it. [82]

Acute bodily pain draws our attention, and makes it very difficult to attend to any thing else, even when attention to the pain serves no other purpose but to aggravate it tenfold

The man who played a game at chess in the agony of the gout, to engage his attention to another object, acted the reasonable part, and consulted his real happiness; but it required a great effort to give that attention to his game which was necessary to produce the effect intended by it.

Even when there is no particular object that draws away our attention, there is a desultoriness of thought in man, and in some more than in others, which makes it very difficult to give that fixed attention to important objects which reason requires.

It appears, I think, from what has been said, that the attention we give to objects is for the most part voluntary; that a great part of wisdom and virtue consists in giving a proper direction to our attention; and that, however reasonable this appears to the judgment of every man, yet, in some cases, it requires an effort of self-command no less than the most heroic virtues.

2. Another operation that may be called *voluntary*, is *Deliberation* about what we are to do or to forbear.

Every man knows that it is in his power to deliberate or not to deliberate about any part of his conduct; to deliberate for a shorter or a longer time, more carelessly or more seriously; and, when he has reason to suspect that his affection may bias his judgment, he may either honestly use the best means in his power to form an impartial judgment, or he may yield to his bias, and only seek arguments to justify what inclination leads him to do. In all these points, he determines, he wills the right or the wrong. [83]

The general rules of deliberation are perfectly evident to reason, when we consider them abstractly. They are axioms in morals.

We ought not to deliberate in cases that are perfectly clear. No man deliberates whether he ought to choose happiness or misery. No honest man deliberates whether he shall steal his neighbour's property. When the case is not clear, when it is of importance, and when there is time for deliberation, we ought to deliberate with more or less care, in proportion to the importance of the action. In deliberation we ought to weigh things in an even balance, and to allow to every consideration the weight which, in sober judgment, we think it ought to have, and no more. This is to deliberate impartially. Our deliberation should be brought to an issue in due time, so that we may not lose the opportunity of acting while we deliberate.

The axioms of Euclid do not appear to me to have a greater degree of self-evidence than these rules of deliberation. And as far as a man acts according to them, his heart approves of him, and he has confidence of the approbation of the Searcher of Hearts.

But though the manner in which we ought to deliberate be evident to reason, it is not always easy to follow it. Our appetites, our affection and passions, oppose all deliberation, but that which is employed in finding the means of their gratification. Avarice may lead to deliberate upon the ways of making money, but it does not distinguish between the honest and the dishonest.

We ought surely to deliberate how far every appetite and passion may be indulged, and what limits should be set to it. But our appetites and passions push us on to the attainment of their objects, in the shortest road, and without delay. [84]

Thus it happens, that, if we yield to their impulse, we shall often transgress those rules of deliberation which reason approves. In this conflict between the dictates of reason, and the blind impulse of passion, we must voluntarily determine. When we take part with our reason, though in opposition to passion, we approve of our own conduct.

What we call a fault of ignorance, is always owing to the want of due deliberation. When we do not take due pains to be rightly informed, there is a fault, not indeed in acting according to the light we have, but in not using the proper means to get light. For if we judge wrong, after using the proper means of information, there is no fault in acting according to that wrong judgment; the error is invincible.

The natural consequence of deliberation on any part of our conduct, is a determination how we shall act; and if it is not brought to this issue it is lost labour.

There are two cases in which a determination may take place—when the opportunity of putting it in execution is present, and when it is at a distance.

When the opportunity is present, the determination to act is immediately followed by the action. Thus, if a man determine to rise and walk, he immediately does it, unless he is hindered by force, or has lost the power of walking. And if he sit still when he has power to walk, we conclude infallibly that he has not determined or willed to walk immediately.

Our determination or will to act, is not always the result of deliberation, it may be the effect of some passion or appetite, without any judgment interposed. And when judgment is interposed, we may determine and act either according to that judgment or contrary to it. [85]

When a man sits down hungry to dine, he eats from appetite, very often without exercising his judgment at all; nature invites, and he obeys the call, as the ox, or the horse, or as an infant does.

When we converse with persons whom we love or respect, we say and do civil things merely from affection or from respect. They flow spontaneously from the heart, without requiring any judgment. In such cases we act as brute-animals do, or as children before the use of reason. We feel an impulse in our nature, and we yield to it.

When a man eats merely from appetite, he does not consider the pleasure of eating, or its tendency to health. These considerations are not in his thoughts. But we can suppose a man who eats with a view to enjoy the pleasure of eating. Such a man reasons and judges. He will take care to use the proper means of procuring an appetite. He will be a critic in tastes, and make nice discriminations. This man uses his rational faculties even in eating. And however contemptible this application of them may be, it is an exercise of which, I apprehend, brute-animals are not capable.

In like manner, a man may say or do civil things to another, not from affection, but in order to serve some end by it, or because he thinks it his duty.

To act with a view to some distant interest, or to act from a sense of duty, seems to be proper to man as a reasonable being; but to act merely from passion, from appetite, or from affection, is common to him with the brute-animals. In the last case there is no judgment required, but in the first there is. [86]

To act against what one judges to be for his real good, upon the whole, is folly. To act against what he judges to be his duty, is immorality. It cannot be denied that there are too many instances of both in human life. *Video meliora proboque, deteriora sequor*, is neither an impossible nor an unfrequent case.

While a man does what he really thinks wisest and best to be done, the more his appetites, his affections, and passions draw him the contrary way, the more he approves of his own conduct, and the more he is entitled to the approbation of every rational being.

3. The *third* operation of mind I mentioned, which may be called voluntary, is, a *Fixed Purpose* or *Resolution* with regard to our future conduct.

This naturally takes place, when any action, or course of action, about which we have deliberated, is not immediately to be executed, the occasion of acting being at some distance.

A fixed purpose to do, some time hence, something which we believe shall then be in our power, is strictly and properly a determination of will, no less than a determination to do it instantly. Every definition of volition agrees to it. Whether the opportunity of doing what we have determined to do be present or at some distance, is an accidental circumstance which does not affect the nature of the determination, and no good reason can be assigned why it should not be called *volition* in the one case, as well as in the other. A purpose or resolution, therefore, is truly and properly an act of will.

Our purposes are of two kinds. We may call the one *particular*, the other *general*. By a *particular* purpose, I mean that which has for its object an individual action, limited to one time and place; by a *general* purpose, that of a course or train of action, intended for some general end, or regulated by some general rule. [87]

Thus, I may purpose to go to London next winter. When the time comes, I execute my purpose, if I continue of the same mind; and the purpose, when executed, is

[85-87]

no more. Thus it is with every particular purpose.

A general purpose may continue for life; and, after many particular actions have been done in consequence of it, may remain and regulate future actions.

Thus, a young man proposes to follow the profession of law, of medicine, or of theology. This general purpose directs the course of his reading and study. It directs him in the choice of his company and companions, and even of his diversions. It determines his travels and the place of his abode. It has influence upon his dress and manners, and a considerable effect in forming his character.

There are other fixed purposes which have a still greater effect in forming the character. I mean such as regard our moral conduct.

Suppose a man to have exercised his intellectual and moral faculties, so far as to have distinct notions of justice and injustice, and of the consequences of both, and, after due deliberation, to have formed a fixed purpose to adhere inflexibly to justice, and never to handle the wages of iniquity.

Is not this the man whom we should call a just man? We consider the moral virtues as inherent in the mind of a good man, even when there is no opportunity of exercising them. And what is it in the mind which we can call the virtue of justice, when it is not exercised? It can be nothing but a fixed purpose, or determination, to act according to the rules of justice, when there is opportunity. [88]

The Roman law defined justice, *A steady and perpetual will to give to every man his due.* When the opportunity of doing justice is not present, this can mean nothing else than a steady purpose, which is very properly called will. Such a purpose, if it is steady, will infallibly produce just conduct; for every known transgression of justice demonstrates a change of purpose, at least for that time.

What has been said of justice, may be so easily applied to every other moral virtue, that it is unnecessary to give instances. They are all fixed purposes of acting according to a certain rule.*

By this, the virtues may be easily distinguished, in thought at least, from natural affections that bear the same name. Thus, benevolence is a capital virtue, which, though not so necessary to the being of society, is entitled to a higher degree of approbation than even justice. But there is a natural affection of benevolence, common to good and bad men, to the virtuous and to the vicious. How shall these be distinguished?

In practice, indeed, we cannot distinguish them in other men, and with difficulty in ourselves; but, in theory, nothing is more easy. The virtue of benevolence is a fixed purpose or resolution to do good when we have opportunity, from a conviction that it is right, and is our duty. The affection of benevolence is a propensity to do good, from natural constitution or habit, without regard to rectitude or duty.

There are good tempers and bad, which are a part of the constitution of the man, and are really involuntary, though they often lead to voluntary actions. A good natural temper is not virtue, nor is a bad one vice. Hard would it be indeed to think, that a man should be born under a decree of reprobation, because he has the misfortune of a bad natural temper. [89]

The physiognomist saw, in the features of Socrates, the signatures of many bad dispositions, which that good man acknowledged he felt within him; but the triumph of his virtue was the greater in having conquered them.

In men who have no fixed rules of conduct, no self-government, the natural temper is variable by numberless accidents. The man who is full of affection and benevolence this hour, when a cross accident happens to ruffle him, or perhaps when an easterly wind blows, feels a strange revolution in his temper. The kind and benevolent affections give place to the jealous and malignant, which are as readily indulged in their turn, and for the same reason, because he feels a propensity to indulge them.

We may observe, that men who have exercised their rational powers, are generally governed in their opinions by fixed principles of belief; and men who have made the greatest advance in self-government, are governed, in their practice, by general fixed purposes. Without the former, there would be no steadiness and consistence in our belief; nor without the latter, in our conduct.

When a man is come to years of understanding, from his education, from his company, or from his study, he forms to himself a set of general principles, a creed, which

* Mr Stewart, ("Philosophy of the Active and Moral Powers," ii. p. 446,) in adopting this doctrine says—"Agreeably to this view of the subject, the ancient Pythagoreans defined virtue to be Ἕξις τοῦ δέοντος, the oldest definition of virtue of which we have any account, and one of the most unexceptionable which is yet to be found in any system of philosophy." The definition to which Mr Stewart refers—ἁ ἀρετὰ ἕξις τίς ἐστι τῶ δέοντος—is that under the name of Theages. The treatise attributed to this philosopher is, however, like the other Pythagorean treatises, spurious. The definition in question, with the whole moral system of its pretended author, is an elegant epitome of Aristotle, who, on the faith of these forgeries, has been commonly viewed as himself the plagiarist. Ethics, I may observe, are thus well denominated *Deontology*.—H.

governs his judgment in particular points that occur.

If new evidence is laid before him which tends to overthrow any of his received principles, it requires in him a great degree of candour and love of truth, to give it an impartial examination, and to form a new judgment. Most men, when they are fixed in their principles, upon what they account sufficient evidence, can hardly be drawn into a new and serious examination of them. [90]

They get a habit of believing them, which is strengthened by repeated acts, and remains immoveable, even when the evidence upon which their belief was at first grounded, is forgot.

It is this that makes conversions, either from religious or political principles, so difficult.

A mere prejudice of education sticks fast, as a proposition of Euclid does with a man who hath long ago forgot the proof. Both indeed are upon a similar footing. We rest in both, because we have long done so, and think we received them at first upon good evidence, though that evidence be quite forgot.

When we know a man's principles, we judge by them, rather than by the degree of his understanding, how he will determine in any point which is connected with them.

Thus, the judgment of most men who judge for themselves is governed by fixed principles; and I apprehend that the conduct of most men who have any self-government, and any consistency of conduct, is governed by fixed purposes.

A man of breeding may, in his natural temper, be proud, passionate, revengeful, and in his morals a very bad man; yet, in good company, he can stifle every passion that is inconsistent with good breeding, and be humane, modest, complaisant, even to those whom in his heart he despises or hates. Why is this man, who can command all his passions before company, a slave to them in private? The reason is plain: He has a fixed resolution to be a man of breeding, but hath no such resolution to be a man of virtue. He hath combated his most violent passions a thousand times before he became master of them in company. The same resolution and perseverance would have given him the command of them when alone. [91]

A fixed resolution retains its influence upon the conduct, even when the motives to it are not in view, in the same manner as a fixed principle retains its influence upon the belief, when the evidence of it is forgot. The former may be called a habit of the *will*, the latter a habit of the *understanding*. By such habits chiefly, men are governed in their opinions and in their practice.

A man who has no general fixed purposes, may be said, as Pope says of most women, (I hope unjustly,) to have no character at all. He will be honest or dishonest, benevolent or malicious, compassionate or cruel, as the tide of his passions and affections drives him. This, however, I believe, is the case of but a few in advanced life, and these, with regard to conduct, the weakest and most contemptible of the species.

A man of some constancy may change his general purposes once or twice in life, seldom more. From the pursuit of pleasure in early life, he may change to that of ambition, and from ambition to avarice. But every man who uses his reason in the conduct of life, will have some end, to which he gives a preference above all others. To this he steers his course; his projects and his actions will be regulated by it. Without this, there would be no consistency in his conduct. He would be like a ship in the ocean, which is bound to no port, under no government, but left to the mercy of winds and tides.

We observed before, that there are moral rules respecting the attention we ought to give to objects, and respecting our deliberations, which are no less evident than mathematical axioms. The same thing may be observed with respect to our fixed purposes, whether particular or general. [92]

Is it not self-evident, that, after due deliberation, we ought to resolve upon that conduct, or that course of conduct, which, to our sober judgment, appears to be best and most approvable?—that we ought to be firm and steady in adhering to such resolutions, while we are persuaded that they are right; but open to conviction, and ready to change our course, when we have good evidence that it is wrong?

Fickleness, inconstancy, facility, on the one hand, wilfulness, inflexibility, and obstinacy, on the other, are moral qualities, respecting our purposes, which every one sees to be wrong. A manly firmness, grounded upon rational conviction, is the proper mean which every man approves and reveres.

CHAPTER IV.

COROLLARIES.

From what has been said concerning the will, it appears—

First, That as some acts of the will are transient and momentary, so others are permanent, and may continue for a long time, or even through the whole course of our rational life.

When I will to stretch out my hand, that will is at an end as soon as the action is done. It is an act of the will which begins and ends in a moment. But when I will to attend to a mathematical proposition, to examine the demonstration, and the consequences that may be drawn from it, this will may continue for hours. It must continue as long as my attention continues; for no man attends to a mathematical proposition longer than he wills.

The same thing may be said of deliberation, with regard, either to any point of conduct, or with regard to any general course of conduct. We will to deliberate as long as we do deliberate; and that may be for days or for weeks. [93]

A purpose or resolution, which we have shewn to be an act of the will, may continue for a great part of life, or for the whole, after we are of age to form a resolution.

Thus, a merchant may resolve, that, after he has made such a fortune by traffic, he will give it up, and retire to a country life. He may continue this resolution for thirty or forty years, and execute it at last; but he continues it no longer than he wills, for he may at any time change his resolution.

There are therefore acts of the will which are not transient and momentary, which may continue long, and grow into a habit. This deserves the more to be observed, because a very eminent philosopher has advanced a contrary principle—to wit, That all the acts of the will are transient and momentary; and from that principle has drawn very important conclusions, with regard to what constitutes the moral character of man.

A *second* corollary is—That nothing in a man, wherein the will is not concerned, can justly be accounted either virtuous or immoral.

That no blame can be imputed to a man for what is altogether involuntary, is so evident in itself, that no arguments can make it more evident. The practice of all criminal courts, in all enlightened nations, is founded upon it.

If it should be thought an objection to this maxim, that, by the laws of all nations, children often suffer for the crimes of parents, in which they had no hand, the answer is easy. [94]

For, *first*, Such is the connection between parents and children, that the punishment of a parent must hurt his children whether the law will or not. If a man is fined, or imprisoned—if he loses life, or limb, or estate, or reputation, by the hand of justice—his children suffer by necessary consequence.

Secondly, When laws intend to appoint any punishment of innocent children for the father's crime, such laws are either unjust, or they are to be considered as acts of police, and not of jurisprudence, and are intended as an expedient to deter parents more effectually from the commission of the crime. The innocent children, in this case, are sacrificed to the public good, in like manner as, to prevent the spreading of the plague, the sound are shut up with the infected in a house or ship that has the infection.

By the law of England, if a man is killed by an ox goring him, or a cart running over him, though there be no fault or neglect in the owner, the ox or the cart is a *deodand*, and is confiscated to the church. The legislature surely did not intend to punish the ox as a criminal, far less the cart. The intention evidently was, to inspire the people with a sacred regard to the life of man.

When the Parliament of Paris, with a similar intention, ordained the house in which Ravilliac was born, to be razed to the ground, and never to be rebuilt, it would be great weakness to conclude, that the wise judicature intended to punish the house.

If any judicature should, in any instance, find a man guilty, and an object of punishment, for what they allowed to be altogether involuntary, all the world would condemn them as men who knew nothing of the first and most fundamental rules of justice. [95]

I have endeavoured to shew, that, in our attention to objects, in order to form a right judgment of them; in our deliberation about particular actions, or about general rules of conduct; in our purposes and resolutions, as well as in the execution of them, the will has a principal share. If any man could be found, who, in the whole course of his life, had given due attention to things that concern him, had deliberated duly and impartially about his conduct, had formed his resolutions, and executed them according to his best judgment and capacity, surely such a man might hold up his face before God and man, and plead innocence. He must be acquitted by the impartial Judge, whatever his natural temper was, whatever his passions and affections, as far as they were involuntary.

A *third* corollary is, That all virtuous habits, when we distinguish them from virtuous actions, consist in fixed purposes of acting according to the rules of virtue, as often as we have opportunity.

We can conceive in a man a greater or a less degree of steadiness to his purposes or resolutions; but that the general tenor of his conduct should be contrary to them, is impossible.

The man who has a determined resolution to do his duty in every instance, and who adheres steadily to his resolution, is a perfect man. The man who has a determined purpose of carrying on a course of action which he knows to be wrong, is a hardened offender. Between these extremes there are many intermediate degrees of virtue and vice. [96]

ESSAY III.

OF THE PRINCIPLES OF ACTION.

PART I.

OF THE MECHANICAL PRINCIPLES OF ACTION.

CHAPTER I.

OF THE PRINCIPLES OF ACTION IN GENERAL.

In the strict philosophical sense, nothing can be called the action of a man, but what he previously conceived and willed or determined to do. In morals we commonly employ the word in this sense, and never impute anything to a man as his doing, in which his will was not interposed. But when moral imputation is not concerned, we call many things actions of the man, which he neither previously conceived nor willed. Hence the actions of men have been distinguished into three classes—the *voluntary*, the *involuntary*, and the *mixed*. By the last are meant such actions as are under the command of the will, but are commonly performed without any interposition of will.

We cannot avoid using the word *action* in this popular sense, without deviating too much from the common use of language; and it is in this sense we use it when we inquire into the principles* of action in the human mind.

By *principles** of action, I understand everything that incites us to act. [98]

If there were no incitements to action, active power would be given us in vain. Having no motive to direct our active exertions, the mind would, in all cases, be in a state of perfect indifference, to do this or that, or nothing at all. The active power would either not be exerted at all, or its exertions would be perfectly unmeaning and frivolous, neither wise nor foolish, neither good nor bad. To every action that is of the smallest importance, there must be some incitement, some motive, some reason.

It is therefore a most important part of the philosophy of the human mind, to have a distinct and just view of the various principles of action, which the Author of our being hath planted in our nature, to arrange them properly, and to assign to every one its rank.

By this it is, that we may discover the end of our being, and the part which is assigned us upon the theatre of life. In this part of the human constitution, the noblest work of God that falls within our notice, we may discern most clearly the character of Him who made us, and how he would have us to employ that active power which he hath given us.

I cannot, without great diffidence, enter upon this subject, observing that almost every author of reputation, who has given attention to it, has a system of his own; and that no man has been so happy as to give general satisfaction to those who came after him.

There is a branch of knowledge much valued, and very justly, which we call knowledge of the world, knowledge of mankind, knowledge of human nature. This, I think, consists in knowing from what principles men generally act; and it is commonly the fruit of natural sagacity joined with experience. [99]

A man of sagacity, who has had occasion to deal in interesting matters, with a great variety of persons of different age, sex, rank, and profession, learns to judge what may be expected from men in given circumstances; and how they may be most effectually induced to act the part which he desires. To know this is of so great importance to men in active life, that it is called knowing men, and knowing human nature.

This knowledge may be of considerable use to a man who would speculate upon the subject we have proposed, but is not, by itself, sufficient for that purpose.

The man of the world conjectures, perhaps with great probability, how a man will act in certain given circumstances; and this is all he wants to know. To enter into a detail of the various principles which influence the actions of men, to give them

* It would have been better to have here substituted another word (as Cause) for the ambiguous term *principle*.—H.

distinct names, to define them, and to ascertain their different provinces, is the business of a philosopher, and not of a man of the world; and, indeed, it is a matter attended with great difficulty from various causes.

First. On account of the great number of active principles that influence the actions of men.

Man has, not without reason, been called an epitome of the universe. His body, by which his mind is greatly affected, being a part of the material system, is subject to all the laws of inanimate matter. During some part of his existence, his state is very like that of a vegetable. He rises, by imperceptible degrees, to the animal, and, at last, to the rational life, and has the principles that belong to all.

Another cause of the difficulty of tracing the various principles of action in man, is, That the same action, nay, the same course and train of action may proceed from very different principles. [100]

Men who are fond of a hypothesis, commonly seek no other proof of its truth, but that it serves to account for the appearances which it is brought to explain. This is a very slippery kind of proof in every part of philosophy, and never to be trusted; but, least of all, when the appearances to be accounted for are human actions.

Most actions proceed from a variety of principles concurring in their direction; and according as we are disposed to judge favourably or unfavourably of the person, or of human nature in general, we impute them wholly to the best, or wholly to the worst, overlooking others which had no small share in them.

The principles from which men act can be discovered only in these two ways—by attention to the conduct of other men, or by attention to our own conduct, and to what we feel in ourselves. There is much uncertainty in the former, and much difficulty in the latter.

Men differ much in their characters; and we can observe the conduct of a few only of the species. Men differ not only from other men, but from themselves at different times, and on different occasions; according as they are in the company of their superiors, inferiors, or equals; according as they are in the eye of strangers, or of their familiars only, or in the view of no human eye; according as they are in good or bad fortune, or in good or bad humour. We see but a small part of the actions of our most familiar acquaintance; and what we see may lead us to a probable conjecture, but can give no certain knowledge of the principles from which they act.

A man may, no doubt, know with certainty the principles from which he himself acts, because he is conscious of them. But this knowledge requires an attentive reflection upon the operations of his own mind, which is very rarely to be found. It is perhaps more easy to find a man who has formed a just notion of the character of man in general, or of those of his familiar acquaintance, than one who has a just notion of his own character. [101]

Most men, through pride and self-flattery, are apt to think themselves better than they really are; and some, perhaps from melancholy, or from false principles of religion, are led to think themselves worse than they really are.

It requires, therefore, a very accurate and impartial examination of a man's own heart, to be able to form a distinct notion of the various principles which influence his conduct. That this is a matter of great difficulty, we may judge from the very different and contradictory systems of philosophers upon this subject, from the earliest ages to this day.

During the age of Greek philosophy, the Platonist, the Peripatetic, the Stoic, the Epicurean, had each his own system. In the dark ages, the Schoolmen and the Mystics had systems diametrically opposite; and, since the revival of learning, no controversy hath been more keenly agitated, especially among British philosophers, than that about the principles of action in the human constitution.

They have determined, to the satisfaction of the learned, the forces by which the planets and comets traverse the boundless regions of space; but have not been able to determine, with any degree of unanimity, the forces which every man is conscious of in himself, and by which his conduct is directed.

Some admit no principle but self-love; others resolve all into love of the pleasures of sense, variously modified by the association of ideas; others admit disinterested benevolence along with self-love; others reduce all to reason and passion; others to passion alone; nor is there less variety about the number and distribution of the passions. [102]

The names we give to the various principles of action, have so little precision, even in the best and purest writers in every language, that, on this account, there is no small difficulty in giving them names, and arranging them properly.

The words *appetite*, *passion*, *affection*, *interest*, *reason*, cannot be said to have one definite signification. They are taken sometimes in a larger, and sometimes in a more limited sense. The same principle is sometimes called by one of those names, sometimes by another; and principles of a very different nature are often called by the same name.

To remedy this confusion of names, it might, perhaps, seem proper to invent new ones. But there are so few entitled to this privilege, that I shall not lay claim to it; but shall endeavour to class the various principles of human action as distinctly as I am able, and to point out their specific differences; giving them such names as may deviate from the common use of the words as little as possible.

There are some principles of action which require no attention, no deliberation, no will. These, for distinction's sake, we shall call *mechanical*. Another class we may call *animal*, as they seem common to man with other animals. A third class we may call *rational*, being proper to man as a rational creature.* [103]

CHAPTER I

INSTINCT.

THE *mechanical* principles of action may, I think, be reduced to two species—*instincts* and *habits*.

By Instinct, I mean a natural blind impulse to certain actions, without having any end in view, without deliberation, and very often without any conception of what we do.

Thus, a man breathes while he is alive, by the alternate contraction and relaxation of certain muscles, by which the chest, and of consequence the lungs, are contracted and dilated. There is no reason to think that an infant new-born knows that breathing is necessary to life in its new state, that he knows how it must be performed, or even that he has any thought or conception of that operation; yet he breathes, as soon as he is born, with perfect regularity, as if he had been taught, and got the habit by long practice.

By the same kind of principle, a new-born child, when its stomach is emptied, and nature has brought milk into the mother's breast, sucks and swallows its food as perfectly as if it knew the principles of that operation, and had got the habit of working according to them.

Sucking and swallowing are very complex operations. Anatomists describe about thirty pairs of muscles that must be employed in every draught. Of those muscles, every one must be served by its proper nerve, and can make no exertion but by some influence communicated by the nerve. The exertion of all those muscles and nerves is not simultaneous. They must succeed each other in a certain order, and their order is no less necessary than the exertion itself. [104]

This regular train of operations is carried on according to the nicest rules of art, by the infant, who has neither art, nor science, nor experience, nor habit.

That the infant feels the uneasy sensation of hunger, I admit; and that it sucks no longer than till this sensation be removed. But who informed it that this uneasy sensation might be removed, or by what means? That it knows nothing of this is evident; for it will as readily suck a finger, or a bit of stick, as the nipple.

By a like principle it is, that infants cry when they are pained or hurt; that they are afraid when left alone, especially in the dark; that they start when in danger of falling; that they are terrified by an angry countenance, or an angry tone of voice, and are soothed and comforted by a placid countenance, and by soft and gentle tones of voice.

In the animals we are best acquainted with, and which we look upon as the more perfect of the brute creation, we see much the same instincts as in the human kind, or very similar ones, suited to the particular state and manner of life of the animal.

Besides these, there are in brute animals instincts peculiar to each tribe, by which they are fitted for defence, for offence, or for providing for themselves, and for their offspring.

It is not more certain that nature hath furnished various animals with various weapons of offence and defence, than that the same nature hath taught them how to use them: the bull and the ram to butt, the horse to kick, the dog to bite, the lion to use his paws, the boar his tusks, the serpent his fangs, and the bee and wasp their sting. [105]

The manufactures of animals, if we may call them by that name, present us with a wonderful variety of instincts, belonging to particular species, whether of the social or of the solitary kind; the nests of birds, so similar in their situation and architecture in the same kind, so various in different kinds; the webs of spiders, and of other spinning animals; the ball of the silkworm; the nests of ants and other mining animals; the combs of wasps, hornets, and bees; the dams and houses of beavers.

The instinct of animals is one of the most delightful and instructive parts of a most pleasant study, that of natural history; and deserves to be more cultivated than it has yet been.

Every manufacturing art among men was invented by some man, improved by others, and brought to perfection by time and experience. Men learn to work in it by long practice, which produces a habit.

* On this classification of Reid, see Mr Stewart's strictures, in his "Philosophy of the Active Powers," i. pp. 14, 16. The division I would prefer, is different from that of either philosopher.—H.

The arts of men vary in every age and in every nation, and are found only in those who have been taught them.

The manufactures of animals differ from those of men in many striking particulars.

No animal of the species can claim the invention. No animal ever introduced any new improvement, or any variation from the former practice. Every one of the species has equal skill from the beginning, without teaching, without experience or habit. Every one has its art by a kind of inspiration. I do not mean that it is inspired with the principles or rules of the art, but with the ability and inclination of working in it to perfection, without any knowledge of its principles, rules, or end. [106]

The more sagacious animals may be taught to do many things which they do not by instinct. What they are taught to do, they do with more or less skill, according to their sagacity and their training. But, in their own arts, they need no teaching nor training, nor is the art ever improved or lost. Bees gather their honey and their wax, they fabricate their combs, and rear their young at this day, neither better nor worse than they did when Virgil so sweetly sung their works.

The work of every animal is indeed like the works of nature, perfect in its kind, and can bear the most critical examination of the mechanic or the mathematician. One example from the animal last mentioned, may serve to illustrate this.

Bees, it is well known, construct their combs with small cells on both sides, fit both for holding their store of honey, and for rearing their young. There are only three possible figures of the cells, which can make them all equal and similar, without any useless interstices. These are the equilateral triangle, the square, and the regular hexagon.

It is well known to mathematicians, that there is not a fourth way possible, in which a plane may be cut into little spaces that shall be equal, similar and regular, without leaving any interstices. Of the three, the hexagon is the most proper, both for conveniency and strength. Bees, as if they knew this, make their cells regular hexagons.

As the combs have cells on both sides, the cells may either be exactly opposite, having partition against partition, or the bottom of a cell may rest upon the partitions between the cells on the other side, which will serve as a buttress to strengthen it. The last way is best for strength; accordingly, the bottom of each cell rests against the point where three partitions meet on the other side, which gives it all the strength possible. [107]

The bottom of a cell may either be one plane perpendicular to the side-partitions, or it may be composed of several planes, meeting in a solid angle in the middle point. It is only in one of these two ways, that all the cells can be similar without losing room. And, for the same intention, the planes of which the bottom is composed, if there be more than one, must be three in number, and neither more nor fewer.

It has been demonstrated, that, by making the bottoms of the cells to consist of three planes meeting in a point, there is a saving of material and labour no way inconsiderable. The bees, as if acquainted with these principles of solid geometry, follow them most accurately; the bottom of each cell being composed of three planes, which make obtuse angles with the side-partitions, and with one another, and meet in a point in the middle of the bottom; the three angles of this bottom being supported by three partitions on the other side of the comb, and the point of it by the common intersection of those three partitions.

One instance more of the mathematical skill displayed in the structure of a honey-comb, deserves to be mentioned.

It is a curious mathematical problem, at what precise angle the three planes which compose the bottom of a cell ought to meet, in order to make the greatest possible saving, or the least expense, of material and labour.

This is one of those problems, belonging to the higher parts of mathematics, which are called problems of *maxima* and *minima*. It has been resolved by some mathematicians, particularly by the ingenious Mr Maclaurin, by a fluxionary calculation, which is to be found in the "Transactions of the Royal Society of London." He has determined precisely the angle required; and he found, by the most exact mensuration the subject could admit, that it is the very angle, in which the three planes in the bottom of the cell of a honey-comb do actually meet. [108]

Shall we ask here, who taught the bee the properties of solids, and to resolve problems of *maxima* and *minima*? If a honey-comb were a work of human art, every man of common sense would conclude, without hesitation, that he who invented the construction must have understood the principles on which it is constructed.

We need not say that bees know none of these things. They work most geometrically, without any knowledge of geometry; somewhat like a child, who, by turning the handle of an organ, makes good music, without any knowledge of music.

The art is not in the child, but in him who made the organ. In like manner, when a bee makes its comb so geometrically, the geometry is not in the bee, but in that great Geometrician who made the bee, and made all things in number, weight, and measure.*

To return to instincts in man; those are most remarkable which appear in infancy, when we are ignorant of everything necessary to our preservation, and therefore must perish, if we had not an invisible guide, who leads us blindfold in the way we should take, if we had eyes to see it.

Besides the instincts which appear only in infancy, and are intended to supply the want of understanding in that early period, there are many which continue through life, and which supply the defects of our intellectual powers in every period. Of these we may observe three classes.

First, There are many things necessary to be done for our preservation, which, even when we will to do, we know not the means by which they must be done. [109]

A man knows that he must swallow his food before it can nourish him. But this action requires the co-operation of many nerves and muscles, of which he knows nothing; and if it were to be directed solely by his understanding and will, he would starve before he learned how to perform it.

Here instinct comes in to his aid. He needs do no more than will to swallow. All the requisite motions of nerves and muscles immediately take place in their proper order, without his knowing or willing anything about them.

If we ask here, whose will do these nerves and muscles obey? Not his, surely, to whom they belong. He knows neither their names, nor nature, nor office; he never thought of them. They are moved by some impulse, of which the cause is unknown, without any thought, will, or intention on his part—that is, they are moved instinctively.

This is the case, in some degree, in every voluntary motion of our body. Thus, I will to stretch out my arm. The effect immediately follows. But we know that the arm is stretched out by the contraction of certain muscles; and that the muscles are contracted by the influence of the nerves. I know nothing, I think nothing, either of nerves or muscles, when I stretch out my arm: yet this nervous influence, and this contraction of the muscles, uncalled by me, immediately produce the effect which I willed. This is as if a weight were to be raised, which can be raised only by a complication of levers, pullies, and other mechanical powers, that are behind the curtain, and altogether unknown to me. I will to raise the weight; and no sooner is this volition exerted, than the machinery behind the curtain falls to work and raises the weight. [110]

If such a case should happen, we would conclude that there is some person behind the curtain who knew my will, and put the machine in motion to execute it.

The case of my willing to stretch out my arm, or to swallow my food, has evidently a great similarity to this. But who it is that stands behind the curtain, and sets the internal machinery a-going, is hid from us; so strangely and wonderfully are we made. This, however, is evident, that those internal motions are not willed nor intended by us, and therefore are instinctive.

A *second* case in which we have need of instinct, even in advanced life, is, When the action must be so frequently repeated, that to intend and will it every time it is done, would occupy too much of our thought, and leave no room for other necessary employments of the mind.

We must breathe often every minute whether awake or asleep. We must often close the eye-lids, in order to preserve the lustre of the eye. If these things required particular attention and volition every time they are done, they would occupy all our thought. Nature, therefore, gives an impulse to do them as often as is necessary, without any thought at all. They consume no time, they give not the least interruption to any exercise of the mind; because they are done by instinct.

A *third case*, in which we need the aid of instinct, is, When the action must be done so suddenly that there is no time to think and determine. When a man loses his balance, either on foot or on horseback, he makes an instantaneous effort to recover it by instinct. The effort would be in vain, if it waited the determination of reason and will. [111]

When anything threatens our eyes, we wink hard, by instinct, and can hardly avoid doing so, even when we know that the stroke is aimed in jest, and that we are perfectly safe from danger. I have seen this tried upon a wager, which a man was to gain if he could keep his eyes open, while another aimed a stroke at them in jest. The difficulty of doing this shews that there may be a struggle between instinct and will; and that it is not easy to resist the impulse of instinct, even by a strong resolution not to yield to it.

Thus the merciful Author of our nature hath adapted our instincts to the defects and to the weakness of our understanding. In infancy we are ignorant of everything; yet many things must be done by us for our preservation: These are done by instinct. When we grow up there are many motions of our limbs and bodies necessary, which can be performed only by a curious

* "Omnia in mensura, et numero, et pondere disposuisti."—(*Wisdom of Solomon*). I forget how it is rendered in our English version.—H.

and complex internal machinery—a machinery of which the bulk of mankind are totally ignorant, and which the most skilful anatomist knows but imperfectly. All this machinery is set a-going by instinct. We need only to will the external motion, and all the internal motions, previously necessary to the effect, take place of themselves, without our will or command.

Some actions must be so often repeated, through the whole of life, that, if they required attention and will, we should be able to do nothing else: These go on regularly by instinct.

Our preservation from danger often requires such sudden exertions, that there is no time to think and to determine: Accordingly we make such exertions by instinct.

Another thing in the nature of man, which I take to be partly, though not wholly, instinctive, is his proneness to imitation. [112]

Aristotle observed, long ago, that man is an imitative animal. He is so in more respects than one. He is disposed to imitate what he approves. In all arts men learn more and more agreeably, by example than by rules. Imitation by the chissel, by the pencil, by description prosaic and poetical, and by action and gesture, have been favourite and elegant entertainments of the whole species. In all these cases, however, the imitation is intended and willed, and therefore cannot be said to be instinctive.

But I apprehend that human nature disposes us to the imitation of those among whom we live, when we neither desire nor will it.

Let an Englishman, of middle age, take up his residence in Edinburgh or Glasgow; although he has not the least intention to use the Scots dialect, but a firm resolution to preserve his own pure and unmixed, he will find it very difficult to make good his intention. He will, in a course of years, fall insensibly, and without intention, into the tone and accent, and even into the words and phrases of those he converses with; and nothing can preserve him from this, but a strong disgust to every Scotticism, which perhaps may overcome the natural instinct.

It is commonly thought that children often learn to stammer by imitation; yet I believe no person ever desired or willed to learn that quality.

I apprehend that instinctive imitation has no small influence in forming the peculiarities of provincial dialects, the peculiarities of voice, gesture, and manner which we see in some families, the manners peculiar to different ranks and different professions; and perhaps even in forming national characters, and the human character in general. [113]

The instances that history furnishes of wild men, brought up from early years, without the society of any of their own species, are so few, that we cannot build conclusions upon them with great certainty. But all I have heard of agreed in this, that the wild man gave but very slender indications of the rational faculties; and, with regard to his mind, was hardly distinguishable from the more sagacious of the brutes.

There is a considerable part of the lowest rank in every nation, of whom it cannot be said that any pains have been taken by themselves, or by others, to cultivate their understanding, or to form their manners; yet we see an immense difference between them and the wild man.

This difference is wholly the effect of society; and, I think, it is in a great measure, though not wholly, the effect of undesigned and instinctive imitation.

Perhaps not only our actions, but even our judgment and belief, is, in some cases, guided by instinct—that is, by a natural and blind impulse.

When we consider man as a rational creature, it may seem right that he should have no belief but what is grounded upon evidence, probable or demonstrative; and it is, I think, commonly taken for granted, that it is always evidence, real or apparent, that determines our belief.

If this be so, the consequence is, that, in no case, can there be any belief, till we find evidence, or, at least, what to our judgment appears to be evidence. I suspect it is not so; but that, on the contrary, before we grow up to the full use of our rational faculties, we do believe, and must believe, many things without any evidence at all. [114]

The faculties which we have in common with brute-animals, are of earlier growth than reason. We are irrational animals for a considerable time before we can properly be called rational. The operations of reason spring up by imperceptible degrees; nor is it possible for us to trace accurately the order in which they rise. The power of reflection, by which only we could trace the progress of our growing faculties, comes too late to answer that end. Some operations of brute-animals look so like reason that they are not easily distinguished from it. Whether brutes have anything that can properly be called belief, I cannot say; but their actions shew something that looks very like it.

If there be any instinctive belief in man, it is probably of the same kind with that which we ascribe to brutes, and may be specifically different from that rational belief which is grounded on evidence; but that there is something in man which we call belief, which is not grounded on evidence, I think, must be granted.

[1°] We need to be informed of many things before we are capable of discerning the evidence on which they rest. Were our belief to be withheld till we are capable, in any degree, of weighing evidence, we should lose all the benefit of that instruction and information, without which we could never attain the use of our rational faculties.

Man would never acquire the use of reason if he were not brought up in the society of reasonable creatures. The benefit he receives from society is derived partly from imitation of what he sees others do, partly from the instruction and information they communicate to him, without which he could neither be preserved from destruction, nor acquire the use of his rational powers.

Children have a thousand things to learn, and they learn many things every day; more than will be easily believed by those who have never given attention to their progress. [115]

Oportet discentem credere is a common adage. Children have everything to learn; and, in order to learn, they must believe their instructors. They need a greater stock of faith from infancy to twelve or fourteen, than ever after. But how shall they get this stock so necessary to them? If their faith depend upon evidence, the stock of evidence, real or apparent, must bear proportion to their faith. But such, in reality, is their situation, that when their faith must be greatest, the evidence is least. They believe a thousand things before they ever spend a thought upon evidence. *Nature supplies the want of evidence, and gives them an instinctive kind of faith without evidence.**

They believe implicitly whatever they are told, and receive with assurance the testimony of every one, without ever thinking of a reason why they should do so.

A parent or a master might command them to believe, but in vain, for belief is not in our power; but, in the first part of life, it is governed by mere testimony in matters of fact, and by mere authority in all other matters, no less than by evidence in riper years.

It is not the words of the testifier, but his belief, that produces this belief in a child: for children soon learn to distinguish what is said in jest, from what is said in good earnest. What appears to them to be said in jest, produces no belief. They glory in shewing that they are not to be imposed on. When the signs of belief in the speaker are ambiguous, it is pleasant to observe with what sagacity they pry into his features, to discern whether he really believes what he says, or only counterfeits belief. As soon as this point is determined, their belief is regulated by his. If he be doubtful, they are doubtful; if he be assured, they are also assured. [116]

It is well known what a deep impression religious principles, zealously inculcated, make upon the minds of children. The absurdities of ghosts and hobgoblins, early impressed, have been known to stick so fast, even in enlightened minds, as to baffle all rational conviction.

When we grow up to the use of reason, testimony, attended with certain circumstances, or even authority, may afford a rational ground of belief; but with children, without any regard to circumstances, either of them operates like demonstration. And as they seek no reason, nor can give any reason, for this regard to testimony and to authority, it is the effect of a natural impulse, and may be called instinct.

[2°] Another instance of belief which appears to be instinctive, is that which children shew even in infancy, *That an event which they have observed in certain circumstances, will happen again in like circumstances.* A child of half a year old, who has once burned his finger by putting it in the candle, will not put it there again. And if you make a shew of putting it in the candle by force, you see the most manifest signs that he believes he shall meet with the same calamity.

Mr Hume hath shewn very clearly, that this belief is not the effect either of Reason or Experience. He endeavours to account for it by the Association of Ideas. Though I am not satisfied with his account of this phænomenon, I shall not now examine it; because it is sufficient for the present argument, that this belief is not grounded on evidence, real or apparent, which I think he clearly proves.

A person who has lived so long in the world as to observe that nature is governed by fixed laws, may have some rational ground to expect similar events in similar circumstances; but this cannot be the case of the child. His belief, therefore, is not grounded on evidence. It is the result of his constitution. [117]

Nor is it the less so, though it should arise from the association of ideas. For what is called the association of ideas is a law of nature in our constitution; which produces its effects without any operation of reason on our part, and in a manner of which we are entirely ignorant.*

* See Stewart's "Philosophy of the Active Powers," ii. p. 341. Reid is not, however, the first who resolved the credulity of children into an original principle. See above, pp. 198, 19[illegible].—H.

* See above, pp. 197-201.—H.

CHAPTER III.

OF HABIT.

Habit differs from Instinct, not in its nature, but in its origin; the latter being natural, the former acquired. Both operate without will or intention, without thought, and therefore may be called *mechanical principles*.

Habit is commonly defined, *A facility of doing a thing, acquired by having done it frequently*. This definition is sufficient for habits of art; but the habits which may, with propriety, be called principles of action, must give more than a facility, they must give an inclination or impulse to do the action; and that, in many cases, habits have this force, cannot be doubted.

How many awkward habits, by frequenting improper company, are children apt to learn, in their address, motion, looks, gesture, and pronunciation. They acquire such habits commonly from an undesigned and instinctive imitation, before they can judge of what is proper and becoming.

When they are a little advanced in understanding, they may easily be convinced that such a thing is unbecoming, they may resolve to forbear it, but when the habit is formed, such a general resolution is not of itself sufficient; for the habit will operate without intention; and particular attention is necessary, on every occasion, to resist its impulse, until it be undone by the habit of opposing it. [118]

It is owing to the force of habits, early acquired by imitation, that a man who has grown up to manhood in the lowest rank of life, if fortune raise him to a higher rank, very rarely acquires the air and manners of a gentleman.

When to that instinctive imitation which I spoke of before, we join the force of habit, it is easy to see, that these mechanical principles have no small share in forming the manners and character of most men.

The difficulty of overcoming vicious habits has, in all ages, been a common topic of theologians and moralists; and we see too many sad examples to permit us to doubt of it.

There are good habits, in a moral sense, as well as bad; and it is certain, that the stated and regular performance of what we approve, not only makes it easy, but makes us uneasy in the omission of it. This is the case, even when the action derives all its goodness from the opinion of the performer. A good illiterate Roman Catholic does not sleep sound if he goes to bed without telling his beads, and repeating prayers which he does not understand.

Aristotle makes Wisdom, Prudence, Good Sense,* Science, and Art, as well as the moral virtues and vices, to be *habits*. If he meant no more, by giving this name to all those intellectual and moral qualities, than that they are all strengthened and confirmed by repeated acts, this is undoubtedly true. I take the word in a less extensive sense, when I consider habits as principles of action. I conceive it to be a part of our constitution, that what we have been accustomed to do, we acquire, not only a facility, but a proneness to do on like occasions; so that it requires a particular will and effort to forbear it, but to do it, requires very often no will at all. We are carried by habit as by a stream in swimming, if we make no resistance. [119]

Every art furnishes examples both of the power of habits and of their utility; no one more than the most common of all arts, the art of speaking.

Articulate language is spoken, not by nature, but by art. It is no easy matter to children to learn the simple sounds of language; I mean, to learn to pronounce the vowels and consonants. It would be much more difficult, if they were not led by instinct to imitate the sounds they hear; for the difficulty is vastly greater of teaching the deaf to pronounce the letters and words, though experience shews that can be done.

What is it that makes this pronunciation so easy at last which was so difficult at first? It is habit.

But from what cause does it happen, that a good speaker no sooner conceives what he would express, than the letters, syllables, and words arrange themselves according to innumerable rules of speech, while he never thinks of these rules? He means to express certain sentiments; in order to do this properly, a selection must be made of the materials, out of many thousands. He makes this selection without any expense of time or thought. The materials selected must be arranged in a particular order, according to innumerable rules of grammar, logic, and rhetoric, and accompanied with a particular tone and emphasis. He does all this as it were by inspiration, without thinking of any of these rules, and without breaking one of them. [120]

This art, if it were not more common, would appear more wonderful than that a man should dance blindfold amidst a thousand burning ploughshares, without being burnt; yet all this may be done by habit.

It appears evident, that as, without instinct, the infant could not live to become

* Νοῦς is here ill translated by *Good Sense*. It corresponds rather to what Reid and others have called *Common Sense*, being the faculty of primary truths—*locus principiorum*.—H.

a man, so, without habit, man would remain an infant through life, and would be as helpless, as unhandy, as speechless, and as much a child in understanding at threescore as at three.

I see no reason to think that we shall ever be able to assign the physical cause, either of instinct, or of the power of habit.*

Both seem to be parts of our original constitution. Their end and use is evident; but we can assign no cause of them, but the will of Him who made us.

With regard to instinct, which is a natural propensity, this will perhaps be easily granted; but it is no less true with regard to that power and inclination which we acquire by habit.

No man can shew a reason why our doing a thing frequently should produce either facility or inclination to do it.

The fact is so notorious, and so constantly in our eye, that we are apt to think no reason should be sought for it, any more than why the sun shines. But there must be a cause of the sun's shining, and there must be a cause of the power of habit.

We see nothing analogous to it in inanimate matter, or in things made by human art. A clock or a watch, a waggon or a plough, by the custom of going, does not learn to go better, or require less moving force. The earth does not increase in fertility by the custom of bearing crops. [121]

It is said, that trees and other vegetables, by growing long in an unkindly soil or climate, sometimes acquire qualities by which they can bear its inclemency with less hurt. This, in the vegetable kingdom, has some resemblance to the power of habit; but, in inanimate matter, I know nothing that resembles it.

A stone loses nothing of its weight by being long supported, or made to move upward. A body, by being tossed about ever so long, or ever so violently, loses nothing of its *inertia*, nor acquires the least disposition to change its state.

* Mr Stewart has made an ingenious attempt to explain sundry of the phenomena referred to the occult principle of habit, in his chapter on Attention, in the first volume of his "Elements of the Philosophy of the Human Mind." It is to be regretted that he had not studied (he even treats it as inconceivable) the Leibnitian doctrine of what has not well been denominated, *obscure perceptions, or ideas*—that is, acts and affections of mind, which, manifesting their existence in their effects, are themselves out of consciousness or *apperception*. The fact of such latent mental modifications, is now established beyond a rational doubt; and on the supposition of their reality, we are able to solve various psychological phenomena otherwise inexplicable. Among these are many of those attributed to Habit.—H.

PART II.

OF ANIMAL PRINCIPLES OF ACTION

CHAPTER I

OF APPETITES.

Having discoursed of the *mechanical* principles of action, I proceed to consider those I called *animal*.*

They are such as operate upon the will and intention, but do not suppose any exercise of judgment or reason; and are most of them to be found in some brute animals, as well as in man.

In this class, the *first* kind I shall call *Appetites*, taking that word in a stricter sense than it is sometimes taken, even by good writers. [122]

The word *appetite* is sometimes limited, so as to signify only the desire of food when we hunger; sometimes it is extended so as to signify any strong desire, whatever be its object. Without pretending to censure any use of the word which custom hath authorized, I beg leave to limit it to a particular class of desires, which are distinguished from all others by the following marks:—

First, Every appetite is accompanied with an uneasy sensation proper to it, which is strong or weak, in proportion to the desire we have of the object. *Secondly*, Appetites are not constant, but periodical, being sated by their objects for a time, and returning after certain periods. Such is the nature of those principles of action, to which I beg leave, in this essay, to appropriate the name of *appetites*. Those that are chiefly observable in man, as well as in most other animals, are *Hunger*, *Thirst*, and *Lust*.

If we attend to the appetite of Hunger, we shall find in it two ingredients, an uneasy sensation and a desire to eat. The desire keeps pace with the sensation,* and ceases when it ceases. When a man is sated with eating, both the uneasy sensation and the desire to eat cease for a time, and return after a certain inverval. So it is with other appetites.

In infants, for some time after they come into the world, the uneasy sensation of hunger is probably the whole. We cannot

* It is observed by Mr Stewart, in reference to the undue latitude with which, in this part of his work, Reid has employed, among others, the term *Animal*, that, in consequence of this, he has been led to rank among our animal principles of action, (that is, among the active principles common to man with the brutes,) not only the desire of knowledge, and the desire of esteem, but pity to the distressed, patriotism, and other benevolent affections.—H.

suppose in them, before experience, any conception of eating, nor, consequently, any desire of it. They are led by mere instinct to suck when they feel the sensation of hunger. But when experience has connected, in their imagination, the uneasy sensation with the means of removing it, the desire of the last comes to be so associated with the first, that they remain through life inseparable. And we give the name of *hunger* to the principle that is made up of both. [123]

That the appetite of hunger includes the two ingredients I have mentioned will not, I apprehend, be questioned. I take notice of it the rather because we may, if I mistake not, find a similar composition in other principles of action. They are made up of different ingredients, and may be analyzed into the parts that enter into their composition.

If one philosopher should maintain that hunger is an uneasy sensation, another, that it is a desire to eat, they seem to differ widely; for a desire and a sensation are very different things, and have no similitude. But they are both in the right; for hunger includes both an uneasy sensation and a desire to eat.

Although there has been no such dispute among philosophers as we have supposed with regard to hunger, yet there have been similar disputes with regard to other principles of action; and it deserves to be considered whether they may not be terminated in a similar manner.

The ends for which our natural appetites are given, are too evident to escape the observation of any man of the least reflection. Two of those I named are intended for the preservation of the individual, and the third for the continuance of the species.

The reason of mankind would be altogether insufficient for these ends, without the direction and call of appetite.

Though a man knew that his life must be supported by eating, reason could not direct him when to eat, or what; how much, or how often. In all these things, appetite is a much better guide than our reason. Were reason only to direct us in this matter, its calm voice would often be drowned in the hurry of business, or the charms of amusement. But the voice of appetite rises gradually, and, at last, becomes loud enough to call off our attention from any other employment. [124]

Every man must be convinced that, without our appetites, even supposing mankind inspired with all the knowledge requisite for answering their ends, the race of men must have perished long ago; but, by their means, the race is continued from one generation to another, whether men be savage or civilized, knowing or ignorant, virtuous or vicious.

By the same means, every tribe of brute animals, from the whale that ranges the ocean to the least microscopic insect, has been continued from the beginning of the world to this day; nor has good evidence been found, that any one species which God made has perished.

Nature has given to every animal, not only an appetite for its food, but taste and smell, by which it distinguishes the food proper for it.

It is pleasant to see a caterpillar, which nature intended to live upon the leaf of one species of plant, travel over a hundred leaves of other kinds without tasting one, till it comes to that which is its natural food, which it immediately falls on, and devours greedily.

Most caterpillars feed only upon the leaf of one species of plant, and nature suits the season of their production to the food that is intended to nourish them. Many insects and animals have a greater variety of food; but, of all animals, man has the greatest variety, being able to subsist upon almost every kind of vegetable or animal food, from the bark of trees to the oil of whales. [125]

I believe our natural appetites may be made more violent by excessive indulgence, and that, on the other hand, they may be weakened by starving. The first is often the effect of a pernicious luxury, the last may sometimes be the effect of want, sometimes of superstition. I apprehend that nature has given to our appetites that degree of strength which is most proper for us; and that whatever alters their natural tone, either in excess or in defect, does not mend the work of nature, but may mar and pervert it.

A man may eat from appetite only. So the brutes commonly do. He may eat to please his taste when he has no call of appetite. I believe a brute may do this also. He may eat for the sake of health, when neither appetite nor taste invites. This, as far as I am able to judge, brutes never do.

From so many different principles, and from many more, the same action may be done; and this may be said of most human actions. From this, it appears that very different and contrary theories may serve to account for the actions of men. The causes assigned may be sufficient to produce the effect, and yet not be the true causes.

To act merely from appetite, is neither good nor ill in a moral view. It is neither an object of praise nor of blame. No man claims any praise because he eats when he is hungry, or rests when he is weary. On the other hand, he is no object of blame, if he obeys the call of appetite when there is no reason to hinder him. In this he acts agreeably to his nature.

From this, we may observe, that the definition of virtuous actions given by the ancient Stoics, and adopted by some modern authors, is imperfect. They defined virtuous actions to be such as are *according to nature*. What is done according to the animal part of our nature, which is common to us with the brute animals, is in itself neither virtuous nor vicious, but perfectly indifferent. Then only it becomes vicious, when it is done in opposition to some principle of superior importance and authority. And it may be virtuous, if done for some important or worthy end. [126]

Appetites, considered in themselves, are neither social principles of action, nor selfish. They cannot be called social, because they imply no concern for the good of others. Nor can they justly be called selfish, though they be commonly referred to that class. An appetite draws us to a certain object, without regard to its being good for us, or ill. There is no self-love implied in it any more than benevolence. We see that, in many cases, appetite may lead a man to what he knows will be to his hurt. To call this acting from self-love, is to pervert the meaning of words. It is evident that, in every case of this kind, self-love is sacrificed to appetite.

There are some principles of the human frame very like to our appetites, though they do not commonly get that name.

Men are made for labour either of body or mind. Yet excessive labour hurts the powers of both. To prevent this hurt, nature hath given to men, and other animals, an uneasy sensation, which always attends excessive labour, and which we call *fatigue*, *weariness*, *lassitude*. This uneasy sensation is conjoined with the desire of rest, or intermission of our labour; and thus nature calls us to rest when we are weary, in the same manner as to eat when we are hungry.

In both cases, there is a desire of a certain object, and an uneasy sensation accompanying that desire. In both cases, the desire is satiated by its object, and returns after certain intervals. In this only they differ, that in the appetites first mentioned, the uneasy sensation arises at intervals without action, and leads to a certain action. In weariness, the uneasy sensation arises from action too long continued, and leads to rest. [127]

But nature intended that we should be active, and we need some principle to incite us to action when we happen not to be invited by any appetite or passion.

For this end, when strength and spirits are recruited by rest, nature has made total inaction as uneasy as excessive labour.

We may call this the principle of *activity*. It is most conspicuous in children, who cannot be supposed to know how useful and necessary it is for their improvement to be constantly employed. Their constant activity, therefore, appears not to proceed from their having some end constantly in view, but rather from this, that they desire to be always doing something, and feel uneasiness in total inaction.

Nor is this principle confined to childhood; it has great effects in advanced life.

When a man has neither hope, nor fear, nor desire, nor project, nor employment of body or mind, one might be apt to think him the happiest mortal upon earth, having nothing to do but to enjoy himself; but we find him, in fact, the most unhappy.

He is more weary of inaction than ever he was of excessive labour; he is weary of the world and of his own existence; and is more miserable than the sailor wrestling with a storm, or the soldier mounting a breach.

This dismal state is commonly the lot of the man who has neither exercise of body nor employment of mind; for the mind, like water, corrupts and putrifies by stagnation, but, by running, purifies and refines.*

Besides the appetites which nature hath given us for useful and necessary purposes, we may create appetites which nature never gave. [128]

The frequent use of things which stimulate the nervous system, produces a languor when their effect is gone off, and a desire to repeat them. By this means, a desire of a certain object is created, accompanied by an uneasy sensation. Both are removed for a time by the object desired; but they return after a certain interval. This differs from natural appetite only in being acquired by custom. Such are the appetites which some men acquire for the use of tobacco, for opiates, and for intoxicating liquors.

These are commonly called habits, and justly. But there are different kinds of habits, even of the active sort, which ought to be distinguished. Some habits produce only a facility of doing a thing, without any inclination to do it. All arts are habits of this kind; but they cannot be called principles of action. Other habits produce a proneness to do an action, without thought or intention. These we considered before as mechanical principles of action. There are other habits which produce a desire of a certain object, and an uneasy sensation till it is obtained. It is this last kind only that I call acquired appetites.

As it is best to preserve our natural appetites in that tone and degree of strength which nature gives them, so we ought to beware of acquiring appetites which nature never gave. They are always useless, and very often hurtful.

---

* The true theory of *Pleasure* and *Pain* affords a solution of this and of many other psychological phænomena.—H.

Although, as was before observed, there be neither virtue nor vice in acting from appetite, there may be much of either in the management of our appetites. [129]

When appetite is opposed by some principle drawing a contrary way, there must be a determination of the will, which shall prevail, and this determination may be, in a moral sense, right or wrong.

Appetite, even in a brute-animal, may be restrained by a stronger principle opposed to it. A dog, when he is hungry and has meat set before him, may be kept from touching it by the fear of immediate punishment. In this case his fear operates more strongly than his desire.

Do we attribute any virtue to the dog on this account? I think not. Nor should we ascribe any virtue to a man in a like case. The animal is carried by the strongest moving force. This requires no exertion, no self-government, but passively to yield to the strongest impulse. This, I think, brutes always do; therefore we attribute to them neither virtue nor vice. We consider them as being neither objects of moral approbation, nor disapprobation.

But it may happen that, when appetite draws one way, it may be opposed, not by any appetite or passion, but by some cool principle of action, which has authority without any impulsive force—for example, by some interest which is too distant to raise any passion or emotion, or by some consideration of decency or of duty.

In cases of this kind, the man is convinced that he ought not to yield to appetite, yet there is not an equal or a greater impulse to oppose it. There are circumstances, indeed, that convince the judgment; but these are not sufficient to determine the will against a strong appetite, without self-government. [130]

I apprehend that brute-animals have no power of self-government. From their constitution, they must be led by the appetite or passion which is strongest for the time.

On this account, they have, in all ages, and among all nations, been thought incapable of being governed by laws, though some of them may be subjects of discipline.

The same would be the condition of man, if he had no power to restrain appetite but by a stronger contrary appetite or passion. It would be to no purpose to prescribe laws to him for the government of his actions. You might as well forbid the wind to blow, as forbid him to follow whatever happens to give the strongest present impulse.

Every one knows that when appetite draws one way, duty, decency, or even interest, may draw the contrary way; and that appetite may give a stronger impulse than any one of these, or even all of them conjoined. Yet it is certain, that, in every case of this kind, appetite ought to yield to any of these principles when it stands opposed to them. It is in such cases that self-government is necessary.

The man who suffers himself to be led by appetite to do what he knows he ought not to do, has an immediate and natural conviction that he did wrong, and might have done otherwise; and therefore he condemns himself, and confesses that he yielded to an appetite which ought to have been under his command.

Thus it appears, that, though our natural appetites have in themselves neither virtue nor vice, though the acting merely from appetite, when there is no principle of greater authority to oppose it, be a matter indifferent; yet there may be a great deal of virtue or of vice in the management of our appetites; and that the power of self-government is necessary for their regulation. [131]

CHAPTER II.

OF DESIRES.

ANOTHER class of animal principles of action in man, I shall, for want of a better specific name, call *desires*.

They are distinguished from appetites by this: That there is not an uneasy sensation proper to each, and always accompanying it; and that they are not periodical, but constant, not being sated with their objects for a time, as appetites are.

The desires I have in view, are chiefly those three—the desire of power, the desire of esteem, and the desire of knowledge.

We may, I think, perceive some degree of these principles in brute-animals of the more sagacious kind; but in man they are much more conspicuous, and have a larger sphere.

In a herd of black cattle, there is a rank and subordination. When a stranger is introduced into the herd, he must fight every one till his rank is settled. Then he yields to the stronger and assumes authority over the weaker. The case is much the same in the crew of a ship of war.

As soon as men associate together, the desire of superiority discovers itself. In barbarous tribes, as well as among the gregarious kinds of animals, rank is determined by strength, courage, swiftness, or such other qualities. Among civilized nations, many things of a different kind give power and rank—places in government, titles of honour, riches, wisdom, eloquence, virtue, and even the reputation of these. All these are either different species of power, or means of acquiring it; and when they are sought for that end, must be considered as instances of the desire of power. [132]

The desire of esteem is not peculiar to man. A dog exults in the approbation and applause of his master, and is humbled by his displeasure. But in man this desire is much more conspicuous, and operates in a thousand different ways.

Hence it is that so very few are proof against flattery, when it is not very gross. We wish to be well in the opinion of others, and therefore are prone to interpret in our own favour, the signs of their good opinion, even when they are ambiguous.

There are few injuries that are not more easy to be borne than contempt.

We cannot always avoid seeing, in the conduct of others, things that move contempt; but, in all polite circles, the signs of it must be suppressed, otherwise men could not converse together.

As there is no quality, common to good and bad men, more esteemed than courage, nor anything in a man more the object of contempt than cowardice, hence every man desires to be thought a man of courage; and the reputation of cowardice is worse than death. How many have died to avoid being thought cowards? How many, for the same reason, have done what made them unhappy to the end of their lives.

I believe many a tragical event, if traced to its source in human nature, might be referred to the desire of esteem, or the dread of contempt. [133]

In brute animals there is so little that can be called knowledge, that the desire of it can make no considerable figure in them. Yet I have seen a cat, when brought into a new habitation, examine with care every corner of it, and anxious to know every lurking place, and the avenues to it. And I believe the same thing may be observed in many other species, especially in those that are liable to be hunted by man or by other animals.

But the desire of knowledge in the human species, is a principle that cannot escape our observation.

The curiosity of children is the principle that occupies most of their time while they are awake. What they can handle they examine on all sides, and often break in pieces, in order to discover what is within.

When men grow up, their curiosity does not cease, but is employed upon other objects. Novelty is considered as one great source of the pleasures of taste, and indeed is necessary, in one degree or other, to give a relish to them all.

When we speak of the desire of knowledge as a principle of action in man, we must not confine it to the pursuits of the philosopher, or of the literary man. The desire of knowledge discovers itself, in one person, by an avidity to know the scandal of the village, and who makes love, and to whom; in another, to know the economy of the next family; in another, to know what the post brings; and, in another, to trace the path of a new comet.

When men shew an anxiety, and take pains to know what is of no moment, and can be of no use to themselves or to others, this is trifling, and vain curiosity. It is a culpable weakness and folly; but still it is the wrong direction of a natural principle, and shews the force of that principle more than when it is directed to matters worthy to be known. [134]

I think it unnecessary to use arguments to shew that the desires of power, of esteem, and of knowledge, are natural principles in the constitution of man. Those who are not convinced of this by reflecting upon their own feelings and sentiments, will not easily be convinced by arguments.

Power, esteem, and knowledge, are so useful for many purposes, that it is easy to resolve the desire of them into other principles. Those who do so must maintain, that we never desire these objects for their own sakes, but as means only of procuring pleasure, or something which is a natural object of desire. This, indeed, was the doctrine of Epicurus; and it has had its votaries in modern times. But it has been observed, that men desire posthumous fame, which can procure no pleasure.

Epicurus himself, though he believed that he should have no existence after death, was so desirous to be remembered with esteem, that, by his last will, he appointed his heirs to commemorate his birth annually, and to give a monthly feast to his disciples, upon the twentieth day of the moon. What pleasure could this give to Epicurus when he had no existence? On this account, Cicero justly observes, that his doctrine was refuted by his own practice.

Innumerable instances occur in life, of men who sacrifice ease, pleasure, and everything else, to the lust of power, of fame, or even of knowledge. It is absurd to suppose that men should sacrifice the end to what they desire only as the means of promoting that end. [135]

The natural desires I have mentioned are, in themselves, neither virtuous nor vicious. They are parts of our constitution, and ought to be regulated and restrained, when they stand in competition with more important principles. But to eradicate them, if it were possible, (and I believe it is not,) would only be like cutting off a leg or an arm—that is, making ourselves other creatures than God has made us.

They cannot, with propriety, be called selfish principles, though they have commonly been accounted such.

When power is desired for its own sake, and not as the means in order to obtain something else, this desire is neither selfish nor social. When a man desires power as the means of doing good to others, this is benevolence. When he desires it only as the means of promoting his own good, this is self-love. But when he desires it for its own sake, this only can properly be called the desire of power; and it implies neither self-love nor benevolence. The same thing may be applied to the desires of esteem and of knowledge.

The wise intention of nature in giving us these desires, is no less evident than in giving our natural appetites.

Without the natural appetites, reason, as was before observed, would be insufficient, either for the preservation of the individual or the continuation of the species; and without the natural desires we have mentioned, human virtue would be insufficient to influence mankind to a tolerable conduct in society.

To these natural desires, common to good and to bad men, it is owing, that a man, who has little or no regard to virtue, may notwithstanding be a good member of society. It is true, indeed, that perfect virtue, joined with perfect knowledge, would make both our appetites and desires unnecessary incumbrances of our nature; but, as human knowledge and human virtue are both very imperfect, these appetites and desires are necessary supplements to our imperfections. [136]

Society, among men, could not subsist without a certain degree of that regularity of conduct which virtue prescribes. To this regularity of conduct, men who have no virtue are induced by a regard to character, sometimes by a regard to interest.

Even in those who are not destitute of virtue, a regard to character is often an useful auxiliary to it, when both principles concur in their direction.

The pursuits of power, of fame, and of knowledge, require a self-command no less than virtue does. In our behaviour towards our fellow-creatures, they generally lead to that very conduct which virtue requires. I say *generally*, for this, no doubt, admits of exceptions, especially in the case of ambition, or the desire of power.

The evils which ambition has produced in the world are a common topic of declamation. But it ought to be observed that, where it has led to one action hurtful to society, it has led to ten thousand that are beneficial to it. And we justly look upon the want of ambition as one of the most unfavourable symptoms in a man's temper.

The desires of esteem and of knowledge are highly useful to society, as well as the desire of power, and, at the same time, are less dangerous in their excesses.

Although actions proceeding merely from the love of power, of reputation, or of knowledge, cannot be accounted virtuous, or be entitled to moral approbation; yet we allow them to be manly, ingenuous, and suited to the dignity of human nature; and, therefore, they are entitled to a degree of estimation superior to those which proceed from mere appetite. [137]

Alexander the Great deserved that epithet in the early part of his life, when ease and pleasure, and every appetite, were sacrificed to the love of glory and power. But when we view him conquered by oriental luxury, and using his power to gratify his passions and appetites, he sinks in our esteem, and seems to forfeit the title which he had acquired.

Sardanapalus, who is said to have pursued pleasure as eagerly as Alexander pursued glory, never obtained from mankind the appellation of *the Great*.

Appetite is the principle of most of the actions of brutes, and we account it brutal in a man to employ himself chiefly in the gratification of his appetites. The desires of power, of esteem, and of knowledge, are capital parts in the constitution of man; and the actions proceeding from them, though not properly virtuous, are human and manly; and they claim a just superiority over those that proceed from appetite. This, I think, is the universal and unbiassed judgment of mankind. Upon what ground this judgment is founded may deserve to be considered in its proper place.

The desires we have mentioned are not only highly useful in society, and in their nature more noble than our appetites—they are likewise the most proper engines that can be used in the education and discipline of men.

In training brute-animals to such habits as they are capable of, the fear of punishment is the chief instrument to be used. But, in training men of ingenuous dispositions, ambition to excel, and the love of esteem, are much nobler and more powerful engines, by which they may be led to worthy conduct, and trained to good habits. [138]

To this we may add, that the desires we have mentioned are very friendly to real virtue, and make it more easy to be acquired.

A man that is not quite abandoned must behave so in society as to preserve some degree of reputation. This every man desires to do, and the greater part actually do it. In order to this, he must acquire the habit of restraining his appetites and passions within the bounds which common decency requires, and so as to make himself a tolerable member of society, if not an useful and agreeable one.

It cannot be doubted that many, from a regard to character and to the opinion of others, are led to make themselves both useful and agreeable members of society, in whom a sense of duty has but a small influence.

Thus men, living in society, especially in polished society, are tamed and civilized by the principles that are common to good and bad men. They are taught to bring their appetites and passions under due restraint before the eyes of men, which makes it more easy to bring them under the rein of virtue.

As a horse that is broken is more easily managed than an unbroken colt, so the man who has undergone the discipline of society is more tractable, and is in an excellent state of preparation for the discipline of virtue; and that self-command, which is necessary in the race of ambition and honour, is an attainment of no small importance in the course of virtue. [139]

For this reason, I apprehend, they err very grossly who conceive the life of a hermit to be favourable to a course of virtue. The hermit, no doubt, is free from some temptations to vice, but he is deprived of many strong inducements to self-government, as well as of every opportunity of exercising the social virtues.*

A very ingenious author† has resolved our moral sentiments respecting the virtues of self-government, into a regard to the opinion of men. This, I think, is giving a great deal too much to the love of esteem, and putting the shadow of virtue in place of the substance; but that a regard to the opinion of others is, in most instances of our external behaviour, a great inducement to good conduct, cannot be doubted. For, whatever men may practice themselves, they will always approve of that in others which they think right.

It was before observed, that, besides the appetites which nature has given us, we may acquire appetites which, by indulgence, become as importunate as the natural. The same thing may be applied to desires.

One of the most remarkable acquired desires is that of money, which, in commercial states, will be found in most men, in one degree or other, and, in some men, swallows up every other desire, appetite, and passion.

The desire of money can then only be accounted a principle of action, when it is desired for its own sake, and not merely as the means of procuring something else.

It is evident that there is in misers such a desire of money; and, I suppose, no man will say that it is natural, or a part of our original constitution. It seems to be the effect of habit. [140]

In commercial nations, money is an instrument by which almost everything may be procured that is desired. Being useful for many different purposes as the means, some men lose sight of the end, and terminate their desire upon the means. Money is also a species of power, putting a man in condition to do many things which he could not do without it; and power is a natural object of desire, even when it is not exercised.

In like manner, a man may acquire the desire of a title of honour, of an equipage, of an estate.

Although our natural desires are highly beneficial to society, and even aiding to virtue, yet acquired desires are not only useless, but hurtful and even disgraceful.

No man is ashamed to own that he loves power, that he loves esteem, that he loves knowledge, for their own sake. There may be an excess in the love of these things, which is a blemish; but there is a degree of it which is natural, and is no blemish. To love money, titles, or equipage, on any other account than as they are useful or ornamental, is allowed by all to be weakness and folly.

The natural desires I have been considering, though they cannot be called *social* principles of action in the common sense of that word, since it is not their object to procure any good or benefit to others, yet they have such a relation to society as to shew most evidently the intention of Nature to be, that man should live in society.

The desire of knowledge is not more natural than is the desire of communicating our knowledge.* Even power would be less valued if there were no opportunity of shewing it to others. It derives half its value from that circumstance. And as to the desire of esteem, it can have no possible gratification but in society. [141]

These parts of our constitution, therefore, are evidently intended for social life; and it is not more evident that birds were made for flying and fishes for swimming, than that man, endowed with a natural desire of power, of esteem, and of knowledge, is made, not for the savage and solitary state, but for living in society.†

* The solitary (says Aristotle) is either a god or a beast.—H.

† Adam Smith.—H.

* Scire tuum nihil est, nisi te scire hoc sciat alter. *Persius*, after Lucilius.—H

† On this subject, what has been best said has been said by Aristotle. See his Politics, Book First.—H.

CHAPTER III.

OF BENEVOLENT AFFECTION IN GENERAL.

We have seen how, by instinct and habit—a kind of mechanical principles—man, without any expense of thought, without deliberation or will, is led to many actions, necessary for his preservation and well-being, which, without those principles, all his skill and wisdom would not have been able to accomplish.

It may perhaps be thought, that his deliberate and voluntary actions are to be guided by his reason.

But it ought to be observed, that he is a voluntary agent long before he has the use of reason. Reason and virtue, the prerogatives of man, are of the latest growth. They come to maturity by slow degrees, and are too weak, in the greater part of the species, to secure the preservation of individuals and of communities, and to produce that varied scene of human life in which they are to be exercised and improved.

Therefore, the wise Author of our being hath implanted in human nature many inferior principles of action, which, with little or no aid of reason or virtue, preserve the species, and produce the various exertions, and the various changes and revolutions which we observe upon the theatre of life. [142]

In this busy scene, reason and virtue have access to act their parts, and do often produce great and good effects; but whether they interpose or not, there are actors of an inferior order that will carry on the play, and produce a variety of events, good or bad.

Reason, if it were perfect, would lead men to use the proper means of preserving their own lives, and continuing their kind. But the Author of our being hath not thought fit to leave this task to reason alone, otherwise the race would long ago have been extinct. He hath given us, in common with other animals, appetites, by which those important purposes are secured, whether men be wise or foolish, virtuous or vicious.

Reason, if it were perfect, would lead men neither to lose the benefit of their active powers by inactivity, nor to overstrain them by excessive labour. But Nature hath given a powerful assistant to reason, by making inactivity a grievous punishment to itself; and by annexing the pain of lassitude to excessive labour.

Reason, if it were perfect, would lead us to desire power, knowledge, and the esteem and affection of our fellow-men, as means of promoting our own happiness, and of being useful to others. Here again, Nature, to supply the defects of reason, hath given us a strong natural desire of those objects, which leads us to pursue them without regard to their utility.

These principles we have already considered; and, we may observe, that all of them have things, not persons, for their object. They neither imply any good nor ill affection towards any other person, nor even towards ourselves. They cannot, therefore, with propriety, be called either *selfish* or *social*. But there are various principles of action in man, which have persons for their immediate object, and imply, in their very nature, our being well or ill affected to some person, or, at least, to some animated being. [143]

Such principles, I shall call by the general name of *affections*, whether they dispose us to do good or hurt to others.

Perhaps, in giving them this general name, I extend the meaning of the word *affection* beyond its common use in discourse. Indeed, our language seems in this to have departed a little from analogy; for we use the verb *affect*, and the participle *affected*, in an indifferent sense, so that they may be joined either with good or ill. A man may be said to be ill affected towards another man, or well affected. But the word *affection*, which, according to analogy, ought to have the same latitude of signification with that from which it is derived, and, therefore, ought to be applicable to ill affections as well as to good, seems, by custom, to be limited to good affections. When we speak of having affection for any person, it is always understood to be a benevolent affection.

Malevolent principles—such as anger, resentment, envy—are not commonly called *affections*, but rather *passions*.

I take the reason of this to be, that the malevolent affections are almost always accompanied with that perturbation of mind which we properly call *passion*; and this passion, being the most conspicuous ingredient, gives its name to the whole.

Even love, when it goes beyond a certain degree, is called a *passion*. But it gets not that name when it is so moderate as not to discompose a man's mind, nor deprive him in any measure of the government of himself. [144]

As we give the name of *passion*, even to benevolent affection when it is so vehement as to discompose the mind, so, I think, without trespassing much against propriety of words, we may give the name of *affection* even to malevolent principles, when unattended with that disturbance of mind which commonly, though not always, goes along with them, and which has made them get the name of *passions*.

The principles which lead us immediately

to desire the good of others, and those that lead us to desire their hurt, agree in this, that persons, and not things, are their immediate object. Both imply our being some way affected towards the person. They ought, therefore, to have some common name to express what is common in their nature; and I know no name more proper for this than *affection*.

Taking affection, therefore, in this extensive sense, our affections are very naturally divided into benevolent and malevolent, according as they imply our being well or ill affected towards their object.

There are some things common to all benevolent affections, others wherein they differ.

They differ both in the feeling or sensation, which is an ingredient in all of them, and in the objects to which they are directed.

They all agree in two things—to wit, That the feeling which accompanies them is agreeable; and, That they imply a desire of good and happiness to their object.

The affection we bear to a parent, to a child, to a benefactor, to a person in distress, to a mistress, differ not more in their object, than in the feelings they produce in the mind. We have not names to express the differences of these feelings, but every man is conscious of a difference. Yet, with all this difference, they agree in being agreeable feelings. [145]

I know no exception to this rule, if we distinguish, as we ought, the feeling which naturally and necessarily attends the kind affection, from those which accidentally, in certain circumstances, it may produce.

The parental affection is an agreeable feeling; but it makes the misfortune or misbehaviour of a child give a deeper wound to the mind. Pity is an agreeable feeling, yet distress, which we are not able to relieve, may give a painful sympathy. Love to one of the other sex is an agreeable feeling; but, where it does not meet with a proper return, it may give the most pungent distress.

The joy and comfort of human life consist in the reciprocal exercise of kind affections, and without them life would be undesirable.

It has been observed by Lord Shaftesbury, and by many other judicious moralists, That even the epicure and the debauchee, who are thought to place all their happiness in the gratifications of sense, and to pursue these as their only object, can find no relish in solitary indulgences of this kind, but in those only that are mixed with social intercourse, and a reciprocal exchange of kind affections.

Cicero has observed that the word *convivium*, which in Latin signifies a feast, is not borrowed from eating or from drinking, but from that social intercourse which, being the chief part of such an entertainment, gives the name to the whole.

Mutual kind affections are undoubtedly the balm of life, and of all the enjoyments common to good and bad men, are the chief. If a man had no person whom he loved or esteemed, no person who loved or esteemed him, how wretched must his condition be! Surely a man capable of reflection would choose to pass out of existence, rather than to live in such a state. [146]

It has been, by the poets, represented as the state of some bloody and barbarous tyrants; but poets are allowed to paint a little beyond the life. Atreus is represented as saying *Oderint dum metuant*—"I care not for their hatred, provided they dread my power." I believe there never was a man so disposed towards all mankind. The most odious tyrant that ever was, will have his favourites, whose affection he endeavours to deserve or to bribe, and to whom he bears some good will.

We may, therefore, lay it down as a principle, that all benevolent affections are, in their nature, agreeable; and that, next to a good conscience, to which they are always friendly, and never can be adverse, they make the capital part of human happiness.

Another ingredient essential to every benevolent affection, and from which it takes the name, is a desire of the good and happiness of the object.

The object of benevolent affection, therefore, must be some being capable of happiness. When we speak of affection to a house, or to any inanimate thing, the word has a different meaning; for that which has no capacity of enjoyment or of suffering, may be an object of liking or disgust, but cannot possibly be an object either of benevolent or malevolent affection.

A thing may be desired either on its own account, or as the means in order to something else. That only can properly be called an object of desire, which is desired upon its own account; and it is only such desires that I call principles of action. When anything is desired as the means only, there must be an end for which it is desired; and the desire of the end is, in this case, the principle of action. The means are desired only as they tend to that end; and, if different, or even contrary means, tended to the same end, they would be equally desired. [147]

On this account, I consider those affections only as benevolent, where the good of the object is desired ultimately, and not as the means only, in order to something else.

To say that we desire the good of others, only in order to procure some pleasure or good to ourselves, is to say that there is no benevolent affection in human nature.

This, indeed, has been the opinion of some philosophers, both in ancient and in later times. I intend not to examine this opinion in this place, conceiving it proper to give that view of the principles of action in man, which appears to me to be just, before I examine the systems wherein they have been mistaken or misrepresented.

I observe only at present, that it appears as unreasonable to resolve all our benevolent affections into self-love, as it would be to resolve hunger and thirst into self-love.

These appetites are necessary for the preservation of the individual. Benevolent affections are no less necessary for the preservation of society among men, without which man would become an easy prey to the beasts of the field.

We are placed in this world by the Author of our being, surrounded with many objects that are necessary or useful to us, and with many that may hurt us. We are led, not by reason and self-love only, but by many instincts, and appetites, and natural desires, to seek the former and to avoid the latter. [148]

But of all the things of this world, man may be the most useful or the most hurtful to man. Every man is in the power of every man with whom he lives. Every man has power to do much good to his fellow-men, and to do more hurt.

We cannot live without the society of men; and it would be impossible to live in society, if men were not disposed to do much of that good to men, and but little of that hurt, which it is in their power to do.

But how shall this end, so necessary to the existence of human society, and consequently to the existence of the human species, be accomplished?

If we judge from analogy, we must conclude that in this, as in other parts of our conduct, our rational principles are aided by principles of an inferior order, similar to those by which many brute animals live in society with their species; and that, by means of such principles, that degree of regularity is observed, which we find in all societies of men, whether wise or foolish, virtuous or vicious.

The benevolent affections planted in human nature, appear therefore no less necessary for the preservation of the human species, than the appetites of hunger and thirst.

CHAPTER IV.

OF THE PARTICULAR BENEVOLENT AFFECTIONS.

HAVING premised these things in general concerning benevolent affections, I shall now attempt some enumeration of them. [149]

1. The *first* I mention is, *that of parents and children, and other near relations.**

This we commonly call *natural* affection. Every language has a name for it. It is common to us with most of the brute-animals; and is variously modified in different animals, according as it is more or less necessary for the preservation of the species.

Many of the insect tribe need no other care of parents, than that the eggs be laid in a proper place, where they shall have neither too little nor too much heat, and where the animal, as soon as it is hatched, shall find its natural food. This care the parent takes, and no more.

In other tribes, the young must be lodged in some secret place, where they cannot be easily discovered by their enemies. They must be cherished by the warmth of the parent's body. They must be suckled, and fed at first with tender food; attended in their excursions, and guarded from danger, till they have learned, by experience, and by the example of their parents, to provide for their own subsistence and safety. With what assiduity and tender affection this is done by the parents, in every species that requires it, is well known.

The eggs of the feathered tribe are commonly hatched by incubation of the dam, who leaves off at once her sprightly motions and migrations, and confines herself to her solitary and painful task, cheered by the song of her mate upon a neighbouring bough, and sometimes fed by him, sometimes relieved in her incubation, while she gathers a scanty meal, and with the greatest dispatch returns to her post. [150]

The young birds of many species are so very tender and delicate, that man, with all his wisdom and experience, would not be able to rear one to maturity. But the parents, without any experience, know perfectly how to rear sometimes a dozen or more at one brood, and to give every one its portion in due season. They know the food best suited to their delicate constitution, which is sometimes afforded by nature, sometimes must be cooked and half digested in the stomach of the parent.

In some animals, nature hath furnished the female with a kind of second womb, into

* Στοργή.—H.

which the young retire occasionally, for food, warmth, and the conveniency of being carried about with the mother.

It would be endless to recount all the various ways in which the parental affection is expressed by brute-animals.

He must, in my apprehension, have a very strange complexion of understanding, who can survey the various ways in which the young of the various species are reared, without wonder, without pious admiration of that manifold wisdom which hath so skilfully fitted means to ends, in such an infinite variety of ways.

In all the brute-animals we are acquainted with, the end of the parental affection is completely answered in a short time; and then it ceases as if it had never been.

The infancy of man is longer and more helpless than that of any other animal. The parental affection is necessary for many years; it is highly useful through life; and therefore it terminates only with life. It extends to children's children, without any diminution of its force.

How common is it to see a young woman, in the gayest period of life, who has spent her days in mirth, and her nights in profound sleep, without solicitude or care, all at once transformed into the careful, the solicitous, the watchful nurse of her dear infant: doing nothing by day but gazing upon it, and serving it in the meanest offices; by night, depriving herself of sound sleep for months, that it may lie safe in her arms. Forgetful of herself, her whole care is centred in this little object. [151]

Such a sudden transformation of her whole habits, and occupation, and turn of mind, if we did not see it every day, would appear a more wonderful *metamorphosis* than any that Ovid has described.

This, however, is the work of nature, and not the effect of reason and reflection. For we see it in the good and in the bad, in the most thoughtless as well as in the thoughtful.

Nature has assigned different departments to the father and mother in rearing their offspring. This may be seen in many brute animals; and that it is so in the human species, was long ago observed by Socrates, and most beautifully illustrated by him, as we learn from Xenophon's *Œconomicks*. The parental affection in the different sexes is exactly adapted to the office assigned to each. The father would make an awkward nurse to a new-born child, and the mother too indulgent a guardian. But both act with propriety and grace in their proper sphere.

It is very remarkable that, when the office of rearing a child is transferred from the parent to another person, nature seems to transfer the affection along with the office. A wet nurse, or even a dry nurse, has commonly the same affection for her nursling as if she had borne it. The fact is so well known that nothing needs be said to confirm it; and it seems to be the work of nature.

Our affections are not immediately in our power, as our outward actions are. Nature has directed them to certain objects. We may do kind offices without affection; but we cannot create an affection which nature has not given. [152]

Reason might teach a man that his children are particularly committed to his care by the providence of God, and, on that account, that he ought to attend to them as his particular charge; but reason could not teach him to love them more than other children of equal merit, or to be more afflicted for their misfortunes or misbehaviour.

It is evident, therefore, that that peculiar sensibility of affection, with regard to his own children, is not the effect of reasoning or reflection, but the effect of that constitution which nature has given him.

There are some affections which we may call *rational*, because they are grounded upon an opinion of merit in the object. The parental affection is not of this kind. For, though a man's affection to his child may be increased by merit, and diminished by demerit, I think no man will say, that it took its rise from an opinion of merit. It is not opinion that creates the affection, but affection often creates opinion. It is apt to pervert the judgment, and create an opinion of merit where there is none

The absolute necessity of this parental affection, in order to the continuance of the human species, is so apparent that there is no need of arguments to prove it. The rearing of a child from its birth to maturity requires so much time and care, and such infinite attentions, that, if it were to be done merely from considerations of reason and duty, and were not sweetened by affection in parents, nurses, and guardians, there is reason to doubt whether one child in ten thousand would ever be reared. [153]

Beside the absolute necessity of this part of the human constitution to the preservation of the species, its utility is very great, for tempering the giddiness and impetuosity of youth, and improving its knowledge by the prudence and experience of age, for encouraging industry and frugality in the parents, in order to provide for their children, for the solace and support of parents under the infirmities of old age; not to mention that it probably gave rise to the first civil governments.

It does not appear that the parental, and other family affections, are, in general, either too strong or too weak for answering their end. If they were too weak, parents would be most apt to err on the side of undue severity; if too strong, of undue indulgence. As they are in fact, I believe no man can say that the errors are more general on one side than on the other.

When these affections are exerted according to their intention, under the direction of wisdom and prudence, the economy of such a family is a most delightful spectacle, and furnishes the most agreeable and affecting subject to the pencil of the painter, and to the pen of the orator and poet.

2. The *next* benevolent affection I mention, is *Gratitude to Benefactors.*

That good offices are, by the very constitution of our nature, apt to produce good will towards the benefactor, in good and bad men, in the savage and in the civilized, cannot surely be denied by any one in the least acquainted with human nature.

The danger of perverting a man's judgment by good deeds, where he ought to have no bias, is so well known that it is dishonourable in judges, in witnesses, in electors to offices of trust, to accept of them; and, in all civilized nations, they are, in such cases, prohibited, as the means of corruption. [154]

Those who would corrupt the sentence of a judge, the testimony of a witness, or the vote of an elector, know well, that they must not make a bargain, or stipulate what is to be done in return. This would shock every man who has the least pretension to morals. If the person can only be prevailed upon to accept the good office, as a testimony of pure and disinterested friendship, it is left to work upon his gratitude. He finds himself under a kind of moral obligation to consider the cause of his benefactor and friend in the most favourable light. He finds it easier to justify his conduct to himself, by favouring the interest of his benefactor, than by opposing it.

Thus the principle of gratitude is supposed, even in the nature of a bribe. Bad men know how to make this natural principle the most effectual means of corruption. The very best things may be turned to a bad use. But the natural tendency of this principle, and the intention of nature in planting it in the human breast, are, evidently to promote good-will among men, and to give to good offices the power of multiplying their kind, like seed sown in the earth, which brings a return, with increase.

Whether there be, or be not, in the more sagacious brutes, something that may be called gratitude, I will not dispute. We must allow this important difference between their gratitude and that of the human kind, that, in the last, the mind of the benefactor is chiefly regarded, in the first, the external action only. A brute-animal will be as kindly affected to him who feeds it in order to kill and eat it, as to him who does it from affection.

A man may be justly entitled to our gratitude, for an office that is useful, though it be, at the same time, disagreeable; and not only for doing, but for forbearing what he had a right to do. Among men, it is not every beneficial office that claims our gratitude, but such only as are not due to us in justice. [155] A favour alone gives a claim to gratitude; and a favour must be something more than justice requires. It does not appear that brutes have any conception of justice. They can neither distinguish hurt from injury, nor a favour from a good office that is due.

3. A *third* natural benevolent affection is *Pity and Compassion towards the Distressed.*

Of all persons, those in distress stand most in need of our good offices. And, for that reason, the Author of nature hath planted in the breast of every human creature a powerful advocate to plead their cause.

In man, and in some other animals, there are signs of distress, which nature hath both taught them to use, and taught all men to understand without any interpreter. These natural signs are more eloquent than language; they move our hearts, and produce a sympathy, and a desire to give relief.

There are few hearts so hard, but great distress will conquer their anger, their indignation, and every malevolent affection.

We sympathise even with the traitor and with the assassin, when we see him led to execution. It is only self-preservation and the public good, that makes us reluctantly assent to his being cut off from among men.

The practice of the Canadian nations towards their prisoners would tempt one to think that they have been able to root out the principle of compassion from their nature. But this, I apprehend, would be a rash conclusion. It is only a part of the prisoners of war that they devote to a cruel death. This gratifies the revenge of the women and children who have lost their husbands and fathers in the war. The other prisoners are kindly used, and adopted as brethren. [156]

Compassion with bodily pain is no doubt weakened among these savages, because they are trained from their infancy to be superior to death, and to every degree of pain; and he is thought unworthy of the name of a man, who cannot defy his tormentors, and sing his death-song in the midst of the most cruel tortures. He who can do this, is honoured as a brave man, though an enemy. But he must perish in the experiment.

A Canadian has the most perfect contempt for every man who thinks pain an intolerable evil. And nothing is so apt to stifle compassion as contempt, and an apprehension that the evil suffered is nothing but what ought to be manfully borne.

It must also be observed, that savages set no bounds to their revenge. Those who find no protection in laws and government never think themselves safe, but in the destruction of their enemy. And one of the chief advantages of civil government is, that it tempers the cruel passion of revenge, and opens the heart to compassion with every human wo.

It seems to be false religion only, that is able to check the tear of compassion.

We are told, that, in Portugal and Spain, a man condemned to be burned as an obstinate heretic, meets with no compassion, even from the multitude. It is true, they are taught to look upon him as an enemy to God, and doomed to hell-fire. But should not this very circumstance move compassion? Surely it would, if they were not taught that, in this case, it is a crime to shew compassion, or even to feel it.

4. A *fourth* benevolent affection is, *Esteem of the Wise and the Good.* [157]

The worst men cannot avoid feeling this in some degree. Esteem, veneration, devotion, are different degrees of the same affection. The perfection of wisdom, power, and goodness, which belongs only to the Almighty, is the object of the last.

It may be a doubt whether this principle of esteem, as well as that of gratitude, ought to be ranked in the order of animal principles, or if they ought not rather to be placed in a higher order.* They are certainly more allied to the rational nature than the others that have been named; nor is it evident that there is anything in brute animals that deserves the same name.

There is indeed a subordination in a herd of cattle, and in a flock of sheep, which, I believe, is determined by strength and courage, as it is among savage tribes of men. I have been informed that, in a pack of hounds, a stanch hound acquires a degree of esteem in the pack; so that, when the dogs are wandering in quest of the scent, if he opens, the pack immediately closes in with him, when they would not regard the opening of a dog of no reputation. This is something like a respect to wisdom.

But I have placed esteem of the wise and good in the order of animal principles, not from any persuasion that it is to be found in brute-animals, but because, I think, it appears in the most unimproved and in the most degenerate part of our species, even in those in whom we hardly perceive any exertion, either of reason or virtue.

I will not, however, dispute with any man who thinks that it deserves a more honourable name than that of an animal principle. It is of small importance what name we give it, if we are satisfied that that there is such a principle in the human constitution. [158]

5. *Friendship* is another benevolent affection.

Of this we have some instances famous in history—few indeed, but sufficient to shew that human nature is susceptible of that extraordinary attachment, sympathy, and affection, to one or a few persons, which the ancients thought alone worthy of the name of friendship.

The Epicureans found it very difficult to reconcile the existence of friendship to the principles of their sect. They were not so bold as to deny its existence. They even boasted that there had been more attachments of that kind between Epicureans than in any other sect. But the difficulty was, to account for real friendship upon Epicurean principles. They went into different hypotheses upon this point, three of which are explained by Torquatus the Epicurean, in Cicero's book, "De Finibus."

Cicero, in his reply to Torquatus, examines all the three, and shews them all to be either inconsistent with the nature of true friendship, or inconsistent with the fundamental principles of the Epicurean sect.

As to the friendship which the Epicureans boasted of among those of their sect, Cicero does not question the fact, but observes that, as there are many whose practice is worse than their principles, so there are some whose principles are worse than their practice, and that the bad principles of these Epicureans were overcome by the goodness of their nature.

6. Among the benevolent affections, the passion of *Love between the Sexes* cannot be overlooked.

Although it is commonly the theme of poets, it is not unworthy of the pen of the philosopher, as it is a most important part of the human constitution. [159]

It is no doubt made up of various ingredients, as many other principles of action are; but it certainly cannot exist without a very strong benevolent affection towards its object, in whom it finds, or conceives, everything that is amiable and excellent, and even something more than human. I consider it here only as a benevolent affection natural to man. And that it is so, no man can doubt who ever felt its force.

It is evidently intended by nature to direct a man in the choice of a mate, with

* See above, p. 551, b, note *.—H.

whom he desires to live, and to rear an offspring.

It has effectually secured this end in all ages, and in every state of society.

The passion of love, and the parental affection, are counterparts to each other; and when they are conducted with prudence, and meet with a proper return, are the source of all domestic felicity, the greatest, next to that of a good conscience, which this world affords.

As, in the present state of things, pain often dwells near to pleasure, and sorrow to joy, it needs not be thought strange that a passion, fitted and intended by nature to yield the greatest worldly felicity, should, by being ill-regulated or wrong directed, prove the occasion of the most pungent distress.

But its joys and its griefs, its different modifications in the different sexes, and its influence upon the character of both, though very important subjects, are fitter to be sung than said; and I leave them to those who have slept upon the two-topped Parnassus. [160]

7. The *last* benevolent affection I shall mention is, what we commonly call *Public Spirit*, that is, *an affection to any community to which we belong.*

If there be any man quite destitute of this affection, he must be as great a monster as a man born with two heads. Its effects are manifest in the whole of human life, and in the history of all nations.

The situation of a great part of mankind, indeed, is such, that their thoughts and views must be confined within a very narrow sphere, and be very much engrossed by their private concerns. With regard to an extensive public, such as a state or nation, they are like a drop to the ocean, so that they have rarely an opportunity of acting with a view to it.

In many, whose actions may affect the public, and whose rank and station lead them to think of it, private passions may be an overmatch for public spirit. All that can be inferred from this is, that their public spirit is weak, not that it does not exist.

If a man wishes well to the public, and is ready to do good to it rather than hurt, when it costs him nothing, he has some affection to it, though it may be scandalously weak in degree.

I believe every man has it in one degree or another. What man is there who does not resent satirical reflections upon his country, or upon any community of which he is a member?

Whether the affection be to a college or to a cloister, to a clan or to a profession, to a party or to a nation, it is public spirit. These affections differ, not in kind, but in the extent of their object. [161]

The object extends as our connections extend; and a sense of the connection carries the affection along with it to every community to which we can apply the pronouns *we* and *our*.

"Friend, parent, neighbour, first it will embrace,
His country next, and then all human race."—*Pope.*

Even in the misanthrope, this affection is not extinguished. It is overpowered by the apprehension he has of the worthlessness, the baseness, and the ingratitude of mankind. Convince him that there is any amiable quality in the species, and immediately his philanthropy revives, and rejoices to find an object on which it can exert itself.

Public spirit has this in common with every subordinate principle of action—that, when it is not under the government of reason and virtue, it may produce much evil as well as good. Yet, where there is least of reason and virtue to regulate it, its good far overbalances its ill.

It sometimes kindles or inflames animosities between communities or contending parties, and makes them treat each other with little regard to justice. It kindles wars between nations, and makes them destroy one another for trifling causes. But, without it, society could not subsist, and every community would be a rope of sand.

When under the direction of reason and virtue, it is the very image of God in the soul. It diffuses its benign influence as far as its power extends, and participates in the happiness of God, and of the whole creation.

These are the benevolent affections which appear to me to be parts of the human constitution. [162]

If any one thinks the enumeration incomplete, and that there are natural benevolent affections, which are not included under any of those that have been named, I shall very readily listen to such a correction, being sensible that such enumerations are very often incomplete.

If others should think that any, or all, the affections I have named, are acquired by education, or by habits and associations grounded on self-love, and are not original parts of our constitution; this is a point upon which, indeed, there has been much subtile disputation in ancient and modern times, and which, I believe, must be determined from what a man, by careful reflection, may feel in himself, rather than from what he observes in others. But I decline entering into this dispute, till I shall have explained that principle of action which we commonly call *self-love.*

I shall conclude this subject with some reflections upon the benevolent affections.

The *first* is, That all of them, in as fa as they are benevolent, in which view only I consider them, agree very much in the conduct they dispose us to, with regard to their objects.

They dispose us to do them good as far as we have power and opportunity; to wish them well, when we can do them no good; to judge favourably, and often partially, of them; to sympathise with them in their afflictions and calamities; and to rejoice with them in their happiness and good fortune.

It is impossible that there can be benevolent affection without sympathy both with the good and bad fortune of the object; and it appears to be impossible that there can be sympathy without benevolent affection. Men do not sympathise with one whom they hate; nor even with one to whose good or ill they are perfectly indifferent. [163]

We may sympathise with a perfect stranger, or even with an enemy whom we see in distress; but this is the effect of pity; and, if we did not pity him, we should not sympathise with him.

I take notice of this the rather, because a very ingenious author,* in his "Theory of Moral Sentiments," gives a very different account of the origin of Sympathy. It appears to me to be the effect of benevolent affection, and to be inseparable from it.

A *second* reflection is, That the constitution of our nature very powerfully invites us to cherish and cultivate in our minds the benevolent affections.

The agreeable feeling which always attends them as a present reward, appears to be intended by nature for this purpose.

Benevolence, from its nature, composes the mind, warms the heart, enlivens the whole frame, and brightens every feature of the countenance. It may justly be said to be medicinal both to soul and body. We are bound to it by duty; we are invited to it by interest; and because both these cords are often feeble, we have natural kind affections to aid them in their operation, and supply their defects; and these affections are joined with a manly pleasure in their exertion.

A *third* reflection is, That the natural benevolent affections furnish the most irresistible proof that the Author of our nature intended that we should live in society, and do good to our fellow-men as we have opportunity; since this great and important part of the human constitution has a manifest relation to society, and can have no exercise nor use in a solitary state.

The *last* reflection is, That the different principles of action have different degrees of dignity, and rise one above another in our estimation, when we make them objects of contemplation. [164]

We ascribe no dignity to instincts or to habits. They lead us only to admire the wisdom of the Creator, in adapting them so perfectly to the manner of life of the different animals in which they are found. Much the same may be said of appetites. They serve rather for use than ornament.

The desires of knowledge, of power, and of esteem, rise higher in our estimation, and we consider them as giving dignity and ornament to man. The actions proceeding from them, though not properly virtuous, are manly and respectable, and claim a just superiority over those that proceed merely from appetite. This, I think, is the uniform judgment of mankind.

If we apply the same kind of judgment to our benevolent affections, they appear not only manly and respectable, but amiable in a high degree.

They are amiable even in brute animals. We love the meekness of the lamb, the gentleness of the dove, the affection of a dog to his master. We cannot, without pleasure, observe the timid ewe, who never shewed the least degree of courage in her own defence, become valiant and intrepid in defence of her lamb, and boldly assault those enemies, the very sight of whom was wont to put her to flight.

How pleasant is it to see the family economy of a pair of little birds in rearing their tender offspring; the conjugal affection and fidelity of the parents; their cheerful toil and industry in providing food to their family; their sagacity in concealing their habitation; the arts they use, often at the peril of their own lives, to decoy hawks, and other enemies, from their dwellingplace; and the affliction they feel when some unlucky boy has robbed them of the dear pledges of their affection, and frustrated all their hopes of their rising family? [165]

If kind affection be amiable in brutes, it is not less so in our own species. Even the external signs of it have a powerful charm.

Every one knows that a person of accomplished good breeding charms every one he converses with. And what is this good breeding? If we analyze it, we shall find it to be made up of looks, gestures, and speeches, which are the natural signs of benevolence and good affection. He who has got the habit of using these signs with propriety, and without meanness, is a well-bred and a polite man.

What is that beauty in the features of the face, particularly of the fair sex, which all men love and admire? I believe it consists chiefly in the features which indicate good affections. Every indication of meekness, gentleness, and benignity, is a beauty. On the contrary, every feature that indi-

* Adam Smith.—H.

cates pride, passion, envy, and malignity, is a deformity.*

Kind affections, therefore, are amiable in brutes. Even the signs and shadows of them are highly attractive in our own species. Indeed they are the joy and the comfort of human life, not to good men only, but even to the vicious and dissolute.

Without society, and the intercourse of kind affection, man is a gloomy, melancholy, and joyless being. His mind oppressed with cares and fears, he cannot enjoy the balm of sound sleep: in constant dread of impending danger, he starts at the rustling of a leaf. His ears are continually upon the stretch, and every zephyr brings some sound that alarms him.

When he enters into society, and feels security in the good affection of friends and neighbours, it is then only that his fear vanishes, and his mind is at ease. His courage is raised, his understanding is enlightened, and his heart dilates with joy. [166]

Human society may be compared to a heap of embers, which when placed asunder, can retain neither their light nor heat, amidst the surrounding elements; but, when brought together, they mutually give heat and light to each other; the flame breaks forth, and not only defends itself, but subdues everything around it.

The security, the happiness, and the strength of human society, spring solely from the reciprocal benevolent affections of its members.

The benevolent affections, though they be all honourable and lovely, are not all equally so. There is a subordination among them; and the honour we pay to them generally corresponds to the extent of their object.

The good husband, the good father, the good friend, the good neighbour, we honour as a good man, worthy of our love and affection. But the man in whom these more private affections are swallowed up in zeal for the good of his country and of mankind, who goes about doing good, and seeks opportunities of being useful to his species, we revere as more than a good man—as a hero, as a good angel.

CHAPTER V.

OF MALEVOLENT AFFECTION.

ARE there, in the constitution of man, any affections that may be called *malevolent?* What are they? and what is their use and end? [167]

* Hence, on this principle of association, some philosophers would exclusively explain the sentiment of the Beautiful. See above, p. [illegible].—H.

To me there seem to be *two* which we may call by that name. They are *Emulation* and *Resentment*. These I take to be parts of the human constitution, given us by our Maker for good ends, and, when properly directed and regulated, of excellent use. But, as their excess or abuse, to which human nature is very prone, is the source and spring of all the malevolence that is to be found among men, it is on that account I call them malevolent.

If any man thinks that they deserve a softer name—since they may be exercised, according to the intention of nature, without malevolence—to this I have no objection.

[I.] By *Emulation*, I mean a desire of superiority to our rivals in any pursuit, accompanied with an uneasiness at being surpassed.*

Human life has justly been compared to a race. The prize is superiority in one kind or another. But the species or forms (if I may use the expression) of superiority among men are infinitely diversified.

There is no man so contemptible in his own eyes as to hinder him from entering the lists in one form or another; and he will always find competitors to rival him in his own way.

We see emulation among brute-animals. Dogs and horses contend each with his kind in the race. Many animals of the gregarious kind contend for superiority in their flock or herd, and shew manifest signs of jealousy when others pretend to rival them.

The emulation of the brute-animals is mostly confined to swiftness, or strength, or favour with their females. But the emulation of the human kind has a much wider field. [168]

In every profession, and in every accomplishment of body or mind, real or imaginary, there are rivalships. Literary men rival one another in literary abilities; artists, in their several arts; the fair sex, in their beauty and attractions, and in the respect paid them by the other sex.

In every political society, from a petty corporation up to the national administration, there is a rivalship for power and influence.

Men have a natural desire of power, without respect to the power of others. This we call *Ambition*. But the desire of superiority, either in power, or in anything we think worthy of estimation, has a respect to rivals, and is what we properly call *emulation*.

* Reid has not properly distinguished *Emulation* from *Envy*. See, among others, Aristotle's "Rhetoric," Book Second, in the chapters on those affections; Butler, Sermon I. "On Human Nature;" Stewart's "Philosophy of the Active Powers," I. p. [illegible], sq.; and other authors quoted by him.—H.

The stronger the desire is, the more pungent will be the uneasiness of being found behind, and the mind will be the more hurt by this humiliating view.

Emulation has a manifest tendency to improvement. Without it life would stagnate, and the discoveries of art and genius would be at a stand. This principle produces a constant fermentation in society, by which, though dregs may be produced, the better part is purified and exalted to a perfection which it could not otherwise attain.

We have not sufficient *data* for a comparison of the good and bad effects which this principle actually produces in society; but there is ground to think of this, as of other natural principles, that the good overbalances the ill. As far as it is under the dominion of reason and virtue, its effects are always good; when left to be guided by passion and folly, they are often very bad. [169]

Reason directs us to strive for superiority only in things that have real excellence, otherwise we spend our labour for that which profiteth not. To value ourselves for superiority in things that have no real worth, or none compared with what they cost, is to be vain of our own folly; and to be uneasy at the superiority of others in such things, is no less ridiculous.

Reason directs us to strive for superiority only in things in our power, and attainable by our exertion, otherwise we shall be like the frog in the fable, who swelled herself till she burst, in order to equal the ox in magnitude.

To check all desire of things not attainable, and every uneasy thought in the want of them, is an obvious dictate of prudence, as well as of virtue and religion.

If emulation be regulated by such maxims of reason, and all undue partiality to ourselves be laid aside, it will be a powerful principle of our improvement, without hurt to any other person. It will give strength to the nerves and vigour to the mind in every noble and manly pursuit.

But dismal are its effects, when it is not under the direction of reason and virtue. It has often the most malignant influence on men's opinions, on their affections, and on their actions.

It is an old observation, that affection follows opinion; and it is undoubtedly true in many cases. A man cannot be grateful without the opinion of a favour done him. He cannot have deliberate resentment without the opinion of an injury; nor esteem without the opinion of some estimable quality; nor compassion without the opinion of suffering.

But it is no less true, that opinion sometimes follows affection—not that it it ought, but that it actually does so, by giving a false bias to our judgment. We are apt to be partial to our friends, and still more to ourselves. [170]

Hence the desire of superiority leads men to put an undue estimation upon those things wherein they excel, or think they excel. And by this means, pride may feed itself upon the very dregs of human nature.

The same desire of superiority may lead men to undervalue those things wherein they either despair of excelling, or care not to make the exertion necessary for that end. "The grapes are sour," said the fox, when he saw them beyond his reach. The same principle leads men to detract from the merit of others, and to impute their brightest actions to mean or bad motives.

He who runs a race feels uneasiness at seeing another outstrip him. This is uncorrupted nature, and the work of God within him. But this uneasiness may produce either of two very different effects. It may incite him to make more vigorous exertions, and to strain every nerve to get before his rival. This is fair and honest emulation. This is the effect it is intended to produce. But, if he has not fairness and candour of heart, he will look with an evil eye upon his competitor, and will endeavour to trip him, or to throw a stumblingblock in his way. This is pure envy, the most malignant passion that can lodge in the human breast; which devours, as its natural food, the fame and the happiness of those who are most deserving of our esteem.*

If there be in some men, a proneness to detract from the character, even of persons unknown or indifferent, in others an avidity to hear and to propagate scandal, to what principle in human nature must we ascribe these qualities? The failings of others surely add nothing to our worth, nor are they, in themselves, a pleasant subject of thought or of discourse. But they flatter pride, by giving an opinion of our superiority to those from whom we detract. [171]

Is it not possible that the same desire of superiority may have some secret influence upon those who love to display their eloquence in declaiming upon the corruption of human nature, and the wickedness, fraud, and insincerity of mankind in general? It ought always to be taken for granted, that the declaimer is an exception to the general rule, otherwise he would rather choose, even for his own sake, to draw a veil over the nakedness of his species. But, hoping that his audience will be so civil as not to include him in the black description, he rises superior by the depression of the species, and

* In this paragraph Reid makes the distinction between Envy and Emulation, which, in the other parts of the chapter, he has not kept in view.—H.

stands alone, like Noah in the antediluvian world. This looks like envy against the human race.

It would be endless, and noways agreeable, to enumerate all the evils and all the vices which passion and folly beget upon emulation. Here, as in most cases, the corruption of the best things is the worst. In brute-animals, emulation has little matter to work upon, and its effects, good or bad, are few. It may produce battles of cocks and battles of bulls, and little else that is observable. But in mankind, it has an infinity of matter to work upon, and its good or bad effects, according as it is well or ill regulated and directed, multiply in proportion.

The conclusion to be drawn from what has been said upon this principle is, that emulation, as far as it is a part of our constitution, is highly useful and important in society; that in the wise and good, it produces the best effects without any harm; but in the foolish and vicious, it is the parent of a great part of the evils of life, and of the most malignant vices that stain human nature. [172]

[2.] We are next to consider *Resentment*.

Nature disposes us, when we are hurt, to resist and retaliate. Besides the bodily pain occasioned by the hurt, the mind is ruffled, and a desire raised to retaliate upon the author of the hurt or injury. This, in general, is what we call *anger* or *resentment*.

A very important distinction is made by Bishop Butler between sudden resentment, which is a blind impulse arising from our constitution, and that which is deliberate. The first may be raised by hurt of any kind; but the last can only be raised by injury real or conceived.

The same distinction is made by Lord Kames in his "Elements of Criticism." What Butler calls *sudden*, he calls *instinctive*.

We have not, in common language, different names for these different kinds of resentment; but the distinction is very necessary, in order to our having just notions of this part of the human constitution. It corresponds perfectly with the distinction I have made between the animal and rational principles of action. For this sudden or instinctive resentment, is an animal principle common to us with brute-animals. But that resentment which the authors I have named call *deliberate*, must fall under the class of rational principles.

It is to be observed, however, that, by referring it to that class, I do not mean, that it is always kept within the bounds that reason prescribes, but only that it is proper to man as a reasonable being, capable, by his rational faculties, of distinguishing between hurt and injury; a distinction which no brute-animal can make.

Both these kinds of resentment are raised, whether the hurt or injury be done to ourselves, or to those we are interested in. [173]

Wherever there is any benevolent affection towards others, we resent their wrongs in proportion to the strength of our affection. Pity and sympathy with the sufferer produce resentment against the author of the suffering, as naturally as concern for ourselves produces resentment of our own wrongs.

I shall first consider that resentment which I call *animal*, which Butler calls *sudden*, and Lord Kames *instinctive*.

In every animal to which nature hath given the power of hurting its enemy, we see an endeavour to retaliate the ill that is done to it. Even a mouse will bite when it cannot run away.

Perhaps there may be some animals to whom nature hath given no offensive weapon. To such, anger and resentment would be of no use; and I believe we shall find that they never shew any sign of it. But there are few of this kind.

Some of the more sagacious animals can be provoked to fierce anger, and retain it long. Many of them shew great animosity in defending their young, who hardly shew any in defending themselves. Others resist every assault made upon the flock or herd to which they belong. Bees defend their hive, wild beasts their den, and birds their nest.

This sudden resentment operates in a similar manner in men and in brutes, and appears to be given by nature to both for the same end—namely, for defence, even in cases where there is no time for deliberation. It may be compared to that natural instinct by which a man, who has lost his balance and begins to fall, makes a sudden and violent effort to recover himself, without any intention or deliberation. [174]

In such efforts, men often exert a degree of muscular strength beyond what they are able to exert by a calm determination of the will, and thereby save themselves from many a dangerous fall.

By a like violent and sudden impulse, nature prompts us to repel hurt upon the cause of it, whether it be man or beast. The instinct before mentioned is solely defensive, and is prompted by fear. This sudden resentment is offensive, and is prompted by anger, but with a view to defence.

Man, in his present state, is surrounded with so many dangers from his own species, from brute-animals, from everything around him, that he has need of some defensive armour that shall always be ready in the moment of danger. His reason is of great use for this purpose, when there is time to apply it. But, in many cases, the mischief would be done before reason could think of the means of preventing it.

The wisdom of nature hath provided two means to supply this defect of our reason. One of these is the instinct* before mentioned, by which the body, upon the appearance of danger, is instantly, and without thought or intention, put in that posture which is proper for preventing the danger, or lessening it. Thus, we wink hard when our eyes are threatened; we bend the body to avoid a stroke; we make a sudden effort to recover our balance, when in danger of falling. By such means we are guarded from many dangers which our reason would come too late to prevent.

But, as offensive arms are often the surest means of defence, by deterring the enemy from an assault, nature hath also provided man, and other animals, with this kind of defence, by that sudden resentment of which we now speak, which outruns the quickest determinations of reason, and takes fire in an instant, threatening the enemy with retaliation. [175]

The first of these principles operates upon the defender only; but this operates both upon the defender and the assailant, inspiring the former with courage and animosity, and striking terror into the latter. It proclaims to all assailants, what our ancient Scottish kings did upon their coins, by the emblem of a thistle, with this motto, *Nemo me impune lacesset*. By this, in innumerable cases, men and beasts are deterred from doing hurt, and others thereby secured from suffering it.

But, as resentment supposes an object on whom we may retaliate, how comes it to pass, that in brutes, very often, and sometimes in our own species, we see it wreaked upon inanimate things, which are incapable of suffering by it?

Perhaps it might be a sufficient answer to this question—That nature acts by general laws, which, in some particular cases, may go beyond or fall short of their intention, though they be ever so well adapted to it in general.

But I confess it seems to me impossible that there should be resentment against a thing which at that very moment is considered as inanimate, and consequently incapable either of intending hurt, or of being punished. For what can be more absurd than to be angry with the knife for cutting me, or with the weight for falling upon my toes? There must, therefore, I conceive, be some momentary notion or conception that the object of our resentment is capable of punishment; and, if it be natural, before reflection, to be angry with things inanimate, it seems to be a necessary consequence, that it is natural to think that they have life and feeling.

Several phænomena in human nature lead us to conjecture that, in the earliest period of life, we are apt to think every object about us to be animated. Judging of them by ourselves, we ascribe to them the feelings we are conscious of in ourselves. So we see a little girl judges of her doll and of her playthings. And so we see rude nations judge of the heavenly bodies, of the elements, and of the sea, rivers, and fountains. [176]

If this be so, it ought not to be said, that by reason and experience, we learn to ascribe life and intelligence to things which we before considered as inanimate. It ought rather to be said—That by reason and experience we learn that certain things are inanimate, to which at first we ascribed life and intelligence.

If this be true, it is less surprising that, before reflection, we should for a moment relapse into this prejudice of our early years, and treat things as if they had life, which we once believed to have it.

It does not much affect our present argument, whether this be or be not the cause why a dog pursues and gnashes at the stone that hurt him; and why a man, in a passion for losing at play, sometimes wreaks his vengeance on the cards or dice.

It is not strange that a blind animal impulse should sometimes lose its proper direction. In brutes this has no bad consequence; in men the least ray of reflection corrects it, and shews its absurdity.

It is sufficiently evident, upon the whole, that this sudden or animal resentment, is intended by nature for our defence. It prevents mischief by the fear of punishment. It is a kind of penal statute, promulgated by nature, the execution of which is committed to the sufferer.

It may be expected, indeed, that one who judges in his own cause, will be disposed to seek more than an equitable redress. But this disposition is checked by the resentment of the other party. [177]

Yet, in the state of nature, injuries once begun will often be reciprocated between the parties, until mortal enmity is produced, and each party thinks himself safe only in the destruction of his enemy.

This right of redressing and punishing

* See Mr Stewart, in "Philosophical Essays," Note (I), who censures Reid for applying the term *instinct* to an acquired dexterity. Reid may be defended, however, on the ground that, though in man there may be *prima facie* reason on which to explain the motions in question as the results of practice, that this is not, at least in a great measure, the case. We see many of the brutes performing these actions from the moment of birth in full perfection; those, to wit, as I have ascertained, who have the cerebellum proportionally to the brain proper, then fully developed; and it is only with the proportional developement of this part of the encephalos, that children obtain the full command of their limbs, the complete power of regulated movement.—H.

our own wrongs, so apt to be abused, is one of those natural rights which, in political society, is given up to the laws, and to the civil magistrate; and this, indeed, is one of the capital advantages we reap from the political union, that the evils arising from ungoverned resentment are in a great degree prevented.

Although deliberate resentment does not properly belong to the class of animal principles; yet, as both have the same name, and are distinguished only by philosophers, and as in real life they are commonly intermixed, I shall here make some remarks upon it.

A small degree of reason and reflection teaches a man that injury only, and not mere hurt, is a just object of resentment to a rational creature. A man may suffer grievously by the hand of another, not only without injury, but with the most friendly intention; as in the case of a painful chirurgical operation. Every man of common sense sees, that to resent such suffering, is not the part of a man, but of a brute.

Mr Locke mentions a gentleman who, having been cured of madness by a very harsh and offensive operation, with great sense of gratitude, owned the cure as the greatest obligation he could have received, but could never bear the sight of the operator, because it brought back the idea of that agony which he had endured from his hands. [178]

In this case, we see distinctly the operation both of the animal and of the rational principle. The first produced an aversion to the operator, which reason was not able to overcome; and probably in a weak mind, might have produced lasting resentment and hatred. But, in this gentleman, reason so far prevailed as to make him sensible that gratitude, and not resentment, was due.

Suffering may give a bias to the judgment, and make us apprehend injury where no injury is done. But, I think, without an apprehension of injury, there can be no deliberate resentment.

Hence, among enlightened nations, hostile armies fight without anger or resentment. The vanquished are not treated as offenders, but as brave men who have fought for their country unsuccessfully, and who are entitled to every office of humanity consistent with the safety of the conquerors.

If we analyze that deliberate resentment which is proper to rational creatures, we shall find that, though it agrees with that which is merely animal in some respects, it differs in others. Both are accompanied with an uneasy sensation, which disturbs the peace of the mind. Both prompt us to seek redress of our sufferings, and security from harm. But, in deliberate resentment, there must be an opinion of injury done or intended. And an opinion of injury implies an idea of justice, and consequently a moral faculty.

The very notion of an injury is, that it is less than we may justly claim; as, on the contrary, the notion of a favour is, that it is more than we can justly claim. Whence, it is evident, that justice is the standard by which both a favour and an injury are to be weighed and estimated. Their very nature and definition consist in their exceeding or falling short of this standard. No man, therefore, can have the idea either of a favour or of an injury, who has not the idea of justice. [179]

That very idea of justice which enters into cool and deliberate resentment, tends to restrain its excesses. For, as there is injustice in doing an injury, so there is injustice in punishing it beyond measure.

To a man of candour and reflection, consciousness of the frailty of human nature, and that he has often stood in need of forgiveness himself, the pleasure of renewing good understanding after it has been interrupted, the inward approbation of a generous and forgiving disposition, and even the irksomeness and uneasiness of a mind ruffled by resentment, plead strongly against its excesses.

Upon the whole, when we consider, That, on the one hand, every benevolent affection is pleasant in its nature, is health to the soul, and a cordial to the spirits; That nature has made even the outward expression of benevolent affections in the countenance, pleasant to every beholder, and the chief ingredient of beauty in the *human face divine*; That, on the other hand, every malevolent affection, not only in its faulty excesses, but in its moderate degrees, is vexation and disquiet to the mind, and even gives deformity to the countenance—it is evident that, by these signals, nature loudly admonishes us to use the former as our daily bread, both for health and pleasure, but to consider the latter as a nauseous medicine, which is never to be taken without necessity; and even then in no greater quantity than the necessity requires. [180]

CHAPTER VI.

OF PASSION.

Before I proceed to consider the rational principles of action, it is proper to observe that there are some things belonging to the mind, which have great influence upon human conduct, by exciting or allaying, inflaming or cooling the animal principles we have mentioned.

Three of this kind deserve particular consideration. I shall call them by the names of *Passion*, *Disposition*, and *Opinion*.

The meaning of the word *Passion* is not precisely ascertained, either in common discourse, or in the writings of philosophers.

I think it is commonly put to signify some agitation of mind, which is opposed to that state of tranquillity and composure in which a man is most master of himself.

The word πάθος, which answers to it in the Greek language, is, by Cicero, rendered by the word *perturbatio*.

It has always been conceived to bear analogy to a storm at sea,* or to a tempest in the air.† It does not therefore signify anything in the mind that is constant and permanent, but something that is occasional, and has a limited duration, like a storm or tempest.

Passion commonly produces sensible effects even upon the body. It changes the voice, the features, and the gesture. The external signs of passion have, in some cases, a great resemblance to those of madness; in others, to those of melancholy. It gives often a degree of muscular force and agility to the body, far beyond what it possesses in calm moments. [181]

The effects of passion upon the mind are not less remarkable. It turns the thoughts involuntarily to the objects related to it, so that a man can hardly think of anything else. It gives often a strange bias to the judgment, making a man quick-sighted in everything that tends to inflame his passion, and to justify it, but blind to everything that tends to moderate and allay it. Like a magic lanthorn, it raises up spectres and apparitions that have no reality, and throws false colours upon every object. It can turn deformity into beauty, vice into virtue, and virtue into vice.

The sentiments of a man under its influence will appear absurd and ridiculous, not only to other men, but even to himself, when the storm is spent and is succeeded by a calm. Passion often gives a violent impulse to the will, and makes a man do what he knows he shall repent as long as he lives.

That such are the effects of passion, I think all men agree. They have been described in lively colours by poets, orators, and moralists, in all ages.* But men have given more attention to the effects of passion than to its nature; and, while they have copiously and elegantly described the former, they have not precisely defined the latter.

The controversy between the ancient Peripatetics and the Stoics, with regard to the passions, was probably owing to their affixing different meanings to the word. The one sect maintained that the passions are good and useful parts of our constitution, while they are held under the government of reason. The other sect, conceiving that nothing is to be called passion which does not, in some degree, cloud and darken the understanding, considered all passion as hostile to reason, and therefore maintained that, in the wise man, passion should have no existence, but be utterly exterminated. [182]

If both sects had agreed about the definition of passion, they would probably have had no difference. But while one considered passion only as the cause of those bad effects which it often produces, and the other considered it as fitted by nature to produce good effects, while it is under subjection to reason, it does not appear that what one sect justified, was the same thing which the other condemned. Both allowed that no dictate of passion ought to be followed in opposition to reason. Their difference therefore was verbal more than real, and was owing to their giving different meanings to the same word.

The precise meaning of this word seems not to be more clearly ascertained among modern philosophers.

Mr Hume gives the name of *passion* to every principle of action in the human mind; and, in consequence of this, maintains that every man is and ought to be led by his passions, and that the use of reason is to be subservient to the passions.

Dr Hutcheson, considering all the principles of action as so many determinations

---

* "Sæpe mihi humanæ meditanti incommoda vitæ,
Speque leves, trepidosque metus, vanosque labores,
Gaudiaque instabili semper fucata sereno,
Non secus ac navis lato jactata profundo,
Quam venti, violensque æstus, cæcusque magister
In diversa trahunt," &c.—Buchanan.

Montaigne alludes to these verses in the tenth chapter of his third book, but without naming his master. He has thus puzzled his commentators.—H.

† "Nubibus atris
Condita nullum
Fundere possunt
Sidera lumen.
Si mare volvens
Turbidus Auster
Misceat æstum,
Vitrea dudum,
Parque serenis
Unda diebus,
Mox resoluto
Sordida cœno
Visibus obstat.
. . . . .
Tu quoque si vis
Lumine claro
Cernere verum,
Tramite recto
Carpere callem;
Gaudia pelle,
Pelle timorem,
Spemque fugato,
Nec dolor adsit.
Nubila mens est,
Vinctaque frenis
Hæc ubi regnant.—Boethius.—H.

* See particularly Aristotle's delineation of the Passions in the second book of his "Rhetoric."—H.

or motions of the will, divides them into the *calm* and the *turbulent*. The turbulent, he says, are our *appetites* and our *passions*. Of the passions, as well as of the calm determinations, he says, that "some are *benevolent*, others are *selfish*; that anger, envy, indignation, and some others, may be either selfish or benevolent, according as they arise from some opposition to our own interests, or to those of our friends, or persons beloved or esteemed."

It appears, therefore, that this excellent author gives the name of *passions*, not to every principle of action, but to some, and to those only when they are turbulent and vehement, not when they are calm and deliberate. [183]

Our natural desires and affections may be so calm as to leave room for reflection, so that we find no difficulty in deliberating coolly, whether, in such a particular instance, they ought to be gratified or not. On other occasions, they may be so importunate as to make deliberation very difficult, urging us, by a kind of violence, to their immediate gratification.

Thus, a man may be sensible of an injury without being inflamed. He judges coolly of the injury, and of the proper means of redress. This is resentment without passion. It leaves to the man the entire command of himself.

On another occasion, the same principle of resentment rises into a flame. His blood boils within him; his looks, his voice, and his gesture are changed; he can think of nothing but immediate revenge, and feels a strong impulse, without regard to consequences, to say and do things which his cool reason cannot justify. This is the passion of resentment.

What has been said of resentment may easily be applied to other natural desires and affections. When they are so calm as neither to produce any sensible effects upon the body, nor to darken the understanding and weaken the power of self-command, they are not called passions. But the same principle, when it becomes so violent as to produce these effects upon the body and upon the mind, is a passion, or, as Cicero very properly calls it, a perturbation.

It is evident, that this meaning of the word *passion* accords much better with its common use in language, than that which Mr Hume gives it. [184]

When he says, that men ought to be governed by their passions only, and that the use of reason is to be subservient to the passions, this, at first hearing, appears a shocking paradox, repugnant to good morals and to common sense; but, like most other paradoxes, when explained according to his meaning, it is nothing but an abuse of words.

For, if we give the name of *passion* to every principle of action, in every degree, and give the name of *reason* solely to the power of discerning the fitness of means to ends, it will be true that the use of reason is to be subservient to the passions.

As I wish to use words as agreeably as possible to their common use in language,* I shall, by the word *passion* mean, not any principle of action distinct from those desires and affections before explained, but *such a degree of vehemence in them*, or in any of them, as is apt to produce those effects upon the body or upon the mind which have been above described.

Our *appetites*, even when vehement, are not, I think, very commonly called *passions*; yet they are capable of being inflamed to rage, and in that case their effects are very similar to those of the passions; and what is said of one may be applied to both.

Having explained what I mean by passions, I think it unnecessary to enter into any enumeration of them, since they differ, not in kind, but rather in degree, from the principles already enumerated.

The common division of the passions into *desire* and *aversion*, *hope* and *fear*, *joy* and *grief*, has been mentioned almost by every author who has treated of them, and needs no explication. But we may observe, that these are ingredients or modifications, not of the passions only, but of every principle of action, animal and rational. [185]

All of them imply the desire of some object; and the desire of an object cannot be without aversion to its contrary; and, according as the object is present or absent, desire and aversion will be variously modified into joy or grief, hope or fear. It is evident that desire and aversion, joy and grief, hope and fear, may be either calm and sedate, or vehement and passionate.

Passing these, therefore, as common to all principles of action, whether calm or vehement, I shall only make some observations on passion in general, which tend to shew its influence on human conduct.

First, It is passion that makes us liable to strong temptations. Indeed, if we had no passions, we should hardly be under any temptation to wrong conduct. For, when we view things calmly, and free from any of the false colours which passion throws upon them, we can hardly fail to see the right and the wrong, and to see that the first is more eligible than the last.

I believe a cool and deliberate preference of ill to good is never the first step into vice.

"When the woman saw that the tree was good for food, and that it was pleasant to the eyes, and a tree to be desired to

* It is not in *all* languages that Reid's limitation of the term *passion* to the more vehement affections, will find a warrant.—H.

make one wise, she took of the fruit thereof and did eat, and gave also to her husband with her, and he did eat; and the eyes of them both were opened." Inflamed desire had blinded the eyes of their understanding. [186]

"Fixed on the fruit she gaz'd, which to behold
Might tempt alone; and in her ears the sound
Yet rung of his persuasive words, impregn'd
With reason to her seeming, and with truth.
——Fair to the eye, inviting to the taste,
Of virtue to make wise: what hinders, then,
To reach, and feed at once both body and mind?"
Milton.

Thus our first parents were tempted to disobey their Maker, and all their posterity are liable to temptation from the same cause. Passion, or violent appetite, first blinds the understanding, and then perverts the will.

It is passion, therefore, and the vehement motions of appetite, that make us liable, in our present state, to strong temptations to deviate from our duty. This is the lot of human nature in the present period of our existence.

Human virtue must gather strength by struggle and effort. As infants, before they can walk without stumbling, must be exposed to many a fall and bruise; as wrestlers acquire their strength and agility by many a combat and violent exertion; so it is in the noblest powers of human nature, as well as the meanest, and even in virtue itself.

It is not only made manifest by temptation and trial, but by these means it acquires its strength and vigour.

Men must acquire patience by suffering, and fortitude by being exposed to danger, and every other virtue by situations that put it to trial and exercise.

This, for anything we know, may be necessary in the nature of things. It is certainly a law of nature with regard to man. [187]

Whether there may be orders of intelligent and moral creatures who never were subject to any temptation, nor had their virtue put to any trial, we cannot without presumption determine. But it is evident that this neither is, nor ever was the lot of man, not even in the state of innocence.

Sad, indeed, would be the condition of man, if the temptations to which, by the constitution of his nature, and by his circumstances, he is liable, were irresistible. Such a state would not at all be a state of trial and discipline.

Our condition here is such that, on the one hand, passion often tempts and solicits us to do wrong; on the other hand, reason and conscience oppose the dictates of passion. The flesh lusteth against the spirit, and the spirit against the flesh. And upon the issue of this conflict, the character of the man and his fate depend.

If reason be victorious, his virtue is strengthened; he has the inward satisfaction of having fought a good fight in behalf of his duty, and the peace of his mind is preserved.

If, on the other hand, passion prevail against the sense of duty, the man is conscious of having done what he ought not and might not have done. His own heart condemns him, and he is guilty to himself.

This conflict between the passions of our animal nature and the calm dictates of reason and conscience, is not a theory invented to solve the phænomena of human conduct; it is a fact, of which every man who attends to his own conduct is conscious.

In the most ancient philosophy of which we have any account—I mean that of the Pythagorean school*—the mind of man was compared to a state or commonwealth, in which there are various powers, some that ought to govern and others that ought to be subordinate. [188]

The good of the whole, which is the supreme law in this, as in every commonwealth, requires that this subordination be preserved, and that the governing powers have always the ascendant over the appetites and passions. All wise and good conduct consists in this; all folly and vice in the prevalence of passion over the dictates of reason.

This philosophy was adopted by Plato; and it is so agreeable to what every man feels in himself, that it must always prevail with men who think without bias to a system.

The governing powers, of which these ancient philosophers speak, are the same which I call the *rational* principles of action, and which I shall have occasion to explain. I only mention them here, because, without a regard to them, the influence of the passions, and their rank in our constitution, cannot be distinctly understood.

A *second* observation is, That the impulse of passion is not always to what is bad, but very often to what is good, and what our reason approves. There are some passions, as Dr Hutcheson observes, that are benevolent, as well as others that are selfish.

The affections of resentment and emulation, with those that spring from them, from their very nature, disturb and disquiet the mind, though they be not carried beyond the bounds which reason prescribes; and therefore they are commonly called passions, even in their moderate degrees. From a similar cause, the benevolent affections, which are placid in their nature, and are

* Of the Pythagorean school and its *particular* doctrines, we know very little with any certainty. The *articulate* accounts we have from the lower Platonists are recent and fabulous, and the treatises under the names of the Pythagorean philosophers themselves, spurious.—H.

rarely carried beyond the bounds of reason, are very seldom called passions. We do not give the name of passion to benevolence, gratitude, or friendship. Yet we must except from this general rule, love between the sexes, which, as it commonly discomposes the mind, and is not easily kept within reasonable bounds, is always called a passion. [189]

All our natural desires and affections are good and necessary parts of our constitution; and passion, being only a certain degree of vehemence in these, its natural tendency is to good, and it is by accident that it leads us wrong.

Passion is very properly said to be blind. It looks not beyond the present gratification. It belongs to reason to attend to the accidental circumstances which may sometimes make that gratification improper or hurtful. When there is no impropriety in it, much more when it is our duty, passion aids reason, and gives additional force to its dictates.

Sympathy with the distressed may bring them a charitable relief, when a calm sense of duty would be too weak to produce the effect.

Objects, either good or ill, conceived to be very distant, when they are considered coolly, have not that influence upon men which in reason they ought to have. Imagination, like the eye, diminisheth its objects in proportion to their distance. The passions of hope and fear must be raised, in order to give such objects their due magnitude in the imagination, and their due influence upon our conduct.

The dread of disgrace and of the civil magistrate, and the apprehension of future punishment, prevent many crimes, which bad men, without these restraints, would commit, and contribute greatly to the peace and good order of society. [190]

There is no bad action which some passion may not prevent; nor is there any external good action, of which some passion may not be the main spring; and it is very probable that even the passions of men, upon the whole, do more good to society than hurt.

The ill that is done draws our attention more, and is imputed solely to human passions. The good may have better motives, and charity leads us to think that it has; but, as we see not the heart, it is impossible to determine what share men's passions may have in its production.

The *last* observation is—That, if we distinguish, in the effects of our passions, those which are altogether involuntary and without the sphere of our power, from the effects which may be prevented by an exertion, perhaps a great exertion, of self-government; we shall find the first to be good and highly useful, and the last only to be bad.

Not to speak of the effects of moderate passions upon the health of the body, to which some agitation of this kind seems to be no less useful than storms and tempests to the salubrity of the air; every passion naturally draws our attention to its object, and interests us in it.

The mind of man is naturally desultory, and when it has no interesting object in view, roves from one to another, without fixing its attention upon any one. A transient and careless glance is all that we bestow upon objects in which we take no concern. It requires a strong degree of curiosity, or some more important passion, to give us that interest in an object which is necessary to our giving attention to it. And, without attention, we can form no true and stable judgment of any object. [191]

Take away the passions, and it is not easy to say how great a part of mankind would resemble those frivolous mortals, who never had a thought that engaged them in good earnest.

It is not mere judgment or intellectual ability that enables a man to excel in any art or science. He must have a love and admiration of it bordering upon enthusiasm, or a passionate desire of the fame, or of some other advantage to be got by that excellence. Without this, he would not undergo the labour and fatigue of his faculties, which it requires. So that, I think, we may with justice allow no small merit to the passions, even in the discoveries and improvements of the arts and sciences.

If the passions for fame and distinction were extinguished, it would be difficult to find men ready to undertake the cares and toils of government; and few perhaps would make the exertion necessary to raise themselves above the ignoble vulgar.

The involuntary signs of the passions and dispositions of the mind, in the voice, features, and action, are a part of the human constitution which deserves admiration. The signification of those signs is known to all men by nature, and previous to all experience.

They are so many openings into the souls of our fellow-men, by which their sentiments become visible to the eye. They are a natural language common to mankind, without which it would have been impossible to have invented any artificial language.

It is from the natural signs of the passions and dispositions of the mind that the human form derives its beauty; that painting, poetry, and music derive their expression; that eloquence derives its greatest force, and conversation its greatest charm. [192]

The passions, when kept within their

proper bounds, give life and vigour to the whole man. Without them man would be a slug. We see what polish and animation the passion of love, when honourable and not unsuccessful, gives to both sexes.

The passion for military glory raises the brave commander, in the day of battle, far above himself, making his countenance to shine, and his eyes to sparkle. The glory of old England warms the heart even of the British tar, and makes him despise every danger.

As to the bad effects of passion, it must be acknowledged that it often gives a strong impulse to what is bad, and what a man condemns himself for, as soon as it is done. But he must be conscious that the impulse, though strong, was not irresistible, otherwise he could not condemn himself.

We allow that a sudden and violent passion, into which a man is surprised, alleviates a bad action; but, if it was irresistible, it would not only alleviate, but totally exculpate, which it never does, either in the judgment of the man himself, or of others.

To sum up all, passion furnishes a very strong instance of the truth of the common maxim, "That the corruption of the best things is worst."*

CHAPTER VII.

OF DISPOSITION.

By *Disposition* I mean a state of mind which, while it lasts, gives a tendency, or proneness, to be moved by certain animal principles, rather than by others; while, at another time, another state of mind, in the same person, may give the ascendant to other animal principles. [193]

It was before observed, that it is a property of our appetites to be periodical, ceasing for a time, when sated by their objects, and returning regularly after certain periods.

Even those principles which are not periodical, have their ebbs and flows occasionally, according to the present disposition of the mind.

Among some of the principles of action, there is a natural affinity, so that one of the tribe naturally disposes to those which are allied to it.

Such an affinity has been observed by many good authors to be among all the benevolent affections. The exercise of one benevolent affection gives a proneness to the exercise of others.

There is a certain placid and agreeable tone of mind which is common to them all, which seems to be the bond of that connection and affinity they have with one another.

The malevolent affections have also an affinity, and mutually dispose to each other, by means, perhaps, of that disagreeable feeling common to them all, which makes the mind sore and uneasy.

As far as we can trace the causes of the different dispositions of the mind, they seem to be in some cases owing to those associating powers of the principles of action which have a natural affinity, and are prone to keep company with one another; sometimes to accidents of good or bad fortune; and sometimes, no doubt, the state of the body may have influence upon the disposition of the mind.

At one time, the state of the mind, like a serene unclouded sky, shews everything in the most agreeable light. Then a man is prone to benevolence, compassion, and every kind affection; unsuspicious, not easily provoked. [194]

The poets have observed that men have their *mollia tempora fandi*,* when they are averse from saying or doing a harsh thing; and artful men watch these occasions, and know how to improve them to promote their ends.

This disposition, I think, we commonly call *good humour;* of which, in the fair sex, Mr Pope says—

> "Good humour only teaches charms to last,
> Still makes new conquests, and maintains the past."

There is no disposition more comfortable to the person himself, or more agreeable to others, than good humour. It is to the mind, what good health is to the body, putting a man in the capacity of enjoying everything that is agreeable in life, and of using every faculty without clog or impediment. It disposes to contentment with our lot, to benevolence to all men, to sympathy with the distressed. It presents every object in the most favourable light, and disposes us to avoid giving or taking offence.

This happy disposition seems to be the natural fruit of a good conscience, and a firm belief that the world is under a wise and benevolent administration; and, when it springs from this root, it is an habitual sentiment of piety.

Good humour is likewise apt to be produced by happy success, or unexpected good fortune. Joy and hope are favourable to it; vexation and disappointment are unfavourable.

The only danger of this disposition seems to be—That, if we are not upon our guard, it may degenerate into levity, and indispose us to a proper degree of caution, and of at-

* *Corruptio optimi pessima.* From Aristotle; who uses it when speaking of pure monarchy—a form of polity which may either be the best or the worst.—H.

* Mollissima fandi Tempora.—VIRGILIUS.
Sola viri molles aditus et tempora noras, ID.—H.

tention to the future consequences of our actions. [195]

There is a disposition opposite to good humour which we call *bad humour*, of which the tendency is directly contrary, and therefore its influence is as malignant as that of the other is salutary.

Bad humour alone is sufficient to make a man unhappy; it tinges every object with its own dismal colour; and, like a part that is galled, is hurt by everything that touches it. It takes offence where none was meant, and disposes to discontent, jealousy, envy, and, in general, to malevolence.

Another couple of opposite dispositions are *elation* of mind, on the one hand, and *depression*, on the other.

These contrary dispositions are both of an ambiguous nature: their influence may be good or bad, according as they are grounded on true or false opinion, and according as they are regulated.

That elation of mind which arises from a just sense of the dignity of our nature, and of the powers and faculties with which God hath endowed us, is true magnanimity, and disposes a man to the noblest virtues, and the most heroic actions and enterprises.

There is also an elation of mind, which arises from a consciousness of our worth and integrity, such as Job felt, when he said—"Till I die, I will not remove my integrity from me. My righteousness I hold fast, and will not let it go; my heart shall not reproach me while I live." This may be called the pride of virtue; but it is a noble pride. It makes a man disdain to do what is base or mean. This is the true sense of honour. [196]

But there is an elation of mind arising from a vain opinion of our having talents, or worth, which we have not; or from putting an undue value upon any of our endowments of mind, body, or fortune. This is pride, the parent of many odious vices; such as arrogance, undue contempt of others, self-partiality, and vicious self-love.

The opposite disposition to elation of mind, is depression, which also has good or bad effects, according as it is grounded upon true or false opinion.

A just sense of the weakness and imperfections of human nature, and of our own personal faults and defects, is true humility. It is, *not to think of ourselves above what we ought to think*—a most salutary and amiable disposition, of great price in the sight of God and man. Nor is it inconsistent with real magnanimity and greatness of soul. They may dwell together with great advantage and ornament to both, and be faithful monitors against the extremes to which each has the greatest tendency.

But there is a depression of mind which is the opposite to magnanimity, which debilitates the springs of action, and freezes every sentiment that should lead to any noble exertion or enterprise.

Suppose a man to have no belief of a good administration of the world, no conception of the dignity of virtue, no hope of happiness in another state. Suppose him, at the same time, in a state of extreme poverty and dependence, and that he has no higher aim than to supply his bodily wants, or to minister to the pleasure, or flatter the pride of some being as worthless as himself. Is not the soul of such a man depressed as much as his body or his fortune? And, if fortune should smile upon him while he retains the same sentiments he is only the slave of fortune. His mind is depressed to the state of a brute; and his human faculties serve only to make him feel that depression. [197]

Depression of mind may be owing to melancholy, a distemper of mind which proceeds from the state of the body, which throws a dismal gloom upon every object of thought, cuts all the sinews of action, and often gives rise to strange and absurd opinions in religion, or in other interesting matters. Yet, where there is real worth at bottom, same rays of it will break forth even in this depressed state of mind.

A remarkable instance of this was exhibited in Mr Simon Brown, a dissenting clergymen in England, who, by melancholy, was led into the belief that his rational soul had gradually decayed within him, and at last was totally extinct. From this belief he gave up his ministerial function, and would not even join with others in any act of worship, conceiving it to be a profanation to worship God without a soul.

In this dismal state of mind, he wrote an excellent defence of the Christian religion, against Tindal's "Christianity as old as the Creation." To the book he prefixed an epistle dedicatory to Queen Caroline, wherein he mentions—"That he was once a man; but, by the immediate hand of God, for his sins, his very thinking substance has, for more than seven years, been continually wasting away, till it is wholly perished out of him, if it be not utterly come to nothing." And, having heard of her Majesty's eminent piety, he begs the aid of her prayers.

The book was published after his death without the dedication, which, however, having been preserved in manuscript, was afterwards printed in the "Adventurer," No. 88. [198]

Thus, this good man, when he believed that he had no soul, shewed a most generous and disinterested concern for those who had souls.

As depression of mind may produce strange opinions, especially in the case of melancholy, so our opinions may have a very considerable influence, either to elevate or to depress the mind, even where there is no melancholy.

Suppose, on one hand, a man who believes that he is destined to an eternal existence; that He who made and who governs the world, maketh account of him, and hath furnished him with the means of attaining a high degree of perfection and glory. With this man, compare, on the other hand, the man who believes nothing at all, or who believes that his existence is only the play of atoms, and that, after he hath been tossed about by blind fortune for a few years, he shall again return to nothing. Can it be doubted, that the former opinion leads to elevation and greatness of mind, the latter to meanness and depression?

CHAPTER VIII.

OF OPINION.

When we come to explain the rational principles of action, it will appear that *Opinion* is an essential ingredient in them. Here we are only to consider its influence upon the animal principles. Some of those I have ranked in that class cannot, I think, exist in the human mind without it.

Gratitude supposes the opinion of a favour done or intended; resentment the opinion of an injury; esteem the opinion of merit; the passion of love supposes the opinion of uncommon merit and perfection in its object. [199]

Although natural affection to parents, children, and near relations is not grounded on the opinion of their merit, it is much increased by that consideration. So is every benevolent affection. On the contrary, real malevolence can hardly exist without the opinion of demerit in the object.

There is no natural desire or aversion which may not be restrained by opinion. Thus, if a man were a-thirst, and had a strong desire to drink, the opinion that there was poison in the cup would make him forbear.

It is evident that hope and fear, which every natural desire or affection may create, depend upon the opinion of future good or ill.

Thus it appears, that our passions, our dispositions, and our opinions, have great influence upon our animal principles, to strengthen or weaken, to excite or restrain them; and, by that means, have great influence upon human actions and characters.

That brute-animals have both passions and dispositions similar, in many respects, to those of men, cannot be doubted. Whether they have opinions is not so clear. I think they have not, in the proper sense of the word. But, waving all dispute upon this point, it will be granted that opinion in men has a much wider field than in brutes. No man will say that they have systems of theology, morals, jurisprudence, or politics; or that they can reason from the laws of nature, in mechanics, medicine, or agriculture.

They feel the evils or enjoyments that are present; probably they imagine those which experience has associated with what they feel. But they can take no large prospect either of the past or of the future, nor see through a train of consequences. [200]

A dog may be deterred from eating what is before him by the fear of immediate punishment, which he has felt on like occasions; but he is never deterred by the consideration of health, or of any distant good.

I have been credibly informed, that a monkey, having once been intoxicated with strong drink, in consequence of which it burnt its foot in the fire, and had a severe fit of sickness, could never after be induced to drink anything but pure water. I believe this is the utmost pitch which the faculties of brutes can reach.

From the influence of opinion upon the conduct of mankind, we may learn that it is one of the chief instruments to be used in the discipline and government of men.

All men, in the early part of life, must be under the discipline and government of parents and tutors. Men who live in society must be under the government of laws and magistrates through life. The government of men is undoubtedly one of the noblest exertions of human power. And it is of great importance that those who have any share, either in domestic or civil government, should know the nature of man, and how he is to be trained and governed.

Of all instruments of government, opinion is the sweetest, and the most agreeable to the nature of man. Obedience that flows from opinion is real freedom, which every man desires. That which is extorted by fear of punishment is slavery, a yoke which is always galling, and which every man will shake off when it is in his power.

The opinions of the bulk of mankind have always been, and will always be, what they are taught by those whom they esteem to be wise and good; and, therefore, in a considerable degree, are in the power of those who govern them. [201]

Man, uncorrupted by bad habits and bad opinions, is of all animals the most tractable; corrupted by these, he is of all animals the most untractable.

I apprehend, therefore, that, if ever civil

government shall be brought to perfection, it must be the principal care of the state to make good citizens by proper education, and proper instruction and discipline.*

The most useful part of medicine is that which strengthens the constitution, and prevents diseases by good regimen; the rest is somewhat like propping a ruinous fabric at great expense, and to little purpose. The art of government is the medicine of the mind, and the most useful part of it is that which prevents crimes and bad habits, and trains men to virtue and good habits by proper education and discipline.

The end of government is to make the society happy, which can only be done by making it good and virtuous.

That men in general will be good or bad members of society, according to the education and discipline by which they have been trained, experience may convince us.

The present age has made great advances in the art of training men to military duty. It will not be said that those who enter into that service are more tractable than their fellow-subjects of other professions. And I know not why it should be thought impossible to train men to equal perfection in the other duties of good citizens. [202]

What an immense difference is there, for the purpose of war, between an army properly trained, and a militia hastily drawn out of the multitude? What should hinder us from thinking that, for every purpose of civil government, there may be a like difference between a civil society properly trained to virtue, good habits, and right sentiments, and those civil societies which we now behold? But I fear I shall be thought to digress from my subject into Utopian speculation.

To make an end of what I have to say upon the animal principles of action, we may take a complex view of their effect in life, by supposing a being actuated by principles of no higher order, to have no conscience or sense of duty, only let us allow him that superiority of understanding and that power of self-government which man actually has. Let us speculate a little upon this imaginary being, and consider what conduct and tenor of action might be expected from him.

It is evident he would be a very different animal from a brute, and, perhaps, not very different, in appearance, from what a great part of mankind is.

He would be capable of considering the distant consequences of his actions, and of restraining or indulging his appetites, desires, and affections, from the consideration of distant good or evil.

He would be capable of choosing some main end of his life, and planning such a rule of conduct as appeared most subservient to it. Of this we have reason to think no brute is capable.

We can, perhaps, conceive such a balance of the animal principles of action as, with very little self-government, might make a man to be a good member of society, a good companion, and to have many amiable qualities. [203]

The balance of our animal principles, I think, constitutes what we call a man's *natural temper*; which may be good or bad, without regard to his virtue.

A man in whom the benevolent affections, the desire of esteem and good humour, are naturally prevalent, who is of a calm and dispassionate nature, who has the good fortune to live with good men and associate with good companions, may behave properly with little effort.

His natural temper leads him, in most cases, to do what virtue requires. And if he happens not to be exposed to those trying situations in which virtue crosses the natural bent of his temper, he has no great temptation to act amiss.

But, perhaps, a happy natural temper, joined with such a happy situation, is more ideal than real, though, no doubt, some men make nearer approaches to it than others.

The temper and the situation of men is commonly such that the animal principles alone, without self-government, would never produce any regular and consistent train of conduct.

One principle crosses another. Without self-government, that which is strongest at the time will prevail. And that which is weakest at one time may, from passion, from a change of disposition or of fortune, become strongest at another time.

Every natural appetite, desire, and affection, has its own present gratification only in view. A man, therefore, who has no other leader than these, would be like a ship in the ocean without hands, which cannot be said to be destined to any port. He would have no character at all, but be benevolent or spiteful, pleasant or morose, honest or dishonest, as the present wind of passion or tide of humour moved him. [204]

* It is not creditable to the people of Great Britain that we are about the last nation of Europe, if not to recognise this principle, at least to carry it into effect. But the spirit of manufactures, which views human beings only in relation to production, and aims exclusively at obtaining them for instruments at the cheapest rate, is diametrically opposed to the spirit of education; in as much as education views the citizen as a subject of intellectual improvement, and, without making him a better instrument, makes him one more costly. Aristotle has signalized this antagonism, which has been overlooked by recent political speculation. But, in ancient times, the prosperity of a state was placed in the moral and intellectual dignity of its citizens; in modern times, in their material riches.—H.

Every man who pursues an end, be it good or bad, must be active when he is disposed to be indolent; he must rein every passion and appetite that would lead him out of his road.

Mortification and self-denial are found not in the path of virtue only—they are common to every road that leads to an end, be it ambition, or avarice, or even pleasure itself. Every man who maintains a uniform and consistent character, must sweat and toil, and often struggle with his present inclination.

Yet those who steadily pursue some end in life, though they must often restrain their strongest desires, and practise much self-denial, have, upon the whole, more enjoyment than those who have no end at all, but to gratify the present prevailing inclination.

A dog that is made for the chase cannot enjoy the happiness of a dog without that exercise. Keep him within doors, feed him with the most delicious fare, give him all the pleasures his nature is capable of, he soon becomes a dull, torpid, unhappy animal. No enjoyment can supply the want of that employment which nature has made his chief good. Let him hunt, and neither pain, nor hunger, nor fatigue seem to be evils. Deprived of this exercise, he can relish nothing. Life itself becomes burdensome.

It is no disparagement to the human kind to say, that man, as well as the dog, is made for hunting, and cannot be happy but in some vigorous pursuit. He has, indeed, nobler game to pursue than the dog; but he must have some pursuit, otherwise life stagnates, all the faculties are benumbed, the spirits flag, and his existence becomes an unsupportable burden.

Even the mere foxhunter, who has no higher pursuit than his dogs, has more enjoyment than he who has no pursuit at all. He has an end in view, and this invigorates his spirits, makes him despise pleasure;* and bear cold, hunger, and fatigue, as if they were no evils. [205]

"Manet sub Jove frigido
Venator, teneræ conjugis immemor,
Seu visa est catulis cerva fidelibus,
Seu rupit teretes Marsus aper plagas."†

* Despise one pleasure for the sake of a higher. In fact, all pleasure is the reflex or concomitant of energy—spontaneous and unimpeded energy. This has been best developed by Aristotle.—H.

† Horace.

[205, 206]

PART III.

OF THE RATIONAL PRINCIPLES OF ACTION.

CHAPTER I.

THERE ARE RATIONAL PRINCIPLES OF ACTION IN MAN.

MECHANICAL principles of action produce their effect without any will or intention on our part. We may, by a voluntary effort, hinder the effect; but, if it be not hindered by will and effort, it is produced without them.

Animal principles of action require intention and will in their operation, but not judgment. They are, by ancient moralists, very properly called *cæcæ cupidines*, blind desires.

Having treated of these two classes, I proceed to the third—the *Rational* principles of action in man; which have that name, because they can have no existence in beings not endowed with reason, and, in all their exertions, require, not only intention and will, but judgment or reason. [206]

That talent which we call *Reason*,* by which men that are adult and of a sound mind are distinguished from brutes, idiots, and infants, has, in all ages, among the learned and unlearned, been conceived to have two offices—*to regulate our belief*, and *to regulate our actions and conduct*.

Whatever we believe, we think agreeable to reason, and, on that account, yield our assent to it. Whatever we disbelieve, we think contrary to reason, and, on that account, dissent from it. Reason, therefore, is allowed to be the principle by which our belief and opinions ought to be regulated.

But reason has been no less universally conceived to be a principle by which our actions ought to be regulated.

To act reasonably, is a phrase no less common in all languages, than to judge reasonably. We immediately approve of a man's conduct, when it appears that he had good reason for what he did. And every action we disapprove, we think unreasonable, or contrary to reason.

A way of speaking so universal among men, common to the learned and the unlearned in all nations and in all languages, must have a meaning. To suppose it to be words without meaning, is to treat, with undue contempt, the common sense of mankind.

Supposing this phrase to have a meaning,

* *Reason* is here used for intelligence in general.—H.

we may consider in what way reason may serve to regulate human conduct, so that some actions of men are to be denominated reasonable, and others unreasonable.

I take it for granted, that there can be no exercise of Reason without Judgment, nor, on the other hand, any judgment of things, abstract and general, without some degree of reason. [207]

If, therefore, there be any principles of action in the human constitution, which, in their nature, necessarily imply such judgment, they are the principles which we may call rational, to distinguish them from animal principles, which imply desire and will, but not judgment.

Every deliberate human action must be done either as the means, or as an end; as the means to some end, to which it is subservient, or as an end, for its own sake, and without regard to anything beyond it.

That it is a part of the office of reason to determine what are the proper means to any end which we desire, no man ever denied. But some philosophers, particularly Mr Hume, think that it is no part of the office of reason to determine the ends we ought to pursue, or the preference due to one end above another. This, he thinks, is not the office of reason, but of taste or feeling.

If this be so, reason cannot, with any propriety, be called a principle of action. Its office can only be to minister to the principles of action, by discovering the means of their gratification. Accordingly, Mr Hume maintains, that reason is no principle of action; but that it is, and ought to be, the servant of the passions.

I shall endeavour to shew that, among the various ends of human actions, there are some, of which, without reason, we could not even form a conception; and that, as soon as they are conceived, a regard to them is, by our constitution, not only a principle of action, but a leading and governing principle, to which all our animal principles are subordinate, and to which they ought to be subject. [208]

These I shall call *rational* principles; because they can exist only in beings endowed with reason, and because, to act from these principles, is what has always been meant by acting according to reason.

The ends of human actions I have in view, are two—to wit, *What is good for us upon the whole*, and, *What appears to be our duty*. They are very strictly connected, lead to the same course of conduct, and co-operate with each other; and, on that account, have commonly been comprehended under one name—that of *reason*. But, as they may be disjoined, and are really distinct principles of action, I shall consider them separately.

CHAPTER II.

OF REGARD TO OUR GOOD ON THE WHOLE.

It will not be denied that man, when he comes to years of understanding, is led, by his rational nature, to form the conception of what is good for him upon the whole.

How early in life this general notion of good enters into the mind, I cannot pretend to determine. It is one of the most general and abstract notions we form.

Whatever makes a man more happy or more perfect, is good, and is an object of desire as soon as we are capable of forming the conception of it. The contrary is ill, and is an object of aversion.

In the first part of life, we have many enjoyments of various kinds; but very similar to those of brute-animals. [209]

They consist in the exercise of our senses and powers of motion, the gratification of our appetites, and the exertions of our kind affections. These are chequered with many evils of pain, and fear, and disappointment, and sympathy with the sufferings of others.

But the goods and evils of this period of life are of short duration, and soon forgot. The mind, being regardless of the past, and unconcerned about the future, we have then no other measure of good but the present desire; no other measure of evil but the present aversion.

Every animal desire has some particular and present object, and looks not beyond that object to its consequences, or to the connections it may have with other things.

The present object, which is most attractive, or excites the strongest desire, determines the choice, whatever be its consequences. The present evil that presses most, is avoided, though it should be the road to a greater good to come, or the only way to escape a greater evil. This is the way in which brutes act, and the way in which men must act, till they come to the use of reason.

As we grow up to understanding, we extend our view both forward and backward. We reflect upon what is past, and, by the lamp of experience, discern what will probably happen in time to come. We find that many things which we eagerly desired, were too dearly purchased, and that things grievous for the present, like nauseous medicines, may be salutary in the issue.

We learn to observe the connexions of things, and the consequences of our actions; and, taking an extended view of our existence, past, present, and future, we correct our first notions of good and ill, and form the conception of what is good or ill upon the whole; which must be estimated, not from the present feeling, or from the present animal desire or aversion, but from a due consideration of its consequences, certain or probable, during the whole of our existence. [210]

That which, taken with all its discoverable connections and consequences, brings more good than ill, I call *good upon the whole*.

That brute-animals have any conception of this good, I see no reason to believe. And it is evident that man cannot have the conception of it, till reason is so far advanced that he can seriously reflect upon the past, and take a prospect of the future part of his existence.

It appears, therefore, that the very conception of what is good or ill for us upon the whole, is the offspring of reason, and can be only in beings endowed with reason. And if this conception give rise to any principle of action in man, which he had not before, that principle may very properly be called a rational principle of action.

I pretend not in this to say anything that is new, but what reason suggested to those who first turned their attention to the philosophy of morals. I beg leave to quote one passage from Cicero, in his first book of "Offices;" wherein, with his usual eloquence, he expresses the substance of what I have said. And there is good reason to think that Cicero borrowed it from Panætius, a Greek philosopher whose books of "Offices" are lost.

"Sed inter hominem et belluam hoc maxime interest, quod hæc tantum, quantum sensu movetur, ad id solum, quod adest quodque præsens est se accommodat, paululum admodum sentiens præteritum aut futurum. Homo autem quoniam rationis est particeps, per quam consequentia cernit, causas rerum videt, earumque progressus et quasi antecessiones non ignorat, similitudines comparat, et rebus præsentibus adjungit atque annectit futuras; facile totius vitæ cursum videt, ad eamque degendam præparat res necessarias." [211]

I observe, in the *next* place—That as soon as we have the conception of what is good or ill for us upon the whole, we are led, by our constitution, to seek the good and avoid the ill; and this becomes not only a principle of action, but a leading or governing principle, to which all our animal principles ought to be subordinate.

I am very apt to think, with Dr Price, that, in intelligent beings, the desire of what is good, and aversion to what is ill, is necessarily connected with the intelligent nature; and that it is a contradiction to suppose such a being to have the notion of good without the desire of it, or the notion of ill without aversion to it. Perhaps there may be other necessary connections between understanding and the best principles of action, which our faculties are too weak to discern. That they are necessarily connected in him who is perfect in understanding, we have good reason to believe.

To prefer a greater good, though distant, to a less that is present; to choose a present evil, in order to avoid a greater evil, or to obtain a greater good, is, in the judgment of all men, wise and reasonable conduct; and, when a man acts the contrary part, all men will acknowledge that he acts foolishly and unreasonably. Nor will it be denied, that, in innumerable cases in common life, our animal principles draw us one way, while a regard to what is good on the whole, draws us the contrary way. Thus the flesh lusteth against the spirit, and the spirit against the flesh, and these two are contrary. That in every conflict of this kind the rational principle ought to prevail, and the animal to be subordinate, is too evident to need, or to admit of proof. [212]

Thus, I think, it appears, that, to pursue what is good upon the whole, and to avoid what is ill upon the whole, is a rational principle of action grounded upon our constitution as reasonable creatures.

It appears that it is not without just cause, that this principle of action has in all ages been called *reason*, in opposition to our animal principles, which in common language are called by the general name of the *passions*.

The first not only operates in a calm and cool manner, like reason, but implies real judgment in all its operations. The second—to wit, the passions—are blind desires of some particular object, without any judgment or consideration, whether it be good for us upon the whole, or ill.

It appears also, that the fundamental maxim of prudence, and of all good morals—That the passions ought, in all cases, to be under the dominion of reason—is not only self-evident, when rightly understood, but is expressed according to the common use and propriety of language.

The contrary maxim maintained by Mr Hume, can only be defended by a gross and palpable abuse of words. For, in order to defend it, he must include under the *passions* that very principle which has always, in all languages, been called *reason*, and never was, in any language, called a *passion*. And from the meaning of the word *reason* he must exclude the most important part of it, by which we are able to discern and to pursue what appears to be good upon the whole. And thus, including the most important part of reason under passion, and making the least important part of reason to be the whole, he defends his favourite paradox, That reason is, and ought to be, the servant of the passions. [213]

To judge of what is true or false in specu-

[210-213]

lative points, is the office of speculative reason; and to judge of what is good or ill for us upon the whole, is the office of practical reason. Of true and false there are no degrees; but of good and ill there are many degrees, and many kinds; and men are very apt to form erroneous opinions concerning them; misled by their passions, by the authority of the multitude, and by other causes.

Wise men, in all ages, have reckoned it a chief point of wisdom, to make a right estimate of the goods and evils of life. They have laboured to discover the errors of the multitude on this important point, and to warn others against them.

The ancient moralists, though divided into sects, all agreed in this—That opinion has a mighty influence upon what we commonly account the goods and ills of life, to alleviate or to aggravate them.

The Stoics carried this so far, as to conclude that they all depend on opinion. Πάντα Ὑπόληψις was a favourite maxim with them.

We see, indeed, that the same station or condition of life, which makes one man happy, makes another miserable, and to a third is perfectly indifferent. We see men miserable through life, from vain fears and anxious desires, grounded solely upon wrong opinions. We see men wear themselves out with toilsome days, and sleepless nights, in pursuit of some object which they never attain; or which, when attained, gives little satisfaction, perhaps real disgust.

The evils of life, which every man must feel, have a very different effect upon different men. What sinks one into despair and absolute misery, rouses the virtue and magnanimity of another, who bears it as the lot of humanity, and as the discipline of a wise and merciful Father in heaven. He rises superior to adversity, and is made wiser and better by it, and, consequently, happier. [214]

It is therefore of the last importance, in the conduct of life, to have just opinions with respect to good and evil; and, surely, it is the province of reason to correct wrong opinions, and to lead us into those that are just and true.

It is true, indeed, that men's passions and appetites too often draw them to act contrary to their cool judgment and opinion of what is best for them. *Video meliora proboque, deteriora sequor*, is the case in every wilful deviation from our true interest and our duty.

When this is the case, the man is self-condemned; he sees that he acted the part of a brute when he ought to have acted the part of a man. He is convinced that reason ought to have restrained his passion, and not to have given the rein to it.

When he feels the bad effects of his conduct, he imputes them to himself, and would be stung with remorse for his folly, though he had no account to make to a superior Being. He has sinned against himself, and brought upon his own head the punishment which his folly deserved.

From this we may see that this rational principle of a regard to our good upon the whole, gives us the conception of a *right* and a *wrong* in human conduct, at least of a *wise* and a *foolish*. It produces a kind of self-approbation, when the passions and appetites are kept in their due subjection to it; and a kind of remorse and compunction when it yields to them. [215]

In these respects, this principle is so similar to the moral principle, or *Conscience*, and so interwoven with it, that both are commonly comprehended under the name of *Reason*. This similarity led many of the ancient philosophers, and some among the moderns, to resolve conscience, or a sense of duty, entirely into a regard to what is good for us upon the whole.

That they are distinct principles of action, though both lead to the same conduct in life, I shall have occasion to shew when I come to treat of *conscience*.

CHAPTER III.

THE TENDENCY OF THIS PRINCIPLE.

It has been the opinion of the wisest men, in all ages, that this principle, of a regard to our good upon the whole, in a man duly enlightened, leads to the practice of every virtue.

This was acknowledged, even by Epicurus; and the best moralists among the ancients derived all the virtues from this principle. For, among them, the whole of morals was reduced to this question? *What is the greatest good?* or, *What course of conduct is best for us upon the whole?*

In order to resolve this question, they divided goods into *three* classes: the *goods of the body*—the *goods of fortune* or *external goods*—and the *goods of the mind*, meaning, by the last, *wisdom* and *virtue*.

Comparing these different classes of goods, they shewed, with convincing evidence, that the goods of the mind are, in many respects, superior to those of the body and of fortune, not only as they have more dignity, are more durable, and less exposed to the strokes of fortune, but chiefly as they are the only goods in our power, and which depend wholly on our conduct. [216]

Epicurus himself maintained, that the wise man may be happy in the tranquillity of his mind, even when racked with pain and struggling with adversity.

They observed very justly, that the goods

of fortune, and even those of the body, depend much on opinion; and that, when our opinion of them is duly corrected by reason, we shall find them of small value in themselves.

How can he be happy who places his happiness in things which it is not in his power to attain, or in things from which, when attained, a fit of sickness, or a stroke of fortune, may tear him asunder?

The value we put upon things, and our uneasiness in the want of them, depend upon the strength of our desires; correct the desire, and the uneasiness ceases.

The fear of the evils of body and of fortune, is often a greater evil than the things we fear. As the wise man moderates his desires by temperance, so, to real or imaginary dangers, he opposes the shield of fortitude and magnanimity, which raises him above himself, and makes him happy and triumphant in those moments wherein others are most miserable.

These oracles of reason led the Stoics so far as to maintain—That all desires and fears, with regard to things not in our power, ought to be totally eradicated; that virtue is the only good; that what we call the goods of the body and of fortune, are really things indifferent, which may, according to circumstances, prove good or ill, and, therefore, have no intrinsic goodness in themselves; that our sole business ought to be, to act our part well, and to do what is right, without the least concern about things, not in our power, which we ought, with perfect acquiescence, to leave to the care of Him who governs the world. [217]

This noble and elevated conception of human wisdom and duty was taught by Socrates, free from the extravagancies which the Stoics afterwards joined with it. We see it in the "Alcibiades" of Plato,* from which Juvenal hath taken it in his tenth satire, and adorned it with the graces of poetry.

"Omnibus in terris quæ sunt a Gadibus usque [1]
Auroram et Gangem, pauci dignoscere possunt
Vera bona atque illis multum diversa, remota
Erroris nebula. Quid enim ratione timemus
Aut cupimus? Quid tam dextro pede concipis ut te
Conatus non pœniteat votique peracti?

. . . .

Nil ergo optabunt homines? Si consilium vis, [346]
Permittes ipsis expendere numinibus, quid
Conveniat nobis rebusque sit utile nostris.
Nam pro jucundis aptissima quæque dabunt Di.
Carior est illis homo quam sibi. Nos animorum
Impulsu, et cæca magnaque cupidine ducti,
Conjugium petimus partumque uxoris; at illis
Notum, qui pueri qualisque futura sit uxor.
[Orandum est, ut sit mens sana in corpore sano.]
Fortem posce animum, mortis terrore carentem,
Qui spatium vitæ extremum inter munera ponat
Naturæ, qui ferre queat quoscunque labores,
Nesciat irasci, cupiat nihil, et potiores
Herculis ærumnas credat sævosque labores
Et Venere, et cœnis, et plumis, Sardanapali.
Monstro, quod ipse tibi possis dare; semita certe
Tranquillæ per virtutem patet unica vitæ.
Nullum numen abest si sit prudentia; nos te
Nos facimus, Fortuna, deam, cœloque locamus."

Even Horace, in his serious moments, falls into this system. [218]

"Nil admirari, prope res est una, Numici,
Solaque quæ possit facere et servare beatum."

We cannot but admire the Stoical system of morals, even when we think that, in some points, it went beyond the pitch of human nature. The virtue, the temperance, the fortitude, and magnanimity of some who sincerely embraced it, amidst all the flattery of sovereign power and the luxury of a court, will be everlasting monuments to the honour of that system, and to the honour of human nature.

That a due regard to what is best for us upon the whole, in an enlightened mind, leads to the practice of every virtue, may be argued from considering what we think best for those for whom we have the strongest affection, and whose good we tender as our own. In judging for ourselves, our passions and appetites are apt to bias our judgment; but when we judge for others, this bias is removed, and we judge impartially.

What is it, then, that a wise man would wish as the greatest good to a brother, a son, or a friend?

Is it that he may spend his life in a constant round of the pleasures of sense, and fare sumptuously every day?

No, surely; we wish him to be a man of real virtue and worth. We may wish for him an honourable station in life; but only with this condition, that he acquit himself honourably in it, and acquire just reputation, by being useful to his country and to mankind. We would a thousand times rather wish him honourably to undergo the labours of Hercules, than to dissolve in pleasure with Sardanapalus. [219]

Such would be the wish of every man of understanding for the friend whom he loves as his own soul. Such things, therefore, he judges to be best for him upon the whole; and if he judges otherwise for himself, it is only because his judgment is perverted by animal passions and desires.

The sum of what has been said in these three chapters amounts to this:—

There is a principle of action in men that are adult and of a sound mind, which, in all ages, has been called *reason*, and set in opposition to the animal principles which we call the *passions*. The ultimate object* of this principle is what we judge to be good upon the whole. This is not the object* of any of our animal principles; they being all directed to particular objects,

* The *Second* Alcibiades: which is not Plato's; as can be shewn on grounds apart from its inferiority to the genuine works of that philosopher.—H.

* The word *object* should not be used for *aim* or *end*, but exclusively for the *materia circa quam*.—H.

without any comparison with others, or any consideration of their being good or ill upon the whole.

What is good upon the whole cannot even be conceived without the exercise of reason, and therefore cannot be an object* to beings that have not some degree of reason.

As soon as we have the conception of this object,* we are led, by our constitution, to desire and pursue it. It justly claims a preference to all objects of pursuit that can come in competition with it. In preferring it to any gratification that opposes it, or in submitting to any pain or mortification which it requires, we act according to reason; and every such action is accompanied with self-approbation and the approbation of mankind. The contrary actions are accompanied with shame and self-condemnation in the agent, and with contempt in the spectator, as foolish and unreasonable. [220]

The right application of this principle to our conduct requires an extensive prospect of human life, and a correct judgment and estimate of its goods and evils, with respect to their intrinsic worth and dignity, their constancy and duration, and their attainableness. He must be a wise man indeed, if any such man there be, who can perceive, in every instance, or even in every important instance, what is best for him upon the whole, if he have no other rule to direct his conduct.

However, according to the best judgment which wise men have been able to form, this principle leads to the practice of every virtue. It leads directly to the virtues of Prudence, Temperance, and Fortitude. And, when we consider ourselves as social creatures, whose happiness or misery is very much connected with that of our fellow-men; when we consider that there are many benevolent affections planted in our constitution, whose exertions make a capital part of our good and enjoyment; from these considerations, this principle leads us also, though more indirectly, to the practice of justice, humanity, and all the social virtues.

It is true, that a regard to our own good cannot, of itself, produce any benevolent affection. But, if such affections be a part of our constitution, and if the exercise of them make a capital part of our happiness, a regard to our own good ought to lead us to cultivate and exercise them, as every benevolent affection makes the good of others to be our own. [221]

* See the last note.

CHAPTER IV.

DEFECTS OF THIS PRINCIPLE.

Having explained the nature of this principle of action, and shewn in general the tenor of conduct to which it leads, I shall conclude what relates to it, by pointing out some of its defects, if it be supposed, as it has been by some philosophers, to be the only regulating principle of human conduct.

Upon that supposition, it would neither be a sufficiently plain rule of conduct, nor would it raise the human character to that degree of perfection of which it is capable, nor would it yield so much real happiness as when it is joined with another rational principle of action—to wit, a disinterested regard to duty.

First, I apprehend the greater part of mankind can never attain such extensive views of human life, and so correct a judgment of good and ill, as the right application of this principle requires.

The authority of the poet before quoted,* is of weight in this point. "Pauci dignoscere possunt vera bona, remotâ erroris nebulâ." The ignorance of the bulk of mankind concurs with the strength of their passions to lead them into error in this most important point.

Every man, in his calm moments, wishes to know what is best for him on the whole, and to do it. But the difficulty of discovering it clearly, amidst such variety of opinions and the importunity of present desires, tempt men to give over the search, and to yield to the present inclination. [222]

Though philosophers and moralists have taken much laudable pains to correct the errors of mankind in this great point, their instructions are known to few; they have little influence upon the greater part of those to whom they are known, and sometimes little even upon the philosopher himself.

Speculative discoveries gradually spread from the knowing to the ignorant, and diffuse themselves over all; so that, with regard to them, the world, it may be hoped, will still be growing wiser. But the errors of men, with regard to what is truly good or ill, after being discovered and refuted in every age, are still prevalent.

Men stand in need of a sharper monitor to their duty than a dubious view of distant good. There is reason to believe, that a present sense of duty has, in many cases, a stronger influence than the apprehension of distant good would have of itself. And it cannot be doubted, that a sense of guilt and demerit is a more pungent reprover

* Juvenal.—H.

than the bare apprehension of having mistaken our true interest.

The brave soldier, in exposing himself to danger and death, is animated, not by a cold computation of the good and the ill, but by a noble and elevated sense of military duty.

A philosopher shews, by a copious and just induction, what is our real good, and what our ill. But this kind of reasoning is not easily apprehended by the bulk of men. It has too little force upon their minds to resist the sophistry of the passions. They are apt to think that, if such rules be good in the general, they may admit of particular exceptions, and that what is good for the greater part, may, to some persons, on account of particular circumstances, be ill.

Thus, I apprehend, that, if we had no plainer rule to direct our conduct in life than a regard to our greatest good, the greatest part of mankind would be fatally misled, even by ignorance of the road to it. [223]

Secondly, Though a steady pursuit of our own real good may, in an enlightened mind, produce a kind of virtue which is entitled to some degree of approbation, yet it can never produce the noblest kind of virtue which claims our highest love and esteem.

We account him a wise man who is wise for himself; and, if he prosecutes this end through difficulties and temptations that lie in his way, his character is far superior to that of the man who, having the same end in view, is continually starting out of the road to it from an attachment to his appetites and passions, and doing every day what he knows he shall heartily repent.

Yet, after all, this wise man, whose thoughts and cares are all centred ultimately in himself, who indulges even his social affections only with a view to his own good, is not the man whom we cordially love and esteem.

Like a cunning merchant, he carries his goods to the best market, and watches every opportunity of putting them off to the best account. He does well and wisely. But it is for himself. We owe him nothing upon this account. Even when he does good to others, he means only to serve himself; and, therefore, has no just claim to their gratitude or affection.

This surely, if it be virtue, is not the noblest kind, but a low and mercenary species of it. It can neither give a noble elevation to the mind that possesses it, nor attract the esteem and love of others. [224]

Our cordial love and esteem is due only to the man whose soul is not contracted within itself, but embraces a more extensive object: who loves virtue, not for her dowry only, but for her own sake: whose benevolence is not selfish, but generous and disinterested: who, forgetful of himself, has the common good at heart, not as the means only, but as the end: who abhors what is base, though he were to be a gainer by it; and loves that which is right, although he should suffer by it.

Such a man we esteem the perfect man, compared with whom he who has no other aim but good to himself is a mean and despicable character.

Disinterested goodness and rectitude is the glory of the Divine Nature, without which he might be an object of fear or hope, but not of true devotion. And it is the image of this divine attribute in the human character that is the glory of man.

To serve God and be useful to mankind, without any concern about our own good and happiness, is, I believe, beyond the pitch of human nature. But to serve God and be useful to men, merely to obtain good to ourselves, or to avoid ill, is servility, and not that liberal service which true devotion and real virtue require.

Thirdly, Though one might be apt to think that he has the best chance for happiness who has no other end of his deliberate actions but his own good, yet a little consideration may satisfy us of the contrary.

A concern for our own good is not a principle that, of itself, gives any enjoyment. On the contrary, it is apt to fill the mind with fear, and care, and anxiety. And these concomitants of this principle often give pain and uneasiness, that overbalance the good they have in view. [225]

We may here compare, in point of present happiness, two imaginary characters: The first, of the man who has no other ultimate end of his deliberate actions but his own good; and who has no regard to virtue or duty, but as the means to that end. The second character is that of the man who is not indifferent with regard to his own good, but has another ultimate end perfectly consistent with it—to wit, a disinterested love of virtue, for its own sake, or a regard to duty as an end.

Comparing these two characters in point of happiness, that we may give all possible advantage to the selfish principle, we shall suppose the man who is actuated solely by it, to be so far enlightened as to see it his interest to live soberly, righteously, and godly in the world, and that he follows the same course of conduct from the motive of his own good only, which the other does, in a great measure, or in some measure, from a sense of duty and rectitude

We put the case so as that the difference between these two persons may be, not in what they do, but in the motive from which they do it; and, I think, there can be no doubt that he who acts from the noblest and most generous motive, will have most happiness in his conduct.

The one labours only for hire, without any love to the work. The other loves the work, and thinks it the noblest and most honourable he can be employed in. To the first, the mortification and self-denial which the course of virtue requires, is a grievous task, which he submits to only through necessity. To the other it is victory and triumph, in the most honourable warfare. [226]

It ought farther to be considered—That although wise men have concluded that virtue is the only road to happiness, this conclusion is founded chiefly upon the natural respect men have for virtue, and the good or happiness that is intrinsic to it and arises from the love of it. If we suppose a man, as we now do, altogether destitute of this principle, who considered virtue only as the means to another end, there is no reason to think that he would ever take it to be the road to happiness, but would wander for ever seeking this object, where it is not to be found.

The road of duty is so plain that the man who seeks it with an upright heart cannot greatly err from it. But the road to happiness, if that be supposed the only end our nature leads us to pursue, would be found dark and intricate, full of snares and dangers, and therefore not to be trodden without fear, and care, and perplexity.

The happy man, therefore, is not he whose happiness is his only care, but he who, with perfect resignation, leaves the care of his happiness to him who made him, while he pursues with ardour the road of his duty.

This gives an elevation to his mind, which is real happiness. Instead of care, and fear, and anxiety, and disappointment, it brings joy and triumph. It gives a relish to every good we enjoy, and brings good out of evil.

And as no man can be indifferent about his happiness, the good man has the consolation to know that he consults his happiness most effectually when, without any painful anxiety about future events, he does his duty.

Thus, I think, it appears—That, although a regard to our good upon the whole, be a rational principle in man, yet if it be supposed the only regulating principle of our conduct, it would be a more uncertain rule, it would give far less perfection to the human character, and far less happiness, than when joined with another rational principle—to wit, a regard to duty. [227]

CHAPTER V.

OF THE NOTION OF DUTY, RECTITUDE, MORAL OBLIGATION.

A BEING endowed with the animal principles of action only, may be capable of being trained to certain purposes by discipline, as we see many brute-animals are, but would be altogether incapable of being governed by law.

The subject of law must have the conception of a general rule of conduct, which, without some degree of reason, he cannot have. He must likewise have a sufficient inducement to obey the law, even when his strongest animal desires draw him the contrary way.

This inducement may be a sense of *interest*, or a sense of *duty*, or both concurring.

These are the only principles I am able to conceive, which can reasonably induce a man to regulate all his actions according to a certain general rule or law. They may therefore be justly called the *rational* principles of action, since they can have no place but in a being endowed with reason, and since it is by them only that man is capable either of political or of moral government.

Without them human life would be like a ship at sea without hands, left to be carried by winds and tides as they happen. It belongs to the rational part of our nature to intend a certain port, as the end of the voyage of life; to take the advantage of winds and tides when they are favourable, and to bear up against them when they are unfavourable. [228]

A sense of interest may induce us to do this, when a suitable reward is set before us. But there is a nobler principle in the constitution of man, which, in many cases, gives a clearer and more certain rule of conduct, than a regard merely to interest would give, and a principle, without which man would not be a moral agent.

A man is prudent when he consults his real interest; but he cannot be virtuous, if he has no regard to duty.

I proceed now to consider this *regard to Duty* as a rational principle of action in man, and as that principle alone by which he is capable either of virtue or vice.

I shall first offer some observations with regard to the *general notion of duty, and its contrary, or of right and wrong in human conduct*, and then consider, *how we come to judge and determine certain things in human conduct to be right, and others to be wrong.*

With regard to the *notion* or *conception*

of Duty, I take it to be too simple to admit of a logical definition.

We can define it only by synonymous words or phrases, or by its properties and necessary concomitants, as when we say that it is *what we ought to do—what is fair and honest—what is approvable—what every man professes to be the rule of his conduct—what all men praise*—and, *what is in itself laudable, though no man should praise it.*

I observe, in the *next* place, That the notion of duty cannot be resolved into that of interest, or what is most for our happiness. [229]

Every man may be satisfied of this who attends to his own conceptions, and the language of all mankind shews it. When I say, This is my interest, I mean one thing; when I say, It is my duty, I mean another thing. And, though the same course of action, when rightly understood, may be both my duty and my interest, the conceptions are very different. Both are reasonable motives to action, but quite distinct in their nature.

I presume it will be granted, that, in every man of real worth, there is a principle of honour, a regard to what is honourable or dishonourable, very distinct from a regard to his interest. It is folly in a man to disregard his interest, but to do what is dishonourable, is baseness. The first may move our pity, or, in some cases, our contempt; but the last provokes our indignation.

As these two principles are different in their nature, and not resolvable into one, so the principle of honour is evidently superior in dignity to that of interest.

No man would allow him to be a man of honour who should plead his interest to justify what he acknowledged to be dishonourable; but to sacrifice interest to honour never costs a blush.

It likewise will be allowed by every man of honour, that this principle is not to be resolved into a regard to our reputation among men, otherwise the man of honour would not deserve to be trusted in the dark. He would have no aversion to lie, or cheat, or play the coward, when he had no dread of being discovered. [230]

I take it for granted, therefore, that every man of real honour feels an abhorrence of certain actions, because they are in themselves base, and feels an obligation to certain other actions, because they are in themselves what honour requires, and this independently of any consideration of interest or reputation.

This is an immediate moral obligation. This principle of honour, which is acknowledged by all men who pretend to character, is only another name for what we call a regard to duty, to rectitude, to propriety of conduct.* It is a moral obligation which obliges a man to do certain things because they are right, and not to do other things because they are wrong.

Ask the man of honour why he thinks himself obliged to pay a debt of honour? The very question shocks him. To suppose that he needs any other inducement to do it but the principle of honour, is to suppose that he has no honour, no worth, and deserves no esteem.

There is, therefore, a principle in man, which, when he acts according to it, gives him a consciousness of worth, and, when he acts contrary to it, a sense of demerit.

From the varieties of education, of fashion, of prejudices, and of habits, men may differ much in opinion with regard to the extent of this principle, and of what it commands and forbids; but the notion of it, as far as it is carried, is the same in all. It is that which gives a man real worth, and is the object of moral approbation. [231]

Men of rank call it *honour*, and too often confine it to certain virtues that are thought most essential to their rank. The vulgar call it *honesty, probity, virtue, conscience.* Philosophers have given it the names of *the moral sense, the moral faculty, rectitude.*

The universality of this principle in men that are grown up to years of understanding and reflection, is evident. The words that express it, the names of the virtues which it commands, and of the vices which it forbids, the *ought* and *ought not* which express its dictates, make an essential part of every language. The natural affections of respect to worthy characters, of resentment of injuries, of gratitude for favours, of indignation against the worthless, are parts of the human constitution which suppose a right and a wrong in conduct. Many transactions that are found necessary in the rudest societies go upon the same supposition. In all testimony, in all promises, and in all contracts, there is necessarily implied a moral obligation on one party, and a trust in the other, grounded upon this obligation.

The variety of opinions among men in points of morality, is not greater, but, as I apprehend, much less than in speculative points; and this variety is as easily accounted for, from the common causes of error, in the one case as in the other; so that it is not more evident, that there is a real distinction between true and false, in matters of speculation, than that there is a real distinction between right and wrong in human conduct.

Mr Hume's authority, if there were any need of it, is of weight in this matter, be-

* This would be true were the term *Honour* used in English in the same latitude as the Latin term *Honestum.*—H.

cause he was not wont to go rashly into vulgar opinions.

"Those," says he, "who have denied the reality of moral distinctions, may be ranked among the disingenuous disputants" (who really do not believe the opinions they defend, but engage in the controversy, from affectation, from a spirit of opposition, or from a desire of shewing wit and ingenuity superior to the rest of mankind); "nor is it conceivable, that any human creature could ever seriously believe that all characters and actions were alike entitled to the regard and affection of every one. [232]

"Let a man's insensibility be ever so great, he must often be touched with the images of RIGHT and WRONG; and let his prejudices be ever so obstinate, he must observe that others are susceptible of like impressions. The only way, therefore, of convincing an antagonist of this kind, is to leave him to himself. For, finding that nobody keeps up the controversy with him, it is probable he will at last, of himself, from mere weariness, come over to the side of common sense and reason." [*Principles of Morals*, § I.]

What we call *right* and *honourable* in human conduct, was, by the ancients, called *honestum*, τὸ καλὸν [καλὸν καὶ ἀγαθὸν, and καλοκἀγαθόν]; of which Tully says, "Quod vero dicimus, etiamsi a nullo laudetur, natura esse laudabile." [*De Officiis*, L. I. c. iv.]

All the ancient sects, except the Epicureans, distinguished the *honestum* from the *utile*, as we distinguish what is a man's duty from what is his interest.

The word *officium*, καθῆκον, extended both to the *honestum* and the *utile*; so that every reasonable action, proceeding either from a sense of duty or a sense of interest, was called *officium*.* It is defined by Cicero to be—"Id quod cur factum sit ratio probabilis reddi potest."† We commonly render it by the word *duty*, but it is more extensive; for the word *duty*, in the English language, I think, is commonly applied only to what the ancients called *honestum*.‡ Cicero, and Panætius before him, treating of offices, first point out those that are grounded upon the *honestum*, and next those that are grounded upon the *utile*.

The most ancient philosophical system concerning the principles of action in the human mind, and, I think, the most agreeable to nature, is that which we find in some fragments of the ancient Pythagoreans,* and which is adopted by Plato, and explained in some of his dialogues. [233]

According to this system, there is a leading principle in the soul, which, like the supreme power in a commonwealth, has authority and right to govern. This leading principle they called *Reason*. It is that which distinguishes men that are adult from brutes, idiots, and infants. The inferior principles, which are under the authority of the leading principle, are our passions and appetites, which we have in common with the brutes.

Cicero adopts this system, and expresses it well in few words. "Duplex enim est vis animorum atque naturæ. Una pars in appetitu posita est, quæ est ὁρμὴ græce, quæ hominem huc et illuc rapit; altera in ratione, quæ docet, et explanat quid faciendum fugiendumve sit. Ita fit ut ratio præsit appetitus obtemperet."—[*De Officiis*, L. I. c. 28.]

This division of our active principles can hardly, indeed, be accounted a discovery of philosophy, because it has been common to the unlearned in all ages of the world, and seems to be dictated by the common sense of mankind.

What I would now observe concerning this common division of our active powers, is, that the leading principle, which is called *Reason*, comprehends both a regard to what is right and honourable, and a regard to our happiness upon the whole.

Although these be really two distinct principles of action, it is very natural to comprehend them under one name, because both are leading principles, both suppose the use of Reason, and, when rightly understood, both lead to the same course of life. They are like two fountains, whose streams unite and run in the same channel.

When a man, on one occasion, consults his real happiness in things not inconsistent with his duty, though in opposition to the solicitation of appetite or passion; and when, on another occasion, without any selfish consideration, he does what is right and honourable, because it is so—in both these cases, he acts reasonably; every man approves of his conduct, and calls it reasonable, or according to reason. [234]

So that, when we speak of reason as a principle of action in man, it includes a regard both to the *honestum* and to the *utile*. Both are combined under one name; and, accordingly, the dictates of both, in the Latin tongue, were combined under the name *officium*, and in the Greek under καθῆκον.

If we examine the abstract notion of

* The Stoics divided καθῆκον (*officium*) into κατόρθωμα (*recte factum—absolutum, sive perfectum, officium*), and καθῆκον μέσον (*commune, sive medium, officium*.)—H.

† This definition does not apply to καθῆκον or *officium*, in general, but only to καθῆκον μέσον, *officium commune*. See Cicero *De Officiis*, L. I. c. iii.—H.

‡ That is, it is limited to the κατόρθωμα or *perfectum officium*.—H.

* Which are, however, all spurious, and written long subsequently to Plato. The moral system of these fragments is also principally accommodated to that of Aristotle.—H.

Duty, or Moral Obligation, it appears to be neither any real quality of the action considered by itself, nor of the agent considered without respect to the action, but a certain relation between the one and the other.

When we say a man ought to do such a thing, the *ought*, which expresses the moral obligation, has a respect, on the one hand, to the person who ought; and, on the other, to the action which he ought to do. Those two correlates are essential to every moral obligation; take away either, and it has no existence. So that, if we seek the place of moral obligation among the categories, it belongs to the category of *relation*.*

There are many relations of things, of which we have the most distinct conception, without being able to define them logically. Equality and proportion are relations between quantities, which every man understands, but no man can define.

Moral obligation is a relation of its own kind, which every man understands, but is, perhaps, too simple to admit of logical definition. Like all other relations, it may be changed or annihilated by a change in any of the two related things—I mean the agent or the action. [235]

Perhaps it may not be improper to point out briefly the circumstances, both in the action and in the agent, which are necessary to constitute moral obligation. The universal agreement of men in these, shews that they have one and the same notion of it.

With regard to the action, it must be a voluntary action, or prestation of the person obliged, and not of another. There can be no moral obligation upon a man to be six feet high. Nor can I be under a moral obligation that another person should do such a thing. His actions must be imputed to himself, and mine only to me, either for praise or blame.

I need hardly mention, that a person can be under a moral obligation, only to things within the sphere of his natural power.

As to the party obliged, it is evident there can be no moral obligation upon an inanimate thing. To speak of moral obligation upon a stone or a tree is ridiculous, because it contradicts every man's notion of moral obligation.

The person obliged must have understanding and will, and some degree of active power. He must not only have the natural faculty of understanding, but the means of knowing his obligation. An invincible ignorance of this destroys all moral obligation.

The opinion of the agent in doing the action gives it its moral denomination. If he does a materially good action, without any belief of its being good, but from some other principle, it is no good action in him. And if he does it with the belief of its being ill, it is ill in him. [236]

Thus, if a man should give to his neighbour a potion which he really believes will poison him, but which, in the event, proves salutary, and does much good; in moral estimation, he is a poisoner, and not a benefactor.

These qualifications of the action and of the agent, in moral obligation, are self-evident; and the agreement of all men in them shews that all men have the same notion, and a distinct notion of moral obligation.

CHAPTER VI.

OF THE SENSE OF DUTY.

We are next to consider, how we learn to judge and determine, that this is right, and that is wrong.

The abstract notion of moral good and ill would be of no use to direct our life, if we had not the power of applying it to particular actions, and determining what is morally good, and what is morally ill.

Some philosophers, with whom I agree, ascribe this to an original power or faculty in man, which they call the *Moral Sense*, the *Moral Faculty*, *Conscience*. Others think that our moral sentiments may be accounted for without supposing any original sense or faculty appropriated to that purpose, and go into very different systems to account for them.

I am not, at present, to take any notice of those systems, because the opinion first mentioned seems to me to be the truth; to wit, That, by an original power of the mind, when we come to years of understanding and reflection, we not only have the notions of right and wrong in conduct, but perceive certain things to be right, and others to be wrong. [237]

The name of the *Moral Sense*, though more frequently given to Conscience since Lord Shaftesbury and Dr Hutcheson wrote, is not new. The *sensus recti et honesti*, is a phrase not unfrequent among the ancients; neither is the *sense of duty*, among us.

It has got this name of *sense*, no doubt, from some analogy which it is conceived to bear to the external senses. And, if we have just notions of the office of the external senses, the analogy is very evident, and I see no reason to take offence, as some have done, at the name of the *moral sense*.*

* The ancients rightly founded the *καλόν* or *honestum* on the *πρέπον* or *decorum*; that is, they considered an action to be virtuous which was performed in harmony with the relations necessary and accidental of the agent.—H.

* On the term *Sense* for *Intelligence*, see Note A.—H.

The offence taken at this name seems to be owing to this, That philosophers have degraded the senses too much, and deprived them of the most important part of their office.

We are taught, that, by the senses, we have only certain ideas which we could not have otherwise. They are represented as powers by which we have sensations and ideas, not as powers by which we judge.

This notion of the senses I take to be very lame, and to contradict what nature and accurate reflection teach concerning them.

A man who has totally lost the sense of seeing, may retain very distinct notions of the various colours; but he cannot judge of colours, because he has lost the sense by which alone he could judge. By my eyes I not only have the ideas of a square and a circle, but I perceive this surface to be a square, that to be a circle. [238]

By my ear, I not only have the idea of sounds, loud and soft, acute and grave, but I immediately perceive and judge this sound to be loud, that to be soft, this to be acute, that to be grave. Two or more synchronous sounds I perceive to be concordant, others to be discordant.

These are judgments of the senses.* They have always been called and accounted such, by those whose minds are not tinctured by philosophical theories. They are the immediate testimony of nature by our senses; and we are so constituted by nature, that we must receive their testimony, for no other reason but because it is given by our senses.

In vain do sceptics endeavour to overturn this evidence by metaphysical reasoning. Though we should not be able to answer their arguments, we believe our senses still, and rest our most important concerns upon their testimony.

If this be a just notion of our external senses, as I conceive it is, our moral faculty may, I think, without impropriety, be called the *Moral Sense*.

In its dignity it is, without doubt, far superior to every other power of the mind; but there is this analogy between it and the external senses, That, as by them we have not only the original conceptions of the various qualities of bodies, but the original judgment that this body has such a quality, that such another; so by our moral faculty, we have both the original conceptions of right and wrong in conduct, of merit and demerit, and the original judgments that this conduct is right, that is wrong; that this character has worth, that demerit.

The testimony of our moral faculty, like that of the external senses, is the testimony of nature, and we have the same reason to rely upon it. [239]

The truths immediately testified by the external senses are the first principles from which we reason, with regard to the material world, and from which all our knowledge of it is deduced.

The truths immediately testified by our moral faculty, are the first principles of all moral reasoning, from which all our knowledge of our duty must be deduced.

By moral reasoning, I understand all reasoning that is brought to prove that such conduct is right, and deserving of moral approbation; or that it is wrong; or that it is indifferent, and, in itself, neither morally good nor ill.

I think, all we can properly call moral judgments, are reducible to one or other of these, as all human actions, considered in a moral view, are either good, or bad, or indifferent.

I know the term *moral reasoning* is often used by good writers in a more extensive sense; but, as the reasoning I now speak of is of a peculiar kind, distinct from all others, and, therefore, ought to have a distinct name, I take the liberty to limit the name of *moral reasoning* to this kind.

Let it be understood, therefore, that in the reasoning I call *moral*, the conclusion always is, That something in the conduct of moral agents is good or bad, in a greater or a less degree, or indifferent.

All reasoning must be grounded on first principles. This holds in moral reasoning, as in all other kinds. There must, therefore, be in morals, as in all other sciences, first or self-evident principles, on which all moral reasoning is grounded, and on which it ultimately rests. From such self-evident principles, conclusions may be drawn synthetically with regard to the moral conduct of life; and particular duties or virtues may be traced back to such principles, analytically. But, without such principles, we can no more establish any conclusion in morals, than we can build a castle in the air, without any foundation. [240]

An example or two will serve to illustrate this.

It is a first principle in morals, That we ought not to do to another what we should think wrong to be done to us in like circumstances. If a man is not capable of perceiving this in his cool moments, when he reflects seriously, he is not a moral agent, nor is he capable of being convinced of it by reasoning.

* Rather, these are judgments, of which the *materials* and the *condition* are afforded by sense. It is, no doubt, true that there can be no sensitive perception without judgment, because there can, in fact, be no consciousness without judgment. But it is not more reasonable to identify sense with judgment, because the former cannot exist without an act of the latter, than it would be to identify the sides and angles of a mathematical figure, because sides and angles cannot exist apart from each other.—H.

From what topic can you reason with such a man? You may possibly convince him by reasoning, that it is his interest to observe this rule; but this is not to convince him that it is his duty. To reason about justice with a man who sees nothing to be just or unjust, or about benevolence with a man who sees nothing in benevolence preferable to malice, is like reasoning with a blind man about colour, or with a deaf man about sound.

It is a question in morals that admits of reasoning, Whether, by the law of nature, a man ought to have only one wife?

We reason upon this question, by balancing the advantages and disadvantages to the family, and to society in general, that are naturally consequent both upon monogamy and polygamy. And, if it can be shewn that the advantages are greatly upon the side of monogamy, we think the point is determined.

But, if a man does not perceive that he ought to regard the good of society, and the good of his wife and children, the reasoning can have no effect upon him, because he denies the first principle upon which it is grounded.

Suppose, again, that we reason for monogamy from the intention of nature, discovered by the proportion of males and of females that are born—a proportion which corresponds perfectly with monogamy, but by no means with polygamy—this argument can have no weight with a man who does not perceive that he ought to have a regard to the intention of nature. [241]

Thus we shall find that all moral reasonings rest upon one or more first principles of morals, whose truth is immediately perceived without reasoning, by all men come to years of understanding.

And this indeed is common to every branch of human knowledge that deserves the name of science. There must be first principles proper to that science, by which the whole superstructure is supported.

The first principles of all the sciences, must be the immediate dictates of our natural faculties; nor is it possible that we should have any other evidence of their truth. And in different sciences the faculties which dictate their first principles are very different.

Thus, in astronomy and in optics, in which such wonderful discoveries have been made, that the unlearned can hardly believe them to be within the reach of human capacity, the first principles are phenomena attested solely by that little organ the human eye. If we disbelieve its report, the whole of those two noble fabrics of science, falls to pieces like the visions of the night.

The principles of music all depend upon the testimony of the ear. The principles of natural philosophy, upon the facts attested by the senses. The principles of mathematics, upon the necessary relations of quantities considered abstractly—such as, That equal quantities added to equal quantities make equal sums, and the like; which necessary relations are immediately perceived by the understanding. [242]

The science of politics borrows its principles from what we know by experience of the character and conduct of man. We consider not what he ought to be, but what he is, and thence conclude what part he will act in different situations and circumstances. From such principles we reason concerning the causes and effects of different forms of government, laws, customs, and manners. If man were either a more perfect or a more imperfect, a better or a worse, creature than he is, politics would be a different science from what it is.

The first principles of morals are the immediate dictates of the moral faculty. They shew us, not what man is, but what he ought to be. Whatever is immediately perceived to be just, honest, and honourable, in human conduct, carries moral obligation along with it, and the contrary carries demerit and blame; and, from those moral obligations that are immediately perceived, all other moral obligations must be deduced by reasoning.

He that will judge of the colour of an object, must consult his eyes, in a good light, when there is no medium or contiguous objects that may give it a false tinge. But in vain will he consult every other faculty in this matter.

In like manner, he that will judge of the first principles of morals, must consult his conscience, or moral faculty, when he is calm and dispassionate, unbiassed by interest, affection, or fashion. [243]

As we rely upon the clear and distinct testimony of our eyes, concerning the colours and figures of the bodies about us, we have the same reason to rely with security upon the clear and unbiassed testimony of our conscience, with regard to what we ought and ought not to do. In many cases moral worth and demerit are discerned no less clearly by the last of those natural faculties, than figure and colour by the first.

The faculties which nature hath given us, are the only engines we can use to find out the truth. We cannot indeed prove that those faculties are not fallacious, unless God should give us new faculties to sit in judgment upon the old. But we are born under a necessity of trusting them.

Every man in his senses believes his eyes, his ears, and his other senses. He believes his consciousness with respect to his own thoughts and purposes; his memory, with regard to what is past; his understanding, with regard to abstract relations of things; and his taste, with regard to what is elegant and beautiful. And he has the same reason, and, indeed, is under the same necessity of believing the clear and unbiassed dictates of his conscience, with regard to what is honourable and what is base.

The sum of what has been said in this chapter is, That, by an original power of the mind, which we call *conscience*, or the *moral faculty*, we have the conceptions of right and wrong in human conduct, of merit and demerit, of duty and moral obligation, and our other moral conceptions; and that, by the same faculty, we perceive some things in human conduct to be right, and others to be wrong; that the first principles of morals are the dictates of this faculty; and that we have the same reason to rely upon those dictates, as upon the determinations of our senses, or of our other natural faculties.* [244]

CHAPTER VII.

OF MORAL APPROBATION AND DISAPPROBATION.

Our moral judgments are not like those we form in speculative matters, dry and unaffecting, but, from their nature, are necessarily accompanied with affections and feelings; which we are now to consider.

It was before observed, that every human action, considered in a moral view, appears to us, good, or bad, or indifferent. When we judge the action to be indifferent, neither good nor bad, though this be a moral judgment, it produces no affection nor feeling, any more than our judgments in speculative matters.

But we approve of good actions, and disapprove of bad; and this approbation and disapprobation, when we analyse it, appears to include, not only a moral judgment of the action, but some affection, favourable or unfavourable, towards the agent, and some feeling in ourselves.

Nothing is more evident than this, That moral worth, even in a stranger, with whom we have not the least connection, never fails to produce some degree of esteem mixed with good will.

The esteem which we have for a man on account of his moral worth, is different from that which is grounded upon his intellectual accomplishments, his birth, fortune, and connection with us.

Moral worth, when it is not set off by eminent abilities and external advantages, is like a diamond in the mine, which is rough and unpolished, and perhaps crusted over with some baser material that takes away its lustre. [245]

But, when it is attended with these advantages, it is like a diamond cut, polished, and set. Then its lustre attracts every eye. Yet these things, which add so much to its appearance, add but little to its real value.

We must farther observe, that esteem and benevolent regard, not only accompany real worth by the constitution of our nature, but are perceived to be really and properly due to it; and that, on the contrary, unworthy conduct really merits dislike and indignation.

There is no judgment of the heart of man more clear, or more irresistible, than this, That esteem and regard are really due to good conduct, and the contrary to base and unworthy conduct. Nor can we conceive a greater depravity in the heart of man, than it would be to see and acknowledge worth without feeling any respect to it; or to see and acknowledge the highest worthlessness without any degree of dislike and indignation.

The esteem that is due to worthy conduct, is not lessened when a man is conscious of it in himself. Nor can he help having some esteem for himself, when he is conscious of those qualities for which he most highly esteems others.

Self esteem, grounded upon external advantages, or the gifts of fortune, is pride. When it is grounded upon a vain conceit of inward worth which we do not possess, it is arrogance and self-deceit. But when a man, without thinking of himself more highly than he ought to think, is conscious of that integrity of heart and uprightness of conduct which he most highly esteems in others, and values himself duly upon this account, this, perhaps, may be called the pride of virtue; but it is not a vicious pride. It is a noble and magnanimous disposition, without which there can be no steady virtue.* [246]

A man who has a character with himself, which he values, will disdain to act in a manner unworthy of it. The language of his heart will be like that of Job—"My righteousness I hold fast, and will not let it go; my heart shall not reproach me while I live."

A good man owes much to his character with the world, and will be concerned to vindicate it from unjust imputations. But he owes much more to his character with

* This theory is virtually the same as that which founds morality on intelligence. The *Practical Reason* of Kant is not essentially different from the *Moral Sense*, the *Moral Faculty* of Reid and Stewart.—H.

* See the fine portraiture of the Magnanimous Man, in Aristotle's "Nicomachian Ethics."—H.

himself. For, if his heart condemns him not, he has confidence towards God; and he can more easily bear the lash of tongues than the reproach of his own mind.

The sense of honour, so much spoken of, and so often misapplied, is nothing else, when rightly understood, but the disdain which a man of worth feels to do a dishonourable action, though it should never be known nor suspected.

A good man will have a much greater abhorrence against doing a bad action, than even against having it unjustly imputed to him. The last may give a wound to his reputation, but the first gives a wound to his conscience, which is more difficult to heal, and more painful to endure.

Let us, on the other hand, consider how we are affected by disapprobation, either of the conduct of others, or of our own.

Everything we disapprove in the conduct of a man lessens him in our esteem. There are, indeed, brilliant faults, which, having a mixture of good and ill in them, may have a very different aspect, according to the side on which we view them. [247]

In such faults of our friends, and much more of ourselves, we are disposed to view them on the best side, and on the contrary side in those to whom we are ill affected.

This partiality, in taking things by the best or by the worst handle, is the chief cause of wrong judgment with regard to the character of others, and of self-deceit with regard to our own.

But when we take complex actions to pieces, and view every part by itself, ill conduct of every kind lessens our esteem of a man, as much as good conduct increases it. It is apt to turn love into indifference, indifference into contempt, and contempt into aversion and abhorrence.

When a man is conscious of immoral conduct in himself, it lessens his self-esteem. It depresses and humbles his spirit, and makes his countenance to fall. He could even punish himself for his misbehaviour, if that could wipe out the stain. There is a sense of dishonour and worthlessness arising from guilt, as well as a sense of honour and worth arising from worthy conduct. And this is the case, even if a man could conceal his guilt from all the world.

We are next to consider the agreeable or uneasy feelings, in the breast of the spectator or judge, which naturally accompany moral approbation and disapprobation.

There is no affection that is not accompanied with some agreeable or uneasy emotion. It has often been observed, that all the benevolent affections give pleasure, and the contrary ones pain, in one degree or another. [248]

When we contemplate a noble character, though but in ancient history, or even in fiction; like a beautiful object, it gives a lively and pleasant emotion to the spirits. It warms the heart, and invigorates the whole frame. Like the beams of the sun, it enlivens the face of nature, and diffuses heat and light all around.

We feel a sympathy with every noble and worthy character that is represented to us. We rejoice in his prosperity, we are afflicted in his distress. We even catch some sparks of that celestial fire that animated his conduct, and feel the glow of his virtue and magnanimity.

This sympathy is the necessary effect of our judgment of his conduct, and of the approbation and esteem due to it; for real sympathy is always the effect of some benevolent affection, such as esteem, love, pity, or humanity.

When the person whom we approve is connected with us by acquaintance, friendship, or blood, the pleasure we derive from his conduct is greatly increased. We claim some property in his worth, and are apt to value ourselves on account of it. This shews a stronger degree of sympathy, which gathers strength from every social tie.

But the highest pleasure of all is, when we are conscious of good conduct in ourselves. This, in sacred scripture, is called the *testimony of a good conscience*; and it is represented, not only in the sacred writings, but in the writings of all moralists, of every age and sect, as the purest, the most noble and valuable of all human enjoyments.

Surely, were we to place the chief happiness of this life (a thing that has been so much sought after) in any one kind of enjoyment, that which arises from the consciousness of integrity, and a uniform endeavour to act the best part in our station, would most justly claim the preference to all other enjoyments the human mind is capable of, on account of its dignity, the intenseness of the happiness it affords, its stability and duration, its being in our power, and its being proof against all accidents of time and fortune. [249]

On the other hand, the view of a vicious character, like that of an ugly and deformed object, is disagreeable. It gives disgust and abhorrence.

If the unworthy person be nearly connected with us, we have a very painful sympathy indeed. We blush even for the smaller faults of those we are connected with, and feel ourselves, as it were, dishonoured by their ill conduct.

But, when there is a high degree of depravity in any person connected with us, we are deeply humbled and depressed by it. The sympathetic feeling has some resemblance to that of guilt, though it be free from all guilt. We are ashamed to see our acquaintance; we would, if possible, disclaim all connection with the guilty person. We wish to tear him from our hearts, and to blot him out of our remembrance.

Time, however, alleviates those sympathetic sorrows which arise from bad behaviour in our friends and connections, if we are conscious that we had no share in their guilt.

The wisdom of God, in the constitution of our nature, hath intended that this sympathetic distress should interest us the more deeply in the good behaviour, as well as in the good fortune of our friends; and that thereby friendship, relation, and every social tie, should be aiding to virtue, and unfavourable to vice.

How common is it, even in vicious parents, to be deeply afflicted when their children go into these courses in which, perhaps, they have gone before them, and, by their example, shewn them the way. [250]

If bad conduct in those in whom we are interested be uneasy and painful, it is so much more when we are conscious of it in ourselves. This uneasy feeling has a name in all languages. We call it *remorse*.

It has been described in such frightful colours, by writers sacred and profane, by writers of every age and of every persuasion, even by Epicureans, that I will not attempt the description of it.

It is on account of the uneasiness of this feeling that bad men take so much pains to get rid of it, and to hide, even from their own eyes, as much as possible, the pravity of their conduct. Hence arise all the arts of self-deceit, by which men varnish their crimes, or endeavour to wash out the stain of guilt. Hence the various methods of expiation which superstition has invented, to solace the conscience of the criminal, and give some cooling to his parched breast. Hence also arise, very often, the efforts of men of bad hearts to excel in some amiable quality, which may be a kind of counterpoise to their vices, both in the opinion of of others and in their own.

For no man can bear the thought of being absolutely destitute of all worth. The consciousness of this would make him detest himself, hate the light of the sun, and fly, if possible, out of existence.

I have now endeavoured to delineate the natural operations of that principle of action in man which we call the *Moral Sense*, the *Moral Faculty*, *Conscience*. We know nothing of our natural faculties, but by their operations within us. Of their operations in our own minds we are conscious, and we see the signs of their operations in the minds of others. Of this faculty, the operations appear to be, the judging ultimately of what is right, what is wrong, and what is indifferent in the conduct of moral agents; the approbation of good conduct, and disapprobation of bad, in consequence of that judgment; and the agreeable emotions which attend obedience, and disagreeable, which attend disobedience to its dictates. [251]

The Supreme Being, who has given us eyes to discern what may be useful and what hurtful to our natural life, hath also given us this light within, to direct our moral conduct.

Moral conduct is the business of every man; and therefore the knowledge of it ought to be within the reach of all.

Epicurus reasoned acutely and justly to shew, that a regard to our present happiness should induce us to the practice of temperance, justice, and humanity. But the bulk of mankind cannot follow long trains of reasoning. The loud voice of the passions drowns the calm and still voice of reasoning.

Conscience commands and forbids with more authority, and in the most common and most important points of conduct, without the labour of reasoning. Its voice is heard by every man, and cannot be disregarded with impunity.

The sense of guilt makes a man at variance with himself. He sees that he is what he ought not to be. He has fallen from the dignity of his nature, and has sold his real worth for a thing of no value. He is conscious of demerit, and cannot avoid the dread of meeting with its reward.

On the other hand, he who pays a sacred regard to the dictates of his conscience, cannot fail of a present reward, and a reward proportioned to the exertion required in doing his duty. [252]

The man who, in opposition to strong temptation, by a noble effort, maintains his integrity, is the happiest man on earth. The more severe his conflict has been, the greater is his triumph. The consciousness of inward worth gives strength to his heart, and makes his countenance to shine. Tempests may beat and floods roar, but he stands firm as a rock in the joy of a good conscience, and confidence of divine approbation.

To this I shall only add, what every man's conscience dictates, That he who does his duty from the conviction that it is right and honourable, and what he ought to do, acts from a nobler principle, and with more inward satisfaction, than he who is bribed to do it merely from the consideration of a reward present or future.

CHAPTER VIII.

OBSERVATIONS CONCERNING CONSCIENCE.

I SHALL now conclude this essay with

some observations concerning this power of the mind which we call *Conscience*, by which its nature may be better understood.

The *first* is, That, like all our other powers, it comes to maturity by insensible degrees, and may be much aided in its strength and vigour by proper culture.

All the human faculties have their infancy and their state of maturity. [253]

The faculties which we have in common with the brutes, appear first, and have the quickest growth. In the first period of life, children are not capable of distinguishing right from wrong in human conduct; neither are they capable of abstract reasoning in matters of science. Their judgment of moral conduct, as well as their judgment of truth, advances by insensible degrees, like the corn and the grass.

In vegetables, first the blade or the leaf appears, then the flower, and last of all the fruit, the noblest production of the three, and that for which the others were produced. These succeed one another in a regular order. They require moisture, and heat, and air, and shelter to bring them to maturity, and may be much improved by culture. According to the variations of soil, season, and culture, some plants are brought to much greater perfection than others of the same species. But no variation of culture, or season, or soil, can make grapes grow from thorns, or figs from thistles.

We may observe a similar progress in the faculties of the mind: for there is a wonderful analogy among all the works of God, from the least even to the greatest.

The faculties of man unfold themselves in a certain order, appointed by the great Creator. In their gradual progress, they may be greatly assisted or retarded, improved or corrupted, by education, instruction, example, exercise, and by the society and conversation of men, which, like soil and culture in plants, may produce great changes to the better or to the worse.

But these means can never produce any new faculties, nor any other than were originally planted in the mind by the Author of nature. And what is common to the whole species, in all the varieties of instruction and education, of improvement and degeneracy, is the work of God, and not the operation of second causes. [254]

Such we may justly account conscience, or the faculty of distinguishing right conduct from wrong; since it appears, and in all nations and ages, has appeared, in men that are come to maturity.

The seeds, as it were, of moral discernment are planted in the mind by him that made us. They grow up in their proper season, and are at first tender and delicate, and easily warped. Their progress depends very much upon their being duly cultivated and properly exercised.

It is so with the power of reasoning, which all acknowledge to be one of the most eminent natural faculties of man. It appears not in infancy. It springs up, by insensible degrees, as we grow to maturity. But its strength and vigour depend so much upon its being duly cultivated and exercised, that we see many individuals, nay, many nations, in which it is hardly to be perceived.

Our intellectual discernment is not so strong and vigorous by nature as to secure us from errors in speculation. On the contrary, we see a great part of mankind, in every age, sunk in gross ignorance of things that are obvious to the more enlightened, and fettered by errors and false notions, which the human understanding, duly improved, easily throws off.

It would be extremely absurd, from the errors and ignorance of mankind, to conclude that there is no such thing as truth; or that man has not a natural faculty of discerning it, and distinguishing it from error.

In like manner, our moral discernment of what we ought, and what we ought not to do, is not so strong and vigorous by nature as to secure us from very gross mistakes with regard to our duty. [255]

In matters of conduct, as well as in matters of speculation, we are liable to be misled by prejudices of education, or by wrong instruction. But, in matters of conduct, we are also very liable to have our judgment warped by our appetites and passions, by fashion, and by the contagion of evil example.

We must not therefore think, because man has the natural power of discerning what is right and what is wrong, that he has no need of instruction; that this power has no need of cultivation and improvement; that he may safely rely upon the suggestions of his mind, or upon opinions he has got, he knows not how.

What should we think of a man who, because he has by nature the power of moving all his limbs should therefore conclude that he needs not be taught to dance, or to fence, to ride, or to swim? All these exercises are performed by that power of moving our limbs which we have by nature; but they will be performed very awkwardly and imperfectly by those who have not been trained to them, and practised in them.

What should we think of the man who, because he has the power by nature of distinguishing what is true from what is false, should conclude that he has no need to be taught mathematics, or natural philosophy, or other sciences? It is by the natural power of human understanding that everything in those sciences has been discovered, and that the truths they contain are discerned. But the understanding, left to itself, without the aid of instruction, training, habit, and exercise, would make very small progress, as every one sees, in persons uninstructed in those matters.

Our natural power of discerning between right and wrong, needs the aid of instruction, education, exercise, and habit, as well as our other natural powers. [256]

There are persons who, as the Scripture speaks, have, by reason of use, their senses exercised to discern both good and evil; by that means, they have a much quicker, clearer, and more certain judgment in morals than others.

The man who neglects the means of improvement in the knowledge of his duty, may do very bad things, while he follows the light of his mind. And, though he be not culpable for acting according to his judgment, he may be very culpable for not using the means of having his judgment better informed.

It may be observed, That there are truths, both speculative and moral, which a man left to himself would never discover; yet, when they are fairly laid before him, he owns and adopts them, not barely upon the authority of his teacher, but upon their own intrinsic evidence, and perhaps wonders that he could be so blind as not to see them before.

Like a man whose son has been long abroad, and supposed dead. After many years, the son returns, and is not known by his father. He would never find that this is his son. But, when he discovers himself, the father soon finds, by many circumstances, that this is his son who was lost, and can be no other person.

Truth has an affinity with the human understanding, which error hath not. And right principles of conduct have an affinity with a candid mind, which wrong principles have not. When they are set before it in a just light, a well disposed mind recognises this affinity, feels their authority, and perceives them to be genuine. It was this, I apprehend, that led Plato to conceive that the knowledge we acquire in the present state, is only reminiscence of what, in a former state, we were acquainted with. [257]

A man born and brought up in a savage nation, may be taught to pursue injury with unrelenting malice, to the destruction of his enemy. Perhaps when he does so, his heart does not condemn him.

Yet, if he be fair and candid, and, when the tumult of passion is over, have the virtues of clemency, generosity, and forgiveness laid before him, as they were taught and exemplified by the divine Author of our religion, he will see that it is more noble to overcome himself, and subdue a savage passion, than to destroy his enemy. He will see, that, to make a friend of an enemy, and to overcome evil with good, is the greatest of all victories, and gives a manly and a rational delight, with which the brutish passion of revenge deserves not to be compared. He will see that hitherto he acted like a man to his friends, but like a brute to his enemies; now he knows how to make his whole character consistent, and one part of it to harmonize with another.

He must indeed be a great stranger to his own heart, and to the state of human nature, who does not see that he has need of all the aid which his situation affords him, in order to know how he ought to act in many cases that occur.

A *second* observation is, That Conscience is peculiar to man. We see not a vestige of it in brute animals. It is one of those prerogatives by which we are raised above them.

Brute animals have many faculties in common with us. They see, and hear, and taste, and smell, and feel. They have their pleasures and pains. They have various instincts and appetites. They have an affection for their offspring, and some of them for their herd or flock. Dogs have a wonderful attachment to their masters, and give manifest signs of sympathy with them. [258]

We see, in brute animals, anger and emulation, pride and shame. Some of them are capable of being trained, by habit, and by rewards and punishments, to many things useful to man.

All this must be granted; and, if our perception of what we ought, and what we ought not to do, could be resolved into any of these principles, or into any combination of them, it would follow, that some brutes are moral agents, and accountable for their conduct.

But common sense revolts against this conclusion. A man who seriously charged a brute with a crime, would be laughed at. They may do actions hurtful to themselves, or to man. They may have qualities, or acquire habits, that lead to such actions; and this is all we mean when we call them vicious. But they cannot be immoral; nor can they be virtuous. They are not capable of self-government; and, when they act according to the passion or habit which is strongest at the time, they act according to the nature that God has given them, and no more can be required of them.

They cannot lay down a rule to themselves, which they are not to transgress, though prompted by appetite, or ruffled by passion. We see no reason to think that they can form the conception of a general rule, or of obligation to adhere to it.

They have no conception of a promise or contract; nor can you enter into any treaty with them. They can neither affirm nor deny, nor resolve, nor plight their faith. If nature had made them capable of these operations, we should see the signs of them in their motions and gestures.

The most sagacious brutes never invented a language, nor learned the use of one before invented. They never formed a plan of government, nor transmitted inventions to their posterity. [259]

These things, and many others that are obvious to common observation, shew that there is just reason why mankind have always considered the brute-creation as destitute of the noblest faculties with which God hath endowed man, and particularly of that faculty which makes us moral and accountable beings.

The *next* [*third*] observation is—That Conscience is evidently intended by nature to be the immediate guide and director of our conduct, after we arrive at the years of understanding.

There are many things which, from their nature and structure, shew intuitively the end for which they were made.

A man who knows the structure of a watch or clock, can have no doubt in concluding that it was made to measure time. And he that knows the structure of the eye, and the properties of light, can have as little doubt whether it was made that we might see by it.

In the fabric of the body, the intention of the several parts is, in many instances, so evident as to leave no possibility of doubt. Who can doubt whether the muscles were intended to move the parts in which they are inserted? Whether the bones were intended to give strength and support to the body; and some of them to guard the parts which they inclose?

When we attend to the structure of the mind, the intention of its various original powers is no less evident. Is it not evident that the external senses are given, that we may discern those qualities of bodies which may be useful or hurtful to us?—Memory, that we may retain the knowledge we have acquired—judgment and understanding, that we may distinguish what is true from what is false? [260]

The natural appetites of hunger and thirst; the natural affections of parents to their offspring, and of relations to each other; the natural docility and credulity of children; the affections of pity and sympathy with the distressed; the attachment we feel to neighbours, to acquaintance, and to the laws and constitution of our country—these are parts of our constitution, which plainly point out their end, so that he must be blind, or very inattentive, who does not perceive it. Even the passions of anger and resentment appear very plainly to be a kind of defensive armour, given by our Maker to guard us against injuries, and to deter the injurious.

Thus it holds generally with regard both to the intellectual and active powers of man, that the intention for which they are given is written in legible characters upon the face of them.

Nor is this the case of any of them more evidently than of conscience. Its intention is manifestly implied in its office; which is, to shew us what is good, what bad, and what indifferent in human conduct.

It judges of every action before it is done. For we can rarely act so precipitately but we have the consciousness that what we are about to do is right, or wrong, or indifferent. Like the bodily eye, it naturally looks forward, though its attention may be turned back to the past.

To conceive, as some seem to have done, that its office is only to reflect on past actions, and to approve or disapprove, is, as if a man should conceive that the office of his eyes is only to look back upon the road he has travelled, and to see whether it be clean or dirty; a mistake which no man can make who has made the proper use of his eyes. [261]

Conscience prescribes measures to every appetite, affection, and passion, and says to every other principle of action—So far thou mayest go, but no farther.

We may indeed transgress its dictates, but we cannot transgress them with innocence, nor even with impunity.

We condemn ourselves, or, in the language of scripture, *our heart condemns us*, whenever we go beyond the rules of right and wrong which conscience prescribes.

Other principles of action may have more strength, but this only has authority. Its sentence makes us guilty to ourselves, and guilty in the eyes of our Maker, whatever other principle may be set in opposition to it.

It is evident, therefore, that this principle has, from its nature, an authority to direct and determine with regard to our conduct; to judge, to acquit, or to condemn, and even to punish; an authority which belongs to no other principle of the human mind.

It is the candle of the Lord set up within us, to guide our steps. Other principles may urge and impel, but this only authorizes. Other principles ought to be controlled by this; this may be, but never ought to be controlled by any other, and never can be with innocence.

The authority of conscience over the other active principles of the mind, I do not consider as a point that requires proof by argument, but as self-evident. For it implies no more than this—That in all cases a man ought to do his duty. He only who does in all cases what he ought to do, is the perfect man. [262]

Of this perfection in the human nature, the Stoics formed the idea, and held it forth in their writings, as the goal to which the race of life ought to be directed. Their *wise man* was one in whom a regard to the *honestum* swallowed up every other principle of action.

The *wise man* of the Stoics, like the *perfect orator* of the rhetoricians, was an ideal character, and was, in some respects, carried beyond nature; yet it was perhaps the most perfect model of virtue that ever was exhibited to the heathen world; and some of those who copied after it, were ornaments to human nature.

The [*fourth* and] *last* observation is—That the Moral Faculty or Conscience is both an Active and an Intellectual power of the mind.

It is an *active* power, as every truly virtuous action must be more or less influenced by it. Other principles may concur with it, and lead the same way; but no action can be called morally good, in which a regard to what is right, has not some influence. Thus, a man who has no regard to justice, may pay his just debt, from no other motive but that he may not be thrown into prison. In this action there is no virtue at all.

The moral principle, in particular cases, may be opposed by any of our animal principles. Passion or appetite may urge to what we know to be wrong. In every instance of this kind, the moral principle ought to prevail, and the more difficult its conquest is, it is the more glorious.

In some cases, a regard to what is right may be the sole motive, without the concurrence or opposition of any other principle of action; as when a judge or an arbiter determines a plea between two different persons, solely from a regard to justice. [263]

Thus we see that conscience, as an active principle, sometimes concurs with other active principles, sometimes opposes them, and sometimes is the sole principle of action.

I endeavoured before to shew, that a regard to our own good upon the whole is not only a rational principle of action, but a leading principle, to which all our animal principles are subordinate. As these are, therefore, two regulating or leading principles in the constitution of man—a regard to what is best for us upon the whole, and a regard to duty—it may be asked, Which of these ought to yield if they happen to interfere?

Some well-meaning persons have maintained—That all regard to ourselves and to our own happiness ought to be extinguished; that we should love virtue for its own sake only, even though it were to be accompanied with eternal misery.

This seems to have been the extravagance of some Mystics, which perhaps they were led into in opposition to a contrary extreme of the schoolmen of the middle ages, who made the desire of good to ourselves to be the sole motive to action, and virtue to be approvable only on account of its present or future reward.

Juster views of human nature will teach us to avoid both these extremes.

On the one hand, the disinterested love of virtue is undoubtedly the noblest principle in human nature, and ought never to stoop to any other. [264]

On the other hand, there is no active principle which God hath planted in our nature that is vicious in itself, or that ought to be eradicated, even if it were in our power.

They are all useful and necessary in our present state. The perfection of human nature consists, not in extinguishing, but in restraining them within their proper bounds, and keeping them in due subordination to the governing principles.

As to the supposition of an opposition between the two governing principles—that is, between a regard to our happiness upon the whole, and a regard to duty—this supposition is merely imaginary. There can be no such opposition.

While the world is under a wise and benevolent administration, it is impossible that any man should, in the issue, be a loser by doing his duty. Every man, therefore, who believes in God, while he is careful to do his duty, may safely leave the care of his happiness to Him who made him. He is conscious that he consults the last most effectually by attending to the first.

Indeed, if we suppose a man to be an atheist in his belief, and, at the same time, by wrong judgment, to believe that virtue is contrary to his happiness upon the whole, this case, as Lord Shaftesbury justly observes, is without remedy. It will be impossible for the man to act so as not to contradict a leading principle of his nature. He must either sacrifice his happiness to virtue, or virtue to happiness; and is reduced to this miserable dilemma, whether it be best to be a fool or a knave.

This shews the strong connection between morality and the principles of natural religion; as the last only can secure a man from the possibility of an apprehension, that he may play the fool by doing his duty. [265]

Hence, even Lord Shaftesbury, in his gravest work, concludes, *That virtue without piety is incomplete.* Without piety, it loses its brightest example, its noblest object, and its firmest support.

I conclude with observing, That conscience, or the moral faculty, is likewise an *intellectual* power.

By it solely we have the original conceptions or ideas of right and wrong in human conduct. And of right and wrong there are not only many different degrees, but many different species. Justice and injustice, gratitude and ingratitude, benevolence and malice, prudence and folly, magnanimity and meanness, decency and indecency, are various moral forms, all comprehended under the general notion of right and wrong in conduct, all of them objects of moral approbation or disapprobation, in a greater or a less degree.

The conception of these, as moral qualities, we have by our moral faculty; and by the same faculty, when we compare them together, we perceive various moral relations among them. Thus, we perceive that justice is entitled to a small degree of praise, but injustice to a high degree of blame; and the same may be said of gratitude and its contrary. When justice and gratitude interfere, gratitude must give place to justice, and unmerited beneficence must give place to both.

Many such relations between the various moral qualities compared together, are immediately discerned by our moral faculty. A man needs only to consult his own heart to be convinced of them. [266]

All our reasonings in morals, in natural jurisprudence, in the law of nations, as well as our reasonings about the duties of natural religion, and about the moral government of the Deity, must be grounded upon the dictates of our moral faculty, as first principles.

As this faculty, therefore, furnishes the human mind with many of its original conceptions or ideas, as well as with the first principles of many important branches of human knowledge, it may justly be accounted an intellectual as well as an active power of the mind. [267]

ESSAY IV.

OF THE LIBERTY OF MORAL AGENTS.

CHAPTER I.

THE NOTIONS OF MORAL LIBERTY AND NECESSITY STATED.

By the *Liberty of a Moral Agent*, I understand, *a power over the determinations of his own Will.**

If, in any action, he had power to will what he did, or not to will it, in that action he is free. But if, in every voluntary action, the determination of his will be the necessary consequence of something involuntary in the state of his mind, or of something in his external circumstances, he is not free; he has not what I call the Liberty of a Moral Agent, but is subject to Necessity.

This Liberty supposes the agent to have Understanding and Will; for the determinations of the will are the sole object about which this power is employed; and there can be no will without such a degree of understanding, at least, as gives the conception of that which we will.

The liberty of a moral agent implies, not only a *conception* of what he wills, but some degree of practical *judgment* or *reason*. [268]

* That is to say, Moral Liberty does not merely consist in the power of *doing what we will*, but (though Reid, p. 611, *infra*, seems to deny it) in the power of *willing what we will*. For a Power over the determinations of our Will supposes an act of Will that our Will should determine so and so; for we can only freely exert power through a rational determination or Volition. This definition of Liberty is right. But then question upon question remains (and this *ad infinitum*)—Have we a power (a will) over such anterior will?—and until this question be definitively answered, which it never can, we must be *unable to conceive the possibility of the fact of Liberty*. But, though inconceivable, this fact is not therefore false. For there are many contradictories (and, of contradictories, *one must*, and *one only can*, be true) of which we are equally unable to conceive the possibility of either. The philosophy, therefore, which I profess, annihilates the theoretical problem—How is the scheme of Liberty, or the scheme of Necessity, to be rendered comprehensible?—by shewing that both schemes are equally inconceivable; but it establishes Liberty practically as a fact, by shewing that it is either itself an immediate *datum*, or is involved in an immediate *datum*, of consciousness. But this by the way. See p. 743 n, 911 b.

I may notice that, among many others, the Platonic definition of Liberty corresponds to that by Reid; Ἐλευθερία, τὸ ἄρχειν αὑτοῦ: and the same condition of self-government is likewise supposed in the various expressions for Liberty—τὸ αὐτεξούσιον—τὸ ἐφ᾽ ἑαυτῷ—τὸ [illegible]—*sui potestas*—*sui juris*, &c.—H.

For, if he has not the judgment to discern one determination to be preferable to another, either in itself or for some purpose which he intends, what can be the use of a power to determine? His determinations must be made perfectly in the dark, without reason, motive, or end. They can neither be right nor wrong, wise nor foolish. Whatever the consequences may be, they cannot be imputed to the agent, who had not the capacity of foreseeing them, or of perceiving any reason for acting otherwise than he did.

We may, perhaps, be able to conceive a being endowed with power over the determinations of his will, without any light in his mind to direct that power to some end. But such power would be given in vain. No exercise of it could be either blamed or approved. As nature gives no power in vain, I see no ground to ascribe a power over the determinations of the will to any being who has no judgment to apply it to the direction of his conduct, no discernment of what he ought or ought not to do.

For that reason, in this Essay, I speak only of the Liberty of Moral Agents, who are capable of acting well or ill, wisely or foolishly, and this, for distinction's sake, I shall call *Moral Liberty*.

What kind or what degree of liberty belongs to brute animals, or to our own species, before any use of reason, I do not know. We acknowledge that they have not the power of self-government. Such of their actions as may be called *voluntary* seem to be invariably determined by the passion, or appetite, or affection, or habit, which is strongest at the time.

This seems to be the law of their constitution, to which they yield, as the inanimate creation does, without any conception of the law, or any intention of obedience. [269]

But of civil or moral government, which are addressed to the rational powers, and require a conception of the law and an intentional obedience, they are, in the judgment of all mankind, incapable. Nor do I see what end could be served by giving them a power over the determinations of their own will, unless to make them intractable by discipline, which we see they are not.

The effect of moral liberty is, *That it is in the power of the agent to do well or ill.* This power, like every other gift of God, may be abused. The right use of this gift of God is to do well and wisely, as far as his best judgment can direct him, and thereby merit esteem and approbation. The abuse of it is to act contrary to what he knows or suspects to be his duty and his wisdom, and thereby justly merit disapprobation and blame.

By *Necessity*, I understand the want of that moral liberty which I have above defined.

If there can be a better and a worse in actions on the system of Necessity, let us suppose a man necessarily determined in all cases to will and to do what is best to be done, he would surely be innocent and inculpable. But, as far as I am able to judge, he would not be entitled to the esteem and moral approbation of those who knew and believed this necessity. What was, by an ancient author, said of Cato, might, indeed, be said of him: *He was good because he could not be otherwise.** But this saying, if understood literally and strictly, is not the praise of Cato, but of his constitution, which was no more the work of Cato than his existence.†

On the other hand, if a man be necessarily determined to do ill, this case seems to me to move pity, but not disapprobation. He was ill, because he could not be otherwise. Who can blame him? Necessity has no law. [270]

If he knows that he acted under this necessity, has he not just ground to exculpate himself? The blame, if there be any, is not in him, but in his constitution. If he be charged by his Maker with doing wrong, may he not expostulate with him, and say—Why hast thou made me thus? I may be sacrificed at thy pleasure, for the common good, like a man that has the plague, but not for ill desert; for thou knowest that what I am charged with is thy work, and not mine.

Such are my notions of moral liberty and necessity, and of the consequences inseparably connected with both the one and the other.

This moral liberty a man may have, though it do not extend to all his actions, or even to all his voluntary actions. He does many things by instinct, many things by the force of habit, without any thought at all, and consequently without will. In the first part of life, he has not the power of self-government any more than the brutes. That power over the determinations of his own will, which belongs to him in ripe years, is limited, as all his powers are; and it is, perhaps, beyond the reach of his understanding to define its limits with precision. We can only say, in general, that it ex-

* The ancient author is Paterculus. (L. II. c. 35.) His words are;—"Homo virtuti simillimus, et per omnia ingenio diis quam hominibus propior; *qui nunquam recte fecit, ut facere videretur, sed quia aliter facere non poterat*; cui id solum visum est rationem habere, quod haberet justitiam; quaque omnibus humanis vitiis immunis, semper fortunam in sua potestate habuit."—H.

† But, in the same sense, God is necessarily good; for, if he became, or could become, evil, he would no longer be God. As Euripides hath it—

Εἰ θεοί τι δρῶσιν αἰσχρὸν οὐκ εἰσὶν θεοί.—H.

[269, 270]

tends to every action for which he is accountable.

This power is given by his Maker, and at his pleasure whose gift it is it may be enlarged or diminished, continued or withdrawn. No power in the creature can be independent of the Creator. His hook is in its nose; he can give it line as far as he sees fit, and, when he pleases, can restrain it, or turn it whithersoever he will. Let this be always understood when we ascribe liberty to man, or to any created being.

Supposing it therefore to be true, *That man is a free agent*, it may be true, at the same time, that his liberty may be impaired or lost, by disorder of body or mind, as in melancholy, or in madness; it may be impaired or lost by vicious habits; it may, in particular cases, be restrained by divine interposition. [271]

We call man a *free* agent in the same way as we call him a *reasonable* agent. In many things he is not guided by reason, but by principles similar to those of the brutes. His reason is weak at best. It is liable to be impaired or lost, by his own fault, or by other means. In like manner, he may be a free agent, though his freedom of action may have many similar limitations.

The liberty I have described has been represented by some philosophers as inconceivable, and as involving an absurdity.

"Liberty, they say, consists only in a power to act as we will; and it is impossible to conceive in any being a greater liberty than this. Hence it follows, that liberty does not extend to the determinations of the will, but only to the actions consequent to its determination, and depending upon the will. To say that we have power to will such an action, is to say, that we may will it, if we will. This supposes the will to be determined by a prior will; and, for the same reason, that will must be determined by a will prior to it, and so on in an infinite series of wills, which is absurd. To act freely, therefore, can mean nothing more than to act voluntarily; and this is all the liberty that can be conceived in man, or in any being."

This reasoning—first, I think, advanced by Hobbes*—has been very generally adopted by the defenders of necessity. It is grounded upon a definition of liberty totally different from that which I have given, and therefore does not apply to moral liberty, as above defined.†

But it is said that this is the only liberty that is possible, that is conceivable, that does not involve an absurdity. [272]

It is strange, indeed, if the word *Liberty* has no meaning but this one. I shall mention *three*, all very common. The objection applies to one of them, but to neither of the other two.

Liberty is sometimes opposed to external force or confinement of the body. Sometimes it is opposed to obligation by law, or by lawful authority. Sometimes it is opposed to necessity.

1. It is opposed to confinement of the body by superior force. So we say a prisoner is set at liberty when his fetters are knocked off, and he is discharged from confinement. This is the liberty defined in the objection; and I grant that this liberty extends not to the will, neither does the confinement, because the will cannot be confined by external force.*

2. Liberty is opposed to obligation by law, or lawful authority. This liberty is a right to act one way or another, in things which the law has neither commanded nor forbidden; and this liberty is meant when we speak of a man's natural liberty, his civil liberty, his Christian liberty. It is evident that this liberty, as well as the obligation opposed to it, extends to the will: For it is the will to obey that makes obedience; the will to transgress that makes a transgression of the law. Without will there can be neither obedience nor transgression. Law supposes a power to obey or to transgress; it does not take away this power, but proposes the motives of duty and of interest, leaving the power to yield to them, or to take the consequence of transgression.†

3. Liberty is opposed to Necessity, and in this sense it extends to the determinations of the will only, and not to what is consequent to the will.‡ [273]

---

* To Hobbes is generally ascribed the honour of first enouncing the modern doctrine of Determinism, in contradistinction to the ancient doctrine of Fatalism; but most erroneously. Hobbes was not the author of this scheme of Necessity, nor is this scheme of Necessity itself modern.—H.

† But how does that definition avoid this absurdity? See above, p. 599, note.—H.

* This is called the *Liberty from Coaction or Violence*—the *Liberty of Spontaneity*—*Spontaneity*—τὸ *Ἑκούσιον*. In the present question, this species of liberty ought to be thrown altogether out of account; it is admitted by all parties; is common equally to brutes and men; is not a peculiar quality of the will; and is, in fact, essential to it, for the will cannot possibly be forced. *The greatest spontaneity* is, in fact, the *greatest necessity*. Thus, a hungry horse, who turns of necessity to food, is said, on this definition of liberty, to do so with freedom, because he does so spontaneously; and, in general, the desire of happiness, which is the most necessary tendency, will, on this application of the term, be the most free.

I may observe, that, among others, the definition of liberty, given by the celebrated advocate of moral freedom, Dr Samuel Clarke, is, in reality, only that of the liberty of Spontaneity—viz., "The power of self-motion or action, which, in all animate agents, is spontaneity, is, in moral or rational agents, what we properly call liberty." (*Fifth Reply to Leibnitz*, §§ 1.—22. and *First Answer to the Gentleman of Cambridge.*) This self motion, absolutely considered, is itself necessary. See below, note on p. [illegible].

† With this description of liberty also, the present question has no concern.—H.

‡ This is variously denominated the *Liberty from*

In every voluntary action, the determination of the will is the first part of the action, upon which alone the moral estimation of it depends. It has been made a question among philosophers, *Whether, in every instance, this determination be the necessary consequence of the constitution of the person, and the circumstances in which he is placed; or whether he had not power, in many cases, to determine this way or that?*

This has, by some, been called the *philosophical* notion of liberty and necessity; but it is by no means peculiar to philosophers. The lowest of the vulgar have, in all ages, been prone to have recourse to this necessity, to exculpate themselves or their friends in what they do wrong, though, in the general tenor of their conduct, they act upon the contrary principle.*

Whether this notion of moral liberty be *conceivable* or not, every man must judge for himself. To me there appears no difficulty in conceiving it.† I consider the determination of the will as an effect. This effect must have a cause which had power to produce it; and the cause must be either the person himself, whose will it is, or some other being. The first is as easily conceived as the last. If the person was the cause of that determination of his own will, he was free in that action,‡ and it is justly imputed to him, whether it be good or bad. But, if another being was the cause of this determination, either by producing it immediately, or by means and instruments under his direction, then the determination is the act and deed of that being, and is solely imputable to him.

But it is said—"That nothing is in our power but what depends upon the will, and therefore, the will itself cannot be in our power."

I answer—That this is a fallacy arising from taking a common saying in a sense which it never was intended to convey, and in a sense contrary to what it necessarily implies. [274]

In common life, when men speak of what is, or is not, in a man's power, they attend only to the external and visible effects, which only can be perceived, and which only can affect them. Of these, it is true that nothing is in a man's power but what depends upon his will, and this is all that is meant by this common saying.

But this is so far from excluding his will from being in his power, that it necessarily implies it. For to say that what depends upon the will is in a man's power, but the will is not in his power, is to say that the end is in his power, but the means necessary to that end are not in his power, which is a contradiction.*

In many propositions which we express universally, there is an exception necessarily implied, and, therefore, always understood. Thus, when we say that all things depend upon God, God himself is necessarily excepted. In like manner, when we say, that all that is in our power depends upon the will, the will itself is necessarily excepted: for, if the will be not, nothing else can be in our power. Every effect must be in the power of its cause. The determination of the will is an effect, and, therefore, must be in the power of its cause, whether that cause be the agent himself, or some other being.

From what has been said in this chapter, I hope the notion of moral liberty will be distinctly understood, and that it appears that this notion is neither inconceivable, nor involves any absurdity or contradiction. [275]

Necessity—Moral Liberty—Philosophical Liberty—Essential Liberty—Formal Liberty—Liberty of Indifference—Liberty of Opposition, &c. The terms *Αὐτεξούσιον, Αὐτοπραγία, Arbitrium, Liberum Arbitrium, Free Will*, though properly limited to the Liberty from Necessity, have not always been applied so as to discriminate it from the Liberty of Spontaneity.—H.

* So Agamemnon:—

Ἐγὼ δ' οὐκ αἴτιός εἰμι,
Ἀλλὰ Ζεὺς καὶ Μοῖρα καὶ ἠεροφοῖτις Ἐριννύς.

This is a favourite topic with Lucian.—H.

† To conceive a *free act*, is to conceive an act which, being a *cause*, is not itself an *effect*; in other words, to conceive an absolute commencement. But is such by us conceivable?—H.

‡ Only if he were not determined to that determination. But is the person an *original undetermined cause* of the determination of his will? If he be not, then is he not a *free* agent, and the scheme of Necessity is admitted. If he be, in the first place, it is impossible to *conceive* the possibility of this; and, in the second, if the *fact*, though inconceivable, be allowed, it is impossible to see how a *cause, undetermined by any motive*, can be a *rational, moral, and accountable, cause*. There is no conceivable medium between *Fatalism & Casualism*; & the contradictory schemes of Liberty and Necessity themselves are inconceivable. For, as we cannot compass in thought an *undetermined cause—an absolute commencement*—the fundamental hypothesis of the one; so we can as little think *an infinite series of determined causes—of relative commencements*—the fundamental hypothesis of the other. The champions of the opposite doctrines are thus at once resistless in assault, and impotent in defence. Each is hewn down, and appears to die under the home-thrusts of his adversary; but each again recovers life from the very death of his antagonist, and, to borrow a simile, both are like the heroes in Valhalla, ready in a moment to amuse themselves anew in the same bloodless and interminable conflict. The doctrine of Moral Liberty cannot be made conceivable, for we can only conceive the determined and the relative. As already stated, all that can be done, is to shew—1°, That, for the *fact* of Liberty, we have, immediately or mediately, the evidence of consciousness; and, 2°, That there are, among the phænomena of mind, many facts which we must admit as actual, but of whose possibility we are wholly unable to form any notion. I may merely observe, that the fact of *Motion* can be shewn to be impossible, on grounds not less strong than those on which it is attempted to disprove the *fact of Liberty*; to say nothing of many contradictories, neither of which can be *thought*, but one of which must, on the laws of Contradiction and Excluded Middle, necessarily be. This philosophy—the *Philosophy of the Conditioned*—has not, however, either in itself, or in relation to its consequences, as yet been developed.—H.

* See above p. 599, note.—H

CHAPTER II.

OF THE WORDS CAUSE AND EFFECT, ACTION, AND ACTIVE POWER.

The writings upon Liberty and Necessity have been much darkened by the ambiguity of the words used in reasoning upon that subject. The words *cause* and *effect*, *action* and *active power*, *liberty* and *necessity*, are related to each other: The meaning of one determines the meaning of the rest. When we attempt to define them, we can only do it by synonymous words which need definition as much. There is a strict sense in which those words must be used, if we speak and reason clearly about moral liberty; but to keep to this strict sense is difficult, because, in all languages, they have, by custom, got a great latitude of signification.

As we cannot reason about moral liberty without using those ambiguous words, it is proper to point out, as distinctly as possible, their proper and original meaning in which they ought to be understood in treating of this subject, and to shew from what causes they have become so ambiguous in all languages as to darken and embarrass our reasonings upon it.

Everything that begins to exist, must have a cause of its existence, which had power to give it existence. And everything that undergoes any change, must have some cause of that change.

That neither existence, nor any mode of existence, can begin without an efficient cause, is a principle that appears very early in the mind of man; and it is so universal, and so firmly rooted in human nature, that the most determined scepticism cannot eradicate it. [276]

It is upon this principle that we ground the rational belief of a deity. But that is not the only use to which we apply it. Every man's conduct is governed by it, every day, and almost every hour, of his life. And if it were possible for any man to root out this principle from his mind, he must give up everything that is called common prudence, and be fit only to be confined as insane.

From this principle it follows, *That everything which undergoes any change, must either be the efficient cause of that change in itself, or it must be changed by some other being.*

In the *first* case, it is said to have *active power*, and to *act* in producing that change. In the *second* case, it is merely *passive*, or is *acted upon*, and the active power is in that being only which produces the change.

The name of a *cause* and of an *agent*, is properly given to that being only, which, by its active power, produces some change in itself, or in some other being. The change, whether it be of thought, of will, or of motion, is the *effect*. Active power, therefore, is a quality in the cause, which enables it to produce the effect. And the exertion of that active power in producing the effect, is called *action*, *agency*, *efficiency*.

In order to the production of any effect, there must be in the cause, not only power, but the *exertion of that power*; for power that is not exerted produces no effect.

All that is necessary to the production of any effect, is power in an efficient cause to produce the effect, and the exertion of that power; for it is a contradiction to say, that the cause has power to produce the effect, and exerts that power, and yet the effect is not produced. The effect cannot be in his power unless all the means necessary to its production be in his power. [277]

It is no less a contradiction to say, that a cause has power to produce a certain effect, but that he cannot exert that power; for power which cannot be exerted is no power, and is a contradiction in terms.

To prevent mistake, it is proper to observe, That a being may have a power at one time which it has not at another. It may commonly have a power, which, at a particular time, it has not. Thus, a man may commonly have power to walk or to run; but he has not this power when asleep, or when he is confined by superior force. In common language, he may be said to have a power which he cannot then exert. But this popular expression means only that he commonly has this power, and will have it when the cause is removed which at present deprives him of it; for, when we speak strictly and philosophically, it is a contradiction to say that he has this power, at that moment when he is deprived of it.

These, I think, are necessary consequences from the principle first mentioned—That every change which happens in nature must have an efficient cause which had power to produce it.

Another principle, which appears very early in the mind of man, is, *That we are efficient causes in our deliberate and voluntary actions.*

We are conscious of making an exertion, sometimes with difficulty, in order to produce certain effects. An exertion made deliberately and voluntarily, in order to produce an effect, implies a conviction that the effect is in our power. No man can deliberately attempt what he does not believe to be in his power. The language of all mankind, and their ordinary conduct in life, demonstrate that they have a conviction of some active power in themselves to produce certain motions in their own and in other bodies, and to regulate and direct their own thoughts. This conviction we have so early in life, that we have no remembrance when, or in what way, we acquired it. [278]

That such a conviction is at first the necessary result of our constitution, and that it can never be entirely obliterated, is, I think, acknowledged by one of the most zealous defenders of Necessity.* "Free Discussion, &c.," p 208. "Such are the influences to which all mankind, without distinction, are exposed that they necessarily refer actions (I mean refer them ultimately) first of all to themselves and others; and it is a long time before they begin to consider themselves and others as instruments in the hand of a superior agent. Consequently, the associations which refer actions to themselves get so confirmed that they are never entirely obliterated; and therefore the common language, and the common feelings, of mankind, will be adapted to the first, the limited and imperfect, or rather erroneous, view of things."

It is very probable that the very conception or idea of active power, and of efficient causes, is derived from our voluntary exertions in producing effects; and that, if we were not conscious of such exertion, we should have no conception at all of a cause, or of active power, and consequently no conviction of the necessity of a cause of every change which we observe in nature.†

It is certain that we can conceive no kind of active power but what is similar or analogous to that which we attribute to ourselves; that is, a power which is exerted by will and with understanding. Our notion, even of Almighty power, is derived from the notion of human power, by removing from the former those imperfections and limitations to which the latter is subjected. [279]

It may be difficult to explain the origin of our conceptions and belief concerning efficient causes and active power. The common theory, that all our ideas are ideas of Sensation or Reflection, and that all our belief is a perception of the agreement or the disagreement of those ideas, appears to be repugnant, both to the idea of an efficient cause, and to the belief of its necessity.

An attachment to that theory has led some philosophers to deny that we have any conception of an efficient cause, or of active power, because efficiency and active power are not ideas, either of sensation or reflection. They maintain, therefore, that a Cause is only *something prior to the effect, and constantly conjoined with it*. This is Mr Hume's notion of a cause, and seems to be adopted by Dr Priestley,* who says, "That a cause cannot be defined to be any thing, but *such previous circumstances as are constantly followed by a certain effect*, the constancy of the result making us conclude that there must be a *sufficient reason*, in the nature of the things, why it should be produced in those circumstances." [*Doctrine of Philosophical Necessity*, p. 11.]

But theory ought to stoop to fact, and not fact to theory. Every man who understands the language knows that neither priority, nor constant conjunction, nor both taken together, imply efficiency. Every man, free from prejudice, must assent to what Cicero has said: *Itaque non sic causa intelligi debet, ut quod cuique antecedat, id ei causa sit, sed quod cuique efficienter antecedat.* [De Fato, c. 15.]

The very dispute, whether we have the conception of an efficient cause, shews that we have. For, though men may dispute about things which have no existence, they cannot dispute about things of which they have no conception. [280]

What has been said in this chapter is intended to shew—That the conception of causes, of action and of active power, in the strict and proper sense of these words, is found in the minds of all men very early, even in the dawn of their rational life. It is therefore probable, that, in all languages, the words by which these conceptions were expressed were at first distinct and unambiguous, yet it is certain that, among the most enlightened nations, these words are applied to so many things of different natures, and used in so vague a manner, that it is very difficult to reason about them distinctly.

This phænomenon, at first view, seems very unaccountable. But a little reflection may satisfy us, that it is a natural consequence of the slow and gradual progress of human knowledge.

And since the ambiguity of these words has so great influence upon our reasoning about moral liberty, and furnishes the strongest objections against it, it is not foreign to our subject to shew whence it arises. When we know the causes that have produced this ambiguity, we shall be less in danger of being misled by it, and the proper and strict meaning of the words will more evidently appear. [281]

* Priestley.—H.

† If this were the case, our notion of *causality* would be of an empirical derivation, and without the quality of universality and necessity. This doctrine is also at variance with the account given of the notion above, (p. 455, sq. et alibi,) where it is viewed as an original and native principle. See p. 323, and note *. It is true, however, that the consciousness of our own efficiency illuminates the dark notion of *causality*, founded, as I conceive, in our impotence to conceive the possibility of an absolute commencement, and raises it from the vague and negative into the precise and positive notion of *power*.—H.

* The same doctrine has found an advocate in Dr Thomas Brown. In this theory, the phænomenon to be saved is silently or in effect evacuated of its principal quality—the quality of *Necessity*; for the real problem is to explain how it is that we *cannot but* think that all which begins to be has not an absolute but only a relative commencement. These philosophers do not *anatomise* but *truncate*.—H.

CHAPTER III.

CAUSES OF THE AMBIGUITY OF THOSE WORDS.

When we turn our attention to external objects, and begin to exercise our rational faculties about them, we find that there are some motions and changes in them, which we have power to produce, and that they have many which must have some other cause. Either the objects must have life and active power, as we have, or they must be moved or changed by something that has life and active power, as external objects are moved by us.

Our first thoughts seem to be, That the objects in which we perceive such motion have understanding and active power as we have.

"Savages," says the Abbé Raynal, "wherever they see motion which they cannot account for, there they suppose a soul."

All men may be considered as savages in this respect, until they are capable of instruction, and of using their faculties in a more perfect manner than savages do.

The rational conversations of birds and beasts in Æsop's "Fables" do not shock the belief of children. They have that probability in them which we require in an epic poem. Poets give us a great deal of pleasure, by clothing every object with intellectual and moral attributes, in metaphor and in other figures. May not the pleasure which we take in this poetical language, arise, in part, from its correspondence with our earliest sentiments? [282]

However this may be, the Abbe Raynal's observation is sufficiently confirmed, both from fact, and from the structure of all languages.

Rude nations do really believe sun, moon, and stars, earth, sea, and air, fountains and lakes, to have understanding and active power. To pay homage to them and implore their favour, is a kind of idolatry natural to savages.

All languages carry in their structure the marks of their being formed when this belief prevailed. The distinction of verbs and participles into active and passive, which is found in all languages, must have been originally intended to distinguish what is really active from what is merely passive; and, in all languages, we find active verbs applied to those objects, in which, according to the Abbé Raynal's observation, savages suppose a soul.

Thus we say, the sun rises and sets, and comes to the meridian; the moon changes; the sea ebbs and flows; the winds blow. Languages were formed by men who believed these objects to have life and active power in themselves. It was therefore proper and natural to express their motions and changes by active verbs.

There is no surer way of tracing the sentiments of nations before they have records, than by the structure of their language, which, notwithstanding the changes produced in it by time, will always retain some signatures of the thoughts of those by whom it was invented. When we find the same sentiments indicated in the structure of all languages, those sentiments must have been common to the human species when languages were invented. [283]

When a few of superior intellectual abilities find leisure for speculation, they begin to philosophize, and soon discover that many of those objects which, at first, they believed to be intelligent and active, are really lifeless and passive. This is a very important discovery. It elevates the mind, emancipates from many vulgar superstitions, and invites to farther discoveries of the same kind.

As philosophy advances, life and activity in natural objects retires, and leaves them dead and inactive. Instead of moving voluntarily, we find them to be moved necessarily; instead of acting, we find them to be acted upon; and nature appears as one great machine, where one wheel is turned by another, that by a third; and how far this necessary succession may reach, the philosopher does not know.

The weakness of human reason makes men prone, when they leave one extreme, to rush into the opposite; and thus philosophy, even in its infancy, may lead men from idolatry and polytheism into atheism, and from ascribing active power to inanimate beings, to conclude all things to be carried on by necessity.

Whatever origin we ascribe to the doctrines of atheism and of fatal necessity, it is certain that both may be traced almost as far back as philosophy; and both appear to be the opposites of the earliest sentiments of men.

It must have been by the observation and reasoning of the speculative *few*, that those objects were discovered to be inanimate and inactive, to which the *many* ascribed life and activity. But while the *few* are convinced of this, they must speak the language of the *many*, in order to be understood. So we see that, when the Ptolemaic system of astronomy, which agrees with vulgar prejudice and with vulgar language, has been universally rejected by philosophers, they continue to use the phraseology that is grounded upon it, not only in speaking to the vulgar, but in speaking to one another. They say, The sun rises and sets, and moves annually through all the signs of the zodiac, while they believe that he never leaves his place. [284]

In like manner, those active verbs and participles which were applied to the inanimate objects of nature, when they were believed to be really active, continue to be applied to them after they are discovered to be passive.

The forms of language, once established by custom, are not so easily changed as the notions on which they were originally founded. While the sounds remain, their signification is gradually enlarged or altered. This is sometimes found, even in those sciences in which the signification of words is the most accurate and precise. Thus, in arithmetic, the word *number* among the ancients, always signified so many units; and it would have been absurd to apply it either to unity or to any part of an unit; but now we call unity, or any part of unity, a *number*. With them, multiplication always increased a number, and division diminished it; but we speak of multiplying by a fraction, which diminishes, and of dividing by a fraction, which increases the number. We speak of dividing or multiplying by unity, which neither diminishes nor increases a number. These forms of expression, in the ancient language, would have been absurd.

By such changes in the meaning of words, the language of every civilized nation resembles old furniture new-modelled, in which many things are put to uses for which they were not originally intended, and for which they are not perfectly fitted.

This is one great cause of the imperfection of language, and it appears very remarkably in those verbs and participles which are active in their form, but are frequently used so as to have nothing active in their signification. [285]

Hence we are authorized by custom to ascribe action and active power to things which we believe to be passive. The proper and original signification of every word, which at first signified action and causation, is buried and lost under that vague meaning which custom has affixed to it.

That there is a real distinction, and perfect opposition, between acting and being acted upon, every man may be satisfied who is capable of reflection. And that this distinction is perceived by all men as soon as they begin to reason, appears by the distinction between active and passive verbs, which is original in all languages, though, from the causes that have been mentioned, they come to be confounded in the progress of human improvement.

Another way in which philosophy has contributed very much to the ambiguity of the words under our consideration, deserves to be mentioned.

The first step into natural philosophy, and what hath commonly been considered as its ultimate end, is the investigation of the causes of the phænomena of nature; that is, the causes of those appearances in nature which are not the effects of human power. *Felix qui potuit rerum cognoscere causas*, is the sentiment of every mind that has a turn to speculation.

The knowledge of the causes of things promises no less the enlargement of human power than the gratification of human curiosity; and, therefore, among the enlightened part of mankind, this knowledge has been pursued in all ages with an avidity proportionate to its importance.

In nothing does the difference between the intellectual powers of man and those of brutes appear more conspicuous than in this. For in them we perceive no desire to investigate the causes of things, nor indeed any sign that they have the proper notion of a cause. [286]

There is reason, however, to apprehend, that, in this investigation, men have wandered much in the dark, and that their success has, by no means, been equal to their desire and expectation.

We easily discover an established order and connection in the phænomena of nature. We learn, in many cases, from what has happened, to know what will happen. The discoveries of this kind, made by common observation, are many, and are the foundation of common prudence in the conduct of life. Philosophers, by more accurate observation and experiment, have made many more; by which arts are improved, and human power, as well as human knowledge, is enlarged.

But, as to the real causes of the phænomena of nature, how little do we know! All our knowledge of things external, must be grounded upon the informations of our senses; but causation and active power are not objects of sense; nor is that always the cause of a phænomenon which is prior to it, and constantly conjoined with it; otherwise night would be the cause of day, and day the cause of the following night.

It is to this day problematical, whether all the phænomena of the material system be produced by the immediate operation of the First Cause, according to the laws which his wisdom determined, or whether subordinate causes are employed by him in the operations of nature; and, if they be, what their nature, their number, and their different offices are? And whether, in all cases, they act by commission, or, in some, according to their discretion? [287]

When we are so much in the dark with regard to the real causes of the phænomena of nature, and have a strong desire to know them, it is not strange that ingenious men should form numberless conjectures and theories, by which the soul, hungering for knowledge, is fed with chaff instead of wheat.

In a very ancient system, love and strife were made the causes of things. In the Pythagorean * and Platonic system, Matter, Ideas, and an Intelligent Mind. By Aristotle, Matter, Form, and Privation. Des Cartes thought that Matter and a certain quantity of Motion given at first by the Almighty, are sufficient to account for all the phænomena of the natural world. Leibnitz, that the universe is made up of Monades, active and percipient, which, by their active power, received at first, produce all the changes they undergo.

While men thus wandered in the dark in search of causes, unwilling to confess their disappointment, they vainly conceived everything they stumbled upon to be a cause, and the proper notion of a cause is lost, by giving the name to numberless things which neither are nor can be causes.

This confusion of various things under the name of causes is the more easily tolerated, because, however hurtful it may be to sound philosophy, it has little influence upon the concerns of life. A constant antecedent or concomitant of the phænomenon whose cause is sought, may answer the purpose of the inquirer, as well as if the real cause were known. Thus a sailor desires to know the cause of the tides, that he may know when to expect high water. He is told that it is high water when the moon is so many hours past the meridian: and now he thinks he knows the cause of the tides. What he takes for the cause answers his purpose, and his mistake does him no harm. [288]

Those philosophers seem to have had the justest views of nature, as well as of the weakness of human understanding, who, giving up the pretence of discovering the causes of the operations of nature, have applied themselves to discover, by observation and experiment, the *rules* or *laws* of nature, according to which the phænomena of nature are produced.

In compliance with custom, or, perhaps, to gratify the avidity of knowing the causes of things, we call the laws of nature causes and active powers. So we speak of the powers of gravitation, of magnetism, of electricity.

We call them causes of many of the phænomena of nature; and such they are esteemed by the ignorant, and by the half learned.

But those of juster discernment see that laws of nature are not agents. They are not endowed with active power, and, therefore, cannot be causes in the proper sense. They are only the rules according to which the unknown cause acts.

Thus it appears that our natural desire to know the causes of the phænomena of nature, our inability to discover them, and the vain theories of philosophers employed in this search, have made the word *cause*, and the related words, so ambiguous, and to signify so many things of different natures, that they have, in a manner, lost their proper and original meaning, and yet we have no other words to express it.

Everything joined with the effect, and prior to it, is called its cause. An instrument, an occasion, a reason, a motive, an end, are called causes.* And the related words *effect*, *agent*, *power*, are extended in the same vague manner. [289]

Were it not that the terms *cause* and *agent* have lost their proper meaning, in the crowd of meanings that have been given them, we should immediately perceive a contradiction in the terms *necessary cause* and *necessary agent*. And, although the loose meaning of those words is authorized by custom, the arbiter of language, and, therefore, cannot be censured, perhaps cannot always be avoided, yet we ought to be upon our guard, that we be not misled by it to conceive things to be the same which are essentially different.

To say that man is a free agent, is no more than to say that, in some instances, he is truly an agent† and a cause, and is not merely acted upon as a passive instrument. On the contrary, to say that he acts from necessity, is to say that he does not act at all, that he is no agent, and that, for anything we know, there is only one agent in the universe, who does everything that is done, whether it be good or ill.

If this necessity be attributed even to

* The less that is said of the Pythagorean system in this relation the better.—H.

* There is no reason why whatever is conceived as necessarily going to the constitution of the phænomenon called the *effect*—in other words, why all and each of its *coefficients*—may not be properly called *causes*, or rather *concauses*; for there must always be more causes than one to an effect. This would be more correct than to give exclusively the name of Cause to any partial constituent or coefficient, even though proximate and principal. In this view, the doctrine of Aristotle, and other ancients, is more rational than that of our modern philosophers —H.

† It is proper to notice, that, as to *live* is to *act* and as man is not free to live or not to live, so neither, absolutely speaking, is he free to act or not to act. As he lives, he is necessarily determined to act or energise—to think and will; and all the liberty to which he can pretend, is to choose between this mode of action and that. In scholastic language, man cannot have the liberty of *exercise*, though he may have the liberty of *specification*. The root of his freedom is thus necessity. Nay, we cannot conceive otherwise even of the Deity. As we must think Him as necessarily existent, and necessarily living, so we must think him as necessarily active. Such are the conditions of human thought. It is thus sufficiently manifest that Dr Clarke's inference of the fact of moral liberty, from the conditions of self-activity, is incompetent. And when he says "*the true definition of Liberty is the Power to Act*," he should have recollected that this power is, on his own hypothesis, absolutely *fatal* if it *cannot but act*. See his "Remarks on Collins," pp. 15, 20, 27.—H.

the Deity, the consequence must be, that there neither is, nor can be, a cause at all; that nothing acts, but everything is acted upon; nothing moves, but everything is moved; all is passion without action; all instrument without an agent; and that everything that is, or was, or shall be, has that necessary existence in its season, which we commonly consider as the prerogative of the First Cause.

This I take to be the genuine and the most tenable system of necessity. It was the system of Spinoza, though he was not the first that advanced it; for it is very ancient. And if this system be true, our reasoning to prove the existence of a first cause of everything that begins to exist, must be given up as fallacious. [290]

If it be evident to the human understanding, as I take it to be, That what begins to exist must have an efficient cause, which had power to give or not to give it existence; and if it be true, that effects well and wisely fitted for the best purposes, demonstrate intelligence, wisdom, and goodness in the efficient cause, as well as power, the proof of a Deity from these principles is very easy and obvious to all men that can reason.

If, on the other hand, our belief, That everything that begins to exist has a cause, be got only by Experience; and if, as Mr Hume maintains, the only notion of a cause be something prior to the effect, which experience has shewn to be constantly conjoined with such an effect, I see not how, from these principles, it is possible to prove the existence of an intelligent cause of the universe.

Mr Hume seems to me to reason justly from his definition of a cause, when, in the person of an Epicurean, he maintains that, with regard to a cause of the universe, we can conclude nothing, because it is a singular effect. We have no experience that such effects are always conjoined with such a cause. Nay, the cause which we assign to this effect, is a cause which no man hath seen, nor can see, and therefore experience cannot inform us that it has ever been conjoined with any effect. He seems to me to reason justly from his definition of a cause, when he maintains, that *anything* may be the cause of anything; since priority and constant conjunction is all that can be conceived in the notion of a cause.

Another zealous defender of the doctrine of necessity[a] says, that, "A cause cannot be defined to be anything but *such previous circumstances as are constantly followed by a certain effect*, the *constancy* of the result making us conclude that there must be a *sufficient reason*, in the nature of things, why it should be produced in those circumstances."

This seems to me to be Mr Hume's definition of a cause in other words, and neither more nor less; but I am far from thinking that the author of it will admit the consequences which Mr Hume draws from it, however necessary they may appear to others. [291]

CHAPTER IV.

OF THE INFLUENCE OF MOTIVES.

THE modern advocates for the doctrine of Necessity lay the stress of their cause upon the influence of *motives*.*

"Every deliberate action, they say, must have a motive. When there is no motive on the other side, this motive must determine the agent: When there are contrary motives, the strongest must prevail. We reason from men's motives to their actions, as we do from other causes to their effects. If man be a free agent, and be not governed by motives, all his actions must be mere caprice, rewards and punishments can have no effect, and such a being must be absolutely ungovernable."

In order, therefore, to understand distinctly, in what sense we ascribe moral liberty to man, it is necessary to understand what influence we allow to motives. To prevent misunderstanding, which has been very common upon this point, I offer the following observations:—

1. I grant that all rational beings are influenced, and ought to be influenced, by motives. But the influence of motives is of a very different nature from that of efficient causes. They are neither causes† nor agents. They suppose an efficient cause, and can do nothing without it. [292] We cannot, without absurdity, suppose a motive either to act, or to be acted upon; it is equally incapable of action and of passion; because it is not a thing that exists, but a thing that is conceived; it is what the schoolmen called an *ens rationis*. Motives, therefore, may *influence* to action, but they do not act.‡ They may be compared to advice,

[a] Priestley.—H.

* A motive, abstractly considered, is called an *end* or *final cause*. It was well denominated in the Greek philosophy, τὸ ἕνεκα οὗ—*that for the sake of which*. A motive, however, in its concrete reality, is nothing apart from the mind; only a mental tendency.—H.

† Not causes; only if the term *cause* be limited to the last or proximate *efficient* cause.—H.

‡ If Motives "*influence* to action," they must co-operate in producing a certain effect upon the agent; and the determination to act, and to act in a certain manner—is that effect. They are thus, on Reid's own view, in this relation, *causes*, and *efficient* causes. It is of no consequence in the argument whether motives be said to determine a man to act or to influence (that is to determine) him to determine himself to act. It does not, therefore, seem consistent to say that motives are *not causes*, and that they *do not act*. See Leibnitz, quoted below, under p. [illegible], *infra*.—H.

or exhortation, which leaves a man still at liberty. For in vain is advice given when there is not a power either to do or to forbear what it recommends. In like manner, motives suppose liberty in the agent, otherwise they have no influence at all.

It is a law of nature with respect to matter, That every motion and change of motion, is proportional to the force impressed, and in the direction of that force. The scheme of necessity supposes a similar law to obtain in all the actions of intelligent beings; which, with little alteration, may be expressed thus:—Every action, or change of action, in an intelligent being, is proportional to the force of motives impressed, and in the direction of that force.

The law of nature respecting matter, is grounded upon this principle: That matter is an inert, inactive substance, which does not act, but is acted upon; and the law of necessity must be grounded upon the supposition, That an intelligent being is an inert, inactive substance, which does not act, but is acted upon.

2. Rational beings, in proportion as they are wise and good, will act according to the best motives; and every rational being who does otherwise, abuses his liberty. The most perfect being, in everything where there is a right and a wrong, a better and a worse, always infallibly acts according to the best motives. This, indeed, is little else than an identical proposition; for it is a contradiction to say, That a perfect being does what is wrong or unreasonable. But, to say that he does not act freely, because he always does what is best, is to say, That the proper use of liberty destroys liberty, and that liberty consists only in its abuse. [293]

The moral perfection of the Deity consists, not in having no power to do ill, otherwise, as Dr Clarke justly observes, there would be no ground to thank him for his goodness to us, any more than for his eternity or immensity; but his moral perfection consists in this, that, when he has power to do everything,* a power which cannot be resisted, he exerts that power only in doing what is wisest and best. To be subject to necessity, is to have no power at all; for power and necessity are opposites. We grant, therefore, that motives have influence, similar to that of advice or persuasion; but this influence is perfectly consistent with liberty, and, indeed, supposes liberty.

3. Whether every deliberate action must have a motive, depends on the meaning we put upon the word *deliberate*. If, by a deliberate action, we mean an action wherein motives are weighed, which seems to be the original meaning of the word, surely there must be motives, and contrary motives, otherwise they could not be weighed. But, if a deliberate action means only, as it commonly does, an action done by a cool and calm determination of the mind, with forethought and will, I believe there are innumerable such actions done without a motive.*

This must be appealed to every man's consciousness. I do many trifling actions every day, in which, upon the most careful reflection, I am conscious of no motive; and to say that I may be influenced by a motive of which I am not conscious, is, in the first place, an arbitrary supposition without any evidence, [?] and then, it is to say, that I may be convinced by an argument which never entered into my thought. [294]

Cases frequently occur, in which an end that is of some importance, may be answered equally well by any one of several different means. In such cases, a man who intends the end finds not the least difficulty in taking one of these means, though he be firmly persuaded that it has no title to be preferred to any of the others.

To say that this is a case that cannot happen, is to contradict the experience of mankind; for surely a man who has occasion to lay out a shilling, or a guinea, may have two hundred that are of equal value, both to the giver and to the receiver, any one of which will answer his purpose equally well. To say, that, if such a case should happen, the man could not execute his purpose, is still more ridiculous, though it have the authority of some of the schoolmen, who determined that the ass, between two equal bundles of hay, would stand still till it died of hunger.†

If a man could not act without a motive,‡ he would have no power at all; for motives are not in our power; and he that has not power over a necessary mean, has not power over the end.

That an action, done without any motive, can neither have merit nor demerit, is much insisted on by the writers for necessity, and triumphantly, as if it were the very hinge

* To do everything consistent with his perfection. But here one of the insoluble contradictions in the question arises; for if, on the one hand, we attribute to the Deity the power of moral evil, we detract from his essential goodness; and if, on the other, we deny him this power, we detract from his omnipotence.—H.

* Mr Stewart ("Active and Moral Powers," pp. 481 and 495) is disposed to concede that no action is performed without some motive; and thinks that Reid has not strengthened his argument by denying this.—H.

† Joannes Buridanus. See above, p. 238, note.—H.

‡ Can we conceive any act of which there was not a sufficient cause or concourse of causes, why the man performed it, and no other? If not, call this cause, or these concauses, the motive, and there is no longer a dispute. See the three following notes.—H.

of the controversy. I grant it to be a self-evident proposition, and I know no author that ever denied it.

How insignificant soever, in moral estimation, the actions may be which are done without any motive, they are of moment in the question concerning moral liberty. For, if there ever was any action of this kind, motives are not the sole causes of human actions. And, if we have the power of acting without a motive, that power, joined to a weaker motive, may counterbalance a stronger. [295]

4. It can never be proved, That when there is a motive on one side only, that motive must determine the action.

According to the laws of reasoning, the proof is incumbent on those who hold the affirmative; and I have never seen a shadow of argument, which does not take for granted the thing in question—to wit, that motives are the sole causes of actions.

Is there no such thing as wilfulness, caprice, or obstinacy, among mankind?* If there be not, it is wonderful that they should have names in all languages. If there be such things, a single motive, or even many motives, may be resisted.

5. When it is said, that of contrary motives the strongest always prevails, this can neither be affirmed nor denied with understanding, until we know distinctly what is meant by the strongest motive.

I do not find that those who have advanced this as a self-evident axiom, have ever attempted to explain what they mean by the strongest motive, or have given any rule by which we may judge which of two motives is the strongest.

How shall we know whether the strongest motive always prevails, if we know not which is strongest? There must be some test by which their strength is to be tried, some balance in which they may be weighed; otherwise, to say that the strongest motive always prevails, is to speak without any meaning. We must therefore search for this test or balance, since they who have laid so much stress upon this axiom, have left us wholly in the dark as to its meaning. I grant, that, when the contrary motives are of the same kind, and differ only in quantity, it may be easy to say which is the strongest. Thus a bribe of a thousand pounds is a stronger motive than a bribe of a hundred pounds. But when the motives are of different kinds—as money and fame, duty and worldly interest, health and strength, riches and honour—by what rule shall we judge which is the strongest motive? [296]

Either we measure the strength of motives merely by their prevalence, or by some other standard distinct from their prevalence.

If we measure their strength merely by their prevalence, and by the strongest motive mean only the motive that prevails, it will be true indeed that the strongest motive prevails; but the proposition will be identical, and mean no more than that the strongest motive is the strongest motive. From this surely no conclusion can be drawn.

If it should be said, That by the strength of a motive is not meant its prevalence, but the cause of its prevalence; that we measure the cause by the effect, and from the superiority of the effect conclude the superiority of the cause, as we conclude that to be the heaviest weight which bears down the scale: I answer, That, according to this explication of the axiom, it takes for granted that motives are the causes, and the sole causes, of actions. Nothing is left to the agent, but to be acted upon by the motives, as the balance is by the weights. The axiom supposes, that the agent does not act, but is acted upon; and, from this supposition, it is concluded that he does not act. This is to reason in a circle, or rather it is not reasoning but begging the question.*

* But are not these all tendencies, and fatal tendencies, to act or not to act? By contra-distinguishing such tendencies from motives, strictly so called, or rational impulses, we do not advance a single step towards rendering liberty *comprehensible*. See following notes. The same may be said of all the other attempts to this end; but in regard to these in general, I conceive it unnecessary to say anything farther.—H.

* On this subject, I shall quote a passage from the controversy between Leibnitz and Clarke:—

"I shall now" (says the former) "come to an objection raised here, against my comparing the weights of a balance with the motives of the Will. It is objected, that a balance is merely passive, and moved by the weights; whereas agents intelligent and endowed with will, are active. To this I answer, that the principle of the want of a sufficient reason, is common both to agents and patients. They want a sufficient reason of their action, as well as of their passion. A balance does not only not act when it is equally pulled on both sides, but the equal weights likewise do not act when they are in an equilibrium, so that one of them cannot go down without the other rising up as much.

"It must also be considered that, properly speaking, motives do not act upon the mind as weights do upon a balance; but it is rather the mind that acts by virtue of the motives, which are its dispositions to act. And, therefore, to pretend, as the author does here, that the mind prefers sometimes weak motives to strong ones, and even that it prefers that which is indifferent before motives—this, I say, is to divide the mind from the motives, as if they were without the mind, as the weight is distinct from the balance, and as if the mind had, besides motives, other dispositions to act, by virtue of which it could reject or accept the motives. Whereas, in truth, the motives comprehend all the dispositions which the mind can have to act voluntarily; for they include not only the reasons, but also the inclinations arising from passions, or other preceding impressions. Wherefore, if the mind should prefer a weak inclination to a strong one, it would act against itself, and otherwise than it is disposed to act. Which shews that the author's notions, contrary to mine, are superficial, and appear to have no solidity in them, when they are well considered.

Contrary motives may very properly be compared to advocates pleading the opposite sides of a cause at the bar. It would be very weak reasoning to say, that such an advocate is the most powerful pleader, because sentence was given on his side. The sentence is in the power of the judge, not of the advocate. It is equally weak reasoning, in proof of necessity, to say, such a motive prevailed, therefore it is the strongest; since the defenders of liberty maintain that the determination was made by the man, and not by the motive.* [297]

We are therefore brought to this issue, that, unless some measure of the strength of motives can be found distinct from their prevalence, it cannot be determined whether the strongest motive always prevails or not. If such a measure can be found and applied, we may be able to judge of the truth of this maxim, but not otherwise.

Everything that can be called a motive, is addressed either to the animal or to the rational part of our nature. Motives of the former kind are common to us with the brutes; those of the latter are peculiar to rational beings. We shall beg leave, for distinction's sake, to call the former, *animal* motives, and the latter, *rational*.

Hunger is a motive in a dog to eat; so is it in a man. According to the strength of the appetite, it gives a stronger or a weaker impulse to eat. And the same thing may be said of every other appetite and passion. Such animal motives give an impulse to the agent, to which he yields with ease; and, if the impulse be strong, it cannot be resisted without an effort which requires a greater or a less degree of self-command. Such motives are not addressed to the rational powers. Their influence is immediately upon the will.* We feel their influence, and judge of their strength, by the conscious effort which is necessary to resist them.

When a man is acted upon by contrary motives of this kind, he finds it easy to yield to the strongest. They are like two forces pushing him in contrary directions. To yield to the strongest, he needs only to be passive. By exerting his own force, he may resist; but this requires an effort of which he is conscious. [298] The strength of motives of this kind is perceived, not by our judgment, but by our feeling; and that is the strongest of contrary motives, to which he can yield with ease, or which it requires an effort of self-command to resist; and this we may call the *animal test* of the strength of motives.

If it be asked, whether, in motives of this kind, the strongest always prevails, I would answer, that in brute-animals I believe it does. They do not appear to have any self-command; an appetite or passion in them is overcome only by a stronger contrary one. On this account, they are not accountable for their actions, nor can they be the subjects of law.

But in men who are able to exercise their rational powers, and have any degree of self-command, the strongest animal motive does not always prevail. The flesh does not always prevail against the spirit, though too often it does. And if men were necessarily determined by the strongest animal motive, they could no more be accountable, or capable of being governed by law, than brutes are.

Let us next consider rational motives, to which the name of *motive* is more commonly and more properly given. Their influence is upon the judgment, by convincing us that such an action ought to be done; that it is our duty, or conducive to our real good, or to some end which we have determined to pursue.

They do not give a blind impulse to the will,† as animal motives do. They convince, but they do not impel, unless, as may often happen, they excite some passion

---

* "To assert, also, that the mind may have good reasons to act, when it has no motives, and when things are absolutely indifferent, as the author explains himself here—this, I say, is a manifest contradiction; for, if the mind has good reasons for taking the part it takes, then the things are not indifferent to the mind."—*Collection of Papers, &c., Leibnitz's Fifth Paper*, §§ 16-16.

The death of Leibnitz terminated his controversy with Clarke; but a defence of the fifth and last paper of Leibnitz against the answer of Clarke, by Thummig, was published, who, in relation to the point in question, says—"The simile of the balance is very unjustly interpreted. No resemblance is intended between scales and motives. . . . . It is of no consequence whether, in their reciprocal relations, the *scales are passive*, while the *mind is active*, since, in this respect, there is no comparison attempted. But, in so far as the principle of *Sufficient Reason* is concerned, that principle applies equally to *actions* and *passions*, as has been noticed by Baron Leibnitz. . . . . . It is to philosophise very crudely concerning mind, and to image every thing in a corporeal manner, to conceive that actuating reasons are something external, which make an impression on the mind, and to distinguish *motives* from the *active principle* (principium actionis) itself."(*In Koehler's German Translation of these Papers*.—H.

* But was the *man* determined by no motive to that determination? Was his specific volition to this or to that without a cause? On the supposition that the sum of influences (motives, dispositions, tendencies) to volition A, is equal to it, and the sum of influences to counter volition B, equal to it—can we conceive that the determination of volition A should not be necessary?—We can only conceive the volition B to be determined by supposing that the man *creates* (calls from non-existence into existence) a certain supplement of influences. But this creation as actual, or, in itself, is inconceivable, and even to conceive the possibility of this inconceivable act, we must suppose *some* cause by which the man is determined to exert it. We thus, *in thought*, never escape determination and necessity. It will be observed, that I do not consider this inability to the *notion*, any disproof of the *fact* of Free Will.—H.

[297, 298]

* This is virtually to identify Desire and Will, which is contrary to truth and our author's own doctrine.—H.

† See the last note.—H.

of hope, or fear, or desire. Such passions may be excited by conviction, and may operate in its aid as other animal motives do. But there may be conviction without passion; and the conviction of what we ought to do, in order to some end which we have judged fit to be pursued, is what I call a *rational motive*. [299]

Brutes, I think, cannot be influenced by such motives. They have not the conception of *ought* and *ought not*. Children acquire these conceptions as their rational powers advance; and they are found in all of ripe age, who have the human faculties.

If there be any competition between rational motives, it is evident that the strongest, in the eye of reason, is that which it is most our duty and our real happiness to follow. Our duty and our real happiness are ends which are inseparable; and they are the ends which every man, endowed with reason, is conscious he ought to pursue in preference to all others. This we may call the *rational test* of the strength of motives. A motive which is the strongest, according to the animal test, may be, and very often is, the weakest according to the rational.

The grand and the important competition of contrary motives is between the animal, on the one hand, and the rational on the other. This is the conflict between the flesh and the spirit, upon the event of which the character of men depends.

If it be asked, Which of these is the strongest motive? the answer is, That the first is commonly strongest, when they are tried by the animal test. If it were not so, human life would be no state of trial. It would not be a warfare, nor would virtue require any effort or self-command. No man would have any temptation to do wrong. But, when we try the contrary motives by the rational test, it is evident that the rational motive is always the strongest.

And now, I think, it appears, that the strongest motive, according to either of the tests I have mentioned, does not always prevail. [300]

In every wise and virtuous action, the motive that prevails is the strongest according to the rational test, but commonly the weakest according to the animal. In every foolish and in every vicious action, the motive that prevails is commonly the strongest according to the animal test, but always the weakest according to the rational.

6. It is true that we reason from men's motives to their actions, and, in many cases, with great probability, but never with absolute certainty. And to infer from this, that men are necessarily determined by motives, is very weak reasoning.

For let us suppose, for a moment, that men have moral liberty, I would ask, what use may they be expected to make of this liberty? It may surely be expected, that, of the various actions within the sphere of their power, they will choose what pleases them most for the present, or what appears to be most for their real, though distant good. When there is a competition between these motives, the foolish will prefer present gratification; the wise the greater and more distant good.

Now, is not this the very way in which we see men act? Is it not from the presumption that they act in this way, that we reason from their motives to their actions? Surely it is. Is it not weak reasoning, therefore, to argue, that men have not liberty, because they act in that very way in which they would act if they had liberty? It would surely be more like reasoning to draw the contrary conclusion from the same premises.

7. Nor is it better reasoning to conclude that, if men are not necessarily determined by motives, all their actions must be capricious.

To resist the strongest animal motives when duty requires, is so far from being capricious that it is, in the highest degree, wise and virtuous. And we hope this is often done by good men. [301]

To act against rational motives, must always be foolish, vicious, or capricious. And, it cannot be denied, that there are too many such actions done. But is it reasonable to conclude, that, because liberty may be abused by the foolish and the vicious, therefore it can never be put to its proper use, which is to act wisely and virtuously?

8. It is equally unreasonable to conclude —That, if men are not necessarily determined by motives, rewards and punishments would have no effect. With wise men they will have their due effect; but not always with the foolish and the vicious.

Let us consider what effect rewards and punishments do really, and in fact, produce, and what may be inferred from that effect upon each of the opposite systems of liberty and of necessity.

I take it for granted that, in fact, the best and wisest laws, both human and divine, are often transgressed, notwithstanding the rewards and punishments that are annexed to them. If any man should deny this fact, I know not how to reason with him.

From this fact, it may be inferred with certainty, upon the supposition of necessity, That, in every instance of transgression, the motive of reward or punishment was not of sufficient strength to produce obedience to the law. This implies a fault in the lawgiver; but there can be no fault in the transgressor, who acts mechanically by the force of motives. We might as well impute a fault to the balance when it does not raise a weight of two pounds by the force of one pound.

Upon the supposition of necessity, there can be neither reward nor punishment, in the proper sense, as those words imply good and ill desert. Reward and punishment are only tools employed to produce a mechanical effect. When the effect is not produced, the tool must be unfit or wrong applied. [302]

Upon the supposition of liberty, rewards and punishments will have a proper effect upon the wise and the good; but not so upon the foolish and the vicious, when opposed by their animal passions or bad habits; and this is just what we see to be the fact. Upon this supposition, the transgression of the law implies no defect in the law, no fault in the lawgiver; the fault is solely in the transgressor. And it is upon this supposition only, that there can be either reward or punishment, in the proper sense of the words, because it is only on this supposition that there can be good or ill desert.

CHAPTER V.

LIBERTY CONSISTENT WITH GOVERNMENT.

WHEN it is said that liberty would make us absolutely ungovernable by God or man; to understand the strength of this conclusion, it is necessary to know distinctly what is meant by *government*. There are two kinds of government, very different in their nature. The one we may, for distinction's sake, call *mechanical* government, the other *moral*. The first is the government of beings which have no active power, but are merely passive and acted upon; the second, of intelligent and active beings. [303]

An instance of mechanical government may be that of a master or commander of a ship at sea. Supposing her skilfully built, and furnished with everything proper for the destined voyage, to govern her properly for this purpose requires much art and attention. And, as every art has its rules, or laws, so has this. But by whom are those laws to be obeyed, or those rules observed? Not by the ship, surely, for she is an inactive being, but by the governor. A sailor may say that she does not obey the rudder; and he has a distinct meaning when he says so, and is perfectly understood. But he means not obedience in the proper, but in a metaphorical sense. For, in the proper sense, the ship can no more obey the rudder than she can give a command. Every motion, both of the ship and rudder, is exactly proportioned to the force impressed, and in the direction of that force. The ship never disobeys the laws of motion, even in the metaphorical sense; and they are the only laws she can be subject to.

The sailor, perhaps, curses her for not obeying the rudder; but this is not the voice of reason, but of passion, like that of the losing gamester when he curses the dice. The ship is as innocent as the dice.

Whatever may happen during the voyage, whatever may be its issue, the ship, in the eye of reason, is neither an object of approbation nor of blame; because she does not act, but is acted upon. If the material, in any part, be faulty, Who put it to that use? If the form, Who made it? If the rules of navigation were not observed, Who transgressed them? If a storm occasioned any disaster, it was no more in the power of the ship than of the master.

Another instance to illustrate the nature of mechanical government may be, that of the man who makes and exhibits a puppet-show. The puppets, in all their diverting gesticulations, do not move, but are moved by an impulse secretly conveyed, which they cannot resist. If they do not play their parts properly, the fault is only in the maker or manager of the machinery. Too much or too little force was applied, or it was wrong directed. No reasonable man imputes either praise or blame to the puppets, but solely to their maker or their governor. [304]

If we suppose for a moment, the puppets to be endowed with understanding and will, but without any degree of active power, this will make no change in the nature of their government; for understanding and will, without some degree of active power, can produce no effect. They might, upon this supposition, be called *intelligent machines;* but they would be machines still as much subject to the laws of motion as inanimate matter, and, therefore, incapable of any other than mechanical government.

Let us next consider the nature of moral government. This is the government of persons who have reason and active power, and have laws prescribed to them for their conduct by a legislator. Their obedience is obedience in the proper sense; it must, therefore, be their own act and deed, and, consequently, they must have power to obey or to disobey. To prescribe laws to them which they have not the power to obey, or to require a service beyond their power, would be tyranny and injustice in the highest degree.

When the laws are equitable, and prescribed by just authority, they produce moral obligation in those that are subject to them, and disobedience is a crime deserving punishment. But, if the obedience be impossible—if the transgression be necessary—it is self-evident that there can be no moral obligation to what is impossible, that there can be no crime in yielding to necessity, and that there can be no justice in punishing a person for what it was not in his power to avoid.* There are first principles in morals, and, to every unprejudiced mind, as self-evident as the axioms of mathematics. The whole science of morals must stand or fall with them. [305]

Having thus explained the nature both of mechanical and of moral government, the only kinds of government I am able to conceive, it is easy to see how far liberty or necessity agrees with either.

On the one hand, I acknowledge that necessity agrees perfectly with mechanical government. This kind of government is most perfect when the governor is the sole agent; everything done is the doing of the governor only. The praise of everything well done is his solely; and his is the blame if there be anything ill done, because he is the sole agent.

It is true that, in common language, praise or dispraise is often metaphorically given to the work; but, in propriety, it belongs solely to the author. Every workman understands this perfectly, and takes to himself very justly the praise or dispraise of his own work.

On the other hand, it is no less evident, that, on the supposition of necessity in the governed, there can be no moral government. There can be neither wisdom nor equity in prescribing laws that cannot be obeyed. There can be no moral obligation upon beings that have no active power. There can be no crime in not doing what it was impossible to do; nor can there be justice in punishing such omission.

If we apply these theoretical principles to the kinds of government which do actually exist, whether human or divine, we shall find that, among men, even mechanical government is imperfect.

Men do not make the matter they work upon. Its various kinds, and the qualities belonging to each kind, are the work of God. The laws of nature, to which it is subject, are the work of God. The motions of the atmosphere and of the sea, the heat and cold of the air, the rain and wind, which are useful instruments in most human operations, are not in our power. So that, in all the mechanical productions of men, the work is more to be ascribed to God than to man. [306]

Civil government among men is a species of moral government, but imperfect, as its lawgivers and its judges are. Human laws may be unwise or unjust; human judges may be partial or unskilful. But, in all equitable civil governments, the maxims of moral government above mentioned, are acknowledged as rules which ought never to be violated. Indeed the rules of justice are so evident to all men, that the most tyrannical governments profess to be guided by them, and endeavour to palliate what is contrary to them by the plea of necessity.

That a man cannot be under an obligation to what is impossible; that he cannot be criminal in yielding to necessity, nor justly punished for what he could not avoid, are maxims admitted, in all criminal courts, as fundamental rules of justice.

In opposition to this, it has been said, by some of the most able defenders of necessity, That human laws require no more to constitute a crime, but that it be voluntary; whence it is inferred that the criminality consists in the determination of the will, whether that determination be free or necessary. This, I think, indeed, is the only possible plea by which criminality can be made consistent with necessity, and, therefore, it deserves to be considered.

I acknowledge that a crime must be voluntary; for, if it be not voluntary, it is no deed of the man, nor can be justly imputed to him; but it is no less necessary that the criminal have moral liberty.* In men that are adult and of a sound mind, this liberty is presumed. But, in every case where it cannot be presumed, no criminality is imputed, even to voluntary actions. [307]

This is evident from the following instances:—*First*, The actions of brutes appear to be voluntary; yet they are never conceived to be criminal, though they may be noxious. *Secondly*, Children in nonage act voluntarily, but they are not chargeable with crimes. *Thirdly*, Madmen have both understanding and will, but they have not moral liberty, and, therefore, are not chargeable with crimes. *Fourthly*, Even in men that are adult and of a sound mind, a motive that is thought irresistible by any ordinary degree of self-command, such as the rack, or the dread of present death, either exculpates or very much alleviates a voluntary action, which, in other circumstances, would be highly criminal; whence it is evident that, if the motive were absolutely irresistible, the exculpation

* St Austin eloquently says—"Utrumne libri hi obscuri mihi scrutandi erant, unde discerem, neminem vituperatione suppliciove dignum, qui aut id velit quod justitia velle non prohibet, aut id non faciat quod facere non potest? Nonne ista cantant et in montibus pastores, et in theatris poetæ, et indocti in circulis, et docti in bibliothecis, et magistri in scholis, et antistites in sacratis locis, et in orbe terrarum genus humanum?"—*De Duabus Animabus*, § 14.—H.

* That is, criminality supposes not merely Liberty of Spontaneity, but also Liberty from Necessity. All imputable actions are spontaneous or voluntary; but all spontaneous or voluntary actions are not imputable.—H.

would be complete. So far is it from being true in itself, or agreeable to the common sense of mankind, that the criminality of an action depends solely upon its being voluntary.

The government of brutes, so far as they are subject to man, is a species of mechanical government, or something very like to it, and has no resemblance to moral government. As inanimate matter is governed by our knowledge of the qualities which God hath given to the various productions of nature, and our knowledge of the laws of nature which he hath established; so brute animals are governed by our knowledge of the natural instincts, appetites, affections, and passions, which God hath given them. By a skilful application of these springs of their actions, they may be trained to many habits useful to man. After all, we find that, from causes unknown to us, not only some species, but some individuals of the same species, are more tractable than others.

Children under age are governed much in the same way as the most sagacious brutes. The opening of their intellectual and moral powers, which may be much aided by proper instruction and example, is that which makes them, by degrees, capable of moral government. [308]

Reason teaches us to ascribe to the Supreme Being a government of the inanimate and inactive part of his creation, analogous to that mechanical government which men exercise, but infinitely more perfect. This, I think, is what we call God's *natural* government of the universe. In this part of the divine government, whatever is done is God's doing. He is the sole cause and the sole agent, whether he act immediately or by instruments subordinate to him; and his will is always done: For instruments are not causes, they are not agents, though we sometimes improperly call them so.

It is therefore no less agreeable to reason, than to the language of holy writ, to impute to the Deity whatever is done in the natural world. When we say of anything, that it is the work of Nature, this is saying that it is the work of God, and can have no other meaning.

The natural world is a grand machine, contrived, made, and governed by the wisdom and power of the Almighty. And, if there be in this natural world, beings that have life, intelligence, and will, without any degree of active power, they can only be subject to the same kind of mechanical government. Their determinations, whether we call them good or ill, must be the actions of the Supreme Being, as much as the productions of the earth. For life, intelligence, and will, without active power, can do nothing, and therefore nothing can justly be imputed to it.

This grand machine of the natural world, displays the power and wisdom of the artificer. But in it, there can be no display of moral attributes, which have a relation to moral conduct in his creatures, such as justice and equity in rewarding or punishing, the love of virtue and abhorrence of wickedness: For, as everything in it is God's doing, there can be no vice to be punished or abhorred, no virtue in his creatures to be rewarded. [309]

According to the system of necessity, the whole universe of creatures is this natural world; and of everything done in it, God is the sole agent. There can be no moral government, nor moral obligation. Laws, rewards, and punishments, are only mechanical engines, and the will of the lawgiver is obeyed as much when his laws are transgressed, as when they are observed. Such must be our notions of the government of the world, upon the supposition of necessity. It must be purely mechanical, and there can be no moral government upon that hypothesis.

Let us consider, on the other hand, what notion of the divine government we are naturally led into by the supposition of liberty.

They who adopt this system conceive that, in that small portion of the universe which falls under our view, as a great part has no active power, but moves as it is moved by necessity, and therefore must be subject to a mechanical government, so it has pleased the Almighty to bestow upon some of his creatures, particularly upon man, some degree of active power, and of reason, to direct him to the right use of his power.

What connection there may be, in the nature of things, between reason and active power, we know not. But we see evidently that, as reason without active power can do nothing, so active power without reason has no guide to direct it to any end. [310]

These two conjoined make moral liberty, which, in how small a degree soever it is possessed, raises man to a superior rank in the creation of God. He is not merely a tool in the hand of the master, but a servant, in the proper sense, who has a certain trust, and is accountable for the discharge of it. Within the sphere of his power, he has a subordinate dominion or government, and therefore may be said to be made after the image of God, the Supreme Governor. But, as his dominion is subordinate, he is under a moral obligation to make a right use of it, as far as the reason which God hath given him can direct him. When he does so, he is a just object of moral approbation; and no less an object of disapprotion and just punishment when he abuses the power with which he is entrusted. And he must finally render an account of the talent committed to him, to the Supreme Governor and righteous Judge.

This is the moral government of God, which, far from being inconsistent with liberty, supposes liberty in those that are subject to it, and can extend no farther than that liberty extends; for accountableness can no more agree with necessity than light with darkness.

It ought, likewise, to be observed, that, as active power in man, and in every created being, is the gift of God, it depends entirely on his pleasure for its existence, its degree, and its continuance; and, therefore, can do nothing which he does not see fit to permit.

Our power to act does not exempt us from being acted upon, and restrained or compelled by a superior power; and the power of God is always superior to that of man.

It would be great folly and presumption in us to pretend to know all the ways in which the government of the Supreme Being is carried on, and his purposes accomplished by men, acting freely, and having different or opposite purposes in their view. For, as the heavens are high above the earth, so are his thoughts above our thoughts, and his ways above our ways. [311]

That a man may have great influence upon the voluntary determinations of other men, by means of education, example, and persuasion, is a fact which must be granted, whether we adopt the system of liberty or necessity. How far such determinations ought to be imputed to the person who applied those means, how far to the person influenced by them, we know not; but God knows, and will judge righteously.

But what I would here observe is, That, if a man of superior talents may have so great influence over the actions of his fellow-creatures, without taking away their liberty, it is surely reasonable to allow a much greater influence of the same kind to Him who made man. Nor can it ever be proved, that the wisdom and power of the Almighty are insufficient for governing free agents, so as to answer his purposes.

He who made man may have ways of governing his determinations, consistent with moral liberty, of which we have no conception. And He who gave this liberty freely, may lay any restraint upon it that is necessary for answering his wise and benevolent purposes. The justice of his government requires that his creatures should be accountable only for what they have received, and not for what was never entrusted to them. And we are sure that the Judge of all the earth will do what is right.

Thus, I think, it appears, that, upon the supposition of necessity, there can be no moral government of the universe. Its government must be perfectly mechanical, and everything done in it, whether good or ill, must be God's doing; and that, upon the supposition of liberty, there may be a perfect moral government of the universe, consistent with his accomplishing all his purposes, in its creation and government. [312]

The arguments to prove that man is endowed with moral liberty, which have the greatest weight with me, are three; *first*, Because he has a natural conviction or belief, that, in many cases, he acts freely; *secondly*, Because he is accountable; and, *thirdly*, Because he is able to prosecute an end by a long series of means adapted to it.

CHAPTER VI.

FIRST ARGUMENT.

We have, by our constitution a natural conviction or belief, that we act freely—a conviction so early, so universal, and so necessary in most of our rational operations, that it must be the result of our constitution, and the work of Him that made us.

Some of the most strenuous advocates for the doctrine of necessity acknowledge that it is impossible to act upon it. They say that we have a natural sense or conviction that we act freely;* but that this is a fallacious sense.†

This doctrine is dishonourable to our Maker, and lays a foundation for universal scepticism. It supposes the Author of our being to have given us one faculty on purpose to deceive us, and another by which we may detect the fallacy, and find that he imposed upon us.‡

* Thus, Hommel, certainly one of the ablest and most decided fatalists—"I myself believe that I have a feeling of Liberty even at the very moment when I am writing against Liberty, upon grounds which I regard as incontrovertible. Zeno was a fatalist only in theory; in practice, he did not act in conformity to that conviction."—H.

† Among others, Reid's friend, Lord Kames, in the first edition of his "Essays on the Principles of Morality and Natural Religion," admitted this natural conviction of freedom from necessity, maintaining it to be illusive. On this melancholy doctrine,
"Man fondly dreams that he is free in act:
Naught is he but the powerless, worthless plaything
Of the blind force that in his Will itself
Works out for him a dread necessity."

‡ All necessitarians do not, however, admit the reality of this deceitful experience, or fallacious feeling of liberty. "Dr Hartley," says Mr Stewart, "was, I believe, one of the first, if not the first, who denied that our consciousness is in favour of free agency;" and in this assertion, he observes, "Hartley was followed by Priestley and Belsham. Speaking of the latter, "We are told," he says, "by Mr Belsham, that the popular opinion that, in many cases, it was in the power of the agent to have chosen differently, the previous circumstances remaining exactly the same,

If any one of our natural faculties be fallacious, there can be no reason to trust to any of them; for He that made one made all.

The genuine dictate of our natural faculties is the voice of God, no less than what he reveals from heaven; and to say that it is fallacious, is to impute a lie to the God of truth.* [313]

If candour and veracity be not an essential part of moral excellence, there is no such thing as moral excellence, nor any reason to rely on the declarations and promises of the Almighty. A man may be tempted to lie, but not without being conscious of guilt and of meanness. Shall we impute to the Almighty what we cannot impute to a man without a heinous affront?

Passing this opinion, therefore, as shocking to an ingenuous mind, and, in its consequences, subversive of all religion, all morals, and all knowledge, let us proceed to consider the evidence of our having a natural conviction that we have some degree of active power.

The very conception or idea of active power must be derived from something in our own constitution. It is impossible to account for it otherwise. We see events, but we see not the power that produces them. We perceive one event to follow another, but we perceive not the chain that binds them together. The notion of power and causation, therefore, cannot be got from external objects.

Yet the notion of causes, and the belief that every event must have a cause which had power to produce it, is found in every human mind so firmly established, that it cannot be rooted out.

This notion and this belief must have its origin from something in our constitution; and that it is natural to man, appears from the following observations.

1. We are conscious of many voluntary exertions, some easy, others more difficult, some requiring a great effort. These are exertions of power. And, though a man may be unconscious of his power when he does not exert it, he must have both the conception and the belief of it, when he knowingly and willingly exerts it, with intention to produce some effect. [314]

2. Deliberation about an action of moment, whether we shall do it or not, implies a conviction that it is in our power. To deliberate about an end, we must be convinced that the means are in our power; and to deliberate about the means, we must be convinced that we have power to choose the most proper.

3. Suppose our deliberation brought to an issue, and that we resolve to do what appeared proper, can we form such a resolution or purpose, without any conviction of power to execute it? No; it is impossible. A man cannot resolve to lay out a sum of money which he neither has nor hopes ever to have.

4. Again, when I plight my faith in any promise or contract, I must believe that I shall have power to perform what I promise. Without this persuasion, a promise would be downright fraud.

There is a condition implied in every promise, *if we live* and *if God continue with us the power which he hath given us.* Our conviction, therefore, of this power derogates not in the least from our dependence upon God. The rudest savage is taught by nature to admit this condition in all promises, whether it be expressed or not. For it is a dictate of common sense, that we can be under no obligation to do what it is impossible for us to do.

If we act upon the system of necessity, there must be another condition implied in all deliberation, in every resolution, and in every promise; and that is, *if we shall be willing.* But the will not being in our power, we cannot engage for it. [315]

If this condition be understood, as it must be understood if we act upon the system of necessity, there can be no deliberation, or resolution, nor any obligation in a promise. A man might as well deliberate, resolve, and

arises either from a mistake of the question, or *from a forgetfulness of the motives by which our choice was determined.*"—(Philosophy of the Active Powers, ii. p. 510.)

To deny, or rather to explain away, the obnoxious phænomenon of a sense of liberty, had, however, been attempted by many Necessitarians before Hartley, and with far greater ingenuity than either he or his two followers displayed. Thus Leibnitz, after rejecting the Liberty of Indifference, says, "Quamobrem ratio illa, quam Cartesius adduxit, ad probandam actionum nostrarum liberarum independentiam, ex jactato quodam *vivido sensu interno*, vim nullam habet. *Non possumus proprie experiri independentiam nostram, nec causas a quibus electio nostra pendet semper percipimus*, utpote sæpe sensum omnem fugientes. [He here refers to his doctrine of latent mental modifications.] Et perinde est ac si *acus magnetica versus polum converti lætaretur; putaret enim, se illuc converti independenter a quacunque alia causa, cum non perciperet motus insensibiles materiæ magneticæ.*" But, previously to Leibnitz, a similar solution and illustration, I find, had been proposed by Bayle—his illustration is a conscious weathercock; but both philosophers are, in argument and example, only followers of Spinoza. Spinoza, after supposing that a certain quantity of motion had been communicated to a stone, proceeds—"Porro concipe jam si placet, lapidem dum moveri pergit cogitare et scire, se quantum potest conari ut moveri pergat. Hic lapis sane, quandoquidem sui tantummodo conatus est conscius et minime indifferens, se liberrimum esse et nulla alia de causa in motu perseverare credet quam quia vult. *Atque hæc humana illa libertas est quam omnes habere jactant, et quæ in hoc solo consistit—quod homines sui appetitus sunt conscii, et causarum a quibus determinantur ignari.*" Chrysippus's Top or Cylinder is the source.—H.

* It can easily be proved to those who are able and not afraid to reason, that the doctrine of Necessity is subversive of religion, natural and revealed; and, Fatalism involving Atheism, the Necessitarian who intrepidly follows out his scheme to its consequences, however monstrous, will consistently reject every argument which proceeds upon the supposition of a Deity and divine attributes.—H.

promise, upon the actions of other men as upon his own.

It is no less evident that we have a conviction of power in other men, when we advise, or persuade, or command, or conceive them to be under obligation by their promises.

5. Is it possible for any man to blame himself for yielding to necessity? Then he may blame himself for dying, or for being a man. Blame supposes a wrong use of power; and, when a man does as well as it was possible for him to do, wherein is he to be blamed? Therefore, all conviction of wrong conduct, all remorse and self-condemnation, imply a conviction of our power to have done better. Take away this conviction, and there may be a sense of misery, or a dread of evil to come; but there can be no sense of guilt or resolution to do better.

Many who hold the doctrine of necessity, disown these consequences of it, and think to evade them. To such, they ought not to be imputed; but their inseparable connection with that doctrine appears self-evident; and, therefore, some late patrons of it* have had the boldness to avow them. "They cannot accuse themselves of having done anything wrong, in the ultimate sense of the words. In a strict sense, they have nothing to do with repentance, confession, and pardon—these being adapted to a fallacious view of things."

Those who can adopt these sentiments, may, indeed, celebrate, with high encomiums, "*the great and glorious doctrine of necessity.*" It restores them, in their own conceit, to the state of innocence. It delivers them from all the pangs of guilt and remorse, and from all fear about their future conduct, though not about their fate. They may be as secure that they shall do nothing wrong as those who have finished their course. A doctrine so flattering to the mind of a sinner, is very apt to give strength to weak arguments. [316]

After all, it is acknowledged, by those who boast of this glorious doctrine, "That every man, let him use what efforts he can, will necessarily feel the sentiments of shame, remorse, and repentance, and, oppressed with a sense of guilt, will have recourse to that mercy of which he stands in need."

The meaning of this seems to me to be, That, although the doctrine of necessity be supported by invincible arguments, and though it be the most consolatory doctrine in the world; yet no man, in his most serious moments, when he sists himself before the throne of his Maker, can possibly believe it, but must then necessarily lay aside this glorious doctrine, and all its flattering consequences, and return to the humiliating conviction of his having made a bad use of the power which God had given him.*

If the belief of our having active power be necessarily implied in those rational operations we have mentioned, it must be coeval with our reason; it must be as universal among men, and as necessary in the conduct of life, as those operations are.

We cannot recollect by memory when it began. It cannot be a prejudice of education, or of false philosophy. It must be a part of our constitution, or the necessary result of our constitution and therefore the work of God.

It resembles, in this respect, our belief of the existence of a material world; our belief that those we converse with are living and intelligent beings; our belief that those things did really happen, which we distinctly remember; and our belief that we continue the same identical persons. [317]

We find difficulty in accounting for our belief of these things; and some philosophers think that they have discovered good reasons for throwing it off. But it sticks fast, and the greatest sceptic finds that he must yield to it in his practice, while he wages war with it in speculation.

If it be objected to this argument, That the belief of our acting freely cannot be implied in the operations we have mentioned, because those operations are performed by them who believe that we are, in all our actions, governed by necessity—the answer to this objection is, That men in their practice may be governed by a belief which in speculation they reject.

However strange and unaccountable this may appear, there are many well-known instances of it.

I knew a man who was as much convinced as any man of the folly of the popular belief of apparitions in the dark; yet he could not sleep in a room alone, nor go alone into a room in the dark. Can it be said, that his fear did not imply a belief of danger? This is impossible. Yet his philosophy convinced him that he was in no more danger in the dark when alone, than with company.

Here an unreasonable belief, which was merely a prejudice of the nursery, stuck so fast as to govern his conduct, in opposition to his speculative belief as a philosopher and a man of sense.

There are few persons who can look down from the battlement of a very high tower without fear, while their reason convinces them that they are in no more danger than when standing upon the ground. [318]

* Priestley. Belsham is still more explicit.—H.

* This is hardly implied. In this the modern Necessitarian, like the ancient Fatalist, only admits—*Hoc quoque Fatale est, sic ipsum expendere Fatum.*—H.

There have been persons who professed to believe that there is no distinction between virtue and vice, yet in their practice they resented injuries, and esteemed noble and virtuous actions.

There have been sceptics who professed to disbelieve their senses and every human faculty; but no sceptic was ever known, who did not, in practice, pay a regard to his senses and to his other faculties.

There are some points of belief so necessary, that, without them, a man would not be the being which God made him. These may be opposed in speculation, but it is impossible to root them out. In a speculative hour they seem to vanish, but in practice they resume their authority. This seems to be the case of those who hold the doctrine of necessity, and yet act as if they were free.

This natural conviction of some degree of power in ourselves and in other men, respects voluntary actions only. For, as all our power is directed by our will, we can form no conception of power, properly so called, that is not under the direction of will.* And therefore our exertions, our deliberations, our purposes, our promises, are only in things that depend upon our will. Our advices, exhortations, and commands, are only in things that depend upon the will of those to whom they are addressed. We impute no guilt to ourselves, nor to others, in things where the will is not concerned.

But it deserves our notice, that we do not conceive everything, without exception, to be in a man's power which depends upon his will. There are many exceptions to this general rule. The most obvious of these I shall mention, because they both serve to illustrate the rule, and are of importance in the question concerning the liberty of man. [319]

In the rage of madness, men are absolutely deprived of the power of self-government. They act voluntarily, but their will is driven as by a tempest, which, in lucid intervals, they resolve to oppose with all their might, but are overcome when the fit of madness returns.

Idiots are like men walking in the dark, who cannot be said to have the power of choosing their way, because they cannot distinguish the good road from the bad. Having no light in their understanding, they must either sit still, or be carried on by some blind impulse.

Between the darkness of infancy, which is equal to that of idiots, and the maturity of reason, there is a long twilight, which, by insensible degrees, advances to the perfect day.

In this period of life, man has but little of the power of self-government. His actions, by nature, as well as by the laws of society, are in the power of others more than in his own. His folly and indiscretion, his levity and inconstancy, are considered as the fault of youth, rather than of the man. We consider him as half a man and half a child, and expect that each by turns should play its part. He would be thought a severe and unequitable censor of manners, who required the same cool deliberation, the same steady conduct, and the same mastery over himself, in a boy of thirteen, as in a man of thirty.

It is an old adage, That violent anger is a short fit of madness.* If this be literally true in any case, a man, in such a fit of passion, cannot be said to have the command of himself. If real madness could be proved, it must have the effect of madness while it lasts, whether it be for an hour or for life. But the madness of a short fit of passion, if it be really madness, is incapable of proof; and therefore is not admitted in human tribunals as an exculpation. And, I believe, there is no case where a man can satisfy his own mind that his passion, both in its beginning and in its progress, was irresistible. The Searcher of hearts alone knows infallibly what allowance is due in cases of this kind. [320]

But a violent passion, though it may not be irresistible, is difficult to be resisted: And a man, surely, has not the same power over himself in passion, as when he is cool. On this account it is allowed by all men to alleviate, when it cannot exculpate; and has its weight in criminal courts, as well as in private judgment.

It ought likewise to be observed, That he who has accustomed himself to restrain his passions, enlarges by habit his power over them, and consequently over himself. When we consider that a Canadian savage can acquire the power of defying death in its most dreadful forms, and of braving the most exquisite torment for many long hours, without losing the command of himself; we may learn from this, that, in the constitution of human nature, there is ample scope for the enlargement of that power of self-command without which there can be no virtue nor magnanimity.

There are cases, however, in which a man's voluntary actions are thought to be very little, if at all, in his power, on account of the violence of the motive that impels him. The magnanimity of a hero, or of a martyr, is not expected in every man, and on all occasions.

If a man trusted by the government with a secret which it is high treason to disclose,

* This explicitly admits what (though seemingly denied) was stated as undeniable, in note at p. 609.—H.

* Ira furor brevis est.—H.

be prevailed upon by a bribe, we have no mercy for him, and hardly allow the greatest bribe to be any alleviation of his crime.

But, on the other hand, if the secret be extorted by the rack, or by the dread of present death, we pity him more than we blame him, and would think it severe and unequitable to condemn him as a traitor. [321]

What is the reason that all men agree in condemning this man as a traitor in the first place, and, in the last, either exculpate him, or think his fault greatly alleviated? If he acted necessarily in both cases, compelled by an irresistible motive, I can see no reason why we should not pass the same judgment on both.

But the reason of these different judgments is evidently this—That the love of money, and of what is called a man's interest, is a cool motive, which leaves to a man the entire power over himself; but the torment of the rack, or the dread of present death, are so violent motives that men who have not uncommon strength of mind, are not masters of themselves in such a situation, and, therefore, what they do is not imputed, or is thought less criminal.

If a man resist such motives, we admire his fortitude, and think his conduct heroical rather than human. If he yields, we impute it to human frailty, and think him rather to be pitied than severely censured.

Inveterate habits are acknowledged to diminish very considerably the power a man has over himself. Although we may think him highly blameable in acquiring them, yet, when they are confirmed to a certain degree, we consider him as no longer master of himself, and hardly reclaimable without a miracle.

Thus we see that the power which we are led, by common sense, to ascribe to man respects his voluntary actions only, and that it has various limitations even with regard to them. Some actions that depend upon our will are easy, others very difficult, and some, perhaps, beyond our power. In different men, the power of self-government is different, and in the same man at different times. It may be diminished, or perhaps lost, by bad habits; it may be greatly increased by good habits. [322]

These are facts attested by experience, and supported by the common judgment of mankind. Upon the system of Liberty they are perfectly intelligible; but, I think, irreconcileable to that of Necessity; for, How can there be an easy and a difficult in actions equally subject to necessity?—or, How can power be greater or less, increased or diminished, in those who have no power?

This natural conviction of our acting freely, which is acknowledged by many who hold the doctrine of necessity, ought to throw the whole burden of proof upon that side; for, by this, the side of liberty has what lawyers call a *jus quæsitum*, or a right of ancient possession, which ought to stand good till it be overturned. If it cannot be proved that we always act from necessity, there is no need of arguments on the other side to convince us that we are free agents.

To illustrate this by a similar case:—If a philosopher would persuade me that my fellow-men with whom I converse are not thinking, intelligent beings, but mere machines, though I might be at a loss to find arguments against this strange opinion, I should think it reasonable to hold the belief which nature gave me before I was capable of weighing evidence, until convincing proof is brought against it. [323]

CHAPTER VII.

SECOND ARGUMENT.

That there is a real and essential distinction between right and wrong conduct, between just and unjust—That the most perfect moral rectitude is to be ascribed to the Deity—That man is a moral and accountable being, capable of acting right and wrong, and answerable for his conduct to Him who made him, and assigned him a part to act upon the stage of life; are principles proclaimed by every man's conscience—principles upon which the systems of morality and natural religion, as well as the system of revelation, are grounded, and which have been generally acknowledged by those who hold contrary opinions on the subject of human liberty. I shall therefore here take them for granted.

These principles afford an obvious, and, I think, an invincible argument, that man is endowed with Moral Liberty.

Two things are implied in the notion of a moral and accountable being—*Understanding* and *Active Power*.

First, He must *understand the law to which he is bound, and his obligation to obey it.* Moral obedience must be voluntary, and must regard the authority of the law. I may command my horse to eat when he hungers, and drink when he thirsts. He does so; but his doing it is no moral obedience. He does not understand my command, and therefore can have no will to obey it. He has not the conception of moral obligation, and therefore cannot act from the conviction of it. In eating and drinking, he is moved by his own appetite only, and not by my authority. [324]

Brute-animals are incapable of moral obligation, because they have not that degree of understanding which it implies. They have not the conception of a rule of conduct, and of obligation to obey it, and therefore, though they may be noxious, they cannot be criminal.

Man, by his rational nature, is capable both of understanding the law that is prescribed to him, and of perceiving its obligation. He knows what it is to be just and honest, to injure no man, and to obey his Maker. From his constitution, he has an immediate conviction of his obligation to these things. He has the approbation of his conscience when he acts by these rules; and he is conscious of guilt and demerit when he transgresses them. And, without this knowledge of his duty and his obligation, he would not be a moral and accountable being.

Secondly, Another thing implied in the notion of a moral and accountable being, is *power to do what he is accountable for*.

That no man can be under a moral obligation to do what it is impossible for him to do, or to forbear what it is impossible for him to forbear, is an axiom as self-evident as any in mathematics. It cannot be contradicted, without overturning all notion of moral obligation; nor can there be any exception to it, when it is rightly understood.

Some moralists have mentioned what they conceived to be an exception to this maxim. The exception is this. When a man, by his own fault, has disabled himself from doing his duty, his obligation, they say, remains, though he is now unable to discharge it. Thus, if a man by sumptuous living has become bankrupt, his inability to pay his debt does not take away his obligation. [325]

To judge whether, in this and similar cases, there be any exception to the axiom above mentioned, they must be stated accurately.*

No doubt a man is highly criminal in living above his fortune, and his crime is greatly aggravated by the circumstance of his being thereby unable to pay his just debt. Let us suppose, therefore, that he is punished for this crime as much as it deserves; that his goods are fairly distributed among his creditors, and that one half remains unpaid. Let us suppose also, that he adds no new crime to what is past, that he becomes a new man, and not only supports himself by honest industry, but does all in his power to pay what he still owes.

I would now ask, Is he further punishable, and really guilty for not paying more than he is able? Let every man consult his conscience, and say whether he can blame this man for not doing more than he is able to do. His guilt before his bankruptcy is out of the question, as he has received the punishment due for it. But that his subsequent conduct is unblameable, every man must allow; and that, in his present state, he is accountable for no more than he is able to do. His obligation is not cancelled, it returns with his ability, and can go no farther.

Suppose a sailor, employed in the navy of his country, and longing for the ease of a public hospital as an invalid, to cut off his fingers, so as to disable him from doing the duty of a sailor; he is guilty of a great crime; but, after he has been punished according to the demerit of his crime, will his captain insist that he shall still do the duty of a sailor? Will he command him to go aloft when it is impossible for him to do it, and punish him as guilty of disobedience? Surely, if there be any such thing as justice and injustice, this would be unjust and wanton cruelty. [326]

Suppose a servant, through negligence and inattention, mistakes the orders given him by his master, and, from this mistake, does what he was ordered not to do. It is commonly said that culpable ignorance does not excuse a fault. This decision is inaccurate, because it does not shew where the fault lies. The fault was solely in that inattention, or negligence, which was the occasion of his mistake. There was no subsequent fault.

This becomes evident, when we vary the case so far as to suppose that he was unavoidably led into the mistake without any fault on his part. His mistake is now invincible, and, in the opinion of all moralists, takes away all blame; yet this new case supposes no change, but in the cause of his mistake. His subsequent conduct was the same in both cases. The fault therefore lay solely in the negligence and inattention which was the cause of his mistake.

The axiom, *That invincible ignorance takes away all blame*, is only a particular case of the general axiom, That there can be no moral obligation to what is impossible; the former is grounded upon the latter, and can have no other foundation.

I shall put only one case more. Suppose that a man, by excess and intemperance, has entirely destroyed his rational faculties, so as to have become perfectly mad or idiotical; suppose him forewarned of his danger, and that, though he foresaw that this must be the consequence, he went on still in his criminal indulgence. A greater crime can hardly be supposed, or more deserving of severe punishment? Suppose him punished as he deserves; will it be said, that the duty of a man is incumbent upon him now, when he has not the faculties of a man, or that he incurs new guilt when he is not a moral agent? Surely we may as

* Such cases are considered and solved on broader grounds by Aristotle. See *Nic. Eth.* L. iii c. 5.—H.

[325, 326]

well suppose a plant. or a clod of earth, to be a subject of moral duty. [327]

The decisions I have given of these cases, are grounded upon the fundamental principles of morals, the most immediate dictates of conscience. If these principles are given up, all moral reasoning is at an end, and no distinction is left between what is just and what is unjust. And it is evident that none of these cases furnishes any exception to the axiom above mentioned. No moral obligation can be consistent with impossibility in the performance.

Active power, therefore, is necessarily implied in the very notion of a moral accountable being. And if man be such a being, he must have a degree of active power proportioned to the account he is to make. He may have a model of perfection set before him which he is unable to reach; but, if he does to the utmost of his power, this is all he can be answerable for. To incur guilt, by not going beyond his power, is impossible.

What was said, in the first argument, of the limitation of our power, adds much strength to the present argument. A man's power, it was observed, extends only to his voluntary actions, and has many limitations, even with respect to them.

His *accountableness* has the same extent and the same limitations.

In the rage of madness he has no power over himself, neither is he accountable, or capable of moral obligation. In ripe age, man is accountable in a greater degree than in non-age, because his power over himself is greater. Violent passions and violent motives alleviate what is done through their influence, in the same proportion as they diminish the power of resistance. [328]

There is, therefore, a perfect correspondence between *power*, on the one hand, and *moral obligation* and *accountableness*, on the other. They not only correspond in general, as they respect voluntary actions only, but every limitation of the first produces a corresponding limitation of the two last. This, indeed, amounts to nothing more than that maxim of common sense, confirmed by Divine authority, "That to whom much is given, of him much will be required."

The sum of this argument is—that a certain degree of active power is the talent which God hath given to every rational accountable creature, and of which he will require an account. If man had no power, he would have nothing to account for All wise and all foolish conduct, all virtue and vice, consist in the right use or in the abuse of that power which God hath given us. If man had no power, he could neither be wise nor foolish, virtuous nor vicious.

If we adopt the system of necessity, the terms *moral obligation* and *accountableness*, *praise* and *blame*, *merit* and *demerit*, *justice* and *injustice*, *reward* and *punishment*, *wisdom* and *folly*, *virtue* and *vice*, ought to be disused, or to have new meanings given to them when they are used in religion, in morals, or in civil government; for, upon that system, there can be no such things as they have been always used to signify. [329]

CHAPTER VIII.

THIRD ARGUMENT.

That man has power over his own actions and volitions appears, because he is capable of carrying on, wisely and prudently, a system of conduct, which he has before conceived in his mind, and resolved to prosecute.

I take it for granted, that, among the various characters of men, there have been some who, after they came to years of understanding, deliberately laid down a plan of conduct, which they resolve to pursue through life; and that of these, some have steadily pursued the end they had in view, by the proper means.

It is of no consequence in this argument, whether one has made the best choice of his main end or not; whether his end be riches, or power, or fame, or the approbation of his Maker. I suppose only, that he has prudently and steadily pursued it; that, in a long course of deliberate actions, he has taken the means that appeared most conducive to his end, and avoided whatever might cross it.

That such conduct in a man demonstrates a certain degree of wisdom and understanding, no man ever doubted; and I say it demonstrates, with equal force, a certain degree of power over his voluntary determinations.

This will appear evident, if we consider, that understanding without power may project, but can execute nothing. A regular plan of conduct, as it cannot be contrived without understanding, so it cannot be carried into execution without power; and, therefore, the execution, as an effect, demonstrates, with equal force, both power and understanding in the cause. [330] Every indication of wisdom, taken from the effect, is equally an indication of power to execute what wisdom planned. And, if we have any evidence that the wisdom which formed the plan is in the man, we have the very same evidence that the power which executed it is in him also.

In this argument, we reason from the same principles as in demonstrating the being and perfections of the First Cause of all things.

The effects we observe in the course of nature require a cause. Effects wisely adapted to an end, require a wise cause. Every indication of the wisdom of the Creator is equally an indication of His power. His wisdom appears only in the works done by his power; for wisdom without power may speculate, but it cannot act; it may plan, but it cannot execute its plans.

The same reasoning we apply to the works of men. In a stately palace we see the wisdom of the architect. His wisdom contrived it, and wisdom could do no more. The execution required both a distinct conception of the plan, and power to operate according to that plan.

Let us apply these principles to the supposition we have made—That a man, in a long course of conduct, has determined and acted prudently in the prosecution of a certain end. If the man had both the wisdom to plan this course of conduct, and that power over his own actions that was necessary to carry it into execution, he is a free agent, and used his liberty, in this instance, with understanding. [331]

But, if all his particular determinations, which concurred in the execution of this plan were produced, not by himself, but by some cause acting necessarily upon him, then there is no evidence left that he contrived this plan, or that he ever spent a thought about it.

The cause that directed all these determinations so wisely, whatever it was, must be a wise and intelligent cause; it must have understood the plan, and have intended the execution of it.

If it be said that all this course of determination was produced by Motives, motives, surely, have not understanding to conceive a plan, and intend its execution.* We must, therefore, go back beyond motives to some intelligent being who had the power of arranging those motives, and applying them in their proper order and season, so as to bring about the end.

This intelligent being must have understood the plan, and intended to execute it. If this be so, as the man had no hand in the execution, we have not any evidence left that he had any hand in the contrivance, or even that he is a thinking being.

If we can believe that an extensive series of means may conspire to promote an end without a cause that intended the end, and had power to choose and apply those means for the purpose, we may as well believe that this world was made by a fortuitous concourse of atoms, without an intelligent and powerful cause.

If a lucky concourse of motives could produce the conduct of an Alexander or a Julius Cæsar, no reason can be given why a lucky concourse of atoms might not produce the planetary system.

If, therefore, wise conduct in a man demonstrates that he has some degree of wisdom, it demonstrates, with equal force and evidence, that he has some degree of power over his own determinations. [332]

All the reason we can assign for believing that our fellow-men think and reason, is grounded upon their actions and speeches. If they are not the cause of these, there is no reason left to conclude that they think and reason.

Des Cartes thought that the human body is merely an engine, and that all its motions and actions are produced by mechanism. If such a machine could be made to speak and to act rationally, we might, indeed, conclude with certainty, that the maker of it had both reason and active power; but, if we once knew that all the motions of the machine were purely mechanical, we should have no reason to conclude that the man had reason or thought.

The conclusion of this argument is—That, if the actions and speeches of other men give us sufficient evidence that they are reasonable beings, they give us the same evidence, and the same degree of evidence, that they are free agents.

There is another conclusion that may be drawn from this reasoning, which it is proper to mention.

Suppose a Fatalist, rather than give up the scheme of necessity, should acknowledge that he has no evidence that there is thought and reason in any of his fellow-men, and that they may be mechanical engines for all that he knows, he will be forced to acknowledge that there must be active power, as well as understanding, in the maker of those engines, and that the first cause is a free agent. We have the same reason to believe this as to believe his existence and his wisdom. And, if the the Deity acts freely, every argument brought to prove that freedom of action is impossible, must fall to the ground. [333]

The First Cause gives us evidence of his power by every effect that gives us evidence of his wisdom. And, if he is pleased to communicate to the work of his hands some degree of his wisdom, no reason can be assigned why he may not communciate some degree of his power, as the talent which wisdom is to employ.

That the first motion, or the first effect, whatever it be, cannot be produced necessarily, and, consequently, that the First Cause must be a free agent, has been demonstrated so clearly and unanswerably by Dr Clarke, both in his "Demonstration of the Being and Attributes of God,"

* On the true signification of Motives, see above, p. 6[illegible], note *, and p. 610, note *.—H.

and in the end of his "Remarks on Collins's Philosophical Enquiry concerning Human Liberty," that I can add nothing to what he has said; nor have I found any objection made to his reasoning, by any of the defenders of necessity.*

CHAPTER IX.

OF ARGUMENTS FOR NECESSITY.

SOME of the arguments that have been offered for Necessity were already considered in this essay.

It has been said, *That human Liberty respects only the actions that are subsequent to Volition; and that power over the determinations of the Will is inconceivable, and involves a contradiction.* This argument was considered in the *first* chapter.

It has been said, *That Liberty is inconsistent with the influence of Motives, that it would make human actions capricious, and man ungovernable by God or man.* These arguments were considered in the *fourth* and *fifth* chapters. [334]

I am now to make some remarks upon *other* arguments that have been urged in this cause. They may, I think, be reduced to *three* classes. They are intended to prove, either [A] that *liberty of determination is impossible*—or, [B] *that it would be hurtful*—or, [C] *that, in fact, Man has no such liberty.*

[A] To prove *that liberty of determination is impossible*, it has been said—That there must be a sufficient reason for everything. *For every Existence, for every Event, for every Truth, there must be a* SUFFICIENT REASON.†

The famous German philosopher Leibnitz boasted much of having first applied this principle to philosophy,‡ and of having, by that means, changed metaphysics from being a play of unmeaning words, to be a rational and demonstrative science. On this account it deserves to be considered.

A very obvious objection to this principle was—That two or more means may be equally fit for the same end; and that, in such a case, there may be a sufficient reason for taking one of the number, though there be no reason for preferring one to another, of means equally fit.

To obviate this objection Leibnitz maintained, that the case supposed could not happen; or, if it did, that none of the means could be used, for want of a sufficient reason to prefer one to the rest. Therefore he determined, with some of the schoolmen—That, if an ass could be placed between two bundles of hay, or two fields of grass equally inviting, the poor beast would certainly stand still and starve; but the case, he says, could not happen without a miracle. [335]

When it was objected to this principle, That there could be no reason but the will of God why the material world was placed in one part of unlimited space rather than another, or created at one point of unlimited duration rather than another, or why the planets should move from west to east, rather than in a contrary direction; these objections Leibnitz obviated by maintaining, That there is no such thing as unoccupied space or duration; that space is nothing but the order of things coexisting, and duration is nothing but the order of things successive; that all motion is relative, so that, if there were only one body in the universe, it would be immovable; that it is inconsistent with the perfection of the Deity, that there should be any part of space unoccupied by body; and, I suppose, he understood the same of every part of duration. So that, according to this system, the world, like its Author, must be infinite, eternal, and immovable; or, at least, as great in extent and duration as it is possible for it to be.

When it was objected to the principle of a sufficient reason, That of two particles of matter perfectly similar, there can be no reason but the will of God for placing *this* here and *that* there; this objection Leibnitz obviated by maintaining, that it is impossible that there can be two particles of matter, or any two things, perfectly similar. And this seems to have led him to another of his grand principles, which he calls, *The Identity of Indiscernibles.**

When the principle of a Sufficient Reason had produced so many surprising discoveries in philosophy, it is no wonder that it should determine the long disputed question about human liberty. This it does in

* It is needless again to say, that, in the preceding three arguments for Liberty, Reid has done nothing to render the scheme of Liberty *conceivable*. But, if our intellectual nature be not a lie—if our consciousness and conscience do not deceive us in the immediate datum of an *Absolute Law of Duty*, (to say nothing of an immediate datum of Liberty itself)—we are *free*, as we are *moral agents*; for morality involves Liberty as its essential condition—as its *ratio essendi*. But this doctrine I cannot now develope.—H.

† The principle of the *Sufficient Reason*, (*p. rationis sufficientis*,)—called, likewise, by Leibnitz, that of the *Determining Reason*, (*p. rationis determinantis*)—of *Convenience*, (*p. convenientiæ*)—of *Perfection*, (*p. perfectionis*)—and of the *Order of Existences*, (*p. existentiarum*)—is one of the most extensive, not to say ambiguous, character. For it is employed to denote, conjunctly and severally, the two metaphysical or real principles—1°, Why a thing *is*, (*principium* or *ratio essendi*;) 2°, Why a thing *becomes* or *is produced*, (*p.* or *r. fiendi*;) and, 3°, the logical or ideal principle, Why a thing is *known* or *conceived*, (*p.* or *r. cognoscendi*.)—H.

‡ First he did not.—H.

* This principle I find enounced in several authors prior to Leibnitz.—H.

a moment. The determination of the will is an event for which there must be a sufficient reason—that is, something previous, which was necessarily followed by that determination, and could not be followed by any other determination; therefore it was necessary. [336]

Thus we see, that this principle of the necessity of a Sufficient Reason for everything, is very fruitful of consequences; and by its fruits we may judge of it. Those who will adopt it, must adopt all the consequences that hang upon it. To fix them all beyond dispute, no more is necessary but to prove the truth of the principle on which they depend.

I know of no argument offered by Leibnitz in proof of this principle, but the authority of Archimedes, who, he says, makes use of it to prove that a balance loaded with equal weights on both ends will continue at rest.

I grant it to be good reasoning with regard to a balance, or with regard to any machine, That, when there is no external cause of its motion, it must remain at rest, because the machine has no power of moving itself. But to apply this reasoning to a man, is to take for granted that the man is a machine, which is the very point in question.*

Leibnitz and his followers would have us to take this principle of the necessity of a sufficient reason for every existence, for every event, for every truth, as a first principle, without proof, without explanation; though it be evidently a vague proposition, capable of various meanings, as the word *reason* is. It must have different meanings when applied to things of so different nature as an event and a truth; and it may have different meanings when applied to the same thing. We cannot, therefore, form a distinct judgment of it in the gross, but only by taking it to pieces, and applying it to different things, in a precise and distinct meaning.

It can have no connection with the dispute about liberty, except when it is applied to the determinations of the will. Let us, therefore, suppose a voluntary action of a man; and that the question is put, Whether was there a sufficient reason for this action or not? [337]

The natural and obvious meaning of this question is—Was there a motive to the action sufficient to justify it to be wise and good, or, at least, innocent? Surely, in this sense, there is not a sufficient reason for every human action, because there are many that are foolish, unreasonable, and unjustifiable.†

If the meaning of the question be—Was there a cause of the action? Undoubtedly there was. Of every event there must be a cause that had power sufficient to produce it, and that exerted that power for the purpose. In the present case, either the *man* was the cause of the action, and then it was a free action, and is justly imputed to him*; or it must have had another cause, and cannot justly be imputed to the man.* In this sense, therefore, it is granted that there was a sufficient reason for the action; but the question about liberty is not in the least affected by this concession.

If, again, the meaning of the question be—Was there something previous to the action which made it to be necessarily produced?—every man who believes that the action was free, will answer to this question in the negative.†

I know no other meaning that can be put upon the principle of a sufficient reason, when applied to the determinations of the human will, besides the three I have mentioned. In the first, it is evidently false; in the second, it is true, but does not affect the question about liberty; in the third, it is a mere assertion of necessity without proof.

Before we leave this boasted principle, we may see how it applies to events of another kind. When we say that a philosopher has assigned a sufficient reason for such a phænomenon, what is the meaning of this? The meaning surely is, that he has accounted for it from the known laws of nature. The sufficient reason of a phænomenon of nature must therefore be some law or laws of nature, of which the phænomenon is a necessary consequence. But are we sure that, in this sense, there is a sufficient reason for every phænomenon of nature? I think we are not. [338]

For, not to speak of miraculous events in which the laws of nature are suspended or counteracted, we know not but that, in the ordinary course of God's providence, there may be particular acts of his administration that do not come under any general law of nature.

Established laws of nature are necessary for enabling intelligent creatures to conduct their affairs with wisdom and prudence, and prosecute their ends by proper means; but still it may be fit that some particular events should not be fixed by general laws,

* See above, p. 610, b, note *.—H.

† But, in regard to the signification of motives, Leibnitz says:—"Non semper sequimur judicium ultimum intellectus practici, dum ad volendum nos determinamus; at ubi volumus, semper sequimur collectionem omnium inclinationum, tam a parte rationum, quam passionum, profectarum; id quod sæpenumero sine expresso intellectus judicio contingit."—(*Theod.* P. I. § 51. Op. I. p. 150.) See also above, p. 608, b, note *, and p. 610, b, note *.—H.

* See above, p. 608, b, note ‡, and p. 611, a, note *—H.

† If it had a cause, (and every effect is the product of more than one cause,) then "was there something previous to the action which made it to be necessarily produced." For, *posita causa, ponitur effectus.*—H.

but be directed by particular acts of the Divine government, that so his reasonable creatures may have sufficient inducement to supplicate his aid, his protection and direction, and to depend upon him for the success of their honest designs.

We see that, in human governments, even those that are most legal, it is impossible that every act of the administration should be directed by established laws. Some things must be left to the direction of the executive power, and particularly acts of clemency and bounty to petitioning subjects. That there is nothing analogous to this in the Divine government of the world, no man is able to prove.

We have no authority to pray that God would counteract or suspend the laws of nature in our behalf. Prayer, therefore, supposes that he may lend an ear to our prayers, without transgressing the laws of nature. Some have thought that the only use of prayer and devotion is, to produce a proper temper and disposition in ourselves, and that it has no efficacy with the Deity. But this is a hypothesis without proof. It contradicts our most natural sentiments, as well as the plain doctrine of Scripture, and tends to damp the fervour of every act of devotion.* [339]

It was, indeed, an article of the system of Leibnitz, That the Deity, since the creation of the world, never did anything, excepting in the case of miracles; his work being made so perfect at first as never to need his interposition. But, in this, he was opposed by Sir Isaac Newton, and others of the ablest philosophers, nor was he ever able to give any proof of this tenet.†

There is no evidence, therefore, that there is a sufficient reason for every natural event; if, by a sufficient reason, we understand some fixed law or laws of nature, of which that event is a necessary consequence.

But what, shall we say, is a sufficient reason for a truth? For our belief of a truth, I think, the sufficient reason is our having good evidence; but what may be meant by a sufficient reason for its being a truth I am not able to guess, unless the sufficient reason of a contingent truth be, That it *is* true; and, of a necessary truth, That it *must be* true. This makes a man little wiser.

From what has been said, I think it appears, that this principle of the necessity of a sufficient reason for everything is very indefinite in its signification. If it mean, that of every event there must be a cause that had sufficient power to produce it, this is true, and has always been admitted as a first principle in philosophy, and in common life.* If it mean that every event must be necessarily consequent upon something (called a sufficient reason) that went before it; this is a direct assertion of universal fatality, and has many strange, not to say absurd, consequences.* But, in this sense, it is neither self-evident, nor has any proof of it been offered. And, in general, in every sense in which it has evidence, it gives no new information; and, in every sense in which it would give new information, it wants evidence. [340]

Another argument that has been used to prove liberty of action to be impossible is, *That it implies "an effect without a cause."*

To this it may be briefly answered, That a free action is an effect produced by a being who had power and will to produce it; therefore it is not an effect without a cause.

To suppose any other cause necessary to the production of an effect than a being who had the power and the will to produce it, is a contradiction; for it is to suppose that being to have power to produce the effect, and not to have power to produce it.

But, as great stress is laid upon this argument by a late zealous advocate for necessity,† we shall consider the light in which he puts it.

He introduces this argument with an observation to which I entirely agree. It is, That, to establish this doctrine of necessity, nothing is necessary but that, throughout all nature, the same consequences should invariably result from the same circumstances.

I know nothing more that can be desired to establish universal fatality throughout the universe. When it is proved that, through all nature, the same consequences invariably result from the same circumstances, the doctrine of liberty must be given up. [341]

To prevent all ambiguity, I grant that, in reasoning, the same consequences, throughout all nature, will invariably follow from the same premises; because good reasoning must be good reasoning in all times and places. But this has nothing to do with the doctrine of necessity. The thing to be

* But, in relation to the last five paragraphs, and the two following, it may be observed, that, of a hyperphysical as well as of a physical event, we must, by a necessary mental law, always suppose a sufficient reason why it *is*, and *is as it is*; and Reid has no ground on which to restrict the Leibnitzian application of that principle to the sphere of the ordinary laws of nature.—H.

† This opinion of Leibnitz stands, however, altogether apart from his doctrine of the Sufficient Reason. That doctrine is equally applicable in the theory of Malebranche, who viewed the Deity as the proximate efficient cause of every effect in nature, and to the theory of Leibnitz himself, who held that the Deity operated in the universe once, and once for all.—H.

* These two positions are, in reality, one and the same. *Sufficient Reason = Sum of Causes.*—H.

† Priestley.—H.

proved, therefore, in order to establish that doctrine, is, That, through all nature, the same events invariably result from the same circumstances.

Of this capital point, the proof offered by that author is, That an event not preceded by any circumstances that determined it to be what it was, would be *an effect without a cause.* Why so? "For," says he, "a *cause* cannot be defined to be anything but *such previous circumstances as are constantly followed by a certain effect;* the constancy of the result making us conclude that there must be a *sufficient reason*, in the nature of things, why it should be produced in those circumstances."*—[*Doctrine of Philosophical Necessity*, p. 11.]

I acknowledge that, if this be the only definition that can be given of a Cause, it will follow that an event not preceded by circumstances that determined it to be what it was, would be (not an *effect* without a cause, which is a contradiction in terms, but) an *event* without a cause, which I hold to be impossible. The matter, therefore, is brought to this issue, Whether this be the only definition that can be given of a cause?

With regard to this point, we may observe, *first*, That this definition of a cause, bating the phraseology of putting a *cause* under the category of *circumstances*, which I take to be new, is the same, in other words, with that which Mr Hume gave, of which he ought to be acknowledged the inventor; for I know of no author before Mr Hume, who maintained that we have no other notion of a cause but that it is something prior to the effect, which has been found by experience to be constantly followed by the effect. This is a main pillar of his system; and he has drawn very important consequences from this definition, which I am far from thinking this author will adopt. [342]

Without repeating what I have before said of causes in the first of these Essays, and in the second and third chapters of this, I shall here mention some of the consequences that may be justly deduced from this definition of a cause, that we may judge of it by its fruits.

First, It follows from this definition of a cause, that night is the cause of day, and day the cause of night. For no two things have more constantly followed each other since the beginning of the world.

Secondly, It follows from this definition of a cause, that, for what we know, anything may be the cause of anything, since nothing is essential to a cause but its being constantly followed by the effect. If this be so, what is unintelligent may be the cause of what is intelligent; folly may be the cause of wisdom, and evil of good; all reasoning from the nature of the effect—to the nature of the cause, and all reasoning from final causes, must be given up as fallacious.

Thirdly, From this definition of a cause, it follows that we have no reason to conclude that every event must have a cause; for innumerable events happen, when it cannot be shewn that there were certain previous circumstances that have constantly been followed by such an event. And, though it were certain that every event we have had access to observe had a cause, it would not follow that every event must have a cause; for it is contrary to the rules of logic to conclude, that, because a thing has *always* been, therefore it *must* be—to reason from what is *contingent* to what is *necessary*. [343]

Fourthly, From this definition of a cause, it would follow that we have no reason to conclude that there was any cause of the creation of this world; for there were no previous circumstances that had been constantly followed by such an effect. And, for the same reason, it would follow from the definition, that whatever was singular in its nature, or the first thing of its kind, could have no cause.

Several of these consequences were fondly embraced by Mr Hume, as necessarily following from his definition of a cause, and as favourable to his system of absolute scepticism. Those who adopt the definition of a cause, from which they follow, may choose whether they will adopt its consequences, or shew that they do not follow from the definition.

A *second* observation with regard to this argument is, That a definition of a cause may be given, which is not burdened with such untoward consequences.

Why may not an Efficient Cause be defined to be *a being that had power and will to produce the effect?* The production of an effect requires active power, and active power, being a quality, must be in a being endowed with that power. Power without will produces no effect; but, where these are conjoined, the effect must be produced.

This, I think, is the proper meaning of the word *cause*, when it is used in metaphysics; and particularly when we affirm, that everything that begins to exist must have a cause; and when, by reasoning, we prove that there must be an eternal First Cause of all things.

Was the world produced by previous circumstances which are constantly followed by such an effect? or, Was it produced by a Being that had power to produce it, and willed its production? [344]

In natural philosophy the word *cause* is often used in a very different sense. When

* See above, p. 608, b, note *.—H.

an event is produced according to a known law of nature, the law of nature is called the cause of that event. But a law of nature is not the efficient cause of any event. It is only the rule, according to which the efficient cause acts. A law is a thing conceived in the mind of a rational being, not a thing that has a real existence; and, therefore, like a motive, it can neither act nor be acted upon, and consequently cannot be an efficient cause. If there be no being that acts according to the law, it produces no effect.

This author takes it for granted, that every voluntary action of man was determined to be what it was by the laws of nature, in the same sense as mechanical motions are determined by the laws of motion; and that every choice, not thus determined, "is just as impossible as that a mechanical motion should depend upon no certain law or rule, or that any other effect should exist without a cause."

It ought here to be observed, that there are two kinds of laws, both very properly called *laws of nature*, which ought not to be confounded. There are *moral* laws of nature, and *physical* laws of nature.* The *first* are the rules which God has prescribed to his rational creatures for their conduct. They respect voluntary and free actions only; for no other actions can be subject to moral rules. These laws of nature ought to be always obeyed, but they are often transgressed by men. There is, therefore, no impossibility in the violation of the moral laws of nature, nor is such a violation an effect without a cause. The transgressor is the cause, and is justly unaccountable for it. [345]

The *physical laws of nature* are the rules according to which the Deity commonly acts in his natural government of the world; and whatever is done according to them, is not done by man, but by God, either immediately or by instruments under his direction. These laws of nature neither restrain the power of the Author of nature, nor bring him under any obligation to do nothing beyond their sphere. He has sometimes acted contrary to them, in the case of miracles, and, perhaps, often acts without regard to them, in the ordinary course of his providence. Neither miraculous events, which are contrary to the physical laws of nature, nor such ordinary acts of the Divine administration as are without their sphere, are impossible, nor are they *effects without a cause*. God is the cause of them, and to him only they are to be imputed.

That the moral laws of nature are often transgressed by man, is undeniable. If the physical laws of nature make his obedience to the moral laws to be impossible, then he is, in the literal sense, *born under one law, bound unto another*, which contradicts every notion of a righteous government of the world.

But though this supposition were attended with no such shocking consequence, it is merely a supposition; and, until it be proved, that every choice or voluntary action of man is determined by the physical laws of nature, this argument for necessity is only the taking for granted the point to be proved.

Of the same kind is the argument for the impossibility of liberty, taken from a balance, which cannot move but as it is moved by the weights put into it. This argument, though urged by almost every writer in defence of necessity, is so pitiful, and has been so often answered, that it scarce deserves to be mentioned.

Every argument in a dispute, which is not grounded on principles granted by both parties, is that kind of sophism which logicians call *petitio principii*; and such, in my apprehension, are all the arguments offered to prove that liberty of action is impossible. [346]

It may farther be observed, that every argument of this class, if it were really conclusive, must extend to the Deity, as well as to all created beings; and necessary existence, which has always been considered as the prerogative of the Supreme Being, must belong equally to every creature and to every event, even the most trifling.

This I take to be the system of Spinosa, and of those among the ancients who carried fatality to the highest pitch.

I before referred the reader to Dr Clarke's argument, which professes to demonstrate that the First Cause is a free agent. Until that argument shall be shewn to be fallacious, a thing which I have not seen attempted, such weak arguments as have been brought to prove the contrary, ought to have little weight.*

* On the ambiguous extent in which the term Nature is employed, see above, p. 216, note †. Etymologically considered, "physical laws of nature" is tautological—*physical* being equivalent to *natural*. It would, perhaps, have been better to have distinguished the one class of laws simply as *moral laws*, or *laws of Intelligence*, the other as *physical laws*, or *laws of Nature*. Nature would thus be restricted to the material universe, as is done by the German philosophers. But it must be admitted that there is no imperative reason why Nature should not be used to comprehend both mind and matter, as was done by the Greek philosophers.—H.

* As I have before observed, the advocates of Liberty and of Necessity are severally successful in proving the doctrine of their antagonists to be, under the law of cause and effect, fundamentally incomprehensible, if not self-repugnant; but it remains to be shewn, on the very conditions of human thought, why these counter schemes are, and must be, unthinkable.—H.

CHAPTER X.

THE SAME SUBJECT.

[B.] With regard to the *second* class of arguments for necessity, which are intended to prove *that liberty of action would be hurtful to man*, I have only to observe, that it is a fact too evident to be denied, whether we adopt the system of Liberty or that of Necessity, that men actually receive hurt from their own voluntary actions, and from the voluntary actions of other men; nor can it be pretended, that this fact is inconsistent with the doctrine of liberty, or that it is more unaccountable upon this system than upon that of necessity. [347]

In order, therefore, to draw any solid argument against liberty, from its hurtfulness, it ought to be proved—That, if man were a free agent, he would do more hurt to himself, or to others, than he actually does.

To this purpose, it has been said, That liberty would make men's actions capricious; that it would destroy the influence of motives; that it would take away the effect of rewards and punishments; and that it would make man absolutely ungovernable.

[C.] These arguments have been already considered in the fourth and fifth chapters of this Essay; and, therefore, I shall now proceed to the *third* class of arguments for necessity, which are intended to prove, *that, in fact, men are not free agents.*

The most formidable argument of this class, and, I think, the only one that has not been considered in some of the preceding chapters, is taken from the *prescience of the Deity.*

God foresees every determination of the human mind. It must, therefore, be what he foresees it shall be; and, therefore, must be necessary.

This argument may be understood *three* different ways, each of which we shall consider, that we may see all its force.

The necessity of the event may be thought to be a just consequence, either *barely from its being certainly future*—or *barely from its being foreseen*—or *from the impossibility of its being foreseen if it was not necessary.*

First, It may be thought, *that, as nothing can be known to be future which is not certainly future; so, if it be certainly future, it must be necessary.* [348]

This opinion has no less authority in its favour than that of Aristotle, who indeed held the doctrine of liberty, but believing, at the same time, that whatever is certainly future must be necessary, in order to defend the liberty of human actions, maintained, *That contingent events have no certain futurity;** but I know of no modern advocate for liberty who has put the defence of it upon that issue.

It must be granted, that, as whatever was, certainly was, and whatever is, certainly is, so whatever shall be, certainly shall be. These are identical propositions, and cannot be doubted by those who conceive them distinctly.

But I know no rule of reasoning by which it can be inferred, that, because an event *certainly shall be*, therefore its production *must be necessary*. The manner of its production, whether free or necessary, cannot be concluded from the time of its production, whether it be past, present, or future. That it shall be, no more implies that it shall be necessarily than that it shall be freely produced; for neither present, past, nor future, have any more connection with necessity than they have with freedom.

I grant, therefore, that, from events being foreseen, it may be justly concluded, that they are certainly future; but from their being certainly future, it does not follow that they are necessary.

Secondly, If it be meant by this argument, *that an event must be necessary, merely because it is foreseen*, neither is this a just consequence; for it has often been observed, That prescience and knowledge of every kind, being an immanent act, has no effect upon the thing known. Its mode of existence, whether it be free or necessary, is not in the least affected by its being known to be future, any more than by its being known to be past or present. The Deity foresees his own future free actions, but neither his foresight nor his purpose makes them necessary. The argument, therefore, taken in this view, as well as in the former, is inconclusive. [349]

A *third* way in which this argument may be understood, is this—*It is impossible that an event which is not necessary should be foreseen; therefore every event that is certainly foreseen must be necessary.* Here the conclusion certainly follows from the antecedent proposition, and therefore the whole stress of the argument lies upon the proof of that proposition.

Let us consider, therefore, whether it can be proved—That no free action can be certainly foreseen. If this can be proved, it will follow, either that all actions are necessary, or that all actions cannot be foreseen.

* See *De Interpretatione*, c. 1x; and there the commentary of Ammonius. By *contingent* is meant what may or may not happen. On this definition, Aristotle, therefore, justly argued, that, of any proposition concerning future contingents, we can only say indefinitely that it may or may not be true; nor is it possible for the human mind to conceive how, without contradiction, a future event can be at once viewed as *certain*, (that is, which cannot, by not happening, possibly falsify the affirmation that it will happen,) and *contingent*, (that is, which may or may not happen.) See Note U.—H.

With regard to the general proposition—*That it is impossible that any free action can be certainly foreseen*, I observe—

First, That every man who believes the Deity to be a free agent, must believe that this proposition not only is incapable of proof, but that it is certainly false. For the man himself foresees, that 'the Judge of all the earth will always do what is right, and that he will fulfil whatever he has promised; and, at the same time, believes, that, in doing what is right, and in fulfilling his promises, the Deity acts with the most perfect freedom.

Secondly, I observe, that every man who believes that it is an absurdity or contradiction that any free action should be certainly foreseen, must believe, if he will be consistent, either that the Deity is not a free agent, or that he does not foresee his own actions; nor can we foresee that he will do what is right, and will fulfil his promises. [350]

Thirdly, Without considering the consequences which this general proposition carries in its bosom, which give it a very bad aspect, let us attend to the arguments offered to prove it.

Dr Priestley has laboured more in the proof of this proposition than any other author I am acquainted with, and maintains it to be, not only a difficulty and a mystery, as it has been called, that a contingent event should be the object of knowledge, but that, in reality, there cannot be a greater absurdity or contradiction. Let us hear the proof of this.

"For," says he, "as certainly as nothing can be known to exist but what does exist; so certainly can nothing be known to *arise from what does exist*, but what does arise from it or depend upon it. But, according to the definition of the terms, a contingent event does not depend upon any previous known circumstances, since some other event might have arisen in the same circumstances."—[*Doctrine of Philosophical Necessity.*]

This argument, when stripped of incidental and explanatory clauses, and affected variations of expression, amounts to this: Nothing can be known to arise from what does exist, but what does arise from it. But a contingent event does not arise from what does exist. The conclusion, which is left to be drawn by the reader, must, according to the rules of reasoning, be—Therefore, a contingent event cannot be known to arise from what does exist.

It is here very obvious, that a thing may arise from what does exist, two ways, freely or necessarily. A contingent event arises from its cause, not necessarily but freely, and so, that another event might have arisen from the same cause, in the same circumstances. [351]

The second proposition of the argument is, that a contingent event does not depend upon any previous known circumstances, which I take to be only a variation of the term of *not arising from what does exist*. Therefore, in order to make the two propositions to correspond, we must understand, by *arising from what does exist*, arising necessarily from what does exist. When this ambiguity is removed, the argument stands thus: Nothing can be known to arise necessarily from what does exist, but what does necessarily arise from it; but a contingent event does not arise necessarily from what does exist; therefore, a contingent event cannot be known to arise necessarily from what does exist.

I grant the whole; but the conclusion of this argument is not what he undertook to prove, and therefore the argument is that kind of sophism which logicians call *ignorantia elenchi*.

The thing to be proved is not, that a contingent event cannot be known to arise necessarily from what exists; but that a contingent future event cannot be the object of knowledge.

To draw the argument to this conclusion, it must be put thus:—Nothing can be known to arise from what does exist, but what arises necessarily from it; but a contingent event does not arise necessarily from what does exist; therefore, a contingent event cannot be known to arise from what does exist.

The conclusion here is what it ought to be; but the first proposition assumes the thing to be proved, and therefore the argument is what logicians call *petitio principii*.

To the same purpose he says, "That nothing can be known at present, except itself or its necessary cause exist at present."

This is affirmed, but I find no proof of it. [352]

Again, he says, "That knowledge supposes an object which, in this case, does not exist." It is true that knowledge supposes an object; and everything that is known is an object of knowledge, whether past, present, or future, whether contingent or necessary.

Upon the whole, the arguments I can find upon this point bear no proportion to the confidence of the assertion, that there cannot be a greater absurdity or contradiction, than that a contingent event should be the object of knowledge.

To those who, without pretending to shew a manifest absurdity or contradiction in the knowledge of future contingent events, are still of opinion that it is impossible that the future free actions of man, a being of imperfect wisdom and virtue, should be certainly foreknown, I would humbly offer the following considerations.

1. I grant that there is no knowledge of this kind in man; and this is the cause that we find it so difficult to conceive it in any other being.

All our knowledge of future events is drawn either from their necessary connection with the present course of nature, or from their connection with the character of the agent that produces them. Our knowledge, even of those future events that necessarily result from the established laws of nature, is hypothetical. It supposes the continuance of those laws with which they are connected. And how long those laws may be continued, we have no certain knowledge. God only knows when the present course of nature shall be changed, and therefore he only has certain knowledge even of events of this kind. [353]

The character of perfect wisdom and perfect rectitude in the Deity, gives us certain knowledge that he will always be true in all his declarations, faithful in all his promises, and just in all his dispensations. But when we reason from the character of men to their future actions, though, in many cases, we have such probability as we rest upon in our most important worldly concerns, yet we have no certainty, because men are imperfect in wisdom and in virtue. If we had even the most perfect knowledge of the character and situation of a man, this would not be sufficient to give certainty to our knowledge of his future actions; because, in some actions, both good and bad men deviate from their general character.

The prescience of the Deity, therefore, must be different not only in degree, but in kind, from any knowledge we can attain of futurity.

2. Though we can have no conception how the future free actions of men may be known by the Deity, this is not a sufficient reason to conclude that they cannot be known. Do we know, or can we conceive, how God knows the secrets of men's hearts? Can we conceive how God made this world without any pre-existent matter? All the ancient philosophers believed this to be impossible: and for what reason but this, that they could not conceive how it could be done? Can we give any better reason for believing that the actions of men cannot be certainly foreseen?

3. Can we conceive how we ourselves have certain knowledge by those faculties with which God has endowed us? If any man thinks that he understands distinctly how he is conscious of his own thoughts; how he perceives external objects by his senses; how he remembers past events—I am afraid that he is not yet so wise as to understand his own ignorance. [354]

4. There seems to me to be a great analogy between the prescience of future contingents, and the memory of past contingents.* We possess the last in some degree, and therefore find no difficulty in believing that it may be perfect in the Deity. But the first we have in no degree, and therefore are apt to think it impossible.

In both, the object of knowledge is neither what presently exists, nor has any necessary connection with what presently exists. Every argument brought to prove the impossibility of prescience, proves, with equal force, the impossibility of memory. If it be true that nothing can be known to arise from what does exist, but what necessarily arises from it, it must be equally true that nothing can be known to have gone before what does exist but what must necessarily have gone before it. If it be true that nothing future can be known unless its necessary cause exist at present, it must be equally true that nothing past can be known unless something consequent, with which it is necessarily connected, exist at present. If the fatalist should say, that past events are indeed necessarily connected with the present, he will not surely venture to say, that it is by tracing this necessary connection that we remember the past.

Why then should we think prescience impossible in the Almighty, when he has given us a faculty which bears a strong analogy to it, and which is no less unaccountable to the human understanding than prescience is? It is more reasonable, as well as more agreeable to the sacred writings, to conclude, with a pious father of the church—"Quocirca nullo modo cogimur, aut, retenta praescientia Dei, tollere voluntatis arbitrium, aut, retento voluntatis ar-

---

* *We have no memory of past contingents.* A past contingent is a contradiction. An event is only contingent as future; in becoming past, it forthwith becomes necessary—it cannot but be. *Ἔχει τὸ γεγονὸς ἀνάγκην*, says Aristotle; and the proverb—*Factum infectum reddere, ne Deus quidem potest*, has been said and sung in a thousand forms. But it is only as past that anything is remembered; whatever, therefore, is known in memory is known as necessary.

Now, so far is it from being true, as Reid soon after says, that "every argument to prove the impossibility of prescience (as the knowledge of future contingents) proves, with equal force, the impossibility of memory," (as the knowledge of past contingents,) that the possibility of a memory of events *as contingent* was, I believe, never imagined by any philosopher—nor, in reality, is it by Reid himself; and, in fact, one of the most insoluble objections to the possibility of a free agency, arises (on the admission that all future events are foreseen by God) from the analogy of prescience to memory; it being impossible for the human mind to reconcile the supposition that an event may or may not occur, and the supposition that one of these alternatives has been foreseen as certain. On this I may say something in Note U.—H.

bitrio, Deum (quod nefas est) negare præscium futurorum; sed utrumque amplectimur, utrumque fideliter et veraciter confitemur: Illud, ut bene credamus; hoc, ut bene vivamus." [AUGUSTINUS, *De Civitate Dei*, L. v. c. 10.]

CHAPTER XI.

OF THE PERMISSION OF EVIL.

ANOTHER use has been made of Divine prescience by the advocates for necessity, which it is proper to consider before we leave this subject.

It has been said—"That all those consequences follow from the Divine prescience which are thought most alarming in the scheme of necessity; and particularly God's being the proper cause of moral evil. For, to suppose God to foresee and permit what it was in his power to have prevented, is the very same thing as to suppose him to will, and directly to cause it. He distinctly foresees all the actions of a man's life, and all the consequences of them. If, therefore, he did not think any particular man and his conduct proper for his plan of creation and providence, he certainly would not have introduced him into being at all."

In this reasoning we may observe, that a supposition is made which seems to contradict itself.

That all the actions of a particular man should be distinctly foreseen, and, at the same time, that that man should never be brought into existence, seems to me to be a contradiction; and the same contradiction there is, in supposing any action to be distinctly foreseen, and yet prevented. For, if it be foreseen, it shall happen; and, if it be prevented, it shall not happen, and therefore could not be foreseen. [356]

The knowledge here supposed is neither prescience nor science, but something very different from both. It is a kind of knowledge, which some metaphysical divines, in their controversies about the order of the Divine decrees, a subject far beyond the limits of human understanding, attributed to the Deity, and of which other divines denied the possibility, while they firmly maintained the Divine prescience.

It was called *scientia media*, to distinguish it from prescience; and by this *scientia media* was meant, not the knowing from eternity all things that shall exist, which is prescience, nor the knowing all the connections and relations of things that exist or may be conceived, which is science, but a knowledge of things contingent, that never did nor shall exist. For instance, the knowing every action that would be done by a man who is barely conceived, and shall never be brought into existence.*

Against the possibility of the *scientia media* arguments may be urged, which cannot be applied to prescience. Thus it may be said, that nothing can be known but what is true. It is true that the future actions of a free agent shall exist, and therefore we see no impossibility in its being known that they shall exist. But with regard to the free actions of an agent that never did nor shall exist, there is nothing true, and therefore nothing can be known. To say that the being conceived, would certainly act in such a way, if placed in such a situation, if it have any meaning, is to say, That his acting in that way is the consequence of the conception; but this contradicts the supposition of its being a free action.

Things merely conceived have no relations or connections but such as are implied in the conception, or are consequent from it. Thus I conceive two circles in the same plane. If this be all I conceive, it is not true that these circles are equal or unequal, because neither of these relations is implied in the conception; yet, if the two circles really existed, they must be either equal or unequal. Again, I conceive two circles in the same plane, the distance of whose centres is equal to the sum of their semidiameters. It is true of these circles, that they will touch one another, because this follows from the conception; but it is not true that they will be equal or unequal, because neither of these relations is implied in the conception, nor is consequent from it. [357]

* The *Scientia Media* (called likewise *Sc. Hypothetica*—*Sc. de futuro conditionato*,) is a scheme excogitated by certain Jesuits about the end of the sixteenth century, and first reduced to system by the Spaniard Molina and his learned countryman Fonseca. It was opposed to another theory, touching the divine decrees, called that of *Predetermination*, which had a little before been introduced among the Spanish Thomists. The former doctrine was generally espoused by the Franciscans and Jesuits; the latter by the Dominicans and Augustinians: a keen theological controversy was the result. Molina regarded the objects of the *divine knowledge* as threefold. They were—1° *things possible*; 2° *actual events*; and, 3° *conditional events*, that is, such as would have existed, had a certain condition been realised. The knowledge of possibilities he denominated the *knowledge of simple intelligence*, (*scientia simplicis intelligentiæ*;) and the knowledge of events which have actually happened in the universe, he called the *knowledge of vision*, (*scientia visionis*.) But as, besides the knowledge of the simply possible and the absolutely actual, there was a third knowledge—that, to wit, of conditional events—Molina conceived that this afforded an intermediate knowledge—*scientia media*—between Vision and Simple Intelligence. A celebrated example of the *scientia media* is that of David consulting the Lord, whether the men of Keilah would deliver him to Saul, *if* Saul came down against the city. The answer was, that they would so deliver him; upon which David, who had intended retiring into Keilah, adopted other plans.—From this it will be seen that Reid is not altogether exact in his statement of the *Scientia Media*; nor is his criticism of it unexceptionable.—H.

In like manner, I can conceive a being who has power to do an indifferent action or not to do it. It is not true that he would do it, nor is it true that he would not do it, because neither is implied in my conception, nor follows from it; and what is not true cannot be known.

Though I do not perceive any fallacy in this argument against a *scientia media*, I am sensible how apt we are to err in applying what belongs to our conceptions and our knowledge, to the conceptions and knowledge of the Supreme Being; and, therefore, without pretending to determine for or against a *scientia media*, I only observe, that, to suppose that the Deity prevents what he foresees by his prescience, is a contradiction, and that to know that a contingent event which he sees fit not to permit would certainly happen if permitted, is not prescience, but the *scientia media*, whose existence or possibility we are under no necessity of admitting.

Waving all dispute about *scientia media*, we acknowledge that nothing can happen under the administration of the Deity, which he does not see fit to permit. The permission of natural and moral evil, is a phænomenon which cannot be disputed. To account for this phænomenon under the government of a Being of infinite goodness, justice, wisdom, and power, has, in all ages, been considered as difficult to human reason, whether we embrace the system of liberty or that of necessity. But, if the difficulty of accounting for this phænomenon upon the system of necessity, be as great as it is upon the system of liberty, it can have no weight when used as an argument against liberty. [358]

The defenders of necessity, to reconcile it to the principles of Theism, find themselves obliged to give up all the moral attributes of God, excepting that of goodness, or a desire to produce happiness. This they hold to be the sole motive of his making and governing the universe. Justice, veracity, faithfulness, are only modifications of goodness, the means of promoting its purposes, and are exercised only so far as they serve that end. Virtue is acceptable to him and vice displeasing, only as the first tends to produce happiness and the last misery. He is the proper cause and agent of all moral evil as well as good; but it is for a good end, to produce the greater happiness to his creatures. He does evil that good may come, and this end sanctifies the worst actions that contribute to it. All the wickedness of men being the work of God, he must, when he surveys it, pronounce it, as well as all his other works, to be very good.

This view of the Divine nature, the only one consistent with the scheme of necessity, appears to me much more shocking than the permission of evil upon the scheme of liberty. It is said, that it requires only *strength of mind* to embrace it: to me it seems to require much strength of countenance to profess it.

In this system, as in Cleanthes' Tablature of the Epicurean System, Pleasure or Happiness is placed upon the throne as the queen, to whom all the virtues bear the humble office of menial servants.—[Cic. *Fin.* ii. 21.]

As the end of the Deity, in all his actions, is not his own good, which can receive no addition, but the good of his creatures; and, as his creatures are capable of this disposition in some degree, is he not pleased with this image of himself in his creatures, and displeased with the contrary? Why then should he be the author of malice, envy, revenge, tyranny, and oppression, in their hearts? Other vices that have no malevolence in them may please such a Deity, but surely malevolence cannot please him. [359]

If we form our notions of the moral attributes of the Deity from what we see of his government of the world, from the dictates of reason and conscience, or from the doctrine of revelation—justice, veracity, faithfulness, the love of virtue and the dislike of vice, appear to be no less essential attributes of his nature than goodness.

In man, who is made after the image of God, goodness or benevolence is indeed an essential part of virtue, but it is not the whole.

I am at a loss what arguments can be brought to prove goodness to be essential to the Deity, which will not, with equal force, prove other moral attributes to be so; or what objections can be brought against the latter, which have not equal strength against the former, unless it be admitted to be an objection against other moral attributes that they do not accord with the doctrine of necessity.

If other moral evils may be attributed to the Deity as the means of promoting general good, why may not false declarations and false promises? And then what ground have we left to believe the truth of what he reveals, or to rely upon what he promises?

Supposing this strange view of the Divine nature were to be adopted in favour of the doctrine of necessity, there is still a great difficulty to be resolved. [360]

Since it is supposed that the Supreme Being had no other end in making and governing the universe but to produce the greatest degree of happiness to his creatures in general, how comes it to pass that there is so much misery in a system made and governed by infinite wisdom and power for a contrary purpose?

The solution of this difficulty leads us necessarily to another hypothesis—That all the misery and vice that is in the world is a necessary ingredient in that system which produces the greatest sum of happiness upon the whole. This connection betwixt the greatest sum of happiness and all the misery that is in the universe must be fatal and necessary in the nature of things, so that even Almighty power cannot break it; for benevolence can never lead to inflict misery without necessity.

This necessary connection between the greatest sum of happiness upon the whole, and all the natural and moral evil that is, or has been, or shall be, being once established, it is impossible for mortal eyes to discern how far this evil may extend, or on whom it may happen to fall; whether this fatal connection may be temporary or eternal, or what proportion of the happiness may be balanced by it.

A world made by perfect wisdom and Almighty power, for no other end but to make it happy, presents the most pleasing prospect that can be imagined. We expect nothing but uninterrupted happiness to prevail for ever. But, alas! when we consider that, in this happiest system, there must be necessarily all the misery and vice we see, and how much more we know not, how is the prospect darkened!

These two hypotheses, the one limiting the moral character of the Deity, the other limiting his power, seem to me to be the necessary consequences of necessity, when it is joined with Theism; and they have, accordingly, been adopted by the ablest defenders of that doctrine. [361]

If some defenders of liberty, by limiting too rashly the Divine prescience, in order to defend that system, have raised high indignation in their opponents; have they not equal ground of indignation against those who, to defend necessity, limit the moral perfection of the Deity, and his Almighty power?

Let us consider, on the other hand, what consequences may be fairly drawn from God's permitting the abuse of liberty in agents on whom he has bestowed it.

It it be asked, Why does God permit so much sin in his creation? I confess, I cannot answer the question, but must lay my hand upon my mouth. He giveth no account of his conduct to the children of men. It is our part to obey his commands, and not to say unto him, Why dost thou thus?

Hypotheses might be framed; but, while we have ground to be satisfied that he does nothing but what is right, it is more becoming us to acknowledge that the ends and reasons of his universal government are beyond our knowledge, and, perhaps, beyond the comprehension of human understanding. We cannot penetrate so far into the counsel of the Almighty as to know all the reasons why it became him, of whom are all things, and to whom are all things, to create, not only machines, which are solely moved by his hand, but servants and children, who, by obeying his commands, and imitating his moral perfections, might rise to a high degree of glory and happiness in his favour; or, by perverse disobedience, might incur guilt and just punishment. In this he appears to us awful in his justice, as well as amiable in his goodness.

But, as he disdains not to appeal to men for the equity of his proceedings towards them when his character is impeached, we may, with humble reverence, plead for God, and vindicate that moral excellence which is the glory of his nature, and of which the image is the glory and the perfection of man. [362]

Let us observe, first of all, that *to permit* hath two meanings. It signifies not to forbid; and it signifies not to hinder by superior power. In the first of these senses, God never permits sin. His law forbids every moral evil. By his laws and by his government, he gives every encouragement to good conduct, and every discouragement to bad. But he does not always, by his superior power, hinder it from being committed. This is the ground of the accusation; and this, it is said, is the very same thing as directly to will and to cause it.

As this is asserted without proof, and is far from being self-evident, it might be sufficient to deny it until it be proved. But, without resting barely on the defensive, we may observe that the only moral attributes that can be supposed inconsistent with the permission of sin, are either goodness or justice.

The defenders of necessity, with whom we have to do in this point, as they maintain that goodness is the only essential moral attribute of the Deity, and the motive of all his actions, must, if they will be consistent, maintain, That to will, and directly to cause sin, much more not to hinder it, is consistent with perfect goodness, nay, that goodness is a sufficient motive to justify the willing, and directly causing it.

With regard to them, therefore, it is surely unnecessary to attempt to reconcile the permission of sin with the goodness of God, since an inconsistency between that attribute and the causing of sin would overturn their whole system.

If the causing of moral evil, and being the real author of it, be consistent with perfect goodness, what pretence can there be to say, that not to hinder it is inconsistent with perfect goodness? [363]

What is incumbent upon them, therefore, to prove, is, That the permission of sin is inconsistent with justice; and, upon this point, we are ready to join issue with them.

But what pretence can there be to say, that the permission of sin is perfectly consistent with goodness in the Deity, but inconsistent with justice?

Is it not as easy to conceive that he should permit sin though virtue be his delight, as that he inflicts misery when his sole delight is to bestow happiness? Should it appear incredible, that the permission of sin may tend to promote virtue, to them who believe that the infliction of misery is necessary to promote happiness?

The justice, as well as the goodness of God's moral government of mankind appears in this—that his laws are not arbitrary nor grievous, as it is only by the obedience of them that our nature can be perfected and qualified for future happiness; that he is ready to aid our weakness, to help our infirmities, and not to suffer us to be tempted above what we are able to bear; that he is not strict to mark iniquity, or to execute judgment speedily against an evil work, but is long-suffering, and waits to be gracious; that he is ready to receive the humble penitent to his favour; that he is no respecter of persons, but in every nation, he that fears God and works righteousness is accepted of him; that of every man he will require an account proportioned to the talents he hath received; that he delights in mercy, but hath no pleasure in the death of the wicked; and, therefore, in punishing, will never go beyond the demerit of the criminal, nor beyond what the rules of his universal government require. [364]

There were, in ancient ages, some who said, the way of the Lord is not equal; to whom the Prophet, in the name of God, makes this reply, which, in all ages, is sufficient to repel this accusation. "Hear now, O house of Israel, is not my way equal, are not your ways unequal? When a righteous man turneth away from his righteousness, and committeth iniquity, for his iniquity which he hath done shall he die. Again, When a wicked man turneth away from his wickedness that he hath committed, and doth that which is lawful and right, he shall save his soul alive. O house of Israel, are not my ways equal, are not your ways unequal? Repent, and turn from all your transgressions, so iniquity shall not be your ruin. Cast away from you all your transgressions whereby you have transgressed, and make you a new heart and a new spirit, for why will ye die, O house of Israel? For I have no pleasure in the death of him that dieth, saith the Lord God."

[364, 365]

Another argument for necessity has been lately offered, which we shall very briefly consider.

It has been maintained that the power of thinking is the result of a certain modification of matter, and that a certain configuration of brain makes a soul; and, if man be wholly a material being, it is said that it will not be denied that he must be a mechanical being; that the doctrine of necessity is a direct inference from that of materialism, and its undoubted consequence.

As this argument can have no weight with those who do not see reason to embrace this system of materialism; so, even with those who do, it seems to me to be a mere sophism.

Philosophers have been wont to conceive matter to be an inert passive being, and to have certain properties inconsistent with the power of thinking or of acting. But a philosopher arises,* who proves, we shall suppose, that we were quite mistaken in our notion of matter; that it has not the properties we supposed, and, in fact, has no properties but those of attraction and repulsion; but still he thinks, that, being matter, it will not be denied that it is a mechanical being, and that the doctrine of necessity is a direct inference from that of materialism. [365]

Herein, however, he deceives himself. If matter be what we conceived it to be, it is equally incapable of thinking and of acting freely. But, if the properties from which we drew this conclusion, have no reality, as he thinks he has proved—if it have the powers of attraction and repulsion, and require only a certain configuration to make it think rationally—it will be impossible to shew any good reason why the same configuration may not make it act rationally and freely. If its reproach of solidity, inertness, and sluggishness be wiped off; and if it be raised in our esteem to a nearer approach to the nature of what we call spiritual and immaterial beings, why should it still be nothing but a mechanical being? Is its solidity, inertness, and sluggishness to be first removed to make it capable of thinking, and then restored in order to make it incapable of acting?

Those, therefore, who reason justly from this system of materialism, will easily perceive that the doctrine of necessity is so far from being a direct inference, that it can receive no support from it.

To conclude this Essay:—Extremes of all kinds ought to be avoided; yet men are prone to run into them; and, to shun one extreme, we often run into the contrary.

Of all extremes of opinion, none are more dangerous than those that exalt the powers

* Priestley is intended.—H.

of man too high, on the one hand, or sink them too low, on the other.* [366]

By raising them too high, we feed pride and vainglory, we lose the sense of our dependence upon God, and engage in attempts beyond our abilities. By depressing them too low, we cut the sinews of action and of obligation, and are tempted to think that, as we can do nothing, we have nothing to do, but to be carried passively along by the stream of necessity.

Some good men, apprehending that to kill pride and vainglory, our active powers cannot be too much depressed, have been led, by zeal for religion, to deprive us of all active power.

Other good men, by a like zeal, have been led to depreciate the human understanding, and to put out the light of nature and reason, in order to exalt that of revelation.

Those weapons which were taken up in support of religion, are now employed to overturn it; and what was, by some, accounted the bulwark of orthodoxy, is become the stronghold of atheism and infidelity.

Atheists join hands with Theologians in depriving man of all active power, that they may destroy all moral obligation, and all sense of right and wrong. They join hands with Theologians in depreciating the human understanding, that they may lead us into absolute scepticism.

God, in mercy to the human race, has made us of such a frame that no speculative opinion whatsoever can root out the sense of guilt and demerit when we do wrong, nor the peace and joy of a good conscience when we do what is right. No speculative opinion can root out a regard to the testimony of our senses, of our memory, and of our rational faculties. But we have reason to be jealous of opinions which run counter to those natural sentiments of the human mind, and tend to shake though they never can eradicate them. [367]

There is little reason to fear that the conduct of men, with regard to the concerns of the present life, will ever be much affected, either by the doctrine of necessity, or by scepticism. It were to be wished that men's conduct, with regard to the concerns of another life, were in as little danger from those opinions.

In the present state, we see some who zealously maintain the doctrine of necessity, others who as zealously maintain that of liberty. One would be apt to think, that a practical belief of these contrary systems should produce very different conduct in them that hold them; yet we see no such difference in the affairs of common life.

The Fatalist deliberates, and resolves, and plights his faith. He lays down a plan of conduct, and prosecutes it with vigour and industry. He exhorts and commands, and holds those to be answerable for their conduct to whom he hath committed any charge. He blames those that are false or unfaithful to him, as other men do. He perceives dignity and worth in some characters and actions, and in others demerit and turpitude. He resents injuries, and is grateful for good offices.

If any man should plead the doctrine of necessity to exculpate murder, theft, or robbery, or even wilful negligence in the discharge of his duty, his judge, though a Fatalist, if he had common sense, would laugh at such a plea, and would not allow it even to alleviate the crime.

In all such cases, he sees that it would be absurd not to act and to judge as those ought to do who believe themselves and other men to be free agents, just as the Sceptic, to avoid absurdity, must, when he goes into the world, act and judge like other men who are not Sceptics. [368]

If the Fatalist be as little influenced by the opinion of necessity in his moral and religious concerns, and in his expectations concerning another world, as he is in the common affairs of life, his speculative opinion will probably do him little hurt. But, if he trust so far to the doctrine of necessity, as to indulge sloth and inactivity in his duty, and hope to exculpate himself to his Maker by that doctrine, let him consider whether he sustains this excuse from his servants and dependants, when they are negligent or unfaithful in what is committed to their charge.

Bishop Butler, in his "Analogy," has an excellent chapter upon *the opinion of necessity considered as influencing practice*, which I think highly deserving the consideration of those who are inclined to that opinion.* [369]

* Could Reid have had the thought of the great Pascal in his view?—"Il est dangereux de trop faire voir à l'homme combien il est égal aux bêtes, sans lui montrer sa grandeur. Il est encore dangereux de lui faire trop voir sa grandeur sans sa bassesse. Il est encore plus dangereux de lui laisser ignorer l'un et l'autre. Mais il est tres avantageux de lui représenter l'un et l'autre." (*Pensées*, I. Partie, Art. iv. § 7.)—H.

* Suetonius of Tiberius observes:—"Circa Deos et religiones negligentior erat, quippe addictus mathematicæ, persuasionisque plenus, omnia fato agi." (c. 69.) And, among others, Eusebius has shewn, in general, that the opinion of Necessity operates practically as a powerful incentive to profligacy, injustice and every vice by which the private and public welfare of mankind is subverted. (*Præp. Evang.*, L. vi. c. 6.)—H.

ESSAY V.

OF MORALS.

CHAPTER I.

OF THE FIRST PRINCIPLES OF MORALS.

MORALS, like all other sciences, must have *first principles*, on which all moral reasoning is grounded.

In every branch of knowledge where disputes have been raised, it is useful to distinguish the first principles from the superstructure. They are the foundation on which the whole fabric of the science leans; and whatever is not supported by this foundation can have no stability.

In all rational belief, the thing believed is either itself a first principle, or it is by just reasoning deduced from first principles. When men differ about deductions of reasoning, the appeal must be to the rules of reasoning, which have been very unanimously fixed from the days of Aristotle. But when they differ about a first principle, the appeal is made to another tribunal—to that of *Common Sense*. [370]

How the genuine decisions of Common Sense may be distinguished from the counterfeit, has been considered in Essay Sixth, on the *Intellectual Powers of Man*, chapter fourth, to which the reader is referred. What I would here observe is, That, as first principles differ from deductions of reasoning in the nature of their evidence, and must be tried by a different standard when they are called in question, it is of importance to know to which of these two classes a truth which we would examine, belongs. When they are not distinguished, men are apt to demand proof for everything they think fit to deny. And when we attempt to prove, by direct argument, what is really self-evident, the reasoning will always be inconclusive; for it will either take for granted the thing to be proved, or something not more evident; and so, instead of giving strength to the conclusion, will rather tempt those to doubt of it who never did so before.

I propose, therefore, in this chapter, to point out some of the first principles of morals, without pretending to a complete enumeration.

The principles I am to mention, relate either [A] to *virtue in general*, or [B] to the different *particular branches of virtue*, or [C] to the *comparison of virtues* where they seem to interfere.

[A] 1. *There are some things in human conduct that merit approbation and praise, others that merit blame and punishment; and different degrees either of approbation or of blame, are due to different actions.*

2. *What is in no degree voluntary, can neither deserve moral approbation nor blame.*

3. *What is done from unavoidable necessity may be agreeable or disagreeable, useful or hurtful, but cannot be the object either of blame or of moral approbation.*

4. *Men may be highly culpable in omitting what they ought to have done, as well as in doing what they ought not.* [371]

5. *We ought to use the best means we can to be well informed of our duty*—by serious attention to moral instruction; by observing what we approve, and what we disapprove, in other men, whether our acquaintance, or those whose actions are recorded in history; by reflecting often, in a calm and dispassionate hour, on our own past conduct, that we may discern what was wrong, what was right, and what might have been better; by deliberating coolly and impartially upon our future conduct, as far as we can foresee the opportunities we may have of doing good, or the temptations to do wrong; and by having this principle deeply fixed in our minds, that, as moral excellence is the true worth and glory of a man, so the knowledge of our duty is to every man, in every station of life, the most important of all knowledge.

6. *It ought to be our most serious concern to do our duty as far as we know it, and to fortify our minds against every temptation to deviate from it*—by maintaining a lively sense of the beauty of right conduct, and of its present and future reward, of the turpitude of vice, and of its bad consequences here and hereafter; by having always in our eye the noblest examples; by the habit of subjecting our passions to the government of reason; by firm purposes and resolutions with regard to our conduct; by avoiding occasions of temptation when we can; and by imploring the aid of Him who made us, in every hour of temptation.

These principles concerning virtue and vice *in general*, must appear self-evident to every man who hath a conscience, and who hath taken pains to exercise this natural power of his mind. I proceed to others that are *more particular*.

[B] 1. *We ought to prefer a greater good, though more distant, to a less; and a less evil to a greater.* [372]

A regard to our own good, though we had no conscience, dictates this principle; and we cannot help disapproving the man that acts contrary to it, as deserving to lose the good which he wantonly threw away, and to suffer the evil which he knowingly brought upon his own head.

We observed before, that the ancient moralists, and many among the modern, have deduced the whole of morals from this principle, and that, when we make a right estimate of goods and evils according to their degree, their dignity, their duration, and according as they are more or less in our power, it leads to the practice of every virtue. More directly, indeed, to the virtues of self-government, to prudence, to temperance, and to fortitude; and, though more indirectly, even to justice, humanity, and all the social virtues, when their influence upon our happiness is well understood.

Though it be not the noblest principle of conduct, it has this peculiar advantage, that its force is felt by the most ignorant, and even by the most abandoned.

Let a man's moral judgment be ever so little improved by exercise, or ever so much corrupted by bad habits, he cannot be indifferent to his own happiness or misery. When he is become insensible to every nobler motive to right conduct, he cannot be insensible to this. And though to act from this motive solely may be called *prudence* rather than *virtue*, yet this prudence deserves some regard upon its own account, and much more as it is the friend and ally of virtue, and the enemy of all vice; and as it gives a favourable testimony of virtue to those who are deaf to every other recommendation.

If a man can be induced to do his duty even from a regard to his own happiness, he will soon find reason to love virtue for her own sake, and to act from motives less mercenary. [373]

I cannot therefore approve of those moralists who would banish all persuasives to virtue taken from the consideration of private good. In the present state of human nature these are not useless to the best, and they are the only means left of reclaiming the abandoned.

2. *As far as the intention of nature appears in the constitution of man, we ought to comply with that intention, and to act agreeably to it.*

The Author of our being hath given us not only the power of acting within a limited sphere, but various principles or springs of action, of different nature and dignity, to direct us in the exercise of our active power.

From the constitution of every species of the inferior animals, and especially from the active principles which nature has given them, we easily perceive the manner of life for which nature intended them; and they uniformly act the part to which they are led by their constitution, without any reflection upon it, or intention of obeying its dictates. Man only, of the inhabitants of this world, is made capable of observing his own constitution, what kind of life it is made for, and of acting according to that intention, or contrary to it. He only is capable of yielding an intentional obedience to the dictates of his nature, or of rebelling against them.

In treating of the principles of action in man, it has been shewn, that, as his natural instincts and bodily appetites are well adapted to the preservation of his natural life, and to the continuance of the species; so his natural desires, affections, and passions, when uncorrupted by vicious habits, and under the government of the leading principles of reason and conscience, are excellently fitted for the rational and social life. Every vicious action shews an excess, or defect, or wrong direction of some natural spring of action, and therefore may, very justly, be said to be unnatural. Every virtuous action agrees with the uncorrupted principles of human nature. [374]

The Stoics defined Virtue to be *a life according to nature*. Some of them more accurately, *a life according to the nature of man, in so far as it is superior to that of brutes*. The life of a brute is according to the nature of the brute; but it is neither virtuous nor vicious. The life of a moral agent cannot be according to his nature, unless it be virtuous. That conscience which is in every man's breast, is the law of God written in his heart, which he can not disobey without acting unnaturally, and being self-condemned.

The intention of nature, in the various active principles of man—in the desires of power, of knowledge, and of esteem, in the affection to children, to near relations, and to the communities to which we belong, in gratitude, in compassion, and even in resentment and emulation—is very obvious, and has been pointed out in treating of those principles. Nor is it less evident, that reason and conscience are given us to regulate the inferior principles, so that they may conspire, in a regular and consistent plan of life, in pursuit of some worthy end.

3. *No man is born for himself only.* Every man, therefore, ought to consider himself as a member of the common society of mankind, and of those subordinate societies to which he belongs, such as family, friends, neighbourhood, country, and to do

as much good as he can, and as little hurt to the societies of which he is a part.

This axiom leads directly to the practice of every social virtue, and indirectly to the virtues of self-government, by which only we can be qualified for discharging the duty we owe to society. [375]

4. *In every case, we ought to act that part towards another, which we would judge to be right in him to act toward us, if we were in his circumstances and he in ours;* or, more generally—*What we approve in others, that we ought to practise in like circumstances, and what we condemn in others we ought not to do.*

If there be any such thing as right and wrong in the conduct of moral agents, it must be the same to all in the same circumstances.

We stand all in the same relation to Him who made us, and will call us to account for our conduct; for with Him there is no respect of persons. We stand in the same relation to one another as members of the great community of mankind. The duties consequent upon the different ranks and offices and relations of men are the same to all in the same circumstances.

It is not want of judgment, but want of candour and impartiality, that hinders men from discerning what they owe to others. They are quicksighted enough in discerning what is due to themselves. When they are injured, or ill-treated, they see it, and feel resentment. It is the want of candour that makes men use one measure for the duty they owe to others, and another measure for the duty that others owe to them in like circumstances. That men ought to judge with candour, as in all other cases, so especially in what concerns their moral conduct, is surely self-evident to every intelligent being. The man who takes offence when he is injured in his person, in his property, in his good name, pronounces judgment against himself if he act so toward his neighbour.

As the equity and obligation of this rule of conduct is self-evident to every man who hath a conscience; so it is, of all the rules of morality, the most comprehensive, and truly deserves the encomium given it by the highest authority, that "*it is the law and the prophets.*" [376]

It comprehends every rule of justice without exception. It comprehends all the relative duties, arising either from the more permanent relations of parent and child, of master and servant, of magistrate and subject, of husband and wife, or from the more transient relations of rich and poor, of buyer and seller, of debtor and creditor, of benefactor and beneficiary, of friend and enemy. It comprehends every duty of charity and humanity, and even of courtesy and good manners.

Nay, I think, that, without any force or straining, it extends even to the duties of self-government. For, as every man approves in others the virtues of prudence, temperance, self-command, and fortitude, he must perceive that what is right in others must be right in himself in like circumstances.

To sum up all, he who acts invariably by this rule will never deviate from the path of his duty, but from an error of judgment. And, as he feels the obligation that he and all men are under to use the best means in his power to have his judgment well-informed in matters of duty, his errors will only be such as are invincible.

It may be observed, that this axiom supposes a faculty in man by which he can distinguish right conduct from wrong. It supposes also, that, by this faculty, we easily perceive the right and the wrong in other men that are indifferent to us; but are very apt to be blinded by the partiality of selfish passions when the case concerns ourselves. Every claim we have against others is apt to be magnified by self-love, when viewed directly. A change of persons removes this prejudice, and brings the claim to appear in its just magnitude. [377]

5. *To every man who believes the existence, the perfections, and the providence of God, the veneration and submission we owe to him is self-evident.* Right sentiments of the Deity and of his works, not only make the duty we owe to him obvious to every intelligent being, but likewise add the authority of a Divine law to every rule of right conduct.

[C.] There is another class of axioms in morals, by which, when there seems to be an *opposition* between the actions that different virtues lead to, we determine to which the *preference* is due.

Between the several virtues, as they are dispositions of mind, or determinations of will, to act according to a certain general rule, there can be no opposition. They dwell together most amicably, and give mutual aid and ornament, without the possibility of hostility or opposition, and, taken altogether, make one uniform and consistent rule of conduct. But, between particular external actions, which different virtues would lead to, there may be an opposition. Thus, the same man may be in his heart, generous, grateful, and just. These dispositions strengthen, but never can weaken one another. Yet it may happen, that an external action which generosity or gratitude solicits, justice may forbid.

That in all such cases, *unmerited generosity should yield to gratitude, and both to justice*, is self-evident. Nor is it less so, that *unmerited beneficence to those who are at ease should yield to compassion to the miserable*, and *external acts of piety to works of mercy*, because God loves mercy more than sacrifice.

At the same time, we perceive, that those acts of virtue which ought to yield in the case of a competition, have most intrinsic worth when there is no competition. Thus, it is evident that there is more worth in pure and unmerited benevolence than in compassion, more in compassion than in gratitude, and more in gratitude than in justice. [378]

I call these *first principles*, because they appear to me to have in themselves an intuitive evidence which I cannot resist. I find I can express them in other words. I can illustrate them by examples and authorities, and perhaps can deduce one of them from another; but I am not able to deduce them from other principles that are more evident. And I find the best moral reasonings of authors I am acquainted with, ancient and modern, Heathen and Christian, to be grounded upon one or more of them.

The evidence of mathematical axioms is not discerned till men come to a certain degree of maturity of understanding. A boy must have formed the general conception of *quantity*, and of *more* and *less* and *equal*, of *sum* and *difference*; and he must have been accustomed to judge of these relations in matters of common life, before he can perceive the evidence of the mathematical axiom—that equal quantities, added to equal quantities, make equal sums.

In like manner, our Moral Judgment or Conscience, grows to maturity from an imperceptible seed, planted by our Creator. When we are capable of contemplating the actions of other men, or of reflecting upon our own calmly and dispassionately, we begin to perceive in them the qualities of honest and dishonest, of honourable and base, of right and wrong, and to feel the sentiments of moral approbation and disapprobation.

These sentiments are at first feeble, easily warped by passions and prejudices, and apt to yield to authority. By use and time, the judgment, in morals, as in other matters, gathers strength, and feels more vigour. We begin to distinguish the dictates of passion from those of cool reason, and to perceive that it is not always safe to rely upon the judgment of others. By an impulse of nature, we venture to judge for ourselves, as we venture to walk by ourselves. [379]

There is a strong analogy between the progress of the body from infancy to maturity, and the progress of all the powers of the mind. This progression in both is the work of nature, and in both may be greatly aided or hurt by proper education. It is natural to a man to be able to walk, or run, or leap; but, if his limbs had been kept in fetters from his birth, he would have none of those powers. It is no less natural to a man trained in society, and accustomed to judge of his own actions and those of other men, to perceive a right and a wrong, an honourable and a base, in human conduct; and to such a man, I think, the principles of morals I have above mentioned will appear self-evident. Yet there may be individuals of the human species so little accustomed to think or judge of anything but of gratifying their animal appetites, as to have hardly any conception of right or wrong in conduct, or any moral judgment; as there certainly are some who have not the conceptions and the judgment necessary to understand the axioms of geometry.

From the principles above mentioned, the whole system of moral conduct follows so easily, and with so little aid of reasoning, that every man of common understanding, who wishes to know his duty, may know it. The path of duty is a plain path, which the upright in heart can rarely mistake. Such it must be, since every man is bound to walk in it. There are some intricate cases in morals which admit of disputation; but these seldom occur in practice; and, when they do, the learned disputant has no great advantage: for the unlearned man, who uses the best means in his power to know his duty, and acts according to his knowledge, is inculpable in the sight of God and man. He may err, but he is not guilty of immorality. [380]

CHAPTER II.

OF SYSTEMS OF MORALS.

If the knowledge of our duty be so level to the apprehension of all men as has been represented in the last chapter, it may seem hardly to deserve the name of a Science. It may seem that there is no need for instruction in morals.

From what cause then has it happened, that we have many large and learned systems of Moral Philosophy, and systems of Natural Jurisprudence, or the Law of Nature and Nations; and that, in modern times, public professions* have been instituted in most places of education for instructing youth in these branches of knowledge?

This event, I think, may be accounted for, and the utility of such systems and professions* justified, without supposing any difficulty or intricacy in the knowledge of our duty.

* Professorships.—H.

I am far from thinking instruction in morals unnecessary. Men may, to the end of life, be ignorant of self-evident truths. They may, to the end of life, entertain gross absurdities. Experience shews that this happens often in matters that are indifferent. Much more may it happen in matters where interest, passion, prejudice, and fashion, are so apt to pervert the judgment.

The most obvious truths are not perceived without some ripeness of judgment. For we see that children may be made to believe anything, though ever so absurd. Our judgment of things is ripened, not by time only, but chiefly by being exercised about things of the same or of a similar kind. [381]

Judgment, even in things self-evident, requires a clear, distinct, and steady conception of the things about which we judge. Our conceptions are at first obscure and wavering. The habit of attending to them is necessary to make them distinct and steady; and this habit requires an exertion of mind to which many of our animal principles are unfriendly. The love of truth calls for it; but its still voice is often drowned by the louder call of some passion, or we are hindered from listening to it by laziness and desultoriness. Thus men often remain through life ignorant of things which they needed but to open their eyes to see, and which they would have seen if their attention had been turned to them.

The most knowing derive the greatest part of their knowledge, even in things obvious, from instruction and information, and from being taught to exercise their natural faculties, which, without instruction, would lie dormant.

I am very apt to think, that, if a man could be reared from infancy, without any society of his fellow-creatures, he would hardly ever shew any sign, either of moral judgment, or of the power of reasoning. His own actions would be directed by his animal appetites and passions, without cool reflection, and he would have no access to improve, by observing the conduct of other beings like himself.

The power of vegetation in the seed of a plant, without heat and moisture, would for ever lie dormant. The rational and moral powers of man would perhaps lie dormant without instruction and example. Yet these powers are a part, and the noblest part, of his constitution; as the power of vegetation is of the seed. [382]

Our first moral conceptions* are probably got by attending coolly to the conduct of others, and observing what moves our approbation, what our indignation. These sentiments* spring from our moral faculty as naturally as the sensations of sweet and bitter from the faculty of taste. They have their natural objects. But most human actions are of a mixed nature, and have various colours, according as they are viewed on different sides. Prejudice against or in favour of the person, is apt to warp our opinion. It requires attention and candour to distinguish the good from the ill, and, without favour or prejudice, to form a clear and impartial judgment. In this we may be greatly aided by instruction.

He must be very ignorant of human nature, who does not perceive that the seed of virtue in the mind of man, like that of a tender plant in an unkindly soil, requires care and culture in the first period of life, as well as our own exertion when we come to maturity.

If the irregularities of passion and appetite be timely checked, and good habits planted; if we be excited by good examples, and bad examples be shewn in their proper colour; if the attention be prudently directed to the precepts of wisdom and virtue, as the mind is capable of receiving them—a man thus trained will rarely be at a loss to distinguish good from ill in his own conduct, without the labour of reasoning.

The bulk of mankind have but little of this culture in the proper season; and what they have is often unskilfully applied; by which means bad habits gather strength, and false notions of pleasure, of honour, and of interest occupy the mind. They give little attention to what is right and honest. Conscience is seldom consulted, and so little exercised that its decisions are weak and wavering. Although, therefore, to a ripe understanding, free from prejudice, and accustomed to judge of the morality of actions, most truths in morals will appear self-evident, it does not follow that moral instruction is unnecessary in the first part of life, or that it may not be very profitable in its more advanced period. [383]

The history of past ages shews that nations, highly civilized and greatly enlightened in many arts and sciences, may, for ages, not only hold the grossest absurdities with regard to the Deity and his worship, but with regard to the duty we owe to our fellow-men, particularly to children, to servants, to strangers, to enemies, and to those who differ from us in religious opinions.

Such corruptions in religion and in morals had spread so wide among mankind, and were so confirmed by custom, as to require a light from heaven to correct them. Revelation was not intended to supersede, but to aid the use of our natural faculties; and I doubt not but the attention given to moral truths, in such systems as we have mentioned, has contributed much to correct the

* *Moral Conceptions* and *Moral Sentiments*, though related, ought not to be used convertibly.—H.

errors and prejudices of former ages, and may continue to have the same good effect in time to come.

It needs not seem strange that systems of morals may swell to great magnitude, if we consider that, although the general principles be few and simple, their application extends to every part of human conduct, in every condition, every relation, and every transaction of life. They are the rule of life to the magistrate and to the subject, to the master and to the servant, to the parent and to the child, to the fellow-citizen and to the alien, to the friend and to the enemy, to the buyer and to the seller, to the borrower and to the lender. Every human creature is subject to their authority in his actions and words, and even in his thoughts. They may, in this respect, be compared to the laws of motion in the natural world, which, though few and simple, serve to regulate an infinite variety of operations throughout the universe. [384]

And as the beauty of the laws of motion is displayed in the most striking manner, when we trace them through all the variety of their effects; so the divine beauty and sanctity of the principles of morals appear most august when we take a comprehensive view of their application to every condition and relation, and to every transaction of human society.

This is, or ought to be, the design of systems of morals. They may be made more or less extensive, having no limits fixed by nature, but the wide circle of human transactions. When the principles are applied to these in detail, the detail is pleasant and profitable. It requires no profound reasoning, (excepting, perhaps, in a few disputable points.) It admits of the most agreeable illustration from examples and authorities; it serves to exercise, and thereby to strengthen, moral judgment. And one who has given much attention to the duty of man, in all the various relations and circumstances of life, will probably be more enlightened in his own duty, and more able to enlighten others.

The first writers in morals, we are acquainted with, delivered their moral instructions, not in systems, but in short unconnected sentences, or aphorisms. They saw no need for deductions of reasoning, because the truths they delivered could not but be admitted by the candid and attentive.

Subsequent writers, to improve the way of treating this subject, gave method and arrangement to moral truths, by reducing them under certain divisions and subdivisions, as parts of one whole. By these means the whole is more easily comprehended and remembered, and from this arrangement gets the name of a system and of a science. [385]

A system of morals is not like a system of geometry, where the subsequent parts derive their evidence from the preceding, and one chain of reasoning is carried on from the beginning; so that, if the arrangement is changed, the chain is broken, and the evidence is lost. It resembles more a system of botany, or mineralogy, where the subsequent parts depend not for their evidence upon the preceding, and the arrangement is made to facilitate apprehension and memory, and not to give evidence.

Morals have been methodised in different ways. The ancients commonly arranged them under the four cardinal virtues of Prudence, Temperance, Fortitude, and Justice;* Christian writers, I think more properly, under the three heads of the Duty we owe to God—to Ourselves—and to our Neighbour. One division may be more comprehensive, or more natural, than another; but the truths arranged are the same, and their evidence the same in all.

I shall only farther observe, with regard to systems of morals, that they have been made more voluminous and more intricate, partly by mixing political questions with morals, which I think improper, because they belong to a different science, and are grounded on different principles; partly by making what is commonly, but I think improperly, called *the Theory of Morals*, a part of the system.

By the Theory of Morals is meant a just account of the structure of our moral powers—that is, of those powers of the mind by which we have our moral conceptions, and distinguish right from wrong in human actions. This, indeed, is an intricate subject, and there have been various theories and much controversy about it in ancient and in modern times. But it has little connection with the knowledge of our duty; and those who differ most in the theory of our moral powers, agree in the practical rules of morals which they dictate.

As a man may be a good judge of colours, and of the other visible qualities of objects, without any knowledge of the anatomy of the eye, and of the theory of vision; so a man may have a very clear and comprehensive knowledge of what is right and what is wrong in human conduct, who never studied the structure of our moral powers. [386]

* This particular distribution was introduced by the Stoics, and adopted from them by Cicero. But a doctrine of four fundamental virtues is to be traced to Plato, and even to Socrates. These, according to the latter, are—Piety (εὐσέβεια), Self-restraint (ἐγκράτεια), Fortitude (ἀνδρία), and Justice (δικαιοσύνη); according to the former—Wisdom (σοφία), Temperance (σωφροσύνη), Fortitude (ἀνδρεία), and Justice (δικαιοσύνη.) Aristotle did not countenance such a reduction.—H.

A good ear in music may be much improved by attention and practice in that art; but very little by studying the anatomy of the ear, and the theory of sound. In order to acquire a good eye or a good ear in the arts that require them, the theory of vision and the theory of sound are by no means necessary, and indeed of very little use. Of as little necessity or use is what we call the theory of morals, in order to improve our moral judgment.

I mean not to depreciate this branch of knowledge. It is a very important part of the philosophy of the human mind, and ought to be considered as such, but not as any part of morals. By the name we give to it, and by the custom of making it a part of every system of morals, men may be led into this gross mistake, which I wish to obviate, That, in order to understand his duty, a man must needs be a philosopher and a metaphysician. [387]

CHAPTER III.

OF SYSTEMS OF NATURAL JURISPRUDENCE.

Systems of Natural Jurisprudence, of the Rights of Peace and War, or of the Law of Nature and Nations, are a modern invention, which soon acquired such reputation as gave occasion to many public establishments for teaching it along with the other sciences. It has so close a relation to morals, that it may answer the purpose of a system of morals, and is commonly put in the place of it, as far, at least, as concerns our duty to our fellow-men. They differ in the name and form, but agree in substance. This will appear from a slight attention to the nature of both.

The direct intention of Morals is to teach the duty of men: that of Natural Jurisprudence to teach the rights of men. Right and Duty are things very different, and have even a kind of opposition; yet they are so related that the one cannot even be conceived without the other; and he that understands the one must understand the other.

They have the same relation which credit has to debt. As all credit supposes an equivalent debt, so all right supposes a corresponding duty. There can be no credit in one party without an equivalent debt in another party; and there can be no right in one party, without a corresponding duty in another party. The sum of credit shews the sum of debt; and the sum of men's rights shews, in like manner, the sum of their duty to one another. [388]

The Word *Right* has a very different meaning, according as it is applied to actions or to persons. A right action is an action agreeable to our duty. But, when we speak of the *rights of men*, the word has a very different and a more artificial meaning. It is a term of art in law, and signifies all that a man may lawfully do, all that he may lawfully possess and use, and all that he he may lawfully claim of any other person.

This comprehensive meaning of the word *right*, and of the Latin word *jus*, which corresponds to it, though long adopted into common language, is too artificial to be the birth of common language. It is a term of art, contrived by Civilians when the Civil Law became a profession.

The whole end and object of Law is to protect the subjects in all that they may lawfully *do*, or *possess*, or *demand*. This threefold object of law, Civilians have comprehended under the word *jus* or *right*, which they define, "*Facultas aliquid agendi, vel possidendi, vel ab alio consequendi:*" "A lawful claim to *do anything*, to *possess anything*, or to *demand some prestation from some other person*." The first of these may be called the right of *liberty*; the second that of *property*, which is also called a *real right*; the third is called *personal right*, because it respects some particular person or persons of whom the prestation may be demanded.

We can be at no loss to perceive the Duties corresponding to the several kinds of Rights. What I have a right to do, it is the duty of all men not to hinder me from doing. What is my property or real right, no man ought to take from me; or to molest me in the use and enjoyment of it. And what I have a right to demand of any man, it is his duty to perform. Between the right, on the one hand, and the duty, on the other, there is not only a necessary connection, but, in reality, they are only different expressions of the same meaning; just as it is the same thing to say, I am your debtor, and to say, You are my creditor; or as it is the same thing to say, I am your father, and to say, You are my son. [389]

Thus we see, that there is such a correspondence between the rights of men and the duties of men, that the one points out the other; and a system of the one may be substituted for a system of the other.

But here an objection occurs. It may be said, *That, although every right implies a duty, yet every duty does not imply a right.* Thus, it may be my duty to do a humane or kind office to a man who has no claim of right to it; and therefore a system of the rights of men, though it teach all the duties of strict justice, yet it leaves out all the duties of charity and humanity, without which the system of morals must be very lame.

In answer to this objection, it may be observed, That, as there is a strict notion of justice, in which it is distinguished from humanity and charity, so there is a more extensive signification of it, in which it includes those virtues. The ancient moralists, both Greek and Roman, under the cardinal virtue of justice, included beneficence; and, in this extensive sense, it is often used in common language. The like may be said of right, which, in a sense not uncommon, is extended to every proper claim of humanity and charity, as well as to the claims of strict justice. But, as it is proper to distinguish these two kinds of claims by different names, writers in natural jurisprudence have given the name of *perfect* rights to the claims of strict justice, and that of *imperfect* rights to the claims of charity and humanity. Thus, all the duties of humanity have imperfect rights corresponding to them, as those of strict justice have perfect rights.

Another objection may be, *That there is still a class of duties to which no right, perfect or imperfect, corresponds.* [390]

We are bound in duty to pay due respect, not only to what is truly the right of another, but to what, through ignorance or mistake, we believe to be his right. Thus, if my neighbour is possessed of a horse which he stole, and to which he has no right, while I believe the horse to be really his, and am ignorant of the theft, it is my duty to pay the same respect to this conceived right as if it were real. Here, then, is a moral obligation on one party without any corresponding right on the other.

To supply this defect in the system of rights, so as to make right and duty correspond in every instance, writers in jurisprudence have had recourse to something like what is called a fiction of law. They give the name of *right* to the claim which even the thief hath to the goods he has stolen, while the theft is unknown, and to all similar claims grounded on the ignorance or mistake of the parties concerned. And to distinguish this kind of right from genuine rights, perfect or imperfect, they call it an *external* right.

Thus it appears, That, although a system of the perfect rights of men, or the rights of strict justice, would be a lame substitute for a system of human duty, yet, when we add to it the imperfect and the external rights, it comprehends the whole duty we owe to our fellow-men.

But it may be asked, *Why should men be taught their duty in this indirect way, by reflection, as it were, from the rights of other men?*

Perhaps it may be thought that this indirect way may be more agreeable to the pride of man, as we see that men of rank like better to hear of obligations of honour than of obligations of duty (although the dictates of true honour and of duty be the same;) for this reason that honour puts a man in mind of what he owes to himself, whereas duty is a more humiliating idea. For a like reason, men may attend more willingly to their rights which put them in mind of their dignity, than to their duties, which suggest their dependence. And we see that men may give great attention to their rights who give but little to their duty. [391]

Whatever truth there may be in this, I believe better reasons can be given why systems of natural jurisprudence have been contrived and put in the place of systems of morals.

Systems of Civil Law were invented many ages before we had any system of Natural Jurisprudence; and the former seem to have suggested the idea of the latter.

Such is the weakness of human understanding, that no large body of knowledge can be easily apprehended and remembered, unless it be arranged and methodised—that is, reduced into a system. When the laws of the Roman people were multiplied to a great degree, and the study of them became an honourable and lucrative profession, it became necessary that they should be methodised into a system. And the most natural and obvious way of methodising law, was found to be according to the divisions and subdivisions of men's rights, which it is the intention of law to protect.

The study of law produced not only systems of law, but a language proper for expressing them. Every art has its terms of art for expressing the conceptions that belong to it; and the civilian must have terms for expressing accurately the divisions and subdivisions of rights, and the various ways whereby they may be acquired, transferred, or extinguished, in the various transactions of civil society. He must have terms accurately defined, for the various crimes by which men's rights are violated, not to speak of the terms which express the different forms of actions at law, and the various steps of the procedure of judicatories. [392]

Those who have been bred to any profession are very prone to use the terms of their profession in speaking or writing on subjects that have any analogy to it. And they may do so with advantage, as terms of art are commonly more precise in their signification, and better defined, than the words of common language. To such persons, it is also very natural to model and arrange other subjects, as far as their nature admits, into a method similar to that of the system which fills their minds.

It might, therefore, be expected that a civilian, intending to give a detailed system of morals, would use many of the terms of civil law, and mould it, as far as it can be done, into the form of a system of law, or of the rights of mankind.

The necessary and close relation of right to duty, which we before observed, justified this. And Moral Duty had long been considered as a *law of nature*; a law, not wrote on tables of stone or brass, but on the heart of man; a law of greater antiquity and higher authority than the laws of particular states; a law which is binding upon all men of all nations, and, therefore, is called by Cicero *the law of nature and of nations.*

The idea of a system of this law was worthy of the genius of the immortal Hugo Grotius, and he was the first who executed it in such a manner as to draw the attention of the learned in all the European nations; and to give occasion to several princes and states to establish public professions for the teaching of this law.

The multitude of commentators and annotators upon this work of Grotius, and the public establishments to which it gave occasion, are sufficient vouchers of its merit.

It is, indeed, a work so well designed, and so skilfully executed; so free from the scholastic jargon which infected the learned at that time; so much addressed to the common sense and moral judgment of mankind; and so agreeably illustrated by examples from ancient history, and authorities from the sentiments of ancient authors, heathen and Christian, that it must always be esteemed as the capital work of a great genius upon a most important subject. [393]

The utility of a just system of natural jurisprudence appears—1. As it is a system of the moral duty we owe to men, which, by the aid they have taken from the terms and divisions of the civil law, has been given more in detail and more systematically by writers in natural jurisprudence than it was formerly. 2. As it is the best preparation for the study of law, being, as it were, cast in the mould, and using and explaining many of the terms of the civil law, on which the law of most of the European nations is grounded. 3. It is of use to lawgivers, who ought to make their laws as agreeable as possible to the law of nature. And as laws made by men, like all human works, must be imperfect, it points out the errors and imperfections of human laws. 4. To judges and interpreters of the law it is of use, because that interpretation ought to be preferred which is founded in the law of nature. 5. It is of use in civil controversies between states, or between individuals who have no common superior. In such controversies, the appeal must be made to the law of nature; and the standard systems of it, particularly that of Grotius, have great authority. And, 6, To say no more upon this point, it is of great use to sovereigns and states who are above all human laws, to be solemnly admonished of the conduct they are bound to observe to their own subjects, to the subjects of other states, and to one another, in peace and in war. The better and the more generally the law of nature is understood, the greater dishonour, in public estimation, will follow every violation of it. [394]

Some authors have imagined that systems of natural jurisprudence ought to be confined to the perfect rights of men, because the duties which correspond to the imperfect rights, the duties of charity and humanity, cannot be enforced by human laws, but must be left to the judgment and conscience of men, free from compulsion. But the systems which have had the greatest applause of the public, have not followed this plan, and, I conceive, for good reasons. *First*, Because a system of perfect rights could by no means serve the purpose of a system of morals, which surely is an important purpose. *Secondly*, Because, in many cases, it is hardly possible to fix the precise limit between justice and humanity, between perfect and imperfect right. Like the colours in a prismatic image, they run into each other, so that the best eye cannot fix the precise boundary between them. *Thirdly*, As wise legislators and magistrates ought to have it as their end to make the citizens good as well as just, we find, in all civilized nations, laws that are intended to encourage the duties of humanity. Where human laws cannot enforce them by punishments, they may encourage them by rewards. Of this the wisest legislators have given examples; and how far this branch of legislation may be carried, no man can foresee.

The substance of the four following chapters was wrote long ago, and read in a literary society,* with a view to justify some points of morals from metaphysical objections urged against them in the writings of David Hume, Esq. If they answer that end, and, at the same time, serve to illustrate the account I have given of our moral powers, it is hoped that the reader will not think them improperly placed here; and that he will forgive some repetitions, and perhaps anachronisms, occasioned by their being wrote at different times, and on different occasions. [395]

* Probably the Philosophical Society in Aberdeen, and, if so, these chapters were written before 1764. See above, pp. 7, a, 61, b.—H.

CHAPTER IV.

WHETHER AN ACTION DESERVING MORAL APPROBATION, MUST BE DONE WITH THE BELIEF OF ITS BEING MORALLY GOOD.

There is no part of philosophy more subtile and intricate than that which is called *The Theory of Morals.* Nor is there any more plain and level to the apprehension of man than the practical part of morals.

In the former, the Epicurean, the Peripatetic, and the Stoic, had each his different system of old; and almost every modern author of reputation has a system of his own. At the same time there is no branch of human knowledge, in which there is so general an agreement among ancients and moderns, learned and unlearned, as in the practical rules of morals.

From this discord in the theory, and harmony in the practical part, we may judge that the rules of morality stand upon another and a firmer foundation than the theory. And of this it is easy to perceive the reason.

For, in order to know what is right and what is wrong in human conduct, we need only listen to the dictates of our conscience when the mind is calm and unruffled, or attend to the judgment we form of others in like circumstances. But, to judge of the various theories of morals, we must be able to analyze and dissect, as it were, the active powers of the human mind, and especially to analyze accurately that conscience or moral power by which we discern right from wrong. [396]

The conscience may be compared to the eye in this as in many other respects. The learned and the unlearned see objects with equal distinctness. The former have no title to dictate to the latter, as far as the eye is judge, nor is there any disagreement about such matters. But, to dissect the eye, and to explain the theory of vision, is a difficult point, wherein the most skilful have differed.

From this remarkable disparity between our decisions in the theory of morals and in the rules of morality, we may, I think, draw this conclusion, That wherever we find any disagreement between the practical rules of morality, which have been received in all ages, and the principles of any of the theories advanced upon this subject, the practical rules ought to be the standard by which the theory is to be corrected, and that it is both unsafe and unphilosophical to warp the practical rules, in order to make them tally with a favourite theory.

The question to be considered in this chapter belongs to the practical part of morals, and therefore is capable of a more easy and more certain determination. And, if it be determined in the affirmative, I conceive that it may serve as a touchstone to try some celebrated theories which are inconsistent with that determination, and which have led the theorists to oppose it by very subtile metaphysical arguments.

Every question about what is or is not the proper object of moral approbation, belongs to practical morals, and such is the question now under consideration :—*Whether actions deserving moral approbation must be done with the belief of their being morally good?* or, *Whether an action, done without any regard to duty or to the dictates of conscience, can be entitled to moral approbation?* [397]

In every action of a moral agent, his conscience is either altogether silent, or it pronounces the action to be *good*, or *bad*, or *indifferent.* This, I think, is a complete enumeration. If it be perfectly silent, the action must be very trifling, or appear so. For conscience, in those who have exercised it, is a very pragmatical faculty, and meddles with every part of our conduct, whether we desire its counsel or not. And what a man does in perfect simplicity, without the least suspicion of its being bad, his heart cannot condemn him for, nor will He that knows the heart condemn him. If there was any previous culpable negligence or inattention which led him to a wrong judgment, or hindered his forming a right one, that I do not exculpate. I only consider the action done, and the disposition with which it was done, without its previous circumstances. And in this there appears nothing that merits disapprobation. As little can it merit any degree of moral approbation, because there was neither good nor ill intended. And the same may be said when conscience pronounces the action to be indifferent.

If, in the *second* place, I do what my conscience pronounces to be bad or dubious, I am guilty to myself, and justly deserve the disapprobation of others. Nor am I less guilty in this case, though what I judged to be bad should happen to be good or indifferent. I did it believing it to be bad, and this is an immorality.

Lastly, If I do what my conscience pronounces to be right and my duty, either I have some regard to duty, or I have none. The last is not supposable; for I believe there is no man so abandoned but that he does what he believes to be his duty, with more assurance and alacrity upon that account. The more weight the rectitude of the action has in determining me to do it, the more I approve of my own conduct. And if my worldly interest, my appetites, or inclinations draw me strongly the contrary way, my following the dictates of my conscience, in opposition to these motives, adds to the moral worth of the action. [398]

When a man acts from an erroneous judgment, if his error be invincible, all agree that he is inculpable. But if his error be owing to some previous negligence or inattention, there seems to be some difference among moralists. This difference, however, is only seeming, and not real. For wherein lies the fault in this case? It must be granted by all, that the fault lies in this and solely in this, that he was not at due pains to have his judgment well informed. Those moralists, therefore, who consider the action and the previous conduct that led to it as one whole, find something to blame in the whole; and they do so most justly. But those who take this whole to pieces, and consider what is blameable and what is right in each part, find all that is blameable in what preceded this wrong judgment, and nothing but what is approvable in what followed it.

Let us suppose, for instance, that a man believes that God has indispensably required him to observe a very rigorous fast in Lent; and that, from a regard to this supposed divine command, he fasts in such manner as is not only a great mortification to his appetite, but even hurtful to his health.

His superstitious opinion may be the effect of a culpable negligence, for which he can by no means be justified. Let him, therefore, bear all the blame upon this account that he deserves. But now, having this opinion fixed in his mind, shall he act according to it or against it? Surely we cannot hesitate a moment in this case. It is evident that, in following the light of his judgment, he acts the part of a good and pious man; whereas, in acting contrary to his judgment, he would be guilty of wilful disobedience to his Maker.

If my servant, by mistaking my orders, does the contrary of what I commanded, believing, at the same time, that he obeys my orders, there may be some fault in his mistake, but to charge him with the crime of disobedience, would be inhuman and unjust. [399]

These determinations appear to me to have intuitive evidence, no less than that of mathematical axioms. A man who is come to years of understanding, and who has exercised his faculties in judging of right and wrong, sees their truth as he sees daylight. Metaphysical arguments brought against them have the same effect as when brought against the evidence of sense: they may puzzle and confound, but they do not convince. It appears, evident, therefore, that those actions only can truly be called virtuous, or deserving of moral approbation, which the agent believed to be right, and to which he was influenced, more or less, by that belief.

If it should be objected, That this principle makes it to be of no consequence to a man's morals, what his opinions may be, providing he acts agreeably to them, the answer is easy.

Morality requires, not only that a man should act according to his judgment, but that he should use the best means in his power that his judgment be according to truth. If he fail in either of these points, he is worthy of blame; but, if he fail in neither, I see not wherein he can be blamed.

When a man must act, and has no longer time to deliberate, he ought to act according to the light of his conscience, even when he is in an error. But, when he has time to deliberate, he ought surely to use all the means in his power to be rightly informed. When he has done so, he may still be in an error; but it is an invincible error, and and cannot justly be imputed to him as a fault. [400]

A *second* objection is, That we immediately approve of benevolence, gratitude, and other primary virtues, without inquiring whether they are practised from a persuasion that they are our duty. And the laws of God place the sum of virtue in loving God and our neighbour, without any provision that we do it from a persuasion that we ought to do so.

The answer to this objection is, That the love of God, the love of our neighbour, justice, gratitude, and other primary virtues, are, by the constitution of human nature, necessarily accompanied with a conviction of their being morally good. We may, therefore, safely presume, that these things are never disjoined, and that every man who practises these virtues does it with a good conscience. In judging of men's conduct, we do not suppose things which cannot happen, nor do the laws of God give decisions upon impossible cases, as they must have done if they supposed the case of a man who thought it contrary to his duty to love God or to love mankind.

But if we wish to know how the laws of God determine the point in question, we ought to observe their decision with regard to such actions as may appear good to one man and ill to another. And here the decisions of scripture are clear: "*Let every man be persuaded in his own mind;*"—"*He that doubteth is condemned if he eat, because he eateth not of faith, for whatsoever is not of faith is sin;*"—"*To him that esteemeth anything to be unclean, it is unclean.*" The Scripture often placeth the sum of virtue in "*living in all good conscience,*" in acting so "*that our hearts condemn us not.*"

The last objection I shall mention is a metaphysical one urged by Mr Hume.

It is a favourite point in his system of morals, *That justice is not a natural but an artificial virtue.* To prove this, he has exerted the whole strength of his reason and eloquence. And as the principle we are considering stood in his way, he takes pains to refute it. [401]

"Suppose," says he, "a person to have lent me a sum of money, on condition that it be restored in a few days. After the expiration of the term, he demands the sum. I ask, what reason or motive have I to restore the money? It will perhaps be said, That my regard to justice and abhorrence of villany and knavery are sufficient reasons for me." And this, he acknowledges, would be a satisfactory answer to a man in his civilized state, and when trained up according to a certain discipline and education. "But, in his rude and more natural condition," says he, "if you are pleased to call such a condition natural, this answer would be rejected as perfectly unintelligible and sophistical.

"For wherein consists this honesty and justice? Not surely in the external action. It must, therefore, consist in the motive from which the external action is derived. This motive can never be a regard to the honesty of the action. For it is a plain fallacy to say, That a virtuous motive is requisite to render an action honest, and, at the same time, that a regard to the honesty is the motive to the action. We can never have a regard to the virtue of an action unless the action be antecedently virtuous."

And, in another place—"To suppose that the mere regard to the virtue of the action is that which rendered it virtuous, is to reason in a circle. An action must be virtuous before we can have a regard to its virtue. Some virtuous motive, therefore, must be antecedent to that regard. Nor is this merely a metaphysical subtility," &c. (*Treatise of Human Nature*, Book III. Part ii. Sect. 1.)

I am not to consider, at this time, how this reasoning is applied to support the author's opinion, That justice is not a natural but an artificial virtue. I consider it only as far as it opposes the principle I have been endeavouring to establish, That, to render an action truly virtuous, the agent must have some regard to its rectitude. And I conceive the whole force of the reasoning amounts to this:— [402]

When we judge an action to be good or bad, it must have been so in its own nature antecedent to that judgment, otherwise the judgment is erroneous. If, therefore, the action be good in its nature, the judgment of the agent cannot make it bad, nor can his judgment make it good if, in its nature, it be bad. For this would be to ascribe to our judgment a strange magical power to transform the nature of things, and to say, that my judging a thing to be what it is not, makes it really to be what I erroneously judge it to be. This, I think, is the objection in its full strength. And, in answer to it—

[1.] *First*, If we could not loose this metaphysical knot, I think we might fairly and honestly cut it, because it fixes an absurdity upon the clearest and most indisputable principles of morals and of common sense. For I appeal to any man whether there be any principle of morality, or any principle of common sense, more clear and indisputable than that which we just now quoted from the Apostle Paul, That, although a thing be not unclean in itself, yet to him that esteemeth it to be unclean, to him it is unclean. But the metaphysical argument makes this absurd. For, says the metaphysician, If the thing was not unclean in itself, you judged wrong in esteeming it to be unclean; and what can be more absurd than that your esteeming a thing to be what it is not, should make it what you erroneously esteem it to be? [403]

Let us try the edge of this argument in another instance. Nothing is more evident than that an action does not merit the name of benevolent, unless it be done from a belief that it tends to promote the good of our neighbour. But this is absurd, says the metaphysician. For, if it be not a benevolent action in itself, your belief of its tendency cannot change its nature. It is absurd that your erroneous belief should make the action to be what you believe it to be. Nothing is more evident than that a man who tells the truth, believing it to be a lie, is guilty of falsehood; but the metaphysician would make this to be absurd.

In a word, if there be any strength in this argument, it would follow, That a man might be, in the highest degree, virtuous, without the least regard to virtue; that he might be very benevolent, without ever intending to do a good office; very malicious, without ever intending any hurt; very revengeful, without ever intending to retaliate an injury; very grateful, without ever intending to return a benefit; and a man of strict veracity, with an intention to lie. We might, therefore, reject this reasoning, as repugnant to self-evident truths, though we were not able to point out the fallacy of it.

2. But let us try, in the *second* place, whether the fallacy of this argument may not be discovered.

We ascribe moral goodness to actions considered abstractly, without any relation to the agent. We likewise ascribe moral goodness to an agent on account of an action he has done; we call it a good action, though, in this case, the goodness is properly in the man, and is only by a figure ascribed to the action. Now, it is to be considered, whether *moral goodness*, when applied to an action considered abstractly, has the same meaning as when we apply it to a man on account of that action; or whether we do not unawares change the meaning of the word, according as we apply it to the one or to the other. [404]

The action, considered abstractly, has neither understanding nor will; it is not accountable, nor can it be under any moral obligation. But all these things are essential to that moral goodness which belongs to a man; for, if a man had not understanding and will, he could have no moral goodness. Hence it follows necessarily, that the moral goodness which we ascribe to an action considered abstractly, and that which we ascribe to a person for doing that action, are not the same. The meaning of the word is changed when it is applied to these different subjects.

This will be more evident, when we consider what is meant by the moral goodness which we ascribe to a man for doing an action, and what by the goodness which belongs to the action considered abstractly. A good action in a man is that in which he applied his intellectual powers properly, in order to judge what he ought to do, and acted according to his best judgment. This is all that can be required of a moral agent; and in this his moral goodness, in any good action, consists. But is this the goodness which we ascribe to an action considered abstractly? No, surely. For the action, considered abstractly, is neither endowed with judgment nor with active power; and, therefore, can have none of that goodness which we ascribe to the man for doing it.

But what do we mean by goodness in an action considered abstractly? To me it appears to lie in this, and in this only, That it is an action which ought to be done by those who have the power and opportunity, and the capacity of perceiving their obligation to do it. I would gladly know of any man, what other moral goodness can be in an action considered abstractly. And this goodness is inherent in its nature, and inseparable from it. No opinion or judgment of an agent can in the least alter its nature.

Suppose the action to be that of relieving an innocent person out of great distress. This surely has all the moral goodness that an action, considered abstractly, can have. Yet, it is evident that an agent, in relieving a person in distress, may have no moral goodness, may have great merit, or may have great demerit. [405]

Suppose, *first*, That mice cut the cords which bound the distressed person, and so bring him relief. Is there moral goodness in this act of the mice?

Suppose, *secondly*, That a man maliciously relieves the distressed person, in order to plunge him into greater distress. In this action, there is surely no moral goodness, but much malice and inhumanity.

If, in the *last* place, we suppose a person, from real sympathy and humanity, to bring relief to the distressed person, with considerable expense or danger to himself—here is an action of real worth, which every heart approves and every tongue praises. But wherein lies the worth? Not in the action considered by itself, which was common to all the three, but in the man who, on this occasion, acted the part which became a good man. He did what his heart approved, and therefore he is approved by God and man.

Upon the whole, if we distinguish between that goodness which may be ascribed to an action considered by itself, and that goodness which we ascribe to a man when he puts it in execution, we shall find a key to this metaphysical lock. We admit that the goodness of an action, considered abstractly, can have no dependence upon the opinion or belief of an agent, any more than the truth of a proposition depends upon our believing it to be true. But, when a man exerts his active power well or ill, there is a moral goodness or turpitude which we figuratively impute to the action, but which is truly and properly imputable to the man only; and this goodness or turpitude depends very much* upon the intention of the agent, and the opinion he had of his action. [406]

This distinction has been understood in all ages by those who gave any attention to morals, though it has been variously expressed. The Greek moralists gave the name of καθῆκον to an action good in itself; such an action might be done by the most worthless. But an action done with a right intention, which implies real worth in the agent, they called κατόρθωμα. The distinction is explained by Cicero in his "Offices." He calls the first *officium medium*, and the second *officium perfectum*, or *rectum*.† In the scholastic ages, an action good in itself was said to be *materially* good, and an action done with a right intention was called *form-*

* It should have been said—"depends altogether," &c.—H.

† The καθῆκον μέσον or *officium medium*, was never called simply either καθῆκον or *officium*; though frequently merely μέσον. Reid was probably led into the mistake by an erroneous reading, (uncountenanced by any MS., and contrary to the universal analogy of the Stoical language), which Pearce, in his edition, introduced into the third chapter of the first book of Cicero's Offices.—H.

ally good. This last way of expressing the distinction is still familiar among Theologians; but Mr Hume seems not to have attended to it, or to have thought it to be words without any meaning.

Mr Hume, in the section already quoted, tells us with great assurance—"In short, it may be established as an undoubted maxim, that no action can be virtuous or morally good, unless there be in human nature some motive to produce it, distinct from the sense of its morality." And upon this maxim he founds many of his reasonings on the subject of morals.

Whether it be consistent with Mr Hume's own system, that an action may be produced merely from the sense of its morality, without any motive of agreeableness or utility, I shall not now inquire. But, if it be true, and I think it evident to every man of common understanding, that a judge or an arbiter acts the most virtuous part when his sentence is produced by no other motive but a regard to justice and a good conscience—nay, when all other motives distinct from this are on the other side;—if this, I say, be true, then that undoubted maxim of Mr Hume must be false, and all the conclusions built upon it must fall to the ground. [407]

From the principle I have endeavoured to establish, I think some consequences may be drawn with regard to the theory of morals.

First, If there be no virtue without the belief that what we do is right, it follows, that a moral faculty—that is, a power of discerning moral goodness and turpitude in human conduct—is essential to every being capable of virtue or vice. A being who has no more conception of moral goodness and baseness, of right and wrong, than a blind man hath of colours, can have no regard to it in his conduct, and therefore can neither be virtuous nor vicious.

He may have qualities that are agreeable or disagreeable, useful or hurtful; so may a plant or a machine. And we sometimes use the word *virtue* in such a latitude as to signify any agreeable or useful quality, as when we speak of the virtues of plants. But we are now speaking of virtue in the strict and proper sense, as it signifies that quality in a man which is the object of moral approbation.

This virtue a man could not have, if he had not a power of discerning a right and a wrong in human conduct, and of being influenced by that discernment. For in so far only he is virtuous as he is guided in his conduct by that part of his constitution. Brutes do not appear to have any such power, and therefore are not moral or accountable agents. They are capable of culture and discipline, but not of virtuous or criminal conduct. Even human creatures, in infancy and non-age, are not moral agents, because their moral faculty is not yet unfolded. These sentiments are supported by the common sense of mankind, which has always determined that neither brutes nor infants can be indicted for crimes. [408]

It is of small consequence what name we give to this moral power of the human mind; but it is so important a part of our constitution as to deserve an appropriated name. The name of *conscience*, as it is the most common, seems to me as proper as any that has been given it. I find no fault with the name *moral sense*, although I conceive this name has given occasion to some mistakes concerning the nature of our moral power. Modern philosophers have conceived of the external senses as having no other office but to give us certain sensations, or simple conceptions, which we could not have without them. And this notion has been applied to the moral sense. But it seems to me a mistaken notion in both. By the sense of seeing, I not only have the conception of the different colours, but I perceive one body to be of this colour, another of that. In like manner, by my moral sense, I not only have the conceptions of right and wrong in conduct, but I perceive *this* conduct to be right, *that* to be wrong, and *that* indifferent. All our senses are judging faculties,* so also is conscience. Nor is this power only a judge of our own actions and those of others—it is likewise a principle of action in all good men; and so far only can our conduct be denominated virtuous as it is influenced by this principle.

A *second* consequence from the principle laid down in this chapter is, that the formal nature and essence of that virtue which is the object of moral approbation consists neither in a prudent prosecution of our private interest, nor in benevolent affections towards others, nor in qualities useful or agreeable to ourselves or to others, nor in sympathizing with the passions and affections of others, and in attuning our own conduct to the tone of other men's passions; but it consists in living in all good conscience—that is, in using the best means in our power to know our duty, and acting accordingly.

Prudence is a virtue, Benevolence is a virtue, Fortitude is a virtue; but the essence and formal nature of Virtue must lie in something that is common to all these, and to every other virtue. And this I conceive can be nothing else but *the rectitude of such conduct and turpitude of the contrary, which is discerned by a good man.* And so far

* See above, p. 589, a, note; *et alibi.*—H.

only he is virtuous as he pursues the former and avoids the latter. [409]

CHAPTER V.

WHETHER JUSTICE BE A NATURAL OR AN ARTIFICIAL VIRTUE.

Mr Hume's philosophy concerning morals was first presented to the world in the third volume of his "Treatise of Human Nature," in the year 1740; afterwards in his "Inquiry concerning the Principles of Morals," which was first published by itself, and then in several editions of his "Essays and Treatises."

In these two works on morals, the system is the same. A more popular arrangement, great embellishment, and the omission of some metaphysical reasonings, have given a preference in the public esteem to the last; but I find neither any new principles in it, nor any new arguments in support of the system common to both.

In this system, the proper object of Moral Approbation is not actions or any voluntary exertion, but qualities of mind—that is, natural affections or passions, which are involuntary, a part of the constitution of the man, and common to us with many brute animals. When we praise or blame any voluntary action, it is only considered as a sign of the natural affection from which it flows, and from which all its merit or demerit is derived.

Moral Approbation or Disapprobation, is not an *Act of the Judgment*, which, like all acts of judgment, must be true or false; it is only a certain *Feeling*, which, from the constitution of human nature, arises upon contemplating certain characters, or qualities of mind, coolly and impartially. [410]

This feeling, when agreeable, is moral approbation; when disagreeable, disapprobation. The qualities of mind which produce this agreeable feeling, are the moral virtues; and those that produce the disagreeable, the vices.

These preliminaries being granted, the question about the foundation of morals is reduced to a simple question of fact—to wit, What are the qualities of mind which produce, in the disinterested observer, the feeling of approbation, or the contrary feeling?

In answer to this question, the author endeavours to prove, by a very copious induction, That all personal merit, all virtue, all that is the object of moral approbation, consists in the qualities of mind which are *agreeable* or *useful* to the person who possesses them, or to others.

The *dulce* and the *utile* is the whole sum of merit in every character, in every quality of mind, and in every action of life. There is no room left for that *honestum* which Cicero thus defines:—*Honestum igitur id intelligimus, quod tale est, ut detracta omni utilitate, sine ullis premiis fructibusve, per seipsum jure possit laudari.*—[DE FINIBUS, ii. 14.]

Among the ancient moralists, the Epicureans were the only sect who denied that there is any such thing as *honestum*, or moral worth, distinct from pleasure. In this, Mr Hume's system agrees with theirs. For the addition of utility to pleasure, as a foundation of morals, makes only a verbal, but no real difference. What is useful only has no value in itself; but derives all its merit from the end for which it is useful. That end, in this system, is agreeableness, or pleasure; so that, in both systems, pleasure is the only end, the only thing that is good in itself, and desirable for its own sake; and virtue derives all its merit from its tendency to produce pleasure. [411]

Agreeableness and utility are not moral conceptions, nor have they any connection with morality. What a man does, merely because it is agreeable, or useful to procure what is agreeable, is not virtue. Therefore the Epicurean system was justly thought, by Cicero, and the best moralists among the ancients, to subvert morality, and to substitute another principle in its room; and this system is liable to the same censure.

In one thing, however, it differs remarkably from that of Epicurus. It allows that there are disinterested affections in human nature; that the love of children and relations, friendship, gratitude, compassion, and humanity, are not, as Epicurus maintained, different modifications of self-love, but simple and original parts of the human constitution; that, when interest, or envy, or revenge, pervert not our disposition, we are inclined, from natural philanthropy, to desire, and to be pleased with the happiness of the human kind.

All this, in opposition to the Epicurean system, Mr Hume maintains with great strength of reason and eloquence, and, in this respect, his system is more liberal and disinterested than that of the Greek philosopher. According to Epicurus, virtue is whatever is agreeable to ourselves—according to Mr Hume, every quality of mind that is agreeable or useful to ourselves or to others.

This theory of the nature of virtue, it must be acknowledged, enlarges greatly the catalogue of moral virtues, by bringing into that catalogue every quality of mind that is useful or agreeable. Nor does there appear any good reason why the useful and agreeable qualities of body and of fortune, as well as those of the mind, should not have a place among moral virtues in this system. They have the essence of virtue; that is, agreeableness and utility—why then should they not have the name? [412]

But, to compensate this addition to the moral virtues, one class of them seems to be greatly degraded and deprived of all intrinsic merit. The useful virtues, as was above observed, are only ministering servants of the agreeable, and purveyors for them; they must, therefore, be so far inferior in dignity as hardly to deserve the same name.

Mr Hume, however, gives the name of *virtue* to both; and, to distinguish them, calls the agreeable qualities *natural* virtues, and the useful *artificial*.

The natural virtues are those natural affections of the human constitution which give immediate pleasure in their exercise. Such are all the benevolent affections. Nature disposes to them, and from their own nature they are agreeable, both when we exercise them ourselves, and when we contemplate their exercise in others.

The artificial virtues are such as are esteemed solely on account of their utility, either to promote the good of society—as justice, fidelity, honour, veracity, allegiance, chastity; or on account of their utility to the possessor—as industry, discretion, frugality, secrecy, order, perseverance, forethought, judgment, and others, of which, he says, many pages could not contain the catalogue.

This general view of Mr Hume's system concerning the foundation of morals, seemed necessary, in order to understand distinctly the meaning of that principle of his, which is to be the subject of this chapter, and on which he has bestowed much labour—to wit, that justice is not a natural but an artificial virtue. [413]

This system of the foundation of virtue is so contradictory in many of its essential points to the account we have before given of the active powers of human nature, that, if the one be true, the other must be false.

If God has given to man a power which we call *conscience*, the *moral faculty*, the *sense of duty*, by which, when he comes to years of understanding, he perceives certain things that depend on his will to be his duty, and other things to be base and unworthy; if the notion of duty be a simple conception, of its own kind, and of a different nature from the conceptions of utility and agreeableness, of interest or reputation; if this moral faculty be the prerogative of man, and no vestige of it be found in brute animals; if it be given us by God to regulate all our animal affections and passions; if to be governed by it, be the glory of man and the image of God in his soul, and to disregard its dictates be his dishonour and depravity—I say, if these things be so, to seek the foundation of morality in the affections which we have in common with the brutes, is to seek the living among the dead, and to change the glory of man, and the image of God in his soul, into the similitude of an ox that eateth grass.

If virtue and vice be a matter of choice, they must consist in voluntary actions, or in fixed purposes of acting according to a certain rule when there is opportunity, and not in qualities of mind which are involuntary.

It is true that every virtue is both agreeable and useful in the highest degree; and that every quality that is agreeable or useful, has a merit upon that account. But virtue has a merit peculiar to itself, a merit which does not arise from its being useful or agreeable, but from its being virtue. This merit is discerned by the same faculty by which we discern it to be virtue, and by no other. [414]

We give the name of *esteem* both to the regard we have for things useful and agreeable, and to the regard we have for virtue; but these are different kinds of esteem. I esteem a man for his ingenuity and learning—I esteem him for his moral worth. The sound of *esteem* in both these speeches is the same, but its meaning is very different.

Good breeding is a very amiable quality; and even if I knew that the man had no motive to it but its pleasure and utility to himself and others, I should like it still; but I would not in that case call it a moral virtue.

A dog has a tender concern for her puppies; so has a man for his children. The natural affection is the same in both, and is amiable in both. But why do we impute moral virtue to the man on account of this concern, and not to the dog? The reason surely is, That, in the man, the natural affection is accompanied with a sense of duty; but in the dog it is not. The same thing may be said of all the kind affections common to us with the brutes. They are amiable qualities; but they are not moral virtues.

What has been said relates to Mr Hume's system in general. We are now to consider his notion of the particular virtue of justice—That its merit consists wholly in its utility to society.

That justice is highly useful and necessary in society, and, on that account, ought to be loved and esteemed by all that love mankind, will readily be granted. And as justice is a social virtue, it is true also, that there could be no exercise of it, and, perhaps, we should have no conception of it, without society. But this is equally true of the natural affections of benevolence, gratitude, friendship, and compassion, which Mr Hume makes to be the natural virtues. [415]

It may be granted to Mr Hume, that men have no conception of the virtue of justice till they have lived some time in society. It is purely a moral conception, and our moral conceptions and moral judgments are not born with us. They grow up by degrees, as our reason does. Nor do I pretend to know how early, or in what order, we acquire the conception of the several virtues. The conception of justice supposes some exercise of the moral faculty, which, being the noblest part of the human constitution, and that to which all its other parts are subservient, appears latest.

It may likewise be granted, that there is no animal affection in human nature that prompts us immediately to acts of justice, as such. We have natural affections of the animal kind, which immediately prompt us to acts of kindness; but none, that I know, that has the same relation to justice. The very conception of justice supposes a moral faculty; but our natural kind affections do not; otherwise we must allow that brutes have this faculty.

What I maintain is, *first*, That when men come to the exercise of their moral faculty, they perceive a turpitude in injustice, as they do in other crimes, and consequently an obligation to justice, abstracting from the consideration of its utility. And, *secondly*, That, as soon as men have any rational conception of a favour, and of an injury, they must have the conception of justice, and perceive its obligation distinct from its utility.

The first of these points hardly admits of any other proof but an appeal to the sentiments of every honest man and every man of honour, Whether his indignation is not immediately inflamed against an atrocious act of villany, without the cool consideration of its distant consequences upon the good of society? [416]

We might appeal even to robbers and pirates, whether they have not had great struggles with their conscience, when they first resolved to break through all the rules of justice; and whether, in a solitary and serious hour, they have not frequently felt the pangs of guilt. They have very often confessed this at a time when all disguise is laid aside.

The common good of society, though a pleasing object to all men, when presented to their view, hardly ever enters into the thoughts of the far greatest part of mankind; and, if a regard to it were the sole motive to justice, the number of honest men must be small indeed. It would be confined to the higher ranks, who, by their education or by their office, are led to make the public good an object; but that it is so confined, I believe no man will venture to affirm.

The temptations to injustice are strongest in the lowest class of men; and, if nature had provided no motive to oppose those temptations, but a sense of public good, there would not be found an honest man in that class.

To all men that are not greatly corrupted, injustice, as well as cruelty and ingratitude, is an object of disapprobation on its own account. There is a voice within us that proclaims it to be base, unworthy, and deserving of punishment.

That there is, in all ingenuous natures, an antipathy to roguery and treachery, a reluctance to the thoughts of villany and baseness, we have the testimony of Mr Hume himself; who, as I doubt not but he felt it, has expressed it very strongly in the conclusion to his "Enquiry," and acknowledged that, in some cases, without this reluctance and antipathy to dishonesty, a sensible knave would find no sufficient motive from public good to be honest. [417]

I shall give the passage at large from the "Enquiry concerning the Principles of Morals," Section 9, near the end.

"Treating vice with the greatest candour, and making it all possible concessions, we must acknowledge that there is not, in any instance, the smallest pretext for giving it the preference above virtue, with a view to self-interest; except, perhaps, in the case of justice, where a man, taking things in a certain light, may often seem to be a loser by his integrity. And, though it is allowed that, without a regard to property, no society could subsist; yet, according to the imperfect way in which human affairs are conducted, a sensible knave, in particular incidents, may think that an act of iniquity or infidelity will make a considerable addition to his fortune, without causing any considerable breach in the social union and confederacy. That *honesty is the best policy*, may be a good general rule, but it is liable to many exceptions; and he, it may perhaps be thought, conducts himself with most wisdom, who observes the general rule, and takes advantage of all the exceptions.

"I must confess that, if a man think that this reasoning much requires an answer, it will be a little difficult to find any which will to him appear satisfactory and convincing. If his heart rebel not against such pernicious maxims, if he feel no reluctance to the thoughts of villany and baseness, he has indeed lost a considerable motive to virtue, and we may expect that his practice

[415-417]

will be answerable to his speculation. But, in all ingenuous natures, the antipathy to treachery and roguery is too strong to be counterbalanced by any views of profit or pecuniary advantage. Inward peace of mind, consciousness of integrity, a satisfactory review of our own conduct—these are circumstances very requisite to happiness, and will be cherished and cultivated by every honest man who feels the importance of them." [418]

The reasoning of the *sensible knave* in this passage, seems to me to be justly founded upon the principles of the "Enquiry" and of the "Treatise of Human Nature," and therefore it is no wonder that the author should find it a little difficult to give any answer which would appear satisfactory and convincing to such a man. To counterbalance this reasoning, he puts in the other scale a reluctance, an antipathy, a rebellion of the heart against such pernicious maxims, which is felt by ingenuous natures.

Let us consider a little the force of Mr Hume's answer to this sensible knave, who reasons upon his own principles. I think it is either an acknowledgment that there is a natural judgment of conscience in man, that injustice and treachery is a base and unworthy practice—which is the point I would establish; or it has no force to convince either the knave or an honest man.

A clear and intuitive judgment, resulting from the constitution of human nature, is sufficient to overbalance a train of subtile reasoning on the other side. Thus the testimony of our senses is sufficient to overbalance all the subtile arguments brought against their testimony. And, if there be a like testimony of conscience in favour of honesty, all the subtile reasoning of the knave against it ought to be rejected without examination, as fallacious and sophistical, because it concludes against a self evident principle; just as we reject the subtile reasoning of the metaphysician against the evidence of sense.

If, therefore, the *reluctance*, the *antipathy*, the *rebellion of the heart* against injustice, which Mr Hume sets against the reasoning of the knave, include in their meaning a natural intuitive judgment of conscience, that injustice is base and unworthy, the reasoning of the knave is convincingly answered; but the principle, *That justice is an artificial virtue, approved solely for its utility*, is given up. [419]

If, on the other hand, the antipathy, reluctance, and rebellion of heart, imply no judgment, but barely an uneasy feeling, and that not natural, but acquired and artificial, the answer is indeed very agreeable to the principles of the "Enquiry," but has no force to convince the knave, or any other man.

The knave is here supposed by Mr Hume to have no such feelings, and therefore the answer does not touch his case in the least, but leaves him in the full possession of his reasoning. And *ingenuous natures*, who have these feelings, are left to deliberate whether they will yield to acquired and artificial feelings, in opposition to rules of conduct, which, to their best judgment, appear wise and prudent.

The *second* thing I proposed to shew was, That, as soon as men have any rational conception of a favour and of an injury, they must have the conception of justice, and perceive its obligation.

The power with which the Author of nature hath endowed us, may be employed either to do good to our fellow-men, or to hurt them. When we employ our power to promote the good and happiness of others, this is a benefit or favour; when we employ it to hurt them, it is an injury. Justice fills up the middle between these two. It is such a conduct as does no injury to others; but it does not imply the doing them any favour. [420]

The notions of a *favour* and of an *injury*, appear as early in the mind of man as any rational notion whatever. They are discovered, not by language only, but by certain affections of mind, of which they are the natural objects. A favour naturally produces gratitude. An injury done to ourselves produces resentment; and even when done to another, it produces indignation.

I take it for granted that gratitude and resentment are no less natural to the human mind than hunger and thirst; and that those affections are no less naturally excited by their proper objects and occasions than these appetites.

It is no less evident, that the proper and formal object of gratitude is a person who has done us a favour; that of resentment, a person who has done us an injury.

Before the use of reason, the distinction between a favour and an agreeable office is not perceived. Every action of another person which gives present pleasure produces love and good will towards the agent. Every action that gives pain or uneasiness produces resentment. This is common to man before the use of reason, and to the more sagacious brutes; and it shews no conception of justice in either.

But, as we grow up to the use of reason, the notion, both of a favour and of an injury, grows more distinct and better defined. It is not enough that a good office be done; it must be done from good will, and with a good intention, otherwise it is no favour, nor does it produce gratitude.

I have heard of a physician who gave

spiders in a medicine to a dropsical patient, with an intention to poison him, and that this medicine cured the patient, contrary to the intention of the physician. Surely no gratitude, but resentment, was due by the patient, when he knew the real state of the case. It is evident to every man, that a benefit arising from the action of another, either without or against his intention, is not a motive to gratitude; that is, is no favour. [421]

Another thing implied in the nature of a favour is, that it be not due. A man may save my credit by paying what he owes me. In this case, what he does tends to my benefit, and perhaps is done with that intention; but it is not a favour—it is no more than he was bound to do.

If a servant do his work and receive his wages, there is no favour done on either part, nor any object of gratitude; because, though each party has benefited the other, yet neither has done more than he was bound to do.

What I infer from this is, That the conception of a favour in every man come to years of understanding, implies the conception of things not due, and consequently the conception of things that are due.

A negative cannot be conceived by one who has no conception of the correspondent positive. Not to be due is the negative of being due; and he who conceives one of them must conceive both. The conception of things due and not due must therefore be found in every mind which has any rational conception of a favour, or any rational sentiment of gratitude.

If we consider, on the other hand, what an injury is which is the object of the natural passion of resentment, every man, capable of reflection, perceives, that an injury implies more than being hurt. If I be hurt by a stone falling out of the wall, or by a flash of lightning, or by a convulsive and involuntary motion of another man's arm, no injury is done, no resentment raised in a man that has reason. In this, as in all moral actions, there must be the will and intention of the agent to do the hurt. [422]

Nor is this sufficient to constitute an injury. The man who breaks my fences, or treads down my corn, when he cannot otherwise preserve himself from destruction, who has no injurious intention, and is willing to indemnify me for the hurt which necessity, and not ill will, led him to do, is not injurious, nor is an object of resentment.

The executioner who does his duty in cutting off the head of a condemned criminal, is not an object of resentment. He does nothing unjust, and therefore nothing injurious.

From this it is evident, that an injury, the object of the natural passion of resentment, implies in it the notion of injustice. And it is no less evident that no man can have a notion of injustice without having the notion of justice.

To sum up what has been said upon this point, a favour, an act of justice, and an injury, are so related to one another that he who conceives one must conceive the other two. They lie, as it were, in one line, and resemble the relations of greater, less, and equal. If one understands what is meant by one line being greater or less than another, he can be at no loss to understand what is meant by its being equal to the other; for, if it be neither greater nor less, it must be equal.

In like manner, of those actions by which we profit or hurt other men, a favour is more than justice, an injury is less; and that which is neither a favour nor an injury is a just action.

As soon, therefore, as men come to have any proper notion of a favour and of an injury; as soon as they have any rational exercise of gratitude and of resentment—so soon they must have the conception of justice and of injustice; and, if gratitude and resentment be natural to man, which Mr Hume allows, the notion of justice must be no less natural. [423]

The notion of justice carries inseparably along with it a perception of its moral obligation. For, to say that such an action is an act of justice, that it is due, that it ought to be done, that we are under a moral obligation to do it, are only different ways of expressing the same thing. It is true, that we perceive no high degree of moral worth in a merely just action, when it is not opposed by interest or passion; but we perceive a high degree of turpitude and demerit in unjust actions, or in the omission of what justice requires.

Indeed, if there were no other argument to prove that the obligation of justice is not solely derived from its utility to procure what is agreeable either to ourselves or to society, this would be sufficient, that the very conception of justice implies its obligation. The morality of justice is included in the very idea of it: nor is it possible that the conception of justice can enter into the human mind, without carrying along with it the conception of duty and moral obligation. Its obligation, therefore, is inseparable from its nature, and is not derived solely from its utility, either to ourselves or to society.

We may farther observe, that, as in all moral estimation, every action takes its denomination from the motive that produces it; so no action can properly be denominated an act of justice, unless it be done from a regard to justice. [424]

If a man pays his debt, only that he may not be cast into prison, he is not a just man, because prudence, and not justice, is his motive. And if a man, from benevolence and charity, gives to another what is really due to him, but what he believes not to be due, this is not an act of justice in him, but of charity or benevolence, because it is not done from a motive of justice. These are self-evident truths; nor is it less evident, that what a man does, merely to procure something agreeable, either to himself or to others, is not an act of justice, nor has the merit of justice.

Good music and good cookery have the merit of utility, in procuring what is agreeable both to ourselves and to society; but they never obtained among mankind the denomination of moral virtues. Indeed, if this author's system be well founded, great injustice has been done them on that account.

I shall now make some observations upon the reasoning of this author, in proof of his favourite principle, That justice is not a natural but an artificial virtue; or, as it is expressed in the "Enquiry," That public utility is the sole origin of justice, and that reflections on the beneficial consequences of this virtue, are the sole foundation of its merit.

1. It must be acknowledged that this principle has a necessary connection with his system concerning the foundation of all virtue; and, therefore, it is no wonder that he hath taken so much pains to support it; for the whole system must stand or fall with it.

If the *dulce* and the *utile*—that is, pleasure, and what is useful to procure pleasure—be the whole merit of virtue, justice can have no merit beyond its utility to procure pleasure. If, on the other hand, an intrinsic worth in justice, and demerit in injustice, be discerned by every man that hath a conscience; if there be a natural principle in the constitution of man by which justice is approved, and injustice disapproved and condemned—then the whole of this laboured system must fall to the ground. [425]

2. We may observe, That, as justice is directly opposed to injury, and as there are various ways in which a man may be injured, so there must be various branches of justice opposed to the different kinds of injury.

A man may be injured, *first*, in his person, by wounding, maiming, or killing him; *secondly*, in his family, by robbing him of his children, or any way injuring those he is bound to protect; *thirdly*, in his liberty, by confinement; *fourthly*, in his reputation; *fifthly*, in his goods, or property; and, *lastly*, in the violation of contracts or engagements made with him. This enumeration, whether complete or not, is sufficient for the present purpose.

The different branches of justice, opposed to these different kinds of injury, are commonly expressed by saying, that an innocent man has a right to the safety of his person and family, a right to his liberty and reputation, a right to his goods, and to fidelity to engagements made with him. To say that he has a right to these things, has precisely the same meaning as to say that justice requires that he should be permitted to enjoy them, or that it is unjust to violate them; for injustice is the violation of right, and justice is to yield to every man what is his right.

These things being understood as the simplest and most common ways of expressing the various branches of justice, we are to consider how far Mr Hume's reasoning proves any or all of them to be artificial, or grounded solely upon public utility. The last of them, fidelity to engagements, is to be the subject of the next chapter, and, therefore, I shall say nothing of it in this. [426]

The four first named—to wit, the right of an innocent man to the safety of his person and family, to his liberty and reputation, are, by the writers on jurisprudence, called *natural* rights of man, because they are grounded in the nature of man as a rational and moral agent, and are by his Creator committed to his care and keeping. By being called *natural* or *innate*, they, are distinguished from acquired rights, which suppose some previous act or deed of man by which they are acquired; whereas natural rights suppose nothing of this kind.

When a man's natural rights are violated, he perceives intuitively, and he feels that he is injured. The feeling of his heart arises from the judgment of his understanding; for, if he did not believe that the hurt was intended, and unjustly intended, he would not have that feeling. He perceives that injury is done to himself, and that he has a right to redress. The natural principle of resentment is roused by the view of its proper object, and excites him to defend his right. Even the injurious person is conscious of his doing injury; he dreads a just retaliation; and, if it be in the power of the injured person, he expects it as due and deserved.

That these sentiments spring up in the mind of man as naturally as his body grows to its proper stature; that they are not the birth of instruction, either of parents, priests, philosophers, or politicians, but the pure growth of nature—cannot, I think, without effrontery, be denied. We find them equally strong in the most savage and in the most civilized tribes of mankind; and nothing can weaken them but an inveterate habit of rapine and bloodshed, which benumbs the conscience, and turns men into wild beasts.

The public good is very properly considered by the judge who punishes a private injury, but seldom enters into the thought of the injured person. In all criminal law, the redress due to the private sufferer is distinguished from that which is due to the public; a distinction which could have no foundation, if the demerit of injustice arose solely from its hurting the public. And every man is conscious of a specific difference between the resentment he feels for an injury done to himself, and his indignation against a wrong done to the public. [427]

I think, therefore, it is evident that, of the six branches of justice we mentioned, four are natural, in the strictest sense, being founded upon the constitution of man, and antecedent to all deeds and conventions of society; so that, if there were but two men upon the earth, one might be unjust and injurious, and the other injured.

But does Mr Hume maintain the contrary?

To this question I answer, That his doctrine seems to imply it; but I hope he meant it not.

He affirms, in general, that justice is not a natural virtue; that it derives its origin solely from public utility; and that reflections on the beneficial consequences of this virtue, are the sole foundation of its merit. He mentions no particular branch of justice as an exception to this general rule; yet justice, in common language, and in all the writers on jurisprudence I am acquainted with, comprehends the four branches above mentioned. His doctrine, therefore, according to the common construction of words, extends to these four, as well as to the two other branches of justice.

On the other hand, if we attend to his long and laboured proof of this doctrine, it appears evident that he had in his eye only two particular branches of justice. No part of his reasoning applies to the other four. He seems, I know not why, to have taken up a confined notion of justice, and to have restricted it to a regard to property and fidelity in contracts. As to other branches he is silent. He nowhere says, that it is not naturally criminal to rob an innocent man of his life, of his children, of his liberty, or of his reputation; and I am apt to think he never meant it. [428]

The only philosopher I know who has had the assurance to maintain this, is Mr Hobbes, who makes the state of nature to be a state of war, of every man against every man; and of such a war in which every man has a right to do and to acquire whatever his power can, by any means, accomplish—that is, a state wherein neither right nor injury, justice nor injustice, can possibly exist.

Mr Hume mentions this system of Hobbes, but without adopting it, though he allows it the authority of Cicero in its favour.

He says, in a note, "This fiction of a state of nature as a state of war was not first started by Mr Hobbes, as is commonly imagined. Plato endeavours to refute an hypothesis very like it, in the 2d, 3d, and 4th books, 'De Republica.' Cicero, on the contrary, supposes it certain and universally acknowledged, in the following passage," &c.—*Pro Sextio*, § 42.

The passage, which he quotes at large from one of Cicero's orations, seems to me to require some straining to make it tally with the system of Mr Hobbes. Be this as it may, Mr Hume might have added, That Cicero, in his orations, like many other pleaders, sometimes says not what he believed, but what was fit to support the cause of his client. That Cicero's opinion, with regard to the natural obligation of justice, was very different from that of Mr Hobbes, and even from Mr Hume's, is very well known. [429]

3. As Mr Hume, therefore, has said nothing to prove the four branches of justice which relate to the innate rights of men, to be artificial, or to derive their origin solely from public utility, I proceed to the fifth branch, which requires us not to invade another man's property.

The right of property is not innate, but acquired. It is not grounded upon the constitution of man; but upon his actions. Writers on jurisprudence have explained its origin in a manner that may satisfy every man of common understanding.

The earth is given to men in common for the purposes of life, by the bounty of Heaven. But, to divide it, and appropriate one part of its produce to one, another part to another, must be the work of men who have power and understanding given them, by which every man may accommodate himself without hurt to any other.

This common right of every man to what the earth produces, before it be occupied and appropriated by others, was, by ancient moralists, very properly compared to the right which every citizen had to the public theatre, where every man that came might occupy an empty seat, and thereby acquire a right to it while the entertainment lasted, but no man had a right to dispossess another.

The earth is a great theatre, furnished by the Almighty, with perfect wisdom and goodness, for the entertainment and employment of all mankind. Here every man has a right to accommodate himself as a spectator, and to perform his part as an actor, but without hurt to others.

He who does so is a just man, and thereby entitled to some degree of moral approbation; and he who not only does no hurt, but employs his power to do good, is a good man, and is thereby entitled to a higher degree of moral approbation. But he who justles and molests his neighbour, who deprives him of any accommodation which his industry has provided without hurt to others, is unjust, and a proper object of resentment. [430]

It is true, therefore, that property has a beginning from the actions of men, occupying, and, perhaps, improving by their industry, what was common by nature. It is true, also, that, before property exists, that branch of justice and injustice which regards property cannot exist. But it is also true, that, where there are men, there will very soon be property of one kind or another, and, consequently, there will be that branch of justice which attends property as its guardian.

There are *two kinds of property* which we may distinguish.

The *first* is *what must presently be consumed to sustain life*; the *second*, which is more permanent, is, *what may be laid up and stored for the supply of future wants*.

Some of the gifts of nature must be used and consumed by individuals for the daily support of life; but they cannot be used till they be occupied and appropriated. If another person may, without injustice, rob me of what I have innocently occupied for present subsistence, the necessary consequence must be, that he may, without injustice, take away my life.

A right to life implies a right to the necessary means of life. And that justice which forbids the taking away the life of an innocent man, forbids no less the taking from him the necessary means of life. He has the same right to defend the one as the other; and nature inspires him with the same just resentment of the one injury as of the other. [431]

The natural right of liberty implies a right to such innocent labour as a man chooses, and to the fruit of that labour. To hinder another man's innocent labour, or to deprive him of the fruit of it, is an injustice of the same kind, and has the same effect, as to put him in fetters or in prison, and is equally a just object of resentment.

Thus it appears, that some kind, or some degree, of property must exist wherever men exist, and that the right to such property is the necessary consequence of the natural right of men to life and liberty.

It has been further observed, that God has made man a sagacious and provident animal, led by his constitution not only to occupy and use what nature has provided for the supply of his present wants and necessities, but to foresee future wants, and to provide for them; and that not only for himself, but for his family, his friends, and connections.

He therefore acts in perfect conformity to his nature, when he stores, of the fruit of his labour, what may afterwards be useful to himself or to others; when he invents and fabricates utensils or machines by which his labour may be facilitated, and its produce increased; and when, by exchanging with his fellow-men commodities or labour, he accommodates both himself and them. These are the natural and innocent exertions of that understanding wherewith his Maker has endowed him. He has therefore a right to exercise them, and to enjoy the fruit of them. Every man who impedes him in making such exertions, or deprives him of the fruit of them, is injurious and unjust, and an object of just resentment.

Many brute-animals are led by instinct to provide for futurity, and to defend their store, and their store-house, against all invaders. There seems to be in man, before the use of reason, an instinct of the same kind. When reason and conscience grow up, they approve and justify this provident care, and condemn, as unjust, every invasion of others, that may frustrate it. [432]

Two instances of this provident sagacity seem to be peculiar to man: I mean the invention of utensils and machines for facilitating labour, and the making exchanges with his fellow-men for mutual benefit. No tribe of men has been found so rude as not to practise these things in some degree. And I know no tribe of brutes that was ever observed to practise them. They neither invent nor use utensils or machines, nor do they traffic by exchanges.

From these observations, I think it evident that man, even in the state of nature, by his powers of body and mind, may acquire permanent property, or what we call *riches*, by which his own and his family's wants are more liberally supplied, and his power enlarged to requite his benefactors, to relieve objects of compassion, to make friends, and to defend his property against unjust invaders. And we know from history, that men, who had no superior on earth, no connection with any public beyond their own family, have acquired property, and had distinct notions of that justice and injustice of which it is the object.

Every man, as a reasonable creature, has a right to gratify his natural and innocent desires, without hurt to others. No desire is more natural, or more reasonable, than that of supplying his wants. When this is done without hurt to any man, to hinder or frustrate his innocent labour, is an unjust violation of his natural liberty. Private utility leads a man to desire property, and to labour for it; and his right to it is only a right to labour for his own benefit. [433]

That public utility is the sole origin, even of that branch of justice which regards property, is so far from being true, that, when men confederate and constitute a public, under laws and government, the right of each individual to his property is, by that confederation, abridged and limited. In the state of nature every man's property was solely at his own disposal, because he had no superior. In civil society it must be subject to the laws of the society. He gives up to the public part of that right which he had in the state of nature, as the price of that protection and security which he receives from civil society. In the state of nature, he was sole judge in his own cause, and had right to defend his property, his liberty, and life, as far as his power reached. In the state of civil society, he must submit to the judgment of the society, and acquiesce in its sentence, though he should conceive it to be unjust

What was said above, of the natural right every man has to acquire permanent property, and to dispose of it, must be understood with this condition, That no other man be thereby deprived of the necessary means of life. The right of an innocent man to the necessaries of life, is, in its nature, superior to that which the rich man has to his riches, even though they be honestly acquired. The use of riches, or permanent property, is to supply future and casual wants, which ought to yield to present and certain necessity.

As, in a family, justice requires that the children who are unable to labour, and those who, by sickness, are disabled, should have their necessities supplied out of the common stock, so, in the great family of God, of which all mankind are the children, justice, I think, as well as charity, requires, that the necessities of those who, by the providence of God, are disabled from supplying themselves, should be supplied from what might otherwise be stored for future wants. [434]

From this it appears, That the right of acquiring and that of disposing of property, may be subject to limitations and restrictions, even in the state of nature, and much more in the state of civil society, in which the public has what writers in jurisprudence call an *eminent dominion* over the property, as well as over the lives of the subjects, as far as the public good requires.

If these principles be well founded, Mr Hume's arguments to prove that justice is an artificial virtue, or that its public utility is the sole foundation of its merit, may be easily answered.

He supposes, *first*, a state in which nature has bestowed on the human race, such abundance of external goods, that every man, without care or industry, finds himself provided of whatever he can wish or desire. It is evident, says he, that, in such a state, the cautious, jealous virtue of justice would never once have been dreamed of.

It may be observed, *first*, That this argument applies only to one of the six branches of justice before mentioned. The other five are not in the least affected by it; and the reader will easily perceive that this observation applies to almost all his arguments, so that it needs not be repeated.

Secondly, All that this argument proves is, That a state of the human race may be conceived wherein no property exists, and where, of consequence, there can be no exercise of that branch of justice which respects property. But does it follow from this, that where property exists, and must exist, that no regard ought to be had to it?

He next supposes that the necessities of the human race continuing tha same as at present, the mind is so enlarged with friendship and generosity, that every man feels as much tenderness and concern for the interest of every man, as for his own. It seems evident, he says, that the use of justice would be suspended by such an extensive benevolence, nor would the divisions and barriers of property and obligation have ever been thought of. [435]

I answer, The conduct which this extensive benevolence leads to, is either perfectly consistent with justice, or it is not. *First*, If there be any case where this benevolence would lead us to do injustice, the use of justice is not suspended. Its obligation is superior to that of benevolence; and, to shew benevolence to one, at the expense of injustice to another, is immoral. *Secondly*, Supposing no such case could happen, the use of justice would not be suspended, because by it we must distinguish good offices to which we had a right, from those to which he had no right, and which therefore require a return of gratitude. *Thirdly*, Supposing the use of justice to be suspended, as it must be in avery case where it cannot be exercised, Will it follow, that its obligation is suspended, where there is access to exercise it?

A *third* supposition is, the reverse of the first, That a society falls into extreme want of the necessaries of life: The question is put, Whether, in such a case, an equal partition of bread, without regard to private property, though effected by power, and even by violence, would be regarded as criminal and injurious? And the author conceives that this would be a suspension of the strict laws of justice.

I answer, That such an equal partition as Mr Hume mentions, is so far from being criminal or injurious, that justice requires it; and surely that cannot be a suspension of the laws of justice which is an act of justice. All that the strictest justice requires in such a case, is, That the man whose life is preserved at the expense of another, and without his consent, should indemnify him when he is able. His case is similar to that of a debtor who is insolvent, without any fault on his part. Justice requires that he should be forborne till he is able to pay. It is strange that Mr Hume should think that an action, neither criminal nor injurious, should be a suspension of the laws of justice. This seems to me a contradiction; for *justice* and *injury* are contradictory terms. [436]

The next argument is thus expressed:—"When any man, even in political society, renders himself, by crimes, obnoxious to the public, he is punished in his goods and person—that is, the ordinary rules of justice are, with regard to him, suspended for a moment, and it becomes equitable to inflict on him what otherwise he could not suffer without wrong or injury."

This argument, like the former, refutes itself. For that an action should be a suspension of the rules of justice, and at the same time equitable, seems to me a contradiction. It is possible that equity may interfere with the letter of human laws, because all the cases that may fall under them, cannot be foreseen; but that equity should interfere with justice is impossible. It is strange that Mr Hume should think that justice requires that a criminal should be treated in the same way as an innocent man.

Another argument is taken from public war. What is it, says he, but a suspension of justice among the warring parties? The laws of war, which then succeed to those of equity and justice, are rules calculated for the advantage and utility of that particular state in which men are now placed.

I answer, when war is undertaken for self-defence, or for reparation of intolerable injuries, justice authorizes it. The laws of war, which have been described by many judicious moralists, are all drawn from the fountain of justice and equity; and everything contrary to justice, is contrary to the laws of war. That justice which prescribes one rule of conduct to a master, another to a servant; one to a parent, another to a child—prescribes also one rule of conduct towards a friend, another towards an enemy. I do not understand what Mr Hume means by the *advantage* and *utility* of a state of war, for which he says the laws of war are calculated and succeed to those of justice and equity. I know no laws of war that are not calculated for justice and equity. [437]

The next argument is this—Were there a species of creatures intermingled with men, which, though rational, were possessed of such inferior strength, both of body and mind, that they were incapable of all resistance, and could never, upon the highest provocation, make us feel the effects of their resentment; the necessary consequence, I think, is, that we should be bound, by the laws of humanity, to give gentle usage to these creatures, but should not, properly speaking, lie under any restraint of justice with regard to them, nor could they possess any right or property, exclusive of such arbitrary lords.

If Mr Hume had not owned this sentiment as a consequence of his Theory of Morals, I should have thought it very uncharitable to impute it to him. However, we may judge of the Theory by its avowed consequence. For there cannot be better evidence that a theory of morals, or of any particular virtue, is false, than when it subverts the practical rules of morals. This defenceless species of rational creatures, is doomed by Mr Hume to have no rights. Why? Because they have no power to defend themselves. Is not this to say—That right has its origin from power; which, indeed, was the doctrine of Mr Hobbes. And to illustrate this doctrine, Mr Hume adds—That, as no inconvenience ever results from the exercise of a power so firmly established in nature, the restraints of justice and property being totally useless, could never have place in so unequal a confederacy; and, to the same purpose, he says, that the female part of our own species owe the share they have in the rights of society, to the power which their address and their charms give them. If this be sound morals, Mr Hume's Theory of Justice may be true. [438]

We may here observe, that, though, in other places, Mr Hume founds the obligation of justice upon its utility to *ourselves* or to *others*, it is here founded solely upon utility to *ourselves*. For surely to be treated with justice would be highly useful to the defenceless species he here supposes to exist. But, as no inconvenience to ourselves can ever result from our treatment of them, he concludes, that justice would be useless, and therefore can have no place. Mr Hobbes could have said no more.

He supposes, in the *last* place, a state of human nature wherein all society and intercourse is cut off between man and man. It is evident, he says, that so solitary a being would be as much incapable of justice as of social discourse and conversation

And would not so solitary a being be as incapable of friendship, generosity, and compassion, as of justice? If this argument prove justice to be an artificial virtue, it

[436 438]

will, with equal force, prove every social virtue to be artificial.

These are the arguments which Mr Hume has advanced in his "Enquiry," in the first part of a long section upon justice.

In the *second* part, the arguments are not so clearly distinguished, nor can they be easily collected. I shall offer some remarks upon what seems most specious in this second part.

He begins with observing—"That, if we examine the particular laws by which justice is directed and property determined, they present us with the same conclusion. The good of mankind is the only object of all those laws and regulations." [439]

It is not easy to perceive where the stress of this argument lies. *The good of mankind is the object of all the laws and regulations by which justice is directed and property determined; therefore, justice is not a natural virtue, but has its origin solely from public utility, and its beneficial consequences are the sole foundation of its merit.*

Some step seems to be wanting to connect the antecedent proposition with the conclusion, which, I think, must be one or other of these two propositions—first, *All the rules of justice tend to public utility*; or, secondly, *Public utility is the only standard of justice, from which alone all its rules must be deduced.*

If the argument be, That justice must have its origin solely from public utility, because all its rules tend to public utility, I cannot admit the consequence; nor can Mr Hume admit it without overturning his own system; for the rules of benevolence and humanity do all tend to the public utility; and yet, in his system, they have another foundation in human nature; so likewise may the rules of justice.

I am apt to think, therefore, that the argument is to be taken in the last sense, That public utility is the only standard of justice, from which all its rules must be deduced; and therefore justice has its origin solely from public utility.

This seems to be Mr Hume's meaning, because, in what follows, he observes, That, in order to establish laws for the regulation of property, we must be acquainted with the nature and situation of man; must reject appearances which may be false though specious; and must search for those rules which are, on the whole, most useful and beneficial; and endeavours to shew, that the established rules which regard property are more for the public good than the system, either of those religious fanatics of the last age who held that saints only should inherit the earth, or of those political fanatics who claimed an equal division of property.

We see here, as before, that, though Mr Hume's conclusion respects justice in general, his argument is confined to one branch of justice—to wit, the right of property; and it is well known that, to conclude from a part to the whole is not good reasoning. [440]

Besides, the proposition from which his conclusion is drawn cannot be granted, either with regard to property, or with regard to the other branches of justice.

We endeavoured before to shew that property, though not an innate but an acquired right, may be acquired in the state of nature, and agreeably to the laws of nature; and that this right has not its origin from human laws, made for the public good, though, when men enter into political society, it may and ought to be regulated by those laws.

If there were but two men upon the face of the earth, of ripe faculties, each might have his own property, and might know his right to defend it, and his obligation not to invade the property of the other. He would have no need to have recourse to reasoning from public good, in order to know when he was injured, either in his property or in any of his natural rights, or to know what rules of justice he ought to observe towards his neighbour.

The simple rule, of not doing to his neighbour what he would think wrong to be done to himself, would lead him to the knowledge of every branch of justice, without the consideration of public good, or of laws and statutes made to promote it. [441]

It is not true, therefore, that public utility is the only standard of justice, and that the rules of justice can be deduced only from their public utility.

Aristides, and the people of Athens, had surely another notion of justice, when he pronounced the counsel of Themistocles, which was communicated to him only, to be highly useful, but unjust; and the assembly, upon this authority, rejected the proposal unheard.* These honest citizens, though subject to no laws but of their own making, far from making utility the standard of justice, made justice to be the standard of utility.

"*What is a man's property?* Anything which it is lawful for him, and for him alone, to use. *But what rule have we by which we can distinguish these objects?* Here we must have recourse to statutes, customs, precedents, analogies, &c."

Does not this imply that, in the state of nature, there can be no distinction of property? If so, Mr Hume's state of nature is the same with that of Mr Hobbes.

It is true that, when men become members of a political society, they subject their

* Had they heard it, there would not probably have been found the same unanimity. The rejection of a vague abstraction is very different from that of a specific reality.—H.

property, as well as themselves, to the laws, and must either acquiesce in what the laws determine, or leave the society. But justice, and even that particular branch of it which our author always supposes to be the whole, is antecedent to political societies and to their laws; and the intention of these laws is, to be the guardians of justice, and to redress injuries.

As all the works of men are imperfect, human laws may be unjust; which could never be, if justice had its origin from law, as the author seems here to insinuate. [442]

Justice requires that a member of a state should submit to the laws of the state, when they require nothing unjust or impious. There may, therefore, be statutory rights and statutory crimes. A statute may create a right which did not before exist, or make that to be criminal which was not so before. But this could never be, if there were not an antecedent obligation upon the subjects to obey the statutes. In like manner, the command of a master may make that to be the servant's duty which, before, was not his duty, and the servant may be chargeable with injustice if he disobeys, because he was under an antecedent obligation to obey his master in lawful things.

We grant, therefore, that particular laws may direct justice and determine property, and sometimes even upon very slight reasons and analogies, or even for no other reason but that it is better that such a point should be determined by law than that it should be left a dubious subject of contention. But this, far from presenting us with the conclusion which the author would establish, presents us with a contrary conclusion. For all these particular laws and statutes derive their whole obligation and force from a general rule of justice antecedent to them—to wit, That subjects ought to obey the laws of their country.

The author compares the rules of justice with the most frivolous superstitions, and can find no foundation for moral sentiment in the one more than in the other, excepting that justice is requisite to the well-being and existence of society.

It is very true that, if we examine *mine* and *thine* by the senses of *sight*, *smell*, or *touch*, or scrutinize them by the sciences of *medicine*, *chemistry*, or *physics*, we perceive no difference. But the reason is, that none of these senses or sciences are the judges of right or wrong, or can give any conception of them any more than the ear of colour, or the eye of sound. Every man of common understanding, and every savage, when he applies his moral faculty to those objects, perceives a difference as clearly as he perceives day-light. When that sense or faculty is not consulted, in vain do we consult every other, in a question of right and wrong. [443]

To perceive that justice tends to the good of mankind, would lay no moral obligation upon us to be just, unless we be conscious of a moral obligation to do what tends to the good of mankind. If such a moral obligation be admitted, why may we not admit a stronger obligation to do injury to no man? The last obligation is as easily conceived as the first, and there is as clear evidence of its existence in human nature.

The last argument is a dilemma, and is thus expressed:—"The dilemma seems obvious. As justice evidently tends to promote public utility, and to support civil society, the sentiment of justice is either derived from our reflecting on that tendency, or, like hunger, thirst, and other appetites, resentment, love of life, attachment to offspring, and other passions, arises from a simple original instinct in the human breast, which nature has implanted for like salutary purposes. If the latter be the case, it follows, That property, which is the object of justice, is also distinguished by a simple original instinct, and is not ascertained by any argument or reflection. But who is there that ever heard of such an instinct," &c.

I doubt not but Mr Hume has heard of a principle called *conscience*, which nature has implanted in the human breast. Whether he will call it a simple original instinct I know not, as he gives that name to all our appetites, and to all our passions. From this principle, I think, we derive the sentiment of justice. [444]

As the eye not only gives us the conception of colours, but makes us perceive one body to have one colour, and another body another; and as our reason not only gives us the conception of true and false, but makes us perceive one proposition to be true and another to be false; so our conscience, or moral faculty, not only gives us the conception of honest and dishonest, but makes us perceive one kind of conduct to be honest, another to be dishonest. By this faculty we perceive a merit in honest conduct, and a demerit in dishonest, without regard to public utility.

That these sentiments are not the effect of education or of acquired habits, we have the same reason to conclude as that our perception of what is true and what false, is not the effect of education or of acquired habits. There have been men who professed to believe that there is no ground to assent to any one proposition rather than its contrary; but I never yet heard of a man who had the effrontery to profess himself to be under no obligation of honour or honesty, of truth or justice, in his dealings with men.

Nor does this faculty of conscience require *innate ideas of property, and of the various ways of acquiring and transferring it, or innate ideas of kings and senators, of praetors, and chancellors, and juries*, any more than the faculty of seeing requires innate ideas of colours, or than the faculty of reasoning requires innate ideas of cones, cylinders, and spheres. [445]

CHAPTER VI.

OF THE NATURE AND OBLIGATION OF A CONTRACT.

The obligation of *Contracts* and *Promises* is a matter so sacred, and of such consequence to human society, that speculations which have a tendency to weaken that obligation, and to perplex men's notions on a subject so plain and so important, ought to meet with the disapprobation of all honest men.

Some such speculations, I think, we have in the third volume of Mr Hume's "Treatise of Human Nature," and in his "Enquiry into the Principles of Morals;" and my design in this chapter is, to offer some observations on the nature of a contract or promise, and on two passages of that author on this subject.

I am far from saying or thinking that Mr Hume meant to weaken men's obligations to honesty and fair dealing, or that he had not a sense of these obligations himself. It is not the man I impeach, but his writings. Let us think of the first as charitably as we can, while we freely examine the import and tendency of the last.

Although the nature of a contract and of a promise is perfectly understood by all men of common understanding; yet, by attention to the operations of mind signified by these words, we shall be better enabled to judge of the metaphysical subtilties which have been raised about them. A promise and a contract differ so little in what concerns the present disquisition, that the same reasoning (as Mr Hume justly observes) extends to both. In a promise, one party only comes under the obligation, the other acquires a right to the prestation promised. But we give the name of a contract to a transaction in which each party comes under an obligation to the other, and each reciprocally acquires a right to what is promised by the other. [446]

The Latin word *Pactum* seems to extend to both: and the definition given of it in the Civil Law, and borrowed from Ulpian, is, *Duorum pluriumve in idem placitum consensus.* Titius, a modern Civilian, has endeavoured to make this definition more complete, by adding the words, *obligationis licitè constituendæ vel tollendæ causa datus.* With this addition, the definition is, that *a Contract is the consent of two or more persons in the same thing, given with the intention of constituting or dissolving lawfully some obligation.*

This definition is, perhaps, as good as any other that can be given; yet, I believe, every man will acknowledge that it gives him no clearer or more distinct notion of a contract than he had before. If it is considered as a strictly logical definition, I believe some objections might be made to it; but I forbear to mention them, because I believe that similar objections might be made to any definition of a contract that can be given.

Nor can it be inferred from this, that the notion of a contract is not perfectly clear in every man come to years of understanding. For this is common to many operations of the mind, that, although we understand them perfectly, and are in no danger of confounding them with anything else; yet we cannot define them according to the rules of logic, by a genus and a specific difference. And when we attempt it, we rather darken than give light to them.

Is there anything more distinctly understood by all men, than what it is to see, to hear, to remember, to judge? Yet it is the most difficult thing in the world to define these operations according to the rules of logical definition. But it is not more difficult than it is useless. [447]

Sometimes philosophers attempt to define them; but, if we examine their definitions, we shall find that they amount to no more than giving one synonymous word for another, and commonly a worse for a better. So, when we define a contract, by calling it a consent, a convention, an agreement, what is this but giving a synonymous word for it, and a word that is neither more expressive nor better understood?

One boy has a top, another a scourge; says the first to the other, If you will lend me your scourge as long as I can keep up my top with it, you shall next have the top as long as you can keep it up. Agreed, says the other. This is a contract perfectly understood by both parties, though they never heard of the definition given by Ulpian or by Titius. And each of them knows that he is injured if the other breaks the bargain, and that he does wrong if he breaks it himself.

The operations of the human mind may be divided into *two* classes, the *Solitary* and the *Social*. As promises and contracts belong to the last class, it may be proper to explain this division.

I call those operations *solitary* which may be performed by a man in solitude, without intercourse with any other intelligent being.

I call those operations *social* which necessarily imply social intercourse with some other intelligent being who bears a part in them. [448]

A man may see, and hear, and remember, and judge, and reason; he may deliberate and form purposes, and execute them, without the intervention of any other intelligent being. They are solitary acts. But, when he asks a question for information, when he testifies a fact, when he gives a command to his servant, when he makes a promise, or enters into a contract, these are social acts of mind, and can have no existence without the intervention of some other intelligent being, who acts a part in them. Between the operations of the mind, which, for want of a more proper name, I have called *solitary*, and those I have called *social*, there is this very remarkable distinction, that, in the solitary, the expression of them by words, or any other sensible sign, is accidental. They may exist, and be complete, without being expressed, without being known to any other person. But, in the social operations, the expression is essential. They cannot exist without being expressed by words or signs, and known to the other party.

If nature had not made man capable of such social operations of mind, and furnished him with a language to express them, he might think, and reason, and deliberate, and will; he might have desires and aversions, joy and sorrow; in a word, he might exert all those operations of mind which the writers in logic and pneumatology have so copiously described; but, at the same time, he would still be a solitary being, even when in a crowd; it would be impossible for him to put a question, or give a command, to ask a favour, or testify a fact, to make a promise, or a bargain.

I take it to be the common opinion of philosophers, That the social operations of the human mind are not specifically different from the solitary, and that they are only various modifications or compositions of our solitary operations, and may be resolved into them.

It is for this reason, probably, that, in enumerating the operations of the mind, the solitary only are mentioned, and no notice at all taken of the social, though they are familiar to every man, and have names in all languages. [449]

I apprehend, however, it will be found extremely difficult, if not impossible, to resolve our social operations into any modification or composition of the solitary; and that an attempt to do this would prove as ineffectual as the attempts that have been made to resolve all our social affections into the selfish. The social operations appear to be as simple in their nature as the solitary. They are found in every individual of the species, even before the use of reason.

The power which man has of holding social intercourse with his kind, by asking and refusing, threatening and supplicating, commanding and obeying, testifying and promising, must either be a distinct faculty given by our Maker, and a part of our constitution, like the powers of seeing and hearing, or it must be a human invention. If men have invented this art of social intercourse, it must follow, that every individual of the species must have invented it for himself. It cannot be taught; for, though, when once carried to a certain pitch, it may be improved by teaching; yet it is impossible it can begin in that way, because all teaching supposes a social intercourse and language already established between the teacher and the learner. This intercourse must, from the very first, be carried on by sensible signs; for the thoughts of other men can be discovered in no other way. I think it is likewise evident, that this intercourse, in its beginning at least, must be carried on by natural signs, whose meaning is understood by both parties, previous to all compact or agreement. For there can be no compact without signs, nor without social intercourse.

I apprehend, therefore, that the social intercourse of mankind, consisting of those social operations which I have mentioned, is the exercise of a faculty appropriated to that purpose, which is the gift of God, no less than the powers of seeing and hearing. And that, in order to carry on this intercourse, God has given to man a natural language, by which his social operations are expressed, and without which, the artificial languages of articulate sounds, and of writing, could never have been invented by human art. [450]

The signs in this natural language are looks, changes of the features, modulations of the voice, and gestures of the body. All men understand this language without instruction, and all men can use it in some degree. But they are most expert in it who use it most. It makes a great part of the language of savages, and therefore they are more expert in the use of natural signs than the civilized.

The language of dumb persons is mostly formed of natural signs; and they are all great adepts in this language of nature. All that we call action and pronunciation, in the most perfect orator, and the most admired actor, is nothing else but superadding the language of nature to the language of articulate sounds. The pantomimes among the Romans carried it to the highest pitch of perfection. For they could act parts of comedies and tragedies in dumbshuw, so as to be understood, not only by those who were accustomed to this entertainment, but by all the strangers that came to Rome, from all the corners of the earth.

For it may be observed of this natural language, (and nothing more clearly demonstrates it to be a part of the human constitution,) that, although it require practice and study to enable a man to express his sentiments by it in the most perfect manner; yet it requires neither study nor practice in the spectator to understand it. The knowledge of it was before latent in the mind, and we no sooner see it than we immediately recognise it, as we do an acquaintance whom we had long forgot, and could not have described; but no sooner do we see him, than we know for certain that he is the very man. [451]

This knowledge, in all mankind, of the natural signs of men's thoughts and sentiments, is indeed so like to reminiscence that it seems to have led Plato to conceive all human knowledge to be of that kind.

It is not by reasoning that all mankind know that an open countenance and a placid eye is a sign of amity; that a contracted brow and a fierce look is the sign of anger. It is not from reason that we learn to know the natural signs of consenting and refusing, of affirming and denying, of threatening and supplicating.

No man can perceive any necessary connection between the signs of such operations, and the things signified by them. But we are so formed by the Author of our nature, that the operations themselves become visible, as it were, by their natural signs. This knowledge resembles reminiscence, in this respect, that it is immediate. We form the conclusion with great assurance, without knowing any premises from which it may be drawn by reasoning.

It would lead us too far from the intention of the present inquiry, to consider, more particularly, in what degree the social intercourse is natural, and a part of our constitution; how far it is of human invention.

It is sufficient to observe, that this intercourse of human minds, by which their thoughts and sentiments are exchanged, and their souls mingle together, as it were, is common to the whole species from infancy.

Like our other powers, its first beginnings are weak, and scarcely perceptible. But it is a certain fact, that we can perceive some communication of sentiments between the nurse and her nursling, before it is a month old. And I doubt not but that, if both had grown out of the earth, and had never seen another human face, they would be able in a few years to converse together. [452]

There appears, indeed, to be some degree of social intercourse among brute-animals, and between some of them and man. A dog exults in the caresses of his master, and is humbled at his displeasure. But there are two operations of the social kind, of which the brute-animals seem to be altogether incapable. They can neither plight their veracity by testimony, nor their fidelity by any engagement or promise. If nature had made them capable of these operations, they would have had a language to express them by, as man has: But of this we see no appearance.

A fox is said to use stratagems, but he cannot lie; because he cannot give his testimony, or plight his veracity. A dog is said to be faithful to his master; but no more is meant but that he is affectionate, for he never came under any engagement. I see no evidence that any brute-animal is capable of either giving testimony, or making a promise.

A dumb man cannot speak any more than a fox or a dog; but he can give his testimony by signs as early in life as other men can do by words. He knows what a lie is as early as other men, and hates it as much. He can plight his faith, and is sensible of the obligation of a promise or contract.

It is therefore a prerogative of man, that he can communicate his knowledge of facts by testimony, and enter into engagements by promise or contract. God has given him these powers by a part of his constitution, which distinguishes him from all brute-animals. And whether they are original powers, or resolvable into other original powers, it is evident that they spring up in the human mind at an early period of life, and are found in every individual of the species, whether savage or civilized.

These prerogative powers of man, like all his other powers, must be given for some end, and for a good end. And if we consider a little farther the economy of nature, in relation to this part of the human constitution, we shall perceive the wisdom of nature in the structure of it, and discover clearly our duty in consequence of it. [453]

It is evident, in the *first* place, that, if no credit was given to testimony, if there was no reliance upon promises, they would answer no end at all, not even that of deceiving.

Secondly, Supposing men disposed by some principle in their nature to rely on declarations and promises; yet, if men found in experience that there was no fidelity on the other part in making and in keeping them, no man of common understanding would trust to them, and so they would become useless.

Hence it appears, *thirdly*, That this

power of giving testimony, and of promising, can answer no end in society, unless there be a considerable degree, both of fidelity on the one part, and of trust on the other. These two must stand or fall together, and one of them cannot possibly subsist without the other.

Fourthly, It may be observed that fidelity in declarations and promises, and its counterpart, trust and reliance upon them, form a system of social intercourse, the most amiable, the most useful, that can be among men. Without fidelity and trust, there can be no human society. There never was a society, even of savages—nay, even of robbers or pirates—in which there was not a great degree of veracity and of fidelity among themselves. Without it man would be the most dissocial animal that God has made. His state would be in reality what Hobbes conceived the state of nature to be—a state of war of every man against every man; nor could this war ever terminate in peace.

It may be observed, in the fifth place, that man is evidently made for living in society. His social affections shew this as evidently as that the eye was made for seeing. His social operations, particularly those of testifying and promising, make it no less evident. [454]

From these observations it follows, that, if no provision were made by nature, to engage men to fidelity in declarations and promises, human nature would be a contradiction to itself, made for an end, yet without the necessary means of attaining it. As if the species had been furnished with good eyes, but without the power of opening their eyelids. There are no blunders of this kind in the works of God. Wherever there is an end intended, the means are admirably fitted for the attainment of it; and so we find it to be in the case before us.

For we see that children, as soon as they are capable of understanding declarations and promises, are led by their constitution to rely upon them. They are no less led by constitution to veracity and candour, on their own part. Nor do they ever deviate from this road of truth and sincerity, until corrupted by bad example and bad company. This disposition to sincerity in themselves, and to give credit to others, whether we call it *instinct*, or whatever name we give it, must be considered as the effect of their constitution.

So that the things essential to human society—I mean good faith on the one part, and trust on the other—are formed by nature in the minds of children, before they are capable of knowing their utility, or being influenced by considerations either of duty or interest.

When we grow up so far as to have the conception of a right and a wrong in conduct, the turpitude of lying, falsehood, and dishonesty, is discerned, not by any train of reasoning, but by an immediate perception. For we see that every man disapproves it in others, even those who are conscious of it in themselves.

Every man thinks himself injured and ill used, and feels resentment, when he is imposed upon by it. Every man takes it as a reproach when falsehood is imputed to him. These are the clearest evidences, that all men disapprove of falsehood, when their judgment is not biassed. [455]

I know of no evidence that has been given of any nation so rude as not to have these sentiments. It is certain that dumb people have them, and discover them about the same period of life in which they appear in those who speak. And it may reasonably be thought, that dumb persons, at that time of life, have had as little advantage, with regard to morals, from their education, as the greatest savages.

Every man, come to years of reflection, when he pledges his veracity or fidelity, thinks he has a right to be credited, and is affronted if he is not. But there cannot be a shadow of right to be credited, unless there be an obligation to good faith. For right on one hand, necessarily implies obligation on the other.

When we see that, in the most savage state that ever was known of the human race, men have always lived in societies greater or less, this of itself is a proof from fact, that they have had that sense of their obligation to fidelity without which no human society can subsist.

From these observations, I think, it appears very evident, that, as fidelity on one part, and trust on the other, are essential to that intercourse of men which we call human society; so the Author of our nature has made wise provision for perpetuating them among men, in that degree that is necessary to human society, in all the different periods of human life, and in all the stages of human improvement and degeneracy.

In early years, we have an innate disposition to them. In riper years, we feel our obligation to fidelity as much as to any moral duty whatsoever. [456]

Nor is it necessary to mention the collateral inducements to this virtue, from considerations of prudence, which are obvious to every man that reflects. Such as, that it creates trust, the most effectual engine of human power; that it requires no artifice or concealment; dreads no detection; that it inspires courage and magnanimity, and is the natural ally of every virtue; so that there is no virtue whatsoever, to which our natural obligation appears more strong or more apparent.

[454-456]

An observation or two, with regard to the nature of a contract, will be sufficient for the present purpose.

It is obvious that the prestation promised must be understood by both parties. One party engages to do such a thing, another accepts of this engagement. An engagement to do, one does not know what, can neither be made nor accepted. It is no less obvious, that a contract is a voluntary transaction.

But it ought to be observed, that the will, which is essential to a contract, is only a will to engage, or to become bound. We must beware of confounding this will with a will to perform what we have engaged. The last can signify nothing else than an intention and fixed purpose to do what we have engaged to do. The will to become bound, and to confer a right upon the other party, is indeed the very essence of a contract; but the purpose of fulfilling our engagement, is no part of the contract at all.

A purpose is a solitary act of mind, which lays no obligation on the person, nor confers any right on another. A fraudulent person may contract with a fixed purpose of not performing his engagement. But this purpose makes no change with regard to his obligation. He is as much bound as the honest man, who contracts with a fixed purpose of performing. [457]

As the contract is binding without any regard to the purpose, so there may be a purpose without any contract. A purpose is no contract, even when it is declared to the person for whose benefit it is intended. I may say to a man, I intend to do such a thing for your benefit, but I come under no engagement. Every man understands the meaning of this speech, and sees no contradiction in it: whereas, if a purpose declared were the same thing with a contract, such a speech would be a contradiction, and would be the same as if one should say, I promise to do such a thing, but I do not promise.

All this is so plain to every man of common sense, that it would have been unnecessary to be mentioned, had not so acute a man as Mr Hume grounded some of the contradictions he finds in a contract, upon confounding a will to engage in a contract with a will or purpose to perform the engagement.

I come now to consider the speculations of that author with regard to contracts.

In order to support a favourite notion of his own, That justice is not a natural but an artificial virtue, and that it derives its whole merit from its utility, he has laid down some principles which, I think, have a tendency to subvert all faith and fair-dealing among mankind.

In the third volume of the "Treatise of Human Nature," p. 40, he lays it down as an undoubted maxim, That no action can be virtuous or morally good, unless there be in human nature, some motive to produce it, distinct from its morality. Let us apply this undoubted maxim in an instance or two. If a man keeps his word, from this sole motive, that he ought to do so, this is no virtuous or morally good action. If a man pays his debt from this motive, that justice requires this of him, this is no virtuous or morally good action. If a judge or an arbiter gives a sentence in a cause, from no other motive but regard to justice, this is no virtuous or morally good action. These appear to me to be shocking absurdities, which no metaphysical subtilty can ever justify. [458]

Nothing is more evident than that every human action takes its denomination and its moral nature from the motive from which it is performed. That is a benevolent action which is done from benevolence. That is an act of gratitude which is done from a sentiment of gratitude That is an act of obedience to God, which is done from a regard to his command. And, in general, that is an act of virtue which is done from a regard to virtue.

Virtuous actions are so far from needing other motives, besides their being virtuous, to give them merit, that their merit is then greatest and most conspicuous, when every motive that can be put in the opposite scale is outweighed by the sole consideration of their being our duty.

This maxim, therefore, of Mr Hume, That no action can be virtuous or morally good, unless there be some motive to produce it distinct from its morality, is so far from being undoubtedly true, that it is undoubtedly false. It was never, so far as I know, maintained by any moralist, but by the Epicureans; and it savours of the very dregs of that sect. It agrees well with the principles of those who maintained, that virtue is an empty name, and that it is entitled to no regard but in as far as it ministers to pleasure or profit.

I believe the author of this maxim acted upon better moral principles than he wrote; and that what Cicero says of Epicurus, may be applied to him:—*Redarguitur ipse a sese, vincunturque scripta ejus probitate ipsius et moribus; et ut alii existimantur dicere melius quam facere, sic ille mihi videtur facere melius quam dicere.* [459]

But let us see how he applies this maxim to contracts. I give you his words from the place formerly cited:—"I suppose," says he, "a person to have lent me a sum of money, on condition that it be restored in a few days; and, after the expiration of the term agreed on, he demands the sum.

I ask, what reason or motive have I to restore the money? It will, perhaps, be said, that my regard to justice, and abhorrence of villany and knavery, are sufficient reasons for me, if I have the least grain of honesty, or sense of duty and obligation. And this answer, no doubt, is just and satisfactory to man in his civilized state, and when trained up according to a certain discipline and education. But, in his rude and more natural condition, if you are pleased to call such a condition natural, this answer would be rejected as perfectly unintelligible and sophistical."

The doctrine we are taught in this passage is this, That, though a man, in a civilized state, and when trained up according to a certain discipline and education, may have a regard to justice and an abhorrence of villany and knavery, and some sense of duty and obligation; yet, to a man in his rude and more natural condition, the considerations of honesty, justice, duty, and obligation, will be perfectly unintelligible and sophistical. And this is brought as an argument to shew that justice is not a natural but an artificial virtue.

I shall offer some observations on this argument.

1. Although it may be true that what is unintelligible to man in his rude state may be intelligible to him in his civilized state, I cannot conceive that what is sophistical in the rude state should change its nature, and become just reasoning when man is more improved. What is a sophism, will always be so; nor can any change in the state of the person who judges make that to be just reasoning which before was sophistical. [460] Mr Hume's argument requires that to man, in his rude state, the motives to justice and honesty should not only appear to be sophistical, but should really be so. If the motives were just in themselves, then justice would be a natural virtue, although the rude man, by an error of his judgment, thought otherwise. But if justice be not a natural virtue, which is the point Mr Hume intends to prove, then every argument, by which man in his natural state may be urged to it, must be a sophism in reality, and not in appearance only; and the effect of discipline and education in the civilized state can only be to make those motives to justice appear just and satisfactory, which, in their own nature, are sophistical.

2. It were to be wished that this ingenious author had shewn us why that state of man, in which the obligation to honesty, and an abhorrence of villany, appear perfectly unintelligible and sophistical, should be his *more natural state*.

It is the nature of human society to be progressive, as much as it is the nature of the individual. In the individual, the state of infancy leads to that of childhood, childhood to youth, youth to manhood, manhood to old age. If one should say that the state of infancy is a more natural state than that of manhood or of old age, I am apt to think that this would be words without any meaning. In like manner, in human society, there is a natural progress from rudeness to civilization, from ignorance to knowledge. What period of this progress shall we call man's natural state? To me they appear all equally natural. Every state of society is equally natural, wherein men have access to exert their natural powers about their proper objects, and to improve those powers by the means which their situation affords. [461]

Mr Hume, indeed, shews some timidity in affirming the rude state to be the more natural state of man; and, therefore, adds this qualifying parenthesis, If you are pleased to call such a condition natural.

But it ought to be observed, That, if the premises of his argument be weakened by this clause, the same weakness must be communicated to the conclusion; and the conclusion, according to the rules of good reasoning, ought to be, That justice is an artificial virtue, if you be pleased to call it artificial.

3. It were likewise to be wished, that Mr Hume had shewn, from fact, that there ever did exist such a state of man as that which he calls his more natural state. It is a state wherein a man borrows a sum of money, on the condition that he is to restore it in a few days; yet, when the time of payment comes, his obligation to repay what he borrowed is perfectly unintelligible and sophistical. It would have been proper to have given, at least, a single instance of some tribe of the human race that was found to be in this natural state. If no such instance can be given, it is, probably, a state merely imaginary; like that state, which some have imagined, wherein men were *ouran outangs*, or wherein they were fishes with tails.

Indeed, such a state seems impossible. That a man should lend without any conception of his having a right to be repaid; or that a man should borrow on the condition of paying in a few days, and yet have no conception of his obligation—seems to me to involve a contradiction.

I grant that a humane man may lend without any expectation of being repaid; but that he should lend without any conception of a right to be repaid, is a contradiction. In like manner, a fraudulent man may borrow without an intention of paying back; but that he could borrow, while an obligation to repay is perfectly unintelligible to him, this is a contradiction. [462]

The same author, in his "Enquiry into the Principles of Morals," § 3, treating of the same subject, has the following note:—

"'Tis evident that the will or consent alone, never transfers property, nor causes the obligation of a promise; (for the same reasoning extends to both;) but the will must be expressed by words or signs, in order to impose a tie upon any man. The expression being once brought in as subservient to the will, soon becomes the principal part of the promise; nor will a man be less bound by his word, though he secretly give a different direction to his intention, and withhold the assent of his mind. But, though the expression makes, on most occasions, the whole of the promise; yet it does not always so; and one who should make use of any expression of which he knows not the meaning, and which he uses without any sense of the consequences, would not certainly be bound by it. Nay, though he know its meaning, yet, if he uses it in jest only, and with such signs as shew evidently he has no serious intention of binding himself, he would not be under any obligation of performance; but it is necessary that the words be a perfect expression of the will, without any contrary signs; nay, even this we must not carry so far as to imagine that one whom, from our quickness of understanding, we conjectured to have an intention of deceiving us, is not bound by his expression or verbal promise, if we accept of it; but must limit this conclusion to those cases where the signs are of a different nature from those of deceit. All these contradictions are easily accounted for, if justice arises entirely from its usefulness to society, but will never be explained on any other hypothesis." [463]

Here we have the opinion of this grave moralist and acute metaphysician, that the principles of honesty and fidelity are at bottom a bundle of contradictions. This is one part of his moral system which, I cannot help thinking, borders upon licentiousness. It surely tends to give a very unfavourable notion of that cardinal virtue without which no man has a title to be called an honest man. What regard can a man pay to the virtue of fidelity, who believes that its essential rules contradict each other? Can a man be bound by contradictory rules of conduct? No more, surely, than he can be bound to believe contradictory principles.

He tells us, "that all these contradictions are easily accounted for, if justice arises entirely from its usefulness to society, but will never be explained upon any other hypothesis."

I know not, indeed, what is meant by accounting for contradictions, or explaining them. I apprehend that no hypothesis can make that which is a contradiction to be no contradiction. However, without attempting to account for these contradictions upon his own hypothesis, he pronounces, in a decisive tone, that they will never be explained upon any other hypothesis.

What if it shall appear that the contradictions mentioned in this paragraph do all take their rise from two capital mistakes the author has made with regard to the nature of promises and contracts; and if, when these are corrected, there shall not appear a shadow of contradiction in the cases put by him?

The first mistake is, That a promise is some kind of will, consent, or intention, which may be expressed, or may not be expressed. This is to mistake the nature of a promise. For no will, no consent, or intention, that is not expressed, is a promise. A promise, being a social transaction between two parties, without being expressed can have no existence. [464]

Another capital mistake that runs through the passage cited is, That this will, consent, or intention, which makes a promise, is a will or intention to perform what we promise. Every man knows that there may be a fraudulent promise, made without intention of performing. But the intention to perform the promise, or not to perform it, whether the intention be known to the other party or not, makes no part of the promise—it is a solitary act of the mind, and can neither constitute nor dissolve an obligation. What makes a promise is, that it be expressed to the other party with understanding, and with an intention to become bound, and that it be accepted by him.

Carrying these remarks along with us, let us review the passage cited.

First, He observes, that the will or consent alone does not cause the obligation of a promise, but it must be expressed.

I answer, The will not expressed is not a promise; and is it a contradiction that that which is not a promise should not cause the obligation of a promise? He goes on, The expression being once brought in as subservient to the will, soon *becomes* a principal part of the promise. Here it is supposed, that the expression was not originally a constituent part of the promise, but it soon *becomes* such. It is brought in to aid and be subservient to the promise which was made before by the will. If Mr Hume had considered that it is the expression accompanied with understanding and will to become bound, that constitutes a promise, he would never have said, that the expression soon becomes a part, and is brought in as subservient.

He adds, Nor will a man be less bound by his word, though he secretly gives a different direction to his intention, and withholds the assent of his mind. [465]

The case here put needs some explication. Either it means, that the man knowingly and voluntarily gives his word, without any intention of giving his word; or that he gives it without the intention of keeping it, and performing what he promises. The last of these is indeed a possible case, and is, I apprehend, what Mr Hume means. But the intention of keeping his promise is no part of the promise, nor does it in the least affect the obligation of it, as we have often observed.

If the author meant that the man may knowingly and voluntarily give his word, without the intention of giving his word, this is impossible: For such is the nature of all social acts of the mind, that, as they cannot be without being expressed, so they cannot be expressed knowingly and willingly, but they must be. If a man puts a question knowingly and willingly, it is impossible that he should at the same time will not to put it. If he gives a command knowingly and willingly, it is impossible that he should at the same time will not to give it. We cannot have contrary wills at the same time. And, in like manner, if a man knowingly and willingly becomes bound by a promise, it is impossible that he should at the same time will not to be bound.

To suppose, therefore, that, when a man knowingly and willingly gives his word, he withholds that will and intention which makes a promise, is indeed a contradiction; but the contradiction is not in the nature of the promise, but in the case supposed by Mr Hume.

He adds, though the expression, for the most part, makes the whole of the promise, it does not always so.

I answer, That the expression, if it is not accompanied with understanding and will to engage, never makes a promise. The author here assumes a postulate, which nobody ever granted, and which can only be grounded on the impossible supposition made in the former sentence. And as there can be no promise without knowledge and will to engage, is it marvellous that words which are not understood, or words spoken in jest, and without any intention to become bound, should not have the effect of a promise? [466]

The last case put by Mr Hume, is that of a man who promises fraudulently with an intention not to perform, and whose fraudulent intention is discovered by the other party, who, notwithstanding, accepts the promise. He is bound, says Mr Hume, by his verbal promise. Undoubtedly he is bound, because an intention not to perform the promise, whether known to the other party or not, makes no part of the promise, nor affects its obligation, as has been repeatedly observed.

From what has been said, I think it evident, that to one who attends to the nature of a promise or contract, there is not the least appearance of contradiction in the principles of morality relating to contracts.

It would, indeed, appear wonderful that such a man as Mr Hume should have imposed upon himself in so plain a matter, if we did not see frequent instances of ingenious men, whose zeal in supporting a favourite hypothesis darkens their understanding, and hinders them from seeing what is before their eyes. [467]

CHAPTER VII.

THAT MORAL APPROBATION IMPLIES A REAL JUDGMENT.

The approbation of good actions, and disapprobation of bad, are so familiar to every man come to years of understanding, that it seems strange there should be any dispute about their nature.

Whether we reflect upon our own conduct, or attend to the conduct of others with whom we live, or of whom we hear or read, we cannot help approving of some things, disapproving of others, and regarding many with perfect indifference.

These operations of our minds we are conscious of every day and almost every hour we live. Men of ripe understanding are capable of reflecting upon them, and of attending to what passes in their own thoughts on such occasions; yet, for half a century, it has been a serious dispute among philosophers, what this approbation and disapprobation is, *Whether there be a real judgment included in it, which, like all other judgments, must be true or false; or, Whether it include no more but some agreeable or uneasy feeling, in the person who approves or disapproves.*

Mr Hume observes very justly, that this is a controversy *started of late*. Before the modern system of Ideas and Impressions was introduced, nothing would have appeared more absurd than to say, that when I condemn a man for what he has done, I pass no judgment at all about the man, but only express some uneasy feeling in myself. [468]

Nor did the new system produce this discovery at once, but gradually, by several steps, according as its consequences were more accurately traced, and its spirit more thoroughly imbibed by successive philosophers.

Des Cartes and Mr Locke went no farther than to maintain that the Secondary Qualities of body—Heat and Cold, Sound, Colour, Taste, and Smell—which we perceive and judge to be in the external object, are mere feelings or sensations in our minds, there being nothing in bodies themselves to which these names can be applied; and that the office of the external senses is not to judge of external things, but only to give us ideas of sensations, from which we are by reasoning to deduce the existence of a material world without us, as well as we can.

Arthur Collier and Bishop Berkeley discovered, from the same principles, that the Primary, as well as the Secondary, Qualities of bodies, such as Extension, Figure, Solidity, Motion, are only sensations in our minds; and, therefore, that there is no material world without us at all.

The same philosophy, when it came to be applied to matters of taste, discovered that beauty and deformity are not anything in the objects, to which men, from the beginning of the world, ascribed them, but certain feelings in the mind of the spectator.

The next step was an easy consequence from all the preceding, that Moral Approbation and Disapprobation are not Judgments, which must be true or false, but barely agreeable and uneasy Feelings or Sensations.

Mr Hume made the last step in this progress, and crowned the system by what he calls his *hypothesis*—to wit, That Belief is more properly an act of the Sensitive than of the Cogitative part of our nature. [469]

Beyond this I think no man can go in this track; sensation or feeling is all, and what is left to the cogitative part of our nature, I am not able to comprehend.

I have had occasion to consider each of these paradoxes, excepting that which relates to morals, in "Essays on the Intellectual Powers of Man;" and, though they be strictly connected with each other, and with the system which has produced them, I have attempted to shew that they are inconsistent with just notions of our intellectual powers, no less than they are with the common sense and common language of mankind. And this, I think, will likewise appear with regard to the conclusion relating to morals—to wit, That moral approbation is only an agreeable feeling, and not a real judgment.

To prevent ambiguity as much as possible, let us attend to the meaning of *Feeling* and of *Judgment*. These operations of the mind, perhaps, cannot be logically defined; but they are well understood, and easily distinguished, by their properties and adjuncts.

Feeling, or sensation, seems to be the lowest degree of animation we can conceive. We give the name of *animal* to every being that feels pain and pleasure; and this seems to be the boundary between the inanimate and animal creation.

We know no being of so low a rank in the creation of God as to possess this animal power only without any other.

We commonly distinguish *Feeling* from *Thinking*, because it hardly deserves the name; and though it be, in a more general sense, a species of thought, is least removed from the passive and inert state of things inanimate. [470]

A feeling must be agreeable, or uneasy, or indifferent. It may be weak or strong. It is expressed in language either by a single word, or by such a contexture of words as may be the subject or predicate of a proposition, but such as cannot by themselves make a proposition. For it implies neither affirmation nor negation; and therefore cannot have the qualities of true or false, which distinguish propositions from all other forms of speech, and judgments from all other acts of the mind.

That I have such a feeling, is indeed an affirmative proposition, and expresses testimony grounded upon an intuitive judgment. But the feeling is only one term of this proposition; and it can only make a proposition when joined with another term, by a verb affirming or denying.

As feeling distinguishes the animal nature from the inanimate; so judging seems to distinguish the rational nature from the merely animal.

Though judgment in general is expressed by one word in language, as the most complex operations of the mind may be; yet a particular judgment can only be expressed by a sentence, and by that kind of sentence which logicians call a *proposition*, in which there must necessarily be a verb in the indicative mood, either expressed or understood.

Every judgment must necessarily be true or false, and the same may be said of the proposition which expresses it. It is a determination of the understanding, with regard to what is true, or false, or dubious.

In judgment, we can distinguish the object about which we judge, from the act of the mind in judging of that object. In mere feeling there is no such distinction. The object of judgment must be expressed by a proposition; and belief, disbelief, or doubt, always accompanies the judgment we form. If we judge the proposition to be true, we must believe it; if we judge it to be false, we must disbelieve it; and if we be uncertain whether it be true or false, we must doubt. [471]

The *toothache*, the *headache*, are words which express uneasy feelings; but to say that they express a judgment would be ridiculous.

That the sun is greater than the earth, is a proposition, and therefore the object of judgment; and, when affirmed or denied, believed or disbelieved, or doubted, it expresses judgment; but to say that it expresses only a feeling in the mind of him that believes it, would be ridiculous.

These two operations of mind, when we consider them separately, are very different, and easily distinguished. When we feel without judging, or judge without feeling, it is impossible, without very gross inattention, to mistake the one for the other.

But in many operations of the mind, both are inseparably conjoined under one name; and when we are not aware that the operation is complex, we may take one ingredient to be the whole, and overlook the other.

In former ages,* that moral power by which human actions ought to be regulated, was called *Reason*, and considered, both by philosophers and by the vulgar, as the power of judging what we ought and what we ought not to do.

This is very fully expressed by Mr Hume, in his "Treatise of Human Nature," Book II. Part iii. § 3. "Nothing is more usual in philosophy, and even in common life, than to talk of the combat of passion and reason, to give the preference to reason, and assert that men are only so far virtuous as they conform themselves to its dictates. Every rational creature, 'tis said, is obliged to regulate his actions by reason; and, if any other motive or principle challenge the direction of his conduct, he ought to oppose it, till it be entirely subdued, or, at least, brought to a conformity to that superior principle. On this method of thinking, the greatest part of moral philosophy, ancient and modern, seems to be founded." [472]

That those philosophers attended chiefly to the judging power of our moral faculty, appears from the names they gave to its operations, and from the whole of their language concerning it.

The modern philosophy has led men to attend chiefly to their sensations and feelings, and thereby to resolve into mere feeling, complex acts of the mind, of which feeling is only one ingredient.

I had occasion, in the preceding Essays, to observe, that several operations of the mind, to which we give one name, and consider as one act, are compounded of more simple acts inseparably united in our constitution, and that, in these, sensation or feeling often makes one ingredient.

Thus, the appetites of hunger and thirst are compounded of an uneasy sensation, and the desire of food or drink. In our benevolent affections, there is both an agreeable feeling, and a desire of happiness to the object of our affection; and malevolent affections have ingredients of a contrary nature.

In these instances, sensation or feeling is inseparably conjoined with desire. In other instances, we find sensation inseparably conjoined with judgment or belief, and that in two different ways. In some instances, the judgment or belief seems to be the consequence of the sensation, and to be regulated by it. In other instances, the sensation is the consequence of the judgment. [473]

When we perceive an external object by our senses, we have a sensation conjoined with a firm belief of the existence and sensible qualities of the external object. Nor has all the subtilty of metaphysics been able to disjoin what nature has conjoined in our constitution. Des Cartes and Locke endeavoured, by reasoning, to deduce the existence of external objects from our sensations, but in vain. Subsequent philosophers, finding no reason for this connection, endeavoured to throw off the belief of external objects as being unreasonable; but this attempt is no less vain. Nature has doomed us to believe the testimony of our senses, whether we can give a good reason for doing so or not.

In this instance, the belief or judgment is the consequence of the sensation, as the sensation is the consequence of the impression made on the organ of sense.

But in most of the operations of mind in which judgment or belief is combined with feeling, the feeling is the consequence of the judgment, and is regulated by it.

Thus, an account of the good conduct of a friend at a distance gives me a very agreeable feeling, and a contrary account would give me a very uneasy feeling; but these feelings depend entirely upon my belief of the report.

In hope, there is an agreeable feeling, depending upon the belief or expectation of good to come; fear is made up of contrary ingredients; in both, the feeling is regulated by the degree of belief.

In the respect we bear to the worthy, and in our contempt of the worthless, there is both judgment and feeling, and the last depends entirely upon the first.

The same may be said of gratitude for good offices and resentment of injuries. [474]

Let me now consider how I am affected when I see a man exerting himself nobly in a good cause. I am conscious that the effect of his conduct on my mind is complex, though it may be called by one name. I look up to his virtue, I approve, I admire it. In doing so, I have pleasure indeed, or

* And by many philosophers since Reid.—H.

an agreeable feeling; this is granted. But I find myself interested in his success and in his fame. This is affection; it is love and esteem, which is more than mere feeling. The man is the object of this esteem; but in mere feeling there is no object.

I am likewise conscious that this agreeable feeling in me, and this esteem of him, depend entirely upon the judgment I form of his conduct. I judge that this conduct merits esteem; and, while I thus judge, I cannot but esteem him, and contemplate his conduct with pleasure. Persuade me that he was bribed, or that he acted from some mercenary or bad motive, immediately my esteem and my agreeable feeling vanish.

In the approbation of a good action, therefore, there is feeling indeed, but there is also esteem of the agent; and both the feeling and the esteem depend upon the judgment we form of his conduct.

When I exercise my moral faculty about my own actions or those of other men, I am conscious that I judge as well as feel. I accuse and excuse, I acquit and condemn, I assent and dissent, I believe and disbelieve, and doubt. These are acts of judgment, and not feelings.

Every determination of the understanding, with regard to what is true or false, is judgment. That I ought not to steal, or to kill, or to bear false witness, are propositions, of the truth of which I am as well convinced as of any proposition in Euclid. I am conscious that I judge them to be true propositions; and my consciousness makes all other arguments unnecessary, with regard to the operations of my own mind. [475]

That other men judge, as well as feel, in such cases, I am convinced, because they understand me when I express my moral judgment, and express theirs by the same terms and phrases.

Suppose that, in a case well known to both, my friend says—*Such a man did well and worthily, his conduct is highly approvable.* This speech, according to all rules of interpretation, expresses my friend's judgment of the man's conduct. This judgment may be true or false, and I may agree in opinion with him, or I may dissent from him without offence, as we may differ in other matters of judgment.

Suppose, again, that, in relation to the same case, my friend says—*The man's conduct gave me a very agreeable feeling.*

This speech, if approbation be nothing but an agreeable feeling, must have the very same meaning with the first, and express neither more nor less. But this cannot be, for two reasons.

First, Because there is no rule in grammar or rhetoric, nor any usage in language, by which these two speeches can be construed so as to have the same meaning. The *first* expresses plainly an opinion or judgment of the conduct of the man, but says nothing of the speaker. The *second* only testifies a fact concerning the speaker—to wit, that he had such a feeling.

Another reason why these two speeches cannot mean the same thing is, that the first may be contradicted without any ground of offence, such contradiction being only a difference of opinion, which, to a reasonable man, gives no offence. But the second speech cannot be contradicted without an affront: for, as every man must know his own feelings, to deny that a man had a feeling which he affirms he had, is to charge him with falsehood. [476]

If moral approbation be a real judgment, which produces an agreeable feeling in the mind of him who judges, both speeches are perfectly intelligible, in the most obvious and literal sense. Their meaning is different, but they are related, so that the one may be inferred from the other, as we infer the effect from the cause, or the cause from the effect. I know, that what a man judges to be a very worthy action, he contemplates with pleasure; and what he contemplates with pleasure must, in his judgment, have worth. But the judgment and the feeling are different acts of his mind, though connected as cause and effect. He can express either the one or the other with perfect propriety; but the speech, which expresses his feeling, is altogether improper and inept to express his judgment, for this evident reason, that judgment and feeling, though in some cases connected, are things in their nature different.

If we suppose, on the other hand, that moral approbation is nothing more than an agreeable feeling, occasioned by the contemplation of an action, the second speech, above mentioned, has a distinct meaning, and expresses all that is meant by moral approbation. But the first speech either means the very same thing, (which cannot be, for the reasons already mentioned,) or it has no meaning.

Now, we may appeal to the reader, whether, in conversation upon human characters, such speeches as the first are not as frequent, as familiar, and as well understood, as anything in language; and whether they have not been common in all ages that we can trace, and in all languages? [477]

This doctrine, therefore, That moral approbation is merely a feeling without judgment, necessarily carries along with it this consequence, that a form of speech, upon one of the most common topics of discourse, which either has no meaning, or a meaning irreconcilable to all rules of grammar or rhetoric, is found to be common and familiar in all languages and in all ages of the world, while every man knows how to express the meaning, if it have any, in plain and proper language.

Such a consequence I think sufficient to sink any philosophical opinion on which it hangs.

A particular language may have some oddity, or even absurdity, introduced by some man of eminence, from caprice or wrong judgment, and followed by servile imitators, for a time, till it be detected, and, of consequence, discountenanced and dropt; but that the same absurdity should pervade all languages, through all ages, and that, after being detected and exposed, it should still keep its countenance and its place in language as much as before, this can never be while men have understanding.

It may be observed, by the way, that the same argument may be applied, with equal force, against those other paradoxical opinions of modern philosophy, which we before mentioned as connected with this; such as, that beauty and deformity are not at all in the objects to which language universally ascribes them, but are merely feelings in the mind of the spectator; that the secondary qualities are not in external objects, but are merely feelings or sensations in him that perceives them; and, in general, that our external and internal senses are faculties by which we have sensations or feelings only, but by which we do not judge. [478]

That every form of speech which language affords to express our judgment, should, in all ages and in all languages, be used to express what is no judgment; and that feelings which are easily expressed in proper language, should as universally be expressed by language altogether improper and absurd, I cannot believe; and, therefore, must conclude, that, if language be the expression of thought, men judge of the primary and secondary qualities of body by their external senses, of beauty and deformity by their taste, and of virtue and vice by their moral faculty.

A truth so evident as this is, can hardly be obscured and brought into doubt, but by the abuse of words. And much abuse of words there has been upon this subject. To avoid this as much as possible, I have used the word *judgment* on one side, and *sensation* or *feeling* upon the other; because these words have been least liable to abuse or ambiguity. But it may be proper to make some observations upon other words that have been used in this controversy.

Mr Hume, in his "Treatise of Human Nature," has employed two sections upon it, the titles of which are, "*Moral Distinctions not derived from Reason*," and "*Moral Distinctions derived from a Moral Sense*."

When he is not, by custom, led unawares to speak of Reason like other men, he limits that word to signify only the power of judging in matters merely speculative. Hence he concludes, "That reason of itself is inactive and perfectly inert;" that "actions may be laudable or blamable, but cannot be reasonable or unreasonable;" that "it is not contrary to reason to prefer the destruction of the whole world to the scratching of my finger;" that "it is not contrary to reason for me to chuse my total ruin to prevent the least uneasiness of an Indian, or of a person wholly unknown to me;" that "reason is, and ought only to be, the slave of the passions, and can never pretend to any other office than to serve and obey them." [479]

If we take the word *reason* to mean what common use, both of philosophers and of the vulgar, hath made it to mean, these maxims are not only false, but licentious. It is only his abuse of the words *reason* and *passion* that can justify them from this censure.

The meaning of a common word is not to be ascertained by philosophical theory, but by common usage; and, if a man will take the liberty of limiting or extending the meaning of common words at his pleasure, he may, like Mandeville, insinuate the most licentious paradoxes with the appearance of plausibility. I have before made some observations upon the meaning of this word, (Essay II., chap. 2, and Essay III., part iii. chap. 1,) to which the reader is referred.

When Mr Hume derives moral distinctions from a Moral Sense, I agree with him in words, but we differ about the meaning of the word *sense*. Every power to which the name of a Sense has been given, is a power of judging of the objects of that Sense,* and has been accounted such in all ages; the moral sense, therefore, is the power of judging in morals. But Mr Hume will have the Moral Sense to be only a power of feeling without judging—this I take to be an abuse of a word.

Authors who place moral approbation in feeling only, very often use the word *Sentiment*, to express feeling without judgment. This I take likewise to be an abuse of a word. Our moral determinations may, with propriety, be called *moral sentiments*. For the word *sentiment*, in the English language, never, as I conceive, signifies mere feeling, but *judgment accompanied with feeling*.† It was wont to signify opinion or judgment of any kind, but, of late, is appropriated to signify an opinion or judgment, that strikes, and produces some agreeable

* See above, p. 300, note.—H.

† This is too unqualified an assertion. The term *Sentiment* is in English applied to the *higher feelings*.—H.

or uneasy emotion. So we speak of sentiments of respect, of esteem, of gratitude; but I never heard the pain of the gout, or any other mere feeling, called a sentiment. [480]

Even the word *judgment* has been used by Mr Hume to express what he maintains to be only a feeling. "Treatise of Human Nature, part iii., page 3:—"The term *perception* is no less applicable to those *judgments* by which we distinguish moral good and evil than to every other operation of the mind." Perhaps he used this word inadvertently; for I think there cannot be a greater abuse of words than to put judgment for what he held to be mere feeling.*

All the words most commonly used, both by philosophers and by the vulgar, to express the operations of our moral faculty—such as, *decision, determination, sentence, approbation, disapprobation, applause, censure, praise, blame*—necessarily imply judgment in their meaning. When, therefore, they are used by Mr Hume, and others who hold his opinion, to signify feelings only, this is an abuse of words. If these philosophers wish to speak plainly and properly, they must, in discoursing of morals, discard these words altogether, because their established signification in the language is contrary to what they would express by them.

They must likewise discard from morals the words *ought* and *ought not*, which very properly express judgment, but cannot be applied to mere feelings. Upon these words Mr Hume has made a particular observation in the conclusion of his first section above mentioned. I shall give it in his own words, and make some remarks upon it.

"I cannot forbear adding to these reasonings an observation which may, perhaps, be found of some importance. In every system of morality which I have hitherto met with, I have always remarked that the author proceeds for some time in the ordinary way of reasoning, and establishes the being of a God, or makes observations concerning human affairs; when, of a sudden, I am surprised to find that, instead of the usual copulations of propositions, *is*, and *is not*, I meet with no proposition that is not connected with an *ought* or an *ought not*. [481] This change is imperceptible, but is, however, of the last consequence. For, as this *ought* or *ought not* expresses some new relation or affirmation, 'tis necessary that it should be observed and explained; and, at the same time, that a reason should be given for what seems altogether inconceivable—how this new relation can be a deduction from others which are entirely different from it. But, as authors do not commonly use this precaution, I shall presume to recommend it to the readers; and am persuaded that this small attention would subvert all the vulgar systems of morality, and let us see that the distinction of vice and virtue is not founded merely on the relations of objects, nor is perceived by reason."

We may here observe, that it is acknowledged that the words *ought* and *ought not* express some relation or affirmation; but a relation or affirmation which Mr Hume thought inexplicable, or, at least, inconsistent with his system of morals. He must, therefore, have thought that they ought not to be used in treating of that subject.

He likewise makes two demands, and, taking it for granted that they cannot be satisfied, is persuaded that an attention to this is sufficient to subvert all the vulgar systems of morals.

The *first* demand is, that *ought* and *ought not* be explained.

To a man that understands English, there are surely no words that require explanation less. Are not all men taught, from their early years, that they ought not to lie, nor steal, nor swear falsely? But Mr Hume thinks, that men never understood what these precepts mean, or rather that they are unintelligible. If this be so, I think indeed it will follow, that all the vulgar systems of morals are subverted. [482]

Dr Johnson, in his Dictionary, explains the word *ought* to signify, *being obliged by duty*; and I know no better explication that can be given of it. The reader will see what I thought necessary to say concerning the moral relation expressed by this word in Essay III., part iii., chap. 5.

The *second* demand is, That a reason should be given why this relation should be a deduction from others which are entirely different from it.

This is to demand a reason for what does not exist. The first principles of morals are not deductions. They are self-evident; and their truth, like that of other axioms, is perceived without reasoning or deduction. And moral truths that are not self-evident are deduced, not from relations quite different from them, but from the first principles of morals.

In a matter so interesting to mankind, and so frequently the subject of conversation among the learned and the unlearned as morals is, it may surely be expected that men will express both their judgments and their feelings with propriety, and consistently with the rules of language. An opinion, therefore, which makes the language of all ages and nations, upon this subject, to be improper, contrary to all rules of lan-

* Mr Hume could easily be defended.—H.

guage, and fit to be discarded, needs no other refutation.

As mankind have, in all ages, understood *reason* to mean the power by which not only our speculative opinions, but our actions ought to be regulated, we may say, with perfect propriety, that all vice is contrary to reason; that, by reason, we are to judge of what we ought to do, as well as of what we ought to believe. [483]

But, though all vice be contrary to reason, I conceive that it would not be a proper definition of vice to say that it is a conduct contrary to reason, because this definition would apply equally to folly, which all men distinguish from vice.

There are other phrases which have been used on the same side of the question, which I see no reason for adopting, such as—*acting contrary to the relations of things—contrary to the reason of things—to the fitness of things—to the truth of things—to absolute fitness.* These phrases have not the authority of common use, which, in matters of language, is great. They seem to have been invented by some authors, with a view to explain the nature of vice; but I do not think they answer that end. If intended as definitions of vice, they are improper; because, in the most favourable sense they can bear, they extend to every kind of foolish and absurd conduct, as well as to that which is vicious.

I shall conclude this chapter with some observations upon the five arguments which Mr Hume has offered upon this point in his "Enquiry."

The *first* is, That it is impossible that the hypothesis he opposes, can, in any particular instance, be so much as rendered intelligible, whatever specious figure it may make in general discourse. "Examine," says he, "the crime of *ingratitude*, anatomize all its circumstances, and examine, by your reason alone, in what consists the demerit or blame, you will never come to any issue or conclusion."

I think it unnecessary to follow him through all the accounts of ingratitude which he conceives may be given by those whom he opposes, because I agree with him in that which he himself adopts—to wit, "That this crime arises from a complication of circumstances, which, being presented to the spectator, excites the sentiment of blame by the particular structure and fabric of his mind." [484]

This he thought a true and intelligible account of the criminality of ingratitude. So do I. And therefore I think the hypothesis he opposes is intelligible, when applied to a particular instance.

Mr Hume, no doubt, thought that the account he gives of ingratitude is inconsistent with the hypothesis he opposes, and could not be adopted by those who hold that hypothesis. He could be led to think so, only by taking for granted one of these two things. Either, *first*, That the *sentiment of blame* is a feeling only, without judgment; or, *secondly*, That whatever is excited by the particular fabric and structure of the mind must be feeling only, and not judgment. But I cannot grant either the one or the other.

For, as to the *first*, it seems evident to me, that both *sentiment* and *blame* imply judgment; and, therefore, that the *sentiment of blame* is a judgment accompanied with feeling, and not mere feeling without judgment.

The *second* can as little be granted; for no operation of mind, whether judgment or feeling, can be excited but by that particular structure and fabric of the mind which makes us capable of that operation.

By that part of our fabric which we call *the faculty of seeing*, we judge of visible objects;* by *taste*, another part of our fabric, we judge of beauty and deformity; by that part of our fabric which enables us to form abstract conceptions, to compare them, and perceive their relations, we judge of abstract truths; and by that part of our fabric which we call the *moral faculty*, we judge of virtue and vice. If we suppose a being without any moral faculty in his fabric, I grant that he could not have the sentiments of blame and moral approbation. [485]

There are, therefore, judgments, as well as feelings, that are excited by the particular structure and fabric of the mind. But there is this remarkable difference between them, That every judgment is, in its own nature, true or false; and, though it depends upon the fabric of a mind, whether it have such a judgment or not, it depends not upon that fabric whether the judgment be true or not. A true judgment will be true, whatever be the fabric of the mind; but a particular structure and fabric is necessary, in order to our perceiving that truth. Nothing like this can be said of mere feelings, because the attributes of true or false do not belong to them.

Thus I think it appears, that the hypothesis which Mr Hume opposes is not unintelligible, when applied to the particular instance of ingratitude; because the account of ingratitude which he himself thinks true and intelligible, is perfectly agreeable to it.

The *second* argument amounts to this: That, in moral deliberation, we must be acquainted before-hand with all the objects and all their relations. After these things are known, the understanding has

* See above, p. 590, note.—H.

no farther room to operate. Nothing remains but to feel, on our part, some sentiment of blame or approbation.

Let us apply this reasoning to the office of a judge. In a cause that comes before him, he must be made acquainted with all the objects, and all their relations. After this, his understanding has no farther room to operate. Nothing remains, on his part, but to feel the right or the wrong: and mankind have, very absurdly, called him a *judge*—he ought to be called a *feeler*. [486]

To answer this argument more directly: The man who deliberates, after all the objects and relations mentioned by Mr Hume are known to him, has a point to determine; and that is, whether the action under his deliberation ought to be done or ought not. In most cases, this point will appear self-evident to a man who has been accustomed to exercise his moral judgment; in some cases it may require reasoning.

In like manner, the judge, after all the circumstances of the cause are known, has to judge whether the plaintiff has a just plea or not.

The *third* argument is taken from the analogy between moral beauty and natural, between moral sentiment and taste. As beauty is not a quality of the object, but a certain feeling of the spectator, so virtue and vice are not qualities in the persons to whom language ascribes them, but feelings of the spectator.

But is it certain that beauty is not any quality of the object? This is indeed a paradox of modern philosophy, built upon a philosophical theory; but a paradox so contrary to the common language and common sense of mankind, that it ought rather to overturn the theory on which it stands, than receive any support from it. And if beauty be really a quality of the object, and not merely a feeling of the spectator, the whole force of this argument goes over to the other side of the question.

"Euclid," he says, "has fully explained all the qualities of the circle, but has not, in any proposition, said a word of its beauty. The reason is evident. The beauty is not a quality of the circle." [487]

By the *qualities of the circle*, he must mean its properties; and there are here two mistakes.

First, Euclid has not fully explained all the properties of the circle. Many have been discovered and demonstrated which he never dreamt of.

Secondly, The reason why Euclid has not said a word of the beauty of the circle, is not, *that beauty is not a quality of the circle*; the reason is, that Euclid never digresses from his subject. His purpose was to demonstrate the mathematical properties of the circle. Beauty is a quality of the circle, not demonstrable by mathematical reasoning, but immediately perceived by a good taste. To speak of it would have been a digression from his subject; and that is a fault he is never guilty of.

The *fourth* argument is, That inanimate objects may bear to each other all the same relations which we observe in moral agents.

If this were true, it would be very much to the purpose; but it seems to be thrown out rashly, without any attention to its evidence. Had Mr Hume reflected but a very little upon this dogmatical assertion, a thousand instances would have occurred to him in direct contradiction to it.

May not one animal be more tame, or more docile, or more cunning, or more fierce, or more ravenous, than another? Are these relations to be found in inanimate objects? May not one man be a better painter, or sculptor, or ship-builder, or tailor, or shoemaker, than another? Are these relations to be found in inanimate objects, or even in brute animals? May not one moral agent be more just, more pious, more attentive to any moral duty, or more eminent in any moral virtue, than another? Are not these relations peculiar to moral agents? But to come to the relations most essential to morality. [488]

When I say that *I ought to do such an action*, that *it is my duty*, do not these words express a relation between me and a certain action in my power; a relation which cannot be between inanimate objects, or between any other objects but a moral agent and his moral actions; a relation which is well understood by all men come to years of understanding, and expressed in all languages?

Again, when in deliberating about two actions in my power, which cannot both be done, I say *this* ought to be preferred to the other—that justice, for instance, ought to be preferred to generosity—I express a moral relation between two actions of a moral agent, which is well understood, and which cannot exist between objects of any other kind.

There are, therefore, moral relations which can have no existence but between moral agents and their voluntary actions. To determine these relations is the object of morals; and to determine relations is the province of judgment, not of mere feeling.

The *last* argument is a chain of several propositions, which deserve distinct consideration. They may, I think, be summed up in these four:—1. There must be ultimate ends of action, beyond which it is absurd to ask a reason of acting. 2. The ultimate ends of human actions can never be accounted for by reason; 3. but recommend themselves entirely to the sentiments and affections of mankind, without any dependence on the intellectual faculties. 4. As virtue is an end, and is desirable on its own account, without fee or reward, merely for the immediate satisfaction it conveys; it is requisite that there should be some sentiment which it touches, some internal taste or feeling, or whatever you please to call it, which distinguishes moral good and evil, and which embraces the one and rejects the other. [489]

To the *first* of these propositions I entirely agree. The ultimate ends of action are what I have called *the principles of action*, which I have endeavoured, in the third essay, to enumerate, and to class under three heads of mechanical, animal, and rational.

The *second* proposition needs some explication. I take its meaning to be, That there cannot be another end, for the sake of which an ultimate end is pursued. For the reason of an action means nothing but the end for which the action is done; and the reason of an end of action can mean nothing but another end, for the sake of which that end is pursued, and to which it is the means.

That this is the author's meaning is evident from his reasoning in confirmation of it. "Ask a man, *why he uses exercise?* he will answer, *because he desires to keep his health.* If you then inquire, *why he desires health?* he will readily reply, *because sickness is painful.* If you push your inquiries further, and desire a reason why he hates pain, it is impossible he can ever give any. This is an ultimate end, and is never referred to any other object." To account by reason for an end, therefore, is to shew another end, for the sake of which that end is desired and pursued. And that, in this sense, an ultimate end can never be accounted for by reason, is certain, because that cannot be an ultimate end which is pursued only for the sake of another end.

I agree therefore with Mr Hume in this second proposition, which indeed is implied in the first. [490]

The *third* proposition is, That ultimate ends recommend themselves entirely to the sentiments and affections of mankind, without any dependence on the intellectual faculties.

By *sentiments* he must here mean feelings without judgment, and by *affections*, such affections as imply no judgment. For surely any operation that implies judgment, cannot be independent of the intellectual faculties.

This being understood, I cannot assent to this proposition.

The author seems to think it implied in the preceding, or a necessary consequence from it, that because an ultimate end cannot be accounted for by reason—that is, cannot be pursued merely for the sake of another end—therefore it can have no dependence on the intellectual faculties. I deny this consequence, and can see no force in it.

I think it not only does not follow from the preceding proposition, but that it is contrary to truth.

A man may act from gratitude as an ultimate end; but gratitude implies a judgment and belief of favours received, and therefore is dependent on the intellectual faculties. A man may act from respect to a worthy character as an ultimate end; but this respect necessarily implies a judgment of worth in the person, and therefore is dependent on the intellectual faculties.

I have endeavoured, in the third Essay before mentioned, to shew that, beside the animal principles of our nature, which require will and intention, but not judgment, there are also in human nature rational principles of action, or ultimate ends, which have, in all ages, been called rational, and have a just title to that name, not only from the authority of language, but because they can have no existence but in beings endowed with reason, and because, in all their exertions, they require not only intention and will, but judgment or reason. [491]

Therefore, until it can be proved that an ultimate end cannot be dependent on the intellectual faculties, this third proposition, and all that hangs upon it, must fall to the ground.

The *last* proposition assumes, with very good reason, That virtue is an ultimate end, and desirable on its own account. From which, if the third proposition were true, the conclusion would undoubtedly follow, That virtue has no dependence on the intellectual faculties. But, as that proposition is not granted, nor proved, this conclusion is left without any support from the whole of the argument.

I should not have thought it worth while to insist so long upon this controversy, if I did not conceive that the consequences which the contrary opinions draw after them are important.

If what we call *moral judgment* be no real judgment, but merely a feeling, it follows that the principles of morals which we have been taught to consider as an immutable law to all intelligent beings, have no other foundation but an arbitrary structure and fabric in the constitution of the human mind. So that, by a change in our structure, what is immoral might become moral, virtue might be turned into vice, and vice into virtue. And beings of a different structure, according to the variety of their feelings, may have different, nay opposite measures of moral good and evil. [492]

It follows that, from our notions of morals, we can conclude nothing concerning a moral character in the Deity, which is the foundation of all religion, and the strongest support of virtue.

Nay, this opinion seems to conclude strongly against a moral character in the Deity, since nothing arbitrary or mutable can be conceived to enter into the description of a nature eternal, immutable, and necessarily existent. Mr Hume seems perfectly consistent with himself, in allowing of no evidence for the moral attributes of the Supreme Being, whatever there may be for his natural attributes.

On the other hand, if moral judgment be a true and real judgment, the principles of morals stand upon the immutable foundation of truth, and can undergo no change by any difference of fabric, or structure of those who judge of them. There may be, and there are, beings, who have not the faculty of conceiving moral truths, or perceiving the excellence of moral worth, as there are beings incapable of perceiving mathematical truths; but no defect, no error of understanding, can make what is true to be false.

[492, 493]

If it be true that piety, justice, benevolence, wisdom, temperance, fortitude, are, in their own nature, the most excellent and most amiable qualities of a human creature; that vice has an inherent turpitude, which merits disapprobation and dislike; these truths cannot be hid from Him whose understanding is infinite, whose judgment is always according to truth, and who must esteem everything according to its real value.

The Judge of all the earth, we are sure, will do right. He has given to men the faculty of perceiving the right and the wrong in conduct, as far as is necessary to our present state, and of perceiving the dignity of the one, and the demerit of the other; and surely there can be no real knowledge or real excellence in man, which is not in his Maker. [493]

We may therefore justly conclude, That what we know in part, and see in part, of right and wrong, he sees perfectly; that the moral excellence, which we see and admire in some of our fellow-creatures is a faint but true copy of that moral excellence which is essential to his nature; and that to tread the path of virtue, is the true dignity of our nature, an imitation of God, and the way to obtain his favour.

A

BRIEF ACCOUNT

OF

ARISTOTLE'S LOGIC,*

WITH REMARKS.

CHAPTER I.

OF THE FIRST THREE TREATISES.

Section I.

OF THE AUTHOR.

ARISTOTLE had very uncommon advantages: born in an age when the philosophical spirit in Greece had long flourished, and was in its greatest vigour; brought up in the court of Macedon, where his father was the king's physician; twenty years a favourite scholar of Plato; and tutor to Alexander the Great, who both honoured him with his friendship, and supplied him with everything necessary for the prosecution of his inquiries.

These advantages he improved by indefatigable study, and immense reading.* He was the first we know,† says Strabo, who composed a library; and in this the Egyptian and Pergamenian kings copied his example. As to his genius, it would be disrespectful to mankind not to allow an uncommon share to a man who governed the opinions of the most enlightened part of the species near two thousand years.‡

If his talents had been laid out solely for the discovery of truth and the good of mankind, his laurels would have remained for ever fresh; but he seems to have had a greater passion for fame than for truth, and to have wanted rather to be admired as the prince of philosophers than to be useful; so that it is dubious whether there be in his character most of the philosopher or of the sophist.§ The opinion of Lord Bacon is

---

* This treatise originally appeared in the second volume of Lord Kames's "Sketches of the History of Man," published in the year 1774. It was written at the earnest solicitation of his Lordship, and forms an appendix to the sketch which he has entitled "Principles and Progress of Reason." From Reid's Correspondence, (*supra*, p. 49, b,) it would appear that he had begun the execution of his task towards the close of the year 1767. Since Reid's death, this work has been once and again published, apart and in the series of the author's philosophical writings, under the title, "Analysis of Aristotle's Logic." But, as the term *Analysis* was applied to it only by the fiat of the bookseller, and may tend to convey an erroneous conception of its purport, I have adhered to the original title, which, not only, good or bad, has a right of occupancy, but is, in fact, far more appropriate to the real character of the work, which is at once more and less than an analysis of the Organon.

From the number of errors, especially in the proper names and terms of art, with which this treatise is deformed, as well in the original as in all the subsequent editions, it is probable that the first impression was not revised by the author, who was, however, it must be owned, at all times rather negligent in this respect. These I shall, in this treatise, silently correct. This I have, indeed, frequently taken the liberty of doing in the other works; but I need not say that such corrections are, in all cases, only of palpable inaccuracies or oversights, and do not extend to a change of even the smallest peculiarity of expression.—H.

* If we take circumstances into account, his activity and research, his erudition and universality, have never been equalled. "For the master of the learned," says Hegel, himself a kindred genius, "the criminal jurisprudence of the Ocean Cumæ or a mythical fable of the founding of a city, were not less attractive than speculations regarding first causes and supreme ends, than discussions on the laws of animal life or the principles of poetry."—H.

† Strabo says, "As far as we know" (ὧν ἴσμεν;) but even this qualification does not render the assertion correct.—H.

‡ This is a very scanty allowance. Others have not been so niggardly. As a specimen:—"*Aristotle*," says Johann von Mueller, "*was the clearest intellect that ever illuminated the world;*" his own rival, Campanella, styles him "*Naturæ Genius;*" and the Christian rigour of St Jerome confesses him *Miraculum Mundi*, and *Humani Intellectus Finis*.—H.

§ In reference to this antithesis, I have great pleasure in quoting a passage from an excellent introductory lecture to a first course of Greek and Latin Philosophy in the *College Royal de France*, by M Barthélemy Saint-Hilaire, to whom we owe an admirable edition, translation, and criticism of the Politics of Aristotle. M. Saint-Hilaire and M. Ravaisson are remarkable manifestations of the spirit of philosophical scholarship, now auspiciously awakened in France by the discipline, example, and

not without probability, That his ambition was as boundless as that of his royal pupil; the one aspiring at universal monarchy over the bodies and fortunes of men, the other over their opinions.* If this was the case, it cannot be said that the philosopher pursued his aim with less industry, less ability, or less success than the hero.†

His writings carry too evident marks of that philosophical pride, vanity, and envy, which have often sullied the character of the learned. He determines boldly things above all human knowledge; and enters upon the most difficult questions, as his pupil entered on a battle, with full assurance of success. He delivers his decisions oracularly, and without any fear of mistake.* Rather than confess his ignorance, he hides it under hard words and ambiguous expressions, of which his interpreters can make what pleases them. There is even reason to suspect that he wrote often with affected obscurity; either that the air of mystery might procure greater veneration,† or that his books might be understood only by the adepts who had been initiated in his philosophy.

His conduct towards the writers that went before him has been much censured. After the manner of the Ottoman princes, says Lord Verulam, he thought his throne could not be secure unless he killed all his brethren.‡ Ludovicus Vives charges him with detracting from all philosophers, that he might derive that glory to himself of which he robbed them.§ He rarely quotes an author but with a view to censure, and is not very fair in representing the opinions which he censures.

The faults we have mentioned are such as might be expected in a man who had the daring ambition to be transmitted to all future ages as the Prince of Philosophers, as one who had carried every branch of human knowledge to its utmost limit, and who was not very scrupulous about the means he took to obtain his end.

We ought, however, to do him the justice to observe, that, although the pride and vanity of the Sophist appear too much in his writings in abstract philosophy, yet, in natural history, the fidelity of his narrations seems to be equal to his industry; and he always distinguishes between what he knew

---

encouragement of the accomplished thinker to whom this edition of Reid is dedicated.

"Depuis Bacon et Des Cartes, il avait été reçu comme une opinion de bon goût et une preuve d'originalité, de dédaigner profondément l'antiquité. Ce dédain appuyé sur l'autorité de ces deux grands exemples, fit fortune en *France* et en *Angleterre*. Aristote surtout en avait été l'objet; et c'est à peine s'il y a quelques années que ce superbe mépris n'a plus de succès parmi nous. Les meilleurs esprits n'avaient pas su se défendre de ce préjugé et de cet aveuglement de l'égoïsme moderne. Reid, le chef de l'école Écossaise, tout circonspect qu'il est, par les habitudes de son caractère et par l'esprit même de sa doctrine, Reid se croit encore tenu d'insulter Aristote, passez-moi le mot car il est vrai, et il va jusqu'à dire qu'il ne sait si, dans le précepteur d'Alexandre, le sophiste ne l'emporte pas sur le philosophe. Chez nous, il y a vingt ans à peine, l'illustre M. de Tracy affirmait, sans réclamation contraire, que jamais doctrine n'avait autant nui que celle d'Aristote à l'esprit humain. Brucker, le grand historien de la philosophie, n'est pas plus équitable que Reid et M. de Tracy. Quand les philosophes eux-mêmes en étaient arrivés à ce point, on peut imaginer sans peine ce que devait être le sentiment de la foule qui, sur ces matières, recevait nécessairement ses opinions toutes faites, des juges compétens. Molière avait raillé Aristote sur la scène; et les sarcasmes de poëts spirituels et vrais, quand il les faisait, parce qu'alors ils pouvaient être dangereux pour lui et utiles à la société, étaient seuls demeurés, dans un siècle où cependant ils n'avaient plus ni sel ni même de signification."

This is not the place to enter into a vindication of the scientific integrity of Aristotle. I shall simply observe, that his works afford no valid ground on which to conclude that he was ever actuated by any other than the generous sentiment which he professes—"that a philosopher, a *lover of wisdom*, is bound, in the cause of Truth, to refute all error, be it the error of himself or of his friends; for, though friends be dear, it is still his hallowed duty to give the higher reverence to Truth; ἀμφοῖν γὰρ ὄντοιν φίλοιν, ὅσιον προτιμᾶν τὴν ἀλήθειαν.—H.

* "For this excellent person, Aristotle, I will think of him, that he learned that humour of his scholar, with whom, it seemeth, he did emulate—the one to conquer all opinions, as the other to conquer all nations. Wherein, nevertheless, it may be, he may, at some men's hands, that are of a bitter disposition, get a like title as his scholar did:—

Felix terrarum prædo, non utile mundo
Editus exemplum, &c.

So—

Felix doctrinæ prædo."

"Advancement of Learning," Book II. See also "De Augmentis Scientiarum," Lib. III. c. 4.

† In fact, were such his aim, he accomplished it with far superior success. The monarchy of Alexander terminated with his death; whereas of Aristotle is pre-eminently true, what has been, not more beautifully than justly, said of the ancients in general—

"*The great of old!*
The dead but sceptred sovrans, who still rule
Our spirits from their urns."

Aristotle governs the opinions of more than are conscious of their allegiance to the Stagirite. His seal is upon all the sciences, and his speculations have mediately or immediately determined those of all subsequent thinkers. Aristotle and Plato are as the two poles of human intelligence, between which the various systems of philosophy still continue to oscillate.—H.

* This assertion is curiously incorrect. On the contrary, Aristotle rarely propounds a categorical decision; his conclusions being usually qualified with an ἴσως, a τάχα, a φαίνεται, &c.—H.

† "Socrates, Aristotle, Galen, were men full of ostentation."—Bacon, *Essay on Vain Glory*. The selection is singular.—H.

‡ "De Augmentis Scientiarum," Lib. III., c. 4. "Advancement of Learning," Book II.

§ The passage of Vives, to which, I presume, Reid refers, is in his Commentary on St Austin; and it is but fair to quote it at large.—*Magnus et admirabilis vir, quique ingenio diligentiaque vicerit plurimos, nemini erat secundus; variarum rerum cognitione Platone magistro superior; artificio, vero, omnes, qui ex omni memoria humanas tractaverunt artes, longo intervallo post se reliquit. Non sunt præterea dolo maligno vel obscurandæ vel interpretandæ. Fuisse cupidiorem gloriæ, avidiorem carpendi alios, fatendum est; at dexteritatem in tradendis artibus nondum est aliquis ab ævo condito consecutus.* De Civ. Dei, L. viii. c. 12.

The accusation of unfairness in his representation of the opinions of others, which owed its origin to the lower Platonists, has now been very generally abandoned.—H.

and what he had by report.* And, even in abstract philosophy, it would be unfair to impute to Aristotle all the faults, all the obscurities, and all the contradictions that are to be found in his writings. The greatest part, and perhaps the best part, of his writings is lost.† There is reason to doubt whether some of those we ascribe to him be really his; and whether what are his be not much vitiated and interpolated. These suspicions are justified by the fate of Aristotle's writings, which is judiciously related, from the best authorities, in Bayle's Dictionary, under the article *Tyrannion*, to which I refer.‡

His books in Logic, which remain, are, 1. One book of the Categories. 2. One of Interpretation. 3. First Analytics, two books. 4. Last Analytics, two books. 5. Topics, eight books. 6. Of Sophisms, one book. Diogenes Laertius mentions many others that are lost.§ Those I have mentioned have commonly been published together, under the name of Aristotle's Organon, or his *Logic*; and, for many ages, Porphyry's‖ Introduction to the Categories has been prefixed to them.

Section II.

OF PORPHYRY'S INTRODUCTION.

In this introduction, which is addressed to Chrysaorius, the author observes, That, in order to understand Aristotle's doctrine concerning the Categories, it is necessary to know what a *Genus* is, what a *Species*, what a *Specific Difference*, what a *Property*, and what an *Accident*; that the knowledge of these is also very useful in Definition, in Division, and even in Demonstration; therefore, he proposes, in this little tract, to deliver shortly and simply the doctrine of the ancients, and chiefly of the Peripatetics, concerning these five *Predicables*, avoiding the more intricate questions concerning them; such as, Whether *genera* and *species* do really exist in nature? or, Whether, they are only conceptions of the human mind? If they exist in nature, Whether they are corporeal or incorporeal? and, Whether they are inherent in the objects of sense, or disjoined from them? These, he says, are very difficult questions, and require accurate discussion; but that he is not to meddle with them.

After this preface, he explains very minutely each of the "*five words*" above mentioned, divides and subdivides each of them, and then pursues all the agreements and differences between one and another through sixteen [seventeen] chapters.*

Section III.

OF THE CATEGORIES.†

The book begins with an explication of what is meant by [*synonymous*‡ or] *univocal* words, what by [*homonymous*, or] *equivocal*, and what by [*paronymous*, or] *denominative*. Then it is observed, that what we say is either simple, without composition or structure, as *man*, *horse*, [*fights*, *runs*;] or it has composition and structure, as a *man fights*, *the horse runs*. Next comes a distinction between a *subject of predication*; that is, a subject of which anything is affirmed or denied, and a *subject of inhesion*. These things are said to be inherent in a subject, which, although they are not a part of the subject,§ cannot possibly exist without it, as figure in the thing figured. Of things that are, says Aristotle, [1°] *some may be predicated of a subject, but are in no subject*;‖ as man may be predicated of James or John, but is not in any subject. [2°] *Some again are in a subject, but can be predicated of no subject.*¶ Thus my knowledge in grammar is in me as its subject, but it can be predicated of no subject; because it is an individual thing. [3°] *Some are both in a subject, and may be predicated of a subject*,** as science, which is in the mind as its subject, and may be predicated of geometry. [4°] Lastly, *Some things can neither be in a subject nor be predicated of any subject.*†† Such are all individual substances, which cannot be predicated, because

* To this, far more than this, ample testimony is borne, among others, by Bacon, Buffon, and Cuvier. But, if so disinterested and indefatigable a worshipper of Truth in the lower walks of science, is it probable that he would sacrifice Truth to Vanity in the higher? —H.

† This is incorrect.—H.

‡ The recent critical examination of the testimonies of Strabo, Plutarch, Athenæus, Suidas, &c., in regard to the fortune of the Aristotelic writings, by Schneider, Brandis, Kopp, and Stahr, has thrown a new light upon this question. It is now proved that various of his most important works were published by Aristotle during his lifetime; and that, at least, the greater number of those now extant were preserved and patent during the two centuries and a half intervening between the death of Aristotle and their pretended publication by Tyrannion.—H.

§ We are not, however, to suppose that Aristotle was the author of all the writings under his name in the lists of Laertius, Suidas, the Anonymus Menagii, &c., or that these were all in reality distinct works.—H.

‖ Porphyry flourished from the middle of the third century.—H.

* Reid follows the *Pacian* distribution of the Organon into chapters. There are two older.—H.

† The book of Categories is rather a metaphysical than a logical treatise; and has therefore improperly been introduced into the Organon.—H.

‡ Synonymes in Logic and Synonymes in Grammar are not the same.—H.

§ It should have been, "which are in a thing, but not in it as a part."—H.

‖ Universal substances.—H.

¶ Individual or Singular Accidents.—H.

** Universal Accidents.—H.

†† Individual or Singular Substances.—H.

they are individuals; and cannot be in a subject, because they are substances. After some other subtleties about Predicates and Subjects, we come to the Categories themselves; the things above mentioned being called by the schoolmen the *antepredicamenta*. It may be observed, however, that, notwithstanding the distinction now explained, the *being in a subject*, and the *being predicated truly of a subject*, are, in the Analytics, used as synonymous phrases;* and this variation of style has led some persons to think that the Categories were not written by Aristotle.

Things which may be expressed without composition or structure are, says the author, reducible to the following heads:—They are either *Substance*, or *Quantity*, or *Quality*, or *Relatives* [or *Posture*], or *Place* [*where*], or *Time* [*when*], or *Having*, or *Doing*, or *Suffering*. These are the Predicaments or Categories. The first four are largely treated of in four chapters; the others are slightly passed over, as sufficiently clear of themselves. As a specimen, I shall give a summary of what he says on the category of Substance.

Substances are either *primary*—to wit, individual substances; or, *secondary*—to wit, the genera and species of substances. Primary substances neither are *in* a subject, nor can be predicated *of* a subject; but all other things that exist, either are in primary substances, or may be predicated of them. For whatever can be predicated of that which is in a subject, may also be predicated of the subject itself. Primary substances are more substances than the secondary; and of the secondary, the species is more a substance than the genus. If there were no primary, there could be no secondary substances.

The properties of Substance are these:—1. No substance is capable of intention or remission. 2. No substance can be in any other thing as its subject of inhesion. 3. No substance has a contrary; for one substance cannot be contrary to another; nor can there be contrariety between a substance and that which is no substance. 4.

* For this statement, Reid has been bitterly reproached by the learned Dr Gillies, and various English writers in his wake, while Mr Stewart only attempts to palliate the error, but not to vindicate the accuracy, of his friend.

"The subject," observes the former in his "New Analysis of Aristotle's Works," "has been strangely perplexed by mistaking Aristotle's language, which is itself highly perspicuous. Τὸ δὲ ἐν ὅλῳ εἶναι, &c. '*To say that one term is contained in another, is the same as saying that the second term be predicated of the first in the full extent of its signification; and one term is predicated of another in the full extent of its signification, when there is no particular denoted by the subject to which the predicate does not apply.*' This remark, which is the foundation of all Aristotle's logic, has been sadly mistaken by many. Among others, the learned and truly respectable Dr Reid writes as follows:—'The being in a subject, and the being truly predicated of a subject, are used by Aristotle in his Analytics as synonymous phrases.' But the two phrases of '*being in a subject*,' and '*being predicated of it*,' are so far from being used as synonymous, that *the meaning of the one is directly the reverse of the meaning of the other*."—P. 83, 4to edition.

On this Mr Stewart, in the second volume of his "Philosophy of the Human Mind," remarks:—"While I readily admit the justness of this criticism on Dr Reid, I must take the liberty of adding, that I consider Reid's error as a mere oversight, or slip of the pen. That he might have accused Aristotle of confounding two things which, although different in fact, had yet a certain degree of resemblance or affinity, is by no means impossible; but it is scarcely conceivable that he could be so careless as to accuse him of confounding two things which he invariably states in direct opposition to each other. I have not a doubt, therefore, that Reid's idea was, that Aristotle used as synonymous phrases, the *being in a thing*, and the *being a subject of which that thing can be truly predicated*; more especially as either statement would equally well have answered his purpose." P. 391.

But even this extenuation Dr Gillies will not admit. In his "Introduction to Aristotle's Rhetoric," after some prefatory comments on the importance of the point, and the heinousness of "*this radical error*"—"I commend," he says, "Mr Stewart for his zeal in the defence of his adopted guide in philosophy, and of so wise and good a man as, from personal acquaintance, I knew Dr Reid to be. But the defence is rendered altogether ineffectual by the words of Dr Reid himself, who subjoins—'Aristotle's distinction between the phrases *being in a subject*, and *being said of a subject*, in the Categories, have led some writers to conclude that the Categories were not written by Aristotle.' Dr Reid's mistake, therefore, being a matter of deliberation, could not proceed from a mere slip of the pen; it runs through the rest of his work, and sometimes becomes the cause of his speaking with much disrespect of the author whose work he professes to illustrate. For this task Dr Reid possessed many requisites—patience, candour, learning, and science. What he wanted was a deeper and more intimate acquaintance with Aristotle's writings," &c., &c. P. 34.

Now, the simple but unsuspected fact is, *That Reid is right and Gillies wrong.* "The *being in a subject*, and the *being predicated of a subject*, are, in the Analytics used as synonymous phrases"—this statement of Reid is literally true. For example, the two following propositions are, in Aristotle's language, convertible:—Τὸ A κατὰ παντὸς B κατηγορεῖσθαι or λέγεσθαι, and τὸ A παντὶ B ὑπάρχειν; (*A is predicated of all B; A is, or inheres, in all B.*) The latter is Aristotle's usual form of expression. What Dr Gillies was thinking of when he said, "*the meaning of the one is directly the reverse of the meaning of the other*," was the inverse relation of an *attributive whole* and *subject part* to each other. To this, and not to the subject of predication, and subject of inhesion, does the quotation he makes from Aristotle apply; and he must, by some inconceivable confusion or oversight, have imagined that Reid's statement was tantamount to the absurdity of saying, that *a species being in a genus*, and *a species being predicated of a genus*, were used by Aristotle as synonymous phrases. To vindicate Aristotle's consistency in this matter, the present is not the occasion.

The exposition of this elementary blunder, is a good illustration of the maxim—*To take nothing upon trust; nothing upon authority.* Mr Stewart was one of the most acute and cautious of reasoners; yet we here find him painfully admitting one erroneous statement, in reliance on the learned accuracy of Dr Gillies; and it may be added, that in the note immediately preceding the one in which the present is contained, we find him accepting another, in deference to the authority of Lord Monboddo. The principle on which his Lordship supposes the whole truth of the syllogism to depend, and the discovery of which he marvellously attributes to a then living author, is one that may be found stated as a common doctrine in almost every system of logic, worthy of the name, for the last fifteen centuries.—H.

The most remarkable property of substance is, that one and the same substance may, by some change in itself, become the subject of things that are contrary. Thus the same body may be at one time hot, at another cold.*

Let this serve as a specimen of Aristotle's manner of treating the categories. After them, we have some chapters, which the schoolmen call *postprædicamenta*; wherein, first, the four kinds of *opposition* of terms are explained; to wit, *relative*, *privative* of *contrariety*, and of *contradiction*. This is repeated in all systems of logic.† Last of all, we have distinctions of the four Greek words which answer to the Latin ones—*prius*, *simul*, *motus*, and *habere*.

Section IV.

OF THE BOOK CONCERNING INTERPRETATION.‡

We are to consider, says Aristotle, what a *Noun* is, what a *Verb*, what *Affirmation*, what *Negation*, [what *Enunciation*,] what *Speech*. *Words* are the signs of what passeth in the mind; *Writing* is the sign of words.§ The signs both of writing and of words are different in different nations, but the operations of mind signified by them are the same. There are some operations of thought which are neither true nor false. These are expressed by nouns or verbs singly, and without composition.

A *Noun* is a sound, which, by compact, signifies something without respect to time, and of which no part has signification by itself. The cries of beasts may have a natural signification, but they are not nouns: we give that name only to sounds which have their signification by compact. The cases of a noun, as the genitive, dative, are not nouns. *Non homo* is not a noun, but, for distinction's sake, may be called a *Nomen Infinitum*.‖

A *Verb* signifies something by compact with relation to time. Thus, *valet* is a verb; but *valetudo* is a noun, because its signification has no relation to time. It is only the present tense of the indicative that is properly called a verb; the other tenses

* These are not all the properties enumerated by Aristotle. Two others are omitted.—H.

† This is hardly correct.—H

‡ The book Περὶ Ἑρμηνείας is absurdly translated *De Interpretatione*. It should be styled in Latin, *De Enunciandi ratione*. In English, we might render it—*On the doctrine of Enouncement—Enunciation*—or the like.—H.

§ "Recte Aristoteles—*Cogitationum tesserae Verba, Verborum Litterae*." Baco *De Augm. Scient.* L. VI. c. 1.—H.

‖ More properly, *Nomen Indefinitum*—ὄνομα ἀόριστον. This mistranslation of Boethius has been the cause of error, among others, to Kant.—H.

and moods are variations* of the verb. *Non valet* may be called a *verbum infinitum*.†

Speech is sound significant by compact, of which some part is also significant. And it is either enunciative, or not enunciative. *Enunciative speech* is that which affirms or denies. As to speech which is *not enunciative*, such as a prayer or wish, the consideration of it belongs to oratory or poetry. Every enunciative speech must have a verb, or some variation of a verb. *Affirmation* is the enunciation of one thing concerning another. *Negation* is the enunciation of one thing from another. *Contradiction* is an affirmation and negation that are opposite. This is a summary of the first six chapters.

The seventh and eighth treat of the various kinds of enunciations or propositions, *universal*, *particular*, *indefinite*, and *singular*; and of the various *kinds of opposition* in propositions, and the *axioms* concerning them. These things are repeated in every system of logic. In the ninth chapter, he endeavours to prove, by a long metaphysical reasoning, that propositions respecting *future contingencies* are not, determinately, either true or false; and that, if they were, it would follow that all things happen necessarily, and could not have been otherwise than as they are. The remaining [five] chapters contain many minute observations concerning the *æquipollency* of propositions both *pure* and *modal*.

CHAPTER II.

REMARKS.

Section I.

ON THE FIVE PREDICABLES.

The writers on logic have borrowed their materials almost entirely from Aristotle's Organon, and Porphyry's Introduction. The Organon, however, was not written by Aristotle as one work. It comprehends various tracts, written without the view of making them parts of one whole, and afterwards thrown together by his editors under one name, on account of their affinity. Many of his books that are lost would have made a part of the Organon, if they had been saved.

The three treatises, of which we have given a brief account, are unconnected with each other, and with those that follow. And although the first was undoubtedly compiled by Porphyry, and the two last

* Πτώσεις: cases, flexions.—H.

† See penult note.—H.

probably by Aristotle, yet I consider them as the venerable remains of a philosophy more ancient than Aristotle. Archytas of Tarentum, an eminent mathematician and philosopher of the Pythagorean school, is said to have wrote upon the ten categories;* and the five predicables probably had their origin in the same school. Aristotle, though abundantly careful to do justice to himself, does not claim the invention of either. And Porphyry, without ascribing the latter to Aristotle, professes only to deliver the doctrine of the ancients, and chiefly of the Peripatetics, concerning them.

The writers on logic have divided that science into *three* parts; the first treating of *Simple Apprehension* and of *Terms*; the second, of *Judgment* and of *Propositions*; and the third, of *Reasoning* and of *Syllogisms*. The materials of the first part are taken from Porphyry's Introduction and the Categories; and those of the second from the book of Interpretation.

A *Predicable*, according to the grammatical form of the word, might seem to signify whatever might be predicated, that is, affirmed or denied, of a subject; and in this sense every predicate would be a predicable. But the logicians give a different meaning to the word. They divide propositions into certain classes, according to the relation which the predicate of the proposition bears to the subject. The first class is that wherein the predicate is the *genus* of the subject, as when we say, "This is a triangle," "Jupiter is a planet." In the second class, the predicate is a *species* of the subject; as when we say, "This triangle is right-angled." A third class is when the predicate is the *specific difference* of the subject; as when we say, "Every triangle has three sides and three angles." A fourth, when the predicate is a *property* of the subject; as when we say, "The angles of every triangle are equal to two right angles." And a fifth class is when the predicate is something *accidental* to the subject; as when we say, "This triangle is neatly drawn."

Each of these classes comprehends a great variety of propositions, having different subjects and different predicates; but in each class the relation between the predicate and the subject is the same. Now, it is to this relation that logicians have given the name of a *predicable*. Hence it is, that, although the number of predicates be infinite, yet the number of predicables can be no greater than that of the different relations which may be in propositions between the predicate and the subject. And if all propositions belong to one or other of the five classes above mentioned, there can be but five predicables—to wit, *genus*, *species*, *differentia*, *proprium*, and *accidens*. These might, with more propriety perhaps, have been called *the five classes of predicates*; but use has determined them to be called *the five predicables*.

It may also be observed, that, as some objects of thought are individuals, such as, *Julius Cæsar*, *the city of Rome*; so others are common to many individuals, as *good*, *great*, *virtuous*, *vicious*. Of this last kind are all things that are expressed by adjectives. Things common to many individuals were by the ancients called *universals*. All predicates are universals, for they all have the nature of adjectives; and, on the other hand, all universals may be predicates. On this account, universals may be divided into the same classes as predicates; and as the five classes of predicates above mentioned have been called the five predicables, so, by the same kind of phraseology, they have been called *the five universals*; although they may more properly be called the *five classes of universals*.

The doctrine of the Five Universals, or Predicables, makes an essential part of every system of logic, and has been handed down without any change to this day. The very name of *predicables* shews, that the author of this division, whoever he was, intended it as a complete enumeration of all the kinds of things that can be affirmed of any subject; and so it has always been understood. It is accordingly implied in this division, that all that can be affirmed of anything whatsoever, is either the *genus* of the thing, or its *species*, or its *specific difference*, or some *property* or *accident* belonging to it.

Burgersdyk, a very acute writer in logic, seems to have been aware that strong objections might be made to the five predicables, considered as a complete enumeration: But, unwilling to allow any imperfection in this ancient division, he endeavours to restrain the meaning of the word *predicable*, so as to obviate objections. Those things only, says he, are to be accounted predicables, which may be *affirmed*—of *many individuals*—*truly*—*properly*—[*naturally*]—and *immediately*. The consequence of putting such limitations upon the word *predicable* is, that, in many propositions, perhaps in most, the predicate is not a predicable. But, admitting all his limitations, the enumeration will still be very incomplete; for of many things we may affirm, truly, pro-

* Archytas is only *said* to have written upon the ten categories, because there is an exposition of these in the treatise on the "Nature of the Universe," under his name, from which copious extracts are preserved by Simplicius, in his Commentaries on the Categories and the Physics of Aristotle. These extracts, however, of themselves, afford sufficient evidence that this treatise is, like the rest of the Pythagorean Fragments, the fabrication of some sophist long subsequent to Aristotle. The unsuspecting admission of these Fragments as genuine remains, is an error, or rather ignorance, of which all British writers on Logic and Philosophy, who have had occasion to refer to them, are guilty.—H

perly, and immediately, their existence, their end, their cause, their effect, and various relations which they bear to other things. These, and perhaps many more, are predicables in the strict sense of the word, no less than the five which have been so long famous.*

Although Porphyry, and all subsequent writers make the predicables to be in number five, yet Aristotle himself, in the beginning of the topics, reduces them to four, and demonstrates that there can be no more.† We shall give his demonstration when we come to the topics,‡ and shall only here observe, that, as Burgersdyk justifies the fivefold division, by restraining the meaning of the word *predicable*, so Aristotle justifies the fourfold division, by enlarging the meaning of the words *property* and *accident*.

After all, I apprehend that this ancient division of predicables, with all its imperfections, will bear a comparison with those which have been substituted in its stead by the most celebrated modern philosophers.

Locke, in his "Essay on the Human Understanding," having laid it down as a principle, That all our knowledge consists in perceiving certain agreements and disagreements between our ideas, reduces these agreements and disagreements to four heads —to wit, 1, *Identity* and *Diversity*; 2, *Relation*; 3, *Co-existence*; 4, *Real Existence*.§ Here are four predicables given as a complete enumeration, and yet not one of the ancient predicables is included in the number.‖

The author of the "Treatise of Human Nature," proceeding upon the same principle, that all our knowledge is only a perception of the relations of our ideas, observes, "That it may perhaps be esteemed an endless task to enumerate all those qualities which admit of comparison, and by which the ideas of philosophical relation are produced; but, if we diligently consider them, we shall find, that, without difficulty, they may be comprised under seven general heads:—1, *Resemblance*; 2, *Identity*; 3, *Relations of Space and Time*; 4, *Relations of Quantity and Number*; 5, *Degrees in Quality*; 6, *Contrariety*; 7, *Causation*."* Here again are seven predicables given as a complete enumeration, wherein all the predicables of the ancients, as well as two of Locke's, are left out.†

The ancients, in their division, attended only to categorical propositions which have one subject and one predicate; and of these to such only as have a general term for their subject. The moderns, by their definition of knowledge, have been led to attend only to relative propositions, which express a relation between two subjects, and these subjects they suppose to be always ideas.‡

Section II.

ON THE TEN CATEGORIES, AND ON DIVISIONS IN GENERAL.

The intention of the *Categories* or *Predicaments* is, to muster every object of human apprehension under ten heads; for the categories are given as a complete enumeration of everything which can be expressed without composition and structure—that is, of everything which can be either the subject or the predicate of a proposition.§ So that, as every soldier belongs to some company, and every company to some regiment, in like manner everything that can be the object of human thought has its place in one or other of the ten categories; and, by dividing and subdividing properly the several categories, all the notions that enter into the human mind may be mustered in rank and file, like an army in the day of battle.‖

* All these, however, fall under one or other of the five words which, it should be observed, are *forms or modes of predication*, and not *things predicated*. Reid seems to have taken the objection from Burgersdyk; he should not have overlooked his solution. —"Quod quidam aiunt, etiam *partem prædicari de toto, causam de effecto, adjunctum externum de subjecto*; ac proinde plura esse prædicabilia quam quinque, nullius prorsus momenti est. Nam pars non prædicatur de toto in casu recto, neque causa de effecto, neque adjunctum externum de subjecto; sed tantum in casu obliquo. Neque enim dicimus, *Animal est caput*, sed, *est capitatum*, aut tale quid: non dicimus etiam, *Eclipsis est interpositio terræ* (nisi improprie) sed, *Fit ob interpositionem terræ*: neque, *Miles est gladius*, sed *est gladiatus*. Et ejusmodi prædicationes revocari debent ad differentiam, proprium aut accidens."—*Institut. Log.*, l. i. c. 10.—H.

† Not absolutely; but only in a certain point of view.—H.

‡ Chapter iv. § 2.—H.

§ Book iv. chap. l.

‖ See note next but one.—H.

* Vol. i. pp. 33 and 125.

† These two paragraphs, independently of the general tenor of the treatise, shew that Reid, like our British philosophers in general, was unaware of the difference between the *Logical* or *Formal*, and the *Metaphysical* or *Real*. He did not consider that the *Predicables* are *forms* or *modes of predication*, and not *things predicated*; in the language of the schools, *second notions*, not *first*. These *real* generalisations of Locke and Hume *may* be brought into comparison with the *Categories* of Aristotle, which are, in truth, a Metaphysical, and not a Logical reduction; but they cannot be brought into comparison with the Five Words, which constitute a purely *formal* generalisation. Why, in brief, was it not objected that the predicables do not contain the predicaments, or the predicaments the predicables?—H.

‡ This observation is out of place.—H.

§ This is incorrect; for from the Categories are excluded many things that form the subject and predicate of a proposition, as *entia rationis* and *notiones secundæ*; while others transcend the classification altogether, as *being*, *one*, *whole*, the *infinite*, &c. In fact, as already noticed, the classification is of a metaphysical, not a logical, purport.—H.

‖ The ten Aristotelic Categories may be thus methodically deduced and simplified:—They are all divisions of *Being*—*Ens*. *Being* is divided into *Ens per se* and *Ens per accidens*. *Ens per se*, corresponds to *Substance*—the first of the Aristotelic Categories;

The perfection of the division of categories into ten heads has been strenuously defended by the followers of Aristotle, as well as that of the five predicables. They are, indeed, of kin to each other; they breathe the same spirit, and probably had the same origin. By the one we are taught to marshal every term that can enter into a proposition, either as subject or predicate; and, by the other, we are taught all the possible relations which the subject can have to the predicate. Thus the whole furniture of the human mind is presented to us at one view, and contracted, as it were, into a nutshell. To attempt, in so early a period, a methodical delineation of the vast region of human knowledge, actual and possible, and to point out the limits of every district, was indeed magnanimous in a high degree, and deserves our admiration, while we lament that the human powers are unequal to so bold a flight.

A regular distribution of things under proper classes or heads is, without doubt, a great help both to memory and judgment. And as the philosopher's province includes all things, human and divine, that can be objects of inquiry, he is naturally led to attempt some general division like that of the categories. And the invention of a division of this kind, which the speculative part of mankind acquiesced in for two thousand years, marks a superiority of genius in the inventor, whoever he was. Nor does it appear that the general divisions which, since the decline of the Peripatetic philosophy, have been substituted in place of the ten categories are more perfect.

Locke has reduced all things to *three* categories—viz., *substances*, *modes*, and *relations*. In this division, *time*, *space*, and *number*, three great objects of human thought, are omitted.*

The author of the "Treatise of Human Nature"† has reduced all things to *two* categories—viz., *ideas* and *impressions*; a division which is very well adapted to his system, and which puts me in mind of another made by an excellent mathematician* in a printed thesis I have seen. In it the author, after a severe censure of the ten categories of the Peripatetics, maintains that there neither are nor can be more than two categories of things—viz., *data* and *quæsita*.

There are two ends that may be proposed by such divisions. The first is, to methodise or digest in order what a man actually knows. This is neither unimportant nor impracticable; and, in proportion to the solidity and accuracy of a man's judgment, his divisions of the things he knows will be elegant and useful. The same subject may admit, and even require, various divisions, according to the different points of view from which we contemplate it; nor does it follow, that, because one division is good, therefore another is naught. To be acquainted with the divisions of the logicians and metaphysicians, without a superstitious attachment to them, may be of use in dividing the same subjects, or even those of a different nature. Thus Quintilian borrows from the ten categories his division of the topics of rhetorical argumentation. Of all methods of arrangement, the most antiphilosophical seems to be the invention of this age;† I mean the arranging the arts and sciences by the letters of the alphabet, in dictionaries and encyclopædias. With these authors the categories are, A, B, C, &c.

Another end commonly proposed by such divisions, but very rarely attained, is to exhaust the subject divided, so that nothing that belongs to it shall be omitted. It is one of the general rules of division, in all systems of logic, That the division should be adequate to the subject divided; a good rule without doubt, but very often beyond the reach of human power. To make a perfect division, a man must have a perfect comprehension of the whole subject at one view. When our knowledge of the subject is imperfect, any division we can make must be like the first sketch of a painter, to be extended, contracted, or mended, as the subject shall be found to require. Yet nothing is more common, not only among the ancient, but even among modern philosophers, than to draw, from their incomplete divisions, conclusions which suppose them to be perfect.

A division is a repository which the philosopher frames for holding his ware in convenient order. The philosopher maintains,

Ens per accidens, comprises the other nine. For it either denotes something *absolute* or something *relative*. If something absolute, it either originates in the *matter* of the substance, and is divisible—*Quantity*, Aristotle's second Category; or in the *form*, and is indivisible—*Quality*, Aristotle's third Category. If something relative, it constitutes *Relation*, the fourth Category; and to Relation the other six may easily be reduced. For the fifth, *Where*, denotes the relation between different objects in space, or the relation between place and the thing placed. The sixth, *When*, denotes the relation between objects in succession, or the relation between time and a thing in time. The seventh, *Posture*, is the relation of the parts of a body to each other. The eighth, *Having*, is the relation of the thing having, and the thing had; while the ninth and tenth, *Action* and *Passion*, are the reciprocal relations between the agent and the patient. There are, on this scheme, one supreme Category—*Being*; two at the first descent—*Ens per se*, *Ens per accidens*; four at the first and second—*Substance*, *Quantity*, *Quality*, *Relation*; and to the dignity of Category, these four are, of Aristotle's ten, pre-eminently, if not exclusively entitled.—H.

* It might be contended that the three latter are contained under the three former.—H.

† Hume.—H.

* Reid's uncle, James Gregory. See above, p. 6, b.—H.

† Not the invention of Reid's age, though in that it was more generally and extensively applied.—H.

that such or such a thing is not good ware, because there is no place in his wareroom that fits it. We are apt to yield to this argument in philosophy, but it would appear ridiculous in any other traffic.

Peter Ramus, who had the spirit of a reformer in philosophy, and who had a force of genius sufficient to shake the Aristotelian fabric in many parts, but insufficient to erect anything more solid in its place, tried to remedy the imperfection of philosophical divisions, by introducing a new manner of dividing.* His divisions always consisted of two members, one of which was contradictory of the other, as if one should divide England into Middlesex and what is not Middlesex. It is evident that these two members comprehend all England; for the Logicians observe, that a term along with its contradictory comprehend all things. In the same manner, we may divide what is not Middlesex into Kent and what is not Kent. Thus one may go on by divisions and subdivisions that are absolutely complete. This example may serve to give an idea of the spirit of Ramean divisions, which were in no small reputation about two hundred years ago.

Aristotle was not ignorant of this kind of division. But he used it only as a touchstone to prove by induction the perfection of some other division, which indeed is the best use that can be made of it. When applied to the common purpose of division, it is both inelegant and burdensome to the memory; and, after it has put one out of breath by endless subdivisions, there is still a negative term left behind, which shews that you are no nearer the end of your journey than when you began.

Until some more effectual remedy be found for the imperfection of divisions, I beg leave to propose one more simple than that of Ramus. It is this—When you meet with a division of any subject imperfectly comprehended, add to the last member an *et cætera*. That this *et cætera* makes the division complete, is undeniable; and therefore it ought to hold its place as a member, and to be always understood, whether expressed or not, until clear and positive proof be brought that the division is complete without it. And this same *et cætera* shall be the repository of all members that may in any future time shew a good and valid right to a property in the subject.†

* There is nothing new whatever in Ramus's Dichotomy by contradiction. It was, in particular, a favourite with Plato. Among others, see Ammonius on the Categories, f. 96, a. ed. Ald. 1546. H.

† Is this "protestation to add and cetera" serious or in joke?—H.

Section III.

ON DISTINCTIONS.

Having said so much of logical divisions, we shall next make some remarks upon distinctions.

Since the philosophy of Aristotle fell into disrepute, it has been a common topic of wit and raillery to inveigh against metaphysical distinctions. Indeed the abuse of them, in the scholastic ages, seems to justify a general prejudice against them; and shallow thinkers and writers have good reason to be jealous of distinctions, because they make sad work when applied to their flimsy compositions. But every man of true judgment, while he condemns distinctions that have no foundation in the nature of things, must perceive, that indiscriminately to decry distinctions, is to renounce all pretensions to just reasoning: for, as false reasoning commonly proceeds from confounding things that are different, so, without distinguishing such things, it is impossible to avoid error or detect sophistry. The authority of Aquinas, or Suarez, or even of Aristotle, can neither stamp a real value upon distinctions of base metal, nor hinder the currency of those that have intrinsic value.

Some distinctions are *verbal*, others are *real*. The first kind distinguish the various meanings of a word, whether proper or metaphorical. Distinctions of this kind make a part of the grammar of a language, and are often absurd when translated into another language. Real distinctions are equally good in all languages, and suffer no hurt by translation. They distinguish the different species contained under some general notion, or the different parts contained in one whole.

Many of Aristotle's distinctions are verbal merely, and therefore more proper materials for a dictionary of the Greek language, than for a philosophical treatise. At least, they ought never to have been translated into other languages, when the idiom of the language will not justify them: for this is to adulterate the language, to introduce foreign idioms into it without necessity or use, and to make it ambiguous where it was not. The distinctions in the end of the categories of the four words, *prius*, *simul*, *motus*, and *habere*, are all verbal.*

The modes or species of *Prius*, according to Aristotle, are five. One thing may be prior to another—first, in point of *time*; secondly, in point of *dignity*; thirdly, in point of *order*; and so forth.† The modes

* These distinctions are all founded on the analogies of real existence, and are all equally valid in other languages as in Greek.—H.

† More accurately: One thing is prior to another

of simul are only three. It seems this word was not used in the Greek with so great latitude as the other, although they are relative terms.*

The modes or species of *Motion* he makes to be six—viz., *generation, corruption, increase, decrease, alteration*, and *change of place*.*

The modes or species of *Having* are [principally] eight. 1. Having a *quality* or habit,† as having wisdom. 2. Having *quantity or magnitude*. 3. Having *things adjacent*, as having a sword. 4. Having *things as parts*, as having hands or feet. 5. Having *in a part or on a part*, as having a ring on one's finger. 6. *Containing*, as a cask is said to have wine. 7. *Possessing*, as having lands or houses. 8. Having *a wife* [or *husband*.]*

Another distinction of this kind is Aristotle's distinction of *Causes*; of which he makes four kinds, *efficient, material, formal*, and *final*. These distinctions may deserve a place in a dictionary of the Greek language; but, in English or Latin, they adulterate the language.‡ Yet so fond were the schoolmen of distinctions of this kind, that they added to Aristotle's enumeration an *impulsive* cause,§ an *exemplary* cause,‖ and I don't know how many more. We seem to have adopted into English a *final* cause; but it is merely a term of art, borrowed from the Peripatetic philosophy, without necessity or use; for the English word *end* is as good as *final cause*, though not so long nor so learned.

Section IV.

ON DEFINITIONS.

It remains that we make some remarks on Aristotle's Definitions, which have exposed him to much censure and ridicule. Yet I think it must be allowed, that, in things which need definition, and admit of it, his definitions are commonly judicious and accurate; and, had he attempted to define such things only, his enemies had wanted great matter of triumph. I believe it may likewise be said in his favour, that, until Locke's essay was wrote, there was nothing of importance delivered by philosophers with regard to definition,* beyond what Aristotle has said upon that subject.

He considers a Definition as *a speech declaring what a thing is*. Every thing *essential* to the thing defined, and nothing more, must be contained in the definition. Now, the essence of a thing consists of these two parts: first, *What is common to it with other things of the same kind*; and, secondly, *What distinguishes it from other things of the same kind*. The first is called the *Genus* of the thing, the second its *Specific Difference*. The definition, therefore, consists of these two parts. And, for finding them, we must have recourse to the ten categories;† in one or other of which everything in nature is to be found. Each category is a *genus*, and is divided into so many species, which are distinguished by their specific differences. Each of these species is again subdivided into so many species, with regard to which it is a genus. This division and subdivision continues until we come to the lowest species, which can only be divided into individuals distinguished from one another, not by any specific difference, but by accidental differences of time, place, and other circumstances.

The category itself, being the highest genus, is in no respect a species, and the lowest species is in no respect a genus; but every intermediate order is a genus compared with those that are below it, and a species compared with those above it. To find the definition of anything, therefore,

---

in the order of *Time*—of *Nature*—of *Arrangement*—of *Dignity*—of *Causation*. This last, which was added by Aristotle, may be well reduced to the second.—H.

* The penult note applies to these.—H.

† It should have been—"Habit, Disposition, or other *Quality*." The others are, in like manner, neither accurately nor adequately stated; *sed non tanti*.—H.

‡ This statement, that Aristotle's quadruple distinction of causes was one not established on the essential nature of things, but founded on a verbal peculiarity of the Greek language, Reid has, in his subsequent writings, once and again repeated. (See above, *Correspondence*, p. 75, a, and 76, b; *Active Powers*, p. 526, a.) It is not, however, correct. The distinction is not found marked out in the Greek language more than in any other; though, from the natural flexibility and analogies of that tongue, it was better suited to express without effort this and other philosophical discriminations. In itself the division is not merely verbal, but proceeds on the natural differences of real things. This, however, is not the place to shew that Aristotle had taken a far juster and more comprehensive view of this subject than the great majority, if not the whole, of our recent philosophers.—H.

§ This is a mistake. The schoolmen added no *impulsive cause* distinct from the *final* and *efficient* causes of Aristotle.—H.

‖ The *exemplary cause* was introduced by *Plato*; and was not adopted by the *schoolmen* as a fifth cause in addition to Aristotle's four.—H.

* This is commonly but erroneously asserted. Locke says little or nothing on the subject of Definition which had not been previously said by philosophers before him, and with whose works he can be proved to have been acquainted. See above, p. 220, a, note †.—H.

† From this and what follows, it would seem that Reid thought that the Aristotelic doctrine of Definition is necessarily relative to the ten Categories; and that, to find the definition of a thing, we must *descend* from the category to the genus and specific difference sought. This, however, is not the case. For, according to Aristotle, there are two methods of "hunting up" the required definition; the one by *division* and descent, the other by induction and ascent.—H.

you must take the genus which is immediately above its place in the category, and the specific difference by which it is distinguished from other species of the same genus. These two make a perfect definition. This I take to be the substance of Aristotle's system, and probably the system of the Pythagorean school,* before Aristotle, concerning definition.

But, notwithstanding the specious appearance of this system, it has its defects. Not to repeat what was before said of the imperfection of the division of things into ten categories, the subdivisions of each category are no less imperfect. Aristotle has given some subdivisions of a few of them; and, as far as he goes, his followers pretty unanimously take the same road. But, when they attempt to go farther, they take very different roads. It is evident, that, if the series of each category could be completed, and the division of things into categories could be made perfect, still the highest genus in each category could not be defined, because it is not a species; nor could individuals be defined, because they have no specific difference.† There are also many species of things, whose specific difference cannot be expressed in language, even when it is evident to sense, or to the understanding. Thus, green, red, and blue, are very distinct species of colour; but who can express in words wherein green differs from red or blue?‡

Without borrowing light from the ancient system, we may perceive that every definition must consist of words that need no definition; and that to define the common words of a language that have no ambiguity is trifling, if it could be done; the only use of a definition being to give a clear and adequate conception of the meaning of a word.

The logicians indeed distinguish between the *definition of a word* and the *definition of a thing*; considering the former as the mean office of a lexicographer, but the last as the grand work of a philosopher. But what they have said about the definition of a thing, if it has a meaning, is beyond my comprehension. All the rules of definition agree to the definition of a word; and if they mean, by the definition of a thing, the giving an adequate conception of the nature and essence of anything that exists, this is impossible, and is the vain boast of men unconscious of the weakness of human understanding.§

The works of God are all imperfectly known by us. We see their outside, or perhaps we discover some of their qualities and relations, by observation and experiment, assisted by reasoning; but we can give no definition of the meanest of them which comprehends its real essence. It is justly observed by Locke, that *nominal essences* only, which are the creatures of our own minds, are perfectly comprehended by us, or can be properly defined;* and even of these there are many too simple in their nature to admit of definition. When we cannot give precision to our notions by a definition, we must endeavour to do it by attentive reflection upon them, by observing minutely their agreements and differences, and especially by a right understanding of the powers of our own minds by which such notions are formed.

The principles laid down by Locke, with regard to definition, and with regard to the abuse of words, carry conviction along with them; and I take them to be one of the most important improvements made in logic, since the days of Aristotle; not so much because they enlarge our knowledge, as because they make us sensible of our ignorance, and shew that a great part of what speculative men have admired as profound philosophy, is only a darkening of knowledge by words without understanding.†

Section V.

ON THE STRUCTURE OF SPEECH.

The few hints contained in the beginning of the book concerning Interpretation relating to the structure of speech, have been left out in treatises of logic, as belonging rather to grammar; yet I apprehend this is a rich field of philosophical speculation. Language being the express image of human

---

* See above, p. 686, note.—H.

† This, of course, is stated by Aristotle himself and other logicians; and it does not affect *his* doctrine of Definition, but marks the necessary limits of Definition in general.—H.

‡ Hence it was expressly stated by the old logicians—*Omnis intuitiva notitia est definitio*.—H.

§ By a *real*, in contrast to a *verbal* or *nominal* definition, the logicians do not intend "*the giving an adequate conception of the nature and essence of a thing*"—that is, of a thing *considered in itself, and apart from the conceptions of it already possessed*. By *verbal* definition, is meant the more accurate determination of the signification of a *word*; by *real*, the more accurate determination of the contents of a *notion*. The one clears up the relation of *words to notions*; the other of *notions to things*. The substitution of *notional* for *real* would, perhaps, remove the ambiguity. But, if we retain the term *real*, the aim of a *verbal* definition being to specify the *thought denoted by the word*, such definition ought to be called *notional*, on the principle on which the definition of a *notion* is called *real*; for this definition is the exposition of what *things are comprehended in a thought*.—H.

* Locke gives the title *Nominal Essence* to the abstract notion marked out by a general term; and *Real Essence* to that (probably unknown) constitution, whereby a thing is as it is. On this definition as the Nominal Essence comprehends all that is conceived it must, of course, comprehend all that can be defined. The *Nominal Essence* of Locke is, in fact, only a new name for the *Logical Essence* of other philosophers.—H.

† See above, p. 690, b, note *.—See also, a paragraph here omitted, at the end of this treatise.—H.

thought, the analysis of the one must correspond to that of the other. Nouns adjective and substantive, verbs active and passive, with their various moods, tenses, and persons, must be expressive of a like variety in the modes of thought. Things that are distinguished in all languages, such as substance and quality, action and passion, cause and effect, must be distinguished by the natural powers of the human mind. The philosophy of grammar, and that of the human understanding, are more nearly allied than is commonly imagined.

The structure of language was pursued to a considerable extent by the ancient commentators upon this book of Aristotle. Their speculations upon this subject, which are neither the least ingenious nor the least useful part of the Peripatetic philosophy, were neglected for many ages, and lay buried in ancient manuscripts, or in books little known, till they were lately brought to light by the learned Mr Harris, in his "Hermes."

The definitions given by Aristotle of a *noun*, of a *verb*, and of *speech*, will hardly bear examination. It is easy in practice to distinguish the various parts of speech; but very difficult, if at all possible, to give accurate definitions of them.

He observes justly, that, besides that kind of speech called a *proposition*, which is always either true or false, there are other kinds which are neither true nor false, such as a prayer or wish; to which we may add, a question, a command, a promise, a contract, and many others. These Aristotle pronounces to have nothing to do with his subject, and remits them to oratory or poetry; and so they have remained banished from the regions of philosophy to this day; yet I apprehend that an analysis of such speeches, and of the operations of mind which they express, would be of real use, and perhaps would discover how imperfect an enumeration the logicians have given of the powers of human understanding, when they reduce them to Simple Apprehension, Judgment, and Reasoning.*

Section VI.

ON PROPOSITIONS.

Mathematicians use the word *Proposition* in a larger sense than Logicians. A problem is called a *proposition* in mathematics, but in logic it is not a proposition; it is one of those speeches which are not enunciative, and which Aristotle remits to oratory or poetry. [?]

A *Proposition*, according to Aristotle, is *a speech wherein one thing is affirmed or denied of another*. Hence, it is easy to distinguish the thing affirmed or denied, which is called *the Predicate*, from the thing of which it is affirmed or denied, which is called *the Subject*; and these two are called *the Terms of the proposition*. Hence, likewise, it appears that propositions are either *affirmative* or *negative*; and this is called *their Quality*. All affirmative propositions have the same quality, so likewise have all negative; but an affirmative and a negative are contrary in their quality.

When the subject of a proposition is a general term, the predicate is affirmed or denied either of the whole, or of a part. Hence propositions are distinguished into *universal* and *particular*. "All men are mortal," is an universal proposition; "Some men are learned," is a particular; and this is called *the Quantity of the proposition*. All universal propositions agree in quantity, as also all particular; while an universal and a particular are said to differ in quantity. A proposition is called *indefinite* when there is no mark either of universality or particularity annexed to the subject: thus, "Man is of few days," is an indefinite proposition; but it must be understood either as universal or as particular, and therefore is not a third species, but, by interpretation, is brought under one of the other two.*

There are also *singular* propositions, which have not a general term, but an individual, for their subject; as, "Alexander was a great conqueror." These are considered by Logicians as universal, because the subject being indivisible, the predicate is affirmed or denied of the whole, and not of a part only. Thus, all propositions, with regard to quality, are either affirmative or negative; and, with regard to quantity, are universal or particular; and, taking in both quantity and quality, they are universal affirmatives, or universal negatives, or particular affirmatives or particular negatives. These four kinds, after the days of Aristotle, came to be named by the names of the four first vowels, A, E, I, O, according to the following distich:—

> Asserit A, negat E, sed universaliter ambo;
> Asserit I, negat O, sed particulariter ambo.†

When the young Logician is thus far instructed in the nature of propositions, he is apt to think there is no difficulty in analyzing any proposition, and shewing its subject and predicate, its quantity and quality; and, indeed, unless he can do this, he will be unable to apply the rules of logic to use. Yet he will find there are some difficulties

* This enumeration was never intended by logicians for a general *psychological* analysis, but merely for a special enumeration of those faculties, the laws of which were proposed to logic, as its object matter.—H.

* The term *indefinite* ought to be discarded in this relation, and replaced by *indesignate*.—H.

† The history of these and the other logical verses is curious, but, I may say, to Logicians unknown.—H.

in this analysis, which are overlooked by Aristotle altogether; and although they are sometimes touched, they are not removed by his followers.* For, 1. There are propositions in which it is difficult to find a subject and a predicate; as in these, "It rains," "It snows." 2. In some propositions, either term may be made the subject or the predicate, as you like best; as in this, "Virtue is the road to happiness." 3. The same example may serve to shew that it is sometimes difficult to say, whether a proposition be universal or particular. 4. The quality of some propositions is so dubious that Logicians have never been able to agree whether they be affirmative or negative; as in this proposition, "Whatever is insentient is not an animal." 5. As there is one class of propositions which have only two terms, viz., one subject and one predicate, which are called *Categorical*† *propositions*, so there are many classes that have more than two terms. What Aristotle delivers in this book is applicable only to categorical propositions; and to them only the rules concerning the conversion of propositions, and concerning the figures and modes of syllogisms, are accommodated. The subsequent writers of logic have taken notice of some of the many classes of complex propositions, and have given rules adapted to them; but, finding this work endless, they have left us to manage the rest by the rules of common sense.

CHAPTER III.

ACCOUNT OF THE FIRST ANALYTICS.

Section I.

OF THE CONVERSION OF PROPOSITIONS.

In attempting to give some account of the Analytics and of the Topics of Aristotle, ingenuity requires me to confess, that, though I have often purposed to read the whole with care, and to understand what is intelligible, yet my courage and patience always failed before I had done. Why should I throw away so much time and painful attention upon a thing of so little real use? If I had lived in those ages when the knowledge of Aristotle's Organon entitled a man to the highest rank in philosophy, ambition might have induced me to employ upon it some years of painful study; and less, I conceive, would not be sufficient. [?] Such reflections as these always got the better of my resolution, when the first ardour began to cool. All I can say is, that I have read some parts of the different books with care, some slightly, and some, perhaps, not at all. I have glanced over the whole often, and, when anything attracted my attention, have dipped into it till my appetite was satisfied. Of all reading, it is the most dry and the most painful, employing an infinite labour of demonstration, about things of the most abstract nature, delivered in a laconic style, and often, I think, with affected obscurity; and all to prove general propositions, which, when applied to particular instances, appear self-evident.*

There is probably but little in the Categories, or in the book of Interpretation, that Aristotle could claim as his own invention [?]; but the whole theory of syllogisms he claims as his own, and as the fruit of much time and labour. And indeed it is a stately fabric, a monument of a great genius, which we could wish to have been more usefully employed. There must be something, however, adapted to please the human understanding, or to flatter human pride, in a work which occupied men of speculation for more than a thousand years. These books are called *Analytics*, because the intention of them is to resolve all reasoning into its simple ingredients.

The *first book* of the *First Analytics*, consisting of *forty-six chapters*, may be divided into *four parts*; the first [A] treating of the *conversion of propositions*; the second, [B,] of the *structure of syllogisms*, in all the different figures and modes; the third, [C,] of the *invention of a middle term*; and the last, [D,] of the *resolution of syllogisms*. We shall give a brief account of each.

[A] *To convert a proposition is to infer from it another proposition, whose subject is the predicate of the first, and whose predicate is the subject of the first.*† This is reduced by Aristotle to three rules:—1. An universal negative may be converted into an universal negative: thus, "No man is a quadruped;" therefore, "No quadruped is a man." 2. An universal affirmative can be converted only into a particular affirmative: thus, "All men are mortal;" therefore, "Some mortal beings are men." 3. A particular affirmative may be converted into a particular affirmative: as, "Some men are just;" therefore, "Some just persons are men." When a proposition may be converted without changing its quantity, this is called *simple conversion*; but when the quantity is diminished, as in the universal affirmative, it is called conversion *per accidens*.

There is another kind of conversion

* The difficulties that follow admit of a very easy solution.—H.

† I was the first, as far as I am aware, who observed that the term [illegible] is, by *Aristotle*, used *only* in the sense of *affirmative*.—H.

* This is unjust. Aristotle attempts no *proof* of these general propositions; he only *shews* that their denial involves a contradiction.—H.

† It might be added, "the quality remaining always the same."—H.

omitted in this place by Aristotle, but supplied by his followers, called *conversion by contraposition*, in which the term that is contradictory to the predicate is put for the subject, and the quality of the proposition is changed;* as, "All animals are sentient;" therefore, "What is insentient is not an animal." A fourth rule of conversion therefore is, That an universal affirmative, and a particular negative, may be converted by contraposition.

Section II.

OF THE FIGURES AND MODES OF PURE SYLLOGISMS.

[B] A SYLLOGISM *is an argument, or reasoning,*† *consisting* [*always, explicitly or implicitly,*] *of three propositions, the last of which, called the* CONCLUSION, *is* [*necessarily*] *inferred from the* [*very statement of the*] *two preceding, which are called the* PREMISES. The conclusion having two terms, a subject and a predicate, its predicate is called the *major term*, and its subject the *minor term*. In order to prove the conclusion, each of its terms is, in the premises, compared with the third term, called the *middle term*. By this means one of the premises will have for its two terms the major term and the middle term; and this premise is called the *major premise*, or the *major proposition* of the syllogism. The other premise must have for its two terms the minor term and the middle term, and it is called the *minor proposition*. Thus the syllogism consists of three propositions, distinguished by the names of the *major*, the *minor*, and the *conclusion*; and, although each of these has two terms, a subject and a predicate, yet there are only three different terms in all. The major term is always the predicate of the conclusion, and is also either the subject or predicate of the major proposition. The minor term is always the subject of the conclusion, and is also either the subject or predicate of the minor proposition. The middle term never enters into the conclusion, but stands in both premises, either in the position of subject or of predicate.

According to the various positions which the Middle Term may have in the premises, syllogisms are said to be of various Figures. Now, all the possible positions of the middle term are only *four*; for, first, it may be the subject of the major proposition, and the predicate of the minor, and then the syllogism is of the first figure; or it may be the predicate of both premises, and then the syllogism is of the second figure; or it may be the subject of both, which makes a syllogism of the third figure; or it may be the predicate of the major proposition, and the subject of the minor, which makes the fourth figure. Aristotle takes no notice of the fourth figure. It was added by the famous Galen,* and is often called *the Galenical Figure.*

There is another division of syllogisms according to their *Modes*. *The Mode of a syllogism is determined by the Quality and Quantity of the propositions of which it consists.* Each of the three propositions must be either an universal affirmative, or an universal negative, or a particular affirmative, or a particular negative. These four kinds of propositions, as was before observed, have been named by the four vowels, A, E, I, O; by which means the mode of a syllogism is marked by any three of those four vowels. Thus, A, A, A, denotes that mode in which the major, minor, and conclusion, are all universal affirmatives; E, A, E, denotes that mode in which the major and conclusion are universal negatives and the minor is an universal affirmative.

To know all the possible modes of syllogism, we must find how many different combinations may be made of three out of the four vowels; and from the art of combination the number is found to be sixty-four. So many possible modes there are in every figure, consequently in the three figures of Aristotle there are one hundred and ninety-two, and in all the four figures two hundred and fifty-six.

Now, the theory of syllogism requires that we shew what are the particular modes in each figure, which do or do not form a just and conclusive syllogism, that so the legitimate may be adopted, and the spurious rejected. This Aristotle has shewn in the first three figures, examining all the modes one by one, and passing sentence upon each; and from this examination he collects some rules which may aid the memory in distinguishing the false from the true, and point out the properties of each figure.

The *first figure* has only four legitimate modes. The major proposition in this figure must be universal, and the minor affirmative; and it has this property, that it yields conclusions of all kinds, affirmative and negative, universal and particular.

The *second figure* has also four legitimate modes. Its major proposition must be universal, and one of the premises must be negative. It yields conclusions both universal and particular, but all negative.

* In this conversion, consider Subject and Predicate as changed into their contradictories, and thus the quality in both propositions remains identical.—H

† Here the genus should be (as Aristotle has it) *a Speech or Enunciation*; for all "argument or reasoning" is a syllogism or series of syllogisms.—H.

* Improbable, though universally believed.—H.

The *third figure* has six legitimate modes. Its minor must always be affirmative; and it yields conclusions both affirmative and negative, but all particular.

Besides the rules that are proper to each figure, Aristotle has given some that are common to all, by which the legitimacy of syllogisms may be tried. These may, I think, be reduced to five. 1. There must be only three terms in a syllogism. As each term occurs in two of the propositions, it must be precisely the same in both: If it be not, the syllogism is said to have four terms, which makes a vitious syllogism. 2. The middle term must be taken universally in one of the premises. 3. Both premises must not be particular propositions, nor both negative. 4. The conclusion must be particular, if either of the premises be particular; and negative, if either of the premises be negative. 5. No term can be taken universally in the conclusion, if it be not taken universally in the premises.

For understanding the second and fifth of these rules, it is necessary to observe, that a term is said to be taken universally, not only when it is the subject of an universal proposition, but when it is the predicate of a negative proposition; on the other hand, a term is said to be taken particularly, when it is either the subject of a particular, or the predicate of an affirmative proposition.

Section III.

OF THE INVENTION OF A MIDDLE TERM.

[C.] The third part of this book contains rules, general and special, for the *invention* [*discovery*] *of a middle term*; and this the author conceives to be of great utility. The general rules amount to this—That you are to consider well both terms of the proposition to be proved; their definition, their properties, the things which may be affirmed or denied of them, and those of which they may be affirmed or denied; these things, collected together, are the materials from which your middle term is to be taken.

The special rules require you to consider the quantity and quality of the proposition to be proved, that you may discover in what mode and figure of syllogism the proof is to proceed. Then, from the materials before collected, you must seek a middle term which has that relation to the subject and predicate of the proposition to be proved, which the nature of the syllogism requires. Thus, suppose the proposition I would prove is an universal affirmative, I know, by the rules of syllogisms, that there is only one legitimate mode in which an universal affirmative proposition can be proved; and that is the first mode of the first figure. I know likewise that, in this mode, both the premises must be universal affirmatives; and that the middle term must be the subject of the major, and the predicate of the minor. Therefore, of the terms collected according to the general rule, I seek out one or more which have these two properties; first, That the predicate of the proposition to be proved can be universally affirmed of it; and, secondly, That it can be universally affirmed of the subject of the proposition to be proved. Every term you can find, which has those two properties, will serve you as a middle term, but no other. In this way, the author gives special rules for all the various kinds of propositions to be proved; points out the various modes in which they may be proved, and the properties which the middle term must have to make it fit for answering that end. And the rules are illustrated, or rather, in my opinion, purposely darkened, by putting letters of the alphabet for the several terms.*

Section IV.

OF THE REMAINING PART OF THE FIRST BOOK.

The resolution of syllogisms requires no other principles but those before laid down for constructing them. However, it is treated of largely, and rules laid down for reducing reasoning to syllogisms, by supplying one of the premises when it is understood, by rectifying inversions, and putting the propositions in the proper order.

Here he speaks also of hypothetical syllogisms;† which he acknowledges cannot be resolved into any of the figures, although there be many kinds of them that ought diligently to be observed, and which he promises to handle afterwards. But this promise is not fulfilled, as far as I know, in any of his works that are extant.

Section V.

OF THE SECOND BOOK OF THE FIRST ANALYTICS.

The second book treats of the *powers* of

---

* The purely *formal* character of logic requires an abstraction from all determinate *matter*; which is best shewn through the application of universal and otherwise unmeaning symbols. This is admirably stated by the Aphrodisian. It would, indeed, have been well had Aristotle always rigidly excluded everything *not formal* from his logical treatises.—H.

† The hypothetical syllogisms of Aristotle were different from our hypothetical syllogisms—which, with the term *Categorical* in its *present* sense, are an inheritance from Theophrastus and Eudemus.—H.

syllogisms, and shews, in *twenty-seven chapters*, how we may perform many feats by them, and what figures and modes are adapted to each. Thus, in some syllogisms, several distinct conclusions may be drawn from the same premises; in some, true conclusions may be drawn from false premises; in some, by assuming the conclusion and one premise, you may prove the other; you may turn a direct syllogism into one leading to an absurdity.

We have likewise precepts given in this book, both to the assailant in a syllogistical dispute, how to carry on his attack, with art, so as to obtain the victory, and to the defendant, how to keep the enemy at such a distance as that he shall never be obliged to yield. From which we learn, that Aristotle introduced in his own school the practice of syllogistical disputation, instead of the rhetorical disputations which the Sophists were wont to use in more ancient times.*

CHAPTER IV.

REMARKS.

Section I.

OF THE CONVERSION OF PROPOSITIONS.

We have given a summary view of the theory of pure syllogisms as delivered by Aristotle, a theory of which he claims the sole invention. And I believe it will be difficult, in any science, to find so large a system of truths of so very abstract and so general a nature, all fortified by demonstration, and all invented and perfected by one man. It shews a force of genius, and labour of investigation, equal to the most arduous attempts. I shall now make some remarks upon it.

As to the conversion of propositions, the writers on logic commonly satisfy themselves with illustrating each of the rules by an example, conceiving them to be self-evident, when applied to particular cases. But Aristotle has given demonstrations of the rules he mentions. As a specimen, I shall give his demonstration of the first rule. "Let A B be an universal negative proposition; I say, that if A is in no B, it will follow that B is in no A. If you deny this consequence, let B be in some A, for example, in C; then the first supposition will not be true; for C is of the Bs." In this demonstration, if I understand it, the third rule of conversion is assumed, *that, if B is in some A, then A must be in some B*, which indeed is contrary to the first supposition. If the third rule be assumed for proof of the first, the proof of all the three goes round in a circle; for the second and third rules are proved by the first. This is a fault in reasoning which Aristotle condemns, and which I would be very unwilling to charge him with, if I could find any better meaning in his demonstration. But it is indeed a fault very difficult to be avoided, when men attempt to prove things that are self-evident.*

---

* Inaccurate: see below, under the translation at the conclusion of chapter iv. § 3.—H.

* This objection does credit to Reid's acuteness: if just, it materially affects the logical impeccability of Aristotle; and, what is remarkable, it is one taken by some of the oldest of the Greek logicians themselves. It is not, however, valid. Alexander of Aphrodisias, the oldest of Aristotle's expositors now extant, tells us, in his commentary on this text, (it is in the Prior Analytics, Book I. ch. ii.), that some doubted, in regard to this demonstration of the first rule of conversion, whether Aristotle had not employed in it the third rule—*that by which particular affirmative propositions are declared simply convertible*; thus committing a twofold violation of the laws of reasoning—1°, In using as a medium of proof what had not yet itself been proved; and, 2°, In thus employing what was itself subsequently proved through the very canon which it is here applied to establish. Besides these charges of *ὕστερον πρότερον* and *δι' ἀλλήλων*, Philoponus records also another; but, as this is, in itself, of little weight, and not relevant to the matter in hand, I will simply translate (with occasional abridgment and emendation, for the text is very corrupt,) the satisfactory answer which Alexander gives to the objection stated. It is as follows:—

"This mode of procedure is confessedly vicious. But Aristotle has not been guilty of it, as they believe. In the sequel, he will undoubtedly manifest (δείξει) the convertibility of particular affirmatives through that of universal negatives; but he does not, at present, evince the convertibility of universal negatives, by assuming that of particular affirmatives. He fairly demonstrates (δείκνυσι) his thesis, and does not employ it as a concession; for, on principles already settled, he shews it manifested and established. These principles are *τὸ κατὰ παντὸς* and *τὸ κατὰ μηδενός*, [the *dictum de omni* and the *dictum de nullo*,] and *τὸ ἐν ὅλῳ* and *τὸ ἐν μηδενί*, [the *dictum in toto* and *dictum in nullo*;] and, by the application of these, does he evince the convertibility of pure universal negatives. 'It being supposed,' he says, 'that A is in [or is predicable of] no B, it follows from this that B is in [or is predicable of] no A; for, if B is in some A, let it be in C. Now, C is contained under the logical whole, A, (ἐν ὅλῳ, *in toto*, A;) A will, therefore, be universally predicated of it, (*κατὰ παντός*, *de omni*.) But C is a part of B; A, therefore, will be predicated of a part of B. But the primary hypothesis was that A is predicable of no B (*de nullo* B;) and the *dictum de nullo* is, that there is no part of B of which A can be predicated.

"Farther, from the very form of the expression, it is manifest that the demonstration does not proceed on the convertibility of particular affirmatives. For he does not say—*If B is in some A, A will be in some B*; for this would have been to demonstrate through the rule of particular affirmatives. But, in the sequel, when he demonstrates the convertibility of particular affirmatives, he employs to that end the convertibility of universal negatives. For he says—'*If B is in no A, A is in no B*;' thus employing the first rule as established and confessed; whereas, in now demonstrating that rule itself, he does not assume as established the convertibility of particular affirmatives. But, there being held out in a concrete individual example, (*ἐκθέμενος*,) C as a part of A, he grounds on this his demonstration—B not being predicated of C as a *particular*, but as a *singular*. It cannot, therefore, be maintained that he employed the reciprocation of particular affirmatives, but the *dictum de omni*

The rules of conversion cannot be applied to all propositions, but only to those that are categorical, and we are left to the direction of common sense in the conversion of other* propositions. To give an example: "Alexander was the son of Philip;" therefore, "Philip was the father of Alexander:" "A is greater than B;" therefore, "B is less than A.†" These are conversions which, as far as I know, do not fall within any rule in logic;‡ nor do we find any loss for want of a rule in such cases.

Even in the conversion of categorical propositions, it is not enough to transpose the subject and predicate. Both must undergo some change, in order to fit them for their new station; for, in every proposition, the subject must be a substantive, or have the force of a substantive; and the predicate must be an adjective, or have the force of an adjective. Hence it follows, that when the subject is an individual, the proposition admits not of conversion.§ How, for instance, shall we convert this proposition, "God is omniscient"?‖

These observations shew, [?] that the

---

and the *dictum in toto*, as his medium of demonstration.

"It is, however, better perhaps, and more agreeable to the context, to hold, that Aristotle made his demonstration to *sense* through the holding up or *exposition* of an individual [ἔκθεσις, *expositio*—hence, singular propositions and syllogisms are called *expository*], and not in the manner previously stated, nor syllogistically. For the *expository* mode of demonstration is brought to bear through sense, and not syllogistically. For C is taken as some *exposed* and sensible part of A, and also as an individual part of B. C is thus a part at once of A and of B; is contained under both these logical wholes; and when A is predicated of C, as its own part, it will also be predicated of a part of B. . . . . Thus, if it be agreed that *Man is in no Horse*, [that *no Horse is a Man*]; and if it be not admitted, *e converso*, that *Horse is in no Man*, [that *no Man is a Horse*]; let us suppose that *Horse is in some Man*, [that *some Man is a Horse*], and let this Man be Theon. Man will therefore be in some Horse, [some Horse will be a Man], for Theon is, *ex hypothesi*, both a Man and a Horse. But this is, as contradictory, impossible; for it was originally agreed, that Man is in no Horse, [that no Horse is a Man]," &c.

It is to be noticed, that the terms which I have usually translated *demonstrate* and *demonstration*, are only δεικνύναι and δεῖξις, and never ἀποδεικνύναι and ἀπόδειξις.

I may notice, before concluding this note, the simpler process by which Theophrastus and Eudemus formally evinced the first rule of conversion; this also is recorded by Alexander. "Let it be supposed that A can be predicated of no B. Now, if not predicable of, it is disjoined from, B. B, therefore, is also disjoined from A; and if disjoined from, is not predicable of, A."—H.

* This is incorrect. *Hypothetical* propositions can be converted *per contrapositionem*; and *Disjunctives*, *per contrapositionem* and *per accidens*.—H.

† These propositions are categorical; they cannot therefore be given as examples of propositions, "*other*" than categorical.—H.

‡ But this simply because they are beyond the sphere of logic, being *material* not *formal* conversions.—H.

§ This is erroneous.—H.

‖ By saying—"Ao, or the, omniscient is God."—H.

doctrine of the conversion of propositions is not so complete as it appears. The rules are laid down without any limitation; yet they are fitted only to one class of propositions—viz., the categorical; and of these only to such as have a general term for their subject.

Section II.

ON ADDITIONS MADE TO ARISTOTLE'S THEORY.

Although the logicians have enlarged the first and second parts of logic, by explaining some technical words and distinctions which Aristotle had omitted, and by giving names to some kinds of propositions which he overlooks, yet, in what concerns the theory of categorical syllogisms, he is more full, more minute and particular, than any of them; so that they seem to have thought this capital part of the Organon rather redundant than deficient.

It is true that Galen [?] added a fourth figure to the three mentioned by Aristotle. But there is reason to think that Aristotle omitted the fourth figure, not through ignorance or inattention, but of design, as containing only some indirect modes, which, when properly expressed, fall into the first figure.

It is true also that Peter Ramus, a professed enemy of Aristotle, introduced some new modes that are adapted to singular propositions; and that Aristotle takes no notice of singular propositions, either in his rules of conversion, or in the modes of syllogism. But the friends of Aristotle have shewn that this improvement of Ramus is more specious than useful. Singular propositions have the force of universal propositions, and are subject to the same rules. The definition given by Aristotle of an universal proposition applies to them; and therefore he might think, that there was no occasion to multiply the modes of syllogism upon their account.*

These attempts, therefore, shew rather inclination than power to discover any material defect in Aristotle's theory.

The most valuable addition made to the theory of categorical syllogisms seems to be the invention of those technical names given to the legitimate modes, by which they may be easily remembered, and which have been comprised in these barbarous verses:—

> *Barbara, Celarent, Darii, Ferio*, dato primæ;
> *Cesare, Camestres, Festino, Baroco*, secundæ;
> Tertia grande sonans recitat *Darapti, Felapton*,
> Adjungens *Disamis, Datisi, Bocardo, Ferison*.†

---

* There are other and better reasons for the omission; but they are not unnoticed by Aristotle.—H.

† This is one of the many variations of these verses but not the original edition.—H.

In these verses, every legitimate mode belonging to the three figures has a name given to it, by which it may be distinguished and remembered. And this name is so contrived as to denote its nature; for the name has three vowels, which denote the kind of each of its propositions.

Thus, a syllogism in *Bocardo* must be made up of the propositions denoted by the three vowels, O, A, O; that is, its major and conclusion must be particular negative propositions, and its minor an universal affirmative; and, being in the third figure, the middle term must be the subject of both premises.

This is the mystery contained in the vowels of those barbarous words. But there are other mysteries contained in their consonants; for, by their means, a child may be taught to reduce any syllogism of the second or third figure to one of the first. So that the four modes of the first figure being directly proved to be conclusive, all the modes of the other two are proved at the same time, by means of this operation of reduction. For the rules and manner of this reduction, and the different species of it, called [*direct* or] *ostensive*, and [*indirect* or] *per impossibile*, I refer to the Logicians, that I may not disclose all their mysteries.

The invention contained in these verses is so ingenious, and so great an adminicle to the dexterous management of syllogisms, that I think it very probable that Aristotle had some contrivance of this kind, which was kept as one of the secret doctrines of his school, and handed down by tradition, until some person brought it to light. This is offered only as a conjecture, leaving it to those who are better acquainted with the most ancient commentators on the Analytics, either to refute or confirm it.*

Section III.

ON EXAMPLES USED TO ILLUSTRATE THIS THEORY.

We may observe, that Aristotle hardly ever gives examples of real syllogisms to illustrate his rules. In demonstrating the legitimate modes, he takes A, B, C, for the terms of the syllogism. Thus, the first mode of the first figure is demonstrated by him in this manner:—"For," says he, "if A is attributed to every B, and B to every C, it follows necessarily, that A may be attributed to every C." For disproving the illegitimate modes, he uses the same manner; with this difference, that he commonly, for an example, gives three real terms, such as *bonum*, *habitus*, *prudentia*; of which three terms you are to make up a syllogism of the figure and mode in question, which will appear to be inconclusive.

The commentators and systematical writers in logic have supplied this defect, and given us real examples of every legitimate mode in all the figures. We acknowledged this to be charitably done, in order to assist the conception in matters so very abstract; but whether it was prudently done for the honour of the art, may be doubted. I am afraid this was to uncover the nakedness of the theory. It has undoubtedly contributed to bring it into contempt; for when one considers the silly and uninstructive reasonings* that have been brought forth by this grand organ of science, he can hardly forbear crying out—

"*Parturiunt montes; nascetur ridiculus mus.*"

Many of the writers of logic are acute and ingenious, and much practised in the syllogistical art; and there must be some reason why the examples they have given of syllogisms are so lean.†

We shall speak of the reason afterwards;

---

* This conjecture, I regret to say, is not borne out.—H.

* This must refer to the concrete examples given by Logicians, in illustration of their rules. Had they given, or attempted to give instruction beyond the bare significance of these rules, they would have been indeed very "silly." See next note. Logic also, it may be observed, is no "*organ of science*," meaning by that, an instrument of discovery.—H.

† Why these examples, instead of being merely *lean*, ought to have been *bare bones*; and the Logicians merit the reproach of having failed in making their skeletons fat, for attempting to give them a garniture of flesh at all. To the symbols of Aristotle they should have stuck. Logic is the *science of the laws of thought as thought*—that is, of the necessary conditions to which thought, considered in itself, is subject. This is technically called its *Form*. Logic, therefore, supposes an abstraction from all consideration of the *matter* of thought—that is, the infinitude of determinate objects in relation to one or other of which it is actually manifested. Now, the principal reproach which can be fairly urged against logical authors, is, that they have never realized to the science its ideal beauty, by reducing it to a purely *formal system*; that they have never yet fully disengaged it from the *material slime* out of which it has so painfully been working its way, and with which it still continues to be soiled. Reid's reproach, on the other hand, and that of many others, is, that Logic is not wholly a *material* science; that it is not an instrument of objective discovery; that its instances are uninstructive—are not an epitome, or complement of the *omne scibile*. He thus reproaches Logic for not being something other than what it is; for not performing what it never professed; nay, for not performing what no single science can effect.—Again, if it be said that Logic, as a formal science, is a lean and barren doctrine—be it so. But this reproach only affects the science through its object. Now, this object is the legislation of thought; and, if the laws and processes which it displays be unimportant and uninteresting, they are the laws and processes by and through which, and which alone, what is nearest to us and noblest in creation executes its marvels. "On earth, there is nothing great but Man; in Man, there is nothing great but Mind." It is not, surely, imagined that there are other laws and processes of thought competent to the human intellect, besides those of which Logic is the exposition. All "discourse of reason" is and must be syllogistic; what is beyond the syllogism is beyond us.—H.

and shall now give a syllogism in each figure as an example.

No work of God is bad;
The natural passions and appetites of men are the work of God;
Therefore, none of them is bad.

In this syllogism, the middle term, "work of God," is the subject of the major, and the predicate of the minor; so that the syllogism is of the first figure. The mode is that called *Celarent;* the major and conclusion being both universal negatives, and the minor an universal affirmative. It agrees to the rules of the figure, as the major is universal, and the minor affirmative; it is also agreeable to all the general rules; so that it maintains its character in every trial. And to shew of what ductile materials syllogisms are made, we may, by converting simply the major proposition, reduce it to a good syllogism of the second figure, and of the mode *Cesare*, thus:—

Whatever is bad is not the work of God;
All the natural passions and appetites of men are the work of God;
Therefore, they are not bad.

Another example:

Every thing virtuous is praiseworthy;
Some pleasures are not praiseworthy;
Therefore, some pleasures are not virtuous.

Here the middle term, "praiseworthy," being the predicate of both premises, the syllogism is of the second figure; and seeing it is made up of the propositions, A, O, O, the mode is *Baroco*. It will be found to agree both with the general and special rules; and it may be reduced into a good syllogism of the first figure, upon converting the major by contraposition, thus:—

What[ever] is not praiseworthy is not virtuous;
Some pleasures are not praiseworthy;
Therefore, some pleasures are not virtuous.

That this syllogism is conclusive, common sense pronounces, and all Logicians must allow; but it is somewhat unpliable to rules, and requires a little straining to make it tally with them.

That it is of the first figure is beyond dispute; but to what mode of that figure shall we refer it?

This is a question of some difficulty; for, in the first place, the premises seem to be both negative, which contradicts the third general rule; and, moreover, it is contrary to a special rule of the first figure, That the minor should be negative. These are the difficulties to be removed.

Some Logicians think that the two negative particles in the major are equivalent to an affirmative; and that, therefore, the major proposition, "What[ever] is not praiseworthy is not virtuous," is to be accounted an affirmative proposition. This, if granted, solves one difficulty; but the other remains. The most ingenious solution, therefore, is this, Let the middle term be "not-praiseworthy." Thus, making the negative particle a part of the middle term, the syllogism stands thus:—

Whatever is *not-praiseworthy* is not virtuous;
Some pleasures are *not-praiseworthy;*
Therefore, some pleasures are not virtuous.

By this analysis, the major becomes an universal negative, the minor a particular affirmative, and the conclusion a particular negative, and so we have a just syllogism in *Ferio*.

We see, by this example, that the quality of propositions is not so invariable, but that, when occasion requires, an affirmative may be degraded into a negative, or a negative exalted to an affirmative.*

Another example:

All Africans are black;
All Africans are men;
Therefore, some men are black.

This is of the third figure, and of the mode *Darapti;* and it may be reduced to *Darii* in the first figure, by converting the minor.

All Africans are black;
Some men are Africans;
Therefore, some men are black.

By this time I apprehend the reader has got as many examples of syllogisms as will stay his appetite for that kind of entertainment.

Section IV.

ON THE DEMONSTRATION OF THE THEORY.

Aristotle and all his followers have thought it necessary, in order to bring this theory of categorical syllogisms to a science, to demonstrate both that the fourteen authorised modes conclude justly, and that none of the rest do. Let us now see how this has been executed.

As to the legitimate modes, Aristotle and those who follow him the most closely, demonstrate the four modes of the first figure directly from an axiom called the *Dictum de omni et nullo*. The amount of the axiom is, *That what is affirmed of a whole genus may be affirmed of all the species and individuals belonging to that genus; and that what is denied of the whole genus may be denied of* [*all*] *its species and individuals.* The four modes of the first figure are evidently included in this axiom. And as to the legitimate modes of the other figures, they are proved by reducing them to some mode

* This is not, *in reality*, the case.—H.

of the first. Nor is there any other principle assumed in these reductions but the axioms concerning the conversion of propositions, and, in some cases, the axioms concerning the opposition of propositions.

As to the illegitimate modes, Aristotle has taken the labour to try and condemn them one by one in all the three figures: But this is done in such a manner that it is very painful to follow him.* To give a specimen: In order to prove that those modes of the first figure, in which the major is particular, do not conclude, he proceeds thus:—"If A is, or is not, in some B, and B in every C, no conclusion follows. Take for the terms in the affirmative case, *good*, *habit*, *prudence*; in the negative, *good*, *habit*, *ignorance*." This laconic style, the use of symbols not familiar,† and, in place of giving an example, his leaving us to form one from three assigned terms, give such embarrassment to a reader, that he is like one reading a book of riddles.

Having thus ascertained the true and false modes of a figure, he subjoins the particular rules of that figure, which seem to be deduced from the particular cases before determined. The general rules come last of all, as a general corollary from what goes before.

I know not whether it is from a diffidence of Aristotle's demonstrations, or from an apprehension of their obscurity, or from a desire of improving upon his method, that almost all the writers in logic I have met with have inverted his order, beginning where he ends, and ending where he begins. They first demonstrate the general rules, which belong to all the figures, from three axioms; then, from the general rules and the nature of each figure, they demonstrate the special rules of each figure. When this is done, nothing remains but to apply these general and special rules, and to reject every mode which contradicts them.‡

This method has a very scientific appearance; and when we consider that, by a few rules once demonstrated, an hundred and seventy-eight false modes are destroyed at one blow, which Aristotle had the trouble to put to death one by one, it seems to be a great improvement. I have only one objection to the three axioms.*

The three axioms are these: 1. Things which agree with the same third agree with one another. 2. When one agrees with the third, and the other does not, they do not agree with one another. 3. When neither agrees with the third, you cannot thence conclude, either that they do, or do not agree with one another. If these axioms are applied to mathematical quantities, to which they seem to relate when taken literally, they have all the evidence that an axiom ought to have; but the Logicians apply them in an analogical sense to things of another nature. In order, therefore, to judge whether they are truly axioms, we ought to strip them of their figurative dress, and to set them down in plain English, as the Logicians understand them. They amount, therefore, to this:—1. If two things be affirmed of a third, or the third be affirmed of them; or if one be affirmed of the third, and the third affirmed of the other; then they may be affirmed one of the other. 2. If one is affirmed of the third, or the third of it, and the other denied of the third, or the third of it, they may be denied one of the other. 3. If both are denied of the third, or the third of them, or if one is denied of the third, and the third denied of the other, nothing can be inferred.

When the three axioms are thus put in plain English, they seem not to have that degree of evidence which axioms ought to have; and, if there is any defect of evidence in the axioms, this defect will be communicated to the whole edifice raised upon them.

It may even be suspected, that an attempt, by any method, to demonstrate that a syllogism is conclusive, is an impropriety somewhat like that of attempting to demonstrate an axiom. In a just syllogism, the connection between the premises and the conclusion is not only real, but immediate; so that no proposition can come between them to make their connection more apparent. The very intention of a syllogism is to leave nothing to be supplied that is necessary to a complete demonstration. Therefore, a man of common understanding, who has a perfect comprehension of the premises, finds himself under a necessity of admitting the conclusion, supposing the premises to be true; and the conclusion is connected with the premises with all the force of intuitive evidence. In a word, an immediate conclusion is seen in the pre-

* It must be recollected that Aristotle was the *founder* of the science; and that it was requisite for him to shew articulately what, in consequence of that manifestation, his successors have been warranted in assuming.—H.

† From the nature and flexion of the prepositive article in Greek, such symbols are far less vague than in our language or in Latin; at the same time, it should be remembered, that those to whom Aristotle addressed himself, were already familiar with the application of such symbols—Mathematics being the first branch of juvenile instruction among the Greeks. It is likely, too, that these letters were relative to diagrams, the loss of which his later commentators have endeavoured to supply. Of the intrinsic propriety of using a symbolical notation in Logic, I have elsewhere spoken.—H.

‡ Each order is proper in its place; the Analytic for the establishment; the Synthetic for the teaching of a science.—H.

* These three axioms are not those employed by Logicians in general; and they have been often, justly, and severely criticised, as a faulty application of Mathematical language to Logical notions.—H.

mises by the light of common sense; and, where that is wanting, no kind of reasoning will supply its place.*

Section V.

ON THIS THEORY, CONSIDERED AS AN ENGINE OF SCIENCE.†

The slow progress of useful knowledge, during the many ages in which the syllogistic art was most highly cultivated as the only guide to science, and its quick progress since that art was disused, suggest a presumption against it; and this presumption is strengthened by the puerility of the examples which have always been brought to illustrate its rules.‡

The ancients seem to have had too high notions, both of the force of the reasoning power in man, and of the art of syllogism as its guide. Mere reasoning can carry us but a very little way in most subjects.§ By observation, and experiments properly conducted, the stock of human knowledge may be enlarged without end; but the power of reasoning alone, applied with vigour through a long life, would only carry a man round like a horse in a mill, who labours hard but makes no progress. There is indeed an exception to this observation in the mathematical sciences. The relations of quantity are so various, and so susceptible of exact mensuration, that long trains of accurate reasoning on that subject may be formed, and conclusions drawn, very remote from the first principles. It is in this science, and those which depend upon it, that the power of reasoning triumphs;* in other matters, its trophies are inconsiderable. If any man doubt this, let him produce, in any subject unconnected with mathematics, a train of reasoning of some length, leading to a conclusion which, without this train of reasoning, would never have been brought within human sight. Every man acquainted with mathematics can produce thousands of such trains of reasoning. I do not say that none such can be produced in other sciences; but I believe they are few, and not easily found; and that, if they are found, it will not be in subjects that can be expressed by categorical propositions, to which alone the theory of figure and mode extends.

In matters to which that theory extends, a man of good sense, who can distinguish things that differ, who can avoid the snares of ambiguous words, and who is moderately practised in such matters, sees at once all that can be inferred from the premises, or finds that there is but a very short step to the conclusion.

When the power of reasoning is so feeble by nature, especially in subjects to which this theory can be applied, it would be unreasonable to expect great effects from it. And hence we see the reason why the examples brought to illustrate it by the most ingenious Logicians have rather tended to bring it into contempt.

If it should be thought that the syllogistic art may be an useful engine in mathematics, in which pure reasoning has ample scope: First, it may be observed, That facts are unfavourable to this opinion: For it does not appear that Euclid, or Apollonius, or Archimedes, or Huygens, or Newton, ever made the least use of this art; and I am even of opinion that no use can be made of it in mathematics.† I would not wish to advance this rashly, since Ari-

---

* The observations contained in this paragraph, which have been adopted and expanded by Mr Stewart, are, in my opinion, without application. There is no Logician I am aware of who has attempted to demonstrate *that a syllogism is conclusive*; though many have taken different modes of scientifically stating the principles which constitute its native evidence and necessity. Aristotle's definition of the syllogism, which has been generally adopted, of itself shows how superfluous are these remarks. As this definition is not given by Reid, I shall quote it:—"A syllogism is a speech, in which certain things [the premises] being supposed, something different from what is supposed [the conclusion] follows *of necessity*; and this solely in virtue of the suppositions themselves." And Alexander, in his commentary on this definition, thus explains—what no logician ever dreamt of doubting—*the formal necessity of the consequence in all syllogisms*:—"But when Aristotle says, '*follows of necessity*,' this does not mean that the conclusion, as a proposition in itself, should necessarily be true; for this is the case only in syllogisms of necessary matter; but *that the conclusion, be its matter what it may—actual, contingent, or necessary—must follow of necessity from the premises*; for, even if the conclusion be (materially considered) contingent, still it cannot but result from propositions standing in syllogistical connection. His words do not, therefore, denote that the conclusion should be a necessary proposition; but the nature of the relation in which the conclusion stands to the premises."—(*On First Book of the Prior Analytics*, f. 8, a. ed. Ald.)—Into Logic ought never to have been introduced a consideration of the differences of Matter at all; it should have been limited exclusively to the Form; and thus would have been avoided the mistakes so prevalent in regard to its object and end.—H.

† As an *engine of science, an instrument of discovery*, logic never, even by the schoolmen, was proposed.—H.

‡ See above, p. [illegible], b, notes.—H.

§ Does "mere reasoning" mean reasoning apart from the conditions of an object matter?—H.

* If, by "*power of reasoning*," be understood mental *force*, that is less exerted in mathematics than in any other intellectual pursuit. As Warburton truly says, "*Mathematical demonstration is the easiest exercise of reason*." In another sense, Reid's observation is correct.—H.

† Mathematical, like all other reasoning, is syllogistic; but, here, *the perspicuous necessity of the matter necessitates the correctness of the form*: we cannot reason wrong. Logic, whether natural or acquired, is thus less exercised in mathematics than in any other department of science; and on this account it is that mathematical study is the very worst gymnastic of the intellect—the very worst preparative for reasoning correctly on matters (and these are only not all the objects of human concernment) in which the mind must actively precede, and not passively follow the evolution of its objects.—H.

stotle has said, that mathematicians reason for the most part in the first figure. What led him to think so was, that the first figure only yields conclusions that are universal and affirmative, and the conclusions of mathematics are commonly of that kind. But it is to be observed, that the propositions of mathematics are not categorical propositions, consisting of one subject and one predicate. They express some relation which one quantity bears to another, and on that account must have three terms. The quantities compared make two, and the relation between them is a third. Now, to such propositions we can neither apply the rules concerning the conversion of propositions, nor can they enter into a syllogism of any of the figures or modes. We observed before, that this conversion, *A is greater than B*, therefore *B is less than A*, does not fall within the rules of conversion given by Aristotle or the Logicians;* and we now add, that this simple reasoning, *A is equal to B, and B to C*, therefore *A is equal to C*, cannot be brought into any syllogism in figure and mode.† There are indeed syllogisms into which mathematical propositions may enter, and of such we shall afterwards speak; but they have nothing to do with the system of figure and mode.

When we go without the circle of the mathematical sciences, I know nothing in which there seems to be so much demonstration as in that part of logic which treats of the figures and modes of syllogism; but the few remarks we have made, shew that it has some weak places [?]; and, besides, this system cannot be used as an engine to rear itself.‡

The compass of the syllogistic system,§ as an engine of science, may be discerned by a compendious and general view of the conclusion drawn, and the argument used, to prove it,* in each of the three figures.

In the first figure, the conclusion affirms or denies something of a certain species or individual; and the argument to prove* this conclusion is, *That the same thing may be affirmed or denied of the whole genus to which that species or individual belongs.*

In the second figure, the conclusion is, That some species or individual does not belong to such a genus; and the argument* is, *That some attribute common to the whole genus does not belong to that species or individual.*

In the third figure, the conclusion is, That such an attribute belongs to part of a genus; and the argument* is, *That the attribute in question belongs to a species or individual which is part of that genus.*

I apprehend that, in this short view, every conclusion that falls within the compass of the three figures, as well as the mean of proof, is comprehended. The rules of all the figures might be easily deduced from it; and it appears that there is only one principle of reasoning in all the three; so that it is not strange that a syllogism of one figure should be reduced to one of another figure.

The general principle in which the whole terminates, and of which every categorical syllogism is only a particular application, is this, *That what is affirmed or denied of the whole genus may be affirmed or denied of every species and individual belonging to it.* This is a principle of undoubted certainty indeed, but of no great depth. Aristotle and all the Logicians assume it as an axiom, or first principle, from which the syllogistic system, as it were, takes its departure; and, after a tedious voyage, and great expense of demonstration, it lands at last in this principle, as its ultimate conclusion.

"*O curas hominum! O quantum est in rebus inane!*"†

Section VI.

ON MODAL SYLLOGISMS.

Categorical propositions, besides their quantity and quality, have another affection, by which they are divided into *pure* and *modal*.‡ In a pure proposition, the

---

* See above, p. 697, a, note ‡.—H.

† Not as it stands; for, as expressed, this reasoning is elliptical. Explicitly stated, it is as follows:—

What are equal to the same, are equal to each other;

A and C are equal to the same (B);

Therefore, A and C are equal to each other.

Dr Reid could have found a rare work in the College Library of Glasgow, which it might have been profitable for him to consult—viz., an edition of the first six books of Euclid, by Herlinus and Dasypodius, in which every demonstration is developed in regular syllogisms. But this development did not render syllogistic what was not syllogistic from the beginning—it only shews that it was always so. A Reasoning is not the less syllogistic, because not formally enounced in two overtly premises and a conclusion. This, however, is the notion that many of those who have written about and against logic, seem to have entertained.—H.

‡ Which is not attempted.—H.

§ "The Compass of the Syllogistic System" is the compass of the reasoning faculty of man. I may notice, however, that Logicians have actually overlooked the better half of Logic; exclusively considering the reasoning in the Whole of *Extension*, and (except in one accidental variety of Syllogism, and the peculiar nature of this also they did not understand) altogether unobservant of that in the Whole of *Comprehension*. But this by the way.—H.

* For "*argument to prove*," &c., read, "*proximate principle which legitimates*."—H.

† The end of all science is the reduction of the many to the one. Is Logic, then, to be derided for accomplishing this end? Astronomy is not an empty, because a simple, science; nor is La Place undervalued for having shewn the universal sufficiency for its phænomena of the single principle of gravitation. But see above, p. 698, b, note †.—H.

‡ The Modality of propositions and syllogisms is a *real* or *Metaphysical*, and not a *Formal* or *Logical*

predicate is barely affirmed or denied of the subject; but, in a modal proposition, the affirmation or negation is modified, by being declared to be *necessary*, or *contingent*, or *possible*, or *impossible*. These are the four modes observed by Aristotle,* from which he denominates a proposition modal. His genuine disciples maintain, that these are all the modes that can affect an affirmation or negation, and that the enumeration is complete. Others maintain, that this enumeration is incomplete; and that, when an affirmation or negation is said to be certain or uncertain, probable or improbable, this makes a modal proposition, no less than the four modes of Aristotle. We shall not enter into this dispute, but proceed to observe, that the epithets of *pure* and *modal* are applied to syllogisms as well as to propositions. A pure syllogism is that in which both premises are pure propositions. A modal syllogism is that in which either of the premises is a modal proposition.

The syllogisms of which we have already said so much, are those only which are pure as well as categorical. But, when we consider, that, through all the figures and modes, a syllogism may have one premise modal of any of the four modes, while the other is pure, or it may have both premises modal, and that they may be either of the same mode, or of different modes, what prodigious variety arises from all these combinations? Now, it is the business of a Logician to shew how the conclusion is affected in all this variety of cases. Aristotle has done this in his first Analytics with immense labour; and it will not be thought strange that, when he had employed only four chapters in discussing one hundred and ninety-two modes, true and false, of pure syllogisms, he should employ fifteen upon modal syllogisms.

I am very willing to excuse myself from entering upon this great branch of logic, by the judgment and example of those who cannot be charged either with want of respect to Aristotle, or with a low esteem of the syllogistic art.

Keckermann, a famous Dantiscan professor, who spent his life in teaching and writing logic,† in his huge folio system of that science, published *anno* 1600, calls the doctrine of the modals the *crux Logicorum*. With regard to the scholastic doctors, among whom this was a proverb, *De modali non gustabit asinus*, he thinks it very dubious whether they tortured most the modal syllogisms, or were most tortured by them. But those crabbed geniuses, says he, made this doctrine so very thorny that it is fitter to tear a man's wits in pieces than to give them solidity. He desires it to be observed, that the doctrine of the modals is adapted to the Greek language. The modal terms were frequently used by the Greeks in their disputations, and, on that account, are so fully handled by Aristotle; but, in [disputations in] the Latin tongue, you shall hardly ever meet with them. Nor do I remember, in all my experience, says he, to have observed any man in danger of being foiled in a dispute, through his ignorance of the modals.*

This author, however, out of respect to Aristotle, treats pretty fully of modal propositions, shewing how to distinguish their subject and predicate, their quantity and quality. But the modal syllogisms he passes over altogether.

Ludovicus Vives, whom I mention, not as a devotee of Aristotle, but on account of his own judgment and learning, thinks that the doctrine of modals ought to be banished out of logic, and remitted to grammar; and that, if the grammar of the Greek tongue had been brought to a system in the time of Aristotle, that most acute philosopher would have saved the great labour he has bestowed on this subject.†

Burgersdyk, after enumerating five classes of modal syllogisms, observes, that they require many rules and cautions, which Aristotle hath handled diligently; but that, as the use of them is not great, and their rules difficult, he thinks it not worth while to enter into the discussion of them; recommending to those who would understand them, the most learned paraphrase of Joannes Monlorius upon the first book of the First Analytics.‡

All the writers of logic for two hundred years back, that have fallen into my hands, have passed over the rules of modal syllogisms with as little ceremony.§ So that this great branch of the doctrine of syllogism, so diligently handled by Aristotle, fell into neglect, if not contempt, even while the doctrine of pure syllogisms continued in the highest esteem. Moved by these authorities, I shall let this doctrine rest in peace, without giving the least disturbance to its ashes.

---

affection. It ought, therefore, as I have shewn, on principle, to be wholly excluded from Logic. See *Edinburgh Review*, vol. lvii. p. 315, sq.—H.

* Aristotle has two enumerations of the *Modes*;—the one now mentioned, and another in the same chapter, comprehending, besides the four stated, also the *true* and the *false*. Modes are indefinite in number; and his Greek expositors contend that Aristotle did not mean to enumerate *all*, but only to signalise the more *important*.—H.

† Keckermann died at the age of thirty-seven, and, besides Systems of Logic, a greater and less, left *Systems of thirteen other sciences*, with various other treatises on particular subjects.—H.

* *Systema Plenius*, L. i. c. 3. *Opera*, i. p. 73.—H.

† Vives *De Causis Corrupt. Artium*, L. iii.—H.

‡ Burgersdicii, *Institut. Log.* L. ii. c. 14.—H.

§ Modals have, indeed, been frequently treated with neglect by Logical writers, but never, at least till lately, formally expelled from the science.—H.

Section VII.

ON SYLLOGISMS THAT DO NOT BELONG TO FIGURE AND MODE.

Aristotle gives some observations upon imperfect syllogisms; such as the *Enthymeme*, in which one of the premises is not expressed, but understood;* *Induction*, wherein we collect an universal from a full enumeration of particulars; and *Example*, which is an imperfect induction. The Logicians have copied Aristotle, upon these kinds of reasoning, without any considerable improvement. But, to compensate the modal syllogisms, which they have laid aside, they have given rules for several kinds of syllogism, of which Aristotle takes no notice. These may be reduced to *two classes*.

The *first* class comprehends the syllogisms into which any *exclusive*, *restrictive*,† *exceptive*, or *reduplicative*† proposition enters. Such propositions are by some called *Exponible*, by others *Imperfectly* [or *Secondarily*] *Modal*. The rules given with regard to these are obvious, from a just interpretation of the propositions.

The *second class* is that of *Hypothetical* syllogisms, which take that denomination from having a hypothetical proposition for one or both premises. Most Logicians give the name of *hypothetical* to all complex propositions which have more terms than one subject and one predicate.‡ I use the word in this large sense, and mean, by hypothetical syllogisms, all those in which either of the premises consists of more terms than two. How many various kinds there may be of such syllogisms, has never been ascertained. The Logicians have given names to some; such as the *copulative*, the *conditional*, (by some called *hypothetical*,) and the *disjunctive*.

Such syllogisms cannot be tried by the rules of figure and mode. Every kind would require rules peculiar to itself. Logicians have given rules for some kinds; but there are many that have not so much as the name.

The *Dilemma* is considered by most Logicians as a species of the disjunctive syllogism.§ A remarkable property of this kind is, that it may sometimes be happily retorted; it is, it seems, like a hand-grenade, which, by dextrous management, may be thrown back, so as to spend its force upon the assailant.* We shall conclude this tedious account of syllogisms with a dilemma mentioned by Aulus Gellius, and from him by many Logicians, as insoluble in any other way.†

"Euathlus, a rich young man, desirous of learning the art of pleading, applied to Protagoras, a celebrated sophist, to instruct him, promising a great sum of money as his reward; one half of which was paid down; the other half he bound himself to pay as soon as he should plead a cause before the judges, and gain it. Protagoras found him a very apt scholar; but, after he had made good progress, he was in no haste to plead causes. The master, conceiving that he intended by this means to shift off his second payment, took, as he thought, a sure method to get the better of his delay. He sued Euathlus before the judges; and, having opened his cause at the bar, he pleaded to this purpose:—'O most foolish young man, do you not see that, in any event, I must gain my point?—for, if the judges give sentence for me, you must pay by their sentence; if against me, the condition of our bargain is fulfilled, and you have no plea left for your delay, after having pleaded and gained a cause.' To which Euathlus answered:—'O most wise master, I might have avoided the force of your argument, by not pleading my own cause. But, giving up this advantage, do you not see that, whatever sentence the judges pass, I am safe? If they give sentence for me, I am acquitted by their sentence; if against me, the condition of our bargain is not fulfilled, by my pleading a cause, and losing it.' The judges, thinking the arguments unanswerable on both sides, put off the cause to a long day."‡

* This is the vulgar opinion regarding Aristotle's Enthymeme, but, as I have shewn, not the correct. See *Edinburgh Review*, vol. lvii. p. 221, sq.—H.

† *Reduplicative*, and *Specificative*, are two species of *Restrictive* propositions.—H.

‡ This abusive employment of the term *Hypothetical*, is not sanctioned by the best Logicians, nor even by the greater number. *Hypothetical* and *Conditional* ought to be used as convertible terms. See *Edinburgh Review*, vol. lvii. p. 212.—H.

§ This is hardly accurate. The greater number of Logicians consider it as an hypothetical (conditional) syllogism; but, in fact, it is both hypothetical and disjunctive, and ought, therefore, to be styled the Hypothetico-Disjunctive Syllogism.—H.

* We must not confound the Dilemma, or Hypothetico-Disjunctive *Syllogism*, and the *Sophism* called the Dilemma.—H.

† Is this not an erratum for "any way?"—H.

‡ This story is, by the Greek authors, generally told of the Rhetorician Corax (Crow) and his pupil Tisias. The puzzled judges, in lieu of a decision on the case, angrily pronounced of plaintiff and defendant—Κακοῦ κόρακος κακὸν ᾠόν, (plaguy egg of a plaguy crow!) Hence the proverb.—H.

CHAPTER V.

ACCOUNT OF THE REMAINING BOOKS OF THE ORGANON.

Section I.

OF THE LAST ANALYTICS.

IN the First Analytics, syllogisms are considered in respect of their *form*; they are now to be considered in respect of their *matter*. The form lies in the necessary connection between the premises and the conclusion; and, where such a connection is wanting, they are said to be informal, or vicious in point of form.

But, where there is no fault in the form, there may be in the matter—that is, in the propositions of which they are composed, which may be *true* or *false*, *probable* or *improbable*.

When the premises are certain,* and the conclusion drawn from them in due form, this is *demonstration*, and produces *science*. Such syllogisms are called *apodictical*, and are handled in the two books of the Last Analytics. When the premises are not certain, but probable only, such syllogisms are called *dialectical*; and of them he treats in the eight books of the Topics. But there are some syllogisms which seem to be perfect both in matter and form, when they are not really so; as, a face may seem beautiful which is but painted. These being apt to deceive, and produce a false opinion, are called *sophistical*; and they are the subject of the book concerning Sophisms.

To return to the Last Analytics, which treat of *demonstration* and of *science*: We shall not pretend to abridge those books, for Aristotle's writings do not admit of abridgement; no man, in fewer words, can say what he says; and he is not often guilty of repetition. We shall only give some of his capital conclusions, omitting his long reasonings and nice distinctions, of which his genius was wonderfully productive.

All demonstration must be built upon principles already known, and these upon others of the same kind; until we come at last to first principles, which neither can be demonstrated, nor need to be, being evident of themselves.

We cannot demonstrate things in a circle, supporting the conclusion by the premises, and the premises by the conclusion. Nor can there be an infinite number of middle terms between the first principle and the conclusion.

In all demonstration, the first principles, the conclusion, and all the intermediate propositions, must be necessary, general, and eternal truths; for, of things fortuitous, contingent, or mutable, or of individual things, there is no demonstration.

Some demonstrations prove only, *that* the thing is thus affected; others prove, *why* it is thus affected. The former may be drawn from a remote cause, or from an effect; but the latter must be drawn from an immediate cause, and are the most perfect.

The first figure is best adapted to demonstration, because it affords conclusions universally affirmative; and this figure is commonly used by the mathematicians.

The demonstration of an affirmative proposition is preferable to that of a negative; the demonstration of an universal to that of a particular; and direct demonstration to that *ad absurdum*.

The principles are more certain than the conclusion.

There cannot be opinion and science of the same thing at the same time.

In the second book, we are taught, that the *questions* that may be put with regard to any thing are four: 1. *Whether the thing be thus affected.* 2. *Why it is thus affected.* 3. *Whether it exists.* 4. *What it is.**

The last of these questions, Aristotle, in good Greek, calls the *What is it* of a thing. The schoolmen, in very barbarous Latin, called this the *quiddity* of a thing. This quiddity, he proves by many arguments, cannot be demonstrated, but must be fixed by a definition. This gives occasion to treat of *definition*, and how a right definition should be formed. As an example, he gives a definition of the number *three*, and defines it to be the first odd number.

In this book he treats also of the four kinds of *causes—efficient*, *material*, *formal*, and *final*.

Another thing treated of in this book is, the manner in which we acquire first principles, which are the foundation of all demonstration. These are not innate, because we may be, for a great part of life, ignorant of them: nor can they be deduced demonstratively from any antecedent knowledge, otherwise they would not be first principles. Therefore he concludes, that first principles are got by induction, from the informations of sense. The senses give us informations of individual things, and from these by induction we draw general conclusions; for it is a maxim with Aristotle, *That there is nothing in the understanding which was not before in some sense.*†

---

* In Demonstration, the premises must not only be *true* and *certain*, but *necessarily* so.—H.

* The natural order of the four questions, and as they are commonly enounced, is:—*An sit*—*Quod sit*—*Quale sit*—*Cur sit*.—H.

† Whether Aristotle admitted the virtual or potential existence of any *a priori* or native judg-

The knowledge of first principles, as it is not acquired by demonstration, ought not to be called science; and therefore he calls it *intelligence* [νοῦς.]

Section II.

OF THE TOPICS.

The professed design of the Topics is, to shew a method by which a man may be able to reason with probability and consistency upon every question that can occur.

Every question is either about the *genus* of the subject, or its *specific difference*, or something *proper* to it, or something *accidental*.

To prove that this division is complete, Aristotle reasons thus. Whatever is attributed to a subject, it must either be, that the subject can be reciprocally attributed to it, or that it cannot. If the subject and attribute can be reciprocated, the attribute either declares what the subject is, and then it is a definition; or it does not declare what the subject is, and then it is a property. If the attribute cannot be reciprocated, it must be something contained in the definition, or not. If it be contained in the definition of the subject, it must be the genus of the subject, or its specific difference; for the definition consists of these two. If it be not contained in the definition of the subject, it must be an accident.

[The instruments by which we may supply ourselves with] the furniture proper to fit a man for arguing dialectically may be reduced to these four heads: 1. [To make choice of] probable propositions of all sorts, which may on occasion be assumed in an argument. 2. [To take] distinctions of words which are nearly of the same signification. 3. [To mark the] distinctions of things which are not so far asunder but that they may be taken for one and the same. 4. [To consider] similitudes.

The second and the five following books are taken up in enumerating the *topics* or heads of argument that may be used in questions about the genus, the definition, the properties, and the accidents of a thing; and occasionally he introduces the topics for proving things to be the same or different; and the topics for proving one thing to be better or worse than another.

In this enumeration of topics, Aristotle has shewn more the fertility of his genius than the accuracy of method. The writers of logic seem to be of this opinion; for I know none of them that has followed him closely upon this subject. They have considered the topics of argumentation as reducible to certain axioms. For instance, when the question is about the genus of a thing, it must be determined by some axiom about genus and species; when it is about a definition, it must be determined by some axiom relating to definition, and things defined; and so of other questions. They have therefore reduced the doctrine of the topics to certain axioms or canons, and disposed these axioms in order under certain heads.

This method seems to be more commodious and elegant than that of Aristotle. Yet it must be acknowledged that Aristotle has furnished the materials from which all the logicians have borrowed their doctrine of topics; and even Cicero, Quintilian, and other rhetorical writers, have been much indebted to the topics of Aristotle.

He was the first, as far as I know, who made an attempt of this kind; and in this he acted up to the magnanimity of his own genius, and that of ancient philosophy. Every subject of human thought had been reduced to ten categories; everything that can be attributed to any subject, to five predicables; he attempted to reduce all the forms of reasoning to fixed rules of figure and mode, and to reduce all the topics of argumentation under certain heads; and by that means to collect, as it were, into one store, all that can be said on one side or the other of every question, and to provide a grand arsenal, from which all future combatants might be furnished with arms, offensive and defensive, in every cause, so as to leave no room to future generations to invent anything new.

The last book of the Topics is a code of the laws according to which a syllogistical disputation ought to be managed, both on the part of the assailant and defendant. From which it is evident, that this philosopher trained his disciples to contend, not for truth merely, but for victory.*

ments, or whether he held that all principles are actually generalisations by induction from experience, is a *vexata quæstio* among his followers; and texts may be produced on both sides of nearly equal weight. See below, pp. 764, b, 771, note.—H.

* The implication here is unfounded, and could easily be shewn to be unjust.—I may notice that there is nothing in regard to which, notions cruder, narrower, or more erroneous prevail, than in regard to Disputation, its nature, its objects, and its ends; nay, I make bold to say, that by no academical degeneracy has the intellectual vigour of youth lost more, than through the desuetude into which, during these latter ages, Disputation, as a regular and daily exercise in our universities, has fallen. Before the invention of printing, when universities could vindicate their necessity as *organs of publication*, Exercise, and Disputation in particular, was still recognised as their grand instrument of education; whereas now, when books are but a drug, our professors too often content themselves with reciting in their class-rooms, what can, with equal profit and far more convenience, be read at home. I cannot, of course, here adduce my reasons, historical and psycholog-

Section III.

OF THE BOOK CONCERNING SOPHISMS.

A syllogism which leads to a false conclusion must be vicious, either in matter or form; for, from true principles, nothing but truth can be justly deduced. If the matter be faulty—that is, if either of the premises be false, that premise must be denied by the defendant. If the form be faulty, some rule of syllogism is transgressed; and it is the part of the defendant to shew what general or special rule it is that is transgressed; so that, if he be an able logician, he will be impregnable in the defence of truth, and may resist all the attacks of the sophist. But, as there are syllogisms which may seem to be perfect both in matter and form, when they are not really so, as a piece of money may seem to be good coin when it is adulterate, such fallacious syllogisms are considered in this treatise, in order to make a defendant more expert in the use of his defensive weapons.

And here the author, with his usual magnanimity, attempts to bring all the *Fallacies* that can enter into a syllogism under *thirteen* heads; of which *six* lie *in the diction* or *language*, and *seven not in the diction*.

The Fallacies in *diction* are, 1. When an ambiguous word is taken at one time in one sense, and at another time in another. 2. When an ambiguous phrase is taken in the same manner. 3. and 4. are ambiguities in syntax; when words are conjoined in syntax that ought to be disjoined, or disjoined when they ought to be conjoined. 5. is an ambiguity in prosody, accent, or pronunciation. 6. An ambiguity arising from some figure of speech.

When a sophism of any of these kinds is translated into another language, or even rendered into unambiguous expressions in the same language, the fallacy is evident, and the syllogism appears to have four terms.

The seven fallacies which are said not to be in the diction, but in the thing [the thought], have their proper names in Greek and in Latin, by which they are distinguished. Without minding their names, we shall give a brief account of their nature.

1. The first is, Taking an accidental conjunction of things for a natural or necessary connection: as, when from an accident we infer a property; when from an example we infer a rule; when from a single act we infer a habit.

2. Taking that absolutely which ought to be taken comparatively, or with a certain limitation. The construction of language often leads into this fallacy; for, in all languages it is common to use absolute terms to signify things that carry in them some secret comparison; or, to use unlimited terms, to signify what from its nature must be limited.

3. Taking that for the cause of a thing which is only an occasion, or concomitant.

4. Begging the question. This is done when the thing to be proved, or something equivalent, is assumed in the premises.

5. Mistaking the question. When the conclusion of the syllogism is not the thing that ought to be proved, but something else that is mistaken for it.

6. When that which is not a consequence is mistaken for a consequence; as if, because all Africans are black, it were taken for granted that all blacks are Africans.

7. The last fallacy lies in propositions that are complex and imply two affirmations, whereof one may be true, and the other false; so that, whether you grant the proposition or deny it, you are entangled; as when it is affirmed that such a man has left off playing the fool. If it be granted, it implies that he did play the fool formerly; if it be denied, it implies, or seems to imply, that he plays the fool still.

In this enumeration, we ought, in justice to Aristotle, to expect only the fallacies incident to categorical syllogisms. And I do not find that the Logicians have made any additions to it when taken in this view, although they have given some other fallacies that are incident to syllogisms of the hypothetical [non-categorical] kind, particularly the fallacy of an incomplete enumeration in disjunctive syllogisms and dilemmas.

The different species of sophisms above mentioned are not so precisely defined by Aristotle, or by subsequent Logicians, but that they allow of great latitude in the application; and it is often dubious under what particular species a sophistical syllogism ought to be classed. We even find the same example brought under one species by one author, and under another species by another. Nay, what is more strange, Aristotle himself employs a long chapter in proving, by a particular induction, that all the seven may be brought under that which we have called *mistaking the question*, and which is commonly called *ignoratio elenchi*. And, indeed, the proof of this is easy, without that laborious detail which Aristotle uses for the purpose; for if you lop off from the conclusion of a sophistical syllogism all

cal, shewing the superior utility of Disputation as an exercise, and the superior utility of Exercise in general as a mean of intellectual development; but I am tempted to quote, in favour of the principle, the testimony of a great philosopher, and great scholar:—"Tacitis meditationibus magis proficere nos, quam altercationibus, verum non est. Etenim sicut lapidum collisione ignis; ita ex disceptationibus elicitur veritas. Quin egomet mecum saepe, diu, multum meditatus—sed incassum, nisi pugnem, infeliciter cadet mihi. A Magistro plus excitamur; at Adversarius, sua vel pertinacia, vel sapientia, mihi duplex magister est."—H

that is not supported by the premises, the conclusion in that case will always be found different from that which ought to have been proved; and so it falls under the *ignoratio elenchi*.

It was probably Aristotle's aim to reduce all the possible variety of sophisms, as he had attempted to do of just syllogisms, to certain definite species; but he seems to he sensible that he had fallen short in this last attempt. When a genus is properly divided into its species, the species should not only, when taken together, exhaust the whole genus, but every species should have its own precinct so accurately defined that one shall not encroach upon another. And when an individual can be said to belong to two or three different species, the division is imperfect; yet this is the case of Aristotle's division of the sophisms, by his own acknowledgment. It ought not, therefore, to be taken for a division strictly logical. It may rather be compared to the several species or forms of action invented in law for the redress of wrongs. For every wrong there is a remedy in law by one action or another; but sometimes a man may take his choice among several different actions. So every sophistical syllogism may, by a little art, be brought under one or other of the species mentioned by Aristotle, and very often you may take your choice of two or three.

Besides the enumeration of the various kinds of sophisms, there are many other things in this treatise concerning the art of managing a syllogistical dispute with an antagonist. And indeed, if the passion for this kind of litigation, which reigned for so many ages, should ever again lift up its head, we may predict, that the Organon of Aristotle will then become a fashionable study; for it contains such admirable materials and documents for this art, that it may be said to have brought it to a science.

The conclusion of this treatise ought not to be overlooked; it manifestly relates, not to the present treatise only, but also to the whole analytics and topics of the author. I shall therefore give the substance of it.—

"Of those who may be called inventors, some have made important additions to things long before begun and carried on through a course of ages; others have given a small beginning to things which, in succeeding times, will be brought to greater perfection. The beginning of a thing, though small, is the chief part of it, and requires the greatest degree of invention; for it is easy to make additions to inventions once begun.

"Now, with regard to the dialectical art,* there was not something done, and something remaining to be done. There was absolutely nothing done; for those who professed the art of disputation had only a set of orations composed,* and of arguments, and of captious questions, which might suit many occasions. These, their scholars soon learned, and fitted to the occasion. This was not to teach you the art, but to furnish you with the materials produced by the art; as if a man professing to teach you the art of making shoes should bring you a parcel of shoes of various sizes and shapes, from which you may provide those who want. This may have its use; but it is not to teach the art of making shoes. And indeed, with regard to rhetorical declamation, there are many precepts handed down from ancient times; but, with regard to the construction of syllogisms, not one.†

"We have, therefore, employed much time and labour upon this subject; and if our system appear to you not‡ to be in the number of those things which, being before carried a certain length, were left to be perfected, we hope for your favourable acceptance of what is done, and your indulgence in what is left imperfect.§

CHAPTER VI.

REFLECTIONS ON THE UTILITY OF LOGIC, AND THE MEANS OF ITS IMPROVEMENT.

Section I.

OF THE UTILITY OF LOGIC.

Men rarely leave one extreme without running into the contrary. It is no wonder, therefore, that the excessive admiration of Aristotle, which continued for so many ages, should end in an undue contempt; and that the high esteem of logic, as the grand engine of science,‖ should at last make way for too unfavourable an opinion, which seems now prevalent, of its being unworthy of a place in a liberal education. Those who think according to the fashion, as the greatest part of men do, will be as prone to go into this extreme as their grandfathers were to go into the contrary.

* Aristotle, in this particular passage, does not allude to the *doctrine of the syllogism in general*, which he does not call Dialectic, but to *dialectic proper*, as contained in his books of Topics and Sophisms.—H.

* This appears to be rather incorrect.—H.

† In this particular passage, *Logic in general* is plainly intended.—H.

‡ Reid is here led into error by a false reading in the common editions.—H.

§ I had meant to have here given a full translation of this remarkable statement of Aristotle in regard to what *Logic* owed to him when first developed, with a parallel testimony of Kant, to what the science now owes him after an assiduous cultivation of two thousand years; but the press is urgent. I shall therefore adjourn these to Note V.—H.

‖ See above, p. 701, a, note †.—H.

Laying aside prejudice, whether fashionable or unfashionable, let us consider whether logic is, or may be made, subservient to any good purpose. Its professed end is, to teach men to think, to judge, and to reason, with precision and accuracy. No man will say that this is a matter of no importance; the only thing, therefore, that admits of doubt is, whether it can be taught.

To resolve this doubt, it may be observed, that our rational faculty is the gift of God, given to men in very different measure. Some have a larger portion, some a less; and where there is a remarkable defect of the natural power, it cannot be supplied by any culture. But this natural power, even where it is the strongest, may lie dead for want of the means of improvement: a savage may have been born with as good faculties as a Bacon or a Newton: but his talent was buried, being never put to use; while theirs was cultivated to the best advantage.

It may likewise be observed, that the chief mean of improving our rational power, is the vigorous exercise of it, in various ways and in different subjects, by which the habit is acquired of exercising it properly. Without such exercise, and good sense over and above, a man who has studied logic all his life may, after all, be only a petulant wrangler, without true judgment or skill of reasoning in any science.

I take this to be Locke's meaning, when, in his "Thoughts on Education," he says, "If you would have your son to reason well, let him read Chillingworth." The state of things is much altered since Locke wrote. Logic has been much improved, chiefly by his writings; and yet much less stress is laid upon it, and less time consumed in it. His counsel, therefore, was judicious and seasonable—to wit, That the improvement of our reasoning power is to be expected much more from an intimate acquaintance with the authors who reason the best, than from studying voluminous systems of logic. But if he had meant that the study of logic was of no use, nor deserved any attention, he surely would not have taken the pains to have made so considerable an addition to it by his "Essay on the Human Understanding" and by his "Thoughts on the Conduct of the Understanding." Nor would he have remitted his pupil to Chillingworth, the acutest logician as well as the best reasoner of his age; and one who, in innumerable places of his excellent book, without pedantry even in that pedantic age, makes the happiest application of the rules of logic, for unravelling the sophistical reasoning of his antagonist.

Our reasoning power makes no appearance in infancy; but as we grow up, it unfolds itself by degrees, like the bud of a tree. When a child first draws an inference, or perceives the force of an inference drawn by another, we may call this *the birth of his reason*; but it is yet like a new-born babe, weak and tender; it must be cherished, carried in arms, and have food of easy digestion, till it gathers strength.

I believe no man remembers the birth of his reason: but it is probable that his decisions are at first weak and wavering; and, compared with that steady conviction which he acquires in ripe years, are like the dawn of the morning compared with noon-day. We see that the reason of children yields to authority, as a reed to the wind; nay, that it clings to it, and leans upon it, as if conscious of its own weakness.

When reason acquires such strength as to stand on its own bottom, without the aid of authority, or even in opposition to authority, this may be called its *manly age*. But, in most men, it hardly ever arrives at this period. Many, by their situation in life, have not the opportunity of cultivating their rational powers. Many, from the habit they have acquired of submitting their opinions to the authority of others, or from some other principle which operates more powerfully than the love of truth, suffer their judgment to be carried along to the end of their days, either by the authority of a leader, or of a party, or of the multitude, or by their own passions. Such persons, however learned, however acute, may be said to be all their days children in understanding. They reason, they dispute, and perhaps write; but it is not that they may find the truth, but that they may defend opinions which have descended to them by inheritance, or into which they have fallen by accident, or been led by affection.

I agree with Mr Locke, that there is no study better fitted to exercise and strengthen the reasoning powers, than that of the mathematical sciences—for two reasons: first, Because there is no other branch of science which gives such scope to long and accurate trains of reasoning;* and, secondly,

* It is not "the length and accuracy of its trains of reasoning" that makes a science a profitable gymnastic of the mind—for this is only the result of the nature and necessity of its matter—but the amount of intellectual effort which it determines in the student. Now mathematics are, as is universally confessed, *the easiest of all sciences*; their perspicuity is excessive; and thus they only conduce to exercise the patience and attention. Mr Stewart, who was an eminent mathematician before he was a distinguished philosopher, in the admirable chapter of his "Philosophy of the Human Mind," entitled "The Mathematician," limits the benefit to be derived from the study of mathematics, in the cultivation of the mental faculties, to the power of continuous attention which it contributes to exercise; and this to the express exclusion of the mechanical process of the algebraic calculus. "This command of attention,"

Because, in mathematics, there is no room for authority, nor for prejudice of any kind, which may give a false bias to the judgment.*

When a youth of moderate parts begins to study Euclid, everything at first is new to him. His apprehension is unsteady; his judgment is feeble, and rests partly upon the evidence of the thing, and partly upon the authority of his teacher. But, every time he goes over the definitions, the axioms, the elementary propositions, more light breaks in upon him; the language becomes familiar, and conveys clear and steady conceptions; the judgment is confirmed; he begins to see what demonstration is; and it is impossible to see it without being charmed with it. He perceives it to be a kind of evidence that has no need of authority to strengthen it. He finds himself emancipated from that bondage, and exults so much in this new state of independence, that he spurns at authority, and would have demonstration for everything, until experience teaches him that this is a kind of evidence which cannot be had in most things; and that, in his most important concerns, he must rest contented with probability.

As he goes on in mathematics, the road of demonstration becomes smooth and easy; he can walk in it firmly, and take wider steps; and at last he acquires the habit, not only of understanding a demonstration, but of discovering and demonstrating mathematical truths.

Thus a man, without rules of logic, may acquire a habit of reasoning justly in mathematics;† and I believe he may, by like means, acquire a habit of reasoning justly in mechanics, in jurisprudence, in politics, or in any other science. Good sense, good examples, and assiduous exercise, may bring a man to reason justly and acutely in his own profession, without rules.

But if any man think, that, from this concession, he may infer the inutility of logic, he betrays a great want of that art by this inference; for it is no better reasoning than this, That because a man may go from Edinburgh to London by the way of Paris, therefore any other road is useless.

There is perhaps no practical art which may not be acquired, in a very considerable degree, by example and practice, without reducing it to rules. But practice, joined with rules, may carry a man on in his art farther, and more quickly, than practice without rules. Every ingenious artist knows the utility of having his art reduced to rules, and by that means made a science. He is thereby enlightened in his practice, and works with more assurance. By rules, he sometimes corrects his own errors, and often detects the errors of others; he finds them of great use to confirm his judgment, to justify what is right, and to condemn what is wrong.

Is it of no use in reasoning to be well acquainted with the various powers of the human understanding, by which we reason? Is it of no use to resolve the various kinds of reasoning into their simple elements, and to discover, as far as we are able, the rules by which these elements are combined in judging and in reasoning? Is it of no use to mark the various fallacies in reasoning, by which even the most ingenious men have been led into error? It must surely betray great want of understanding, to think these things useless or unimportant. These are the things which Logicians have attempted, and which they have executed; not, indeed, so completely as to leave no room for improvement, but in such a manner as to give very considerable aid to our reasoning powers. That the principles laid down with regard to definition and division, with regard to the conversion and opposition of propositions, and the general rules of reasoning, are not without use, is sufficiently apparent from the blunders committed by those who disdain any acquaintance with them.*

he says, "it may be proper to add, is to be acquired, not by practice of the modern methods, but by the study of the Greek geometry; more particularly, by accustoming ourselves to pursue long trains of demonstration, without availing ourselves of the aid of any sensible diagrams; the thoughts being directed solely to those ideal delineations which the powers of conception and of memory enable us to form."

Reid likewise, in what he now says in favour of Mathematics as an intellectual exercise, contemplates exclusively the ostensive or geometric method. This is manifest, not only from the necessary meaning of his words, but also from his "Essay on Quantity," in which he says: "Long deductions in algebra are, for the most part, made, not so much by a train of reasoning in the mind, as by a kind of artificial [mechanical?] operation which is built on a few principles," &c. On the pernicious influence of the modern analysis, in an educational point of view, many philosophers and practical instructors have recorded their emphatic testimonies. On this subject, see *Edinburgh Review*, No. 126, art. 7.—H.

* There is, in fact, no room for difference of opinion. But it is difficult to see how we can be trained to reason *right*, by a science in which there is no reasoning wrong.—H.

† A man is made "to reason justly in mathematics," in the same manner in which a man is made to walk straight in a ditch.—H.

* "I am aware," says Baron Degerando, "that in presenting the syllogism as the primary and essential form of reasoning, I run counter to the opinions of modern metaphysicians. I am aware that the very name of *Syllogism* is enough, at the present day, to throw a sort of ridicule on any philosophical work in which it ventures to appear. Men have reasoned frequently so ill in mood and figure, that syllogism seems to have for ever lost its credit. Nevertheless, I am not afraid to oppose myself to these prepossessions; and I make bold to maintain that, on this occasion, *our predecessors have analysed better than we*. The moderns have considered reasoning only as clothed in the external and sensible forms of speech; the ancients have observed it as it exists in the mind. The abuse that has been made of syllogism, proves nothing against its necessity because the connection of signs is not enough to

Although the art of categorical syllogism is better fitted for scholastic litigation than for real improvement in knowledge, it is a venerable piece of antiquity, and a great effort of human genius. We admire the pyramids of Egypt, and the wall of China, though useless burdens upon the earth; we can bear the most minute description of them, and travel hundreds of leagues to see them: if any person should, with sacrilegious hands, destroy or deface them, his memory would be had in abhorrence. The predicaments and predicables, the rules of syllogism, and the topics, have a like title to our veneration as antiquities; they are uncommon efforts, not of human power, but of human genius; and they make a remarkable period in the progress of human reason.

The prejudice against logic has probably been strengthened by its being taught too early in life. Boys are often taught logic as they are taught their creed, when it is an exercise of memory only, without understanding. One may as well expect to understand grammar before he can speak, as to understand logic before he can reason. It must even be acknowledged, that commonly we are capable of reasoning in mathematics more early than in logic. The objects presented to the mind in this science are of a very abstract nature, and can be distinctly conceived only when we are capable of attentive reflection upon the operations of our own understanding, and after we have been accustomed to reason. There may be an elementary logic, level to the capacity of those who have been but little exercised in reasoning; but the most important parts of this science require a ripe understanding, capable of reflecting upon its own operations. Therefore, to make logic the first branch of science that is to be taught, is an old error that ought to be corrected.*

Section II.

OF THE IMPROVEMENT OF LOGIC.

In compositions of human thought, expressed by speech or by writing, whatever is excellent and whatever is faulty fall within the province, either of grammar, or of rhetoric, or of logic. Propriety of expression is the province of grammar; grace, elegance, and force, in thought and in expression, are the province of rhetoric; justness and accuracy of thought are the province of logic.

The faults in composition, therefore, which fall under the censure of logic, are obscure and indistinct conceptions, false judgment, inconclusive reasoning, and all improprieties in distinctions, definitions, division, or method. To aid our rational powers in avoiding these faults, and in attaining the opposite excellencies, is the end of logic; and whatever there is in it that has no tendency to promote this end, ought to be thrown out.

The rules of logic being of a very abstract nature, ought to be illustrated by a variety of real and striking examples taken from the writings of good authors. It is both instructive and entertaining to observe the virtues of accurate composition in writers of fame: we cannot see them without being drawn to the imitation of them, in a more powerful manner than we can be by dry rules. Nor are the faults of such writers less instructive or less powerful monitors. A wreck left upon a shoal, or upon a rock, is not more useful to the sailor than the faults of good writers, when set up to view, are to those who come after them. It was a happy thought in a late ingenious writer of English grammar, to collect under the several rules examples of bad English found in the most approved authors. It were to be wished that the rules of logic were illustrated in the same manner. By this means, a system of logic would become a repository, wherein whatever is most acute in judging and in reasoning, whatever is most accurate in dividing, distinguishing, and defining, should be laid up and disposed in order for our imitation, and wherein the false steps of eminent authors should be recorded for our admonition.

After men had laboured in the search of truth near two thousand years by the help of syllogisms, Lord Bacon proposed the method of induction, as a more effectual engine for that purpose. His "Novum Organum" gave a new turn to the thoughts

guarantee the concatenation of ideas, and thus, as we are about to see, the mind may err in a reasoning the best conformed to rule. Though it may be useless to enounce, in terms, a proposition in itself evident and simple, this does not prove that such proposition ought not to be presented to the mind when reasoning, in order to establish the connection of the notions which it compares. Let those who would reduce all reasoning to the Enthymeme, ask themselves how a first proposition could conduct them to a second, if the understanding did not, by a secret operation, apprehend the nexus of their terms. Let them propose their enthymeme to a child, or a man of limited understanding, and they will soon, by being compelled to restore, in their discourse, the omitted proposition, be made to see that its presence in the intellect was necessary all along, and that, though not expressed by them, it was always understood."

I quote this acknowledgment as valuable from a philosopher of the school of Condillac. To adduce testimonies from the followers of Leibnitz or Kant, would be superfluous. In Germany, Logic has always been estimated at its proper value.—H.

* On the absurdity of entering on the study of the sciences of *reflection* before concluding the study of those of *observation*, see above, p. [illegible], a, note †. To Mr Stewart's testimony there quoted, might be added that of almost every competent authority in education. See Note W.—H

and labours of the inquisitive, more remarkable and more useful than that which the "Organon" of Aristotle had given before, and may be considered as a second grand era in the progress of human reason.*

The art of syllogism produced numberless disputes, and numberless sects who fought against each other with much animosity, without gaining or losing ground, but did nothing considerable for the benefit of human life. The art of induction, first delineated by Lord Bacon, produced numberless laboratories and observatories, in which nature has been put to the question by thousands of experiments, and forced to confess many of her secrets that before were hid from mortals; and, by these, arts have been improved, and human knowledge wonderfully increased.

In reasoning by syllogism from general principles, we descend to a conclusion virtually contained in them. The process of induction is more arduous, being an ascent from particular premises to a general conclusion.† The evidence of such general conclusions is probable only, not demonstrative: but when the induction is sufficiently copious, and carried on according to the rules of art, it forces conviction no less than demonstration itself does.

The greatest part of human knowledge rests upon evidence of this kind. Indeed we can have no other for general truths which are contingent in their nature, and depend upon the will and ordination of the Maker of the world. He governs the world he has made by general laws: The effects of these laws in particular phænomena are open to our observation; and, by observing a train of uniform effects with due caution, we may at last decipher the law of nature by which they are regulated.

Lord Bacon has displayed no less force of genius in reducing to rules this method of reasoning, than Aristotle did in the method of syllogism. [?] His "Novum Organum" ought therefore to be held as a most important addition to the ancient logic.‡ Those who understand it, and enter into its spirit, will be able to distinguish the chaff from the wheat in philosophical disquisitions into the works of God. They will learn to hold in due contempt all hypotheses and theories, the creatures of human imagination, and to respect nothing but facts sufficiently vouched, or conclusions drawn from them by a fair and chaste interpretation of nature.

Most arts have been reduced to rules, after they had been brought to a considerable degree of perfection by the natural sagacity of artists; and the rules have been drawn from the best examples of the art that had been before exhibited; but the art of philosophical induction was delineated by Lord Bacon in a very ample manner, before the world had seen any tolerable example of it.* This, although it adds greatly to the merit of the author, must have produced some obscurity in the work, and a defect of proper examples for illustration. This defect may now be easily supplied from those authors who, in their philosophical disquisitions, have the most strictly pursued the path pointed out in the "Novum Organum." Among these, Sir Isaac Newton appears to hold the first rank; having, in the third book of his "Principia," and in his "Optics," had the rules of the "Novum Organum" constantly in his eye.

I think Lord Bacon was also the first who endeavoured to reduce to a system the prejudices or biasses of the mind, which are the causes of false judgment, and which he calls *the idols of the human understanding*. Some late writers of logic have very properly introduced this into their system; but it deserves to be more copiously handled, and to be illustrated by real examples.

It is of great consequence to accurate reasoning to distinguish first principles which are to be taken for granted, from propositions which require proof. All the real knowledge of mankind may be divided into two parts: The first consisting of self-evident propositions; the second, of those which are deduced by just reasoning from self-evident propositions. The line that divides these two parts ought to be marked as distinctly as possible; and the principles that are self-evident reduced, as far as can be done, to general axioms. This has been done in mathematics from the beginning, and has tended greatly to the emolument of that science. It has lately been done in natural philosophy: and by this means that science has advanced more in an hundred and fifty years, than it had done before in two thousand. Every science is in an unformed state until its first principles are ascertained; after which, it advances regularly, and secures the ground it has gained.

* The Organon of Aristotle and the Organum of Bacon stand in relation, but the relation of contrariety: the one considers the laws under which *the subject* thinks; the other the laws under which *the object* is to be known. To compare them together is therefore, in reality, to compare together quantities of different species. Each proposes a different end: both, in different ways, are useful; and both ought to be assiduously studied.—H.

† Induction is always a syllogism. But we must distinguish two inductions—a *formal* and a *material*. The confusion of these has led to great confusion. But of this not here.—H.

‡ It is not of a logical argument at all, if we limit the domain of logic to the *form of thought*.—H.

* One of the most perfect examples of a genuine induction is that afforded by Bacon's contemporary, Galileo; but Galileo's practice was anterior to Bacon's precept.—H.

Although first principles do not admit of direct proof, yet there must be certain marks and characters by which those that are truly such may be distinguished from counterfeits. These marks ought to be described and applied to distinguish the genuine from the spurious.

In the ancient philosophy, there is a redundance, rather than a defect, of first principles. Many things were assumed under that character without a just title That nature abhors a *vacuum*; that bodies do not gravitate in their proper place; that the heavenly bodies undergo no change; that they move in perfect circles, and with an equable motion: such principles as these were assumed in the Peripatetic philosophy without proof, as if they were self-evident.

Des Cartes, sensible of this weakness in the ancient philosophy, and desirous to guard against it in his own system, resolved to admit nothing until his assent was forced by irresistible evidence. The first thing which he found to be certain and evident was, that he thought, and reasoned, and doubted. He found himself under a necessity of believing the existence of those mental operations of which he was conscious; and having thus found sure footing in this one principle of consciousness, he rested satisfied with it, hoping to be able to build the whole fabric of his knowledge upon it; like Archimedes, who wanted but one fixed point to move the whole earth. But the foundation was too narrow; and in his progress he unawares assumes many things less evident than those which he attempts to prove. Although he was not able to suspect the testimony of consciousness, yet he thought the testimony of sense, of memory, and of every other faculty, might be suspected, and ought not to be received until proof was brought that they are not fallacious. Therefore he applies these faculties, whose character is yet in question, to prove, That there is an infinitely perfect Being, who made him, and who made his senses, his memory, his reason, and all his faculties; that this Being is no deceiver, and therefore could not give him faculties that are fallacious; and that on this account they deserve credit.

It is strange that this philosopher, who found himself under a necessity of yielding to the testimony of consciousness, did not find the same necessity of yielding to the testimony of his senses, his memory, and his understanding; and that, while he was certain that he doubted and reasoned, he was uncertain whether two and three made five, and whether he was dreaming or awake. It is more strange that so acute a reasoner should not perceive that his whole train of reasoning, to prove that his faculties were not fallacious, was mere sophistry; for, if his faculties were fallacious, they might deceive him in this train of reasoning; and so the conclusion, That they were not fallacious, was only the testimony of his faculties in their own favour, and might be a fallacy.

It is difficult to give any reason for distrusting our other faculties, that will not reach consciousness itself.* And he who distrusts the faculties of judging and reasoning which God hath given him, must even rest in his scepticism till he come to a sound mind, or until God give him new faculties to sit in judgment upon the old. If it be not a first principle, that our faculties are not fallacious, we must be absolute sceptics; for this principle is incapable of a proof; and if it is not certain, nothing else can be certain.

Since the time of Des Cartes, it has been fashionable with those who dealt in abstract philosophy, to employ their invention in finding philosophical arguments, either to prove those truths which ought to be received as first principles, or to overturn them: and it is not easy to say, whether the authority of first principles is more hurt by the first of these attempts, or by the last; for such principles can stand secure only upon their own bottom; and to place them upon any other foundation than that of their intrinsic evidence, is in effect to overturn them.

I have lately † met with a very sensible and judicious treatise, wrote by Father Buffier about fifty years ago, concerning first principles and the source of human judgments, which, with great propriety, he prefixed to his treatise of logic. And indeed I apprehend it is a subject of such consequence, that, if inquisitive men can be brought to the same unanimity in the first principles of the other sciences as in those of mathematics and natural philosophy, (and why should we despair of a general agreement in things that are self-evident ?) this might be considered as a third grand era in the progress of human reason

* Two things must be distinguished in Consciousness—the reality of the phenomenon, and the truth of what the phenomenon vouches. Of the former, scepticism is impossible, because the doubt implies a contradiction. Of the latter, scepticism is always possible, because it does not immediately subvert itself. See below, p. 744.—H.

† This would seem to prove that Reid was not aware of Buffier's treatise on First Truths, when he wrote his "Inquiry;" as indeed, from internal evidence, is probable.—H.

OMISSION.

NOTE.—*The following paragraph should have formed the conclusion of Chapter II., Section 4*—On Definitions. *It had been omitted in the editions of this treatise published apart from Lord Kames's "Sketches." One of these was the copy given to the printer; the proof was, however, always collated with the two authentic editions, and the various unauthorized changes which had been subsequently introduced into the text carefully expunged. It was found impossible, however, to restore this passage to its connection, without deranging several sheets which had been set up together.*—H.

If Aristotle had understood those principles, many of his definitions, which furnish matter of triumph to his enemies, had never seen the light; let us impute them to the times rather than to the man. The sublime Plato, it is said, thought it necessary to have the definition of a man, and could find none better than *Animal implume bipes*; upon which Diogenes sent to his school a cock with his feathers plucked off, desiring to know whether it was a man or not.

AN

ESSAY

ON

QUANTITY;*

OCCASIONED BY READING A TREATISE

IN WHICH

SIMPLE AND COMPOUND RATIOS

ARE APPLIED TO

VIRTUE AND MERIT.

Since it is thought that mathematical demonstration carries a peculiar evidence along with it, which leaves no room for further dispute, it may be of some use, or entertainment at least, to inquire to what subjects this kind of proof may be applied.

Mathematics contain properly the *doctrine of measure*; and the object of this science is commonly said to be *Quantity*; therefore, quantity ought to be defined, *what may be measured*. Those who have defined quantity to be *whatever is capable of more or less*, have given too wide a notion of it, which, it is apprehended, has led some persons to apply mathematical reasoning to subjects that do not admit of it. Pain and pleasure admit of various degrees, but who can pretend to measure them?

Whatever has quantity, or is measurable, must be made up of parts, which bear proportion to each other, and to the whole; so that it may be increased by *addition* of like parts, and diminished by *subtraction*, may be *multiplied* and *divided*, and, in short, may bear any proportion to another quantity of the same kind, that one line or number can bear to another. That this is essential to all mathematical quantity, is evident from the first elements of algebra, which treats of quantity in general, or of those relations and properties which are common to all kinds of quantity. Every algebraical quantity is supposed capable, not only of being increased and diminished, but of being exactly doubled, tripled, halved, or of bearing any assignable proportion to another quantity of the same kind. This, then, is the characteristic of quantity; whatever has this property may be adopted into mathematics; and its quantity and relations may be measured with mathematical accuracy and certainty.

---

* This Essay was originally published in the Transactions of the Royal Society of London, vol. xlv., anno, 1748. On the occasion of the paper, see above, p. 5; and Stewart's Elements, II. 539.

This is Reid's earliest publication; and it is curious that Kant should, in the preceding year, have also ushered into the world his first regular work, and on a similar subject; that work, too, containing a refutation of the Leibnitzian estimate of velocity. I refer to his "Thoughts on the True Measure of Living Forces."

This is not the only parallel between the two philosophers, who, with sundry striking contrasts, presented still more remarkable similarities. The doctrines of both, however different in external character and in particular opinions, were of a kindred spirit: they had a common origin, as recoils against the scepticism of Hume; the same dominant result, in the establishment of certain ultimate laws of speculation and practice; and the same tendency, in restraining the intellectual pride, and elevating the moral dignity of man. Each, in a different sphere, was at the head of a great scientific determination; both were distinguished rather for philosophical originality and independence, than for the extent of their philosophical learning; and, finally, (may I add?) both were Scotchmen—Reid by birth, Kant (Cant) by proximate descent.—H.

There are some quantities which may be called *proper*, and others *improper*. This distinction is taken notice of by Aristotle; but it deserves some explanation. That *properly* is quantity which is *measured by its own kind*; or which, of its own nature, is capable of being doubled or tripled, without taking in any quantity of a different kind as a measure of it.

Improper quantity is that which *cannot be measured by its own kind*; but to which we assign a measure by the means of some proper quantity that is related to it. Thus velocity of motion, when we consider it by itself, cannot be measured. We may perceive one body to move faster, another slower; but we can have no distinct idea of a proportion or ratio between their velocities, without taking in some quantity of another kind to measure them by. Having, therefore, observed, that by a greater velocity a greater space is passed over in the same time, by a less velocity a less space, and by an equal velocity an equal space; we hence learn to measure velocity by the space passed over in a given time, and to reckon it to be in exact proportion to that space: and having once assigned this measure to it, we can then, and not till then, conceive one velocity to be exactly double, or half, or in any other proportion to another; we may then introduce it into mathematical reasoning without danger of confusion or error, and may also use it as a measure of other improper quantities.

All the kinds of proper quantity we know, may perhaps be reduced to these four, *extension*, *duration*, *number*, and *proportion*. Though *proportion* be measurable in its own nature, and, therefore, has proper quantity, yet as things cannot have proportion which have not quantity of some other kind, it follows, that whatever has quantity must have it in one or other of these three kinds, *extension*, *duration*, or *number*. These are the measures of themselves, and of all things else that are measurable.

Number is applicable to some things, to which it is not commonly applied by the vulgar. Thus, by attentive consideration, lots and chances of various kinds appear to be made up of a determinate number of chances that are allowed to be equal; and by numbering these, the values and proportions of those which are compounded of them may be demonstrated.

Velocity, the *quantity of motion*, *density*, *elasticity*, the *vis insita* and *impressa*, the various kinds of *centripetal forces*, and different orders of *fluxions*, are all improper quantities; which, therefore, ought not to be admitted into mathematics, without having a measure of them assigned. The measure of an improper quantity ought always to be included in the definition of it; for it is the giving it a measure that makes it a proper subject of mathematical reasoning. If all mathematicians had considered this as carefully as Sir Isaac Newton appears to have done, some labour had been saved both to themselves and to their readers. That great man, whose clear and comprehensive understanding appears even in his definitions, having frequent occasion to treat of such improper quantities, never fails to define them so as to give a measure of them, either in proper quantities, or in such as had a known measure. This may be seen in the definitions prefixed to his "Principia Philosophiæ Naturalis Mathematica."

It is not easy to say how many kinds of improper quantity may, in time, be introduced into mathematics, or to what new subjects measures may be applied; but this, I think, we may conclude, that there is no foundation in nature for, nor can any valuable end be served, by applying measure to anything but what has these *two properties*:—First, *It must admit of degrees of greater and less*; Secondly, *It must be associated with or related to something that has proper quantity, so as that when one is increased, the other is increased; when one is diminished, the other is diminished also; and every degree of the one must have a determinate magnitude or quantity of the other corresponding to it.*

It sometimes happens, that we have occasion to apply different measures to the same thing. Centripetal force, as defined by Newton, may be measured in various ways; he himself gives different measures of it, and distinguishes them by different names, as may be seen in the above-mentioned definitions.

In reality. Dr M.* conceives, that the applying of measures to things that properly have not quantity, is only a fiction or artifice of the mind, for enabling us to conceive more easily, and more distinctly to express and demonstrate, the properties and relations of those things that have real quantity. The propositions contained in the first two books of Newton's "Principia" might perhaps be expressed and demonstrated without those various measures of motion, and of centripetal and impressed forces which he uses; but this would occasion such intricate and perplexed circumlocutions, and such a tedious length of demonstrations, as would frighten any sober person from attempting to read them.

From the nature of quantity, we may see what it is that gives mathematics such advantage over other sciences, in clearness and certainty; namely, that quantity ad-

* The author, Reid himself.—H.

mits of a much greater variety of relations than any other subject of human reasoning; and, at the same time, every relation or proportion of quantities may, by the help of lines and numbers, be so distinctly defined as to be easily distinguished from all others, without any danger of mistake. Hence it is that we are able to trace its relations through a long process of reasoning, and with a perspicuity and accuracy which we in vain expect in subjects not capable of mensuration.

Extended quantities, such as lines, surfaces, and solids, besides what they have in common with all other quantities, have this peculiar, that their parts have a particular place and disposition among themselves: a line may not only bear any assignable proportion to another, in length or magnitude, but lines of the same length may vary in the disposition of their parts; one may be straight, another may be part of a curve of any kind or dimension, of which there is an endless variety. The like may be said of surfaces and solids. So that extended quantities admit of no less variety with regard to their form, than with regard to their magnitude; and as their various forms may be exactly defined and measured, no less than their magnitudes, hence it is that geometry, which treats of extended quantity, leads us into a much greater compass and variety of reasoning than any other branch of mathematics. Long deductions in algebra, for the most part, are made, not so much by a train of reasoning in the mind, as by an artificial kind of operation, which is built on a few very simple principles; but in geometry we may build one proposition on another, a third upon that, and so on, without ever coming to a limit which we cannot exceed. The properties of the more simple figures can hardly be exhausted, much less those of the more complex ones.

It may be deduced from what has been said above, that mathematical evidence is an evidence *sui generis*, not competent to any proposition which does not express a relation of things measurable by lines or numbers. All proper quantity may be measured by these, and improper quantities must be measured by those that are proper.

There are many things capable of more and less, which, perhaps, are not capable of mensuration. Tastes, smells, the sensations of heat and cold, beauty, pleasure, all the affections and appetites of the mind, wisdom, folly, and most kinds of probability, with many other things too tedious to enumerate, admit of degrees, but have not yet been reduced to measure, nor, perhaps, ever can be.* I say, most kinds of probability, because one kind of it—viz., the probability of chances—is properly measurable by number, as observed above.

Though attempts have been made to apply mathematical reasoning to some of these things, and the quantity of virtue and merit in actions has been measured by simple and compound ratios; yet Dr M. does not think that any real knowledge has been struck out this way; it may, perhaps, if discreetly used, be a help to discourse on these subjects, by pleasing the imagination, and illustrating what is already known; but till our affections and appetites shall themselves be reduced to quantity, and exact measures of their various degrees be assigned, in vain shall we essay to measure virtue and merit by them. This is only to ring changes on words, and to make a show of mathematical reasoning, without advancing one step in real knowledge.

Dr M. apprehends that the account given of the nature of proper and improper quantity, may also throw some light on the controversy about the force of moving bodies, which long exercised the pens of many mathematicians, and, perhaps, is rather dropped than ended, to the no small scandal of mathematics, which has always boasted of a degree of evidence inconsistent with debates that can be brought to no issue.

Though philosophers on both sides agree with each other and with the vulgar in this, that the force of a moving body is the same while its velocity is the same, is increased when its velocity is increased, and diminished when that is diminished; but this vague notion of force, in which both sides agree, though perhaps sufficient for common discourse, yet is not sufficient to make it a subject of mathematical reasoning: in order to that, it must be more accurately defined, and so defined as to give us a measure of it, that we may understand what is meant by a double or a triple force. The ratio of one force to another cannot be perceived but by a measure; and that measure must be settled, not by mathematical reasoning, but by a definition. Let any one consider force without relation to any other quantity, and see whether he can conceive one force exactly double to another; I am sure I cannot, says he, nor shall, till I shall be endowed with some new faculty; for I know nothing of force but by its effects, and therefore can measure it only by its effects. Till force then is defined, and by that definition a measure of it assigned, we fight in the dark about a vague idea, which is not sufficiently determined to be admitted into any mathematical proposition. And when such a definition is given, the controversy will presently be ended.

Of the Newtonian Measure of Force.—You say, the force of a body in motion is as

* What would Reid now say to the *Herbartian* Psychology?—H.

its velocity: either you mean to lay this down as a definition, as Newton himself has done; or you mean to affirm it as a proposition capable of proof. If you mean to lay it down as a definition, it is no more than if you should say, I call that a double force which gives a double velocity to the same body, a triple force which gives a triple velocity, and so on in proportion. This he entirely agrees to; no mathematical definition of force can be given that is more clear and simple, none that is more agreeable to the common use of the word in language. For, since all men agree that the force of the body being the same, the velocity must also be the same; the force being increased or diminished, the velocity must be so also—what can be more natural or proper than to take the velocity for the measure of the force?

Several other things might be advanced to shew that this definition agrees best with the common popular notion of the word force. If two bodies meet directly with a shock, which mutually destroys their motion, without producing any other sensible effect, the vulgar would pronounce, without hesitation, that they met with equal force; and so they do, according to the measure of force above laid down; for we find by experience, that in this case their velocities are reciprocally as their quantities of matter. In mechanics, where by a machine two powers or weights are kept *in equilibrio*, the vulgar would reckon that these powers act with equal force, and so by this definition they do. The power of gravity being constant and uniform, any one would expect that it should give equal degrees of force to a body in equal times, and so by this definition it does. So that this definition is not only clear and simple, but it agrees best with the use of the word force in common language, and this is all that can be desired in a definition.

But if you are not satisfied with laying it down as a definition, that the force of a body is as its velocity, but will needs prove it by demonstration or experiment, I must beg of you, before you take one step in the proof, to let me know what you mean by force, and what by a double or a triple force. This you must do by a definition which contains a measure of force. Some primary measure of force must be taken for granted, or laid down by way of definition; otherwise we can never reason about its quantity. And why then may you not take the velocity for the primary measure as well as any other? You will find none that is more simple, more distinct, or more agreeable to the common use of the word force: and he that rejects one definition that has these properties, has equal right to reject any other. I say then, that it is impossible, by mathematical reasoning or experiment, to prove that the force of a body is as its velocity, without taking for granted the thing you would prove, or something else that is no more evident than the thing to be proved.

Of the Leibnitzian Measure of Force.—Let us next hear the Leibnitzian, who says, that the force of a body is as the square of its velocity. If he lays this down as a definition, I shall rather agree to it than quarrel about words, and for the future shall understand him, by a quadruple force to mean that which gives a double velocity; by nine times the force, that which gives three times the velocity; and so on in duplicate proportion. While he keeps by his definition, it will not necessarily lead him into any error in mathematics or mechanics. For, however paradoxical his conclusions may appear, however different in words from theirs who measure force by the simple ratio of the velocity, they will in their meaning be the same: just as he who would call a foot twenty-four inches, without changing other measures of length, when he says a yard contains a foot and a half, means the very same as you do, when you say a yard contains three feet.

But, though I allow this measure of force to be distinct, and cannot charge it with falsehood, for no definition can be false, yet I say, in the *first* place, It is less simple than the other: for why should a duplicate ratio be used where the simple ratio will do as well? In the *next* place, This measure of force is less agreeable to the common use of the word force, as has been shewn above; and this indeed is all that the many laboured arguments and experiments, brought to overturn it, do prove. This also is evident, from the paradoxes into which it has led its defenders.

We are next to consider the pretences of the Leibnitzian, who will undertake to prove by demonstration, or experiment, that force is as the square of the velocity. I ask him first, what he lays down for the first measure of force? The only measure I remember to have been given by the philosophers of that side, and which seems first of all to have led Leibnitz into his notion of force, is this: the height to which a body is impelled by any impressed force, is, says he, the whole effect of that force, and therefore must be proportional to the cause: but this height is found to be as the square of the velocity which the body had at the beginning of its motion.

In this argument I apprehend that great man has been extremely unfortunate. For, *first*, whereas all proof should be taken from principles that are common to both sides, in order to prove a thing we deny, he assumes a principle which we think farther from the truth; namely, that the height to which the body rises is the whole effect of the impulse, and ought to be the whole measure of it. *Secondly*, His reasoning serves as well against him as for him; for may I not plead with as good reason at least thus? The velocity given by an impressed force is the whole effect of that impressed force; and therefore the force must be as the velocity. *Thirdly*, Supposing the height to which the body is raised to be the measure of the force, this principle overturns the conclusion he would establish by it, as well as that which he opposes. For, supposing the first velocity of the body to be still the same; the height to which it rises will be increased, if the power of gravity is diminished; and diminished, if the power of gravity is increased. Bodies descend slower at the equator, and faster towards the poles, as is found by experiments made on pendulums. If then a body is driven upwards at the equator with a given velocity, and the same body is afterwards driven upwards at Leipsic with the same velocity, the height to which it rises in the former case will be greater than in the latter; and therefore, according to his reasoning, its force was greater in the former case; but the velocity in both was the same; consequently the force is not as the square of the velocity any more than as the velocity.

Reflections on this Controversy.—On the whole, I cannot but think the controvertists on both sides have had a very hard task; the one to prove, by mathematical reasoning and experiment, what ought to be taken for granted; the other by the same means to prove what might be granted, making some allowance for impropriety of expression, but can never be proved.

If some mathematician should take it in his head to affirm that the velocity of a body is not as the space it passes over in a given time, but as the square of that space; you might bring mathematical arguments and experiments to confute him, but you would never by these force him to yield, if he was ingenious in his way; because you have no common principles left you to argue from, and you differ from each other not in a mathematical proposition, but in a mathematical definition.

Suppose a philosopher has considered only that measure of centripetal force which is proportional to the velocity generated by it in a given time, and from this measure deduces several propositions. Another philosopher in a distant country, who has the same general notion of centripetal force, takes the velocity generated by it, and the quantity of matter together, as the measure of it. From this he deduces several conclusions, that seem directly contrary to those of the other. Thereupon a serious controversy is begun, whether centripetal force be as the velocity, or as the velocity and quantity of matter taken together. Much mathematical and experimental dust is raised, and yet neither party can ever be brought to yield; for they are both in the right, only they have been unlucky in giving the same name to different mathematical conceptions. Had they distinguished these measures of centripetal force as Newton has done, calling the one *vis centripeta quantitatis acceleratrix*, the other, *quantitatis motrix*; all appearance of contradiction, had ceased, and their propositions, which seem so contrary, had exactly tallied.

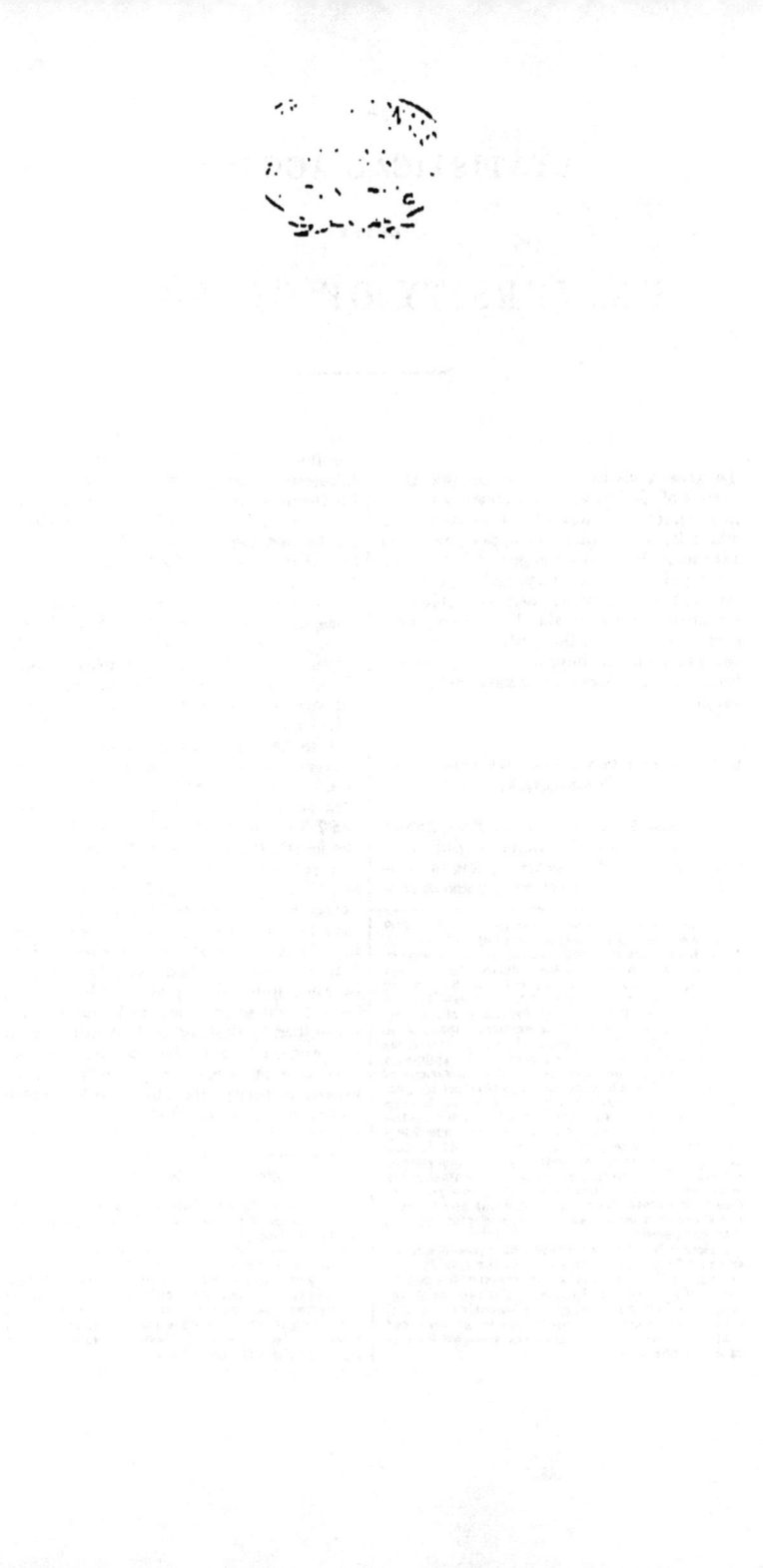

A

STATISTICAL ACCOUNT

OF THE

UNIVERSITY OF GLASGOW.*

INTRODUCTION.

To give a distinct account of the University of Glasgow, it is necessary to distinguish two periods of its existence, in which its constitution and appearance were extremely different—the period before the reformation from Popery, and that which followed it; to which may be subjoined, the present state of the University, with such alterations in the mode of conducting education as the improvements in literature, and the state of society, have suggested.

I. HISTORY OF THE UNIVERSITY BEFORE THE REFORMATION.

Origin.—At the request of King James II., Pope Nicolas V. granted a Bull, constituting a "*studium generale, tam in theologia, ac jure canonico et civili, quam in artibus, et quavis alia licita facultate*,"* to continue in all time to come in the city of Glasgow, as being a notable place, and fit for the purpose, by the temperature of the air, and the plenty of all kinds of provisions for human life; and, by his apostolical authority, ordained, That its doctors, masters, readers, and students, shall enjoy all the privileges, liberties, honours, exemptions, and immunities granted to the *studium generale* of his city of Bononia [Bologna.] He likewise appointed William Turnbull, then Bishop of Glasgow, and his successors in that see, to be the Rectors,† called Chancellors, of the said *studium*; and to have the same authority over the doctors, masters, and scholars, as the Rectors [of the schools] have in the *Studium Bononiense*.‡ This Bull is dated at Rome the 7th of the month of January 1450, and the fourth year of his pontificate.

Establishment.—By the care of the bishop and his chapter, a body of statutes was prepared, and an university established in the year 1451; consisting, besides the Chancellor, of a Rector, Doctors, and Masters of the four faculties, who had taken their degrees in other universities; and students, who, after a course of study and examination, prescribed by their several faculties, might be promoted to academical degrees.—That this institution might open with the greater celebrity, the bishop had procured and published a Bull from the Pope, granting an *universal indulgence* to all faithful

---

* This Account was published in the last or 21st volume of the "Statistical Account of Scotland," in 1799, three years after the death of Reid. It was not communicated by the author himself to Sir John Sinclair, nor probably during his life, but, as the title bears, was "Transmitted by Professor Jardine in Name of the Principal and Professors of the University." In the "Statistical Account," there is no indication afforded in regard to the writer: but it has always been attributed to our author. It exhibits his character of thought and style, and even various of his peculiarities of expression (as *professions* for *professorships*); and, as I am informed by my learned friend, Dr Lee, was produced and founded on as the work of Reid, in an action maintained, some thirty years ago, by sundry of his colleagues, (Mr Jardine among the number,) in regard to their collegiate privileges. From internal evidence, it appears that the Account itself was drawn up in 1794, two years before Reid's death; but the "Additions and Corrections" are of a more recent date, and probably by a different hand.

Before I became aware that this Account was the work of Reid, I had been struck by the singular correctness of the view that is here taken of the constitution of the ancient University, and this, as it appears, not from any analogical knowledge of the history of the European universities in general, but abstracted from the records of the Glasgow Faculty of Arts alone.—H.

* This quotation has been corrected from the Bull.—H.

† The term *Rector* is here used generically. *The Rector*, the proper head of the University, was by the University elected.—H.

‡ The origin and nature of the office of Chancellor, in relation to the ancient universities, is a very curious subject, and one not at all known; but, as it cannot be explained in a few words, I must not speak of it at present.—I may observe, in general, that there is nothing in the privileges and regulations of the University of Glasgow but what is common, I may say, to all the older Universities.—H.

Christians*, who should visit the cathedral church of Glasgow, in the year 1451. We have no account of the solemnity and ceremony of the first establishment; but it appears that David Cadzow, licentiate in canon-law, and canon of Glasgow, was the first rector, (probably appointed by the bishop;) and that he was, by election, continued in 1452. There are more than 100 members mentioned, as incorporated by him in these two years; and most of them not young men; but secular or regular ecclesiastics, canons, rectors, vicars, and presbyters, abbots, priors, and monks.* Andrew Stewart, brother to King James II., was incorporated in 1456, being then sub-dean of Glasgow.

Exemptions.—The clergy would perhaps be the more disposed to attend the University, as, while they were incorporated members, they were, by royal charters and acts of Parliament, exempted from all taxes and public burdens. And Bishop Turnbull, in the year 1453, ordained, That the beneficed clergy in his diocese, who were regents or students in his university, or willing to study while they were teachable, should, upon asking his license, be exempted from residence in their cures, providing they took care to have the religious offices duly performed.

Royal Charter.—King James II., in the year 1453, at the request of Bishop Turnbull, granted a charter in favour of the University of Glasgow; by which the Rector, the Deans of the Faculties, the Procurators of the *four nations*, the Masters, Regents, and Scholars, studying in the said university, providing they be not prelates, as well as the Beadals, Writers, Stationers, and Parchment-makers,† are exempted *ab omnibus tributis, muneribus, exactionibus, taxationibus, collectis, vigiliis, et pedagiis, aliquo modo infra regnum nostrum statuendis et levandis.*

Privileges and Powers.—The same privilege was renewed by subsequent sovereigns, and confirmed by acts of Parliament. And even in taxes of an eighth part of all ecclesiastical livings, for the defence of the nation against an invasion of the English, the clergy in the University of Glasgow, on pleading their privilege, were exempted. This right of exemption from taxation, was pleaded by this University before the Lords of Council and Session, on the 20th of November 1633, and was sustained.

To these privileges, which the bishops of Glasgow obtained from the Crown and Parliament, they added others which were in their own power, in consequence of the ample civil and criminal jurisdiction which they possessed within their own diocese—to wit, The privilege of buying, selling, and transporting provisions, within the jurisdiction of the bishop, free of tolls and customs; the fixing the rent of houses or lodgings, possessed by persons belonging to the university, by a jury, the one half citizens, the other half persons belonging to the university; the obliging the magistrates of Glasgow, upon their election, to swear that they shall observe, and cause to be observed, the immunities, liberties, and statutes of the university; the granting the rector the next place, in precedence to the bishop, in all ceremonies and processions; the granting the privileges of incorporated members to all the servants of the university; the *self-denying* clause in the chancellor's oath, [?] and which still makes a clause in it—"*Se nihil in academiæ negotiis sine moderatorum et magistrorum assensione tentaturum*"—and particularly, the granting to the Rector, at first, the jurisdiction in all civil and pecuniary questions, respecting members of the university, and in crimes less atrocious; and afterwards, the extending it to all causes and crimes whatsoever; the power also, of inflicting ecclesiastical censure, even that of excommunication.

Capital Trial.—There is, however, only one instance on record of a capital trial before the rector's court, and that so late as the year 1670. That year, Robert Bartoune, a student, was indicted for murder, before Sir William Fleming, rector; but was acquitted by the jury.

II. ANCIENT CONSTITUTION.

The constitution of this learned body will appear, by taking a view of the parts into which it was divided, and the powers and obligations of each.

I. *Election of Office-Bearers, &c.*—The whole incorporated members, students, as well as doctors and masters, were divided into four parts, called the *Quatuor Nationes*, according to the place of their nativity. The whole realm of Scotland, and the Isles, was distinguished into four districts, under the names of *Clydesdale*, *Teviotdale*, *Albany*, and *Rothesay*. A meeting of the whole University was annually called, on the day next after St Crispin's day. This meeting

* This circumstance was probably the cause why the election of Rector was conceded to all the members of the University, and not limited to the graduated alone. In this particular, the custom of the Italian schools was preferred to that of Paris, by the example of which most of the transalpine universities were regulated. This, with the circumstance that only one college arose within the University, enabled the regents of that college more easily to usurp from the graduates at large the rights of academical teaching and legislation—to sink the public university in the private pædagogium.—H.

† These were all the common supposts (suppositi) of a university; and the following are only the immunities and privileges in the usual form granted to every other institution of the kind over Europe.—H.

was called the *Congregatio Universitatis*; and, being divided into the four Nations, each nation, by itself, chose a Procurator and an Intrant; and the intrants, meeting by themselves, made choice of a Rector and a *Deputatus* of each nation, who were assistants and Assessors to the Rector.*

Functions.—The *Rector* and *Deputati* had several functions.

1st, They were judges in all civil and criminal causes, wherein any member of the University was a party. Every mem- who either sued or answered before any other court, was guilty of perjury, and incurred the penalty of expulsion. The ecclesiastics in the University, to whatever dioceses they belonged, could not be called before their rural deans.

2dly, All members were incorporated by the rector and *deputati*, after taking an oath to obey the rector and his successors, to observe the statutes, and preserve the privileges of the University, and not to reveal its secrets to its prejudice, to whatever station they should arive.

3dly, The rector and *deputati* were the council of the University; who deliberated upon, and digested all matters to be brought before the congregation of doctors and masters. And the determinations of the doctors and masters, in such cases, were accounted, in respect of authority, next to the statutes. Sometimes the *congregatio universitatis* was called occasionally for weighty matters; such as the making or repealing of statutes, or for an embassy to the higher powers, in name of the University. In such cases, each nation chose three or four *deputati*, who were joined with the rector and his *deputati*, to transact the business committed to them.

Two other office-bearers were chosen annually, on the morrow after St Crispin's day; a *Bursarius*, who kept the university purse, and accounted for what he received and expended; and a *Promotor*, whose office was to see that the statutes were observed, and to bring delinquents before the Rector's court, which had power to enforce the statutes, or to dispense with them in cases that were not declared to be indispensible.

II. *Faculties.*—A second division of the University was into its different *Faculties*. The Pope's Bull mentions four by name—to wit, *Theology*, *Canon Law*, *Civil Law*, and *the Arts*. All others are comprehended in a general clause, *et in quavis alia licita facultate*.——In the dark ages, the professions of theology, canon, and civil law, were called the three learned professions; as being the only professions in which learning was expected or thought necessary. They fitted men for the most honourable and lucrative employments; for the highest dignities in the church; for the councils of kings; for the offices of judges at home; and of ambassadors to foreign courts. To train men to eminence in these professions, was the first intention of universities. The Arts, under which was comprehended logic, physics, and morals, were considered as a necessary introduction to the learned professions, and, therefore, a necessary part of study in every university.

Their Plan.—The plan upon which universities were incorporated by the Popes, was very like to that of incorporated towns and boroughs, and perhaps was borrowed from it. The university corresponds to the whole incorporation of the borough; the different faculties to the different companies of the trades or crafts into which the borough is divided. A company is a smaller incorporation, subordinate to that of the borough; has the power of choosing its own head, or deacon; and an authority over those who are in the course of being trained to the same craft. The companies in the incorporated towns were anciently called *collegia*, or colleges; and the whole incorporation, comprehending all the companies, was called the *universitas* of that town. These names were, by analogy, applied to corporations of the learned professions, and at last appropriated to them. The word used in Pope Nicolas' Bull is not *universitas* but *studium generale*; and the university of Bononia he calls *Studium Bononiense*; but, in the charter of King James II. in 1453, we have—*Alma universitas Glasguensis, filia nostra dilecta*.*

Government.—The government of a faculty was very similar to that of the University. Each faculty had its own statutes, determining the time of study, and the exercises and examinations requisite for attaining degrees in that faculty. Each chose annually its own dean, its own *bursarius*, and sometimes four *deputati* as a council to the dean. We know very little of the three higher faculties in this University, as there is no record extant, either of their statutes or of their transactions. There are only two memorandums relating to them in the University record. In the first, we are told, that, on the 29th of July 1460, the venerable David Cadzow, then rector of the University, began, in the chapter house of the predicant friars, the clergy and masters being there convened, to read the rubric in the canon law, *de vita et honestate clericorum*; and that he con-

* See above, note, 721, b.—H.

* *Universitas*, as originally used, is simply a word for an incorporated generality. It has nothing to do with any complement of studies. *Collegium* is ambiguous in its academical employment; sometimes being applied to denote the public sub-incorporation of a faculty; sometimes a private incorporation of certain individuals of the university.—H.

tinued according to the pleasure of the hearers; and that, on the same day, and in the same place, William de Levenax began a title in the civil law. But we are not told how long it pleased the hearers that these lectures should be continued.——In another memorandum we are told, that, on the 23d of March, in the year 1521, Robert Lile, bachelor in theology, and prior of the convent of predicant friars in Glasgow, began, *pro forma*, to read a lecture on the fourth book of the sentences, in the monastery; in presence of the rector, dean of faculty, and the rest of the masters; John Ade, professor of theology, and provincial of the order in Scotland, presiding at the time.

III. *Degrees.*—A third division was according to the academical degree of every member. The highest degree in theology, canon, and civil law, was that of *Doctor;* and in the arts, that of *Master*. In some universities, *Masters of Arts* are called *Doctors of Philosophy;* but in most they are distinguished by the name of *Master*, from those who have the highest degree in any of the higher faculties.* A master, however, might be chosen to be rector, or a *deputatus*, as well as doctor. In all the faculties, there were two degrees by which a man rose to the highest; these were Bachelor and Licentiate.† The degree of Licentiate, as well as that of Doctor or Master, was conferred only by the chancellor or vice-chancellor. The requisites to all the degrees was a certain time of study, and the having heard certain books prelected upon, and certain exercises and examinations; in Bachelors of the Arts fifteen years of age, and in Masters twenty. It was forbidden, under a heavy penalty, to give any man the title of Master, by word or writing, who had not attained that degree; and the penalty was still more heavy if any man took it to himself before he had lawfully obtained it. Academical degrees were considered as of *divine* institution, (probably because instituted by Popes, who were thought to be inspired by the Holy Ghost); and, therefore, the chancellor or vice-chancellor conferred them *authoritate divina, et in nomine Patris, Filii, et Spiritûs Sancti.*

IV. *Teaching.*—The last division we shall mention, is into *teachers*, and those who *were taught*. On this part of the constitution, the records that are extant leave us much in the dark. We know that four faculties were established; because, in the oath taken by masters of arts, they swore to promote peace among the four faculties, especially with the faculty of theology. A school of canon law is mentioned as being in disrepair, and to be repaired out of the university purse; and it appears that degrees were conferred both in that faculty and in theology. Andreas de Garlies, *Doctor in Medicinis*, was incorporated in 1469; but his name is never mentioned again, nor anything else that relates to medicine. It is probable, therefore that there was no faculty of medicine, nor any teaching in that science. Of the teaching in the faculty of arts we have more full information, from two manuscripts in parchment;—one of which contains the statutes of that faculty, and its conclusions; and the other the minutes of its meetings, and transactions, from 1451 to 1509, and from 1535 to 1555. These manuscripts were transcribed by order of the University in 1769.

Pædagogium.—Some years after the University was founded, many of the students were young men, to whom tuition, as well as teaching, was necessary; and, therefore, provision was made that they should live and eat in one house, which was called *Pædagogium*, or the College of Arts; where they were taught and governed by certain masters, who were called *Regentes in Artibus.** This college was at first on the south side of the Rotten-row, and probably was a part of the property of the bishop and chapter; but afterwards a tenement was bequeathed by Lord Hamilton, for the College of Arts, where the college now stands.

Regents.—At first there were three regents in the arts; to wit, Alexander Geddes, a Cistertian monk; Duncan Bunch; and William Arthurlie. Afterwards, we find sometimes two, and sometimes but one. It seems to have been the most laborious and least coveted office in the University. Besides teaching and presiding in disputations *omni die legibili*, they lived within the College, eat at a common table with the students of arts, visited the rooms of the students before nine at night, when the gates were shut, and at five in the morning, and assisted in all examinations for degrees in arts. In the beginning of every session, they proposed to the faculty the books they intended to prelect upon, and had their

* Originally Magister, Doctor, and Professor were convertible terms.—H.

† The *Licence* was originally properly granted by the Chancellor, and usually preceded the highest Degree, or admission in a Faculty, by a year. This function of the Chancellor—who, in the older universities was always the Ecclesiastical Ordinary or his mandatory—was the continuance of a right exercised prior to the origin of universities, in the eleventh and twelfth centuries.—H.

* A *Regens in Artibus* was not a title appropriated to a teacher in the pædagogium or college. This was only a house into which certain members of the university were admitted, and where they were maintained; and among these certain graduates, under the condition of there teaching in their faculty. *Regere*, or *regere scholas*, meant simply and in general, to teach; and *Magister Regens*, or *Doctor Regens*, denoted a graduate who actually exercised his duty or his privilege of lecturing, &c. There were, at least there might have been, many other graduates *regenting*, besides those who had appointments in the pædagogium.—H.

permission. There was no salary for this office for many years; and the fees paid by the bearers were very small. Twice we find a regent presented by the chancellor, and one of these he turned off for insufficiency in two or three years. Once, the faculty turned one out for insufficiency, and put two in his place, with power to choose a third, with the consent of the faculty, if they found it proper. All that had this office, excepting two, continued in it but a few years; and very often one who was not a member of the faculty was called to this office, and made a regent immediately upon being incorporated. From these particulars, it is probable that there was no competition either for this office or for the patronage of it; but rather some difficulty to find persons qualified who were willing to take it.

Books.—The books which students were obliged to hear read, before taking the degree of Bachelor, were prescribed by statute. They were, "Porphirie's Introduction to certain books of Aristotle," and "Petrus Hispanus." The fee to be paid for hearing each was also fixed.[a] When they had these, and the other requisites, they were presented by their regent to a meeting of the Faculty, which, by statute, was appointed to be held annually the day after *All-Saints*.

Examinations.—When they were found to have all the *requisita*, or wanted only such as the faculty saw cause to dispense with, four examinators, called *temptatores*, were elected, to examine them, within ten days. Of the four *temptatores*, two were regents, (when there were two,) and the other two non-regents. The examinators, after examination, wrote, signed, and sealed their report; which contained not only the name of those whom they found worthy, but their order, according to their merit; and, in this order, the dean conferred the degree of *Bachelor of Arts*. The examinators, when they were chosen, took an oath to make a faithful report, and not to reveal the secrets of the examination. The candidates were also sworn not to reveal the secrets of the examination; nor to shew any resentment, by word or deed, against any fellow-candidate, by whom they had been refuted in the course of the examination. The examination for the degrees of *Licentiate* and of *Master* was carried on in the same way.

Obligation.—In the oath taken by one who took the degree of Master, he came under an obligation *de lectura ad biennium*; but this, which implied not only his continuing his studies in the College for two years, but his giving lectures during that time, was very often dispensed with upon paying a fine.*

---

[a] This fee was called the *Pastus*. It was exigible by all unsalaried graduates for their prelections. But when the custom of giving salaries to certain graduates, i. e. of endowing certain chairs, was introduced, *so far could be legally demanded*; the endowment was in lieu of the pastus, a boon to the public and the poor; and it was only after these salaried graduates, who in time came to be called *professors*, had, by their gratuitous instruction, rendered the lectures of the graduates at large a profitless vocation—I say it was only when other lectures were discontinued, competition thus removed, and the whole instruction, and often even the whole regulation, of the university allowed to fall into their hands, that, by slow and imperceptible degrees, fees were again introduced, and in different schools and countries, by different means, sometimes legally, more frequently illegally, raised to the footing of compulsory exactions. The records of the University of Glasgow shew the progress of the innovation in that institution. In the earlier ages, and when the salaried graduates—the regents of the pædagogium—were very inadequately provided for, honoraria, or voluntary offerings, by the richer students, were naturally made. These gradually became customary; were, in time, looked upon as a due; and, by sanction of the *Moderators*, (not Professors,) a graduated scale was, from time to time, fixed, according to which students of different ranks were expected to contribute. The poorer scholars were always declared free, and those educated for the church being generally of that description, no custom of honoraries was ever introduced into the theological classes. The city of Glasgow had been a considerable benefactor of the college; and the corporation, till a late period, took care that its citizens should enjoy their original privilege of gratuitous instruction, or, at least, pay only such fees as they themselves deemed reasonable; for, at every new regulation touching "*scholliages*," or "*honoraries*," it is stated, either that the children of the citizens shall be entitled to gratuitous education, or that they shall be liable in payment only "in such proportions and rates as the Town Council and Moderators, after conference, shall agree upon." At length, since the commencement of the present century, the Professors seem to have taken upon themselves, to double and treble the previous rate of fees without the sanction of the Moderators, far less the consent of the city. The Commissioners of Inquiry into the state of the Universities of Scotland animadvert severely upon the impropriety of the high amount of fees thus exacted; whereby, in the faculty of arts, the poor student is obliged to pay as high (and in one class even higher) to the well endowed professors of a provincial university, as he does to those of the metropolitan university, who enjoy no salaries worth taking into account. But, while commenting on the impropriety of the proceeding, it is singular that the Commissioners have not adverted to its palpable illegality. If the city of Glasgow should vindicate its right of control, this might be exerted not merely as a salutary check on the irregular imposition of fees, but indirectly be employed as a mean of raising the character of the university itself, by extorting a reform in the present mode of its academical patronage—that by self-election. See above, p. 43, a, note *.—H.

* This statement is quite correct. This interval was the period of what, in the older universities, was called the *necessary regency*. I see that this matter is mistaken in the able Report relative to the University of Glasgow, by the Commissioners on the Universities and Colleges of Scotland. The phrase is there supposed to mean, only a continuation of *study* in the Faculty for two years subsequent to the degree of A. M. In the English universities the dispensation is still in use; and, on the supposition that they are then actually teaching, Masters, during this interval, have certain privileges in the university which they may not afterwards enjoy. The practice was originally universal. In the first place, it was necessary to ensure instruction in the department of the faculty; and, in the second place, our ancestors knew, it seems, better than we the value of intellectual exercise, and, in particular, that the most effective means of learning is to teach.

Lectures.—The statutes of this faculty suppose that every master is to give prelections; for they enjoin, that, on the day in which the dean is chosen the masters, according to their seniority, shall name the book upon which they are to prelect; and that, if two masters choose the same book, the senior be preferred, unless there be so many hearers that both may prelect on the same book, at the same time, in different schools. But, in the minutes of faculty, there is no mention of any such lectures being proposed or given by any master but the *magistri regentes*.*

The manner of teaching and of hearing is, by the statutes, ordained to be the same as in *Bononia* and in *Pisa*. In many other things, the practice of some one of the foreign universities is made the rule; but those of England are never mentioned.

Discipline.—Corporal punishment was sometimes inflicted upon students in the College of Arts. For some faults, the statutes order the punishment to be inflicted *caligis laxatis*.

Property.—It may appear strange that this University was founded without any property in lands, houses, or rents. It came into the world as *naked* as every individual does. The *congregatio universitatis* was always held at the cathedral. Sometimes the doctors and masters met at the convent of the Dominicans, or Predicators, as they were called. All the lectures we find mentioned in theology, canon or civil law, were read there. There was an university purse, into which some perquisites, paid at incorporation, and at examinations, and promotions to degrees, were put. From this purse, caps of ceremony were furnished. after some years: but, to defray the expense of a silver rod or mace, to be carried before the rector at certain solemnities, it was found necessary to tax all the incorporated members; and, on that occasion, we are told that David Cadzow, who was then rector, gave twenty nobles.

Two or three chaplainries were bequeathed, under the patronage of the university, by some of its first members. The duty of the chaplain was to perform certain masses, at such an altar, for the souls of the founder and his friends; for which he had a small annuity. These chaplainries were commonly given to some of the regents of the college of arts; perhaps because they were the poorest of the sacerdotal order in the university. This patronage and this purse, as far as appears, were all the property which the university ever possessed. Nor does it appear that the faculties of theology, canon or civil law, ever had any property. The individuals had rich livings through all parts of the nation—abbacies, priories, prebends, rectories, and vicarages; but the community had nothing. Its privileges were the inducement to bring rich ecclesiastics into a society, in which they lived at ease, free of all taxes, and subject to no authority but that of their own rector.

The *College of Arts*, however, being perhaps thought the most useful part of the whole, and entitled to public favour, as entrusted with the education of youth, soon came to have some property. In the year 1459, James Lord Hamilton bequeathed to Mr Duncan Bunch, principal regent of the College of Arts, and his successors, regents, for the use of the said College—a tenement, with the pertinents, lying on the north side of the church and convent of the Predicators, together with four acres of land in the Dow hill.* From this time we find the purse of the faculty of arts, which appears, to have been heavier than that of the University, employed in repairing and adding to the buildings of the College; furnishing rooms for the regents and students; and things necessary for the kitchen, and a common table.

In the year 1466, another tenement, adjoining to the College, was bequeathed by Mr Thomas Arthurlie. By this time, many of the students of arts were the youth of the nation, whose good education was a matter of importance to the public. They were distinguished, according to their rank, into sons of noblemen, of gentlemen, and of those of meaner rank; and, in the expense of their education, were taxed accordingly.

Such, as far as we can learn, was the constitution of the University of Glasgow before the Reformation. There is reason to think, that, when the zeal in favour of a new institution began to cool, the three higher faculties gradually declined into inactivity.

Defects.—From the year 1490, we find frequent complaints, of masters not attending university meetings; of statutes having fallen into disuse; of bachelors and licenti-

As it was proverbially said—

Discere si quæris, doceas; sic ipse doceris:
Nam studio tali tibi proficis atque sodali.

Those graduates who not merely performed their *obligation* during the years of necessary regency, but exercised their *privilege* of teaching when that period was at an end, were called voluntary regents, (regentes ad placitum.)—H.

* In regard to the term *Magistri regentes*, see above p. 7/4, b, *. This practice of arranging the books to be prelected on *in ordinary* (ordinarie) by the regent masters, was general in the European schools. We have some curious lists of the books, and of the various rates of *pastus* at which the lectures on them were stated, in the histories of the universities of Vienna and Ingolstadt.—H.

* In this deed, the regents and students are required, every day after dinner and after supper, to stand up and pray for the souls of James Lord Hamilton, founder of the college; of Euphemia his spouse, Countess of Douglas; of his ancestors and successors; and of all from whom he has received any benefit, for which he has not made a proper return.

ates not proceeding in their degrees; of the jurisdiction of the University not being respected. Sometimes, at the election of a rector, not one of the *nation of Albany* was present; and once, none either of *Albany* or of *Teviotdale*. There seems only to have been one dean in the University for some time before the Reformation, to wit, the dean of the faculty of arts; and, therefore, it is probable the other faculties had no meetings. In the later minutes of the University he is called *Decanus Facultatis*, without addition; whereas, more early, he is always *Decanus Facultatis Artium*.* This style, of *Dean of Faculty of the University*, which we see was a considerable time before the Reformation, continues to be used to this day; there being only one dean of faculty in that University, who is considered not as the head of one particular faculty, but in the light of an university officer, as the rector is.

There seem to have been two obvious defects in the ancient constitution of the University. The first, that no salaries were provided for regular lectures in the high faculties. It was not to be expected, that the laborious work of teaching should be performed by those who could not live by it; and who could not, by their industry and eminence in their profession, rise to some degree of respect proportioned to what their talents and learning might have raised them in another line of life. The second defect—That there was not sufficient power over the University to remedy disorders, when these became general, and infected the whole body. The chancellor had, by his oath already mentioned, divested himself of the power which the Pope's Bull gave him; and neither royal nor parliamentary visitations, so frequent afterwards, were then introduced.†

III. HISTORY AFTER THE REFORMATION.

The reformation in religion, established by act of Parliament in the year 1560, brought the University of Glasgow almost to annihilation. The dignitaries of the church and convents, of whom its doctors and masters were composed, were no more. The Chancellor, James Beaton, fled to France, and carried with him the plate of the cathedral, with the bulls, charter, and rights both of the see and of the University, which he deposited partly in the Convent of the Carthusians, and partly in the Scotch College at Paris, (where they lately were,) to be restored when Popery should be re-established. It ought to be observed, to the honour of that college, that they have always been ready to give extracts from the originals deposited with them, as well as to gratify the curious by the inspection of them. The late Principal Gordon, of that college, made a present to the University of Glasgow of a copy of the chartulary of the Chapter of Glasgow, notorially attested.

All that was now to be seen of the University was that small part, called the *College of Arts*, or *Pædagogium*;* the least in dignity, though perhaps not the least useful. This small part, with its small property—probably much impaired by the confusion of the times, and the loss of rights—remained as a relic of the ancient University, and a seed of a reformed University, dependent for its subsistence and growth on future benefactions. The rich fabric of the Popish hierarchy, in Scotland, was pulled down with more zeal than prudence, by a fierce nation, long oppressed, and little accustomed to regular government. All who had power or interest scrambled for

---

* This conjecture is confirmed by a notarial instrument of the foundation of a chaplainry, by Mr Thomas Leiss, while he was on a sick-bed, but sound in his mind. This instrument was taken, the 8th day of March, in the year 1509, before respectable witnesses, five of whom signed it with the notary. In it the notary says—*Constituti dominum rectorem Universitatis Glasguensis et decanum facultatis ejusdem, indubitatos patronos.* From this, it appears, that only one dean existed at that time in the University, or was expected to exist; and we know that a dean of the faculty of arts was chosen annually, till the year 1555. [see p. 719, note.—H.]

† Whatever were the causes of declension in this University before the Reformation, the annals of literature mention very few of its members who made any considerable figure in the learned world. One, however, deserves to be mentioned. William Elphinston, who had been a canon of Glasgow, and had borne the offices both of rector of the University, and dean of the faculty of arts, was eminent in the knowledge both of the canon and civil law. He was made Bishop of Aberdeen, and Chancellor of Scotland; and was employed in several embassies to foreign courts. He founded the University of Old Aberdeen, in the year 1494; and, either from the experience of what he had seen in the University of Glasgow, or from a deeper knowledge of human nature, he supplied, in his university, both the defects we have observed in that of Glasgow, for he gave salaries (not illiberal for the times) to those who were to teach theology, canon and civil law, medicine, languages, and philosophy, and pensions to a certain number of poor students; and likewise appointed a visitorial power, reserving to himself, as chancellor, and to his successors in that office, a dictatorial power, to be exercised occasionally according to the report of the visitors.

James Beaton, the last Popish Archbishop of Glasgow, deserves also to be mentioned with honour. His fidelity in depositing everything he carried away, that belonged to the Archbishopric or to the University, to the Convent of the Carthusians, or to the Scotch College at Paris, was never questioned. His political ability appears by his having been appointed one of the Scottish ambassadors, at the court of France, for settling the articles of the Queen's marriage with the Dauphin; his having been again appointed her ambassador at that court, and continuing in that office from the time of the Reformation till her death; and, after that tragical event, his being appointed King James's ambassador at the same court, and holding that office till the time of his own death in 1603, when King James came to be King of England. This archbishop left several monuments of his learning in manuscript, which are preserved in the Scotch College at Paris, to which he bequeathed the greatest part of his effects at his death.

* Not synonymous. See above, p. 713, b, note a —H.

the wreck. The crown, the nobility, and the cities, were enriched by it; some *crumbs* came, by second hand, to the universities.

Queen Mary's Charter.—The first who had compassion on the University of Glasgow, in its depressed state, was the famous and the unfortunate Queen Mary. In a charter granted by her, and to which her privy seal is appended, dated the 13th of July 1560, there is the following narrative:—"Forasmuch as, within the citie of Glasgow, ane colledge and universitie was devysit to be hade, &c., of the whilke colledge ane part of the scoles and chalmers being *bigget*, the rest thairof, alsweil dwellings as provision for the poor burrars and maisters to teach, ceasit, swa that the samyn appeared rather to be the decay of ane university, nor oniewaye to be reckonit ane estabiisht foundation." Therefore, for the zeal she bore to letters, &c., she founds five poor children bursars within the said college, to be called, in all times to come, *bursars of her foundation*; and for their *sustentation*, she gives to the Masters of the said college and university the manse and kirk of the Friars Predicators, with thirteen acres of ground adjacent, and several other rents and annuities therein named, which had belonged to the said friars.*

Burgh Charter.—The next benefaction made to this college is contained in a charter, granted by Sir John Stewart of Mynto, provost, with the bailies, council, and community of the city of Glasgow, in the year 1572, and ratified by the Parliament the same year. They, considering that, besides other detriment their town sustained, their schools and colleges were utterly ruined; and their youth, who were wont to be trained to probity and good morals, left to be corrupted by idleness and wantonness; and, being earnestly desirous to remedy so great an evil, by the exhortation, counsel, and aid of the most respectable Master Andrew Hay, Rector of the church of Renfrew, and Vice-Superintendent, and Rector for the time, of their University of Glasgow—resolved to restore, renew, and give a new foundation to the *Pædagogium Glasguense, quod pro sumptuum inopia pene corruerat, et in quo, pro nimia paupertate, disciplinarum studia extincta jacebant.* For this purpose, they annex to the said college, and to the regents and students aftername, residing within it, being fifteen persons in all, "for their honest and commodious sustentation, all and sundry the lands, tenements, houses, biggings, kirks, chapels, yards, orchards, crofts, annual-rents, fruits, duties, profits and emoluments, mails, obit-silver, and anniversaries whatsoever, which pertained to whatsoever chappels, altarages, prebendaries, founded in whatever kirk or college within the said city; or of the places of all the friars of the same city, according to the gift made to them by the Queen, under the Great Seal, the 26th March 1566." They likewise will and declare, that the said College, the fifteen persons before mentioned, and all others who shall be students in the same, and their servants, shall be exempted *ab omni jurisdictione ordinaria; necnon ab omnibus custumis, et exactionibus pedariis, intra civitatem nostram impositis, vel imponendis.* It is understood to be in consequence of this charter, that the magistrates of Glasgow, or a deputation from them, still continue annually to inspect the accompts of the old revenue of the College in which the particulars of this donation were comprehended,* though the greatest part of it, which consisted of small ground annuals, is now lost.

One might think, that, when to the former revenue of the College were added these donations of Queen Mary, and of the city of Glasgow, it must have been completely endowed for the maintenance of fifteen persons; yet it was soon found necessary to increase the revenue, and to diminish the number of persons to be maintained by it. For, although the property of the Dominican Friars in Glasgow was certainly very considerable before the Reformation, yet all that the College could make effectual of that, and all their funds taken together, amounted only, by their rental, to £300 Scotch money.†

A more effectual benefaction was made to this poor society, in the year 1577, by King James VI., in his minority, with the advice and consent of the Earl of Morton,

* The name of *bursar*, or *bursarius*, was anciently given to the treasurer of an university or of a college, who kept the common purse of the community. We see that, in Queen Mary's time, this name had come to be given to poor students, probably because they were pensioners on the *common purse.* Her gift is the first we have met with, that was destined particularly for the support of a certain number of such poor students, whom she appoints to be called *bursars of her foundation.*

* Hence, too, the privilege of the citizens of Glasgow, to which I have alluded in a previous note.—H.

† The reason why donations, in appearance liberal, turned out to so small account, was, partly, that the Popish ecclesiastics, secular and regular, though their form of worship was totally abolished through the whole nation, continued to enjoy their temporalities for life, subject to a taxation of a third part to the Crown, out of which the clergy of the reformed church were to be maintained; partly, that those incumbents, during their life, practised many arts to alienate their revenues to laymen, either from friendship or for their own profit, by pretended feu-contracts, perpetual or long leases, and many other means, which their private interest, their regard to relations, or their hatred of the new religion, suggested.

Some of these pretended alienations, made to the hurt of the college, were afterwards reduced and annulled by the courts of law, some by arbitration. Probably many more might have been reduced; but that very often the subject was *too small* to bear the expense of a lawsuit, or the man in possession *too powerful* to be sued by the college.

Regent of the kingdom. That was the rectory and vicarage of the parish of Govan, of which the incumbent was lately dead, and the value reckoned about twenty-four chalders. It was found, however, that the late incumbent had, before his death, given a nineteen years' lease of the temporality to a friend, and that friend had transferred his right to a man in power. By this and some other incumbrances, all that the College could draw from it, for about twenty years, was only 300 merks yearly.

IV. MODERN CONSTITUTION.

New Royal Charter.—With this gift, King James gave a *charter of foundation* to the College, which, in its most essential articles, has continued in force to this day. It is commonly called the *nova erectio*; all subsequent changes being superstructures upon this foundation. The charter proceeds upon this narrative.—*Intelligentes quod annua proficua et reditus collegii, seu Pædagogii Glasguensis, tam exigua sunt, ut hac nostra ætate minime sufficientia sint ad sustentandum principalem, magistros regentes, bursarios, et officiarios necessarios in quovis collegio; nec ad adminiculandum sustentationi et reparationi ejusdem.* And afterwards—*Dum animum nostrum adjecerimus ad colligendas reliquias academiæ Glasguensis; quam præ inopia languescentem, ac jam pene confectam reperimus.*—The persons founded by this charter are twelve; a Principal, three Regents, four Bursars, an *Œconomus* or Steward, a Cook, a Porter, and a Servant to the Principal.

Establishment.—The Principal was to teach Theology one day, and Hebrew and Syriac the next alternately, through the week; and to preach in the church of Govan on Sunday. Of the Regents, one was to teach Greek and Rhetoric; another, Dialectics, Morals, and Politics, with the elements of Arithmetic and Geometry; and the third, who was also Sub-Principal, was to teach all the branches of Physiology and Geography, Chronology and *Astrology*. The Principal to be presented by the Crown; the Regents to be elected by the Rector, Dean of Faculty, and the Principal. The Regents were not, as was the custom of other Scottish universities, to carry on their students through the three years' course; but to keep by one profession; so that the student had a new Regent every year. The Bursars were to be maintained for three years and a half within the College; that being the time required in the Scottish universities for acquiring the degree of Master of Arts. The Steward was to collect the whole revenues, and to provide all necessaries for the College table; and to give an account, every day, to the Principal and Regents, of his disbursements. The Rector, the Dean of Faculty, and the Minister of Glasgow, are authorized to visit the College four times in the year, to examine and authenticate the public accounts, and to see that all things be carried on according to the intention of this foundation, and to correct what was not.

Privileges and Exemptions.—All donations formerly made to the College, by whatsoever person or persons, of whatsoever rank, are ratified. And the whole revenue formerly belonging to, or now granted, the King declares and ordains, for him and his successors, shall be enjoyed by the said College, free from any taxation of a third part, or any other taxation whatsoever; any law, custom, act, or ordinance of Parliament, notwithstanding. Finally, he wills and declares, That the College and University of Glasgow shall enjoy all the privileges and immunities, by his ancestors, by him, or any other way, granted to any university in his kingdom, as freely, peaceably, and quietly as if it had enjoyed them from ancient times before the memory of men. This charter was ratified by the King, after he came to the years of majority, and confirmed by act of Parliament, in the year 1587.

Government.—In Glasgow, the whole property and revenue pertaining to the University, is vested in the college, and is administrated by a meeting of the Principal and Professors, commonly called *the College Meeting*, and very often, though perhaps with less propriety, *the Faculty Meeting*. The record of this meeting is visited and authenticated by the Rector, Dean of Faculty, and the Minister of the High Church of Glasgow. Other business of the University, besides matters of revenue, and the discipline of the students, is managed in what is called *an University-Meeting*, or *Senate*; in which the Rector and Dean of Faculty sit, along with the Principal and Professors. Indeed, besides the College, all that remains of the University is a Chancellor, Rector, and Dean. We see that the *Nova Erectio* supposes their existence; but makes no change with regard to their powers, except in giving to the two last, together with the Minister of Glasgow, a visitorial power over the College. The Rector and Dean are chosen annually much in the same manner as they were from the first foundation of the University.* The Rector always names the Principal and

* The Dean—the Dean of the Faculty of Arts, he is not. He was originally, and, on the constitutional principle of the University, he ought now, to be elected by the whole body of graduates of this Faculty of Arts, (for they constitute that faculty which is an *universitas*, not a *college* incorporation,) and not by the Professors only, *i. e.*, the collegiate or salaried

Professors to be his Assessors; and, with them, occasionally forms a court of law, for judging in pecuniary questions, and less atrocious crimes, wherein any member of the University was party. The University has always maintained its exemption from all jurisdiction of the City Magistrates, but not of the Sheriff or Court of Session.

This may suffice for a general view of the *constitution* of the university, since the reformation from Popery. As to the state of its *revenues* during that period, it has been much indebted both to our princes and to subjects. Its declension before the reign of James VI. was not more remarkable than its progress since that period. From the small beginning derived from the bounty of that prince, it continued to prosper to the era of the Restoration; having, at that time, besides a Principal, eight Professors, a Librarian, with a tolerable Library, the number of its Bursars increased, and an additional number of other Students of all ranks. A renewal of the fabric (which had been ruinous) was begun and carried on, with great enlargement, in an elegant manner for the time; but not finished.

V. DONATIONS.

Soon after the new foundation, in the year 1581, the Archbishop gave to the College the customs of the city of Glasgow, by which it was enabled to found a fourth regent. A new body of statutes was formed about this time, which are extant. By them it appears that the Principal and four regents were put to very hard and constant labour; and the students kept under very strict discipline. Of the Regents, the first and highest was Professor of Physiology, and Sub-Principal; the second was Professor of Moral Philosophy; the third of Logic and Rhetoric; and the fourth of Greek. Their salaries rose in gradation; and, when any of the higher offices became vacant, those who were in the lower were commonly advanced a step; and the new chosen Regent had the profession of Greek for his department.

In this state, the College continued for a long time; excepting that, in the year 1621, by a meeting of the visiters, in which the Archbishop was present, the principal was freed from the duty of preaching in the church of Govan. A minister was appointed to have the pastoral charge of that parish, to whom a stipend was provided out of the teinds of the parish; the patronage of the church being reserved to the University, and the minister being obliged "to read some public lecture in the common schools of the college, as shall be prescribed to him by the officers of the University, and Masters of the College." This change they were enabled to make, from having, by an act of Parliament, in the year 1616, been vested in the tithes of the parishes of Kilbride and Renfrew; burdened with the payment of stipends to the ministers of these two parishes, which are modified by the act; and likewise burdened with the life-rent of the persons who were at that time titulars of these tithes. In the year 1637, it appears that a Master or Professor, Humaniorum Literarum, commonly called Professor of Humanity, had been founded.*

In the year 1641, Charles I., by his signature, gave to the College the temporality of the bishopric of Galloway; reserving to himself the power of burdening it with the sum of £100 sterling, to any person he should name. This gift was confirmed by an act of Parliament the same year. The office of Chancellor of the University becoming vacant by the abolition of Episcopal government in the church, James Marquis of Hamilton was chosen chancellor, and was the first layman who bore that office. After him, William Earl of Glencairn was chosen, in the year 1660.

Though the greatest part of the Masters submitted with reluctance to the government of Oliver Cromwell, and wished a restoration of the monarchy, under proper limitations, the Principal, Mr Patrick Gillespie, was a zealous republican; and, by the interest he had with Oliver, obtained great favours for the University. The Protector and his counsel renewed all its immunities and privileges; adding that of printing bibles, and all sorts of books belonging to the liberal sciences, and licensed by the University. He confirmed all former founda-

Masters, who are only members of it *qua* Masters; for, on principle, no one is eligible to a Professorship who is not a graduate in the relative faculty. In like manner, the other faculties ought severally to have their own Deans elected in the same way by their graduates at large; a *Dean of Faculties* is an academical solecism. Each Faculty also should confer its proper degrees apart from every other; and establish its own by-laws and statutes. The *college* is not the *university*, though they are now so confusedly mixed up together. As to the right of the graduates at large to constitute the university, and to ratify its laws; this was recognised in Glasgow, so late as the year 1727, when, as I remember noticing in the academical records, which I had occasion some years ago to examine, it was found necessary, in conformity to principle and practice, (not then forgotten,) to summon a Congregation of Graduates, in order to legalise the statutes proposed by the Visitation of that date. All constitutional principles have, however, in this as in our other British universities, been so long violated with impunity, that they are now conscientiously ignored.—H

* In the year 1637, a meeting of the Visiters, the Archbishop being present, appointed Mr Robert Mayne, then Professor of Logic, to be Professor of Medicine, and to give lectures in that science. At the same time, the Professor of Greek was advanced to the profession of Logic; the Professor of Humanity to the profession of Greek; and a new Professor of Humanity was chosen.

tions, mortifications, and donations made in its favour, particularly that of the bishopric of Galloway; to which he added the vacant stipends of the parishes which had been in the patronage of the bishop of Galloway, for seven years to come; and also, in perpetuity, the revenues of the deanery and sub-deanery of Glasgow. This last gift, however, was accompanied with several limitations and restrictions, by which the College had not the possession of the subjects while his power lasted; and, his acts being rescinded at the Restoration, it fell, of course, and had no effect.

The re-establishment of Episcopal government in the church after the restoration of Charles II. gave a severe check to the prosperity of the University; by depriving it at once of the best part of its revenue—to wit, that of the bishopric of Galloway. Before arrangements could be made, suited to this impoverished state, a great debt was contracted. Of the eight professions which had been established, three were sunk; and those that remained were reduced to a very short allowance. The College now consisted of a Principal, a Professor of Theology, and four Regents; a very scanty revenue, sunk in debt; and a large fabric unfinished.

A visitation of the universities was appointed by Parliament, in the year 1664. The noblemen, gentlemen, and clergy, who visited the College of Glasgow, after a strict examination of their revenue, report—"That the sum of three thousand nine hundred and forty-one pounds Scotch, yearly, will be necessar to be speedily provided for unto the University, or otherways it must quickly decay and ruine."* Besides this, they found it had a great load of debt; and that many professions were wanting which it ought to have, but cannot for the present possibly have for want of revenue. In this report the visiters were unanimous.

In this state the University remained till after the Revolution. It is true that, in this interval, it received several considerable donations and mortifications; but these were all appropriated, by the donors, either to the carrying on of the building, or to the foundation of bursars; and were faithfully applied to these purposes. So that it must have required great economy in the professors, as well as great lenity in their creditors, to preserve them from bankruptcy, during this long interval.

In the year 1693, each of the Scottish universities obtained a gift of £300 a-year out of the bishops' rents in Scotland. The sum payable to the University of Glasgow, was allocated upon the income of the archbishopric of Glasgow; and soon after, still better to secure the payment, the College obtained a lease of the whole rent of the archbishopric for nineteen years, which lease has from time to time been renewed by the Crown.

The University began now to raise her head, after a long period of depression, by debt and poverty, and by the diminution of her professors. The exertions which were made about this time were encouraged by the great number of her students. Principal Stirling, in his diary, says, that in the year 1702 the students of Theology, Greek, and Philosophy, amounted to upwards of four hundred and two. The great demand for clergymen, to fill the vacant benefices, immediately after the establishment of the Presbyterian government, occasioned the attendance of a greater number of students about the beginning of this century, than at any former period.

In the year 1706, the profession of Humanity was revived; and Mr Andrew Rose was appointed professor.

In the year 1708, her Majesty Queen Anne was pleased to grant the University £210 sterling yearly, payable out of the Exchequer; one part of which was appropriated for salaries to a Professor of Anatomy and Botany, and to a Professor of Oriental Languages; and another part of it for augmenting the salaries of the Principal and Professors, according to a scheme of division mentioned in the deed. This gift has been renewed by all the subsequent sovereigns.

The gift of £300 per annum, by King William, was for some time directed to be applied for extinguishing the college debts, and supporting four Bursars. By a subsequent deed of Queen Anne, in the year 1713, part of it was continued for the said purposes; and the remainder appropriated for salaries to a Professor of Civil Law, and a Professor of Medicine.

His Majesty King George I. was pleased to grant, out of the rents of the archbishopric, a new gift of £170 per annum; which was appropriated for a salary to a Professor of Ecclesiastical History, and for augmenting the smaller salaries of the other professors. By these royal donations, the whole of the rent paid by the College, for the lease of the archbishopric, is exhausted; and regular accompts thereof are transmitted to the Exchequer.

Since that time, there has been one profession added to this University, by the bounty of King George II.

Alexander Macfarlane, Esq., of Jamaica, had erected an astronomical observatory in that island for his own use. At his death, he bequeathed his astronomical apparatus to the College of Glasgow, on condition that

* The visiters of the college of Glasgow were, the Archbishop of Glasgow, the Bishop of Galloway; of the nobility, Hamilton, Montrose, Argyle, Kilmarnock, Cochran; besides gentlemen and clergy.

they should build an observatory, and appoint an observer. The College very readily accepted the condition, and built an observatory; and, in the year 1760, his Majesty was pleased to grant a presentation to Dr Alexander Wilson, to be Professor of Practical Astronomy and Observer, with a salary of £50 yearly out of the Exchequer.

It will not be expected that we should enumerate the donations made by subjects: of books or prints to the public library, or money to purchase books—of money for prizes to the more deserving students in the several classes—of money for carrying on the buildings—of money, or land, for the foundation of bursars in philosophy, in theology, and in medicine. The names of many of these benefactors are now little known but in the annals of the University of Glasgow, where they will always be preserved. Some may be mentioned, whose attention to the interest of this society does them honour. Among these are, Anne Duchess of Hamilton; Rahina, Countess of Forfar; William Earl of Dundonald; the Duke of Chandos; the Duke of Montrose; Dr Robert Leighton, Archbishop of Glasgow; and Boulter, Archbishop of Armagh. Of commoners—Mr Snell, Dr Williams, Dr Walton, and the late Dr William Hunter, are distinguished by the largeness of their donations.

VI. PRESENT STATE.

From the foregoing statement, it appears that the ancient constitution of the University of Glasgow, in the distribution of sciences and modes of teaching, as well as in the form of its government, was very similar to that of all the other universities of Europe. The alterations which it has undergone, in later times, are such as might be expected from the changes of opinion with respect to literary objects, and from other varying circumstances. The progress of knowledge, and the increasing demand for literature, have produced many additional departments of science, to those which were originally thought worthy of a particular teacher. What is called the *curriculum*, or ordinary course of public education, comprehends at present five branches—the Latin and Greek languages, Logic, Moral Philosophy, and Natural Philosophy. These branches are understood to require the study of five separate sessions.

During their attendance upon these courses of languages and philosophy, and particularly before they enter the class of natural philosophy, the students are expected to acquire a knowledge of Mathematics and Algebra, for which there is a separate Professor, and which is understood to be subservient to natural philosophy, and to many of the practical arts. There is also a Professor of Practical Astronomy, whose business is to make observations, for the improvement of that great branch of physics.

After the course of general education, above-mentioned, a provision is made for what are called the three learned professions—Divinity, Law, and Medicine. For the peculiar education of Churchmen, there are four Professors: the Principal, who is Primarius Professor of Theology, and has, besides, the superintendence of the whole University; and the respective Professors of Theology, of Oriental Languages, and of Church History. This last is also lecturer in Civil History.

In Law there is only one professor.

There are, by the constitution, no more than two professors allotted to the faculty of *Medicine*—to wit, a professor of the Theory and Practice of Medicine, and a professor of Anatomy and Botany. But the University, out of its funds, and with the assistance of private donations, has made an annual provision for three additional lecturers—in Chemistry, in Materia Medica, and in Midwifery.

The University has now the prospect of a great and important addition being soon made to the faculty of Medicine. The late Rev. Dr Walton, of Upton, in Huntingdonshire, about twenty years ago, in a tour to Scotland, visited the University of Glasgow; and, approving of its constitution and mode of conducting education, gave to the University £400 sterling; the interest of which, at his death, he appropriated for the support of a medical student during the course of his education. About five years ago, the same generous benefactor mortified the additional sum of £1000 sterling, at his death, to the University, for the purpose of supporting a lecturer in any branch of medicine, or of science connected with medicine, which the University should judge most expedient or necessary. By the Doctor's death, which happened about three years ago, both these donations now take effect.

Miss Christian Brisbane, sister of the late Dr Brisbane, Professor of Medicine in this University, mortified the sum of £1000 sterling; the interest of which she appropriated for the support of a medical student, two years at this University, and other two years at any other celebrated school of medicine in Britain, or on the Continent, as the University shall direct.

The late celebrated Dr William Hunter, of London, formerly an alumnus of this University, and, during the whole of his life, warmly attached to its interests, bequeathed to the University, at his death, the whole of his Museum, one of the most valuable collections in Europe, of Natural

History, Medals, Anatomical Preparations, Books, &c. When this collection has continued a certain number of years at London, he has, by his will, directed it to be carried to the University of Glasgow. And, for the purpose of building a house for the reception of this noble donation, and establishing such new professions in medicine as the University should judge expedient, he bequeathed £8000 sterling, bearing interest from his death; the one-half of which he directed to be applied for the support of the said Museum, while it continues in London—the other, to increase the principal sum, till the period arrive when both principal and interest shall be appropriated, by the University, for the above-mentioned purposes specified in the deed of donation.

Infirmary.—The progress of a medical school, in this University, has been hitherto much retarded by the want of an infirmary in Glasgow. But there is at present a prospect of that obstacle being immediately removed. A very considerable sum of money has been lately raised, by voluntary subscription, for the purpose of erecting and supporting an infirmary in Glasgow. A royal charter has been obtained, and a grant from the Crown, of the site of the Archbishop's Castle, for the buildings; which, according to a beautiful design, given by the late Robert Adam, Esq., are now finished.

Appointments of the Professors.—The Principal, and the Professors of Church History, Law, Medicine, Anatomy and Botany, and Astronomy, are nominated by the King. The Professors of Theology, Oriental Languages, Humanity, Greek, Logic, Moral Philosophy, Natural Philosophy, and Mathematics, and the Lecturers on Chemistry, Materia Medica, and Midwifery, are nominated by the College. The average number of students, of all denominations, attending the different classes, is considerably above six hundred.

Salaries, &c.—From the state of the university funds, the professors are allowed very moderate salaries; so as to depend chiefly for subsistence upon the *honorariums*, or fees of their students. This, it is believed, has greatly promoted their zeal and their diligence in their several professions. In seminaries of literature, possessed of rich endowments, and where there is access to large ecclesiastical benefices, by seniority, the business of lecturing has generally gone into disuse, or been reduced to a mere matter of form; as few persons are willing to labour, who, by doing little, or by following their amusement, find themselves in easy and comfortable circumstances. The department of teaching is likely, in such a case, to be devolved upon the junior members of the society, who discharge the office of private tutors; and who, from the moment they enter upon their office, are ready to consider it as a passing state, and to look forward to that period when they shall, in their turn, be freed from the drudgery of teaching. In such circumstances, when neither the tutor nor pupil is under the immediate eye of the public, instead of struggling for distinction and superiority in their respective stations, they will be too apt to indulge the laziness, and to gratify the peculiar humour of each other. In the Scottish universities, and particularly that of Glasgow, where the professors have no benefices in the church, nor any emoluments of any kind independent of their labour, nor anything that can be called preferment within their reach, that radical defect in the conduct of education is altogether removed. There is likely to grow up with them, in these circumstances, a habitual liking to their objects and occupations, and that interest and zeal in the discharge of their duty, which are most likely to call forth the activity and industry of their pupils.

It may be thought, perhaps, that, as necessity is the parent of labour, it would be a still greater improvement, that professors in colleges should have no salaries at all. This would be indisputable, if all other employments were left to the natural profit which they can produce, and were not peculiarly rewarded by fixed appointments from the public. But if one trade, or art, is allowed a bounty, another must, upon this account, have also some compensation. The peculiar premiums given by Government to other professions, particularly to the church and the law, seem to require, that, for maintaining some kind of balance, a degree of similar encouragement should be given to the teaching of the liberal arts and sciences. Without this, a private academy can seldom collect a sufficient number of well qualified teachers, so as to prevent a single individual from undertaking too many branches, and becoming what is vulgarly called a *Jack of all trades.*

Time of Lecturing, &c.—The uniform assiduity of the professors in the University of Glasgow, and the length of time which they employ in lecturing, will afford an illustration of these remarks. The annual session for teaching, in the university, begins, in the ordinary *curriculum*, on the tenth of October; and ends, in some of the classes, about the middle of May, and in others continues to the tenth of June. The lectures, in all the other branches, commence on the first of November, and end about the beginning of May. The class of Botany begins on the first of May.

During this period, the business of the College continues without interruption. The Professors of Humanity, or Latin, and of

Greek, lecture and examine their students, receive and correct exercises, three hours every day, and four hours for two days every week: the professors of Logic, Moral Philosophy, and Natural Philosophy, two hours every day, and three hours during a part of the session; excepting on Saturdays, when, on account of a general meeting of the public students, there is only one lecture given. The other professors lecture, in general, one hour every day; the Professor of Mathematics, two hours every day, except on Saturdays; the Professor of Law, in his public department, two hours. The Professor of Practical Astronomy gives no public lecture.

Advantages of Public Lecturing.—In those universities where the professors are uniformly employed in lecturing, it may be expected that the matter of their lectures will correspond, in some measure, to the general progress of science and literature in their several departments. A professor whose consequence and livelihood depend upon the approbation given by the public to his lectures, will find it necessary to study the principal authors upon the subject: he will imbibe, in some degree, the taste of the age in which he lives, and avail himself of the increase of knowledge and new discovery: he will find it expedient to model his instructions in the manner most likely to suit the purposes and to promote the interest of his students. By going frequently over the same subject, he has a chance to correct the erroneous opinions which he might formerly have admitted; and, according to the scale of his understanding, to attain the most liberal and comprehensive views of his science. If he is possessed, at the same time, of taste and abilities, he can hardly avoid acquiring an enthusiastic attachment to the objects of his profession, and an ardent desire of propagating those improvements in it which appear to him of importance.

In colleges where no lectures are given, and where the reading and prelecting on certain books, in a private manner, make the chief object of the teacher, the same dispositions and views will seldom occur. The professor, having little temptation to study, in any particular manner, that science with which he is *nominally* connected, will be apt to possess but a superficial knowledge of it, and to have little zeal in communicating new ideas or discoveries concerning it. In such a situation, the prejudices and contracted views of literature, which formerly prevailed, and which were natural upon the immediate revival of letters, may remain to the present day; and the name of *scholar* be restricted to a mere proficient in the Greek and Roman languages, the *vehicles* only of taste and knowledge: the pursuits of philosophy may be regarded as idle and chimerical; and every attempt to dissipate the clouds of ancient ignorance, or to correct the errors and prejudices of a former period, may be reprobated as a *dangerous innovation*.

The distribution of science, and the course of lectures, formerly established in all the universities of Europe, were almost exclusively adapted to the education of churchmen, and proceeded upon a much more limited state of knowledge than that which obtains at present. To accommodate instruction, therefore, to the purposes and views of the nation at large, and to render the academical course useful in every situation, it is frequently necessary, in those universities where any part of the old plan is retained, that the professors should now treat their respective subjects in a different manner, and that what is comprehended under particular branches should be greatly varied and extended.

Latin.—In the University of Glasgow, the students, who attend the Humanity lectures, are supposed to have acquired the elements of the Latin tongue, in public or private schools; and the Professor is employed in reading, explaining, and prelecting upon such Roman authors as are most suited to carry on their progress in that language. To a class of more advanced students, the Professor reads a course of lectures on the peculiarities and beauties of the Roman language, on the principles of classical composition, and on Roman antiquities.

Greek.—In the ancient state of the University, it was probably not usual for any person to study under the professor of Greek, until he had acquired some previous knowledge of the Greek language. But, as Greek is now seldom regularly taught in public schools, the Professor is under the necessity of instructing a great number in the very elements of that language. To a second set, who have made some proficiency in that respect, he is employed in reading, explaining, and prelecting upon those classical authors from an acquaintance with whom his hearers are most likely to imbibe a knowledge of Greek, and, at the same time, to improve their taste in literary composition. To a still more advanced set of students, he also delivers a course of lectures on the higher branches of Greek literature, introducing a variety of disquisitions on the general principles of grammar, of which the regular structure of that language affords such copious illustration.

Philosophy.—In the threefold distribution of Philosophy, in the academical course,

Logic has, in general, preceded the other two in the order of teaching, and has been considered as a necessary preparation for them. Before the student entered upon the subjects of moral and natural philosophy, it was thought proper to instruct him in the art of reasoning and disputation; and the syllogsitic art, taken from the Analytics of Aristotle, was, for many ages, considered as the most effectual and infallible instrument for that purpose. It was supposed to afford a mechanical mode of reasoning, by which, in all cases, truth and falsehood might be accurately distinguished. [?] But the change of opinions on the subjects of literature, and on the means of comprehending them, has occasioned a correspondent alteration in the manner of treating this part of the academical course. The present Professor, after a short analysis of the powers of the understanding, and an explanation of the terms necessary to comprehend the subjects of his course, gives a historical view of the rise and progress of the art of reasoning, and particularly of the syllogistic method, which is rendered a matter of curiosity by the universal influence which for a long time it obtained over the learned world; and then dedicates the greater part of his time to an illustration of the various mental operations, as they are expressed by the several modifications of speech and writing; which leads him to deliver a system of lectures on general grammar, rhetoric, and belles lettres. This course, accompanied with suitable exercises and specimens, on the part of the students, is properly placed at the entrance to philosophy: no subjects are likely to be more interesting to young minds, at a time when their taste and feelings are beginning to open, and have naturally disposed them to the reading of such authors as are necessary to supply them with facts and materials for beginning and carrying on the important habits of reflection and investigation.

Moral Philosophy.—The lectures in the *Moral Philosophy* class consist of three principal divisions. The first comprehends natural theology; or the knowledge, confirmed by human reason, concerning the being, perfections, and operations of God. The second comprehends ethics; or inquiries concerning the active powers of man, and the regulation of them, both in the pursuit of happiness, and in the practice of virtue; and, consequently, those questions that have been agitated concerning good and evil, right and wrong. The third comprehends natural jurisprudence, or the general rules of justice, which are founded upon the rights and the condition of man; whether considered as an individual, or as a member of a family, or as a member of some of those various forms of government which have arisen from the social combinations of mankind.

Natural Philosophy.—The lectures in *Natural Philosophy* comprehend a general system of *physics*; and are calculated, in like manner, to keep pace with those leading improvements and discoveries, in that branch of science, by which the present age is so much distinguished. The theoretical and experimental parts make the subjects of two separate courses. The apparatus for conducting the latter is believed not to be inferior to any in Europe.

Mathematics.—The Professor of *Mathematics* has three separate courses. The first comprehends the elements of geometry and algebra; the second, the higher parts of those sciences; the third, the general principles of geometry and astronomy. To teach the application of the speculative doctrines to the various practical arts, makes a very important object in this useful department of education.

Theology.—In the faculty of Theology, the respective Professors of *Theology*, *Church History*, and *Oriental Languages*, deliver a system of lectures on natural and revealed religion, on the history of the church, and on the Hebrew language. In this faculty, no *honorarium* or *fee* is paid by the students.* If this regulation had been extended to all the sciences, it would probably have been fatal to academical activity; but, being limited to a single branch, it has been counteracted by the influence of the general industry and exertion which pervade the society. No deficiency, therefore, is imputable to the professors in this department, either with respect to their zeal in teaching, or with respect to those liberal and tolerating principles which are so conformable to the spirit and genius of Christianity.

Law.—The improvement of *Law* in this university, seems to have excited less attention from government than that of the other sciences, as this profession was not established till a late period, and as no provision has hitherto been made for dividing this branch of education among separate professors. The want of competition appears to have had the usual effects; and the custom of lecturing in Latin was longer retained in this than in the other sciences. The predecessor of the present professor was the first who prelected on Justinian's "Institutes," in English; and this example has, for many years, been followed in the prelections upon the pandects. It may be mentioned, as a strong instance of prepossession in favour of ancient usages, that, upon this last innovation, the Faculty of Advocates made application to the University of Glasgow, requesting "that the old practice of teaching the civil law in Latin

* Why, see above, p. 725, a. note *.—H.

might be restored." The Professor of Law, besides lecturing regularly upon the Institutes and Pandects of Justinian, delivers annually a course of lectures on the principles of civil government, including a particular account of the British constitution; and, every second year, a course of lectures on the law of Scotland.

Medicine.—The professors and lecturers in the medical department, it would appear, have been less limited than those in some of the other parts of literature, by the effect of old institutions and prejudices. They have thus been enabled to accommodate their lectures to the progress of knowledge and discovery, and to those high improvements which have of late years been introduced into all the sciences connected with the art of medicine. The progress of botany and natural history, and the wonderful discoveries in chemistry, have now extended the sphere of these useful branches beyond the mere purposes of the physician, and have rendered a competent knowledge of them highly interesting to every man of liberal education.

Improvements.—The University of Glasgow, as has been already observed, was anciently possessed of a jurisdiction similar to that of the other universities of Europe, and exercised a similar discipline and authority over its members. A great part of the students were accommodated with lodgings in the college, and dined at a common table, under the inspection of their teachers. While this mode of living continued, almost everything was the subject of restrictions and regulations. But, for a long time, this practice has been discontinued, and the severity of the ancient discipline has been a good deal relaxed. The lodgings in the college rooms, after the disuse of the common table, became less convenient; and, at present, no students live within the college, but a few of considerable standing, whose regularity of conduct is perfectly known and ascertained.

These deviations from the ancient usage were introduced from the experience of many inconveniences attending it. The common table, by collecting a multitude of students so frequently together, afforded encouragement and temptations to idleness and dissipation; and, though the masters sat at table along with the students, yet few advantages of conversation could be attained. Contrivances were fallen upon to remedy that defect, by appointing one of the students (generally a bursar, or servitor) to read a portion of Scripture, or of some useful book, while the rest of the students were at table. But this practice, it is obvious, in such circumstance, was more likely to bring ridicule upon the subjects, or at least to occasion indifference or contempt, than to be productive of improvement. Besides, from a general alteration in the habits and manners of the people, the academical rules, in these matters, were found troublesome both to the teachers and the students. Hence, attendance at the common table became a kind of drudgery to the masters, from which they endeavoured to escape, or to which they submitted in their turns with reluctance; while the students procured dispensations, or permissions to have their commons in their own apartments. This latter was found to be a source of expense and dissipation, not more unfriendly to literature than to morals. The common table, it is said, became a source of mismanagement and imposition, which could not easily be remedied.

This change in the mode of living has been attended with much comfort and satisfaction to all the members of the University, by superseding many strict regulations, and of course rigorous penalties, which, in the former situation, had been thought necessary: neither has it produced any bad effect upon the manners and behaviour of the students. When teachers are attentive to perform their duty, and discover an anxiety to promote the interests of their scholars, who are above the age of mere boys, it requires very little authority to enforce respect and propriety of behaviour. The most certain and effectual mode of discipline, or rather the best method of rendering discipline in a great measure useless, is by filling up regularly and properly the time of the student, by interesting him in the objects of his studies and pursuits, and by demanding, regularly and daily, an account of his labours.

Boarding.—In the present state of the University of Glasgow, such of the students as can afford the expense, frequently live in the families of the Principal and Professors; where they have, together with the opportunity of prosecuting their studies, the advantages of proper society and private tuition. It is, at the same time, in the power of every Professor, to be acquainted with the behaviour, the application, and the abilities of almost every one of his students. And the knowledge of this is likely to be much more effectual in exciting their exertions, and producing regular attention to their studies, than the endless penalties which may be contrived for every species of misdemeanour. A complicated and rigorous discipline, extending to innumerable frivolous observances, can hardly fail, in this age, to become contemptible; and, if students are treated like *children*, it is not to be expected that they will behave like *men*.

Weekly Meeting.—Every Saturday there is a general meeting of all the public or *gowned* students, which is attended by the Principal and their respective Professors. A Latin oration is delivered by the higher students, in their turns: after which, all smaller matters of discipline are discussed. By this weekly meeting, the whole of the students are brought, in a more particular manner, under the inspection of the teachers; and a good opportunity is regularly afforded of mutual information, respecting the studies and deportment of their scholars.

Tests not required.—No oaths, or subscriptions, or *tests* of any kind, are required of students, at their admission to the University; as it is deemed highly improper that young persons, in prosecuting a general course of academical education, should bind themselves to any particular system of tenets or opinions.

Bursaries. — Besides the salaries bestowed upon professors, additional encouragement has been often given to universities, by the mortification of certain funds for the maintenance of students; as also by requiring that a certain attendance shall be given, in those seminaries, by such as obtain academical degrees, accompanied with various exclusive privileges.

It has of late been remarked, that such institutions and regulations, though intended to promote the interest of those incorporated societies, have proved, in some degree, hurtful to them, by forcing an attendance from a greater number of students, and consequently tending to supersede the industry and abilities of the respective teachers. But the number of this description of students, commonly called *bursars*, at the University of Glasgow, cannot have any considerable tendency of this nature, as their *honorariums* make but a small part of the professor's income; and, it must not be overlooked, that the payment of fees to the professors supposes that lectures are to be given: so that this establishment encourages, at least, the practice of lecturing, however it may tend to produce carelessness in the performance. One good effect of it is obvious. Several of these bursaries are in the gift of the college; so that the principal and professors have it in their power to bestow them upon students of superior genius and industry, but who have not the means of prosecuting their studies. The character of a bursar does not, in the University of Glasgow, carry with it any external marks of servility, or degradation of any kind. Several names might be here mentioned, that would do great honour to the University, who were supported, during the course of their studies, by funds appropriated for that purpose.

The foundation by Mr Snell deserves particularly to be mentioned, as perhaps one of the largest and most liberal in Britain. That gentleman, in the year 1688, bequeathed a considerable estate in Warwickshire for the support of *Scotch students* at Baliol College, Oxford, who had studied for some years at the University of Glasgow. By the rise in the value of lands, and the improvements which have, from time to time, been made on that estate, that fund now affords £70 per annum, for ten years, to each of ten exhibitioners. Another foundation, at the same college, of £20 per annum, to each of four Scotch students, though under a different patronage, is generally given to the Glasgow *exhibitioners*; so that four of them have a stipend of £90 per annum, continuing for ten years. The University have the sole nomination or appointment of these exhibitioners.

Rules for obtaining Degrees.—The candidates for degrees in arts, are, by express regulations, obliged to attend the hours of lecture, and the separate hours of examination, in the *curriculum*, or public course already mentioned; and the laws of the church oblige all students to pass the same *curriculum* before they can be enrolled students of theology. But no such qualification is requisite for entering upon the study of law or medicine. Such students, in short, as are not upon any public foundation, or who do not intend to qualify themselves for the church, may attend any of the lectures which they think most suited to their views; though, in case of their deviating from the *curriculum*, they have not the benefit of the regular examinations and exercises of the public students.

The rules, for conferring degrees, were formerly much the same in the University of Glasgow as in the other ancient universities. In those days, when the art of disputation was considered as the ultimate object of academical education, the candidates were obliged, after a certain standing, or residence at the University, to compose and print a thesis, and to defend it in a public syllogistic disputation. But experience discovered that mode of trial to be inadequate to the purpose for which it was intended. It, by degrees, degenerated into a mere matter of form and ceremony. The same subjects of disputation, the same arguments of attack and defence, were preserved and handed down among the students; the public disputations were not attended:—so that degrees became not the rewards of abilities and diligence, but merely the marks of standing, or residence at the University. These circumstances gave occasion for a material change, in the rules for conferring degrees, in the University of Glasgow. The composing and defending a thesis have now become optional on the part of the candidate. The same standing is still required; and the candidates for degrees in arts are obliged to undergo a minute examination, in the Greek and Roman classics, in the different branches of philosophy which compose the *curriculum*, and by each of the professors in their respective branches: an examination which, in the manner it is conducted, gives the best opportunity of judging of the proficiency and literature of the candidates.

Degrees in Theology and Law.—Degrees in theology, having no privileges in the church attached to them, under the Presbyterian form of government, are, without any regard to standing in the University, conferred on clergymen respectable for their abilities and literature.—Degrees in law are either bestowed upon eminent men as marks of respect; or upon students of a certain standing, after a regular examination of the candidate.——The University of Glasgow admits students who have passed a part of their academical course in other universities, *ad eundem*, as it is commonly called: that is, whatever part of their academical course is finished at any other university, upon proper certificates, is admitted, as a part of their standing, in the University of Glasgow; so that, without again beginning their course, they can pass forward to degrees, and be enrolled students of theology.

Medical Degrees.—Degrees in medicine are conferred, after having finished the medical course, at the University; or, upon proper certificates of having finished it at some eminent school of physic: but the candidates are obliged to undergo both a private and public examination, on all the different branches of medicine, before they can receive that honour. It is very common also for them, though not absolutely required, to defend a thesis in the common hall.

Prizes.—The institution of *Prizes*, or rewards of literary merit, either in books or medals, to students, during the course of their education, has now been tried for many years in the University of Glasgow, and has been attended with the best effects. Every effort has been made to correct the common defects and irregularities in the distribution of prizes, and to render the competition fair and equal. Subjects of competition are prescribed, calculated to give scope to every kind of genius, and accommodated to the standing of the different students.

Library.—The University *Library*, to which all the students have easy access, is a large and valuable collection of books, among which are many now become very scarce. As it was founded about two centuries ago, it is enriched with many early editions; and proper attention has been paid, from time to time, to supply it with the more elegant and improved productions of the press, particularly in the classical departments. The funds which are destined for its support and increase, are considerable; and many private donations of books have been made to it from time to time. It was of late greatly enriched, in the mathematical department, by the library of the late celebrated Dr Robert Simson, professor of mathematics. By the ingenuity of the late Dr Wilson & Sons, type-founders, and the care and accuracy of the late Messrs Foulis, printers to the University, the Library contains some of the most elegant editions of many valuable books. It will soon receive an important addition, by a collection of many rare and splendid editions of books, in all the different departments of science, but particularly in the medical department, bequeathed by the late Dr William Hunter.

Antiquities.—In an adjoining apartment, the college has placed a number of *mile-stones*, *altars*, and other *remains of antiquity*, which have been discovered in the ancient Roman wall between the Forth and the Clyde.

Worship.—During the session, there is public worship every Sunday in the college chapel. Three or four preachers are annually appointed out of the number of those students who continue at the university after they have received their license. The Principal, and such of the Professors as have been ordained, or have received licenses, occasionally preach in the college chapel during the session.

Landed Property, &c.—The college, though in some measure surrounded by the houses of the town, is possessed of more than twenty acres of ground adjacent to its buildings. Upon the most distant part of this ground, and upon a small eminence, is erected the Observatory, properly fitted up, and supplied with the most improved instruments for the purposes of the Professor of Practical Astronomy. The college buildings, though not splendid, are neat and commodious. The Principal and all the Professors possess convenient houses contiguous to the other public buildings. These buildings are surrounded by a *garden* of about ten acres, appropriated to the use of the members of the University, and some part of it for exercise to the younger classes of students.

VII. CONCLUSION.

Upon the whole, this University, after experiencing many revolutions and turns of fortune, has, by favourable conjunctures, and by the bounty of the sovereign and of the public, been raised to prosperous circumstances: and has, as an academical foundation, become possessed of some conspicuous advantages. *Its local situation*, in the neighbourhood of an industrious city, and at some distance from the capital; by which it is not exposed to the dissipation arising from a number of amusements; nor too remote from the topics of speculation, suggested by the progress of philosophy, and the interesting business of society. *The state of its revenue*, sufficient, with economy, in the management of the society, to promote useful improvements; but not so large as to be productive of idleness, and the luxury of learned indolence. *Its institutions and government*, by which no sort of monopoly is created in favour of particular sects, or particular branches of science; but persons of all persuasions are at liberty to follow that course of study which they find suited to their various pursuits and prospects. Lastly, *Its moderate discipline*, endeavouring to regulate the behaviour of the students by a regard to interest and reputation, more than by *authority*; and substituting the anxious watchfulness of a parent, in place of the troublesome and vexatious interpositions of a prying and, perhaps, unpopular magistrate.

ADDITIONS.*

Infirmary.—The medical school in this University was long retarded by the want of an infirmary at Glasgow. But that obstacle is now completely removed. In the year 1790, a voluntary subscription was opened, for the purpose of erecting and supporting an infirmary, in this place, for the western districts of Scotland. This scheme met with the most liberal encouragement, from the charitable and well-disposed in the city of Glasgow, and in the adjoining counties, and was, in particular, much promoted by the activity and influence of the members of the University. In the year 1791, upon the petition of the subscribers, a royal charter was obtained from the Crown, together with a grant of the site of the Archbishop's castle and garden, for the purpose of erecting the buildings. During the years 1792 and 1793, the buildings were erected, according to a most beautiful design given by the late Robert Adam, Esq., architect, at an expense of about £8000; and it is believed, that, in point of situation, good air, abundance of water, and convenient accommodation for the patients, this infirmary is not excelled by any other establishment of the same kind in Britain. The infirmary was opened for the reception of patients on the 8th December 1794; and since that time, the beneficial and salutary effects of it have been so much felt that it is now considered as a public benefit and blessing to this part of the country. Among other advantages, the number of medical students is greatly increased since it was opened; and there is every reason to believe, that this institution will contribute, in a great degree, to the further extension and improvement of the medical school in this University.

P. 732, b: The Rev. Dr Walton's first donation was *anno* 1767, and his second *anno* 1788. P. 736, a, l. 8: After *Scotland*, add, "to which is now added a course of lectures on English law."

* Not by Reid.—H

DISSERTATIONS,

HISTORICAL, CRITICAL,

AND

SUPPLEMENTARY,

BY

THE EDITOR.

SUPPLEMENTARY DISSERTATIONS;

OR

EXCURSIVE NOTES,

CRITICAL AND HISTORICAL.

NOTE A.

ON THE PHILOSOPHY OF COMMON SENSE;

OR

OUR PRIMARY BELIEFS

CONSIDERED AS THE ULTIMATE CRITERION OF TRUTH.

§ I.—*The meaning of the doctrine, and purport of the argument, of Common Sense.*

§ II.—*The conditions of the legitimacy, and legitimate application, of the argument.*

§ III.—*That it is one strictly philosophical and scientific.*

§ IV.—*The essential characters by which our primary beliefs, or the principles of Common Sense, are discriminated.*

§ V.—*The nomenclature, that is, the various appellations by which these have been designated.*

§ VI.—*The universality of the philosophy of Common Sense; or its general recognition, in reality and in name, shown by a chronological series of testimonies from the dawn of speculation to the present day.*

[References.—On *Common Sense* from Inq. 96 b, 209 b, I. P. 233 a, 421 b, 468 b, see passim, and § V. i. 1—§ VI. No. 63;—on *Instinct* from Inq. 184 b, &c., see § V. ii. 3;—on *Belief* from Inq. 95 b, &c., see § V. ii. 3;—on *Reason* from Inq. 100 b, 108 a, 127 ab, see § V. ix. 7.]

§ *I.—The meaning of the doctrine, and purport of the argument, of Common Sense.*

In the conception and application of the doctrine of Common Sense, the most signal mistakes have been committed; and much unfounded prejudice has been excited against the argument which it affords, in consequence of the erroneous views which have been held in regard to its purport and conditions. What is the veritable character of this doctrine, it is, therefore, necessary to consider.

Our cognitions, it is evident, are not all at second hand. Consequents cannot, by an infinite regress, be evolved out of antecedents, which are themselves only consequents. Demonstration, if proof be possible, behoves to repose at last on propositions, which carrying their own evidence, necessitate their own admission; and which being, as primary, inexplicable, as inexplicable, incomprehensible, must consequently manifest themselves less in the character of cognitions than of *facts*, of which consciousness assures us under the simple form of *feeling* or *belief*.

Without at present attempting to determine the character, number, and relations—waiving, in short, all attempt at an articulate analysis and classification of the primary elements of cognition, as carrying us into a discussion beyond our limits, and not of indispensable importance for the end we have in view;* it is sufficient to have it conceded, in general, *that such elements there are*; and this concession of their existence being supposed, I shall proceed to hazard some observations, principally in regard to their authority as warrant and criteria of truth. Nor can this assumption of the existence of some original bases of knowledge in the mind itself, be refused by any. For even those philosophers who profess to derive all our knowledge from experience, and who admit no universal truths of intelligence but such as are generalized from individual truths of fact—even these philosophers are forced virtually to acknowledge, at the root of the several acts of observation from which their generalization starts, some law or principle to which they can appeal as guaranteeing the procedure, should the validity of these primordial acts themselves be called in question. This acknowledgment is, among others, made even by Locke; and on such fundamental guarantee of induction he even bestows the name of Common Sense. (See below, in Testimonies, No. 51.)

Limiting, therefore, our consideration to the question of authority; how, it is asked, do these primary propositions—these cognitions at first hand—these fundamental facts, feelings, beliefs, certify us of their own veracity? To this the only possible answer is—that as elements of our mental constitution—as the essential conditions of our knowledge—they *must* by us be accepted as true. To suppose their falsehood, is to suppose that we are created capable of intelligence, in order to be made the victims of delusion; that God is a deceiver, and the root of our nature a lie. But such a supposition, if gratuitous, is manifestly illegitimate. For, on the contrary, the data of our original consciousness must, it is evident, *in the first instance*, be presumed true. It is only if proved false, that their authority can, in *consequence of that proof*, be, in the second instance, disallowed. Speaking, therefore, generally, to argue from common sense, is simply to show, that the denial of a given proposition would involve the denial of some original datum of consciousness; but as every original datum of consciousness is to be presumed true, that the proposition in question, as dependent on such a principle, must be admitted.

But that such an argument is competent and conclusive, must be more articulately shown.

Here, however, at the outset, it is proper to take a distinction, (to which in the foot-notes I have once and again adverted,) the neglect of which has been productive of considerable error and confusion. It is the distinction between the data or deliverances of consciousness considered sim-

* Such an analysis and classification is however in itself certainly one of the most interesting and important problems of philosophy; and it is one in which much remains to be accomplished. Principles of cognition, which now stand as ultimate, may, I think, be reduced to simpler elements; and some which are now viewed as direct and positive, may be shewn to be merely indirect and negative; their cogency depending not on the immediate necessity of thinking them—for if carried unconditionally out they are themselves incogitable—but in the impossibility of thinking something to which they are directly opposed, and from which they are the immediate recoils. An exposition of the axiom—That positive thought lies in the limitation or conditioning of one or other of two opposite extremes, neither of which, as unconditioned, can be realized to the mind as possible, and yet of which, as contradictories, one or other must, by the fundamental laws of thought, be recognised as necessary;—the exposition of this great but unnoticed axiom would show that some of the most illustrious principles are only its subordinate modifications, as applied to certain primary notions, intuitions, data, forms, or categories of intelligence, as Existence, Quantity, (protensive, Time—extensive, Space—intensive, Degree) Quality, &c. Such modifications, for example, are the principles of Cause and Effect, Substance and Phænomenon, &c.

I may here also observe, that though *the primary truths of fact*, and the *primary truths of intelligence* (the *contingent* and *necessary* truths of Reid) form two very distinct classes of the original beliefs or intuitions of consciousness; there appears no sufficient ground to regard their sources as different, and therefore to be distinguished by different names. In this I regret that I am unable to agree with Mr Stewart. See his Elements, vol. ii., ch. 1, and his Account of Reid, supra, p. 77 b.

ply, *in themselves, as apprehended facts or actual manifestations*, and those deliverances considered *as testimonies to the truth of facts beyond their own phænomenal reality*.

Viewed under the former limitation, they are above all scepticism. For as doubt is itself only a manifestation of consciousness, it is impossible to doubt that, what consciousness manifests, it does manifest, without, in thus doubting, doubting that we actually doubt; that is, without the doubt contradicting and therefore annihilating itself. Hence it is that the facts of consciousness, as mere phænomena, are by the unanimous confession of all Sceptics and Idealists, ancient and modern, placed high above the reach of question. Thus, *Laertius*, in Pyrrh. L. ix., seg. 103;—*Sextus Empiricus*, Pyrrh. Hypot. L. i. cc. 4, 10, et passim;—*Descartes*, Med., ii., pp. 13, and iii., p. 16, ed. 1658;—*Hume*, Treatise on Human Nature, vol. i., pp. 123, 370, et alibi, orig. ed.;—*Schulze*, Aenesidemus, p. 24, Kritik, vol. i., p. 51;—*Platner*, Aphor., vol. i. § 708;—*Reinhold*, Theorie, p. 190;—*Schad*, in Fichte's Philos. Jour., vol. x., p. 270. See also *St. Austin*, Contra Academ., L. iii., c. 11; De Trin. L. xv, c. 112;—*Scotus*, in Sent., L. i., dist. 3, qu. 4, 10;—*Buffier*, Prem. Verit., § 9—11, 40;—*Mayne's* Essay on Consciousness, p. 177, *sq.*;—*Reid*, p. 442, b. et alibi;—*Cousin*, Cours d' Hist. de la Philosophie Morale, vol. ii., pp 220, 236.

On this ground, St Austin was warranted in affirming—*Nihil intelligenti tam notum esse quam se sentire, se cogitare, se velle, se vivere;* and the *cogito ergo sum* of Descartes is a valid assertion, that in so far as we are *conscious* of certain modes of existence, in so far we possess an absolute certainty that we really exist. (*Aug.*, De Lib. Arb. ii., 3; De Trin., x., 3; De Civ. Dei., xi., 26; *Desc.*, ll. cc., et passim.)

Viewed under the latter limitation, the deliverances of consciousness do not thus peremptorily repel even the possibility of doubt. I am conscious, for example, in an act of sensible perception, 1°, of myself, the subject knowing; and, 2°, of some thing given as different from myself, the object known. To take the second term of this relation:—that I am conscious in this act of an object given, *as a non-ego*—that is, *as not a modification of my mind*—of this, *as a phænomenon*, doubt is impossible. For, as has been seen, we cannot doubt the actuality of a fact of consciousness without doubting, that is subverting, our doubt itself. To this extent, therefore, all scepticism is precluded. But though it cannot but be admitted that the object of which we are conscious in this cognition is given, not *as* a mode of self, but *as* a mode of something different from self, it is however possible for us to suppose, without our supposition at least being *felo de se*, that, though *given as* a non-ego, this object may, *in reality, be* only a *representation* of a *non-ego*, in and by the *ego*. Let this therefore be maintained: let the *fact* of the testimony be admitted, but the *truth* of the testimony, to aught beyond its own ideal existence, be doubted or denied. How in this case are we to proceed? It is evident that the doubt does not in this, as in the former case, refute itself. It is not suicidal by self contradiction. The idealist, therefore, in denying the existence of an external world, as more than a subjective phænomon of the internal, does not advance a doctrine ab initio null, as a scepticism would be which denied the phænomena of the internal world itself. Yet many distinguished philosophers have fallen into this mistake; and, among others, both Dr Reid, probably, and Mr Stewart, certainly. The latter in his Philosophical Essays (pp. 6, 7) explicitly states, "that the belief which accompanies consciousness, as to the present existence of its appropriate phænomena, rests on no foundation more solid than our belief of the existence of external objects." Reid does not make any declaration so explicit, but the same doctrine seems involved in various of his criticisms of Hume and of Descartes (Inq pp. 100 a., 129, 130; Int. Pow., pp. 269 a., 442 b.) Thus (p. 100 a) he reprehends the latter for maintaining that consciousness affords a higher assurance of the reality of the internal phænomenn, than sense affords of the reality of the external. He asks—Why did Descartes not attempt a proof of the existence of his thought? and if consciousness be alleged as avouching this, he asks again,—Who is to be our voucher that consciousness may not deceive us? My observations on this point, which were printed above three years ago, in the foot-notes at pp. 129 and 442 b., I am happy to find confirmed by the authority of M. Cousin. The following passage is from his Lectures on the Scottish School, constituting the second volume of his "Course on the History of the Moral Philosophy of the Eighteenth Century," delivered in the years 1819, 1820, but only recently published by M. Vacherot. "It is not (he observes in reference to the preceding strictures of Reid upon Descartes) as a fact attested by consciousness, that Descartes declares his personal existence beyond a doubt; it is because the negation of this fact would involve a contradiction." And after quoting the relative passage from Descartes: —"It is thus by a reasoning that Descartes establishes the existence of the thinking subject; if he admit this existence, it is not because it is guaranteed by consciousness; it is for this reason, that when he thinks —let him deceive himself or not—he exists in so far as he thinks." P. 236. See also p. 219, *sq.*

It is therefore manifest that we may throw wholly out of account the phænomena of consciousness, considered merely in themselves; seeing that scepticism in regard to them, under this limitation, is confessedly impossible; and that it is only requisite to consider the argument from Common Sense, as it enables us to vindicate the truth of these phænomena, viewed as attestations of more than their own existence, seeing that they are not, in this respect, placed beyond the possibility of doubt.

When, for example, consciousness assures us that, in perception, we are immediately cognizant of an external and extended non-ego; or that, in remembrance, through the imagination, of which we are immediately cognizant, we obtain a mediate knowledge of a real past; how shall we repel the doubt—in the former case, that what is given as the extended reality itself is not merely a representation of matter by mind;—in the latter, that what is given as a mediate knowledge of the past, is not a mere present phantasm, containing an illusive reference to an unreal past? We can do this only in one way. The legitimacy of such gratuitous doubt necessarily supposes that the deliverance of consciousness *is not to be presumed true.* If therefore it can be shown, on the one hand, that the deliverances of consciousness must philosophically be accepted, *until* their certain or probable falsehood has been positively evinced; and if, on the other hand, it cannot be shown that any attempt to discredit the veracity of consciousness has ever yet succeeded; it follows that, as philosophy now stands, the testimony of consciousness must be viewed as high above suspicion, and its declarations entitled to demand prompt and unconditional assent.

In the first place, as has been said, it cannot but be acknowledged that the veracity of consciousness must, at least in the first instance, be conceded. "Neganti incumbit probatio." Nature is not gratuitously to be assumed to work, not only in vain, but in counteraction of herself; our faculty of knowledge is not, without a ground, to be supposed an instrument of illusion; man, unless the melancholy fact be proved, is not to be held organized for the attainment, and actuated by the love, of truth, only to become the dupe and victim of a perfidious creator.

But, in the second place, though the veracity of the primary convictions of consciousness must, in the outset, be admitted, it still remains competent to lead a proof that they are undeserving of credit. But how is this to be done? As the ultimate grounds of knowledge, these convictions cannot be redargued from any higher knowledge; and as original beliefs, they are paramount in certainty to every derivative assurance. But they are many; they are, in authority, co-ordinate; and their testimony is clear and precise. It is therefore competent for us to view them in correlation; to compare their declarations; and to consider whether they contradict, and, by contradicting, invalidate each other. This mutual contradiction is possible, in two ways. 1°, It may be that the *primary data themselves* are directly or immediately contradictory of each other; 2°, it may be that they are mediately or indirectly contradictory, in as much as the *consequences* to which they *necessarily* lead, and for the truth or falsehood of which they are therefore responsible, are mutually repugnant. By evincing either of these, the veracity of consciousness will be disproved; for in either case consciousness is shown to be inconsistent with itself, and consequently inconsistent with the unity of truth. But by no other process of demonstration is this possible. For it will argue nothing against the trustworthiness of consciousness, that all or any of its deliverances are inexplicable—are incomprehensible; that is, that we are unable to conceive through a higher notion, how that is possible, which the deliverance avouches actually to be. To make the comprehensibility of a datum of consciousness the criterion of its truth, would be indeed the climax of absurdity. For the primary data of consciousness, as themselves the conditions under which all else is comprehended, are necessarily themselves incomprehensible. We know, and can know, only—*That* they *are*, not—*How* they *can* be. To ask how an immediate fact of consciousness is possible, is to ask how consciousness is possible; and to ask how consciousness is possible, is to suppose that we have another consciousness, before and above that human consciousness, concerning whose mode of operation we inquire. Could we answer this, "verily we should be as gods."*

To take an example:—It would be unreasonable in the Cosmothetic or the Absolute Idealist, to require of the Natural Realist† a reason, through which to understand how a self can be conscious of a not-self—how an unextended subject can be cognizant of an extended object; both of which are given us as facts by consciousness, and, as such, founded on by the Natural Realist. This is unreasonable, because it is incompetent to demand the explanation of a datum of consciousness, which, as original and simple, is necessarily beyond analysis and explication. It is still further unreasonable, in as much as all philosophy being only a development of the primary data of consciousness, any philosophy, in not accepting the truth of these, pro tanto surrenders its own possibility—is felo de se. But at the hands of the Cosmothetic Idealists—and they constitute the great majority of philosophers—the question is peculiarly absurd; for before proposing it, they are themselves bound to afford a solution of the far more insuperable difficulties which their own hypothesis involves—difficulties which, so far from attempting to solve, no Hypothetical Realist has ever yet even articulately stated. For the illustration of this, I must refer the reader to an article "On the Philosophy of Perception," Edinburgh Review, vol. lii., p. 175—181; to be found also in Cross's Selections, and Peisse's Fragments.

This being understood, the following propositions are either self-evident, or admit of easy proof:—

1. The end of philosophy is truth; and consciousness is the instrument and criterion of its acquisition. In other words, philosophy is the development and application of the constitutive and normal truths which consciousness immediately reveals.

2. Philosophy is thus wholly dependent upon consciousness; the possibility of the former supposing the trustworthiness of the latter.

3. Consciousness is to be presumed trustworthy, until proved mendacious.

4. The mendacity of consciousness is proved, if its data, immediately in themselves, or mediately in their necessary consequences, be shown to stand in mutual contradiction.

5. The immediate or mediate repugnance of any two of its data being established, the presumption in favour of the general veracity of consciousness is abolished, or rather reversed. For while, on the one hand, all that is not contradictory is not therefore true; on the other, a positive proof of falsehood, in one instance, establishes a presumption of probable falsehood in all; for the maxim, "*falsus in uno, falsus in omnibus*," must determine the credibility of consciousness, as the credibility of every other witness.

6. No attempt to show that the data of consciousness are (either in themselves, or in their necessary consequences) mutually contradictory, has yet succeeded: and the presumption in favour of the truth of consciousness and the possibility of philosophy has, therefore, never been redargued. In other words, an original, universal, dogmatic subversion of knowledge has hitherto been found impossible.

7. No philosopher has ever formally denied the truth or disclaimed the authority of consciousness; but few or none have been content implicitly to accept and consistently to follow out its dictates. Instead of humbly resorting to consciousness, to draw from thence his doctrines and their proof, each dogmatic speculator looked only into consciousness, there to discover his preadopted opinions. In philosophy, men have abused the code of natural, as in theology, the code of positive, revelation; and the epigraph of a great protestant divine, on the book of scripture, is certainly not less applicable to the book of consciousness:

"*Hic liber est in quo quærit sua dogmata quisque; Invenit, et pariter dogmata quisque sua.*"

8. The first and most obtrusive consequence of this procedure has been, the multiplication of philosophical systems in every conceivable aberration from the unity of truth.

9. The second, but less obvious, consequence has been, the virtual surrender, by each several system, of the possibility of philosophy in general. For, as the possibility of philosophy supposes the absolute truth of consciousness, every system which proceeded on the hypothesis, that even a single deliverance of consciousness is untrue, did, however it might eschew the

* From what has now been stated, it will be seen how far and on what grounds I hold, at one with Dr Reid and Mr Stewart, that our original beliefs are to be established, but their authority not to be canvassed; and with M. Jouffroy, that the question of their authority is not to be absolutely withdrawn, as a forbidden problem, from philosophy.—*See Preface*

† On these terms, see in the sequel of this § p. 748, b. sq. and Note C, § 1.

overt declaration, thereby invalidate the general credibility of consciousness, and supply to the sceptic the premises be required to subvert philosophy, in so far as that system represented it.

10. And yet, although the past history of philosophy has, in a great measure, been only a history of variation and error (*variasse erroris est*); yet the cause of this variation being known, we obtain a valid ground of hope for the destiny of philosophy in future. Because, since philosophy has hitherto been inconsistent with itself, only in being inconsistent with the dictates of our natural beliefs—

"For Truth is catholic and Nature one;"

it follows, that philosophy has simply to return to natural consciousness, to return to unity and truth.

In doing this we have only to attend to the three following maxims or precautions:—

1°, That we admit nothing, not either an original datum of consciousness, or the legitimate consequence of such a datum;

2°, That we embrace all the original data of consciousness, and all their legitimate consequences; and

3°, That we exhibit each of these in its individual integrity, neither distorted nor mutilated, and in its relative place, whether of pre-eminence or subordination.

Nor can it be contended that consciousness has spoken in so feeble or ambiguous a voice, that philosophers have misapprehended or misunderstood her enouncements. On the contrary, they have been usually agreed about the fact and purport of the deliverance, differing only as to the mode in which they might evade or qualify its acceptance.

This I shall illustrate by a memorable example—by one in reference to the very cardinal point of philosophy. In the act of sensible perception, I am conscious of two things;—of *myself* as the *perceiving subject*, and of an *external reality*, in relation with my sense, as the *object perceived*. Of the existence of both these things I am convinced: because I am conscious of knowing each of them, not mediately, in something else, *as represented*, but immediately in itself, *as existing*. Of their mutual independence I am no less convinced; because each is apprehended equally, and at once, in the same indivisible energy, the one not preceding or determining, the other not following or determined; and because each is apprehended out of, and in direct contrast to, the other.

Such is the fact of perception, as given in consciousness, and as it affords to mankind in general the conjunct assurance they possess, of their own existence, and of the existence of an external world. Nor are the contents of the deliverance, considered *as a phænomenon*, denied by those who still hesitate to admit the truth of its testimony. As this point, however, is one of principal importance, I shall not content myself with assuming the preceding statement of the fact of perception as a truth attested by the internal experience of all; but, in order to place it beyond the possibility of doubt, quote in evidence, more than a competent number of authoritative, and yet reluctant, testimonies, and give articulate references to others.

Descartes, the father of modern Idealism, acknowledges, that in perception we suppose the qualities of the external realities to be themselves apprehended, and not merely represented, by the mind, in virtue or on occasion of certain movements of the sensuous organism which they determine. "Putamus nos *videre ipsam tædam, et audire ipsam campanam:* non vero solum sentire motus qui ab ipsis proveniunt." De Passionibus art. xxiii. This, be it observed, is meant for a statement applicable to our perception of external objects in general, and not merely to our perception of their secondary qualities.

De Raei, a distinguished follower of Descartes, frequently admits, that what is commonly rejected by philosophers is universally believed by mankind at large—"*Res ipsas secundum se in sensum incurrere.*" De Mentis Humanæ Facultatibus, Sectio II. § 41, 70, 89. De Cognitione Humana, § 15, 39, et alibi.

In like manner, *Berkeley*, contrasting the belief of the vulgar, and the belief of philosophers on this point, says:—"The former are of opinion that *those things they immediately perceive are the real things;* and the latter, that the things immediately perceived are ideas which exist only in the mind." Three Dialogues, &c., Dial. III. prope finem. His brother idealist, *Arthur Collier*, might be quoted to the same purport; though he does not, like Berkeley, pretend that mankind at large are therefore idealists.

Hume frequently states that, in the teeth of all philosophy, "men are carried by a blind and powerful instinct of nature to *suppose the very images presented by the senses to be the external objects*, and never entertain any suspicion that the one are nothing but representations of the other." Enquiry concerning Human Understanding, Sect. XII., Essays, ed. 1788, vol. II.

p. 154. Compare also ibid. p. 157; and Treatise of Human Nature, vol. i., B. i., P. iv., Sect. 2., pp. 330, 338, 353, 358, 361, 369.

Schelling, in many passages of his works, repeats, amplifies, and illustrates the statement, that "*the man of common sense believes, and will not but believe, that the object he is conscious of perceiving is the real one.*" This is from his Philosophische Schriften, I. p. 274; and it may be found with the context, translated by Coleridge —but given as his own—in the "Biographia Literaria," I. p. 262. See also among other passages, Philos. Schr., I. pp. 217, 238; Ideen zu einer Philosophie der Natur, Einleit. pp. xix, xxvi, first edition, (translated in Edinb. Rev. vol. lii., p. 202.); Philosophisches Journal von Fichte und Niethhammer, vol. vii., p. 244. In these passages Schelling allows that it *is only on the believed identity of the object known and of the object existing, and in our inability to discriminate in perceptive consciousness the representation from the thing, that mankind at large believe in the reality of an external world.*

But to adduce a more recent writer, and of a different school.—"From the natural point of view" says *Stiedenroth*, "the representation (Vorstellung) is not in sensible perception distinguished from the object represented; for it appears as if the sense actually apprehended the things out of itself, and in their proper space." (Psychologie, vol. i. p. 244.) "The things—the actual realities are not in our soul. Nevertheless, from the psychological point of view on which we are originally placed by nature, we do not suspect that our representation of external things and their relations is nought but representation. Before this can become a matter of consideration, the spatial relations are so far developed, that it seems as if the soul apprehended out of itself—as if it did not carry the images of things within itself, but perceived the things themselves in their proper space," (p. 267.) "This belief (that our sensible percepts are the things themselves,) is so strong and entire, that a light seems to break upon us when we first learn, or bethink ourselves, that we are absolutely shut in within the circle of our own representations. Nay, it costs so painful an effort, consistently to maintain this acquired view, in opposition to that permanent and unremitted illusion, that we need not marvel, if, even to many philosophers, it should have been again lost," (p. 270.)

But it is needless to accumulate confessions as to a fact which has never, I believe, been openly denied; I shall only therefore refer in general to the following authorities, who, all in like manner, even while denying the *truth* of the natural belief, acknowledge the *fact* of its existence. *Malebranche*, Recherche, L. iii. c. 1.; *Tetens*, Versuche, vol. i. p. 375.; *Fichte*, Bestimmung des Menschen, p. 56, ed. 1825; and in Philos. Journal, VII. p. 35.; *Tennemann*, Geschichte der Philosophie, vol ii. p. 294, (translated in Edinb. Rev., vol. lii. p. 202.); *Fries*, Neue Kritik, Vorr. p. xxviii. sec. ed.; *Herbart*, Allgemeine Metaphysik, II Th., § 327.; *Gerlach*, Fundamental Philosophie, § 33.; *Beneke*, Das Verhaeltniss von Seele und Leib, p. 23; and Kant und die Philosophische Aufgabe unserer Zeit, p. 70.; *Stoeger*, Pruefung, &c., p. 504. To these may be added, *Jacobi*, Werke, vol. i. p. 119; and in vol. ii., his "David Hume" passim, of which see a passage quoted infra in Testimonies, No. 87 c. Reid's opinion will be adduced in Note C, § II.

The contents of the *fact* of perception, *as given* in consciousness, being thus established, what are the consequences to philosophy, according as the *truth* of its testimony (I.) *is*, or (II.) *is not, admitted?*

I. On the *former* alternative, the veracity of consciousness, in the fact of perception, being unconditionally acknowledged, we have established at once, without hypothesis or demonstration, the reality of mind, and the reality of matter; while no concession is yielded to the sceptic, through which he may subvert philosophy in manifesting its self-contradiction. The *one* legitimate doctrine, thus possible, may be called *Natural Realism* or *Natural Dualism.*

II. On the *latter* alternative, *five* great variations from truth and nature may be conceived—and all of these have actually found their advocates—according as the testimony of consciousness, in the fact of perception, (A) is *wholly*, or (B) is *partially*, rejected.

A. If *wholly* rejected, that is, if nothing but the phænomenal reality of the fact itself be allowed, the result is *Nihilism.* This may be conceived either as a dogmatical or as a sceptical opinion; and Hume and Fichte have competently shown, that if the truth of consciousness be not unconditionally recognized, Nihilism is the conclusion in which our speculation, if consistent with itself, must end.

B. On the other hand, if *partially* rejected, *four* schemes emerge, according to the way in which the fact is tampered with.

i. If the veracity of consciousness be allowed to the equipoise of the subject and object in the act, but disallowed to the reality of their antithesis, the system of *Absolute Identity* (whereof Pantheism is the corollary) arises, which reduces mind and matter to phænomenal modifications of the same common substance.

ii., iii. Again, if the testimony of consciousness be refused to the equal originality and reciprocal independence of the subject and object in perception, two Unitarian schemes are determined, according as the one or as the other of these correlatives is supposed the prior and genetic. Is the object educed from the subject? *Idealism*; is the subject educed from the object? *Materialism*, is the result.

iv. Finally, if the testimony of consciousness to our *knowledge* of an external world existing be rejected with the Idealist, but with the Realist the *existence* of that world be affirmed; we have a scheme which, as it by many various hypotheses, endeavours, on the one hand, not to give up the reality of an unknown material universe, and on the other, to explain the ideal illusion of its cognition, may be called the doctrine of *Cosmothetic Idealism*, *Hypothetical Realism*, or *Hypothetical Dualism*. This last, though the most vacillating, inconsequent, and self-contradictory of all systems, is the one which, as less obnoxious in its acknowledged consequences, (being a kind of compromise between speculation and common sense,) has found favour with the immense majority of philosophers.*

From the rejection of the fact of consciousness in this example of perception, we have thus, in the first place, multiplicity, speculative variation, error; in the second, systems practically dangerous; and in the third, what concerns us exclusively at present, the incompetence of an appeal to the common sense of mankind by any of these systems against the conclusions of others. This last will, however, be more appropriately shown in our special consideration of the conditions of the argument of Common Sense, to which we now go on.

* See, in connexion with this more general distribution of philosophical systems from the whole fact of consciousness in perception, other more special divisions, from the relation of the object to the subject of perception, in Note C, § 1.

§ *II.—Conditions of the legitimacy, and legitimate application, of the argument from Common Sense.*

From what has been stated, it is manifest that the argument drawn from Common Sense, for the truth or falsehood of any given thesis, proceeds on two suppositions—

1°. *That the proposition to be proved is either identical with, or necessarily evolved out of, a primary datum of consciousness*; and,

2°. *That the primary data of consciousness are, one and all of them, admitted, by the proponent of this argument, to be true.*

From this it follows, that each of these suppositions will constitute a condition, under which the legitimate application of this reasoning is exclusively competent. Whether these conditions have been ever previously enounced, I know not. But this I know, that while their necessity is so palpable, that they could never, if explicitly stated, be explicitly denied; that in the hands of philosophers they have been always, more or less violated, implicitly and in fact, and this often not the least obtrusively by those who have been themselves the loudest in their appeal from the conclusions of an obnoxious speculation to the common convictions of mankind. It is not therefore to be marvelled at if the argument itself should have sometimes shared in the contempt which its abusive application so frequently and so justly merited.

1. That the first condition—that of *originality*—is indispensable, is involved in the very conception of the argument. I should indeed hardly have deemed that it required an articulate statement, were it not that, in point of fact, many philosophers have attempted to establish, on the principles of common sense, propositions which are not original data of consciousness; while the original data of consciousness, from which their propositions were derived, and to which they owed their whole necessity and truth—these data the same philosophers were (strange to say!) not disposed to admit. Thus, when it is argued by the Cosmothetic Idealists—"The external world exists, because we naturally believe it to exist;" the illation is incompetent, in as much as it erroneously assumes that our belief of an external world is a primary datum of consciousness. This is not the case. That an outer world exists is given us, not as a "miraculous revelation," not as a "cast of magic," not as an "instinctive feeling," not as a "blind belief." These expressions, in

which the Cosmothetic Idealists shadow forth the difficulty they create, and attempt to solve, are wholly inapplicable to the real fact. Our belief of a material universe is not ultimate; and that universe is not unknown. This belief is not a supernatural inspiration; it is not an infused faith. We are not compelled by a blind impulse to believe in the external world, as in an unknown something; on the contrary, we believe it to exist only because we are immediately cognisant of it as existing. If asked, indeed —How we know that we know it?—how we know that what we apprehend in sensible perception is, as consciousness assures us, an object, external, extended, and numerically different from the conscious subject?—how we know that this object is not a mere mode of mind, illusively presented to us as a mode of matter?—then indeed we must reply, that we do not in propriety *know* that what we are compelled to perceive as not-self, is not a perception of self, and that we can only on reflection *believe* such to be the case, in reliance on the original necessity of so believing, imposed on us by our nature,

'Quæ nisi sit veri, ratio quoque falsa fit omnis.'

That this is a correct statement of the fact has been already shown; and if such be the undenied and undeniable ground of the natural belief of mankind, in the reality of external things, the incompetence of the argument from common sense in the hands of the Cosmothetic Idealist is manifest, in so far as it does not fulfil the fundamental condition of that argument.

This defect of the argument may, in the present example indeed, be easily supplied, by interpolating the medium which has been left out. But this cannot consistently be done by the Cosmothetic Idealist, who is reduced to this dilemma—that if he adhere to his hypothesis, he must renounce the argument; and if he apply the argument, he must renounce his hypothesis.

2. The second condition, that of *absolute truth*, requires that he who applies the argument of common sense, by appealing to the veracity of consciousness, should not himself, directly or indirectly, admit that consciousness is ever false; in other words, he is bound, in applying this argument, to apply it thoroughly, impartially, against himself no less than against others, and not according to the conveniences of his polemic, to approbate and reprobate the testimony of our original beliefs. That our immediate consciousness, if competent to prove any thing, must be competent to prove every thing it avouches, is a principle which none have been found, at least openly, to deny. It is proclaimed by Leibnitz: "Si l'expérience interne immédiate pouvait nous tromper, il ne saurait y avoir pour moi aucune vérité de fait, j'ajoute, ni de raison." And by Lucretius:—

'Denique ut in fabrica si prava 'st Regula prima,
Omnia mendose fieri atque obstipa necessum 'st;
Sic igitur Ratio tibi rerum prava necesse 'st,
Falsaque sit, falsis quæcunque ab Sensibus orta 'st.'

Compare *Plotinus*, En. V. Lib. v. c. 1—*Buffier*, Pr. Ver., § 71—*Reid*, Inq., p. 183, b. I. P., p. 260, b.

Yet, however notorious the condition, that consciousness unless held trustworthy in all its revelations cannot be held trustworthy in any; marvellous to say, philosophers have rarely scrupled, on the one hand, quietly to supersede the data of consciousness, so often as these did not fall in with their preadopted opinions;—and on the other, clamorously to appeal to them, as irrecusable truths, so often as they could allege them in corroboration of their own, or in refutation of a hostile, doctrine.

I shall again take for an example the fact of perception, and the violation of the present condition by the Cosmothetic Idealists—1°, in the constitution of their own doctrine; 2°, in their polemic against more extreme opinions.

In the first place, in the constitution of their doctrine, nothing can be imagined more monstrous than the procedure of these philosophers, in attempting to vindicate the reality of a material world, on the ground of an universal belief in its existence; and yet rejecting the universal *belief in the knowledge* on which the universal *belief in the existence* is exclusively based. Here the absurdity is twofold. Firstly, in postulating a conclusion though rejecting its premises; secondly, in founding their doctrine partly on the veracity, and partly on the mendacity, of consciousness.

In the second place, with what consistency and effect do the Hypothetical Realists point the argument of common sense against the obnoxious conclusions of the thorough-going Idealist, the Materialist, the Absolutist, the Nihilist?

Take first their vindication of an external world against the Idealist.

To prove this, do they, like Dr Thomas Brown, simply found on the natural belief of mankind in its existence? But they themselves, as we have seen, admitting the untruth of one natural belief—the belief in our immediate knowledge of external things—have no right to presume upon the truth of any other; and the absurdity is carried to its climax, when the natural belief, which they regard as false, is the sole ground of the natural belief which they would assume and found upon as true. Again, do they, like Descartes, allege that God would be a deceiver, were we constrained by nature to believe in the reality of an unreal world? But the Deity, on their hypothesis, is a deceiver; for that hypothesis assumes that our natural consciousness deludes us in the belief, that external objects are immediately, and in themselves, perceived. (See 747 a.) Either therefore maintaining the veracity of God, they must surrender their hypothesis; or, maintaining their hypothesis, they must surrender the veracity of God.

Against the Materialist, in proof of our Personal Identity, can they maintain, that consciousness is able to identify self, at one period, with self, at another; when, in their theory of perception, consciousness mistaking self for not-self, is unable, they virtually assert, to identify self with self, even at the same moment of existence?

How, again, can they maintain the substantial Individuality and consequent Immateriality of the thinking principle, on the unity of consciousness, when the duality given in consciousness is not allowed substantially to discriminate the object from the subject in perception?

But to take a broader view. It is a maxim in philosophy,—*That substances are not to be multiplied without necessity;* in other words,—*That a plurality of principles are not to be assumed, when the phænomena can possibly be explained by one.* This regulative principle, which may be called the law or maxim of Parcimony, throws it therefore on the advocates of a scheme of psychological Dualism, to prove the necessity of supposing more than a single substance for the phænomena of mind and matter.—Further, we know nothing whatever of mind and matter, considered as substances; they are only known to us as a twofold series of phænomena: and we can only justify, against the law of parcimony, the postulation of two substances, on the ground, that the two series of phænomena are, reciprocally so contrary and incompatible, that the one cannot be reduced to the other, nor both be supposed to coinhere in the same common substance. Is this ground shown to be invalid?—the presumption against a dualistic theory at once recurs, and a unitarian scheme becomes, in the circumstances, philosophically necessary.

Now the doctrine of Cosmothetic Idealism, in abolishing the incompatibility of the two series of phænomena, subverts the only ground on which a psychological Dualism can be maintained. This doctrine denies to mind a knowledge of aught beyond its own modifications. The qualities, which we call material—Extension, Figure, &c. —*exist for us,* only as they are *known by us;* and, on this hypothesis, they are known by us, *only as modes of mind.* The two series of phænomena, therefore, so far from being really, as they are apparently, opposed, are, on this doctrine, in fact, admitted to be all only manifestations of the same substance.

So far, therefore, from the Hypothetical Dualist being able to resist the conclusion of the Unitarian—whether Idealist, Materialist, or Absolutist; the fundamental position of his philosophy—*that the object immediately known is in every act of cognition identical with the subject knowing* —in reality, establishes any and every doctrine but his own. On this principle, the Idealist may educe the object from the subject; the Materialist educe the subject from the object; the Absolutist carry both up into indifference; nay the Nihilist subvert the substantial reality of either:—and the Hypothetical Dualist is doomed to prove, that, while the only salvation against these melancholy results is an appeal to the natural convictions of mankind, that the argument from common sense is, in his hands a weapon, either impotent against his opponents, or fatal equally to himself and them.

§ *III.—The argument from Common Sense is one strictly philosophical and scientific.*

We have thus seen, though the argument from common sense be an appeal to the natural convictions of mankind, that it is not an appeal from philosophy to blind feeling. It is only an appeal, from the heretical conclusions of particular philosophies, to the catholic principles of all philosophy. The prejudice, which, on this supposition, has sometimes been excited against the argument, is groundless.

Nor is it true, that the argument from common sense denies the decision to the judgment of philosophers, and accords it to the verdict of the vulgar. Nothing can be more erroneous. We admit—nay we maintain, as D'Alembert well expresses it, "that the truth in metaphysic, like the truth in matters of taste, is a truth of which all minds have the germ within themselves; to which indeed the greater number pay no attention, but which they recognise the moment it is pointed out to them. . . But if, in this sort, all are able to understand, all are not able to instruct. The merit of conveying easily to others true and simple notions is much greater than is commonly supposed; for experience proves how rarely this is to be met with. Sound metaphysical ideas are common truths, which every one apprehends, but which few have the talent to develope. So difficult is it on any subject to make our own what belongs to every one." (Melanges, t. iv. § 6.) Or, to employ the words of the ingenious Lichtenberg—"Philosophy, twist the matter as we may, is always a sort of chemistry (Scheidekunst.) The peasant employs all the principles of abstract philosophy, only *inveloped*, *latent*, *engaged*, as the men of physical science express it; the Philosopher exhibits the *pure* principle." (Hinterlassene Schriften, vol. ii, p. 67.)

The first problem of Philosophy—and it is one of no easy accomplishment—being thus to seek out, purify, and establish, by intellectual analysis and criticism, the elementary feelings or beliefs, in which are given the elementary truths of which all are in possession; and the argument from common sense being the allegation of these feelings or beliefs as explicated and ascertained, in proof of the relative truths and their necessary consequences;—this argument is manifestly dependent on philosophy, as an art, as an acquired dexterity, and cannot, notwithstanding the errors which they have so frequently committed, be taken out of the hands of the philosophers. Common Sense is like Common Law. Each may be laid down as the general rule of decision; but in the one case it must be left to the jurist, in the other to the philosopher, to ascertain what are the contents of the rule; and though in both instances the common man may be cited as a witness, for the custom or the fact, in neither can he be allowed to officiate as advocate or as judge.

Μηδέποτε κρίνειν ἀδαήμονας ἄνδρας ἰάσεις·
Τὴν σοφίην σοφὸς ἰθύνει, τέχνας δ' ὁμότεχνος.

PHOCYLIDES.

It must be recollected, also, that in appealing to the consciousness of mankind in general, we only appeal to the consciousness of those not disqualified to pronounce a decision. "In saying (to use the words of Aristotle) simply and without qualification, that this or that *is a known truth*, we do not mean that it is in fact recognized by all, but only by such as are of a sound understanding; just as in saying absolutely, that a thing is wholesome, we must be held to mean, to such as are of a hale constitution." (Top. L. vi., c. 4, § 7.)—We may, in short, say of the true Philosopher what Erasmus, in an epistle to Hutten, said of Sir Thomas More:—"Nemo minus ducitur *vulgi judicio*; sed rursus nemo minus abest a *sensu communi*."

When rightly understood, therefore, no valid objection can be taken to the argument of common sense, considered in itself. But it must be allowed that the way in which it has been sometimes applied was calculated to bring it into not unreasonable disfavour with the learned. (See C. L. Reinhold's Beytræge zur leichtern Uebersicht des Zustandes der Philosophie, i. p. 61; and Niethhammer in his Journal, i. p 43 sq.) In this country in particular, some of those who opposed it to the sceptical conclusions of Hume did not sufficiently counteract the notion which the name might naturally suggest; they did not emphatically proclaim that it was no appeal to the undeveloped beliefs of the unreflective many; and they did not inculcate that it presupposed a critical analysis of these beliefs by the philosophers themselves. On the contrary, their language and procedure might even, sometimes, warrant an opposite conclusion. This must be admitted without reserve of the writings of Beattie, and more especially, of Oswald. But even Reid, in his earlier work, was not so explicit as to prevent his being occasionally classed in the same category. That the strictures on the "Scottish Philosophy of Common Sense" by Feder, Lambert, Tetens, Eberhard, Kant, Ulrich, Jacob, &c., were inapplicable to Reid, is sufficiently proved by the more articulate exposition of his doctrine, afterwards given in his Essays on the Intellectual and Active Powers. But these criticisms having been once recorded, we need not wonder at their subsequent repetition, without qualification or exception, by philosophers and historians of philosophy.

To take, as an example, the judgment of the most celebrated of these critics. "It is not (says Kant, in the preface to his Prolegomena) without a certain painful feeling, that we behold how completely Hume's opponents, Reid, Oswald, Beattie, and, at last, Priestley, missed the point of his problem; and whilst they, on the one hand, constantly assumed the very positions which he did not allow, and on the other, demonstrated warmly, and often with great intemperance, what he had never dreamt of calling into question, they so little profited by the hint which he had given towards better things, that all remained in the same position as if the matter had never been agitated at all. The question mooted, was not—*Whether the notion of Cause were right, applicable, and, in relation to all natural knowledge, indispensable*; for of this Hume had never insinuated a doubt; but—*Whether this notion were by the mind excogitated a priori, whether it thus possessed an intrinsic truth, independent of all experience, and consequently a more extensive applicability, one not limited merely to objects of experience*: on this Hume awaited a disclosure. In fact, the whole dispute regarded the origin of this notion, and not its indispensability in use. If the former be made out, all that respects the conditions of its use, and the sphere within which it can be validly applied, follow as corollaries, of themselves. In order satisfactorily to solve the problem, it behoved the opponents of this illustrious man to have penetrated deeply into the nature of the mind, considered as exclusively occupied in pure thinking: but this did not suit them. They, therefore, discovered a more convenient method, in an appeal to the common understanding of mankind (gemeiner Menschenverstand)"—and so forth; showing that Kant understood by the common sense of the Scottish philosophers, only good sense, sound understanding, &c. (Prolegomena, p. 10.)

I will not object to the general truth of the statements in this passage; nor to their bearing in so far as they are applied to the British philosophers in general. For Reid, however, I must claim an exemption; and this I shall establish with regard to the very notion of Cause to which Kant refers.

That from the limited scope of his earlier work the "*Inquiry*," Reid had not occasion to institute a critical analysis of the notion of Causality, affords no ground for holding that he did not consider such analysis to be necessary in the establishment of that and the other principles of common sense. This, indeed, he in that very work, once and again, explicitly declares. "We have taken notice of several original principles of belief in the course of this inquiry; and when *other faculties* of the mind are examined we shall find *more*. * * * A *clear explication and enumeration* of the principles of common sense, is *one of the chief desiderata* in Logic. We have *only* considered such of them as occurred in the examination of the *five senses*." p. 209 ab. See also p. 96 a. And accordingly in his subsequent and more extensive work, the "Essays on the Intellectual Powers," published within two years after Kant's "Prolegomena," we find the notion of Causality, among others, investigated by the very same critical process which the philosopher of Koenigsberg so successfully employed; though there be no reason whatever for surmising that Reid had ever heard the name, far less seen the works, of his illustrious censor. The criterion—the index by which Kant discriminates the notions of *pure* or *a priori* origin from those elaborated from experience, is their quality of *necessity*; and its quality of necessity is precisely the characteristic by which Reid proves that, among others, the notion of causality cannot be an educt of experience, but must form a part of the native cognitions of the mind itself. It is doubtful indeed whether Reid, like Kant, was even indebted to Leibnitz for his knowledge of this touchstone; but the fact of its familiar employment by him in the discrimination and establishment of the fundamental principles of thought, more especially in his later works, sufficiently shows, that the reproach of an uncritical application of the argument from common sense, made against the Scottish philosophers in general, was, at least in reference to him, unfounded. Reid however—and to his honour be it spoken—stands alone among the philosophers of this country in his appreciation and employment of the criterion of necessity. See Note T.

[Since writing the above, I have met with the following passage in the "Lettere Philosophiche" of Baron Galluppi, one of the two most distinguished of the present metaphysicians of Italy.

"The philosopher of Koenigsberg makes Hume thus reason:—'Metaphysical Causality is not in the objects observed; it is, therefore, a product of imagination engendered upon custom.'—This reasoning, says Kant, is inexact. It ought to have proceeded thus.—'Causality is not in the things observed; it is therefore in the observer.' But here Kant does not apprehend Hume's meaning, whose reasoning, as I have stated in the eighth letter, is altogether different. Metaphysical causality, he argues, is not in the things observed; it cannot therefore be in the observer, in whom all is derived from the things observed. Reid fully understands the purport of Hume's argument, and meets it precisely and conclusively with this counter-reasoning;—'Metaphysical Causality is a fact in our intellect; it is not derived from the things observed, and is therefore a subjective law of the observer.' Kant objects, that Reid has not attended to the state of the question. There is no dispute, he says, about the existence of the notion of metaphysical causality; the only doubt regards its origin. This is altogether erroneous. Hume being unable to find the origin of the notion in experience, denied its existence. Kant's criticism of Reid is therefore unjust." P. 225.

Kant, I think, is here but hardly dealt with. Hume did not, certainly, deny the existence of the notion of causality, meaning thereby its existence as a mental phænomenon; he only (on the hypothesis of the then dominant doctrine of sensualism) shewed that it had no objective validity—no legitimate genesis. In different points of view, therefore, Hume may be said to deny, and not to deny, its reality. The dispute is a mere logomachy. See Note Q.—Kant also stands clear of injustice towards Reid, when it is considered that his strictures on the Scottish philosophers were prior to the appearance of the "Essays on the Intellectual Powers," the work in which Reid first expounded his doctrine of causality.]

§ IV. *On the Essential Characters by which the principles of Common Sense are discriminated.*

It now remains to consider what are the essential notes or characters by which we are enabled to distinguish our original, from our derivative, convictions. These characters, I think, may be reduced to four;—1°, their *Incomprehensibility*—2°, their *Simplicity*—3°, their *Necessity* and *absolute Universality*—4°, their *comparative Evidence* and *Certainty*.

1. In reference to the first;—A conviction is incomprehensible when there is merely given us in consciousness—*That its object is* (*Ὅτι ἔστι*); and when we are unable to comprehend through a higher notion or belief, *Why or How it is* (*Διότι ἔστι*). When we are able to comprehend why or how a thing is, the belief of the existence of that thing is not a primary datum of consciousness, but a subsumption under the cognition or belief which affords its reason.

2. As to the second;—It is manifest that if a cognition or belief be made up of, and can be explicated into, a plurality of cognitions or beliefs, that, as compound, it cannot be original.

3. Touching the third;—Necessity and Universality may be regarded as coincident. For when a belief is necessary it is, *eo ipso*, universal; and that a belief is universal, is a certain index that it must be necessary. (See Leibnitz, Nouveaux Essais, L. I. § 4. p. 32.) To prove the necessity, the universality must, however, be absolute; for a relative universality indicates no more than custom and education, howbeit the subjects themselves may deem that they follow only the dictates of nature. As St Jerome has it—"Unaquaeque gens hoc legem naturae putat, quod didicit."

It is to be observed, that the necessity here spoken of, is of two kinds. There is one necessity, when we cannot construe it to our minds as possible, that the deliverance of consciousness should not be true. This logical impossibility occurs in the case of what are called necessary truths—truths of reason or intelligence; as in the law of causality, the law of substance, and still more in the laws of identity, contradiction, and excluded middle. There is another necessity, when it is not unthinkable, that the deliverance of consciousness may possibly be false, but at the same time, when we cannot but admit, that this deliverance is of such or such a purport. This is seen in the case of what are called contingent truths or truths of fact. Thus, for example, I can theoretically suppose that the external object I am conscious of in perception, may be, in reality, nothing but a mode of mind or self. I am unable however to think that it does not appear to me—that consciousness does not compel me to regard it—*as* external—*as* a mode of matter or not-self. And such being the case, I cannot practically believe the supposition I am able speculatively to maintain. For I cannot believe this supposition, without believing that the last ground of all belief is not to be believed; which is self-contradictory. "Nature," says Pascal, "confounds the Pyrrhonist;" and, among many similar confessions, those of Hume, of Fichte, of Hommel may suffice for an acknowledgement of the impossibility which the Sceptic, the Idealist, the Fatalist finds in practically believing the scheme which he views as theoretically demonstrated.—The argument from common sense, it may be observed, is of principal importance in reference to the class of contingent truths. The others, from their converse being absolutely incogitable, sufficiently guard themselves.

As this criterion of Necessity and Universality is signalised by nearly the whole series of authorities adduced in the sequel, it would be idle to refer to any in particular. See however Reid, p. 233, a.; and on the quality of Necessity as a criterion of the originality of a cognition, Note T, with the relative places. Buffier's second and third essential qualities of primary truths may be reduced to this. See in Testimonies n. 63.

4. The fourth and last character of our original beliefs is their comparative Evidence and Certainty. This along with the third is well stated by Aristotle.—"What *appears to all* that we affirm *to be*; and he who rejects this belief will assuredly advance *nothing better deserving of credence*." And again:—"If we know and believe through certain original principles, we must know and believe these with *paramount certainty*, for the very reason that we know and believe all else through them." And such are the truths in regard to which the Aphrodisian says,—"though some men may verbally dissent, all men are in their hearts agreed." This constitutes the first of Buffier's essential qualities of primary truths, which is, as he expresses it,—"to be so clear, that if we attempt to prove or to disprove them, this can be done only by propositions which are manifestly *neither more evident nor more certain*." Testimonies nn. 3, 10, 63. Compare the others, passim.

A good illustration of this character is afforded by the assurance—to which we have already so frequently referred—that in perception mind is immediately cognisant of matter. *How* self can be conscious of not-self, *how* mind can be cognisant of matter, we do not know; but we know as little *how* mind can be percipient of itself. In both cases we only know the fact, on the authority of consciousness; and when the conditions of the problem are rightly understood—when it is established that it is only the *primary* qualities of body which are apprehended in themselves, and this only in so far as they are in immediate relation to the organ of sense, the difficulty in the one case is not more than in the other. This in opposition to the simple Idealists. But the Cosmothetic Idealists—the Hypothetical Realists are far less reasonable; who, in the teeth of consciousness, on the ground of inconceivability, deny to mind all cognisance of matter, yet bestow on it the more inconceivable power of representing, and truly representing, to itself the external world which, ex hypothesi, it does not know. These theorists do not substitute, in place of the simple fact which they repudiate, another more easy and intelligible. On the contrary they gratuitously involve themselves in a maze of unwarrantable postulates, difficulties, improbabilities, and self-contradictions, of such a character, that we well may wonder, how the doctrine of Cosmothetic Idealism has been able to enlist under its banners, not a few merely, but the immense majority of modern philosophers. The Cosmothetic Idealists, in truth, violate in their hypothesis every condition of a legitimate hypothesis. But for the illustration of this, I must again refer to the article on the Philosophy of Perception, Edinburgh Review, vol. lii. p. 178–181.

§ V.—*The Nomenclature, that is the various appellations by which the principles of Common Sense have been designated.*

It is evident that the foundations of our knowledge cannot properly be themselves the objects of our knowledge; for as by them we know all else, by nought else can they themselves be known. We know them indeed, but only in the fact, that with and through them we know. This it is which has so generally induced philosophers to bestow on them appellations marking out the circumstance, that in different points of view, they may and they may not, be regarded as cognitions. They appear as cognitions, in so far as we are conscious *that* (ὅτι) they *actually* are; they do not appear as cognitions, in so far as in them we are not conscious *how* (διότι) they *possibly* can be. Philosophers accordingly, even when they view and designate them as cognitions, are wont to qualify their appellation, under this character, by some restrictive epithet. For example, Cicero styling them *intelligentiæ* does not do so simply; but *i. inchoatæ*, *i. adumbratæ*, *i. obscuræ*, &c. A similar limitation is seen in the terms *ultimate facts*, *primary data*, &c. *of consciousness*; for these and the analogous expressions are intended to show, that while their existence is within our *apprehension*, the reason or ground of their existence is beyond our *comprehension*.

On the other hand we see the prevalence of the opposite point of view in the nomenclatures which seem to regard them not as cognitions wholly within consciousness, but as the bases of cognition, and therefore partly without, and partly within, consciousness. Such is the scope of the analogical designations applied to them of *Senses*, *Feelings*, *Instincts*, *Revelations*, *Inspirations*, *Suggestions*, *Beliefs*, *Assents*, *Holdings*, &c. It is the inexplicable and equivocal character which the roots of our knowledge thus exhibit, to which we ought to attribute the inadequacy, the vacillation and the ambiguity of the terms by which it has been attempted to denote them; and it is with an indulgent recollection of this, that we ought to criticise all and each of these denominations,—which, after this general observation, I proceed to consider in detail. In doing this I shall group them according to the principal points of view from which it would seem they were imposed.

I. The first condition, the consideration of which seems to have determined a certain class of names, is that of *Immediacy*. In our primitive cognitions we apprehend existence at once, and without the intervention of aught between the apprehending mind and the existence apprehended.

Under this head the first appellations are those which, with some qualifying attribute, apply to these cognitions the name of —*Sense*.

It is hardly necessary to observe that the words corresponding to the term Sense and its conjugates have in no language been limited to our perceptions of the external world, or to the feeling of our bodily affections. In every language they have been extended to the operations of the higher faculties;—indeed it can be shown, in almost every instance, that the names which ultimately came to be appropriated to the purest acts of intelligence were, in their origin, significant of one or other of the functions of our organic sensibility. Such among others is the rationale of the terms *moral sense (sensus boni) logical sense (sensus veri) aesthetical sense (sensus pulchri)*, which, even in modern philosophy, have been very commonly employed, though not employed to denote any thing lower than the apprehensive faculty of intelligence in these different relations. On this transference of the term Sense, see *Aristotle*, (De Anima, L. iii. c. 3)—*Quintilian*, (Instit. L. viii. c. 5)—*Budaeus*, (in Pandectas, Tit. i.)—*Salmasius*, (ad Solinum, p. 141.)—*Grotius*, (ad Acta Apostolorum, vii. 32, and I. Petri, i. 12.)—*Claubergius*, (Exercitationes, 83-88)—*Burmannus*, (ad Phaedrum, L. ii. Ep. 13.)—*Gronovius*, (Diatribe ad Statium, c. 43.)—*J. A. Fabricius*, (Programma De Gustatu Pulcri, p. 5.) &c. &c.

This being, in general, premised we have now to consider in particular, 1°, the ancient term *Common Sense*; and, 2°, the modern term *Internal Sense*, as applied to our elementary consciousness.

1. SENSE *Common, (sensus communis, sensus communes, sensus publicus, sens commun, senso comune, Gemeinsinn,) principles, axioms, maxims, truths, judgments*, &c. of.

The Greek tongue was for a long period destitute of any word to denote *Consciousness;* and it was only after both the philosophy and language of Greece had passed their prime, that the terms *συναισθάνομαι* and *συναίσθησις* were applied not merely to denote the apperception of sense but the primary condition of knowledge in general. (See Note I.) The same analogy explains how in the Latin tongue the term *Sensus Communis* came, from a very ancient period, to be employed with a similar latitude; and as Latin, even after its extinction as a living language, was long the exclusive vehicle of religion and philosophy throughout western Europe, we need not wonder that the analysis and its expression, the thing and the word, passed not only into the dialects in which the Romanic, but into those also in which the Teutonic, element was predominant. But as the expression is not unambiguous it is requisite to distinguish its significations.

The various meanings in which the term Common Sense is met with, in ancient and modern times, may I think be reduced to *four;* and these fall into *two* categories, according as it *is*, or *is not, limited to the sphere of sense proper*.

As restricted to sense proper.

a.—Under this head Common Sense has only a single meaning; that to wit which it obtained in the Peripatetic philosophy and its derivative systems. Common Sense (*κοινὴ αἴσθησις*) was employed by Aristotle to denote the faculty in which the various reports of the several senses are reduced to the unity of a common apperception. This signification is determinate. The others are less precisely discriminated from each other.

(I may observe, however, that a second meaning under this category might be found in the *Conaesthesis, common feeling* or *sensation*, by which certain German physiologists have denominated the *sensus vagus* or vital sense, and which some of them translate by common sense (Gemeinsinn). But as the term in this signification has been employed recently, rarely, abusively, and without imposing authority, I shall discount it.)

As not limited to the sphere of sense proper, it comprises three meanings.

b.—The second signification of Common Sense is when it denotes the complement of those cognitions or convictions which we receive from nature; which all men therefore possess in common; and by which they test the truth of knowledge, and the morality of actions. This is the meaning in which the expression is now emphatically employed in philosophy, and which may be, therefore, called its *philosophical* signification. As authorities for its use in this relation, Reid (I. P. p. 423–425) has adduced legitimate examples from Bentley, Shaftesbury, Fenelon, Buffier, and Hume. The others which he quotes from Cicero and Priestley can hardly be considered as more than instances of the employment of the words; for the former, in the particular passage quoted, does not seem to mean by "*sensus communes*" more than the faculty of *apprehending sensible relations* which all possess; and the latter explicitly states, that he uses the words in a meaning (the third) which we are hereafter to consider. Mr Stewart (Elements, vol ii., c. 7, sect. 3, p. 76) to the examples of Reid adds only a single, and that not an unambiguous, instance—from Bayle. It therefore still remains to show that in this signification its employment is not only of authorised usage, but, in fact, one long and universally established. This is done in the series of testimonies I shall adduce in a subsequent part of this note,—principally indeed to prove that the *doctrine* of Common Sense, notwithstanding many schismatic aberrations, is the one catholic and perennial philosophy, but which also concur in showing that this too is the *name* under which that doctrine has for two thousand years been most familiarly known, at least, in the western world. Of these Lucretius, Cicero, Horace, Seneca, Tertullian, Arnobius, and St Augustin, exhibit the expression as recognised in the language and philosophy of ancient Rome; while some fifty others prove its scientific and colloquial usage in every country of modern Europe. (See Nos 5—8, 12, 13, 15, 23, 25, 27—29, 31, 32, 34–36, 38–44, 47, 48, 51—53, 55, 56, 58—69, 71—75, 78—85, 90.)

The objections to the term Common Sense in this its philosophical application are obvious enough. It is not unambiguous. To ground an objection it has sometimes unintentionally, more frequently wilfully, been taken in the third signification (v. p. 758 b); and its employment has even afforded a ground for supposing that Reid and other Scottish philosophers proposed under it a certain peculiar sense, distinct from intelligence, by which truth is apprehended or revealed. See *Fries*, in Testimonies No. 95, and *Franke*, Leben des Gefuehls, § 42.

On the other hand, besides that no other expression, to which valid objection may not be taken, has yet been proposed; and besides, that it has itself been ratified by ancient and general usage; the term Common Sense is not inappropriately applied to denote an original source of knowledge common to all mankind—a fountain of truths intelligible indeed, but like those of the senses revealed immediately as facts to be believed, but not as possibilities to be explained and understood. On this ground the term Sense has found favour, in this application, with the most ancient and the most recent philosophers. For example—*Aristotle* (Eth. Nic. L. vi. c. 11. and Eth. Eud. L. v. c. 11) says that νοῦς, Intelligence proper, the faculty of first principles is, in certain respects, a Sense; and the ancient Scholiast, Eustratius, in his commentary on the former work (f. 110, b) explains it by observing, "that Intelligence and Sense have this exclusively in common—they are both *immediate cognitions*." Hence it is that Aristotle (Metaph. xii. 7), Theophrastus (see Test. No. 4), and Plotinus (En. vi. L. vii, cc. 36, 39, L. ix. c. 7) assimilate intellection, the noetic energy, to *touching* in particular.* In

* Among the Greeks the expression "Common Intellect" was, however, rarely, if ever, used for Common Sense in this its second, or philosophical, meaning. The learned Mr Harris (in a note on his Dialogue concerning Happiness) in stating the doctrine of the Greek philosophers, says—"The recognition of self evident truths, or at least the ability to recognise them is called *κοινὸς νοῦς*, "*common sense*," as being a sense common to all, except lunatics and idiots." This is inaccurate; for his statement of what was usual among the Greeks is founded (I presume, for he does not allege any authority,) on a single, and singular, example of such usage. It is that of Epictetus (Diss. Arriani, L. iii. c. 6). This philosopher seems in that passage to give the name of common intellect (*κοινὸς νοῦς* which H. Wolfius and Upton translate by *sensus communis*) to the faculty of those common notions possessed by all who are of sound mind. Now were the epithet *common* here applied to intellect *because* intellect is the repository of such common notions or in as much as it is common to all men—this, however likely a usage, is, I am confident, the only, or almost the only, example to be found in antiquity of such a nomenclature; for though the expression in question is frequent among the Greek writers, I do not recollect to have elsewhere met with it in a similar import. It is employed in two significations.—1°, with νοῦς in its stricter meaning, for the highest faculty of mind, *κοινὸς* is used to mark its imperson-

reference to the apprehension of primary truths, 'the soul,' says Dr John Smith, 'has its senses, in like manner as the body' (Select Discourses); and his friend Dr Henry More designates the same, by the name of *intellectual sense*. (Test. n. 45.) Jacobi defines Vernunft, his faculty of 'intellectual intuitions' as 'the sense of the supersensible.' (Test. n. 87.) De la Mennais could not find a more suitable expression whereby to designate his theological system of *universal consent* or *general reason*, than that of *Common Sense*; and Borger in his classical work 'De Mysticismo' prefers *sensus* as the least exceptionable word by which to discriminate those notions, of which, while we are conscious of the existence, we are ignorant of the reason and origin. 'Cum igitur, qui has notiones sequitur, illum *sensum* sequi dicimus, hoc dicimus, illas notiones non esse ratione [ratiocinatione] quaesitas, sed omni argumentatione antiquiores. Eo autem majori jure eos *sensus* vocabulo complectimur, quod, adeo obscurae sunt, ut eorum ne distincte quidem nobis conscii simus, sed eas *esse*, ex efficacia earum intelligamus, i. e. ex vi qua animum afficiunt' (P. 259, ed 2.) See also of Testimonies the numbers already specified.

c.—In the third signification, Common Sense may be used with emphasis on the adjective or on the substantive.

In the former case, it denotes such an ordinary complement of intelligence, that, if a person be deficient therein, he is accounted mad or foolish.

Sensus communis is thus used in Phaedrus, L. i. 7;—but Horace, Serm i. iii. 66, and Juvenal Sat. viii. 73, are erroneously, though usually, interpreted in this signification. In modern Latinity (as in Milton contra Salmasium, c. 8) and in most of the vulgar languages, the expression in this meaning is so familiar that it would be idle to adduce examples. Sir James Mackintosh (Dissertations, &c., p. 387 of collected edition) indeed, imagines that this is the only meaning of *common sense*; and on this ground censures Reid for the adoption of the term; and even Mr Stewart's objections to it seem to proceed on the supposition, that this is its proper or more accredited signification. See Elements ii. ch. 1, sec. 2; et supra 27 b. This is wrong; but Reid himself, it must be acknowledged, does not sufficiently distinguish between the second and third acceptations; as may be seen from the tenor of the second chapter of the sixth Essay on the Intellectual Powers, but especially from the concluding chapter of the Inquiry. (p. 209 b.)

In the latter case, it expresses native, practical intelligence, natural prudence, mother wit, tact in behaviour, acuteness in the observation of character, &c., in contrast to habits of acquired learning, or of speculation away from the affairs of life. I recollect no unambiguous example of the phrase, in this precise acceptation, in any ancient author. In the modern languages, and more particularly in French and English, it is of ordinary occurrence. Thus, Voltaire's saying, 'Le sens commun n'est pas si commun;'—which, I may notice, was stolen from Buffier. (Metaphysique, § 69.)

With either emphasis it corresponds to the κοινὸς λογισμὸς of the Greeks, and among them to the ὀρθὸς λόγος of the Stoics, to the *gesunde Menschenverstand* of the

---

ality, its unity, its general identity in men, or in man and God. 2°, With νοῦς, in its looser meaning for mind in general, it denotes a community of opinion or a community of social sentiment, corresponding to Sensus Communis among the Romans, to be spoken of as the fourth signification. The only second instance, I believe, that can be brought, is from the Aphrodisian. (On the Soul, f. 138 ed. Ald.) But there the epithet *common* is given to the natural in opposition to the acquired intellect, exclusively from the circumstance that the former is possessed by all of sound mind, the latter only by some; nay from a comparison of the two passages it is evident, that Alexander in his employment of the expression *had Epictetus and this very instance* immediately in his eye. But it is in fact by no means improbable that Epictetus here uses the expression only in the first of its two ordinary significations—as a Stoic, to denote the individual intellect, considered as a particle of the universal; and this even the commentators are inclined to believe. See Upton, ad locum. In illustration of this:—Plutarch in his treatise 'On Common Notions against the Stoics,' uses (after παρὰ or κατὰ) τὰς κοινὰς ἐννοίας or τῆς κοινῆς ἐννοίας at least *twenty-three* times, and without the adjective τὰς ἐννοίας or τῆς ἐννοίας, at least *twenty-one* times; which last, by the bye, Xylander always renders by 'Sensus Communis.' Now how many times does Plutarch use as a synonyme, κοινὸς νοῦς? Not once. He does, indeed, once employ it and κοινὰς φρένας (p. 1077 of the folio editions); but in the sense of an agreement in thought with others—the sense which it obtains also in the only other example of the expression to be found in his writings. (P. 529 D.)

I see Forcellini (voce Sensus) has fallen into the same inaccuracy as Harris.

I may here notice that Aristotle does not apply the epithet *common* to *intellect* at all; for τοῦ κοινοῦ (De An. i 4. § 5) does not, as Themistius supposes, mean 'of the common [intellect]' but 'of the composite,' made up of soul and body.

Germans, to the *Bons Sens* of the French, and to the *Good Sense* of the English. The two emphases enable us to reconcile the following contradictions:—'Le bon sens (says Descartes) est la chose du monde la mieux partagée;' 'Good sense (says Gibbon) is a quality of mind hardly less rare than genius.'

d.—In the fourth and last signification, Common Sense is no longer a natural quality; it denotes an acquired perception or feeling of the common duties and proprieties expected from each member of society,—a gravitation of opinion—a sense of conventional decorum—communional sympathy—general *bienséance*—public spirit, &c. In this signification—at least as absolutely used—it is limited to the language of ancient Rome. This is the meaning in which it occurs in Cicero, De Orat. l. 3, ii. 16—Or. pro Domo 37—in Horace, Serm. l. iii. 66—in Juvenal, Sat. viii. 73—in Quintilian, Instit. i. 2—and in Seneca, Epp. 5, 105, whose words in another place (which I cannot at the moment recover) are—'Sic in beneficio *sensus communis*, locum, tempus, personam observet.' Shaftesbury and others, misled probably by Casaubon, do not seize the central notion in their interpretation of several of these texts. In this meaning the Greeks sometimes employed *κοινὸς νοῦς* —an ambiguous expression, for which Antoninus seems to have coined as a substitute, *κοινονοημοσύνη*.—To this head may be referred Hutcheson's employment of Sensus Communis for Sympathy. Synopsis Metaphysicae, P. ii. c. 1.

2.—Sense *inmost, interior, internal, (sensus intimus, interior, internus, sens intime, interne.)* This was introduced, as a convertible term with *Consciousness* in general, by the philosophers of the Cartesian school; and thus came to be frequently applied to denote the source, complement, or revelation of immediate truths. It is however not only in itself vague, but liable to be confounded with *internal sense*, in other very different significations. We need not therefore regret, that in this relation, it has not (though Hutcheson set an example) been naturalized in British Philosophy.

The third appellation determined by the condition of Immediacy is that of

3.—Intuitions—Intuitive *cognitions, notions, judgments, (Intuitiones—Intuitus—cognitio Intuitiva—Intuitions—faculté Intuitive—Anschauungen.* We may add, *ἐπιβολαί—γνῶσις κατὰ πρώτην ἐπιβολήν.*) In this sense *αὐτοπτικός, ἐποπτικός* are rare.

The term Intuition is not unambiguous. Besides its original and proper meaning (as a visual perception), it has been employed to denote a kind of *apprehension*, and a kind of *judgment*.

Under the former head, Intuition, or intuitive knowledge, has been used in the six following significations:—

a.—To denote a perception of the actual and present, in opposition to the 'abstractive' knowledge which we have of the possible in imagination, and of the past in memory.

b.—To denote an immediate apprehension of a thing in itself, in contrast to a representative, vicarious, or mediate, apprehension of it, in or through something else. (Hence by Fichte, Schelling, and others, Intuition is employed to designate the *cognition*, as opposed to the *conception*, of the Absolute.)

c.—To denote the knowledge which we can adequately represent in imagination, in contradistinction to the 'symbolical' knowledge which we cannot image, but only think or conceive, through and under a sign or word. (Hence probably Kant's application of the term to the forms of the Sensibility—the imaginations of Space and Time—in contrast to the forms or categories of the Understanding).

d.—To denote perception proper (the objective), in contrast to sensation proper (the subjective), in our sensitive consciousness.

e.—To denote the simple apprehension of a notion, in contradistinction to the complex apprehension of the terms of a proposition.

Under the latter head, it has only a single signification; viz.

f.—To denote the immediate affirmation by the intellect, that the predicate does or does not pertain to the subject, in what are called self-evident propositions.

All these meanings, however, with the exception of the fourth, have this in common, that they express the condition of an immediate, in opposition to a mediate, knowledge. It is therefore easy to see, how the term was suggested in its application to our original cognitions; and how far it marks out their distinctive character. It has been employed in this relation by Descartes, Leibnitz, Locke, Hemsterhuis, Beattie, Jacobi, Ancillon, Degerando, Thurot, and many others.

II. The second condition, which, along with their Immediacy, seems to have determined a class of names, is the *Incomprehensibility* or *Inexplicability* of our original cognitions.

Under this head there are two appellations which first present themselves —*Feeling* and *Belief*; and these must be considered in correlation.

A thing mediately known is conceived under a representation or notion, and therefore only known as possibly existing; a thing immediately known is apprehended in itself, and therefore known as actually existing.

This being understood, let us suppose an act of immediate knowledge. By external or internal perception I apprehend a phænomenon, of mind or matter, as existing; I therefore affirm it to be. Now if asked how I know, or am assured, that what I apprehend as a mode of mind, may not be, in reality, a mode of matter, or that what I apprehend as a mode of matter, may not, in reality, be a mode of mind; I can only say, using the simplest language, 'I know it to be true, because I *feel* and *cannot but* feel,' or 'because I *believe* and *cannot but* believe, it so to be.' And if farther interrogated, how I know or am assured, that I thus *feel*, or thus *believe*, I can make no better answer than, in the one case, 'because I *believe* that I *feel*,' in the other, 'because I *feel* that I *believe*.' It thus appears, that when pushed to our last refuge, we must retire either upon Feeling, or upon Belief, or upon both indifferently. And accordingly, among philosophers we find that a great many employ one or other of these terms by which to indicate the nature of the ultimate ground to which our cognitions are reducible; while some employ both, even though they may accord a preference to one.

1.—Feeling in English (as *Sentiment* in French, *Gefuehl* in German &c.) is ambiguous:—And in its present application (to say nothing of its original meaning in relation to Touch) we must discharge that signification of the word by which we denote the phænomena of pain and pleasure. Feeling is a term preferable to Consciousness, in so far as the latter does not mark so well the simplicity, ultimacy, and incomprehensibility of our original apprehensions, suggesting, as it does, always something of thought and reflection. In other respects, Consciousness—at least with a determining epithet—may be the preferable expression. In the sense now in question, Feeling is employed by Aristotle, Theophrastus, Pascal, Malebranche, Bossuet, Leibnitz, Buffier, D'Aguesseau, Berkeley, Hume, Kames, Hemsterhuis, Jacobi, Schulze, Bouterweck, Fries, Köppen, Ancillon, Gerlach, Franke, and a hundred others. In this meaning it has been said, and truly, that 'Reason is only a developed Feeling.'

2.—Belief or Faith, (Πίστις, *Fides*, *Croyance*, *Foi*, *Glaube*, &c.) Simply, or with one or other of the epithets *natural*, *primary*, *instinctive*, &c., and some other expressions of a similar import as *Conviction*, *Assent*, *Trust*, *Adhesion*, *Holding for true or real* &c. (Συγκατάθεσις, *Assensus*, *Fuerwahr-und-wirklichhalten*, &c.) have, though not unobjectionable, found favour with a great number of philosophers, as terms whereby to designate the original warrants of cognition. Among these may be mentioned Aristotle, Lucretius, Alexander, Clement of Alexandria, Proclus, Algazel, Luther, Hume, Reid, Beattie, Hemsterhuis, Kant, Heidenreich, Fichte, Jacobi, Bouterweck, Köppen, Ancillon, Hermes, Blunde, Esser, Elvanich, &c. &c.

Nor can any valid objection be taken to the expression.—St Austin accurately says—"We *know*, what rests upon *reason*; we *believe*, what rests upon *authority*." But reason itself must rest at last upon authority; for the original data of reason do not rest on reason, but are necessarily accepted by reason on the authority of what is beyond itself. These data are, therefore, in rigid propriety, Beliefs or Trusts. Thus it is, that in the last resort, we must, perforce, philosophically admit, that belief is the primary condition of reason, and not reason the ultimate ground of belief. We are compelled to surrender the proud *Intellige ut credas* of Abelard, to content ourselves with the humble *Crede ut intelligas* of Anselm.

3.—A third denomination, under this head, is that of

Instincts, *rational* or *intellectual* (*Instinctus*, *Impetus spontanei*, *Instinctus intelligentiæ*, *rationales*.)

Instinctive *beliefs*, *cognitions*, *judgments*, &c.

These terms are intended to express not so much the light as the dark side which the elementary facts of consciousness exhibit. They therefore stand opposed to the conceivable, the understood, the known.

> 'Notre faible Raison se trouble et se confond;
> Oui, la Raison se tait, mais l'Instinct vous répond.'

Priestley (Examination, &c., passim) has attempted to ridicule Reid's use of the terms Instinct and Instinctive, in this relation, as an innovation, not only in philosophy, but in language; and Sir James Mackintosh (Dissert. p. 388) considers the term Instinct not less improper than the term Common Sense.

As to the impropriety, though like most other psychological terms these are not unexceptionable, they are however less so than many, nay than most, others. An Instinct is an agent which performs blindly and ignorantly a work of intelligence and knowledge. The terms *Instinctive belief,—judgment—cognition* are therefore expressions not ill adapted to characterise a belief, judgment, cognition, which, as the result of no anterior consciousness, is, like the products of animal instinct, the intelligent effect of (as far as we are concerned) an unknowing cause. In like manner, we can hardly find more suitable expressions to indicate those incomprehensible spontaneities themselves, of which the primary facts of consciousness are the manifestations, than *rational* or *intellectual Instincts.* In fact if Reason can justly be called a developed Feeling, it may with no less propriety be called an illuminated Instinct:—in the words of Ovid,

Et quod nunc Ratio est, Impetus ante fuit.

As to an innovation either in language or philosophy, this objection only betrays the ignorance of the objector. Mr Stewart (Essays, p. 87 4to ed.) adduces Boscovich and D'Alembert as authorities for the employment of the terms Instinct and Instinctive in Reid's signification. But before Reid he might have found them *thus* applied by Cicero, Scaliger, Bacon, Herbert, Descartes, Rapin, Pascal, Poiret, Barrow, Leibnitz, Musaeus, Feuerlin, Hume, Bayer, Kames, Reimarus, and a host of others; while subsequent to the 'Inquiry into the Human Mind,' besides Beattie, Oswald, Campbell, Fergusson, among our Scottish philosophers, we have, with Hemsterhuis in Holland, in Germany Tetens, Jacobi, Bouterweck, Neeb, Köppen, Ancillon, and many other metaphysicians who have adopted and defended the expressions. In fact, Instinct has been for ages familiarised as a philosophical term in the sense in question, that is, in application to the higher faculties of mind, intellectual and moral. In proof of this, take the article from the 'Lexicon Philosophicum' of Micraelius, which appeared in 1653:—'*Instinctus* est rei ad aliquid tendentis inclinatio; estque alius materialis in corporibus; *alius rationalis in mente;*' and Chauvin is to the same purport, whose 'Lexicon Philosophicum' was first published in 1691. In a moral relation, as a name for the natural tendencies to virtue, it was familiarly employed even by the philosophers of the sixteenth century (v. F. Picolominei 'Decem Gradus,' &c. Gr. iii. c. 1. *sq.*); and in the seventeenth, it had become, in fact, their usual appellation (v. Velthuysen De Principiis Justi, &c. p. 73 *sq.*)

4.—Revelations—Inspirations.—These expressions are intended metaphorically to characterise the incomprehensible manner in which we are made suddenly aware of existence; and, perhaps, to indicate that our knowledge rests ultimately on a testimony which ought to be implicitly believed, however unable we may be explicitly to demonstrate, on rational grounds, its credibility. They have been thus employed, one or both, by Reid, Stewart, Degerando, Cousin, and others, but most emphatically by Jacobi.

5.—Suggestions, (*Suggestiones, Suggestus.*)—This term with some determining epithet is a favourite word of Reid, and in a similar signification. So also was it of St Augustin and Tertullian.—By the νοῦς of Aristotle the latter says—"non aliud quid intelligimus quam *suggestum* animæ ingenitum et insitum et nativitus proprium. De Anima c. 12. See also Testimonies, *infra,* No. 12 d; and, supra, p. 111 a, note.

6.—Facts—Data (*ultimate—primary—original* &c.) of *Consciousness* or *Intelligence.* These expressions have found favour with many philosophers, among whom Fergusson, Fichte, Creuzer, Krug, Ancillon, Gerlach, Cousin, Bautain, may be mentioned. They are well adapted to denote, that our knowledge reposes upon what ought to be accepted as actually true, though why, or in what manner it is true, be inexplicable.

III.—The third quality, in reference to which our primary cognitions have obtained certain appellations, is their *Originality.* Under this head:

1.—First — Primary — Primitive — Primordial — Ultimate, as epithets applied to *truths, principles of thought, laws of intelligence, facts or data of consciousness, elements of reason,* &c., are expressions which require no comment.

2.—Principles ('Αρχαί, *Principia,* literally commencements—points of departure) *Principles of Common Sense—first, proper, authentic* (κυριώτατοι) *Principles of thought, reason, judgment, intelligence—Initia naturæ,* &c.

Without entering on the various meanings of the term Principle, which Aristotle defines, in general, *that from whence any thing exists, is produced, or is known,* it is sufficient to say that it is always used for that on which something else depends; and thus both for an original *law*, and for an original *element*. In the former case it is a *regulative*, in the latter a *constitutive*, principle; and in either signification it may be very properly applied to our original cognitions. In this relation, Mr Stewart would impose certain restrictions on the employment of the word. But admitting the propriety of his distinctions, in themselves,—and these are not new—it may be questioned whether the limitation he proposes of the generic term be expedient, or permissible. See his Elements ii. c. 1. particularly pp. 59, 93 of 8vo. editions.

3.—Anticipations—Presumptions—Prenotions, (προλήψεις, προϋπάρχουσα γνῶσις, *anticipationes, praesumptiones, praenotiones, informationes anteceptæ, cognitiones anticipatæ*, &c.) with such attributes as *common, natural, native, connate, innate*, &c., have been employed to indicate that they are the antecedents, causes, or conditions of all knowledge. These are more especially the terms of ancient philosophy.—To this group may be added the expression *Legitimate Prejudices*, borrowed from the nomenclature of theology, but which have sometimes been applied by philosophers, in a parallel signification.*

4.—A priori—*truths, principles, cognitions, notions, judgments*, &c.

The term *a priori*, by the influence of Kant and his school, is now very generally employed to characterise those elements of knowledge which are not obtained *a posteriori*,—are not evolved out of experience as factitious generalizations; but which, as native to, are potentially in, the mind antecedent to the act of experience, on occasion of which (as constituting its subjective conditions) they are first actually elicited into consciousness. These like many—indeed most—others of his technical expressions, are old words applied in a new signification. Previously to Kant the terms *a priori* and *a posteriori* were, in a sense which descended from Aristotle, properly and usually employed,—the former to denote a reasoning from cause to effect—the latter, a reasoning from effect to cause. The term *a priori* came, however, in modern times to be extended to any abstract reasoning from a given notion to the conditions which such notion involved; hence, for example, the title *a priori* bestowed on the ontological and cosmological arguments for the existence of the deity. The latter of these, in fact, starts from experience—from the observed contingency of the world, in order to construct the supposed notion on which it founds. Clarke's cosmological demonstration, called *a priori*, is therefore, so far, properly an argument *a posteriori*.

5.—Categories *of thought, understanding, reason*, &c.

The Categories of Aristotle and other philosophers were the highest classes (under Being) to which the objects of our knowledge could be generalized. Kant contorted the term Category from its proper meaning of attribution; and from an objective to a subjective application; bestowing this name on the ultimate and necessary laws by which thought is governed in its manifestations. The term, in this relation, has however found acceptation; and been extended to designate, in general, all the *a priori* phaenomena of mind, though Kant himself limited the word to a certain order of these.

6. Transcendental *truths, principles, cognitions, judgments, &c.*

In the Schools *transcendentalis* and *transcendens* were convertible expressions, employed to mark a term or notion which *transcended*, that is, which rose above, and thus contained under it, the categories, or summa genera, of Aristotle. Such, for example is Being, of which the ten categories are only subdivisions. Kant, according to his wont, twisted these old terms into a new signification. First of all, he distinguished them from each other *Transcendent* (transcendens) he employed to denote what is wholly beyond experience, being given neither as an a posteriori nor as an a priori element of cognition—what therefore transcends every category of thought. *Transcendental* (transcendentalis) he applied to signify the a priori or necessary cognitions which, though manifested in, as affording the conditions of, experience, transcend the sphere of that contingent or adventitious knowledge which we acquire by experience. Transcendental is not therefore what transcends, but what in fact constitutes, a category of thought. This term, though probably from another quarter, has found favour with Mr Stewart; who proposes to ex-

* As by Trembley of Geneva. It is manifest, though I have not his treatise at hand, that he borrowed this, not over-fortunate, expression from the *Préjugés Légitimes contre les Calvinistes* of Nicole, the work in which originated the celebrated controversy in which Pajon, Basnage, &c. were engaged. Of this Mr Stewart does not seem to be aware. See p 27 b.

change the expression *principles of common sense* for, among other names, that of *transcendental truths*.

7. Pure (rein) is another Kantian expression (borrowed with a modification of meaning from previous philosophers*) for cognitions, in which there is mingled nothing foreign or adventitious, that is, nothing from experience, and which consequently are wholly native to the mind, wholly a priori. Such elements however, it is evident, are obtained only by a process of sundering and abstraction. In actual, or concrete, thinking, there is given nothing pure; the native and foreign, the a priori and a posteriori are there presented in mutual fusion.

IV. The fourth determining circumstance, is that the cognitions in question are *natural* not conventional, *native* not acquired. Hence their most universal denominations:

1 Nature (*Φύσις natura*); as, common *Nature of man—light of Nature*†—*primary hypotheses of Nature—initia Naturae*, &c.

Natural (*Φυσικός, naturalis*) as conjoined with cognitions, *notions, judgments, anticipations, presumptions, prenotions, beliefs, truths, criteria*, &c.

2. Native, Innate, Connate, Implanted, &c. (*ἐνὸν, ἔμφυτος, σύμφυτος, innatus, ingenitus, congenitus, insitus*, &c.) as applied to *cognitions, notions, conceptions, judgments, intellections, beliefs*, &c. These terms may be used either to express a correct or an erroneous doctrine.

V. The fifth ground of nomenclature, is the *Necessity* of these cognitions, constituting as they do the indispensable *foundations* and *elementary* ingredients of every act of knowledge and thought. Hence they have been called in the one point of view,

Fundamental—*truths, laws of belief, principles of knowledge, intelligence, reason*, &c.; in the other,

Essential or Constituent elements *of reason—Original* Stamina, *of reason*—Elemental *laws of thought*, &c. These are Mr Stewart's favourite denominations.

VI. The sixth circumstance is, that they afford the conditions and regulative principles of all knowledge. Hence they obtain the name of,

Laws, or Canons—*fundamental, ultimate, elemental, necessary*, &c. of *human belief, knowledge, thought*, &c.

VII. The seventh circumstance is their *Universality*; this being at once the consequence of their necessity, and its index. Hence to designate them the attributes of—

Common — Universal — Catholic — Public, &c. (*κοινός, communis, καθολικός, universalis, publicus*) applied to *sense, reason, intelligence*—to *cognitions, notions, conceptions, judgments, intellections, prenotions, anticipations, presumptions, principles, axioms, beliefs, nature of man*, &c., &c. I may observe, however, that a principle, &c, may be called common for one or other, or for all of three reasons:—1°, because common to all men (philosophers in general); 2°, because common to all sciences, (Aristotle, Anal. Post. L. i. c. ii. § 5); 3°, by relation to the multitude of conclusions dependent from it, (Calovius, Nool. c. 2.)

VIII. The eighth, is their presumed *Trustworthiness*, either as veracious enouncements, or as accurate tests, of truth. Hence, in the one relation, they have been styled—

1. Truths (*veritates*) *first, primary, a priori, fundamental*, &c.; and in the other,

2. Criteria (*κριτήρια, normae*) *natural, authentic*, &c.

IX. The ninth, is that the principles of our knowledge must be themselves *Knowledges*.*

If viewed as cognitions, in general, they have been called

1. a. Cognitions or Knowledges (*γνώσεις, cognitiones, notitiae, informationes*, &c.) with the discriminative attri-

* *Pure knowledge* (cognitio pura) was a term employed by the Cartesians and Leibnitians to denote that knowledge in which there was no mixture of *sensible images*, being purely intellectual. Using the term *Intellect* less precisely than the Aristotelians, the Cartesians found it necessary to employ, in ordinary, for the sake of discrimination, the expression *pure Intellect* (intellectus purus) in contrast to Sense and Imagination. This term was however borrowed from the Schools; who again borrowed it, through the medium of St. Augustine, from the Platonists.—See Scoti Comm. Oxon. in Sent. L. i. dist. iii. qu. 4. § 22. Op. V. p. 491.

† *Light of Nature*, or *Lumen naturale* (intellectus sc. agentis) a household expression with the Schoolmen, was however used to denote the natural revelation of intelligence, in opposition to the supernatural light afforded through divine inspiration. The analogy of the *active* Intellect and light, was suggested by Aristotle. —(De An. iii. § 1.)

* *Knowledges*, in common use with Bacon and our English philosophers till after the time of Locke, ought not to be discarded. It is however unnoticed by any English Lexicographer.

butes, *first, primary, ultimate, original, fundamental, elemental, natural, common, pure, transcendental, a priori, native, innate, connate, implanted,* &c.

2. b.—CONSCIOUSNESS (*conscientia, conscience, Bewusstseyn*) *facts, data, revelations,* &c. of, have been very commonly employed; while

CONSCIOUSNESSES (*conscientiae, consciences,*) with, or without, an epithet, as *connate, innate,* has the authority of Tertullian, Keckermann, D'Aguesseau, Hunber, and many others.

If viewed as *incomplex* cognitions, they have more properly obtained the names of

3.—NOTIONS, CONCEPTIONS, PRENOTIONS (ἔννοιαι, ἐννοήματα, νοήματα, προλήψεις, notiones, conceptiones, conceptus, &c.) sometimes simply, but more usually limited by the same attributes; though these terms were frequently extended to complex cognitions likewise.

If viewed as *complex* cognitions, they have been designated, either by the general name of

4.—JUDGMENTS, PROPOSITIONS (judicia, ἀποφάνσεις, προτάσεις, effata, pronunciata, enunciata, &c.) qualified by such adjectives as *self-evident, intuitive, natural, common, a priori,* &c.;—or by some peculiar name. Of these last there are two which deserve special notice—Axiom and Maxim.

5.—AXIOMS, (ἀξιώματα, *dignitates, pronunciata honoraria, effata fide digna, propositiones illustres, κύριαι δόξαι, ratae, firmae sententiae,* &c.)

The term Axiom is ambiguous; the history of its employment obscure, and uninvestigated; and the received accounts of its signification, and the reasons of its signification, very erroneous.—I am aware of *three* very different meanings in which it has been used. Of these the first and second are of ancient, the third of modern, usurpation. The verb ἀξιόω, originally and properly, means *to rate a thing at a certain worth or value, to appreciate, to estimate.* Now it is evident, that from this central signification it might very easily be deflected into two collateral meanings.

a.—To rate a thing at its value, seems to presuppose that it has some value to be rated; hence the verb came very naturally to signify—*I deem worthy,* &c. From it in this signification we have ἀξίωμα, *worth, dignity, authority;* and, applied in a logical relation, a *worthy,* an *authoritative, proposition.* But why worthy?—why authoritative? Either because a proposition worthy of acceptance (πρότασις ἀξιόπιστος); or because a proposition commanding and obtaining acceptance (κυρία δόξα, pronunciatum honorarium, illustre.) But of what nature are the propositions worthy of, or which command, universal credence? Manifestly not, at least primarily, those which, though true, and even admitted to be true, shine in a reflected light of truth, as dependent on other propositions for their evidence; but those out of which the truth beams directly and immediately, which borrow not the proof from any which they afford to all, which are deserving of credit on their own authority—in a word, *self-evident propositions* (προτάσεις αὐτοπίστοι.) Hence the application of the term to judgments true, primary, immediate, common. To this result converge the authorities of Aristotle, Theophrastus, Alexander, Themistius, Proclus, Ammonius Hermiae, and Philoponus.

In this signification, as I can recollect, the oldest example of the word is to be found in Aristotle. That this philosopher limited the expression Axiom to those judgments which, on occasion of experience, arise naturally and necessarily in the conscious mind, and which are therefore virtually prior to experience, cannot, I think, be reasonably doubted. 'Of the immediate principles,' he says, 'of syllogism, that which cannot be demonstrated, but which it is not necessary to possess as the prerequisite of all learning, I call *Thesis;* and that *Axiom,* which he who would learn aught must himself bring, [and not receive from his instructor]. For some such principles there are; and it is to these that we are accustomed to apply this name.' (Anal. Post., L. i. c. 1, § 14.) And again, distinguishing the Axiom from the Hypothesis and Postulate, of the two latter he says—'Neither of these of itself necessarily exists, and necessarily manifests its existence in thought.' (Ibid. c. 10, § 7.) He, consequently, supposes that an Axiom is not only something true, but something that we *cannot but think to be true.* All this is confirmed by sundry other passages (Of these, some will be seen in Testimonies, n. 3; where also, in a note, is given a solution of what may be said in opposition to the attribution of this doctrine to the Stagirite.) The same is confirmed, also, by the ancient interpreters of the Posterior Analytics—Themistius, (f. 2. a. ed. Ald.) and Philoponus, or rather Ammonius Hermiae, (f. 9. b., ed. Ald.) These harbour no doubt in regard to the purport of the texts now quoted;—and the same construction is given to Aristotle's doctrine on this point, by Alexander, elsewhere, but especially in his Commentary on the Topics (p. 12, ed. Ald.), and by Proclus in his Commentaries on Euclid. (Libb. ii. iii.)

The following definition by Theophrastus is preserved by Themistius (l. c.) I translate the context, cautioning the reader that it is impossible to determine whether the latter part of the passage belongs to Theophrastus, or, what is more probable, to Themistius himself. 'Theophrastus thus defines an Axiom:—An axiom is a certain kind of opinion [or judgment,] one species of which is [valid] of all things of the same class, as [under the category, Quantity]—*If equals be taken from equals, the remainders are equal;* while another is [valid] of all things indifferently, as—*Between affirmation and negation there is no medium.* For these are, as it were, connate and common to all. Whence also the reason of the denomination Axiom, [worth, dignity, authority.] For what is set over, either all things absolutely, or certain classes of things universally, that we judge to have precedence, authority, by reference to them.'

In this sense the word is universally supposed to have been technically employed by the mathematicians, from a very ancient period. But whether it was so prior to Aristotle, I should be vehemently disposed to doubt; both from the tenor of the former passage of the Posterior Analytics, just quoted, in which the philosopher seems to attribute to himself this application of the term, and from the absence of all evidence to prove its earlier introduction. I am aware indeed of a passage in the Metaphysics, (L. iii. [iv.] c. 3,) which, at first sight, and as it has always been understood, might appear unfavourable to this surmise; for mention is there made of 'what in mathematics (*ἐν τοῖς μαθήμασι*) are called Axioms.' But this text is, I suspect, misunderstood, and that it ought to be translated—'what in our "Mathematics" are called Axioms.' But did Aristotle write on this subject? He did, one, if not two treatises; as appears from the lists of Laertius (L. v. § 24) and the Anonymus Menagii. In the former we have Μαθηματικὸν, α', '*On Mathematics, one book;*' in the latter—Περὶ τῆς ἐν τοῖς μαθήμασιν οὐσίας, '*On the existence treated of in Mathematics.*' Nay, the term is not to be found in the writings we possess of those geometricians who ascend the nearest to the age of Aristotle. Euclid, what may surprise the reader, does not employ it. There it stands, certainly, in all the editions and translations of the Elements, in ordinary use. But this is only one of the many tamperings with his text, for which the perfidious editors and translators of Euclid are responsible; and in the present instance the Aristotelizing commentary of Proclus seems to have originally determined the conversion of 'Common Notions' into 'Axioms.' Archimedes (De Sphaera et Cylindro, sub initio) is, after Aristotle, the oldest authority extant for the term, in a mathematical relation; though Archimedes, who only *once* employs it, does not apply it in the Aristotelic limitation, as equivalent to the Common Notions of Euclid, and exclusive of Postulates and Definitions. On the contrary, with him *axiom* is, if not convertible with *definition*, used only in the second or Stoical sense, for an *enunciation* in general. Turning indeed to the works of the other Greek Mathematicians which I have at hand, I cannot find the term in Apollonius of Perga, in Serenus, Diophantus, Pappus, Eutocius, Hero, or the Samian Aristarchus. Sextus Empiricus, in all his controversy with the Mathematicians, knows it not; nor, except in the second technical meaning, is it to be found in Plutarch. Its application in mathematics was therefore, I surmise, comparatively late, and determined by the influence of Aristotle. This is not the only instance by which it might be shown that the Mathematicians are indebted to the Stagirite for their language; who, if he borrowed a part of his Logical nomenclature from Geometry, amply repaid the obligation.

This first meaning is that which Axiom almost exclusively obtains in the writings of the Aristotelian, and (though Plato does not philosophically employ the term) of the Platonic school.

b.—To rate a thing at its value, that is, to attribute or not to attribute to it a certain worth, is a meaning which would easily slide into denoting the affirmation or negation of qualities in regard to a subject; for its qualities determine, positively or negatively, the value of any thing. Hence, in general, *to be of opinion, to think so and so, to judge.* (In like manner, among other analogical examples, the Latin verb *existimo* (that is *ex-æstimo*), its primary meaning falling into desuetude, was at last almost exclusively employed in the secondary, as—*I think that*, or *I opine.*) From this signification of the verb flowed a second logical meaning of the substantive; Axiom being applied to denote, in general, an *enunciation* or *proposition*, (properly a categorical), *whether true or false.* In this sense it was used, sometimes by Aristotle (v. Top. L. viii ce, 1, 3—if this work be his—et ibi, Alexandrum), and, as far as I am aware, to say nothing of the Epicureans and Sceptics, *always* by the Stoics—though Simplicius (ad. Epict. Ench. c. 58) asserts, that they occasionally employed it, like the Aristotelians, in the first. Laelius, Varro, Cicero, Sergius, Agellius, Apuleius, Donatus, Martianus Capella, &c., render it by various Latin terms, in all of which however the present meaning, exclusively, is embodied; and in the same signification the Greek term *axioma* itself was, in modern times, adopted by Ramus and his school, as their common logical expression for 'proposition.'

Thus in neither of its logical significations, I make bold to say, is the word Axiom to be found in any writing extant, prior to Aristotle; and in its second, only in a work, the Topics, which is not with absolute certainty the production of the Stagirite.—I may observe, that there is another account given of the logical applications of the word, but to this I think it wholly needless to advert.

c.—The third and last meaning is that imposed upon the word by Bacon. He contorted Axiom to designate any higher proposition, obtained by generalisation and induction from the observation of individual instances—the enunciation of a general fact—an empirical law.

So much for the meanings of the term Axiom itself—now for its translation.

Dignitas was employed by Boethius to render Axioma in its first or Aristotelic meaning; and from him came, in this application, into general use among the Latin schoolmen. But before Boethius, and as a translation of the term in its second or Stoical meaning, I find *Dignitas* employed by Priscian, (Instit. Grammat. L. xvii. c. 1.) No lexicographer, however, no philologist has noticed these authorities for the word, while Latin was still a living language. It has, indeed, till this hour, been universally taken for granted by philologers that *dignitas* in this relation is a mere modern barbarism. 'Inepte faciunt (says Muretus) qui ἀξιώματα *dignitates* vocant; cujus pravae consuetudinis Hermolaus Barbarus auctor fuit.' (Variae Lectiones, L. vi. c. 2.) This is wrong, more especially as regards the author and æra of the custom: nay H. Barbarus is only reprehensible for not always, instead of rarely, translating the term, as it occurs in Themistius, by *Dignitas*, if translated into Latin it must be; for his usual version by *Proloquium* or *Pronuntiatum*—expressions which only render the word in its Stoical meaning—has been the cause of considerable error and confusion among subsequent logicians, who, unable to resort to the one rare edition of the original, were thus led to suppose that the nomenclature of Theophrastus and Themistius were different from that of Aristotle. The authority of Muretus has obtained, however, for his mistake a universal acceptation; and what is curious, Nicolaus Loensis (Misc. Epiph. L. I. c. 1.) in his criticism of the very chapter in which it occurs, omitting this solitary error, stupidly or perfidiously inculpates Muretus for assertions, which that illustrious scholar assuredly never dreamt of hazarding.

6. MAXIMS—(*maximae*, *propositiones maximae*, *supremae*, *principales*, &c.)

In Maxim we have the example of a word which all employ, but of whose meaning none seem to know the origin or reason.* Extant in all the languages of Christendom, this term is a bequest of that philosophy, once more extensive than Christianity itself, through which Aristotle, for a thousand years, swayed at once and with almost equal authority, the theology of the Bible and the Koran. But it was not original to the scholastic philosophy. The schoolmen received it from Boethius, who is the earliest author to whom I trace the expression. He propounds it in his two works—'In Topica Ciceronis,' and 'De Differentiis Topicis.' The following is one of his definitions:—'Maximas propositiones [which he also styles propositiones supremae principales, indemonstrabiles, per se notae, &c.] vocamus quae et universales sunt, et ita notae atque manifestae, ut probatione non egeant, eaque potius quae in dubitatione sunt

* I have had the curiosity to see how far this ignorance extended. Our English Lexicographers, Johnson, Todd, Webster, are in outer darkness. They only venture to hint at some unknown relation between *maxim* and "*maximum*, *the greatest!*" Richardson is not positively wrong. He is aware (probably from Furetiere or his copyist the Dictionaire de Trevoux, for there is a verbal coincidence in all three) that *maxima* was in low Latin used in a similar signification; but his explanation of the reason is not only defective but erroneous. In other dictionaries, real and verbal, if we find the word noticed at all, we find nothing beyond a bare statement of its actual meaning; as may be seen in those of Goclenius, Micraelius, Martinius, Ducange, the Zedlerian Lexicon, to say nothing of our more modern Encyclopedias Even the great Selden (On Fortescue, c. 8) in attempting to explain the term in its legal application, betrays his unacquaintance with its history and proper import.

probent. Nam quae indubitatae sunt, ambiguorum demonstrationi solent esse principia; qualis est—*Omnem numerum vel parem vel imparem*, et—*Aequalia relinqui si aequalibus aequalia detrahuntur*, caeteraeque de quarum nota veritate non quaeritur.'

With Boethius *maxima propositio* (maxima he never uses absolutely) is thus only a synonyme for axiom or self-evident judgment. He however applies the term specially to denote those dialectical principles, axioms, or canons, those catholic judgments which constitute what in Logic and Rhetoric have since Aristotle been called *common places*; that is, the sources or receptacles of arguments applicable to every matter, and proper to none.* Such propositions, he says, are styled *maximae* or *greatest*, because as universal and primary they implicitly contain the other propositions, (minores posterioresque,) and determine the whole inference of a reasoning; (reliquas in se propositiones complectuntur, et per eas fit consequens et rata conclusio.) But he also sometimes indicates that they are entitled to this epithet, because, as evident in themselves and independent of all others, they afford to the unintuitive judgments they support, their primary proof, (antiquissimam probationem,) and their greatest certainty, (maximam fidem.) Compare In Top. Cic. L. i. Op. p. 765—De Diff. Top. L. i. p. 859 L. ii. p. 865 sq. Boethius had likewise perhaps Aristotle's saying in his thought—'that principles, though what are least in magnitude, are what are *greatest* in power.'

Maxima propositio, as a dialectical expression, was adopted from Boethius by his friend and brother consul, the patrician Cassiodorus; and from those 'ultimi Romanorum' it passed to the schoolmen, with whom so soon as it became established as a common term of art, *propositio* was very naturally dropt, and *maxima* thus came to be employed as a substantive—by many at last, who were not aware of the origin and rationale of its meaning. Finally, from the Latinity and philosophical nomenclature of the schools, it subsided, as a household word, into all the vernacular languages of Europe; with this restriction however—that in them it is not usually applied except in a practical relation; denoting a moral apophthegm, a rule of conduct, an ethical, a political, a legal, canon, &c., and this too, enouncing, not so much what is always and necessarily, but what is for the most part and probably, true. It sounds strange in our ears to hear of a mathematical or logical maxim, in the sense of axiom, self-evident principle, or law—though this is the sense in which it was commonly employed, among others, by Locke and Leibnitz. To this restriction, its special employment in Dialectic (the logic of contingent matter) probably prepared the way; though by the schoolmen, as by Boethius, it continued to be used as convertible with axiom. '*Dignitas* dicitur (says Albertus Magnus) quia omnibus dignior est, eo quod omnibus influit cognitionem et veritatem; et dicitur *Maxima*, eo quod virtute influentiae lucis et veritatis omnia excedit immediata principia.' (In i. Post. Anal. c. 1.) St Thomas and Scotus, might be adduced to the same effect; see also P. Hispanus (Summulae, tr. v. c. 3. et ibi Versor.) At an early period, it was borrowed as a term of art, into the Common Law of England; *Maxims* there denoting what by the civilians were technically denominated *Regulae Juris*. (Fortescue, De Laudibus legum Angliae c. 8.—Doctor and Student. c. 8.) By Kant Maxim was employed to designate a subjective principle, theoretical or practical, i. e. one not of objective validity, being exclusively relative to some interest of the subject. Maxim and Regulative principle are, in the Critical philosophy, opposed to Law and Constitutive principle.

---

* Thus in arguing, *that a wise, is not an intemperate, man*, by the syllogism—

He is wise who controls his passions;
He is intemperate who does not control his passions;

Therefore a wise, is not an intemperate, man; the whole reasoning is contained under, and therefore presupposes, the proposition *To what the definition is inapplicable, to that is inapplicable the thing defined*, (*cui non convenit definitio, non convenit definitum.*) This proposition (one of six co-ordinates which make up the common place called of Definition) as containing under it a multitude of others (e. g. Cui non convenit definitio *sapientis*, nec convenit nomen; cui non convenit definitio *justi*, *pulchri*, *timidi*, &c. &c., nec nomen) is not inappropriately styled *p. maxima*. I may observe, however, that, as thus employed, *maxima* can only, in strict propriety, qualify a proposition relatively, not absolutely, greatest. For every maxim of every dialectical Place is itself contained within the sphere of one or other of the four logical laws of Identity, Contradiction, Excluded Middle, and Reason and Consequent, of which it is only a subordinate modification. Thus the maxim adduced, is only a special application of the law of Contradiction. To the four laws therefore the name of *propositiones maximae* should be exclusively applicable, if this expression were intended to denote an unconditioned universality.

Besides the preceding designations under this head, names have been given to the original deliverances of Consciousness, considered as the manifestations of some special faculty; that is, Consciousness as performing this peculiar function has obtained a particular name. In this respect it has been called *Reason*, and, with greater propriety, *Intellect* or *Intelligence*.

7. REASON, (λόγος, *ratio*, *raison*, *Vernunft*,) *truths*, *principles*, *beliefs*, *feelings*, *intuitions*, &c. of.

Reason is a very vague, vacillating, and and equivocal word. Throwing aside various accidental significations which it has obtained in particular languages, as in Greek denoting not only the *ratio* but the *oratio* of the Latins; throwing aside its employment, in most languages, for *cause*, *motive*, *argument*, *principle of probation*, or *middle term of a syllogism*, and considering it only as a philosophical word denoting a faculty or complement of faculties;—in this relation it is found employed in the following meanings, not only by different individuals, but frequently, to a greater or less extent, by the same philosopher.

a.—It has both in ancient and modern times been very commonly employed, like *understanding* and *intellect*, to denote our intelligent nature in general (λογικὸν μέρος); and this usually as distinguished from the lower cognitive faculties, as sense, imagination, memory—but always, and emphatically, as in contrast to the feelings and desires. In this signification, to follow the Aristotelic division, it comprehends—1°, *Conception*, or *Simple Apprehension* (ἔννοια, νόησις τῶν ἀδιαιρέτων, conceptus, conceptio, apprehensio simplex, das Begreifen);—2°, the *Compositive and Divisive process*, *Affirmation and Negation*, *Judgment*, (σύνθεσις καὶ διαίρεσις, ἀπόφανσις, judicium);—3°, *Reasoning* or the *Discursive faculty* (διάνοια, λόγος, λογισμός, τὸ συλλογίζεσθαι, discursus, ratiocinatio);—4°, *Intellect* or *Intelligence* proper, either as the intuition, or as the place, of principles or self-evident truths (νοῦς, intellectus, intelligentia, mens.)

b.—In close connexion with the preceding signification, from which perhaps it ought not to be separated, is that meaning in which *reason*, the *rational*, the *reasonable*, is used to characterize the legitimate employment of our faculties in general, in contradistinction to the irregular or insubordinate action of one or more even of our rational faculties, which, if exercised out of their proper sphere, may be viewed as opposed to *reason*. Thus the plain sense of one of Moliere's characters complains—

> Raisonner est l'emploi de toute ma maison,
> Et le *raisonnement* en bannit la *raison*.

c.—It has not unfrequently been employed to comprehend the *third* and *fourth* of the special functions above enumerated—to wit, the dianoetic and noetic. In this meaning it is taken by Reid in his *later* works. Thus in the Intellectual Powers (p. 425 ab.) he states, that Reason, in its first office or degree, [the noetic,] is identical with Common Sense, in its second, [the dianoetic,] with Reasoning.

d.—It has very generally, both in ancient and modern philosophy, been employed for the *third* of the above special functions;—λόγος and λογισμός, Ratio and Ratiocinatio, Reason and Reasoning being thus confounded. Reid thus applied it in his *earlier* work the Inquiry. See pp. 100, b., 108, a., 127, a. b.

e.—In the ancient systems it was very rarely used exclusively for the *fourth* special function, the noetic, in contrast to the dianoetic. Aristotle, indeed, (Eth. Nic. L. vi. c. 11 (12), Eth. Eud. L. v. c. 8) expressly says that Reason is not the faculty of principles, that faculty being Intelligence proper. Boethius (De Cons. Phil. L. v. Pr. 5) states that Reason or Discursive Intellect belongs to man, while Intelligence or Intuitive Intellect is the exclusive attribute of Divinity. '*Ratio* humani tantum generis est, sicuti *Intelligentia* sola divini;' while Porphyry somewhere says 'that we have Intelligence in common with the Gods, and Reason in common with the brutes.' Sometimes however it was apparently so employed. Thus St Augustine seems to view Reason as the faculty of intuitive truths, and as opposed to Reasoning:—'*Ratio* est quidam mentis adspectus, quo, per seipsam non per corpus, verum intuetur; *Ratiocinatio* autem est rationis inquisitio, a certis ad incertorum indagationem nitens cogitatio.' (De Quant. An. § 53—De Immort. An. §§ 1, 10.) This, however, is almost a singular exception.

In modern times, though we frequently meet with Reason, as a general faculty, distinguished from Reasoning, as a particular; yet until Kant, I am not aware that Reason (Vernunft) was ever exclusively, or even emphatically, used in a signification corresponding to the noetic faculty, in its strict and special meaning, and opposed to understanding (Verstand) viewed as comprehending the other functions of thought—unless Crusius (Weg, &c. § 62 sq.) may be regarded as Kant's forerunner in this innovation. Indeed the Vernunft of Kant, in its special signification, (for he also uses it for Reason in the first or more general meaning, as indeed nothing can be more vague and various than his employment of the word,) cannot without considerable qualification be considered analogous to Νοῦς, far less to Common Sense; though his usurpation of the term for the faculty of principles, probably determined Jacobi (who had originally, like philosophers in general, confounded Vernunft with Verstand, Reason with Reasoning,) to appropriate the term Reason to what he had at first opposed to it, under the name of Belief (Glaube.) Accordingly in his maturer writings, '*Vernunft*, Reason—' *Vernunft-Glaube*,' Belief of Reason —' *Vernunft-Gefuehl*,' Feeling of Reason —' *Rationale Anschauung*,' Rational Intuition—' *Sinn, Organ fuer das Uebersinnliche*,' Sense or Organ of the Supersensible, &c. are the terms by which we may roundly say that Jacobi denominates the noetic faculty or common sense.

Kant's abusive employment of the term Reason, for the faculty of the Unconditioned, determined also its adoption, under the same signification, in the philosophy of Fichte, Schelling, and Hegel; though Νοῦς, Intellectus, Intelligentia, which had been applied by the Platonists in a similar sense, were (through Verstand, by which they had been always rendered into German) the only words suitable to express that cognition of the Absolute, in which subject and object, knowledge and existence, God and man, are supposed to be identified. But even in this, to add to the confusion, no consistency was maintained. For though that absolute cognition was emphatically the act of *Reason*, it was yet by Fichte and Schelling denominated the Intuition *of Intellect* (intellectuale Anschauung.) F. Schlegel was therefore justified in his attempt to reverse the relative superiority of Vernunft and Verstand. What were his reasons I know not: but as they have excited no attention, they were probably of little weight.

Though Common Sense be not therefore opposed to Reason, except perhaps in its fourth signification, still the term Reason is of so general and ambiguous an import, that its employment in so determinate a meaning as a synonyme of Common Sense ought to be avoided. It is only, we have seen, as an expression for the noetic faculty, or Intellect proper, that Reason can be substituted for Common Sense; and as the former is hardly allowable, still less is the latter.

Besides the more precise employment of Reason as a synonyme for Common Sense by the recent German philosophers, it will be found more vaguely applied in the same meaning—usually, however, with some restrictive epithet, like *common*, *universal*, *fundamental*, &c.—by many older authorities, of whom Heraclitus, the Stoics, Turretin, Lyons, Bentley, Shaftesbury, De La Mennais, are among the Testimonies adduced in the sequel.

8.—INTELLECT, INTELLIGENCE, (νοῦς,* *intellectus, intelligentia, mens, entendement, intelligence, intellect, Verstand*,) *truths, principles, axioms, dicta, intuitions*, &c., of.

INTELLECTIONS, (νοήσεις, *intellectiones, intelligentiæ, intellections, intelligences*,) *primary, natural, common*, &c.

By Aristotle, from whom it finally obtained the import which it subsequently retained, the term Νοῦς is used in two principal significations. In the one (like Reason in its first meaning) it denotes, in general, our higher faculties of thought and knowledge; in the other it denotes, in special, the faculty, habit, place, of principles, that is, of self-evident and self evidencing notions and judgments. The schoolmen, following Boethius, translated it by *intellectus* and *intelligentia*;† and some of them appropriated the former of these terms to its first, or general, signification, the latter to its second or special. Cicero does not employ the term *intellectus*; and the Ciceronian epidemic prevalent after the revival of letters, probably induced the Latin translators of the Greek philosophers to render it more usually by the term *mens*. In one and all of our modern languages the words derived from, or corresponding to, Intellectus, Intellectio, Intelligentia, have been so loosely and variously employed, that they offer no temptation to substitute them for that of Common Sense. The case is different with the adjective *noetic*. The correlatives *noetic* and *dianoetic* would afford the best philosophical designations—the former for an intuitive principle, or truth at first hand; the latter for a demonstra-

* See above, p. 757 b, note.

† *Intelligentia* (like *Intellectio*) properly denotes the *act* or *energy* of *Intellectus*. How it came that the term *Intelligentiæ* was latterly applied to denote the higher order of created existences, as angels, &c., is explained by Aquinas (S. Th. P. I., qu. 79, art. 10,) as an innovation introduced by certain translations from the Arabic. I shall not commemorate the distinction of *Intellectus* and *Intelligentia* given in the contradictory farrago attributed to St Augustine, under the title *De Spiritu et Anima*. See cc. 37, 38.

tive proposition, or truth at second hand. *Noology* and *Noological, Dianoialogy* and *Dianoialogical* would be also technical terms of much convenience in various departments of philosophy. On the doctrine of first principles as a department of 'Gnostology,' the philosophy of knowledge, we have indeed during the seventeenth century, by German authors alone, a series of special treatises, under the titles —of '*Noologia*,' by Calovius, 1651, Mejerus, 1662, Wagnerus, 1670, and Zeidlerus, 1680,—and of '*Intelligentia*,' by Gutkius, 1625, and Geilfussius, 1662. '*Archelogia*,' again, was the title preferred for their works upon the same subject by Alstedius, 1620, and Micraelius, 1658. Of these treatises, in so far as I have seen them, the execution disappoints the curiosity awakened by the title and attempt.

In this sense, besides the ordinary employment of *Intellectus*, and *Intelligentia* by the ancient and modern Aristotelians; Cicero, St Austin, and others, in like manner, use *Intelligentiæ*, either simply, or with some differential epithet, as *inchoatæ, adumbratæ, complicatae, involutae, primae, communes*, &c.; as is done likewise by Pascal and other French philosophers with the terms *Intelligence* and *Intelligences*.

X. The tenth and last circumstance is, that the native contributions by the mind itself to our concrete cognitions have, prior to their elicitation into consciousness through experience, only a *potential*, and in actual experience only an *applied, engaged*, or *implicate*, existence. Hence their designation of—

Habits, (possessions,) Dispositions, Virtualities &c., with some discriminating epithet. Thus, by Aristotle, noetic Intelligence is called the (natural) *Habit of principles* (ἕξις τῶν ἀρχῶν); and principles themselves are characterised by Leibnitz, as *natural Habits, Dispositions, Virtualities*. As prior to experience, Galen styles them things *occult* or *delitescent* (κεκρυμμένα,) in contrast to the manifestations made in experience itself (φαινόμενα.) Cicero and others call them *Intelligentiae obscuras, inchoatae, complicatae, involutae*, &c. To the same head are to be referred the metaphorical denominations they have obtained of—*Seeds* (λόγοι σπερματικοί, *semina scientiae, semina aeternitatis*, &c.,)—or *Sparks* (*scintillae, igniculi*, ζώπυρα, ἐναύσματα, σπινθῆρες, &c.)

§ VI. *The Universality of the philosophy of Common Sense; or its general recognition, in Reality and in Name, shewn by a chronological series of Testimonies, from the dawn of speculation to the present day.**

1.—Hesiod thus terminates his Works and Days:—

Φήμη δ' οὔτις πάμπαν ἀπόλλυται, ἥν τινα πολλοὶ
Λαοὶ φημίζουσι· θεός νύ τίς ἐστι καὶ αὐτή.

'The Word proclaimed by the concordant voice
Of mankind fails not; for in Man speaks God.'

Hence the adage?—Vox Populi, vox Dei.

2.—Heraclitus.—The doctrine held by this philosopher of a Common Reason, (ξυνὸς λόγος,) the source and the criterion of truth, in opposition to individual wisdom, (ἰδία φρόνησις,) the principle of opinion and error, may be regarded as one of Common Sense. Its symbol—τὰ κοινῇ φαινόμενα πιστά—Sextus Empiricus thus briefly expounds:—'What appears to all, that is to be believed; for it is apprehended by the Reason which is Common and Divine: whereas, what is presented to individual minds, is unworthy of belief, and for the counter cause.'—I. Adv. Log. § 131.

In so far, however, as our scanty sources of information enable us to judge, Heraclitus mistook the import, and transgressed the boundaries of the genuine doctrine, in the same way as is done in the system of 'Common Sense,' 'Universal Consent,' or 'Common Reason,' so ingeniously maintained by the eloquent Abbé De La Mennais, (No. 101.) Both vilipend all private judgment as opinion; and opinion both denounce as a disease. Both sacrifice the intelligence of individual men at the shrine of the common reason of mankind; and both celebrate the apotheosis of this Common Reason or Sense, as an immediate ray of the divinity. Both, finally,

* In throwing together these testimonies, I had originally in view, merely to adduce such as bore explicitly and directly on the doctrine of Common Sense, word and thing; subsequently I found it proper to take in certain others, in which that doctrine is clearly, though only implicitly or indirectly, asserted. These last, I have admitted, in preference, from those schools which ascribe the least to the mind itself, as a fountain of knowledge, and a criterion of truth; and have, in consequence, taken little or nothing from the Platonic. I have also been obliged to limit the testimonies, almost exclusively, to Common Sense, considered on its speculative side. On its practical, there could have been no end.

in proclaiming—'that we ought to follow the Common,' (δεῖν ἕπεσθαι τῷ ξυνῷ,) mean, that we should resort to this, not merely as a catholic criterion, or a source of elementary truths, but as a magazine of ready fabricated dogmas Heraclitus and La Mennais are the first and last philosophers in our series: philosophy would thus seem to end as it began.—In relation to the former, see Schleiermacher, in Wolf und Buttmann's Museum, i. pp. 313, seq.; and Brandis Geschichte der Philosophie, i., § 44. In relation to the latter, see his Catechisme du Sens Commun—Essais sur L'Indifference, &c., *passim*: with Bautain, Psychologie, i., Disc. Prelim., pp. xliv. seq.; and Biunde, Fund. Phil. pp. 129, seq. 166. (To these is now to be added the Esquisse d' une Philosophie par F. Lamennais, 1840, L. I. ch. 1. Here the doctrine in question is presented in a far less objectionable form; but as its previous statements are not withdrawn, I have not thought it necessary to cancel the preceding observations, which were written before I had received this remarkable work.)

3.—ARISTOTLE.—He lays it down in general as the condition of the possibility of knowledge that it do not regress to infinity, but depart from certain primary *facts, beliefs*, or *principles*—true, and whose truth commands assent, through themselves, and themselves alone. These, as the foundations, are not objects, of Science; as the elements of Demonstration, they are themselves indemonstrable. The fountains of certainty to all else, they are themselves pre-eminently certain; and if denied in words, they are still always mentally admitted. The faculty of such principles is not Reason, the discursive or *dianoetic* faculty, (λόγος, διάνοια,) but Intellect or Intelligence proper, the *noetic* faculty, (νοῦς.) Intellect as an immediate apprehension of what is, may be viewed as a *Sense* (αἴσθησις.) Compare Analyt. Post. L. I. cc. 2, 3, 10, 32—L. ii. c. ult.—Top. L. i. c. 1—Metaph. L. i. c. 7—L. ii. (A minor) c. 2—L. ii. (ill. Duvallio) cc. 3, 4, 6—L. iii. (iv.) c. 6—Eth. Nic. L. vi. cc. 6, 11 (12)—Eth. End. L. v. cc. 6, 8—L. vii. c. 14.—Mag. Mor. L. i. c. 35.—See also above. p. 764 b.

In particular, that Aristotle founds knowledge on belief, and the objective certainty of science on the subjective necessity of believing, is, while not formally enounced, manifest from many passages—though he might certainly have been more explicit. Compare Post. Anal. L. I. c. 2, §§ 1, 2, 16, 17, 18; c 10, § 7; c 31, § 3; Top. L. I. c. 1, § 6, &c.; Eth. Nic. vii. c. 3; Magn. Mor. L. ii. c. 6.

'Since Aristotle,' says the profound Jacobi (Werke ii p. 11) 'there has been manifested a continual and increasing tendency in the philosophical schools to subordinate, in general, immediate to mediate knowledge—the powers of primary apprehension, on which all is founded, to the powers of reflexion as determined by abstraction—the prototype to the ectype—the thing to the word—the Reason [Vernunft—Aristotle's noetic faculty or Intellect] to the Intellect [Verstand—Aristotle's dianoetic faculty or Reason]; nay to allow the former to be wholly subjugated and even lost.'—In this Jacobi (and to Jacobi may be added Fries) does Aristotle the most signal injustice; for there is no philosopher who more emphatically denounces the folly of those 'who require a reason of those things of which there is no reason to be given, not considering that the principle of demonstration is not itself demonstrable.' Metaph. iii. 6. See No. 4 a. In fact Jacobi's own doctrine in its most perfect form will be found to bear a wonderful analogy to that of Aristotle. See No. 87 d In determining indeed the question whether Aristotle does or does not derive all our knowledge from experience and induction, there is some difficulty, from the vagueness with which the problem has usually been stated. In so far, however, as it concerns the doctrine of Common Sense, the opinion of Aristotle admits of no reasonable doubt.*

---

* The doctrine of those passages (as Post. An. L. ii. c. ult. Eth. Nic. L. vi. c. 3. Eth. Eud. L. v. c. 3, &c.) in which Aristotle asserts that our knowledge of principles is derived from sense, experience, induction, may be reconciled with the doctrine of those others in which he makes the intellect itself their source (see above, p. 764 b, and quotations a. b c. that follow)—in two ways.

The first is that adopted by a majority of his Greek and Latin expositors. They suppose that our knowledge of principles is dependent on both, but in different manners, and in different degrees On the intellect this knowledge is principally dependent, as on its proximate, efficient, essential cause (αἰτία γεννητική, ποιητική, causa, causa per se, origo, &c.) On sense, experience, induction, it is dependent, as on its exciting, disponent, permissive, manifestive, subsidiary, instrumental, occasional cause (ἀφορμή, ἐφορμή, πρόφασις, αἰτία ὑπουργὸς, λύτρον, ὑπηρέτης, &c.) Of the Greek interpreter, see Alexander in Top pp 12. 47, 48, ed Ald. (Test. n. 10)—Themistius in Post. An. ff. 2. 14, 15, and De An. f. 90, ed. Ald.—Philoponus, (or Ammonius) in Post. An. f. 100, ed. Ald. and De Anima, Proem.—Eustratius in Post An.

But to adduce some special testimonies. These I shall translate; and for the original of the more essential parts of sundry of the following passages, see foot-note at p. 328.

a.—Top. L. i. c. 1. § 6.—'First truths are such as are believed, not through aught else, but through themselves alone. For in regard to the principles of science we ought not to require the reason *Why* [but only the fact *That* they are given]; for each such principle behoves to be itself a *belief* in and of itself.'

b.—Pr. Analyt. L. i. c. 3. § 4.—Maintaining against one party, that demonstrative science is competent to man and against another, that this science cannot itself be founded on propositions which admit of demonstration, Aristotle says—'We assert not only that science does exist, but also that there is given a certain beginning or principle of science, *in so far as* [or on another interpretation of the term ᾗ—'*by which*'] we recognize the import of the terms.' On the one interpretation the meaning of the passage is—'We assert not only that [demonstrative] science does exist, but also that there is given a certain [indemonstrable] beginning or principle of science, [that is, Intellect which comes into operation] so soon as we apprehend the meaning of the terms.' For example, when we once become aware of the sense of the terms *whole* and *part*, then the intellect of itself spontaneously enounces the axiom—*The whole is greater than its part.*—On the other interpretation;—'We assert not only that [demonstrative science does exist, but also that there is given a certain [indemonstrable] beginning or principle of science [viz. intellect] by which we recognize the import of the terms,' i. e. recognize them in their necessary relation, and thereupon explicitly enounce the axiom which that relation implies.

c.—Anal. Post. L. i. c. 2. § 16.—'But it is not only necessary that we should be endowed with an antecedent knowledge of first principles—all or some—but that this knowledge should, likewise, be of paramount certainty. For whatever communicates a quality to other things must itself possess that quality in a still higher degree; as that on account of which we love all objects that partake of it, cannot but be itself, pre-eminently, an object of our love. Hence, if we know and believe through certain first principles, we must know and believe these themselves in a superlative degree, for the very reason that we know and believe [all] secondary truths through them.'

In connexion herewith, compare the passages quoted above, p. 764 b.

d.—Rhet. L. i. c. 1.—'By nature man is competently organized for truth; and truth, in general, is not beyond his reach.'

e.—Metaph. L. ii (A minor) c. 1.—'The theory of Truth is in one respect difficult, in another easy; as shown indeed by this—that while enough has been denied to any, some has been conceded to all.'

f.—Eth. Nic. L. x. c. 2.—Arguing against a paradox of certain Platonists, in regard to the Pleasureable, he says—'But they who oppose themselves to Eudoxus, as if what all nature desiderates were not

---

f. 63. sq., ed. Ald. in Eth. Nic. f 80 b., ed. Ald. Of the Latin expositors, among many, Fonseca, in Metaph. L. i. c. 1, q. 4—Conimbricenses, Org. Post. Anal. L. i. c. 1. q. 1—Sonerus in Metaph L. i. c. 1, p. 67, sq. Of Testimonies infra, see nos. 10, 20, 21, 22. On this interpretation, Aristotle justly views our knowledge as chronologically commencing with Sense, but logically originating in Intellect. As one of the oldest of his modern antagonists has incomparably enounced it—'Cognitio nostra omnis a *Mente* primam *originem*, a *Sensibus exordium* habet primum;'—a text on which an appropriate commentary may be sought for in the opening chapter of Kant's Critique of pure Reason, and in the seventeenth Lecture of Cousin upon Locke.

The second mode of reconciling the contradiction, and which has not I think been attempted, is—that on the supposition of the mind virtually containing, antecedent to all actual experience, certain universal principles of knowledge, in the form of certain necessities of thinking; still it is only by repeated and comparative experiment, that we compass the certainty—on the one hand, that such and such cognitions cannot but be thought, and are, therefore, as necessary, native generalities;—and, on the other, that such and such cognitions may or may not be thought, and are, therefore, as contingent, factitious generalizations. To this process of experiment, analysis and classification, through which we attain to a scientific knowledge of principles, it might be shown that Aristotle, not improbably, applies the term Induction.

In regard to the passage (De An. L. iii. c. 5) in which the intellect prior to experience is compared to a tablet on which nothing has actually been written, the context shows that the import of this simile is with Aristotle very different from what it is with the Stoics; to whom, it may be noticed, and not, as is usually supposed, to the Stagirite, are we to refer the first enouncement of the brocard—*In Intellectu nihil est, quod non prius fuerit in Sensu.*

In making intellect a source of knowledge, Aristotle was preceded by Plato. But the Platonic definition of '*Intellection*' is '*The principle of science*;' and Aristotle's merit is not the abolition of intellect as such, but its reduction from a sole to a conjunct principle of science.

a good, talk idly. For what *appears to all*, that we affirm *to be*; and he who would subvert this *belief*, will himself assuredly advance nothing more deserving of credit.' —Compare also L. vii. c. 13 (14 Zuing.)

In his paraphrase of the above passage the Pseudo-Andronicus (Heliodorus Prusensis) in one place uses the expression *common opinion*, and in another all but uses (what indeed he could hardly do in this meaning as an Aristotelian, if indeed in Greek at all) the expression *common sense*, which D. Heinsius in his Latin version actually employs. 'But, that what all beings desire is a good, this is manifest to every one endowed with sense'—(*πᾶσι τοῖς ἐν αἰσθήσει*, 'omnibus communi sensu praeditis.') See No. 31.

g.—Eth. Eud. L. i. c. 6.—'But of all these we must endeavour to seek out rational grounds of belief, by adducing manifest testimonies and examples. For it is the strongest evidence of a doctrine, if all men can be adduced as the manifest confessors of its positions; because every individual has in him a kind of private organ of the truth. . . . Hence we ought not always to look only to the conclusions of reasoning, but frequently rather to what appears [and is believed] to be.' See Nos. 10, 30.

h.—Ibid. L. vii. c. 14.—'The problem is this;—What is the beginning or principle of motion in the soul? Now it is evident, that as God is in the universe, and the universe in God, that [I read *κινεῖν καὶ*] the divinity in us is also, in a certain sort, the universal mover of the mind. For the principle of Reason is not Reason, but something better. Now what can we say is better than even science, except God?'—The import of this singular passage is very obscure. It has excited, I see, the attention, and exercised the ingenuity, of Pomponatius, J. C. Scaliger, De Raei, Leibnitz, Leidenfrost, Jacobi, &c. But without viewing it as of pantheistic tendency, as Leibnitz is inclined to do, it may be interpreted as a declaration, that Intellect, which Aristotle elsewhere allows to be pre-existent and immortal, is a spark of the Divinity; whilst its data (from which, as principles more certain than their deductions, Reason, Demonstration, Science must depart) are to be reverenced as the revelation of truths, which would otherwise lie hid from man. That, in short,

'The voice of Nature is the voice of God.'

By the bye, it is remarkable that this text was not employed by any of those Aristotelians who endeavoured to identify the Active Intellect with the Deity.

i.—Phys. L. viii. c. 3.—Speaking of those who from the contradictions in our conception of the possibility, denied the fact, of motion:—'But to assert that all things are at rest, and to attempt a proof of this by reasoning, throwing the testimony of sense out of account, is a sign not of any strength, but of a certain imbecility of reason.' And in the same chapter—'Against all these reasonings there suffices the belief [of sense] alone.' See Simplicius ad locum, ed. Ald. ff. 276, 277.

k.—De Gen. Anim. L. iii. c. 10.—'We ought to accord our belief to sense, in preference to reasoning; and of reasonings, especially to those whose conclusions are in conformity with the phænomena.' And somewhere in the same work he also says, 'Sense is equivalent to, or has the force of, science.'

l.—See also De Coelo L. i. c. 3, text 22.

m.—Ibid. L. iii. c. 7, text 61.

n.—Meteor., L. i. c. 13.

4.—THEOPHRASTUS.—a.—Metaph. c. 8, (ed. Sylb. p. 260, Brand. p. 310.) The following testimony of this philosopher (if the treatise be indeed his) is important both in itself, and as illustrative of the original peripatetic doctrine touching the cognition of first principles, which he clearly refuses to Sense and induction, and asserts to Intelligence and intuition. It has however been wholly overlooked; probably in consequence of being nearly unintelligible in the original from the corruption of the common text, and in the version of Bessarion—also from a misapprehension of his author's meaning.

Having observed that it was difficult to determine up to what point and in regard to what things the investigation of causes or reasons is legitimate;—that this difficulty applies to the objects both of Sense and of Intelligence, in reference to either of which a regress to infinity is at once a negation of them as objects of understanding and of philosophy;—that Sense and Intelligence, severally furnish a point of departure, a principle, the one relative, or to us, the other absolute, or in nature;—and that each is the converse of the other, the first in nature being the last to us;—he goes on to state what these counter processes severally avail in the research, or, as he calls it, after Aristotle, the speculation, of principles. 'Up to a certain point, taking our departure from the Senses, we are able, rising from reason to reason, to carry on the speculation of principles; but when we arrive at those which are [not merely comparatively prior but] absolutely supreme and primary, we can no more; because, either that a reason is no longer to be found, or of our own imbecility, unable, as it were to look from mere excess of light. [Compare Arist. Metaph. A minor, c. 1; which supports the reading, φανώτατα.] But the other procedure is probably the more authentic, which accords the speculation of principles to the *touch*, as it may be called, and *feeling* of Intelligence (τῷ νῷ θίγοντι καὶ οἷον ἀψαμένῳ.) [Comp. Aristot. Metaph. xii. 7.] For in this case there is no room for illusion in regard to these.' He then observes—' That it is even in the sciences of detail, of great, but in the universal sciences, of paramount, importance, to determine wherein, and at what point the limit to a research of reasons should be fixed.' And why? '*Because* [*they who require a reason for every thing,*] *subvert, at once, the foundations of reason and of knowledge.*']

b.—See above, p. 765 a, where from his doctrine in regard to first principles it appears that Theophrastus, like Aristotle, founds knowledge on natural Belief.

5.—Lucretius.—De Rerum Natura, L. i. v. 423, sq.

> ' Corpus enim per se communis deliquat esse
> *Sensus*; que nisi prima *fides* fundata valebit,
> Haud erit, occultis de rebus que referentes,
> Confirmare animi quicquam ratione queamus.'

Sensus Communis here means Sense, strictly so called, as testifying not only in all men, but in all animals. It is a translation of the expression of Epicurus—ἡ αἴσθησις ἐπὶ πάντων (Laert. x. 39); and as in the Epicurean philosophy all our knowledge is merely an educt of Sense, the truth of the derived, depends wholly upon the truth of the original evidence. See L. iv., vv. 480, sq.

6.—Cicero.—a.—De Fin. L. iv. c. 19.—Speaking of the Stoical paradoxes, (' recte facta omnia aequalia,—omnia peccata paria,' &c.) he says—' Quae cum magnifice primo dici videntur, considerata, minus probantur. *Sensus* enim *cujusque*, [i.e. S. communis] et natura rerum, atque ipsa veritas clamat, quodam modo, non posse adduci, ut inter eas res quas Zeno exaequaret, nihil interesset.' (See No. 7.)

b.—Tusc. Disp. L. i. c. 13—' Omni autem in re consensio omnium gentium lex naturae putanda est.' Compare also c. 15.

c.—De Nat. Deor., L. i. c. 16.—The Epicurean Velleius there speaking the doctrine of his sect:—' Intelligi necesse est, esse Deos, quoniam insitas eorum, vel potius innatas cognitiones habemus.* *De quo autem, omnium natura consentit, id verum esse necesse est.* Esse igitur Deos confitendum est.' Compare Plato, De Legibus, L. x.; Aristotle. De Cœlo, L. i. c. 3.; Plutarch, Amatores; Seneca, Epistolæ, 117.

d.—For ' *Sensus Communis*, and ' *Sensus Communes*,' as the sources of moral judgment, see the Orations Pro Cluentio 6.—Pro Plancio, 13, 14.—Pro Domo, 36.

e.—For ' *Sensus Communis*' as criterion of judgment in the arts, see De Orat., L. iii. c. 50; quoted by Reid, p. 424, b; compare L. i. c. 3.

7.—Horace.—Sermones, I. iii. 96. Speaking like Cicero (No. 6, a.) of the Stoical paradox, he says—

> ' Queis paria esse fere placuit peccata, laborant,
> Quum ventum ad verum est; *Sensus* moresque repugnant.'

That is, as Acro (to say nothing of Torrentius, Baxter, and other moderns,) interprets it—' *communis hominum sensus*.' †

8.—Seneca.—a.—Epist. 117.—' Multum dare solemus praesumptioni omnium hominum. Apud nos veritatis argumentum est, aliquid omnibus videri.'

b.—Ep. 9. ' Ut scias autem hos *sensus communes* esse, natura scilicet dictante, apud poetam comicum invenies,

> " Non est beatus, esse se qui non putet."

* It is not to be supposed that the κοιναὶ ἔννοιαι, φυσικαὶ προλήψεις, of the Stoics, far less of the Epicureans (however, as in the present instance, styled *innate* or *implanted*,) were more than generalisations *a posteriori*. Yet this is a mistake, into which, among many others, even Lipsius and Leibnitz have fallen, in regard to the former. See Manud. ad Stoic. Philos. L. ii. diss. 11; and Nouv. Ess. Pref.

† This gloss of Acro is not to be found in any of the editions of the two Horatian scholiasts. But I am in possession of extracts made by the celebrated William Canter, from a more complete MS. of these commentators, than any to which Fabricius and their other editors had access. This codex belonged to Canter himself; and he gives its character, and a few specimens of its *anecdota*, in his *Novae Lectiones*. The copy of Horace (one of the first edition of Lambinus) in which these extracts are found, contains also the full collation of Canter's ' Manuscripti Codices Antiquissimi' of the poet, (*two* only, I can prove, not three, as the Novae Lectiones, fallaciously state,) and which, from the many remarkable readings to be found exclusively in them, must, in all probability, have perished—perhaps in the inundation by which Canter's celebrated library was, in a great measure, destroyed.

a.—Ep 120. 'Natura *semina* nobis scientiae dedit, scientiam non dedit.'

9.—PLINY the Younger.—Paneg. c. 64. —'Melius omnibus quam singulis creditur. Singuli enim decipere et decipi possunt: nemo omnes, neminem omnes fefellerunt.'

9*.—QUINTILIAN.—Inst., L. v. c. 10. § 12.—'Pro certis habemus ea, in quae communi opinione consensum est.'

10.—ALEXANDER OF APHRODISIAS, the oldest and ablest of the interpreters of Aristotle whose writings have come down to us, follows his master, in resting truth and philosophy on the natural convictions of mankind.

a.—On Fate, § 2, edd. Lond. et Orell. Οὐ κενὸν οὐδ' ἄστοχον τ' ἀληθοῦς ἡ κοινὴ τῶν ἀνθρώπων φύσις, κ.τ.λ. 'The common nature of man is neither itself void of truth, nor is it an erring index of the true;* in virtue whereof all men are on certain points mutually agreed, those only excepted, who, through preconceived opinions, and a desire to follow these out consistently, find themselves compelled verbally † to dissent.' And he adds, that 'Anaxagoras of Clazomene, however otherwise distinguished as a physical philosopher, is undeserving of credit, in opposing his testimony touching fate to the common belief of mankind.' This he elsewhere calls their '*common presumptions*,' their '*common and natural notions*.' See §§ 8, 14, 26, of the same work, and the chapter on Fate in the second book of his treatise On the Soul, f. 161. ed. Ald. 1534.

b.—On the Topics of Aristotle, (p. 48, ed. Ald.) 'The induction useful in the employment of axioms is useful for illustrating the application to particulars of the axiomatic rule, [read περὶ λαμβανομένα,] but not in demonstrating its universality; for this, as an object of intellect, is self-evident, nor can it, in propriety, be proved by induction at all.' Compare also p. 12.

11.—CLEMENT OF ALEXANDRIA—Stromata. After stating (L. v. Op. ed. 1688, p. 544,) that there is neither knowledge without belief, nor belief without knowledge, and having shown (L. viii. p. 771,) after Aristotle and others, that the supposition of proof or demonstration being founded on propositions themselves capable of being proved, involves the absurdity of an infinite regress, and therefore subverts the possibility of demonstration, he says—'Thus the philosophers confess that the beginnings, the principles of all knowledge, are indemonstrable; consequently if demonstration there be, it is necessary that there should be something prior, *believable of itself*, something first and indemonstrable. All demonstration is thus ultimately resolved into an *indemonstrable belief*.'

12.—TERTULLIAN.—a.—De Testimonio Animae adversus Gentes, c. 5.—'Hæc testimonia animae, quanto vera tanto simplicia, quanto simplicia tanto vulgaria, quanto vulgaria tanto communia, quanto communia tanto naturalia, quanto naturalia tanto divina; non putem cuiquam frivolum et frigidum videri posse, si recogitet naturæ majestatem, ex qua censetur auctoritas animae. Quantum dederis magistrae, tantum adjudicabis discipulæ. Magistra natura, anima discipula. Quicquid aut illa edocuit, aut ista perdidicit, a Deo traditum est, magistro scilicet ipsius magistrae. Quid anima possit de principali institutore praesumere, in te est aestimare de ea quae in te est. . . . Sed qui ejusmodi eruptiones animae non putavit doctrinam esse naturae, et congenitae et ingenitae *conscientiae** tacita commissa, dicet potius de ventilatis in vulgus opinionibus, publicatarum litterarum usum jam, et quasi vitium, corroboratum taliter sermocinandi. Certe prior anima quam littera, et prior sermo quam liber, et prior sensus quam stylus, et prior homo ipse quam philosophus et poeta. Nunquid ergo credendum est ante litteraturam et divulgationem ejus, mutos absque hujusmodi pronunciationibus homines vixisse? . . . Et unde ordo ipsis litteris contigit, nosse, et in usum loquelae disseminare, quae nulla unquam mens conceperat, aut lingua protulerat, aut auris exceperat!'—He alludes to I. Corinthians ii. 9, &c.

b.—De Resurrectione Carnis, c. 3.—'Est quidem et de *communibus sensibus* sapere in Dei rebus. . . . Utar et *conscientia** populi, contestantis Deum Deorum; utar et reliquis *communibus sensibus*, etc. . . *Communes* enim *sensus* simplicitas ipsa commendat, et compassio sententiarum, et familiaritas opinionum, eoque fideliores existimantur, quia nuda et aperta et omnibus nota definiunt. *Ratio* enim divina in medulla est, non in superficie, et plerumque aemula manifestis.'

c.—Ibid. c. 5.—'Igitur quoniam et rudes quique de *communibus* adhuc *sensibus* sapiunt,' &c.

* See Aristotle, No. 3, d.

† *Verbally*, not mentally. He has Aristotle (Anal Post. L. i. c. 10. § 7,) in view. See Buffier, No. 63.

* Tertullian is the only *ancient* writer who uses the word *Conscientia* in a psychological sense, corresponding with our *Consciousness*. See note I.

d.—De Anima, c 2.—Speaking of the sources from which a merely human philosophy had derived its knowledge of the mind, he concludes—'Sed et natura pleraque suggeruntur quasi de *publico sensu*, quo animam Deus dotare dignatus est.' See above, p. 111 b, note.

e.—Praescr. 28. 'Quod apud multos unum invenitur, non est erratum sed traditum.'

13.—Arnobius.—Adversus Gentes, L. ii. p. 92. ed. 1651. 'Quid est a nobis factum contra *sensum* judiciumque *commune*, si majora et certiora delegimus, nec sumus nos passi falsorum religionibus attineri?' Add., pp. 66, 127.

14.—Lactantius.—Institut. L. iii. c. 5.—'Debuit ergo Arcesilaus siquid saperet, distinguere, quae sciri possent, quaeve nesciri. Sed si id fecisset, ipse se in populum redigisset. Nam vulgus interdum plus sapit, quia tantum, quantum opus est, sapit.'

Quaere—Had Lactantius the line of Martial in his eye?

'Quisquis plus justo non sapit, ille sapit;'

or the precept of St Paul?—'Non plus sapere quam oportet sapere, sed sapere ad sobrietatem.'

15.—St Augustin.—a.—De duabus Animabus, c. 10. 'Quivis enim homines, quos modo a *communi sensu* generis humani nulla disrupisset amentia,' &c.

b.—De Trinitate. Lib. xiii. c. 1.—'Novimus certissima scientia, et clamante Conscientia.' That is, Conscience, not Consciousness, as sometimes supposed.

c.—De Magistro, c. 11.—'Ait Propheta, [Is. vii. 9.] *Nisi credideritis non intelligetis*; quod non dixisset profecto, si nihil distare judicasset. Quod ergo intelligo, id etiam credo; at non omne quod credo, etiam intelligo. Omne autem quod intelligo scio; non omne quod credo scio.—Quare pleraque cum sciro non possim, quanta tamen utilitate credantur scio.'

16.—Proclus (In Platonis Theologiam, Lib. i. c. 25,) has still more remarkable declarations of the truth, that *Belief* is the foundation of knowledge. Speaking of the faith of the gods, which he describes as anterior to the act of cognition, (προτέραν τῆς γνωστικῆς ἐνεργείας,) he says that it is not only to be distinguished from our belief, or rather error, in regard to things sensible; but likewise from the belief we have of what are called Common Notions, with which it, however, agrees, in that these common notions command assent, prior to all reflection or reasoning: (καὶ γὰρ ταῖς κοιναῖς ἐννοίαις πρὸ παντὸς λόγου πιστεύομεν.) See below, Hermes, No. 99.

Among other Platonists the same doctrine is advanced by the pseudo Hermes Trismegistus, L. xvi. sub fine, p. 436, ed. Patricii, 1593.

17.—Ammonius Hermiae (as extracted and interpolated by Philoponus) in his Commentary on Aristotle 'On the Soul,' Introduction, p. 1-3, ed. Trincavelli, 1535. 'The function of Intellect (νοῦς) is by immediate application [or intuition, ἁπλαῖς προσβολαῖς,] to reach or compass reality, and this end it accomplishes more certainly than through the medium of demonstration. For as Sense, by applying itself at once to a coloured or figured object, obtains a knowledge of it better than through demonstration—for there needs no syllogism to prove that this or the other thing is white, such being perceived by the simple appliance of the sense; so also the Intellect apprehends its appropriate object by a simple appliance, [a simple intuitive jet, ἁπλῇ ἐπιβολῇ,] better than could be done through any process of demonstration.' . . .

'I say that the rational soul has in, and co-essential with, it the reasons (λόγους) of things; but, in consequence of being clothed in matter, they are, as it were, oppressed and smothered, like the spark which lies hid under the ashes. And as, when the ashes are slightly dug into, the spark forthwith gleams out, the digger not however making the spark, but only removing an impediment; in like manner, Opinion, excited by the senses, elicits the reasons of existences from latency into manifestation. Hence they [the Platonists] affirm that teachers do not infuse into us knowledge, but only call out into the light that which previously existed in us, as it were, concealed. . . . It is however more correct to say that these are Common Notions or adumbrations of the Intellect; for whatever we know more certainly than through demonstration, that we know in a common notion.' . . . . Such common notions are—'Things that are equal to the same are equal to one another,'—'If equals be taken from equals the remainders are equal,'—'Every thing must be either affirmed or denied.''

18.—St Anselm professes the maxim—'Crede ut intelligas;' which became celebrated in the schools, as opposed to the 'Intellige ut credas' of Abelard.

19.—Algazel of Bagdad, 'the Imaum of the world,' somewhere (in his Destruction of the Philosophers, if I recollect aright) says, as the Latin version gives it—'Radix cognitionis fides.'

20.—St Thomas Aquinas.—a.—De veritate fidei catholicae contra Gentiles. L. I. c. 7. § 1. 'Ea quae naturaliter rationi insita, verissima esse constat; intantum, ut nec ea falsa esse possibile cogitare. . . . . . Principiorum *naturaliter* notorum cognitio nobis *divinitus* est indita, cum ipse Deus sit auctor nostrae naturae. Haec ergo principia etiam divina sapientia continet. Quicquid igitur principiis hujusmodi contrarium est, est divinae sapientiae contrarium; non igitur a Deo esse potest. Ea igitur quae ex revelatione divina per fidem tenentur, non possunt naturali cognitioni esse contraria.'

b.—Expositio in Libb. Metaph. Aristot. Lect. v.—'Et quia talis cognitio principiorum (those of Contradiction and of Excluded Middle) inest nobis *statim a natura*, concludit,' &c.

c.—Summa Theologiae, P. i. Partis ii. Qu. 51, art. 1.—'Intellectus principiorum dicitur esse *habitus naturalis*. Ex ipsa enim natura animae intellectualis convenit homini, quod, statim cognito quid est totum et quid est pars, cognoscat quod omne totum est majus sua parte, et simile in caeteris. Sed quid sit totum et quid sit pars cognoscere non potest, nisi per species intelligibiles a phantasmatibus acceptas, et propter hoc Philosophus, in fine Posteriorum, ostendit quod cognitio principiorum provenit ex sensu.'

d.—De Veritate, Qu. xi. De Magistro, conclusio—'Dicendum est similiter de scientiae acquisitione, quod praeexistunt in nobis principia quae statim *lumine intellectus agentis* cognoscuntur, per species a sensibilibus abstractas, sive sint complexa ut *dignitates*, sive incomplexa sicut *entis* et *unius* et hujusmodi quae statim intellectus apprehendit. Ex istis autem principiis universalibus omnia principia sequuntur, sicut ex quibusdam *rationibus seminalibus*,' &c.

e.—Summa Theologiae, P. i. Partis ii. Qu. 5. art. 3. 'Quod ab omnibus dicitur non potest totaliter falsum esse. Videtur enim naturale quod in pluribus est; natura autem non totaliter deficit.' Compare Nos. 1 and 3, f.

21.—JOANNES DUNS SCOTUS holds a doctrine of *Common Sense*, with reference, more especially, to necessary truths, in which the genuine doctrine of Aristotle is admirably enounced, and cogently defended.

On the one hand, he maintains (against Averroes) that principles are not, in a certain sense, innate in the Intellect; *i. e.* not as actual cognitions chronologically anterior to experience.—'Dicendum quod non habet aliquam cognitionem naturalem secundum naturam suam, neque simplicium, neque complexorum, quia omnis nostra cognitio ortum habet ex sensu. Primo enim movetur sensus ab aliquo simplici non complexo, et a sensu moto movetur intellectus et intelligit simplicia, quod est primus actus intellectus; deinde post apprehensionem simplicium, sequitur alius actus, qui est componere simplicia ad invicem; post illam autem compositionem, habet intellectus ex *lumine naturali* quod assentiat illi veritati complexorum, si illud complexum sit principium primum.' Quaestt. super libros Metaph. L. ii. q. 1. § 2

On the other hand, he maintains (against Henry of Ghent) that, in a different sense, principles are naturally inherent in the mind. For he shews that the intellect is not dependent upon sense and experience, except accidentally, in so far as these are requisite, in affording a knowledge of the terms, to afford the occasion on which, by its native and proper light, (in other words, by the suggestion of common sense,) it actually manifests the principles which it potentially contained; and that these principles are certain, even were those phaenomena of sense illusive, in reference to which they are elicited. 'Respondeo, quod quantum ad istam notitiam, (principiorum sc.) intellectus non habet sensum *pro causa* [vel *origine*, as he elsewhere has it,] sed tantum *pro occasione*: quia intellectus non potest habere notitiam simplicium nisi acceptam a sensibus, illa tamen accepta potest simplicia virtute sua componere et, si ex ratione talium simplicium sit complexio evidenter vera, intellectus virtute propria et terminorum assentiet illi complexioni, non virtute sensus, a quo accipit terminos exterius. Exemplum;—si ratio *totius* et ratio *majoritatis* accipiantur a sensu, et intellectus componat istam—*Omne totum est maius sua parte*, intellectus virtute sui et istorum terminorum assentiet indubitanter isti complexioni, et non tantum quia vidit terminos conjunctos in re, sicut assentit isti—*Socrates est albus*, quia vidit terminos in re uniri. Immo dico, quod si omnes sensus essent falsi,' &c. In libros Sent. Comm. Oxon. L. i., Dist. 3, qu. 4, § 8.—See also §§ 12, 23; and Quaestt. super Metaph., L. i. qu. 4. §§ 3, 4, 5, 11, 12, 14, 16; L. ii. qu. 1. §§ 2, 3, et alibi; where it is frequently repeated that sense and experience are not the *cause* or *origin*, but only the *occasion* on which the *natural light of Intellect* reveals its principles or first truths.

I may observe, that like Locke, the *Subtle Doctor* divides our acquisition of knowledge between two sources, *Sense* and

Reflection.—'*Nihil est in intellectu quin prius fuerit in sensu*, vera est de eo quod est primum intelligibile, scilicet *quod quid est* [τὸ ὅτι] rei materialis, non autem de omnibus per se intelligibilibus; nam multa per se intelliguntur, non quia speciem faciunt in *Sensu*, sed per *Reflexionem intellectus*.' Quaestt. super Univ. Porph. q 3. But what Locke was sometimes compelled virtually to confess, in opposition to the general tenor of his doctrine, (see No. 51,) Scotus professedly lays down as the very foundation of his—that Reflection finds in the mind, or intellect itself, principles, or necessary cognitions, which are not the educts of experience, howbeit not actually manifested prior to, or except on occasion of, some empirical act of knowledge.*

22.—ANTONIUS ANDREAS, an immediate disciple of Scotus,—the Doctor Dulcifluus. Quaestt. super libros Metaph. L. ii. qu. 1.—'Respondeo, et dico duo.

'PRIMUM;—*Quod notitia Primorum Principiorum non est nobis a natura*; quia omnis nostra cognitio intellectiva habet ortum a sensu, et, per consequens, non inest a natura. . . Primo enim motu movetur sensus ab objecto simplici non complexo; et a sensu moto movetur intellectus, et intelligit simplicia, qui est primus actus intellectus. Deinde post apprehensionem simplicium sequitur alius actus, qui est componere simplicia ad invicem; et post istam compositionem habet intellectus, *ex lumine naturali* ut assentiat illi veritati complexae, si illud complexum sit primum principium.

'SECUNDUM;—*Quod notitia Primorum Principiorum* [*recte*] *dicitur nobis inesse naturaliter*, quatenus, *ex lumine naturali* intellectus, sunt nobis inesse nota, habita notitia simplici terminorum, quia "principia cognoscimus inquantum terminos cognoscimus," (ex primo Posteriorum.)'

To this schoolman we owe the first enouncement of the Principle of Identity.

Those who are curious in this matter will find many acute observations on the nature of principles in the other schoolmen; more especially in Averroes on the Analytics and Metaphysics, in Albertus Magnus on the Predicables and Pr. Analytics, and in Hales, 3d and 4th books of his Metaphysics.

23.—BUDAEUS.—In Pandectas, Tit. i. —'Ista igitur fere quae juri naturali ascribuntur, id est, quae natura docuisse nos creditur, versantur in *Sensu Communi*,' &c.

24.—LUTHER.—Weisheit, Th. iii. Abth. 2.—'All things have their root in *Belief*, which we can neither perceive nor comprehend. He who would make this Belief visible, manifest, and conceivable, has sorrow for his pains.'

25.—MELANCHTHON.—a.—De Dialectica, ed. Lugd. 1542, p. 90.—Speaking of the Dicta de Omni et de Nullo—'Nec opus est procul quaerere harum regularum interpretationem; si quis *sensum communem* consuluerit, statim intelliget eas. Nam ut Arithmetica et aliae artes initia sumunt a *sensu communi*, ita Dialecticae principia nobiscum nascuntur.'

b.—Ibid., p. 103.—Speaking of the process in the Expository Syllogism,—'Habet causam haec consequentia in natura positam quandam *κοινὴν ἔννοιαν*, ut vocant, hoc est, sententiam quam omnis natura docet, de qua satis est *sensum communem* consulere.' And again—'Est et hujus consequentiae ratio sumpta a *communi sensu*.'

c.—Erotemata Dialectica L. iv. in Loco, ab Absurdo, p. 1040, ed. 3, Strigelii, 1579 —'*Absurdum* in Philosophia vocatur opinio pugnans cum *Sensu Communi*. id est vel cum principiis naturae notis, vel cum universali experientia.' Reid (see n. 79 a) says repeatedly the very same.

d.—Ibid., p. 853.—'Quare Principia sunt certa? I. Quia notitia principiorum est *lumen naturale*, insitum humanis mentibus divinitus. II. Quia dato opposito sequitur destructio naturae.' See also pp. 798, 857, and the relative commentary of Strigelius. What Melanchthon states in regard to the cognition of Principles and Light of Nature is borrowed from the schoolmen. See above, Nos. 20, 21, 22. Consult also his treatise *De Anima* in the chapters *De Intellectu*; more especially that entitled—*Estne verum dictum, notitias aliquas nobiscum nasci?*

26.—JULIUS CAESAR SCALIGER.—De Subtilitate, Exerc. cccvii. § 18.—'Sunt cum anima nostra quaedam *cognatae notitiae*, quae idcirco *νοῦς* dicuntur a Philosopho. Nemo enim tam infans est, quem cognitio lateat pluris et paucioris. Infanti duo poma apponito. Uno recepto, alterum item poscet. Ab his principiis actus Mentis, a sensilibus excitatus.'—Such principles, he contends, are innate in the

* The edition I use, is that by the Irish Franciscans, Lyons, 1639, of the Opera Omnia of Scotus, 12 vols. in folio. This is the only edition in which the Subtle Doctor can be conveniently studied. His editor and commentators of course maintain him to be a countryman; but the patriotism of Father Maurice (t. iii. p. 254,) makes no scruple in holding him out as actually inspired;—'Suppono, cum Moyse in monte hoc vidit, aut cum Paulo ad tertium cœlum ascendit, aut certe cum alio Joanne supra pectus sapientiae recubuit.'

human Intellect, precisely as the *instincts* of the lower animals are innate in their highest power. They may therefore be denominated Intellectual Instincts. Compare §§ 21, 22.

The doctrine of this acute philosopher was adopted and illustrated, among others, by his two expositors Rodolphus Goclenius of Marburg, and Joannes Sperlingius of Wittemberg; by the former in his Adversaria ad Scaligeri Exercitationes, 1594 (qq. 41, 51, 60); by the latter, not indeed in his Meditationes ad Scaligeri Exercitationes, but in his Physica Anthropologica, 1668 (L. i. c. 3, § 8.) In these the arguments of Gassendi and Locke for the counter opinion, are refuted by anticipation; though, in fact, Locke himself is at last, as we shall see, obliged to appeal to *Common Sense*, identical with the *Intellectus*, *Mens* and *Lumen Naturale* of these and other philosophers. (No. 51.) Otto Casmann, the disciple of Goclenius, may also be consulted in his Psychologia Anthropologica, 1594. (c. 5, § 5.)

27.—Omphalius.—Nomologia, f. 72 b. 'Non eget his praeceptis [dictis scilicet de omni et de nullo] qui *Sensum Communem* consulit. Natura siquidem plerasque *κοινὰς ἐννοίας* animis nostris insevit quibus rerum naturam pervidemus.'

28.—Antonius Goveanus.—Pro Aristotele Responsio adversus Petri Rami Calumnias. Opera Omnia, ed. Meermanniana, p. 802 a.—'An non ex *hominum communi sensu* desumptae enunciationum reciprocationes hae videntur? . . . Sumpta haec, Rame, sunt e *communi hominum intelligentia*, cujus cum mater natura sit, quid est, quaeso, cur negemus naturae decreta haec et praecepta esse?'

29. — Nonnesius.— De Constitutione Dialecticae, f. 56, b. ed. 1554.—'Sed cum Dialectica contenta sit *Sensu Communi*,' &c.

30.—Murerus.—In Aristotelis Ethica ad Nicomachum Commentarius, 1583. Opera Omnia, Ruhnkenii, t. iii. p. 230.

In proof of the immortality of the soul, in general, and in particular, in disproof of an old and ever-recurring opinion—one, indeed, which agitates, at the present moment, the divines and philosophers of Germany—that the intellect in man, as a merely passing manifestation of the universal soul, the Absolute, can pretend to no individual, no personal, existence beyond the grave; he adduces the argument drawn from the common sense of mankind, in the following noble, though hitherto unnoticed, passage:—touching the eloquence of which, it should be borne in mind, that what is now read as a commentary was originally listened to by a great and mingled auditory, as improvisations from the mouth of him, for whose equal as a Latin orator we must ascend to Cicero himself.

'Neque laborandum est etiamsi haec [nisi] naturalibus argumentis probare nequeamus, neque fortassis dissolvere rationes quasdam, quas afferunt ii, qui contrarias opiniones tuentur. Naturalis enim omnium gentium consensus multo plus ponderis apud nos, quam omnia istorum argumenta, habere debet. Neque quicquam est aliud gigantum more bellare cum diis, quam repugnare naturae,* et insitas ab ea in omnium animis opiniones acutis ac fallacibus conclusiunculis velle subvertere. Itaque ut senes illi Trojani, apud Homerum, dicebant, pulchram quidem esse Helenam, sed tamen ablegandum ad suos, ne exitio esset civitati; ita nos, si quando afferetur nobis ab istis acutum aliquod argumentum, quo colligatur . . . . animos interire una cum corporibus, aut si quid supersit, commune quiddam esse, et ut unum solem,† ita unam esse omnium mentem, . . . respondeamus:—Ingeniosus quidem es, o bone, et eruditus, et in disputando potens; sed habe tibi istas praeclaras rationes tuas; ego eas, ne mihi exitiosae sint, admittere in animum meum nolo. Accipite, enim, gravissimi viri, . . . studiosissimi adolescentes, . . . praeclaram, et immortali memoria dignam, summi philosophi Aristotelis sententiam, quam in omnibus hujus generis disputationibus teneatis, quam sequamini, ad quam sensus cogitationesque vestras perpetuo dirigatis. Ex illius enim divini hominis pectore, tanquam ex augustissimo quodam sapientiae sacrario, haec prodierunt, quae primo Ethicorum ad Eudemum leguntur—Προσέχειν οὐ δεῖ πάντα τοῖς διὰ τῶν λόγων, ἀλλὰ πολλάκις μᾶλλον τοῖς φαινομένοις. Convertam haec in Latinum sermonem, utinamque possem in omnes omnium populorum linguas convertere, atque in omnium hominum animis, ita ut nun-

* Cic. De Sen. c. 2. Quid enim est aliud gigantum more bellare cum diis, nisi naturae repugnare?

† Had Muretus the following passage of Bessarion in his eye?—'*Intellectum deforis advenire*, [Aristotle's dictum,] Theophrastus, Alexander, Themistius, Averroes, ita accipiunt, ut jam quisque ortus, illico intellectus sibi applicatam excipiat portionem, ita extinctus relinquat in commune; non aliter, ac si quis *Sole, nascens, participare dicatur, moriens, privari*; et non esse animam particularem, quae deforis advenit, sed ex communi acceptam applicationem.' In Calumn. Plat. L. iii. c. 27.—The simile of the sun is however to be found in Plotinus, and—I think—in Themistius.

quam delerentur, insculpere:—*Non semper, neque omnibus in rebus, assentiendum est iis quae rationibus et argumentis probantur; immo potius ea plerumque tenenda, quae communi hominum sententia comprobantur.* Quid enim est tam falsum, tamque abhorrens a vero, ut non ad id probandum ab ingeniosis et exercitatis hominibus argumenta excogitari queant? . . . Vidistisne unquam in tenebrosa nocte accensam aliquam facem e longinquo loco micantem? Illam, igitur, quamvis dissitam, videbatis; neque tamen quicquam, in illo longo, interjecto inter oculum vestrum et facem, densis obsito tenebris spatio, videre poteratis. Idem putatote animis accidere. Saepe animus noster veritatem alicujus enunciationis tanquam eminus fulgentem ac collucentem videt, etiamsi propter illam, qua circumfusus est, caliginem, videre ea quae intermedia sunt, et per quae ad eam pervenitur, non potest. . . . Si iter aliquod ingressurus, duas videres vias, quae eodem ferrent; unam expeditam, planam, tutam, et eo quo constituisses, sine ulla erratione, ducentem; alteram tortuosam, asperam, periculosam, et quam qui sequerentur, propter varios et multiplices anfractus, saepe aberrarent;—dubitares utram potius eligeres? Duae sunt viae quibus homines ad aliquam cognitionem Dei et animi sui pervenire posse se putant. Aut enim eo contendunt disputando, et cur quicquam ita sit subtiliter inquirendo; aut sine dubitatione ulla assentiendo iis, quae majores summo consensu, partim naturali lumine cognita, partim divinitus inspirata, tradiderunt. Illam qui secuti sunt, omnibus saeculis in multiplices errores inciderunt. At haec illorum signata est vestigiis, quos in coelum sublatos veneramur et colimus.'*

31.—GIPHANIUS.—Commentarii in libros Ethicorum ad Nicomachum, L. x. c. 2.—'Quod omnibus videtur, id (inquit Aristoteles) esse dicimus. Nam *communis* hominum *sensus* et judicium est tanquam lex naturae.' See n. 3. f.

32.—MARIANA. De Rege et Regis institutione, L. i. c. 6. 'Et est *communis sensus* quasi quaedam naturae vox [lex?] mentibus nostris indita, auribus insonans lex, [vox?] qua a turpi honestum secernimus.'

33.—SIR JOHN DAVIES. Of the Immortality of the Soul, 1 ed. 1599, pp. 63, 97.

'If then all souls, both good and bad, do teach,
With general voice, that souls can never die;
'Tis not man's flattering gloss, but nature's speech,
Which, like God's oracle, can never lie.'

* * * * *

'But how can that be false, which every tongue
Of every mortal man affirms for true?
Which truth has in all ages stood so strong,
That, loadstone-like, all hearts it ever drew.
For not the Christian or the Jew alone,
The Persian or the Turk, acknowledge this;
This mystery to the wild Indian known,
And to the Cannibal and Tartar is.'

These latter stanzas were probably suggested by a passage in the first Dissertation of Maximus Tyrius. This 'learned poet' requires, and eminently deserves, a commentary.

34.—KECKERMANNUS. (Systema Logicum, L. iii. c. 13.) treating of Necessary Testimony:—'Testimonium necessarium est vel Dei vel Sensuum.' Having spoken of the former, he proceeds: 'Restat testimonium *sensuum*, quod suum cuique sensus dictat. Estque vel *externum* vel *internum*. Internum est, quod leges naturae, tam *theoreticas* quam *practicas* dictant; itemque *conscientia*. Externum est, quod sensus externi, ut visus, auditus, &c., recte dispositi, adeoque ipsa sensualis observatio, et experientia comprobat.' In illustration of the testimony of Internal Sense, *Conscientia*, he says: 'Magna est vis testimonii Conscientiae in utramque partem; et sicut leges seu principia naturae duplicia sunt—theoretica, ut *totum est major sua parte*—et practica, ut, *quod tibi fieri non vis, alteri ne feceris*: ita duplex est Conscientia, *theoretica* nimirum et *practica*, per quam conclusiones theoreticae et practicae firmiter nobis probantur.'

The employment here of *Conscientia*, for the noetic faculty or faculty of principles, is (if we except the single precedent of Tertullian) unexampled, as far as I have observed, previous to the extension given to the word by Descartes. The *internal* and *external sense* of Keckermann are,

* Of none of the great scholars of the 16th century—the second golden age of Latin letters—have the works been so frequently republished, so learnedly annotated, so industriously collected, as those of the pattern critic, the incomparable Muretus. There however still remains a considerable gleaning. I have myself taken note of some twenty scattered *anecdota*, in prose and verse, in Greek, Latin, and French, which, if the excellent edition (excellent, even after that of Ruhnkenius) of the *Opera Omnia*, by Professor Frotscher of Leipsic, now unfortunately interrupted, be not finally abandoned, I should have great pleasure in communicating to the learned editor.—How is it, that whilst Italy, Germany, and Holland have, for centuries, been emulating each other in paying homage to the genius of Muretus, France has done absolutely nothing to testify her admiration of so illustrious a son?

taken together, nearly equivalent to the expression *common sense*, in the meaning under consideration; an expression, it may be added, which this author had himself, in the same work, previously employed. (L. i. c. 5.)

35.—Lord Herbert of Cherbury.—In 1624, at Paris and London, was first published his work 'De Veritate;' and to the third edition, London, 1645, was annexed his correlative treatise 'De Causis Errorum.' These works, especially the former, contain a more formal and articulate enouncement of the doctrine of common sense, than had (I might almost say than has) hitherto appeared. It is truly marvellous, that the speculations of so able and original a thinker, and otherwise of so remarkable a man, should have escaped the observation of those, who, subsequently, in Great Britain, philosophized in a congenial spirit; yet he is noticed by Locke, and carefully criticised by Gassendi. The following is an abstract of his doctrine—strictly in reference to our present subject. The edition I use is the third, that of 1645.

Lord Herbert makes a fourfold distribution of the human faculties;—into *Natural Instinct*—*Internal Sense*—*External Sense*—and the *Discursive faculty*, (Discursus) p. 37. These names he employs in significations often peculiar to himself. Each of these powers is the guarantee of a certain class of truths; and there is given no truth, which is not made known to us through one or other of these attesting faculties. Let us not, therefore, be wise beyond our powers. *(Ne sapiamus ultra facultates.)*

But of these there is one whose truths are of a relatively higher order, as commanding universal assent, and therefore of indubitable certainty. This faculty, which he calls *Natural Instinct*, (Instinctus Naturalis,) might with more discriminative propriety have been styled *Intellectual Instinct;* and it corresponds, as is manifest, with the Νοῦς of Aristotle, the Intelligentia of the schoolmen, and the Common Sense of philosophers in general. Natural Instinct may be considered, either as a faculty, or as the manifestation of a faculty. In the former signification, Instinct or the Noetic faculty is the proximate instrument of the universal intelligence of God; in fact, a certain portion thereof ingrafted on the mind of man. In the latter signification, Natural Instincts are those Catholic Cognitions or Common Notions, (*κοιναὶ ἔννοιαι*, notitiae communes,) which exist in every human being of sound and entire mind; and with which we are naturally or divinely furnished, to the end that we may truly decide touching the objects with which we are conversant during the present life, (pp. 27, 29, 44.) These Instincts or Common Notions, he denominates also *Primary Truths*—*Common Principles*—*Received Principles of Demonstration*—*Sacred Principles against which it is unlawful to contend*, &c. These are so far from being mere products of experience and observation, that, without some of them, no experience or observation is possible, (pp. 28, 48, 54.) But, unless excited by an object, they remain silent; have then a virtual, not an actual, existence, (pp. 39, 42.) The comparison of the mind to a *tabula rasa* or blank book, on which objects inscribe themselves, must be rejected; but it may be resembled to a *closed book, only opened on the presentation of objects*, (p. 54.) The sole criterion by which we can discriminate principles, natural or divine, is *universal agreement;* though, at the same time, the higher and more necessary the truth, the more liable is it to be alloyed with error, (p. 52.) Our Natural Instincts operate irrationally; that is, they operate without reasoning or discursion; and Reason, (Ratio,) which is the deduction of these common notions to their lower and lowest applications, has no other appeal, in the last resort, except to them, (p. 42.)

The primary truths, or truths of Instinct, are discriminated from secondary truths, (those, to wit, which are not obtained without the intervention of the Discursive faculty,) by six characters.

1°. By their *Priority*. For Natural Instinct is the first, Discursion the last, of our faculties.

2°. By their *Independence*. For if a truth depend upon a common notion, it is only secondary; whereas a truth is primary, which itself hanging upon no superior truth, affords dependence to a chain of subordinate propositions.

3°. By their *Universality*. Universal consent is indeed the most unequivocal criterion of an instinctive truth. The Particular is always to be suspected as false, or, at least, as partially erroneous; whereas Common Notions, drawn as it were from the very wisdom of nature, are, in themselves, universal, howbeit, in reasoning, they may be brought down and applied to particulars.

4°. By their *Certainty*. For such is their authority, that he who should call them into doubt, would disturb the whole constitution of things, and, in a certain sort, denude himself of his humanity. It is, therefore, unlawful to dispute against these principles, which, if clearly understood, cannot possibly be gainsaid. (Compare No. 25, d.)

5°. By their *Necessity*. For there is none which does not conduce to the conservation of man.

6°. By the *Manner of their Formation or Manifestation*. For they are elicited, instantaneously and without hesitation, so soon as we apprehend the significance of the relative objects or words. The discursive understanding, on the other hand, is in its operations slow and vacillating—advancing only to recede—exposed to innumerable errors—in frequent confliction with sense—attributing to one faculty what is of the province of another, and not observing that each has its legitimate boundaries, transcending which, its deliverances are incompetent or null, (pp. 60, 61.) *

36.—Joannes Camero, the celebrated theologian.—De Ecclesia iv., Op. ed. 1642, p. . 'Sensus Communis seu Ratio,' &c.

37.—Descartes proclaims as the leading maxim of philosophy a principle which it would have been well for his own doctrine had he always faithfully applied. (v. p. 749 a.) 'Certum autem est, nihil nos unquam falsum pro vero admissuros, si tantum iis assensum praebeamus quae *clare et distincte* percipiemus. Certum, inquam, quia *cum Deus non sit fallax, facultas percipiendi, quam nobis dedit* [*sive Lumen Naturae*], *non potest tendere in falsum*; ut neque etiam facultas assentiendi, cum tantum ad ea, quae clare percipiuntur, se extendit. Et quamvis hoc nulla ratione probaretur, ita omnium animis a natura impressum est, ut quoties aliquid clare percipimus, ei sponte assentiamur, et nullo modo possimus dubitare quin sit verum.' Princ. i. § 43, with §§ 30, 45—De Meth. § 4—Med. iii. and iv.—Resp. ad Obj. ii. passim. What Descartes, after the schoolmen, calls the 'Light of Nature' is only another term for Common Sense (see Nos. 20, 21, 22, 25); and Common Sense is the name which Descartes' illustrious disciple, Malebranche, subsequently gave it. See No. 60. There are some good observations on Descartes' *Light of Nature*, &c. in Gravii Specimina Philosophiae Veteris, L. ii. c. 16; and in Regis, Metaphysique, L. i. P. i. ch. 12, who identifies it with consciousness.

That Descartes did not hold the crude and very erroneous doctrine of innate ideas which Locke took the trouble to refute, I may have another opportunity of more fully showing. 'Nunquam scripsi vel judicavi (he says) mentem indigere ideis innatis, quae sint *aliquid diversum ab ejus facultate cogitandi*.' Notae in Programma (Regii) § 12.—Compare § 13 with Responsiones et Objectiones iii. rr. 5, 10. By innate ideas in general, Descartes means simply the innate faculty we possess of forming or eliciting certain manifestations in consciousness (whether of necessary or contingent truths) on occasion of, but wholly different from, both the qualities of the reality affecting, and the movements of the organism affected; these manifestations or ideas being nothing else than states of the conscious substance itself. On this ground he occasionally calls the *secondary* qualities innate; in so far as they are, actually, mere modes of mind, and, potentially, subjective predispositions to being thus or thus modified.

His doctrine in regard to principles, when fully considered, seems identical with that of Aristotle, as adopted and expounded by the schoolmen; and I have no doubt that had he and Locke expressed themselves with the clearness and precision of Scotus, their opinions on this subject would have been found coincident both with each other and with the truth.

38.—Sir Thomas Brown (Religio Medici, First Part, sect. 36.) has '*Common Sense*,' word and thing.

39.—Balzac in Le Barbon, (Sallengre Histoire de Pierre de Montmaur, t. ii. p. 88, and Œuvres de Balzac,) 'Sens Commun,' word and thing.

40.—Chanet, (Traité de l'Esprit, p. 15) notices that the term *Common Sense* had in French a meaning different from its Scholastic or Aristotelic signification, 'being equivalent to *common* or *universal reason*, and by some denominated *natural logic*.'

41.—P. Irenaeus a Sancto Jacobo, a Thomist philosopher, and Professor of Theology at Rennes.—Integra Philosophia, 1655; Logica c. iv. sectio 4. § 2.—In reference to the question, 'Quid sit habitus ille *primorum principiorum*?' he says—'Probabilior apparet sententia dicentium habitum primorum principiorum esse *lu-*

* I was surprised to find an eloquent and very just appreciation of Herbert (for he it is who is referred to,) by a learned and orthodox theologian of Cambridge—Nathaniel Culverwell, in his 'Discourse of the Light of Nature,' written in 1646, p. 93. Culverwell does not deserve the oblivion into which he has fallen; for he is a compeer worthy of More, Spencer, Smith, Cudworth, and Taylor—the illustrious and congenial band by which that university was illustrated, during the latter half of the seventeenth century.

men naturale, seu naturaliter inditum (Intellectus sc.) . . . Favet *communis omnium sensus*, qui diffiteri nequit aliqua esse naturaliter et seipsis cognoscibilia; ergo principium talis cognitionis debet censeri signatum super nos *naturae lumen*.'

42.—Lescalopier.—Humanitas Theologica, &c. L. i. p. 87.—'Quid gravius in sentiendo, quod sequamur, habere possumus, quam constans naturae judicium, aetatum omnium cana sapientia et perpetuo suffragio confirmatum? Possunt errare singuli; labi possunt viri sapientes sibi suoque arbitrio permissi; at totam hominis naturam tanta erroris contagio invadere non potest. . . . Quod in communibus hominum sensibus positum, id quoque in ipsa natura situm atque fixum esse, vel ipse Orator coram judice non diffitetur. [Pro Cluentio, c. 6.] Itaque *communis* ille *sensus*, naturae certissima vox est; immo, 'vox Populi,' ut trito fertur adagio, 'vox Dei.'

43.—Pascal.—Pensées; editions of Bossut and Renouard.

a.—Partie i. art. x. § 4. (ch. 31 old editions,) 'Tout notre raisonnement se réduit à céder au *Sentiment*.' This feeling he, before and after, calls '*Sens Commun*.' Art. vi. § 17, (ch. 25)—art. xi. § 2, (wanting in old editions.)

b.—Partie ii. art. i. § 1 (ch 21.) Speaking the doctrine of the Sceptics—'Nous n'avons aucun certitude de la vérité des *principes* (hors la foi et la revelation) sinon en ce que nous les *sentons naturellement en nous*.' . . . . And having stated their principal arguments why this is not conclusive, he takes up the doctrine of the Dogmatists.

'L'unique fort des Dogmatistes, c'est qu'en parlant de bonne foi et sincèrement, on ne peut douter des *principes naturels*. Nous connoissons, disent-ils, la vérité, non seulement par raisonnement, mais aussi par *sentiment, et par une intelligence vive et lumineuse;* et c'est de cette dernière sorte que nous connoissons les *premiers principes*. C'est en vain que le raisonnement, qui n'y a point de part, essaie de les combattre. Les Pyrrhoniens, qui n'ont que cela pour objet, y travaillent inutilement. Nous savons que nous ne rêvons point, quelque impuissance où nous soyons de le prouver par raison [which he uses convertibly with *raisonnement*.] Cette impuissance ne conclut autre chose que la foiblesse de notre raison, mais non pas l'incertitude de toutes nos connoissances, comme ils le pretendent: car la connoissance des premiers principes, comme, par exemple, qu'il y a *espace, temps, mouvement, nombre, matière*, est aussi ferme qu'aucune de celles que nos raisonnements nous donnent. Et c'est sur ces connoissances *d'intelligence et de sentiment* qu'il faut que la raison s'appuie, et qu'elle fonde tout son discours. Je *sens* qu'il y a trois dimensions dans l'espace, et que les nombres sont infinis; et la raison démontre ensuite qu'il n'y a point deux nombres carrés dont l'un soit double de l'autre. Les *principes se sentent; les propositions se concluent;* le tout avec certitude, quoique par differentes voies. Et il est aussi ridicule que la raison demande au *sentiment et a l'intelligence* des preuves de ces premiers principes pour y consentir, qu'il seroit ridicule que *l'intelligence* demandât à la raison un *sentiment* de toutes les propositions qu'elle démontre. Cette impuissance ne peut donc servir qu'à humilier la raison qui vondroit juger de tout, mais non pas à combattre notre certitude, comme s'il n'y avoit que la raison capable de nous instruire. Plût à Dieu que nous n'en eussions au contraire jamais besoin, et que nous connussions toutes choses par *instinct* et par *sentiment!* Mais la nature nous a refusé ce bien et elle ne nous a donné que très peu de connoissances de cette sorte; toutes les autres ne peuvent être acquises que par le raisonnement.' . . .

'Qui démêlera cet embrouillement? La nature confond les Pyrrhoniens, et la raison confond les Dogmatistes. Que deviendrez vous donc, ô homme, qui cherchez votre veritable condition par votre raison naturelle? Vous ne pouvez fuir une de ces sectes, ni subsister dans aucune. Voilà ce qu'est l'homme à l'égard de la verite.'

44.—La Chambre.—Systeme de l'Ame, L. ii. c. 3.—'*Sens Commun*' word and thing.

45.—Henry More.—Confutatio Cabbalae; Opera Omnia, p. 528. 'Hoc Externus Sensus, corporeave Imaginatio non dictat, sed *Sensus Intellectualis, innataque ipsius mentis sagacitas*, inter cujus notiones communes seu axiomata, noematice vel immediate vera, supra numeratum est.'—Compare Epistola H. Mori, ad. V. C. § 17, Opera, p. 117, and Enchiridion Ethicum, L. i. cc. 4, 5.

46.—Rapin.—Comparaison de Platon et d'Aristote, ch. vii. § 11.—'Ce consentement general de tous les peuples, est un *instinct de la nature* qui ne peut estre faux, estant si universel.'

47.—Duhamel.—Philosophia Burgundiae, t. l. Disp. ii. in Categ. qu. 4, art. 2. '*Communis Sensus*,' name and thing.

Grotius - D.J.B. ac P. I. 1. § XII

48.—MALEBRANCHE.—Recherche de la Verité—Entretiens sur la Metaphysique—Traité de Morale, &c. passim.

He holds, 1°, that there is a supreme absolute essential Reason or Intelligence, an eternal light illuminating all other minds, containing in itself and revealing to them the necessary principles of science and of duty; and manifesting also to us the contingent existence of an external, extended universe. This Intelligence is the Deity; these revelations, these manifestations, are Ideas. He holds, 2°, that there is a natural Reason common to all men—an eye, as it were, fitted to receive the light, and to attend to the ideas in the supreme Intelligence; in so far therefore an infallible and '*Common Sense.*' But, 3°, at the same time, this Reason is obnoxious to the intrusions, deceptions, and solicitations of the senses, the imagination, and the passions; and, in so far, is personal, fallible, and factitious. He opposes objective knowledge, 'par idée,' to subjective knowledge, 'par conscience,' or 'sentiment interieur.' To the latter belong all the Beliefs; which, when necessary, as determined by Ideas in the Supernal Reason, are always veracious.—It could, however, easily be shown that, in so far as regards the representative perception of the external world, his principles would refute his theory.—A similar doctrine in regard to the infallibility and divinity of our Intelligence or Common Sense was held by Bossuet.

49.—POIRET.—The objects of our cognitions are either things themselves—*realities*; or the representations of realities, their shadows, pictures,—*ideas*. Realities are divided into two classes; *corporeal* things, and *spiritual* things. Each of these species of object has an appropriate faculty by which it is cognised. 1°, Corporeal realities are perceived by the *animal* or *sensual Intellect*—in a word by *Sense*; this is merely passive. 2°, Spiritual realities—original truths—are perceived by the *passive* or *receptive Intellect* which may be called *Intelligence*; it is the sense of the supersensible. [This corresponds not to the passive intellect of Aristotle, but to his intellect considered as the place of principles and to Common Sense; it coincides also with the Vernunft of Jacobi and other German philosophers, but is more correctly named.]—These two faculties of apprehension are veracious, as God is veracious. 3°, The faculty of calling up and complicating Ideas is the *active—ideal—reflective Intellect*, or *human Reason*. [This answers not to the active or efficient, but to the discursive or dianoetic, intellect of Aristotle and the older philosophers in general, also to the Verstand of Kant, Jacobi, and the recent philosophers of Germany, but is more properly denominated.] (De Eruditione Solida, &c. ed. 2. Meth. P. I. § 43–50, and Lib. I. § 4–7, and Lib. II. § 3–8, and Def. p. 408 sq.—Cogitationes Rationales, &c. ed. 2. disc. pr. § 45. L. II. c. 4. § 2.—Fides et Ratio, &c. p. 28 sq p. 81. sq. p. 131 sq.—Defensio Methodi &c. Op. post. p. 113 sq.—Œconomia Divina, L. iv. c. 20–25.—Vera et Cognita, passim.)—'Innate principles' he indifferently denominates 'Instincts.' (Fides et Ratio, Pr. pp. 13. 45.—Def. Meth. Op. post. pp. 131, 133, 136, 172.—Vindiciae, ibid. p. 602.)

This profound but mystical thinker has not yet obtained the consideration he deserves from philosophers and historians of philosophy;—why, is sufficiently apparent.

50.—BOSSUET.—Œuvres inédites. Logique, L. iii. c. 22.—'*Le Sentiment de genre humain* est considéré comme la voix de toute la nature, et par consequent en quelque façon, comme celle de Dieu. C'est pourquoi la preuve est invincible.'—Alibi.

51.—LOCKE.—Essay, B. i. c. 3. § 4. 'He would be thought void of *common sense*, who asked, on the one side, or on the other, went to give, a reason, why it is impossible for the same thing to be or [and] not to be.' In other words—Common Sense or intellect, as the source, is the guarantee, of the principle of contradiction.—There is here a confession, the importance of which has been observed neither by Locke nor his antagonists. Had Locke, not relying exclusively on Gassendi, prepared himself by a study of the question concerning the origin of our knowledge in the writings of previous philosophers, more especially of Aristotle, his Greek commentators, and the Schoolmen (see Nos. 3, 10, 20, 21, 22, 25, 26, &c.); and had he not been led astray in the pursuit of an ignis fatuus, in his refutation, I mean, of the Cartesian theory of Innate Ideas, which, certainly, as impugned by him, neither Descartes, nor the representatives of his school, ever dreamt of holding; he would have seen, that in thus appealing to common sense or intellect, he was, in fact, surrendering his thesis—that all our knowledge is an educt from experience. For in admitting, as he here virtually does, that experience must ultimately ground its procedure on the laws of intellect, he admits that intellect contains principles of judgment, on which experience being dependent, cannot possibly be their precursor or their cause. Compare Locke's language with that of the intellectualist, Price, as given in No. 78. They are, in substance, identical.—What Locke here calls Common Sense, he elsewhere by another ordinary synonyme denominates *Intuition* (B. iv. c. 2. § 1, c. 3. § 8 et alibi); also *Self-evidence* (B. iv. c. 7. § 1. sq.) As I have already observed, had Descartes and Locke expressed themselves on the subject of innate ideas and principles with due precision, the latter would not so have misunderstood the former, and both would have been found in harmony with each other and with the truth.

52.—Bentley.—Quoted by Reid, I. P. p. 423 a. 'Common Sense,' word and thing.

53.—Serjeant, Locke's earliest antagonist.—Solid Philosophy Asserted, p. 206.—'These ideas of Act and Power are so natural that *common sense* forces us to acknowledge them.' &c. So alibi.

53.*—Abercromby.—Fur Academicus, Sectt. 2, 30.—'*Communis hominum Sensus*,'—name and thing.

54.—Leibnitz.—This great philosopher held a doctrine, on the point in question, substantially corresponding to that of Aristotle, the Schoolmen, and Descartes. It is most fully evolved in his posthumous work the Nouveaux Essais; which I refer to in the original edition by Raspe.—Leibnitz admitted innate truths, which he explains to be cognitions not actually, but only virtually, existent in the mind, anterior to experience; by which they are occasioned, excited, registered, exemplified, and manifested, but not properly caused or contributed, or their infallibility and eternal certainty demonstrated, (pp. 5, 6, 37.) For, as necessary to be thought, and therefore absolutely universal, they cannot be the product of sense, experience, induction; these at best being only competent to establish the relatively general, (pp. 5, sq. 36, 116.) See also Opera by Dutens, t. v. p. 358 and t. vi. p. 274. These truths are consequently given 'as natural habitudes, that is, dispositions, aptitudes, preformations, active and passive, which render the intellect more than a mere *tabula rasa*,' (p. 62.) Truths thus innate are manifested in two forms; either as *Instincts*, or as the *Light of Nature*, (p. 48.) But both become known to us as facts of consciousness, that is, in an immediate, internal experience; and if this experience deceive us, we can have no assurance of any truth, be it one *of fact*, or be it one *of reason*, (p. 197.)—Leibnitz's *Natural Light* and *Instinct* are, together, equivalent to *Common Sense*.

55.—Toland.—Christianity not Mysterious, Sect. i. ch. i. p. 9. '*Common Sense*, or Reason in general.' See Leibnitz (Opera, t. v. p. 143.) This testimony belongs perhaps rather to the third signification of the term.

56.—Christian Thomasius gave 'Fundamenta Juris Naturae et Gentium ex *Sensu Communi* deducta;' and in his introductory chapter, § 26, he says—'Rogo ut considerent, quod ubique mihi posuerim sequi *sensum communem*, atque non stabilire intenderim sententias, quae multis subtilibus abstractionibus opus habent, sed quarum veritatem quilibet, si modo paululum attentior esse velit, *intra se sentit*.' Compare also his Philosophia Aulica. c. v. §§ 26, 35.

57.—Rydiger, in 1709 published his work '*De Sensu Veri et Falsi*.' By this he does not, however, designate the Common Sense of mankind as a natural principle, but the dexterity, 'qua quid in unaquaque re sit verum, falsumve, sentire queamus.'

58.—Fauerlin.—De genuina ratione probandi a consensu gentium existentiam Dei.—'Haec est praecipui argumenti facies:—Ad cujuscunque rei existentiam agnoscendam mentes humanae, [ab *instinctu naturali*, to wit, as he frequently states] peculiarem habent inclinationem, ea vere existit,' &c. p. 28.

59.—A. Turretinus.—Cogitationes et Disputationes Theologicae, Vol. i. p. 46, sq.

'De Sensu Communi.

§ xv. Religio *sensum communem* supponit; nec enim truncos, aut bruta, aut ebrios, aut mente captos, sed homines sui compotes, alloquitur.

§ xvi. In artibus omnibus atque disciplinis, non modo licet, sed et necesse est adhibere *sensum communem*. Quis capiat eam solam artem, eam solam disciplinam, quae omnium praestantissima est, *sensus communis* usum adimere?

§ xvii. Nisi supponatur *sensus communis*, nulla fides, nulla religio, consistere potest: Etenim, quo organo res sacras percipimus, veraque a falsis, aequas ab iniquis, utiles a noxiis, dignoscimus, nisi ope *sensus communis*?

§ xviii. Quomodo gentes notitiam Dei habuerunt, nisi ope *sensus communis*?—Quid est 'Lex in cordibus scripta,' de qua Paulus (Rom. ii.), nisi ipsemet *sensus communis*, quatenus de moribus pronuntiat?

§ xix. Divinitas Scripturae, quibus argumentis probari potest, nisi argumentis e *sensu communi* depromptis?

§ xx. Sensus Scripturae, quibus regulis erui potest, nisi regulis a *sensu communi* subministratis?

§ xxi. Scriptura perpetuo provocat ad *sensum communem*: etenim quotiescunque ratiocinatur, toties supponit *sensum communem* esse in nobis, et *sensu communi* utendum esse.

§ xxii. In syllogismis theologicis pene omnibus, quis nescit praemissarum alteram, imo saepissime utramque, a *sensu communi* desumptam esse?

§ xxiii. Divinae veracitati non minus repugnat, *sensum communem* nos fallere, quam Scripturam Sacram aliquid falsum docere; etenim *sensus communis* non minus opus Dei quam Scriptura Sacra.

§ xxiv. Pessimum est indicium, cum aliquis non vult de suis placitis ex *sensu communi* judicari.

§ xxv. Nullus est error magis noxius, magisque Religioni injurius, quam is qui statuit, Religioni credi non posse, quin *sensui communi* nuntius mittatur.

§ xxvi. Nulla datur major absurditas, quam ea quae nullis non absurditatibus portam aperit, quaeque ad eas revincendas omnem praecludit viam: atque talis est eorum sententia, qui nolunt *sensum communem* adhiberi in Religione.

§ xxvii. Quae hactenus diximus de *sensu communi*, a nemine, ut quidem putamus, improbabuntur: at si loco *Sensus Communis*, vocem *Rationis* subjiciamus, multi illico caperata fronte et torvis oculis nos adspicient. Quid ita? cum *sensus communis*, *lumen naturale*, et *ratio*, unum idemque sint.'

60. — Fenelon. — De l' Existence de Dieu. Partie ii. ch. 2.—'Mais qu' est-ce que le *Sens Commun?* N' est-ce pas† les premières notions que tous les hommes ont également des mêmes choses? Ce Sens Commun qui est toujours et par-tout le même, qui prévient † tout examen, qui rend l' examen même de certaines questions ridicule, qui réduit l' homme à ne pouvoir douter† quelque effort qu' il fit pour se mettre dans un vrai doute; ce Sens Commun qui est celui de tout homme; ce Sens, qui n' attend que d'être consulté, qui se montre au premier coup-d'œil, et qui découvre aussitôt l' evidence ou l' absurdité de la question; n' est-ce pas ce que j' appelle mes idées? Les voilà donc ces idées ou notions générales que je ne puis ni contredire ni examiner, suivant lesquelles au contraire j' examine et je décide tout; en sort que je ris au lieu de répondre, toutes les fois qu' on me propose ce qui est clairement opposé à ce que ces idées immuables me representent.

'Ce principe est constant, et il n'y auroit que son application qui pourroit être fautive: c' est-à-dire qu' il faut sans hésiter suivre toutes mes *idées claires*; mais qu' il faut bien prendre garde de ne prendre jamais pour idée clair celle qui renferme quelque chose d' obscur. Aussi veux-je suivre exactement cette régle dans les choses que je vais mediter.'

Common Sense is declared by Fenelon to be identical with the *Natural Light* of Descartes. See No 37. The preceding passage is partly quoted by Reid from a garbled and blundering translation, (p. 424.) The obeli mark the places where the principal errors have been committed. Like Melanchthon, Reid, &c. (Nos. 25, 79,) Fenelon calls what is contrary to common sense, the *absurd*.

61.—Shaftesbury.—Quoted by Reid, I. P. p. 424 a., '*Common sense*,' word and thing.

62.—D'Aguesseau.—Meditations Metaphysiques, Med. iv. Œuvres, 4o t. xi. p. 127.—'Je m' arrête donc à ces deux principes, qui sont comme la conclusion générale de tout ce que jo viens d' établir sur l' assurance où l' homme peut être d' avoir découvert la vérité.

'L'un, que cet état de certitude n' est en lui-même qu' un *sentiment* ou une *conscience interieure*.

'L' autre, que les trois causes que j' en ai distinguées se réduisent encore à un autre *sentiment*.

'Sentiment simple, qui se prouve lui-même comme dans ces vérités, *j' existe, je pense, je veux, je suis libre*, et que je puis appeller un *sentiment de pure conscience*.

'Sentiment justifié, ou sentiment de l' evidence qui est dans le chose même, ou de cette proposition, que *tout ce qui est evident est vrai*, et je l' appellerai un *sentiment d' evidence*.

'Enfin, sentiment que peut aussi être appellé, un sentiment justifié par le poids du témoignage qui l' excite, et qui a pour fondement une evidence d' autorité. Je l' appellerai donc par cette raison, *le sentiment d' une autorité evidente*.'

62.*—Berkeley.—Quoted by Reid, I. P. pp. 283, 284; compare p. 423 a. '*Common Sense*,' name and reality.

63.—Buffier's 'Traité des Premières Véritez' was first published in 1717, his 'Elemens de Metaphysique' in 1724. If we except Lord Herbert's treatise 'De Veritate,' these works exhibit the first regular and comprehensive attempt to found philosophy on certain primary truths, given in certain primary sentiments or feelings. These feelings, and the truths of which they are the sources, he distinguishes into two kinds. One is *Internal Feeling* (sentiment intime), the self-consciousness of our existence, and of what passes in our minds. By this he designates our conviction of the facts of consciousness in themselves, as merely present and ideal phænomena. But these phænomena, as we have seen, (p. 743 sq.) testify also to the reality of what lies beyond themselves; and to our instinctive belief in the truth of this testimony, he gives, by perhaps an arbitrary limitation of words, the name of *common natural feeling* (sentiment commun de la nature), or, employing a more familiar expression, *Common Sense* (sens commun.)—Buffier did not fall into the error of Mr Stewart and others, in holding that we have the same evidence for the objective reality of the external world, as we have for the subjective reality of the internal. 'If,' he says, 'a man deny the truths of *internal feeling*, he is self-contradictory; if he deny the truths of *common sense*, he is not self-contradictory—he is only mad.'

Common Sense he thus defines:—'J'entens donc ici par le Sens Commun la disposition que la nature a mise dans tous les hommes ou manifestment dans la plupart d' entre eux; pour leur faire porter, quand ils ont ateint l' usage de la raison; un jugement commun et uniforme, sur des objets diférens du sentiment intime de leur propre perception; jugement qui n' est point la consequence d'aucun principe interieur.'—Prem. Vér. § 33. And in his 'Metaphysique,'—'Le sentiment qui est manifestement le plus commun aux hommes de tous les temps et de tous les pays, quand ils ont ateint l'usage de la raison, et des choses sur quoi ils portent leur jugement.' § 67.

He then gives in both works not a full enumeration, but examples, of First Truths or sentiments common to all men. These are more fully expressed in the 'Metaphysique,' from which as the later work, and not noticed by Reid (p. 467 h), I quote, leaving always the author's orthography intact.

'1. Il est quelque chose qui existe hors de moi; et ce qui existe hors de moi, est autre que moi.

2. Il est quelque chose que j'apelle *âme*, *esprit*, *pensée*, dans les autres hommes et dans moi, et la pensée n'est point ce qui s'apelle *corps* ou matière.

3. Ce qui est connu par le sentiment ou par l'experience de tous les hommes, doit être reçu pour vrai; et on n'en peut disconvenir sans se brouiller avec le sens commun.'—§ 78.

[These three he calls 'véritez externes, qui soient des sentiments communs à tous les hommes.' The third is not given in the 'Traité des Premiéres Véritez.']

4. Il est dans les hommes quelque chose qui s'apelle *raison* et qui est oposé à *l'extravagance*; quelque chose qui s'apelle *prudence*, qui est oposé a *l'imprudence*; quelque chose qui s'apelle *liberté*, opusé à *la necessité d' agir*.

5. Ce qui réunit un grand nombre de parties diférentes pour un efet qui revient reguliérement, ne sauroit être le par effet du hazard; mais c'est l'efet de ce que nous apellons une intelligence.

6. Un fait atesté par un très grand nombre de gens sensés, qui assurent en avoir été les temoins, ne peut sensement être revoqué en doute.' § 82.

These examples are not beyond the reach of criticism.

In the Treatise on First Truths he gives a statement and exposition of their three essential characters. The statement is as follows:—

'1. Le premier de ces caractères est, qu'elles soient si claires, que quand on entreprend de les prouver, ou de les ataquer, on ne le puisse faire que par des propositions, qui, manifestement, ne sont ni plus claires ni plus certaines.

2. D'être si universellement reçues parmi les hommes en tous tems, en tous lieux, et par toutes sortes d'esprits; que ceux qui les ataquent se trouvent dans le genre humain, être manifestement moins d'un contre cent, ou même contre mille.

3. D'être si fortement imprimées dans nous, que nous y conformions notre conduite, malgré les rafinemens de ceux qui imaginent des opinions contraires; et qui eux-memes agissent conformément, non à leurs opinions imaginées, mais aux premières véritez universellement reçues.'—§ 51–52. Compare Alexander, n. 10 a.*

* We are now only considering the natural data of consciousness in their most catholic relations,—and it would be out of place to descend to any discussion of them in a subordinate point of view. But, though alluding to matters beyond our present purpose, I cannot refrain from doing, by the way, an act of justice to this acute philosopher, to whom, as to Gassendi, his countrymen have never, I think, accorded the attention he deserves.

No subject, perhaps, in modern speculation, has excited an intenser interest or more vehement controversy, than Kant's famous distinction of *Analytic* and *Synthetic judgments a priori*, or, as I think they might with far less of ambiguity be denominated, *Explicative* and *Ampliative* judgments. The interest in the distinction

I should not have deemed it necessary to make any comment on Buffier's doctrine of Common Sense, were it not that it is proper to warn my readers against the misrepresentations of the anonymous English translator of his Treatise on Primary Truths; for not only have these never been exposed, but Mr Stewart has bestowed on that individual an adventitious importance, by lauding his 'acuteness and intelligence,' while acquiescing in his 'severe but just animadversions' on Dr Beattie. (Elements vol. ii. c. 1, sect. 3, p. 87, 89, 2 ed.)

Buffier does not reduce Reason (which he employs for the complement of our higher faculties in general) to Reasoning; he does not contra-distinguish Common Sense from Reason, of which it is constituent; but while he views the former as a natural sentiment, he views it as a sentiment of our rational nature; and he only requires, as the condition of the exercise of common sense in particular, the actual possession of Reason or understanding in general, and of the object requisite to call that Reason into use. Common Sense, on Buffier's doctrine, is thus the primary, spontaneous, unreasoning, and, as it were, instinctive, energy of our rational constitution. Compare Pr. Vér. §§ 41, 66—72, 93. Met. §§ 65, 72, 73.

The translator to his version, which appeared in 1780, has annexed an elaborate Preface, the sole purport of which is to inveigh against Reid, Beattie, and Oswald—more especially the two last—for at once *stealing* and *spoiling* the doctrine of the learned Jesuit.

In regard to the *spoiling*, the translator is the only culprit. According to him, Buffier's 'Common Sense is a disposition of mind not natural but acquired by age and time,' (pp. iv. xxxiv.) 'Those first truths which are its object require experience and meditation to be conceived, and the judgments thence derived are the result of exercising reason,' (p. v.) 'The use of Reason is Reasoning;' and 'Common Sense is that degree of understanding in all things to which the generality of mankind are capable of attaining by the exertion of their rational faculty.' (p. xvii.) In fact Buffier's *first* truths, on his translator's showing, are *last* truths; for when 'by time we arrive at the knowledge of an infinitude of things, and by the use of reason (i. e. by reasoning) form our judgment on them, *those judgments are then justly to be considered as first truths*'!!! (p. xviii.)

But how, it will be asked, does he give any colour to so unparalleled a perversion? By the very easy process of—1° throwing out of account, or perverting, what his author does say;—2° of interpo-

itself was naturally extended to its history. The records of past philosophy were again ransacked; and, for a moment, it was thought, that the Prussian sage had been forstalled, in the very groundwork of his system, by the Megaric Stilpo. But the originality (I say nothing of the truth) of Kant's distinction still stands untouched; the originality of its author, a very different question, was always above any reasonable doubt. Kant himself is disposed, indeed, to allow, that Locke (B. iv. ch. 3. § 9, sq.) had, perhaps, a glimpse of the discrimination; but looking to the place referred to, this seems, on the part of Kant, an almost gratuitous concession. Locke, in fact, came far nearer to it in another passage (B. i. ch. 2, §§ 19, 20); but there although the examples on which the distinction could have been established are stated, and even stated in contrast, the principle was not apprehended, and the distinction, consequently, permitted to escape.

But this passage and its instances seem to have suggested, what was overlooked by Locke himself, to Buffier; who although his name has not, as far as I am aware, ever yet been mentioned in connexion with this subject, may claim the honour of having been the first to recognize, to evolve, and even to designate, this celebrated distinction, almost as precisely as the philosopher who erected on it so splendid an edifice of speculation. I cannot now do more than merely indicate the fact of the anticipation; mentioning only that, leaving to Kant's *analytic* judgment its previous title of *identical*, Buffier preoccupies Kant's designation of *synthetic* in that of *conjunctive* (or logical) judgment, which he himself proposes. Those interested in the question will find the exposition in the 'Vérites de Consequence,' Log. ii. Art. xxi.

I may farther, however, when on this matter, notice, that before Kant, another philosopher had also signalised the same distinction. I refer to Principal Campbell of Aberdeen, in the chapter on intuitive evidence, of his Philosophy of Rhetoric (B. i. c. 5 S. i. P. 1.)—first published in 1776, and therefore four years prior to the Critique on Pure Reason; for the distinction in question is to be found, at least explicitly, neither in the treatise 'Ueber die Evidenz,' nor in the Dissertation 'De Mundi Sensibilis atque Intelligibilis forma et principiis,' which appeared in 1763 and 1770. But Campbell manifestly only repeats Buffier, (with whose works he was intimately acquainted, and from which he frequently borrows,) and with inferior precision; so that, if we may respect the shrewdness, which took note, and appreciated the value, of the observation, we must condemn the disingenuity which palmed it on the world as his own. Campbell's doctrine, I may finally observe, attracted the attention of Mr Stewart (El. ii. p. 32 sq.); but he was not aware either of its relation to Buffier or of its bearing upon Kant.

lating what his author not only does not say, but what is in the very teeth of his assertions; and 3° by founding on these perversions and interpolations as on the authentic words of his author.

As to the *plagiarism*, I may take this opportunity of putting down, once and for ever, this imputation, although the character of the man might have well exempted Reid from all suspicion of so unworthy an act. It applies only to the 'Inquiry;' and there the internal evidence is almost of itself sufficient to prove that Reid could not, prior to that publication, have been acquainted with Buffier's Treatise. The strongest, indeed the sole, presumption arises from the employment, by both philosophers, of the term Common Sense, which, strange to say, sounded to many in this country as singular and new; whilst it was even commonly believed, that before Reid Buffier was the first, indeed the only philosopher, who had taken notice of this principle, as one of the genuine sources of our knowledge. See Beattie, n. 82; Campbell's Philosophy of Rhetoric, B. I. c. 5, part 3; and Stewart's Account of Reid, supra, p. 27 b.

After the testimonies now adduced, and to be adduced, it would be the apex of absurdity to presume that none but Buffier could have suggested to Reid either the principle or its designation. Here are given *forty-eight* authorities, ancient and modern, for the philosophical employment of the term Common Sense, *previous to Reid*, and from any of those Reid may be said to have borrowed it with equal justice as from Buffier; but, taken together, they concur in proving that the expression, in the application in question, was one in general use, and free as the air to all and each who chose thus to employ it.—But, in fact, what has not been noticed, we know, from an incidental statement of Reid himself—and this, be it noticed, prior to the charge of plagiarism,—that he only became acquainted with the treatise of Buffier, after the publication of his own Inquiry. For in his Account of Aristotle's Logic, written and published some ten years subsequently to that work, he says—'I have *lately* met with a very judicious treatise written by Father Buffier,' &c., p. 713, b. Compare also Intellectual Powers, p. 468, b. In this last work, however, published *after* the translation of Buffier, though indirectly defending the less manifestly innocent partners in the accusation, from the charge advanced, his self-respect prevents him from saying a single word in his own vindication.

64.—Lyons.—About the year 1720 was published the first edition of the following curious, and now rare, work :—

'The Infallibility of Human Judgment, its Dignity and Excellence. Being a New Art of Reasoning, and discovering Truth, by reducing all disputable cases to general and self evident propositions. Illustrated by bringing several well known disputes to such self-evident and universal conclusions. With the Supplement answering all objections which have been made to it and the design thereby perfected, in proving this method of Reasoning to be as forcibly conclusive and universal as Arithmetick and as easie. Also a Dissertation on Liberty and Necessity. The fourth edition. To which is now added a Postscript obviating the complaints made to it, and to account for some things which occurred to it and the author. By Mr Lyons. London. 1724.'

He gives (p. 83-94) 'A Recapitulation of the whole work, being the principles of a Rationalist reduced to certain stated articles containing the Laws of Reason, the Elements of Religion, of Morals, and of Politicks; with the Art of reducing all disputes to universal determinations.' From these articles (twenty-three in number) I extract the first three.

1. '*Reason* is the distinguishing excellency, dignity, and beauty of mankind.

2. 'There is no other use of Reason—than to judge of Good and Bad, Justice and Injustice, Wisdom and Folly, and the like; that a man may thereby attain Knowledge to distinguish Truth from Error, and to determine his Actions accordingly.

3. 'This Reason is known to us also by the names of *Judgment*, *Light of Nature*, *Conscience*, and *Common Sense*; only varying its name according to its different uses and appearances, but is one and the same thing.'

The conclusion of the whole is given in the maxim—'*Exert with Diligence and Fortitude the Common Use of Common Sense*.'

It is probable that Lyons was not unacquainted with the treatise of Turretini.

65.—Amherst.—Terræ Filius, No. 21.—'*Natural reason* and *common sense*,' used as convertible terms.

66.—Wollaston.—Religion of Nature Delineated, (ed. 1721, p. 23.) 'They who deduce the difference between good and evil from the *Common Sense* of mankind, and certain *principles that are born with us*, put,' &c.

67.—VULPIUS (Volpi).—Scholae Duae, p. 45. 'Non certe quod putaret Aristoteles, summos illos viros (Parmenidem et Melissum) tam longe a *communi sensu* abhorruisse, ut opinarentur nullam esse omnino rerum dissimilitudinem,' &c.

68.—VICO frequently employs the terms '*communis sensus*' and '*senso commune*' for our primary beliefs. See his Latin and Italian works, passim.

69. — WOLFIUS.—Ontologia, § 125.— 'Veritates ad *sensum communem* reducimus, dum in notiones resolvuntur, quas ad judicandum utitur ipsum vulgus imperitum naturali quodam acumine, quae distincte enunciata maxime abstracta sunt, in rebus obviis confuse percipiens. . . . Id igitur in Philosophia prima agimus, ut notiones quae confusae vulgo sunt, distinctas reddamus, et terminis generalibus enunciemus: ita enim demum in disciplinis caeteris, quae sublimia sunt, et a cognitione vulgi remota, ad notiones eidem familiares revocare, sicque ad *Sensum Communem* reducere licebit.' . . . § 245. . . . 'Nemo miretur, quod notiones primas, quas fundamentales merito dixeris, cum omnis tandem nostra cognitio iisdem innitatur, notionibus vulgi conformes probemus. Mirandum potius esset, quod non dudum de reductione philosophiae ad notiones communes cogitaverint philosophi, nisi constaret singulare requiri acumen, ut, quid notionibus communibus insit, distincte et pervidere, et verbis minime ambiguis enunciare valeamus, quod nonnisi peculiari et continuo quodam exercitio obtinetur in Psychologia exponendo.'—See also a curious letter of Wolf among the '*Epistolae Physicae*' of Krazenstein, regarding Common Sense.

70.—HUBER.—In 1732 appeared the first edition of *Le Monde Fou preféré au Monde Sage*. This treatise is anonymous, but known to be the work of Mademoiselle Huber. Its intrinsic merit, independently of its interest as the production of a Lady, might have saved it from the oblivion into which it seems to have fallen.—Consciousness (conscience) is considered as the faculty of 'uncreated, primary, simple, and universal truths,' in contrast to 'truths created, particular, distinct, limited,' (i. pp. 180, 220.) Consciousness is superior to Reasoning; and as primitive is above all definition, (i. pp. 103, 130, 140). 'Les vérites les plus simples sont, par leur rélation avec la verité primitive si fort au-dessus des preuves, qu' elles ne paroissent douteuses que tarce qu' on entrepend de les prouver; leur idée seule, ou le sentiment que l' on en a, prouve qu' elles existent; l'existence de la Conscience, par example, est prouvé par son langage même; elle se fait entendre, donc elle est; son témoignage est invariablement droit, donc il est infaillible, donc les vérites particulières qu' il adopte sont indubitables, par cela seul qu' elles n' ont pas besoin d' autres preuves, (i. p. 180.)

71.—GENOVESI.— Elementorum Metaphysicae, Pars Prior, p. 94. In reference to our moral liberty, he says—'Appello ad *sensum*, non plebeiorum modo, ne tantas res judicio imperitorum judicari quis opponat, sed philosophorum maxime, *communem*, quem qui erroris reprehendere non veretur, is vecors sit oportet.' See also Pars Altera, p. 160, et alibi.

72.—HUME.—Quoted by Reid, p. 424 b. '*Common Sense*,' word and thing.

73.—CRUSIUS.—a.—Weg zur Gewissheit, § 256, et alibi. 'The highest principle of all knowledge and reasoning is—*That which we cannot but think to be true, is true; and that which we absolutely cannot think at all,* [?] *or cannot but think to be false, is false.*'

b.—Entwurf nothwendigen Vernunftwahrheiten, Pref. 2 ed. 'The Leibnitio-Wolfian system does not quadrate with the *common sense* of mankind (sensus communis.)' His *German* expression is 'gemeiner Menscheosinn.'

74.—D'ALEMBERT holds that philosophy is an evolution from, and must, if legitimate, be conformed to, the primary truths of which all men are naturally in possession. The complement of these truths is '*sens commun*.' Compare Melanges, t. iv. §§ 4, 6, pp. 28, 46 t. v. § 76, p. 269, ed. Amst. 1763.

75.—OETINGER.—Inquisitio in *Sensum Communem* et Rationem, necnon utriusque regulas, pro dijudicandis philosophorum theoriis, &c. Tubingae, 1753.—'*Sensus Communis*' is defined (§ 11), 'Viva et penetrans perceptio objectorum, toti humanitati obviorum, ex immediato *tactu* et *intuitu* eorum, quae sunt simplicissima, utilissima et maxime necessaria,' &c.—§ 18. . . 'Objecta *Sensus Communis* sunt veritates omni tempore et loco omnibus utiles, apprehensu faciles, ad quas conservandas Deus illos secreto impulsu indesinenter urget, ut sunt moralia,' &c. &c.—So far, so well. The book however turns out but a vague and mystical farrago. The author appears to have had no knowledge of Buffier's treatise on First Truths. Solomon and Confucius are his staple authorities. The former affords him all his rules; and even materials for a separate publication on the same subject, in the same year—'Die Wahrheit des *Sensus Communis* in den erklaerten Spruechen Salomonis.' This I have not seen.

76.—Eschenbach.—Sammlung, &c. 1756. In the appendix to his translation of the English Idealists Berkeley and Collier, after showing that the previous attempts of philosophers to demonstrate the existence of an external world were inconclusive, the learned Professor gives us his own, which is one of common sense. —'How is the Idealist to prove his existence as a thinking reality? He can only say—*I know that I so exist, because I feel that I so exist.*' This feeling being thus the only ground on which the Idealist can justify the conviction he has of his existence, as a mind, our author goes on to show, that the same feeling, if allowed to be veracious, will likewise prove the existence, immediately, of our bodily organism, and, through that, of a material world. p. 549–552.

77.—Gesner, prelecting on his 'Isagoge in Eruditionem Universalem,' § 808, speaking of Grotius, says:—'De jure gentium eleganter scripsit, et auctor classicus est. Imprimis, quod reprehendunt imperiti, laudandum in eo libro est hoc, quod omnia veterum auctorum locis ac testimoniis probat. Nam ita provocatur quasi ad totum genus humanum. Nam si videmus, illos viros laudari, et afferri eorum testimonia, qui dicuntur *sensum communem* omnium hominum habuisse; si posteri dicant, se ita sentire, ut illi olim scripserint: est hoc citare genus humanum. Proferuntur enim illi in medium, quos omnes pro sapientibus habuerunt. Verum est, potest unusquisque stultus dicere: 'Ego habeo *sensum communem*:' sed *sensus communis* est, quod consensu humano dictum sit per omnia secula. Ita etiam in religione naturali videndum est, quid olim homines communi consensu dixerint: neo ea ad religionem et theologiam naturalem referenda sunt, quae aliunde accepimus. Sic egit Grotius in opere praestantissimo. Ostendit, hoc Romanorum, hoc Gallorum, legatos dixisse; hoc ab omni tempore fuisse jus gentium, hoc est, illud jus, ex quo totae gentes judicari, et agi secum, voluerint. Sermo est de eo jure quod toti populi et illi sapientissimi scriptores nomine et consensu populorum totorum, pro jure gentium habuere; de eo, quo gentes inter se teneantur; non de jure putativo, quod unusquisque sibi excogitavit. Haec enim est labes, hoc est vitium saeculi nostri, quod unusquisque ponit principium, ex quo deducit deinde conclusiones. Bene est, et laudandi sunt, quod in hoc cavent sibi, ut in fine conveniant in conclusionibus; quod ex diversis principiis efficiunt easdem conclusiones: Sed Grotius provocat simpliciter ad consensum generis humani et *sensum communem*.'

78.—Price, in his Review of the principal Questions on Morals, 1 ed. 1758, speaking of the necessity of supposing a cause for every event, and having stated examples, says—'I know nothing that can be said or done to a person who professes to deny these things, besides referring him to *common sense* and *reason*,' p. 35. And again; 'Were the question—whether our ideas of number, diversity, causation, proportion, &c., represent truth and reality perceived by the understanding, or particular impressions made by the object to which we ascribe them on our minds; —were this, I say, the question; would it not be sufficient to appeal to *common sense*, and to leave it to be determined by every person's private *consciousness?*' p. 65. See also 2 ed. p. 81 note; 'Common sense, the faculty of self-evident truths.'

79.—Reid.—a.—Inquiry, &c., p. 108 b. —'If there be certain principles, as I think there are, which the constitution of our nature leads us to believe, and which we are under a necessity to take for granted in the common concerns of life, without being able to give a reason for them; these are what we call the *principles of common sense*; and what is manifestly contrary to them is what we call *absurd*.'—See also p. 209, b. Compare Melanchthon n. 25, c., Fenelon, n. 60, Buffier n. 63.

b.—Intellectual Powers, p. 425, a. b.—'It is absurd to conceive that there can be any opposition between Reason and Common Sense. Common Sense is indeed the first-born of Reason; and they are inseparable in their nature.—We ascribe to Reason two offices or two degrees. The first is *to judge of things self-evident*; [this is Intellect, νοῦς.] The second is to *draw conclusions that are not self-evident from those that are*; [this is Reasoning, or διάνοια.] The first of these is the province, and the sole province of Common Sense; and therefore it coincides with Reason in its whole extent, and is only another name for one branch or one degree of Reason.—I have already observed that of these offices, the former (Common Sense) might be well denominated the *noetic* function of Reason, or rather Intellect, and the latter (Reasoning) its *dianoetic* or discursive. See p. 769 b

80.—HILLER.—Curriculum Philosophiae, 1705. Pars iii. § 34.—'*Sensus Communis*' used in its philosophical meaning.

81.—HEMSTERHUIS, 'the Batavian Plato,' founds his philosophy on the original feelings or beliefs of our intelligent nature, as on ultimate facts. Feeling, or the faculty of primitive intuition (sentiment, sensation, faculté intuitive) is prior to reasoning; on which it confers all its validity, and which it supplies with the necessary conditions of its activity. It is not logical inference which affords us the assurance of any real existence; it is *belief—feeling—the instinctive judgment of the intuitive faculty*. (This he sometimes calls common sense—*sens commun*). Demonstration is the ladder to remoter truths. But demonstrations can yield us information, neither as to the ground on which the ladder rests, nor as to the points on which it is supported.—Of his works, see in particular, 'Sophyle' and 'Lettre sur l' Homme et ses Rapports,' passim.

82.—BEATTIE.—Essay on Truth, 1773, p. 40. 'The term *Common Sense* hath, in modern times, been used by philosophers, both French and British, to signify that power of the mind which perceives truth, or commands belief, not by progressive argumentation, but by an instantaneous, instinctive, and irresistible impulse; derived neither from education nor from habit, but from nature; acting independently of our will, whenever its object is presented, according to an established law, and therefore properly called *Sense*; and acting in a similar manner upon all, or at least upon a great majority of mankind, and therefore properly called *Common Sense*.'

I should hardly have thought it necessary to quote Beattie's definition of common sense any more than those of Campbell, Oswald, Fergusson, and other Scottish philosophers in the train of Reid, were it not to remark that Mr Stewart, (Elements, vol. ii. c. 1, sect. 3), contrary to his usual tone of criticism, is greatly too unmeasured in his reprehension of this and another passage of the same Essay. In fact if we discount the identification of Reason with Reasoning—in which Beattie only follows the great majority of philosophers, ancient and modern—his consequent distinction of Reason from Common Sense, and his error in regard to the late and limited employment of this latter term, an error shared with him by Mr Stewart, there is far more in this definition to be praised than censured. The attack on Beattie by the English translator of Buffier is futile and false. Mr Stewart's approbation of it is to me a matter of wonder. See No. 63.

83.—VON STORCHENAU.—Grundsaetze der Logik, 1774. *Common Sense* (der allgemeine Menschensinn) defined and founded on, as an infallible criterion of truth, in reference to all matters not beyond its sphere.

84.—STATTLER.—Dissertatio Logica de valore Sensus Communis, 1780.—A treatise chiefly in reference to the proof of the being of a God from the general agreement of mankind.—See also his Logica.

85.—HENNERT.—Aphorismi philosophici Utrecht, 1781.—'*Sensus communis*, seu sensus immediatae evidentiae, intimus est sensus,' § 112. '*Sensus communis* est cos et norma omnis veri,' § 2. 'Natura mortalibus tribuit *sensum communem*, qui omnes edocet quibus in rebus consentire debeant,' &c. § 1.

86.—KANT is a remarkable confessor of the supreme authority of natural belief; not only by reason of his rare profundity as a thinker, but because we see him, by a signal yet praiseworthy inconsequence, finally re-establishing in authority the principle, which he had originally disparaged and renounced. His theoretical philosophy, which he first developed, proceeds on a rejection, in certain respects, of the necessary convictions of mankind; while on these convictions his practical philosophy, the result of his maturer contemplations, is wholly established. As Jacobi well expresses it—'The Critical philosophy, first out of love to science, theoretically subverts metaphysic; then—when all is about to sink into the yawning abyss of an absolute subjectivity—it again, out of love to metaphysic, subverts science,' (Werke ii. p. 44). The rejection of the common sense of mankind as a criterion of truth, is the weakest point of the speculative philosophy of Kant. When he says—'Allowing idealism to be as dangerous as it truly is, it would still remain a scandal to philosophy and human reason in general, to be forced to accept the existence of external things on the testimony of mere belief,' (Cr. d. r. V. Vorr.): yet, that very belief alone is what makes the supposition of an external world incumbent; and the proof of its reality which Kant attempted, independently of that belief, is now admitted by one and all of his disciples, to be so inconsequent, that it may reasonably be doubted, whether he ever intended it for more than an exeteric disclaimer of the esoteric Idealism of his doctrine. But the philosopher who deemed it 'a scandal to philosophy and human reason' to found the proof of a material world—in itself to us a matter of supreme indifference—on belief; on belief, on feeling, afterwards established the proof of all the highest objects of our interest—God—Free Will—and Immortality. In the character he ascribes to this Feeling and Belief, Kant indeed erred. For he ought to have regarded it, not as a mere spiritual craving, but as an immediate manifestation to intelligence; not as a postulate, but as a datum; not as an interest in certain truths, but as the fact, the principle, the warrant, of their cognition and reality. Kant's doctrine on this point is too prominent and pervading, and withal too well known, to render any quotation necessary; and I only refer to his Critique of Practical Reason and his moral treatises in general.—See also on Kant's variation in this respect, among others, Jacobi's Introduction to his collected philosophical writings (Werke vol. ii. p. 3-126), with the Appendix on Transcendental Idealism (ibid. p. 289-309); and Platner's Philosophical Aphorisms (vol. I. Pref. p. vi.); to which may be added Schoppenhauer's letter in Preface to the first volume of Kant's collected works by Rosenkrantz and Schubert.

87.—Jacobi.—The philosophy of Jacobi—who from the character and profundity of his speculations merited and obtained the appellation of the Plato of Germany—in its last and most perfect exposition establishes two faculties immediately apprehensive (vernehmend, wahrnehmend) of reality; *Sense* of corporeal existence, *Reason* (Vernunft) of supersensible truths.* Both as primary are inconceivable, being only cognitions of the *fact*. Both are therefore incapable of definition, and are variously and vaguely characterised as *revelations, intuitions, feelings, beliefs, instincts*.

The resistless belief or feeling of reality which in either cognition affords the surrogate of its truth, is equivalent to the common sense of Reid. Reid was an especial favourite with Jacobi; and through Jacobi's powerful polemic we may trace the influence of the Scottish philosophy on the whole subsequent speculation of Germany. See Preface.

a.—Die Lehre des Spinoza, &c. 1785, p. 162 sq.—Werke, vol. iv. p. 210. 'Dear Mendelsohn, we are all born in belief (Glaube*), and in belief we must remain, as we were all born in society, and in society must remain. How can we strive after certainty, were certainty not already known to us; and known to us, how can it be, unless through something which we already know with certainty? This leads to the notion of an immediate certainty, which not only stands in need of no proof, but absolutely excludes all proof, being itself, and itself alone, the representation (Vorstellung†) corresponding with the represented thing, and therefore having its sufficient reason within itself. The conviction, through proof or demonstration, is a conviction at second hand; rests upon comparison; and can never be altogether sure and perfect. If, then, all *assent*, all *holding for true*, (Fuerwahrhalten,) not depending on such grounds of reasoning, be a *belief*; it follows, that the conviction from reasoning itself, must spring out of belief, and from belief receive all the cogency it possesses.

'Through belief we know that we have a body, and that, external to us, there are found other bodies, and other intelligent existences. A truly miraculous [marvellous!] revelation! For we have only a sensation (Empfinden) of our body, under this or that modification; and whilst we have a sensation of our body thus modified, we are at the same time, aware or percipient, not only of its changes, but likewise of—what is wholly different from

---

* This last corresponds to the νοῦς proper of the Greek philosophers; and the employment of the term Reason in this limitation by Jacobi in his later works (to which he was manifestly led by Kant), is not a fortunate nomenclature. In his earlier writings he does not discriminate Reason from Understanding (Verstand), viewing it as a faculty of mediate knowledge, and as opposed to Belief, in which Jacobi always held that we obtain the revelation of all reality—all original cognition. See pp. 768, 769.

* The Germans have only this one word for philosophical *Belief* and theological *Faith*. Hence much scandal, confusion, and misrepresentation, on its first employment by Jacobi.

† *Vorstellung* in this place might perhaps be rendered *presentation*. But I adhere to the usual translation; for Jacobi never seems to have risen to the pure doctrine of Natural Realism.

‡ The Germans have only one word, *Wunder*, *wunderbar*, to express marvel and *miracle*, *marvellous* and *miraculous*. Hence often confusion and ambiguity in their theology. The superiority we have over them in the two instances noticed in this and the penult note is, however, rare. The making perception a *revelation* and not an *apprehension* of existence belongs also to a Cosmothetic Idealism, struggling into Natural Realism.

mere sensation, or a mere thought—we are aware or percipient of other real things, and this too with a certainty, the same as that with which we are percipient of our own existence; for without a *Thou* an *I* is impossible. [?—See above, p. 742 sq.]

'We have thus a revelation of nature, which does not recommend merely, but compels, all and each of us to believe, and, through belief, to receive those eternal truths which are vouchsafed to man.'

P. 223.—'V. We can only demonstrate similarities (coincidences, conditioned necessary truths) in a series of identical propositions. Every proof supposes, as its basis, something already established, the principle of which is a revelation.

'VI. The element of all human knowledge and activity is Belief.'

P. 103. (Given as an aphorism of Spinoza)—'An immediate cognition, considered in and for itself, is without representation—is a Feeling.'—The three last words do not appear in the original edition; and I cannot find their warrant in Spinoza.

h.—From the Dialogue entitled 'David Hume upon Belief, or Idealism and Realism,' which appeared two years later (1787), Werke, vol. ii. p. 143, sq.

'*I.*—That things appear *as* external to us, requires no argument. But that these things are not mere appearances *in us*—are not mere modifications of our proper self, and consequently null *as representations of aught external to ourselves; but that, as representations in us*, they have still reference to something really external and self-existent, which they express, and from which they are taken—in the face of this, not only is doubt possible, it has been even often satisfactorily demonstrated, that such doubt cannot be solved by any process of reasoning strictly so denominated. Your immediate certainty of external things would, therefore, on the analogy of my Belief, be *a blind certainty*.'

(After defending the propriety of the term *Glaube* employed by him in his previous writings (which, in consequence of the word denoting in German both positive faith and general belief, had exposed him to the accusation of mysticism,) by examples of a similar usage of the word *Belief*, in the philosophical writings of Hume, Reid, &c.; he proceeds to vindicate another term he had employed—*Offenbarung*, revelation.)

'*I.*—In so far as the universal usage of language is concerned, is there required any special examples or authorities? We say commonly in German, that objects *offenbaren*, reveal, i. e. manifest, themselves through the senses. The same expression is prevalent in French, English, Latin, and many other languages. With the particular emphasis which I have laid on it, this expression does not occur in Hume;—among other reasons because he leaves it undetermined, whether we perceive things really *external* or only *as* external. . . . The decided Realist, on the contrary, who unhesitatingly accepts an external existence, on the evidence of his senses, considers this certainty as an original conviction, and cannot but think, that on this fundamental experience, all our speculation touching a knowledge of the external world, must rest—such a decided Realist, how shall he denominate the mean through which he obtains his certainty of external objects, as of existences independent of his representation of them? He has nothing on which his judgment can rest, except the things themselves—nothing but the fact, that the objects stand there, actually before him. In these circumstances, can he express himself by a more appropriate word, than the word Revelation.* And should we not rather inquire, regarding the *root* of this word, and the origin of its employment?

'*He.*—So it certainly appears.

'*I.*—That this Revelation deserves to be called *truly miraculous* [marvellous] follows of course. For if we consider sufficiently the reasons for the proposition—"That consciousness is exclusively conversant with the modifications of our proper self," Idealism will appear in all its force, and as the only scheme which our speculative reason can admit. Suppose, however, that our Realist, notwithstanding, still remains a Realist, and holds fast by the belief that—for example—this object here, which we call a table, is no mere sensation—no mere existence found only in us, but an existence external and independent of our representation, and by us only perceived; I would boldly ask him for a more appropriate epithet for the Revelation of which he boasts, in as much as he maintains that something external to him is presented (sich darstelle) to his consciousness. For the presented existence (Daseyn) of such a thing external to us, we have no other proof than the presented existence of this thing itself; and we must admit it to be wholly inconceivable, how that existence can possibly be perceived by us. But still, as was said, we maintain that we do perceive it; main-

* This looks very like Natural Realism.

tain with the most assured conviction, that things there are, extant really out of us, that our representations and notions are conformed to these external things, and not that the things which we only *fancy* external are conformed to our representations and notions. I ask on what does this conviction rest? In truth on nothing, except on a revelation, which we can denominate no otherwise than one *truly miraculous* [marvellous.]'

c. — Allwills Briefsammlung, 1792. Werke, vol. i. p. 120.—' We admit, proceeded Allwill, freely and at once, that we do not comprehend how it is that, through the mere excitation and movement of our organs of sense, we are not only sensitive but sensitive of something;—become aware of, perceive, something wholly different from us; and that we comprehend, least of all, how we distinguish and apprehend our proper self, and what pertains to our internal states, in a manner wholly different from all sensitive perception. But we deem it more secure here to appeal to an original *Instinct*, with which every cognition of truth *begins*, than, on account of that incomprehensibility, to maintain—that the *mind can perceive and represent in an infinitely various fashion not itself, and not other things, but, exclusively and alone, what is neither itself, nor any other thing*.' *

d.—From the Preface to the second volume of his Works, forming the 'Introduction to the author's collected philosophical writings;' this was published in 1815, and exhibits the last and most authentic view of the Jacobian doctrine.

P. 58 sq.—' Like every other system of cognitions, Philosophy receives its *Form* exclusively from the Understanding (Verstand) as, in general, the faculty of Concepts (Begriffe). Without notions or concepts there can be no reconsciousness, no consciousness of *cognitions*, consequently no discrimination and comparison, no separation and connexion, no weighing, reweighing, estimating, of these; in a word, no seizing possession (Besitzergreifung) of any truth whatever. On the other hand the contents—the peculiar contents, of philosophy are given exclusively by the Reason (Vernunft),† by the faculty, to wit, of cognitions, independent of sense, and beyond its reach. The Reason fashions no concepts, builds no systems, pronounces no judgments, but, *like the external senses*, it merely reveals, it merely announces the fact.

' Above all, we must consider—that as there is a sensible intuition, an *intuition* through the *Sense*, so there is likewise a rational *intuition* through the *Reason*. Each, as a peculiar source of knowledge, stands counter to the other; and we can no more educe the latter from the former, than we can educe the former from the latter. So likewise, both hold a similar relation to the Understanding (Verstand), and consequently to demonstration. Opposed to the *intuition of sense* no demonstration is valid; for all demonstration is only a reducing, a carrying back of the concept to the *sensible intuition* (empirical or pure), which affords its guarantee: and this, in reference to physical science, is the first and the last, the unconditionally valid, the absolute. On the same principle, no demonstration avails in opposition to the *intuition of reason*, which affords us a knowledge of supersensible objects, that is, affords us assurance of their reality and truth.*

' We are compelled to employ the expression *rational intuition*, or *intuition of reason* (Vernunft-Anschauung), because the language possesses no other to denote the mean and the manner, in which the understanding is enabled to take cognisance of what, unattainable by the sense, is given by *Feeling* alone, and yet, not as a subjective excogitation, but as an objective reality.

' When a man says—*I know*, we have a right to ask him—*Whence he knows?* And in answering our question, he must, in the end, inevitably resort to one or other of these two sources—either to the *Sensation of Sense* (Sinnes-Empfindung), or to the *Feeling of the Mind* (Geistes-Gefuehl). Whatever we know from mental *feeling*, that, we say, we *believe*. So speak we all. Virtue—consequently, Moral Liberty—consequently, Mind and God—these can only be *believed*. But the Sensation on which knowledge in the intuition of sense—knowledge properly so called—reposes, is as little superior to the Feeling on which the *knowledge in belief* is founded, as the brute creation is to the human, the material to the intellectual world, nature to its creator.†

* And to be represented, a thing must be known. But *ex hypothesi*, the external reality is unknown; it cannot therefore be represented.

† See note at p. 793 a, and references.

* Compare this with Aristotle's doctrine, No. 3, especially a. b. c. f., and p. 771, b.

† As will be seen from what follows, Jacobi applies the terms *Feeling* and *Belief* to both Sense and Reason. *Sensation*, as properly the mere consciousness of a subjective sensual state,—of the agreeable or disagreeable in our

'The power of Feeling, I maintain, is the power in man paramount to every other; it is that alone which specifically distinguishes him from the brutes, that is, which, affording a difference not merely in degree but in kind, raises him to an incomparable eminence above them; it is, I maintain, one and the same with Reason; or, as we may with propriety express ourselves—what we call Reason, what transcends *mere* understanding, understanding solely applied to nature, springs exclusively and alone out of the power of Feeling. As the senses refer the understanding to Sensation, so the Reason refers it to Feeling. The consciousness of that which Feeling manifests, I call *Idea*.'*

P. 107.—'As the reality, revealed by the external senses, requires no guarantee, itself affording the best assurance of its truth; so the reality, revealed by that deep internal sense which we call Reason, needs no guarantee, being, in like manner, alone and of itself the most competent witness of its veracity. Of necessity, man believes his senses; of necessity, he believes his reason; and there is no certainty superior to the certainty which this belief contains.

'When men attempted to demonstrate scientifically the truth of our representations (Vorstellungen) of a material world, existing beyond, and independent of, these representations, the object which they wished to establish vanished from the demonstrators; there remained nought but mere subjectivity, mere *sensation*: they found Idealism.

'When men attempted to demonstrate scientifically the truth of our representations of an immaterial world, existing beyond these representations,—the truth of the substantiality of the human mind,—and the truth of a free creator of the universe, distinct from the universe itself, that is, an administrator, endowed with consciousness, personality, and veritable providence; in like manner the object vanished from the demonstrators; there remained for them mere logical phantasms: they found—Nihilism.

'All reality, whether corporeal, revealed by the senses, or spiritual, revealed by the reason, is assured to us alone by Feeling;† beyond and above this there is no guarantee.'

Among those who have adopted the principles of Jacobi, and who thus philosophize in a congenial spirit with Reid, besides Koeppen and Ancillon (Nos. 96, 97), I may refer, in general, to Bouterwek, Lehrb. d. philos. Wissensch. i. § 26, 27, and Lehrb. d. philos. Vorkent. §§ 12, 27.—Neeb, Verm. Schr., vol. i. p. 154 sq. vol. ii. p. 18, 70, 245 sq. 251, vol. iii. p. 141 sq.

88.—Heidenreich, one of the most distinguished of the older Kantians. Betrachtungen, &c., P. i. p. 213, 227.—'In as much as the conviction of certain cognitions (as of our own existence, of the existence of an external world, &c.,) does not depend upon an apprehension of reasons, but is exclusively an immediate innate reliance of the subject on self and nature, I call it *natural belief* (Naturglaube). Every other cognition, notion, and demonstration, reposes upon this natural belief, and without it cannot be brought to bear.'

89.—L. Creuzer.—Skeptische Betrachtungen, &c., p. 110.—'We accord reality to the external world because our consciousness impels us so to do. . . . That we are unable to explain, conceive, justify all this, argues nothing against its truth. Our whole knowledge rests ultimately on facts of consciousness, of which we not only cannot assign the reason, but cannot even think the possibility.' He does not however rise above Hypothetical Realism; see p. 108.

90.—Platner.—Philosophische Aphorismen, 2d ed. Pref. p. vi.—'There is, I am persuaded, only one philosophy; and that the true; which in the outset of its inquiries departs from the principle, that the certainty of human knowledge is demonstrable, only relatively to our faculty of knowing, and which, at the end of its speculative career, returns within the thoughts—Experience, *Common Sense*, and Morality—the best results of our whole earthly wisdom.'

91.—Fichte is a more remarkable, because a more reluctant, confessor of the paramount authority of Belief than even Kant. Departing from the principle common to Kant and philosophers in general, that the mind cannot transcend itself, Fichte developed, with the most admirable rigour of demonstration, a scheme of idealism, the purest, simplest, and most consistent which the history of philosophy exhibits. And so confident was Fichte in the necessity of his proof, that on one occasion he was provoked to imprecate eternal damnation on his head, should he ever swerve from any, even the

corporeal organism, is a term that ought to have been here avoided.

* Without entering on details, I may observe that Jacobi, like Kant, limits the term Idea to the highest notions of pure intellect, or Reason.

† In regard to the term Feeling, see p. 760 a

least of the doctrines which he had so victoriously established. But even Fichte in the end confesses that natural belief is paramount to every logical proof; and that his own idealism he could not believe.

In the foot note at page 129 b, I have given the result as stated by himself of his theoretical philosophy—Nihilism. After the passage there quoted, he thus proceeds:—'All cognition strictly so called (Wissen) is only an effigiation (Abbildung), and there is always in it something wanted, that to which the image or effigies (Bild) corresponds. This want can be supplied through no cognition; and a system of cognitions is necessarily a system of mere images, destitute of reality, significance, or aim.' These passages are from the conclusion of the second book of his 'Bestimmung des Menschen,' entitled 'Wissen,' pp. 130, 132, ed. 1825.

But in his Practical Philosophy Fichte became convinced that he had found an organ by which to lay hold on the internal and external worlds, which had escaped from him in his Theoretical. 'I have discovered, he says, the instrument by which to seize on this Reality, and therewith, in all likelihood, on every other. Knowledge (das Wissen) is not this instrument: no cognition can be its own basis, and its own proof; every cognition supposes another still higher, as its reason, and this ascent has no termination. The instrument I mean, is *Belief* (Glaube).' (Ib. book third, entitled 'Glaube,' p. 146) —'All my conviction is only Belief, and it proceeds from Feeling or Sentiment (Gesinnung), not from the discursive Understanding (Verstand).' (Ib. p. 147). 'I possess, when once I am aware of this, the touchstone of all truth and of all conviction. The root of truth is in the Conscience (Gewissen) alone.' (Ib. p. 148). Compare St Austin, supra, No. 15, b.—See also to the same effect Fichte's 'System der Sittenlehre,' p. 18;—his work 'Ueber den Begriff der Wissenschaftslehre, p. 21, sq.;—and the 'Philosophische Journal, vol. x. p. 7. Still more explicit is the recognition of 'internal sense' and 'belief' as an irrecusable testimony of the reality of our perception of external realities, subsequently given by Fichte in his lectures at Erlangen in 1805, and reported by Gley in his 'Essai sur les Elements de la Philosophie,' p. 141, sq., and in his 'Philosophia Turonensis,' vol. i. p. 237.—I regret that I have not yet seen Fichte's 'Hinterlassene Schriften,' lately published by his son.

After these admissions it need not surprise us to find Fichte confessing, that 'How evident soever may be the demonstration that every object of consciousness (Vorstellung) is only illusion and dream, I am unable to believe it;' and in like manner maintaining, that Spinoza never could have believed the system which he deduced with so logical a necessity. (Philos. Journ. vii. p. 35.)

93.—Krug.—The Transcendental Synthetism of this philosopher is a scheme of dualism founded on the acceptance of the original datum of consciousness, that we are immediately cognisant, at once, of an internal, and of an external world. It is thus a scheme of philosophy, really, though not professedly, founded on Common Sense. Krug is a Kantian; and as originally promulgated in his 'Entwurf eines neuen Organons,' 1801, (§ 5), his system was, like Kant's, a mere Cosmothetic Idealism; for while he allowed a *knowledge* of the internal world, he only allowed a *belief* of the external. The polemic of Schulze against the common theory of sensitive representation, and in professed conformity with Reid's doctrine of perception, was published in the same year; and it was probably the consideration of this that determined Krug to a fundamental change in his system. For in his treatise 'Ueber die verschiedenen Methoden,' &c. 1802 (p. 44), and still more explicitly in his 'Fundamental Philosophie,' 1803 (§ 68), the mere belief in the unknown existence of external things is commuted into a cognition, and an immediate perception apparently allowed, as well of the phaenomena of matter, as of the phaenomena of mind. See also his pamphlet 'Ueber das Verhaeltniss der Philosophie zum gesunden Menschenverstande,' 1835, in reference to Hegel's paradox,—'That the world of Common Sense, and the world of Philosophy, are, to each other, worlds upside down.'

94.—Degerando.—Histoire comparée des Systemes de Philosophie t. iii. p. 343, original edition. 'Concluons: la realité de nos connaissances [of the external world] ne se démontre pas; elle se reconnait. Elle se reconnait, par l'effet de cette même *conscience* qui nous révèle notre connaissance elle-même. Tel est le privilége de l' intelligence humaine. Elle aperçoit les objets, elle s'aperçoit ensuite elle-même, elle aperçoit qu'elle a aperçu. Elle est toute lumière, mais une lumière qui réfléchit indéfiniment sur elle-même. On nous opposera ce principe abstrait: *qu'une sensation ne peut nous instruire que de notre propre existence*. . . Sans doute lorsqu' on commence par confondre la *sensation* avec la *perception*, par définir celle-ci *une manière d'être du moi*, on ne peut leur attribuer d'autre instruction que celle dont notre propre existence est l' objet. Mais évitons ici les disputes de mots; il s'agit seulement de constater un fait; savoir, si dans certains cas, en réfléchissant sur nos opérations, en démêlant toutes leurs circonstances, nous n' y découvrons pas la perception immédiate et primitive d'une existence étrangère, perception à la quelle on donnera tel nom qu' on jugera convenable. Si ce fait est exact, constant, universel, si ce fait est primitif, il est non seulement inutile, mais absurde, d'en demander le *pourquoi* et le *comment*. Car nous n'avons aucune donnée pour l'expliquer.'

95.—FRIES, a distinguished philosopher of the Kantian school, but whose opinions have been considerably modified by the influence of the Jacobian philosophy of belief, professes in his *Feeling of Truth* (Wahrheitsgefuehl) a doctrine of common sense. This doctrine is in every essential respect the same as Reid's; for Fries is altogether wrong in the assertion which, in different works, he once and again hazards that, under Common Sense, Reid had in view a special organ of truth—a peculiar sense, distinct from reason or intelligence in general. See in particular his Krit. vol. i. § 85.—Metaph. § 17.—Gesch. d. Phil. vol. ii. § 172. Anthr. vol. i. § 52. ii. Vorr. p. xvi.—Log. § 84.

96.—KOEPPEN—a philosopher of the school of Jacobi.—Darstellung des Wesens der Philosophie, § 11.—'Human knowledge, (Wissen) considered in its totality, exhibits a twofold character. It is either *Apprehension* (Wahrnehmung) or *Conception* (Begriff); either an immediate conviction, or a mediate insight, obtained through reasons. By the former we are said to *believe*, by the latter to *conceive* [or comprehend]' After an articulate exposition of this, and having shown, with Jacobi and Hume, that *belief* as convertible with *feeling* constitutes the ultimate ground both of action and cognition, he proceeds:—'In a philosophical sense, *believed* is tantamount to *apprehended*. For all apprehension is an immediate conviction which cannot be founded upon reflection and conception. In our human individuality we possess a double faculty of apprehension—*Reason* [intelligence, νοῦς] and *Sense*. What, therefore, through reason and sense is an object of our apprehension is *believed*. . . . The belief of reason and the belief of sense, are our guarantees for the certainty of what we apprehend. The former relies on the testimony of reason, the latter on the testimony of sense. Is this twofold testimony false, there is absolutely no truth of apprehension. The combinations of conceptions afford no foundation for this original truth.—*Belief* is thus the *first* in our cognition, because apprehension is the first; *conception* is the *second*, because it regards the relations of what is given through apprehension. If, then, I exclusively appropriate to the result of conceptions the name of *knowledge* (Wissen)—still all knowledge presupposes belief, and on belief does the truth of knowledge repose. Belief lays hold on the originally given; knowledge developes the relations of the given, in conformity with the laws of thought,' &c.

97.—ANCILLON (the Son).—German by birth, French by lineage, writing in either language with equal elegance, and representing in himself the highest and most peculiar qualities of both his nations; we have still farther to admire in the prime minister of Prussia, at once, the metaphysician and moralist, the historian and statesman, the preacher and man of the world. He philosophised in the spirit of Jacobi; and from his treatise Ueber Glaube (On Belief), one of his later writings, I translate the following passages:—

P. 36. 'Existences, realities, are *given us* We apprehend them by means of an internal *mental intuition* (geistige Anschauung) which, in respect of its clearness, as in respect of its certainty, is as evident as universal, and as resistless and indubitable as evident.

'Were no such internal, immediate, mental intuition given us, there would be given us no existence, no reality. The universe—the worlds of mind and matter—would then resolve themselves into apparency. All realities would be mere appearances, appearing to another mere appearance—Man; whilst no answer could be afforded to the ever-recurring questions—*What is it that appears?* and *To whom is the appearance made?* Even language resists such assertions, and reproves the lie.

'Had we no such internal, immediate, mental intuition, existences would be beyond the reach of every faculty we possess. For neither our abstractive nor reflective powers, neither the analysis of notions, nor notions themselves, neither synthesis, nor reasoning, could ever lead us to reality and existence.'*

(Having shown this in regard to each of these in detail, he proceeds: p. 40.)—'This root of all reality, this ground of existence, is the Reason (Vernunft),† out of which all reasonings proceed, and on which alone they repose.

'The Reason of which I here speak is not an instrument which serves for this or that performance, but a true productive force, a creative power, which has its own revelation; which does not show what is already manifested, but, as a primary consciousness, itself contemplates existence; which is not content to collect data, and from these data to draw an inference, but which itself furnishes Reality as a datum. This Reason is no arithmetical machine, but an active principle; it does not reach the truth after toil and time, but departs from the truth, because it finds the truth within itself.

'This Reason, this internal eye,‡ which immediately receives the light of existence, and apprehends existences, as the bodily eye the outlines and the colours of the sensuous world, is an immediate *sense* which contemplates the invisible.

'This Reason is the ground, the principle, of all knowledge (Wissen); for all knowledge bears reference to reality and existences.

'All knowledge must, first or last, rest on *facts* (Thatsachen,) universal facts, necessary facts, of the internal sense;—on facts which give us ourselves, our own existence, and a conviction of the existence of other supersensible beings.

'These facts are for us *mental intuitions*. In as much as they give us an instantaneous, clear, objective perception of reality, they are entitled to the name of *Intuition* (Anschauung); in as much as this intuition regards the objects of the invisible world, they deserve the attribute of *mental*.

'Such an intuition, such a mental feeling (Gefuehl), engenders *Philosophical Belief*. This belief consists in the immediate apprehending of existences wholly concealed and excluded from the senses, which reveal themselves to us in our inmost consciousness, and this too with a necessary conviction of their objectivity (reality.)

'Belief, in the philosophical sense, means, the apprehension without proof, reasoning or deduction of any kind, of those higher truths which belong to the supersensible world, and not to the world of appearances.' . . . . .

P. 43. 'Philosophical belief apprehends existences which can neither be conceived nor demonstrated. Belief is therefore a knowledge conversant about existences, but it does not know existences, if under knowledge be understood—demonstrating, comprehending, conceiving.' . . .

P. 44.—'The internal intuition which affords us the apprehension of certain existences, and allows us not to doubt in regard to the certainty of their reality, does not inform us concerning their nature. This internal intuition is given us in *Feeling* and through Feeling.' . . . .

P. 48.—'This internal universal *sense*, this highest power of mental vision in man, seems to have much in it of the *instinctive*, and may therefore appropriately be styled *intellectual Instinct*. For on the one hand it manifests itself through sudden, rapid, uniform, resistless promptings; and on the other hand, these promptings relate to objects, which lie not within the domain of the senses, but belong to the supersensible world.

'Let no offence be taken at the expression *Instinct*. For, &c.' . . .

P. 50.—'Had man not an intellectual Instinct, or a reason giving out, revealing, but not demonstrating, truths rooted in itself, for want of a point of attachment and support, he would move himself in all directions, but without progress; and on a level, too, lower than the brutes, for he could not compass that kind of perfection which the brute possesses, and would be disqualified from attaining any other.

'The *immediate Reason* elicits internal *mental intuitions*; these intuitions have an evidence, which works on us like an *intellectual instinct*, and generates in us a *philosophical belief*, which constitutes the foundation of our knowledge. To which soever of these expressions the preference be accorded, all their notions have a common character, and are so interlinked together, that they all equally result in the same very simple proposition:—*There is either no truth, or there are fundamental truths, which admit as little of demonstration as of doubt.*' . . .

P. 51.—'Had we not in ourselves an active principle of truth, we should have

* Fichte says the same:—'From cognition to pass out to an object of cognition—this is impossible; we must therefore depart from the reality, otherwise we should remain forever unable to reach it.'

† On the employment of the word *Reason* by the German philosophers, supra, p. 768, sq.

‡ Plato, Aristotle, and many philosophers after them, say this of Intelligence, νοῦς.

neither a rule, nor a touchstone, nor a standard, of the true. Had we not in ourselves the consciousness of existences, there would be for us no means of knowing, whether what comes from without be not mere illusion, and whether what the mind itself fashions and combines be aught but an empty play with notions. In a word—the truth must be in us, as a constitutive, and as a regulative, principle; or we should never attain to truth. Only with determinate points of commencement and termination, and with a central point of knowledge, from which every thing departs, and to which every things tends to return, are other cognitions possible; failing this primary condition, nothing can be given us to know, and nothing certain can exist.'

And in the Preface (p. xi.) he had said:—'The Reason invents, discovers, creates, in propriety, nothing; it enounces only what it harbours, it only reveals what God himself has deposited within it; but so soon as it is conscious to itself of this, it speaks out with a force which inspires us with a rational belief, a faith of reason (Vernunftglaube),—a belief which takes priority of every other, and which serves to every other as a point of departure and of support. How can we believe the word of God, if we do not already believe that a God exists?'

Compare also his 'Zur Vermittlung der Extreme,' vol. ii. p. 253, sq., and his 'Moi Humain' passim.

98.—Gerlach.—Fundamental Philosophie, § 16.—'So soon as a man is convinced of any thing—be his conviction of the True, of the Good, or of the Beautiful—he rests upon his Consciousness; for in himself and in his Consciousness alone does he possess the elements which constitute the knowledge of things, and it is herein alone that he finds the necessity of all and each of his judgments. In a word, that only has an existence for us of which we are conscious.'

99.—Hermes, the late illustrious ornament of the Catholic faculty of Theology in Bonn, a thinker of whom any country may well be proud, is the author of a philosophy of cognition which, in its fundamental principles, is one of Common Sense. It is contained in the first volume of his 'Introduction to Christian Catholic Theology,' a work which, since the author's death, has obtained a celebrity, apart from its great intrinsic merits, through the agitation consequent on its condemnation at Rome, for doctrines, which, except on some notoriously open questions, the Hermesians—in Germany, now a numerous and able school strenuously deny that it contains.

To speak only of his theoretical philosophy.—For the terms *Feeling of Truth*, *Belief*, &c., Hermes substitutes the term *Holding-for-true* (Fuerwahrhalten) which is only inadequately expressed by the Latin *assensus*, *assensio*, *adhæsio*, the Greek *συγκατάθεσις*, or any English term. *Holding-for-true* involves in it a duplicity;—viz., a Holding-for-*true* of the *knowledge*, and a Holding-for-*real* (Fuerwirklichhalten) of the *thing known*. Both of these parts are united in the decision—that the knowledge and the thing known coincide.

Holding-for-real is not consequent on reflection; it is not the result of a recognition; it is the concomitant, not the consequent of apprehension. It is a constituent element of the primary consciousness of a perception external or internal; it is what, in the language of the Scottish philosophers, might be called an instinctive belief. 'This holding-for-real (says Hermes) is manifestly given in me *prior* to all Reflection: for with the first consciousness, with the consciousness 'that I know,' from which all Reflection departs, the consciousness is also there, 'that I hold the thing known for real,'' Einl. vol. i. p. 182. See Nos. 3, 15* (at end), 16, &c.

The *necessity* we find of assenting or holding is the last and highest security we can obtain for truth and reality. The necessary holding of a thing for real is not itself reality; it is only the instrument, the mean, the surrogate, the guarantee, of reality. It is not an objective, it is only a subjective, certainty. It constitutes, however, all the assurance or certainty of which the human mind is capable. 'The [necessary] Holding,' says Hermes, 'of something known [for real,] can afford no other certainty of the objective existence of what is known but this—*that I (the subject) must hold the thing known for objectively existent*; or (meaning always by the word *subjective* what is *in me*, *in the subject*,)—of the *objective existence* of a thing known there can possibly be given only the highest *subjective certainty*. But no one who knows what he would be at, will ever ask after any other certainty; not merely because it is unattainable, but because it is contradictory for human thought: in other words, can a subject be any otherwise certain than that *it* is certain—than that *itself, the subject*, is certain? To be *objectively* certain (taking the term *objective* in a sense corresponding to the term *subjective* as here employed) the subject must, in fact, no longer remain the subject, it must also be the object, and, as such, be able to become certain; and yet in conformity to our notion of certainty (Gewissheit) — or whatever more suitable expression may be found for it—all questions concerning certainty must be referred to the subject (to the Ego): the attempt to refer them to the object involves a contradiction.' Ibid. p. 186.

This is clearly and cogently stated; and it would seem as if we had only to appeal to the subjective certainty we have, in our being compelled to hold that in perception the *ego*, is immediately cognisant, not only of itself as subject but of a *non-ego* as object—to prove that the *external world* being actually known as existing, actually exists. (See above, p. 745, sq.) This Hermes does not, however, do. He seems not, indeed, to have contemplated the possibility of the mind being conscious or immediately cognitive of aught but self; and only furnishes us with an improved edition of the old and inconclusive reasoning, that an external world must be admitted, as the necessary ground or reason of our internal representation of it.

100. — COUSIN. — Fragmens Philosophiques, third edition, Vol. I.

a. — P. 243.—'Philosophy is already realized, for human thought is there.

'There is not, and there cannot be, a philosophy absolutely false; for it would behove the author of such a philosophy to place himself out of his own thought, in other words, out of his humanity. This power has been given to no man.

'How then may philosophy err?—By considering thought only on a single side, and by seeing, in that single side, the totality of thought. There are no false, but many incomplete systems;—systems true in themselves, but vicious in their pretensions, each to comprise that absolute truth which is only found distributed through all.

'The incomplete, and by consequence, the exclusive—this is the one only vice of philosophy, or rather, to speak more correctly, of philosophers, for philosophy rises above all the systems. The full portrait of the real, which philosophy presents, is indeed made up of features borrowed from every several system; for of these each reflects reality; but unfortunately reflects it under a single angle.*

* The like has been said by Leibnitz and Hegel; but not so finely.

'To compass possession of reality full and entire, it is requisite to sist ourselves at the centre. To reconstitute the intellectual life, mutilated in the several systems, it behoves us to re-enter Consciousness, and there, weaned from a systematic and exclusive spirit, *to analyse thought into its elements, and all its elements, and to seek out in it the characters, and all the characters, under which it is at present manifested to the eye of consciousness.*'—Du Fait de Conscience.

b.—P. 181.—'The fundamental principle of knowledge and intellectual life is *Consciousness*. Life begins with consciousness, and with consciousness it ends: in consciousness it is that we apprehend ourselves; and it is in and through consciousness that we apprehend the external world. Were it possible to rise above consciousness, to place ourselves, so to speak, behind it, to penetrate into the secret workshop where intelligence blocks out and fabricates the various phaenomena, there to officiate, as it were, at the birth, and to watch the evolution of consciousness;—then might we hope to comprehend its nature, and the different steps through which it rises to the form in which it is first actually revealed. But, as all knowledge commences with consciousness, it is able to remount no higher. *Here a prudent analysis will therefore stop, and occupy itself with what is given.*'

Other testimonies might easily be quoted from the subsequent writings of M. Cousin—were this not superfluous; for I presume that few who take an interest in philosophical inquiries can now be ignorant of these celebrated works.

101.—DE LA MENNAIS.—See No. 2.

OMITTED.

9**. — AELIUS ARISTIDES. — Platonic Oration, ii. (Opera, ed. Canter. t. iii. p. 249 ed. Jebb. t. ii. p. 150)—'That the Many are not to be contemned, and their opinion held of no account; but that in them, too, there is a presentiment, an unerring instinct, which, by a kind of divine fatality, seizes darkling on the truth;—this we have Plato himself teaching, and, ages earlier than Plato, this old Hesiod, with posterity in chorus, in these familiar verses sang:

The Fame, born of the many-nation'd voice
Of mankind, dies not; for it lives as God.'

For Hesiod, see No. 1. These verses are likewise adduced by Aristotle as proverbial. (Eth. Nic. vii. 13 [14.]) They may be also rendered thus:

'*The Word, forth sent by the conformant voice*
Of mankind, errs not; for its truth is God's.'

Fame (Public Opinion) had her temple in Athens. See Pausanias.

Plato is referred to in the Laws, (L. xii § 5. ed. Bekk. t. ii. p. 950, ed Steph.) Another passage, in the Crito, which Canter indicates, is irrelevant. In the former, Plato attributes to mankind at large a certain divine sense or vaticination of the truth (θεῖόν τι καὶ εὔστοχον), by which, in our natural judgments, we are preserved from error. I did not, however, find the statement sufficiently generalized to quote the context as a testimony.

15*.—Theodoret.—The Curative of Greek Affections, Sermon I., On Belief. (Opera, ed. Sirmondi, t. iv. p. 478.)—'Belief [or Faith], therefore, is a matter of the greatest moment. For, according to the Pythagorean Epicharmus,

Mind, it seeth; Mind, it heareth;
All beside is deaf and blind;

and Heraclitus, in like manner, exhorts us to submit to the guidance of belief, in these words;—*Unless ye hope, ye shall not find the unhoped for, which is inscrutable and impermeable.* . . . And let none of you, my friends, say aught in disparagement of belief. For belief is called by Aristotle the *Criterion of Science;* whilst Epicurus says, that it is the *Anticipation of Reason,* and that anticipation, having indued Knowledge, results in Comprehension.—But, as we define it, Belief is—*a spontaneous assent or adhesion of the mind,*—or *the intuition of the unapparent,*—or *the taking possession of the real* (περὶ τὸ ὂν ἐμβατευσις—v. Bud. in Pand. et Com. L. G.), *and natural apprehension of the unperceivable,*—*or an unvacillating propension established in the mind of the believer.*—But, on the one hand, Belief requires knowledge, as on the other, Knowledge requires belief. For there can subsist, neither belief without knowledge, nor knowledge without belief. Belief precedes knowledge, knowledge follows belief; while desire is attendant upon knowledge, and action consequent upon desire. For it is necessary,—to believe first; then to learn; knowing, to desire; and desiring, to act. . . . .—Belief, therefore, my friends, is a concern common to all; . . . for all who would learn any thing must first believe. [So Aristotle.] Belief is, therefore, the foundation and basis of Science. For your philosophers have defined Belief—*a voluntary assent or adhesion of the mind;* and Science—*an immutable habit, accompanied with reason.*'—This is a testimony which I should regret to have totally forgotten. Compare Nos. 3, 11, 15, 16, 18, 19, 24, 81, 86, 87, 91, 96, 97, 99, &c.

17*.—Simplicius.—Commentary on the Manual of Epictetus; and there speaking in the language of the Porch, rather than in that of the Lyceum or the Academy.

a.—C. 33, Heins. 23, Schweigh.—'The Common Notions of men concerning the nature of things, according to which, in place of varying from each other, they are in opinion mutually agreed, (as, that *the good is useful, and the useful good,* that *all things desiderate the good,* that *the equal is neither surpassing nor surpassed,* that *twice two is four*)—these notions, and the like, suggested in us by right reason, and tested by experience and time, are true, and in accordance with the nature of things; whereas the notions proper to individual men are frequently fallacious.'

b.—C. 72, Heins. 48, Schweigh.—'But Reason, according to the proverb, is a Mercury common to all; for, although, as in us individually, reasons are plural, or numerically different, they are in species one and the same; so that, by reason all men follow after the same things as good, and eschew the same things as bad, and think the same things to be true or to be false.'

In these passages, *Reason,* in the vaguer meaning of the Stoics, is employed, where *Intellect,* in the precise acceptation of the Aristotelians and Platonists, might have been expected from Simplicius. But he is here speaking by accommodation to his author.

As a chronological Table was luckily omitted at the head of the Series, I here append, ethnographically subarranged, the following—

LIST OF THE PRECEDING TESTIMONIES.

Greek.—1, Hesiod; 2, Heraclitus; 3, Aristotle; 4, Theophrastus; 9**, Aelius Aristides, see at end; 10, Alexander Aphrodisiensis; 11, Clemens Alexandrinus; 15, Theodoret, see at end; 16, Proclus; 17, Ammonius Hermiae; 17*, Simplicius, see at end.

ROMAN.—5, Lucretius; 6, Cicero; 7, Horace; 8, Seneca; 9, Pliny, younger; 9*, Quintilian; 12, Tertullian; 13, Arnobius; 14, Lactantius; 15, St Augustin.

ARABIAN.—19, Algazel.

ITALIAN.—18, St Anselm (ambiguously French); 20, Aquinas; 26, Julius Cæsar Scaliger; 67, Vulpius; 68, Vico; 71, Genovesi.

SPANISH.—22, Antonius Andreas; 28, Antonius Goveanus (*Portuguese*); 29, Nunnesius; 32, Mariana.

FRENCH.—23, Budaeus; 27, Omphalius; 30, Muretus; 37, Descartes; 39, Balzac; 40, Chanet; 41, Irenaeus a Sancto Jacobo; 42, Lescalopier; 43, Pascal; 44, La Chambre; 46, Le Pere Rapin; 47, Du Hamel; 48, Malebranche; 49, Poiret; 50, Bossuet; 59, John Alphonso Turretini (*Genevese*); 60, Fenelon; 62, D'Aguesseau; 63, Buffier; 70, Huber; 74, D'Alembert; 94, Degerando; 100, Cousin; 101, De La Mennais.

BRITISH.—21, Duns Scotus; 33, Sir John Davies; 35, Lord Herbert; 36, Cameron; 38, Sir Thomas Brown; 45, Henry More; 51, Locke; 52, Bentley; 53, John Serjeant; 53*, Abercromby; 55, Toland; 61, Shaftesbury; 62*, Berkeley; 64, Lyons; 65, Amherst; 66, Wollaston; 72, Hume; 78, Price; 79, Reid; 82, Beattie. (Of these, 21, [?] 36. 53*, 72, 79, 82, are *Scottish*.)

GERMAN.—24, Luther; 25, Melanchthon; 34, Keckermann; 54, Leibnitz; 56, Christian Thomasius; 57, Ridiger; 58, Feuerlin; 69, Christian Wolf; 73, Crusius; 75, Oetinger; 76, Eschenbach; 77, John Matthew Gesner; 80, Hiller; 83, Storchenau; 84, Stattler; 86, Kant; 87, Jacobi; 88, Heidenreich; 89, Leonhard Creuzer; 90, Platner; 91, Fichte; 93, Krug; 95, Fries; 96, Koeppen; 97, Ancillon, the son; 98, Gerlach; 99, George Hermes.

BELGIAN.—31, Giphanius; 81, Hemsterhuis; 85, Hennert.

In all one hundred and six Witnesses

NOTE B.

OF PRESENTATIVE AND REPRESENTATIVE KNOWLEDGE.

§ I.—*The distinction of Presentative, Intuitive or Immediate, and of Representative or Mediate cognition; with the various significations of the term Object, its conjugates and correlatives.*

§ II.—*Errors of Reid and other philosophers, in reference to the preceding distinctions.*

[References.—From Inq. 106 a, from I. P. 226 b, 283 a, 292 a b, 293 b, 298 b, 305 a, 339 b, 351 b, 357 a, 368 b, 369 a b, 373 a, 427 a.]

§ I.—*The distinction of Presentative, Intuitive or Immediate, and of Representative or Mediate cognition; with the various significations of the term Object, its conjugates and correlatives.*

The correlative terms, *Immediate* and *Mediate*, as attributes of *knowledge* and its modifications, are employed in more than a single relation. In order, therefore, to obviate misapprehension, it is necessary, in the first place, to determine in what signification it is, that we are at present to employ them.

In apprehending an individual thing, either itself through sense or its representation in the phantasy, we have, in a certain sort, an absolute or irrespective cognition, which is justly denominated *immediate*, by contrast to the more relative and *mediate* knowledge which, subsequently, we compass of the same object, when, by a comparative act of the understanding we refer it to a class, that is, think or recognise it, by relation to other things, under a certain notion or general term. With this distinction we have nothing now to do. The discrimination of *immediate* and *mediate* knowledge, with which we are at present concerned, lies within and subdivides what constitutes, in the foregoing division, the branch of *immediate* cognition; for we are only here to deal with the knowledge of individual objects absolutely considered, and not viewed in relation to aught beyond themselves.

This distinction of immediate and mediate cognition it is of the highest importance to establish; for it is one without which the whole philosophy of knowledge must remain involved in ambiguities. What, for example, can be more various, vacillating, and contradictory, than the employment of the all-important terms *object* and *objective*, in contrast to *subject* and *subjective*, in the writings of Kant?—though the same is true of those of other recent philosophers. This arose from the want of a preliminary determination of the various, and even opposite, meanings of which these terms are susceptible,—a selection of the one proper meaning,—and a rigorous adherence to the meaning thus preferred. But, in particular, the doctrine of Natural Realism cannot, without this distinction, be adequately understood, developed, and discriminated. Reid, accordingly, in consequence of the want of it, has not only failed in giving to his philosophy its precise and appropriate expression, he has failed even in withdrawing it from equivocation and confusion;—in so much, that it even remains a question, whether his doctrine be one of Natural Realism at all. —The following is a more articulate developement of this important distinction than that which I gave, some ten years ago; and since, by more than one philosopher adopted. See Edinburgh Review, vol. lii. p 160, sq.; Cross's Selections from Ed. Rev. vol. iii. p. 200 sq.; Peisse, Fragments Philosophiques, p. 75 sq.

For the sake of distinctness, I shall state the different moments of the distinction in separate *Propositions;* and these for more convenient reference I shall number.

1.—A thing is known *immediately* or *proximately*, when we cognise it *in itself;* *mediately* or *remotely*, when we cognise it *in or through something numerically different from itself.* Immediate cognition, thus the knowledge of a thing in itself, involves the *fact* of its existence; mediate cognition, thus the knowledge of a thing in or through something not itself, involves only the *possibility* of its existence.

2.—An immediate cognition, in as much as the thing known is *itself presented* to observation, may be called a *presentative;* and in as much as the thing presented, is, as it were, *viewed by the mind face to face*, may be called an *intuitive*,* cognition.—A mediate cognition, in as much as the thing known is *held up or mirrored to the mind in a vicarious representation*, may be called a *representative* † cognition.

3.—A *thing known* is called an *object* of knowledge.

4.—In a presentative or immediate cognition there is *one sole object;* the thing (immediately) known and the thing existing being one and the same.—In a representative or mediate cognition there may be discriminated *two objects;* the thing (immediately) known, and the thing existing being numerically different.

5.—A thing known *in itself* is the (sole) *presentative* or *intuitive object* of knowledge, or the (sole) object of a *presentative* or *intuitive knowledge.*—A thing known *in and through something else* is the *primary, mediate, remote*,* *real*,† *existent*, or *represented, object* of (mediate) knowledge,—*objectum quod;* and a thing *through which something else is known* is the *secondary, immediate, proximate*,*

* On the application of the term *Intuitive*, in this sense, see in the sequel of this Excursus, p. 812 a b.

† The term *Representation* I employ always strictly, as in contrast to *Presentation*, and, therefore, with exclusive reference to individual objects, and not in the vague generality of *Repraesentatio* or *Vorstellung* in the Leibnitian and subsequent philosophies of Germany, where it is used for any cognitive act, considered, not in relation to what knows, but to what is known; that is, as the genus including under it Intuitions, Perceptions, Sensations, Conceptions, Notions, Thoughts proper, &c. as species.

* The distinction of *proximate* and *remote* object is sometimes applied to perception in a different manner. Thus Colour (the White of the Wall, for instance,) is said to be the *proximate* object of vision, because it is seen immediately; the coloured thing (the Wall itself for instance) is said to be the *remote* object of vision, because it is seen only through the mediation of the colour. This however is inaccurate. For the Wall, that in which the colour inheres, however mediately *known*, is never mediately *seen*. It is not indeed an *object of perception* at all; it is only the *subject* of such an object, and is reached by a cognitive process, different from the merely perceptive.

† *On the term Real.*—The term *Real* (realis), though always importing *the existent*, is used in various significations and oppositions. The following occur to me:—

1. As denoting *existence*, in contrast to the *nomenclature* of existence,—the *thing*, as contradistinguished from its *name*. Thus we have definitions and divisions *real*, and definitions and divisions *nominal or verbal*.

2. As expressing the *existent* opposed to the *non-existent*,—a *something* in contrast to a *nothing*. In this sense the diminutions of existence, to which reality, in the *following* significations, is counterposed, are *all real*.

3. As denoting *material* or *external*, in contrast to *mental*, *spiritual* or *internal*, existence. This meaning is improper; so, therefore, is the term *Realism*, as equivalent to *Materialism*, in the nomenclature of some recent philosophers.

4. As synonymous with *actual;* and this a.) as opposed to *potential*, b.) as opposed to *possible*, existence.

5. As denoting *absolute* or *irrespective*, in opposition to *phænomenal* or *relative*, existence; in other words, as denoting things in themselves and out of relation to all else, in contrast to things in relation to, and as known by, intelligences, like men, who know only under the conditions of plurality and difference. In this sense, which is rarely employed and may be neglected, the Real is only another term for the Unconditioned or Absolute,—*τὸ ὄντως ὄν*.

6. As indicating existence considered as a *subsistence in nature*, (*ens extra animam, ens naturae*,) it stands counter to an existence considered as a *representation in thought*. In this sense, *realis*, in the language of the older philosophy (Scholastic, Cartesian, Gassendian,) as applied to *esse* or *ens*, is opposed to *intentionale*, *notionale*, *conceptibile*, *imaginarium*, *rationis*, *cognitionis*, *in anima*, *in intellectu*, *prout cognitum*, *ideale*, *&c.;* and corresponds with *a parte rei*,

*ideal,** *vicarious* or *representative*, *object* of (mediate) knowledge,—*objectum quo*, or *per quod*. The former may likewise be styled *objectum entitativum*.

6.—The Ego as the subject of thought and knowledge is now commonly styled by Philosophers simply *The Subject*; and *Subjective* is a familiar expression for what pertains to the mind or thinking principle. In contrast and correlation to these, the terms *Object* and *Objective* are, in like manner, now in general use to denote the Non-ego, its affections and properties,—and in general the Really existent as opposed to the Ideally known. These expressions, more especially Object and Objective, are ambiguous; for though the Non-Ego may be the more frequent and obtrusive object of cognition, still a *mode of mind* constitutes an *object* of thought and knowledge, no less than a mode of matter. Without, therefore, disturbing the preceding nomenclature, which is not only ratified but convenient, I would propose that, when we wish to be precise, or where any ambiguity is to be dreaded, we should employ—on the one hand, either the terms *subject-object* or *subjective object*, (and this we could again distinguish as *absolute* or as *relative*)—on the other, either *object-object*, or *objective object*.*

as opposed to *a parte intellectus*, with *subjectivum*, as opposed to *objectivum*, (see p. 806 b, sq. note), with *proprium*, *principale* and *fundamentale*, as opposed to *vicarium*, with *materiale*, as opposed to *formale*, and with *formale in seipso*, and *entitativum*, as opposed to *representativum*, &c. Under this head, in the vacillating language of our more recent philosophy, *real* approximates to, but is hardly convertible with, *objective*, in contrast to *subjective* in the signification there prevalent, (see p. 808 ab, note.)

7. In close connexion with the sixth meaning, *real*, in the last place, denotes an identity or difference founded on the conditions of the existence of a thing in itself, in contrast to an identity or difference founded only on the relation or point of view in which the thing may be regarded by the thinking subject. In this sense it is opposed to *logical* or *rational*, the terms being here employed in a peculiar meaning. Thus a thing which *really* (*re*) or in itself is one and indivisible may *logically* (*ratione*) by the mind be considered as diverse and plural, and, vice versa, what are *really* diverse and plural may *logically* be viewed, as one and indivisible. As an example of the former;—the sides and angles of a triangle (or trilateral), as mutually correlative—as together making up the same simple figure—and as, without destruction of that figure, actually inseparable from it, and from each other, are *really* one; but in as much as they have peculiar relations which may, in thought, be considered severally and for themselves, they are *logically* twofold. In like manner take apprehension and judgment. These are *really* one, as each involves the other, (for we apprehend only as we judge something to be, and we judge only, as we apprehend the existence of the terms compared), and as together they constitute a single indivisible act of cognition; but they are *logically* double, in as much as, by mental abstraction, they may be viewed each for itself, and as a distinguishable element of thought. As an example of the latter;—individual things, as John, James, Richard, &c., are *really* (numerically) different, as co-existing in nature only under the condition of plurality; but, as resembling objects constituting a single class or notion (man) they are, *logically* considered, (generically or specifically) identical and one.

* I eschew, in general, the employment of the words *Idea* and *Ideal*—they are so vague and various in meaning. (See Note G.) But they cannot always be avoided, as the conjugates of the indispensable term *Idealism*. Nor is there, as I use them, any danger from their ambiguity; for I always manifestly employ them simply for subjective—(what is in or of the mind), in contrast to objective—(what is out of, or external to, the mind.)

* *The terms Subject and Subjective, Object and Objective.*—I have already had occasion to shew, that, in the hands of recent philosophers, the principal terms of philosophy have not only been frequently changed from their original meanings and correlations, but those meanings and correlations sometimes even simply reversed. I have again to do this in reference to the correlatives *subjective* and *objective*, as employed to denote what Aristotle vaguely expressed by the terms τὰ ἐν ἡμῖν and τὰ ἐν φύσει—*the things in us*, and *the things in nature*.

The terms *subject and object* were, for a long time, not sufficiently discriminated from each other.—Even in the writings of Aristotle τὸ ὑποκείμενον is used ambiguously for *id in quo*, the *subject proper*, and *id circa quod*, the *object proper*;—and this latter meaning is unknown to Plato. The Greek language never, in fact, possessed any one term of equal universality, and of the same definite signification, as object. For the term ἀντικείμενον, which comes the nearest, Aristotle uses, like Plato, in the plural, to designate, in general, the various kinds of *opposites*; and there is, I believe, only a single passage to be found in his writings, (De An. ii. c. 4,) in which this word can be adequately translated by *object*. The reason of this, at first sight, apparent deficiency may have been that as no language, except the Greek, could express, not by a periphrasis, but by a special word, the object of every several faculty or application of mind, (as αἰσθητόν, φανταστόν, νοητόν, γνωστόν, ἐπιστητόν, δοξαστόν, ὁρατόν, βουλευτόν, ποιητόν, &c. &c.,) so the Greek philosophers alone found little want of a term precisely to express the abstract notion of *objectivity* in its indeterminate universality, which they could apply, as they required it, in any determinate relation. The schoolmen distinguished the *subjectum occupationis*, from the *subjectum inhaesionis*, *praedicationis*, &c., limiting the term *objectum* (which in classical Latinity had

7.—If the representative object be supposed (according to one theory) a mode of the conscious mind or self, it may be distinguished as *Egoistical*; if it be supposed (according to another) something numerically different from the conscious mind or self, it may be distinguished as, *Non-Egoistical*. See Note C. The former

---

never been naturalised as an absolute term, even by the philosophers) to the former; and it would have been well had the term *subjectum*, in that sense, been, at the same time, wholly renounced. This was not, however, done. Even to the present day, the word *subject* is employed, in most of the vernacular languages, for the *materia circa quam*, in which signification the term *object* ought to be exclusively applied. But a still more intolerable abuse has recently crept in; *object* has, in French and English, been for above a century vulgarly employed for *end*, *motive*, *final cause*. But to speak of these terms more in detail.

The term *object* (objectum, id quod objicitur cognitioni, &c.) involves a twofold element of meaning. 1°, It expresses something absolute, something in itself that is; for before a thing can be presented to cognition, it must be supposed to exist. 2°, It expresses something relative; for in so far as it is presented to cognition, it is supposed to be only as it is known to exist. Now if the equipoise be not preserved, if either of these elements be allowed to preponderate, the word will assume a meaning precisely opposite to that which it would obtain from the preponderance of the other. If the first element prevail, *object* and *objective* will denote that which exists of its own nature, in contrast to that which exists only under the conditions of our faculties;—the *real* in opposition to the *ideal*. If the second element prevail, *object* and *objective* will denote what exists only as it exists in thought;—the *ideal* in contrast to the *real*.

Now both of these counter meanings of the terms *object* and *objective* have obtained in the nomenclature of different times and different philosophies,—nay in the nomenclature of the same time and even the same philosophy. Hence great confusion and ambiguity.

In the Scholastic philosophy in which, as already said, *object* and *objective*, *subject* and *subjective*, were first employed in their high abstraction, and as absolute terms, and, among the systems immediately subsequent, in the Cartesian and Gassendian schools, the latter meaning was the one exclusively prevalent. In these older philosophies, *objectivum*, as applied to *ens* or *esse*, was opposed to *formale* and *subjectivum*; and corresponded with *intentionale*, *vicarium*, *repraesentativum*, *rationale* or *rationis*, *intellectuale* or *in intellectu*, *prout cognitum*, *ideale*, &c., as opposed to *reale*, *proprium*, *principale*, *fundamentale*, *prout in seipso*, &c.

In these schools the *esse subjectivum*, in contrast to the *esse objectivum*, denoted a thing considered as inhering in its subject, whether that subject were mind or matter, as contradistinguished from a thing considered as present to the mind only as an accidental object of thought. Thus the faculty of imagination, for example, and its acts, were said to have a *subjective* existence in the mind; while its several images or representations had, *qua* images or objects of consciousness, only an *objective*. Again, a material thing, say a horse, *qua* existing, was said to have a *subjective* being out of the mind; *qua* conceived or known, it was said to have an *objective* being in the mind. Every thought had thus a *subjective* and an *objective* phasis;—of which more particularly as follows:—

1. The *esse subjectivum*, *formale*, or *proprium* of a *notion*, *concept*, *species*, *idea*, *&c.*, denoted it as considered absolutely for itself, and as distinguished from the thing, the real object, of which it is the notion, species, &c.; that is, simply as a mode inherent in the mind as a subject, or as an operation exerted by the mind as a cause. In this relation, the *esse reale* of a notion, species, &c., was opposed to the following.

2. The *esse objectivum*, *vicarium*, *intentionale*, *ideale*, *repraesentativum* of a *notion*, *concept*, *species*, *idea*, &c., denoted it, not as considered absolutely for itself, and as distinguished from its object, but simply as vicarious or representative of the thing thought. In this relation the *esse reale* of a notion, &c., was opposed to the mere negation of existence—only distinguished it from a simple *nothing*.

Hitherto we have seen the application of the term *objective* determined by the preponderance of the second of the two counter elements of meaning; we have now to regard it in its subsequent change of sense as determined by the first.

The cause of this change I trace to the more modern Schoolmen, in the distinction they took of *conceptus* (as also of *notio* and *intentio*) into *formalis* and *objectivus*,—a distinction both in itself and in its nomenclature, inconsistent and untenable.—A *formal* concept or notion they defined—'the immediate and actual representation of the thing thought;' an *objective* concept or notion they defined—'the thing itself which is represented or thought.'—Now, in the first place, the second of these, is, either not a concept or notion at all, or it is indistinguishable from the first. (A similar absurdity is committed by Locke in his employment of *Idea* for its object—the reality represented by it—the *Ideatum*.)—In the second place, the terms *formal* and *objective* are here used in senses precisely opposite to what they were when the same philosophers spoke of the *esse formale* and *esse objectivum* of a notion.

This distinction and the terms in which it was expressed came however to be universally admitted. Hence, though proceeding from an error, I would account, in part, but in part only, for the general commutation latterly effected in the application of the term *objective*. This change began, I am inclined to think, about the middle of the seventeenth century—and in the German schools. Thus Calovius—'Quicquid *objective* fundamentaliter in natura existit,' &c., (Scripta Philosophica, 1651, p. 72.) In the same sense it is used by Leibnitz;

theory supposes *two* things numerically different: 1°, the object represented,—2°, the representing and cognisant mind:—the latter, *three*;—1°, the object represented,—2°, the object representing,—3°, the cognisant mind. Compared merely with each other, the former, as simpler, may, *by contrast* to the latter, be consi-

e. g. N. Essais, p. 187; and subsequently to him by the Leibnitio-Wolfians and other German philosophers in general. This application of the term, it is therefore seen, became prevalent among his countrymen long before the time of Kant; in the 'Logica' of whose master Knutzen, I may notice, *objective*, and *subjective*, in their modern meaning are employed in almost every page. The English philosophers, at the commencement of the last century, are found sometimes using the term *objective* in the old sense,—as Berkeley in his 'Siris,' § 292; sometimes in the new,—as Norris in his 'Reason and Faith,' (ch. 1.) and Oldfield in his 'Essay towards the improvement of Reason,' (Part II. c. 19,) who both likewise oppose it to *subjective*, taken also in its present acceptation.

But the cause, why the general terms *subject* and *subjective*, *object* and *objective*, came, in philosophy, to be simply applied to a certain special distinction; and why, in that distinction, they came to be opposed as contraries—this is not to be traced alone to the inconsistencies which I have noticed; for that inconsistency itself must be accounted for. It lies deeper. It is to be found in the constituent elements of all knowledge itself; and the nomenclature in question is only an elliptical abbreviation, and restricted application of the scholastic expressions by which these elements have for many ages been expressed.

All knowledge is a relation—a relation between that which knows, (in scholastic language, the *subject* in which knowledge inheres), and that which is known, (in scholastic language, the *object* about which knowledge is conversant); and the contents of every act of knowledge are made up of elements, and regulated by laws, proceeding partly from its object and partly from its subject. Now philosophy proper is principally and primarily the *science of knowledge*; its first and most important problem being to determine—*What can we know?*—that is, what are the conditions of our knowing, whether these lie in the nature of the object, or in the nature of the subject, of knowledge?

But Philosophy being the *Science of Knowledge*; and the science of knowledge supposing, in its most fundamental and thorough going analysis, the distinction of the *subject and object of knowledge*; it is evident, that *to philosophy* the *subject of knowledge* would be, by pre-eminence, *The Subject*, and the *object of knowledge* by preeminence, *The Object*. It was therefore natural that the *object* and the *objective*, the *subject* and the *subjective* should be employed by philosophers as simple terms, compendiously to denote the grand discrimination, about which philosophy was constantly employed, and which no others could be found so precisely and promptly to express. In fact, had it not been for the special meaning given to *objective* in the Schools, their employment in this their natural relation would probably have been of a much earlier date; not however that they are void of ambiguity, and have not been often abusively employed. This arises from the following circumstance:—The subject of knowledge is exclusively the Ego or conscious mind. *Subject* and *subjective*, considered in themselves, are therefore little liable to equivocation. But, on the other hand, the *object* of knowledge is not necessarily a phænomenon of the Non-Ego; for the phænomena of the Ego itself constitute as veritable, though not so various and prominent, objects of cognition, as the phænomena of the Non-Ego. *Subjective* and *objective* do not, therefore, thoroughly and adequately discriminate that which *belongs to mind*, and that which *belongs to matter*; they do not even competently distinguish what is *dependent*, from what is *independent*, *on the conditions of the mental self*. But in these significations they are and must be frequently employed. Without therefore discarding this nomenclature, which, as far as it goes, expresses, in general, a distinction of the highest importance, in the most apposite terms; these terms may by qualification easily be rendered adequate to those subordinate discriminations, which it is often requisite to signalise, but which they cannot simply and of themselves denote.

Subject and *subjective*, without any qualifying attribute, I would therefore employ, as has hitherto been done, to mark out what inheres in, pertains to, or depends on, the knowing mind whether of man in general, or of this or that individual man in particular; and this in contrast to *object* and *objective*, as expressing what does not so inhere, pertain, and depend. Thus, for example, an art or science is said to be *objective*, when considered simply as a system of speculative truths or practical rules, but without respect of any actual possessor; *subjective* when considered as a habit of knowledge or a dexterity, inherent in the mind, either vaguely of any, or precisely of this or that, possessor.

But, as has been stated, an *object* of knowledge may be a mode of mind, or it may be something different from mind; and it is frequently of importance to indicate precisely under which of these classes that object comes. In this case by an internal developement of the nomenclature itself, we might employ, on the former alternative, the term *subject-object*; on the latter, the term *object-object*.

But the *subject-object* may be either a mode of mind, of which we are conscious as absolute and for itself alone,—as, for example, a pain or pleasure; or a mode of mind, of which we are conscious, as relative to, and representative of, something else,—as, for instance, the imagination of something past or possible. Of these we might distinguish, when necessary, the one, as the *absolute* or the *real subject-object*, the other, as the *relative* or the *ideal* or the *representative subject-object*.

dered, but still inaccurately, as an immediate cognition.* The latter of these as limited in its application to certain faculties, and now in fact wholly exploded, may be thrown out of account.

8.—*External Perception* or *Perception* simply, is the faculty *presentative* or *intuitive* of the phaenomena of the Non-Ego or Matter—if there be any *intuitive* apprehension allowed of the Non-Ego at all. *Internal Perception* or *Self-Consciousness* is the faculty *presentative* or *intuitive* of the phaenomena of the Ego or Mind.

9.—*Imagination* or *Phantasy*, in its most extensive meaning, is the faculty *representative* of the phaenomena both of the external and internal worlds.

10.—A representation considered as an *object* is logically, not really, different from a representation considered as an *act*. Here object and act are merely the same indivisible mode of mind viewed in two different relations. Considered by reference to a (mediate) object represented, it is a representative object; considered by reference to the mind representing and contemplating the representation, it is a representative act. A representative *object* being viewed as posterior in the order of nature, but not of time, to the representative *act*, is viewed as a *product*; and the representative act being viewed as prior in the order of nature, though not of time, to the representative object, is viewed as a *producing process*. (v. I. P. 305 a.) The same may be said of Image and Imagination. (Prop. 21, and p. 813, a b, and note.)

11.—A thing to be known *in itself* must be known as *actually existing* (Pr. 1.) and it cannot be known as actually existing unless it be known as existing in its *When* and its *Where*. But the When and Where of an object are *immediately* cognisable by the subject, only if the When be now (i. e. at the same moment with the cognitive act,) and the Where be *here*, (i. e. within the sphere of the cognitive faculty); therefore a presentative or intuitive knowledge is only competent of an object *present* to the mind, both in *time* and in *space*.

12.—E converso—whatever is known, but not as *actually* existing *now* and *here*, is known not in itself, as the presentative object of an intuitive, but only as the remote object of a representative, cognition.

13.—A representative object, considered irrespectively of what it represents, and simply as a mode of the conscious subject, is an intuitive or presentative object. For it is known in itself, as a mental mode, actually existing now and here.*

Finally it may be required to mark whether the *object-object* and the *subject-object* be immediately known as present, or only as represented. In this case we must resort, on the former alternative to the epithet *presentative* or *intuitive*; on the latter, to those of *represented*, *mediate*, *remote*, *primary*, *principal*, &c.

* This observation has reference to Reid. See sequel of this note, § ii., and note C § ii. A, 4.

* Propositions 10-13 may illustrate a passage in Aristotle's treatise on Memory and Reminiscence (c. 1), which has been often curiously misunderstood by his expositors; and as it, in return, serves to illustrate the doctrine here stated, I translate it:—

'Of what part of the soul memory is a function, is manifest;—of that, to wit, of which imagination or phantasy is a function. [And imagination had been already shown to be a function of the common sense.]

'And here a doubt may be started—Whether the affection [or mental modification] being present, the reality absent, that which is not present can be remembered [or, in general, known.] For it is manifest that we must conceive the affection, determined in the soul or its proximate bodily organ, through sense, to be, as it were, a sort of portrait, of which we say that memory is the habit [or retention]. For the movement excited [to employ the simile of Plato] stamps, as it were, a kind of impression of the total process of perception† [on the soul or its organ], after the manner of one who applies a signet to wax. . . .

'But if such be the circumstances of memory,—Is remembrance [a cognition] of this affection, or of that from which it is produced? For if, of the latter, we can have no remembrance [or cognition] of things absent: if of the former, how, as percipient [or conscious] of this [present affection], can we have a remembrance [or cognition] of that of which we are not percipient [or conscious]—the absent [reality]?—Again?—supposing there to be a resembling something, such as an impression or picture, in the mind; the perception [or consciousness] of this—Why should it be the remembrance [or cognition] of another thing, and not of this something itself?—for in the act of remembrance we contemplate this mental affection, and of this [alone] are we percipient [or conscious]. In these circumstances, how is a remembrance [or cognition] possible of what is not present? For if so, it would seem that what is not present might, in like manner, be seen and heard.

'Or is this possible, and what actually occurs? And thus:—As in a portrait the thing painted is an animal and a representation (εἰκών) [of an animal], one and the

---

† Αἰσθόμενος:—this comprehends both the objective presentation—αἰσθητόν, and the subjective energy—αἴσθησις.

‡ I read ἔνι εἴ τι. Themistius has ἔνεστι.

14.—*Consciousness* is a knowledge *solely of what is now and here present* to the mind. It is therefore only intuitive, and its objects exclusively presentative. Again, Consciousness is a knowledge of *all that is now and here present* to the mind: every immediate object of cognition is thus an object of consciousness, and every intuitive cognition itself, simply a special form of consciousness. See Note H.

15.—*Consciousness comprehends every cognitive act*; in other words, whatever we are not conscious of, that we do not know. But consciousness is an immediate cognition. Therefore *all our mediate cognitions are contained in our immediate.*

16.—The *actual* modifications—the *present acts* and affections of the *Ego*, are objects of immediate cognition, as themselves objects of consciousness. (Pr. 14.) The *past* and *possible* modifications of the Ego are objects of mediate cognition, as represented to consciousness in a present or actual modification.

17.—The *Primary Qualities** of *matter* or *body*, *now* and *here*, that is in proximate relation to our organs, are objects of immediate cognition to the Natural Realists,† of mediate, to the Cosmothetic Idealists:† the former, on the testimony of consciousness, asserting to mind the capability of intuitively perceiving what is not itself; the latter denying this capability, but asserting to the mind the power of representing, and truly representing, what it does not know.—To the Absolute Idealists† matter has no existence as an object of cognition, either immediate or mediate.

18.—The *Secondary Qualities** of body *now* and *here*, as only present affections of the conscious subject, determined by an unknown external cause, are, on every theory, now allowed to be objects of immediate cognition. (Pr. 16.)

19.—As not *now present in time*, an immediate knowledge of the *past* is impossible. The past is only mediately cognisable in and through a present modification relative to, and representative of, it, as having been. To speak of an immediate knowledge of the past involves a contradiction *in adjecto*. For to know the past immediately, it must be known in *itself*;—and to be known in itself it must be known as *now existing*. But the past is just a negation of the now existent: its very notion therefore excludes the possibility of its being immediately known.—So much for Memory, or Recollective Imagination.

20.—In like manner, supposing that a knowledge of the *future* were competent, this can only be conceived possible, in and through a now present representation; that is, only as a mediate cognition. For as *not yet existent* the future cannot be known in itself, or as *actually* existent. As *not here present*, an immediate knowledge of an object *distant in space* is likewise impossible.* For, as beyond the sphere of our organs and faculties, it cannot be known by them in itself; it can only therefore, if known at all, be known through something different from itself, that is mediately, in a reproductive or a constructive act of imagination.

21.—A *possible* object—an *ens rationis*—is a mere fabrication of the mind itself; it exists only ideally in and through an act of imagination, and has only a logical existence, apart from that act with which it is really identical. (Pr. 10, and p 813 a b, with note.) It is therefore an intuitive object in itself: but in so far, as not involving a contradiction, it is conceived as prefiguring something which may possibly exist some-where and some-when,—this something, too, being constructed out of elements which had been

---

same being, at once, both; (for, though in reality both are not the same, in thought we can view the painting, either [absolutely] as animal, or [relatively] as representation [of an animal]); in like manner, the phantasm in us, we must consider, both absolutely, as a phænomenon (θεώρημα) in itself, and relatively, as a phantasm [or representation] of something different from itself. Considered absolutely, it is a [mere] phænomenon or [irrespective] phantasm; considered relatively, it is a representation or recollective image. So that when a movement [or mental modification] is in present act;—if the soul perceive [or apprehend] it as absolute and for itself, a kind of [irrespective] concept or phantasm seems the result; whereas, if as relative to what is different from itself, it views it (as in the picture) for a representation, and a representation of Coriscus, even although Coriscus has not himself been seen. And here we are differently affected in this mode of viewing [the movement, as painted representation,] from what we are when viewing it, as painted animal; the mental phænomenon, in the one case, is, so to say, a mere [irrelative] concept; while in the other, what is remembered is here [in the mind,] as there [in the picture,] a representation.'

* On the distinction of the Primary and Secondary Qualities of Matter—its history and completion, see Note D.

† On these designations, see above, Note A. § I. pp. 746, 747 and below, Note C. § I.

* On the assertions of Reid, Stewart, &c., that the mind is *immediately* percipient of *distant* objects, see § II. of this Note, and Note C § II.

previously given in Presentation—it is Representative. See Note C. § i.

Compared together, these two cognitions afford the following *similarities* and *differences*.

A Compared by reference to their *simplicity or complexity, as Acts.*

22.—Though both as really considered, (re, non ratione), are equally one and indivisible; still as logically considered, (ratione, non re,) an Intuitive cognition is *simple*, being merely intuitive; a Representative, *complex*, as both representative and intuitive of the representation.

B. Compared by reference to the *number of their Objects.*

23—In a Presentative knowledge there can only be a *single* object, and the term object is here therefore univocal.—In a Representative knowledge *two* different things are viewed as objects, and the term object, therefore, becomes equivocal; the secondary object within, being numerically different from the primary object without, the sphere of consciousness, which it represents.

C. Compared by reference to the *relativity of their Objects, known in consciousness.*

24.—In a presentative cognition, the object known in consciousness, being relative only to the conscious subject, may, by contrast, be considered as *absolute* or *irrespective*. In a representative cognition, the object known in consciousness, being, besides the necessary reference to the subject, relative to, as vicarious of, an object unknown to consciousness, must, in every point of view, be viewed as *relative* or *respective*. Thus, it is on all hands admitted, that in Self consciousness the object is subjective and absolute; and, that in Imagination, under every form, it is subjective and relative. In regard to external Perception, opinions differ. For, on the doctrine of the Natural Realists, it is objective and absolute; on the doctrine of the Absolute Idealists, subjective and absolute; on the doctrine of the Cosmothetic Idealists, subjective and relative. See Note C. § I.

D. Compared by reference to the *character of the existential Judgments* they involve.

25—The judgment involved in an Intuitive apprehension is *assertory*; for the fact of the intuition being dependent on the fact of the present existence of the object, the existence of the object is unconditionally enounced as actual.—The judgment involved in a Representative apprehension is *problematic*; for here the fact of the representation not being dependent on the present existence of the object represented, the existence of that object can be only modally affirmed as possible.

E. Compared by reference to their *character as Cognitions.*

26.—Representative knowledge is admitted on all hands to be exclusively *subjective* or *ideal*; for its proximate object is, on every theory, *in* or *of* the mind, while its remote object, in itself, and, except in and through the proximate object, is unknown.—Presentative knowledge is, on the doctrine of the Natural Realists, *partly subjective and ideal, partly objective and real*; inasmuch as its sole object may be a phaenomenon either of *self* or of *not-self*: while, on the doctrine of the Idealists (whether Absolute or Cosmothetic) it is *always subjective or ideal*; consciousness, on their hypothesis, being cognisant only of mind and its contents.

F. Compared in respect of their *Self-sufficiency or Dependence.*

27.—a.—In *one* respect, Representative knowledge is *not self-sufficient*, in as much as every representative cognition of an object supposes a previous presentative apprehension of that same object. This is even true of the representation of an imaginary or merely possible object; for though the object, of which we are conscious in such an act, be a mere figment of the phantasy, and, as a now represented whole, was never previously presented to our observation; still that whole is nothing but an assemblage of parts, of which, in different combinations, we have had an intuitive cognition.—Presentative knowledge, on the contrary, is, in this respect, *self-sufficient*, being wholly independent on Representative for its objects.

28.—b.—Representative knowledge, in *another* respect, is *not self-sufficient*. For in as much as all representation is only the repetition, simple or modified, of what was once intuitively apprehended; Representative is dependent on Presentative knowledge, as (with the mind) the concause and condition of its possibility.—Presentative knowledge, on the contrary, is in this respect *independent* of Representative; for with our intuitive cognitions, commences all our knowledge.

29.—c.—In a *third* respect Representative knowledge is *not self-sufficient*; for it is only deserving of the name of knowledge in so far as it is conformable with the intuitions which it represents.—Presentative knowledge, on the contrary, is, in this respect, *all-sufficient*; for in the last resort it is the sole vehicle, the exclusive criterion and guarantee of truth.

30.—d.—In *a fourth* respect, Representative knowledge is *not self-sufficient*, being wholly dependent upon Intuitive; for the object represented is only known through an intuition of the subject representing. Representative knowledge always, therefore, involves presentative, as its condition.—Intuitive knowledge, on the contrary, is, in this respect, *all-sufficient*, being wholly independent of representative, which it, consequently, excludes. Thus in different points of view Representative knowledge contains and is contained in, Presentative, (Pr. 15.)

G.—Compared in reference to their *intrinsic Completeness and Perfection.*

31.—a.—In *one* respect Intuitive knowledge is *complete and perfect*, as irrespective of aught beyond the sphere of consciousness; while Representative knowledge is *incomplete* and *imperfect*, as relative to what transcends that sphere.

32.—b.—In *another* respect, Intuitive knowledge is *complete* and *perfect*, as affording the highest certainty of the highest determination of existence—the Actual—the Here and Now existent;—Representative, *incomplete* and *imperfect*, as affording only an inferior assurance of certain inferior determinations of existence—the Past, the Future, the Possible—the not Here and not Now existent.

33.—c.—In a *third* respect, Intuitive knowledge is *complete* and *perfect*, its object known being at once real, and known as real;—Representative knowledge, *incomplete* and *imperfect*, its known object being unreal, its real object unknown.

The precise distinction between Presentative and Representative knowledge, and the different meanings of the term Object,—the want of which has involved our modern philosophy in great confusion,—I had long ago evolved from my own reflection, and before I was aware that a parallel distinction had been taken by the Schoolmen, under the name *Intuitive* and *Abstract* knowledge (*cognitio Intuitiva* et *Abstractiva*, or *Visionis* et *Simplicis Intelligentiae.*) Of these, the former they defined—*the knowledge of a thing present as it is present, (cognitio rei praesentis, ut praesens est)*; the latter—*the knowledge of a thing not as it is present, (cognitio rei non ut praesens est.)* This distinction remounts, among the Latin Schoolmen, to at least the middle of the eleventh century; for I find that both St Anselm and Hugo a Sancto Victore notice it. It was certainly not borrowed from the Arabians; for Averroes, at the end of the following century, seems unaware of it. In fact, it bears upon its front the indication of a Christian origin; for, as Scotus and Ariminensis notice, the term *Intuitive* was probably suggested by St Paul's expression, '*facie ad faciem*,' as the Vulgate has it, (1 Corinth. xiii. 12.) For intuitive, in this sense, the lower Greeks sometimes employed the terms ἐποπτικός, and αὐτοπτικός—a sense unknown to the Lexicographers;—but they do not appear to have taken the counter distinction. The term *abstract* or *abstractive* was less fortunately chosen than its correlative; for besides the signification in question, as opposed to *intuitive*, in which case we look away from the existence of a concrete object; it was likewise employed in opposition to *concrete*, and, though improperly, as a synonyme of *universal*, in which case we look away from each and every individual subject of inhesion. As this last is the meaning in which *abstract* as it was originally, is now exclusively, employed, and as *representative* is, otherwise, a far preferable expression, it would manifestly be worse than idle to attempt its resuscitation in the former sense.

The propriety and importance of the distinction is unquestionable; but the Schoolmen—at least the great majority who held the doctrine of intentional species—wholly spoiled it in application; by calling the representative perception they allowed of external things, by the name of an intuitive cognition, to say nothing of the idle thesis which many of them defended—that by a miracle we could have an intuitive apprehension of a distant, nay even of a non-existent, object. This error, I may notice, is the corollary of another of which I am soon to speak—the holding that external things, though known only through species, are immediately known in themselves, (see p. .)

§ *II.—The errors of Reid and other philosophers, in reference to the distinction of Presentative or Immediate and Representative or Mediate knowledge, and of Object Proximate and Remote.*

The preceding distinction is one which, for the Natural Realist, it is necessary to establish, in order to discriminate his own peculiar doctrine of perception from those of the Idealists, Cosmothetic and Absolute, in their various modifications. This, however, Reid unfortunately did not do;

and the consequence has been the following imperfections, inaccuracies, and errors.

A. In the first place he has, at least in words, *abolished the distinction of presentative and representative cognition.*

1°, He asserts, in general, that every object of thought must be an immediate object, (I. P. 427 b.)

2°, He affirms, in particular, not only of the faculties whose objects are, but of those whose objects are not, actually present to the mind,—that they are all and each of them immediate knowledges. Thus he frequently defines memory (in the sense of recollective imagination) 'an immediate knowledge of things past,' (I. P. 339 a, 351 b, 357 a); he speaks of an immediate knowledge of things future, (I. P. 340 b); and maintains that the immediate object in our conception (imagination) of a distant reality is that reality itself (I. P. 374 b.) See above, Propp. 10, 11, 12, 19, 20, 21.

Now the cause why Reid not only did not establish, but even thought to abolish, the distinction of mediate cognition with its objects proximate and remote was, 1°, his error, which we are elsewhere to consider, (Note C. § ii.,) in supposing that philosophers in the proximate object of knowledge, had in view, always, a *tertium quid* different both from the reality represented and the conscious mind (Inq. 106 a, I. P. 226 b, 369 ab); and 2°, his failing to observe that the rejection of this complex hypothesis of non-egoistical representation, by no means involved either the subversion of representative knowledge in general, or the establishment of presentative perception in particular. (See Prop. 7, and Note C. § i.)

But Reid's doctrine in this respect is perhaps imperfectly developed, rather than deliberately wrong; and I am confident that had it been proposed to him, he would at once have acquiesced in the distinction of presentative and representative knowledge, above stated, not only as true in itself, but as necessary to lay a solid foundation for a theory of intuitive perception, in conformity with the common sense of mankind.

B. In the *second* place, Reid maintains *that in our cognitions there must be an object (real or imaginary) distinct from the operation of the mind conversant about it; for the act is one thing and the object of the act another.* (I. P. 292 b, 305 a, also 298 b, 373 a, 374 b.)

This is erroneous—at least it is erroneously expressed. Take an imaginary object, and Reid's own instance—a centaur. Here he says, 'The sole object of conception (imagination) is an animal which I believe never existed.' It 'never existed;' that is never really, never in nature, never externally, existed. But it is 'an object of imagination.' It is not therefore a mere non-existence; for if it had no kind of existence, it could not possibly be the positive object of any kind of thought. For were it an absolute nothing, it could have no qualities (*non-entis nulla sunt attributa*); but the object we are conscious of, as a Centaur, has qualities,—qualities which constitute it a determinate something, and distinguish it from every other entity whatsoever. We must, therefore, per force, allow it some sort of imaginary, ideal, representative, or (in the older meaning of the term) *objective*, existence in the mind. Now this existence can only be one or other of two sorts; for such object in the mind, either *is*, or *is not*, *a mode of mind*. Of these alternatives the latter cannot be supposed; for this would be an affirmation of the crudest kind of non-egoistical representation—the very hypothesis against which Reid so strenuously contends. The former alternative remains—that it is a mode of the imagining mind;—that it is in fact the plastic act of imagination considered as representing to itself a certain possible form—a Centaur. But then Reid's assertion—that there is always an object distinct from the operation of the mind conversant about it, the act being one thing, the object of the act another—must be surrendered. For the *object* and the *act* are here only one and the same thing in two several relations. (Prop. 21.) Reid's error consists in mistaking a logical for a metaphysical difference—a distinction of relation for a distinction of entity. Or is the error only from the vagueness and ambiguity of expression? *

* In what manner many of the acutest of the later Schoolmen puzzled themselves likewise, with this, apparently, very simple matter, may be seen in their discussions touching the nature of *Entia Rationis*. I may mention in general Fonseca, Suarez, Mendoza, Ruvius, Murcia, Oviedo, Arriaga, Carleton, &c., on the one hand; and Biel, Mirandulanus, Jandunus, Valesius, Erice. &c., on the other. I may here insert, though only at present, for the latter paragraph in which Reid's difficulty is solved, the following passage from Biel. It contains important observations to which I must subsequently refer:—

'Ad secundum de figmentis dicitur, quod (intelligendo illam similitudinem quam anima fingit, i.e. abstrahit a rebus) sic figmenta sunt actus intelligendi, qui habent esse verum et subjectivum (v. p. 807 a b, note) in anima.

C. In the *third* place, to this head we may refer Reid's *inaccuracy in regard to the precise object of perception.* This object is not, as he seems frequently to assert, any distant reality; (Inq. 104 b, 158 b, 159 a b, 160 a, 186 b.—I. P. 299 a, 302 a, 303 a, 304 a, et alibi); for we are percipient of nothing but what is in proximate contact, in immediate relation, with our organs of sense. Distant realities we reach, not by perception, but by a subsequent process of inference founded thereon: and so far, as he somewhere says, (I. P. 284 b,) from all men who look upon the sun perceiving the same object, in reality, every individual, in this instance, perceives a different object, nay, a different object in each several eye. The doctrine of Natural Realism requires no such untenable assumption for its basis. It is sufficient to establish the simple fact, that we are competent, as consciousness assures us, immediately to apprehend through sense the non-ego in certain limited relations; and it is of no consequence whatever, either to our certainty of the reality of a material world, or to our ultimate knowledge of its properties, whether by this primary apprehension we lay hold, in the first instance, on a larger or a lesser portion of its contents.

Mr Stewart also (Elem. vol. i. ch. i. sect. 2, p. 79 sq. 6 ed.), in arguing against the counter doctrine in one of its accidental forms, maintains, in general, that we may be percipient of distant objects. But his observations do not contemplate, therefore do not meet, the cardinal questions;—Is perception a presentative cognition of the non-ego, or only a representative cognition of it, in and through the ego?—and if the former,—Can we apprehend a thing immediately and not know it in itself?—Can we apprehend it as actually existing?—and, Can we apprehend it as actually existing, and not apprehend it in the When and Where of its existence, that is, only as present?

A misapprehension analogous to that of Reid and Stewart, and of a still more obtrusive character, was made by a majority of those Schoolmen who, as non-egoistical representationists, maintained the hypothesis of intentional species, as media of sensitive perception, imagination, &c. They, in general, held, *that the species is not itself perceived, but the reality through the species;*—and on the following as the principal grounds:—The present objects we perceive by sense, or the absent objects we imagine, are extended, figured, coloured, &c.; but the species are not themselves extended, figured, coloured, &c., they are only representative of these qualities in external objects; the species are not, therefore, themselves objects of knowledge, or, as they otherwise expressed it, do not themselves terminate the cognition.* See, instar omnium, De Raconis, Physica, Disp. iii. de An. Sens. App. sect. ii. qu 4. art 3.—Irenaeus, De Anima, c. 2. sect. 3. § 3.

The error of this doctrine did not, however, escape the observation of the acuter even of those who supported the theory of intentional species. It is exposed by Scaliger the father; and his exposition is advanced as a 'very subtle' speculation. Addressing Cardan, whose work 'De Subtilitate' he is controverting, he says:—

'Cum tam praeclare de visu sentires, maximam omisisti subtilitatem. Doce me prius sodes—Quid est id quod video? Dices, "Puerilem esse interrogationem—*Rem* enim esse, quae videatur." At doce quaeso nos pueros per salebras hasce Naturae perreptantes. *Si sensio est receptio; nec recipitur Res;* demonstrabitur certissima

---

Sunt enim qualitates animae inhaerentes; et hi actus sunt naturales similitudines rerum a quibus formantur, quae sunt objecta eorum; nec oportet ponere aliquod objectum medium inter cognitionem intellectivam actus, et realo ejus objectum.

'Dicuntur autem hujusmodi actus figmenta, quia tales sunt *in repraesentando* rem, quales sunt res repraesentatae. Non autem talia in *existendo*, i.e. in qualitatibus realibus; quia sunt qualitates spirituales, objecta vero frequenter res materiales; sunt autem naturaliter *similes in repraesentando*, quia repraesentant res distincte cum suis habitudinibus sicut sunt realiter; non autem sunt *similes in essendo*, i.e. quod actus [actu] haberent esse reale ejusdem speciei cum suis objectis.

'Quod additur de Chimaera; patet quod aliter chimaera dicitur figmentum, et aliter cognitio rei possibilis. Verum conceptus chimaerae, id est actus cognoscendi correspondens huic voci '*chimaerae*,' est vera qualitas in mente: tamen illud quod significat nihil est.' In i. Sent. Dist. ii. Qu. 8.

The author of the preceding passage, it must be remembered, allowed no *intentional species*, that is, no representative entities different from the operations of the mind itself.

* This doctrine his recent and very able biographer (M. Huet) finds maintained by the great Henry of Ghent, and he adduces it as both an original opinion of the Doctor Solennis, and an anticipation of one of the truths established by the Scottish school. There was, however, nothing new in the opinion; and if an anticipation, it was only the anticipation of an error. Recherches, &c., pp. 130, 119

demonstratione sic;—*ergo non sentitur Res*. Aiunt—"Rem videri per Speciem." Intelligo; et concludo:—*Species ergo sentitur* Rem ipsam haud percipit sensus. Species ipsa non est ea res, cujus est species. Isti vero ausi sunt ita dicere;—"Non videri speciem, sed Rem *per* Speciem. Speciem vero esse videndi rationem." Audio verba; rem haud intelligo. Non enim est species ratio videndi, ut Lux. Quid igitur?—"Per speciem (inquiunt) vides rem; non potes autem videre speciem, quia necesse esset ut, per speciem, videres." Quae sententia est omnium absurdissima. Dico enim jam;—*Rem non videri, sed Speciem*. Sensus ergo recipit speciem; quam rei similem judicat Intellectus, atque sic rem cognoscit per reflexionem.' (De Subtilitate, Ex. cccxviii. § 14.)

But in correcting one inconsistency Scaliger here falls into another. For how can the reflective intellect judge the species to resemble, that is, correctly to represent, the external reality, when, ex hypothesi, the reality itself is unknown; unknown in its qualities, unknown even in its existence? This consideration ought to have led 'the Master of Subtilties' to doubt concerning the doctrine of perception by species altogether.

But long before Scaliger, the error in question had been refuted by certain of those Schoolmen who rejected the whole doctrine of intentional species. I was surprised to find the distinction between an immediate and a mediate object, in our acts cognitive of things not actually present to apprehension, advanced by Gregory of Rimini, in a disputation maintained by him against a certain 'Joannes Scotus,'—not the Subtle Doctor, who was already gone, but—a Scotsman, who appears to have been a fellow Regent with Gregory in the University of Paris. This doctrine did not, however, obtain the acceptation which it merited; and when noticed at all, it was in general noticed only to be redargued—even by his brother Nominalists. Biel rejects the paradox, without naming its author. But John Major, the last of the regular Schoolmen, openly maintains on this point, against the Authentic Doctor, the thesis of his earlier countryman, Joannes—a thesis also identical with the doctrine of his later countryman, Reid. 'Dico (he says, writing in Paris,) quod notitiam abstractivam quam habeo pinnaculi Sanctae Genovefes in Scotia, in Sancto Andrea, ad pinnaculum *immediate terminatur*; verum, ob notitiae imperfectionem et naturam, nescio certitudinaliter an sit dirutum exustumve, sicut olim tonitruo conflagravit.'* In Sent. L. i. dist. 3. qu. 2.

I have omitted however to notice, that the vulgar doctrine of the Schools in regard to the immediate cognition of real objects, through their species or representations, was refuted, in anticipation, by Plotinus, who observes—'That if we receive the impressed forms (τύπους) of objects perceived, it cannot be that we really perceive the things which we are said to perceive, but only their images or shadows; so that the things existing are one distinct order of beings, the objects perceived by us, another.' (Ennead. v. L. vi. c. 1.) His own doctrine of perception is however equally subjective as that which he assails; it is substantially the same with the Cartesian and Leibnitian hypotheses.

Representationists (Note C. § i.) are not however always so reluctant to see and to confess, that their doctrine involves a surrender of all immediate and real knowledge of an external world. This too is admitted by even those who, equally with Reid, had renounced ideas as representative entities, different, either from the substance of mind, or from the act of cognition itself. Arnauld frankly acknowledges this of his own theory of perception; which he justly contends to be identical with that of Descartes. (See above, p. 296 a, n. †) Other Cartesians, and of a doctrine equally pure, have been no less explicit. 'Nota vero, (says Flender, whose verbosity I somewhat abridge,) mentem nostram percipere vel cognoscere *immediate tantum seipsam* suasque facultates, per intimam sui conscientiam; sed *alias res a se distinctas, non nisi mediate*, scilicet per ideas. . . Nota porro, quod *perceptio* seu *idea rei* spectari dupliciter: vel *in se ipsa*, prout est *modus cogitandi* cujus mens est conscia,—quo modo a mente ut causa efficiente fluit; vel *relata ad objectum* quod per eam representatur, prout est cogitatio intellectus hanc vel illam rem representans,—quo modo forma seu essentia ideae consistit *in representatione rei*, sive in eo *quod sit representamen* vel imago ejus rei quam concipimus.' (Phosph. Philos. § 5.)

---

* The existence of a Pinnacle of St Genevieve in St Andrews is now unknown to our Scottish Antiquaries; and this, I may notice, is one of a thousand curious anecdotes relative to his country, scattered throughout Major's writings, and upon matters to which allusions from a Doctor of the Sorbonne, in a Commentary on the Sentences, were least to be expected.

NOTE C.

ON THE VARIOUS THEORIES OF EXTERNAL PERCEPTION.

---

§ I.—*Systematic Schemes, from different points of view, of the various theories of the relation of External Perception to its Object; and of the various systems of Philosophy founded thereon.*

§ II.—*What is the character, in this respect, of Reid's doctrine of Perception?*

[References.—From Inq. 106 a, 128 a b, 130 b, 210 a, I. P. 226 a b, 257 b, 269 a, 274 a, 277 b, 278 a b, 293 b, 299 a, 305 a, 318 b, 427 a b.]

---

§ *I.—Systematic Schemes, from different points of view, of the various theories of the relation of External Perception to its Object, and of the various systems of Philosophy founded thereon.**

Scheme I.—*Table of distribution. General and Special.*—In the perception of the external world, the object of which we are conscious may be considered—either, (I.) as *absolute* and *total*—or, (II.) as *relative* and *partial*, i. e. *vicarious* or *representative* of another and principal object, beyond the sphere of consciousness. Those who hold the former of these doctrines may be called *Presentationists* or *Intuitionists*; those who hold the latter, *Representationists*.† Of these in their order.

I.—The *Presentationists* or *Intuitionists* constitute the object, of which we are conscious in perception, into a sole, absolute, or total, object; in other words, reduce perception to an act of immediate or intuitive cognition: and this—either (A) by abolishing any immediate, ideal, subjective object, representing;—or, (B) by abolishing any mediate, real, objective object, represented.

A.—The former of these, viewing the one total object of perceptive consciousness as *real*, as existing, and therefore, in this case, as material, extended, external, are Realists, and may distinctively be called *Intuitional* or *Presentative Realists*, and *Real Presentationists* or *Intuitionists*; while, as founding their doctrine on the datum of the natural consciousness, or common sense, of mankind, they deserve the names of *Natural Realists* or *Natural Dualists*. Of this scheme there are no subordinate varieties; except in so far as a difference of opinion may arise, in regard to—what qualities are to be referred to the object perceived, or non-ego,—what qualities to the percipient subject, or ego. Presentative Realism is thus divided (i.) into a philosophical or developed form—that, to wit, in which the Primary Qualities of body, the Common Sensibles, (see Note D.) constitute the objective object of perception; and (ii.) into a vulgar or undeveloped form—that, to wit, in which

---

* Compare the more comprehensive evolution of Philosophical Systems from the total fact of Consciousness in Perception, given above, p. 746 a, sq. An acquaintance with that distribution is here supposed.

† On the terms *Intuition* and *Representation*, and on the distinction of *immediate* and *mediate*, of *ideal* and *real*, *object*, see Note B. § I.

not only the primary qualities, (as Extension and Figure,) but also the secondary, (as Colour, Savour, &c.,) are, as known to us, regarded equally to appertain to the non-ego.

B.—The latter of these, viewing the object of consciousness in perception as ideal, (as a phænomenon in or of mind,) are Idealists; and as denying that this ideal object has any external prototype, they may be styled *Absolute Idealists*, or *Idealist Unitarians*.—They are to be again divided into two subaltern classes, as the Idea—(i.) is,—or (ii.) is not, considered a modification of the percipient mind.

i.—If the Idea be regarded as a mode of the human mind itself, we have a scheme of *Egoistical Idealism*; and this again admits of a twofold distinction, according as the idea is viewed—(a) as having no existence out of the momentary act of presentative consciousness, with which it is, in fact, identical;—or (b) as having an (unknown) existence, independent of the present act of consciousness by which it is called up, contemplated, but not created. Finally, as in each of these the mind may be determined to present the object either—(1.) by its own natural laws,—or (2.) by supernatural agencies, each may be subdivided into a *Natural* and *Supernatural* variety.

ii.—If, on the other hand, the Idea be viewed not as a mode of the human mind, there is given the scheme of *Non-Egoistical Idealism*, which, in all its forms, is necessarily hyperphysical. It admits, in the first place, of a twofold distinction, according as the ideal object is supposed—(a) to be,—or (b) not to be, in the percelving mind itself.

a.—Of these the former may again be subdivided according as the ideas are supposed—(1.) to be connate with the mind and existent in it out of consciousness;—or (2.) infused into it at the moment of consciousness,—(α) immediately by God,—(β) by some lower supernatural agency.

b.—The latter supposes that the human mind is conscious of the idea, in some higher intelligence, to which it is intimately present; and this higher mind may either be—(1.) that of the deity, or—(2) that of some inferior supernatural existence.

All these modifications of Non-Egoistical Idealism admit, however, in common, of certain subordinate divisions, according as the qualities (primary and secondary) and the phænomena of the several senses may be variously considered either as *objective* and *ideal* or as *subjective* and *sensational*.*

II.—The *Representationists*, as denying to consciousness the cognisance of aught beyond a merely subjective phænomenon, are likewise Idealists; yet as positing the reality of an external world, they must be distinguished as *Cosmothetic Idealists*. But, as affirming an external world, they are also Realists, or Dualists. Since, however, they do not, like the Natural Realists, accept the existence of an external world directly on the natural testimony of consciousness, as something known, but endeavour to establish its unknown existence by a principal and sundry subsidiary hypotheses; they must, under that character, be discriminated as *Hypothetical Realists* or *Hypothetical Dualists*. This Hypothesis of a Representative perception has been maintained under one or other of two principal forms,—a finer and a cruder,—according as the representation—either, (A) is,—or (B) is not, supposed to be a mode of the percipient subject itself. (And, be it observed, this distinction, in reference to Reid's philosophy, ought to be carefully borne in mind.)

A.—If the immediate, known, or representative, object be regarded as a modification of the mind or self, we have one variety of representationism, (the simpler

---

* The general approximation of thorough-going Realism and thorough-going Idealism here given, may, at first sight, be startling. On reflection, however, their radical affinity will prove well grounded. Both build upon the same fundamental fact—that the extended object immediately perceived is identical with the extended object actually existing;—for the truth of this fact, both can appeal to the common sense of mankind;—and to the common sense of mankind Berkeley did appeal not less confidently, and perhaps more logically, than Reid. Natural Realism and Absolute Idealism are the only systems worthy of a philosopher; for, as they alone have any foundation in consciousness, so they alone have any consistency in themselves. The scheme of Hypothetical Realism or Cosmothetic Idealism, which supposes that behind the non-existent world perceived, there lurks a correspondent but unknown world existing, is not only repugnant to our natural beliefs, but in manifold contradiction with itself. The scheme of Natural Realism may be ultimately difficult—for, like all other truths, it ends in the inconceivable; but Hypothetical Realism—in its origin—in its development—in its result, although the favourite scheme of philosophers, is philosophically absurd. See Philosophy of Perception, Ed. Rev. vol. lii. p. 175-181.

and more refined) which may be characterised as the *Egoistical Representationism.* This finer form is, however, itself again subdivided into a finer and a cruder; according as the subjective object—(i.) is—or (ii.) is not, identified with the percipient act.

i.—In the former case, the immediate or ideal object is regarded, as only logically distinguished from the perceptive act; being simply the perceptive act itself, considered in one of its relations,—its relation, to wit (not to the subject perceiving, in which case it is properly called a *perception,* but) to the mediate object, the reality represented, and which, in and through that representation alone, is objectified to consciousness and perceived.

ii.—In the latter case, the immediate object is regarded, as a mode of mind, existent out of the act of perceptive consciousness, and, though contemplated in, not really identical with, that act. This cruder form of egoistical representationism substantially coincides with that finer form of the non-egoistical, which views the vicarious object as spiritual (II. B, i. h.) I have therefore found it requisite to consider these as identical; and accordingly in speaking of the finer form of representation, be it observed, I exclusively have in view the form of which I have last spoken, (II. A, i.)

This form, in *both* its degrees, is divided into certain subaltern genera and species, according as the mind is supposed to be determined to represent by causes—either, (a) natural, physical,—or, (b) supernatural, hyperphysical.

a.—Of these, the *natural* determination to represent, is—either, (1.) one foreign and external, (by the action of the material reality on the passive mind, through sense);—or (2.) one native and internal, (a self determination of the impassive mind, on occasion of the presentation of the material object to sense);—or finally, (3.) one partly both, (the mind being at once acted on, and itself reacting.)

b.—The *hyperphysical* determination, again, may be maintained—either to be, (1.) immediate and special; whether this be realized—(α) by the direct operation or concourse of God (as in a scheme of Occasional Causes)—or (β) by the influence of inferior supernatural agencies:—or (2.) mediate and general, (as by the predetermined ordination of God, in a theory of Pre-established Harmony.)

B.—If the representative object be viewed as something in, but not a mere mode of, mind;—in other words, if it be viewed as a tertium quid numerically different both from the subject knowing and the object represented; we have a second form of Representationism, (the more complex and cruder,) which may be distinguished as the *Non-egoistical.* This also falls into certain inferior species: for the ideal or vicarious object has been held (i.) by some to be spiritual;—(ii.) by others to be corporeal;—while (iii.) others, to carry hypothesis to absurdity, have regarded it, as neither spiritual nor corporeal, but of an inconceivable nature, intermediate between, or different from, both.

i.—*Spiritual.* Here the vicarious object may be supposed—either, (a) to be some supernatural intelligence, to which the human mind is present; and this—either (1.) the divine,—or (2.) not the divine:—or (b) in the human mind; and if so—either (1.) connate and inexistent, being elicited into consciousness, on occasion of the impression of the external object on the sensual organ;—or, (2.) infused on such occasions, and this—either (α) by God,—or (β) by other supernatural intelligences,—and of these different theorists have supposed different kinds.

ii.—*Corporeal,* in the common sensory (whether brain or heart.) This—either (a) as a propagation from the external reality—(1.) of a grosser;—(2.) of a more attenuated nature:—or (b) a modification determined in the sensory itself—(1.) as a configuration;—(2.) as a motion, (and this last—either (α) as a flow of spirits—or (β) as a vibration of fibres—or (γ) as both a flow and a vibration);—or (3.) as both a configuration and a motion.

iii.—*Neither spiritual nor corporeal.* This might admit, in part, of similar modifications with B, i. and B, ii.

All these species of Representationism may be, and almost all of them have been, actually held. Under certain varying restrictions, however, in as much as a representative object may be postulated in perception for all, or only for some of the senses, for all or only for some of the qualities made known to us in the perceptive act. And this latter alternative which has been most generally adopted, again admits of various subdivisions, according to the particular senses in which, and the particular qualities of which, a vicarious object is allowed.

SCHEME II.—*Table of General distribution; with references for details to Scheme I.*

The object of Consciousness in Perception is a quality, mode or phaenomenon—either (I.) *of an external reality,* in immediate relation to our organs;—or (II.) *not of an external reality*, but either of the mind itself, or of something in the mind, which internal object, let us on either alternative, here call *Idea*.

I. The former opinion is the doctrine of *real presentative* perception. (I. A.)

II. The latter is the doctrine of *ideal* perception; which either—

A—supposes that the Idea is an original and absolute presentment, and thus constitutes the doctrine of *ideal presentative* perception (I. B); or

B—supposes that the Idea only represents the quality of a real object; and thus constitutes the doctrine of *ideal representative* perception (II.)

SCHEME III.—Merely *General Table*.

In relation to our perception of an external world, philosophers are (I.) *Realists*; (II.) *Idealists*.

I. The Realists are (A) *Natural*; (B) *Hypothetical*, (= Cosmothetic Idealists.)

II. The Idealists are (A) *Absolute* or *Presentative*; (B) *Cosmothetic* or *Representative*, (= Hypothetical Realists.) See above, p. 817 b, and 747 a.

Such is a conspectus in different points of view of all the theories touching perception and its object; and of the different systems of philosophy founded thereon, which, as far as they occur to me, have been promulgated during the progress of philosophy. But it is at present only requisite for the student of philosophy to bear in mind the more general principles and heads of distribution. To enumerate the individual philosophers by whom these several theories were originated or maintained, would require a far greater amplitude of detail than can be now afforded; and, though of some historical interest, this is not required for the purposes which I am here exclusively desirous of accomplishing. Similar tables might be also given of the opinions of philosophers, touching the object of *Imagination* and of *Intellect*. But the relation of these faculties to their object does not, in like manner, afford the fundamental principles of difference, and therefore a common starting point, to the great philosophical systems; while a scheme of the hypotheses in regard to them, would, at least in the details, be little more than an uninteresting repetition of the foregoing distribution. There is therefore little inducement to annex such tables; were they not, in other respects, here completely out of place. I have only, at present, two ends in view. Of these the primary, is to display, to discriminate, and to lay down a nomenclature of, the various theories of Perception, actual and possible. This is accomplished. The secondary, is to determine under which of these theories the doctrine of Reid is to be classed. And to this inquiry I now address myself.

§ II.—*Of what character, in the preceding respect, is Reid's doctrine of Perception?*

As in this part of his philosophy, in particular, Mr Stewart closely follows the footsteps of his predecessor, and seems even to have deemed all further speculation on the subject superfluous; the question here propounded must be viewed as common to both philosophers.

Now, there are only *two* of the preceding theories of perception, with one or other of which Reid's doctrine can possibly be identified. He is a Dualist;—and the only doubt is—whether he be a *Natural Realist*, (I. A,) or a *Hypothetical Realist*, under the finer form of *Egoistical Representationism*, (II. A, i.)

The cause why Reid left the character of his doctrine ambiguous on this the very cardinal point of his philosophy, is to be found in the following circumstances.

1°, That, in general, (although the same may be said of all other philosophers,) he never discriminated either speculatively or historically the three theories of Real Presentationism, of Egoistical, and of Non-Egoistical, Representationism.

2°, That, in particular, he never clearly distinguished the first and second of these, as not only different, but contrasted, theories; though on one occasion (I. P. p. 297 a b) he does seem to have been obscurely aware that they were not identical.

3°, That, while right in regarding philosophers, in general, as Cosmothetic Idealists, he erroneously supposed that they were all, or nearly all, Non-Egoistical Representationists. And—

4°, That he viewed the theory of Non-Egoistical Representationism as that form alone of Cosmothetic Idealism which when carried to its legitimate issue ended in Absolute Idealism; whereas the other form of Cosmothetic Idealism, the theory of Egoistical Representationism, whether speculatively or historically considered, is, with at least equal rigour, to be developed into the same result.

Dr Thomas Brown considers Reid to be, like himself, a Cosmothetic Idealist, under the finer form of egoistical representationism; but without assigning any reason for this belief, except one which, as I have elsewhere shewn, is altogether nugatory.* For my own part, I am decidedly of opinion, that, as the great end—the governing principle of Reid's doctrine was to reconcile philosophy with the necessary convictions of mankind, that he intended a doctrine of natural, consequently a doctrine of presentative, realism; and that he would have at once surrendered, as erroneous, every statement which was found at variance with such a doctrine. But that the reader should be enabled to form his own opinion on the point, which I admit not to be without difficulty; and that the ambiguities and inconsistencies of Reid, on this the most important part of his philosophy, should, by an articulate exposition, be deprived of their evil influence: I shall now enumerate — (A) the statements, which may, on the one hand, be adduced to prove that his doctrine of perception is one of *mediate* cognition under the form of *egoistical representationism*;—and (B) those which may, on the other hand, be alleged to shew, that it is one of *immediate* cognition, under the form of *real presentationism*. But as these counter statements are only of import, in as much as they severally imply the conditions of mediate or of immediate cognition; it is necessary that the reader should bear in mind the exposition, which has been given of these conditions, in Note B. § I.

A.—*Statements conformable to the doctrine of a mediate perception, under the form of an egoistical representation, and inconsistent with that of immediate perception, under the form of a real presentation, of material objects.*

1. On the testimony of consciousness, and in the doctrine of an intuitive perception, the mind, when a material existence is brought into relation with its organ of sense, obtains two concomitant, and immediate, cognitions. Of these, the one is the consciousness (sensation) of certain subjective modifications in us, which we refer, as effects, to certain unknown powers, as causes, in the external reality; the secondary qualities of body: the other is the consciousness (perception) of certain objective attributes in the external reality itself, as, or as in relation to our sensible organism;—the primary qualities of body. Of these cognitions the former is admitted, on all hands, to be subjective and ideal: the latter, the Natural Realist maintains, against the Cosmothetic Idealist, to be objective and real. But it is only objective and real, in so far as it is immediate; and immediate it cannot be, if—either, 1° dependent on the former, as its cause or its occasion—or, 2° consequent on it, as on a necessary antecedent. But both these conditions of a presentative perception Reid and Stewart are seen to violate; and therefore they may be held, virtually, to confess, that their doctrine is one only of representative perception. See Note D. § I. No. 23.

Touching the former condition: Reid states, that the primary qualities of material existences Extension, Figure, &c., are *suggested* to us through the secondary, which, though not the sufficient causes of our conception, are the *signs*,* on occasion of which, we are made to 'conceive' the primary. (Inq. 188 a, 122 a, 123 b, 128 b note). The secondary qualities, as mere sensations, mere consciousness of certain subjective affections, afford us no immediate knowledge of aught different from self. If, therefore, the primary qualities be only '*suggestions*,' only '*conceptions*,' (Inq. 183 a, I. P. 318 a b), which are, as it were, 'conjured up by a kind of natural magic,' (Inq. 122 a), or 'inspired by means unknown,' (Inq. 188 a); these conceptions are only representations, which the mind is, in some inconceivable manner, blindly determined to form of what it does not know; and, as perception is only a consciousness of these conceptions, perception is, like sensation, only an immediate cognition of certain modes of self. Our knowledge of the external world, on this footing, is wholly subjective or ideal;

* Edinb. Rev. vol. lii. p. 173-175;—also in Cross and Peisse. In saying, however, on that occasion, that Dr Brown was guilty of 'a reversal of the real and even *unambiguous* import' of Reid's doctrine of perception, I feel called upon to admit, that the latter epithet is too strong;—for on grounds, totally different from the untenable one of Brown, I am now about to shew, that Reid's doctrine, on this point, is doubtful. This admission does not, however, imply that Brown is not, from first to last,—is not in one and all of his strictures on Reid's doctrine of perception, as there shewn, wholly in error

* This application of the term *sign* suits the Cosmothetic Idealist, as the Cartesian Bossuet (Connaissance de Dieu, &c., ch. 3, § 8), or the Absolute Idealist, as Berkeley (passim), but not the Natural Realist. In this doctrine of natural signs, I see Reid was, in a manner, also preceded by Hutcheson, (Syn. Met P. ii. c. 1—Syst. of Mor B. i. ch. 1, p. 5).

and if such be Reid's doctrine, it is wholly conformable to that enounced in the following statement of the Cartesian representationism by Silvain Regis:—'We may thus, he says, affirm, that the cognition we have of any individual body which strikes the sense is composed of two parts,—of a *sensation* (sentiment), and of an *imagination*; an imagination, which represents the extension of this body under a determinate size; and a sensation of colour and light, which renders this extension visible.' (Metaph. L. ii. P. i. ch. 5. Cours, t. i. p. 162, ed. 1691). This statement may stand equally for an enouncement of the Kantian doctrine of perception; and it is, perhaps, worth noticing, that Regis anticipated Kant, in holding the imagination of space to be the a priori form or subjective condition of perception. 'L' Idée de l' Entendue (he says) est née avec l' âme,' &c., (ibid. c. 9, p. 171 et alibi.)—This theory of Suggestion, so explicitly maintained in the 'Inquiry,' is not repeated in the 'Essays on the Intellectual Powers.' Reid, therefore, as I have already observed, (p. 129 a, note,) may seem to have become doubtful of the tendency of the doctrine advanced in his earlier work; and we ought not, at all events, to hold him rigorously accountable for the consequences of what, if he did not formally retract in his later writings, he did not continue to profess.

Touching the latter condition:—Reid in stating, that 'if sensation be produced, the corresponding perception *follows* even when there is no object,' (I. P. 320 b,)—and Stewart in stating, that 'sensations are the constant *antecedents* of our perceptions,' (El. i. c. 1, p. 93, e d. 6,) manifestly advance a doctrine, which if rigidly interpreted, is incompatible with the requisites of an intuitive perception.

2. It is the condition of an intuitive perception, that a sensation is actually felt there, where it is felt to be. To suppose that a pain, for instance, in the toe, is felt really in the brain, is conformable only to a theory of representationism. For if the mind cannot be conscious of the secondary qualities, except at the centre of the nervous organism, it cannot be conscious of the primary, in their relation to its periphery; and this involves the admission, that it is incompetent to more than a subjective or ideal or representative cognition of external things. But such is the doctrine which Reid manifestly holds. (I. P. 319 b, 320 a b.)

3. On the doctrine of Natural Realism, that the ego has an intuitive perception of the non-ego in proximate relation to its organs, a knowledge and a belief of the existence of the external world, is clearly given in the fact of such intuitive perception. In this case, therefore, we are not called upon to explain such knowledge and belief by the hypothesis, or, at least, the analogy, of an inspired notion and infused faith. On the doctrine of Cosmothetic Idealism, on the contrary, which supposes that the mind is determined to represent to itself the external world, which, ex hypothesi, it does not know; the fact of such representation can only be conceived possible, through some hyperphysical agency; and therefore Reid's rationale of perception, by an inspiration or kind of magical conjuration, as given in the Inquiry, (122 a, 188 a; Stewart, El. i. 64, 93), may seem to favour the construction, that his doctrine is a representationism. In the Essays on the Intellectual Powers he is, however, more cautious; and the note I have appended in that work at p. 257 a, is to be viewed in more especial reference to the doctrine of the Inquiry; though in the relative passage 'the will of God' may, certainly, seem called as a Deus ex machina, to solve a knot which the doctrine of intuitive perception does not tie.

4. The terms *notion* and *conception* are, in propriety, only applicable to our mediate and representative cognitions.—When Reid, therefore, says that 'the Perception of an object consists of, or implies, a *conception* or *notion* of it,' (Inq. 183 a, 188 a, I. P. 258 a b, 318 b, 319 a, et alibi); there is here, either an impropriety of language, or perception is, in his view, a mediate and representative knowledge. The former alternative is, however, at least equally probable as the latter; for Consciousness, which, on all hands, is admitted to be a knowledge immediate and intuitive, he defines (I. P. 327 a) 'an immediate *conception* of the operation of our own minds,' &c. Conception and Notion, Reid seems, therefore, to employ, at least sometimes, for cognition in general.

5. In calling imagination of the past, the distant, &c., an immediate knowledge, Reid, it may be said, could only mean by *immediate*, a knowledge effected not through the supposed intermediation of a vicarious object, numerically different from the object existing and the mind knowing, but through a representation of the past, or real, object, in and by the mind itself; in other words, that by *mediate* knowledge he denoted a *non-ego-*

istical, by *immediate* knowledge an *egoistical*, representation. (Note B. § 1. Pr. 7. p. 805 a). This being established it may be further argued—1°, that in calling *Perception* an *immediate* knowledge, he, on the same analogy, must be supposed to deny, in reference to this faculty, only the doctrine of non-egoistical representation. This is confirmed—2°, by his not taking the distinction between perception as a presentative, and Memory, for instance, (i. e. recollective imagination) as a representative, cognition; which he ought to have done, had he contemplated, in the former, more than a faculty, through which the ego represents to itself the non-ego, of which it has no consciousness—no true objective and immediate apprehension. This, however, only proves that Reid's Perception *may be* representative, not that it actually is so.

6. The doctrine maintained by Reid (I. P. 109 a, 298 b, 299 a, 302 a, 305 b) and by Stewart (Elem. vol. i. c. I, sect. 2) that perception is possible of distant objects, is, when sifted, found necessarily to imply, that perception is not, in that case, an apprehension of the object in its place in space—in its Where; and this again necessarily implies, that it is not an apprehension of the object, as existing, or in itself. But if not known as existing, or in itself, a thing is, either not known at all, or known only in and through something different from itself. Perception, therefore, is, on this doctrine, at best a mediate or representative cognition;—of the simpler form of representation, the egoistical, it may be, but still only vicarious and subjective. See Note B.

7. In some places our author would seem to hold that Perception is the result of an inference, and that what is said to be perceived is the remote *cause* and therefore not the *immediate object* of Perception. If this be so, Perception is not a presentative knowledge. (Inq. 125 a, I. P. 310 a b, 319 a.) In other passages, that perception is the result of inference or reasoning is expressly denied. (I. P. 259 b, 260 a b, 309 b, 326 a, 328 b, &c.)

8. On the supposition, that we have an immediate cognition or consciousness of the non-ego, we must have, at the same time, involved as part and parcel of that cognition, a *belief* of its existence. To view, therefore, our belief of the existence of the external world, as any thing apart from our knowledge of that world,—to refer it to instinct—to view it as unaccountable—to consider it as an ultimate law of our constitution, &c., as Reid does, (Inq. 188 a b, I. P. 258 b, 309 b, 326 a, 327 a, et alibi), is, to say the least of it, suspicious; appearing to imply, that our cognition of the material world, as only mediate and subjective, does not, at once and of itself, necessitate a belief of the existence of external things.

B. *Counter statements, conformable to the doctrine of a real presentation of material objects, and inconsistent with that of a representative perception.*

1. Knowledge and existence only infer each other when a reality is known in itself or as existing; for only in that case can we say of it,—on the one hand, *it is known, because it exists*,—on the other, *it exists, since it is known.* In propriety of language, this constitutes, exclusively, an *immediate*, *intuitive* or *real*, cognition. This is at once the doctrine of philosophers in general, and of Reid in particular. 'It seems,' he says, 'admitted as a first principle, by the learned and the unlearned, that what is really perceived must exist, and that to perceive what does not exist is impossible. So far the unlearned man and the philosopher agree.' (I. P. p. 274 b.) This principle will find an articulate illustration in the three proximately following statements, in all of which it is implied.

2. The *idea* or *representative object*, all philosophers, of whatever doctrine, concur in holding to be, in the strictest sense of the expression, itself immediately apprehended; and that, as thus apprehended, it necessarily exists. That Reid fully understands their doctrine, is shown by his introducing a Cosmothetic Idealist thus speaking:—'I perceive an image, or form, or idea, in my own mind, or in my brain. I am certain of the existence of the idea; because I immediately perceive it.' (Ibid.) Now then, if Reid be found to assert—that, on his doctrine, we perceive material objects not less immediately, than, on the common doctrine of philosophers, we perceive ideal objects; and that therefore his theory of perception affords an equal certainty of the existence of the external reality, as that of the Cosmothetic Idealist does of the existence of its internal representation;—if Reid, I say, do this, he unambiguously enounces a doctrine of presentative, and not of representative, perception. And this he does. Having repeated, for the hundredth time, the deliverance of common sense, that we perceive material things immediately, and not their ideal representations, he proceeds:—'I shall only here observe that if external objects be perceived immediately, we have

the same reason to believe their existence as philosophers have to believe the existence of ideas, while they hold them to be the immediate objects of perception.' (I. P. 446 a b. See also 263 b, 272 b.)

3 Philosophers—even Sceptics and Idealists—concur in acknowledging, that mankind at large believe that the external reality is itself the immediate and only object in perception. (Note A. p. 745 sq.) Reid is of course no exception. After stating the principle, previously quoted (B, st 1.) 'that what is really perceived must exist,' he adds;—'the unlearned man says, I perceive the external object and I perceive it to exist. Nothing can be more absurd than to doubt it.' (I. P. 274 b). —Again:—'The vulgar undoubtedly believe, that it is the external object which we immediately perceive, and not a representative image of it only. It is for this reason, that they look upon it as perfect lunacy to call in question the existence of external objects.' (Ibid.) Again: —'The vulgar are firmly persuaded, that the very identical objects which they perceive continue to exist when they do not perceive them; and are no less firmly persuaded, that when ten men look at the sun or the moon they all see the same individual object.'* (I. P. 284 b). Again, speaking of Berkeley:—'The vulgar opinion he reduces to this,—that the very things which we perceive by our senses do really exist. This he grants.' (I. P. 284 a). Finally, speaking of Hume:—'It is therefore acknowledged by this philosopher to be a natural instinct or prepossession, an universal and primary opinion of all men, that the objects which we immediately perceive, by our senses, are not images in our minds, but external objects, and that their existence is independent of us and our perception.' (I. P. 299 b; see also 275 a, 298 b, 299 a b, 302 a b).

It is thus evinced, that Reid, like other philosophers, attributes to men in general the belief of an intuitive perception. If then he declare that his own opinion coincides with that of the vulgar, he will, consequently, declare himself a Presentative Realist. And he does this; emphatically too. Speaking of the Perception of the external world:—'We have here a remarkable conflict between two contradictory opinions, wherein all mankind are engaged. On the one side stand all the vulgar, who are unpractised in philosophical researches, and guided by the uncorrupted primary instincts of nature. On the other side, stand all the philosophers, ancient and modern; every man, without exception, who reflects. In this division, to my great humiliation, *I find myself classed with the vulgar.*' (I. P. 302 b).

4. All philosophers agree that self-consciousness is an immediate knowledge, and therefore affords an absolute and direct certainty of the existence of its objects. Reid (with whom consciousness is equivalent to self-consciousness,) of course maintains this; but he also maintains, not only that perception affords a sufficient proof, but as valid an assurance of the reality of material phænomena, as consciousness does of the reality of mental. (I. P. 263 b, 269 a, 373, et alibi.) In this last assertion I have shewn that Reid (and Stewart along with him) is wrong; for the phænomena of self-consciousness cannot possibly be doubted or denied (p. 741 b, sq.); but the statement, at least tends to prove, that his perception is truly immediate,—is, under a different name, a consciousness of the non-ego.

5. Arnauld's doctrine of external perception is a purely egoistical representationism; and he has stated its conditions and consequences, with the utmost accuracy and precision. (I. P. 295-298). Reid expresses both his content and discontent with Arnauld's theory of perception, which he erroneously views as inconsistent with itself, (297 a b). This plainly shews that he had not realised to himself a clear conception of the two doctrines of Presentationism and Egoistical Representationism, in themselves and in their contrasts. But it also proves that when the conditions and consequences of the latter scheme, even in its purest form, were explicitly enounced, that he was then sufficiently aware of their incompatibility with the doctrine which he himself maintained—a doctrine, therefore, it may be fairly contended, (though not in his hands clearly understood, far less articulately developed,) substantially one of Natural Realism.*

To Reid's inadequate discrimination —common to him with other philoso-

---

* The inaccuracy of this statement (see p. 814 a) does not affect the argument.

* It will be observed that I do not found any argument on Reid's frequent assertion, that *perception* affords an *immediate knowledge* and *immediate belief* of external things, (e. g. I. P.

phers—of the different theories of Perception, either as possible in theory, or as actually held, is, as I have already noticed, to be ascribed the ambiguities, and virtual contradictions, which we have now been considering.

In the first place, (what was of little importance to the Hypothetical, but indispensably necessary for the Natural Realist), he did not establish the fact of the two cognitions, the presentative and representative;—signalise their contents;—evolve their several conditions;—consider what faculties in general were to be referred to each;—and, in particular, which of these was the kind of cognition competent, in our Perception of the external world.

In the second place, he did not take note, that representation is possible under two forms—the egoistical, and non-egoistical; each, if Perception be reduced to a representative faculty, affording premises of equal cogency to the absolute idealist and sceptic. On the contrary, he seems to have overlooked the egoistical form of representationism altogether (compare Inq. 106 a, 128 a b, 130 b, 210 a, I. P. 226 a b, 256 a b, 257 a b, 269 a, 274 a, 277 b, 278 a b, 293 b, 299 a, 318 b, 427 a b.); and confounded it either with the non-egoistical form, or with the counter doctrine of real presentationism. In consequence of this, he has been betrayed into sundry errors, of less or greater account. On the one hand;—to the confusion of Presentationism and Egoistical representationism, we must attribute the inconsistencies, we have just signalised, in the exposition of his own doctrine. These are of principal account. On the other hand;—to the confusion of Egoistical and Non-egoistical representationism, we must refer the less important errors;—1°, of viewing many philosophers who held the former doctrine, as holding the latter; and 2°, of considering the refutation of the non-egoistical form of representation, as a subversion of the only ground on which the sceptic and absolute idealist established, or could establish their conclusions.

269 b, 260 a b, 267 a, 300 b, 326 b). For if he call memory an immediate knowledge of the past—meaning thereby, in reference to it, only a negation of the doctrine of non-egoistical representation—he may also call Perception an immediate knowledge of the outward reality, and still not deny that it is representative cognition, in and by the mind itself.

NOTE D.

DISTINCTION OF THE PRIMARY AND SECONDARY QUALITIES OF BODY.

§ I.—*Historically considered.*

§ II.—*Critically considered.*

[References.—From Inq. 123 a, 205. From I. P. 316 a, 319 a.]

The developed doctrine of Real Presentationism, the basis of Natural Realism, asserts the consciousness or immediate perception of certain essential attributes of matter objectively existing; while it admits that other properties of body are unknown in themselves, and only inferred as causes to account for certain subjective affections of which we are cognisant in ourselves. This discrimination, which to other systems is contingent, superficial, extraneous, but to Natural Realism necessary, radical, intrinsic, coincides with what, since the time of Locke, has been generally known as the distinction of the Qualities of Matter or Body, using these terms as convertible, into Primary and Secondary.

Of this celebrated analysis, I shall here, in the first place, attempt an *historical survey*; and in the second, endeavour to place it on its proper footing by a *critical analysis*; without however in either respect proposing more than a contribution towards a more full and regular discussion of it in both.

§ I.—*Distinction of the Primary and Secondary Qualities of Body considered Historically.*

In regard to its History—this, as hitherto attempted, is at once extremely erroneous, if History may be called the incidental notices in regard to it of an historical import, which are occasionally to be met with in philosophical treatises.—Among the most important of these, are those furnished by Reid himself, and by M. Royer Collard.

The distinction of the real and the apparent, of the absolute and the relative, or of the objective and the subjective qualities of perceived bodies is of so obtrusive a character, that it was taken almost at the origin of speculation, and can be shown to have commanded the assent even of those philosophers by whom it is now commonly believed to have been again formally rejected. For in this, as in many other cases, it will be found that while philosophers appear to differ, they are, in reality, at one.

1.—Leucippus and Democritus are the first on record by whom the observation was enounced, that the Sweet, the Bitter, the Cold, the Hot, the Coloured, &c., are wholly different, in their absolute nature, from the character in which they come manifested to us. In the latter case, these qualities have no real or independent existence (οὐ κατὰ ἀλήθειαν.) The only existence they can pretend to, is merely one phaenominal in us; and this in virtue of a law or relation (νόμῳ), established between the existing body and the percipient mind; while all that can be denominated Quality in the external reality, is only some modification of Quantity, some particular configuration, position, or co-arrangement of Atoms, in conjunction with the Inane. (*Aristoteles*, Metaph. L. i. c. 4—Phys. Ausc. L. i. c. 5—De Anima, L. iii. c. 1—De Sensu et Sensili, c. 4—De Gen. et Corr. L. i. cc. 2. 7. 8.;—*Theophrastus*, De Sensu, §§ 63. 65. 67. 69. 73, ed. Schneid.;—*Sextus Empiricus*, adv. Math. vii. § 135—Hypot. i. § 213;—*Galenus*, De Elem. L. i. c. 2.;—*Laertius*, L. ix. seg. 44.;—*Plutarchus*, adv. Colot. p. 1110, ed. Xyl.;—*Simplicius*, in Phys. Ausc. ff. 7. 10, 106, 119. ed. Ald.;—*Philoponus*, De Gen. et Corr. f. 32. ed. Ald.)

2, 3.—This observation was not lost on PROTAGORAS or on PLATO. The former on this ground endeavoured to establish the absolute relativity of all human knowledge; the latter the absolute relativity of our sensible perceptions. (Theaetetus, passim.)

4.—By the CYRENAIC philosophers the distinction was likewise adopted and applied. (*Cic.* Qu. Acad. iv. c. 24.)

5.—With other doctrines of the older Atomists it was transplanted into his system by EPICURUS. (Epist. ad Herod. apud *Laert.* L. x. seg. 54. *Lucret.* L. ii. v. 729—1021.)

6.—In regard to ARISTOTLE, it is requisite to be somewhat more explicit. This philosopher might seem, at first sight, to have rejected the distinction (De Anima, L. iii. c. 1.); and among many others, Reid has asserted that Aristotle again ignored the discrimination, which had been thus recognised by his predecessors. (Inq. 123 a, I. P. 313 b.) Nothing, however, can be more erroneous than the accredited doctrine upon this point. Aristotle does not abolish the distinction;—nay, I am confident of showing, that to whatever merit modern philosophers may pretend in this analysis, all and each of their observations are to be found, clearly stated, in the writings of the Stagirite.

In the *first* place, no philosopher has discriminated with greater, perhaps none with equal, precision, the difference of corporeal qualities considered *objectively* and *subjectively*. These relations he has not only contrasted, but has assigned to them distinctive appellations. In his Categories, (c. viii. § 10, Pacian division, by which, as that usually adopted, I uniformly quote,) speaking of Quality, he says:—' A third kind of Quality [Suchness] is made up of the *Affective Qualities* and *Affections* (παθητικαὶ ποιότητες, πάθη.) Of this class are Sweetness, Bitterness, Sourness, and the like, also Heat and Cold, Whiteness and Blackness, &c. That these are qualities [suchnesses] is manifest. For the subjects in which they are received, are said to be such and such by relation to them. Thus honey is called sweet, as recipient of sweetness, body, white, as recipient of whiteness, and so of the rest. They are called *affective* [i. e. causing passion or affection*] not because the

* The active-potential term, *παθητικός*, primarily and properly denotes that which *can in itself suffer or be affected*; it is here employed in a secondary and abusive sense (for *πάσχειν* is intransitive), but which subsequently became the more prevalent,—to signify that which *can cause suffering or affection in something else*. The counter passivo-potential form, *παθητός*, is not, I venture to assert, ever used by Aristotle, though quoted from him, and from this very treatise, by all the principal lexicographers for the last three centuries; nay, I make further bold to say, there is no authority for it, (Menander's is naught,) until long subsequently to the age of the Stagirite. [The error, I suspect, originated thus:—Tusanus, in his Lexicon (1552), says, under the word,—' Vide Fabrum Stapulensem apud Aristotelem in Prædicamentis;' meaning, it is probable (for I have not the book at hand), to send us to Faber's Introduction to the Categories, for some observations on the term. The Lexicon Septemvirale (1563), copying Tusanus, omits Faber, and simply refers ' Aristoteli, in Prædicamentis,' as to an authority for the word; and this error propagated through Stephanus, Constantine, Scapula, and subsequent compilers, stands uncorrected to the present day.] But this term, even were it of Aristotelic usage, could not, without violence, have been twisted to denote, in conjunction with *ποιότης*, what the philosopher less equivocally, if less symmetrically, expresses by *πάθος*, *affection*.—*Patibilis*, like most Latin verbals of its class, indiscriminately renders the two potentials, active and passive, which the Greek tongue alone so admirably contradistinguishes. But, in any way, the word is incompetent to Aristotle's meaning in the sense of *affective*. For it only signifies, either that which *can suffer*, or that which *can be suffered*; and there is not, I am confident, a single ancient authority to be found for it, in the sense of that which *can cause to suffer*,—the sense to which it is contorted by the modern Latin Aristotelians. But they had their excuse—necessity; for the terms, *passivus*, used in the ' Categoriæ Decem' attributed to St Augustine, and *passibilis*, employed by Boethius in his version of the present passage, are even worse. The words *affective* and *affection* render the Greek adjective and substantive tolerably well.

This distinction by Aristotle is very commonly misunderstood. It is even reversed by Gassendi; but with him, of course, only from inadvertence. Phys. Sect. i. Lib. vi. c. 1.

things to which these qualities belong, have been themselves affected in any way; (for it is not because honey, or the like, has been somehow affected that it is called sweet, and in like manner heat and cold are not called affective qualities because the bodies in which they inhere have undergone any affection;) but they are called *affective*, because each of the foresaid qualities has the power of causing an affection in the sense. For sweetness determines a certain affection in tasting, heat in touching, and in like manner the others.'

Nothing can be juster than this distinction, and it is only to be regretted that he should have detracted from the precision of the language it which it is expressed by not restricting the correlative terms, *Affective Qualities* and *Affections*, to the discrimination in question alone. In this particular observation, it is proper to notice, Aristotle had in view the secondary qualities of our modern philosophy exclusively. It suffices, however, to show that no philosopher had a clearer insight into the contrast of such qualities, as they *are*, and as they are *perceived*; and, were other proof awanting, it might also of itself exonerate him from any share in the perversion made by the later Peripatetics of his philosophy, in their doctrine of Substantial Forms;—a doctrine which, as Reid (I. P. 316) rightly observes, is inconsistent with the distinction in question as taken by the Atomic philosophers, but which in truth, is not less inconsistent with that here established by Aristotle himself.* It may be here likewise observed that Andronicus, as quoted by Simplicius (Categ. f. 55 ed. Velsii), explicitly states, that the Affective Qualities are, in strict propriety, not *qualities* but *powers* (οὐ ποιὰ ἀλλὰ ποιητικά.) Aristotle himself, indeed, accords to these, apart from perception, only a potential existence; and the Peripatetics in general held them to be, in their language not *παθητικῶς, formally, subjectively*, but *ἐνεργητικῶς, virtually, eminently*, in the external object. Locke has thus no title whatever to the honour generally accorded to him of first promulgating the observation, that the secondary qualities, as in the object, are not so much *qualities* as *powers*. This observation was, however, only borrowed by Locke from the Cartesians. But of this hereafter.

In the *second* place, Aristotle likewise notices the ambiguity which arises from languages not always affording different terms by which to distinguish the *potential* from the *actual*, and the *objective* from the *subjective* phases, in our perception by the different senses. Thus, he observes (De Anima, L. iii. c. 1.) that, 'Though the actuality or energy of the *object of sense* and of the *sense itself* be one and indivisible, the nature, the essence, of the energy is, however, not the same in each; as, for example, *sound* in energy, and *hearing* in energy. For it may happen, that what has the power of hearing does not now hear, and that what has the power of

* The theory of what are called Substantial Forms, that is, qualities viewed as entities conjoined with, and not as mere dispositions or modifications of, matter, was devised by the perverse ingenuity of the Arabian philosophers and physicians. Adopted from them, it was long a prevalent doctrine in the Western schools, among the followers of Aristotle and Galen; to either of whom it is a gross injustice to attribute this opinion. It was the ambiguity of the word *οὐσία*, by which the Greeks express what is denoted (to say nothing of Arabic) by both the Latin terms *essentia* and *substantia*, that allowed of, and principally occasioned, the misinterpretation.

I may, likewise, notice, by the way, that Aristotle's doctrine of the assimilation, in the sensitive process, of that which perceives with that which is perceived, may reasonably be explained to mean, that the object and subject are then, so brought into mutual relation, as, by their coefficient energy, to constitute an act of cognition one and indivisible, and in which the reality is to us, as we perceive it to be. This is a far easier and a far more consistent interpretation of his words, than the monstrous doctrine of *intentional forms* or *species*;—a doctrine founded on one or two vague or metaphorical expressions, and for which the general analogy of his philosophy required a very different meaning. For example, when Aristotle (De Anima, iii. 1.) in showing that an objection was incompetent, even on its own hypothesis, dialectically admits—'that what sees colour is, in a certain sort, itself coloured;'—is this more than a qualified statement of what modern philosophers have so often, far less guardedly, asserted—that colour is not to be considered merely as an attribute of body, since, in a certain respect, it is an affection of mind?—And when he immediately subjoins the reason,—'for each organ of sense is receptive of its appropriate object,' or, as he elsewhere expresses it, 'receptive of the form without the matter;' what is this but to say—that our organs of sense stand in relation to certain qualities of body, and that each organ is susceptible of an affection from its appropriate quality; such quality, however, not being received by the sense in a material efflux from the object, as was held by Democritus and many previous philosophers? Yet this is the principal text on which the common doctrine of Intentional Species is attributed to Aristotle.

sounding does not always sound. But when what has the faculty of hearing, on the one hand, operates, and what has the faculty of sounding, on the other, sounds, then the actual hearing and the actual sounding take place conjunctly; and of these the one may be called *Audition*, the other *Sonation*;'—the subjective term, *hearing*, and the objective term, *sound*, as he afterwards states, being twofold in meaning, each denoting ambiguously both the actual and the potential.—'The same analogy,' he adds, 'holds good in regard to the other senses and their respective objects. For as affection and passion are realized in the patient, and not in the efficient, so the energy of the *object* of sense (αἰσθητόν), and the energy of the *faculty* of sense (αἰσθητικόν) are both in the latter;—but whilst in certain of the senses they have obtained distinct names, (as Sonation and Audition), in the rest, the one or the other is left anonymous. For Vision denotes the energy of the visual faculty, whereas the energy of colour, its object, is without a name; and while Gustation expresses the act of what is *able to taste*, the act* of that *capable of being tasted* is nameless. But seeing that of the object, and of the faculty, of sense the energy is one and the same, though their nature be different, it is necessary, that hearing and sound, as actual, (and the same is the case in the other senses), should subsist and perish together; whereas this is not necessary, in so far as these are considered as potentially existing.'

He then goes on to rectify, in its statement, the doctrine of the elder physical philosophers; in whom Philoponus (or Ammonius) contemplates Protagoras and his followers, but Simplicius, on better grounds, the Democriteans. 'But the earlier speculators on nature were not correct in saying, that there is nothing white or black, apart from sight, and nothing sapid, apart from taste. This doctrine is, in certain respects, right, in certain respects, wrong. For *sense*, and the *object of sense*, having each a twofold signification, in as much as they may severally mean either what is *potentially*, or what is *actually*, existent; in the latter case, what is here asserted, takes place, but not so in the former. These speculators were therefore at fault, in stating absolutely what is only true under conditions.' (De Anima, iii. c. 1.)

This criticism, it is evident, so far from involving a rejection of the distinction taken by Leucippus and Democritus, is only an accommodation of it to the form of his own philosophy; in which the distinction of the *Potential* and *Actual* contains a great, perhaps an exaggerated importance. And it is sufficiently manifest that the older philosophers exclusively contemplated the latter.

But, in the *third* place, not only did Aristotle clearly establish the difference between qualities considered absolutely, as in the existing object, and qualities considered relatively, as in the sentient subject; and not only did he signalize the ambiguity which arises from the poverty of language, employing only a single word to denote these indifferently;—he likewise anticipated Descartes, Locke, and other modern philosophers, in establishing, and marking out by appropriate terms, a distinction precisely analogous with that taken by them of the *Primary and Secondary Qualities of Matter*. The Aristotelic distinction which, *in its relation to the other*, has been wholly overlooked, is found in the discrimination of the *Common and Proper Percepts, Sensibles, or objects of Sense* (αἰσθητὰ κοινὰ καὶ ἴδια.) It is given in the two principal psychological treatises of the philosopher; and to the following purport.

Aristotle (De Anima L. ii. c. 2, L. iii. c. 1. and De Sensu et Sensili, c. 1.) enumerates five *percepts* common to all or to a plurality of the senses,—viz, *Magnitude (Extension), Figure, Motion, Rest, Number*. To these in one place (De Anima iii. 1.) he adds *Unity*; and in another (De Sensu et Sensili c. 4), he states, as common, at least to sight and touch, besides Magnitude and Figure, the *Rough* and the *Smooth*, the *Acute* and the *Obtuse*. Unity however he comprises under Number; and the Rough and Smooth, the Acute and Obtuse, under Figure. Nay, of the five common sensibles or percepts, he gives us (De Anima iii. 1.) a further reduction, resolving Figure into Magnitude; while both of these, he says, as well as Rest and Number, are known through

---

* In English and in most other languages there are not distinct words to express as well the objective, as the subjective, coefficient in the senses, more particularly of Tasting and Smelling; and we are therefore obliged ambiguously to apply the terms *taste* and *smell* (which are rather subjective in signification) in an objective sense, and the terms *savour*, *flavour*, &c. (which have perhaps now more of an objective meaning) in a subjective signification. In reference to the sense of touch, the same word is often equivocally used to denote, objectively, a primary quality, and subjectively, a secondary. As *hardness*, *roughness*, &c

Motion; which last, as he frequently repeats, necessarily involves the notion of Time; for motion exists only as in Time. (Compare Phys. Ausc. L. iv. passim.) His words are—'All these we perceive by Motion.* Thus Magnitude (Extension) is apprehended by motion; wherefore also Figure, for figure is a kind of magnitude; what is at Rest by not being moved; Number, by a negation of the continuous,† even in the sensations proper to the several senses, for each of these is itself percipient of what is one.'—This attempt at simplification was followed out by his disciples. Thus St Thomas (Summa Theologiæ P. i. Qu. 78, art. 3), in shewing that the common sensibles do not primarily, and of themselves, act upon and affect the sense, carries them all up into modifications of Quantity (Quantitatis);—and in another book (De Sensu et Sensibili, Lect. ii.) by a variation of the expression (for in both cases he contemplates only the Extended) into species of the Continuous. To quote the latter:—'Sensibilia communia omnia pertinent aliquo modo ad *Continuum*; vel secundum mensuram ejus, ut *Magnitudo*; vel secundum divisionem, ut *Numerus*; vel secundum terminationem, ut *Figura*; vel secundum distantiam et propinquitatem, ut *Motus*.'

Aristotle indeed (De Anima, L. ii. c. 6.) virtually admits, that the *common* are abusively termed *sensibles* at all: for he says, 'the proper alone are accurately, or pre-eminently, objects of sense' (τὰ ἴδια κυρίως ἐστὶ αἰσθητά); and the same seems also to be involved in his doctrine, that the *common* percepts (which in one place he even says are only apprehended *per accidens*) are, in fact, within the domain of sense, merely as being the concomitants or consequents (ἀκολουθοῦντα, ἑπόμενα) of the proper.* (Ibid. L. iii. cc. 1, 4.) See

* This doctrine of Aristotle is rejected by Theophrastus, as we learn from the fragments concerning Sense preserved in the rare and neglected treatise of Priscianus Lydus, p. 285. Many modern philosophers when they attempted to explain the origin of our notion of extension from motion, and, in particular, the motion of the hand, were not aware that they had the Stagirite at their head. It is to be remembered, however, that Aristotle does not attempt, like them, to explain by motion our necessary concept of space, but merely our contingent perception of the relative extension of this or that particular object.

This, however, takes it for granted, that by motion, (κινήσεως,) Aristotle intends *local motion*. But motion is with him a generic term, comprising under it four, or six, species; and, in point of fact, by motion Aristotle may here, as in many, if not most, other places of his psychological writings, mean a subjective mutation (ἀλλοιώσεως) or modification of the percipient. This, too, is the interpretation given to the passage by the great majority, if not the whole, of the ancient expositors—by Plutarchus of Athens, Ammonius or Philoponus, Simplicius, and Priscianus Lydus;—Themistius alone is silent. I say nothing of the sequacious cloud of modern commentators. It is therefore remarkable that Dr Trendelenburg, in his late valuable edition of the De Anima, should have apparently contemplated the interpretation by local motion, as the only one proposed or possible. This may, however, adduce in its favour the authority of Theophrastus, among the ancients—among the moderns, of the subtle Scaliger.—From both interpretations, however, a defensible meaning can be elicited.

† This explicitly shews that, by Number, Aristotle means only the necessary attribution of *either unity or plurality* to the object of sense. *Divisibility* (in extension, intension, protension,) is thus contained under Number. Number in the abstract is, of course, a merely intellectual concept, as Aristotle, once and again, notices. See Philoponus on 63 text of second book De Anima, Sign. i. 8 ed. Trinc. 1535. Of this again under Locke, No. 19; and Royer Collard, No. 25.

* I have already noticed (p. 124) that Hutcheson, in saying that 'Extension, Figure, Motion, and Rest, seem to be more properly ideas accompanying the sensations of Sight and Touch than the sensations of either of these senses' only, mediately or immediately, repeats Aristotle; to whom is therefore due all the praise which has been lavished on the originality and importance of the observation [I might have there added, however, that Hutcheson does not claim it as his own. For in his System of Moral Philosophy (which is to be annexed to the other references) he speaks of 'what *some* call the Concomitant ideas of Sensation.' (B. i. c. 1, p. 6)]. Dr Price extols it as 'a very just observation of Hutcheson' (Rev. p. 56, ed. 1). Mr Stewart calls it 'a remark of singular acuteness,'—'a very ingenious and original remark,'—and 'a sentence which, considering the period at which the author (Hutcheson) wrote, reflects the highest honour on his metaphysical acuteness.' (Essays pp. 31, 46, 551, 4th ed.) M. Royer Collard says,—'Hutcheson est le premier des philosophes modernes qui ait fait cette observation aussi fine que juste quo,' &c. (Oeuvres de Reid, t. iii. p. 431).

I may here observe that Philippson (Ὕλη ἀνθρωπίνη p. 335) is misled by an ambiguous expression of Aristotle in stating that he assigned the *common sensibles* as objects to the *Common Sense*. See the Commentaries of Philoponus and of Simplicius on the 134 common text of third book *De Anima*. But compare also Alexander in his treatise on the Soul, first Book, in the chapter on the Common Sense, f. 134 ed. Ald

also Alexander On the Soul. (A. ff. 130 b, 134 a b—B. ff. 152, 153, ed. Ald.)

The more modern Schoolmen (followed sometimes unwittingly by very recent philosophers) have indeed contended, that on the principles of Aristotle the several common sensibles are in reality apprehended by other and higher energies than those of sense. Their argument is as follows:—*Motion* cannot be perceived without the collation of past and present time, without acts of memory and comparison. *Rest*, says Aristotle, is known as a privation, but sense is only of the positive; let it, however, be considered as a state, and as opposed to motion, still this supposes comparison. *Number* in like manner as a negation, a negation of the continuous, is beyond the domain of sense; and while Aristotle in one treatise (Phys. iv. 14) attributes the faculty of numeration to intelligence; in another (Problem. sect. 30 § 5, if this work be his,) he virtually denies it to sense, in denying it to the brutes. *Magnitude* (extension), if considered as comparative, is likewise manifestly beyond the province of mere sense; Aristotle, indeed, admits that its apprehension, in general, presupposes Motion. Finally, *Figure*, as the cognition of extension terminated in a certain manner, still more manifestly involves an act of comparison. (*Scaliger*, De Subtilitate, Ex. lxvi. and cccviii. § 15.—*Toletus*, in lib. de Anima L. ii. c. 6.—*Conimbricences*. Ibid.—*Irenaeus*, De An. p. 40.—Compare *Gassendi*, Phys. Sect. iii. Memb. Post. L. vi. c. 2—*Du Hamel*, Philos. Vetus et Nova, Phys. P. iii. c. 4.—and *Royer Collard*, in Œuvres de Reid, t. iii. p. 428 sq.—to be quoted in the sequel, No. 25.

The common sensibles thus came, in fact, to be considered by many of the acutest Aristotelians, as not so much perceptions of sense (in so far as sensible perception depends on corporeal affection) as concomitant cognitions to which the impression on the organ by the proper sensible only afforded the occasion. 'Sensibile Commune dicitur (says Compton Carleton) quod vel percipitur pluribus sensibus, vel ad quod cognoscendum, ab intellectu vel imaginatione desumitur *occasio* ex variis sensibus; ut sunt Figura, Motus, Ubicatio, Duratio, Magnitudo, Distantia, Numerus,' &c. (Philosophia Universa, De Anima Disp. xvi. Sect 2. § 1.)

But before leaving Aristotle, I should state, that he himself clearly contemplated, in his distinction of Common and Proper Sensibles, a classification correspondent to that of the Primary and Secondary Qualities of bodies, as established by the ancient atomists. This is expressly shewn in a passage wherein he notices that 'Democritus, among others, *reduced the proper sensibles to the common*, in explaining, for example, the differences of colour by differences of roughness and smoothness in bodies, and the varieties of savour by a variety in the configuration of atoms.' (De Sensu et Sensili, c. 4.)

Of a division by Aristotle, in a physical point of view, of the Qualities of body into *Primary* and *Secondary*, I shall speak in the sequel, when considering this nomenclature, as adopted, and transferred to the psychological point of view, by Locke, No. 19.

7.—Galen, whose works are now hardly more deserving of study by the physician than by the philosopher, affords me some scattered observations which merit notice, not merely in reference to the present subject. Sensitive perception, he well observes, consists not in the passive affection of the organ, but in the discriminative recognition—the dijudication of that affection by the active mind. "Ἔστι δὲ αἴσθησις οὐκ ἀλλοίωσις, ἀλλὰ διάγνωσις ἀλλοιώσεως. This function of diagnostic apprehension he accords to the dominant principle (τὸ ἡγεμονικόν,) that is, the imaginative, recollective and ratiocinative mind. (De Placit. Hipp. et Plat. L. vii cc. 14, 16, 17).*—Again:—'The objects in propriety called Sensible, are such as require for their discriminative recognition no other faculty but that of sensitive perception itself; whereas those objects are improperly called sensible, whose recognition, besides a plurality of the senses, involves memory and what is called the compositive and collective (generalising) reason. [I read συνθετικῷ and κεφαλαιωτικῷ.] Thus Colour is an object proper of sense, and Savour and Odour and Sound; so likewise are Hardness and Softness, Heat and Cold, and, in a word, all the Tactile qualities.' Then, after stating that no concrete object of sense—an apple for instance—is fully cognisable by sense alone, but, as Plato has it, by opinion with the aid of sense; and having well shewn how this frequently becomes a source of illusion,—in all which he is closely followed by Nemesius,—he goes on:—'But to carry sense into effect in all its

* The annotators of Nemesius have not observed that this philosopher is indebted to Galen, really and verbally, for the whole of his remarkable doctrine of sense. See his treatise De Nat. Hom. c. 6-11. ed. Matthiae.

various applications, is impossible without the co-operation of *memory* and *connumeration* (*συναρίθμησις*), and this, which likewise obtains the name of *summation* (*συγκεφαλαίωσις*, conceiving, thinking under a class,) is an act neither of sense nor of memory, but of the discursive or dianoetic faculty of thought. (Com. I. in Hipp. Lib. De Medici Officina, text. 3.)—In another work we have the same doctrine applied to solve the question—By what faculty is Motion apprehended? and it affords the result,—'That all motion is manifestly recognised, not by a mere act of sensitive perception, not even by sense with the aid of memory, but principally by a compositive act of thought' (*συλλογισμῷ*). This is a fourth synonyme for the three other convertible terms which occur in the previous passage. They are Platonic. (De Dignoscendis Pulsibus, L. iii. c. 1.)

8.—A remarkable but neglected passage relative to the present subject is to be found in the Saggiatore of Galileo, a work first published in 1623. Mamiani della Rovere is the only philosopher, as far as I am aware, who has ever alluded to it. Galileo there precedes Descartes in the distinction, and anticipates Locke in its nomenclature. The following is an abstract of his doctrine, which coincides with that of the ancient Atomists, in some respects, and with that of Kant, in others.

In conceiving *matter* or corporeal substance we cannot but think that it is somehow terminated, and therefore of such and such a figure; that in relation to other bodies it is large or small; that it exists in this or that place; in this or that time; that it is in motion or at rest; that it does or does not touch another body; that it is single or composed of parts; and these parts either few or many. Those are conditions from which the mind cannot in thought emancipate the object. But that it is white or red, bitter or sweet, sonorous or noiseless, of a grateful or ungrateful odour;—with such conditions there is no necessity for conceiving it accompanied.* Hence Tastes, Odours, Colours, &c., considered as qualities inherent in external objects, are merely names; they reside exclusively in the sentient subject. Annihilate the animal percipient of such qualities, and you annihilate such qualities themselves; and it is only because we have bestowed on them particular names different from those by which we designate the other *primary and real affections of matter* (primi e reali accidenti), that we are disposed to believe that the former are in objects truly and really different from the latter.

Having illustrated this doctrine at considerable length in relation to the senses of Touch, Taste, Smell, and Hearing; and, in imitation of Aristotle, shewn the analogy which these severally hold to the elements of Earth, Water, Fire, and Air, he adds:—'Ma che ne' corpi esterni per eccitare in noi i sapori, gli odori, e i suoni, si richiegga altro, que grandezze, figure, moltitudini, e movimenti tardi o veloci, io non lo credo. Io stimo, che tolti via gli orecchi, le lingue, e i nasi, restino bene le figure, i numeri, e i moti, ma non già gli odori, nè i sapori, nè i suoni, li quali fuor dell' animal vivente, non credo che sieno altro che nomi, come appunto altro che nome non è il solletico, e la titillazione, rimosse l' ascelle, e la pelle intorno al naso; e come a i quattro sensi considerati hanno relazione i quattro elementi, così credo, che per la vista, senso sopra tutti gli altri eminentissimo, abbia relazione la luce, ma non quella proporzione d' eccellenza, qual' è tra 'l finito, e l' infinito, tra 'l temporaneo, e l' instantaneo, tra 'l quanto, e l' indivisibile, tra la luce, e le tenebre.'

He then applies this doctrine to the case of Heat and says,—'Ma che oltre alla figura, moltitudine, moto, penetrazione, o toccamento, sia nel fuoco altra qualità, e che questa sia caldo, io non lo credo altrimenti, e stimo, che questo sia talmente nostro, che rimosso il corpo animato, e sensitivo, il calore non resti altro che un semplice vocabolo.' (Opere, t. ii. p. 340 sq. ed. Padov. 1744.)

9.—Descartes is always adduced as the philosopher by whom the distinction in question was principally developed; and by whom, if not first established, it was, at least in modern times, first restored. In truth, however, Descartes originated nothing. He left the distinction as he found it. His only merit is that of signalizing more emphatically than had previously been done, the different character of the knowledge we are conscious of in reference to the two contrasted classes;

* But, as Aristotle has observed, we cannot imagine body without *all* colour, though we can imagine it without *any one*. In like manner where the qualities are mutual contradictories, we cannot positively represent to ourselves an object without a determination by one or other of these opposites. Thus we cannot conceive a body which is not either sapid or tasteless, either sonorous or noiseless, and so forth. This observation applies likewise to the first class

although this difference is not, as he thinks, to be explained by a mere gradation in the clearness of our perceptions. But neither of the one nor of the other is his enumeration of the contents exhaustive; nor did he bestow distinctive appellations on the counter classes themselves.—His 'Meditationes' were first published in 1641, his 'Principia' in 1644; and in these works his doctrine upon this matter is contained.

In the latter, he observes—'Nos longe alio modo cognoscere quidnam sit in viso corpore Magnitudo, vel Figura, vel Motus, (saltem localis, philosophi enim alios quosdam motus a locali diversos affingendo, naturam ejus sibi minus intelligibilem reddiderunt,) vel Situs, vel Duratio, vel Numerus, et similia, quae in corporibus clare percipi jam dictum est; quam quid in eodem corpore sit Color, vel Dolor, vel Odor, vel Sapor, vel quid aliud ex iis, quae ad sensus dixi esse referenda. Quamvis enim videntes aliquod corpus, non magis certi simus illud existere, quatenus apparet figuratum, quam quatenus apparet coloratum; longe tamen evidentius agnoscimus, quid sit in eo esse figuratum, quam quid sit esse coloratum.' (Princ. i. § 69.)

Of the *former* class we find enumerated by a collation of different passages, Magnitudo (or Extension in length, breadth, and thickness), Figure, Locomotion, Position, Duration, Number, Substance, and the like;—all (with the exception of Substance, which is erroneously and only once enumerated) corresponding with the Common Sensibles of the Peripatetics. Of the *latter* class, he instances Colours, Sounds, Odours, Savours, the Tactile qualities * in general, specially enumerating, as examples, Heat, Cold, Pain, Titillation, and (N. B.) Hardness, Weight;—all conformable to the Proper Sensibles of Aristotle.—In the one class we have an idea of the property, such as it exists, or may exist, ('ut sunt, aut saltem esse possunt,') in the external body; in the other, we have only an obscure and confused conception of a something in that body which occasions the *sensation* of which we are distinctly conscious in ourselves, but which sensation does not represent to us aught external—does not afford us a real knowledge of any thing beyond the states of the percipient mind itself. (Princ. P. i. §§. 70, 71. P. iv. §§ 191, 197, 199. —Medit. iii. p. 22. vi. pp. 43, 47, 48.—Resp. ad. Med. vi. p. 194, ed. 1658.) Of these two classes, the attributes included under the latter, in so far as they are considered as residing in the objects themselves of our sensations, Descartes, like Democritus and Galileo, held to be only modifications of those contained under the former. 'Exceptis Magnitudine, Figura et Motu, quae qualia sint in unoquoque corpore explicui, nihil extra nos positum sentitur nisi Lumen, Color, Odor, Sapor, Sonus, et Tactiles qualitates; quae nihil aliud esse in objectis, quam *dispositiones quasdam in Magnitudine, Figura et Motu consistentes*, hactenus est demonstratum. (Princ. P. iv. § 199.—Med. Resp. vi. p. 194.) This distinction, by their master, of the two classes of quality, was, as we shall see, associated by the Cartesians with another, taken by themselves,—between *Idea* and *Sensation*.

I have previously shown, that Aristotle expressly recognises the coincidence of his own distinction of the proper and common sensibles with the Democritean distinction of the apparent and real properties of body. I have now to state that Descartes was also manifestly aware of the conformity of his distinction with those of Aristotle and Democritus. Sufficient evidence, I think, will be found—of the former, in the Principia P. iv. §. 200, and De Homine §. 42;—of the latter, in the Principia P. iv. §. 200–203. All this enhances the marvel, that the identity of these famous classifications should have hitherto been entirely overlooked.

10.—The doctrine of DIGBY—an acute and independent thinker, who died in 1664—coincides with that of Aristotle and his genuine school; it is very distinctly and correctly expressed. Sensible qualities, he says, may be considered in two aspects; as they are in the *sensible object*, and as they are in the *sentient animal*. As in the latter, they exist *actually* and *formally*, constituting certain affections agreeable or disagreeable, in a word, sensations of such or such a character. The feeling of Heat is an example. As in the former, they exist only *virtually* or *potentially*; for, correctly speaking, the fire does not contain heat, and is,

* I am not aware that Descartes, any where, gives a full and formal list of the Tactile qualities. In his treatise De Homine, under the special doctrine of Touch (§§. 29, 30) we have Pain, Titillation, Smoothness, Roughness, Heat, Cold, Humidity, Dryness, Weight, '*and the like*.' He probably acquiesced in the Aristotelic list, the one in general acceptation,—viz., the Hot and Cold, Dry and Moist, Heavy and Light, Hard and Soft, Viscid and Friable, Rough and Smooth, Thick and Thin. De Gen. et Corr. ii. 2.

therefore, *not hot*, but only *capable of heating*. 'Ignis itaque, proprie loquendo, non habere calorem, atque adeo non esse *calidum* sed *calorificum*;* nisi vocabulum *caloris* sumatur pro virtute producendi calorem in animali. Sed philosophi (he refers to the scholastic Aristotelians with their substantial Forms, and Intentional Species, though among them were exceptions)—sed philosophi sunt prorsus inexcusabiles, qui volunt calorem, sumptum pro virtute calefaciendi, quae est in igne, aut potius identificatur cum ipso igne, et calorem productum in animali, esse ejusdem speciei, naturae et essentiae; nam calor moderatus productus in animali consistit in aliqua passione et quasi titillatione grata quae sentitur ab animali, quae passio non potest esse in igne.' And so forth in regard to the other senses. (Philos. Contr. Phys. p. 199.)

11.—I may adduce to the same purport GLANVILLE, who, in his 'Vanity of Dogmatizing' (1661 p. 88 sq.), and in his 'Scepsis Scientifica' (1665 p. 65 sq.), though a professed, and not overscrupulous antagonist of Aristotle, acknowledges, in reference to the present question, that 'the Peripatetic philosophy teaches us, that Heat is not in the body of the sun, as *formally* considered, but only *virtually*, and as *in its cause*.' I do not know whether Glanville had Aquinas specially in view; but the same general statement and particular example are to be found in the Summa contra Gentes, L. i. cc. 29, 31, of the Angelic Doctor.

12.—It is remarkable that MR BOYLE's speculations in regard to the classification of corporeal Qualities should have been wholly overlooked in reference to the present subject; and this not only on account of their intrinsic importance, but because they probably suggested to Locke the nomenclature which he has adopted, but, in adopting, has deformed.

In his treatise entitled 'The origin of Forms and Qualities,' published at Oxford in 1666, Boyle denominates 'Matter and Motion' 'the most Catholic Principles of bodies.' (P. 8.) 'Magnitude (Size, Bulk, or Bigness), Shape (Figure), Motion or Rest,' to which he afterwards adds 'Texture,' he styles 'the *Primitive Moods* or *Primary Affections of bodies*, to distinguish them from those less simple Qualities (as Colours, Tastes, Odours, and the like) that belong to bodies upon their account,' (p. 10). The former of these, he likewise designates '*the Primitive* or *more Catholic Affections of Matter*,' (pp. 43, 44); and in another work, (Tracts 1671, p. 18), '*the Primary and most Simple Affections of Matter*.' To the latter he gives the name of '*Secondary Qualities*, if (he says) I may so call them,' (p. 44).

In reference to the difficulty, 'That whereas we explicate colours, odours, and the like sensible qualities, by a relation to our senses, it seems evident that they have an absolute being irrelative to us; for snow (for instance) would be white, and a glowing coal would be hot, though there were no man or any other animal in the world,' (p. 42). And again (p. 49):—'So if there were no sensitive Beings, those bodies that are now the objects of our senses, would be so *dispositively*, if I may so speak, endowed with Colours, Tastes, and the like, but *actually* only with those more catholic affections of bodies, Figure, Motion, Texture, &c.' Is this intended for an Aristotelic qualification of the Democritean paradox of Galileo?

In his 'Tracts, published at Oxford 1671—in that entitled 'History of particular Qualities,' he says;—'I shall not inquire into the several significations of the word *Quality*, which is used in such various senses, as to make it ambiguous enough. But thus much I think it not amiss to intimate, that there are some things that have been looked upon as Qualities, which ought rather to be looked on as States of Matter or complexions of particular Qualities; as animal, inanimal, &c., Health, Beauty. And there are some other attributes — namely, Size, Shape, Motion, Rest, that are wont to be reckoned among Qualities, which may more conveniently be esteemed the *Primary Modes* of the parts of Matter, since from these *Simple Attributes* or *Primordial Affections*, all the Qualities are derived,' (p. 3). This is accurate; and it is to be regretted that Locke did not profit by the caution.

13.—DE LA FORGE, whose able treatise 'De l' Esprit de l' Homme' was first published in 1666, contributes little of importance to the observation of Descartes, of whose psychology he there exhibits a systematic view. To the ideas of the primary attributes, enumerated by Descartes, he inconsistently adds those of

* The chemists have called *Caloric* what they ought to have called *Calorific*. The Lavoisierian nomenclature, whatever it merits in other respects, is a system of philological monstrosities, in which it is fortunate when the analogies of language are only violated, and not reversed.

Solidity and Fluidity; and among the secondary he mentions the sensations of the Dry and the Humid, (ch. 10). In shewing that our sensations of the secondary qualities afford us no knowledge of what these are, as in the external object; and in explanation of the theories of Aristotle and Descartes, he says;—'Mais sans examiner ici lequel a le mieux rencontré, je ne pense pas qu' aucun des sectateurs de l' un ni de l' autre fassent difficulté d' avoüer que le *Sentiment* qu' excitent en lui les corps chauds ou froids, et l' *Idée* qu' il en a ne lui représente rien de tout cela.' He thus correctly places the Aristotelians and Cartesians on a level, in admitting that both equally confess our ignorance of what the secondary qualities are in themselves,—an ignorance which is commonly regarded as a notable discovery of Descartes alone.

14.—Geulinx, a Cartesian not less distinguished than De la Forge, and who with him first explicitly proclaimed the doctrine of Occasional Causes, died in 1669; but his 'Annotata' and 'Dictata' on the 'Principia' of Descartes were only published in 1690, and 1691. In these works, like most other Cartesians, he uses the term *Idea*, in reference to body, exclusively to denote the representations of its primary qualities; but he adopts the scholastic term *Species*, instead of *Sensatio* (sensation, sentiment) as employed by them, to express our consciousness of the secondary. (*Species*, De la Forge had made a better use of, in relieving an ambiguity in the philosophical language of Descartes, who had sometimes abusively usurped the word *idea* for the organic motion in the brain, to which the idea proper—the intellectual representation in the mind itself was by the law of union attached.) Geulinx is the Cartesian who, from the occasional paradox of his expression, has afforded the most valid foundation for the charge so frequently, but so erroneously, preferred against the sect, of denying all objective reality to the secondary qualities of matter.

15.—Rohault, another illustrious Cartesian whose 'Physique,' was first published in 1671, (and which continued until about the middle of last century to be a *College* text-book of philosophy in the University of Newton) may be adduced in disproof of this accusation—an accusation which will be further refuted in the sequel by the testimonies of Malebranche and Sylvain Regis.—Speaking of Heat and Cold, he says,—'Ces deux mots ont chacun deux significations. Car, premièrement, par la Chaleur et par la Froideur on entend deux *sentimens* particuliers qui sont en nous, et qui ressemblent en quelque façon à ceux qu' on nomme douleur et chatouillement, tels que les sentimens qu on a quand on approche du feu, ou quand on touche de la glace. Secondement, par la Chaleur et par la Froideur on entend le *pouvoir* que certains corps ont de causer en nous ces deux sentimens dont je viens de parler.' He employs likewise the same distinction in treating of Savours (ch. 24)—of Odours (ch. 25)—of Sound (ch. 26)—of Light and Colours (ch. 27.)

16.—Duhamel.—I quote the following passage without the comment, which some of its statements might invite, from the treatise 'De Corpore Animato,' 1673, of this learned and ingenious philosopher. It contains the most explicit (though still a very inadequate) recognition of the merits of Aristotle, in reference to our present subject, with which I am acquainted.—'Quocirca, ut id, quod sentio, paucis aperiam. Corpus omne sensibile *vim* habet in se, qua sensum moveat; sed *forma* ipsa, qua percipimus, vel est motus, vel effluvium, vel quidam substantiæ modus, quem possumus *qualitatem* appellare. Nec sensibilis solius qualitatis prædicamento continetur, sed per omnia fere vagatur genera. Corporum enim Figuræ, Dimensiones, Motus, et variæ Positiones sensum impellunt. Itaque Humor Siccitas, Duritics, Figura, atque alii modi, tales sunt, quales a nobis percipiuntur. Rotunditas enim circuli, vel terræ siccitas a sensuum cognitione non pendet. Idem fortassis erit de Colore, Luce, atque aliis activis qualitatibus judicium. Sonus vero nihil est quam percussio organi ex motione aëris, aut conflictu corporum orta. Sapor item et Odor positi sunt in sola sensus impressione. Tolle animalia, nullus erit sapor, nullus odor. Quanquam, ut mihi videtur, *rem totam optime distinguit Aristoteles, cum Patibilem Qualitatem vocat id quod in objecto est sensibili, Passionem vero eandem vocat qualitatem, ut a nobis percipitur.*' (Lib. i. c. 3, § 11.)

17.—In the following year (1674) was first published the celebrated 'Recherche de la Verité' of Malebranche. The admissions already quoted of his immediate predecessor might have guarded him, at least on the point under consideration, from the signal injustice of his attack on Aristotle, the philosophers, and mankind in general, *as confounding our subjective sensations with the objective qualities of matter;* and it is only by a not unmerited retribution, that he likewise has been made the object of a counter accusation, equally unfounded, by authorities hardly inferior to himself. Buffier,* Reid,† Royer Collard,‡ and many beside, reproach Descartes, Malebranche, Locke, and others, with advancing it, without qualification, as a new and an important truth, *that the sensible or secondary qualities have no existence in external objects, their only existence being as modes of the percipient mind.* The charge by Malebranche in the following passage, has been already annihilated, through what has been previously adduced; and the passage itself sufficiently disproves the charge *against* Malebranche.—'As regards the terms expressive of Sensible ideas, there is hardly any one who recognises that they are equivocal. On this Aristotle and the ancient philosophers have not even bestowed a thought. [!] What I state will be admitted by all who will turn to any of their works, and who are distinctly cognisant of the reason why these terms are equivocal. For there is nothing more evident, than that philosophers have believed on this subject quite the contrary of what they ought to have believed. [!!]

'For example, when the philosophers say that fire is hot, the grass green, the sugar sweet, &c., they mean, as children and the vulgar do, that the fire contains what they feel when they warm themselves; that the grass has on it the colours which they believe to be there; that the sugar contains the sweetness which they taste in eating it; and thus of all the objects of the different senses. It is impossible to doubt of it in reading their writings. They speak of sensible qualities as of sensations; they mistake motions for heat; and they thus confound, by reason of the ambiguity of these terms, the modes in which bodies with the modes in which minds, exist. [!!!]

'It is only since the time of Descartes that those confused and indeterminate questions whether fire be hot, grass green, sugar sweet, &c., have been answered by distinguishing the ambiguity of the terms in which they are expressed. If by heat, colour, savour, you understand such or such a motion of the insensible parts, then fire is hot, grass green, and sugar sweet. But if by heat and the other sensible qualities, you mean what I feel when near the fire, what I see when I look at the grass, &c., in that case the fire is not hot, nor the grass green, &c.; for the heat I feel and the colour I see are only in the soul.' (Recherche, Liv. vi. P. ii. c. 2.)

Malebranche contributed to a more precise discrimination between the objective or primary, and the subjective or secondary qualities, by restricting the term *Idea* to the former, and the term *Sensation* to the latter. For though the other Cartesians soon distinguished, more accurately than Descartes himself, Idea from Sensation, and coincided with Malebranche, in their application of the second; yet in allowing *Ideas* of the modes, both of *extension* and of *thought*, they did not so precisely oppose it to *sensation* as Malebranche, who only allowed *ideas* of *extension* and its modes. (See Recherche, L. iii. P. ii. cc. 6, 7, and relative Eclaircissement.) It has not, I believe, been observed that Locke and Leibnitz, in their counter criticisms of Malebranche's theory, have both marvellously overlooked this his peculiar distinction, and its bearing on his scheme; and the former has moreover, in consequence of neglecting the Cartesian opposition of Idea and Sensation altogether, been guilty of an egregious *mutatio elenchi* in his strictures on the Cartesian doctrine of Extension, as the essential attribute of body. (Essay, B. ii. c. 13. § 25.

18.—The 'Système de Philosophie' of the celebrated Cartesian SYLVAIN REGIS appeared in 1690. The following, among other passages of a similar import, deserve quotation from the precision with which the whole ambiguity of the terms expressive of the secondary qualities in their subjective and objective relations, is explained and rectified.

'It is evident that savours, taken *formally*, are nothing else than certain sensations (sentimens) or certain perceptions of the soul, which are in the soul itself; and that savours, taken for the *physical cause* of formal savours, consist in the particles themselves of the savoury bodies, which according as they differ in size, in figure, and in motion, diversely affect the nerves of the tongue, and thereby cause the sensation of different savours in the soul in virtue of its union with the body.' This doctrine, as the author admits, is conformable to that of Aristotle, though not to that of his scholastic followers, 'who maintain that savour in the savoury body is something similar to the sensation which we have of it.' (Phys. L. viii. P. ii. ch. 4.)

* Logique, § 222. Cours, p. 819.

† P. 131 a, second paragraph, from which there should have been a reference to the present Note.

‡ Œuvres de Reid, t. iii. pp. 380, 447.

The same, mutatis mutandis, is repeated in regard to Odours (ch. 5), and to Sounds (ch. 7); and so far, the distinction with its expression of *formal* as opposed to *virtual* is wholly borrowed from the Aristotelians.

But a more minute analysis and nomenclature are given in regard to Light and to Colour.

'The word Light is not less equivocal than those of Savour, Smell, and Sound; for it is employed sometimes to express the peculiar *sensation* which the soul receives from the impression made by luminous bodies on the eye, and sometimes to denote *what there is in those bodies by which they cause* in the soul this peculiar sensation.

'Moreover, as luminous bodies are not applied immediately to the eye, and as they act by the intervention of certain intermediate bodies, as air, water, glass, &c., whatsoever that may be which they impress on these media is also called Light, but light *Secondary* and *Derived*, to distinguish it from that which is in the luminous body, which last is styled *Primitive* or *Radical* Light.' (ch. 9.)

'We call the Sensation of Colour, *Formal* colour; the quality in bodies causing this Sensation, *Radical* colour; and what these bodies impress on the medium, *Derivative* colour.' (ch. 17.)

But this acute subdivision of objective Light and Colour into *primitive* or *radical*, and into *secondary* or *derivative*, is not original with Regis, nor indeed with any Cartesian at all. It is evidently borrowed from the following passage of Gassendi:—'Lumen, ut Simplicius ait, est quasi baculus qui uno sui extremo a sole motus, alio extremo oculum moveat: sicque motio in ipso sole (non movit quippe nisi moveatur) est ipsa *radicalis* et quasi *fontana* lux;—motio vero perspicui per omnia spatia a sole ad terram extensa, est lux diffusa *derivataque*;—et motio in oculo est *perceptio conspectiova* ipsius lucis.' (Animadv. in x. lib. Diog. Laertii. p 851.) Though apparently the whole sentence is here given as a quotation from Simplicius (or, as I suspect, Priscianus) in his commentary on the *De Anima* of Aristotle; the comparison of the staff (or more correctly of the lever) is alone his; and therefore the merit of the distinction in question would belong to Gassendi, were it not that the term *radical* was an expression common in the Schools as a synonyme of *fundamental*, and as opposed to *actual* or *formal*. The distinction is thus substantially Aristotelian.

19.—The Essay of LOCKE on the Human Understanding was published in the same year with the Système de Philosophie of Regis,—in 1690. His doctrine in regard to the attributes of bodies, in so far as these have power to produce sensations, or perceptions, or simple ideas in us, contains absolutely nothing new; and it is only in consequence of the prevalent ignorance in regard to the relative observations of previous philosophers, that so much importance has been attached to Locke's speculations on this matter. The distinction is, however, far more correctly given by him than by many of those who subsequently employed it.

Neglecting what Locke calls qualities mediately perceivable, but which lie altogether beyond the sphere of sense, being in reality powers, which, from the phænomena manifested in certain bodies, we infer to exist in other bodies of producing these phænomena as their effects—neglecting these, the following is an abstract of the doctrine given, at great length, and with much repetition, in the eighth chapter of the second book of the Essay.

a.—Locke discriminates the attributes of sensible objects into the same two classes which had been established by all his predecessors.

b.—To the one of these he gives the name of *Primary*, to the other that of *Secondary*, Qualities;* calling likewise the former *Real* or *Original*, the latter *Imputed*, Qualities.

Remark.—In this nomenclature, of which Locke is universally regarded as the author, there is nothing new. Primary or Original and Secondary or Derived Qualities had been terms applied by Aristotle and the Peripatetics to mark a distinction in the attributes of matter;—a distinction, however, not analogous to that of Locke, for Aristotle's Primary and Secondary qualities are exclusive of Locke's Primary.† But Galileo had bestowed the

* The term *Quality* ought to have been restricted to the attributes of the second class; for these are the properties of body as such or such body, (corporis ut tale corpus), whereas the others are the properties of body as body, (corporis ut corpus); a propriety of language which Locke was among the first to violate.

† Corporeal qualities, in a physical point of view, were according to *Aristotle*, (De Gen. et Corr. L. ii. and Meteor. L. iv.)—and the distinction became one classical in the Schools,—divided into *Primary* and *Secondary*; the former being original, the latter, derived.

The *Primary* are four in number, and all tactile,—Hot and Cold, Humid (Liquid) and Dry;

names of Primary or Real on the same class of attributes with Locke, leaving, of course, the correlative appellations of Secondary, Intentional, Ideal, &c. to be given to the other; while Boyle had even anticipated him in formally imposing the names of Primary and Secondary on the counter classes. It is indeed wholly impossible to doubt, from many remarkable coincidences of thought and expression, that Locke had at least the relative treatises of his countryman, friend and correspondent under his eye; and it is far more probable, that by Boyle, than by either Aristotle or Galileo, were the names suggested, under which Locke has had the honour of baptising this classical distinction.

o.—To the *first* class belong Extension (or Bulk), Solidity (or Impenetrability), Figure, Motion and Rest (or Mobility), Number;* and to these five (or six) which he once and again formally enumerates, he afterwards, without comment, throws in Situation and Texture.

Remark.—In all this there is nothing original. To take the last first:—Situation (relative Position or Ubication) was one of the Common Sensibles current in the Schools. Texture is by Boyle, in like manner, incidentally enumerated, though neither formally recognised as a co-ordinate quality, nor noticed as reducible to any other. Solidity or Impenetrability is, to go no higher, borrowed from Gassendi; De la Forge's Solidity is only the contrast of Fluidity. But Solidity and Extension ought not thus to be contra-distinguished, being attributes of body only, as constituting its one total property—that of occupying space.† The other attributes

---

and are subdivided into two classes,—the two former being *active*, the two latter, *passive*.

The *Secondary* are either less, or more, properly secondary.—The former are common to elementary and to mixed bodies; and are all potentially objects of touch. Of these Aristotle enumerates fourteen,—the Heavy and Light, the Dense and Rare, the Thick and Thin, (Concrescent and Fluid), the Hard and Soft, the Viscid and Friable, the Rough and Smooth, the Tenacious and Slippery.—The latter are Colour, Savour, Odour, [to which ought to be added Sound],—the potential objects of the senses of Sight, Taste, Smell, [and Hearing.]

This whole distinction of Qualities Primary and Secondary, is exclusive of Locke's class of Primary. To these, Aristotle would not indeed have applied the term *Quality* at all.

Cicero also may have given the hint.—'Qualitatum aliae *principes* (vel *primae*,) aliae ex iis ortae,' &c. The former are the corporeal elements, the latter the bodies constituted by them. (Acad. i. 7.)

* Locke borrowed Number (i. e. Unity or Plurality) from the Cartesians,—Descartes, from Aristotle. It corresponds in a sort with Divisibility, for which it has latterly been exchanged. See Nos. 20, 21, 22, 23, 24, 25. Locke is not therefore primarily liable to Mr Stewart's censure for the introduction of Number among the Primary Qualities, were that censure in itself correct. But it is not; for Mr Stewart (with M. Royer Collard, No 25) has misapprehended the import of the expression. (Essays p. 95 4° ed.) For Number is not used only for the measure of discrete quantity, but likewise for the continuation (unity) or discontinuation (plurality) of a percept. The former is an abstract notion; the latter is a recognition through sense. See above p. 820 a, note † and Note D. * § 1

† The term *Solidity* (τὸ στερεόν, solidum), as denoting an attribute of body, is a word of various significations; and the non-determination and non-distinction of these have given rise to manifold error and confusion.

First Meaning.—In its most unexclusive signification the Solid is that which *fills or occupies space*, (τὸ ἐπέχον τόπον.) In this meaning it is simply convertible with Body; and is opposed, 1°, to the unextended in all or in any of the three dimensions of space, and 2° to mere extension or empty space itself. This we may call *Solidity*, simply.

But the filling of space may be viewed in different phases. The conditions it involves, though all equally essential and inseparable, as all involving each other, may, however, in thought, be considered apart; from different points of view the one or the other may even be regarded as the primary; and to these parts or partial aspects, the name of the unexclusive whole may be conceded. The occupation of space supposes two necessary conditions;—and each of these has obtained the common name of Solidity, thus constituting a second and a third meaning.

Second Meaning.—What is conceived, as occupying space, is necessarily conceived *as extended in the three dimensions of space* (τὸ τριχῇ διαστατόν.) This is the phasis of Solidity which the Geometer exclusively contemplates. Trinal extension has accordingly, by mathematicians, been emphatically called the Solid; and this first partial Solidity we may therefore distinguish as the *Mathematical*, or rather, the *Geometrical*.

Third Meaning.—On the other hand, what is conceived as occupying space, is necessarily conceived as *what cannot be eliminated from space*. But this supposes a power of resisting such elimination. This is the phasis of solidity considered exclusively from the physical point of view. Accordingly, by the men of natural science the impossibility of compressing a body from an extended to an unextended has been emphatically styled Solidity; and this second partial solidity we may therefore distinguish as the *Physical*. The resisting force here involved has been called the *Impenetrability of matter*; but most improperly and most

are those of Aristotle, Descartes, and the philosophers in general;—their legitimacy will be considered in the sequel.

d.—The principle which constitutes the preceding qualities into a separate class, is that the mind finds it impossible to think any particle of matter, as divested of such attributes.

---

ambiguously. It might more appropriately be termed its *Ultimate* or *Absolute Incompressibility*.

In each of these its two partial significations, Solidity denotes an essential attribute of body; and whichsoever of these attributes be sisted as the prior, the other follows, as a necessary consequent. In regard to their priority, opinions are divided. Precedence is accorded to *trinal extension* by Descartes, at the head of one body of philosophers; to *impenetrability* by Leibnitz, at the head of another. Both parties are right; and both are wrong. Each is right as looking from its peculiar point of view; each is wrong, in not considering that its peculiar, is only a partial, point of view, and neither the one sole, nor even the one absolutely preferable.—From the *psychological* point of view, Descartes is triumphant; for extension is first in the order of thought.—From the *physical* point of view, Leibnitz is victorious; for impenetrability is the more distinctive attribute of body. The two properties, the two points of view, ought not, in truth, to be disjoined; and the definitions of body by the ancients are, as least exclusive, still the most philosophical that have been given;—τὸ τριχῇ διαστατόν, and τὸ τριχῇ διαστατὸν μετ' ἀντιτυπίας, and ὄγκος ἀντίτυπος ὅσον ἐφ' ἑαυτῷ.

Locke is therefore wrong, really and verbally.—*Really* he is wrong, in distinguishing trinal extension and impenetrability (or ultimate incompressibility) as two primary and separate attributes, instead of regarding them only as one-sided aspects of the same primary and total attribute—the occupying of space. Each supposes the other. The notion of a thing trinally extended, eo ipso, excludes the negation of such extension. It therefore includes the negation of that negation. But this is just the assertion of its ultimate incompressibility. Again, the notion of a thing as ultimately incompressible, is only possible under the notion of its trinal extension. For body being, ex hypothesi, conceived or conceivable only as that which occupies space; the final compression of it into what occupies no space goes to reduce it, either from an *entity* to a *non-entity*, or from an *extended* to an *unextended entity*. But neither alternative can be realised in thought. Not the former; for annihilation, not as a mere change in an effect, not as a mere resumption of creative power in a cause, but as a taking out from the sum total of existence, is positively and in itself incogitable. Not the latter; for the conception of matter, as an unextended entity, is both in itself inconceivable, and ex hypothesi absurd.—*Verbally*, Locke is wrong, in bestowing the name of solidity, without a qualification, exclusively on the latter of these two phases; each being equally entitled to it with the other, and neither so well entitled to it, without a difference, as the total attribute of which they are the partial expressions.—But these inaccuracies of Locke are not so important as the errors of subsequent philosophers, to which, however, they seem to have afforded the occasion. For under the term Solidity, and on the authority of Locke, there have been introduced as primary, certain qualities of body to which in common language the epithet Solid is applied, but which have no title whatever to the rank in question. Against this abuse, it must be acknowledged, Locke not only guarded himself, but even, to a certain extent, cautioned others; for he articulately states, that Solidity, in his sense, is not to be confounded with Hardness. (B. ii. c. 4 § 4.) It must, however, also be confessed, that in other passages he seems to identify Solidity and Cohesion; while on Solidity he, at the same time, makes 'the mutual impulse, resistance and protrusion of bodies to depend.' (Ibid. § 5.) But I am anticipating.

In a psychological point of view—and this is that of Locke and metaphysicians in general—no attribute of body is primary which is not necessary in thought; that is, which is not necessarily evolved out of, as necessarily implied in, the very notion of body. And such is Solidity, in the one total and the two partial significations heretofore enumerated. But in its *physical* application, this term is not always limited to denote the ultimate incompressibility of matter. Besides that necessary attribute, it is extended, in common language, to express other powers of resistance in bodies, of a character merely contingent in reference to thought. (See § ii.) These may be reduced to the five following:—

Fourth Meaning.—The term Solid is very commonly employed to denote not merely the absolutely, but also the relatively, incompressible, the Dense, in contrast to the relatively compressible, the Rare, or Hollow.—(In Latin moreover, *Solidus* was not only employed, in this sense, to denote that a thing fully occupied the space comprehended within its circumference; but likewise to indicate, 1° its *entireness in quantity*—that it was whole or complete; and, 2°, its *entireness in quality*—that it was pure, uniform, homogeneous. This arose from the original identity of the Latin *Solidum* with the Oscan *sollum* or *solum*, and the Greek ὅλον. See Festus or Verrius Flaccus, vv. *Solitaurilia* and *Solla*; also J. C. Scaliger, De Subtilitate, ex. 76.)

Fifth Meaning.—Under the *Vis Inertiae*, a body is said to be Solid, i.e. Inert, Stable, Immoveable, in proportion as it, whether in motion or at rest, resists, in general, a removal from the place it would otherwise occupy in space.

Sixth Meaning.—Under *Gravity*, a body is said to be Solid, i.e. Heavy, in proportion as it resists, in particular, a displacement by being lifted up.

The two following meanings fall under *Cohesion*, the force with which matter resists the distraction of its parts; for a body is said in a

Seventh Meaning, to be Solid, i.e. Hard, in contrast to Soft; and in an—

Remark.—In this criterion Locke was preceded by Galileo. But it does not, alone, suffice to discriminate the primary from the secondary qualities. For, as already noticed, of two contradictory qualities, one or other must, on the logical principle of excluded middle, be attributed to every object. Thus, odorous or inodorous, sapid or tasteless, &c., though not primary qualities, cannot both be abstracted in thought from any material object; and, to take a stronger example, colour, which, psychologically speaking, contains within itself such contradictions (for light and darkness, white and black, are, in this relation, all equally colours) is thus a necessary concomitant of every perception, and even every imagination, of extended substance; as has been observed by the Pythagoreans, Aristotle, Themistius, and many others.

e.—These attributes really exist in the objects, as they are ideally represented to our minds.

Remark.—In this statement Locke followed Descartes; but without the important qualification, necessary to its accuracy, under which Descartes advances it. On the doctrine of both philosophers, we know nothing of material existence in itself; we know it only as represented or in idea. When Locke, therefore, is asked, how he became aware that the known idea truly represents the unknown reality; he can make no answer. On the first principles of his philosophy, he is wholly and necessarily ignorant, whether the idea does, or does not, represent to his mind the attributes of matter, as they exist in nature. His assertion is, therefore, confessedly without a warrant; it transcends, ex hypothesi, the sphere of possible knowledge. Descartes is more cautious. He only says, that our ideas of the qualities in question represent those qualities as they are, or as they may exist;—'ut sunt, vel saltem esse possunt.' The Cosmothetic Idealist can only assert to them a problematical reality.

f.—To the *second* class belong those qualities which, as in objects themselves, are nothing but various occult modifications of the qualities of the former class; these modifications possessing, however, the power of determining certain manifest sensations or ideas in us. Such for example are colours, sounds, tastes, smells, &c.,—all, in a word, commonly known by the name of Sensible Qualities. These qualities, *as in the reality*, are properly only *powers;* powers to produce certain sensations in us. *As in us*, they are only *sensations*, and cannot, therefore, be considered as attributes of external things.

Remark.—All this had, long before Locke, become mere philosophical commonplace. With the exception of the dogmatical assertion of the hypothetical fact, that the subjective sensations of the secondary, depend exclusively on the objective modifications of the primary, qualities, this whole doctrine is maintained by Aristotle; while that hypothetical assertion itself had been advanced by the ancient Atomists and their followers the Epicureans, by Galileo, by Descartes and his school, by Boyle, and by modern philosophers in general. That the secondary qualities, as in objects, are only powers of producing sensations in us—this, as we have seen, had been explicitly stated, after Aristotle, by almost every theorist on the subject. But it was probably borrowed by Locke from the Cartesians.

It is not to be forgotten, that Locke did not observe the propriety of language introduced by the Cartesians, of employing the term *Idea*, in relation to the primary, the term *Sensation*, in relation to the secondary, qualities. Indeed Locke's whole philosophical language is beyond measure vague, vacillating, and ambiguous; in this respect, he has afforded the worst of precedents, and has found only too many among us to follow his example.

20.—Purchot's doctrine on this subject deserves to be noticed—which it never has been. It struck me from its correspondence, in certain respects, with that which I had myself previously thought out. The first edition of his Institutiones Philosophicae did not appear at Paris until a year or two after the publication of Locke's Essay,—the second was in 1698;

Eighth Meaning, to be Solid, i.e. Concrete, in opposition to Fluid.

The term Solidity thus denotes besides the absolute and necessary property of occupying space, simply and in its two phases of Extension and Impenetrability, also the relative and contingent qualities of the Dense, the Inert, the Heavy, the Hard, the Concrete; and the introduction of these latter, with their correlative opposites, into the list of Primary Qualities was facilitated, if not prepared, by Locke's vacillating employment of the vague expression Solid; in partial designation of the former. By Kames, accordingly, Gravity and Inertia were elevated to this rank; while Cohesion, in its various modifications and degrees, was, by Kames, Reid, Fergusson, Stewart, Royer Collard, and many others, not only recognised as Primary, but expressly so recognised as in conformity with the doctrine of Locke. See the sequel of this §, and § II.

but the French cursualist does not appear to have been aware of the speculations of the English philosopher, nor does he refer to Boyle. His doctrine—which is not fully stated in any single place of his work—is as follows:

a.—The one *Primary Affection* or *Attribute* of Body is *Extension*. Without this, matter cannot be conceived. But in the notion of Extension as an attribute is immediately involved that of *Solidity* or *Impenetrability*, i. e. the capacity of filling space to the exclusion of another body.

b.—But extended substance (eo ipso, solid or impenetrable)—

1°, Necessarily exists under some particular mode of Extension, in other words it has a certain *Magnitude*; and is *Divisible* into parts;

2°, Is necessarily thought as capable of *Motion* and *Rest*;

3°, Necessarily supposes a certain *Figure*; and in relation to other bodies a certain *Position*.

These five, 1, *Magnitude* or measure of extension, involving *Divisibility*; 2, Motion; 3, Rest; 4, Figure; 5, *Position* or *Situation*, he styles the *simple and secondary attributes, affections* or *qualities* which flow immediately from the nature of Body, i. e. Extension.

c.—Out of these Primary Affections of Body there are educed, and as it were compounded, other affections to which the name of *Quality* in a more emphatic and appropriate sense belongs; such among others are *Light, Colours, Sounds, Odours, Tastes*, and the *Tactile qualities, Heat Cold, Moisture, Dryness*, &c. These he denominates the *secondary and composite qualities or affections of Body*. (Instit. Philos. t. ii. Phys. Sect. i. iv. v. pp. 87, 205, 306, ed 4)

21.—Le Clerc does not borrow his doctrine on this head from his friend Locke; and his point of view is not purely psychological. The five properties common to all bodies—Extension—Divisibility—Solidity (Impenetrability)—Figure—Mobility—he very properly does not denominate *Qualities*, but reserves that name for what serves to distinguish bodies from each other Under this restriction, he divides Qualities into *Primitive* and *Derivative*. By Primitive he designates those occult qualities in body which are known to us only in their effects; as, for example, the cause of Solidity. The Derivative, he says, are those which flow from the Primitive and affect our senses, as colour, savour, odour, &c. His doctrine is, however, neither fully evolved nor unambiguously expressed. (Clerici Opera Philos. Phys. L. v. cc. 1, 6.)

22.—Lord Kames, in the *first* edition of his 'Essays on the principles of Morality and Natural Religion,' (1751,) touches only incidentally on the present subject. He enumerates *Softness, Hardness, Smoothness, Roughness*, among the Primary Qualities (p. 248); and he was, I am confident, the only philosopher before Reid, by whom this amplification was sanctioned, although Mr Stewart has asserted that herein Reid only followed the classification of most of his immediate predecessors.* (Essays, p. 91.) The *second* edition I have not at hand. In the *third* and last, (1779,) there is introduced a chapter expressly on the distinction, which is treated of in detail. He does not here repeat his previous enumeration; but to *Size, Figure, Solidity* (which he does not define) and *Divisibility*, he adds, as primary qualities, *Gravity*, the *Vis Inertiae*, and the *Vis Insita*; the two last being the Vis Insita or Vis Inertiae of Kepler and Newton divided into a double power. See Reid's Correspondence, pp. 55, 56. Kames unwittingly mixes the psychological and physical points of view; and, otherwise, his classification, in so far as original, is open to manifold objections. See the foot-note † at p. 837 c, and § ii.

23.—Reid.—We have seen that Descartes and Locke, to say nothing of other metaphysicians, admitted a fundamental difference between the primary and the secondary qualities: the one problematically, the other assertorily, maintaining, that the primary qualities, as known, correspond with the primary qualities, as existent; whereas that the secondary qualities, as sensations in us, bear no analogy to these qualities as inherent in matter. On the general doctrine, however, of these philosophers, both classes of qualities, as known, are confessedly only states of our own minds; and, while we have no right from a subjective affection to infer the existence, far less the corresponding character of the existence, of any objective reality, it is evident that their doctrine, if fairly evolved, would result in a dogmatic, or in a sceptical, negation of the primary, no less than of the secondary

* Mr Stewart also says that Berkeley 'employs the word Solidity as synonymous with Hardness and Resistance.' This is not correct. Berkeley does not consider hardness and resistance as convertible; and these he mentions as two only out of three significations in which, he thinks, the term Solidity is used.

qualities of body, as more than appearances in and for us. This evolution was accordingly soon accomplished; and Leibnitz, Berkeley, Hume, Condillac, Kant, Fichte, and others, found no difficulty in demonstrating, on the principles of Descartes, and Locke, and modern Representationists in general, that our notions of Space or Extension, with its subordinate forms of Figure, Motion, &c., have no higher title to be recognized as objectively valid, than our sensations of Colour, of Savour, of Odour; and were thus enabled triumphantly to establish their several schemes of formal or virtual idealism. Hence may we explain the fact that this celebrated distinction is overlooked or superseded in the speculation, not of some merely, but of all the more modern German Schools.

It is therefore manifest that the fundamental position of a consistent theory of dualistic realism is—that our cognitions of Extension and its modes are not wholly ideal;—that although Space be a native, necessary, a priori, form of imagination, and so far, therefore, a mere subjective state, that there is, at the same time, competent to us, in an *immediate* perception of external things, the *consciousness* of a really existent, of a really objective, *extended* world. To demonstrate this was therefore prescribed, as its primary problem to a philosophy which, like that of Reid, proposed to re-establish the philosophy of natural realism—of common sense, on a refutation of every idealism overt or implied. Such is the problem. It remains for us to see how it was dealt with.

Reid's doctrine, in regard to the Primary and Secondary Qualities, is to be found in the Inquiry, ch. 5, sect. 4–6, p. 123–126, and in the Intellectual Powers Essay ii. ch. 17, p. 313–318.

In his enumeration of the Primary qualities Reid is not invariable; for the list in the Inquiry is not identical with that in the Essays. In the former, without professing to furnish an exhaustive catalogue, he enumerates *Extension, Figure, Motion, Hardness* and *Softness, Roughness* and *Smoothness*. The four last are, as we have seen, to be found, for the first time, in the earliest edition of Lord Kames's Essays on Morality, which preceded Reid's Inquiry by thirteen years. In the latter he gives another list, which he does not state to be an altered edition of his own, but which he apparently proposes as an enumeration identical with Locke's. 'Every one,' he says, 'knows that *Extension, Divisibility, Figure, Motion, Solidity, Hardness, Softness*, and *Fluidity*, were by Locke called primary qualities of body.' In reference to himself—this second catalogue omits *Roughness* and *Smoothness*, which were contained in his first: and introduces, what were omitted in the first, *Divisibility* (which Kames had also latterly added), *Solidity* and *Fluidity*. In reference to Locke—this and the former list are both very different from his. For, allowing *Divisibility* to replace *Number*, and saying nothing in regard, either to the verbal inaccuracy of making *Motion* stand for *Mobility*, or to the real inaccuracy of omitting *Rest* as the alternative of *Motion*; we find in both lists a series of qualities unrecognized as primary by Locke; or, as far as I know, by any other philosopher previous to Lord Kames and himself. These are *Roughness* and *Smoothness*, in the Inquiry; *Fluidity* in the Essays; and *Hardness* and *Softness* in both. But these five qualities are not only not to be ascribed to the list of primary qualities by Locke; they ought not to be viewed as co-ordinate with *Extension, Solidity* (which Reid more rigorously than Locke limits to the ultimate incompressibility of matter), *Figure, Mobility*, and *Divisibility*, i.e. not as primary qualities at all. Of these five qualities, the last three, as he himself states (p. 314 a), are only different degrees of *Cohesion*; and the first two are only modifications of *Figure* and *Cohesion* combined. But Cohesion, as will be shewn (§ ii.), is not a character necessarily involved in our notion of body; for though Cohesion, (and we may say the same of Inertia,) in all its modes, necessarily supposes the occupation of space, the occupation of space while it implies a continuity does not necessarily imply a cohesion of the elements (whatever they may be) of that which occupies space. At the same time, the various resistances of cohesion and of inertia cannot be reduced to the class of Secondary qualities. It behoves us therefore, neither with Locke and others, to overlook them; nor to throw them in without qualification or remark, either with Descartes among the Secondary, or with Reid among the Primary, qualities. But of this again.

Independently of these minor differences, and laying also out of account Reid's strictures on the cruder forms of the representative hypothesis, as held by Descartes and Locke, but which there is no sufficient ground to suppose that Descartes, at least, adopted; Reid's doctrine touching the present distinction corresponds, in all essential respects, with that maintained by these two philosophers. He does not adopt, and even omits to notice, the erroneous criterion of inseparability in thought, by which Locke attempts to discriminate the primary qualities from the secondary. Like Descartes, he holds that our notions of the primary qualities are clear and distinct; of the secondary, obscure and confused; and, like both philosophers, he considers that the former afford us a knowledge of what the corresponding qualities are (or, as Descartes cautiously interpolates *may be*) in themselves, while the latter only point to the unknown cause or occasion of sensations of which we are conscious ourselves. Reid therefore calls the notion we have of the primary qualities, *direct*; of the secondary, *relative*. (I. P. 313 b.) On this subject there is, thus, no important difference of opinion between the three philosophers. For if we modify the obnoxious language of Descartes and Locke; and, instead of saying that the ideas or notions of the primary qualities *resemble*, merely assert that they *truly represent*, their objects, that is, afford us such a knowledge of their nature as we should have were an immediate intuition of the extended reality in itself competent to man,—and this is certainly all that one, probably all that either philosopher, intended,—Reid's doctrine and theirs would be found in perfect unison. The whole difficulty and dispute on this point is solved on the old distinction of *similarity in existence*, and *similarity in representation*, which Reid and our more modern philosophers have overlooked. Touching this, see, as stated above, the doctrine of those Schoolmen who held the hypothesis of species, (p. 814 b); and of those others who, equally with Reid, rejected all representative entities different from the act itself of cognition, (p. 813 b. note.)

But much more than this was called for at Reid's hands. His philosophy, if that of Natural Realism, founded in the common sense of mankind, made it incumbent on him to shew, that we have not merely a notion, a conception, an imagination, a subjective representation—of Extension, for example, 'called up or *suggested*,' in some incomprehensible manner to the mind, on occasion of an extended object being presented to the sense; but that in the perception of such an object, we really have, as by nature we believe we have, an immediate knowledge or consciousness of that external object, *as extended*. In a word, that in sensitive perception the extension, as known, and the extension, as existing, are convertible; known, because existing, and existing, since known.

Reid however, unfortunately, did not accomplish—did not attempt this. He makes no articulate statement, even, that in perception we have an immediate knowledge—an objective consciousness, of an extended non-ego, actually existing; as in imagination we have a subjective consciousness of a mode of the ego, representing such an extended non-ego, and thereby affording us a mediate knowledge of it as possibly existing. On the contrary were we to interpret his expressions rigidly, and not in liberal conformity with the general analogy of his philosophy, we might, as repeatedly noticed, found on the terms in which he states his doctrine of the primary qualities, and, in particular, his doctrine concerning our cognition of extension, a plausible argument that his own theory of perception is as purely subjective, and therefore as easily reducible to an absolute Idealism, as that of any of the philosophers whom he controverts.

Thus when Reid, for example, (Inq. 123 b.) states 'that Extension is a quality *suggested* to us by certain sensations,' i. e. by certain merely subjective affections; and when (324 b.) he says 'that Space [Extension] whether tangible or visible, is not so properly an object of sense as a necessary *concomitant* of the objects both of sight and touch;' he apparently denies us all immediate perception of any extended reality. But if we are not percipient of any extended reality, we are not percipient of body as existing; for body exists, and can only be known immediately and in itself, *as extended*. The material world, on this supposition, sinks into something unknown and problematical; and its existence, if not denied, can, at best, be only precariously affirmed, as the occult cause, or incomprehensible occasion, of certain subjective affections we experience in the form, either of a sensation of the secondary quality, or of a perception of the primary. Thus interpreted, what is there to distinguish the doctrine of Reid from the undeveloped idealism of Descartes or of Kant? See Note C. § ii. p. 820 b, sq.

Having noticed the manifest incongruity of Reid's doctrine on this point with the grand aim of his philosophy,—an incongruity which I am surprised has not been long ago adverted to either by friend or foe,—I may take this opportunity of modifying a former statement, (p. 123 b, note *)—that, according to Reid, Space is a notion a posteriori, the result of experience. On reconsidering more carefully his different statements on this subject, (Inq. 123 sq. I. P. 324 sq.), I am now inclined to think that his language implies no more than the chronological posteriority of this notion; and that he really held it to be a native, necessary, a priori form of thought, requiring only certain prerequisite conditions to call it from virtual into manifest existence. I am confirmed in this view by finding it is also that of M. Royer Collard. Mr Stewart is however less defensible, when he says, in opposition to Kant's doctrine of Space—'I rather lean to the common theory which supposes our first ideas of Space or Extension to be *formed* by *other* qualities of matter.' (Dissertation, &c. p. 281, 2d ed.)

Passing over the less important observations of several intermediate philosophers in the wake of Reid, I proceed to the most distinguished of his disciples.

24.—Stewart, while he agrees with his master in regard to the contrast of Primary and Secondary Qualities, proposes the following subdivision, and change of nomenclature in reference to the former. 'I distinguish,' he says, 'Extension and Figure by the title of *the mathematical affections of matter*; restricting the phrase *primary qualities* to Hardness and Softness, Roughness and Smoothness, and other properties of the same description. The line which I would draw between *primary* and *secondary* qualities is this; that the former necessarily involve the notion of *extension*, and consequently of *externality* or *outness*; whereas the latter are only conceived as the unknown causes of known sensations; and when *first apprehended by the mind* do not imply the existence of any thing locally distinct from the subjects of its own self-consciousness.' (Essays, p. 94.)

The more radical defects of this ingenious reduction are, as they appear to me, the following:

1°, That it does not depart from the central notion of body—from Solidity Absolute, the occupying of space. (See p. 837 c, note †) In logical propriety Extension and Figure are not proximately attributes of body but of space; and belong to body only as filling space. Body supposes them; they do not suppose body; and the inquiry is wholly different in regard to the nature of extension and figure as space, and of the extended and figured as body.

2°, This original defect in the order of evolution, has led, however, to more important consequences. Had Mr Stewart looked at Extension (Solidity Mathematical), as a property of body, in virtue of body filling space, he would not only not have omitted, but not have omitted as an attribute co-ordinate with extension, the Ultimate Incompressibility or Impenetrability of body, (Solidity Physical.)

3°, But while omitting this essential property, the primary qualities which, after Reid, he enumerates, (Hardness, Softness, Roughness, Smoothness,) are, as already noticed, and to be hereafter shewn, not primary, not being involved in the necessary notion of body. For these are all degrees or modifications of Cohesion; but a Cohesion of its ultimate elements it is not necessary to think as a condition or attribute of matter at all. See § ii. Moreover, Roughness and Smoothness, as more than the causes of certain *sensations* in us, therefore only *secondary* qualities, are modifications, not only of Cohesion, but of Figure, and would, therefore, on Mr Stewart's distribution, fall under the category of the Mathematical Affections of Body.

As regards the great problem of Natural Realism,—to prove that we have an immediate perception of the primary qualities of body,—this was left by Mr Stewart where it was left by Reid.

25.—The last philosopher to be adduced is the illustrious founder of the Scoto-Gallican School, M. Royer Collard. The sum of his doctrine touching the Primary Qualities is given in the following passage, which I translate from the Fragments of his Lectures, published by M. Jouffroy as Appendices to his version of the Works of Reid, (Vol. iii. p. 429 sq.);—Fragments which, with M. Jouffroy's general Preface, I have reason to hope will be soon given to the British public by a translator eminently qualified for the task. My observations I find it most convenient to subjoin in the form of notes; and admiring as I do both the attempt itself and the ability of its author, I regret to differ here so widely, not only from the doctrines which M. Royer Collard holds in common with other philosophers, but from those which are peculiar to himself. On the former, however, in so far as, with his more immediate predecessors, he confounds in one class qualities which I think ought to be discriminated into two, I deem it unnecessary to make any special comment; as this matter, which has been already once and again adverted to, is to be more fully considered in the sequel. (§ ii.) As to the latter, it will be seen that the more important differences arise from the exclusive point of view from which M. Royer Collard has chosen to consider the Qualities in question.

'Among the Primary Qualities, that of *Number* is peculiar to Locke.* It is evident that Number, far from being a quality of matter, is only an abstract notion, the work of intellect and not of sense.†

'*Divisibility* is proper to Reid.‡ On this quality and *Mobility* I will observe, that neither ought to have been placed among the qualities manifested through sense; and yet this is what Reid understands by the Primary Qualities, for he distinguishes them from the Secondary by this—that we have of the former a direct notion.§ *Divisibility* is known to us by division; and a body divided is known to us, as such, by memory. For did we not recollect that it had previously been one, we should not know that it is at present two; we should be unable to compare its present with its past state; and it is by this comparison alone that we become aware of the fact of division. Is it said that the notion of *Divisibility* is not acquired by the fact of division, but that it presents itself immediately to the mind prior to experience? In this case it is still more certain that it is not a cognition proper to sense.¶

'As to the notion of *Mobility* it is evidently posterior to that of motion;†† that of motion supposes not less evidently the exercise of memory and the idea of time; it is thus not derived exclusively from sense.‡‡ As Divisibility also supposes motion, this again is an additional proof that the notion of divisibility is not immediate.

'*Figure* is a modification of *Extension*.

'*Solidity*, *Impenetrability*, *Resistance*, are one and the same thing; §§ *Hardness*, *Softness*, *Fluidity*, are modifications of Solidity and its different degrees; while the *Roughness* and *Smoothness* of surfaces express only sensations attached to certain perceptions of Solidity.

'The Primary Qualities may be thus generalized, if I may so express myself, into *Extension* and *Solidity*.'

---

* Number is, with Locke, common to Aristotle and the Aristotelians, Galileo, Descartes, and the Cartesians, &c.

† Number, as an abstract notion, is certainly not an object of sense. But it was not as an abstract notion intended by the philosophers to denote an attribute of Body. This misprision was expressly guarded against by the Aristotelians See Toletus in Aristotelem De Anima, L. ii. c. 6, qu. 15. Number may be said to correspond to Divisibility; see p. 829 a, and p. 837 a. If it cannot be said that sense is percipient of objects as many, it cannot be said to be percipient of an object as one. Perception, moreover, is a consciousness, and consciousness is only realised under the condition of plurality and difference. Again, if we deny that through sense we perceive a plurality of colours, we must deny that through sense we perceive a figure or even a line. See Note E. And if three bodies are not an object of sense, neither is a triangle. Sense and intellect cannot thus be distinguished. See Note D*, § 1.

‡ Sundry philosophers preceded Reid in making Divisibility (which corresponds also to Number) one of the Primary Qualities. See Nos. 20, 21, 22.

§ M. Royer Collard not only takes his point of view exclusively from Sense; but sense he so limits, that, if rigorously carried out, no sensible perception, as no consciousness, could be brought to bear. See Note D*, § 1. The reason he gives why Reid must be held as of the same opinion, I do not understand. Psychologically speaking, an attribute would not be *primary* if it could be thought away from body; and the notion of body being supposed given, every primary quality is to be evolved out of that notion, as necessarily involved in it, independently altogether of any experience of sense. In this respect, such quality is an object of intellect. At the same time, a primary quality would not be an attribute of body, if it could not, contingently, to some extent, at least, be apprehended as an actual phaenomenon of sense. In this respect, such quality is an object of perception and experience.

¶ I am afraid that this, likewise, is a misapprehension of the meaning of the philosophers. Divisibility, in their view, has nothing to do with the process of dividing. It denotes either the alternative attribute, applicable to all body, of unity or plurality; or the possibility that every single body may, as extended, be sundered into a multitude of extended parts Every material object being thus, though actually one, always potentially many, it is thus convertible with Number; see foot-note †.

†† *Mobility*, as applied in this relation, is merely a compendious expression for the alternative attributions of *motion or rest*; and both of these, as possible attributes, are involved in the notion of body. See § ii. of this Excursus.

‡‡ Compare above pp. 830 a, 831 a. But Perception can no more be separated from all memory than from all judgment; for consciousness involves both. See Note D*, § 1.

§§ This is only correct from M. Royer Collard's exclusive point of view—from sense alone. On the various meanings of the term *Solidity*, see p. 837, note †. The confusion also resulting from the ambiguity of the word *Impenetrability* as denoting both a resistance absolute and insuperable, and a resistance relative and superable, both what is necessary, and what is contingent to body, is here shown, either in the reduction to a single category of qualities of a wholly heterogeneous character, or in the silent elimination of the higher.

The distinction of these different classes of material qualities has, as already noticed, no real importance, no real foundation, on the hypothesis of Idealism, whether absolute or cosmothetic,—in no philosophy, indeed, but that of Natural Realism; and its recognition, in the systems of Descartes and Locke, is, therefore, with them a superficial observation, if not a *hors d'œuvre*. It was, accordingly, with justice formally superseded, because virtually null, in the philosophy of Leibnitz, the complement of the Cartesian, and in the philosophy of Condillac, the complement of the Lockian. The Kantian system, again, is built on its positive negation, or rather its positive reversal. For Kant's transcendental Idealism not only contains a general assertion of the subjectivity of all our perceptions; its distinctive peculiarity is, in fact, its special demonstration of the absolute subjectivity of Space or Extension, and in general of the primary attributes of matter; these constituting what he calls the *Form*, as the Secondary constitute what he calls the *Matter*, of our Sensible intuitions. (See, in particular, Proleg., § 13, Anm. 2.) This, I repeat, may enable us to explain why the discrimination in question has, both in the intellectualism of Germany and in the sensualism of France, been so generally overlooked; and why, where in relation to those philosophers by whom the distinction has been taken, any observations on the point have been occasionally hazarded, (as by Tetens with special reference to Reid,) that these are of too perfunctory a character to merit any special commemoration.*

Such, then, are the forms under which the distinction of the Primary and Secondary Qualities of Body has been presented, from its earliest promulgation to its latest development. In this historical survey, I have to acknowledge no assistance from the researches of preceding inquirers; for what I found already done in this respect was scanty and superficial, even when not positively erroneous. Every thing had thus anew to be explored and excavated. The few who make a study of philosophy in its sources, can appreciate the labour of such a research; and from them, at least, I am sure of indulgence for the imperfections of what I offer, not as a history, but as a hasty collection of some historical materials.

§ II.—*Distinction of the Primary and Secondary Qualities of Body critically considered.*

From what has been said in the foregoing section, it will be seen that I am by no means satisfied with the previous reduction of the Qualities of Body to two classes of Primary and Secondary. Without preamble, I now go on to state what I deem their true and complete classification; limiting the statement, however, to little more than an enouncement of the distribution and its principles, not allowing myself to enter on an exposition of the correlative doctrine of perception, and refraining, in general, from much that I might be tempted to add, by way of illustration and support.

The Qualities of Body I divide into *three* classes.

Adopting and adapting, as far as possible, the previous nomenclature—the first of these I would denominate the class of *Primary*, or *Objective*, Qualities; the second, the class of *Secundo-Primary*, or *Subjectivo-Objective*, Qualities; the third, the class of *Secondary*, or *Subjective*, Qualities.

* To this also are we to attribute it, that the most elaborate of the recent histories of philosophy among the Germans, slur over, if they do not positively misconceive, the distinction in question. In the valuable expositions of the Cartesian doctrine by the two distinguished Hegelians, Feuerbach and Erdmann, it obtains from the one no adequate consideration, from the other no consideration at all. In the Lectures on the History of Philosophy by their illustrious master, a work in which the erudition is often hardly less remarkable than the force of thought, almost every statement in reference to the subject is, to say the least of it, inaccurate. Hegel, as he himself employs, apparently makes Aristotle and Descartes employ, the term Solidity simply for Hardness. This, however, neither one nor other ever does; while by Locke, the terms are even expressly distinguished. (Vol. iii. pp 360, 431.) He confounds Descartes' distinction (baptised by Locke that) of the Primary and Secondary qualities, with Descartes' distinction of the Primitive and Derivative attributes of body; distinctions not coincident, though not opposed. Figure, for example, in the one is primary, but not in the other primitive. In regard to his criticism of Locke, (p. 431,) suffice it to say, that Locke, so far from opposing, in fact *follows* Descartes in making "Figure and so forth" primary qualities; nor does Descartes denominate any class of qualities "secondary."—(pp. 350, 430.) Finally, Aristotle's distinction of "external qualities" into primary and secondary, if this be referred to, corresponds with that so styled by Locke only in the name.

The general point of view from which the Qualities of Matter are here considered is not the *Physical*, but the *Psychological*. But, under this, the ground or principle on which these qualities are divided and designated is, again, twofold. There are, in fact, within the psychological two special points of view; that of *Sense*, and that of *Understanding*. Both of these ought to be taken, but taken separately, into account in a classification like the present; and not, as has been often done, either one only adopted or both fortuitously combined. Differing, however, as these widely do from each other, they will be found harmoniously to conspire in establishing the threefold distribution and nomenclature of the qualities in question which I have ventured to propose.

The point of view chronologically prior, or first to us, is that of *Sense*. The principle of division is here the different circumstances under which the qualities are originally and immediately *apprehended*. On this ground, as apprehensions or immediate cognitions through Sense, the *Primary* are distinguished as *objective*, not subjective,* as *percepts proper*, not sensations proper; the *Secundo-primary*, as *objective and subjective*, as *percepts proper and sensations proper*; the *Secondary*, as *subjective*, not objective, cognitions, as *sensations proper*, not percepts proper.

The other point of view chronologically posterior, but first in nature, is that of *Understanding*. The principle of division is here the different character under which the qualities, already apprehended, are *conceived* or construed to the mind in thought. On this ground, the *Primary*, being thought as *essential* to the notion of Body, are distinguished from the *Secundo-primary* and *Secondary*, as *accidental*; while the *Primary* and *Secundo-primary*, being thought as *manifest or conceivable in their own nature*, are distinguished from the *Secondary*, as in *their own nature occult and inconceivable*. For the notion of Matter having been once acquired, by reference to that notion, the Primary Qualities are recognized as its a priori or necessary constituents; and we clearly conceive how they must exist in bodies in knowing what they are objectively in themselves; the Secundo-primary Qualities, again, are recognized as a posteriori or contingent modifications of the Primary, and we clearly conceive how they do exist in bodies in knowing what they are objectively in their conditions; finally, the Secondary Qualities are recognized as a posteriori or contingent accidents of matter, but we obscurely surmise how they may exist in bodies only as knowing what they are subjectively in their effects.

It is thus apparent that the Primary Qualities may be *deduced a priori*, the bare notion of matter being given; they being, in fact, only evolutions of the conditions which that notion necessarily implies: whereas the Secundo-primary and Secondary must be *induced a posteriori*; both being attributes contingently superadded to the naked notion of matter. The Primary Qualities thus fall more under the point of view of Understanding, the Secundo-primary and Secondary, more under the point of view of Sense.

Deduction of the Primary Qualities.—Space or Extension is a necessary form of thought. We cannot think it as non-existent; we cannot but think it as existent. But we are not so necessitated to imagine the reality of aught occupying space; for while unable to conceive as null the space in which the material universe exists, the material universe itself we can, without difficulty, annihilate in thought. All that exists in, all that occupies, space, becomes, therefore, known to us by experience: we acquire, we construct, its notion. The notion of space is thus native or *a priori*; the notion of what space contains, adventitious or *a posteriori*. Of this latter class is that of Body or Matter.

But on the hypothesis, always, that body has been empirically apprehended, that its notion has been acquired;—What are the a priori characters in and through which we *must* conceive that notion, if conceived it be at all, in contrast to the a posteriori characters under which we *may*, and probably *do*, conceive it, but under which, if we conceive it not, still the notion itself stands unannihilated? In other words, what are the necessary or essential, in contrast to the contingent or

* *All* knowledge, in one respect, is *subjective*; for all knowledge is an energy of the Ego. But when I perceive a quality of the Non-Ego, of the object-object, as in immediate relation to my mind, I am said to have of it an *objective* knowledge; in contrast to the *subjective* knowledge, I am said to have of it when supposing it only as the hypothetical or occult cause of an affection of which I am conscious, or thinking it only mediately through a subject object or representation in, and of, the mind. But see below, in footnote to Par. 15, and first footnote to Par. 16.

accidental properties of Body, as apprehended and conceived by us? The answer to this question affords the class of Primary, as contradistinguished from the two classes of Secundo-primary and Secondary Qualities.

Whatever answer may be accorded to the question—How do we come by our knowledge of Space or trinal extension? it will be admitted on all hands, that whether given solely a priori as a native possession of the mind, whether acquired solely a posteriori as a generalization from the experience of sense, or whether, as I would maintain, we at once must think Space as a necessary notion, and do perceive the extended in space as an actual fact; still, on any of these suppositions, it will be admitted, that we are only able to conceive Body as that which (I.) *occupies space*, and (II.) *is contained in space.*

But these catholic conditions of body, though really simple, are logically complex. We may view them in different aspects or relations, which, though like the sides and angles of a triangle, incapable of separation, even in thought, supposing as they do each other, may still, in a certain sort, be considered for themselves, and distinguished by different appellations.

I.—The property of *filling space* (Solidity in its unexclusive signification, *Solidity Simple*) implies two correlative conditions: (A) the *necessity of trinal extension, in length, breadth, and thickness,* (*Solidity geometrical*;) and (B) the corresponding *impossibility of being reduced from what is to what is not thus extended,* (*Solidity Physical, Impenetrability.*)

A.—Out of the absolute attribute of Trinal Extension may be again explicated three attributes, under the form of necessary relations:—(i.) *Number* or *Divisibility;* (ii.) *Size, Bulk,* or *Magnitude;* (iii.) *Shape* or *Figure.*

i.—Body necessarily exists, and is necessarily known, either as one body or as many bodies. *Number,* i. e. the alternative attribution of unity or plurality, is thus, in a first respect, a primary attribute of matter. But again, every single body is also, in different points of view, at the same time one and many. Considered as a *whole,* it is, and is apprehended, as actually one; considered as an *extended* whole, it is, and is conceived, potentially many. Body being thus necessarily known, if not as already divided, still as always capable of division, *Divisibility* or *Number* is thus likewise, in a second respect, a primary attribute of matter. (See pp. 829 a, 837 a.)

ii.—Body (multo majus this or that body) is not infinitely extended. Each body must therefore have a certain finite extension, which by comparison with that of other bodies must be less, or greater, or equal; in other words, it must by relation have a certain Size, Bulk, or Magnitude; and this, again, as estimated both (a) by the quantity of space occupied, and (b) by the quantity of matter occupying, affords likewise the relative attributes of *Dense* and *Rare.*

iii.—Finally, bodies, as not infinitely extended, have, consequently, their extension bounded. But bounded extension is necessarily of a certain *Shape or Figure.*

B.—The negative notion—the impossibility of conceiving the compression of body from an extended to an unextended, its elimination out of space—affords the positive notion of an insuperable power in body of resisting such compression or elimination. This force, which, as absolute, is a conception of the understanding, not an apprehension through sense, has received no precise and unambiguous name; for *Solidity,* even with the epithet *Physical,* and *Impenetrability* and *Extreity* are vague and equivocal.—(See p. 837 b, note †.) We might call it, as I have said, *Ultimate* or *Absolute Incompressibility.* It would be better, however, to have a positive expression to denote a positive notion, and we might accordingly adopt, as a technical term, *Autantitypy.* This is preferable to *Antitypy* (ἀντιτυπία,) a word in Greek applied not only to this absolute and essential resistance of matter, *qua* matter, but also to the relative and accidental resistances from cohesion, inertia, and gravity.

II.—The other most general attribute of matter—that of *being contained in space*—in like manner affords, by explication, an absolute and a relative attribute: viz., (A) the *Mobility,* that is the possible motion, and, consequently, the possible rest, of a body; and (B) the *Situation, Position, Ubication,* that is, the local correlation of bodies in space. For

A.—Space being conceived as infinite, (or rather being inconceivable as not infinite,) and the place occupied by body as finite, body in general, and, of course, each body in particular, is conceived capable either of remaining in the place it now holds, or of being translated from that to any then unoccupied part of space. And

B.—As every part of space, i.e., every potential *place,* holds a certain position relative to every other, so, consequently, must bodies, in so far as they are all contained in space, and as each occupies, at one time, one determinate place.

To recapitulate:—The necessary constituents of our notion of Matter, the Primary Qualities of Body, are thus all evolved from the two catholic conditions of matter—(I.) the occupying space, and (II.) the being contained in space. Of these the former affords (A) *Trinal Extension*, explicated again into (i.) *Divisibility*, (ii.) *Size*, containing under it *Density* or *Rarity*, (iii.) *Figure;* and (B) *Ultimate Incompressibility:* while the latter gives (A) *Mobility;* and (B) *Situation*. Neglecting subordination, we have thus eight proximate attributes; 1, Extension; 2, Divisibility; 3, Size; 4, Density, or Rarity; 5, Figure; 6, Incompressibility absolute; 7, Mobility; 8, Situation.

The primary qualities of matter thus develope themselves with rigid necessity out of the simple datum of—*substance occupying space*. In a certain sort, and by contrast to the others, they are, therefore, notions *a priori*, and to be viewed, *pro tanto*, as products of the understanding. The others, on the contrary, it is manifestly impossible to *deduce*, i.e., to evolve out of such a given notion. They must be *induced*, i.e., generalized from experience; are, therefore, in strict propriety, notions *a posteriori*, and, in the last resort, mere products of sense. The following may be given as consummative results of such induction in the establishment of the two classes of the Secundo-primary and Secondary Qualities.

Induction of the Class of Secundo-primary Qualities.—This terminates in the following conclusions.—These qualities are modifications, but contingent modifications, of the Primary. They suppose the Primary; the Primary do not suppose them. They have all relation to space, and motion in space; and are all contained under the category of Resistance or Pressure. For they are all only various forms of a relative or superable resistance to displacement, which, we learn by experience, bodies oppose to other bodies, and, among these, to our organism moving through space;—a resistance similar in kind (and therefore clearly conceived) to that absolute or insuperable resistance, which we are compelled, independently of experience, to think that every part of matter would oppose to any attempt to deprive it of its space, by compressing it into an inextended.

In so far, therefore, as they suppose the primary, which are necessary, while they themselves are only accidental, they exhibit, on the one side, what may be called a quasi primary quality; and, in this respect, they are to be recognised as percepts, not sensations, as objective affections of things, and not as subjective affections of us. But, on the other side, this objective element is always found accompanied by a secondary quality or sensorial passion. The Secundo-primary qualities have thus always two phases, both immediately apprehended. On their Primary or objective phasis they manifest themselves as *degrees* of resistance opposed to our locomotive energy; on their secondary or subjective phasis, as *modes* of resistance or pressure affecting our sentient organism. Thus standing between, and, in a certain sort, made up of the two classes of Primary and Secondary qualities, to neither of which, however, can they be reduced; this their partly common, partly peculiar nature, vindicates to them the dignity of a class apart from both the others, and this under the appropriate appellation of the Secundo-primary qualities.

They admit of a classification from two different points of view. They may be *physically*, they may be *psychologically*, distributed.—Considered *physically*, or in an objective relation, they are to be reduced to classes corresponding to the different sources in external nature from which the resistance or pressure springs. And these sources are, in all, three:—(I.) that of *Co-attraction;* (II.) that of *Repulsion;* (III.) that of *Inertia*.

I.—Of the resistance of *Co-attraction* there may be distinguished, on the same objective principle, two subaltern genera; to wit (A) that of *Gravity*, or the co-attraction of the particles of body in general; and (B) that of *Cohesion*, or the co-attraction of the particles of this and that body in particular.

A.—The resistance of Gravity or Weight according to its degree, (which, again, is in proportion to the Bulk and Density of ponderable matter,) affords, under it, the relative qualities of *Heavy* and *Light* (absolute and specific.)

B.—The resistance of Cohesion (using that term in its most unexclusive universality) contains many species and counter-species. Without proposing an exhaustive, or accurately subordinated, list;—of these there may be enumerated, (i.) the *Hard* and *Soft;* (ii.) the *Firm* (Fixed, Stable, Concrete, Solid,) and *Fluid* (Liquid,) the Fluid being again subdivided into the *Thick* and *Thin;* (iii.) the

Viscid and *Friable*; with (iv.) the *Tough* and *Brittle* (Irruptile and Ruptile); (v.) the *Rigid* and *Flexible*; (vi.) the *Fissile* and *Infissile*; (vii.) the *Ductile* and *Inductile* (Extensible and Inextensible); (viii.) the *Retractile* and *Irretractile* (Elastic and Inelastic); (ix.) (combined with Figure) the *Rough* and *Smooth*; (x.) the *Slippery* and *Tenacious*.

II.—The resistance from *Repulsion* is divided into the counter qualities of (A.) the (relatively) *Compressible* and *Incompressible*; (B.) the *Resilient* and *Irresilient* (Elastic and Inelastic.)

III.—The resistance from *Inertia* (combined with Bulk and Cohesion) comprises the counter qualities of the (relatively) *Moveable* and *Immoveable*.

There are thus, at least, fifteen pairs of counter attributes which we may refer to the Secundo-primary Qualities of Body;—all obtained by the division and subdivision of the resisting forces of matter, considered in an objective or physical point of view. (Compare Aristotle, Meteor. L. iv., c. 8.)

Considered *psychologically*, or in a subjective relation, they are to be discriminated, under the genus of the *relatively Resisting*, (I.) according to the *degree* in which the resisting force might counteract our locomotive faculty or muscular force; and, (II.) according to the *mode* in which it might affect our capacity of feeling or sentient organism. Of these species, the former would contain under it the gradations of the quasi-primary quality, the latter the varieties of the secondary quality—these constituting the two elements of which, in combination, every Secundo-primary quality is made up. As, however, language does not afford us terms by which these divisions and subdivisions can be unambiguously marked, I shall not attempt to carry out the distribution, which is otherwise sufficiently obvious, in detail.—So much for the induction of the Secundo-primary qualities.

But it has sometimes been said of the Secundo-primary qualities as of the Primary, that they are necessary characters in our notion of body; and this has more particularly been asserted of Gravity, Cohesion, and Inertia. This doctrine, though never brought to proof, and never, I believe, even deliberately maintained, it is, however, necessary to show, is wholly destitute of foundation.

That Gravity, Cohesion, Inertia, and Repulsion, in their various modifications, are not conceived by us as necessary properties of matter, and that the resistances through which they are manifested do not therefore, psychologically, constitute any primary quality of body;—this is evident, 1°, from the historical fact of the wavering and confliction of philosophical opinion, in regard to the nature of these properties; and, 2°, from the response afforded to the question by our individual consciousness. These in their order:—

1.—The vacillation of philosophical opinion may be shown under two heads, to wit, from the Psychological, and from the Physical, point of view.

As to the *Psychological point of view*, the ambiguous, and at the same time the unessential, character of these qualities, is shown by the variation of philosophers in regard to which of the two classes of Primary or Secondary they would refer them; for the opinion, that philosophers are in this at one, is an error arising from the perfunctory manner in which this whole subject has hitherto been treated. Many philosophers in their schemes of classification, as Galileo, Boyle, Le Clerc, overlook, or at least omit to enumerate these qualities. In point of fact, however, they undoubtedly regarded them as *Sensible*, and therefore, as we shall see, as *Secondary*, qualities. The great majority of philosophers avowedly consider them as secondary. This is done, implicitly or explicitly, by Aristotle and the Aristotelians, by Galen, by Descartes * and his school, by Locke,† by Purchot, &c.; for these philosophers refer Hardness, Softness, Roughness, Smoothness, and the like, to the Tactile qualities—the sensible qualities of Touch; while they identify the sensible qualities in general, that is, the sensations proper of the several senses, with the class of Secondary, the percepts

* See, besides what is said under Descartes, No. 9, Regis, Phys. L. viii. P. ii., ch. 2. Spinoza, Princ. Philos. Cartes. P. ii., Lem. 2, pr. 1.

† Compare Essay B. ii., c 3, § 1, and c. 4, § 4, and c. 8, §§ 14, 23; with Lee's Notes B. ii., c. 8, § 4, p. 56. Looking superficially at certain casual ambiguities of Locke's language, we may, with Kames, Reid, and philosophers in general, suppose him to have referred the qualities in question to the class of Primary. Looking more closely, we may hold him to have omitted them altogether, as inadvertently stated at p. 841 b. But, looking critically to the whole analogy of the places now quoted, and, in particular, considering the import of the term "sensible qualities," as then in ordinary use, we can have no doubt that, like the Peripatetics and Descartes, he viewed them as pertaining to the class of Secondary.

common to more than a single sense, with the class of Primary, qualities. In this Aristotle, indeed, is found not always in unison with himself; or rather, at different times he views as proximate the different phases presented by the qualities in question. For though in general he regards the Rough and the Smooth as sensations proper to Touch, (De Gen. et Corr. ii. 2, et alibi,) on one occasion he reduces these to the class of common percepts, as modifications of Figure. (De Sensu et Sensili, c. 4.) Recently, however, without suspecting their confliction with the older authorities, nay, even in professed conformity with the doctrine of Descartes and Locke, psychologists have, with singular unanimity, concurred in considering the qualities in question as Primary. For to say nothing of the anomalous and earlier statements of De La Forge and Du Hamel, (Nos. 13, 14,) and passing over, as hardly of psychological import, the opinion of Cotes, (Praef. ad Newtoni Princ. ed. 2,) this has been done by Kames, Reid, Fergusson, Stewart, and Royer Collard—philosophers who may be regarded as the authors or principal representatives of the doctrine now prevalent among those by whom the distinction is admitted.

Looking, therefore, under the surface at the state of psychological opinion, no presumption, assuredly, can be drawn from the harmony of philosophers against the establishment of a class of qualities different from those of Primary and Secondary. On the contrary, the discrepancy of metaphysicians not only with each other, but of the greatest even with themselves, as to which of these two classes the qualities I call Secundo-primary should be referred, does, in fact, afford a strong preliminary probability that these qualities can with propriety be reduced to neither; themselves, in fact, constituting a peculiar class, distinct from each, though intermediate between both.

As to the *Physical point of view*, I shall exhibit in detail the variation of opinion in relation to the several classes of those qualities which this point of view affords.

a.—*Gravity*. In regard to weight, this, so far from being universally admitted, from the necessity of its conception, to be an essential attribute of body, philosophers, ancient and modern, very generally disallow all matter to be heavy; and many have even dogmatically asserted to certain kinds of matter a positive levity. This last was done by Aristotle, and his Greek, Arabian, and Latin followers; i.e., by the philosophic world in general for nearly two thousand years. At a recent period, the same doctrine was maintained, as actually true, by Gren and other advocates of the hypothesis of Phlogiston, among many more who allowed its truth as possible; and Newton had previously found it necessary to clothe his universal æther with a quality of negative gravity, (or positive lightness,) in order to enable him hypothetically to account for the phænomenon of positive gravity in other matter.

Of Gravity, some, indeed, have held the cause to be internal and essential to matter. Of these we have the ancient atomists, (Democritus, Leucippus, Epicurus, &c.,) with Plato and a few individual Aristotelians, as Strato and Themistius; and in modern times a section of the Newtonians, as Cotes, Freind, Keill, with Boscovich, Kant, Kames, Schelling, and Hegel. But though holding (physically) weight to be, de facto, an essential property of matter, these philosophers were far from holding (psychologically) the character of weight to be an essential constituent of the notion of matter. Kant, for example, when speaking psychologically, asserts that weight is only a synthetic predicate which experience enables us to add on to our prior notion of body, (Cr. d. r. Vern. p. 12, ed. 2.—Proleg. § 2, p. 25, ed. 1.); whereas, when speaking physically, he contends that weight is an universal attribute of matter, as a necessary condition of its existence. (Met. Anfangsgr. d. Naturwiss. p. 71, ed. 2.)

But the latter opinion—that weight is only, in reality, as in thought, an accident of body—is that adopted by the immense majority, not only of philosophers but of natural philosophers. Under various modifications, however; some, for example, holding the external cause of gravity to be physical, others to be hyperphysical. Neglecting subordinate distinctions, to this class belong Anaxagoras, Democritus, Melissus, Diogenes of Apollonia, Aristotle and his school, Algazel, Avicembron, Copernicus, Bruno, Keppler, Gilbert, Berigardus, Digby, Torricelli, Descartes, Gassendi, Lana, Kircher, Andala, Malebranche, Rohault, De Guericke, Perrault, H. More, Cudworth, Du Hamel, Huygens, Sturmius, Hooke, Is. Vossius, Newton, S. Clarke, Halley, Leibnitz, Saurin, Wolf, Mueller, Bilfinger, the Bernoullis James and John, Canz, Hamberger, Varignon, Viliemot, Fatio, Euler, Baxter, Colden, Saussure, Le Sage,

L'Huillier, Prevost, De Luc, Monboddo, Horsley, Drummond, Playfair, Blair, &c. In particular, this doctrine is often and anxiously inculcated by Newton — who seems, indeed, to have sometimes inclined even to an immaterial cause; but this more especially after his follower, Cotes, had ventured to announce an adhesion to the counter theory, in his preface to the second edition of the 'Principia,' which he procured in 1713. See Newton's letter to Boyle, 1678 — Letters, second and third, to Bentley, 1693;—Principia, L. I. c. 5. L. iii. reg. 3, alibi;—in particular, Optics, ed. 1717, B. iii. Qu. 21.

b. — *Cohesion*, comprehending under that term not only Cohesion proper, but all the specific forces, (Adhesion, Capillarity, Chemical Affinity, &c.,) by which the particles of individual bodies tend to approach, and to maintain themselves in union—Cohesion is even less than Gravity, than the force by which matter in general attracts matter, a character essential to our notion of body. Upon Gravity, indeed, a majority of the earlier Newtonians maintained Cohesion, in some inexplicable manner, to depend; and the other hypotheses of an external agency, all proceed upon the supposition that it is merely an accident of matter. Cohesion, the cause of which Locke wisely regarded as inconceivable, Descartes attempted to explain by the quiescence of the adjoining molecules; Malebranche, (as an occasional cause,) by the agitation of a pervading invisible matter; Stair, by the pressure (whence, he does not state) of the physical points, his supposed constituents of body, to a common centre; and James Bernoulli, by the pressure of a circumambient fluid,—an hypothesis to which Newton likewise seems to have inclined: while a host of others, following Algazel and Avicembron, Biel and D'Ailly, spurned all mechanical media, these being themselves equally inexplicable as the phænomenon in question, and resorted to the immediate agency of an immaterial principle. The psychologists, therefore, who (probably from confounding hardness with solidity, solidity with impenetrability) have carried up the resistance of cohesion into the class of primary qualities, find but little countenance for their procedure, even among the crude precedents of physical speculation.

c.—*Vis Inertiæ*. But if, on the ground of philosophical agreement, Gravity and Cohesion are not to be regarded as primary qualities of matter; this dignity is even less to be accorded to that force by which bodies resist any change of state, whether that be one of quiescence or of motion. This, variously known under the names of Vis Inertiæ, Inertia, Vis Insita Resistentiæ, Resistentia Passiva, &c., was, indeed, if not first noticed, only first generalized at a comparatively recent period—to wit, by Keppler; while the subsequent controversies in regard to its nature and comprehension, equally concur in showing that there is no necessity for thinking it as an essential attribute of matter. The Cartesians, among others, viewed it as a quality not only derivative but contingent; and even those Newtonians who, in opposition to Newton, raised Gravity to the rank of a primary quality, did not, however, venture to include inertia under the same category. (See Cotes's Preface to the second edition of the Principia.) Leibnitz, followed, among others, by Wolf, divided this force into two;—discriminating the *vis activa* or *motrix*, from the *vis passiva* or *inertia*. The former they held not to be naturally inherent in, but only supernaturally impressed on, matter. Without reference to Leibnitz, a similar distinction was taken by D'Alembert, in which he is followed by Destutt de Tracy; a distinction, as we have seen, which also found favour with Lord Kames, who in this, however, stands alone, among metaphysicians, that he places both his *vis inertiæ* and *vis incita* among the primary qualities of body.

Finally, Physical speculators, in general, distinguish Inertia and Weight, as powers, though proportional, still distinct. Many, however, following Wiedeburg, view the former as only a modification or phasis of the latter.

d.—*Repulsion*, meaning by that term more than the resistance of impenetrability, gravity, cohesion, or inertia, has, least of all, authority to plead in favour of its pretension to the dignity of a primary quality. The dynamical theories of matter, indeed, view Attraction and Repulsion not merely as fundamental qualities, but even as its generic forces; but the ground of this is the necessity of the hypothesis, not the necessity of thought.

2.—But the voice of our individual consciousness is a more direct and cogent evidence than the history of foreign opinion;—and this is still less favourable to the claim in question. The only resistance which we think as necessary to the conception of body, is a resistance to the occupation of a body's space—the resistance of ultimate incompressibility. The others, with their causes, we think only as contingent, because, one and all of them we can easily annihilate in thought.

Repulsion (to take them backwards)—a resistance to the approximation and contact of other matter—we come only by a late and learned experience to view as an attribute of body, and of the elements of body; nay, so far is it from being a character essential in our notion of matter, it remains, as apparently an *actio in distans*, even when forced upon us as a fact, still inconceivable as a possibility. Accordingly, by no philosopher has the resistance of Repulsion been psychologically regarded as among the primary qualities.

Nor has *Inertia* a greatly higher claim to this distinction. There is no impossibility, there is little difficulty, in imagining a thing, occupying space, and therefore a body; and yet, without attraction or repulsion for any other body, and wholly indifferent to this or that position, in space, to motion and to rest; opposing, therefore, no resistance to any displacing power. Such imagination is opposed to experience, and consequently to our acquired habitudes of conceiving body; but it is not opposed to the necessary conditions of that concept itself.

It was on this psychological ground that Descartes reduced inertia to a mere accident of extension. Physically reasoning, Descartes may not perhaps be right; but Kames is certainly, as he is singularly, wrong, in psychologically recognizing Inertia as a primary attribute of body.

Of the two attractions, *Cohesion* is not constituent of the notion of what occupies, or is trinally extended in, space This notion involves only the supposition of parts out of parts; and although what fills an uninterrupted portion of space, is, pro tanto, considered by us as one thing; the unity which the parts of this obtain in thought, is not the internal unity of cohesion, but the external unity of continuity or juxtaposition. Under the notion of repletion of space, a rock has not in thought a higher unity than a pile of sand. Cohesion, consequently, is not, in a psychological view, an essential attribute of body. [In saying this, I may notice parenthetically, that I speak of cohesion only as between the ultimate elements of body, *whatever these may be;* and fortunately our present discussion does not require us to go higher, that is to regard cohesion in reference to our conception of these considered in themselves. In forming to ourselves such concept, two counter inconceivabilities present themselves:—inconceivabilities from the one or other of which, as speculators have recoiled, they have embraced one or other of the counter theories of Atomism and Dynamism.] But if cohesion be not thought as an essential attribute of body, Kames, Reid, Fergusson, Stewart, Royer Collard, and other recent philosophers, were wrong to introduce the degrees of cohesive resistance among the primary qualities; either avowedly, under the explicit titles of the Hard, the Soft, &c., or covertly, under the ambiguous head of Solidity. But though Locke did not, as they believe, precede them in this doctrine, his language, to say the least of it, is unguarded and inaccurate. For he employs *cohesion* and *continuity* as convertible terms; and states, without the requisite qualification, that 'upon the solidity [to him the impenetrability or ultimate incompressibility] of bodies depend their mutual impulse, resistance and protrusion.' (ii. 4, 5.)

As to *Weight*,—we have from our earliest experience been accustomed to find all tangible bodies in a state of gravitation; and, by the providence of nature, the child has, even anteriorly to experience, an instinctive anticipation of this law in relation to his own. This has given weight an advantage over the other qualities of the same class; and it is probably through these influences, that certain philosophers have been disposed to regard gravity, as, physically and psychologically, a primary quality of matter. But instinct and consuetude notwithstanding, we find no difficulty in imagining the general co-attraction of matter to be annihilated; nay, not only annihilated, but reversed. For as attraction and repulsion seem equally *actiones in distans*, it is not more difficult to realize to ourselves the notion of the one, than the notion of the other.

In reference to both Cohesion and Gravity, I may notice, that though it is only by experience we come to attribute an internal unity to aught continuously extended, that is, consider it as a system or constituted whole; still, in so far as we do so consider it, we think the parts as held together by a certain force, and the whole, therefore, as endowed with a power of resisting their distraction. It is, indeed, only by finding that a material continuity resists distraction, that we view it as more than a fortuitous aggregation of many bodies, that is, as a single body. The material universe, for example, though not de facto continuously extended, we consider as one system, in so far, but only in so far, as we find all bodies tending together by reciprocal attraction. But here I may add, that though a love of unity may bias us, there is no necessity for supposing this co-attraction to be the effect of any single force. It may be the result of any plurality of forces, provided that these co-operate in due subordination. Thus we are not constrained to view the universe of matter as held together by the power of gravity alone. For though gravity be recognised as the prime, proximate, and most pervading principle of co-attraction, still, until the fact be proved, we are not required to view it as the sole. We may suppose that a certain complement of parts are endowed with weight; and that the others, immediately and in themselves indifferent to gravitation, are mediately drawn within its sphere, through some special affinity or attraction subsisting between them and the bodies immediately subjected to its influence. Let the letters A, B, C, x, y, z, represent in general the universe of matter; the capital letters representing, in particular, the kinds of matter possessed of, the minor letters representing the kinds of matter destitute of, weight. Of themselves, A, B, C will, therefore, gravitate; x, y, z will not. But if x have a peculiar affinity for A, y for B, and z for C; x, y, z, though in themselves weightless, will, through their correlation to A, B, C, come mediately under the influence of gravitation, and enter along with their relatives, as parts, into the whole of which gravity is the proximate bond of unity. To prove, therefore, a priori, or on any general principle whatever, that no matter is destitute of weight, is manifestly impossible. All matter may possibly be heavy; but until experiment can decide, by showing, in detail, that what are now generally regarded as imponderable fluids, are either in truth ponderable substances, or not substances at all, we have no data on which to infer more than a conjectural affirmative of little probability. On the dynamical theories of matter, the attempts made from Boscovich to Hegel to demonstrate, that weight is a catholic property, as a fundamental condition, of matter, are all founded on petitory premises. This is justly acknowledged by Hegel himself of the Kantian deduction, (Werke, Vol. vii. P. i. § 202); and, were the proof of psychological concernment, the same might no less justly be demonstrated of his own.*

Induction of the Secondary Qualities. — Its results are the following.—The Secondary as manifested to us, are not,

* Since writing the above, I am indebted to the kindness of Mr Whewell for his 'Demonstration that all Matter is Heavy,' published in the Transactions of the Cambridge Philosophical Society, Vol. vii., Part II.;—an author whose energy and talent all must admire, even while convinced the least by the cogency of his reasoning. As this demonstration proceeds not on a mere physical ground, but on the ground of a certain logical or psychological law, and as it is otherwise diametrically opposed to the whole tenor of the doctrine previously maintained, I shall briefly consider it in its general bearing;—which Mr Whewell thus states, afterwards illustrating it in detail:—

'The question then occurs, whether we can, by any steps of reasoning, point out an inconsistency in the conception of matter without weight. This I conceive we may do, and this I shall attempt to show.—The general mode of stating the argument is this:—The quantity of matter is measured by those sensible properties of matter [Weight and Inertia] which undergo quantitative addition, subtraction, and division, as the matter is added, subtracted, and divided. The quantity of matter cannot be known in any other way. But this mode of measuring the quantity of matter, in order to be true at all, must be universally true. If it were only partially true, the limits within which it is to be applied would be arbitrary; and, therefore, the whole procedure would be arbitrary, and, as a method of obtaining philosophical truth, altogether futile.' [But this is not to be admitted. 'We must suppose the rule to be universal. If any bodies have weight all bodies must have weight.']

1°. This reasoning assumes in chief that we cannot but have it in our power, by some means or other, to ascertain the quantity of matter as a physical truth. But gratuitously. For why may not the quantity of matter be one of that multitude of problems, placed beyond the reach, not of human curiosity, but of human determination?

2°. But, subordinate to the assumption that some measure we *must* have, the reasoning further supposes that a measure of the weight (and inertia) is the *only* measure we *can* have of the quantity of matter. But is even this correct? We may, certainly, attempt to estimate the quantity of matter by the quantity of *two*, at least, of the properties of matter; to wit—a) by the quantity of space of which it is found to resist the occupation; and—b) by the quantity of weight (and inertia), which it manifests. We need not enquire, whether, were these measures harmonious in result, they would, in combination, supply a competent criterion; for they are at variance; and, if either, one must be exclusively selected. Of the two, the former, indeed, at first sight,

in propriety, qualities of Body at all. As apprehended, they are only subjective affections, and belong only to bodies in so far as these are supposed furnished with the powers capable of specifically determining the various parts of our nervous apparatus to the peculiar action, or rather passion, of which they are susceptible; which determined action or passion is the quality of which alone we are immediately cognisant, the external concause of that internal effect remaining to perception altogether unknown. Thus, the Secondary qualities (and the same is to be said, mutatis mutandis, of the Secundo-primary) are, considered subjectively, and considered objectively, affections or qualities of things diametrically opposed in nature—of the organic and inorganic, of the sentient and insentient, of mind and matter: and though, as mutually correlative, and their several pairs rarely obtaining in common language more than a single name, they cannot well be considered, except in conjunction, under the same category or general class; still their essential contrast of character must be ever carefully borne in mind. And in speaking of these qualities, as we are here chiefly concerned with them on their subjective side, I request it may be observed, that I shall employ the expression *Secondary qualities* to denote those phænomenal affections determined in our sentient organism by the agency of external bodies, and not, unless when otherwise stated, the occult powers themselves from which that agency proceeds.

Of the Secondary qualities, in this relation, there are various kinds; the variety principally depending on the differences of the different parts of our nervous apparatus. Such are the proper sensibles, the idiopathic affections of our several organs of sense, as Colour, Sound, Flavour, Savour, and Tactual sensation; such are the feelings from Heat, Electricity, Galvanism, &c.; nor need it be added, such are the muscular and cutaneous sensations which accompany the perception of the Secundo-primary qualities. Such, though less directly the result of foreign causes, are Titillation, Sneezing, Horripilation, Shuddering, the feeling of what is called Setting-the-teeth-on-edge, &c., &c.; such, in fine, are all the various sensations of bodily pleasure and pain determined by the action of external stimuli.—So much for the induction of the Secondary Qualities in a subjective relation.

It is here, however, requisite to add some words of illustration.—What are denominated the secondary qualities of body, are, I have said, as apprehended, not qualities of body at all; being only idiopathic affections of the different portions of our nervous organism—affections which, however uniform and similar in us, may be determined by the most dissimilar and multiform causes in external things. This is manifest from the physiology of our senses and their appropriate nerves. Without entering on details, it is sufficient to observe, that we are endowed with

---

recommends itself as the alone authentic. For the quantity of matter is, on all hands, admitted to be in proportion to the quantity of space it fills, extension being necessarily thought as the essential property of body; whereas it is not universally admitted that the quantity of matter is in proportion to its amount of weight and inertia; these being, on the contrary, conceivable, and generally conceived, as adventitious accidents, and not, therefore, as necessary concomitants of matter.—But, then, it may be competently objected,—The cubical extension of compressed bodies cannot be taken as an authentic measure of the quantity of space they fill, because we are not assured that the degree of compressing force which we can actually apply is an accurate index of what their cubical extension would be, in a state of ultimate or closest compression. But though this objection must be admitted to invalidate the certainty of the more direct and probable criterion, it does not, however, leave the problem to be determined by the other; against which, indeed, it falls to be no less effectually retorted. For as little, at least, can we be assured that there is not (either separately, or in combination with gravitating matter) substance occupying space, and, therefore, material, but which, being destitute of weight, is, on the standard of ponderability, precisely as if it did not exist. This supposition, be it observed, the experiments of Newton and Bessel do not exclude. Nay, more; there are, in fact, obtruded on our observation a series of apparent fluids, (as Light or its vehicle, the Calorific, Electro-galvanic and Magnetic agents,) which, in our present state of knowledge, we can neither, on the one hand, denude of the character of substance, nor, on the other, clothe with the attribute of weight.

3°. This argument finally supposes, as a logical canon, that a presumption from analogy affords a criterion of truth, subjectively necessary, and objectively certain. But not the former; for however inclined, we are never necessitated, a posteriori, to think, that because *some are*, therefore *all* the constituents of a class *must be*, the subjects of a predicate a priori contingent. Not the latter; for though a useful stimulus and guide to investigation, analogy is, by itself, a very doubtful guarantee of truth

various assortments of nerves; each of these being astricted to certain definite functions; and each exclusively discharging the function which specially belongs to it. Thus there are nerves of feeling, (comprehending under that term the sensations of cutaneous touch and feeling proper, of the muscular sense, and of the vital sense, or sensus vagus, in all its modifications,) of seeing, of hearing, of smelling, of tasting, &c.

The nerves of feeling afford us sensations to which, in opposite extremes, we emphatically, if not exclusively, attribute the qualities of pain and pleasure. Acute pain—pain from laceration may, indeed, be said to belong exclusively to these; for the nerves appropriated to the other and more determinate senses, are like the brain in this respect altogether insensible, and it is even probable that the pain we experience from their over-excitement is dependent on the nerves of feeling with which they are accompanied. Now pain and pleasure no one has ever attributed as qualities to external things: feeling has always been regarded as purely subjective, and it has been universally admitted that its affections, indicating only certain conscious states of the sentient animal, afforded no inference even to definite causes of its production in external nature. So far there is no dispute.

The case may, at first sight, seem different with regard to the sensations proper to the more determinate senses; but a slight consideration may suffice to satisfy us that these are no less subjective than the others;—as is indeed indicated in the history already given of the distinction of Primary and Secondary qualities. As, however, of a more definite character, it is generally, I believe, supposed that these senses, though they may not precisely convey material qualities from external existence to internal knowledge, still enable us at least to infer the possession by bodies of certain specific powers, each capable exclusively of exciting a certain correlative manifestation in us. But even this is according greatly too large a share in the total sensitive effect to the objective concause. The sensations proper to the several senses depend, for the distinctive character of their manifestation, on the peculiar character of the action of their several nerves; and not, as is commonly supposed, on the exclusive susceptibility of these nerves for certain specific stimuli. In fact every the most different stimulus (and there are many such, both extra and intra-organic, besides the one viewed as proper to the sense,) which can be brought to bear on each several nerve of sense, determines that nerve only to its one peculiar sensation. Thus the stimulus by the external agent exclusively denominated Light, though the more common, is not the only, stimulus which excites in the visual apparatus the subjective affection of light and colours. Sensations of light and colours, are determined among other causes, *from within*, by a sanguineous congestion in the capillary vessels of the optic nerve, or by various chemical agents which affect it through the medium of the blood; *from without*, by the application to the same nerve of a mechanical force, as a blow, a compression, a wound, or of an imponderable influence, as electricity or galvanism. In fact, the whole actual phænomena of vision might be realized to us by the substitution of an electro-galvanic stimulus, were this radiated in sufficient intensity from bodies, and in conformity with optical laws. The blind from birth are thus rarely without all experience of light, colour and visual extension, from stimulation of the interior organism.—The same is the case with the other senses. Apply the aforementioned or other extraordinary stimuli to their several nerves; each sense will be excited to its appropriate sensation, and its appropriate sensation alone. The passion manifested (however heterogeneous its external or internal cause) is always,—of the auditory nerves, a sound, of the olfactory, a smell, of the gustatory, a taste. But of the various common agencies which thus excite these several organs to their idiopathic affection, we are manifestly no more entitled to predicate the individual colour, sound, odour, or savour of which, in each case, we have a sensation, than we are to attribute the pain we feel to the pin by which we are pricked. But if this must per force be admitted of the extraordinary external causes of these sensations, it is impossible to deny it of the ordinary.

In this respect Aristotle, (and the same may also be said of Theophrastus,) was far in advance of many of our modern philosophers. In his treatise on Dreams, to prove that sensation is not a purely objective cognition, but much more a subjective modification or passion of the organ, he shows, and with a detail very unusual to him, that this sensible affection does not cease with the presence, and, therefore, does not manifest the quality, of the external object. 'This (he says) is apparent so often as we have the sensation of a thing for a certain continuance. For then, divert as we may the sense from one object to another, still the affection from the first accompanies the second; as (for example) when we pass from sunshine into shade. In this case we at first see nothing, because of the movement in the eyes still subsisting, which had been determined by the light. In like manner if we gaze for a while upon a single colour, say white or green, whatever we may now turn our sight on will appear of that tint. And if, after looking at the sun or other dazzling object, we close our eyelids, we shall find, if we observe, that, in the line of vision, there first of all appears a colour such as we had previously beheld, which then changes to red, then to purple, until at last the affection vanishes in black;'—with more to the same effect. (C. 2.) And in the same chapter he anticipates modern psychologists in the observation—that 'Sometimes, when suddenly awoke, we discover, from their not incontinently vanishing, that the images which had appeared to us when asleep are really movements in the organs of sense; and to young persons it not unfrequently happens, even when wide awake, and withdrawn from the excitement of light, that moving images present themselves so vividly, that for fear they are wont to hide themselves under the bed-cloaths.' (C. 2.) See also *Ockham*, in Sent. L. ii. qq. 17, 18.—*Biel*, in Sent. L. ii. Dist. iii. q. 2.—*Berigardus*, Circulus Pisanus P. vi. Circ. 12, ed. 2.—*Hobbes*, Human Nature, ch. ii. § 7-10.—*Boerhaave*, Prælectiones in proprias Institutiones, §§ 284, 579.—*Sprengel*, Semiotik § 770-773; Pathelogie, vol. ii. § 719.—*Gruithuisen*, Anthropologie, § 449.—*Sir Charles Bell*, An Idea, &c. (in Shaw's Narrative, p. 35, sq.;) The Hand, &c., p. 175, sq.—*Plateau*, Essai d'une Theorie, &c., p. .—*J. Mueller*, Physiology, Book v., Preliminary Considerations, p. 1059, sq., Engl. Transl.

Such being the purely subjective character of the Secondary qualities, as apprehended or immediately known by us, we must reject as untenable the doctrine on this point, however ingeniously supported, of the celebrated Neapolitan philosopher, Baron Galluppi; who, while, justly I think, dissatisfied with the opinion of Reid, that the perception of the primary qualities is a conception instinctively suggested on occasion of our sensation of the secondary, errs on the opposite extreme, in his attempt to show that this sensation itself affords us what is wanted,—an immediate cognition, an objective apprehension, of external things. The result of his doctrine he thus himself states:—'*Sensation is of its very nature objective; in other words, objectivity is essential to every sensation.*' Elementi di Filosofia, vol. i. c. 10, ed. 4. Florence, 1837. The matter is more amply treated in his Critica della Conoscenza, L. ii. c. 6, and L. iv.—a work which I have not yet seen. Compare Bonelli, Institutiones Logico-Metaphysicæ, t. i. pp. 184, 222, ed. 2, 1837.

Such is a general view of the grounds on which the psychological distinction of the Qualities of Body, into the three classes of Primary, Secundo-primary, and Secondary is established. It now remains to exhibit their mutual differences and similarities more in detail. In attempting this, the following order will be pursued.—I shall state of the three relative classes,—(A) *What they are, considered in general;* then, (B) *What they are, considered in particular.* And under this latter head I shall view them, (1°) *as in Bodies;* (2°) *as in Cognition;* and this (a) *as in Sensitive Apprehension;* (b) *as in Thought;* (c) *as in both.*—For the conveniency of reference the paragraphs will be numbered.

A.—*What they are in general.*

1. The Primary are less properly denominated Qualities (Suchnesses,) and deserve the name only as we conceive them to distinguish body from not-body,—corporeal from incorporeal substance. They are thus merely the attributes of *body as body,—corporis ut corpus.* The Secundo-primary and Secondary, on the contrary, are in strict propriety denominated Qualities, for they discriminate body from body. They are the attributes of *body as this or that kind of body,—corporis ut tale corpus.**

2. The Primary arise from the universal relations of body to itself; the Secundo-primary from the general relations of this body to that; the Secondary from the special relations of this kind of body to this kind of animated or sentient organism.

3. The Primary determine the possibility of matter absolutely; the Secundo-

* Thus, in the Aristotelic and other philosophies, the title *Quality* would not be allowed to those fundamental conditions on which the very possibility of matter depends, but which modern philosophers have denominated its Primary Qualities.

primary, the possibility of the material universe as actually constituted; the Secondary, the possibility of our relation as sentient existences to that universe.

4. Under the Primary we apprehend modes of the Non-ego; under the Secundo-primary we apprehend modes both of the Ego and of the Non-ego; under the Secondary we apprehend modes of the Ego, and infer modes of the Non-ego. (See par. 15.)

5. The Primary are apprehended as they are in bodies; the Secondary, as they are in us; the Secundo-primary, as they are in bodies, and as they are in us. (See par. 15.)

6. The term *quality* in general, and the names of the several qualities in particular, are—in the case of the Primary, univocal, one designation unambiguously marking out one quality;*—in the case of the Secundo-primary and Secondary, equivocal, a single term being ambiguously applied to denote two qualities, distinct though correlative—that, to wit, which is a mode of existence in bodies, and that which is a mode of affection in our organism.† (See par. 24.)

7. The Primary, and also the Secundo-primary qualities, are definite in number and exhaustive; for all conceivable relations of body to itself, or of body to body merely, are few, and all these found actually existent. The Secondary, on the contrary, are in number indefinite; and the actual hold no proportion to the possible. For we can suppose, in an animal organism, any number of unknown capacities of being variously affected; and, in matter, any number of unknown powers of thus variously affecting it;‡ and this though we are necessarily unable to imagine to ourselves what these actually may be.

B.—*What they are in particular; and* 1°, *Considered as in Bodies.*

8. The Primary are the qualities of body in relation to our organism, as a body simply; the Secundo-primary, are the qualities of body in relation to our organism, as a propelling, resisting, cohesive body; the Secondary are the qualities of body in relation to our organism, as an idiopathically excitable and sentient body. (See p. 854 b—856 a.)

9. Under this head we know the Primary qualities immediately as objects of perception; the Secundo-primary, both immediately as objects of perception and mediately as causes of sensation, the Secondary, only mediately as causes of sensation. In other words:—The Primary are known immediately in themselves; the Secundo-primary, both immediately in themselves and mediately in their effects on us; the Secondary, only mediately in their effects on us. (See par. 15.)

10. The Primary are known under the condition of sensations; the Secundo-primary, in and along with sensations; the Secondary, in consequence of sensations. (See par. 20.)

11. The Primary are thus apprehended objects; the Secondary, inferred powers; the Secundo-primary, both apprehended objects and inferred powers.

12. The Primary are conceived as necessary and perceived as actual; the Secundo-primary are perceived and conceived as actual; the Secondary are inferred and conceived as possible.

13. The Primary are perceived as conceived. The Secundo-primary are conceived as perceived. The Secondary are neither perceived as conceived, nor conceived as perceived;—for to perception they are occult, and are conceived only as latent causes to account for manifest effects. (See par. 15, and footnote.)*

14. The Primary may be roundly characterized as mathematical; the Secundo-primary, as mechanical; the Secondary, as physiological.

2°. *Considered as Cognitions; and here* (*a*) *As in Sensitive Apprehension, or in relation to Sense.*

15. In this relation the Primary qualities are, as apprehended, unambiguously

* For example, there is no subjective Sensation of Magnitude, Figure, Number, &c., but only an objective Perception. (See par. 15–19.)

† Thus, in the Secundo-primary the term Hardness, for instance, denotes both a certain resistance, of which we are conscious, to our motive energy, and a certain feeling from pressure on our nerves. The former, a Perception, is wholly different from the latter, a Sensation; and we can easily imagine that we might have been so constituted, as to apprehend Resistance as we do Magnitude, Figure, &c., without a corresponding organic passion. (See par. 18.)—In the Secondary the term Heat, for example, denotes ambiguously both the quality which we infer to be in bodies and the quality of which we are conscious in ourselves.

‡ Sextus Empiricus, Montaigne, Voltaire, Hemsterhuis, Krueger, &c., notice this as possible; but do not distinguish the possibility as limited to the Secondary Qualities.

objective (object-objects); the Secondary, unambiguously subjective (subject-objects); * the Secundo-primary, both objective and subjective (object-objects and subject-objects). In other words:—We are conscious, as objects, in the Primary qualities, of the modes of a not-self; in the Secondary, of the modes of self; * in the Secundo-primary, of the modes of self and of a not-self at once.†

16. Using the terms strictly, the apprehensions of the Primary are perceptions, not sensations; of the Secondary, sensations, not perceptions; of the Secundo-primary, perceptions and sensations together. (See par. 15, footnote *.)

17. In the Primary there is, thus, no concomitant Secondary quality; in the Secondary there is no concomitant primary quality; in the Secundo-primary, a secondary and quasi-primary quality accompany each other.

18. In the apprehension of the Primary qualities the mind is primarily and principally active; it feels only as it knows. In that of the Secondary, the mind is primarily and principally passive; it knows only as it feels.‡ In that of the Secundo-

* How much this differs from the doctrine of Reid, Stewart, &c., who hold that in every sensation there is not only a subjective object of sensation, but also an objective object of perception, see Note D*, § I.

† In illustration of this paragraph, I must notice a confusion and ambiguity in the very cardinal distinction of psychology and its terms—the distinction I mean of *subjective* and *objective*, which, as far as I am aware, has never been cleared up, nay, never even brought clearly into view.

Our nervous organism, (the rest of our body may be fairly thrown out of account,) in contrast to all exterior to itself, appertains to the concrete human Ego, and in this respect is *subjective, internal;* whereas, in contrast to the abstract immaterial Ego, the pure mind, it belongs to the Non-ego, and in this respect is *objective, external.* Here is one source of ambiguity sufficiently perplexing; but the discrimination is here comparatively manifest, and any important inconvenience from the employment of the terms may, with proper attention, be avoided.

The following problem is more difficult. Looking from the mind, and not looking beyond our animated organism, are the phænomena of which we are conscious in that organism all upon a level, i.e., equally objective or equally subjective; or is there a discrimination to be made, and some phænomena to be considered as objective, being modes of our organism viewed as a mere portion of matter, and in this respect a Non-ego, while other phænomena are to be considered as subjective, being the modes of our organism as animated by or in union with the mind, and therefore states of the Ego? Without here attempting to enter on the reasons which vindicate my opinion, suffice it to say, that I adopt the latter alternative; and hold further, that the discrimination of the sensorial phænomena into objective and subjective, coincides with the distinction of the qualities of body into Primary and Secondary, the Secundo-primary being supposed to contribute an element to each. Our nervous organism is to be viewed in two relations;—1°, as a body simply, and—2°, as an animated body. As a body simply it can possibly exist, and can possibly be known as extent, only under those necessary conditions of all matter, which have been denominated its Primary qualities. As an animated body it actually exists, and is actually known to exist, only as it is susceptible of certain affections, which, and the external causes of which, have been ambiguously called the Secondary qualities of matter. Now, by a law of our nature, we are not conscious of the existence of our organism, consequently not conscious of any of its primary qualities, unless when we are conscious of it, as modified by a secondary quality, or some other of its affections, as an animated body. But the former consciousness requires the latter only as its negative condition, and is neither involved in it as a part, nor properly dependent on it as a cause. The object in the one consciousness is also wholly different from the object in the other. In that, it is a contingent passion of the organism, as a constituent of the human self; in this, it is some essential property of the organism, as a portion of the universe of matter, and though apprehended by, not an affection proper to, the conscious self at all. In these circumstances, the secondary quality, say a colour, which the mind apprehends in the organism, is, as a passion of self, recognised to be a *subjective object;* whereas the primary quality, extension, or figure, or number, which, when conscious of such affection, the mind therein at the same time apprehends, is, as not a passion of self, but a common property of matter, recognized to be an *objective object.* (See par. 16–19, with footnote†, and par. 18, with footnote‡.)

‡ Thus in vision the secondary quality of colour is, in the strictest sense, a passive affection of the sentient ego; and the only activity the mind can be said to exert in the sensation of colours, is in the recognitive consciousness that it is so and so affected. It thus knows as it feels, in knowing that it feels.

But the apprehension of extension, figure, divisibility, &c., which, under condition of its being thus affected, simultaneously takes place, is, though necessary, wholly active and purely spiritual; in as much as extension, figure, &c., are, directly and in their own nature, neither, subjectively considered, passions of the animated sensory, nor, objectively considered, efficient qualities in things by which such passion can be caused. The perception of parts out of parts is not given in the mere affection of colour, but is obtained by

primary the mind is equally and at once active and passive; in one respect, it feels as it knows, in another, it knows as it feels.*

19. Thus Perception and Activity are at the maximum in the Primary qualities; at the minimum in the Secondary; Sensation and Passivity are at the minimum in the Primary, at the maximum in the Secondary; while, in the Secundo-primary, Perception and Sensation, Activity and Passivity, are in equipoise.—Thus too it is, that the most purely material phænomena are apprehended in the most purely inorganic energy.†

---

a reaction of the mind upon such affection. It is merely the recognition of a relation. But a relation is neither a passion nor a cause of passion; and, though apprehended through sense, is, in truth, an intellectual not a sensitive cognition;—unless under the name of sensitive cognition we comprehend, as I think we ought, more than the mere recognition of an organic passion. (See Note D*, § 1.) The perception of Extension is not, therefore, the mere consciousness of an affection—a mere sensation.—This is still more manifest in regard to Figure, or extension bounded. Visual figure is an expanse of colour bounded in a certain manner by a line. Here all is nothing but relation. '*Expanse of colour*' is only coloured extension; and extension, as stated, is only the relation of parts out of parts. '*Bounded in a certain manner*,' is also only the expression of various relations. A thing is '*bounded*,' only as it has a limited number of parts; but *limited*, *number*, and *parts*, are, all three, relations; and, farther, '*in a certain manner*' denotes that these parts stand to each other in one relation and not in another. The perception of a thing as bounded, and bounded in a certain manner, is thus only the recognition of a thing under relations. Finally, '*by a line*' still merely indicates a relation; for a line is nothing but the negation of each other, by two intersecting colours. Absolutely considered, it is a nothing; and so far from there being any difficulty in conceiving a breadthless line, a line is, in fact, not a line (but a narrow surface between two lines) if thought as possessed of breadth. (See Note E.)—In such perceptions, therefore, if the mind can be said to feel, it can be said to feel only in being conscious of itself as purely active; that is, as spontaneously apprehensive of an object-object or mode of the non-ego, and not of a subject-object or affection of the ego. (See par. 16—19, and relative footnote †.)

The application of the preceding doctrine to the other primary qualities is even more obtrusive.

To prevent misunderstanding, it may be observed, that in saying *the mind is active, not passive, in a cognition*, I do not mean to say that the mind is free to exert or not to exert the cognitive act, or even not to exert it in a determinate manner. The mind energises as it lives, and it cannot choose but live; it knows as it energises, and it cannot choose but energise. An object being duly presented, it is unable not to apprehend it, and apprehend it, both in itself, and in the relations under which it stands. We may evade the presentation, not the recognition of what is presented. But of this again.

* This is apparent when it is considered that under the cognition of a secundo-primary quality are comprehended both the apprehension of a secondary quality, i.e. the sensation of a subjective affection, and the apprehension of a quasi-primary quality, i.e. the perception of an objective force. Take, for example, the Secundo-primary quality of Hardness. In the sensitive apprehension of this we are aware of two facts. The first is the fact of a certain affection, a certain feeling, in our sentient organism, (Muscular and Skin senses.) This is the *sensation*, the apprehension of a feeling consequent on the resistance of a body, and which in one of its special modifications constitutes Hardness, viewed as an affection in us;—a sensation which we know, indeed, by experience to be the effect of the pressure of an unyielding body, but which we can easily conceive might be determined in us independently of all internal movement, all external resistance; while we can still more easily conceive that such movement and resistance might be apprehended, independently of such concomitant sensation. Here, therefore, we know only as we feel, for here we only know, that is, are conscious, that we feel.—The second is the fact of a certain opposition to the voluntary movement of a limb—to our locomotive energy. Of this energy we might be conscious, without any consciousness of the state, or even the existence, of the muscles set in motion; and we might also be conscious of resistance to its exertion, though no organic feeling happened to be its effect. But as it is, though conscious of the sensations connected both with the active state of our muscular frame determined by its tension, and of the passive state in our skin and flesh determined by external pressure; still, over and above these animal sensations, we are purely conscious of the *fact*, that the overt exertion of our locomotive volition is, in a certain sort, impeded. This consciousness is the *perception*, the objective apprehension, of resistance, which in one of its special modifications constitutes Hardness, as an attribute of body. In this cognition, if we can be said with any propriety to feel, we can be said only to feel as we know, because we only feel, i.e., are conscious, that we know. (See par 18, footnote ‡, and par. 25, first footnote, Part I.)

† The doctrine of paragraphs 16–19 seems to have been intended by Aristotle (see above, p. 829 b) in saying that the Common Sensibles (—the Primary Qualities) are percepts *concomitant* or consequent on the sensation of the Proper (—the Secondary Qualities), and on one occasion that the Common Sensibles are, in a certain sort, only to be considered as apprehensions of sense *per accidens*. For this may be interpreted to mean, that our appre-

20. In the Primary, a sensation of organic affection is the condition of perception, a mental apprehension; in the Secundo-primary, a sensation is the concomitant of the perception; in the Secondary, a sensation is the all in all which consciousness apprehends. (See par. 10.)

21. In the Primary, the sensation, the condition of the perception, is not itself caused by the objective quality perceived; in the Secundo-primary, the concomitant sensation is the effect of the objective quality perceived; in the Secondary, the sensation is the effect of an objective quality supposed, but not perceived. In other words:—In the apprehension of the Primary, there is no subject-object determined by the object-object; in the Secundo-primary, there is a subject-object

---

hension of the common sensibles is not, like that of the proper, the mere consciousness of a subjective or sensorial passion, but, though only exerted when such passion is determined, is in itself the spontaneous energy of the mind in objective cognition.

Tending towards, though not reaching to, the same result, might be adduced many passages from the works of the Greek interpreters of Aristotle. In particular, I would refer to the doctrine touching the Common Sensibles, stated by Simplicius in his Commentary on the De Anima, (L. ii., c. 6, f. 35 a, L. iii., c. 1, f. 51 a, ed. Ald.,) and by Priscianus Lydus, in his Metaphrase of the Treatise of Theophrastus on Sense, (p. 274, 275, 285, ed. Basil. Theoph.):—but (as already noticed) these books ought, I suspect, from strong internal evidence, both to be assigned to Priscianus as their author; while the doctrine itself is probably only that which Iamblichus had delivered, in his lost treatise upon the Soul. It is to this effect:—The common sensibles might appear not to be sensibles at all, or sensibles only per accidens, as making no impression on the organ, and as objects analogous to, and apprehended by, the understanding or rational mind alone. This extreme doctrine is not, however, to be admitted. As sensibles, the common must be allowed to act somehow upon the sense, though in a different manner from the proper. Comparatively speaking, the proper act primarily, corporeally, and by causing a passion in the sense; the common, secondarily, formally, and by eliciting the sense and understanding to energy. But though there be, in the proper more of passivity, in the common more of activity, still the common are, in propriety, objects of sense per se; being neither cognised (as substances) exclusively by the understanding, nor (as is the sweet by vision) accidentally by sense.

A similar approximation may be detected in the doctrine of the more modern Aristotelians. (See p. 830 a.) Expressed in somewhat different terms, it was long a celebrated controversy in the schools, whether a certain class of objects, under which common sensibles were included, did or did not modify the organic sense; and if this they did, whether primarily and of themselves, or only secondarily through their modification of the proper sensibles, with which they were associated. Ultimately, it became the prevalent doctrine, that of Magnitude, Figure, Place, Position, Time, Relation in general, &c., 'nullam esse efficaciam vel actionem:' that is, these do not, like the affective qualities (qualitates patibiles) or proper sensibles, make any real, any material impress on the sense; but if they can be said to act at all, act only, either, as some held, spiritually or intentionally, or as others, by natural resultance, (vel spiritualiter sive intentionaliter, vel per naturalem resultantiam.) See *Toletus*, Comm. De Anima, L. ii., c. 6, qq. 14, 15;—*Zabarella*, Comm De Anima, L. ii., Text. 65; De Rebus Naturalibus, p. 939 sq., De Sensu Agente, cc. 4, 5;—*Goclenius*, Adversaria, q. 55;—*Suarez*, Metaphysicae Disputationes, disp. xviii., sec. 4;—*Scheibler*, Metaphysica, L. ii., c. 5, art. 5, punct. 1; De Anima, P. ii., disp. ii., § 24; Liber Sententiarum, Ex. vi., ax. 4, Ex. vii., ax. 10.

The same result seems, likewise, confirmed indirectly, by the doctrine of those philosophers who, as Condillac in his earlier writings, Stewart, Brown, Mill, J. Young, &c., hold that extension and colour are only mutually concomitant in imagination, through the influence of inveterate association. In itself, indeed, this doctrine I do not admit; for it supposes that we could possibly be conscious of colour without extension, of extension without colour. Not the former; for we are only, as in sense, so in the imagination of sense, aware of a minimum visible, as of a luminous or coloured point, in contrast to and out of a surrounding expanse of obscure or differently coloured surface; and a visual object, larger than the minimum, is, ex hypothesi, presented, or represented, as extended. (See also Note E.)—Not the latter; for, as I have already observed, psychologically speaking, the sensation of colour comprehends contradictory opposites; to wit, both the sensation of positive colour, in many modes, and the sensation of a privation of all colour, in one. But of contradictory predicates one or other must, by the logical law of excluded middle, be attributed in thought to every object of thought. We cannot, therefore, call up in imagination an extended object, without representing it either as somehow positively coloured, (red, or green, or blue, &c.,) or as negatively coloured, (black.) But though I reject this doctrine, I do not reject it as absolutely destitute of truth. It is erroneous I think; but every error is a truth abused; and the abuse in this case seems to lie in the extreme recoil from the counter error of the common opinion,—that the apprehension through sight of colour, and the apprehension through sight of extension and figure, are as inseparable, identical cognitions of identical objects.—See Reid, Inq. 145.

determined by the object-object; in the Secondary, a subject-object is the only object of immediate cognition.

22. In the Primary, the sensation of the secondary quality, which affords its condition to the perception of the primary, is various and indefinite;* in the Secundo-primary, the sensation of the secondary quality, which accompanies the perception of the quasi primary, is, under the same circumstances, uniform and definite; in the Secondary, the sensation is itself definite, but its exciting cause, the supposed quality in bodies, various and indefinite. (See p. 854 b—856 a.)

23. The Primary and Secondary qualities

* The opinions so generally prevalent, that through touch, or touch and muscular feeling, or touch and sight, or touch, muscular feeling, and sight,—that through these senses, exclusively, we are percipient of extension, &c., I do not admit. On the contrary, I hold that all sensations, whatsoever, of which we are conscious, as one out of another, eo ipso, afford us the condition of immediately and necessarily apprehending extension; for in the consciousness itself of such reciprocal outness is actually involved a perception of difference of place in space, and, consequently, of the extended. Philosophers have confounded what supplies the condition of the more prompt and precise perception of extension, with what supplies the condition of a perception of extension at all.

And be it observed, that it makes no essential difference in this doctrine, whether the mind be supposed proximately conscious of the reciprocal outness of sensations at the central extremity of the nerves, in an *extended sensorium commune*, where each distinct nervous filament has its separate locality, or at the peripheral extremity of the nerves, in the places themselves where sensations are excited, and to which they are referred. From many pathological phænomena the former alternative might appear the more probable. In this view, each several nerve, or rather, each several nervous filament, (for every such filament has its peculiar function, and runs isolated from every other,) is to be regarded merely as one sentient *point*; which yields one indivisible sensation, out of and distinct from that of every other, by the side of which it is arranged; and not as a sentient *line*, each point of which, throughout its course, has for itself a separate local sensibility. For a stimulus applied to any intermediate part of a nerve, is felt not as there, but as if applied to its peripheral extremity; a feeling which continues when that extremity itself, nay, when any portion of the nerve, however great, has been long cut off. Thus it is that a whole line of nerve affords, at all its points, only the sensation of one determinate point. One point, therefore, physiologically speaking, it is to be considered. (See *Plutarch*, De Plac. Philos. L. iv. c. 23;—*Nemesius*, De Hom., c. 8;—*Fabricius Hildanus*, Obs. Cent. iii. obs. 15;—*Descartes*, Princ. P. iv. § 196;—*Blancard*, Coll. Med. Phys. cent. vii. obs. 15;—*Stuart*, De Motu Musc. c. 5;—*Knaw Boerhaave*, Imp. fac. § 368 sq.;—*Sir Ch. Bell*, Idea, &c. p. 12; The Hand, p. 159;—*Magendie*, Journ. t. v. p. 33;—*Mueller*, Phys. pp. 694-696, Engl. tr.)

Take for instance a man whose leg has been amputated. If now two nervous filaments be irritated, the one of which ran to his great, the other to his little, toe—he will experience two pains, as in these two members. Nor is there, in propriety, any deception in such sensations. For his toes, as all his members, are his only as they are to him sentient; and they are only sentient and distinctively sentient, as endowed with nerves and distinct nerves. The nerves thus constitute alone the whole sentient organism. In these circumstances, the peculiar nerves of the several toes, running isolated from centre to periphery, and thus remaining, though curtailed in length, unmutilated in function, will, if irritated at any point, continue to manifest their original sensations; and these being now, as heretofore, manifested out of each other, must afford the condition of a perceived extension, not less real than that which they afforded prior to the amputation.

The hypothesis of an extended sensorium commune, or complex nervous centre, the mind being supposed in proximate connexion with each of its constituent nervous terminations or origins, may thus be reconciled to the doctrine of natural realism; and therefore what was said at p. 821 a, No. 2, and relative places, with reference to a sensorium of a different character, is to be qualified in conformity to the present supposition.

It is, however, I think, more philosophical, to consider the nervous system as one whole, with each part of which the animating principle is equally and immediately connected, so long as each part remains in continuity with the centre. To this opinion may be reduced the doctrine of *Aristotle*, that the soul contains the body, rather than the body the soul, (De An., L. i., c. 9, § 4);—a doctrine on which was founded the common dogma of the *Schools*, that the Soul is all in the whole body, and all in every of its parts, meaning thereby, that the simple, unextended mind, in some inconceivable manner, present to all the organs, is percipient of the peculiar affection which each is adapted to receive, and actuates each in the peculiar function which it is qualified to discharge. See also *St Gregory of Nyssa*, (De Hom. Opif. cc. 12, 14, 15), the oldest philosopher I recollect, by whom this dogma is explicitly enounced. Compare *Galen*. De Sympt. Causis. L. i. c. 4. Of modern authorities to the same result, are—*Perrault* (Du Mouv. des Yeux, p. 591, and Du Toucher, p. 531); *Tabor* (Tract iii. c. 3); *Stuart* (De Motu Musc. c. 5); *Leidenfrost* (De Mente Humana, c. iii. §§ 11, 14, 15); *Tiedemann* (Psychologie, p. 309. sq.); *Berard*, (Rapports &c. ch. 1 § 2); *C. G. Carus* (Vorles. ueb. Psychologie, passim); *Umbreit* (Psychologie, c. 1, and Beilage, passim); *F. Fischer* (Ueb. d. Sitz d. Seele, passim, and Psy-

are, in this relation, simple and self-discriminated. For, in the perception of a primary, there is involved no sensation of a secondary with which it can be mixed up; while in the sensation of a secondary there is no perception of a primary at all. Thus prominent in themselves, and prominently contrasted as mutual extremes, neither class can be overlooked, neither class can be confounded with the other.

---

chologie, c. 4). The two last seem to think that their opinion on this matter is something new! Rosmini also maintains the same doctrine, but as I have not yet obtained his relative works, I am unable to refer to them articulately.—See Bibl. Univ. de Genève, No. 76, June 1842, p. 241, sq.

As to the question of materialism this doctrine is indifferent. For the connexion of an unextended with an extended substance is equally incomprehensible, whether we contract the place of union to a central point, or whether we leave it co-extensive with organization.

The causes why the sensations of different parts of the nervous apparatus vary so greatly from each other in supplying the conditions of a perception of extension, &c., seem to me comprehended in two general facts, the one constituting a physiological, the other a psychological, law of perception;—laws, neither of which, however, has yet obtained from philosophers the consideration which it merits.

The *Physiological* law is—*That a nervous point yields a sensation felt as locally distinct, in proportion as it is isolated in its action from every other.* Physiological experiment has not yet been, and probably never may be able, to prove anatomically the truth of this law which I have here ventured to enounce; physiologists, indeed, seem hitherto to have wholly neglected the distinction. So far, however, is it from being opposed to physiological observation, it may appeal in its confirmation to the analogy of all the facts to which such observation reaches, (see par. 25, first note, III.;) while the psychological phænomena are such as almost to necessitate its admission. To say nothing of the ganglionic fusions, which are now disproved, the softness and colliquescence of the olfactory nerves and nervous expansion, for example, correspond with the impossibility we experience, in smell, of distinctly apprehending one part of the excited organism as out of another; while the marvellous power we have of doing this in vision, seems, by every more minute investigation of the organic structure, more clearly to depend upon the isolation, peculiar arrangement, and tenuity of the primary fibrils of the retina and optic nerve; though microscopical anatomy, it must be confessed, has not as yet been able to exhibit any nervous element so inconceivably small as is the minimum visibile. Besides the older experiments of Porterfield, Haller, &c., see *Treviranus*, Beytraege, 1835, p. 63 sq.—*Volkmann*, Neue Beytraege, 1836, pp. 61 sq., 197 sq.;—*Mueller*, Phys. 1840, pp. 1073 sq. 1121 sq. Engl tr.;—also *Baer*, Anthropologie, 1824, § 163.—Of Touch and Feeling I am to speak immediately.

And here I may say a word in relation to a difficulty which has perplexed the physiologists, and to which no solution, I am aware of, has been attempted.—The retina, as first shown by Treviranus, is a pavement of perpendicular rods, terminating in papillæ; a constitution which may be roughly represented to imagination by the bristles of a thick set brush. The retina is, however, only the terminal expansion of the optic nerve; and the rods which make up its area, after bending behind to an acute angle, run back as the constituent, but isolated, fibrils of that nerve, to their origin in the brain. On the smaller size of the papillæ and fibrils of the optic nerve, principally depends, as already stated, the greater power we possess, in the eye, of discriminating one sensation as out of another, consequently of apprehending extension, figure, &c.—But here the difficulty arises: Microscopic observations on the structure of the retina give the diameter of the papillæ as about the eight or nine thousandth part of an inch. Optical experiments, again, on the ultimate capacity of vision, show that a longitudinal object (as a hair) viewed at such a distance that its breadth, as reflected to the retina, is not more than the six hundred thousandth or millionth of an inch, is distinctly visible to a good eye. Now there is here—1° a great discrepancy between the superficial extent of the apparent ultimate fibrils of the retina, and the extent of the image impressed on the retina by the impinging rays of light, the one being above a hundred times greater than the other; and, 2°, it is impossible to conceive the existence of distinct fibrils so minute as would be required to propagate the impression, if the breadth of the part affected were actually no greater than the breadth of light reflected from the object to the retina. To me the difficulty seems soluble if we suppose, 1°, that the ultimate fibrils and papillæ are, in fact, the ultimate units or minima of sensation; and, 2°, that a stimulus of light, though applied only to part of a papilla, idiopathically affects the whole. This theory is confirmed by the analogy of the nerves of feeling, to which I shall soon allude. The objections to which it is exposed I see; but I think that they may easily be answered. On the discussion of the point I cannot however enter.

The *Psychological* law is—*That though a perception be only possible under condition of a sensation; still, that above a certain limit the more intense the sensation or subjective consciousness, the more indistinct the perception or objective consciousness.*

On this, which is a special case of a still higher law, I have already incidentally spoken and shall again have occasion to speak. (See Note D*.) It is at present sufficient to notice—

1°. That we are only conscious of the existence of our organism as a physical body, under our consciousness of its existence as an animal

The Secundo-primary qualities, on the contrary, are, at once, complex and confusive. For, on the one hand, as perceptions approximating to the primary, on the other, as sensations identified with the secondary, they may, if not altogether overlooked, lightly be, as they have always hitherto been, confounded with the one or with the other of these classes. (See pp. 849 b, 860 a.)

---

body, and are only conscious of its existence as an animal body under our consciousness of it as somehow or other sensitively affected.

2°. That though the sensation of our organism as animally affected, is, as it were, the light by which it is exhibited to our perception as a physically extended body; still, if the affection be too strong, the pain or pleasure too intense, the light blinds by its very splendour, and the perception is lost in the sensation. Accordingly, if we take a survey of the senses, we shall find, that exactly in proportion as each affords an idiopathic sensation more or less capable of being carried to an extreme either of pleasure or of pain, does it afford, but in an inverse ratio, the condition of an objective perception more or less distinct. In the senses of Sight and Hearing, as contrasted with those of Taste and Smell, the counter proportions are precise and manifest; and precisely as in animals those latter senses gain in their objective character as means of knowledge, do they lose in their subjective character as sources of pleasurable or painful sensations. To a dog, for instance, in whom the sense of smell is so acute, all odours seem, in themselves, to be indifferent. In Touch or Feeling the same analogy holds good, and within itself; for in this case, where the sense is diffused throughout the body, the subjective and objective vary in their proportions at different parts. The parts most subjectively sensible, those chiefly susceptible of pain and pleasure, furnish precisely the obtusest organs of touch; and the acutest organs of touch do not possess, if ever even that, more than an average amount of subjective sensibility. I am disposed, indeed, from the analogy of the other senses, to surmise, that the nerves of touch proper (the more objective) and of feeling proper (the more subjective) are distinct; and distributed in various proportions to different parts of the body. I should also surmise, that the ultimate fibrils of the former run in isolated action from periphery to centre, while the ultimate fibrils of the latter may, to a certain extent, be confounded with each other at their terminal expansion in the skin; so that for this reason, likewise, they do not, as the former, supply to consciousness an opportunity of so precisely discriminating the reciprocal outness of their sensations. The experiments of Weber have shown, how differently in degree different parts of the skin possess the power of touch proper; this power, as measured by the smallness of the interval at which the blunted points of a pair of compasses, brought into contact with the skin, can be discriminated as double, varying from the twentieth of an English inch at the tip of the tongue, and a tenth on the volar surface of the third finger, to two inches and a half over the greater part of the neck, back, arms, and thighs.—(De Pulsu, &c., p. 44-81, in particular p. 58. An abstract, not altogether accurate, is given by Mueller, Phys. p. 700.) If these experiments be repeated with a pair of compasses not very obtuse, and capable, therefore, by a slight pressure, of exciting a sensation in the skin, it will be found, that whilst Weber's observations, as to the remarkable difference of the different parts in the power of tactile discrimination, are correct; that, at the same time, what he did not observe, there is no corresponding difference between the parts in their sensibility to superficial pricking, scratching, &c. On the contrary, it will be found that, in the places where, objectively, touch is most alive, subjectively feeling is, in the first instance at least, in some degree deadened; and that the parts the most obtuse in discriminating the duplicity of the touching points, are by no means the least acute to the sensation excited by their pressure.

For example;—The tip of the tongue has *fifty*, the inferior surface of the third finger *twenty five*, times the tactile discrimination of the arm. But it will be found, on trial, that the arm is more sensitive to a sharp point applied, but not strongly, to the skin, than either the tongue or the finger, and (depilated of course) at least as alive to the presence of a very light body, as a hair, a thread, a feather, drawn along the surface. In the several places the phænomena thus vary;—In those parts where touch proper prevails, a subacute point, lightly pressed upon the skin, determines a sensation of which we can hardly predicate either pain or pleasure, and nearly limited to the place on which the pressure is made. Accordingly, when two such points are thus, at the same time, pressed upon the skin, we are conscious of two distinct impressions, even when the pressing points approximate pretty closely to each other.—In those parts, on the other hand, where feeling proper prevails, a subacute point, lightly pressed upon the skin, determines a sensation which we can hardly call indifferent; and which radiates, to a variable extent, from the place on which the pressure is applied. Accordingly, when two such points are thus, at the same time, pressed upon the skin, we are not conscious of two distinct impressions, unless the pressing points are at a considerable distance from each other; the two impressions running, as it were, together, and thus constituting one indivisible sensation. The discriminated sensations in the one case, depend manifestly on the discriminated action, through the isolated and unexpanded termination of the nervous fibrils of touch proper; and the indistinguishable sensation in the other, will, I have no doubt, be ultimately found by microscopic anatomy to depend, in like manner, on

24. In the same relation a Primary or a Secondary quality, as simple, has its term univocal. A Secundo-primary, on the contrary, being complex, its term, as one, is necessarily equivocal. For, viewed on one side, it is the modification of a primary; on the other, it is, in reality, simply a secondary quality.—(How, in a more general point of view, the Secondary qualities are no less complex, and their terms no less ambiguous than the Secundo-primary, see par. 6.)

25. All the senses, simply or in combination, afford conditions for the perception of the Primary qualities, (par. 22, note;) and all, of course, supply the sensations themselves of the Secondary. As only various modifications of resistance, the Secundo-primary qualities are all, as percepts proper, as quasi-primary qualities, apprehended through the locomotive faculty,* and our consciousness of its energy; as sensations, as secondary qualities, they are apprehended as modifications

---

the nervous fibrils of feeling proper being, as it were, fused or interlaced together at their termination, or rather, perhaps, on each ultimate fibril, each primary sentient unit being expanded through a considerable extent of skin. The supposition of such expansion seems, indeed, to me necessitated by these three facts: —1°, that every point of the skin is sensible; 2°, that no point of the skin is sensible except through the distribution to it of nervous substance; and, 3°, that the ultimate fibrils, those minima, at least, into which anatomists have, as yet, been able to analyse the nerves, are too large, and withal too few, to carry sensation to each cutaneous point, unless by an attenuation and diffusion of the finest kind.—Within this superficial sphere of cutaneous apprehension, the objective and subjective, perception and sensation, touch proper and feeling proper, are thus always found to each other in an inverse ratio.

But take the same places, and puncture deeply. Then, indeed, the sense of pain will be found to be intenser in the tongue and finger than in the arm; for the tongue and finger are endowed with comparatively more numerous nerves, and consequently with a more concentrated sensibility, than the arm; though these may either, if different, lie beneath the termination of the nerves of touch, or, if the same, commence their energy as feeling only at the pitch where their energy as touch concludes. Be this, however, as it may, it will be always found, that in proportion as the internal feeling of a part becomes excited, is it incapacitated, for the time, as an organ of external touch.

I do not therefore assert, without a qualification, that touch and feeling are every where manifested in an inverse ratio; for both together may be higher, both together may be lower, in one place than another. But whilst I diffidently hold that they are dependent upon different conditions—that the capacity of pain and pleasure, and the power of tactual discrimination, which a part possesses, are not the result of the same nervous fibres; I maintain, with confidence, that these senses never, in any part, coexist in exercise in any high degree, and that wherever the one rises to excess, there the other will be found to sink to a corresponding deficiency.

In saying, in the present note, that touch is more objective than feeling, I am not to be supposed to mean, that touch is, in itself, aught but a subjective affection—a feeling—a sensation. Touch proper is here styled objective, not absolutely, but only in contrast and in comparison to feeling proper; 1°, in as much as it affords in the cycle of its own phænomena a greater amount of information; 2°, as it affords more frequent occasions of perception or objective apprehension; and, 3°, as it is feebly, if at all, characterized by the subjective affections of pain and pleasure.

* I.—*On the Locomotive Faculty and Muscular Sense, in relation to Perception.*—I say that the Secundo-primary qualities, in their quasi-primary phasis, are apprehended through the *locomotive faculty*, and not through the *muscular sense*; for it is impossible that the state of muscular feeling can enable us to be immediately cognisant of the existence and degree of a resisting force. On the contrary, supposing all muscular feeling abolished, the power of moving the muscles at will remaining, however, entire, I hold (as will anon be shown) that the consciousness of the mental motive energy, and of the greater or less intensity of such energy requisite, in different circumstances, to accomplish our intention, would of itself enable us always to perceive the fact, and in some degree to measure the amount, of any resistance to our voluntary movements; howbeit the concomitance of certain feelings with the different states of muscular tension, renders this cognition not only easier, but, in fact, obtrudes it upon our attention. Scaliger, therefore, in referring the apprehension of weight, &c., to the locomotive faculty, is, in my opinion, far more correct than recent philosophers, in referring it to the muscular sense. (See II. of this footnote.)

We have here to distinguish three things.

1°. The still immanent or purely mental act of will: what for distinction's sake I would call the *hyperorganic* volition to move;—the *actio elicita* of the schools. Of this volition we are conscious, even though it do not go out into overt action.

2°. If this volition become transeunt, be carried into effect, it passes into the mental effort or nisus to move. This I would call the *enorganic volition*, or, by an extension of the scholastic language, the *actio imperata*. Of this we are immediately conscious. For we are conscious of it, though by a narcosis or stupor of the sensitive nerves we lose all feeling of the movement of the limb;—though by a paralysis of the motive nerves, no move-

of touch proper, and of cutaneous and muscular feeling.*

b)—As in Thought; as in relation to Intellect.

26. As modes of matter, the Primary qualities are thought as necessary and universal; the Secundo-primary, as contingent and common; the Secondary, as contingent and peculiar.

27. Thought as necessary, and immediately apprehended as actual, modes of matter, we conceive the Primary qualities in what they objectively are. The Secundo-primary, thought in their objective phasis, as modifications of the Primary,

---

ment in the limb follows the mental effort to move;—though by an abnormal stimulus of the muscular fibres, a contraction in them is caused even in opposition to our will.

3°. Determined by the enorganic volition, the cerebral influence is transmitted by the motive nerves; the muscles contract or endeavour to contract, so that the limb moves or endeavours to move. This motion or effort to move I would call the *organic movement*, the *organic nisus*; by a limitation of the scholastic term, it might be denominated the *actio imperata*.

It might seem at first sight,—1°, that the organic movement is immediately determined by the enorganic volition; and, 2°, that we are immediately conscious of the organic nisus in itself. But neither is the case.—Not the former: for even if we identify the contraction of the muscles and the overt movement of the limb, this is only the mediate result of the enorganic volition, through the action of the nervous influence transmitted *from* the brain. The mind, therefore, exerts its effort to move, proximately in determining this transmission; but we are unconscious not only of the mode in which this operation is performed, but even of the operation itself.—Not the latter: for all muscular contraction is dependent on the agency of one set of nerves, all feeling of muscular contraction on another. Thus, from the exclusive paralysis of the former, or the exclusive stupor of the latter, the one function may remain entire, while the other is abolished; and it is only because certain muscular feelings are normally, though contingently, associated with the different muscular states, that, independently of the consciousness of the enorganic volition, we are indirectly made aware of the various degrees of the organic nisus exerted in our different members.* But though indirect, the information thus forced upon us is not the less valuable. By the associated sensations our attention is kept alive to the state of our muscular movements; by them we are enabled to graduate with the requisite accuracy the amount of organic effort, and to expend in each movement precisely the quantum necessary to accomplish its purpose. Sir Charles Bell records the case of a mother who, while nursing her infant, was affected with paralysis or loss of muscular motion on one side of her body, and by stupor or loss of sensibility on the other. With the arm capable of movement she could hold her child to her bosom; and this she continued to do so long as her attention remained fixed upon the infant. But if surrounding objects withdrew her observation, there being no admonitory sensation, the flexor muscles of the arm gradually relaxed, and the child was in danger of falling. (The Hand, p. 204.)

These distinctions in the process of voluntary motion, especially the two last, (for the first and second may be viewed as virtually the same,) are of importance to illustrate the double nature of the secundo-primary qualities, each of which is, in fact, the aggregate of an objective or quasi-primary quality, apprehended in a perception, and of a secondary or subjective quality caused by the other, apprehended in a sensation. Each of these qualities, each of these cognitions, appertains to a different part of the motive process. The quasi-primary quality and its perception, depending on the enorganic volition and the nerves of motion; the secondary quality and its sensation, depending on the organic nisus and the nerves of sensibility.

The quasi-primary quality is, always, simply a resistance to our enorganic volition, as realized in a muscular effort. But, be it remem-

---

* I must here notice an error of inference, which runs through the experiments by Professor Weber of Leipsic, in regard to the shares which the sense of touch proper and the consciousness of muscular effort have in the estimation of weight, as detailed in his valuable 'Annotationes de Pulsu, Resorptione, Auditu et Tactu,' 1834, pp. 81-113, 134, 159-161.—Weight he supposes to be tested by the Touch alone, when objects are laid upon the hand, reposing, say, on a pillow. Here there appears to me a very palpable mistake. For without denying that different weights, up to a certain point, produce different sensations on the nerves of touch and feeling, and that consequently an experience of the difference of such sensation may help us to an inference of a difference of weight; it is manifest, that if a body be laid upon a muscular part, that we estimate its weight proximately and principally by the amount of lateral pressure on the muscles, and this pressure itself, by the difficulty we find in lifting the body, however imperceptibly, by a contraction or bellying out of the muscular fibres. When superincumbent bodies, however different in weight, are all still so heavy as to render this contraction almost or altogether impossible; it will be found, that our power of measuring their comparative weights becomes, in the one case feeble and fallacious, in the other null.

and, in both their objective and subjective phases, immediately apprehended, we conceive them in what they objectively, as well as in what they subjectively, are. The Secondary being neither thought as necessary, nor immediately apprehended in their external reality, we conceive adequately what they are in their subjective effects, but inadequately what they are as objective causes.

---

bered, there may be muscular effort, even if a body weighs or is pressed upon a part of our muscular frame apparently at rest. (See footnote * of page 865.)—And how is the resistance perceived? I have frequently asserted, that in perception we are conscious of the external object immediately and in itself. This is the doctrine of Natural Realism. But in saying that a thing is known in itself, I do not mean that this object is known in its absolute existence, that is, out of relation to us. This is impossible; for our knowledge is only of the relative. To know a thing in itself or immediately, is an expression I use merely in contrast to the knowledge of a thing in a representation, or mediately. (See Note B.) On this doctrine an external quality is said to be known in itself, when it is known as the immediate and necessary correlative of an internal quality of which I am conscious. Thus, when I am conscious of the exertion of an enorganic volition to move, and aware that the muscles are obedient to my will, but at the same time aware that my limb is arrested in its motion by some external impediment;—in this case I cannot be conscious of myself as the resisted relative without at the same time being conscious, being immediately percipient, of a not-self as the resisting correlative. In this cognition there is no sensation, no subjective-organic affection. I simply know myself as a force in energy, the not self as a counter force in energy.—So much for the quasi-primary quality, as dependent on the enorganic volition.

But though such pure perception may be detected in the simple apprehension of resistance, in reality it does not stand alone; for it is always accompanied by sensations, of which the muscular nisus or quiescence, on the one hand, and the resisting, the pressing body, on the other, are the causes. Of these sensations, the former, to wit the feelings connected with the states of tension and relaxation, lie wholly in the muscles, and belong to what has sometimes been distinguished as the muscular sense. The latter, to wit the sensations determined by the foreign pressure, lie partly in the skin, and belong to the sense of touch proper and cutaneous feeling, partly in the flesh, and belonging to the muscular sense. These affections, sometimes pleasurable, sometimes painful, are, in either case, merely modifications of the sensitive nerves distributed to the muscles and to the skin; and, as manifested to us, constitute the secondary quality, the sensation of which accompanies the perception of every secundo-primary.

Although the preceding doctrine coincide, in result, with that which M. Maine de Biran, after a hint by Locke, has so ably developed, more especially in his 'Nouvelles Considerations sur les Rapports du Physique et du Moral de l'Homme;' I find it impossible to go along with his illustrious editor, M. Cousin, (p. xxv. of Preface,) in thinking that his examination of Hume's reasoning against the deduction of our notion of Power from the consciousness of efficacy in the voluntary movement of our muscles, 'leaves nothing to desire, and nothing to reply.' On the contrary, though always dissenting with diffidence from M. Cousin, I confess it does not seem to me, that in any of his seven assaults on Hume, has De Biran grappled with the most formidable objections of the great sceptic. The *second*, *third*, and *seventh*, of Hume's arguments, as stated and criticised by Biran, are not proposed, as arguments, by Hume at all; and the *fourth* and *fifth* in Biran's array constitute only a single reasoning in Hume's. Of the three arguments which remain, the *first* and *sixth* in Biran's enumeration are the most important. —But, under the *first*, the examples alleged by Hume, from cases of sudden palsy, Biran silently passes by; yet these present by far the most perplexing difficulties for his doctrine of conscious efficacy. In another and subsequent work (Réponses, &c., p. 366) he, indeed, incidentally considers this objection, referring us back for its regular refutation to the strictures on Hume, where, however, as stated, no such refutation is to be found. Nor does he in this latter treatise relieve the difficulty. For as regards the argument from our non consciousness of loss of power, prior to an actual attempt to move, as shown in the case of paralysis supervening during sleep,—this, it seems to me, can only be answered from the fact, that we are never conscious of force, as unexerted or in potentia, (for the ambiguous term *power*, unfortunately after Locke employed by Hume in the discussion, is there equivalent to *force*, *vis*, and not to mere *potentiality* as opposed to *actuality*,) but only of force, as in actu or exerted. For in this case, we never can possibly be conscious of the absence of a force, previously to the effort made to put it forth.—The purport of the *sixth* argument is not given, as Hume, notwithstanding the usual want of precision in his language, certainly intended it;—which was to this effect;—Volition to move a limb, and the actual moving of it, are the first and last in a series of more than two successive events; and cannot, therefore, stand to each other, immediately, in the relation of cause and effect. They may, however, stand to each other in the relation of cause and effect, mediately. But, then, if they can be known in consciousness as thus mediately related, it is a necessary condition of such knowledge, that the intervening series of causes and effects, through which the final movement of the limb is supposed to be mediately dependent on the primary volition to move, should be known to consciousness immediately under that relation. But this intermediate, this connecting series

28. Our conceptions of the Primary are clear and distinct; of the Secundo-primary, both as secondary and quasi-primary qualities, clear and distinct; of the Secondary, as subjective affections, clear and distinct, as objective, obscure and confused. For the Primary, Secundo-primary, and Secondary, as subjective affections, we can represent in imagination; the Secondary, as objective powers, we cannot.

29. Finally—The existential judgments

---

is, confessedly, unknown to consciousness at all, far less as a series of causes and effects. It follows therefore, a fortiori, that the dependency of the last on the first of these events, as of an effect upon its cause, must be to consciousness unknown. In other words:—having no consciousness that the volition to move is the efficacious force (power) by which even the event immediately consequent on it (say the transmission of the nervous influence from brain to muscle) is produced, such event being in fact itself to consciousness occult; multo minus can we have a consciousness of that volition being the efficacious force, by which the ultimate movement of the limb is mediately determined? This is certainly the argument which Hume intended, and as a refutation of the doctrine, that in our voluntary movements at least, we have an apprehension of the causal nexus between the mental volition as cause and the corporeal movement as effect, it seems to me unanswerable. But as stated, and easily refuted, by De Biran, it is only tantamount to the reasoning—That as we are not conscious *how* we move a limb, we cannot be conscious of the feeling *that* we do exert a motive force. But such a feeling of force, action, energy, Hume did not deny.

II.—*Historical notices touching the recognition of the Locomotive Faculty as a medium of perception, and of the Muscular Sense.*—That the recognition of the Locomotive Faculty, or rather, the recognition of the Muscular Sense as a medium of apprehension, is of a recent date, and by psychologists of this country, is an opinion in both respects erroneous.—As far as I am aware, this distinction was originally taken by two Italian Aristotelians, some three centuries ago; and when the observation was again forgotten, both France and Germany are before Scotland in the merit of its modern revival.

It was first promulgated by Julius Cæsar Scaliger about the middle of the sixteenth century (1557.) Aristotle, followed by philosophers in general, had referred the perception of weight (the heavy and light) to the sense of Touch; though, in truth, under Touch, Aristotle seems to have comprehended both the Skin and Muscular senses. See Hist. An. L 4. De Part. An. ii. 1, 10. De Anima, ii. 11. On this particular doctrine, Scaliger, inter alia, observes: 'Et sane sic videtur. Namque gravitas et levitas tangendo deprehenditur. Ac nemo est, qui non putet, attrectatione sese cognoscere gravitatem et levitatem. Mihi tamen haud persuadetur. Tactu motum deprehendi fateor, gravitatem nego. Est autem maximum argumentum hoc. Gravitas est objectum motivæ potestatis: cui sane competit *actio*. At tactus non fit, nisi *patiendo*. Gravitas ergo percipitur a motiva potestate, non a tactu. Nam duo cum sint instrumenta (de nervis atque spiritibus loquor,) ad sensum et ob motum, a se invicem distincta; male confunderemus, quod est motricis objectum, cum objecto motæ. Movetur enim tactus, non agit. Motrix autem movet grave corpus, non autem movetur ab eo. Idque manifestum est in paralysi. Sentitur calor, non sentitur gravitas. Motrici namque instrumenta sublata sunt.—An vero *sentitur* gravitas? Sentitur quidem a motrice, atque ab ea judicatur: quemadmodum difficile quippiam enunciatu [enunciatur?] ab ipsa intellectus vi: quæ tamen agit, non patitur, cum enunciat. Est enim omnibus commune rebus nostratibus hisce, quæ pendent a materia: ut agendo patiantur.—Poterit aliquid objici de compressione. Nam etc. . . . Sunt præterea duæ rationes. Quando et sine tactu sentimus gravitatem, et quia tactu non sentimus. Nempe cuipiam gravi corpori manus imposita contingit illud: at non sentit gravitatem. Sine tactu, vero, virtus motrix sentiet. Appensum filo plumbum grave sentitur. Manus tamen filum, non plumbum tangit. Deinde hoc. Brachium suo pondere cum deorsum fertur, sentitur grave. At nihil tangit.' (De Subtilitate, contra Cardanum, ex. 109.)

It should, however, be noticed, that Scaliger may have taken the hint for the discrimination of this and another sense, from Cardan. This philosopher makes Touch fourfold. One sense apprehending the four primary qualities, the Hot and Cold, the Dry and Humid; a second the Pleasurable and Painful; a third the Venereal sensations; a fourth the *Heavy* and *Light*. (De Subtilitate, L. xiii.)

This doctrine did not excite the attention it deserved. It was even redargued by Scaliger's admiring expositor Goclenius. (Adversaria, p. 75—80); nor do I know, indeed, that previous to its revival in very recent times, with the exception to be immediately stated, that this opinion was ever countenanced by any other philosopher. Towards the end of the seventeenth century it is indeed commemorated by Chauvin, no very erudite authority, in the *first* edition of his Lexicon Philosophicum (vv. *Tactile* and *Gravitas*) as an opinion that had found supporters; but it is manifest from the terms of the statement, for no names are given, that Scaliger and Scaliger only is referred to. In the subsequent edition the statement itself is omitted.

By another philosophical physician, the celebrated Cæsalpinus of Arezzo, it was afterwards (in 1569) still more articulately shown, that only by the exercise of the motive power are we percipient of those qualities which I denominate the Secundo-Primary; though he can hardly be said, like Scaliger, to have discriminated that power as a faculty of perception or active apprehension, from touch as a

are of the Primary assertory; of the Secundo-primary, in both their aspects, assertory; of the Secondary, as modes of mind, assertory, as modes of matter, problematic. (See par. 11, 12, 13.)

e)—*As both in Sensitive Apprehension and in Thought; as in relation both to Sense and Intellect.*

80. In the order of nature and of ne-

---

capacity of sensation or mere consciousness of passion. It does not indeed appear that Cæsalpinus was aware of Scaliger's speculation at all.

'Tactus igitur si unus est sensus, circa unam erit contrarietatem, reliquæ autem ad ipsam reducentur. [Compare Aristotle, De Anima, ii. 11.] Patet autem Calidum et Frigidum maxime proprie ipsius tactus esse; solum enim tangendo comprehenduntur. Humidum autem et Siccum (Fluid and Solid), Durum et Molle, Grave et Leve, Asperum et Lene, Rarum et Densum, aliaque hujusmodi, ut tactu comprehendantur, *non satis est ea tangere, sed necesse est motum quendam adhibere*, aut comprimendo, aut impellendo, aut trahendo, aut alia ratione patiendi potentiam experiendo Sic enim quod proprium terminum non retinet, et quod facile dividitur, Humidum esse cognoscimus; quod autem opposito modo se habet, Siccum: et quod cedit comprimenti, Molle, quod non cedit, Durum. Similiter autem et reliquæ tactivæ qualitates sine motu non percipiuntur. Idcirco et a reliquis sensibus cognosci possunt, ut a visu. [But not immediately.] Motus enim inter communia sensibilia ponitur. [There is here through ambiguity a mutatio elenchi.] Nihil autem refert, an motus in organo an in re fiat.' [?] (Quæstiones Peripateticæ, L. iv. qu. 1.)

In more recent times, the action of the voluntary motive faculty and its relative sense in the perception of Extension, Figure, Weight, Resistance, &c., was in France brought vaguely into notice by Condillac, and subsequently about the commencement of the present century more explicitly developed, among others, by his distinguished follower M. Destutt de Tracy, who established the distinction between *active* and *passive* touch. The speculations of M Maine de Biran on muscular effort (from 1803,) I do not here refer to; as these have a different and greatly higher significance. (*Condillac*, Traité des Sensations, P. ii. cc. 3, 12. —*De Tracy*, Idéologie, t. i. cc. 9–13; t. iii. cc. 5, 9.—Compare *Degerando*, Histoire des Systèmes, t. iii. p. 343, sq. orig. ed., and *Laboulinière*, Précis, p. 321, sq.)—In Germany, before the conclusion of the last century, the same analysis was made, and the active touch there first obtained the distinctive appellation of the Muscular Sense (Muskel Sinn.) The German physiologists and psychologists not only—what had been previously done—professedly demonstrated the share it had in the empirical apprehension of Space, &c., and established its necessity as a condition even of the perceptions of Touch proper—the Skin Sense; they likewise for the first time endeavoured to show how in vision we are enabled to recognise not only figure, but distance, and the third dimension of bodies, through the conscious adjustment of the eye. (*Tittel*, Kantische Denkformen, (1787,) p. 183, sq.—*Tiedemann*, in Hessische Beytraege (1789,) St. i. p. 119, sq.; Theaetet (1794,) passim; Idealistische Briefe (1798,) p. 84, sq.; Psychologia (1804,) p. 405, sq.—*Schulz*, Pruefung (1791,) i. p. 182, sq.—*Engel*, in Mémoires de l'Academie de Berlin (1802.)—*Gruithuisen*, Anthropologie (1810,) pp. 130, sq. 361, sq. and the subsequent works of *Herbart*, *Hartmann*, *Lenhossek*, *Tourtual*, *Beneke*, and a host of others.) But see Reid, 188, b.

Britain has not advanced the enquiry which, if we discount some resultless tendencies by Hartley, Wells, and Darwin, she was the last in taking up; and it is a curious instance of the unacquaintance with such matters prevalent among us, that the views touching the functions of the will, and of the muscular sense, which constitute, in this relation certainly, not the least valuable part of Dr Brown's psychology, should to the present hour be regarded as original, howbeit these views, though propounded as new, are manifestly derived from sources with which all interested in psychological disquisitions might reasonably be presumed familiar. This is by no means a solitary instance of Brown's silent appropriation; nor is he the only Scottish metaphysician who has borrowed, without acknowledgment, these and other psychological analyses from the school of Condillac. De Tracy may often equally reclaim his own at the hands of Dr John Young, Professor of Philosophy in Belfast College, whose frequent coincidences with Brown are not the marvels he would induce us to believe, when we know the common sources from which the resembling doctrines are equally derived. It must be remembered, however, that the Lectures of both Professors were posthumously published; and are therefore not to be dealt with as works deliberately submitted to general criticism by their authors. Dr Young, it should likewise be noticed, was a pupil of the late Professor Mylne of Glasgow, whose views of mental philosophy are well known to have closely resembled those of M. De Tracy. I see from M. Mignet's eloquent *eloge* that this acute philosopher was, like Kant, a Scotsman by descent, and 'of the clan Stutt,' (Stott?)

These notices of the gradual recognition of the sense of muscular feeling, as a special source of knowledge, are not given on account of any importance it may be thought to possess as the source from which is derived our notion of Space or Extension. This notion, I am convinced, though first manifested in, cannot be evolved out of, experience; and what was observed by Reid (Inq. p. 126, a,) by Kant (Cr. d. r. V. p. 38,) by Schulz (Pruef. i p. 114,) and by Stewart (Essays, p. 564,) in regard to the attempts which had previously been made to deduce it from the operations of sense, and, in particular, from the motion of the hand, is equally true of those subsequently repeated. In all these attempts, the exper-

cessary thought, the Primary qualities are prior to the Secundo-primary and Secondary; but in the order of empirical apprehension, though chronologically simultaneous, they are posterior to both. For it is only under condition of the Sensation of a Secondary, that we are percipient of any Primary, quality.

31. The apprehension of a Primary quality is principally an intellectual cogni-

---

ence itself is only realized through a substitution of the very notion which it professes to generate; there is always a concealed petitio principii. Take for example the deduction so laboriously essayed by Dr Brown, and for which he has received such unqualified encomium. (Lectt. 23 and 24.)—Extension is made up of three dimensions; but Brown's exposition is limited to length and breadth. These only, therefore, can be criticised.

As far as I can find his meaning in his cloud of words, he argues thus:—The notion of Time or succession being supposed, that of *longitudinal* extension is given in the succession of feelings which accompanies the gradual contraction of a muscle; the notion of this succession constitutes, ipso facto, the notion of a certain length; and the notion of this length [he quietly takes for granted] is the notion of longitudinal extension sought, (p. 146. a.) —The paralogism here is transparent.—Length is an ambiguous term; and it is length in space, extensive length, and not length in time, protensive length, whose notion it is the problem to evolve. To convert, therefore, the notion of a certain kind of length (and that certain kind being also confessedly only length in time) into the notion of a length in space, is at best an idle begging of the question.—Is it not? Then I would ask, whether the series of feelings of which we are aware in the gradual contraction of a muscle, involve the consciousness of being a succession or length, (1) in time alone? or (2) in space alone? —or (3) in time and space together? These three cases will be allowed to be exhaustive. If the first be affirmed, if the succession appear to consciousness a length in time exclusively, then nothing has been accomplished; for the notion of extension or space is in no way contained in the notion of duration or time.—Again, if the second or the third be affirmed, if the series appear to consciousness a succession or length, either in space alone, or in space and time together, then is the notion it behoved to generate employed to generate itself.

In the deduction of the notion of *superficial* extension he is equally illogical; for here, too, his process of evolution only in the end openly extracts what in the commencement it had secretly thrown in. The elements, out of which he constructs the notion of extension, in the second dimension, he finds in the consciousness we have of several contemporaneous series of muscular feelings or lengths, standing in relation to each other, as *proximate, distant, intermediate*, &c.—Proximate! In What? In time? No; for the series are supposed to be in time coexistent; and were it otherwise, the process would be unavailing for proximity in time does not afford proximity in space. In space, then? Necessarily. On this alternative, however, the notion of space or extension is already involved doubly deep in the elements themselves, out of which it is proposed to construct it; for when two or more things are conceived as proximate in space, they are not merely conceived as in different places or out of each other, but over and above this elementary condition in which extension simply is involved, they are conceived as even holding under it a secondary and more complex relation. But it is needless to proceed, for the petition of the point in question is even more palpable if we think the series under the relations of the *distant*, the *intermediate* &c.—The notion of Space, therefore, is not shown by this explanation of its genesis to be less a native notion than that of Time, which it admits. Brown's is a modification of De Tracy's deduction, the change being probably suggested by a remark of Stewart (l. n.); but though both involve a paralogism, it is certainly far more shrewdly cloaked in the original.

III.—*Historical notices in regard to the distinction of Nerves and nervous Filaments into Motive and Sensitive; and in regard to the peculiarity of function, and absolute isolation, of the ultimate nervous Filaments.*—The important discovery of Sir Charles Bell, that the spinal nerves are the organs of motion through their anterior roots, of sensation through their posterior; and the recognition by recent physiologists, that each ultimate nervous filament is distinct in function, and runs isolated from its origin to its termination;—these are only the last of a long series of previous observations to the same effect,—observations, in regard to which (as may be inferred from the recent discussions touching the history of these results) the medical world is, in a great measure, uninformed. At the same time, as these are the physiological facts with which psychology is principally interested; as a contribution towards this doctrine and its history, I shall throw together a few notices, which have for the most part fallen in my way when engaged in researches for a different purpose.

The cases of paralysis without narcosis (stupor,) and of narcosis without paralysis—for the ancient propriety of these terms ought to be observed—that is, the cases in which either motion or sensibility, exclusively, is lost, were too remarkable not to attract attention even from the earliest periods; and at the same time, too peremptory not to necessitate the conclusion, that the several phænomena are, either the functions of different organs, or, if of the same, at least regulated by different conditions. Between these alternatives all opinions on the subject are divided; and the former was the first, as it has been the last, to be adopted.

No sooner had the nervous system been recognised as the ultimate organ of the animal and vital functions, and the intracranial me-

tion, in so far as it is, in itself, a purely mental activity, and not the mere sensation of an organic passion; and secondarily, a sensible cognition, in so far as it is the perception of an attribute of matter, and, though not constituted by, still not realized without, the sensation of an organic passion.—The apprehension of a Secondary quality is solely a sensible cognition; for it is nothing but the sen-

---

dulla or encephalos (*encephalon* is a modern misnomer) ascertained to be its centre, than *Erasistratus* proceeded to appropriate to different parts of that organism the functions which, along with Herophilus, he had distinguished, of sensibility and voluntary motion. He placed the source—of the former in the meninges or membranes, of the latter in the substance, of the encephalos in general, that is, of the Brain-proper and After-brain or Cerebellum. And while the nerves were, mediately or immediately, the prolongations of these, he viewed the nervous membranes as the vehicle of sensation, the nervous substance as the vehicle of motion. (Rufus Ephesius, L. i. c. 22; L. ii cc. 2, 17.) This theory which is remarkable, if for nothing else, for manifesting the tendency from an early period to refer the phænomena of motion and sensation to distinct parts of the nervous organism, has not obtained the attention which it even intrinsically merits. In modern times, indeed, the same opinion has been hazarded, even to my fortuitous knowledge, at least thrice. Firstly by Fernelius (1550, Physiologia, v. 10, 15;) secondly by Rosetti (1722, Raccolta d'Opuscoli, &c., t. v. p. 272 sq.;) thirdly by Le Cat (1740, Traité des Sensations, Œuv. Phys. t. i. p. 124, and Diss. sur la Sensibilité des Meninges, § 1.)—By each of these the hypothesis is advanced as original. In the two last this is not to be marvelled at; but it is surprising how the opinion of Erasistratus could have escaped the erudition of the first. I may observe, that Erasistratus also anticipated many recent physiologists in the doctrine, that the intelligence of man, and of animals in general, is always in proportion to the depth and number of the cerebral convolutions, that is, in the ratio of the extent of cerebral surface, not of cerebral mass.

The second alternative was adopted by *Galen*, who while he refutes apparently misrepresents the doctrine of Erasistratus; for Erasistratus did not, if we may credit Rufus, an older authority than Galen, derive the nerves from the membranes of the encephalos, to the exclusion of its substance; or if Galen be herein correct, this is perhaps the early doctrine which Erasistratus is by him said in his maturer years to have abandoned;—a doctrine, however, which, under modifications, has in modern times found supporters in Rondoletius and others. (Laurentii Hist. Anat. iv. qu. 13.)—Recognising, what has always indeed been done, the contrast of the two phænomena of sensibility and motion, Galen did not, however, regard them as necessarily the products of distinct parts of the nervous system, although, de facto, different parts of that system were often subservient to their manifestation. As to the problem—Do the nerves perform their double function by the conveyance of a corporeal fluid, or through the irradiation of an immaterial power?—Galen seems to vacillate; for texts may be adduced in favour of each alternative. He is not always consistent in the shares which he assigns to the heart and to the brain, in the elaboration of the animal spirits; nor is he even uniform in maintaining a discrimination of origin, between the animal spirits and the vital. Degrading the membranes to mere envelopments, he limits every peculiar function of the nervous organism to the enveloped substance of the brain, the after brain, the spinal chord and nerves. But as the animal faculty is one, and its proximate vehicle the animal spirits is homogeneous, so the nervous or cerebral substance which conducts these spirits is in its own nature uniform and indifferently competent to either function; it being dependent upon two accidental circumstances, whether this substance conduce to motion, to sensation, or to motion and sensation together.

The first circumstance is the degree of hardness or softness; a nerve being adapted to motion, or to sensation, in proportion as it possesses the former quality or the latter. Nerves extremely soft are exclusively competent to sensation. Nerves extremely hard are pre-eminently, but not exclusively, adapted to motion; for no nerve is wholly destitute of the feeling of touch. The soft nerves, short and straight in their course, arise from the anterior portion of the encephalos (the Brain proper;) the hard, more devious in direction, spring from the posterior portion of the brain where it joins the spinal chord, (Medulla oblongata?) the spinal chord being a continuation of the After-brain, from which no nerve immediately arises; the hardest originate from the spinal chord itself, more especially towards its inferior extremity. A nerve soft in its origin, and, therefore, fitted only for sense, may, however, harden in its progress, and by this change become suitable for motion.

The second circumstance is the part to which a nerve is sent; the nerve being sensitive or motive as it terminates in an organ of sense, or in an organ of motion—a muscle; every part being recipient only of the virtue appropriate to its special function.

This theory of Galen is inadequate to the phænomena. For though loss of motion without the loss of sense may thus be accounted for, on the supposition that the innervating force is reduced so low as not to radiate the stronger influence required for movement, and yet to radiate the feebler influence required for feeling; still this leaves the counter case (of which, though less frequently occurring, Galen has himself recorded some illustrious

sation of an organic passion.—The apprehension of a Secundo-primary quality is, equally and at once, an intellectual and sensible cognition; for it involves both the perception of a quasi-primary quality, and the sensation of a secondary. (See par. 15, sq., and Note D*, § 1.)

---

examples) not only unexplained, but even renders it inexplicable. In this theory Galen is, likewise, not always consistent with himself. The distinction of hard and soft, as corresponding with the distinction of motory and sensitive, nerves, though true in general, is, on his own admission, not absolutely throughgoing. (I must observe, however, that among other recent anatomists this is maintained by Albinus, Malacarne, and Reil.) And to say nothing of other vacillations, Galen, who in one sentence, in consistency with his distinction of cerebral and (mediately) cerebellar nerves, is forced to accord exclusively to those of the spine the function of motion; in another finds himself compelled, in submission to the notorious fact, to extend to these nerves the function of sensation likewise. But if Galen's theory be inadequate to their solution, it never leads him to overlook, to dissemble, or to distort, the phænomena themselves; and with these no one was ever more familiarly acquainted. So marvellous, indeed, is his minute knowledge of the distribution and functions of the several nerves, that it is hardly too much to assert, that, with the exception of a few minor particulars, his pathological anatomy of the nervous system is practically on a level with the pathological anatomy of the present day (De Usu Partium, l. 7, v. 9, 7, 14, viii. 3, 6, 10, 12, ix. 1, xii. 10, 11, 15. xiii. 8, xvi. 1, 3, 5, xvii. 2, 3.—De Causis Sympt. i. 5.—De Motu Musc. l. 13.—De Anat. Adm. vii. 8.—Ars parva, 10, 11.—De Locis Aff. i. 6, 7, 12. iii. 6, 12.—De Diss. Nerv. 1.—De Plac. Hipp. et Plat. ii. 12, vii. 3, 4, 5, 8.)

The next step was not made until the middle of the fourteenth century subsequent to Galen's death; when *Rondeletius* (c. 1550,) reasoning from the phænomena of paralysis and stupor, enounced it as an observation never previously made, that 'All nerves, from their origin in the brain, are, even in the spinal marrow itself, isolated from each other. The cause of paralysis is therefore not so much to be sought for in the spinal marrow as in the encephalic heads of the nerves; Galen himself having, indeed, remarked, that paralysis always supervenes when the origin of the nerve is obstructed or diseased.' (Curandi Methodus, c. 82.)

This observation did not secure the attention which it deserved; and some thirty years later (1595,) another French physiologist, another celebrated professor in the same university with Rondelet, I mean *Laurentius* of Montpellier, advanced this very doctrine of his predecessor, as 'a new and hitherto unheard-of observation.' This anatomist has, however, the merit of first attempting a sensible demonstration of the fact, by resolving, under water, the spinal cord into its constituent filaments. 'This new and admirable observation,' he says, 'explains one of the obscurest problems of nature; why it is that from a lesion, say of the cervical medulla, the motion of the thigh may be lost, while the motions of the arms and thorax shall remain entire.' In the second edition of his Anatomy, Dulaurens would seem, however, less confident, not only of the absolute originality, but of the absolute accuracy, of the observation. Nor does he rise above the Galenic doctrine, that sensibility and motion may be transmitted by the same fibre. In fact, rejecting the discrimination of hard and soft nerves, he abolishes even the accidental distinction which had been recognised by Galen. (Compare Hist. Anat., later editions, iv. c. 18, qq. 9, 10, 11; x. c. 12, with the relative places in the first.)

The third step was accomplished by *Varolius*, (1572,) who showed Galen to be mistaken in holding that the spinal chord is a continuation of the After-brain alone. He demonstrated, against all previous anatomists, that this chord is made up of *four* columns, severally arising from *four* encephalic roots; two roots or trunks from the Brain-proper being prolonged into its anterior, and two from the After-brain into its posterior, columns. (Anatomia, L. iii: De Nervis Opticis Epistolæ.)

At the same time, the fact was signalized by other contemporary anatomists, (as *Coiter*, 1572, *Laurentius*, 1595,) that the spinal nerves arise by double roots; one set of filaments emerging from the anterior, another from the posterior, portion of the chord. It was in general noticed, too, (as by *Coiter*, and *C. Bauhinus*, 1590,) that these filaments, on issuing from the chord, passed into a knot or ganglion; but, strange to say, it was reserved for the second Monro, (1783,) to record the special observation, that this ganglion is limited to the fibres of the posterior root alone

Such was the state of anatomical knowledge touching this point at the close of the sixteenth century; and it may now seem marvellous, that aware of the independence of the motory and sensitive functions,—aware that of these functions the cerebral nerves were, in general, limited to one, while the spinal nerves were competent to both,—aware that the spinal nerves, the nerves of double function, emerged by double roots and terminated in a twofold distribution,—and, finally, aware that each nervous filament ran distinct from its peripheral extremity through the spinal chord to its central origin;—aware, I say, of all these correlative facts, it may now seem marvellous that anatomists should have stopped short, should not have attempted to lay fact and fact together, should not have surmised that in the spinal nerves difference of root is correspondent with difference of function, should not have instituted experiments, and anticipated by two centuries the most remarkable physiological discovery of the present day. But our wonder will be enhanced, in finding the most illustrious of the more modern schools of medicine teaching the same doctrine in greater detail, and yet never proposing to itself the question—May not the double roots correspond with the double function of the spinal nerves? But so has it been with all the most momentous discoveries. When Harvey proclaimed the circulation of the blood, he only proclaimed a doctrine necessitated by the discovery of the venous valves; and the Newtonian theory of the heavens was but a final generalization, prepared by foregone observations, and even already partially enounced.

The school I refer to is that of *Leyden*—the school of Boerhaave and his disciples.—*Boerhaave* held with Willis that the Brain-proper is the organ of animality; a distinct part thereof being destined to each of its two functions, sense and voluntary motion;—that the After-brain is the organ of vitality, or the involuntary motions;—and that the two encephalic organs are prolonged, the former into the anterior, the latter into the posterior, columns of the spinal chord. In his doctrine, all nerves are composite, being made up of fibrils of a tenuity, not only beyond our means of observation, but almost beyond our capacity of imagination. Some nerves are homogeneous, their constituent filaments being either for a certain kind of motion alone, or for a certain kind of sensation alone; others are heterogeneous, their constituent fibrils being some for motion, some for sensation;—and of this latter class are the nerves which issue from the spine. On Boerhaave's doctrine, however, the spinal nerves, in so far as they arise from the anterior column, are nerves both of sensation and voluntary motion—of animality; in so far as they arise from the posterior column, are nerves of involuntary motion—of vitality. A homogeneous nerve does not, as a totality, perform a single office; for every elementary fibril of which it is composed runs from first to last isolated from every other, and has its separate sphere of exercise. As many distinct spheres of sensation and motion, so many distinct nervous origins and terminations; and as many different points of local termination in the body, so many different points of local origin in the brain. The Sensorium Commune, the centre of sensation and motion, is not therefore an indivisible point, not even an undivided place; it is, on the contrary, the aggregate of as many places (and millions of millions there may be) as there are encephalic origins of nervous fibrils. No nerve, therefore, in propriety of speech, gives off a branch; their sheaths of dura mater alone are ramified; and there is no intercourse, no sympathy between the elementary fibrils, except through the sensorium commune. That the nerves are made up of fibrils is shown, though inadequately, by various anatomical processes; and that these fibrils are destined for distinct and often different purposes, is manifested by the phænomena of disjoined paralysis and stupor. (De Morbis Nervorum Prælectiones, by Van Eems, pp. 261, 490-497, 696, 713-717. Compare *Kaau Boerhaave*, Impetum faciens, § 197-200.)

The developed doctrine of Boerhaave on this point is to be sought for, neither in his Aphorisms, nor in his Institutions and his Prelections on the Institutions—the more prominent works to which his illustrious disciples, *Haller* and *Van Swieten*, appended respectively a commentary.—The *latter* adopts, but does not advance, the doctrine of his master. (Ad Aph. 701, 711, 774, 1057, 1060.)—The *former*, who in his subsequent writings silently abandoned the opinion, that sensation and motion are conveyed by different nervous fibrils, in two unnoticed passages of his annotations on Boerhaave, (1740,) propounds it as a not improbable conjecture—that a total nerve may contain within its sheath a complement of motory and of sensitive tubules, distinct in their origin, transit, and distribution, but which at their peripheral extremity communicate; the latter, like veins, carrying the spirits back to the brain, which the former had, like arteries, carried out. (Ad Boerh. Instit. § 288, n. 2, § 293, n. 2.)

The doctrine of the school of Leyden, on this point, was however still more articulately evolved by the younger (Bernard Siegfried) *Albinus*; not in any of his published works, but in the prelections he delivered for many years, in that university, on Physiology. From a copy in my possession of his dictata in this course, very fully taken, after the middle of the century, by Dr William Grant, (of Rothiemurcus,) subsequently a distinguished medical author and practical physician in London, compared with another very accurate copy of these dictata, taken by an anonymous writer, in the year 1741; I am enabled to present the following general abstract of the doctrine taught by this celebrated anatomist, though obliged to retrench both the special cases, and the reasoning in detail by which it is illustrated and confirmed.

The nerves have a triple destination as they minister (1.) to voluntary motion, (2.) to sensation, (3.) to the vital energies—secretion, digestion, &c. Albinus seems to acquiesce in the doctrine, that the Brain-proper is the ultimate organ of the first and second function, the After-brain, of the third.

Nerves, again, are of two kinds. They are either such in which the function of each ultimate fibril remains isolated in function from centre to periphery (the cerebro-spinal nerves); or such in which these are mutually confluent (the ganglionic nerves.)

To speak only of the cerebro-spinal nerves, and of these only in relation to the functions of motion and sensation;—they are to be distinguished into three classes according as destined, (1.) to sense, (2.) to motion, (3) to both motion and sensation. Examples—of the first class are the olfactory, the optic, the auditory, of which last he considers the portio mollis and the portio dura to be, in propriety, distinct nerves;—of the second class, are the large portion of those passing to muscles, as the fourth and sixth pairs;—of the third class, are the three lingual nerves, especially the ninth pair, fibrils of which he has frequently traced, partly to the muscles, partly to the gustatory papillæ of the tongue, and the subcutaneous nerves, which are seen to give off branches, first to the muscles, and thereafter to the tactile papillæ of the skin. The nervous fibres which minister to motion are distinct in origin, in transit, in termination, from those which minister to sensation. This is manifest, in the case of those nerves which run from their origin in separate sheaths, either to an organ of sense (as the olfactory and optic), or to an organ of motion, (as the fourth and sixth pairs, which go to the muscles of the eye); but it is equally, though not so obtrusively, true, in the case where a nerve gives off branches partly to muscles, partly to the cutaneous papillæ. In this latter case, the nervous fibrils or fistulæ are, from their origin in the medulla oblongata to their final termination in the skin, perfectly distinct.—The Medulla Oblongata is a continuation of the encephalos; made up of two columns from the Brain-proper, and of two columns from the After-brain. Immediately or mediately, it is the origin, as it is the organ, of all the nerves. And in both respects it is double; for one part, the organ of sense, affords an origin to the sensitive fibrils; whilst another, the organ of motion, does the same by the motory. In their progress, indeed, after passing out, the several fibrils, whether homogeneous or not, are so conjoined by the investing membranes as to exhibit the appearance of a single nerve; but when they approach their destination they separate, those for motion ramifying through the muscles, those for sensation going to the cutaneous papillæ or other organs of sense. Examples of this are afforded --in the ninth pair, the fibres of which (against more modern anatomists) he holds to arise by a double origin in the medulla, and which, after running in the same sheath, separate according to their different functions and destinations;—and in the seventh pair, the hard and soft portions of which are respectively for motion and for sensation, though these portions, he elsewhere maintains, ought rather to be considered as two distinct nerves than as the twofold constituents of one.

The proof of this is of various kinds.—In the *first* place, it is a theory forced upon us by the phænomena; for only on this supposition can we account for the following facts:—(1) That we have distinct sensations transmitted to the brain from different parts of the same sensitive organ (as the tongue) through which the same total nerve is diffused. (2) That we can send out from the brain a motive influence to one, nay, sometimes to a part of one, muscle out of a plurality, among which the same total nerve (e. g. the ischiatic) is distributed. (3) That sometimes a part is either, on the one hand, paralysed, without any loss of sensibility; or, on the other, stupified, without a diminution of its mobility.

In the *second* place, we can demonstrate the doctrine, proceeding both from centre to periphery, and from periphery to centre.—Though ultimately dividing into filaments beyond our means of observation, we can still go far in following out a nerve both in its general ramifications, and in the special distribution of its filaments, for motion to the muscles and for sensation to the skin, &c.; and how far soever we are able to carry our investigation, we always find the least fibrils into which we succeed in analysing a nerve, equally distinct and continuous as the chord of which they were constituent.—And again, in following back the filaments of motion from the muscles, the filaments of sensation from the skin, we find them ever collected into larger and larger bundles within the same sheath, but never losing their individuality, never fused together to form the substance of a larger chord.—The nerves are thus not analogous to arteries, which rise from a common trunk, convey a common fluid, divide into branches all similar in action to each other and to the primary trunk. For every larger nerve is only a complement of smaller nerves, and every smallest nerve only a fasciculus of nervous fibrils; and these not only numerically different, but often differing from each other in the character of their functions.

In the *third* place, that in the nerves for both motion and sensation are enveloped distinct nerves or fibrils for these several functions—this is an inference supported by the analogy of those nerves which are motive or sensitive, exclusively. And in regard to these latter, it becomes impossible, in some cases, to conceive why a plurality of nerves should have been found necessary, as in the case of the two portions of the seventh pair, in reality distinct nerves, if we admit the supposition that each nerve, each nervous fibril, is competent to the double office.

In the *fourth* place, the two species of nerve are distinguished by a difference of structure. For he maintains the old Galenic doctrine, that the nerves of motion are, as compared with those of sensation, of a harder and more fibrous texture;—a diversity which he does not confine to the homogeneous nerves, but extends to the counter filaments of the heterogeneous.—This opinion, in modern times, by the majority surrendered rather than refuted, has been also subsequently maintained by a small number of the most accurate anatomists, as Malacarne and Reil; and to this result the recent observations of Ehrenberg and others seem to tend. (See Memoirs of the Berlin Academy for 1836, p. 605, sq.; Mueller's Phys. p. 598.)

Finally, to the objection—Why has nature not, in all cases as in some, enclosed the motive and the sentient fibrils in distinct sheaths?—as answer, and *fifth* argument, he shows, with great ingenuity, that nature does precisely what, in the circumstances, always affords the greatest security to both, more especially to the softer, fibrils; and he might have added, as a *sixth* reason and second answer—with the smallest expenditure of means.

The subtilty of the nervous fibres is much greater than is commonly suspected; and there is probably no point of the body to which they are not distributed. What is the nature of their peripheral terminations it is, however, difficult to demonstrate; and the doctrines of Ruysch and Malpighi in this respect are, as he shows, unsatisfactory.

The doctrine of Albinus, indeed, of the whole school of Boerhaave, in regard to the nervous system, and, in particular, touching the distinction and the isolation of the ultimate nervous filaments, seems during a century of interval not only to have been neglected but absolutely forgotten; and a counter opinion of the most erroneous character, with here and there a feeble echo of the true, to have become generally prevalent in its stead. For, strange to say, this very doctrine is that recently promulgated as the last consummation of nervous physiology by the most illustrious physiologist in Europe. "That the primitive fibres of all the cerebro-spinal nerves are to be regarded as isolated and distinct from their origin to their termination, and as radii issuing from the axis of the nervous system," is the grand result, as stated by himself, of the elaborate researches of *Johann Mueller*; and to the earliest discovery of this general fact he carefully vindicates his right against other contemporary observers, by stating that it had been privately communicated by him to Van der Kolk, of Utrecht, so long ago as the year 1830. (Phys. p. 596–603.)

In conclusion, I may observe that it is greatly to be regretted that these Prelections of Albinus were never printed. They present not only a full and elegant digest of all that was known in physiology at the date of their delivery, (and Albinus was celebrated for the uncommon care which he bestowed on the composition of his lectures;) but they likewise contain, perdue, many original views, all deserving of attention, and some which have been subsequently re-produced to the no small celebrity of their second authors. The speculation, for example, of John Hunter and Dr Thomas Young, in regard to the self-contractile property of the Chrystalline lens is here anticipated; and that pellucidity and fibrous structure are compatible, shown by the analogy of those gelatinous mollusca, the medusæ or sea blubbers, which are not more remarkable for their transparency, than for their contractile and dilative powers.

As I have already noticed, the celebrity of the Leyden School far from commanding acceptance, did not even secure adequate attention to the doctrine of its illustrious masters; and the Galenic theory, to which Haller latterly adhered, was, under the authority of Cullen and the Monros, that which continued to prevail in this country, until after the commencement of the present century. Here another step in advance was then made by *Mr Alexander Walker*, an ingenious Physiologist of Edinburgh; who, in 1809, first started the prolific notion, that in the spinal nerves the filaments of sensation issue by the one root, the filaments of motion by the other. His attribution of the several functions to the several roots—sensation to the anterior, motion to the posterior — with strong presumption in its favour from general analogy, and its conformity with the tenor of all previous, and much subsequent, observation, is, however, opposed to the stream of later and more precise experiment. Anatomists have been long agreed that the anterior column of the spinal marrow is in continuity with the brain-proper, the posterior, with the after-brain. To say nothing of the Galenic doctrine, Willis and the School of Boerhaave had referred the automatic, Heboken and Pontean the automatic and voluntary, motions to the cerebellum. Latterly, the experiments of Rolando, Flourens, and other physiologists, would show that to the after-brain belongs the power of regulated or voluntary motion; while the parallelism which I have myself detected, between the relative development of that part of the encephalos in young animals and their command over the action of their limbs, goes, likewise, to prove that such motion is one, at least, of the cerebellic functions. (See Monro's Anatomy of the Brain, 1831, p. 4—9.) In contending, therefore, that the nervous filaments of sensation ascend in the anterior rachitic column to the brain-proper, and the nervous filaments of motion in the posterior, to the after-brain; Mr Walker originally proposed, and still maintains, the alternative which, independently of precise experiment, had the greatest weight of general probability in its favour. (Archives of Science for 1809; The Nervous System, 1834, p. 50, sq.)

In 1811, *Sir Charles Bell*, holding always the connexion of the brain proper with the anterior, of the after-brain with the posterior, column of the spinal chord, proceeding, however, not on general probabilities, but on experiments expressly instituted on the roots themselves of the spinal nerves, first advanced the counter doctrine, that to the filaments ascending by the posterior roots belongs exclusively the function of sensation; and thereafter, but still, as is now clearly proved, previously to any other physiologist, he further established by a most ingenious combination of special analogy and experiment, the correlative fact, that the filaments descending by the anterior roots are the sole vehicles of voluntary motion. These results, confirmed as they have been by the principal physiologists throughout Europe, seem now placed above the risk of refutation. It still, however, remains to reconcile the seeming structural connexion, and the manifest functional opposition, of the after-brain and posterior rachitic column; for the decussation in the medulla oblongata, observed, among others, by Rolando and Solly, whereby the cerebellum and anterior column are connected, is apparently too partial to reconcile the discordant phænomena. (*Bell's* Nervous System; *Shaw's* Narrative; *Mueller's* Physiology, &c.)

As connected with the foregoing notices, I may here call attention to a remarkable case reported by M. Rey Regis, a medical observer, in his 'Histoire Naturelle de l'Ame.' This work, which is extremely rare, I have been unable to consult, and must therefore rely on the abstract given by M. de Biran in his 'Nouvelles Considerations,' p. 96, sq. This case, as far as I am aware, has escaped the observation of all subsequent physiologists. In its phænomena, and in the inferences to which they lead, it stands alone; but whether the phænomena are themselves anomalous, or that experiments, with the same intent, not having been made in like cases, they have not in these been brought in like manner into view, I am unable to determine.—A man lost the power of movement in one half of his body, (one lateral half, probably, but in De Biran's account the paralysis is not distinctly stated as hemiplegia;) while the sensibility of the parts affected remained apparently entire. Experiments, various and repeated, were, however, made to ascertain with accuracy, whether the loss of the motive faculty had occasioned any alteration in the capacity of feeling: and it was found that the patient, though as acutely alive as ever to the sense of pain, felt, when this was secretly inflicted, as by compression of his hand under the bed-clothes, a sensation of suffering or uneasiness, by which, when the pressure became strong, he was compelled lustily to cry out; but a sensation merely general, he being altogether unable to localise the feeling, or to say from whence the pain proceeded. It is unfortunately not stated whether he could discriminate one pain from another, say the pain of pinching from the pain of pricking; but had this not been the case, the notice of so remarkable a circumstance could hardly, I presume, have been overlooked. The patient, as he gradually recovered the use of his limbs, gradually also recovered the power of localizing his sensations.—It would be important to test the value of this observation by similar experiments, made on patients similarly affected. Until this be done, it would be rash to establish any general inferences upon its facts.

I may notice also another problem, the solution of which ought to engage the attention of those who have the means of observation in their power. Is the sensation of heat dependent upon a peculiar set of nerves? This to me seems probable; 1°, because certain sentient parts of the body are insensible to this feeling; and, 2°, because I have met with cases recorded, in which, while sensibility in general was abolished, the sensibility to heat remained apparently undiminished.

NOTE D.*

PERCEPTION;

PERCEPTION PROPER AND SENSATION PROPER.*

I.—*Principal momenta of the Editor's doctrine of Perception, (A) in itself, and (B) in contrast to that of Reid, Stewart, Royer Collard, and other philosophers of the Scottish School.*

II.—*Historical notices in regard to the distinction of Perception proper and Sensation proper.*

[References.—From Inq. 182 b; from I. P. 729 a, 813 ab; from Supplementary Dissertations, passim.]

---

§ I.—*Principal momenta of the Editor's doctrine of Perception.*

A)—*In itself:*

I.—*Perception in general.*

1. *Sensitive Perception*, or *Perception* simply, is that act of Consciousness whereby we apprehend in our body,

a.) Certain *special affections*, whereof as an *animated* organism it is contingently susceptible; and

b.) Those *general relations of extension* under which as a *material* organism it necessarily exists.

---

* A word as to the various meanings of the terms here prominent—*Perception, Sensation, Sense.*

I.—*Perception* (Perceptio; Perception; Percezione; Percepcion, Wahrnehmung) has different significations; but under all and each of these, the term has a common ambiguity, denoting as it may, either 1° the perceiving Faculty, or 2° the perceiving Act, or 3° the Object perceived. Of these the only ambiguity of importance is the last; and to relieve it I would propose the employment, in this relation, of *Percept*, leaving *Perception* to designate both the faculty and its act; for these it is rarely necessary to distinguish, as what is applicable to the one is usually applicable to the other.

But to the significations of the term, as applied to *different* faculties, acts, and objects; of which there are in all four:—

1. *Perceptio*—which has been naturalised in all the principal languages of modern Europe, with the qualified exception of the German, in which the indigenous term Wahrnehmung has again almost superseded it—Perceptio, in its primary philosophical signification, as in the mouths of Cicero and Quintilian, is vaguely equivalent to Comprehension, Notion, or Cognition in general.

2. From this first meaning it was easily deflected to a second, in which it corresponds to an apprehension, a becoming aware of, in a word, a consciousness. In this meaning, though long thus previously employed in the schools, it was brought more prominently and distinctively forward in the writings of Descartes. From him it passed, not only to his own disciples, but, like the term Idea, to his antagonist, Gassendi, and, thereafter, adopted equally

Of these Perceptions, the former, which is thus conversant about a *subject-object*, is *Sensation proper*; the latter, which is thus conversant about an *object-object*, is *Perception proper*. (See 808 b, 858 a.)

2. All Perception is an act of Consciousness; no Perception, therefore, is possible except under the conditions under which Consciousness is possible. (See Note H.) The eight following conditions are partly common to Perception with the other acts of Consciousness; partly proper to it as a special operation.

3. The first is a certain *concentration* of consciousness on an object of sense;—an act of *Attention*, however remiss.*

---

by Locke and Leibnitz, it remained a household word in every subsequent philosophy, until its extent was farther limited, and thus a third signification given to it.

Under this second meaning it is, however, proper to say a word in regard to the special employment of the term in the Cartesian and Leibnitio-Wolfian philosophies.—Perception the Cartesians really identified with *Idea* (using this term in its unexclusive universality, but discounting Descartes' own abusive application of it to the organic movement in the brain, of which the mind has, ex hypothesi, no consciousness) and allowed them only a logical distinction;—the same representative act being called Idea, in as much as we regard it as a representation, i. e. view it in relation to what through it, as represented, is mediately known, and Perception, in as much as we regard it as a consciousness of such representation, i. e. view it in relation to the knowing mind.—The Leibnitio-Wolfians, on the other hand, distinguished three acts in the process of representative cognition:—1° the act of representing a (mediate) object to the mind; 2° the representation, or, to speak more properly, representamen, itself as an (immediate or vicarious) object exhibited to the mind; 3° the act by which the mind is conscious, immediately of the representative object, and, through it, mediately of the remote object represented. They called the first *Perception*; the last *Apperception*; the second *Idea—sensual*, to wit, for what they styled the *material* Idea was only an organic motion propagated to the brain, which, on the doctrine of the pre-established harmony, is in sensitive cognition the arbitrary concomitant of the former, and, of course, beyond the sphere of consciousness or apperception.

3. In its third signification, Perception is limited to the apprehensions of Sense alone. This limitation was first formally imposed upon the word by Reid, for no very cogent reason besides convenience (222 b;) and, thereafter by Kant. Kant, again, was not altogether consistent; for he employs '*Perception*' in the second meaning, for the consciousness of any mental presentation, and thus in a sense corresponding to the *Apperception* of the Leibnitians, while its vernacular synonyme '*Wahrnehmung*' he defines in conformity with the third, as the consciousness of an empirical intuition. Imposed by such authorities, this is now the accredited signification of these terms, in the recent philosophies of Germany, Britain, France, Italy, &c.

4. But under this third meaning it is again, since the time and through the authority of Reid, frequently employed in a still more restricted acceptation, viz. as Perception (proper) in contrast to Sensation (proper.) The import of these terms, as used by Reid and other philosophers on the one hand, and by myself on the other, is explained in the text.

II.—*Sensation* (Sensatio; Sensation, Sentiment; Sensazione; Empfindung) has various significations; and in all of these, like Perception, Conception, Imagination, and other analogous terms in the philosophy of mind, it is ambiguously applied;—1°, for a Faculty—2°, for its Act—3°, for its Object. Here there is no available term like Percept, Concept, &c., whereby to discriminate the last.

There are two principal meanings in which this term has been employed.

1. Like the Greek *aisthesis*, it was long and generally used to comprehend the process of sensitive apprehension both in its subjective and its objective relations.

2. As opposed to Idea, Perception, &c. it was limited, first in the Cartesian school, and thereafter in that of Reid, to the subjective phasis of our sensitive cognitions; that is, to our consciousness of the affections of our animated organism,—or on the Neo-Platonic, Cartesian, and Leibnitian hypotheses, to the affections of the mind corresponding to, but not caused by, the unknown mutations of the body. Under this restriction, Sensation may, both in French and English, be employed to designate our corporeal or lower feelings, in opposition to Sentiment, as a term for our higher, i.e., our intellectual and moral, feelings.

III.—*Sense* (Sensus; Sens; Senso; Sinn) is employed in a looser and in a stricter application.

Under the former head it has two applications;—1°, a psychological, as a popular term for Intelligence; 2°, a logical, as a synonyme for Meaning.

Under the latter head, Sense is employed ambiguously;—1°, for the Faculty of sensitive apprehension; 2°, for its Act; 3°, for its Organ.

In this relation, Sense has been distinguished into External and Internal; but under the second term, in so many vague and various meanings, that I cannot here either explain or enumerate them.

On the analogical employments of the word, see above, p. 756 sq.

* St Jerome—'Quod mens videat et mens audiat, et quod nec audire quidpiam nec videre possumus, nisi sensus in ea quæ cernimus et audimus *intentus*, vetus sententia.' (Adv. Jovin. ii., 9.) See Aristotle, (Probl. xi., 33,) whom Jerome manifestly had in his eye; Strato Physicus as quoted by Plutarch, (De Sol. An. Opera, t. ii., p. 961;) and Plutarch himself, (ibid.)

4. The second is (independently of the necessary contrast of a subject and an object,) a *plurality, alteration, difference* on the part of the perceived object or objects, and of a recognition or discrimination thereof on the part of the perceiving subject.*—This supposes the following:—*Quality proper; Quantity, Protensive* (Time,) *Extensive* (Space,) *Intensive* (Degree;) and *Relation*. Therefore—

5. The third is *Quality*, quality strictly so called. For one affection is distinguished from another as it is, or is not, such and such; in other words, as it has, or has not, this or that quality (suchness.)

6. The fourth is *Time;* which supposes *Memory*, or, to speak more correctly, a certain *continuous representation* of the late and latest past, known with and in contrast to our apprehension of the passing present. For without such continuity of consciousness, no consciousness is possible.

7. The fifth is *Space*. For we are only conscious of perceiving, as we are conscious of perceiving something as discriminated from other co-existent things. But this in perception is to be conscious of one thing as out of another, that is, as extended, that is, as in Space.

8. The sixth is *Degree*. For all sensations are, though possibly of any, actually of one definite intensity; and distinguished not only by differences in Quality, Time, Space, but also by differences in Degree.

9. The seventh is *Relation*. For discrimination, which all perception supposes, is a recognition of a relation, the relation of contrast; and differences in Quality, Time, Space, Degree, are only so many various kinds of such relativity.

10. Finally, the eighth is an *Assertory Judgment*, that within the sphere of sense an object (a) *exists*, and (b) exists *thus or thus conditioned*.† All consciousness is realized in the enunciation—*That is there* (or *This is here*.) All Perception consequently enounces—*That is there;* but in this case, there is especially understood by the *That*—an object manifested through one or more qualities, Secondary, Secundo-primary, Primary; and by the *is there*—apprehended in, or in immediate relation to, our organism.‡

11. Such being the general conditions of Perception, it is manifestly impossible to discriminate with any rigour Sense from Intelligence. Sensitive apprehension is, in truth, only the recognition by Intelligence of the phænomena presented in or through its organs.‖

---

* It has been well said by Hobbes, in regard to the former,—'*Sentire semper idem, et non sentire*, ad idem recidunt,' (Elem. Philos. P. iv c. 25, § 5;) and by Galen and Nemesius in reference to the latter,—'Sensation is not an alteration, (affection, modification,) but the recognition of an alteration.' See p. 830 b.

† Aristotle in various passages asserts that Sensitive perception is a discrimination or a *judgment*. (Anal. Post. L. ii., c. 19, § 5.—Top. L. ii., c. 4, § 2.—De An. L. iii., c. 1, § 10; c. 10, § 1; alibi.) And the Aphrodisian:—'Although sensation be only brought to bear through certain corporeal passions, yet Sensation itself is not a passion, but a *judgment*.' (On the Soul, f. 138 b, ed. Ald.) Reid has the merit among modern philosophers of first approximating to the recognition of judgment as an element or condition of consciousness in general, in laying it at the root of Perception, Sensation, Memory, and (Self) Consciousness; though he unfortunately fell short of the truth in refusing an existential judgment also to the acts of the representative faculty, his Conception, Imagination, or Simple Apprehension.

‡ In this qualitative judgment there is only the consciousness of the quality perceived in itself as a distinct object. The judgment, again, by which it is recognised of such a class or such a name, is a higher energy, and ought not, as is sometimes done, to be styled Perception; it is *Judgment*, emphatically so called, a simple act of, what I would call, the elaborative, or dianoetic, or discursive faculty, the faculty of relations, or comparison.

‖ Tertullian:—'Non enim et sentire intelligere est, et intelligere, sentire.—At *quid erit Sensus, nisi ejus rei quæ sentitur intellectus?* Quid erit intellectus, nisi ejus rei quæ intelligitur sensus? Unde ista tormenta cruciandæ simplicitatis, et suspendendæ veritatis? Quis mihi exhibebit sensum non intelligentem quod sentit; aut intellectum non sentientem quod intelligit?'—(De Anima, c. 18; compare De Carne Christi, c. 12.)—To the same effect St Gregory of Nyssa (De Opif. Hom. cc. 6, 10; and De Anima et Resur., Opera, t. ii. p 623 ed. Paris, 1615.)—See also St Jerome as quoted in note * 877.—But this doctrine we may trace back to Aristotle and his school, and even higher. 'There is extant,' says Plutarch, 'a discourse of Strato Physicus, demonstrating—*That a Sensitive apprehension is wholly impossible without an act of Intellect*.' (Op. Mor p. 961.) And as to Aristotle himself:—'To divorce (he says) Sensation from Understanding, is to reduce Sensation to an insensible process; wherefore it has been said—*Intellect sees, and Intellect hears*.' (Probl. xi. 33.)

This saying, as recorded by Aristotle, constitutes in the original (a difference of dialect discounted) the first hemistich of the famous verse of Epicharmus:—

Νοῦς ὁρῇ καὶ Νοῦς ἀκούει, τἆλλα κωφὰ καὶ τυφλά.

Mind it seeth, Mind it heareth; all beside is deaf and blind;

12. All Perception is an *immediate* or *presentative* cognition: and has, therefore, in either form, only one univocal object; that, to wit, which it apprehends as *now* and *here* existent. (See Note B. § I. 4, 8, 11.)

13. All Perception is a *sensitive* cognition; it, therefore, apprehends the existence of no object out of its organism, or not in immediate correlation to its organism; for thus only can an object exist, *now* and *here*, to sense.

ii.—Sensation proper and Perception proper, in correlation.

14. In Perception proper there is a higher energy of intelligence, than in

---

or less literally—

What sees is Mind, what hears is Mind;
The ear and eye are deaf and blind.

Though overlooked as a quotation, by both the commentators on the Problems, by Erasmus, and many others, it has never been suspected that these words, as quoted, are not a quotation from the Syracusan poet. This negative I, however, venture to maintain, at least, as a probable thesis; for I am inclined to think that the line, however great its merit, does not ascend to Epicharmus, but was forged and fathered on him in an age considerably later than Aristotle's. My reasons are these:—

1. Epicharmus was a Pythagorean philosopher and a Doric poet. But to fabricate Pythagorean treatises in the Doric dialect seems to have become in the latter ages a matter of exercise and emulation among the Greek Sophists and Syncretists. In fact, of the numerous fragments under the names of Pythagoras, Theano, Timæus, Ocellus, Archytas, Hippodamus, Euryphamus, Hipparchus, Thrages, Metopus, Clinias, Crito, Polus, Lysis, Melissa, Mya, &c.; there are hardly any to a critical eye not manifestly spurious, and none whatever exempt from grave suspicion. On general grounds, therefore, forgeries on Epicharmus are not only not improbable, but likely.

2. And that such were actually committed we are not without special evidence. We know from Athenæus (L. xiv.) that there were many *Pseudepicharmia* in circulation. Besides Apollodorus, he cites, as authorities for this, Aristoxenus (who was a scholar of Aristotle) in the eighth book of his Polity, and Philochoros (who lived about a century later) in his treatise on Divination. Among the more illustrious fabricators, the former of these commemorates Chrysogonus the flute-player; the latter, Axiopistus of Locrus or Sicyon, with the names of his two supposititious works, the *Canon* and the *Gnomæ*. Of either of these, judging from their title, the line in question may have formed a part; though it is not improbably of a still more recent origin.

3. The words (and none could be more direct and simple) which make up the first hemistich of the verse, we find occasionally quoted as a proverbial philosopheme, subsequently to the time of Plato. To Plato's doctrine, and his language, I would indeed attribute its rise; for it is idle to suppose, with Jacobs, that Sophocles (Œd. T. 389) and Euripides (Hel. 118) had either the verse or dogma in their eye. Aristotle, at least, the author of the Problems, is the oldest testimony for such a usage; and long after Aristotle, after, indeed, the line had been already fathered on Epicharmus, we have Pliny (H. N. xi. 37,) Cassius Felix (Pr. 22,) St Jerome (Adv. Jovin. ii. 9,) the *manuscripts* of Stobæus (iv. 42,) and the Scholiast of Aristophanes (Pl. 43,) all adducing it only as an adage. It is not, however, till nearly *six centuries after Epicharmus*, and considerably more than *four centuries after Aristotle*, that we find the saying either fully cited as a verse, or the verse ascribed to the Syracusan. But from the time of Plutarch, who himself thrice alleges it, its quotation in either fashion becomes frequent; as by Tertullian, Clement of Alexandria, Maximus Tyrius, Julian, Theodoret, Olympiodorus (twice,) and Tzetzes (four times.) Porphyry (thrice) records it—but as a saying of Pythagoras; and Iamblichus, as a dictum of the Pythagorean school. These authors both had learning, though neither, certainly, was ever critical in its application. Their statements can only, therefore, be held to favour the opinion that they were unaware of any decisive evidence to vindicate the verse to Epicharmus.

4. But if improbable, even at first sight, that such a verse of such an author should not, if authentic, have been adduced by any writer now extant, during the long period of six hundred years, the improbability is enhanced when we come to find, that during that whole period it is never quoted, even under circumstances when, had it been current as a line of Epicharmus, it could not but have been eagerly appealed to. Plato, as observed by Alcimus and Laertius, was notoriously fond of quoting Epicharmus; and there were at least two occasions—in the Theætetus (§ 102, sq.,) and in the Phædo (§ 25 [11 Wytt.])—when this gnome of his favourite poet would have confirmed and briefly embodied the doctrine he was anxiously inculcating. Could he fail to employ it? In fact, it comes to this;—these passages must either be held to follow, or to found, the philosopheme in question.—In like manner Cicero, in his exposition of the first passage, (Tusc. i. 20,) could hardly have avoided associating Epicharmus with Plato, as Tertullian and Olympiodorus have done in their expositions of the second—had the line been recognised in the age of the former, as it was in the age of the two latter. Nor could such an apophthegm of such a poet have been unknown to Cicero,—to Cicero, so generally conversant with Hellenic literature,—and who, among other sayings of Epicharmus himself, adduces in Greek, as his brother Quintus paraphrases in Latin, the no less celebrated maxim—

Sensation proper. For though the latter be the apprehension of an affection of the Ego, and therefore, in a certain sort, the apprehension of an immaterial quality; still it is only the apprehension of the *fact* of an organic passion; whereas the former, though supposing Sensation as its condition, and though only the apprehension of the attributes of a material Non-ego, is, however, itself without corporeal passion, and, at the same time, the recognition not merely of a fact, but of *relations*. (See 22, 29, and p. 858, notes † and ‡.)

15. Sensation proper is the *conditio sine qua non* of a Perception proper of the Primary qualities. For we are only aware of the existence of our organism, in being sentient of it, as thus or thus affected; and are only aware of it being the subject of extension, figure, division, motion, &c., in being percipient of its affections, as like or as unlike, and as out of, or locally external to, each other.

16. Every Perception proper has a Sensation proper as its condition; but every Sensation has not a Perception proper as its conditionate — unless, what I think ought to be done, we view the general consciousness of the locality of a sensorial affection as a Perception proper. In this case, the two apprehensions will be always coexistent.

17. But though the fact of Sensation proper and the fact of Perception proper imply each other, this is all; — for the two cognitions, though coexistent, are not proportionally coexistent. On the contrary, although we can only take note of, that is perceive, the special relations of sensations, on the hypothesis that these sensations exist; a sensation, in proportion as it rises above a low degree of intensity, interferes with the perception of its relations, by concentrating consciousness on its absolute affection alone. It may accordingly be stated as a general rule — *That, above a certain point, the stronger the Sensation, the weaker the Perception; and the distincter the perception the less obtrusive the sensation*; in other words — *Though Perception proper and Sensation proper exist only as they coexist, in the degree or intensity of their existence they are always found in an inverse ratio to each other*. (See 862 b, sq.)

18. The organism is the field of apprehension, both to Sensation proper and Perception proper; but with this difference:—that the former views it as of the Ego, the latter, as of the Non-ego; that the one draws it within, the other shuts it out from, the sphere of self. As animated, as the subject of affections of which I am conscious, the organism belongs to me; and of these affections, which I recognise as mine, Sensation proper is the apprehension. As material, as the subject of extension, figure, divisibility, and so forth, the organism does not belong to me, the conscious unit; and of these properties, which I do not recognise as mine, Perception proper is the apprehension.* (See 38, 39, and p. 858 a †.)

19. The affections in Sensation proper are determined, (a) by certain intra-organic, or (b) by certain extra-organic, causes. The latter, as powers in bodies, beyond the sphere of perception, and their effects in us, the objects of Sensation, are both (therefore ambiguously) denominated, either, in the language of modern philosophers, the *Secondary Qualities of Matter*, or, in the language of Aristotle and his school, the *Proper Sensibles*. (Note D.)

Be sober, and to doubt inclin'd;
These are the very joints of mind;

or on the other reading—

Be cool, and ake to doubt propense;
These are the sinews of good sense.

---

* It may appear, not a paradox merely, but a contradiction, to say, that the organism is, at once, within and without the mind; is at once, subjective and objective; is, at once, Ego and Non-ego. But so it is; and so we must admit it to be, unless, on the one hand, as Materialists, we identify mind with matter, or, on the other, as Idealists, we identify matter with mind. The organism, as animated, as sentient, is necessarily ours; and its affections are only felt as affections of the indivisible Ego. In this respect, and to this extent, our organs are not external to ourselves. But our organism is not merely a sentient subject, it is at the same time an extended, figured, divisible, in a word, a material, subject; and the same sensations which are reduced to unity in the indivisibility of consciousness are in the divisible organism recognised as plural and reciprocally external, and, therefore, as extended, figured, and divided. Such is the fact: but how the immaterial can be united with matter, how the unextended can apprehend extension, how the indivisible can measure the divided,—this is the mystery of mysteries to man. "Modus (says the Pseudo-Augustin)—Modus quo corporibus adhærent spiritus, omnino mirus est, nec comprehendi ab hominibus potest; et hoc ipse homo est." Thus paraphrased by Pascal:—"Man is, to himself, the mightiest prodigy of nature. For he is unable to conceive what is Body, still less what is Mind, and, least of all, how there can be united a body and a mind. This is the climax of his difficulties; yet this is his peculiar nature."

20. Sensation proper has no object but a *subject-object*, i.e. the organic affection of which we are conscious. The cause of that affection, whether without the organism or within, that is, whether or not a secondary quality of body, is immediately or in its own nature unknown; being known only, if known it ever be, mediately, by observation, induction, inference, conjecture. Even in the perception of the Secundo-primary qualities, where there is the perception proper of a quasi-primary quality, in some degree of resistance, and the sensation proper of a secondary quality, in some affection of the sentient organism, its effect; still to Sensation proper there is no other object but the subjective affection; and even its dependence, as an effect, upon the resistance, as a cause, is only a conclusion founded on the observed constancy of their concomitance. (See 36, 37, and p. 857 b, sq.)

21. Nay, the Perception proper, accompanying a sensation proper, is not an apprehension, far less a representation, of the external or internal stimulus, or concause, which determines the affection whereof the sensation is the consciousness. —Not the former; for the stimulus or concause of a sensation is always, in itself, to consciousness unknown. Not the latter; for this would turn Perception into Imagination — reduce it from an immediate, and assertory, and objective, into a mediate, and problematic, and subjective, cognition. In this respect, Perception proper is an apprehension of the relations of sensations to each other, primarily in Space, and secondarily in Time and Degree. (See 31.)

iii.—Sensation proper.

22. Sensation proper, viewed on one side, is a passive affection of the organism; but viewed on the other, it is an active apperception, by the mind, of that affection. And as the former only exists for us, in as much as it is perceived by us; and as it is only perceived by us, in as much as it is apprehended, in an active concentration, discrimination, judgment, of the mind;—the latter, an act of intelligence, is to be viewed as the principal factor in the percipient process, even in its lower form, that of Sensation proper.* (See 4, 10, 11, 14, with notes.)

iv.—Perception proper.

23. In Perception proper the object-object perceived is, always, either a *Primary* quality, or the *quasi-Primary* phasis of a Secundo-primary. (See p. 857 b, sq.)

24. The Primary qualities are perceived as *in our organism;* the Quasi-primary phasis of the Secundo-primary as *in correlation to our organism.* (See 866 a.)

25. Thus a perception of the Primary qualities does not, originally and in itself, reveal to us the existence, and qualitative existence, of aught beyond the organism, apprehended by us as extended, figured, divided, &c.

26. The primary qualities of things external to our organism we do not perceive, i.e., *immediately know.* For these we only learn to *infer*, from the affections which we come to find that they determine in our organs;—affections which, yielding us a perception of organic extension, we at length discover, by observation and induction, to imply a corresponding extension in the extra-organic agents.

27. Further, in no part of the organism have we any apprehension, any

* This is the true doctrine of Aristotle and his school, who are, however, not unfrequently misrepresented, by relation to the extreme counter-opinion of the Platonists, as viewing in the cognitions of Sense a mere passion;—a misrepresentation to which, undoubtedly, a few of the Latin Schoolmen have afforded grounds. It is, indeed, this twofold character of the Sensitive process that enables us to reconcile the apparent confliction of those passages of Aristotle, where (as De Anima, L. ii. c. 4. § 8; c. 5. § 2; c. 11. § 14; c. 12. § 1; De Sensu et Sensili, c. 1. § 5; Physica, L. vii. c. 3. § 12. Pacian division) he calls Sensation a passion or alteration of the Sentient; and those others where (as De Anima, L. iii. c 6. § 2) he asserts that in Sensation the Sentient is not passively affected. In the former passages the sentient faculty is regarded on its organic side, in the latter on its mental. Compare De Somno et Vigilia, c. 1. § 6, where it is said, that "Sensation is a process belonging exclusively neither to the soul nor to the body, but, as energy, a motion of the soul, through the [medium of the] body;"—a text which, however, may still be variously expounded.—See Alexander, in note † p 878; who, with the other Greek interpreters, Ammonius, Simplicius, Philoponus, solves the difficulty by saying, that it is not the sentient *mind* that suffers, but the sentient *organ*. To the same effect are Galen and Nemesius, as quoted in note * p. 878. Reid is partly at one with the Peripatetics; with whose doctrine, indeed, he is more frequently in accordance than he is always himself aware. (Inq. 114 a.)

immediate knowledge, of extension in its true and absolute magnitude; perception noting only the fact given in sensation, and sensation affording no standard, by which to measure the dimensions given in one sentient part with those given in another. For, as perceived, extension is only the recognition of one organic affection in its outness from another;—as a minimum of extension is thus to perception the smallest extent of organism in which sensations can be discriminated as plural;—and as in one part of the organism this smallest extent is, perhaps, some million, certainly some myriad, times smaller than in others; it follows that, to perception, the same real extension will appear, in this place of the body, some million or myriad times greater than in that.* Nor does this difference subsist only as between sense and sense; for in the same sense, and even in that sense which has very commonly been held exclusively to afford a knowledge of absolute extension, I mean Touch proper, the minimum, at one part of the body, is some fifty times greater than it is at another. (See p. 863 ab, note.)

28. The existence of an extra-organic world is apprehended, not in a perception of the Primary qualities, but in a perception of the quasi-primary phasis of the Secundo-primary; that is, in the consciousness that our locomotive energy is resisted, and not resisted by aught in our organism itself. For in the consciousness of being thus resisted is involved, as a correlative, the consciousness of a resisting something external to our organism. Both are, therefore, conjunctly apprehended. (See p. 866 a, note.)—This experience presupposes, indeed, a possession of the notions of space and motion in space.

29. But on the doctrine that space, as a necessary condition, is a native element of thought; and, since the notion of any one of its dimensions, as correlative to, must inevitably imply the others; it is evident that every perception of sensations out of sensations will afford the occasion, in apprehending any one, of conceiving all the three extensions; that is, of conceiving space. On the doctrine, and in the language, of Reid, our original cognitions of space, motion, &c., are instinctive; a view which is confirmed by the analogy of those of the lower animals which have the power of locomotion at birth. It is truly an idle problem to attempt imagining the steps by which we may be supposed to have acquired the notion of extension; when, in fact, we are unable to imagine to ourselves the possibility of that notion not being always in our possession.

30. We have, therefore, a twofold cognition of space: a) an *a priori* or *native* imagination of it, in general, as a necessary condition of the possibility of thought; and b,) under that, an *a posteriori* or *adventitious* percept of it, in particular, as contingently apprehended in this or that actual complexus of sensations.*

B.) *Editor's doctrine of Perception, in contrast to that of Reid, Stewart, Royer Collard, and other philosophers of the Scottish School.*†

31. Perception (proper) is the *Notion* or *Conception* of an object, *instinctively suggested, excited, inspired,* or, as it were, *conjured up, on occasion or at the sign of*

---

* This difference, in the power of discriminating affections, possessed by different parts of the body, seems to depend partly on the minuteness and isolation of the ultimate nervous fibrils, partly on the sensation being less or more connected with pleasure and pain. In this respect the eye greatly transcends all the other organs. For we can discriminate in the retina sensations, as reciprocally external, more minutely than we can in touch—as over the greater part of the body, two millions five hundred thousand fold—as at the most sensitive place of the hand, a hundred thousand fold—as at the tip of the tongue, where tactile discrimination is at its maximum, fifty thousand fold. I am, however, inclined to think for reasons already given, that we must reduce millions to myriads. (See p. 862, note.)

* This doctrine agrees with that of Kant and Reid in the former; it differs certainly from that of Kant, and probably from that of Reid, in the latter. But see B.

† I here contrast my own doctrine of perception with that of the philosophers in question, not because their views and mine are those at farthest variance on the point, but, on the contrary, precisely because they thereon approximate the nearest. I have already shown that the doctrine touching Perception held by Reid, (and in the present relation he and his two illustrious followers are in almost all respects at one) is ambiguous. For while some of its statements seem to harmonize exclusively with the conditions of natural presentationism, others, again, appear only compatible with those of an egoistical representationism.—(See 820-823; also 812-815.) Maintaining, as I do, the former doctrine, it is, of course, only the positions conformable to the latter, which it is, at present, necessary to adduce.

a Sensation (proper.*) *Reid*, Inq. 111 b, 121 a, 122 a, 123 b, 128 b note 130 b, 159 a, 183 a, 188 a. I. P. 258 ab, 259 b, 260 b, 318 ab, 327 a;—*Stewart*, El. vol. i. pp. 92, 93;—*Royer Collard*, in Jouffroy's Reid, vol. iii. pp. 402, 403.—(Compare 820 b, 821 ab.)

On the contrary, I hold, in general, that as Perception, in either form, is an immediate or presentative, not a mediate or representative, cognition, that a Perception proper is not, and ought not to be called, a Notion or Conception. And, I hold, in particular, that, on the one hand, in the consciousness of sensations, out of each other, contrasted, limited, and variously arranged, we have a Perception proper, of the primary qualities, in an externality to the mind, though not to the nervous organism, as an immediate cognition, and not merely as a notion or concept, of something extended, figured, &c.; and, on the other, as a correlative contained in the consciousness of our voluntary motive energy resisted, and not resisted by aught within the limits of mind and its subservient organs, we have a Perception proper of the secundo-primary quality of resistance, in an extraorganic force, as an immediate cognition, and not merely as a notion or concept, of a resisting something external to our body;—though certainly in either case there may be, and probably is, a concomitant act of imagination, by which the whole complex consciousness on the occasion is filled up. (See 21, and Note B § ii.)

32. On occasion of the Sensation (proper,) along with the notion or conception which constitutes the Perception (proper,) of the external object, there is *blindly created* in us, or *instinctively determined*, an invincible *belief* in its existence. (Reid, Inq. 159 a, 122 ab, 183 a, I. P. 258 a, 327 a, alibi; *Stewart* and *Royer Collard*, ll. cc.)

On the contrary, I hold, that we only believe in the existence of what we perceive, as extended, figured, resisting, &c., in as much as we believe that we are conscious of these qualities as existing; consequently, that a belief in the existence of an extended world external to the mind, and even external to the organism, is not a faith blindly created or instinctively determined, in supplement of a representative or mediate cognition, but exists in, as an integral constituent of, Perception proper, as an act of intuitive or immediate knowledge.

33. The object of Perception (proper) is a *conclusion*, or *inference*, or *result*, (instinctive, indeed, not ratiocinative,) from a Sensation proper. (*Reid*, Inq. 125 a, 186 b, I. P. 310 ab, 319 a;—*Royer Collard*, l. c.)

On the contrary, I hold, that the object of Perception proper is given immediately in and along with the object of Sensation proper. (See 822 a 7.)

34. Sensation (proper) *precedes*, Perception (proper) *follows*. (*Reid*, Inq. 186 b, 187 b. I. P. 320 b; *Stewart* and *Royer Collard*, ll. cc.)

On the contrary, I hold, that though Sensation proper be the condition of, and therefore anterior to, Perception proper in the order of nature, that, in the order of time, both are necessarily coexistent;—the latter being only realised in and through the present existence of the former. Thus visual extension cannot be perceived, or even imagined, except under the sensation of colour; while colour, again, cannot be apprehended or imagined without, respectively, a concomitant apprehension or phantasm of extension.

35. Sensation (proper) is not only an antecedent, but an *arbitrary antecedent*, of Perception (proper.) The former is only a sign on occasion of which the latter follows; they have no necessary or

* This is not the doctrine, at least not the language of the doctrine, of real presentationism. It is the language, at best, of an egoistical representationism; and, as a doctrine, it coincides essentially with the theory of mediate perception held by the lower Platonists, the Cartesians, and the Leibnitians—as properly understood. The Platonising Cudworth, in different parts of his works, gives, in fact, nearly in the same terms, the same account of the process of Sensitive Perception. He signalises, firstly, the bodily affection, determined by the impression of an external something, [precisely as Reid;] secondly, the sympathetic recognition thereof by the soul, [Reid's Sensation;] thirdly, to quote his expressions, 'whereby according to *nature's instinct*, it hath several *Seemings* or *Appearances* begotten in it of those resisting objects, without it at a distance, in respect of colour, magnitude, figure, and local motion,' [Reid's Conceptions or Notions of which Perception is made up.] (Imm. Mor. B. v. ch. 2. § 3. Compare B. iii. ch. 1. § 5.) See also, above, the Neoplatonic doctrine, as stated, p. 262 b. note *; the Cartesian Sylvain Regis, as quoted, p. 821 a; and the Cartesian Andala, as quoted, p. 257, b. note *; and to these may be added the Aristotelian Compton Carlton, (who did not reject the doctrine of a *representative* perception of the Common Sensibles,) as quoted, p. 830 a.—But that Reid might possibly employ the terms *notion* and *conception* in a vague and improper sense, for cognition in general, see p. 821, b. 4.

even natural connexion; and it is only by the will of God that we do not perceive the qualities of external objects independently of any sensitive affection. This last, indeed, seems to be actually the case in the perception of visible extension and figure. (*Reid*, Inq. 111 b, 121 a, 143 b, 122 a, 123 b, 187 b, 188 a. I. P. 257 b, 260 b, alibi; *Stewart* and *Royer Collard*, ll. cc.)

On the contrary, I hold that Sensation proper is the universal condition of Perception proper. We are never aware even of the existence of our organism except as it is somehow affected; and are only conscious of extension, figure, and the other objects of Perception proper, as realized in the relations of the affections of our sentient organism, as a body extended, figured, &c. As to colour and visible extension, neither can be apprehended, neither can be even imagined, apart from the other. (V. 831 a, footnote, et alibi; but especially Note E, § 1.)

36. In a Sensation (proper) of the secondary qualities, as affections in us, we have a *Perception (proper) of them as properties in objects* and causes of the affections in us. (*Reid*, I. P. 310 ab, and Inq. passim; *Royer Collard*, l. c.)

On the contrary, I hold, that as Perception proper is an immediate cognition; and as the secondary qualities, in bodies, are only inferred, and therefore only mediately known to exist as occult causes of manifest effects; that these, at best only objects of a mediate knowledge, are not objects of Perception. (See 20, 21, and p 858.)

37. In like manner, in the case of various other bodily affections, as the toothache, gout, &c., we have not only a Sensation proper of the painful feeling, but a conception and belief, i.e., *a Perception (proper) of its cause*. (*Reid*, I. P. 319 a, alibi.)

On the contrary, and for the same reason, I hold, that there is in this case no such Perception.

38. Sensation (proper) is an affection *purely of the mind*, and not in any way an affection of the body. (*Reid*, Inq. 105 a, 159 ab, 187 a, I. P. 229 ab, 310.)

On the contrary, I hold with Aristotle, (De An. I. 5, De Som. c. I. § 6,) indeed, with philosophers in general, that Sensation is an affection neither of the body alone nor of the mind alone, but of the composite of which each is a constituent; and that the subject of Sensation may be indifferently said to be in our organism (as animated) or in our soul (as united with an organism.) For instance, hunger or colour are, as apprehended, neither modes of mind apart from body, nor modes of body apart from mind. (See 18.)

39. Sensations (proper) as merely affections of the mind, have *no locality* in the body, no locality at all. (*Reid*, I. P. 319 ab, 320 ab.) From this the inference is necessary, that, though conscious of the relative place and reciprocal outness of sensations, we do not in this consciousness apprehend any real externality and extension.

On the contrary, I hold, that Sensation proper being the consciousness of an affection, not of the mind alone, but of the mind as it is united with the body, that in the consciousness of sensations, relatively localized and reciprocally external, we have a veritable apprehension, and, consequently, an immediate perception of the affected organism, as extended, divided, figured, &c. This alone is the doctrine of Natural Realism, of Common Sense. (See 18.)

40. In the case of Sensation (proper) and the Secondary qualities, there is a *determinate quality in certain bodies*, exclusively competent to cause a determinate sensation in us, as colour, odour, savour, &c.; consequently, that from the fact of a similar internal effect we are warranted to infer the existence of a similar external concause. (*Reid*, Inq. 137–142. I. P. 315, 316, alibi.)

On the contrary, I hold, that a similar sensation only implies a similar idiopathic affection of the nervous organism; but such affection requires only the excitation of an appropriate stimulus; while such stimulus may be supplied by manifold agents of the most opposite nature, both from within the body and from without. (See 854, b—856, a.)

41. Perception excludes *memory*; Perception (proper) cannot therefore be apprehensive of *motion*. (*Royer Collard*, supra, 844, ab.)

On the contrary, I hold, that as memory, or a certain continuous representation, is a condition of consciousness, it is a condition of Perception; and that motion, therefore, cannot, on this ground, be denied as an object apprehended through sense. (See 6, and Note H.)

42. An *apprehension of relations* is not an act of Perception (proper.) (*Royer Collard* [apparently,] ibid.)

On the contrary, I hold, in general, that as all consciousness is realised only in the apprehension of the relations of plurality and contrast; and as perception is a consciousness; that the apprehension of relation cannot, simpliciter, be denied to perception: and, in particular, that unless we annihilate Perception proper, by denying to it the recognition of its peculiar objects, Extension, Figure, and the other primary qualities, we cannot deny to it the recognition of relations; for, to say nothing of the others, Extension is perceived only in apprehending sensations out of sensations—a relation; and Figure is only perceived in apprehending one perceived extension as limited, and limited in a certain manner by another—a complexus of relations. (See 9, pp. 844 a, 859 a, and infra Note E.)

43. *Distant* realities are objects of Perception (proper.) (*Reid*, Inq. 104 b, 145 a, 158 b, 159 ab, 160 a, 186 b; I. P. 299 a, 302 a, 303 a, 304 a, 305 b; *Stewart*, El. i. 79 sq.)

On the contrary, I hold, that the mind perceives nothing external to itself, except the affections of the organism as animated, the reciprocal relations of these affections, and the correlative involved in the consciousness of its locomotive energy being resisted. (See 814 a, 822 ab.)

44. Objects not in contact with the organs of sense are perceived by a *medium*. (*Reid*, Inq. 104 b, 186 ab, 187 b; I. P. 247 ab.)

On the contrary, I hold, that the only object perceived is the organ itself, as modified, or what is in contact with the organ, as resisting. The doctrine of a medium is an error, or rather a confusion, inherited from Aristotle, who perverted, in this respect, the simpler and more accurate doctrine of Democritus.

45. *Extension* and *Figure* are first perceived through the sensations of *Touch*. (*Reid*, Inq. 123–125. 188 a; I. P. 331; *Stewart*, El. i. 349, 357; Ess. 564.)

On the contrary, I hold, that (unless by Extension be understood only extension in the three dimensions, as Reid in fact seems to do, but not Stewart,) this is erroneous, for an extension is apprehended in the apprehension of the reciprocal externality of all sensations. Moreover, to allow even the statement as thus restricted to pass, it would be necessary to suppose, that under Touch it is meant to comprehend the consciousness of the Locomotive energy and of the Muscular feelings. (See 864 b, sq.)

46. *Externality* is exclusively perceived on occasion of the sensations of *Touch* (*Reid*, Inq. 123, 124, 188. a; I. P. 332 and alibi; *Royer Collard*, Jouffroy's Reid, iii. 412.)

On the contrary, I hold, that it is, primarily, in the consciousness of our locomotive energy being resisted, and, secondarily, through the sensations of muscular feeling, that the perception of Externality is realised. All this, however, might be confusedly involved in the Touch of the philosophers in question. (See 28.)

47. *Real* (or absolute) *magnitude* is an object of perception (proper) through *Touch*, but through touch only. (*Reid*, I. P. 303.)

On the contrary, I hold, that the magnitude perceived through touch is as purely relative as that perceived through vision or any other sense; for the same magnitude does not appear the same to touch at one part of the body and to touch at another. (303 b, note; 863 ab, note; and n. 27.)

48. *Colour*, though a secondary quality, is an object not of Sensation (proper) but of Perception (proper); in other words, we perceive Colour, not as an affection of our own minds, but as a quality of external things. (*Reid*, Inq. 137 ab, 138 a; I. P. 319 b.)

On the contrary, I hold, that colour, in itself, as apprehended or immediately known by us, is a mere affection of the sentient organism; and therefore like the other secondary qualities, an object not of Perception, but of Sensation, proper. The only distinguishing peculiarity in this case, lies in the three following circumstances:—a) That the organic affection of colour, though not altogether indifferent, still, being accompanied by comparatively little pleasure, comparatively little pain, the apprehension of this affection, qua affection, i. e., its Sensation proper, is, consequently, always at a minimum.—b) That the passion of colour first rising into consciousness, not from the amount of the intensive quantity of the affection, but from the amount of the extensive quantity of the organism affected, is necessarily apprehended under the condition of extension.—c) That the isolation, tenuity, and delicacy, of the ultimate filaments of the optic nerve, afford us sensations minutely and precisely distinguished, sensations realised in consciousness only as we are conscious of them as out of each other in space.—These circumstances show, that while in vision Perception proper is at its maximum, and Sensation proper at its minimum, (17,) the sensation of colour cannot be realised apart from the perception of extension: but they do not warrant the assertions, that colour is not, like the other secondary qualities, apprehended by us as a mere sensorial affection, and, therefore, an object not of Sensation proper but of Perception proper. (See 855 ab, 858 ab.)

§ II.—*Historical notices in regard to the distinction of Perception proper and Sensation proper.*

This distinction is universally supposed to be of a modern date; no one has endeavoured to carry it higher than Malebranche; and, in general, the few indications of it noticed previous to Reid, have been commemorated as only accidental or singular anticipations.* This is altogether erroneous; the distinction is ancient; and adopting, for the standard, my own opinion of what the distinction ought to be, I find it taken more simply and less incorrectly by Aristotle, than by any modern philosopher whatever.

Aristotle's discrimination of the Common and Proper Sensibles or Percepts (which has been already explained, 828 b sq.) embodies not only the modern distinction of the Primary and Secondary Qualities of matter, but also the modern distinction of the two Perceptions, Perception proper and Sensation proper. The generalisation of these two correlative distinctions into one, constitutes indeed, the first peculiar merit of Aristotle's analysis and nomenclature. But a second is, that in his hands at least, the Common Sensibles, the immediate objects of Perception proper, are viewed as the *object-objects* of an intuitive, and not perverted into the *subject-objects* of a representative cognition. For in the writings of Aristotle himself I can find no ground for regarding him as other than a presentationist or natural realist. In this respect his doctrine stands distinguished from all the others in which the distinction in question has been recognised; for the Neo-Platonic, the Neo-Aristotelic, the Scholastic (with certain exceptions) and the Cartesian, all proceed on the ideality or representative character of the objects of which we are conscious in Perception proper. Even Reid himself, as we have seen, and the Scottish School in general, can only with doubt and difficulty be held as qualified exceptions. (See § I., B of this Note, and § II. of Note C.)

Nay, the canon I have endeavoured to establish of the universal co-existence in an inverse ratio of Perception proper and Sensation proper (and in general of Feeling and Cognition) though not enounced in its abstract universality by Aristotle, may still be detected as supposed and specially applied by him. In his treatise On the Soul (ii. 9. 1.) speaking of the sense of Smell, and of the difficulty of determining the nature and quality of its objects—odours, he says:—'The cause is, that we do not possess this sense in any high degree of accuracy, but are, in this respect, inferior to many of the brutes; for man smells imperfectly, and has no perception of things odorous, unaccompanied by either pain or pleasure; the organ of this sense not being nicely discriminative.' And the same is implied, in what he adds touching the vision of the sclerophthalma. Does not this manifestly suppose the principle—that in proportion as a sense rises as a mean of information, it sinks as a vehicle of pleasure and pain?—Galen, I may notice, has some remarkable observations to the same effect. In considering 'the causes of pleasure and pain in the several senses;' and after stating, in general, the order of intensity in which these are susceptible of such affections, to wit, Touch or Feeling—Taste—Smell—Hearing—Vision; he goes on to treat of them in detail. And here it is evident, that he also deems the

* The only attempt of which I am aware, at any historical account of the distinction in hand, is by Mr Stewart, in Note F of his Essays. It contains, however, notices, and these not all pertinent, only of Hutcheson, Crousaz, Baxter, and D'Alembert, and none of these have any title to an historical commemoration on the occasion. For Hutcheson (as already once and again mentioned, 124 ab, 829 b) only repeats, indeed, only thought of repeating, Aristotle; while the others, at best, merely re-echo Malebranche and the Cartesians.

I may here observe, that in that Note, as also repeatedly in the Dissertation, Mr Stewart (who has been frequently followed) is wrong in stating, unexclusively, that Reid's writings were anterior to Kant's; founding thereon a presumption against the originality of the latter. The priority of Reid is only true as limited to the 'Inquiry;' but, on the ground of this alone there could be proved, between the philosophers, but little community of thought, on points where either could possibly claim any right of property. But though Kant's first 'Critik' and 'Prolegomena' preceded Reid's 'Essays' by several years, no one will assuredly suspect any connexion whatever between these several works. In general, I must be allowed to say, that the tone and tenor of Mr Stewart's remarks on the philosopher of Koenigsberg are remarkable exceptions to the usual cautious, candid and dignified character of his criticism.

capacity of pain and pleasure in a sense to be inversely as its power of cognitive discrimination. For, inter alia, he says of Hearing:—'The pleasurable is more conspicuous in this sense [than in that of Vision,] because it is of a coarser nature and constitution; but the pleasurable becomes even more manifest in the sensations of Smell, because the nature and constitution of this sense is coarser still.' (De Sympt. causis L. i. c. 6.)

The distinction of the Common and Proper Sensibles, and virtually therefore, the distinction in question, was continued, with some minor developments, by the Greek and Latin Aristotelians. (See 830 a, 860 ab.) As to the interesting doctrine, on this point, of those Schoolmen who rejected *intentional species* in Perception, I may refer, instar omnium, to Biel. (Collect. L. ii. dist. 3. qu. 2.)

Sensation proper and Perception proper were, however, even more strongly contradistinguished in the system of the lower Platonists. They discriminated, on the one hand, in the body, the organic passion and its recognition—that is Sensation proper; and on the other, in the impassive soul, the elicitation into consciousness (through some inscrutable instinct or inspiration) of a *gnostic reason*, or subjective form, representative of the external object affecting the sense—that is Perception proper. (See 262 b Note *.) There might also be shown, in like manner, an analogy between the distinction in question, and that by the Schoolmen of the *species impressa et expressa*; but on this I shall not insist. Nor on the Neo-Platonic theory of Perception which has rarely been touched upon, and when touched on almost always misrepresented (even Mr Harris, for instance, has wholly misconceived the nature of the *gnostic reasons*;)—nor on this can I now enter, though, as recently noticed, it bears a striking analogy to one phasis of the doctrine of Reid. In special reference to the present distinction I may, however, refer the reader to a passage of Plotinus. (Enn. III. vi. 2.)

In the Cartesian philosophy, the distinction was virtually taken by Descartes, but first discriminated in terms by his followers. In general, Perception proper, and the Primary qualities as perceived, they denoted by *Idea*; Sensation proper, and the Secondary qualities as felt, by *Sensation* (sensatio, sentiment). See *De Rari*, (Clavis, &c., p. 290 alibi, ed. 1677;) —*De la Forge*, (De l'Esprit, ch. 10, p. 109 sq., ch. 17, p. 276, ed. Amst. et supra 834 a;)—*Geulinx*, (Dictata in Principia. pp. 45, 48, alibi, et supra 834 a;)—*Rohault*, (Physique, passim;)—*Malebranche* (Recherche, L. iii. P. ii. ch. 6 and 7, with Eeclairc. on last, et supra 835 h;)—*Silvain Regis*, (Cours, t. i. pp. 60, 61, 72, 145;—*Bossuet*, (Connaissance de Dieu, ch. iii art. 8;)—while *Buffier*, *S' Gravesande*, *Crousaz*, *Sinsert*, *Keranflech*, *Genovesi*, with a hundred others, might be adduced as showing that the same distinction had been very generally recognised before Reid; who, far from arrogating to himself the credit of its introduction, remarks that it had been first accurately established by Malebranche. (265 b.)

As already noticed, (835 h,) it is passing strange that Locke, hot truly marvellous that Leibnitz, should have been ignorant of the Cartesian distinction of Sensation and Idea (Sentiment, Idée.) Locke's unacquaintance is shown in his 'Essay,' besides other places, in B. ii. ch. 13, § 25, but, above all, in his 'Examination of P. Malebranche's Opinion;' and that of Leibnitz, elsewhere, and in L. ii. ch. 8 of his 'Nouveaux Essais,' but more particularly in the 'Examen du Sentiment du P. Malebranche,' both of which works he wrote in opposition to the relative treatises of Locke. As for Locke, he seems wholly unaware that any difference subsisted in the Cartesian school, between *Idea* and *Sensation*; while Leibnitz actually thinks that Malebranche 'entend par *sentiment* une perception d'imagination'! In his own philosophy, Leibnitz virtually supersedes the discrimination. I am, therefore, doubly surprised at the observation of M. Royer Collard, that 'Malebranche is the first among modern philosophers, and, *with Leibnitz*, perhaps the only one before Reid, who accurately distinguished perception from the sensation which is its forerunner and sign. (Jouffroy's Reid, iii. 329.)

In the Kantian school, and generally in the recent philosophy of Germany, the distinction is adopted, and marked out by the terms *Anschauung* or *Intuitio*, for the one apprehension, and *Empfindung* or *Sensatio* for the other. In France and Italy, on the other hand, where the distinction has been no less universally recognised, Reid's expressions, *Perception* and *Sensation*, have become the prevalent; but their ambiguity, I think, ought to have been avoided, by the addition of some such epithet as—*proper*.

Since generalizing the *Law of the coexistence, but the co-existence in an inverse ratio, of Sensation and Perception, of the subjective and objec'ive, and, in general, of feeling and cognition;* I have noticed, besides those adduced above from Aristotle and Galen, other partial observations tending to the same result, by sundry modern philosophers.—*Sulzer*, in a paper published in 1759 (Vermischte Schriften, vol. i. p. 113,) makes the remark, that 'a representation manifests itself more clearly in proportion as it has less the power of exciting in us emotion;' and confirms it by the analogy observed in the gradation of the agreeable and disagreeable sensations.—*Kant* in his Anthropologie (1798, § 14,) in treating of the determinate or organic senses (Sensus fixi,) says:—'Three of these are rather objective than subjective—i. e., as empirical intuitions, they conduce more to the cognition of the external object, than they excite the consciousness of the affected organ; but two are rather subjective than objective—i. e., the representation they mediate is more that of enjoyment [or suffering] than of the cognition of the external object. . . . . The senses of the former class are those—1) of *Touch* (tactus,) 2) of *Sight* (visus,) 3) of *Hearing* (auditus;) of the latter, those—a) of *Taste* (gustus,) b) of *Smell* (olfactus.)'—This and the Galenic arrangement will appear less conflictive, if we recollect, that under Touch Galen comprehends Feeling proper, whereas Feeling proper is by Kant relegated to his vital sense or sensus vagus, the cœnæsthesis or common sense of others. See also *Meiners*, Untersuchungen, i. p. 64; *Wetzel*, Psychologie, i. § 225; *Fries*, N. Kritik, i. § 14-19; Anthropologie, i. §§ 27, 28, &c. &c.

M. Ravaisson, in an article of great ability and learning on the 'Fragments de Philosophie' which M. Peisse did me the honour to translate, when speaking of the reform of philosophy in France, originating in *Maine de Biran's* recoil against the Sensualistic doctrine, has the following passage:—'Maine de Biran commence par séparer profondément de la passion l'activité, que Condillac avait confondue avec elle sous le titre commun de Sensation. La sensation proprement dite est une affection toute passive; l'être qui y serait réduit irait se perdre, s'absorber dans toutes ses modifications; il deviendrait successivement chacune d'elles, il ne se trouverait pas, il ne se distinguerait pas, et jamais ne se connaîtrait lui-même. Bien loin que la connaissance soit la sensation seule, la sensation, en se mêlant à elle, la trouble et l'obscurcit, et elle éclipse à son tour la sensation. De là, la loi que M. Hamilton a signalée dans son remarquable article sur la theorie de la perception: *la sensation et la perception, quoique inséparables, sont en raison inverse l'une de l'autre.* Cette loi fondamentale, Maine de Biran l'avait découverte près de trente ans auparavant, et en avait suivi toutes les applications; il en avait surtout approfondi le principe, savoir, que la sensation résulte de la passion, et que la perception résulte de l'action.' (Revue des Deux Mondes, Nov. 1840.)—It is perhaps needless for me to say, that when I enounced the law in question (in 1830,) I had never seen the printed memoir by De Biran, which, indeed, from the circumstances of its publication, was, I believe, inaccessible through the ordinary channels of the trade, and to be found in no library in this country; and now I regret to find that, through procrastination, I must send this note to press before having obtained the collective edition of his earlier works which has recently appeared in Paris. All that I know of De Biran is comprised in the volume edited in 1834 by M. Cousin, from whose kindness I received it. In this, the 'Nouvelles Considérations sur les Rapports du Physique et du Moral de l'Homme,' the treatise in which, as his editor informs us, the full and final development of his doctrine is contained, was for the first time published. But neither in that, nor in any other of the accompanying pieces, can I discover any passage besides the following, that may be viewed as anticipating the law of coexistence and inversion:—'Souvent une impression perçue à tel degré cesse de l'être à un degré plus élevé ou lorsqu'elle s'avive au point d'absorber la conscience ou le *moi* luimême qui la *devient*. Ainsi plus la sensation serait éminemment *animale*, moins elle aurait le charactère vrai d'une perception humaine.'

NOTE D.**

CONTRIBUTION TOWARDS
A HISTORY
OF THE DOCTRINE OF
MENTAL SUGGESTION OR ASSOCIATION.

[References omitted, and to be supplied from pp. 294, 886, &c.]

THE doctrine of, what is most familiarly styled, the *Association of Ideas*, would be an interesting subject for historical inquiry.—The importance of this principle has, in later times, been fully recognised,—sometimes, perhaps, exaggerated; but to the older philosophers, and to the schoolmen in particular, the *Excitatio Specierum* afforded, likewise, a peculiar object of interest and speculation. Poncius, for example, pronounces it—"ex difficilioribus naturæ arcanis;" and Oviedo,—"maximum totius philosophiæ sacramentum, nunquam ab aliquo satis explicandum." Joseph Scaliger informs us, that touching two things especially, his proud and subtle father professed curiosity and ignorance;—the cause of *reminiscence* and the cause of *gravity*. Association and Gravitation, indeed, present, in themselves, a striking parallel; in the history of their exposition, a striking contrast.

Each (as observed by Hume) is a species of Attraction; and the effects which, in the mental world, are referred to the one, are not less multiform, extraordinary, and important, than those which, in the material, are referred to the other. The causes of both are equally occult; the speculation of these causes equally unphilosophical; and each is to be reduced to science only by observing its effects, and carrying up its phænomena into universal facts or fact, laws or law. But in the progress of this reduction the analogy ceases;—it is actually reversed. For whilst the laws of Gravitation were only slowly developed by the labours of successive generations, and their application only gradually extended from the earth to the universe of matter; the not more obtrusive laws of Association, whose evolution modern philosophers fondly arrogated to themselves, are, after these have tried and tired themselves in the attempt, found already developed and applied,—I may say, indeed, even generalized into unity,—at a single jet, by a single philosopher of antiquity, who, for this—but not alone for this—stands the Copernicus and Kepler and Newton of the intellectual world.

The singular circumstances of this inverted history have not, however, found a competent historian;—nay, the circumstances themselves have yet to be signalised and verified. Some attempts have indeed been made under the name of *Histories of the Association of Ideas*: but comparing what has been, with what ought to be, accomplished; these, at best, are only fragmentary contributions by writers, unaware of the real authors of even the most remarkable movements, and compensating their omissions, or their meagre and inaccurate notices of important matters, by tedious excursions on others of no interest or difficulty. These inadequate attempts have been also limited to *Germany*; and, in Germany, to the treatises of *three* authors; for the historical notices on this doctrine, found in the works of other German psychologists, are wholly borrowed from them. I refer—to the "Geschichte" of *Hismann* (1777); to the "Paralipomena" and "Beytræge" of *Maass* (1787, 1792); and to the "Vestigia" of *Goerenz*, (1791). In England, indeed, we have a chapter in Mr Coleridge's "Biographia Literaria," entitled, "*On the law of Association—its history traced from Aristotle to Hartley*;" but this, in so far as it is of any value, is a plagiarism, and a blundering plagiarism, from Maass;* the whole chapter exhibiting, in fact, more mistakes than paragraphs. We may judge of Mr Coleridge's competence to speak of Aristotle, the great philosopher of ancient times, when we find him referring to the *De Anima* for his speculations on the associative principle; opposing the *De Memoria* and *Parva Naturalia* as distinct works; and attributing to Aquinas, what belongs exclusively and notoriously to the Stagirite. We may judge of his competence to speak of Descartes, the great philosopher of modern times, when telling us, that *Idea*, in the Cartesian philosophy, denotes merely a configuration of the brain; the term, he adds, being first extended by Locke, to denote the immediate object of the mind's attention or consciousness. But, in truth, it might be broadly asserted, that every statement in regard to the history of this doctrine hazarded by British philosophers, to say nothing of others, is more or less erroneous.—Priestley, for example, assigns to *Locke* the honour of having *first* observed the fact of Association, (Hartley's Theory by P. Intr. p. xxv.); and Hume, as we have seen, arrogates *to himself* the glory of *first* generalising its laws.* (Hum. Und. sect. iii.)—Mr Stewart, but at second hand, says, that "*something like an attempt* to enumerate the laws of Association is to be found in Aristotle."—Sir James Mackintosh, again, founding on his own research, affirms that Aristotle and his disciples, among whom Vives is specified, confine the application of the law of association "*exclusively to the phenomena of recollection*, without any glimpse of a more general operation, extending to all the connections of *thought and feeling*;" while the enouncement of a general theory of Association, thus denied to the genius of Aristotle, is, all, and more than all, accorded to the sagacity of *Hobbes*. The truth, however, is, that in his whole doctrine upon this subject, name and thing, Hobbes is simply a silent follower of the Stagirite; inferior to his master in the comprehension and accuracy of his general views; and not superior, even on the special points selected, either to Aristotle or to Vives.† (Dissertation, &c. Note T.)

* To be added to my friend Professor Ferrier's "Plagiarisms of S. T. Coleridge;" in Blackwood's Magazine, March 1840. This paper is remarkable for the sagacity which tracks, through the "Hercynian brakes" of philosophy and poetry, the footsteps of the literary reaver; whose ignorance of French alone freed France from contribution. Coleridge's systematic plagiarism is, perhaps, the most remarkable on record,—taking all the circumstances into account, the foremost of which, certainly, is the natural ability of the culprit. But sooth to say, Coleridge had in him more of the ivy than of the oak,—was better able to clothe than to create. The publication of his literary Table-Talk, &c., shews that he was in the habit of speaking, as his Biographia, &c., show that he was in the habit of writing, the opinions of others,—as his own.

* Among his other dreaming errors, Coleridge charges Hume with plagiarising from Aquinas (who, by the way, herein only repeats Aristotle) his whole doctrine of Association. But Coleridge charging plagiarism! "Quis tulerit Gracchum, de seditione querentem?"—See my ingenious friend, Mr Burton's excellent Biography of David Hume, lately published.

† Let it not be supposed, that, in these observations, I would insinuate aught like a charge of plagiarism, against The Philosopher of Malmesbury; or that, though disinclined to many of his opinions, I am a lukewarm admirer of his philosophical talent. It is an egregious error to consider Hobbes as an unlearned man; or, as one, who wove only what he spun and grew. Among English,—among modern philosophers, he towers a shrewd and intrepid, an original and independent thinker. But these qualities are exhibited, not so much in the discovery of new materials, as in the new elaboration of old. He is essentially an eclectic. But he chooses and rejects freely; illustrating the principles he adopts with admirable ingenuity, and carrying them out with unshrinking consistency to their most startling results. This is more especially true of his psychology; which is original rather for what it omits, than for what it contains. It is, in substance, an Aristotelic doctrine, retrenched, not to say mutilated. Of the writings of the Stagirite himself, Hobbes was even a zealous student; of which his "*Briefe of the Art of*

But, that Aristotle's merits in regard to the theory of Association have not, as yet, been fully recognised by philosophers, is not to be marvelled at; when we consider the extra brevity and occasional corruption of the treatise in which his doctrine on that subject is contained, and when it is known that the editors, translators, and expositors of that treatise have all misapprehended its theory of Association in the most important points. Without, therefore, attempting aught like a history of this doctrine, for which, the materials I have collected, it is, at present, impossible to employ; I shall confine myself to the principal object of such a history—endeavour to *render justice to the great author of that theory;* by translating, from his treatise on Memory and Reminiscence, all that has any bearing on the subject; at the same time, restoring the text from its corruptions, and illustrating its veritable import.—I shall likewise translate what, (but *only what*,) of any moment, is to be found in the relative commentary of *Themistius;* because this, both in itself and in reference to Aristotle, is, on the matter in question, a valuable, though wholly neglected, monument of ancient philosophy;—because, from the rarity of its one edition, it is accessible to few even of those otherwise competent to read it;—but, above all, because we herein discover the origin of those misconceptions, which, bequeathed by the first, have been inherited by the last, of Aristotle's interpreters.

In other respects, I shall neglect no *subsidia* within reach; and my Aristotelic collection is tolerably full, more complete, indeed, than that extant in any public library in this country. Though statements may therefore sometimes appear sweeping, the reader should not believe that I hazard them without an adequate foundation.*

Rhetorique" is only one of many proofs that could be shown: and though he occasionally abuses the schoolmen when in his way, he was neither ignorant of, nor unindebted to, their writings. There is, however, another philosopher whose relation to Hobbes has never been observed, but whose influence, if not on the general character of his speculation, at least on the adoption of several of his more peculiar opinions, appears to me almost demonstrable. I mean the Frenchman *Berigardus*, (Beauregard;) who, when Hobbes visited Pisa, in 1637, was in the meridian of his academic reputation, and who, in his great work, the "*Circulus Pisanus*," first published in 1643, takes, or rather makes, an occasion to speak of the English philosopher, then known only by his recent work "De Cive," in terms manifestly the suggestion of personal regard. The counter alternative will hardly be maintained,—that it was Hobbes who privately acted upon Berigard.

I may be permitted to take this opportunity of acknowledging for myself the obligation which Sir William Molesworth has conferred upon all who take an interest in philosophical pursuits, by his recent edition of the collected works of this illustrious thinker;—an undertaking in which he has not only done honour to himself, but taken off a reproach which has long weighed heavily upon our country.

* 1°.—Of *commentators* on the *De Memoria* I have the following.—The Greek Paraphrasis of *Themistius* which dates from the fourth century.—The only edition is that of Aldus in 1534.—The Greek commentary of *Michael Ephesius*, in points of difficulty seldom more than a transcript of Themistius, is of a comparatively recent, but uncertain, date. If Allatius (De Psellis, § 32.) be right in his plausible conjecture, and the Scholiast and the Ex-Emperor Michael Ducas, who died Archbishop of Ephesus, be the same, it will not ascend higher than the latter part of the eleventh century. Of this, also, there is only one edition—the Aldine, of 1527.—I am well acquainted with the scholastic commentaries of *Averroes*, (†1206,) *Albertus Magnus*, (†1280,) and *Aquinas*, (†1274.)—Subsequent to the revival of letters, I have the expositions of—*Faber Stapulensis*, 1500,—*Leonicus*, 1520,—*Janellus*, 1540,—*Schegkius*, 1546,—*Labittus* (in MS.), 1553,—*Gesner*, c. 1560, but only printed 1586,—*Simonius*, 1566,—*Crippa*, 1567,—the *Coimbra Jesuits*, 1600,—*Pacius*, 1600,—*Havenreuter*, 1600.—Of these the commentary of *Leonicus* is of especial moment; not for any original merit of its own, but as the principal medium through which the views of the Greek expositors, on the *Parva Naturalia*, were propagated in the west.—To these are to be added illustrations of this treatise occasionally met with in psychological writings of the Aristotelic school; of which it is only necessary to notice one—the remarkable work "De Anima" of *Vives*, 1538.—The Paraphrase of the Greek Monk, Theodorus Metochita, († 1332,) has escaped me.

2°. Of *versions*, some of which have the authority of MSS., I have those of *Leonicus*, *Schegkius*, *Vatablus*, *Perionius*, *Labittus*, *Simonius*, *Crippa*, and the *anonymous* version extant in the Venice editions of the combined works of Aristotle and Averroes. That of *Alcyonius* I have not seen. *Taylor's* English translation is mere rubbish.

3°. In regard to the *text itself*, besides *Bekker's* admirable recension, with the variations of six MSS., in the edition of the Berlin Academy, I shall compare, when requisite, the *Camotio-Aldine*, *Erasmian*, *Morellian*, *Simo-*

By *Memory* (ἡ μνήμη, τὸ μνημονεύειν,) Aristotle, in his treatise on that subject, does not simply denote the conservative power of mind—*mere retention*. He there employs it, proximately to designate the faculty of reproduction, in so far as that is direct and immediate—*simple remembrance or recollection;* while, to the process of *mediate or indirect reproduction* of something heretofore in memory, but which we cannot now call up, except through the intervention of something else, he gives the name of *Reminiscence*, (ἡ ἀνάμνησις.)

But though the term Reminiscence be properly and principally applied to this intentional process of recovery, and which it is the purpose of the present treatise to consider; he extends it also to the *obtrusion* of thoughts on our remembrance, through the course of *spontaneous suggestion*, of which, however, he has here occasion only to speak incidentally.—This is enough to prepare the reader for the Aristotelic extract which follows; and this, though divided, for the sake of illustration, into segments, ought, in the first instance, to be read continuously and by itself.

§ 1. Aristotle here enounces the one proximate cause or condition of Reminiscence—the *determined consecution of thought on thought.* (And, be it observed, that I shall here employ the term *thought* in its widest signification, for *every conscious mode of mind.*)

ARISTOTLE.

"*Reminiscences* take place,* in virtue of that constitution of our mind, whereby *each mental movement** is determined

---

nian, *Sylburgian*, *Casaubonian*, *Pacian* and *Duvallian* editions; but above all, the quotations in *Themistius*, and the ῥήσεις in *Michael Ephesius*.

When not otherwise stated in the notes, the text of Bekker is that from which the translation will be made.

* "Oblivio imperfecta," (says Vives,) "instauratione, indiget, ut vestigatione, et quasi gradibus, ad id veniatur quod quærimus: ut ab *annulo* in *aurifabrum;* ex hoc in *monile reginæ;* hinc in *bellum quod gesserit vir ejus;* a bello in *duces;* a ducibus ad *eorum progenitores* aut *liberos;* hinc ad *disciplinas quibus studebant;*—in quo nulla est ad sistendum meta.—Gradus hi per omnia argumentorum genera late sese diffundunt:—a *causa* ad *effectum;* ab hoc ad *instrumentum;* a *parte* ad *totum;* ab isto ad *locum;* a loco ad *personam;* a persona ad *priora* ejus et *posteriora;* ad *contraria;* ad *similia;*—in quo discursu non est finis—Et sunt transitus quidam longissimi—immo saltus. Ut ex *Scipione* venio in cogitationem *potentiæ Turcicæ*, propter victorias ejus de Asia, in qua regnabat Antiochus: ex nomine *Ciceronis* venit in recordationem *Lactantius*, qui fuit ejus imitator; et ex hoc de *chalcographia* [cogitamus,] nam ejus liber dicitur formulis æneis excusus, vel primus, vel de primis." (De Anima, L ii. c. De Mem. et Rem.)

** It is necessary to say a word in regard to the Aristotelic employment of the term *motion or movement*, (κίνησις,) in a psychological relation. It has been generally either mistaken or inadequately understood.—Hissmann supposes that Aristotle means by it some *local motion*, akin to the vibrations of certain nervous fibres, or the flow of certain nervous spirits, by which so many ancient and modern physiologists have pretended to explain the phænomena of thought. Maass and Goerenz reject, for the Stagirite, this mechanical hypothesis; but, unacquainted with the general analogy of Aristotle's language, they have not established their rejection on its broad and proper basis.

Change or Mutation, (μεταβολή) according to Aristotle, is a genus containing under it four (or six) species;—each species affecting a subject pertaining to a different category—1°. If in Substance, (κατὰ τὸ τί or τόδε,) it is *generation* and *destruction*, (γένεσις, φθορά.)—2°. If in Quantity, (κατὰ τὸ ποσόν,) it is *augmentation* and *diminution*, (αὔξησις, φθίσις:)—3° If in Quality, (κατὰ τὸ ποιόν, or πάθος,) it is *variation*, (ἀλλοίωσις;)—4°. If in Place, (κατὰ τὸ ποῦ, or τόπον.) it is *local motion*, (φορά.) (Metaph. xii. 2.)

Now Aristotle, sometimes makes *motion* convertible with *change*, and thus a genus containing under it the same four species,—(as in Phys. III. 1.;)—sometimes he makes it a subgenus to *change*, containing under it only the last three species, (as in Metaph. XI. 11, 12. Phys. V. 1. 2—VII. 3. De Anima, I. 3.—in which last the species of motion are called four, *increase* and *diminution* being counted as two.)

Now, by the generic term *motion*, or *movement*, Aristotle, in its psychological application, simply means to denote *change in quality*, or the species *variation*,—the nature of which he more than once expounds, (Gen. et Corr. I. 4 text 23. Phys. VII. 2.); and variation, to accommodate a more ancient to a more modern nomenclature, may be fairly translated by the more familiar expression—*modification*. In this, Aristotle only follows the example of Plato; who, in the Timæus and Parmenides, constituting two species of simple motion, *lation* and *variation* (τὸ φέρεσθαι and τὸ ἀλλοιοῦσθαι) commonly employs the generic term for the latter species, in designating the mental modes. As a psychological substitute for these terms, Aristotle also very commonly employs *affection* or *passion* (πάθος).

These *three* terms, then, Aristotle uses in

to arise, as the sequel of a certain other." *

THEMISTIUS.

"What, then, is Reminiscence, has been shewn;—it is *the renovation of Memory.* How this is brought to bear is also manifest." Having quoted the preceding text, he proceeds:—"For as in a chain,

---

differently to denote both the activities and the passivities of mind; and (De Anima ii. 5 § 6) he explains "how the same [mental phænomenon, in different points of view,] is variously styled *affection*, or *movement*, or *passion*, or *energy*."—Further, "Sensitive perception (he says) consists in a certain *movement* and *affection*, for it seems to be a kind of *variation*." (De An. ii. 5. § 2. See also Phys. vii. 3. § 12.)—"The phantasm, the object represented in imagination, is an *affection*—a *movement* of the common sense." (De Mem. 1. § 8—De Ins. 2. §§ 16, 17, 20.)—But as "there is no intelligence possible except by relation to a phantasm," (De An. iii. 8. §§ 5. 8. 9 § 4. De Mem. 1. § 8;) and as memory is, along with phantasy, a function of the common sense, "we remember our intellections only secondarily and accidentally, through our remembrance of the relative phantasms." (De Mem. 1. §§ 8, 11.)—These intro-sensitive movements thus proximately constituting our whole suggestive series of thought.—To these movements are to be referred our Feelings. "Pleasures and Pains are *movements* caused by a sensible object—are *variations* of the sensitive part of the soul," (Phys. vii. 4, § 10;) while, in regard to the Appetencies,—(the desires, emotions, and affections proper, "of which pain and pleasure are the concomitants,")—there is no room for question. (Eth. Nic. ii. 4 Magn. Mor. i, 13.)

It is thus, in the *first* place, manifest, that in employing the term *movement*, in this, as in his other psychological treatises, Aristotle never dreamt of insinuating any mechanical hypothesis, by which to explain the phænomena of thought and suggestion; and, in the *second*, that he here and elsewhere employs it, as a general word, by which to denote all the various modifications of the conscious mind.—Under this last, a word in reference to Sir James Mackintosh.

"What," (says Sir James,) "Mr Coleridge has not told us is, that the Stagirite confines the application of this law *exclusively to the phænomena of recollection*, without any glimpse of a more general operation extending to all connections of thought and feeling." And he adds, that the illustrations "of Ludovicus Vives, as quoted by Mr Coleridge, extend no farther."—(L. c.) This, I must be pardoned in saying, is altogether erroneous.

In the *first* place—Sir James is wrong, in asserting, that Aristotle attempts to reduce to law "the phænomena of recollection alone," meaning by that, the phænomena of intentional reminiscence; for (see § 5, and relative notes,) Aristotle declares that the same laws govern the voluntary, and the spontaneous, course of thought.

In the *second* place, he is wrong, in saying, that Aristotle "had no glimpse of a more general operation, extending to all connections of thought and feeling;" for, we have now shewn, that the term *movement*, as employed by the philosopher, comprehends, indifferently, every mental mode, be it one of cognition, whether a presentation, representation, or thought proper,—one of feeling, whether painful or pleasurable,—one of appetency, whether a volition or a desire.—Hobbes's "train *of imaginations or conceptions or thoughts*," and Locke's "association of *ideas*," are objectionable expressions, because, in propriety, only applicable to the phænomena of cognition; to which it is certain, that Locke, at least, had no thought of restricting the connection. On the contrary, Aristotle's "train of *mental movements*" states the fact, and his view of the fact, fully and unambiguously.

In the *third* place, in regard to Vives, though Sir James be right, in so far as he limits his assertion to "Vives, as quoted by Mr Coleridge;" yet as Coleridge only quotes the scraps which he chanced to find in Maass, it is proper to state that any negative presumption founded upon these would be erroneous; for in other passages, the Spanish Aristotelian extends the principle of association "to all the connections of thought and feeling."—Thus:—"Ad aspectum *loci*, de eo venit in mentem quod *in loco* scimus *evenisse*, aut *situm esse*. Quando etiam cum *voce*, aut *sono* aliquo quippiam contingit lætum, eodem *sono audito*, *delectamur*; si triste, *tristamur*. Quod in *brutis* quoque est annotare; quæ, si quæ sono vocata, gratum aliquid acceipiunt, rursum, ad eundem sonum facile ac libenter accurrunt; sin cædantur, sonitum eundem deinceps reformidant, ex plagarum recordatione.—Eundem in modum, de *sapore*, de *odore*. Puer, quum Valentiæ *febri* laborarem, et, depravato gustu, *cerasa* edissem, multis post annis, quoties id pomum gustabam, toties, non solum *de febri meminieram*, sed *habere mihi illam videbam*." (L. 1.) I am unable to find in Hobbes (whom Sir James Mackintosh would elevate not only above Vives, but above Aristotle) any passage which shews that he had taken so comprehensive a view of the influence of the associative principle as the Spanish philosopher.—On the other hand, the reader may compare Cartesii, Epist. i. 36, and Locke, Essay ii. 33. § 7.

* By τόδε μετὰ τόδε,—by μεθ' ἑτέραν ἐκείνην, and the like, Aristotle here and in the sequel, (see n. †, p. 894, b, &c.) denotes the following of *this* determinate mode *of consciousness upon that other*, and not merely the following of some one upon some other, or, as Hobbes expresses it, of "*any thing to any thing*." This the commentators have strangely overlooked, and in consequence thereof, as we shall see, (§ 5,) sadly perverted Aristotle's doctrine.

If one ring be lifted, the link therewith connected will of necessity be moved, and through that the next again, and so forth;* this likewise is the case, in those impressions of which the soul is the subject. For if the soul be once moved by an impression, forthwith, the one thereon following, and then the other after that, move it likewise. For example:—I have seen *Coriscus*, the musician, with *his lyre;* and there has remained impressed in my mind an image, both of the lyre and of Coriscus. Thereafter, let us say, I behold *Socrates holding a lyre*. Incontinently, I am reminiscent of the *lyre* of Coriscus, and then of *Coriscus* himself.—Again:—I have heard a *person* singing [the religious song, (?)]

> ' *Two souls the body leaving,*
> *One to the other said:—*
> *Ah! whither now to wend us,*
> [*And join the happy dead!*']

After a season, I hear *another* singing the *same air*, but to words of a different character, as [in the amatory ditty,(?)]

> ' *My heart to hope uplifts me,*
> *Then sinks me to despair.*' †

Though now moved by the melody alone, there yet rises therewith a reminiscence of the former words, ' *Two souls the body leaving*,' and of the *person* by whom they were sung."‡

§ 2. Thought being only manifested as consecutive and determined, the law of consecution, absolutely considered, is thus universal and necessary. But by relation to the following of *this individual thought on that*, there is a distinction to be taken; for in this respect, the sequence is either *necessary* or *habitual*.

ARISTOTLE.

" If the consecution be *necessary*,* it is manifest that, whenever the mind is determined to that individual movement, it will, also, be determined to this."†

" If, again, the consecution be not of necessity, but only the *effect of habit;* the [individual] movement will follow, not as the invariable, but only as the ordinary, rule."‡

THEMISTIUS.

" Some impressions are consequent to each other, *necessarily*. For he who is reminiscent of *Fire*, must at the same time have an imagination of *Heat;* and he who was *struck by Socrates*, in the reminiscence of Socrates, cannot but be correminiscent, that by him *he was struck*, and in *such or such a place* §

---

* Before Themistius, Carneades had compared the consecution of thoughts to "a *chain*, in which one link is dependent on another." (Sext. Emp. adv. Math L. vii. §. 176.) It is resembled by our countryman, Joannes Major, to a *cobbler's bristle and thread;* "una notitia aliam trahit, ut seta sutoris, filum;" (In Sent. L. i. d. 3. q 3.) Hobbes likens it to the *following of water* upon a table whithersoever it is guided by the finger." (Hum. Nat. ch. 3, and Lev. ch. 3.) Hume, finally, compares it to *attraction*, and represents the attraction of association in the mental, as analogous to the attraction of gravitation in the material, world. (Hum Nat. B 1 P. 1. S 4.)—On these see § 9, note 1st.

† This and the preceding fragment have escaped the collectors of Greek Scolia

‡ Michael Ephesius says—" We are first reminiscent of the former *words*, then of the former *place*, and then of the former *singer*."

* By necessary or natural consecution Aristotle probably means the dependence subsisting between notions, one of which cannot be thought, without at the same time our thinking the other; as all Relations, Cause and Effect, Means and End, Premises and Conclusion, &c. (See nn. p. 894, a, b.) He did not, it may be observed, fall into the error of many modern philosophers, in confounding the natural and necessary, with the habitual and acquired connections of thought. He makes no fruitless attempt to shew the genesis of the former; far less does he attempt to evolve the laws under which we think, from the tendencies generated by thinking. Locke, indeed, very properly limits the term "association of ideas" to their habitual or subjective connection, to the exclusion of their logical or objective or "natural connection." (Essay, B ii. ch. 33, § 5.) Mr Stewart, again, (Elem. i. p. 291, takes a distinction, corresponding to this of Aristotle, as "*important*," but one "which," he says, "as far as I am aware, has *not hitherto* attracted the attention of philosophers."

† The expositors not observing that Aristotle does not here relax the condition of determined consecution absolutely, but only the determined consecution *of this particular thought on that*, (see n. *, p. 893, b &c ;) have all of them been led, as will be seen, to the actual reversal of his doctrine, in supposing him to admit the possibility of thought arising without suggestion—at least without suggestion according to the laws which he lays down. See § 5.

‡ This applies to the consecution of any two individual thoughts, not necessarily connected, as well in *different persons*, as in the *same person*, at different times, under different circumstances, in different frames of mind.

§ These examples are unfortunate. If we think *Fire* and *Heat*, in the relation of Cause

"Other impressions, again, are not connected of necessity, but in virtue of *habit* or *custom*; and of these, the subsequent follow the antecedent, not always, but only for the most part. An example will illustrate this. It frequently happened, that wishing to employ *lycabas*, [archaic word for year,] I could not recall it. To remedy this I accustomed myself to connect it in thought with the familiar term *lycos* [wolf], both words commencing with the common syllable *ly*[c.] Obtaining thus a starting impulse from *lycos*, I henceforward was enabled easily to recollect *lycabas*. Another finding it difficult to remember *Tauromenitas* [inhabitant of Tauromenium], used himself to think of *tauros* [a bull]; and a third was wont, by departing from *pleura* [the side], to call up *Pleuron* [the town.] But in these the antecedent is *not always* followed by the consequent; we often, for example, think of *pleura* [the side] without any reminiscence of *Pleuron* [the town.]"—See § 9, Themistius.

§ 3. The necessary consecution or concomitancy of individual thoughts, being involved in the very fact of the several thoughts themselves, (the conception of each being only realised through the conception of the other); this requires and admits of no farther explanation. To the habitual consecution, therefore, Aristotle exclusively confines himself. And here, before proceeding to enounce the laws by which the habitual consecution is governed, he indicates, in the *first* place, the circumstances by which, in different minds variously constituted, and in the same mind under different affections, thoughts are more or less promptly associated, and consequently the general or abstract laws of association modified in their particular or concrete applications. These have by modern philosophers been sometimes treated as *secondary laws of association*; but from their contingent, variable, indefinite, and latescent character, they cannot be reduced to rule, and are, therefore, undeserving of the name of *Laws*. In doing this, he shows that by the term *habit* he does not mean merely to express the result of a frequent repetition of the same action or passion, but generally the *simple fact of association*, whether that be the effect of such repetition, or of some extraordinarily intense attention, determined by peculiar circumstances upon certain objects.—Text emended.

ARISTOTLE.

"But [in regard to habit it is to be observed, that] with certain things, certain minds* become more habitual-

---

and Effect, in that case, certainly, the notion of the one necessarily suggests the notion of the other. But it is only by experience of their coadjacency in time and space, and by habit, that we come to think them under this relation. The other example is one of a strong habitual, (in Aristotle's sense of the word habit,) but not of a necessary connection. The example by St Thomas is better. The thought of *Socrates*, he says, necessarily suggests the thought of *Man*, and the thought of man necessarily suggests the thought of *Animal*. But this too is exceptionable; for it may be said, that animal, being a part of man, man of Socrates, the former notion is not properly *suggested by* the latter, but already *given in* it. This may indeed be applied to all relatives. For a relation being an indivisible thought, made up of two or more terms, to say, that one relative term suggests another, is improper; for, in point of fact, neither exists, neither can exist, in thought apart from, or prior to, the other. (See nn. p. 900, a, b.)—As examples of *necessary* suggestion, take the following:—We are aware of a phenomenon. That it exists—only as known—only as a phenomenon—only as an absolute relative, we are unable to realise in thought; and there is necessarily suggested the notion of an unimaginable something, in which the phenomenon inheres,—a Subject, or Substance.—Again;—a thing appears, as beginning to be. Think we cannot, aught absolutely to commence—to start of itself from nonentity into being; and there is necessarily suggested the notion of something (vague perhaps and undetermined) in which the complement of existence, appearing to begin, is thought as having previously been realised in a different form, and as now only relatively commencing under a novel aspect,—a Cause.—The impossibility we find of imagining extension without colour—not to say colour without extension—is also an example.

* All the editions and collated MSS. have ἐνίους; one Vatican codex, however, exhibiting ἔνια (and the correlative ἕτερα) as a variation or a correction. The natural and obvious meaning of ἐνίους is some persons or minds; but, among the commentators, Michael Ephesius supposes the ellipsis may be of τύπους, impressions. Themistius with ἐνίους, reads, instead of ἄλλους, (or ἑτέρους for the MSS. vary,) ἑτέρας and κινουμένας.—All this manifests the well-founded discontent with the present lection, which affords a sense inadequate to that required; while the causal dependence, by δὲ of the following sentence, or clause, from the present, is, as the text stands, inept. I therefore read—ἐνίους ἔνια. This affords the meaning desiderated; and at the cheapest rate. For in transcription nothing is more

ised,* at the first movement, than other minds, though this be frequently repeated. Hence is it that some objects which we have seen but once, are more perfectly remembered by us, than others which we have oftentimes beheld."

THEMISTIUS

Reads :—" '*But certain minds become more habitualised with this movement at once, than with that, though frequently repeated.*' " No illustration given.

§ 4. In the *second* place, Aristotle proceeds to enounce the general laws of the habitual consecution, suggestion, or association, on which Reminiscence is dependent. This he does first in relation to Reminiscence *intentional* or *voluntary*, and then in relation to Reminiscence *unintentional* or *spontaneous* ;—in regard to both of which it is shewn, that these laws are absolutely identical.

In regard to *intentional* Reminiscence he generalises *one* supreme or universal

---

likely than the omission of one or other of such semi identical words.

* By *habit* (ἔθος) is commonly understood a certain quality generated by *custom* ; (i e. the frequent iteration of the same action or passion)—though these words are frequently commuted; in English, and in Greek, the same term stands for both. Aristotle here, however, uses the term in a less limited sense; and it might, perhaps, at present, be more adequately translated by *Association* than by *Habit*. In like manner Aristotle often uses the term ἕξις, (which we inadequately translate by habit or possession,) not only for the acquired, but also for the natural. Aristotle means simply to state the fact,—that two mental movements having once coexisted, each tends, if reproduced, to reproduce the other; the force of this tendency being in proportion, 1°, to the frequency of their co-existence, and 2°, to their mutual affinity;—this affinity being dependent on the greater power of attention and retention natural or acquired for this or that class of objects, and on the temporary states of mind, in which certain things and thoughts exert a stronger influence than they do in others.

This *Vives* thus illustrates; and his observations comprise, in brief, nearly all of principal moment that has been said upon this subject, either before or since. "(1.) Nec memoriam habent omnes pariter ad omnia. Sunt qui *verba*, sunt qui *res* meminerunt facilius; ut Themistocles rerum, Hortensius verborum recordatione dicuntur valuisse; quod exemplum positum sit pro toto et hominum et rerum in genere. Nam alii *curiosa*, alii *recta et simplicia*, alii *publica*, alii *privata*, alii *vetera*, alii *nova*, alii *sua*, alii *aliena*, alii *vitia*, alii *virtutes* recordantur citius et melius; ut est cujusque ingenii pronitas, et attendit ad hæc aut illa libentius.—(2.) Memoriæ plurimum confert naturalis *contemperatio corporis*, quali fuisse præditos illos credibile est quorum magnitudo memoriæ monumentis literarum celebratur—Themistocles, Cyrus, Cineas, Hortensius.—(3.) Adjuvatur tota ratione *victus*, . . . (4.) Alte descendunt in memoriam, quæ *attente* sunt a primo accepta et cum cura; quo fit ut ingeniosissimi sæpe homines et bona memoria prolixe instructi non tam recordentur multa, quam qui illis non sunt pares his dotibus, quod neglectim multa vident, legunt, audiunt.—(5.) Si se *adfectus* aliquis concitatus, primæ rei cujusque memoriæ admiscuit, recordatio est deinceps facilior, promptior, diuturnior; ut quae maxima lætitia vel dolore sunt in animum ingressa, horum longissima est memoria; eaque de causa mos est quarundam gentium in statuendis agrorum limitibus acriter cædere pueros qui adsint, ut firmius et diutius recordentur illorum finium. [Does Vives allude to what takes, or took, place in the perambulation of the *English* parishes?]—(6.) *Exercitatione et meditatione crebra* magnum memoria sumit robur. Fit enim et ad accipiendum prompta, et ad plura capienda latior, et tenacior ad continendum; nec est ulla in toto animo functio, quæ perinde cultum sui desideret, . . . —(7.) Quæ *vacuo animo et tranquillo* accepimus, facilius hærent in mente, si modo attente animum applicamus. Qua de causa, quæ prima ætate vidimus atque audivimus ea diutius recordamur et integrius. Est enim tunc soluta curis et cogitationibus mens.—(8.) Tum etiam attendimus diligentior; quippe ætate illa admiramur omnia tanquam *nova*, at quæ *admirationem* nobis movent ea solicite spectamus, alteque in animum descendunt," &c.—Aristotle, or whoever was the author of the Problems, makes a similar observation, and adds that—" In like manner we remember best what first occurs to us in the morning, our memory falling off as the day advances, in consequence of the multitude of objects by which we are distracted."—(Sect. XXX. § 5.)

An instance of the way in which our habitudes of thought and feeling regulate the points of view in which we contemplate objects and consequently determine—often capriciously—the course of our reminiscence, is unwittingly afforded, in himself, by the Lutheran commentator, Simon Simonius of Lucca. This is the general example of consecution which he proposes :—" *Hydræ*, ab Hercule sagittis et igne interfectæ, memoria *Papæ* mihi memoriam suggerit; hæc *Romæ* ; qua deinceps *Babylonis*, reminiscor." Compare Shylock, (Merchant of Venice, Act I. Scene 1.) " My wind, cooling my broth," &c. The Ethology and Pathology in the second book of Aristotle's Rhetoric, more especially the chapters on the different tendencies of the different ages and conditions of life, supply a rich magazine of observations on the practical influence of association and habit. Add John Barclay's Icon Animarum.

law, divided into *three* special or subordinate laws. The *one universal law*,—to which I would give the name of *Redintegration*—is: *Thoughts which have, at any time, recent or remote, stood to each other in the relation of coexistence or immediate consecution, do when severally reproduced tend to reproduce each other;* in other words: *The parts of any total thought when subsequently called into consciousness are apt to suggest, immediately, the parts to which they were proximately related, and, mediately, the whole of which they were co-constituent.* The terms in which this great law is enounced by Aristotle, have not been understood by his expositors; and the law itself has, in consequence, altogether escaped their observation. Text, therefore, explicated.

The three laws, of which the one preceding is an absolute expression, are the law of *Similars*, the law of *Contraries*, and the law of *Co-adjacents;* for to these three heads may be reduced all the relations into which a thing, having once been thought as a relative, tends subsequently to relapse; and thus to recall into consciousness all else with which it had then stood in correlation.—What is the import of these terms, is considered in the notes.

ARISTOTLE.

"When, therefore, we accomplish an act of Reminiscence, we pass through a certain series of precursive movements, until we arrive at a movement, on which the one we are in quest of is habitually consequent. Hence too it is, that we hunt* through the mental train,* excogitating [what we seek] from [its *Concomitant* in] THE PRESENT† OR SOME OTHER‡

* "For as dogs," (says Longinus,) "having once found the footsteps of their game, follow from trace to trace, deeming it already all but caught; so he, who would recover his past cognitions from oblivion, must speculate the parts which remain to him of these cognitions, and the circumstances with which they chance to be connected, to the end that he may light on something which shall serve him for a starting-point, from whence to follow out his recollection of the others." See the interesting chapter on Memory, in the rhetorical treatise, restored by Ruhnkenius from Apsines to Longinus; (Rhetores Græci—of Aldus, p 719;—of Walz. t ix. p. 574.) It is not amongst the fragments in Weiske's Longinus.

Vives, too, compares the process of reminiscence to the tracing by dogs, and also to the ascending the steps of a ladder or stair.

"The term θηρεύειν (says Sir James Mackintosh, speaking of the passage in the text,) is as significant as if it had been chosen by Hobbes.' In point of fact, it was chosen by Hobbes, and in illustration of this very process;—but borrowed from Aristotle, along with the correlative terms, *seeking*, *beginning*, &c. (See Hum. Nat. ch. iii. §§ 3, 4.—Lev. P. i. ch. 3)

* The expressions τὸ ἐφεξῆς and ἡ κίνησις μετὰ ταῦτα, commonly rendered by Aristotle's Latin translators—*motuum animæ*, &c. *consequentia*, *series*, *sequela*, *insecutio*, &c. were among others adopted by Hobbes; whose "*consequentia vel series imaginationum*," in Latin, and in English, "*consequence*, *series*, *train*, *succession of imaginations*, *conceptions or thoughts*," have been often ignorantly supposed expressions original to himself. Even Hissmann and Maass seem guilty of this. Subsequently to Aristotle, Carneades employed the term συνδρομὴ τῶν φαντασιῶν; but, with him, this is not to be viewed as simply convertible with what we understand by the mental train. (Sext. Emp. adv. Math. l. vii. § 176–182.

† *The Present* (τὸ νῦν) is not of course to be taken rigidly for the infinitesimal point of transition from the past, but (as might even be shewn from Aristotle's previous discussion) in its common signification,—for a certain latter portion of the past. In fact, before we are conscious of the Now, in its strict signification, it is already fled. *Concomitance*, or *Simultaneity*, is also to be taken in a certain latitude;—viz, not only for that which is strictly coexistent, but also for that which is proximately antecedent or consequent.

I find, however, that all Aristotelians have not been so blind to Aristotle's meaning, in this passage, as his regular commentators. Timpler seems to have fairly, if not fully, understood it. "Adjuvans causa (recordationis) est consideratio, partim *circumstantiarum, præsertim temporis præteriti*, quo homo rem, vel per sensum, vel per intellectum, cognovit; partim *similium et affinium*, partim *contrariorum*. (Empsychologia L. iii. c 3. pr. 17.)—I should observe also, that Maass, who, if we are to judge from one and all of his Greek quotations, could not pretend to a knowledge even of the alphabet of that language, was yet too forward in philosophy, not to see, at once, what, in this instance, Aristotle's meaning must necessarily be. Aristotle has been here so long mis-apprehended, only because he was so far a head of his expositors. Nor is there a higher testimony to his genius than that it required a progress in philosophy of two thousand years, before philosophers were prepared to apprehend his meaning, when the discovery of that meaning was abandoned to their own intelligence

‡ The Commentators and Translators of this treatise have, one and all, here marvellously mistaken Aristotle's meaning, and thus misrepresented his doctrine in its most important point. They have not perceived that ἄλλου

[TIME],* and from its SIMILAR or CON-

τινος means—"*or some other* TIME," and not "*or some other* THING" Looking to the preceding words, the sub-intelligence of χρόνου or καιροῦ is demanded, as a correlative, by τὸ νῦν; and looking to the context, before and after, it is demanded, as that which alone satisfies the natural, and even necessary, sense The interpretation of the Commentators, on the other hand, is, at once, grammatically perverse, and philosophically absurd. It does violence to Aristotle's language. And to what end? To prevent him from consummating the theory of association in the enouncement of its universal law Nay more—actually to make him throw up the attempt at reducing the phænomena of Suggestion to determinate laws at all. Aristotle, in their view, appends to an imperfect series of four stated causes of association, a *fifth*, under the title of a "*some other*,"—thus literally, and in sober earnest, making him forestall Dean Aldrich in his joke:—

"Si bene quid speculor, causæ sunt *quinque* Bibendi:
Hospitis adventus; præsens sitis; atque futura;
Et vini probitas; *et quælibet altera causa*."

* The law, I style that of Redintegration, and which is here enounced by Aristotle, may be viewed as a corollary of his doctrine of Imagination and Memory. The representations of Imagination or Phantasy he views as merely the movements continued in the organ of internal sense after the moving object itself has been withdrawn, (De Insom. c. 1. § 9—c. ii. §§ 11, 15. 16, 18, 20, ed. Pac.;) and though there are passages which would shew, that he considered sensible perception as something more than the mere recognition of a subjective affection; he yet, when popularly speaking, defines imagination to be—a kind of feeble or decaying sense, (Rhet. l. 1 c 11.;)—a definition which Des Cartes and Hobbes adopt without qualification, and in scientific rigour.—Again:—Memory Aristotle does not view as a faculty distinct from imagination; but simply as the recalling those impressions, these movements into consciousness, of which Phantasy is the complement In these circumstances, as there is no reason, why the movements should hold any other co-arrangement when in, than they held when *coming into*, the mind; and as there is no reason, why they should be recalled to consciousness, in any other co-ordination, than what they held previously to such revocation;—the law of Redintegration is, consequently, a rule which follows naturally and of itself.

To *Hobbes*, who had, pro tanto, adopted Aristotle's doctrine of Imagination, this law would, of course, present itself; but it might also present itself, as a consectary of the mechanical theory of cognition which he had espoused. "All fancies are motions within us, relics of those made in the sense; and *those motions that immediately succeeded one another in the sense continue also together after sense; in so much, as the former coming again to take place, and be predominant the latter followeth*, by coherence of the matter moved, in such manner as water upon a plane table is drawn which way any one part of it is guided by the finger." (Lev. P. I. ch. 3.—compare also Hum. Nat. ch. 4, § 2, and Elem. Philos. c. 25, § 8.)

But while it is impossible, to hold with Sir James Mackintosh, that Hobbes, as opposed to Aristotle, is the original discoverer "of this fundamental law, of this prolific truth which forms the basis of all true psychology;" it is even impossible to allow him the priority of such inadequate generalisation of this principle as his materialism allowed, in competition with many subsequent philosophers.

Passing over St Augustine, whose doctrine of Reminiscence is too important to be here spoken of by the way, this law is, after Aristotle, explicitly enounced by *Vives*.—"*Quæ simul sunt a Phantasia comprehensa, si alterutrum occurrat, solet secum alterum repræsentare.*" (L. c.)

Omitting others,—prior also to Hobbes, whose "Human Nature," "Leviathan," and "Elementa Philosophiæ," appeared in 1650, 1651, and 1655, this law was enounced by three of his own immediate contemporaries and *friends*;—philosophers from whose mechanical hypotheses of perception and memory it flowed equally as from his own, and who, howbeit their names have not hitherto been adduced in connection with the doctrine of Association, proclaimed it—two of them at least—not less clearly than himself. These are Berigard, Digby, and White

In 1643, Berigard, in the course of a discussion, otherwise well deserving of attention, states the law of Redintegration, as regulating the current of our thoughts;—"quæ *sicut necessario acquiruntur, ita et moventur; frus*traque fingimus [NB.] internam aliquam facultatem quæ incumbat in cogitationem quamdiu vult, mox ad aliam sese transferat, etenim illæ omnes sunt simulacrorum motus, qui se necessario consequuntur," &c. (Circ Pis. P. vi c 19)

"We see," says Sir Kenelm Digby, in 1644, "that things of quite different natures, *if they come in together, are remembered together;* upon which principle the whole art of memory dependeth, &c." (Treatise of Bodies, ch 31, § 3.)

Finally, in 1647, Thomas White (De Albiis or Anglus;)—"*Since those things which enter together and at once must necessarily attain a kind of connection; when, by any means, they are again brought to the fountain of sensation,* [consciousness?] *they must needs meet there together, and in a kind of order.*" (Instit. Peripat. Lib. ii. Lect. 20, § 6. English translation.)

In conclusion of this matter I may briefly notice, in supplement and correction of what has been stated by the German historians:—

1°. That Malebranche, whom Hissman very erroneously considers as the original discoverer of the law of Redintegration, can be shewn to have borrowed it from the illustrious father to whom he is indebted for many other of his opinions. I mean St Austin; a philosopher whose merits, in regard to the doctrine of Association, have been, marvellous to

PART OF COADJACENT.* | "Through this process Reminiscence is

—

say, wholly overlooked. See his Confessions, L. x. cc. 8—19, and especially this last; De Musica, L. vi. c. 8. § 22.

2° That Wolf, whom Maass considers (for the "Nouveaux Essais" of Leibnitz were then unpublished) as "the first who not only clearly promulgated the universal law of Association, but also recognised its importance for Psychology and Morals;" was, certainly, herein anticipated by his contemporary, and brother Leibnitian, the celebrated Bilfinger—whose merits in this respect have, also, remained altogether unnoticed. See of this latter the "Dilucidationes," §§ 254, 255, and "Oratio de Reductione Philosophica," § 2; both some three years prior to the very earliest work of Wolf, enouncing the law in question.

* An important, but altogether neglected question, is,—In what comprehension are these three terms employed by Aristotle?

i. The SIMILAR (τὸ ὅμοιον) affords little difficulty, and may pass without comment. It comprehends, of course, not merely *simple*, but also *analogical*, resemblance.

ii. The CONTRARY (τὸ ἐναντίον) is not an unambiguous expression: for Aristotle sometimes usurps it even for the opposition of possession and privation (ἕξις, στέρησις); sometimes he does not carry it beyond the opposition of genus and genus, of species and species; and sometimes he restricts it to the opposition of incompatible attributes. But I recollect no instance, in which he uses it for *the opposition of relatives proper*. With this exception, we may presume, that Aristotle does not here mean to employ the term in any exclusive rigour; and may, therefore safely apply it in its most extensive meaning. Themistius thrice renders it by τὸ ἀντικείμενον, *the opposite*; but what comprehension he gave to that equally vague term, he does not explain.

iii. The COADJACENT (τὸ σύνεγγυς) is of some difficulty; for I do not now think it probable, that Aristotle by this intended to denote mere *vicinity in space*. It is evident, that it must comprehend all that is not comprehended in the other two; but it is not easy to see how it is to do so much, and yet not comprehend these also.

It is manifest, in general, that Aristotle, under this head, intended to include whatever stands, *as part and part of the same whole*. Of these there are various kinds:—

1°—We must admit that the *integrant parts* of an *integrate whole* suggest each other, as coadjacent. The thought of any thing which we had previously known as such a part, is not usually, when reproduced, viewed as an irrespective object, but tends to call up the other, and, in particular, the proximately adjacent parts, jointly with it constituent of a certain total object. Such parts may be either coadjacent in *space* or coadjacent (coexistent or immediately consecutive) in *time*; and, in both cases, may possess either, a.) an *objective unity* in themselves, (as the parts of a house or poem)—a unity, however, subjectively recognised by us; or b.) *objectively unconnected* and even incongruous in themselves, (as the parts of any common view,) they may obtain a subjective unity for, and from, us, as forming the partial objects of some totalising act of our cognition.—To this head are to be reduced Hume's "*Contiguity in time or place*," and his "*Cause or Effect*," in so far as the latter does not fall under the category of *necessary* suggestion.

2°—We may safely also refer to this head the parts of a *formal* or *comprehensive whole*: the several qualities and the several relations of the same subject, suggesting each other as coadjacent.—For example: The Sagacity of Socrates calls up his Justice, his Fortitude, and so forth; and thinking him as Son, we are prone to think him as Father, Husband, Citizen, &c. Here the attributes and relations are mutually suggestive, in virtue of their proximity, as parts of a system or systems, of which Socrates is the centre and principle of union.

3°—The parts of a *universal* or *extensive whole* may be likewise viewed as suggesting each other, from their coadjacency. For, though the coospecies of a genus are formed by the combined principles of Similarity and Contrast;—yet, once formed, they arrange themselves in scientific thought, as the coordinate parts of a common whole, and can thus mutually suggest each other as coadjacents. Accordingly, Dog may suggest Wolf as its coadjacent. But this, only in one point of view; for, in another, it may do this as its *similar*, and in a third, again, as its *contrary*.

4°—The parts of an *essential whole*,—*matter* and *form*, *subject* and *accident*,—may suggest each other, as coadjacents; although this they may do also as *contraries*.

5°—The different *signs of the same significate*, and the different *significates of the same sign*, are also reciprocally suggestive, as coadjacents; for, in different respects they constitute parts of a certain whole or common system of thought.

6°—To this head, and on the same principle, also belong things, viewed not only as different parts of the same whole, but as *different wholes of the same part*—viewed not only as different effects of the same cause, but as *different causes of the same effect*—viewed not only as different accidents of the same subject, but as *different subjects of the same accident*. These are all reciprocally suggestive, in as much as they are cogitable as parts of the same total thought.

7°—The mutual suggestion of *conjugates*—the *abstract* and *concrete*—is to be referred also to coadjacency.

8°—The *whole* suggests the *parts*, the *parts* suggest the *whole*, as coadjacent;—in truth, they are only the same thought, viewed in different relations.

9°—The *sign* and the *thing signified* are mu-

effected.* For the movements [which, and by which, we recollect,] are, in these cases, sometimes the SAME, sometimes at the SAME TIME, sometimes PARTS OF THE SAME WHOLE;† so that [having, from one or other of these, obtained a commencement,] the subsequent movement is already more than half accomplished."‡

---

tually suggestive, as coadjacent,—if the signification be not in virtue of a natural resemblance. In this case, it may be referred more properly to the head of *similarity*

10mo—Are the *terms of a relation* suggestive of each other, as coadjacent? It is manifest, that all relatives being cogitable, only through each other, and thus constituting only parts of the same thought, fall naturally under the class of coadjacents; and it is also manifest, that there are relatives which cannot, with any propriety, be reduced to either of the other two classes,—the similars or the contraries. Such are what have obtained the name of *relatives proper*. Socrates, for example, suggesting his father Sophroniscus or his wife Xantippe, and Tobias suggesting his Dog, cannot, without violence, be said to do so in virtue either of similarity or of contrast. But if such relatives are to be brought exclusively under the class of coadjacents, the question arises,—Why not simply reduce all relatives, whether of similarity or of contrast, to coadjacents, likewise? Nor is it easy to give a satisfactory answer to this question. For if, on the one hand, we admit all relatives to be coadjacents,—the special law of Coadjacency then absorbs the other two, and rises to a level with the universal law of Redintegration; and on the other, if we do not, there then only remains an arbitrary line of demarcation between the laws of Similarity and Contrast and the law of Coadjacency.

But if, considered in itself, Aristotle's reduction be not above criticism; compared with that of others—with Hume's, for instance, which is at once redundant, defective, and erroneous—it shows almost as perfect.—See Reid, pp. 294, b., 386, ab. I may only notice, that besides a host of the older psychologists, who professed only to follow in his steps; sundry of our more recent philosophers, though incognisant of his higher law, have had the shrewdness to borrow (but not the candour to confess the obligation) Aristotle's three special principles of association. This, for instance, has been done by Dr Gerard, under the names of *Resemblance*, *Contrariety*, and *Vicinity*; and that this distribution, in contrast to Hume's, is alone exhaustive and complete, he has shewn with considerable ingenuity. Nor, in his case, can there be any presumption of originality on the ground of ignorance; for in the same work, but in reference to other matters, he quotes among the other Aristotelic treatises that on Memory.—("Essay on Genius," pp. 109, 267.) Of the later British philosophers, indeed, there is hardly to be found another, who has studied the works of Aristotle more attentively and to better effect.

Themistius, as synonymes for the coadjacent, uses the terms τὰ ἐγγύς, τὰ ἑξῆς, τὰ σύστοιχα.

* Were we to adopt the distribution and combination of this and the preceding sentence, as given by Themistius, for the true reading, the antithesis and relative supremacy of the law of Redintegration would be more emphatically signalized. In the text he quotes, διὰ τοῦτο commences, and γίνεται ἡ ἀνάμνησις concludes a sentence, of which καὶ——σύνεγγυς constitutes the middle.

† If it be held (as may plausibly be done, and as I was originally inclined to do, (p 294, b. n. †) that the first—concomitancy in time—is only one of four co-ordinate laws; this clause suffices, however, to shew, that Aristotle was perfectly aware of the higher principle: for he here states that Concomitant, Similar, Contrary, Coadjacent modifications suggest each other, because, *wholly or partially, they had already coexisted in the mind.*

‡ On the general doctrine in this §, I must here make two observations—one *cautionary*, the other *supplementary*:—

The *first* is, that Aristotle is not to be understood as meaning, that things thought *as* Coexistent, Similar, Contrary, Coadjacent, are *habitually* suggestive of each other; for, in this case, being thought as the terms of a relation, they have, eo ipso, already been thought together, and thus fall under the category of *necessary* consecution; but, that things which *may* stand to each other in such relations, and having, once at least, been thought together as so standing, if afterwards introduced into the mind, as absolute and sole, do, in virtue of custom, tend again to fall back into relation, and consequently to reproduce the objects with which they had been formerly correlative. For example: If we think Socrates *as* son or *as* husband, we cannot but think of a parent or a wife, say Sophroniscus or Xantippe. But while we can think Socrates, without thinking him in any domestic relation, the thought of Socrates is not necessarily suggestive of parent or wife, of Sophroniscus or Xantippe; though, in proportion as we have been used to think the philosopher under the filial or marital relations, will the thought of Socrates tend more habitually to run into one or other of these channels, and thus to suggest the thought of the correlatives. The preceding explication applies to the statements made, on this head, by other philosophers as well as by Aristotle.

The *second* observation is, that thoughts associated and mutually suggestive do not suggest each other with equal certainty and force. The rule is this:—*Of two thoughts, the one is suggested by the other, in proportion*—1°, *to its comparative importance, the thoughts being considered in themselves; and*, 2°, *to its comparative interest (be it from love or loathing) the thoughts being considered in relation to us.* Thus, the Foot suggests the Head more promptly than the Head suggests the Foot; and the

THEMISTIUS

Quotes Aristotle from "When"—to—"WHOLE;" and the following (see n. *, p. 900 b) he reads thus remarkably co-arranged:—"'OTHER [TIME.] *Through this process, and from its* SIMILAR *or* CONTRARY or COADJACENT, *Reminiscence is effected.*'"—He then proceeds:—"For example, I see a *painted lyre*, and moved by this, as the prior and leading image, I have the reminiscence of a *real lyre*; this suggests* the *musician*; and the musician, the *song* I heard him play. Frequently, however, this result is determined '*by some other' thing*. For should it have happened, that, in connection with the original impression of the song, there was impressed the image, say, of a certain *Column*, the view or representation of the column will suggest the recollection of the *Song*.

"From the SIMILAR and the CONTRARY:—[In the former case,] as when from the *portrait of Socrates*, I become reminiscent of *Socrates* himself; [in the latter,] as when the *black* suggests the *white*, the *hot* suggests the *cold*. From the CO-ADJACENT:—As when the one clause—'*Ye would count, I think, no cost, O men of Athens*,' calls up the other:—'*were it shewn, that the measures now before you are, indeed, for the welfare of the state*.' †

"Now, the beginning [according to the proverb,] is the better part of the whole; and this once discovered, what follows thereon is, comparatively, a small matter. Hence, [in the case of reminiscence,] having obtained a principle or originating movement, the other movements follow in a concatenated train.

"We ought not, however, to marvel, should it happen that, though a beginning be found, and the first part of the series set in motion, the movement is not propagated farther. For when an impression is completely vanished, it has, of course, no longer any consecution."

§ 5. Having stated what were the laws of *habitual* consecution, in reference to those reminiscences, accomplished, *intentionally, or through an act of will*; Aristotle proceeds, in the *second* place, to shew, that the same laws equally govern the other class of Reminiscences—those which arise *spontaneously, or without any intentional effort, any conscious volition*. And, in subordination hereto, he eliminates, as superfluous, the question, as to the mode in which, when seeking to recall one thing, others, wholly foreign to our quest, obtrude themselves on our remembrance;—this being manifestly only a particular case of spontaneous suggestion, and one exclusively governed by the the general rules.

It is, in consequence of his very manifest meaning having been here, not merely misunderstood, but actually reversed, by his interpreters, that Aristotle's doctrine did not exert its merited influence; and that he himself has not, as yet, been universally acknowledged, at once, the founder and finisher of the *theory* of Association.—Text illustrated.

ARISTOTLE.

"In this manner [reminiscence is brought to bear] when we [intentionally] seek out a remembrance.‡ But also,

---

sight of Tobias's Dog calls up the image of Tobias in the mind of his mother, with a far greater vehemence, than does the sight of Tobias call up in her mind the image of the Dog. This, I should notice, did not escape the observation of *Vives*:—"Illud non evenit, ut ex re minore veniat nobis de majore in mentem sæpius, non a contrario." (§ 9.)

* Let it not be supposed, that the terms *suggest* and *suggestion* (which in translating from an ancient, I thus venture to employ) are, in their psychological relation, of recent, or even modern, application; for so applied they are old—the oldest we possess.—In this relative signification, *Suggero*, the verb, ascends to Cicero; and *suggestio*, the noun, is a household expression of Tertullian and St Augustine. Among the earlier modern philosophers, and in this precise application, they were, of course, familiar words;—as is shewn, among five hundred others, by the writings of Hermolaus Barbarus, the elder Scaliger, Melanchthon, Simonius, Campanella—to say nothing of the Schoolmen, &c. They were no strangers to Hobbes and Locke;—and so far is Berkeley from having first employed them in this relation, as Mr Stewart seems to suppose, Berkeley only did not discontinue what he found established and in common use.—I may notice, that Association, under the name of *Suggestion*, was styled in the theology of the schools, "The Logic of Lucifer" or "The Devil's Dialectic," (Luciferi Logica, Diaboli Dialectica.) Why?—is manifest.

† Opening of first (or third) Olynthiac.

‡ Ζητοῦσι μὲν οὖν, οὕτω. Themistius, though leading the subsequent expositors astray in the following sentence, is here exclusively correct. They all view ζητοῦσι as the verb, and connect with it οὕτω: he, again, regards the former as the participle, and connects the latter with γίνεται ἡ ἀνάμνησις, understood

when we do not so seek, it is still, in this same manner, that we are [unintentionally] reminiscent,* so often as this particular movement follows upon that particular antecedent. But it is the usual case, [though there are exceptions in the spontaneous as in the intentional reminiscence, from special causes to be immediately noticed,] that the particular movement does ensue, when the relative movements, of the nature we have specified, actually precede.† [The laws stated, are therefore universal, applying both to the voluntary, and to the spontaneous, current of thought.]

" Nor is there any necessity to consider

---

* Καὶ μὴ ζητοῦντες δέ, οὕτως ἀναμιμνήσκονται ;—thus I punctuate. Themistius, and all the other expositors, connecting ζητοῦντες δ' οὕτως, make Aristotle say—" But also when we do not so seek (*i.e.* from the *concomitant*, the *similar*, &c.) still are we reminiscent," there being further understood—" though from none of these causes of suggestion."—But—1°. Looking to the consecution of the immediate words, this interpretation is constrained; for had Aristotle intended so to speak, he would have naturally said, καὶ μὴ οὕτως ζητοῦντες.—2°. It renders the remainder of the clause, " so often," &c., an idle superfluity; and is altogether inconsistent with the whole sequel of the paragraph.—3°. Looking to the general meaning which it affords, such is odious and *strictissimi juris*. For it makes Aristotle, without reason, nay, in opposition to the whole analogy of the context, not only limit, but frustrate his reduction of the phænomena of reminiscence to necessary and universal laws.

In looking again over the commentators, to be assured that my sweeping statement in regard to them is not inaccurate, I find that *Havenreuter* ought perhaps to be excepted—who says,—" Itaque recordamur, si vel alterum ex altero inquirimus, vel si non inquirimus; *attamen alterum post alterum movetur*." But this is ambiguous.

Before him, however, *Vives* seems to have had a clear perception of the truth. He says—" Reminiscentia hæc vel *naturalis* est, cogitatione ultro ab aliis ad alia transeunte; seu *jussa*, quum animus in recordationem rei alicujus conatur pervenire."

It has not been noticed, I think, that *Hobbes* varies in regard to the universality of the law of connected consecution. In his " Human Nature," 1650, he divides the " series, succession, or consequence " of conceptions in the mind, " into *casual* or *incoherent*, and into *orderly* or *coherent*." In the latter case, the antecedent thought is the cause of the consequent; in the former it is not. The casual succession prevails in dreams; the orderly in our waking hours. To this last exclusively, he gives the name of *Discursion*, which he divides and subdivides, in a confused manner. See ch. iv. § 3; ch. v. § 1. In his Leviathan, published in the subsequent year, when treating of the " Consequence or Train of Thoughts, or the Mental Discourse," he says nothing of any casual or incoherent succession, whether awake or sleeping; on the contrary, he asserts that " we have no transition from one imagination to another, whereof we have never had the like before in our senses " This determined sequence he divides into the *unguided* and the *regulated*. So also in the Elementa Philosophiæ, 1655, (c. 25, § 8.) In his earlier doctrine, Hobbes thus harmonises with the erring expositors of Aristotle; in his later, with Aristotle himself. In the Leviathan, he says:—

" This train of thoughts or mental discourse, is of two sorts. The *first* is *unguided*, without design and inconstant; wherein there is no passionate thought, to govern and direct those that follow, to itself, as the end and scope of some desire, or other passion: in which case, the thoughts are said to wander and seem *impertinent* one to another, as in a dream. . . . And yet in this wild ranging of the mind, a man may oft-times perceive the way of it, and the dependence of one thought upon another. For in a discourse of *our present civil war*, what could seem more impertinent, [see Aristotle, § 8,] than to ask, as one did, what was the value of a *Roman penny?* Yet the coherence to me was manifest enough. For the thought of the *war*, introduced the thought of *the delivering up the king to his enemies*; the thought of that, brought in the thought of the *delivering up of Christ*; and that again the thought of the *thirty pence*, which was the price of that treason; and thence easily followed that malicious question, and all this in a moment of time; for *thought is quick*. [See Aristotle, § 8.]

" The *second* is more constant; as being *regulated* by some desire and design, &c."—(Lev P. i. ch. 3.)

† It is to be noted, that Aristotle does not here, as the commentators suppose, admit the non universality of the law of determined consecution, contending for it merely as the ordinary rule. He admits the non universality of the consecution, only of *that individual consequent* (ἥδε ἡ κίνησις) upon *this individual antecedent* (ἑτέρα κίνησις); as, for example, of the thought of Tobias, on the sight or imagination of his Dog, which, though it usually, does not always, take place. As Aristotle afterwards explains, (§ 9.) the same thought, having more than a single association, may at one time suggest one consequent, at another time, another; and howbeit the thoughts, in themselves most strongly associated, will, in general, call up each other, still, in particular circumstances, an association weaker in itself may obtain, for the moment, a higher relative intensity, and consequently prevail over another, absolutely considered, more powerful. But still there is always suggestion,—suggestion according to law.

things remote* [and irrelevant,]—how these rise into memory; but only the matters coadjacent [and pertinent to our inquiry]. For it is manifest that the mode is still the same,—that, to wit, of consecution,†—[in which a thing recurs to us, when] neither pre-intentionally seeking it, nor voluntarily reminiscent. For [*here too*], *by custom, the several movements are concomitant of one another—this determinately following upon that.*‡

THEMISTIUS.

"'*In this manner, when we [intentionally] seek out a remembrance,*' is reminiscence effected from the sources enumerated,—the *similar*, the *opposite*, or the *continuous* (τῶν ἑξῆς). But when a reminiscence takes place without our thus intentionally seeking to remember aught, it is determined by none of these. For if remembering a *song*, we haply become reminiscent of *Socrates*; in this case, the reminiscence is caused neither by the *similar*, nor the *opposite*, nor the *adjacent*, (τῶν ἐγγύς) But this is rare. For in most cases, the reminiscence follows as the sequel of certain antecedent movements.§

"'*Nor is there any necessity*' for those treating of Reminiscence, '*to consider things remote*' [in space?] and old, [in time,] '*how these rise into memory, but only things adjacent*,'‖ and which we have recently observed or learned; for, by reason of their proximity, the latter are more conducive to instruction than the former. The mode of reminiscence, in both, is one and the same. For as, in matters proximate and recent, starting on our search from some internal principle or point of departure, we evolve and are reminiscent of a certain subsequent train of thought; [so also in matters distant in time or space]. '*For*, (as observed,) *by custom the several movements are concomitant of one another—this determinately following upon that.*' But the same takes place, when we call into reminiscence those cognitions which we had long previously acquired."¶

§ 6. Aristotle now returns from the *involuntary* Reminiscence, on which he has only touched incidentally, in consequence of its relation to the *voluntary* Reminiscence,—the professed and special object of this treatise. The transition here has also been mistaken. Here, along with the result, he enounces *two* corollaries of the theory previously established; both having reference to the *perfection* of Reminiscences, as determined by *the relation of the subjective to the objective*.

The *first*,—that Reminiscence is perfect, in proportion as the principle and consecution of the reminiscent thoughts run parallel with the principle and evolution of the existences to be remembered.

The *second*,—that Reminiscence is perfect, in proportion as the objects to be recollected exhibit a definite arrangement.

ARISTOTLE.

"When, therefore, we are desirous to accomplish an act of Reminiscence we

---

* Τὰ πάλαι.—By this the interpreters, after Themistius, all suppose that Aristotle means *old thoughts* in contrast to recent. This error is a corollary of the misprision of Aristotle's general doctrine, in regard to the involuntary train. And yet, the no-meaning which their interpretation, here again, affords, might have rendered them suspicious of its validity; whereas, independently of its own evidence, the light which the interpretation I propose, receives from, and reflects back on, that general doctrine, is a satisfactory confirmation of the truth of both. *Veritas, index sui et falsi.*

† I read πρότερον, πῶς (λέγω δὲ τὸ ἐφεξῆς) τὸ &c.; both as that which affords the best sense, and that towards which the MSS. and editions, taken together, all gravitate. Most of the editions, as those of Moreil, Sylburgius, Simonius, Casaubon, Pacius, Duval, give a second πῶς after δὲ. Bekker (apparently with half his MSS.) omits it altogether. Again, if λέγω be read with Themistius and Michael, half the MSS., the Erasmian and Camotio-Aldine editions, and the versions in general, a tolerable sense is obtained, to this extent: "For it is manifest, that the mode is here the same as that in which a man repeats some rote, without forethought or active reminiscence."

‡ It is to be observed that this latter paragraph, likewise, exhibits a sense incompatible with the interpretation, given by the commentators of Aristotle's doctrine. Themistius it will be seen, in reference to the last sentence, (to say nothing of his other misrepresentations,) exactly reverses Aristotle's application.

§ Themistius, (followed by Michael, Leoneus, and the commentators in a body,) thus *makes Aristotle admit the non-universality of the law of connected consecution.* So Hobbes, in his earlier work:—See note *, p. 902, a.

‖ "*Adjacent*," ἐγγύς; *σύνεγγυς*, *co-adjacent*, is the reading of Michael and of all the MSS. and editions.

¶ Themistius, in these two latter sentences, just inverts Aristotle's statement: applying proximately to the one, what the philosopher applies proximately to the other.

will do this,—endeavour to find that principle or initiatory movement, in the train whereof the one of which we are in quest will turn up.

"The Reminiscences most prompt and perfect are therefore those which are evolved from principles, which are as their objects;* for the same dependency of prior and posterior, that obtains among objects, obtains among the relative mental movements.

"Such things, also, as display an orderly arrangement are well and easily remembered.—Mathematics, for example: while others [confusedly disposed] are imperfectly [retained] and with difficulty [recollected.]"†

§ 7. Distinction of *Reminiscence* and *Relearning*.

ARISTOTLE.

"And Reminiscence is hereby distinguished from learning anew; that, as reminiscent, the mind exerts, in some sort, a power of self-determined motion, in relation to a certain pre-originated train; whereas, when it has not this power, but receives its direction from without, it is no longer said to remember."

§ 8. Question mooted and solved:—Why essaying we do not (though absolutely competent) always accomplish a Reminiscence? One corollary; two incidents. Text restored.

ARISTOTLE.

"It however often happens that the mind attempts, and is foiled in, a Reminiscence. But it has the power of seeking; and seeking it at last finds. This it does when, essaying many various movements, it at length excites the movement of which the matter sought is a sequel. For to recollect‡ is to have potentially § the moving faculty [or inceptive motion] within; and moreover, as already said, to be self-moved, and to movements which itself contains. But [in this casting about] it is necessary always to start from some primary movement—some principle or other.‖ Hence we sometimes become reminiscent from principles,

---

* The term ἀρχή, *principle*, has here an emphatic and special meaning. All reminiscence, according to Aristotle, proceeds from a beginning or principle of movement, that is, from a certain mode of mind, which originates the evolution of a certain subsequent series of dependent modes; the dependence however, being, perhaps, only determined by some personal or subjective association. But here, Aristotle, as the following sentence manifests, intends not a merely subjective principle, but a principle, which, though subjective, has an objective correlation and validity. But he could hardly employ the word in this restricted meaning, without, at least, some premonition. Perhaps the word πραγμάτων originally stood after ἀρχῆς; or rather ἀναμνήσεως was followed by the words ὡς τὰ πράγματα—words, which, from their proximate repetition, were very likely to be omitted in transcription.

† Aquinas (Lectio v. ad locum)—"Sic ergo ad bene memorandum vel reminiscendum, ex præmissis, *quatuor* documenta utilia addiscere possumus. Quorum *primum* est, ut studeat quæ vult retinere in aliquem ordinem deducere: *secundo*, ut profunde et intente eis mentem apponat: *tertio*, ut frequenter meditetur secundum ordinem: *quarto*, ut incipiat reminisci à principio."

‡ Μιμνῆσθαι.—Themistius and Michael seem to have read *ἀναμιμνήσκεσθαι*, in the sense of which, at least, the other must here be taken.

§ Δυνάμει;—Thus Bekker after half his MSS. The common reading is *δύναμιν*, which Themistius and Michael exhibit, but explain in conformity to the other.

‖ "Necesse est (says Javellus) reminiscentem incipere ab aliquo principio, quod memoria tenetur, et ab illo procedere ad aliquod memorandum, et ab illo ad aliud, donec deveniamus ad principale quod desideramus ad memoriam reduci. Quod quidem principium aliquando est *res* memoria retenta, aliquando *tempus*, aliquando *locus*. . . . Exemplum *temporis*:—Volo reminisci, *quo die*, constitutus in itinere, *fui Bononiæ*, et incipio sic;—heri fui Parmæ, nudiustertius Mutinæ, et illo per diem quievi, deinde itineratus sum, et non pernoctavi extra Bononiam, ergo, *quarta die jam elapsa*, fui Bononiæ. Exemplum *loci*:—Volo reminisci, constitutus in itinere, *quo loco perdidi pecuniam*, et incipio sic;—in tali loco habebam pecuniam, quoniam solvi cœnam in hospitio, et in tali habebam, quoniam solvi equitaturam, et in tali habebam quoniam emi panes, in tali autem loco non habebam, quoniam non potui solvere in hospitio; ergo, in tanta distantia cecidit bursa, et tunc, facta reminiscentia, incipio quærere deperditam pecuniam." (Epit. Parv. Nat. tr. ii. c 3.)

From this Hobbes seems to have taken the hint in the following passages; which, at any rate afford a good amplification of Aristotle's meaning.

"There is yet another kind of Discursion beginning with the appetite to recover something lost, proceeding from the Present backward, from the thought of the Place where we miss at, to the thought of the place from whence we came last; and from the thought of that, to the thought of a place before, till we have in our mind some place, wherein we had the thing we miss: and this is called *Reminiscence*." (Hum. Nat. ch. 4.)

"Sometimes a man seeks what he hath lost

which [in relation to the result] appear impertinent and absurd.* The reason of this is the rapidity with which the mind passes from thought to thought; as from *milk* to *white*, from white to the [*clear*] *atmosphere*, from that to *wet weather*, which finally suggests *autumn*;—this season being what we are supposed seeking to remember, [but which, at first sight, would seem to have no conceivable connection with the principle from which it has been evolved.]

"But it would seem in general, that the exordial movement or principle, is also the central movement of a series. For if not before, we shall, on this being suggested, either find in itself the object to be recollected, or obtain from it exclusively the media of recollection. For example, let the letters

A, B, C, D, E, F, G, H,

represent a series of thoughts. If, then, [on the suggestion of] D E, we do not find what we would remember, we shall find it on [traversing] E - - - - H; for from the centre, we may be moved either backwards by D, or forwards by E. But, if we are seeking none of those [in the forward series, in the backward,] coming on C, [C being suggested as a centre?] we shall accomplish our recollection in it; or, if seeking B or D, [through it,] in them. But if none of these be what we seek, this we shall find at all events on [reaching] A. And thus is it always."†

THEMISTIUS.

. . . "'*To be reminiscent is to have the moving faculty within.*' By faculty, I understand the inexistent principle; for this excites the discursive faculty to an analysis [read resumption ‡] of the rest. . . . . "Therefore '*it is necessary always to start from some primary movement—some principle or other;*' on which account, we appear most rapidly '*sometimes to be reminiscent from places.*' § '*Places;*'—meaning either [1°] the principles or primary movements which, we said, behoved to be inexistent in the soul; ‖ or [2°] such heads, as Conjugates, Similars, Opposites, treated of in Dialectic [and Rhetoric]; or [3°] external localities, and the positions therein. ¶

and from that Place and Time, wherein he misses it, his mind runs back, from place to place, and time to time, to find where, and when he had it; that is to say, to find some limited time and place, in which to begin a method of seeking. Again, from thence his thoughts run over the same places and times to find what action, or other occasion might make him lose it. This we call *Remembrance*, or *calling to mind*; the Latins call it *Reminiscentia*, as it were a *Re-conning* of our former actions. Sometimes a man knows a Place determinate, within the compass whereof he is to seek; and then his thoughts run over all the parts thereof, in the same manner as one would sweep a room to find a jewel; or as a spaniel ranges the field till he find a scent; or as a man should run over the alphabet to start a rhyme." (Lev. P. I ch. 3.)

An excellent illustration of Aristotle's doctrine, in another view, is to be found in Plautus, Trinummus, Act IV. scene II., v. 65—78.

* The reading, hitherto received, is ἀπὸ τόπων, "*from places;*" and the commentators have been more anxious to enumerate all the meanings which this expression could possibly bear, than to show how any one of these could possibly be tolerated in the present passage. In this relation all are indeed absurd; and the expositors needed only to pronounce Aristotle's righteous judgment on their attempts—ἄτοπα!—and they had recovered Aristotle's veritable words (ἀπ' ἀτόπων.) This emendation, I make no scruple of proposing, as absolutely certain. For, by the mere change of an τ into an α—and be it remembered, that words were anciently written continuously—the whole passage, previously unintelligible and disjointed, becomes pregnant with sense, every part of it supporting and illustrating every other. No better elucidation of the truth and necessity of this correction can be given, than the passage, (in n *, p. 902, b.) from Hobbes, who in this whole doctrine is an *alter ego* of Aristotle.

† In the preceding paragraph, Aristotle's meaning in general,—in so far at least as it can interest us at present, is sufficiently apparent. But it is probable that something has been lost in the details of his illustration. In the readings also, more especially of the symbols, the Greek expositors, the manuscripts and the editions, are all at variance. The text I have chosen affords, I think, as good a meaning as can be purchased at as cheap a rate; but to assign the reasons of preference—non tanti. Those curious to see in how many phases the notion of Aristotle can be viewed, may consult the various hypotheses of Themistius, Faber, Amerbach, Crippa, Simonius, Havenreuter, &c.

‡ In Themistius, we now have ἀνάλυσιν; and that this is an old reading, is shown by Michael, who gives it also. Can there be a doubt that ἀνάληψιν is the true lection?

§ Themistius not only mistakes the purport but reverses the order of Aristotle's thought.

‖ Νοῦς, *Intellect*, is called in the Aristotelic philosophy the *Place of Principles*. Aristotle, however, never styles principles, intellections, native or a priori cognitions, &c., by the name of *places*.

¶ To these *three* alternative possibilities

"'*But it would seem, in general, that the exordial movement, or principle, is also the central movement of a series;*' and the discovery of this is of capital importance, leading us, as it does, to the apprehension of what we seek. To illustrate this process, let us typify it by letters, correspoding in number, and proportional to the thoughts set in movement towards the retrievement of a lurking remembrance.

A, B, C, D, E, F, G, H.

Now as E is here the central thought, (?) If, in finding it, we do not recover what we seek, we shall certainly do so when we arrive at H. For, the centre once gained, we may, from thence, move either backwards or forwards in the series. Nor is there any thing to prevent a suggestion of the thoughts *per saltum*, or in any *perverse order*;—to think, for instance, H immediately after E, and, after H, to think, first F, and then G.—If, then, the thought we seek lie in the progressive series, we shall consequently, as already said, find it [at furthest] on reaching H. If, on the contrary, it lie in the regressive series, it will be found [certainly] on attaining A. The thoughts denoted by the symbols, we shall say, are—

Athens [A]—*the Lycian Suburb** [B]—*the House of Plato* [C]—*the time of New Moon* [D]—*the Banquet* [E]—*Socrates* [F]—*the being struck* by Socrates [G]—*the Lyre* [H]."

MICHAEL EPHESIUS

Thus continues:—"Nothing prevents us, on recollecting the *Banquet*, to recollect, first, the *Lyre* and then the *being struck*, consequently, that it was by *Socrates*; although, in the order supposed, the recollection of *Socrates* follows immediately on that of the *Banquet*, then the *being struck*, and, last of all, the *Lyre*. For we may suppose, that the person was struck with the lyre and not with a stick. In saying, that '*the exordial seems also the central movement*,' he assigns the reason,—'*because from the centre we may be moved either forwards or backwards*;' for E is the road to the series subsequent —F, G, H, and to the series preceding—D, C, B, A. And it is competent for us, at will, as from H, to call up either G or F, so, from A, to call up any one of the series consequent upon it. If E, however, be not the centre, but C; in the suggestion of C we shall terminate our reminiscence; or, if C be not our end, we shall find it in A, in like manner, as E, not contenting us itself, did so by helping us on to H."

§ 9. Question mooted and solved:—Why the same principle does not always effectuate the same result?—Collateral observations.—Text restored.

ARISTOTLE.

"The reason why, though departing from the same principle or inceptive movement, the same thing is sometimes recalled to mind, and sometimes not, is to be found in the circumstance, that the same principle, [having more than a single connection,] can determine a resuscitating movement upon one or other of a *plurality*.† If for example, [F and D be both dependent upon C,] from C the resusci-

---

Simonides, followed by Pacius, adds, and prefers a *fourth*; the places, to wit, so called, employed in the Art of Memory—Mnemonic.

* *Λύκειον*. If we suppose this an error for *Λυκεῖον*, Lyceum, Themistius is guilty of an anachronism, (see Plutarch, Op. Mor. Xyl. p. 790;) and, at any rate, the *Lyceum* was not the place where *Plato's house* either would or could be. I therefore suppose, that by this is meant the extra mural quarter designated from the temple of Apollo Lycius. (See Pausanias.) And does this give us the true locality of Plato's residence?

† The fact,—that the same one thought may, and commonly has, many connections, and consequently may suggest, and be suggested by, many different movements, (N ‡, p. 900, b;) shows that the old and familiar simile of a Chain is inadequate to the phænomenon. (See N. *, p. 894, a.) For it implies—1° Coexistence, to the exclusion of succession in consciousness; 2° equal and reciprocal suggestion. But these vices are common; the chain has others peculiar to itself. For, 3° It would lead us to suppose, that the mind could run only backwards and forwards, on one simple series; each consequent thought having, like the link of a simple chain, only a single determinate connection, before and after; whereas, the concatenations with every ring of the mental series, are indefinitely numerous. In this respect, instead of a mere chain, the simile of a hauberk, or *chain web*, would be better; and better still, *a sphere of chainwork*. But one defect there is in all of these similitudes:—any ring being moved, moves, and that *equally*, *all* the rings attached to it; which is not the case in the momenta of the mental dependency.

Association of Ideas is an expression the introduction of which is universally attributed to Locke; but erroneously. For some twenty years previous to the publication of the Essay, another philosophical physician, M. La

tating movement may tend, either upon F or upon D. Should the movement, then, not be through *a natural necessity*,* [in which case, as there is no alternative,

---

Chambre, in his "Systeme de l'Ame," (L. iv. c. 2, art. 9,) speaks of "the *Union* and *Connection of Images* (*l'Union* et la *Liaison des Images*,) as an integrant action in our knowledge by Imagination and Understanding,' &c. With the writings of this author, which were, in that age, not undeservedly, popular, Locke could hardly fail to be acquainted; though we cannot presume that he was aware of "the *mutually consecutive movements*" of Aristotle. But of these three terms, the first and second are, in both their parts, objectionable.

Like the Chain—*Association, Union, Connection*—is faulty.—1°. It implies coexistence; a connection between coexistences actually known.—2°. It implies a bilateral—an equal correlation. If B is associated with A, A is no less associated with B. But in the mental train, it is rare that any two thoughts call each other up with equal force; and this inequality may vary, from perfect equilibrium, to a maximum in the one co suggestive, and a minimum in the other. Thus A suggests B, far more strongly than B suggests A; thus the Dog suggests Tobit, far more strongly than Tobit suggests the Dog. (See n. †, p. 900, b. a.) For the same reasons the simile of *Attraction*, by Themistius (§ 9,) and Hume (n *, p. 894, a.) is at fault. Major's homely illustration (ibid.,) by a *cobbler's bristle and thread*, is better, as more unilateral; whereas, that of Hobbes (ibid.,) by *the following of water through the guidance of the finger*, is, on all accounts, as bad as can be. In the third, on the contrary, *Mutual Consequence*, (ἀκολουθία ἀλλήλαις,) states the phænomenon more accurately than any of the others,—though not yet accurately enough.

The expressions, Association, Union, Connection, of *Ideas* or *Images*, are (as already noticed of Hobbes' language, p. 893, b. note, and p. 898, b. note,) objectionable, inasmuch as these terms are apt (even though not intended by their authors) to limit the dependency to modes of Cognition, to the exclusion of those of Appetency and of Feeling. It has, indeed, been held, even by some recent and acute philosophers, that the secondary or suggested movement is always a cognition—an idea. That a representative cognition is here necessary, is indubitable. But that suggestion is *only* of cognitions, must be denied; for how, under this limitation, can the numerous phænomena be saved, like what Van Swieten commemorates of himself? He never passed, he says, a place, where he had once seen and smelt the putrid carcase of a dog, without a recurrence of sickness. See also Vives in note p. 893, b. On the other hand, Aristotle's word *Movement*, (n. *, p. 892, b.) as comprehending cognitions, feelings, and appetencies, is praiseworthy.

The term *Subnotion*, (*Subnotio*,) as expressive of the present phænomenon, is good; but would require (what cannot here be given) explanation, along with a statement of the remark able but neglected doctrine of the ingenious philosopher, and more illustrious poet, by whom it was propounded.

The words of Aristotle, and the Greek Aristotelians—*Movement, Train, Series, Chain, Concatenation, Mutual Consecution, Subsequence, Dependence, Determined Sequence, Resumption, Subsumption, Seeking, Hunting, Discursion, Principle, Precursive Series, Beginning, Inceptive, Prior, Leading Movements*, &c., and their correlatives—words which mediately, but generally have been adopted by modern philosophers, are the oldest, and in so far as they denote nothing but the simple fact, are, to say the least of them, not exposed to objection. (N. *, p. 897.)

Upon the whole, as among the earliest, so I think, perhaps the *best* terms for the process of reproduction are to be found in *Suggest, Suggestion, Suggestive, Co-suggestive*, with their conjugates. These were terms, in this relation familiar to the Fathers and the Schoolmen,—to say nothing of modern psychologists. The metaphor implied is not inappropriate; but, in English at least, the tropical have long subsided into proper terms. (N. *, p. 901, a.)

The other scholastic, and almost equivalent, expressions (which Locke and others also employ,)—*Excite, Excitation*, &c., are likewise laudable. (P. 889, a.)

* μὴ διὰ παλαιοῦ. Thus, all the manuscripts, editions, translators, commentators;—with the exception of Themistius and two MSS. which with him omit the negative—and (strange to say!) without either injuring or improving the sense.—In regard to the import of παλαιοῦ, opinions are also divided. Some, as Themistius and Michael, explain it by "*old and worn out*"—*effete*. Leonicus, the echo of the Greek expositors, seems, in copying the latter of these, to have read νόσους συνήθεις, instead of νόσους ἀσυνήθεις, or to have so found it in his MS.; for, be it observed, neither Greek commentary was then printed. Leonicus, accordingly, interprets it "*old and worn in*"—*inveterate*; in which he is followed by Simonius, Crippa, and others. Nor is this latter exposition, though founded on a blunder, a whit inferior to the former; the two opposites, here again, affording each just the same minimum of sense—maximum of non-sense. The expositors and translators, indeed, seem, in general sensible of this; and prudently pass by the difficulty altogether. It is, however, easily solved. Μὴ διὰ παλαιοῦ is manifestly a false reading; and I think it equally manifest, that the true is found in μὴ δι' ἀσυνήθους. This, exactly, and exclusively, supplies the meaning which the context impetrates—and for which the previous discussion had prepared us, (§ 2;) while it is obtained at the expense of only an interchange of two and three easily commutable letters. This conjectural lection I have accordingly adopted in the translation, as indubitable.

there is no question,] it will be turned, among different objects, on that which has to it the strongest habitual affinity. For Habit obtains in a certain sort the force of Nature. Hence, those things on which we frequently think, we easily remember. For, as in nature, this consequent follows [pronely] that antecedent, so also in the operations or energy of mind.* But an iteration of the same, at length generates a nature. As some things, however, occur, even in the works of nature [proper,] beside [the course of] nature, from the intervention of accidental causes, [as in the case of monsters]; this will happen still more frequently in the formations of habit, in which [the acquired] nature is not of a determination equally intense. Thus it is, that the mind may be sometimes moved at once in one direction and another; and this especially when something † [like] shall turn it aside from the course on which it was proceeding. This, [for instance,] is the reason why, when we have occasion to call up a name, we are apt to call up another somewhat similar, and so blunder in a sort,‡ with regard to that of which we are in quest."

THEMISTIUS.

"If, for example, from *pleura*, [the side, strictly, the membrane lining the chest,] we be moved towards, both *pleuritis* [inflammation of that membrane—pleurisy,] and *Pleuronia*, [Pleuron, Pleurone, the town];—should, then, *pleuritis* be more familiar than *Pleuronia*, it will attract ¶ towards itself the mind, in the same manner as the more brilliant colours draw upon themselves the sight. [§ 2. Themistius.]

"But in the case, that one of the impressions is *old*, the other *new*: the new will prevail in moving its own reminiscence, by preference; unless the old has been deeply inscribed on the mind, as part of a scientific acquirement, and be, likewise, the more familiar. For thus, it is, as it were, renovated, every time we have occasion to turn our attention on it.

"But, '*as in Nature, this consequent follows that antecedent*;' (for, in the natural reminiscence, the thought of *heat* follows, necessarily, that of *fire*, and the thought of *light*, that of the *sun*; ‖) '*so also in Habit*.'** For, through the force of Habit, there are things, which, on their own reminiscence, forthwith cause the concomitant reminiscence of certain others. But what we are frequently accustomed to, becomes, as it were, a [second] nature. And as, among the products of nature itself, aberrations may occur from the rule of nature; this also is possible in the operations of habit. It may, therefore, easily happen, that starting correctly from the prior and suggestive thought, we shall fall out, in consequence of a deflective movement, in passing to the subsequent and suggested; as when, [departing from *pleura*,] *pleuritis* attracts the movement

---

* For ἐνεργείᾳ, Themistius seems to read ἔθει.—But on the common reading, does Energy mean *act of mind*? or, (as the interpreters in general suppose,) *act of habit*? If the latter be preferred, the meaning will be this:—"For as in [the works of] nature this consequent follows [pronely and invariably] upon that antecedent, so in the operations of habit." I decidedly prefer the former: both as the one meaning which the context requires; and because, while Aristotle could hardly by ἐνέργεια simply mean to denote *habit*, (which is a *power*, as opposed to energy,) it was the natural expression whereby to denote an *act* of mind—a cognition, thought, &c.

† For τι, which is otiose, I would read τι, that is, "something [similar.]" which, at any rate, must be understood.

‡ "Quoniam Similitudo" (says Vives.) "ex multis velut unum reddit, facilis est et usitatus, non memoriæ solum, sed cogitationis quoque *error*, *ut a simili transeat ad simile*. Pro *Gregorio*, sumimus *Georgium*, pro *enthymemate*, *prolemma*, *Pindarus* pro *Pandaro*; Quæ similitudo est in vocis, ex medio, principio, fine: Tum in exacte, ex eo quod in illis attentio consideraret: ut *Xenocratem*, pro *Aristotele*, in philosophia et discipulus Platonis; *Scipionem* pro *Q. Fabio* in bellis Punicis; *Irum* pro *Codro*, in paupertate; *Demosthenem* pro *Cicerone*, in eloquentia; *Narcissum* pro *Adonide* in pulchritudine; *allium* pro *cepis*, in odore. Eodem modo, de loco, tempore, de actionibus aut qualitatibus, quorum exempla patent latissime.—Hoc vitium vel in *prima attentione* nascitur, quod intelligentia non satis animadvertit quæ offeruntur, ut integra ea distinctaque posset memoriæ commendare; vel in ipsa *memoria*, quæ parum sincera fide custodiit; vel in *secunda attentione*, quum perperam ea quæ integra erant in memoria reposita depromit. Perturbatur item *consideratio* vel *secunda attentio*, quum jussa aliquid quærere, aut depromere objicitur extrinsecus, diversum quid vel alienum. Salutavit me heri in foro *Petrus Toletanus*, nec satis animadverti, nec satis memini. Si quis ex me quærat,—*Quis te in foro heri salutarit?* si nihil addat facilius respondere quam si dicat—*Joannes Manricusne an Ludovicus Abylensis?*" (L. I.)

¶ See Hume; (n.*, p 894, a.)

‖ See n. §, p 894. ** See n. *, p. 906.

from *Pleuronia* to itself. '*For this reason, when we have occasion to call up a name, we are apt to call up another somewhat similar, and so blunder in a sort, with regard to that of which we are in quest.*' Wishing, for example, to recollect *Leophanes*, we recollect *Leosthenes*, and [substituting this,] thus blunder in relation to *Leophanes*."

§ 10. After other observations, which it is not necessary to adduce, Aristotle goes on to show, that Reminiscence—reminiscence *intentional* or *proper*,—is to a certain extent, a *rational*—*discursive* procedure.

ARISTOTLE.

. . . . "That, in the same individual, the power of Memory and the power of Reminiscence stand in no mutual proportion, has been already stated.—And, independently of the difference of their manifestation, in the order of time;* Reminiscence is distinguished from Memory in this,—that of memory, many of the other animals are participant, whereas, it may be safely affirmed, that, of the animals known to us, man alone is endowed with Reminiscence.† The reason is, that Reminiscence is, as it were, a kind of syllogism or mental discourse. For he who is reminiscent, that he has formerly seen or heard or otherwise perceived, any thing, virtually performs an act of syllogism. Here also there is instituted, as it were, a question and inquiry. But inquiry is competent, only as deliberation is competent; while deliberation, in like manner, is a sort of syllogism."

THEMISTIUS.

. . . . "'*Of the animals known to us, man alone is endowed with Reminiscence;*' because to whom reminiscence is competent, to the same syllogism is competent. For as, in the act of syllogising, this [minor] proposition is connected with that [major]; so in the act of reminiscence we connect lesser [movements] with greater. But the power of syllogising implies the power of inquiry, [for we only syllogise as we inquire]; and the power of inquiry implies the power of deliberation, [for we only inquire as we deliberate.] [The power of reminiscence, therefore,

* Reminiscence, chronologically considered is both *prior* and *posterior* to Memory (in Aristotle's meaning of this term.) For reminiscence starts from a Memory, which affords it a principle or point of departure; and it results in a Memory, as its end this being a memory of the matter sought.

† This Aristotle also states in his History of Animals, (Book I ch 2.) The expositors do not, I think, fully or correctly apprehend Aristotle's view. Themistius, for example, supposes that Reminiscence is a rational procedure, because, like syllogism, it connects a lesser with a greater. But Memory, or simple recollection, equally connects a lesser with a greater; and this Aristotle accords to the brutes, whilst he denies them intentional reminiscence. At any rate, this subordination is, in reminiscence, one merely accidental; for the same two thoughts, in alternately suggesting each other, are alternately to each other as the greater and the less. Aristotle I presume, refers to the analogy subsisting between the acts of Reminiscence and Reasoning, in both being processes to a certain end; both being processes from the known to the unknown;—and in both evolving their conclusion, under certain laws, and from certain general sources;—Reminiscence, contingently educing the thing to be recollected, in conformity to the laws, and out of the common places, of Mnemonic, as universal principles or inceptive movements, by a process of investigation, and subjective suggestion of the connected by the connected;—Reasoning, necessarily educing the thing to be proved, in conformity to the laws, and out of the common places of *Logic*, as universal principles or major propositions, by a process of investigation, and objective subsumption of the contained under the containing

Aristotle, though he assimilates, does not identify rational or logical subsumption, with voluntary, far less with spontaneous, suggestion. At most he only shews that reminiscence, *qua intentional*, as it involves an application of means to end, involves deliberation, which again involves discursion.

This discursion of Reminiscence the Latin commentators, in general, refer, not to the inorganic Intellect, not to *Λόγος*, *Διάνοια*, or *Ratio* proper, but to that *Analogon Rationis* or *Particular Reason*, possessed, in some measure, by the brutes; and which among other Arabian Aristotelians, Averroes introduced as one of the internal senses, under the name of *Cogitativa* "Ex quibus patet, (says Javellus,) quod in reminiscendo, syllogizamus et discurrimus, non quidem per propositiones universales, id enim est proprium intellectus, sed per singulares Discurrimus enim ab uno singulari memorato ad aliud memorando; et ideo fit a cogitativa quæ dicitur ratio particularis apud commentatorem."—Now, if we *discard the higher faculty of thought*, and *admit, exclusively, the lower*, we have at once the scheme of *Hobbes*. It should be also noticed, that while Aristotle and his followers limit, and properly, the expression "*mental discourse*" to the *intentional* process of reminiscence, Hobbes, borrowing the term, unwarrantably extends it to the *spontaneous* train of thought

implies the power of deliberation]. But man alone deliberates; man, therefore, alone, is reminiscent. That Reminiscence, consequently, is a function of the discursive intellect, (διανοίας,) is demonstrated; for deliberation is an act of intellect, (νοῦ); [and Themistius had previously stated, that] *discursion is only the energy of intellect and imagination combined*—οὐδὲν ἕτερον ἐστιν ἢ διάνοια ἢ νοῦ μετὰ φαντασίας ἐνέργεια."

NOTE D.***

OUTLINE OF A THEORY OF MENTAL REPRODUCTION, SUGGESTION, OR ASSOCIATION.

---

§ I.—*Laws of Mental Succession, as General.—(A.) Not of Reproduction proper, uniform.—(B.) Of Reproduction proper, not uniform: as possible; as actual; as direct,—Abstract or Primary law of Repetition; as indirect,—Abstract or Primary law of Redintegration, Concrete or Secondary law of Preference.*

§ II.—*Laws of Mental Succession, as Special.—Of Reproduction:—(A.) Abstract or Primary,—modes of the laws of Repetition and Redintegration, one or both;—(B.) Concrete or Secondary,—modes of the law of Preference.*

[References omitted, and to be supplied from pp. 294, 386, &c.]

---

§ I.—*General Laws of Mental Succession.*

A—As not of Reproduction proper.

Human Consciousness being realised, (see Note H,) only under the two conditions of *contrast* and *continuity in time*, is necessarily astricted to a *ceaseless variation of state*; and its variations (called likewise more or less adequately *mental modifications, modes, states, movements, thoughts, activities, passivities, &c.,*) are thus successive, and uninterruptedly successive. The two highest laws of thought are, therefore,

i.—The Law of Succession:—*That we are only conscious, as conscious of succession*; and

ii.—The Law of Variation:—*That we are only conscious of succession, as conscious of successive variation.*

But these successive variations do not follow on each other in a row, as isolated phænomena, related only as before and after on the thread of time; nor is their manifestation determined always by causes, external to the series itself, although this be frequently the case. On the contrary, the train, though ever changing, is ever continuous; each antecedent movement running into each consequent; and, abstracting from the intervention of foreign influences, each antecedent standing to each consequent as its cause. Thought is thus evolved, not only in a chronological, but in a causal sequence; and another of its Laws is, therefore,

III.—The Law of DEPENDENCE or DETERMINED CONSECUTION:—*That every consequent modification in the mental train is the effect of that immediately antecedent.*

IV.—*Thoughts are dependent on each other, only as they stand together as the relative parts of the same common whole.* This may be called the Law of RELATIVITY or INTEGRATION.

But this whole is of *two* kinds. It is either an *objective* (necessary and essential) unity, constituted by, and intrinsic to, the thoughts themselves; or it is a *subjective* (contingent and accidental) unity, extrinsic to themselves, and imposed on them by the mind—the mind in general. In the former case, a certain thought being given, it necessarily, of, and along with itself, evolves a certain one, exclusive, other; in the latter, a certain thought being given, it only moves the mind, according to definite subjective laws, to pass on to this or that of a certain plurality of others. In the one instance, there is a determination to an individual consequent; in the other, only a determination to a class of consequents, the preference of this or that class, of this or that individual under it, being regulated by circumstances, external to the nature of the antecedent thought itself. The former constitutes what may be called the *logical* or *objective*; the latter, what may be called the *psychological* or *subjective* train of thought.

The *logical* consecution is shewn in those thoughts, which, though denoted by a single and separate expression, implicitly contain a second; which second, the process of thinking explicates but does not determine to succeed. Such are all relatives. The conception of the one term of a relation necessarily implies that of the other; it being of the very nature of a relative, to be thinkable, only through the conjunct thought of its correlative. For a relation is, in truth, a thought, one and indivisible; and while the thinking a relation, necessarily involves the thought of its two terms, so is it, with equal necessity, itself involved in the thought of either. It is therefore improper to say, that the thought of one relative *follows*, or is *consequent on*, the thought of the other,—if thereby be denoted a succession in time; since the thought of both is, in truth, already given in the thought of each. Aristotle expressly says of relatives, that they are things which exist *together* (ἅμα) in the mind. It is consequently also improper to say of such terms, that they are *associated* or mutually *suggestive*. Not the former, for this supposes that they can be dissociated; not the latter, for this supposes them not to be given as necessary reciprocals. Such are whole and parts, means and end, cause and effect, reason and consequent, substance and accident, like and unlike, great and small, parent and child, husband and wife, &c. &c.

To this head, I may simply notice, though I cannot now explain, are to be referred those compulsory relatives, imposed upon thought by that great, but as yet undeveloped, law of our intellectual being, which I have elsewhere denominated the Law of the CONDITIONED:—*That all positive thought lies between two extremes, neither of which we can conceive as possible, and yet, as mutual contradictories, the one or the other we must recognise as necessary.* From this impotence of intellect, we are unable to think aught as absolute. Even absolute relativity is unthinkable. But to this I merely allude, that I may shew to what head such compulsory connections are to be referred. See, however, p. 743, n. *, p. 800n. *. Logical consecution is thus governed by:—

V.—The Law of INTRINSIC or OBJECTIVE RELATIVITY:—*That one relative term being thought, there is virtually thought also its correlative.*

General Laws of Mental Succession.

B—As of Reproduction proper.

The other kind of dependence, the *psychological* consecution, is that which subsists between two thoughts, the one of which preceding, entails the sequence of the other, not necessarily, or in virtue of its own intrinsic relativity, but of a certain extrinsic relativity, of a contingent imposition and indefinite obtrusive force which inclines them, though perhaps unequally, to call each other into consciousness, and which, when not counteracted by a stronger influence, inevitably operates its end. The terms (chronological) *suggestion*, *association*, *succession*, are properly applied to this dependence alone;—for under it, exclusively, have the thoughts a before and after, in the order of time, or in themselves any separate and irrespective existence. Psychological consecution is equivalent to *Reproduction*. [I may parenthetically observe, that the power of reproduction (into consciousness,) supposes a power of retention (out of consciousness) To this conservative power I confine exclusively the term Memory; with this, however, we have at present nothing to do.]

There are *three subjective unities, wholes* or *identities*, each of which affords a ground of chronological succession, and reciprocal suggestion, to the several thoughts which they comprehend in one. In other words, Reproduction has *three sources*.

These are:—1° the unity of thoughts, differing in *time* and *modification*, in a co-identity of SUBJECT;—2° the unity of thoughts, differing in time, in a co-identity of MODIFICATION;—3° the unity of thoughts, differing in *modification*, in a co-identity of TIME.

Of these, the *first* affords a common principle of the possibility of association, or mutual suggestion for all our mental movements, however different in their character as modifications, however remote in the times of their occurrence; for all, even the most heterogeneous and most distant, are reproducible, co-*suggestible*, or *associable*, as, and only as, phænomena of the same unity of consciousness—affections of the same indivisible Ego. There thus further emerges:—

vi.—The Law of ASSOCIABILITY or POSSIBLE CO-SUGGESTION:—*All thoughts of the same mental subject are associable, or capable of suggesting each other.*

But the unity of subject, the fundamental condition of the associability of thought in general, affords no reason why this particular thought should, *de facto*, recall or suggest that. We require, therefore, besides a law of possible, a law or laws of *actual reproduction*. Two such are afforded in the *two* other unities—those of *Modification* and of *Time*.

And now let us, for the sake of subsequent reference, pause a moment to state the following symbolic illustration:—

A B C
A'
A"

Here the same letter, repeated in perpendicular order, is intended to denote the same mental mode, brought into consciousness, represented, at different times.

Here the different letters, in horizontal order, are supposed to designate the partial thoughts integrant of a total mental state, and therefore co-existent, or *immediately* consequent, at the moment of its actual realization.

This being understood, we proceed:—

Of these two unities that of *modification* affords the ground, why, for example, an object determining a mental modification of a certain complement and character, to-day, this presentation tends to call up the representation of the same modification determined by that object, yesterday. Or suppose, as in our symbols, the three As to typify the same thought, determined at three different times, be the determining movement of a presentation or a representation. On the second occasion, A' will suggest the representation of A. This, it will not be denied, that it can do; for, on the possibility hereof, depends the possibility of *simple remembrance*. The total thought, after this suggestion, will be A' + A; and on the third occasion, A" may suggest A' and A; both on this principle, and on that other which we are immediately to consider, of co-identity in time. We have thus, as a first general law of actual Reproduction, Suggestion, or Association:—

vii.—The Law of REPETITION, or of DIRECT REMEMBRANCE:—*Thoughts coidentical in modification, but differing in time, tend to suggest each other.*

The law which I here call that of Repetition, seems to be the principle of remembrance referred to by Aristotle, in saying, that "the movements [which and by which, we recollect] are, in these cases, sometimes THE SAME," &c. (See above, p. 900 a.) If this be correct, Aristotle has here again made a step a-head of subsequent philosophers; for, if I be not mistaken, we must recur to Repetition as an ultimate principle of reproduction, and not rest satisfied, as has been done, with that of Redintegration alone. But of this anon.

The unity of *time* affords the ground, why thoughts, different in their character as mental modes, but having once been proximately coexistent, (including under coexistence immediate consecution,) as the parts of some total thought, and a totality of thought is determined even by a unity of time; do, when recalled into consciousness, tend immediately to suggest each other, as co-constituents of that former whole, and mediately, that whole itself. Thus, let (A, B, C, D, E, F,) be supposed a complement of such concomitant thoughts. If A be recalled into consciousness, A will tend to reawaken B, B to reawaken C, and so on, until the whole formerly coexistent series has been reinstated—or the mind diverted by some stronger movement, on some other train. We have thus as a second general law of actual Reproduction, Suggestion, or Association,—

viii.—The Law of REDINTEGRATION, of INDIRECT REMEMBRANCE, or of REMINISCENCE:—*Thoughts once coidentical in time, are, however different as mental modes, again suggestive of each other, and that in the mutual order which they originally held.*

To this law of Redintegration can easily be reduced Aristotle's second and third suggestives—"the movements [which and by which, we recollect,] . . . are sometimes AT THE SAME TIME, sometimes PARTS OF THE SAME WHOLE, &c. (See p. 900, a.)

Philosophers, in generalising the phænomena of reproduction, have, if our exception of Aristotle be not admitted, of these two, exclusively regarded the law of Redintegration. That of Repetition was, however, equally worthy of their consideration. For the excitation of the same by the same, differing in time, is not less marvellous, than the excitation of the different by the different, identical in time. It was a principle, too, equally indispensable, to explain the phænomena. For the attempts to reduce these to the law of Redintegration alone will not stand the test of criticism; since the reproduction of thought by thought, as disjoined in time, cannot be referred to the reproduction of thought by thought, as conjoined in time. Accordingly, we shall find in coming to detail, that some phænomena are saved by the law of Repetition alone, while others require a combination of two laws of Repetition and Redintegration.

Movements thus suggest and are suggested, in proportion to the strictness of the dependency between that prior and this posterior. But such general relation between two thoughts—and on which are founded the two Abstract or Primary laws of Repetition and Redintegration—is frequently crossed, is frequently superseded, by another, and that a particular relation, which determines the suggestion of a movement not warranted by any dependence on its antecedent. To complete the general laws of reproduction, we must therefore recognise a Secondary or Concrete principle—what may be styled, (under protest, for it is hardly deserving of the title Law):—

ix.—The Law of PREFERENCE:—*Thoughts are suggested, not merely by force of the general subjective relation subsisting between themselves, they are also suggested, in proportion to the relation of interest (from whatever source,) in which these stand to the individual mind.*

§ II.—*Special Laws of Mental Succession. Those of Reproduction.*

A.—*Primary; modes of the laws of Repetition and Redintegration.*

The first special law under this head is—

x.—The Law of SIMILARS:—*Things—thoughts resembling each other (be the resemblance simple or analogical) are mutually suggestive.*

From Aristotle downwards, all who have written on Suggestion, whether intentional or spontaneous, have recognized the association of similar objects. But whilst all have thus fairly acknowledged the effect; none, I think, (if Aristotle be not a singular exception,) have speculated aright as to the cause.

In general, Similarity has been lightly assumed, lightly laid down, as one of the ultimate principles of associations. Nothing, however, can be clearer than that resembling objects—resembling mental modifications, being, *to us*, in their resembling points, *identical;* they must, on the principle of Repetition, call up each other. This, of course, refers principally to suggestion *for the first time*. Subsequently, Redintegration co-operates with Repetition; for *now*, the resembling objects have formed, together, *parts of the same mental whole;* and are, moreover, associated both as *similar* and as *contrasted*.

It is, however, more important to prove, that the law of Similarity cannot be reduced to the law alone of Redintegration. This reduction has often been assumed; seldom a demonstration of it propounded. Discounting Wolf, who cannot *properly* be adduced, I recollect only *four* philosophers who have attempted such probative reduction. As two of these, however, are only repeaters of a third, there are found, in reality, among them, only *two* independent arguments; and these, though both aiming at the same end, endeavour to accomplish it on different principles.—The one is by Maass, (followed by Hoffbauer and Biunde;) the other by Mr James Mill.

Of these, the former is as follows:—"Similar representations," says Maass, "can only be associated, in as much as they, or their constituent characters, belong to the same total representation; and this, without exception, is the case with them. The two representations, A and B resemble each other, in so far as both contain the common character *b*. If then, B, to which belong the characters *b d e*, is associated with A, to which belong the characters *b a c*, in that case *a c* are associated with *b* [B ?], and these consequently, taken together, are all parts of the same total representation."—There seems to be here so egregious a *petitio principii*, that I am almost doubtful whether I correctly apprehend the purport of the argument.—No doubt, "*if B is associated with A*," all will follow as stated. For *after* one representation has, in virtue of their similarity, been associated with, and has suggested another; they become associated *anew* as parts of the total representation which that original suggestion caused; and may, of course, *subsequently* re-suggest each other, simply on the principle of Redintegration, and apart from their similarity altogether. But the question here to be answered is—"How do the similar representations B and A *become* associated or mutually suggestive ?—on the hypothesis, always, that they have not been previously associated, as mentally coexistent; —and the reasoning violates the hypothesis.

Mr Maass goes on :—"Further, the Similarity of two representations could not, in itself, be any reason of their association. For Similarity is an objective relation, subsisting between them; but from this there follows not in the least their subjective inter-dependence in imagination." (Versuch, &c., § 20.)—Here again, I can hardly think that I understand aright. Is it intended to be said,—that we know, or can know aught of objective Similarity in things, except through our subjective consciousness, or feeling, of the partial sameness of certain subjective movements determined by them in us ?—that *representations* are in themselves aught but subjective modifications, and that the consciousness or feeling of them, and their identity or difference, are not also purely subjective ?

On the statements of Hoffbauer, who manifestly, and of Biunde, who professedly, adopts the preceding reasoning from Maass, it is unnecessary to make any observation. They are as follows :—"We call things," says the former, "reciprocally similar when certain attributes are common to them. The [common] attribute which is found in one of these must therefore also be met with in the others. In the representation of the object A, which resembles another object, B, there is involved the representation of the common attribute, found also in B, and this is likewise contained in a total representation along with B." (Naturlehre, &c., Br. 23.)—"Were there," says the latter, "in similar (and analogous) representations no coexistence, the representations, as Maass rightly observes, would be without any internal bond of connection, and no conceivable reason could be any longer assigned, why a representation should awaken its co-similars and not rather any other representation." (Versuch, &c , § 70.)

The other attempt at such a reduction is by the late Mr Mill, in his ingenious "Analysis of the Phenomena of the Human Mind ;" who thus, after Hobbes and Hartley, enounces what I have called the law of Redintegration as the general law of association, with its causes: "Our *ideas* spring up or exist, *in the order* in which the *sensations* existed, of which they are the copies." He adds :—"The causes of strength in association seem all to be resolvable into *two*; the *vividness* of the associated feelings and the *frequency* of the association." (I. pp. 56, 61.) Again, treating of Hume's principles of association, he thus endeavours to recall that of Resemblance to these causes :—"I believe it will be found that we are *accustomed* to see like things *together*. When we see a tree, we generally see more trees than one; when we see an ox, we generally see more oxen than one; a sheep, more sheep than one; a man, more men than one. From this observation, I think, we may refer *resemblance* to the law of *frequency*, of which it seems to form only a particular case." (I. p. 79.)—I confess myself unable to perceive the cogency of this reasoning,—if I rightly apprehend its tenor. Admitting, "that we are accustomed to *see* like things together," (though are we not far more accustomed to things *unlike* together ?); the following objections occur to this. as a ground on which to reduce the principle of similarity exclusively to the principle of accustomed mental concomitance.

1°. It could only enable us to explain the mutual suggestion of those things which have actually been seen together. But there are innumerable cases of similars suggesting similars, in which the objects having never previously been witnessed in conjunction, nor even mentally compared together, the fact of their association cannot be thus accounted for

2°. Even in relation to things usually seen together, the pervading Similarity [will not] serve as a principle for their reciprocal suggestion. The sheep, or ox, or man A does not suggest the sheep, or ox, or man B, on the score of any generic similarity. For such suggestion, this generic similarity is as zero. It is only similarity in the midst of difference that associates; and instead of being in proportion to the frequency, it is strong exactly in proportion to the rarity, of its occurrence.*

3°, The association of similarity is comparatively strong; that of coexistence comparatively weak. The latter cannot, therefore, afford the reason of the former.

4°, Many of the very strongest suggestions by resemblance are of, and by, objects which have never before been mentally coexistent.

* * * * * * * *

The Law of Analogy.†

* * * * * * * *

The Law of Affinity.†

* * * * * * * *

xi.—The Law of Contrast.‡

1°, All contrast is of things contained under a common notion. Qualities are contrasted only as they are similar. A good horse and a bad syllogism have no contrast. Virtue and vice agree as moral attributes; great and little agree as quantities, and as extraordinary deflections from ordinary quantity. Even existence and non-existence are not opposed as of different genera, but only as species of

* This argument may be illustrated by the remark of Hume (Treat. of Hum. Nat. B. i. P. i. s. 5),—'Though resemblance be necessary to all philosophical relation, it does not follow that it always produces a connexion or association of ideas. When a quality becomes very general, and is common to a great many individuals, it leads not the mind directly to any one of them, but, by presenting at once too great a choice, does thereby prevent the imagination from fixing on any single object.'—Ed.

† Of these laws the titles only have been found among the Author's papers: the further account of them, if ever written, has been lost. It is probable, however, that the Author finally intended to include them under the Law of Similars; for which reason they have not been numbered as xi. and xii.—Ed.

‡ The following historical notices concerning the Law of Contrast are extracted from the Author's Common-Place Book. The views of Stiedenroth have been mainly followed in the fragmentary remarks printed in the text.—Ed.

The Law of Contrast has been reduced—

1. To Frequency, or Frequency and Vividness, by Mr James Mill. [Analysis, &c. i. p. 80. 'A dwarf suggests the idea of a giant. How? We call a dwarf a dwarf, because he departs from a certain standard. We call a giant a giant, because he departs from the same standard. This is a case, therefore, of resemblance—that is, of frequency. Pain is said to make us think of pleasure; and this is considered a case of association by contrast. There is no doubt that pain makes us think of relief from it; because they have been conjoined, and the great vividness of the sensations makes the association strong. Relief from pain is a species of pleasure; and one pleasure leads to think of another, from the resemblance. This is a compound case, therefore, of vividness and frequency. All other cases of contrast, I believe, may be expounded in a similar manner.']

2. To Resemblance under a higher notion, by Stiedenroth. [Psychologie, p. 92. 'Doch ist es merkwuerdig, dass die Erinnerung mehr von der widrigen Seite des Contrastes nach der entgegengesetzten geht, als umgekehrt, obgleich auch dieser Gang sich allerdings findet. Wie wird sich diese ganze Erscheinung mit der Aehnlichkeit vergleichen? Vor allen Dingen darf nicht vergessen werden, dass es keinen Contrast giebt, ausgenommen unter demselben hoeheren Begriff. Eine reiche Gegend und Geistesarmuth bilden an und fuer sich keinen Contrast. Die contrastirenden Vorstellungen sind also immer theilweise einerlei; sie sind Gegensaetze unter demselben hoeheren Begriff, und zwar Gegensaetze, die, wenn gleich concret, dennoch durch Contradiction schlechthin gedacht werden. Nun ist der Begriff und seine Verneinung zugleich, und dieses Verhaeltniss wurde daher frueher zu den naechsten psychologisch aehnlichen gezaehlt. Wird daher ein Begriff vorausgesetzt, so involvirt eine besondere Fassung unter ihm zugleich mit dem Hauptbegriff in dieser Fassung, d. h. mit dem Begriff, der die Fassung des Besonderen vorzugsweise bestimmt, den Gegensatz. Daher wird begreiflich seyn, wie Contraste an einander erinnern koennen, und wie sich dieses Verhaeltniss der Aehnlichkeit keineswegs entzieht.'] So Alexander Aphrodisiensis (in Top. i. 18) makes contrariety equivalent to similarity, inasmuch as contraries, &c., have common attributes.

3. To a mixture of Causation and Resemblance, by Hume. [Essay on the Association of Ideas. 'Contrast or contrariety is also a connection among ideas; but it may, perhaps, be considered as a mixture of Causation and Resemblance. When two objects are contrary, the one destroys the other—that is, [is] the cause of its annihilation, and the idea of the annihilation of an object implies the idea of its former existence.']

4. To Simultaneity and Interest of Understanding or Feeling, by Schulze. [Anthropologie, § 72, p. 156, 3d. ed. 1826. 'Die Folge der Bilder in der Einbildungskraft nach dem so genannten Gesetze des Contrastes ist, in den meisten Faellen, eine durch den Einfluss des forschenden Verstandes oder des Hanges des Herzens zu gewissen Gefuehlen auf jene Folge nach dem Gesetze der Gleichzeitigkeit bestimmte Verbindung. Sie entsteht naemlich hauptsaechlich dadurch, dass man Dinge vermittelst der Vergleichung mit ihrem Gegentheile aufzuklaeren, von unangenehmen Gefuehlen aber durch die Vorstellung erheiternder Gegenstaende sich zu befreien sucht.']

existence—positive existence and negative existence. Conspecies thus (as wolf and dog) may be associated either as similars or as contraries — similars as opposed to animals of other genera—contraries, as opposed to each other. [Contraries are] thus united under a higher notion.

But 2°, Affirmation of any quality involves the negation of its contradictory—the affirmation of goodness is virtually the negation of badness; and many terms for the contradictory qualities are only negations and affirmations—just, unjust—finite, infinite—partial, impartial. Hence logical contradictory opposition is even a stronger association than logical contrariety, because only between two.

3°, Contrast is a relation—the knowledge of contraries is one. So in passive feeling—pain—pleasure.

4°, Consciousness is only of the distinguishable. *Ergo*, contrast most clearly distinguished must heighten consciousness.

N.B.- Consciousness is activity of mind rising above a certain *degree* or *intension*. Where it is dissipated—divided—falling under this degree, there is *unconsciousness*. Unconsciousness is not equal to inactivity of mind, but to [that which is below] this degree of activity.

[xii. The Law of COADJACENCY.]

Cause and Effect—Whole and Parts—Substance and Attribute—Sign and Signified.*

B—*Secondary; modes of the Law of Preference.*

Under the laws of possibility, one thought being associated with a plurality, and each of that plurality being therefore suggestible, it suggests one in preference to another, according to two laws.

1°, By relation to *itself*, the one most strictly associated with itself.

2°, By relation to the mind, the thought most easily suggestible.

That there must be two laws is shown, because two associated thoughts do not suggest each other with equal force. B may be very strongly associated with A, but A very slightly associated with B. This twofold, 1° in order of time, 2° in order of interest.

[Under the first head, that of suggestion by relation to the thought suggesting, may be stated the following special laws:—

xiii.—The Law of IMMEDIACY.]

Of two thoughts, if the one be immediately, the other mediately connected [*with a third*], *the first will be suggested* [*by the third in preference to the second*].

[xiv.—The Law of HOMOGENEITY.]

A thought will suggest another of the same order [*in preference to one of a different order*].

Thus, a smell will suggest a smell, a sight a sight, an imagination an imagination [in preference to a thought of a different class].*

[Under the second head, that of suggestion by relation to the mind, may be stated as a special law.

xv.—The Law of FACILITY.]

A thought easier to suggest will be roused in preference to a more difficult one.

The easier are—

a.—Those more clearly, strongly impressed, than the reverse.† [Such are ideas] more undistractedly, attentively, [received]; in youth, in the morning; [assisted by] novelty, wonder, passion, &c. [See above, p. 896, n.*] Hence, also, sights are more easily suggested than smells, imaginations than thoughts, &c.‡

b.—Those more recent, than older (cæteris paribus).§

c.—Those more frequently repeated (cæteris paribus).‖

d.—Those which stand more isolated from foreign and thwarting thoughts.¶

e.—Those which are more connected with homogeneous and assisting thoughts.**

f.—Those more interesting to (1.) na-

---

* From p. 899, n.*, it seems probable that the Author intended to include these relations, the titles of which are given in his papers, under the general head of Coadjacency. This law has accordingly been supplied. In reference to this classification, it should be observed that, though Cause and Effect, Whole and Parts, &c., when considered generally as relative notions, fall under the Law of Relativity or Integration (see above, p. 911), yet when considered specially as regards the suggestion of this particular effect by this particular cause, &c., they are instances of association proper, and may be fitly considered in this place. See p. 900, n. ‡.—ED.

* Fries, Neue Kritik (1807), p. 110. Schmid, Metaphysik der inneren Natur, p. 243.

† Ueberwasser, [Anweisungen zum regelmaessigen Studium der Empirischen Psychologie, 1787], p. 122. Cf. Biunde, Empir. Psychol. i. p. 326; Baumgarten, Metaph., § 422.

‡ Fracastorius, f. 123 D. [Turrius, sive de Intellectione, Fracastorii Opera, Venet. 1584.—ED.]

§ Ueberwasser, p. 125. Cf. Biunde, p. 330. Baumgarten, § 422.

‖ Ueberwasser, p. 126, Brown, Lecture xxxvii. p. 236, ed. 1830. Cf. Biunde, p. 331.

¶ Ueberwasser, p. 130. Cf. Biunde, p. 334.

** Ueberwasser, p. 132. Cf. Biunde, p. 333.

tural cognitive powers, talents; (2.) acquired habits of cognition, studies; (3.) temporary line of occupation.

g.—Those more in harmony with affective dispositions, (1.) natural; (2.) habitual; (3.) temporary.

* * * * *

[The above fragments are all that the Editor has been able to put together from the papers apparently intended for the completion of Note D. * * * Another exposition of the Author's views on Association, more finished in writing, though less developed in thought, will be found in the Lectures on Metaphysics, Lect. xxxi. xxxii.—Ed.]

NOTE E.

ON THE CORRELATIVE APPREHENSIONS OF COLOUR, AND OF EXTENSION AND FIGURE.

---

§ I.—*On the Correlation of Colour with Extension and Figure in visual Perception and Imagination.*

§ II.—*On the Philosophy of the Point, the Line, and the Surface: in illustration of the reality, nature, and visual perception of breadthless lines.*

[References.—From Inq. 145 a b; from Supplementary Dissertations, 844 a, 859 a, 860 b, 885 a, et alibi.]

---

§ I.—*On the Correlation of Colour with Extension and Figure in visual Perception and Imagination.*

There may be here mooted *four* questions, in reference to both cognitions. In reference to the former, we may ask, Can there be *seen*—

1°, Extension without colour?
2°, Figure without colour?
3°, Colour without extension?
4°, Colour without figure?

The same questions, if the response be negative in regard to vision, may be further asked in regard to imagination; but if the answer be affirmative in the former case, *multo magis* must it be affirmative in the latter.

The first question (*Can we see, can we imagine, Extension apart from Colour?*) must, I think, be at once negatived in reference to both. For there is no actual, no conceivable, object of vision which is not coloured. Which is thus demonstrated:—*Physically* speaking, Colour is coextensive with Light. As a genus containing under it, as species, the various modifications of light, it excludes, of course, the privation of light. The black or dark is not therefore, physically considered, a colour. But *psychologically* speaking, as we are at present, and in common language, this is not the case. For *colour* is used as a word equivalent with *visual state*, and as a genus (or, perhaps, more properly as an equivocal term) contains under it every mode of our visual organism, whether one of excitement (a positive affection or colour, as the white, blue, red, yellow, &c.), or one of non-excitement (a negative affection or colour, as the black or dark). In this relation, colour thus comprises two contradictory or repugnant opposites. But if so, every visible object must be seen, every visible object must be imagined, with the attribute of colour; for on the laws of contradiction and excluded middle, of two repugnant predicates, the one or the other must be affirmed of every object of thought. The same holds true of the other senses. But in these, there being no generic or equivocal term, as in vision, comprising both their excitements and non-excitements—both their positive and negative states—there is no ambiguity which stands in need of explanation. The terms *sonorous*, *sapid*, *odorous*, *tactile*, *&c.*, denote only the positive, to the exclusion of the privative, alternative; but had we words to denote at once the sonorous and noiseless, the sapid and tasteless, &c., these words we could apply, these words (if we thought thoroughly) we could not but apply, as predicates to every sensible object, precisely as at present we must (on the same bypothesis) attribute to every such object one or other of the contradictory epithets they would contain. Why this difference should have arisen between the nomenclature of the objects and affections of vision, and of the other senses, it is not difficult to discover.

This is the simple solution of a difficulty which has perplexed so many philosophers, and of the objection which has so often been triumphantly advanced to the quality of necessity as the ground and index of our native notions, in contradistinction from our acquired. If Space and Time (it has been said) are to be held as *a priori* concepts, because we are unable not to think them, Colour, on the same criterion, must be held as also *a priori*, because we are equally unable to imagine the extended in space, or even space itself, as uncoloured. But to return.

This doctrine is no novelty of mine. It was held by Aristotle; who, while he recognises colour as the proper sensible of vision, maintains also "that colour and magnitude (extension) always accompany each other." (De Anima, L. iii. c. 1, § 5 [11]; De Sensu et Sensili, c. 1, § 9; c. 3, §§ 6, 8, 14.) It was, however, more explicitly enounced by the Aristotelic Themistius, among others, in the following passage of his Paraphrase on the Posterior Analytics: "It is impossible to find in nature, or to realise in thought, a surface destitute of colour." (Opera, ed. Ald., f. 78 b.) Hence it was that, as noticed by Aristotle, "the Pythagoreans called the *Surface* of bodies by the name of *Colour*" (De Sensu et Sensili, c. 3); a statement reversed by the Pseudo-Plutarch, who says, that they called *Colour* by the name of *Surface*. (De Plac. Philos. L. i. c. 15.) Both statements, however, may be right; for it is probable that the terms (ἐπιφάνεια, χροιά) were used indifferently; and the former, be it remarked, the common Greek term for surface, itself denotes a surface only by relation to the apprehension of sight.

Mr Fearn has exaggerated this truth into an error, in asserting unconditionally that "*we think in colours*." He is also mistaken in supposing that the fact, as limited to the imagination of extended objects, had been first noticed by himself; though I am far from doubting the personal originality of this perverse, but acute, psychologist. (*First Lines*, and *Manual of Mind*, passim.) *

As for Reid (Inq. 145 b), in holding, under the second question, that the visual perception of *Figure* is not necessarily dependent upon a sensation of *Colour*, he must, *a majore*, maintain the same, under this, of the visual perception of *Extension*.

The second question (*Can we see Figure apart from Colour?*) is affirmed by Reid (l. c.); and on valid grounds denied by Stewart, in the passage from his Dissertation, quoted in the relative footnote,† although it be impossible to reconcile this with his other and earlier statements, to which I shall immediately refer. This second question, however, receives its solution in that of the two last, to which I, therefore, proceed.

---

* The following authorities, who maintain that we cannot imagine extension without colour, are added from the Author's Common-Place Book. *Berkeley*, Theory of Vision, § 130; Princ. of Hum. Knowledge, P. i. § 10;—*Hume*, Treat. of Hum. Nat., B. i. P. ii. s. 3;—*D'Alembert*, Disc. Prél., Mélanges, &c., t. i. p. 30;—*Tourtual*, Die Sinne des Menschen (Muenster, 1827), p. 23;—*Royer Collard*, Jouffroy's Reid, t. iii. p. 427.—Ed.

† See p. 144, n. †.—Ed.

The third question (*Can we see Colour apart from Extension?*) and the fourth (*Can we see Colour apart from Figure?*) are to be taken together, as the answer to either involves the answer to both. It is likewise evident, that to answer these two questions in regard to sense, we must answer them in regard to imagination;—for as a colour can or cannot be imagined visible apart from extension and figure, it can or cannot be visible, in reality, apart from these.

These questions have, by philosophers in general, either not been proposed at all, or peremptorily answered in the negative. The doctrine of Aristotle seems to have been that silently recognised by philosophers. Not only has the perception or imagination of extension and figure been supposed to imply that of colour, the perception or the imagination of colour has been equally supposed to imply that of extension and figure. By a small number of philosophers they have, however, been mooted; and by a still smaller, decided in the affirmative.

Of these last, the first I am aware of is Condillac, in his work *On the Origin of Human Knowledge;* but in his later writings he apparently abandons the paradox which he had originally maintained.*

The next is Reid (l. c.); but, in like manner, the doctrine advanced in his Inquiry is silently withdrawn in his Essays. It is certain that he did not borrow this opinion from Condillac, with whose works he seems never to have been acquainted; but it is not, I think, impossible that it may have been suggested to him by a passage in Berkeley's *New Theory of Vision*, § cxxx.

In this opinion Reid is followed by Mr Stewart; but, also, only in his writings previous to the Dissertation, in which it is manifestly, though not professedly, surrendered. In these works this philosopher admits the fact, as a constant, though contingent, experience,—that we never do actually perceive colour apart from extension; and on this ground he endeavours in various passages to account by association for our inability to imagine colour apart from extension. To quote one:—"I formerly had occasion to mention several instances of very intimate associations formed between two ideas which have *no necessary connexion* with each other. One of the most remarkable is, that which exists in every person's mind between the notions of *colour* and *extension*. The former of these words expresses, at least in the sense in which we commonly employ it, a sensation in the mind; the latter denotes a quality of an external object; so that there is, in fact, no more connexion between the two notions than between those of pain and of solidity. And yet, in consequence of our always perceiving extension at the same time at which the sensation of colour is excited in the mind, we find it impossible to think of that sensation, without conceiving extension along with it." (Elem., i. 349.* Compare also pp. 73, 74, 575-579, octavo edition; Essays, pp. 100, 563, 564, quarto edition.†)

The view which Reid and Stewart thus originally countenanced was adopted, and, according to his wont, without acknowledgment, by Brown, who has attempted an elaborate, but unsuccessful, argument in its favour. (Lect. xxix.) It has likewise found favour with other psychologists of this country, among whom I have to mention a philosopher of great acuteness, Mr James Mill, in his *Analysis of the Human Mind* (vol. i. pp. 72, 265), and Dr John Young, in his *Lectures on Intellectual Philosophy* (p. 121 sq.).

This paradox appears to me untenable. We are conscious of the affection of colour either as one colour, or as a plurality of colours. On the former alternative, one homogeneous colour occupies the whole field of vision; on the latter, this field is divided among several.

To take the second first: the very statement of the supposition implies a negation of the paradox.

For, in the first place, we are only aware of the coexistence of a plurality of colours in being aware of them as exterior to each other; but such reciprocal exteriority supposes a relation between them of extension.

---

* It is in his later work, the *Traité des Sensations* (part i. ch. xi.; part ii. ch. iv. v.), that Condillac maintains the opinion mentioned in the text; and it is against this work that the arguments of Daube, mentioned below, are directed. In his earlier work, the *Origine des Connoissances Humaines*, Condillac maintained the opposite opinion, that the idea of colour necessarily involves that of extension. (Part i. sect. 6.) In his later view, Condillac has been anticipated by Berkeley, against whom the arguments in his earlier work are directed. Compare *Lectures on Metaphysics*, vol. ii. p. 160, and the editor's note, p. 161, in which Condillac's view is further explained.—Ed.

* Collected Works, vol. ii. p. 306.—Ed.

† Collected Works, vol. ii. pp. 98, 496-497; vol. v. pp. 119, 431, 432.—Ed.

But, in the second place, the several colours themselves are necessarily apprehended as extended. For they limit each other; this limitation constitutes a line; and this line, if it return upon itself, constitutes a figure. But a line and a figure are both extensions; and that which constitutes a line or figure must itself be extended. This simple refutation of the paradox in question is not new. I find it in D'Alembert, who had probably Condillac's earlier doctrine in his eye; and it is marvellous how it should have escaped, in particular, the notice of Mr Stewart, by whom D'Alembert's philosophical writings were held in the highest esteem. "La vision seule nous donne l'idée de la couleur des objects. *Supposons maintenant des parties de l'espace, différemment colorées, et exposées a nos yeux ; la différence des couleurs nous fera remarquer nécessairement les bornes ou limites qui séparent deux couleurs voisines, et par conséquent nous donnera une idée de figure ; car on conçoit une figure dès qu'on conçoit des bornes en tous sens.*" *Elémens de Philosophie*, Eclaircissemens, § vii. [Mélanges, t. v. p. 110.]

Subsequently, the same fact is alleged, expressly in refutation of Condillac, by Daube, in his *Essai d'Idéologie* (p. 66).* "On ne peut voir à la fois plusieurs couleurs, sans voir leur limites. Or, voir les limites des couleurs, c'est avoir la sensation de figure." A similar doctrine was, however, apparently intended by Zeno, the stoic, in saying "that colours are the primary figurations of matter" (Pseudo-Plutarch, *De Plac. Philos.* L. i. c. 15; Pseudo-Galen, *Hist. Philos.* c. 15); and by the elder Scaliger in the statement—"Corpus videmus quia coloratum; figuram quia coloratæ superficiei terminus est." (De Subtilitate, Exerc. cccxviii. § 15; compare Exerc. lxvi. § 2.) Mr Fearn applies the same fact in refutation of the paradox of Reid and Stewart; but he overrates the importance, as well as novelty, of the observation, and is still more grievously mistaken, in supposing that a disproof of this individual opinion (which the latter seems ultimately, and of his own accord, to have abandoned), is equivalent to a subversion of the general doctrine of perception held by these philosophers.†

[The other alternative,—that we can be conscious of a single colour without extension,—is equally untenable.] In the first place, while, on the one hand, we are conscious of extension only as we are conscious of one affection as out of another, so, on the other, we cannot be conscious of one sensation as out of another, without being, *ipso facto*, conscious of extension. But in vision, where every affection is an affection of colour, we cannot be conscious of a colour, without being conscious of that colour in contrast to, and therefore out of, another colour,—without, therefore, being conscious of the extended. For we are only conscious of a homogeneous affection or single colour, as occupying either, 1) a part, or 2) the whole, of the field of vision.

In the former case the part may be either (a) a smallest part—a minimum visibile, or (b) not a smallest part. If a smallest part, this minimum is, and is apprehended to be, only as it excludes, or is the negation of, other colour or colours (positive or negative), by which it is surrounded. But in all this, reciprocal outness, extension, is involved. Again, the same is still more manifest on the supposition that the single colour is not a minimum; for in this case the colour is not merely apprehended as out of other colour or colours by which it is limited—the hypothesis itself, that it is not a minimum, involves the apprehension itself of parts exterior to parts.

The apprehension of parts exterior to parts is, in like manner, but even more obtrusively, involved in the latter case, where a homogeneous colour is supposed to occupy the whole field of vision. For this field has a right and a left, an upper and an under side, and may be divided into halves, quarters, &c., indefinitely.

[The above portion of this Note probably represents very nearly, if not exactly, the form in which it would ultimately have been published. Another dissertation on the above and some cognate questions, will be found in the Lectures on Metaphysics, Lect. xxvii. and xxviii. The remainder of the Note is left incomplete, but the following fragments seem to have been intended for the second part of it.—ED.]

---

* See above, p. 919 a, n. *. Compare also Daube, p. 242, where Condillac's arguments are examined more at length.—ED.

† Mr Stewart seems latterly to have tacitly renounced the opinion in which he had originally coincided with Reid; for the passage from his Dissertation quoted above (p. 144, n. †), cannot, I think, be reconciled with the doctrine of his earlier publications. [This note in the MS. concludes with an account of Mr Fearn's controversy with Stewart, which has been already published in a corrected form in the Author's edition of Stewart's works. Vol. I., Advertisement, p. ix.—ED.]

§ II.—*On the Philosophy of the Point, the Line, and the Surface: in illustration of the reality, nature, and visual perception of breadthless lines.*

1. The Superficies, Line, Point, are not positive entities, but negations. They do not constitute extension, but are themselves constituted by its cessation; the cessation of extension in solidity being the superficies, in superficiality the line, in linearity the point.

2. The Superficies, Line, Point, are the limits of extension, but in the sense not of causes, but of effects of limitation; for they emerge only by the sublation of one extended by the position of another.

3. The Superficies, Line, Point, do not exist of themselves, but only as in something else; they are not substances, but accidents.

4. Again, of accidents, they are not qualities, neither are they in propriety quantities; they are relations—the reciprocal relations of two extensions, each limiting the other.

5. But a limitation is a negation, and a reciprocal negation is in itself a nothing. Considered absolutely, or in themselves, they are therefore nonentities.

* * * * * * *

In illustration of the preceding doctrine in regard to the mere negativity of our perception of terminal lines, I may refer to some confirmatory opinions held by previous speculators.

Of these, the first I shall adduce is Aristotle's; and his doctrine, in so far as it was developed, is apparent from the following passages.

In his Metaphysics (L. x., (or xi., or xiii.), c. 2), objecting, to those who would make lines and surfaces the constitutive principles of things,* that these are not separate or separable, not self-subsistent entities, but either mere "sections and divisions," or mere "terminations," he says:—"A Surface is the mere section or termination of a body (or solid), as a Line is of a surface, which again is either cut or terminated by a Point. All these are only as they are in something else; apart and by themselves, they are nonentities." In the same work (L. ii. (or iii.), c. 5), the same doctrine is, though less explicitly, asserted, where, on a similar occasion, he maintains that the Surface, the Line, the Point, "seem all to be only divisions of body, one in breadth, another in depth, a third in length." And in his De Anima, (L. iii. c. 6), he further says, that "a Point, and whatever is as a division, itself indivisible, is manifested to the mind as a privation." Another speculation of Aristotle on this subject is imperfectly preserved by Sextus Empiricus (Adv. Geom. § 57-59; I. Adv. Phys. § 412), probably from his lost treatise or treatises on Mathematics. But is it not an error for Apollonius?*

* Compare also (against the Platonists and Pythagoreans) De Cœlo, iii. 1; De Gen. et Corr. i. 2; De Lin. Insec.; Phys. vi. 1, 2.

* Additional notes from Aristotle on Lines, &c.

1. In his Problems (xxv. 3), speaking of the air as superincumbent on the water, he supposes "their extremes to be together, and thus one plane (or surface) to be common to both."—Cf. Phys. iv. 6, § 9.

2. Phys. v. 3, § 2. — "Things are said to be, locally considered, *together*, in as much as they coexist in one primary or proximate place [i.e. are in the same space]; *apart*, in as much as they exist in different places. Things touch each other in so far as their extremes exist together" [i.e. are in the same space]. But if so, not extended—not corporeal.

3. Ibid. § 5, 6.—"The coherent is what, while it follows, is in contact. . . . . . . The continuous is a species of the coherent; for I say that things are continuous when their several limits, in which they coalesce or touch each other, become one and the same"—in other words, when each immediately limits the other.

4. Ibid. iv. 11, § 12.—"A point in a certain sort continues length, and limits it; for it is the beginning of one [length] and the end of another." So Phys. viii. 8, texts 68, 69, where it is expressly said that "one point is common to two continuous lines, being the end of the one, the beginning of the other."—Simplicius, f. 32, perverts Aristotle's doctrine. So Averroes.

5. Categ. c. 6.—After dividing quantity into continuous and discrete, defining the former that which does, the latter that which does not, consist of parts having a position to each other, and enumerating, as species of the continuous, a line, a surface, a solid, and also place (or space) and time—he proceeds to consider these in detail. "But a line is continuous; for we can take in it a common limit [or common limits] at which its parts coalesce or mutually touch — a point [or points]. In like manner in a surface [we may take] a line; for the parts of a plane coalesce at a certain common limit. So likewise in a body [or solid] you may take a common limit, to wit, a line or surface, at which the parts of the body coalesce. Of the same class are time and place [or space]. For the time Now coalesces with both the Past and the Future. And on the other hand place [space] is a quantity continuous; for the parts of body occupy a certain place [space], and these parts coalesce at a certain common limit; consequently the parts of place [space] which each of these parts of body occupy, coalesce at the same limit at which the parts of body coalesced. Place [space] will, therefore, likewise be continuous; for its parts coalesce at one common limit." The parts and limits here spoken of

The preceding doctrine received no explication of any consequence until the time of Proclus; in whose commentary on the elements of Euclid there is contained, in relation to the Second Definition, the following memorable statement. After noticing the mode in which Apollonius and his followers explain the formation of our conception of a Line—by measuring the length alone of a road or wall, he subjoins:—"But we may obtain the sensible perception of a line by looking at the discriminations of lighted from shaded places, or on the moon and on the earth. (The text is here imperfect.) For this medium *in respect of breadth is unextended;* but it has length, that, to wit, which co-extends with the light and the shade." (Ed. Basil. 1533, f. 28.)

The same observation, but more explicitly stated, is found in the Commentary of Ammonius Hermiæ, the disciple of Proclus, on the Categories of Aristotle. It is not, however, unlikely that Proclus and Ammonius only followed Aristotle in his work, not now extant, on the Existence treated of in Mathematics. In the chapter on Quantity, speaking of a line and its mathematical definition, he says:—"That the existence of *length without breadth* is not a figment of our understandings, but that such also exists in the nature of things—this is clearly shown by the discrimination of light and shade. For if the sunshine fall, for instance, on, and partially illuminate a wall, it is necessary that what discriminates the shiny from the shady portion should be *a length destitute of breadth.* For grant that it have breadth; the breadth behoves to be either shine or shade, as between these there is no medium. But if the former, it will fall in with the shiny, if the latter, with the shady part. Betwixt these, however, a line is clearly seen, extended only in length and dividing the surface in the light from the surface in the shade. For if these are discriminated from each other, it must be, that there is something beside themselves, by which they are discriminated, and which itself is neither shiny nor shady. But this will be without breadth. For that has breadth which is necessarily either shine or shade. It is, however, neither of these, being their mutual distinction. Wherefore it is absolutely necessary, that the discrimination of the shiny from the shady parts *should be a length without breadth—that is, a line.* . . . . . . Again if a line be not infinite but bounded, there is an absolute necessity that its termination should have one extension less than itself possesses. But as a line possesses only a single extension (viz. in length), its termination will, consequently, have no extension (whether in breadth or depth). But such is a point; the distinction of which, accordingly, is—what has no part." (f. 68 b., ed. Ald., 1546.)

There is only one inaccuracy in this passage—an inaccuracy, however, perhaps rather of expression than of thought; viz. where it is said that, besides the light and shade, there must be something different from both, by which they are mutually distinguished. This is erroneous, if by this something be meant aught absolute or positive. For the line is nothing but a negation of the light by the shade, and of the shade by the light. Each discriminates itself from the other. Apart from both or from either, the line has no existence, even in thought. It is nothing absolute, being only a relation; it is nothing positive, being only a privation. But independently of this inaccuracy, neither Proclus nor Ammonius have sufficiently generalised the phænomenon by showing, 1°, that (to say nothing of a point) a Line is merely the negation of superficial extension: and, 2°, that in so far as visible, it is only the reciprocal limitation of two contrasting colours.

The inaccuracy here noticed was not committed by the Nominalists, whose reasonings I have next to notice; but, on the other hand, they did not, like the two Platonists, approve their arguments by the evidence of a sensible demonstration.

Occam, in his Quodlibeta (i. qu. 9), in his Logic (under the category of Quantity), and more fully in his Treatise on the Eucharist (cc. 1, 2), maintains with all his usual subtlety, that a Surface, a Line, a Point are nothing positive out of the mind, and neither *really* distinguished from each

are potential and not necessarily actual. For in Phys. iv. 5, § 2:—"Some things are in place [space] potentially, others actually. Wherefore, when that whose parts are reciprocally similar is continuous, its parts exist potentially in place [space]; whereas when they are separate but in mutual contact, as a heap, they exist actually."

The counter doctrine is also to be found in Aristotle, but only in those works in which he adopts vulgar opinions by accommodation. Thus, in the Topics (L. vi. c. 4, § 3; cf. L. i. c. 18, § 13), it is assumed that absolutely, in the order of nature, a point is prior to a line, a line to a surface, a surface to a solid. I see that Professor Trendelenburg adheres to this (Logische Untersuchungen, i. p. 224). But I am surprised that so learned an Aristotelian should quote the Topica, as a work from the examples in which we could infer the genuine doctrine of Aristotle.

other nor from the essence of body (corporeitas): that these are merely privations of extended substance in its threefold dimensions; a surface being simply the negation of the farther continuation of a Solid, a Line simply the negation of the farther continuation of a Surface, a Point simply the negation of the farther continuation of a Line. The same doctrine was ably supported by Durandus, and, with some unessential modifications, by Gregory of Rimini, in their several Commentaries on the Sentences (L. ii. dist. 2. qu. 4. § 13, sq., and L. ii. dist. 2. qu. 2. art. 1). But the arguments, theological and philosophical, of the Venerable Inceptor, of the most Resolute and Authentic Doctors, did not secure to their opinion a favourable reception among either their contemporaries or successors: it remained, indeed, a doctrine not merely peculiar to the Nominalists, but peculiar to a small number of them. With the exception of Scheglius (Comm. in Organ. p. 362), who seems inclined to this opinion, I do not recollect any of the Aristotelians, subsequent to the revival of letters, by whom it was adopted; while, among other later philosophers the question seems never to have been agitated at all. On modern mathematicians, who have in general been guiltless of metaphysics, the observation of the philosophical expositor of Euclid was thrown away. Clavius, indeed, and one or two geometers beside, may slavishly repeat from Proclus the individual illustration, but without expansion, far less a perception of its general bearing; and Euclid's definition of a line—length without breadth—is to the present hour laboriously and erroneously expounded as only a theoretical abstraction of intellect, though, in truth, at every turn practically realised by observation even through sense. I am aware only of one, and that a qualified exception; though I speak with hesitation, for I take no particular interest in mathematical and physical literature. In the "Lectures on Natural Philosophy," by the late Dr Thomas Young, published in 1807, there is at least the indication of a sounder doctrine; this indication has, however, likewise remained unnoticed. After defining a Solid as "a portion of space limited in magnitude on all sides"—a Surface as "the limit of a Solid"—a Line as "the limit of a Surface"—a Point as "the limit of a Line"—he adds the following scholium, illustrated by two triangular figures; the first appearing as a black spot upon a white ground, the second described, in the usual manner of mathematical diagrams, by narrow strokes. "The paper of which this figure [the first] covers a part, is an example of a Solid; the shaded portion represents a portion of Surface; the boundaries of that Surface are Lines; and the three terminations or intersections of those Lines are Points. In conformity with this more correct conception, these definitions are illustrated by representation of the respective portions of space of which the limits are considered; and also [in the second figure] by the more usual method of denoting a Line by a narrow surface, and a Surface by such a line surrounding it." (Vol. ii. p. 8.)

It is hardly to be supposed that this ingenious and learned physician had any knowledge of the observation of Proclus and Ammonius, far less of the speculations of the Nominalists. This is shown, indeed, by the comparative vagueness and inaccuracy of his language, which we are compelled to blame, in order to allow him credit for the thought he would express. His definition of a Solid is not only inexact but erroneous. It is trinal extension, and not omnilateral limitation, which determines the notion of Solidity simply; for space, or what occupies space, body, though not conceived as limited, would still necessarily be conceived as solid—as trinally extended. Limitation is thus the accident, not the essence of solidity; and Euclid's definition of a Solid by length, breadth, and thickness is exclusively correct. Euclid's is also the definition which alone gives us a distinct notion of the thing defined; for Young's is only significant to him who already knows what space is and how many dimensions it has. Further, the definition of a Surface, of a Line, of a Point, by the term *limit*, is, without a definition, inexplicit, if not wrong. For it leaves us to suppose that this limit may be something more than a mere negation of that which it is said to limit. In other respects, the whole statement is so meagre and cursory, that we are left in doubt whether the doctrine be not what the author partially stumbled on, rather than fully understood.

Mr Fearn is the only modern philosopher I am aware of, who clearly apprehended the truth of the doctrine in its full extent; and his merit is the greater, inasmuch as there is no reason whatever for surmising that he is indebted for any hint to any previous speculator. It will be found stated in almost all his various writings; and these I may recommend as worthy the attention of all those who can appreciate a rare metaphysical talent though unendowed with even an ordinary faculty of expression.

NOTE F.

ON LOCKE'S NOTION OF THE CREATION OF MATTER.*

[Reference.—From I. P. 286 b.]

[In the interpretation of Locke (*Essay*, B. iv. c. 10, § 18)] Stewart does not coincide with Reid. In quoting the same passage of Locke, he says of it, that "when considered in connection with some others in his writings, it would almost tempt one to think that a theory concerning *matter*, somewhat analogous to that of Boscovich, had occasionally passed through his mind;" and then adduces various reasons in support of this opinion, and in opposition to Reid's. (Philosophical Essays, Ess. ii. ch. i. p. 63. Collected Works, vol. v., p. 94.)

The whole arcanum in the passage in question is, however, revealed by *M. Coste*, the French translator of the Essay, and of several other of the works of Locke, *with whom the philosopher lived in the same family, and on the most intimate terms, for the last seven years of his life;* and who, though *he has never been consulted*, affords often the *most important information in regard to Locke's opinions.* To this passage there is in the *fourth* edition of Coste's translation, a very curious note appended, of which the following is an abstract :—"Here Mr Locke excites our curiosity without being inclined to satisfy it. Many persons, having imagined that he had communicated to me this *mode of explaining the creation of matter*, requested, when my translation first appeared, that I would inform them what it was ; but I was obliged to confess that Mr Locke had not made *even me* a partner in the secret. At length, long after his death, *Sir Isaac Newton*, to whom I was accidentally speaking of this part of Mr Locke's book, *discovered to me the whole mystery.* He told me, smiling, that it was he himself who had imagined this manner of explaining the creation of matter, and that the thought had struck him one day, when this question chanced to turn up in a conversation between himself, Mr Locke, and the late Earl of Pembroke. The following is the way in which he explained to them his thought: '*We may be enabled* (he said) *to form some rude conception of the creation of matter, if we suppose that God, by his power, had prevented the entrance of anything into a certain portion of pure space, which is of its nature penetrable, eternal, necessary, infinite ; for henceforward this portion of space would be endowed with impenetrability, one of the essential qualities of matter : and as pure space is absolutely uniform, we have only again to suppose that God communicated the same impenetrability to another portion of space, and we should then obtain in a certain sort the notion of the mobility of matter, another quality which is also very essential to it.*' Thus, then, we are relieved of the embarrassment of endeavouring to discover what it was that Mr Locke had deemed it advisable to conceal from his readers ; for the above is all that gave him occasion to tell us—'If we would raise our thoughts as far as they could reach, we might be able to aim at some dim and seeming conception how matter might at first be made,'" &c. This suffices to show what was the general purport of Locke's expressions, and that Mr Stewart's conjecture is at least nearer to the truth than Dr Reid's. Compare Newtoni Opt., qu. 31.

* The following Note is reprinted from the Author's *Discussions*, pp. 201, 202.—Ed.

NOTE G.

ON THE HISTORY OF THE WORD IDEA.

[References.—From Inq., 204 a; from I. P. 224 b, 267 a, 296 a, 360 a; from Supplementary Dissertations, 806 a.]

In regard to the precise signification of the terms employed, it is requisite to say a word.

Idea may be used to denominate merely a Notion,—properly a simple thought, in opposition to a composite thought or judgment. In this sense, *ideal* will mean merely what exists subjectively in our thought, contrasted with *real*—that is, what exists objectively in the universe (internally of mind, externally of matter).

But this is not the acceptation in which the words *idea* and *ideal* are specially employed by philosophers, and particularly in the polemic of Reid, of Stewart, and in general of the Scottish school. In their mouths, the *Ideal Theory* designates the theory of cognition brought to bear through the hypothesis of ideas, in one or more of the faculties of knowledge; and *idea* designates distinctively a vicarious, mediate, or representative object, through which we take cognisance of a mode of matter or mind, which, though really existing, is not, as existing, that is, in itself, immediately or presentatively by us known. To refute the Ideal Theory, to them means simply to evince that cognition, *pro tanto*, is not dependent on the hypothesis of ideas; or that, *pro tanto*, an immediate or presentative knowledge of a mode of matter or mind, as existing in itself, is competent to man.*

The history of the word *idea* seems completely unknown. Previous to the age of Descartes, as a philosophical term, it was employed exclusively by the Platonists,—at least exclusively in a Platonic meaning;* and this meaning was *precisely the reverse* of that attributed to the word by Dr Brown;—the idea *was not an object of perception*,—the idea *was not derived from without*. In the schools, so far from being a current *psychological* expression, as he imagines, it had no other application than a *theological*.† Neither, after the revival of letters, was the term extended by the Aristotelians even to the objects of *intellect*. Melanchthon, indeed (who was a kind of semi-Platonist), uses it, on *one* occasion, as a synonym for notion or intelligible species (De Anima, p. 187, ed. 1555); but it was even to this solitary instance, we presume, that Julius Scaliger alludes (De Subtilitate, vi. 4), when he castigates such an application of the word as neoteric and abusive. "*Melanch.*" is on the margin. Goclenius also probably

---

* The preceding paragraph is from a paper written in the autumn of 1855. The two next paragraphs, with the exception of the notes, are reprinted from *Discussions*, p. 70.—Ed.

* On the word *idea* before Plato, see Brandis, Gesch. d. Phil., pp. 242, 299, 307. Theognis is quoted by Goclenius (Lex. Phil. Gr. v. *Idea*), as using the word in sense of *species animo concepta*,—

πολλάκι γὰρ γνώμην ἐξαπατῶσ' ἰδέαι,

[l. 128, where, however, the word seems to be used in its ordinary sense of *visible appearance*.—Ed.]

† The word is used by the Schoolmen, after Augustin, only in a theological, not in a psychological sense, for the reasons of things in the intelligence of God, by whose exemplar the world was formed, and in whose image the universe is contemplated. "Mundum mente gerens, similique in imagine formans." [*Boethius*, De Consol. Phil., Lib. iii. metr. ix. Cf. *Heereboord*, Meletemata Philosophica, p. 290 sq.—Ed.]

founded his usage on Melanchthon.* We should have distinctly said that, previous to its employment *by Descartes himself*, the expression had never been used as a comprehensive term for the immediate objects of thought, had we not in remembrance the Historia Animæ Humanæ of our countryman, David Buchanan. This work, originally written in French, had for some years been privately circulated previous to its publication at Paris in 1636.† Here we find the word *idea* familiarly employed, in its most extensive signification, to express the objects not only of intellect proper, but of memory, imagination, sense; and this is the *earliest* example of such an employment. For the Discourse on Method, in which the term is usurped by Descartes in an equal latitude, was at least a year later in its publication—viz. in June 1637. Adopted soon after also by Gassendi,‡ the word, under such imposing patronage, gradually won its way into general use. In England, however, Locke may be said to have been the first who naturalised the term in its Cartesian universality. Hobbes employs it, and that historically, only once or twice.§ Henry More and Cudworth are very chary of it, even when treating of the Cartesian Philosophy; Willis rarely uses it; while Lord Herbert, Reynolds, and the English philosophers in general, between Descartes and Locke, do not apply it psychologically at all. When in common language employed by Milton and Dryden, *after* Descartes, as *before* him, by Sidney, Spenser, Shakspeare, Hooker, &c., the meaning is Platonic. Our Lexicographers are ignorant of the difference.

The fortune of this word is curious. Employed by Plato to express the real forms of the intelligible world, in lofty contrast to the unreal images of the sensible, it was lowered by Descartes, who extended it to the objects of our consciousness in general. When, after Gassendi, the school of Condillac had analysed our highest faculties into our lowest, the *idea* was still more deeply degraded from its high original. Like a fallen angel, it was relegated from the sphere of divine intelligence to the atmosphere of human sense; till at last *Idéologie* (more correctly *Idéalogie*), a word which could only *properly* suggest an *a priori* scheme, deducing our knowledge from the intellect, has in France become the name peculiarly distinctive of that philosophy of mind which exclusively derives our knowledge from the senses.—Word and thing, *ideas* have been the *crux philosophorum*, since Aristotle sent them packing (χαιρέτωσαν ἰδέαι), to the present day.

* 'Ideæ sumuntur nonnunquam pro conceptionibus seu notionibus animi communibus.'—Goclenii Lexicon Philosophicum (Lat.) v. *Idea*.—Ed.

† See the Dedication prefixed to the first Latin edition (Paris, 1637). This Dedication is dated "Octavo Calendas Apriles Gregorianas anno æræ Christianorum vulgaris, 1636."—Ed.

‡ Inst. Log. Pars I., Opera, I. p. 92.—Ed.

§ Hobbes uses the word *idea*, both in Latin and English, in the sense of phantasm or image in the mind, or even in the sense. See his Elementa Philosophiæ, Pars I. c. i. § 3—c. ii. § 14—c. v. §§ 8, 9; and his Leviathan, Part iv. c. 45, p. 649, ed Molesworth. Previously, in the "Objectiones Tertiæ in Meditationes Cartesii," which were written by Hobbes, the word *idea* is frequently used in the same sense, which Descartes notices as different from his own.—Ed.

[The following references, extracted from the Author's Common-Place Book, will shew how carefully he had studied the subject, and represent probably the greater part of the materials which would have been employed, had he lived to re-write the above note in the form contemplated for the present work.—Ed.]

On history of opinions about Ideas, see *Zimmermann*, Dial. de Idearum Natura, Opuscula, t. i. p. 604 sq., Tiguri, 1751; *Hillerus*, Logica, § 33; *Lossius*, Real-Lexikon, v. Angeborne Begriffe.

That *idea* used for *notion in intellect* rarely before Descartes, (Mem. Melanchthon and Fracastorius, below), see *Ruiz*, Comm. et Disp. de Scientia, [Disp. lxxxi. § 1, ed. 1629]; *Goclenius*, Lex. Phil. (Lat.) v. Idea; *Scharfius*, Metaph. Exempl. [L. i. c. i. p. 19, ed. 1628]; *Schegkius*, Comm. in Arist. Organ. [pp. 91, 344, 411 sq., ed. 1570]. Compare also *Micraelius*, Lex. Phil., v. Idea; who, with the Peripatetics, makes it equivalent to *general notion*.

[*Historical notices of the use of the term Idea.*]

1.—Theognis is said to have used Ἰδέα for *phantasm*. See *Goclenius*, Lex. Phil. (Græc.), v. Idea. [But see above, p. 925 b, n. *.—Ed.]

2.—Aristotle, De Cœlo, I. 7, for *form*, *figure*. See *Patricius*, Discuss. Peripatet. p. 327.

3.—Melanchthon, once for *intelligible species*, or *general notion*, De Anima, ed. Lugd. 1555, p. 187. [' Noticia est mentis actio, qua rem adspicit, quasi formans imaginem rei quam cogitat. Nec aliud sunt *imagines illæ seu ideæ*, nisi actus intelligendi.'] But see Erotemata Dialectica, p. 60-3, ed. 3, Strigelii, 1579; De Dialectica, pp. 11, 76, ed. Lugd. 1542. Compare *J. C. Scaliger*, De Subtilitate, Exerc. vi. § 4.

4.—FRACASTORIUS, likewise in same sense. De Intellectione, L. i. Opera, 3 ed., 1584, f. 130 A. ['Sicut autem e lacte et nive universale albedinis fit, ita et conjunctorum *sua universalia et ideæ* extrahuntur. Quare et universale loci, et figuræ, et quantitatis, et numeri, et aliorum conficitur. Propter quod potentia hæc animæ, quæ *ideis* est plena, divina quodammodo est, et solus hic intellectus appellatur.']

5.—SIR JOHN DAVIES, Nosce Teipsum (1599), never uses 'idea;' but 'form,' 'image.'

6.—CHARRON, De la Sagesse (1601)—'images,' 'espèces;' never 'idées.'

7.—BACON never [psychologically]; but contradistinguishes and contrasts '*humanæ* mentis *idola* et *divinæ* mentis *ideæ*.' Nov. Organ. aph. 23, et alibi pluries.

8.—CASPAR BAUHINUS, Theatrum Anatomicum (Basileæ, 1621), L. iii. c. 40, p. 402, speaking of the retina, says:—'Et rerum visibilium *ideas* ad cerebrum tanquam judicem deferat.' Compare Ibid. c. 42, pp. 408, 410.

9.—DAVID BUCHANAN, Hist. Animæ Humanæ (Paris, 1637), in full extent—before Descartes. [See pp. 39, 113-14, 214 sq., et alibi pluries.—ED.]

10.—DESCARTES. His 'De la Méthode' first published in 1637; and *idea* there used, as well as in the subsequent Latin translation; and in 'Meditationes,' 1641.

N.B.—The Cartesians did not apply the term *idea* to *smells, tastes, &c.* See *Regis*, Cours entier de Philosophie, t. i. p. 145, ed. 1691; *Malebranche* [Recherche, L. iii. P. ii. c. 7, and relative Eclaircissement]. Locke (Essay, B. ii. c. 13. § 25) wrong in thinking they did. Compare *Bayle*, Lettre à M. Coste, Œuvres, t. iv. p. 831; and *Coste's* Locke (ed. 1755), p. 131, note.

11.—GASSENDI used *idea*, but only in works after Descartes.

12.—HOBBES seldom uses the word; but 'species,' 'phantasm,' 'image,' 'apparition,' 'conception,' 'visible show,' 'aspect,' 'notice,' 'imagination,' &c. Only once in Treatise of Human Nature (1640*) c. i., *idea* mentioned as a synonym. ['The Imagery and Representations of the qualities of the things without, is that we call our Conception, Imagination, *Ideas*, Notice, or Knowledge of them.'] And in Elementa Philosophiæ (Lond. 1655) p. 224, [Para. iv. c. 25, § 1,] *idea* occurs as an equivalent for *phantasma*. [The latter is thus explained, §§ 2, 3]:—'Sensio est ab origine sensorii conatu ad extra, qui generatur a conatu ab objecto versus interna, eoque aliquamdiu manente per reactionem factum Phantasma * * * Phantasma enim est sentiendi actus; neque differt a sensione aliter quam *fieri* differt a *factum esse*; quæ differentia in instantaneis nulla est. Fit autem Phantasma in instante.' *

13.—REYNOLDS, Treatise of the Passions and Faculties of the Soul of Man (1640). *Ideas* not used.

14.—SIR KENELM DIGBY, On the Nature of Bodies, &c. (1644). Term not used.

15.—LORD HERBERT OF CHERBURY (1645), not 'idea;' but 'notitia,' 'conceptus,' 'apparentia,' 'species,' 'ectypus.'

16.—FROMONDUS, De Anima (1649), never uses *idea*.

17.—DE LA CHAMBRE, Système de l'Ame (1664).—After Descartes. Only 'image,' 'espèce,' &c.

18.—GLANVILL used term *idea* in its Cartesian sense, before Locke. See Vanity of Dogmatising (London, 1661), pp. 91, 97, et alibi. [P. 91: 'I would not that the *Idea* of our passions should be applied to anything without us, when it hath its subject nowhere but in ourselves.'—P. 97: 'When we would conceive a triangle, man, horse, or any other sensible, we figure it in our Phancies, and stir up there its sensible *Idea*.'] Cf. also his Scepsis Scientifica (London, 1665), pp. 67, 71, et alibi.

19.—LOCKE appears, from the author † of 'Solid Philosophy, asserted against the Fancies of the Ideists, Lond. 1697,' p. 3, to have been the first to introduce the use of the word in England. And Locke himself acknowledges that it is new. (Reply to the Bishop of Worcester, Works, vol. i. p. 410.) But Glanvill before him.

20.—HENRY MORE, chary in use, even when speaking of the Cartesian philosophy.

21.—HON. ROBERT BOYLE, Discourse of Things above Reason (1681), uses it, passim, in the vaguest way for image of Imagination, or notion of Understanding.

22.—SIDNEY, SPENSER (Sonnet 45), SHAKSPEARE, HOOKER, MILTON, DRYDEN, &c., use it in Platonic sense. [See quotations in Johnson's Dict., v. Idea.]

---

* The dedication is dated 1640, but the work was not actually published till 1650.—ED.

* For further notices of Hobbes see above, p. 928 d, n. †.—ED.

† John Sergeant. See *Discussions*, p. 80 n *.—ED.

Poiret (Cogitationes Rationales, p. 175 note, 3 ed. 1715) gives five different extensions of the term *Idea*. [The following is the passage referred to:—(1.) 'Sunt quibus *idea* et perceptio unum et idem significant; atque his licet dicere Dei Mentisque ideas dari, Deumque Mentemque per ideas suas agnosci; (2.) Sunt quibus non perceptio aut conscientia mera, sed perceptio contemplativa vel intuitiva, ut sic loquar, et intellectiva sit idem ac idea: atque his dolor, verbi gratia, colores, passiones animæ, non dicuntur *idea* directe cognosci seu percipi, sed *sensu* et *conscientia*: quod utique ipsis ita efferre licet; modo et aliis permittant sua quemque uti nomenclatura; (3.) Sunt qui solam perceptionem, cujus terminus extra nos, ideam vocant: et hoc sensu *Animæ* cujusque suæ perceptio *idea* non erit nominanda; (4.) Si quibusdam perceptionem solam rei finitæ et limitatæ placeat ideam vocare, his *idea* Dei non veniet nuncupanda; (5.) Denique illi quibus perceptionem solam, cujus terminus extra nos est corporeus, *ideam* dicere volupe est, solius corporis et rerum huc spectantium ideas dare concedent: cetera vero dicent alio modo, sensu nempe sive conscientia vel conjectura, cognosci.'—ED.]

[*As a psychological term,* idea *has been used*]—

1. Of an individual object, whether in perception or imagination,—equivalent to the German *Anschauung*.—*Baumgarten*, Acr. Log. § 51 (v. *Bolzano*, Wissenschaftslehre, i. p. 344).

2. Exclusive of object of perception, and always of the past,—equivalent to both *image* and *notion*.—*Hume*, Essays, &c., vol. ii. p. 29.

3. Equivalent to *image*—representation of past perception, and opposed to *notion*. —*Daube*, Essai d'Idéologie, p. 61; *Sam. Johnson* (Life by Boswell, p. 560, ed. Croker, 1848); *Gleig*, Encycl. Brit., 7th ed., art. Metaphysics, p. 601; *Author*[*] of 'Two Dissertations concerning Sense and the Imagination,' [pp. 58, 104-107]; *Ernesti*, Init. Doctr. Solid. [De Mente Humana c. i. § 35] p. 134.

4. Equivalent to *notion*, and opposed to *image*.—*Leibnitz*, Œuvres Philosophiques, ed. Raspe, pp. 93, 219-21, 503; *Spinoza*, Eth. Pars i. [Op. Posth. 1677], p. 87; *Seyner*, Specimen Logicæ universaliter demonstratæ, Sect. i. def. 1; *Toussaint*, De la Pensée, p. 155 sq.; *Burthogge*, Essay upon Reason and the Nature of Spirits, p. 10.

5. Inclusive of past and present, general and particular,—equivalent to 'repraesentatio rei quatenus objective consideratur.' —*Wolf*, Psych. Emp. § 48; *Descartes*,[*] Resp. et Obj. Tertiæ R. v. Medit. p. 114; *Reusch*, Syst. Metaph. § 325; *Wyttenbach*, Præc. Phil. Log. P. i. c. 3. p. 31 (ed. 1810).

6. Of extension and primary qualities, as opposed to *sensation* of secondary qualities.—*Malebranche* [Recherche, L. iii. P. ii. c. 7, and relative Eclaircissement.]

7. Including all the phænomena of consciousness, or modifications of the conscious subject.—*Bonnet*, Essai Analytique, t. i. pp. 14, 170 (but he distinguishes *ideas* and *notions*); *Destutt Tracy*, Elém. d'Idéol., i. pp. 27-29, 419; *Thurot*, Introd. à l'Etude de la Philosophie, Disc. Prél., t. i. p. xxxvi.; *Laromiguière* (v. Toussaint, De la Pensée, p. 158; Jacquier, Elémens, &c., p. 64); *Cardaillac*, Etudes Elém., t. ii. p. 185; *Degerando*, Des Signes, t. i. p. 84. 'Je comprendrai sous le nom général d'*idées*, et ces images et les éléments ou rapports que l'esprit apperçoit en elles, et les circonstances qui les accompagnent; en un mot, j'y comprendrai tout ce qu'on imagine.'

Gassendi (Instit. Log. P. i., Opera, t. i. p. 92), uses *Idea* for image or representation of aught in the mind, comprehending *species*, *imago*, *notio*, *prænotio*, *anticipatio*, *anticipata notio*, *conceptus*, *phantasma*,—in a word, any incomplex object of cognition. So Locke applied the term to every modification of mind as an object of thought.[†] (*Essay*, Introd. § 8; B. ii. c. 8. § 8.) So also Descartes and the Port Royal Logicians. (See *Jacquier*, Elémens, &c., p. 64.)[‡]

---

[*] Probably Zachary Mayne.—See *Discussions*, pp. 46, 48.—ED.

[*] But he varies. Holds it properly for *image*, but not merely in imagination, also in intellect. (See *Gassendi*, Opera, t. iii. p. 322.) He allowed also ideas of colour and other secondary qualities.—Principia, P. i. § 68.

[†] That Locke made passions, feelings, sensations, &c., in presenti, of which we are conscious, ideas, like the Vorstellungen of Wolf, see *Hume*, Essays, &c., Note [A], vol. ii. p. 545, ed. 1788. Locke's ambiguity and vacillation in the use of the term *idea*, is castigated by *Sergeant* (Solid Philosophy Asserted, p. 8), *Z. Mayne* (Two Dissertations, &c. p. 186), and *Bishop Browne* (Procedure, Extent, and Limits of Human Understanding, pp. 72, 133, et alibi).

[‡] On Locke and Descartes, see Baxter's Enquiry, &c., vol. ii. p. 261.

NOTE H.

ON CONSCIOUSNESS.

§ I.—*Reid's reduction of Consciousness to a special faculty.*

§ II.—*Conditions and Limitations of Consciousness.*

[References.—From I. P. 223 a, 231 b, 297 b; from Supplementary Dissertations, 810 a, 877 b, 884 b, 910 a.]

§ I.—*Reid's reduction of Consciousness to a special faculty.*

In all legitimate speculation with regard to the phænomena of mind, it is Consciousness which affords us at once, (1.) the capacity of knowledge; (2.) the means of observation; (3.) the point from whence our investigation should depart; (4.) the limit of our inquiry; (5.) the measure of its validity; and, (6.) the warrant of its truth.

1. Consciousness is not to be considered merely as a separate and specific faculty of self-knowledge,—as that power which is conversant about the other intellectual operations and passions, from which it is distinguished, as about its peculiar objects; but, on the contrary, it is to be regarded as a general expression for the primary and fundamental condition of all the energies and affections of our mind, inasmuch as these are known to exist. For while knowledge, feeling, and desire, in all their various modifications, can only exist as the knowledge, feeling, and desire of some determined subject, and as this subject can only know, feel, desire, inasmuch as he is conscious that he knows, feels, and desires, it is therefore manifest that all the acts and passions of the intellectual self involve Consciousness as their generic and essential quality. On the other hand, as there exists no intuitive or immediate knowledge of self as the absolute subject of thought, feeling, and desire, but, on the contrary, there is only possible a deduced, relative, and secondary knowledge of self, as the permanent basis of those transient modifications of which we are directly conscious,—it follows that, independently of the particular present energies and affections of our minds, Consciousness can have no possible existence as a distinct, peculiar, and co-ordinate faculty.

And, therefore, while Consciousness, in reference to the subaltern capacities of the intellectual subject, may be considered as their absolute and universal form, so these subordinate capacities, in reference to this universal concomitant of their existence, may with propriety be regarded as the relative and special modifications of Consciousness. And in particular,—to speak only at present with regard to our faculties of knowledge, which have necessarily reference to something different from the conscious subject,—as all existences different from our mind are only known in reference to the intellectual self, as the subject and condition of that knowledge, and by self as conscious of its own activity; and, on the other hand, as we are only conscious of self as existing in some particular state, which state again is always relative to something foreign, which, mediately or immediately, determines its existence as its cause,—it follows that all knowledge is to a certain extent necessarily self-knowledge, and that again all self-knowledge involves Consciousness of a correlative, actually or possibly, really or hypothetically, different from our mind. The distinction between consciousness and our particular faculties of knowledge, consists, not in any real intrinsic difference of themselves, but only in the order in which we ourselves contemplate the terms of the same relation.

For, if, looking from the concentric unity of the subject, we consider only the particular and multifarious modifications of Consciousness in excentric relation to the world without, we shall naturally view it as separated into an infinite number of different acts, corresponding to the infinity of its objects, and to the various relations, direct or mediate, in which these may stand connected with the thinking subject. *I see this house, I hear this sound, I feel this pain, I imagine this chimera*, are examples. These constitute the individual facts of Consciousness, and are infinite as their objects. But if these individual facts are considered only in what they possess in common, or in that quality of activity by which several of them are arranged in Consciousness together, these facts, as thus conjoined, then obtain the character of a general fact; and the species of conscious activity which afforded the principle of their classification receives the name of a faculty. *I perceive, I feel, I imagine*, &c., are examples of concrete expressions for the general facts; and *perception, feeling, imagination*, &c., are abstract expressions for the faculties. These facts are, however, only facts of consciousness; and the several faculties are only special forms of the activity of Consciousness in excentric relation to what is different from self.

On the other hand, if, looking from the multifarious and complicated modifications of thought, as determined by the various relations of mind to the external objects of its knowledge, we regard these modifications only in their concentric identity in the unity of the conscious subject, we naturally view these different faculties of knowledge as essentially one, and to this single principle we give the general name of *Consciousness*. But as this distinction between absolute Consciousness and its relative modifications, as subordinate faculties of knowledge, is only a logical and not a real difference, it is evident, on the one hand, that an act of Consciousness is only possible through some particular energy of a subordinate faculty, and on the other, that every simple act of a subordinate faculty is a simple, though relative, energy of Consciousness. Consciousness may therefore be univocally predicated of all our faculties of knowledge, and in relation to all their objects, as it is coextensive with the sphere and determines the boundaries of our knowledge. Thus the propositions, *I feel pain or pleasure, I perceive an external object, I imagine an existence, I remember an occurrence*, &c., are only shorter expressions for the following facts of Consciousness,—I am conscious of an absolute affection of self, which I call pain or pleasure,—I am conscious of something as existing different from self,—I am conscious of a certain modification of mind, not as absolute in itself, but as representing, and therefore relative to, the possible existence of an external something,—I am conscious of a modification of mind, not as absolute in itself, but as representative of the object of a former consciousness.

How Consciousness in general is possible; and how, in particular, the consciousness of self, and the consciousness of something different from self, are possible; in what manner we can have a consciousness of any absolute affection of the thinking subject, and a consciousness of self in representative relation either to an external possibility or to a previous act of consciousness:—all these questions are equally unphilosophical, as they all equally suppose the possibility of a faculty exterior to Consciousness and conversant about its operations. But all philosophy of mind, if it does not wander into the region of hypothesis, must employ Consciousness as the only instrument of observation. Consciousness gives us the existence both of the absolute and of the relative affections of the mind; and it gives all these as facts equally ultimate and inexplicable.*

* * * * * * *

Reid seems to have borrowed his narrow limitation of Consciousness as a special faculty from Hutcheson, (Synopsis

* The preceding dissertation appears to have been left unfinished. The following notes on Reid's doctrine, which were probably intended as materials for its conclusion, have been extracted from the Author's Common-Place Book. —ED.

Metaphysicæ, pars ii. c. 2),* or Malebranche.†

Locke is directly opposed to Reid, making Consciousness the condition of all thought (*Essay*, B. ii. ch. i. § 19, *Works*, i. p. 37): "If they say, the man thinks always, but is not always conscious of it, they may as well say his body is extended without having parts. For it is altogether as intelligible to say that a body is extended without parts, as that anything thinks without being conscious of it, or perceiving that it does so. . . . If they say that a man is always conscious to himself of thinking, I ask how they know it? *Consciousness is the perception of what passes in a man's own mind.* Can another man perceive that I am conscious of anything, when I perceive it not myself? No man's knowledge here can go beyond his experience, &c." So Descartes, &c.‡ But Monboddo agrees with Reid. (*Antient Metaphysics*, B. ii. ch. 2, vol. ii. p. 87.) On the question generally, see *De Vries*, De Ideis Innatis, Sect. iii. p. 26.

"Non sentimus nisi sentiamus nos sentire," say the learned. And Aristotle, *Probl.* sect. xi. § 33—χωρισθεῖσα δὲ αἴσθησις διανοίας καθάπερ ἀναίσθητον πόνον ἔχει, ὥσπερ εἴρηται τό, Νοῦς ὁρᾷ καὶ νοῦς ἀκούει.§ Compare *De Anima*, L. iii. c. 2, texts 136, 137; and there Themistius (p. 88), Philoponus, and the Conimbricenses (p. 370 sq.) Aristotle had no word for Consciousness;‖ but here he shews the absurdity of holding a faculty for the act which is not also of the object. Even the word for *Attention* was first introduced by Philoponus. (*Conimbricenses*, Comm. De Anima, p. 371.)

Aristotle's doctrine as to sense (*De Anima*, l. c.) is well applied by Plotinus to intellect. Enn. ii. L. ix. c. 1. Compare Proclus, Instit. Theol. §§ 83, 168. On Aristotle's intellect conscious of itself, see De Anima, L. iii. c. 4, texts 8, 15, and Conimbricenses, p. 503. Compare Philoponus, In De Anima, Sign. A. iv., ed. Venet., 1535, quoted by Monboddo, Antient Metaphysics, vol. i. p. 136.

On the whole controversy, whether the senses know their own operations, see Conimbricenses, p. 369 sq. Plato (Theætetus*) says that sense feels that it feels, and that it does not feel. See also Alex. Aphrod., De Anima, f. 135.

St Augustin (quoted in *De la Forge*, Traité, &c. Préf. p. xi.) shews that, in the perception of an object, the mind has not only a knowledge of that object, but also of the operation by which it perceives.† See also a long and curious passage in De la Forge. (Préf. p. xiv.)

Strato (*De la Forge*, Préf. p. xxxviii.) of sense. [See Plutarch, De Solert. Animal. c. 3.—Ed.]

Varii, in De Villemandy, Scepticismus Debellatus, pp. 121, 122.

---

* The passage of Hutcheson is as follows:—"Altera percipiendi vis est Sensus quidam internus, aut Conscientia; cujus ope nota sunt ea omnia, quæ in mente geruntur. Novit quisque sensationes suas, judicia, ratiocinia, volitiones, desideria, et consilia: neque hæc mentem, cui insunt, latere possunt. Hac animi vi se novit quisque; et sui habet perceptionem: atque in se et actiones suas, animum convertere potest. Unde et spirituum æque plena potest esse notitia ac corporum: intima latet natura; notæ sunt utriusque affectiones."—Ed.

† For Malebranche, see Recherche, L. iii. P. ii. ch. 7, and Eclaircissement xi. He held that we perceive the affections of our mind directly by consciousness, while we are cognisant of bodies by ideas in God. Hence it may, perhaps, be inferred that we have no direct consciousness of the objects, but only of the acts, of intelligence.—Ed.

‡ Principia, i. 9: "Cogitationis nomine intelligo illa omnia quæ nobis consciis in nobis fiunt, quatenus eorum in nobis conscientia est."—Ed.

§ See *Chauvin*, Lex. Phil. v. Sensatio; and *Clauberg*, Exerc. lxxxvii. § 3

‖ Tennemann (Gesch d. Philosophie, iii. p. 194) notices the want in the Greek language of a word for consciousness, and the inconvenience thereof. See also Gillies, Introduction to Aristotle's Rhetoric, p. 193.

* The reference to the Theætetus is given by the Conimbricenses (In Arist. De Anima, ii. 2.) The passage referred to is probably Theæt. p. 192. Ἀδύνατον ὃ αἰσθάνεταί γε, ἕτερόν τι ὧν αἰσθάνεται οἰηθῆναι εἶναι, καὶ ὃ αἰσθάνεται, ὧν τι μὴ αἰσθάνεται, κ.τ.λ. This passage, however, is not exactly in point. Compare *Lectures on Metaphysics*, vol i. p. 196.—Ed.

† De Libero Arbitrio, L. ii. c. iv.: "Arbitror etiam illud esse manifestum, sensum illum interiorem non ea tantum sentire quæ acceperit a quinque sensibus corporis, sed etiam ipsos ab eo sentiri. . . . Quod si adhuc obscurum est, elucescet, si animadvertas quod, exempli gratia, sat est in uno aliquo sensu, veluti in visu. Namque aperire oculum, et movere aspiciendo ad id quod videre appetit, nullo modo posset, nisi oculo clauso vel non ita moto se id non videre sentiret. Si autem sentit se non videre dum non videt, necesse est etiam sentiat se videre dum videt; quia cum eo appetitu non movet oculum videns, quo movet non videns, indicat se utrumque sentire." Another passage to the same effect is quoted by De la Forge from the spurious work De Spiritu et Anima, c. 32.—Ed.

§ II.—*Conditions and Limitations of Consciousness.*

We are only conscious as conscious of some mode, of such or such a quality or qualities. But to be conscious of such or such a quality, is virtually to affirm that what we are conscious of is *this*, to the negation of *that*. Consciousness, therefore, necessarily supposes a *discrimination*, and consequently a *judgment*. As Hobbes has well expressed it,—"Sentire semper idem et non sentire ad idem recidunt."* The first law of thought — using that word in its widest sense as coextensive with consciousness—is, therefore, what we may call

I. The Law of *Variety* — that we are conscious only as we are conscious of difference. This variety may be either simultaneous or successive. Without denying that we are actually conscious of different phænomena at once, were there no successive variation, or were we unable to compare our actual consciousness with our past, it could hardly be said that we were conscious at all. Another law of thought is therefore

II. The Law of *Succession*—that we are conscious only as we are conscious of a present in contradistinction to a past. But contradistinction supposes an apprehension, comparison, and judgment of that which is distinguished; and consciousness is only of the actual or present. How, therefore, can consciousness apprehend, compare, and judge, what is not actual or present—the past? This would be impossible, were nothing left in the mind of the various modes or movements, of which it is the subject, beyond the actual now of their existence; in other words, were the consciousness, determined by a present external cause, the only cognition of which the mind is capable. But the modes or movements of which we have been conscious do not cease to exist, so soon as we cease to be conscious of their existence; they remain, when out of consciousness, as it were in an obscured or rather a subdormant state; ready, however, to be re-aroused, by the appropriate agency, to that pitch of vivacity which shall reinstate them anew within the sphere of consciousness; nor is there any reason to suppose that a movement once determined in the mental ego is, absolutely considered, ever again utterly abolished. In virtue, however, of this constitution it is that Consciousness is able, in a certain sort, to re-present its past energies in its present, to contrast them with each other, and thus to realise itself. Consciousness thus involves a retentive, a reproductive, and a re-manifestative power; in other words, it supposes in its subject the faculties of Memory, of Suggestion and Reminiscence, and of Imagination—by faculties always understanding no separate operations, but only different relations of the same indivisible activity. Consciousness also is not to be regarded as aught different from the mental modes or movements themselves. It is not to be viewed as an illuminated place, within which objects coming are presented to, and passing beyond are withdrawn from, observation; nor is it to be considered even as an observer—the mental modes as phænomena observed. Consciousness is just the movements themselves, rising above a certain degree of intensity. Consciousness is thus not coextensive with the attributes of mind; for the movements beyond the conscious range are still properties—and effective properties, of the mental ego.

Consciousness, being thus realised only under the laws of *variety* and *succession*, is necessarily astricted to a *ceaseless variation*. But the same condition is also imposed upon it by the disproportion between what we are actually conscious of at any given moment, and what we may potentially be conscious of at successive times.

Consciousness is very limited. It is only a comprehensive word for those mental movements which rise at once above a certain degree of intension; and as the extensive quantity of such movements is always in the inverse ratio of its intensive, that consciousness will be most perfect which is concentrated within the smallest sphere. But while Consciousness is thus of its very nature limited to the very smallest complement of actual cognitions, the sum of our potential cognitions—those which may be recalled from latency into consciousness—is almost infinite. It is, therefore, only by succession—and rapid succession, that the signal disproportion between our intellectual possessions and our capacity of employing them can be diminished.

But, further, the same condition of ceaseless variation is involved in the fact that Consciousness is only realised in a certain degree. But it is a general law, that the protension or continuance of a mental energy is in the inverse ratio of its intension or degree, its degree, as already stated, in the inverse ratio of its extension or complexity. The stronger the exertion, the sooner is lassitude induced; the more

* See above, p. 878 a, n. *.—ED.

vehement the pleasure, the more prompt is the alternation of disgust. Thus the various movements, after rising to the conscious pitch, tend naturally of themselves to a gradual remission, the result of which is their relapse into a state of latent subactivity; while in proportion as they cease to occupy the disposable amount of conscious energy, this is transferred to other movements, which, rising in consequence from latency, maintain unbroken the consecutive series of thought.

But this effect of ceaseless variation is determined not only by the tendency of the movements in consciousness to evacuate their place: it is equally determined by the tendency of the movements out of consciousness to occupy their room.

• • • • • • •

[The preceding fragment, treating of the general conditions under which Consciousness is possible, may be regarded as introductory to the following, which treats of the special characteristics of Consciousness as actually manifested. The transition, however, from the one to the other, is abrupt, and some intermediate remarks would be required to connect them into a whole.—ED.]

1. *Consciousness is the necessary condition of all knowledge—all knowledge is a consciousness; knowledge, e converso, is the necessary condition of all consciousness—all consciousness is a knowledge.* Consciousness and knowledge are, in fact, the same thing considered in different relations, or from different points of view. Knowledge is consciousness viewed in relation to its object; Consciousness is knowledge viewed in relation to its subject. The one signalises that *something is known* (by me); the other signalises that *I know* (something). These different points of view determine, however, a difference in signification.*

2. Consciousness is a more limited term than knowledge. For Knowledge is a knowledge, 1°, either immediate or mediate; 2°, either potential or actual: whereas Consciousness is a knowledge only immediate, and only actual. It may be said *an object is known*, though only known or knowable in a representation, and though not now before the mind either in itself or in its representation. But it cannot be said that *I am conscious of an object*, unless that object be immediately and actually known. But though the term consciousness is thus less extensive than the term knowledge, the truth of the proposition—that all knowledge supposes consciousness—is not invalidated. For all knowledge of a mediate or represented object exists only in and through the consciousness of an immediate object or representation; and a potential knowledge is only a knowledge in so far as it is, or may be, realised in an actual. In asking, therefore, what are the conditions of knowledge, we simplify the problem in asking only what are the conditions of consciousness; and from what has been now said, the four first or most general limitations are already manifest. These, however, it may be proper to restate articulately in their order.*

3. The *first* limitation of Consciousness is—*that it is a knowledge.* For whether I be conscious—that I know,—that I feel a pain or pleasure—or that I will or desire; in all these different classes of the mental phænomena there is one common and essential quality. They exist only as they are *known.*

4. The *second* limitation of Consciousness is—*that it is a knowledge known by me*—by an Ego, a Self, a Subject of knowledge.

5. The *third* limitation of Consciousness is—*that it is an immediate not a mediate knowledge.*

6. The *fourth* limitation of Consciousness is—*that it is an actual not a potential knowledge.*

7. The *fifth* condition of Consciousness is—*that it is an apprehension.* For to know we must know something; and immediately and actually to know anything is to know it as now and here existing, that is, to apprehend it.

8. The *sixth* condition of Consciousness is—*that it is a discrimination*, and supposes therefore plurality and difference. For we cannot apprehend a thing unless we distinguish the apprehending subject from the apprehended object.—I find this condition explicitly taken in the Wolfian School. *Wolf*, Vernunftige Gedanken, §§ 728, 733; Psychologia Rationalis, § 10-13;—*Bilfinger*, Dilucidationes, §§ 242, 269;—*Thummig*, Psychol. Rat. § 171;—*Canz*, Psychol. § 31;—*Baumgarten*, Log. § 3.

9. The *seventh* condition of Consciousness is—*that it is a judgment.* For we cannot apprehend a thing, without, *pro tanto*, affirming it to exist. Though this condition be virtually contained in the preced-

* See *Lectures on Metaphysics*, vol. i. p 193.—ED.

* With these limitations of Consciousness, compare *Lectures on Metaphysics*, vol. i. p. 201 sq.—ED.

ing, Reid has the merit of being, among modern philosophers, the first who trenched upon a recognition of this truth. Of Consciousness (to him a special faculty of self-consciousness), Sensation, Perception, and Memory, he once and again says, that judgment is involved in, or necessarily accompanies, their acts (Inq. 106 b, 107 a; I. P. 414 b; alibi); but this again he explicitly denies in regard to the operation of the faculty, which he variously denominates Conception, Imagination, and Simple Apprehension. (I. P. 223 a, 243 a, 375 a, 414 a b.) This limitation is incorrect; though it is easy to see how Reid, contemplating only a judgment affirmative of objective or real existence, was led to overlook the judgment affirmative of subjective or ideal existence in which all consciousness is realised.

10. The *eighth* condition of Consciousness is — *that whatever is thought is thought under the attribute of existence;* existence being a notion *a priori* or native to the mind, and the primary act of consciousness an existential judgment. For if we are only conscious as we apprehend an object, and only apprehend it as we affirm it to exist, existence must be attributed to the object by the mind. But such could not be done unless this predicate were a notion which had a virtual pre-existence in the mind. For suppose it derived from, and not merely elicited on the occasion of, experience; suppose, in a word, with Locke, "that existence is an idea [not native but] suggested to the understanding by every object without, and every idea within;"* in this case it must perforce be admitted that what suggests the notion of existence is itself an object of consciousness; for what we are not conscious of, that can suggest nothing. But where is the object of consciousness not already thought under the very attribute which this doctrine would maintain it originally to suggest? Till this question be answered—till the possibility of its being answered can be even conceived, we may safely reject the hypothesis that would contingently evolve the notion of existence out of an antecedent knowledge, instead of making the notion of existence the condition which all knowledge necessarily supposes. *Ens*, accordingly, has been viewed as the *primum cognitum* by a large proportion, if not the majority of philosophers, more or less prominently, on stronger or on weaker grounds; as by Aristotle, Alexander, Themistius, Simplicius implicitly, and explicitly by Avicenna, Averroes, Albertus Magnus, St Thomas with the whole Thomist school, and many other of the principal Schoolmen and Aristotelians. In more recent ages, without enumerating a long list of names, I may state in general that no philosopher has admitted the doctrine of cognitions *a priori*, who has been found to disallow the pre-eminent claims to this distinction which the notion of existence may prefer. Among contemporary metaphysicians, the Abbate Rosmini merits commemoration; who has, with great ingenuity and perseverance, endeavoured to develop this notion into a systematic, and in many respects, an original, philosophy of mind. This attempt would, I am confident, have been more successful, had it taken the following lower limitation of consciousness as its point of departure.

11. The *ninth* limitation of Consciousness is—*that while only realised in the recognition of existence, it is only realised in the recognition of the existent as conditioned;* and even this requires a still further limitation, for we are conscious of the conditioned itself only as not unconditionally conditioned. Of the unconditioned, of the absolute or the infinite, we have no cognition, no conception,—in a word, no consciousness; and these, in themselves incognisable and inconceivable, we can talk about only as negations of what is positively cognisable and conceivable—the conditioned in its various phases of the relative, the finite, &c. The development of this limitation would constitute a philosophy of the Conditioned in direct antithesis to the philosophy of the Absolute, maintained under diverse forms by many of the profoundest thinkers of the last half-century, among whom Fichte, Schelling, Hegel, and my illustrious friend M. Cousin, are the most distinguished. This I may hereafter attempt; not certainly presuming to mete my own strength with that of such opponents, but confiding solely in the strength of the cause itself which I maintain. Of the nature of the present limitation, and of the polemical relations of a philosophy of the unconditioned, some indications may be found in an article by me, entitled, "The Philosophy of the Absolute, &c.," in immediate reference to M. Cousin, in the *Edinburgh Review*, vol. L. p. 194 sq.;* to be found also in Cross's "Selections," and in the "Fragmens Philosophiques, &c.," trans-

* Essay, B. ii. ch. 7. § 7.

* Reprinted in *Discussions*, p. 1 sq.—Ed.

lated by M. Peisse, whose preface to the volume is on this subject especially worthy of attention. At present I can only enounce the principle to shew its place in an evolution of the conditions of Consciousness; and, where ample illustrations would be requisite, I can with difficulty afford room for a few scattered hints in regard to one or two of its [manifold applications.]

The principle, that we are conscious only of the conditioned, and only of the conditionally conditioned, is valuable as an important truth: it is likewise valuable as affording a genesis of some of the most momentous, and at the same time most contested, phænomena of mind. For example, in the principle of the Conditioned, the two great principles, the law of Substance and Accident, and the law of Cause and Effect, find their origin and explanation. They are no longer to be regarded as ultimate data of intelligence; they appear now as merely particular cases, merely special applications, of this higher principle. Take the former—the law of Substance. I am aware of a phænomenon—a phænomenon be it of mind or of matter; that is, I am aware of a certain relative, consequently a conditioned, existence. This existence is only known, and only knowable, as in relation. Mind and matter exist for us only as they are known by us; and they are so known only as they have certain qualities relative to certain faculties of knowledge in us, and we certain faculties of knowledge relative to certain qualities in them. All our knowledge of mind and matter is thus relative, that is, conditioned; and so far in conformity with the principle that we are conscious only of existence as conditioned. But further;—I am aware of a certain phænomenon, be it of mind or matter. This phænomenon,—a manifestation of what exists for me only as known by me, and of what as known by me exists only in relativity to my faculties,—how is it that I cannot even conceive it to exist solely in the relativity in which solely it is known, that I cannot suppose it to be a mere phænomenon, an appearance of nothing but itself as appearing, but am compelled by a necessity of my nature to think that out of this relativity it has an absolute or irrelative existence—*i. e.*, an existence, as absolute or irrelative, unknown, and incomprehensible? why, in short, am I constrained to suppose that it is the known phænomenon of an unknown Substance? Philosophers answer and say—it is an ultimate law of mind. I answer and say—it is a particular case of the general law which bears that not only the unconditioned simply, but even the unconditioned of the conditioned, is unthinkable. Take an object; strip it by abstraction of all its qualities, of all its phænomena, of all its relativities; reduce it to a mere unconditioned, irrelative, absolute entity, a mere substance; and now try to think this substance. You cannot. For either in your attempt to think you clothe it again with qualities, and thus think it as a conditioned; or you find that it cannot be thought,—except as a negation of the thinkable. This is an instance of the unconditioned simply, and an ordinary application of the law.

Take now of the same object a quality or phænomenon. A phænomenon is a relative — ergo, a conditioned — ergo, a thinkable. But try to think this relative as absolutely relative, this conditioned as unconditionally conditioned, this phænomenon as a phænomenon and nothing more. You cannot; for either you do not realise it in thought at all, or you suppose it to be the phænomenon of something that does not appear; you give it a basis out of itself; you think it not as the absolutely, but as the relatively relative; not as the unconditionally, but as the conditionally conditioned; in other words, you conceive it as the Accident of a Subject or Substance. This is an instance of the Conditioned, and constitutes the special case, the particular law, of Substance and Phænomenon. The law of Cause and Effect is another subordinate application of the same general principle; but in connection with another limitation of Consciousness, which it is necessary [to state before proceeding.] *

* * * * * * *

[12. The *tenth* limitation of Consciousness is that of *Time.*] This is the necessary condition of every conscious act; thought is only realised to us as in succession, and succession is only conceived by us under the concept of Time. Existence, and existence in Time, is thus an elementary form of our intelligence. But we do not conceive existence in time absolutely or infinitely,—we conceive it only as conditioned in time; and Existence conditioned in Time expresses, at once and in relation, the three categories of thought, which afford us in combination

* The Author's MS. breaks off here. What follows has been supplied, partly from his *Lectures on Metaphysics*, vol. ii. p. 390, and partly from his *Discussions*, p. 618.—Ed.

the principle of Causality. What does *existence* [*conditioned or*] *relative in time* imply? It implies, 1°, that we are unable to realise in thought: on the one pole of the irrelative, either an *absolute* commencement, or an *absolute* termination of time; as on the other, either an *infinite* non-commencement, or an *infinite* non-termination of time. It implies, 2°, That we can think, neither, on the one pole, an *absolute* minimum, nor, on the other, an *infinite* divisibility of time. Yet these constitute two pairs of contradictory propositions; which, if our intelligence is not all a lie, cannot both be true, whilst, at the same time, either the one or the other necessarily must. But, as *not relatives*, they are not cogitables.

Now the phenomenon of Causality seems nothing more than a corollary of the law of the Conditioned, in its application to a thing thought under the form or mental category of *Existence Relative in Time*. We cannot know, we cannot think a thing, except under the attribute of *Existence*; we cannot know or think a thing to exist, except as *in Time*; and we cannot know or think a thing to exist in Time, and think it *absolutely to commence or terminate*.* Now this at once imposes on us the judgment of causality. Unable positively to think an absolute commencement, our impotence to this drives us backwards on the notion of *Cause*; unable positively to think an absolute termination, our impotence to this drives us forwards on the notion of *Effect*. More articulately thus:—An object is given us, either by our presentative, or by our representative, faculty. As given, we cannot but think it Existent, and existent in Time. But to say, that we cannot but think it to exist, is to say, that we are unable to think it non-existent,—to think it away,—to annihilate it in thought. And this we cannot do. We may turn away from it; we may engross our attention with other objects; we may, consequently, exclude it from our thought. That we need not think a thing is certain; but thinking it, it is equally certain that we cannot think it not to exist. So much will be at once admitted of the present; but it may probably be denied of the past and future. Yet if we make the experiment, we shall find the mental annihilation of an object equally impossible under time past, and present, and future. To obviate, however, misapprehension, a very simple observation may be proper. In saying that it is impossible to annihilate an object in thought, in other words, to conceive as non-existent, what had been conceived as existent,—it is of course not meant, that it is impossible to imagine the object wholly changed in form. We can represent to ourselves the elements of which it is composed, divided, dissipated, modified in any way; we can imagine anything of it, short of annihilation. But the complement, the quantum, of existence, thought as constituent of an object,—*that* we cannot represent to ourselves, either as increased, without abstraction from other entities, or as diminished, without annexation to them. In short, we are unable to construe it in thought, that there can be an atom absolutely added to, or absolutely taken away from, existence in general. Let us make the experiment. Let us form to ourselves a concept—an image of the universe. Now, we are unable to think, that the quantity of existence, of which the universe is the conceived sum, can either be amplified or diminished. We are able to conceive, indeed, the creation of a world; this in fact as easily as the creation of an atom. But what is our thought of creation? It is not a thought of the mere springing of nothing into something. On the contrary, creation is conceived, and is by us conceivable, only as the evolution of existence from possibility into actuality, by the fiat of the Deity.* Let us place ourselves in imagination at its very crisis. Now, can we construe it to thought, that, the moment after the universe flashed into material reality, into manifested being, there was a larger complement of existence in the universe and its author together than, the moment before, there subsisted in the Deity alone? This we are unable to imagine. And what is true of our concept of creation, holds of our

* How easily the difficulty from the *simultaneity* of Cause and Effect, or rather from the identity of Causation and Effectuation, is solved on this theory, and on this theory alone, it would be out of bounds here to explain. I may notice, however, that the whole difficulty is developed by Aenesidemus, in Sextus Empiricus; and that those who have recognised it in modern times, seem to have been wholly unaware of the most ingenious speculation of the ancient sceptic.

* The creation *A Nihilo* means only: that the universe, when created, was not merely put into form, an original chaos, or complement of brute matter, having preceded a plastic energy of intelligence; but, that the universe was called into actuality from potential existence by the Divine fiat. The Divine fiat, therefore, was the proximate cause of the creation; and the Deity containing the cause, contained, potentially, the effect.

concept of annihilation. We can think no real annihilation,—no absolute sinking of something into nothing. But, as creation is cogitable by us, only as a putting forth of Divine power, so is annihilation by us only conceivable, as a withdrawal of that same power. All that is now *actually* existent in the universe, this we think and must think, as having, prior to creation, *virtually* existed in the creator; and in imagining the universe to be annihilated, we can only conceive this, as the retractation by the Deity of an overt energy into latent power.—In short, it is impossible for the human mind to think what it thinks existent, lapsing into absolute non-existence, either in time past or in time future.

Our inability to think, what we have once conceived existent *in Time*, as in time becoming non-existent, corresponds with our inability to think, what we have conceived existent *in Space*, as in space becoming non-existent. We cannot realise it to thought, that a thing should be extruded, either from the one quantity or from the other. Hence, under extension, the law of *Ultimate Incompressibility*; under protension, the law of *Cause and Effect*.

I have hitherto spoken only of one inconceivable pole of the conditioned, in its application to existence in time,—of the *absolute* extreme, as absolute commencement and absolute termination. The counter or *infinite* extreme, as infinite regress or non-commencement, and infinite progress or non-termination, is equally unthinkable. With this latter we have, however, at present nothing to do. Indeed, as not obtrusive, the Infinite figures far less in the theatre of mind, and exerts a far inferior influence in the modification of thought, than the Absolute. It is, in fact, both distant and delitescent; and in place of meeting us at every turn, it requires some exertion on our part to seek it out. It is the former and more obtrusive extreme,—it is the Absolute alone which constitutes and explains the mental manifestation of the causal judgment. An object is presented to our observation which has phænomenally begun to be. But we cannot construe it to thought, that the object, that is, *this determinate complement of existence*, had really no being at any past moment; because, in that case, once thinking it as existent, we should again think it as non-existent, which is for us impossible. What then can we—must we do? That the phænomenon presented to us, did, *as a phænomenon*, begin to be, — this we know by experience; but that the elements, the constituents of its existence only began, when the phænomenon which they make up came into manifested being,—this we are wholly unable to think. In these circumstances how do we proceed? There is for us only one possible way. We are compelled to believe, that the object, (that is the certain *quale* and *quantum* of being, whose *phænomenal* rise into existence we have witnessed,) did *really* exist, prior to this rise, under other forms; (and by *form*, be it observed, I mean any mode of existence, conceivable by us or not.) But to say, that a thing previously existed under different forms, is only to say, in other words, that *a thing had causes*. (It would be here out of place, to refute the error of philosophers, in supposing that anything can have a *single* cause;—meaning always by a cause that without which the effect would not have been. I speak of course only of second causes, for of the Divine causation we can pretend to no conception.)

I must, however, now cursorily observe, that nothing can be more erroneous in itself, or in its consequences more fertile in delusion, than the common doctrine, that the causal judgment is elicited, only when we apprehend objects in consecution, and uniform consecution. No doubt, the observation of such succession prompts and enables us to assign particular causes to particular effects. But this assignation ought to be carefully distinguished from the judgment of causality, absolutely. This consists, not in the empirical and contingent attribution of this phænomenon, as cause, to that phænomenon, as effect; but in the *universal necessity* of which we are conscious, to think causes for every event, whether that event stand isolated by itself, and be by us referable to no other, or whether it be one in a series of successive phænomena, which, as it were, spontaneously arrange themselves under the relation of effect and cause. Of no phænomenon, as observed, need we think *the* cause; but of every phænomenon must we think *a* cause. The former we *may* learn, through a process of induction and generalisation; the latter we *must* always and at once admit, constrained by the Condition of Relativity. On this, not sunken, rock, Dr Brown and others have been shipwrecked.*

* The above extracts, being the exposition of the Author's theory of causation, have been supplied as necessary to the completion of the present Note. For some further remarks in support of the theory as compared with others, see *Discussions*, p. 672, and *Lectures on Metaphysics*, vol ii. p. 409.—Ed.

[The following references from the Author's Common-Place Book relate to the second portion of the present Note.—Ed.]

I.—*On the conditions of Consciousness.*

Plotinus (Enn. vi. L. vii. c. 39) states admirably the conditions of knowledge, which he makes five in number: 1°, Change; 2°, Diversity; 3°, [Comparison; 4°, Relation; 5°, Multiplicity.] * [The passage is as follows: — Διὸ καὶ ὀρθῶς ἑτερότητα λαμβάνει, ὅπου νοῦς καὶ οὐσία. Δεῖ γὰρ τὸν νοῦν ἀεὶ ἑτερότητα καὶ ταὐτότητα λαμβάνειν, εἴπερ νοήσει· ἑαυτόν τε γὰρ οὐ διακρινεῖ ἀπὸ τοῦ νοητοῦ, τῇ πρὸς αὐτὸ ἑτέρου σχέσει, τά τε πάντα οὐ θεωρήσει, μηδεμιᾶς ἑτερότητος γενομένης, εἰς τὸ πάντα εἶναι· οὐδὲ γὰρ ἂν οὐδὲ δύο. Ἔπειτα εἰ νοήσει οὐ δήπου ἑαυτὸν μόνον νοήσει, εἴπερ ὅλως νοήσει· διὰ τί γὰρ οὐχ ἅπαντα; ἢ ἀδυνατήσει; ὅλως δὲ οὐχ ἁπλοῦς γίνεται νοῶν ἑαυτόν, ἀλλὰ δεῖ τὴν νόησιν τὴν περὶ αὐτοῦ ἑτέρου εἶναι, εἴ τι ὅλως δύναται νοεῖν αὐτό· ἐλέγομεν δὲ, ὅτι οὐ νόησις τοῦτο, εἰ δὴ ἄλλον αὐτὸν ἐθέλει ἰδεῖν † νοήσας δὲ αὐτὸς, πολὺς γίνεται, νοητὸς, νοῶν, κινούμενος, καὶ ὅσα ἄλλα προσήκει νῷ. Πρὸς δὲ ταύταις κἀκεῖνο ὁρᾶν προσήκει, ὅπερ εἴρηται ἤδη ἐν ἄλλοις, ὡς ἑκάστη νόησις, εἴπερ νόησις ἔσται, ποικίλον τι δεῖ εἶναι· τὸ δὲ ἁπλοῦν καὶ τὸ αὐτὸ πᾶν οἷον κίνημα, εἰ τοιοῦτον εἴη οἷον ἐπαφή, οὐδὲν νοερὸν ἔχει. Τί οὖν; οὔτε τὰ ἄλλα οὔτε αὐτὸν εἰδήσει, ἀλλὰ σεμνὸν ἑστήξεται; τὰ μὲν οὖν ἄλλα ὕστερα αὐτοῦ, καὶ ἦν πρὸ αὐτῶν ὃ ἦν, κ. τ. λ.]

So Jordanus Brunus (De Imaginum Signorum et Idearum Compositione, Dedicatio, p. iv.): 'Intelligere nostrum (id est, operationes nostri intellectus) aut est phantasia, aut non sine phantasia. Rursum, non intelligimus nisi phantasmata speculemur. Hoc est quod non in simplicitate quadam, statu, et unitate, sed in compositione, collatione, terminorum pluralitate, mediante discursu atque reflexione, comprehendimus.'

Cicero, De Natura Deorum, L. i. c. 29: ['Si una omnium (sc. Deorum) facies est, florere in cœlo Academiam necesse est. Si enim nihil inter deum et deum differt, nulla est apud deos cognitio, nulla perceptio.']

Burthogge, Essay upon Reason and the Nature of Spirits (London, 1694), pp. 4, 5: ['Consciousness seems to me to arise, ordinarily, from the distinction and difference that is in Conceptions; for, should any person have his eye perpetually tied to one object, without ever closing of, or turning it to another, he would no more be sensible that he saw that object, or know any more what it was to see, than if he had been blind from his birth. For since consciousness of seeing is nothing but a perceiving by the eye, that one is affected, or otherwise affected than he was, with the appearance of Light or Colour; if a person had never seen but one thing, and never but seen it, he could have no perceivance (that) he is so affected, that is, he could not be sensible or conscious (that) he did see. . . . I conclude, that as difference of conception arises from different affections of the faculties by objects, so Consciousness, or Sense of Conception, arises from the difference of Conceptions, &c.']

See also, to the same effect, Brown's Philosophy of the Human Mind, Lect. xi. p 66 (ed. 1830).

II. *On acts of mind beyond the sphere of Consciousness.**

Are there acts of mind beyond the sphere of consciousness?

Affirmative: Leibnitz, Nouv. Ess., Avant-propos, p. 8-9, and L. ii. cc. 1, 2, p. 69-72 (ed. Raspe); Monad. §§ 14, 20-23; Princ. de la Nature et de la Grace, § 4; alibi;—*Bilfinger*, De Harmonia Præstabilita, Sect. vi. § 68, pp. 182, 183 (3d edition); — *Canz*, Philosophia Wolfiana, Psych. L. i. § 36 (ed. 1737); Med. Phil. § 830 (Tubingae, 1750);—*Feuerlin*, Phil. Saetze von klaren und dunkeln Begriffen, B. ii. Th. i. pp. 39, 69 sq.;—*Kames*, Essays, &c., P. ii. Ess. iv., On Matter and Spirit, p. 289 to end (3d edition);—*Schaubert*, Diss. de Idearum in Anima Conservatione (Altorfii Noricorum, 1744), omnino;—*Platner*, Phil. Aph., i. p. 70;—*Tetens*, Phil. Versuche, i. p. 265, quodammodo;—*Beausobre*, Ueber die Natur und ueber die Nothwendigkeit dunkler Ideen (in Hissmann's 'Magazin fuer die Philo-

* It is evident that the Author intended to enumerate the five conditions given in the summary of Ficinus, from which the last three have been supplied. It may be questioned, however, whether these can be fairly inferred from the text of Plotinus.—Ed.

† So Creuzer. Ficinus seems to have read εἰ μὴ ὡς ἄλλον αὐτὸν ἐθέλοι ἰδεῖν. He renders, "Diximus autem hoc ipsum non esse intelligentiam, nisi se contueatur ut alium."—Ed.

* See above, pp. 962, 963. This question has been partly discussed in the Author's *Lectures on Metaphysics*, Lectt. xviii. xix. It is probable that he contemplated a fuller treatment in the present work, for which the following references would have served as materials.—Ed.

sophie und ihre Geschichte,' v. p. 145 sq.);—*Sulzer*, Verm. Schriften, i. pp. 99 sq., 109 (ed. 1808);—*Boerhaave*, De Morb. Nerv. t. ii. p. 860 sq.;—*Maass*, Versuch, &c., § 24, p. 65 sq. (ed. 1797);—*Kant*, Anthrop., § 5;—*Fries*, N. Kritik, i. §§ 23, 30; Anthrop., § 24, ed. 1820 (§ 20, ed. 1837);—*Jacob*, Erkl. des Grundr. der Emp. Psych., § 49;—*Schwab*, Ueb. d. dunkeln Vorstellungen (Stuttgart, 1813);—*Meiners*, Untersuchungen, &c., i. pp. 56, 57; —*Graevell*, Der Mensch, pp. 73, 135;—*Schulze*, Phil. Wissenschaften, i. p. 16-17; Anthropologie, § 61;—*Denzinger*, Instit. Log. § 260, t. i. p. 226 (ed. 1824);—*Beneke*, Lehrb. d. Psych., § 96 sq. p. 72 (ed. 1833); Psych. Skizzen, i. p. 353-360;—*Hibbert*, Sketches of the Philosophy of Apparitions, P. iv. ch. 5, p. 284 sq. (2d edition); —*Cardaillac*, Etudes Element. de Phil., t. ii. p. 124 sq. (See *Damiron*, Ess. sur l'Hist. de Phil., Supplément, p. 460 sq.);—*H. Schmid*, Versuch, &c., pp. 23, 232 sq.; *Damiron*, Cours, &c., i. p. 190 (ed. 1834); *Géruzez*, N. Cours de Phil., p. 67;—*Biunde*, Versuch, &c., i. p. 345 sq.;—*Reinhold*, Theorie d. mensch. Erkenntniss u. Metaph., i. p. 279 sq.

Negative: *Locke*, Essay, B. ii. ch. i. § 10; *Condillac*, Sur l'Orig. des Connoiss. Hum., Sect. ii. c. 1. § 4-13 (On him see Merian in Hissmann's 'Magazin,' t. vi. p. 199);—*Merian*, Ueber die Apperzeption (Hissmann's 'Magazin,' i. p. 156 sq.);—*Tiedemann*, Untersuchungen, i. p. 40 sq.; Psychologie (1804), p. 28-29;—*Galluppi*, Elementi di Filosofia, i. § 105 (ed. 1837); —*Stewart*, Elements, [Part i. ch. ii.—Coll. Works, vol. ii. p. 120 sq.]

On the question generally, see the following authorities, in addition to those above referred to. *Walch*, Lexikon, i. p. 2034-5;—*Caesar*, De Animi et Obscurarum Idearum Natura (Lipsiae, 1789) omnino;—*Ancillon*, Mélanges, t. i. p. 40-41;—*Hennings*, Von Geistern und Geistersehern (Leipzig, 1780) p. 3-5;—*Feuerbach*, Darstellung Entwicklung und Kritik der Leibnitz'schen Philosophie, §§ 6, 7, p. 54 sq.

On Obscure Ideas before Leibnitz, see *Feuerbach*, Darstellung, &c., Anmerk., pp. 217, 224, ed. 1837. [Feuerbach refers to the Pythagorean saying, *πᾶν γὰρ τὸ φαινόμενον ἐξ ἀφανῶν ὀφείλει συνίστασθαι . . . . ὡς γὰρ τὰ τῆς λέξεως στοιχεῖα οὐκ εἰσὶ λέξεις, οὕτω καὶ τὰ τῶν σωμάτων στοιχεῖα οὐκ ἔστι σώματα* (v. *Sext. Emp.*, Adv. Phys. L. ii. §§ 250, 253, pp. 674, 675, ed. 1718), and to Cudworth's Dissertation on the Plastic Nature, Intell. Syst. B. i. ch. iii. sect. 37, subs. 17. 'It is certain that our human souls themselves are not always conscious of whatever they have in them. . . . . We have all experience of our doing many animal actions non-attendingly, which we reflect upon afterwards; as also that we often continue a long series of bodily motions by a mere virtual intention of our minds, and as it were by half a cogitation.'—Ed.] Arnauld (Oeuvres, t. xl. p. 173) attacks the hypothesis of thoughts of which we are not conscious, as held by *Malebranche*. That the Stahlians held obscure perceptions, see Camerarius, De Unione An. cum Corp., in Bilfinger, De Harm. Praestab., p. 273.

That Descartes denied Obscure Ideas, see *Leibnitz*, Principia Philosophiae, (Monadologie) §§ 14, 20-23, and *Cans*, Psychologia, p. 320. Compare *Descartes* himself, Resp. ad Medit. iv. p. 158 (ed. 1658):—'Quod autem nihil in mente, quatenus est res cogitans, esse possit, cujus non sit conscia, per se notum mihi videtur, quia nihil in illa sic spectata esse intelligimus quod non sit cogitatio, vel a cogitatione dependens, alioqui enim ad mentem, quatenus est res cogitans, non pertineret; nec ulla potest in nobis esse cogitatio, cujus, eodem illo momento quo in nobis est, conscii non simus. Quamobrem non dubito quin mens, statim atque infantis corpore infusa est, incipiat cogitare, simulque sibi suae cogitationis conscia sit, etsi postea ejus rei non recordetur, quia species istarum cogitationum memoriae non inhaerent.'

NOTE I.

ON THE HISTORY OF THE TERMS

CONSCIOUSNESS, ATTENTION, AND REFLECTION.

---

§ I.—*Extracts explanatory of Sir W. Hamilton's view of the distinction between Consciousness, Attention, and Reflection, with special reference to the opinions of Reid and Stewart.*

§ II.—*Historical Notices of the use of the terms Consciousness, Attention, and Reflection.*

[References.—From I. P. 232 a, 239 b, 346 b, 347 b; from Supplementary Dissertations, 756 b, 775 b.]

[*N.B.*—From the reference at p. 231 b, it appears that the Author had originally intended to include the history of Consciousness in Note H. Subsequently, however, he seems to have transferred it to Note I.—Ed.]

[The materials collected for this Note comprise only a few historical extracts and references, which are given below, under § II. In relation to these, it is important that the reader should be aware of the Author's critical opinion on the distinction indicated by the above terms, as it may be gathered from previous publications. Extracts for this purpose have accordingly been prefixed, as § I.—Ed.]

§ I.—*Extracts explanatory of Sir W. Hamilton's view of the distinction between Consciousness, Attention, and Reflection, with special reference to the opinions of Reid and Stewart.*

(1.) From *Lectures on Metaphysics*, vol. I. pp. 232, 233.

"Mr Stewart seems inadvertently to have misrepresented the opinion of Dr Reid in regard to the meaning and difference of Attention and Reflection. Reid either employs these terms as synonymous expressions, or he distinguishes them only by making attention relative to the consciousness and perception of the present; reflection, to the memory of the past.* . . . . Mr Stewart, in the chapter on Attention in the first volume of his *Elements*,† says, 'Some important observations on the subject of attention occur in different parts of Dr Reid's writings; particularly in his *Essays on the Intellectual Powers of Man*, p. 62, and his *Essays on the Active Powers of Man*, p. 78 *et seq.*‡ To this ingenious author we are indebted for the remark, that attention to things external is properly called *observation*; and attention to the subjects of our consciousness, *reflection*.'" §

---

* For instances of this use of the terms in Reid, Sir. W. Hamilton refers to *Intellectual Powers*, Essay ii. ch. 5, and Essay vi. ch. I. (See above, pp. 258, 420.) The latter of these passages seems to show that the two terms are used by Reid as convertible. The same conclusion may be inferred from a passage in the *Active Powers*, Essay iii. ch. 3, p. 537. The distinction noticed by Stewart is, however, accepted by Sir W. Hamilton, though not as Reid's.—Ed.

† *Collected Works*, vol. ii. pp. 122, 123.

‡ Pp. 246, 537 of the present edition.—Ed.

§ This distinction has been attempted by others. See *Keckermann*, Syst. Phys., L. iv. c. 5. (Opera, t. i. p. 1612); *Goclenius*, Lex. Phil. (Lat.) v. Reflexus; *Maine de Biran* [Oeuvres Philosophiques, tome iv. p. 394]. On the other hand, see *Wolf*,

(2.) From *Lectures on Metaphysics*, vol. i. pp. 236, 237.

"Taking, however, Attention and Reflection for acts of the same faculty, and supposing, with Mr Stewart, that reflection is properly attention directed to the phænomena of mind—observation, attention directed to the phænomena of matter; the main question comes to be considered, Is attention a faculty different from consciousness, as Reid and Stewart maintain?* . . . . Dr Reid has rightly said that attention is a voluntary act. This remark might have led him to the observation, that attention is not a separate faculty, or a faculty of intelligence at all, but merely an act of will or desire, subordinate to a certain law of intelligence. This law is, that the greater the number of objects to which our consciousness is simultaneously extended, the smaller is the intensity with which it is able to consider each, and consequently the less vivid and distinct will be the information it obtains of the several objects.† This law is expressed in the old adage,

'Pluribus intentus minor est ad singula sensus.'

Such being the law, it follows that, when our interest in any particular object is excited, and when we wish to obtain all the knowledge concerning it in our power, it behoves us to limit our consideration to that object, to the exclusion of others. This is done by an act of volition or desire, which is called *attention*. But to view attention as a special act of intelligence, and to distinguish it from consciousness, is utterly inept. Consciousness may be compared to a telescope, attention to the pulling out or in of the tubes in accommodating the focus to the object; and we might, with equal justice, distinguish, in the eye, the adjustment of the pupil from the general organ of vision, as, in the mind, distinguish attention from consciousness as separate faculties. Not, however, that they are to be accounted the same. Attention is consciousness and something more. It is consciousness voluntarily applied, under its law of limitations, to some determinate object; it is consciousness concentrated."

(3.) From *Lectures on Metaphysics*, vol. i. pp. 247, 248.

"I think Reid and Stewart incorrect in asserting that attention is only a voluntary act, meaning by the expression *voluntary*, an act of free will. I am far from maintaining, as Brown and others do, that all will is desire; but still I am persuaded that we are frequently determined to an act of attention, as to many other acts, independently of our free and deliberate volition. Nor is it, I conceive, possible to hold that, though immediately determined to an act of attention by desire, it is only by the permission of our will that this is done; consequently, that every act of attention is still under the control of our volition. This I cannot maintain. Let us take an example:—When occupied with other matters, a person may speak to us, or the clock may strike, without our having any consciousness of the sound; but it is wholly impossible for us to remain in this state of unconsciousness intentionally and with will. We cannot determinately refuse to hear by voluntarily withholding our attention; and we can no more open our eyes, and, by an act of will, avert our mind from all perception of sight, than we can, by an act of will, cease to live. We may close our ears or shut our eyes, as we may commit suicide; but we cannot, with our organs unobstructed, wholly refuse our attention at will. It, therefore, appears to me the more correct doctrine to hold that there is no consciousness without attention,—without concentration, but that attention is of three degrees or kinds. The first, a mere vital and irresistible act; the second, an act determined by desire, which, though involuntary, may be resisted by our will; the third, an act determined by a deliberate volition. An act of attention,—that is, an act of concentration,—seems thus necessary to every exertion of consciousness, as a certain contraction of the pupil is requisite to every exercise of vision. We have formerly noticed, that discrimination is a condition of consciousness; and a discrimination is only possible by a concentrative act, or act of attention. This, however, which corresponds to the lowest degree,—to the mere vital or automatic act of attention, has been refused the name; and *attention*, in contradistinction to this mere automatic contraction, given to the two other degrees, of which, however, Reid only recognises the third.

"Attention, then, is to consciousness, what the contraction of the pupil is to sight; or to the eye of the mind, what the

---

Psych. Emp., § 257; Caus, Medit., § 841 (who makes Reflection twofold—external and internal); *Destutt Tracy*, Elémens d'Idéologie, t. i. pp. 61, 234, 443; *Ancillon*, Essais Philos., t. ii. p. 184.

* For Reid, see above, p. 239. For Stewart, see *Collected Works*, vol. ii. p. 134.—Ed.

† Cf. Steeb, Ueber den Menschen, ii. 673; Fries, Anthropologie, i. 83; and Schulze, Ueber die menschliche Erkenntniss, p. 65.

microscope or telescope is to the bodily eye. The faculty of attention is not, therefore, a special faculty, but merely consciousness acting under the law of limitation to which it is subjected. But, whatever be its relations to the special faculties, attention doubles all their efficiency, and affords them a power of which they would otherwise be destitute. It is, in fact, as we are at present constituted, the primary condition of their activity."

[The following translation from the Commentary of Philoponus on the *De Anima*, (L. iii. c. 2,) has been found among the Author's papers. This passage is noticed in *Discussions*, p. 51, *Lectures on Metaphysics*, i. p. 201, as "the first indication in the history of philosophy, of that false analysis which has raised Attention into a separate faculty."—ED.]

"But the more recent interpreters, standing not in awe of the frown of Alexander, not listening to Plutarchus, and even repelling Aristotle himself, have devised a new interpretation. They say that it is the function of the attentive part (τοῦ προσεκτικοῦ μέρους) of the rational soul to take cognisance of the energies of sense. For, according to them, the rational soul not only comprehends the faculties of intelligence (νοῦς), thought (διάνοια), opinion (δόξα), will (βούλησις), and election (προαίρεσις), they also thrust into it another sixth faculty, which they call that of Attention. The attention, they say, assists in all that goes on in man. It is that which pronounces *I understand*, *I think*, *I opine*, *I resent*, *I desire*. The attentive function of the rational soul, in fact, pervades in all the powers without exception —the rational, the irrational, and the vegetative. If then, they proceed, the attentive faculty be thus thorough-going, why not let it accompany the sensations and pronounce of them, *I see*, *I hear*, &c.? for to do this is the peculiar office of what is recognisant of the several energies. If, therefore, it be the attention which pronounces this, attention will be the power which takes note of the energies of sense. For it behoves that what takes note of all should itself be indivisible and *one*; seeing also at the same time that the subject of all these operations, *Man*, is one. For, if this faculty took cognisance of these objects, that faculty of those others, it would be, as he himself [Aristotle] elsewhere says, as if you perceived that, I this. That, therefore, must be one to which the attentive function appertains; for this function is conversant with the faculties—both the cognitive and the vital [practical?].* In so far as it is conversant with the cognitive energies it is called Attention. Hence, when we would correct a person whose mind is wandering from any intellectual occupation, we call out to him, Attend! When, on the other hand, it has to do with the life [and moral action?] it is called Conscience (σύνεσις, not σύνοιδος). Hence in the tragedy,

[*Men.*—'How now? What illness quells thee?
Orest.]—Intelligence! for I am conscious of my dreadful deed.'†

Attention is therefore that which is cognisant of our sensitive energies. And Plutarchus (they say) falsely attributed this function to opinion (δόξα). For what is cognisant of the operations of all the faculties behoves to be one. But opinion does not take cognisance of the energies of intelligence (νοῦς). For opinion does not say *I intelligise* (ἐνόησα), or even *I reason* (διενοήθην); for although it may say *I opine*, *I am indignant*, it is unable to contemplate the energies of the higher faculties."—[Sign. O. v., ed. Venet. 1535.]

§ II.—*Historical notices of the use of the terms Consciousness, Attention, Reflection.*

[Nothing appears to have been written on this subject, except what has been already published in the Lectures on Metaphysics, vol. i. pp. 196, 201, and pp. 234, 235. The following references have been found among the Author's papers.—ED.]

Συναίσθησις—συναισθάνομαι.

1°. Sympathy, fellow-feeling, to feel along with.

Plutarch, Solon, Opera, i. p. 88 (ed. 1599).

[De Adul. et Amici Discr.], ii. p. 63.

Clemens Alex., Strom. L. i. p. 282 (ed. 1688); L. ii. p. 383.

2°. Having a common knowledge with others.

Plutarch, Agis et Cleon, Opera, i. 822.

[De Adul. et Amici Discr.], ii. 54.

3°. To feel as a bodily affection—a

---

* By *vital* (ζωτικῶν) Philoponus means appetent. See Introduction. [Προοίμιον, f. 2 a. τῶν δὲ ὀρεκτικῶν καὶ ζωτικῶν ἡ μὲν ἐστὶ θυμός, ἡ δὲ ἐπιθυμία.—ED.]

† Euripides, Orest., 395:—

MEN. Τί χρῆμα πάσχεις; τίς σ' ἀπόλλυσιν νόσος;

OP. Ἡ ξύνεσις, ὅτι σύνοιδα δείν' εἰργασμένος.—ED.

poison acting—a disease—equivalent to consciousness of sensations.

a.—As a medical term—

Plutarch, Dom., Opera, i. 859.

Galen, De Diff. Puls., L. iv. c. 11.*

Therapeut. L. xiii. c. 1. There συναίσθησις said to be *proprius sensus*, self-perception of a symptom, in contrast to its perception by others.

Dioscorides, viii. 2.

b.—Of sense strictly—

Alex. Aphrod., [De Anima, L. i. c. 22. f. 135.]

Hierocles, apud Steph. Thesaur. v. συναίσθησις.

4°. To become discriminating—aware of—perceive.

Plutarch, Aratus, Opera, i. 1021.

[De Profect. Virt. Sent.], ii. 75, 76.

[De Sanitate Tuenda], ii. 123.

[De Solertia Animalium], ii. 977, 983.

Theodoti Epit., apud Clem. Alex. p. 795.

5°. Conscious,—consciousness, and of supersensibles.

Plutarch, [De Profect. Virt. Sent.] Opera, ii. 82 (may be 4°.)

Antoninus, De Rebus Suis, L. vii. § 24,—τοῦ ἁμαρτάνειν (may be 4°).

Epictetus, Diss., L. ii. c. 11. (may be 4°).

Hierocles, In Carm. Pyth. p. 213, ed. 1654.

Dionysius Alexandrinus, apud Eusebium, Præp. Evang. 778 d.

Dionysius Theologus (which?) apud Budæum, Comm. Ling. Græcæ, p. 528.

1. συνειδός—for 'conscience.'

Plutarch, Poplicola, Opera, i. 99.

De Sera Num. Vind., ii. 554, 556.

[De Profect. Virt. Sent.], ii. 84, 85.

Demosthenes, p. 263, Reiske. [De Corona, c. 32. Here, however, it rather means Consciousness in sense of 'common knowledge with others.'—Ed.]

Orphica, [Hymn. lxiii. (62), 5, p. 332, ed. Hermann.—Ed.]

Hierocles, In Carm. Pyth. p. 213, ed. 1654.

Pythagoras apud Stobæi Flor. T. 24, 8.

Epictetus [Fragm. 97, vol. iv. p. 98, ed. Schweigh.—Ed.]

Plutarch apud Stobæi Flor. T. 24, 15 [De Animi Tranquillitate, c. 19, Opera, ii. p. 476. Stobæus quotes τὸ συνειδός; but the word in Plutarch is σύνεσις, introduced by the line of Euripides, Orestes, 395, as referred to below.—Ed.]

Σύνεσις—for conscience.

Menander apud Stobæi Flor. T. 24, 3.

Clemens Alex., Strom. L. ii. p. 371, ed. 1688.

Herodian, L. iv. c. 7, but some MSS. have συνείδησις. [Vide Gale, Philosophia Generalis, 1676, p. 867.—Ed.]

Euripides, [Orestes, 395], quoted by Plutarch, as above, and by Clemens Alex., Strom. L. vii. p. 714.

Συνίημι.

Not used for 'to be morally conscious,' though sometimes 'to be aware of in relation to self,' as Lucian [Dial. Door., ii. 1, quoted by Gale, l. c.—Ed.]

Συνετός—συνετής—ἀσύνετος—ἀσυνεσία—εὐσύνετος—εὐσυνεσία, &c.

Not used in relation to conscience.

Πρόσεξις.

Used only once by Plato, Rep. iii. p. 407, Steph.

Προσέχω.

Used commonly with νοῦν, to mean 'attend,' sometimes by itself. Out of 36 times in Plato, 27 with νοῦν, and 9 absolutely in this sense. N. B.—Plato only joins νοῦν with it, and never γνώμην or διάνοιαν.

Προσοχή.

Not used by Plato; but by Lucian, ii. 63 [Quomodo Hist. Conscr. Sit, § 53], Suidas [v. εἰσβολή], Psellus [De Omnifaria Doctr., § 46], Plutarch [De Garrulitate, c. 23, and elsewhere. See Wyttenbach's Index.—Ed.]

Προσεκτικός.

Used for 'attentive' by Aristotle, (Rhet. iii. 14), but never by Plato.

[The following references from the Author's Common-Place Book have been added, as relating to the same subject.]

---

* Galen has no name for consciousness of sensations, &c., though he uses συναίσθησις in a medical sense (v. Hofmann, Comm. in Galenum, p. 185). This (sc. consciousness of sensations) he attributes to τὸ ἡγεμονικόν—i. e. the imagining, recollecting, and reasoning mind—might be called common sense. See Hofmann, pp. 179, 182.

I.—CONSCIOUSNESS.

On Consciousness in general, see *Z. Mayne*, Two Dissertations, &c., [p. 141 sq.]; *Sulzer*, Vermischte Schriften [i. p. 201 sq.]; *C. L. Reinhold*, Das menschliche Erkenntnissvermoegen, pp. 108 sq., 227 sq.; *Dalberg* [Von dem Bewusstseyn als allgemeinem Grunde der Weltweisheit], omnino. Add *Weiss*, Ueber d. Wesen und Wirken d. Seele, § 29, p. 134 sq.; *Tiedemann*, Psychologie, p. 24; Untersuchungen, &c., i. p. 53 sq.

Reinhold (ll. cc.) gives the meaning affixed to the expression by Descartes (p. 227), Leibnitz (228), Wolf (229), Locke (231), Hume (235), Kant (237), Reinhold himself (old opinion, 239—new opinion, 109), Fichte (242), Schelling (244), Fries (244), Bouterwek (245).

Wolf distinguishes, 1. *Perception*—act of mind representing object, *i.e.* forming idea. This may be without consciousness or apperception. 2. *Apperception*—act by which mind conscious of its perceptions, representations, ideas. 3. *Cogitation*—thought, including the two former. *Wolf*, Psych. Emp. §§ 23-26, 48; Psych. Rat. § 12; *Baumeister* [Philosophia Recens Controversa, Deff. 660, 662], p. 104.

*Συναίσθησις**—*συναισθάνομαι*.

1.—PROCLUS.—Instit. Theol., c. 39—of consciousness in general.

2.—ALEXANDER APHRODISIENSIS gives *συναίσθησις* to the common sense. De Anima, L. i. c. 22, f. 135 a, ed. Ald. 1534; Quæst. Nat. f. 22 b, ed. Trincav. 1536.

3.—SIMPLICIUS.—a.—In Arist. De Anim. f. 52, ed. Ald. 1527 uses these words to express Aristotle's meaning of sense knowing its own operations. He makes *συναίσθησις* cognisant not only of the presence and absence of the object of perception, and perception itself, and non-perception, but of the attempt at perception. This *συναίσθησις* he attributes not only to the common sense (though this has it purer and better), but also to the several senses. His translator, Asulanus, renders by *conscientia* and *consensus*. So Budæus has *conscientia morbi* in a medical sense. Comm. Ling. Græc., p. 528.

b.—In Epicteti Enchiridion, c. i. p. 28, Heinsii (p. 49, Schweigh.)—*συναίσθησις τοῦ θέλειν καὶ μὴ θέλειν, κ. τ. λ.*

4.—EUGENIOS OF BULGARIA.—*Λογικὴ* (1766), p. 113, *συναίσθησις* for consciousness.*

That *συναίσθησις* belongs only to rational beings, see Anon. ap. Cramer, Anecd. Græc. Paris. vol. iv. p. 390.

Συνείδησις—*σύνοιδα*.

PLATO.—Ion, p. 533. 'Ἀλλ' *ἐκεῖνο ἐμαυτῷ σύνοιδα ὅτι, κ. τ. λ.*, 'sed illius mihi conscius sum quod,' &c.—Ficini. On this use of *σύνοιδα*, &c., v. omnino Wyttenbach ad Phædonem (Platonis Opera, ed. Valpy, vol. v. p. 298).

DIOG. LAERT., vii. 85 [*πρῶτον οἰκεῖον λέγων εἶναι παντὶ ζῴῳ τὴν αὑτοῦ σύστασιν, καὶ τὴν ταύτης συνείδησιν*], referred to in Harris' Philological Enquiries, ch. xvii. But there *σύνθεσιν* appears to be the right reading. [See *Lectures on Metaphysics*, vol. i. p. 199.—ED.]

Ξύννοια—for 'consciousness.'

HIPPOCRATES, De Morb. Epidem., L. vi. § 8, *τῆς γνώμης ξύννοια αὐτὴ καθ' ἑαυτήν.*

Conscientia—*conscius*, &c.

1.—TERTULLIAN has conscientia for 'consciousness.' a.—De Carne Christi adversus IV. Hæreses, c. 3. Arguing, against Marcion, that the birth and body of Christ were real and not phantastic,—he supposes Marcion to say, that Christ's subjective belief of his body was enough. 'Sed satis erat illi, inquis, *conscientia* sua. Viderint homines, si natum putabant, quia hominem videbant.' (This argument he had used before.) 'Quanto ergo dignius, quantoque constantius humanam sustinuisset existimationem vere natus, eandem existimationem etiam non natus subiturus cum injuria *conscientiæ* suæ, quam tu ad fiduciam reputas, ut non natus adversus *conscientiam* suam natum se existimari sustineret! Quid tanti fuit,

---

* [As a psychological term] *συναίσθησις* may be used—

1. For simple perception, see Hofmann, Comm. in Galenum, p. 155.

2. For the perception of two things, either actually or potentially. Thus sight may be said *συναισθάνεσθαι* colour and magnitude, darkness and light. See Themistius, Opera, ed. Venet. 1534, ff. 84 b, 98 b.

3. For sensitive apperception, see Alexander Aphrod., De Anima, L. i. c. 22, f. 135 a, and Quæst. Nat. f. 22 b.

4. For consciousness in general, and is thus applied to intellect. This frequent after it came into use. See the authorities referred to in the text.

* Eugenios uses *συνείδησις* and *συνειδὸς* in the same sense. *Λογική*, ibid. Compare his *Ψυχολογία* (18[illegible]), p. 5.

edoce, ut consciens Christus quid esset, esse se quod non erat, exhiberet.' *

b.—De Testimonio Animæ, c. 5. Speaking of the natural testimonies of the mind, he says:—'Qui ejusmodi eruptiones animæ non putavit doctrinam esse naturæ, et congenitæ et ingenitæ *conscientiæ* tacita commissa, dicet, &c.' Afterwards, in the same chapter, conscientia is used for the place of principles—the faculty of native cognitions.

c.—De Anima, c. 18. 'Conscientia communis' of sense, opposed to a higher consciousness of intelligence.

But all these examples of conscientia in Tertullian may be translated by '*knowledge*.'

2.—St Augustin.—De Trinitate, L. x. c. 7. (Opera, ed. Benedict., t. viii. p. 894). 'Et quia sibi bene *conscia* est [mens] principatus sui quo corpus regit; hinc factum est, &c.'

3.—Petrarch, De Contemptu Mundi, Dial. i., Opera, ed. Basileæ 1581, pp. 334, 335, has *conscientia*, [but in a moral sense for *conscience*.]

4.—Keckermann.—Opera, t. i. pp. 342, 731, 798. He says there is a practical and a speculative consciousness. See also his Organi Aristotelis Analysis, pp. 103, 158, 159.

5.—Descartes was the first to give currency to the word in his definition of thought as everything of which we are conscious, *i.e.* equivalent to consciousness. [Princ. P. i. § 9. 'Cogitationis nomine intelligo illa omnia quæ nobis consciis in nobis fiunt, quatenus eorum in nobis *conscientia* est.']

Conscience (French and English)—

Used as convertible with 'pensée' by De la Forge, Traité de l'Esprit, p. 14. ['Je vous dirai donc que je prens ici la Pensée pour cette perception, *conscience*, ou connoissance intérieure que chacun de nous ressent immédiatement par soi même, quand il s'aperçoit de ce qu'il fait ou de ce qui se passe en lui.']

On French 'Conscience,' see foot-note in Coste's Translation of Locke's Essay, B. ii. ch. 27, § 9, [p. 264, 5th ed. 1755.]

Hooker, Eccles. Polity, ii. 7. § 2, speaks of the '*conscience* of their own ignorance' as in the 'simpler sort.'

Conscioisité—

Used by Leibnitz, to express *consciousness*. Nouv. Essais, Liv. ii. ch. xxvii. §§ 9, 16, 18—Oeuvres Phil., ed. Raspe, pp. 194, 195, 199, 200.

* See Barthius, Adversaria [L. xxix. c. 1.], p. 1348, who notices this as a peculiar use of *conscientia*.

II.—Attention.

[Attention is recognised as a special faculty by]

1.—Philoponus.—In Arist. De Anima, p. 167 [Lat. Transl., Lugd. 1544; Sign. O. v., Gr. ed. Venet. 1535], where is noticed at length the opinion of 'some recent interpreters,' with whom he agrees touching τὸ προσεκτικὸν (μέρος), which, in their view, includes both Consciousness and Attention—if not Reflection. [See above, p. 942 a.—Ed.]

2.—Michael Ephesius (or Eustratius).—In Arist. Eth. Nic. L. ix. c. 9 (f. 160 b, ed. Gr. 1536; p. 388, ed. Feliciani, 1542.)

3.—By Michael Psellus, προσοχὴ is mentioned as a middle faculty of mind. De Omnifaria Doctrina, § 46. Προσοχὴ δέ ἐστι καθ' ἣν προσέχομεν τοῖς ἔργοις οἷς πράττομεν καὶ τοῖς λόγοις οἷς λέγομεν.

Mr Stewart (Elem. i. c. 2—Coll. Works, vol. ii. p. 122) thinks that no psychologist has treated of Attention as a separate faculty. But see Wolf, Condillac, Canzius (Meditationes, 709), Bonnet, Contzen, among modern philosophers, and of ancient as above. [Compare *Lectures on Metaphysics*, vol. i. p. 235-6.—Ed.]

On Attention as faculty of directing and concentrating Consciousness, see *De Raei*, Clavis Philosophiæ Naturalis, p. 273 (where Scaliger, Aristotle, and Descartes); *Fries*, Anthropologie, i. p. 83 sq.; *Kant*, Anthropologie, [§ 3 sq.; and Menschenkunde, ed. Starke, p. 53.—Ed.]

On Attention in general, see *St Augustin* (in Duhamel, p. 488).* He notices well

* The passage of St Augustin is from the De Musica, L. vi. c. 5. 'Et ne longum faciam, videtur mihi anima, cum sentit in corpore, non ab illo aliquid pati, sed in ejus passionibus attentius agere, et has actiones, sive faciles propter convenientiam, sive difficiles propter inconvenientiam, non eam latere: et hoc totum est quod sentire dicitur. . . . . . . Cum autem ab eisdem suis operationibus aliquid patitur, a seipsa patitur, non a corpore; sed plane cum se accommodat corpori: et ideo apud se ipsam minus est, quia corpus semper minus quam ipsa est. Conversa ergo a Domino suo ad servum suum, necessario deficit: conversa item a servo suo ad Dominum suum, necessario proficit, et præbet eidem servo facillimam vitam, et propterea minime operosam et negotiosam, ad quam propter summam quietem nulla detorquetur attentio; sicut est affectio corporis quæ sanitas dicitur: nulla quippe attentione nostra opus habet, non quia nihil tunc agit anima in corpore, sed quia nihil facilius agit. Nam in omnibus operibus nostris tanto quidquam attentius, quanto difficilius operamur.' Quoted by *Duhamel*, De Corpore Animato, Lib. i. cap. 2.—Ed.

that in health no attention to state of body—so '*tanto attentius quanto difficilius operamur.*' See also *Vives*, De Anima, L. ii., p. 54, ed. 1555*—*Steeb*, Ueber den Menschen, ii. 675 — *Tiedemann*, Untersuchungen, i. p. 98; Psychologie, p. 121 — *Irwing*, Erfahrungen und Untersuchungen ueber den Menschen, i. § 107; ii. § 147-50.

St Augustin, De Trinitate, L. xi c. 2, makes 'animi intentio' (equivalent to 'animi voluntas') a necessary element in every act of Perception. See *Fromondus*, Phil. Christ. de Anima, p. 557 sq.

Hieronymus, Adv. Jovin. ii. 9. 'Quod mens videat et mens audiat, et quod nec audire quidpiam nec videre possimus, nisi sensus in ea quæ cernimus et audimus fuerit *intentus*, vetus quoque sententia est.'

Plinius, Hist. Nat., L. xi. c. 54. 'Animo autem videmus, animo cernimus: oculi, ceu vasa quædam, visibilem ejus partem accipiunt atque transmittunt, &c.'

Cicero, Acad. Quæst. iv. c. 10. 'Mens ipsa quæ sensuum fons est, naturalem vim habet, quam intendit ad ea quibus movetur.' (Quoted in Mazure, Etudes, &c. i. p. 77.)

Laromiguière makes Attention a power of intellect. Cousin reprehends this (*De Biran*, Nouv. Consid., préf., p. xxix.) and makes it a power of will.

Πρόσεξις, συντονία ψυχῆς πρὸς τὸ καταμαθεῖν. Definitiones Platonicæ.

III.—Reflection.

Mr Stewart (Dissertation, Note Y—Coll. Works, vol. i. p. 556; compare Essays, Part i. Ess. i. ch. 1—Coll. Works, vol. v. p. 56) says that 'Mr Locke seems to have considered the use of the word *reflection* as peculiar to himself;' and does not himself know that it is common to the whole School philosophy.†

1.—St Augustin (in De la Forge, De l'Esprit, préf., p. xiv.; who himself uses 'réflexion,' préf., p. xi.) This passage of St Augustin probably suggested to Leibnitz his acute rejoinder to the argument against innate principles—'nisi intellectus ipse.'*

2.—Duns Scotus, Super Universalibus Porphyrii, qu. iii., where our knowledge is said to be either from sense or from reflection, just as Locke. ['Ad tertium dico quod illa propositio Aristotelis, nihil est in intellectu quin prius fuerit in sensu, vera est de eo quod est primum intelligibile, quod est scilicet quod quid est rei materialis, non autem de omnibus per se intelligibilibus; quia multa per se intelliguntur, non quia speciem faciunt in sensu, sed per *reflexionem* intellectus.']†

3.—Durandus, In Sent. L. ii. Disp. iii. qu. 6. § 21, says that Reflection on the operations of our minds affords *certain knowledge*, and that it is *experimental*.

4.—J. C. Scaliger, De Subtilitate, Exerc. cccvii. § 2.‡ ['Intellectus noster non intelligit se per speciem sicuti cetera entia materialia, sed per *reflexionem*,' &c.] See also §§ 18, 28; and Exerc. cccxcviii. § 14.

5.—Melanchthon, De Anima, ed. Lugd. 1555, p. 183. ['Intellectus est potentia cognoscens, judicans, et ratiocinans, . . . habens et actum *reflexum* quo suas actiones cernit et judicat, et errata emendare potest.']

6.—Fracastorius, De Intellectione, L. ii., Opera, f. 137. '*Reflectente* se intellectu super conceptus factos.'

7.—Gul. Camerarius, Select. Disp. Philos. (Paris, 1630), p. 27, discusses the question whether *entia rationis—relationes rationis* are made by a direct or by a reflex act of the intellect. That made by a reflex act held by the Thomists.

---

* Vives says:—'Et ut necessarium est ad cernendum, ut sit oculus apertus; ita et intelligentiæ, ad intelligendum, necessaria est attentio, seu adversio quædam animi, quod Græcis dicitur προσέχειν τὸν νοῦν. Hæc est veluti mentis quædam apertio, ad recipiendum quod offertur.'—Ed.

† We have the scholastic dictum—'Reflexiva cogitatio facilis est deflexiva'—pointing at the difficulty of turning inwards upon self.—Keckermann, Opera, t. i. p. 408.—[Compare *Lectures on Metaphysics*, i. p. 234.—Ed.]

* The passage of Augustin is from the spurious treatise, De Spiritu et Anima, c. 32: 'Mens ergo cui nihil seipsa præsentius est, quadam interiori, non simulata, sed vera præsentia, videt se in se. Nihil enim tam novit mens quam id quod sibi præsto est; nec menti quidquam magis præsto est, quam ipsa sibi. Nam cognoscit se vivere, se meminisse, se intelligere, se velle, cogitare, scire, judicare. Hæc omnia novit in se, nec imaginatur, quasi extra se illa aliquo sensu corporis tetigerit, sicut corporalia quæque tanguntur. Ex quorum cogitationibus si nihil sibi affingat, ut tale aliquid sese putet; quidquid ei de se remanet, hoc solum ipsa est. Nihil enim tam in mente est, quam ipsa mens; nec quidquam sic mentem cognoscit, quemadmodum mens, &c.'—Cf. De Trinitate, L. x. c. 8.—Ed.

† By the Scotists the act of intellect was regarded as threefold—*rectus*, *reflexus*, and *collativus*. See Constantius (a Sarnano), Tract. de Secundis Intentionibus, ad calcem Scoti Operum, p. 452, and Castanæus, Distinctiones Philosophicæ, Lugd. Bat. 1651, pp. 11, 151.

‡ Compare Goclenius, Adversaria ad Scaligeri Exercitationes (1594), p. 192.

8.—Bernardus, Thes. Plat., vv. Intellectus, Conversio, Circulus.

9.—Jordanus Brunus, De Imaginum Signorum et Idearum Compositione, Dedicatio, p. iv. [See above, p. 938 a.—Ed.]

10.—Philippus Mocenicus, Contemplationes Philosophicæ (1581), has the word in all its forms, passim.

11.—Keckermann, Systema Physicum, L. iv. cc. 3, 5 (Opera, ed. 1614, t. i. pp. 1600, 1612.)

12.—Goclenius, Lexicon Philosophicum (Lat.), ed. Francof. 1613, v. Reflexus. 'Reflecti, 1°, Proprie est vel rursus seu iterum flecti, vel retro flecti. 2°, Translate est revocari, reprimi, sedari, cui opponitur incitari. Sic Cicero usurpavit, vide Nizolium. 3°, Tralatitium etiam est, quod Physici Reflexionem intellectui tribuunt. Reflexio enim intellectus eis est, cum, postquam intellectus concepit rem aliquam, rursus concipit se concepisse eam, et considerat ac metitur, qua certitudine et modo illam cognoverit, et, si opus fuerit, iterum atque iterum convertit se seu revertitur ad se et ad actus suos. (Hoc dicunt Scholastici reflecti supra actus ipsos reflexos.) Quod argumento est, intellectum esse divinum at immaterialem. Breviter, Reflexio intellectus est intima actio, qua recognoscit tum seipsum, tum suos actus et suas species.

'Itaque Reflecti metaphorice etiam tribuitur motui mentis, quo mens quasi in se redit. Aliud est intelligere rem, et aliud intelligere ipsam intentionem intellectam, (id est, similitudinem acceptam in intellectu de re intellecta, quam verba exteriora significant,) quod intellectus facit dum supra opus suum reflectitur.' This passage is commented on by Wolf, Psych. Emp. § 257; Wolf wrong.

13.—D. Buchanan, Hist. An. Hum. (Paris, 1637), pp. 114, 250—that reflection necessarily of an inorganic faculty.

14.—Descartes (in Gruyer, Essais Philosophiques, t. iv. p. 118). [Epist. P. ii. ep. 6.—Ed.]

15.—Gassendi, Physica, Sect. iii., Memb. Post., L. ix. c. 3 (Opera, Leyden, 1658, t. ii. p. 451): 'Ad secundam vero operationem præsertim spectat ipsa intellectus ad suam operationem attentio, reflexiove illa supra actionem propriam, qua se intelligere intelligit, cogitatve se cogitare.'

16.—Duhamel, Philosophia Burgundiæ, t. i. pp. 617, 621, 651, 652, 655, (4th ed. Lond. 1685.)

The origin of the word *Reflection* may perhaps be traced to Aristotle's comparison of a straight and spiral or crooked line—De Anima, L. iii. c. 4, text 10: compared with Averroes, in locum (Aristotelis Opera, Venetiis, 1560, t. vii. p. 108), and Ant. Andreas, Quæst. Metaph., L. vii. qu. 13.

Ἡ ἐπιστροφὴ πρὸς ἑαυτό—τὸ πρὸς ἑαυτὸ ἐπιστρεπτικόν—τὸ πρὸς ἑαυτὸ ἐπιστρέψαι. [Used by] Plotinus, Enn. v. L. iii. c. 1, 8, et alibi; Proclus, Institut. Theol. [cc. 15, 32, 33, 42, 43, et alibi]; Philoponus, In Arist. De Anima, Sign. A. iv.;* compare Sign. B. v., ed. Venet. 1535; Simplicius, In Arist. De Anima, f. 52, ed. Ald. 1527.†

Phrases:—Plotinus, Enn. i. L. iv. c. 10—Ἡ ἀντίληψις ἔοικεν εἶναι καὶ γίγνεσθαι, ἀνακάμπτοντος τοῦ νοήματος, καὶ τοῦ ἐνεργοῦντος τοῦ κατὰ τὸ ζῆν τῆς ψυχῆς, οἷον ἀπωσθέντος πάλιν, κ. τ. λ. St Augustin, De Immortalitate Animæ, c. 4 (Opera, ed. Benedict., t. i. p. 390),—'*Intentionem* in ante cogitata *reflectere*.' Balde, Lyrica, L. i. Ode 22,—'Mira potentiæ Figura mens in se *reflexa*.' Ficinus (in Bernardi Thes. Plat., v. Circulus),—'*Animadversio mentis* in seipsam.'

Immateriality and immortality of the mind proved from power of reflecting on self:—

Plotinus, ut supra; *Proclus*, Inst. Theol.

---

* Οὐδὲν τῶν σωμάτων αὐτὸ ἑαυτὸ γιγνώσκει, οὐδὲ πρὸς ἑαυτὸ ἐπιστρέφεται· οὐ γὰρ οἶδεν ἑαυτὴν ἡ χείρ, ἢ ἄλλό τι τῶν σωμάτων. Ἀλλ' οὐδὲ αἱ ἄλογοι δυνάμεις, καίτοι ἀσώματοι οὖσαι, ἑαυτὰς ἴσασιν· οὐ γὰρ οἶδεν ἑαυτὴν ἡ ὄψις ἢ ἡ ἀκοὴ ἢ ἁπλῶς ἡ αἴσθησις, οὐδὲ ζητεῖ ποίας ἐστὶ φύσεως· ἀλλ' ὁ λόγος ἐστὶν ὁ περὶ αὐτῶν ζητῶν. Ἡ μέντοι ψυχὴ ἡ λογικὴ αὐτὴ ἑαυτὴν γινώσκει· αὕτη γοῦν ἐστιν ἡ ζητοῦσα, αὕτη ἡ ζητουμένη, αὕτη ἡ εὑρίσκουσα, αὕτη ἡ εὑρισκομένη, ἡ γινώσκουσα καὶ γινωσκομένη· ἀσώματος ἄρα ἐναργῶς ἀποδέδεικται. —Ed.

† Τὸ δὲ αἰσθάνεσθαι ὅτι αἰσθανόμεθα, ἀνθρώπου μοι μόνον ἴδιον εἶναι δοκεῖ· λογικῆς γὰρ ζωῆς ἔργον τὸ πρὸς ἑαυτὴν ἐπιστρεπτικόν. Καὶ δείκνυται διὰ τοῦδε καὶ μέχρι τῆς αἰσθήσεως ἡμῶν τὸ λογικὸν διῆκον· εἴγε καὶ αἴσθησις ἡ ἀνθρωπεία ἑαυτῆς ἀντιληπτική· γιγνώσκει γάρ πως ἑαυτὸ τὸ αἰσθανόμενον, ὅτε αἰσθανόμενον ἑαυτὸ γνωρίζει· καὶ διὰ τοῦτο ἐπιστρέφον πρὸς ἑαυτὸ καὶ αὐτὸ ἑαυτοῦ ὄν—and then he shews that this is a power higher than a bodily faculty, and therefore separable from body; for the particles of body, lying each without the other, cannot be converged (συννεύειν) on self.

cc. 15, 16, 43, 82, 83, 187, 188 (See Eugenios, Psych., p. 78 sq.); *Philoponus*, In Arist. De Anima, Procem. Sign. A. iv.; *Aonius Palearius*, De Immortalitate Animorum, L. ii. v. 125 sq.; *D. Heinsius*, De Contemptu Mortis, L. ii. v. 315 (Poemata, ed. 1640, p. 397); *D. Buchanan*, Hist. An. Hum., p. 534.; *Gassendi*, Physica, Sect. iii., Memb. Post., L. ix. c. 2; *Henry More*, [Ψυχαθανασία Platonica, or a Platonicall Poem of the Immortality of Souls, &c. (Cambridge, 1642), Book ii. Cant. iii. Stanza 27; Book iii. Cant. ii., Stanza 23-25]; *Sir John Davies*, Poem on the Immortality of the Soul, [Sect. ii.]; *Goclenius*, Lex. Phil., v. Reflexus (Wolf, Psych. Emp., § 257); *Descartes*, passim [See Epist. P. ii. ep. 2, 6.—ED.]; *De la Forge*, in note on Descartes' De Homine, art. 77, et alibi pluries; *Glanvill*, Defence of the Vanity of Dogmatising (1665), p. 20; *Mayne*, Essay on Consciousness, p. 217.

NOTE K.

THAT THE TERMS IMAGE, IMPRESSION, TYPE, ETC., IN PHILOSOPHICAL THEORIES OF PERCEPTION, ARE NOT TO BE TAKEN LITERALLY.

[References.—From I. P. 254 a, 256 b, 257 a, 353 b, 355 a.]

[This Note does not appear to have been written. The following fragment relates to one of the subjects intended to be discussed in it. See above, p. 353, note †.—ED.]

Reid is wrong in stating, that Aristotle imputes the defect of memory in children and old persons, to the brain, in the one case, being 'too soft to retain impressions,' and, in the other, 'too hard to receive them.' In the *first* place, the primary sensorium, where these impressions are to be made, is not, in Aristotle's doctrine, the *brain*, but the *heart*. In the *second*, Reid and other philosophers do Aristotle, here and elsewhere, injustice, in taking his expressions in a strictly literal signification. His statement, on the subject in question, is found in the first chapter of his treatise *On Memory and Reminiscence*. Themistius, in his paraphrase on this chapter, literally following the Aphrodisian (Περὶ Ψυχῆς—κεφ. περὶ Φαντασίας), and literally followed by Michael of Ephesus (εἰς τὸ περὶ Μνήμης καὶ Ἀναμνήσεως—προοίμ.), declares it to be the doctrine of Aristotle and the Peripatetics—that the term *impress* (τύπος) is one *abusively* employed, from the poverty of the language, and that it serves only to indicate, vaguely and in general, a certain organic affection, not, as it would properly imply, any depression, eminence, and figure in the sensorium. For what, they ask, would be the figure of *white*, or in general of *colour*? What the figure of the objects of *smell*, *taste*, and *hearing*? This reduces it to Reid's own opinion; for he, equally with Gassendi, admits the dependence of memory on some organic disposition of the sensorium, (p. 354 b). It is, perhaps, hardly worthy of notice that Brown (Lect. xxx. p. 191) attempts to refute the doctrine of Species, only by fastening on it the very absurdity ridiculed by the most illustrious interpreters of Aristotle; he was also ignorant that the common opinion, even of the Latin Schoolmen, denied species to every sense, except those of *sight*, and *hearing*, &c.

[The following translations of the passages of Alexander, above referred to, have been found among the Author's papers. They are from the treatise Περὶ Ψυχῆς, printed at the end of the works of Themistius, Ald. 1534, ff. 135 b, 136 a.—Ed.]

'Now what Phantasy (or Imagination) is, we may thus explain: Let us conceive that from the energies about objects of sense, there is formed, as it were, some type or impress (τύπος), and picture (ἀναζωγράφημα), in the primary sensory (i.e. that part of the body with which the sensitive part of the soul is connected), being a relict of the motion determined by the sensible object—a relict which, when the sensible object is no longer present, remains, and is preserved, as a kind of image (εἰκὼν) thereof, and which, in consequence of being thus preserved, becomes the cause to us of memory. Now, such type or impress, as it were, is called Phantasy (φαντασία, but I would read φάντασμα); and therefore Phantasy is defined an impression (τύπωσις) in the soul, and an impression in the mind (ἐν ἡγεμονικῷ). The type or impress itself is not, however, to be called imagination; for imagination is properly the energy of the imaginative faculty about this impress as its object, &c. . . .

'It is necessary to understand the term *type* or *impress* (τύπος) in a looser signification in reference to Imagination. In its proper meaning, this word conveys the notion of elevation and depression, or the figure made by something impressing something impressed, as we see exemplified in the case of a seal and wax. But the relicts in us from sensible objects are not of this nature; for the correspondent apprehensions in the primary acts of sense were not realised through any figure. For of what figure is white, or in general colour? or, again, of what figure is smell? It was, however, necessary, from the want of any proper appellation, to employ a metaphorical expression to denote the vestige and relict which remains in us from sensible objects.'

Following Alexander, like cautions are given by two other of the Greek Interpreters of Aristotle in regard to the same or similar expressions—viz., by *Themistius* in his Commentary on the Third Book De Anima, f. 93 a, ed. Ald. 1534, and in his Commentary on the De Memoria et Reminiscentia, f. 96 b; and by *Michael Ephesius* in his Commentary on the latter work, f. 127 b, ed. Ald. 1527.

In like manner Plotinus guards against misconception in the employment of such terms, by observing that the things they denote have no magnitude, no configuration, no elevation or depression, and even in some cases are not produced by impulse. Enn. iv. L. iii. c. 26.*

[The following additional references from the Author's Common-Place Book relate to the subject of this note.—Ed.]

Excellent passage of *Simon Simonius* (De Mem. et Rem. p. 290 D.), to show that words, *image*, *impression*, &c., only metaphorical and from penury of language, as Themistius also notices.†

See also *De Villemandy*, Scepticismus Debellatus, &c., p. 184. ['Sed hæc omnia sunt metaphorica vereque typica. In hisce imaginibus nullus fere color, qui splendeat; in his umbris nullus est lucis radius, qui emicet. Verum cum nulli succurrant nobis characteres, quibus earum conditionem circumscriptius definiamus, necesse est his simus contenti, &c.']

---

* The words of Plotinus are: 'Αλλὰ πρῶτον μὲν οἱ τύποι οὐ μεγέθη· οὐδ' ὥσπερ αἱ ἐνσφραγίσεις, οὐδ' ἀντερείσεις, ἢ τυπώσεις, ὅτι μηδ' ὠθισμὸς, μηδ' ὥσπερ ἐν κηρῷ, ἀλλ' ὁ τρόπος οἷον νόησις, καὶ ἐπὶ τῶν αἰσθητῶν.—Ed.

† The passage of Simonius is as follows. Substantially, though not verbally, it is taken from Themistius. 'Quare cum sentimus, idem fere accidit, quod cum aliquid sigillo obsignatur. Namque sicuti effigies tantum, quæ a sigillo imprimitur, in cera manet, sigillum vero ipsum abjungitur, ita a rebus extrinsecus objectis quasi effigies et figura quædam mediis sensibus exterioribus in primo Aestheterio, nempe corde, qui sensus origo et fons est, pingitur et insculpitur, in quo demum effigies et figura illa, quamvis res ipsa sensilis abjungatur, manet. *Hanc figuram et effigiem, nunc speciem, nunc simulacrum, aliquando imaginem, aliquando impressionem, nonnunquam motionem, tensionem, et passionem vocare solemus, non tamen proprie, ut Themistius monuit, sed penuria aptiorum vocabulorum*,' &c.—Ed.

NOTE L.

ON THE PLATONIC DOCTRINE OF PERCEPTION.

[References.—From I. P. 296 a, 368 b.]

[No part of this Note appears to have been written. The following extracts from the Author's Common-Place Book exhibit some of the materials which would probably have been employed for it. A few further remarks may be found in the Lectures on Metaphysics, vol. ii. p. 32.—Ed.]

On the Platonic doctrine of Perception, see *Bernardus*, Seminarium Philosophiæ Platonicæ, p. 821; *Tennemann*, Plat. Phil., ii. pp. 15-36, 156 sq.; Gesch. der Phil., ii. p. 248.

The *εἴδωλα* only modifications of the mind itself, determined by the impressions (*κινήσεις*) of the external something (*τινος*) on the organ of sense, as affected by them—*πάθος*, *παθήματα*. N.B.—Sense (in mind) is not an alteration—affection—passion, but the recognition of it in the living organ of sense.*

On Plato's theory of vision, see *Galen*, De Plac. Hippocr. et Plat., L. vii. c. 6, ed. Chart.

Empedocles and Plato (though not constant) held that vision accomplished by light going out of the eye, as from a lantern; *Aristotle*, De Sensu et Sensili, [c. 2, § 6], who refutes them. Compare *Simon Simonius* [Comm. in eundem librum], p. 63. Galen adopted the same theory, and is abused for it by Scaliger, (*De Subtilitate*, Exerc. cccxcviii., § 16); also the ancient Mathematicians or Opticians in general, who are attacked by Aristotle (*De Sensu et Sensili*, c. 2, § 14), and by Alexander Aphrodisiensis on that book (f. 98, ed. Ald.) See an excellent discussion on this in Simon Simonius, p. 82 sq.

St Augustin (De Quant. Animæ, c. 23) platonises on Vision, but is not consistent. See De Trinitate, L. xi. c. 2.

That Plato did not really hold so absurd an opinion, (which is given up by Ficinus), see *Scaliger*, De Subtilitate, Exerc. cccxxv.

On Platonic ideas, see *Balforeus*, in Arist. Organ., p. 65; *Norris*, Miscellanies, p. 435, ed. 1687; *A. Smith*, Essays, p. 119, ed. 1795; *Herbart*, Lehrbuch zur Einleitung in die Philosophie, § 120-25, p. 207 sq., 3 ed. 1834.

The Platonists do not explain (do they not?) how maintaining the mind to be *merely active* in sensation, and only operating about affection in organ—how the mind is determined, without being affected, to act thus—what is the mode of connection between the suggestion of the *λόγος* and the bodily passion.

In treating of Plato's theory of perception (*αἴσθησις*) we have nothing to do with his theory of the higher powers (viz., *διάνοια*, reason, and *φρόνησις* or *νοῦς*, intellect)—nothing to say to the relation of sensation to the intellect and reason; and the *εἴδωλα* of the senses have nothing to do with the objects of the higher powers. It is nothing to our present purpose that Plato held that the senses give us no real knowledge, *i.e.*, no representation of the essences of things in themselves. *Tennemann*, Plat. Phil., ii. p. 200.

* The remark of Galen. See De Plac. Hippocr. et Plat., L. vii. c. 6, ed. Chart. Οὔκουν ἀλλοίωσίς ἐστιν ἡ αἴσθησις, ὥς ἔνιοί φασιν, ἀλλὰ διάγνωσις ἀλλοιώσεως.—Ed.

NOTE M.

ON THE DOCTRINE OF SPECIES, AS HELD BY ARISTOTLE AND THE ARISTOTELIANS.

[References.—From I. P. 254 a, 267 a, 268 a, 271 b, 296 a, 313 a, 326 b, 368 b.]

The hypothesis, that the immediate object of perception is something different both from the external object and from the mind itself, owes its origin not merely to a metaphysical opinion in regard to the impossibility of an immediate communication between two substances so opposite as Mind and Matter; but has been likewise introduced as a physical supposition, to account for the communication between the external object and the mind. And, as a physical hypothesis, it has been used, not merely in the infancy of natural science, to afford a medium of communication between the external object and the sense; but it has likewise been employed by some philosophers, who limited the mind to the region of the brain, to connect the intellectual perception with the affection of the organ.

By Democritus and Epicurus,* who both believed only in the existence of Matter, the medium of communication between the organ and the object, and the whole process of sensation and thought, was transacted by the intervention of certain fine images or exuviæ (*εἴδωλα, ἀπόρροιαι, ἀποστάσεις, exuviæ, imagines species, simulacra rerum*), which were continually thrown off from the surfaces of bodies.*

> 'Esse ea quæ rerum simulacra vocamus,
> Quæ, quasi membranæ summo de corpore rerum
> Dereptæ, volitant ultro citroque per auras.'—
> [Lucretius, iv. 34.]

This theory found little favour among the other philosophers of Greece; and Aristotle, to whom a similar opinion is commonly attributed, contented himself with

* Leucippus and Empedocles—see *Aristotle*, De Sensu et Sensili, [c. 2, § 10; where, among the theories of Empedocles regarding sight, is mentioned one which ascribes it ταῖς ἀπορροίαις ταῖς ἀπὸ τῶν ὁρωμένων. (Cf. *Plato*, Meno, p. 76.) Empedocles and Leucippus, as well as Democritus, are also probably among the ἀρχαίοι, mentioned in c. 3, § 15, in connection with the same theory. More express mention of all these philosophers is made in De Gen. et Corr., L. i. c. 8. See also *Theophrastus*, De Sensu, §§ 7, 50; *Pseudo-Plutarch*, De Plac. Phil., iv. 8, 9. For Epicurus, see *Lucretius*, iv. 33, 726; *Diog. Laert.*, x. 49. All these philosophers held the soul to be material, and, consequently, adopted the theory of representative effluxes, not to account for the intercourse between mind and matter, but to explain the mode of communication between the organ of sense and its object.—Ed.]

* The species (ἀπόρροιαι, ῥεύματα) of Democritus and Epicurus were only given by these philosophers in *sight*. The other senses had qualities of things themselves for objects. See *Gassendi*, Opera, ii. p. 338, and i. p. 448, &c. [This distinction must be understood as relating not to the emanations themselves, but only to their representative character. This is expressed in the words of Gassendi:—'Atque hæc quidem fuisse causa videtur, quamobrem Epicurus et alii species seu spectra, et imagines simulacrave rerum ita dixerint ac descripserint, ut res visibiles solum attinerent; supponentes videlicet pertingere ad cæteros sensus non imagines sonorum, sed sonos, non simulacra odorum, sed odores.'—Ed.]

the observation, that the mind obtains a perception of external objects through an impression on the organs of sense, without determining the nature of this impression, or explaining the connection between the sensual affection and the intellectual knowledge.* But, although Aristotle had not attempted to expound the origin of our perception of external objects after the manner of Democritus, nevertheless the greater number of those who professed themselves his followers, deceived by a mistaken interpretation of his language, and believing, as their master had taught, that all sensation was a passive affection of the mind, [held] that, consequently, it was necessary to suppose, for the causes of this affection,—more especially where the object was at a distance from the sense,—certain effluxes from the object, which, penetrating the organ, might affect the soul, and determine it to a mediate and representative perception of the outward reality.

According to the opinion which generally prevailed among the Peripatetic philosophers of the middle ages, our faculties of knowledge required for their activity a certain representative medium, different both from the mind itself and from the external object of thought. These intermediate and vicarious objects were called *Intentional Species*;—*Species* (*formæ*, *similitudines*, *simulacra*, *idola*), because they represented the object to the mind—*intentional*,* to express the relative and accidental nature of their manifestation. These intentional species were held to be the formal or virtual similitudes of their object, and which

* [See De Anima, ii. 7, § 11. Πάσχοντος γάρ τι τοῦ αἰσθητικοῦ γίνεται τὸ ὁρᾶν, κ. τ. λ. In the same work (ii. 12, § 1), the impression is compared to that of a seal on wax, which communicates its form without its matter. Ἡ μὲν αἴσθησίς ἐστι τὸ δεκτικὸν τῶν αἰσθητῶν εἰδῶν ἄνευ τῆς ὕλης, οἷον ὁ κηρὸς τοῦ δακτυλίου ἄνευ τοῦ σιδήρου καὶ τοῦ χρυσοῦ δέχεται τὸ σημεῖον, λαμβάνει δὲ τὸ χρυσοῦν ἢ τὸ χαλκοῦν σημεῖον, ἀλλ' οὐχ ᾗ χρυσὸς ἢ χαλκός· ὁμοίως δὲ καὶ ἡ αἴσθησις ἑκάστου ὑπὸ τοῦ ἔχοντος χρῶμα ἢ χυμὸν ἢ ψόφον πάσχει, ἀλλ' οὐχ ᾗ ἕκαστον ἐκείνων λέγεται, ἀλλ' ᾗ τοιονδί, καὶ κατὰ τὸν λόγον. The point of the comparison seems to be, that each sense perceives, not the entire nature of the individual object, but only certain qualities, such as colour, savour, &c., adapted to the sense in question. Thus interpreted, it affords no foundation for the doctrine of sensible species. Sir W. Hamilton's opinion, that Aristotle is a natural realist (see above, pp. 827, 886), is also that of M. St Hilaire. See the preface to his Translation of the De Anima, p. xxii.—ED.] That Aristotle did not hold the doctrine of species usually attributed to him, see *Gassendi*, Opera, i. p. 443, ii. pp. 339, 373; *Piccolomineus*, Physica, p. 1306 [De Humana Mente, L. iii. c. 8]; *Th. Albius* (*White*), Sciri, in answer to Glanvill. Zabarella, Comm. in De Anima p. 405, says, 'Species recepta nihil aliud est, quam cognitio ipsa.' Cf. De Rebus Naturalibus, p. 928 sq.

* On the meaning of *intention* and *intentional*, see Zabarella, De Rebus Naturalibus, Francof., 1607, p. 871. 'Ego dico intentionem nil aliud esse, quam attentionem ac diligentiam animæ in alicujus rei consideratione, quo fit ut intentum etiam sumamus pro attento. Hæc est vere Latina hujus vocis significatio, sed traducta postea a philosophis nostris hæc vox est ad omnem animi conceptum significandum, etiamsi absque diligentia fiat, et omnem speciem, sive sensilem sive intellectilem; hæc enim, quatenus est species spiritalis realis objectum repræsentans, dicitur esse ejus intentio, id est, imago in anima: hinc orta est distinctio illa, qua omnes utuntur, primarum et secundarum intentionum. . . . . Sed postea traducta est hujus vocis significatio etiam extra animam, ut id quod est imago alterius repræsentativa, etiamsi non sit in anima, dicatur ens intentionale; hujusmodi est species objecti sensilis in medio, ut species coloris in aere, sive etiam in solido aliquo corpore recepta.' Compare Stier, Quæstiones Controversæ (1652), p. 91. 'Species sensiles vocantur intentionales, non quasi non sint reales, quo sensu entia rationis dicuntur habere esse intentionale; sed quia: 1, habent esse aliquod incompletum et imminutum, degenerans a realitate objectorum quæ repræsentant: . . . . 2, quia hæ species requiruntur ad cognitionem quæ vocatur *intentio*: 3, quia sunt id quo potentia tendit in sua objecta.' Irenæus a Sancto Jacobo, In Arist. De Anima (1655), p. 45, gives several explanations, 'Dicuntur intentionales, ut ostendatur discrimen talis manifestationis ab ea quam faceret objectum per seipsum: enimvero objectum tunc alio non tenderet quam ad seipsum; species autem illæ non tendunt ad seipsas, sed ad objectum, cujus sunt species. Vel iterum sic denominantur, quod habeant esse quoddam diminutum, et admodum simile *intentioni*, . . . non quod sint entia fictitia, sed accedant proxime ad esse spirituale, ideoque videantur similes actibus intellectus et voluntatis, quos appellant *intentiones*. Vel iterum sic dicuntur, quod secum vehendo objecti *effigiem*, *formam*, ac *speciem*, tribuant tali objecto in potentia modum existendi, quem non habet in se; quemadmodum intellectus cogitando de rebus, illis tribuit quædam attributa, v. g. quod sint subjectum, prædicatum, genus, species, &c., quibus carent citra considerationem mentis: unde fit, ut sicuti Logici appellant ista attributa *intentiones*, quasi fabricationes intellectus *tendentis in rem illam*; ita Animastici vocant esse datum objecto per tales species, *intentionale*, id est, non fictum, sed reale diminutum, ut jam diximus.'

likeness they impressed on the particular faculty of knowledge to which they belonged, whether that faculty were the intellect or the sense, and whether the sense were the external or internal.*

These Species were distinguished, both in the intellect and in the sense, either as *species impressæ* or as *species expressæ*.† A *species impressa* was the vicarious existence itself, as emitted by the object, as impressed on the particular faculty, and as concurring with that faculty in its operation. A *species expressa* was the operation itself, elicited by the faculty and the impressed species together; that is, a perception or an intellection, as including both the object and the act.‡ The *species impressa* was the partial cause of the cognition as co-operating with the mind; the *species expressa* was the result and consummation of the act: the former was to the mind the virtual, the latter the formal, similitude of the object. A species fitted to affect the sense, was called a *sensible species* (species sensibilis): it proceeded immediately from the object, either by instantaneous transition or by continuous propagation, to the sense; § and, if not altogether immaterial, was of an intermediate nature between matter and spirit. The senses were either the external—sight, hearing, &c.—or the internal. These were generally accounted four:—the common sense (sensus communis), the imagination (phantasia), the sensitive judgment (potentia æstimativa or cogitativa), the sensitive memory (memoria sensitiva). Many, however, counted only three, not distinguishing the sensitive judgment from the imagination; some acknowledged only two, the common sense and the imagination; while others again admitted only the common sense.* The species of the intellect were called *intelligible species* (species intelligibiles), and were altogether immaterial.

The intellect was twofold—the Active (agens), and the Passive or Possible (passibilis, patiens, vel possibilis), which a few held to be distinct principles, many to be distinct powers, and some to be the same power manifested in different relations. The function of the Active Intellect was, on occasion of the species in the internal senses, to fabricate from itself *species impressæ* for the Passive Intellect. These intelligible species were

* See Irenæus, In Arist. De Anima, p. 45. 'Per *species intentionales* intelliguntur minimæ quædam entitates, quæ similitudinem objecti, a quo exeunt, continent, imprimuntque cognoscitivæ potentiæ, ad quam tendunt: sive ea potentia sit intellectus; sive sensus, sive internus aut externus. Dixi *cognoscitivæ*, nam de iis solum potentiis nunc agimus: utrum vero etiam dentur respectu voluntatis et appetitus sensitivi, constabit ex dicendis de modo, quo intellectus movet voluntatem, et phantasia appetitum.'

† 'Species alia impressa, quam objectum imprimit in potentia; alia expressa, quam potentia in se exprimit et format. Existimo eam ita vocari quia exprimit objectum; *exprimo* enim opponitur verbo *adumbro;* hoc significat obumbratam sive umbra tectam figuram, illud vero claram et apertam.' Hurtado de Mendoza, Universa Philosophia, p. 553. 'Species impressa est qualitas quæ loco objecti præbetur potentiæ cognoscitivæ, ut simul cum illa concurrat ad actum,' Ibid., p. 610.

‡ Irenæus, In Arist. De Anima, p. 45, 'Appellantur quoque *species impressæ*, ad distinctionem aliarum, quas vocant *species expressas*. *Impressæ* sunt illæ, quas objecta emittunt, seu imprimunt potentiæ pro elicienda operatione. *Expressæ*, sunt ipsemet operationes elicitæ a potentia et impressa specie, id est, sensationes et intellectiones. Quæritur utrum dentur ejusmodi impressæ species? Quid sint? Quodnam illarum munus proprium?'

§ See Gassendi, Opera i. p. 448. [Cf. Biel, In ii Sent. Dist. iii. qu. 2, C.—Ed.]

* The following note has been compiled from memoranda in the Author's Common-Place Book. On the Internal Senses, and the different divisions, and number of them, given by different Schoolmen, see *Toletus*, In Arist. de Anima, L. iii. c. 3, qu. 6; *Piccolomineus*, Physica, p. 1190 sq.; *Conimbricenses*, In Arist. De Anima, L. iii. c. 3, qu. 1, art. 1; *Eustachius*, Summa Philosophiæ, Phys., P. iii. tract. ii. disp. 3, qu. 1; *Irenæus*, In Arist. De An., p. 66; *Gassendi*, Phys., Sect. iii., Memb. Post., L. viii. cc. 1, 2; *La Chambre*, Système de l'Ame, L. ii. c. 8, p. 111 (ed. 1664); *Tosca*, Comp. Phil., t. vii. p. 194; *Krug*, Lexikon, v. Sinn.—Avicenna, Algazel, Albertus Magnus, and Jandunus (see Toletus, l. c.) agree in giving *five: Sensus Communis, Imaginatio, Æstimatio* (ὑπόληψις), *Phantasia*, and *Memoria;* but differ in their account of them (in re). St Thomas (Summ. Theol., P. i. qu. 78, art. 4) and Averroes (In De Anima, L. iii. comm. 6) give *four: Sensus Communis, Imaginatio, Æstimatio* (quæ in Homine est *Cogitatio*), and *Memoria*. Toletus (l. c.) and Zabarella (Comm. De Anima, L. ii. c. 12) hold *three: Sensus Communis, Phantasia* (vel *Imaginatio* vel *Æstimatio*), and *Memoria;* and the former thinks that Aristotle and the Greeks held as he does (but see Gassendi, l. c.). Galen and his followers (Conimbricenses, La Chambre, ll. cc.) also give *three: Imaginatio, Cogitativa*, and *Memoria*.—Averroes (De Anima, L. ii. comm. 63, and L. iii. comm. 6, 20) first (?) distinguished Cogitatio from Phantasia and Memoria. This faculty of Cogitatio versant about particulars, comparing them together; different from *Mens*. See *Simon Simonius*, De Mem. et Rem., p. 269. On Cogitativa, as a material faculty, called also *Ratio particularis*, v. *Bernardi* Sem. Phil. Arist., p. 261.—Ed.

not, however, formed or abstracted from the phantasmata or sensible species, because the intellect, as wholly immaterial and not conversant about matter, as it could not contemplate, so it could not fabricate from the material species of the internal senses, an immaterial species proportioned to its nature and qualified to concur in an act of intellectual knowledge.* By a conversion of the Active Intellect towards the phantasms or sensible species, a certain similitude of the external object, abstracted from its individual conditions, is occasioned in the Passive Intellect, which similitude constitutes its impressed species,—the *species intelligibilis impressa*.† It was the common opinion that intelligible species were wholly the work of the mind itself. The function of the Passive or Possible Intellect is to receive the *species impressæ* from the Active Intellect and to co-operate with them unto a perfect act of knowledge—an intellection—a *species intelligibilis expressa*. It was not, therefore, called *passive*, as if without an energy, but as receiving the species produced by the Active Intellect, by which, as it were impregnated, it could produce an actual cognition. In point of fact, its activity, though subsequent, is of a higher and more enduring character than that of the subordinate and ministering intellect specially denominated *active*,—constituting, as it does, the supreme energy of conscious intellection.‡

We should err, however, if we should suppose that this was the doctrine universally received among the Schools; for the opinions were various, and contradictory, in regard to all the details of the theory, and there were not a few who regarded the whole hypothesis as a fiction. No doubt, indeed, can possibly arise in regard to the existence of the *species expressæ*, in so far as they are viewed as acts of knowledge,—as phænomena of consciousness. But the case is different with the *species impressæ*, as these are not revealed to us as facts, but only excogitated as hypotheses. Nor was this doctrine ever universally admitted. So erroneous, indeed, is the belief in regard to its exclusive prevalence during the middle ages, that some of the acutest Schoolmen regarded them entirely, in Sense and Intellect, as an idle theory, unsupported by the authority either of reason or of Aristotle;* while a still greater number rejected them in part. For some, allowing them for Sense, disallowed them for Intellect;† while

* Those who held the absolute immateriality of sensible species of course held their immediate contemplation by the intellect, which was then said, not *converti supra phantasmata*, but *speculari phantasmata*. We shall have to notice the correspondence of this doctrine with that of Descartes.

† Vide S. Thomam, apud Irenæum, p. 140. [The passage referred to is from Summa, P. i. Qu. lxxxv. art. 1. 'Phantasmata cum sint similitudines individuorum, et existant in organis corporis, non habent eundem modum existendi quem habet intellectus humanus, ut ex dictis patet, et ideo non possunt sua virtute imprimere in intellectum possibilem. Sed virtute intellectus agentis resultat quædam similitudo in intellectu possibili ex conversione intellectus agentis supra phantasmata, quæ quidem est repræsentativa eorum quorum sunt phantasmata, solum quantum ad naturam speciei. Et per hunc modum dicitur abstrahi species intelligibilis a phantasmatibus.'—ED.]

‡ On a passive and active intellect, the former as the holder of principles unevolved in consciousness, the latter as the thinking principle by which they are evolved, as held by Plato, and as affording Aristotle the hint for his active and passive intellects, see Tennemann, Gesch. d. Phil., ii. p. 307. These only two relations of the same faculty.—(*Note in Author's Common-Place Book.*)

* Both sensible and intelligible species are denied by *Ockam*, (In ii. Sent., Qu. 15, 18), by his epitomator, *Biel*, (In ii. Sent., Dist. iii. qu. 2), by *Durandus*, (In ii. Sent., Dist. iii. qu. 6), and by *Adam*, On the Sentences, (see Capreolus, In ii. Sent., Dist. iii. qu. 2, p. 176); also by *Buccaferreus*, (apud Piccolominei Physica, p. 1304), and by *Piccolomineus* himself, (p. 1308). Cf. Lalemandet, Cursus Philosophicus, p. 558. Nor did the Nominalists allow that in their opinion touching species they were opposed by the authority of Aristotle. 'As to the texts of the philosopher quoted in support of this hypothesis, where he says, for example, that Intellect is receptive of species,—and the place of species,—that a stone itself is not in the mind, but its species, &c., we answer;—That by species Aristotle means simply the cognitive acts themselves, which are called species, because involving a similitude (a representation) of the object cognised. For a stone is not in the mind of him who thinks of a stone, but the cognition (or act representative) thereof, during which the intellect is in the state of understanding a stone; and of these cognitions (representations) the mind is the place.' Biel, [In ii. Sent., Dist. iii. qu. 2, BB, KK]; compare Ockam, In ii. Sent., Qu. 17, R. [For Durandus, see *Conimbricenses*, In Arist. De Anima, p. 188, ed. 1617, and the extracts quoted in a note to the Author's *Lectures on Metaphysics*, vol. ii. p. 36. For Plato's and Aristotle's theories, see above, pp. 262 b, n. *, 827, n. *, and *Lectures on Metaphysics*, l. c.—ED.]

† This was done by those who held the phantasms to be sufficient, without the aid of intelligible species. This view was maintained by

others admitting them for Intellect, denied them for Sense.* Some again, according them in Sense, limited their admission to the external senses;† while in these, few allowed them in all; smell, taste, and touch being usually supposed to require nothing vicarious of their objects.‡

Opinions touching the Intelligible Species were divided into two hostile classes, according as the many maintained the *intelligible species* and the *intellection* to be two things really distinguished from each other, in nature and in time; while the few denied intelligible species as aught really different from, or existent before or after, intellection.§

In the former class, however, opinions differed; some holding that the intellect had a peculiar species, as a peculiar operation, of its own; while others maintained, that, though it energised after its own fashion, it did this only in turning towards the phantasmata or species of internal sense, which thus served, in a sort, as vicarious objects to the higher as to the lower faculties of cognition.* According to the former opinion, (which was the one generally adopted, and of which Aquinas and Scotus were illustrious leaders), the *species impressa* is something superadded to the intellect, being a certain spiritual accident elaborated by the active intellect from the rude material of phantasms, and impressed in the passive intellect as its subject; and, while preceding the act of intellection in the order of time, is preserved in the faculty after the cessation of its act, ready to be anew called out of habit into consciousness,—the intellection and the impressed species constituting together the *species expressa intellectus*—*verbum mentis*. According to the latter opinion, (of which Henry of Ghent and Joannes Bacconius were the original representatives), there is no species impressed in, no new quality superadded to, the passive intellect; the phantasms alone, as sublimated by the active intellect, and (by reference to the phantasy) under the name of *species expressæ*, being held sufficient to cause or to occasion intellection.†

As to the modes of the operations of the Active Intellect on the phantasms, in spiritualising the material, in denuding the singular of its individuating conditions—processes necessary, on either opinion, to assimilate the faculty and its object—as was to be expected, all is vague, and varying, and controversial.‡ [This indeed is the case with the details of the theory in general, as regards both sensible and intelligible species: the following varieties of opinion may be cited as instances.]

Some held that the mind had the power within itself of suggesting or creating the species, when determined to this act by the external affection of the senses.

Some held that the mind had innate

Joannes Bacconius, (In i. Sent. Prolog qu. 2, art. 2, § 5;)—*Godfredus*, (Quodl. ix. qu. 19;)—*Henricus Gandavensis*, (Quodl. iv. qu. 7, 8; Quodl. v. qu. 14.) See Conimbricenses (In De Anima, p. 429), who also refer to *Theophrastus*, *Themistius*, and *Avempace*, as holding a similar view. Cf. Capreolus, l. c., and Zabarella, De Rebus Naturalibus, p. 982. Henricus (Quodl. v. qu. 14) allows the *species expressa*, but denies the *species impressa*; see Capreolus, t. ii. p. 153. Compare Casmann, Psychologia Anthropologica, p. 101.

* See *Gregorius Ariminensis*, In i. Sent., Dist. iii. qu. 2; In ii. Sent., Dist. vii. qu. 3. Cf. Dandinus, De Corpore Animato, ff. 1153, 1981. For various theories, see Philippus a S. Trinitate, Summa Philosophica, Lugd. 1648, p. 561. [He mentions, as denying species in sense, *Galen*, *Plotinus*, and others; in intellect, *Themistius* and others; in both, *Ockam*, *Biel*, *Durandus*, and others. See also Toletus, In Arist. De Anima, L. ii. qu. 23; L. iii. qu. 21.—Ed.]

† This is partially done by *F. Bonæ Spei*, (Physica, Pars iv. Disp. vi. § 32; Disp. x. § 2,) who allows species in the sense of sight, while he agrees with the nominalists in rejecting them for the internal senses. On the other hand, they are maintained in both by *Suarez*, *Hurtado*, *Arriaga*, *Oviedo*, *Telles*, *Murcia*, *Poncius*, *Fremondus*, and, in general, by the *Thomists* and *Scotists*. [The nominalist doctrine, however, as regards the internal senses, has been variously represented. See Toletus, In Arist. De Anima, Lib. ii. qu. 23; Dandinus, De Corpore Animato, f. 1152. —Ed.]

‡ See Arriaga, Curs. Phil., De Anima, Disp. iv.; Hurtado de Mendoza, Universa Philosophia, De Anima, Disp. xii. Sect. 1. Cf. Vallesius, Controv. Medic. et Philos., L. ii. c. 31. Thus in those senses in which objective perception predominates, species were usually given; in those in which subjective sensation predominates, they were usually denied.

§ That species (intelligible) are only modifications of the mind itself, see Melanchthon, De Anima, [De Intellectu, p. 187, ed. Lugd. 1555]; Piccolomineus, De Mente Humana, L. iii. c. 7. Some of the Schoolmen held them to have no entity, and that intellectual cognition was only a habit or certain relation to an object present. See Casmann, Psychol. Anthropol., p. 101. (*Note in Author's Common-Place Book.*)

* See Conimbricenses, In Arist. De Anima, pp. 429, 430.—Ed.

† See above, p. 954, note †.

‡ See on this point Zabarella, De Rebus Naturalibus, p. 1003.

species, which were merely excited by the impression of the outward object.*

Some held, with St Austin, in regard to intelligible species, that we know everything in the divine intellect, *rationibus æternis*, like Malebranche.†

Some held that the Active Intellect did not exist.‡

The Nominalists in general held the Active and Passive Intellects to be only the same power in two different relations. Indeed, after Scotus and St Austin, they allowed the various faculties to be neither really distinct from the soul nor from each other, but all to be only the same indivisible principle operating differently only as operating in different respects.§

Some held the substantial distinction of the Active and Passive Intellects; and of these, some held that the Active Intellect is a substance distinct from the human mind, and that it is one and the same in all men, and not different from God;‖ while others maintained the unity of the passive or possible intellect really separate from the mind of the individual, but assisting it and conjoined by the images in the phantasy: from these images, illuminated by its light, they held that the intellect receives the intelligible species, by which 'consignatus,' it obtains a knowledge of things.*

Some held that species were not the natural effluxions from the objects, but the supernatural production of some higher power.†

Questions without number were agitated concerning the nature of the species: whether immediately or mediately produced; whether substance or accident, or between both; whether possessing real or only representative existence; whether themselves the objects or only the conditions of perception; whether formally or really different from their objects; whether those of the sense were material or spiritual; whether material *in subjecto* and spiritual *in modo*; whether virtual or formal in their similitude; whether divisible objectively or subjectively; whether they multiply themselves in the external medium; whether proper to the cognitive faculties, or common also to those of will, &c., &c.

The doctrine, however, of Intentional Species continued, notwithstanding its manifest incongruities, to be the dominant and orthodox opinion in the schools of philosophy until after the middle of the seventeenth century, when it sunk under the new spirit of inquiry which at that period had been excited in all the departments of human knowledge. It was chiefly to the arguments of Hobbes, Gassendi, Berigard, and Descartes, that we owe the final refutation of this doctrine; and the theory was perhaps the more easily abandoned, that the new hypothesis of a subjective representation in our perception of material objects, which was then introduced by the last of these philosophers, afforded, as it seemed, a more intelligible explanation of the great problem in regard to the origin of our knowledge of an external world. Traces of the ancient theory may still be found in some of the philosophical speculations of a later age, but from the period of Des-

---

* *Avicenna* and other Arabians, *Albertus Magnus* in some degree. See Genuensis, Elementa Metaphysicæ (Venet. 1748), Pars ii. pp. 143, 144.

† Genuensis, l. c. [who cites *St Thomas*, Summa, Pars i. Qu. 84, art. 5. But see below, Note P.—Ed.]

‡ *Durandus*, *Joannes Narbonensis*, and others. [See Conimbricenses, In De Anima, p. 417.—Ed.]

§ See *St Augustin*, De Trinitate, L. x. c. 11. 'Hæc tria, memoria, intelligentia, voluntas, quoniam non sunt tres vitæ, sed una vita; nec tres mentes, sed una mens; consequenter utique nec tres substantiæ sunt, sed una substantia.' Cf. *Pseudo-Augustin*, De Spiritu et Anima, c. 13. 'Dicitur anima, dum vegetat; spiritus, dum contemplatur; sensus, dum sentit; animus, dum sapit; dum intelligit, mens; dum discernit, ratio; dum recordatur, memoria; dum consentit, voluntas. Ista tamen non differunt in substantia, quemadmodum in nominibus; quoniam omnia ista una anima est: proprietates quidem diversæ, sed essentia una.' The same view is maintained by *Scotus*, In ii. Sent., Dist. xvi. qu. 1; and, among the Nominalists, by *Occam*, In ii. Sent. qu. 24; *Gregorius Ariminensis*, In ii. Sent., Dist. xvi. qu. 3; *Biel*, In ii. Sent., Dist. xvi. qu. 1. Other authorities are also quoted by P. Bonæ Spei, Physica, Pars iv. Disp. iii. § 4.—Ed.

‖ *Alexander Aphrodisiensis*, *Priscianus Lydus*, also *Avicenna*, *Avempace*, and *Marinus*, a Greek mentioned by Philoponus. (These three last however did not identify it with God.)—*Cajetanus* and *Zabarella*. [See Conimbricenses, In De Anima, p. 417; Genuensis, Elem. Metaph., ii. p. 145.—Ed.]

* *Averroes*, apud Conimbricenses, In De Anima, p. 107. A similar view was held by *Themistius*, De Anima, Lib. i. cont. 60; Lib. iii. cont. 30. [ff. 70, 90, ed. Ald.] *Simplicius*, not very different; see Simpl. In De Anima, Lib. iii. cont. 2. [f. 62, ed. Ald.] On these, compare Cardan, De Animarum Immortalitate, Opera, Lugd. 1663, vol. ii. p. 505, who notices some differences of detail between them. [See also Zabarella, De Rebus Naturalibus, p. 962.—Ed.]

† *Buccaferreus* made heaven the cause of species; *Suessanus*, God. See Berigard, Circulus Pisanus (1661), p. 656. [The opinions of Suessanus and Buccaferreus are examined at some length by Zabarella, De Rebus Naturalibus, p. 833.—Ed.]

cartes we may confidently affirm that the hypothesis of a representative perception —where the immediate object was something different from the mind—had been almost universally superseded by the representative hypothesis, in which the vicarious object was held only for a modification of the mind itself.* The nomenclature of the ancient theory was not, however, abandoned along with the reality; and many even of the followers of Descartes continued to employ the terms *species*, *image*, &c., when the acceptation in which they had been originally employed had become obsolete.†

* * * * * * * *

[This Note has been put together from different papers containing separate outlines, all left unfinished. The following translations and abridgments of passages exhibiting the nominalist doctrine of species, were probably intended for the same Note. The language adopted is generally that of Biel.—Ed.]

A. In reference to the lower cognitive faculties,—the SENSIBILITY, External and Internal.

1. "That by the represented object there is caused in the medium between it and the organ a species wholly diverse in nature from itself and previous to the act of sensitive perception—this is disproved on the principle that a plurality of causes is not to be postulated without necessity. For there is no necessity to warrant the hypothesis of such species; it being impossible to assign any manifest and sufficient reason for its adoption. Such a reason must proceed, either on the ground of experience, or of some self-evident principle *a priori*. Not the former —for as the advocates of this theory admit, that Species are not themselves perceived, we have consequently no possible experience of their existence, as a fact. Not the latter — for the principle that the mover and the moved must coexist in reciprocal propinquity, is incompetent to legitimate the assumption. For," &c. —the demonstration I must omit. Ockam, In Sent. L. ii. qu. 18 F.; Biel, In Sent. L. ii. dist. iii. qu. 2 E. Compare also Durandus, In Sent. L. ii. dist. iii. qu. 6, § 15.

2. "That in the outer sense, either organ or faculty, there is impressed a Species previous to the sensitive act and necessary for its causation, is disproved, like the foregoing assumption, on the score of its gratuity. For to determine such an act in the organ of the external sense, there is required alone the material object and the unimpeded sensitive power." Ockam, Biel, ll. cc.; Durandus l. c. § 21.

3. "Moreover, if such Species were admitted as a concause with the sensitive power in producing the act of sensitive perception, it would be a natural cause. Suppose then that by God it were preserved in the sense, the object represented by it being annihilated. On this hypothesis, the Species would, along with the power, continue to cause the act of sensitive perception, seeing that it remains unchanged either in its existence or in its nature. But the act of sensitive perception is an *intuitive* cognition, and there would thus naturally be determined an intuitive cognition of a non-existent object; which is impossible." Ockam, Biel, ll. cc.*

* On the ambiguity in the Cartesian use of the term *idea*, see above, p. 273. On the subordinate question, whether the mental modification has any existence apart from the act of consciousness, the opinion of Descartes was variously interpreted by his followers. See *Discussions*, p. 74. Some exceptions may also be noted in those philosophers, such as Newton and Clarke, who maintained the hypothesis of images in the brain. See above, p. 273, and *Discussions*, p. 80.—Ed.

† De la Forge occurs first to my recollection; but the following passage from Chauvin, who flourished not long posterior to Descartes, may supply the place of other references. 'Sunt tamen inter Recentiores philosophos non pauci qui retinent nomenclationes speciei impressæ et expressæ. Illis autem species impressa nihil aliud est, quam motus aliquis ab objectis mediate, vel immediate, exterioribus corporis partibus impressus, indeque per nervos ad cerebrum transmissus; vel certa fibrarum cerebri commotio, ex spirituum animalium, in cerebro decurrentium, agitatione procedens: quæ, cum nullam habeant cum rebus objectis naturæ similitudinem, nulla alia de causa earum habentur repræsentamina, quam quod ipsorum occasione mens res sibi faciat præsentes, easdemque in ideis suis exinde nascentibus contempletur. . . . . . . Expressa vero species nihil aliud quicquam est, præter eam animi notionem, quæ ad speciei impressæ præsentiam exprimitur, cujusque attentione et intuitu res ipsa cognoscitur.' Lexicon Rationale, sive Thesaurus Philosophicus, v. *Species Intelligibilis*.

* It should have been added — there would thus also be rendered problematical the existence of an external world; but Idealism, as such a consequence, was not yet developed.—It ought, however, to have been shewn, that the hypothesis of Species in sensible perception is in truth a negation of a true intuitive, or immediate, apprehension of external things. But the same objection might have been brought against Ockam's own doctrine of perception; nor did this escape the observation of another acute nominalist and

4. "Nor for the internal sense, or Imagination, is there need of supposing any Species distinct from the cognitive energy. For," (and this is a profound observation in which modern philosophers are anticipated,) "along with the act of intuitive cognition in external perception, there is always a concomitant act of abstractive (representative) cognition by the phantasy, which, when the external object is removed, tends ever, through the well-known influence of habit, to repeat itself; consequently, to explain the phænomena of imagination and memory, there is no necessity of resorting to the idle hypothesis of representative entities, distinct from the mind, and remaining in it after the conclusion of its acts." Ockam and Biel, ll. cc. [Ockam, Qu. 15 H. L, 17 N.; Biel, L. ii. dist. iii. qu. 2 H.]

5. "That thing through which, as a representative, the knowing faculty is carried to another thing, is necessarily first known itself. But, for example, the species of colour in the eye is not first known or seen by the eye, nay in no manner of way is it ever seen or known at all; consequently it is impossible that through it, as through a representative, the visive faculty can be conducted to aught else. The major is thus proved:—Whatever stands in the relation of an object (objective se habet) to a knowing faculty, as knowing, is necessarily knowable or known by it. But whatever represents anything to a knowing faculty holds to that faculty the relation of an object, (for it is vicarious of the thing it represents, which, were it itself present, would hold the relation of an object to the knowing faculty); therefore every such representative entity is necessarily knowable or known. And since it conduces to the knowledge of another, it is consequently known pre-

---

even more thoroughgoing expugnator of Species than himself,—I mean Durandus.

In reference to his doctrine, that the first act of abstractive (representative) knowledge in imagination is a simultaneous concomitant of the act of intuitive cognition in perception or intellection, Ockam says:—"In regard to the first abstractive cognition, that which accompanies the intuitive, it is to be observed, that the former cognition is caused by the latter, whether in Intellect or Sense, in conjunction with the imaginative power, and to the exclusion of the object of the intuition, albeit the contrary may have been previously stated. Because, were the intuitive cognition to subsist, its object being absolutely annihilated, the abstractive cognition would subsist also. These two partial causes are of themselves sufficient to determine the first act of imagination, of which the external object is not a cause, but only a cause of its cause. For, were God to destroy the external object of sense, conserving, however, in sense the intuitive cognition thereof, the power of phantasy would still be competent to an imaginative act in reference to that object. But if the intuitive cognition were destroyed, whether the external object remain or not, it is impossible that the act of imagination could, except supernaturally, be brought to bear." Ockam, Qu. 16 G. G., and Biel, l. c. H. The real object being, on this doctrine, excluded from the sphere of consciousness in perception, that object is consequently not intuitively, or in itself, apprehended; the object of which we are conscious in perception is therefore only a vicarious object; and a scheme of representationism, though in its simpler form, emerges. Now, though the Venerable Inceptor be not named in the following strictures, I make no doubt that his doctrine is the one which the Most Resolute Doctor had in his eye. "But some one may say . . . . that the cognition alone of a thing in a cognitive faculty makes that object present to the faculty, not in the capacity of a thing existent, but in the capacity of a thing apprehended (non in ratione existentis, sed in ratione agniti). For the act alone constitutes this presence, and no other presence of the object is required for its cognition, except when the cognition is determined as an effect by the object; because, in this case, there is certainly required the actual presence of the object in its real existence, for what is not really in act cannot possibly operate. But God can do immediately of himself, what he does mediately by the object. Therefore it is manifest that God can cause in the intellect the knowledge of a thing not present to the intellect, and this, too, immediately according to its actual existence, and not through any medium or species.

"This doctrine, in its very statement, may seem passing marvellous. For, according to it, God can cause the eye to see a colour not really present to it, nay, not even extant in the universe of things; a corollary whereof is, that the act of a faculty does not require any real existence of an object when that object does not move the faculty to act, which is tantamount to saying, that God might supply the place of the motive object. On this ground it could be asserted, that the sight can see a colour which is not, the hearing hear a sound which is not, the taste taste a savour which is not, and the feeling feel a heat which is not,—a doctrine that many would regard as impossible." Durandus, In Prolog. Sent. Qu. 3, §§ 13, 14.

Durandus, I may notice, seems to deny, like Reid (see p. 801), absolutely and without reserve, the affection of sense by the agency of the object. He requires only the mutual approximation of the sense and its object; and then ensues the sensitive perception, simply because the one is capable of perceiving, the other capable of being perceived. See L. ii. dist. iii. qu. 6, § 21, and dist. viii. qu. 4, §§ 2, 3, 4. This doctrine is only correct if limited to the primary qualities; but it is a nearer approximation to the truth than, before Reid, was accomplished by any modern philosopher.

viously to that other, in the order of time or of nature. Such is the major: the minor is self-evident. For the species of colour in the eye, is by the eye neither seen, nor in any way capable of being seen, as the experience of every one testifies; therefore, &c." Durandus, In Sent. L. ii. dist. iii. qu. 6. § 10.

6. "Further, if such a Species lead to the knowledge of aught else, it can only do this by reason of its similarity. Hence it is that the Species is generally described as the likeness of the thing. It thus performs the part and holds the relation of an image. But an image, in leading to the knowledge of that of which it is the image, is itself previously known; this cannot, however," (as is indeed admitted), "be said of the Species in question; therefore, &c. And in truth it appears self-evidently absurd that the faculty knowing should be conducted to the knowledge of aught by a representative to it utterly unknown; whereas it is most certain that only by the known can it be led to a knowledge of the unknown." § 11.

B. In regard to the higher cognitive faculty,—the INTELLECT.

"Species are only supposed, to account, 1°, for the assimilation of an immaterial intellect with a material object; 2°, for the representation of what cannot be known in itself; 3°, for the determination of the faculty to energy; 4°, for the bringing into union when reciprocally remote, that which moves with that which is moved." Ockam, In Sent. L. ii. qu. 14, 15 T.; Biel, In Sent. L. ii. dist. iii., qu. 2 L.

1°. *Assimilation.*—It has been an almost universal assumption of philosophers, that the relation of knowledge infers similarity of nature between the object known and the subject knowing. Hence the common ground on which the advocates and opponents of species contend. Among other arguments under this head, I select the following:—

a.) "The object is a substance, the intellect is a substance, whereas the species, if admitted, will be an accident. The intellect and object, therefore, as substances, are already more assimilated to each other than either to the proposed medium of assimilation; and it is, therefore, easier to suppose the intellect representing to itself the object, than to suppose this represented by a Species." Ockam, Biel, ll. cc.

b.) "The Species are either material or immaterial; for these are mutual contradictories. But if immaterial, how can a material object be assimilated by an immaterial Species with which it holds no analogy, to an immaterial intellect when the extreme assimilated behoves the rather to be assimilated to the mean by which, than to the extreme to which, it is assimilated?" Ockam, Biel, ll. cc.

2°. *Representation.* — a.) "Species are not necessary for representation. For, while the object is present, it needs nothing vicarious of itself; and when representation is required, there is implied a previous knowledge of the thing represented, and the representation only leads to a recollective cognition thereof, &c. Hence *to represent* is convertible with *to present again.* Species, therefore, as supposed pre-existent to cognition, cannot be proposed as representative of objects." Ockam, Biel, ll. cc. Compare Durandus, ibid. § 12.

3°. *Determination.*—a.) "Nor is it necessary to suppose Species, to account for the determination of the power to act. For every passive or recipient power is sufficiently determined by a competent active or impressive power; and this more especially when the passive power itself is also active, as in the case in question. For the intellect is an active power recipient in itself of intellection, and, along with the object, co-operating to the production of this energy." Ockam, Biel, ll. cc. Compare Durandus, ibid. § 13.

b.) "Nor ought we to suppose Species, in order to account for the causation of intellection, on the ground, which they maintain, that the corporeal cannot act upon the incorporeal, and therefore that the admission of Species is necessary as a medium of operation between the material object and the immaterial intellect. But, on their own shewing, their hypothesis is idle. For the intellectual Species is as immaterial as the intellect its subject. Therefore, as the material object cannot with the passive intellect be the immediate concause of its intellection, so it cannot co-operate with the active intellect in the production of intelligible Species — a product not less spiritual than intellection itself." Ockam, Biel, ll. cc.

4°. *Union of the Motor and the Moved* —"Nor need we suppose Species, in order to explain the union of a remote object with the relative power, on the principle that the distant cannot act upon the distant,—in other words, that a thing cannot operate where it is not. This principle, as necessitating the hypothesis of sensible Species, has already been disproved."

(This omitted as involved in the Ockamist theory of perception.) "But, in reference to the immediate question, it is incompetent, because the object is as distant from the intelligible Species as from the act of intellection; for both are in the intellect. In these circumstances, the object either acts by *immediately* causing the intelligible Species, on which alternative the principle is surrendered, the approximation of agent and patient not being required. Or again the object acts by causing the intelligible Species through the mediation of another Species. On this alternative, the Species present in the intellect has, prior and immediately determining its existence, another Species; this Species again another; and so on indefinitely to the object. But this is false. For the Species prior to the last or intelligible Species behove to be either material or immaterial. If material, they would then not be of the same nature (ejusdem rationis) with that which is present to the intellect, for material and immaterial are opposed in Species. They could not therefore be multiplied the one by the other; for the condition of this multiplication is identity of nature; and thus the immaterial Species in the intellect could not, as is supposed, be produced by the material Species in the medium. If again it be supposed that the previous Species are spiritual, then these immaterial and indivisible accidents will proceed from, and inhere in, a material and divisible subject; which is not to be without necessity presumed, &c." Biel, l. c., with Ockam, l. c.

Hence, concludes Ockam, it is manifest that certain cognitive Habits in the intellect are to be admitted, in order to save the phænomena, but not Species.

To these arguments of Ockam and his expositor—for the latter ought not to be regarded as a mere abbreviator—may be added the more summary mode of reasoning adopted by Durandus.

"That this hypothesis of Species is as inept in reference to the Intellect as to the Sense is manifest, and for the same reason—viz., that it behoves the Species to be known prior to the reality it represents, but this we all experience to be the converse of the truth.

"Again, the intellect is the faculty of reflection (virtus reflexiva), and it knows itself and its contents with certainty, and, as it were, by observation and experiment. Thus we know by experience that we understand, and have in us a principle by which we understand. If then there existed in our intellect any such Species, it appears that we could not but know with certainty that such there were; as we know with certainty of the existence of our other intellectual furniture, whether these be acts or habits. But we do not. There seems, therefore, no better reason to suppose, in intellect, Species representative of its objects, than in sense; and in regard to sense we have already proved that there was none." Durandus, ibid. §§ 12, 13.

The ἀπόρροιαι, *effluxus*, of Democritus and Epicurus, are decidedly non-egoistical and material; but the *species* of the Aristotelian schoolmen in their various modifications cannot be simply referred to the class either of corporeal or incorporeal, though there can be no doubt that in general they belong to the category of non-egoistical media. The same of the Cartesian *ideas*, as of Malebranche. The *cognitive reasons* (λόγοι γνωστικοί) of the lower Platonists appear again to belong to the forms of egoistical representationism, as do the *ideas* of Arnauld and many of the Cartesian school.

NOTE N.

THE CARTESIAN THEORY OF PERCEPTION AND IDEAS.

[References.—From I. P. 256 a, 267 a, 269 a, 274 a, 296 a b, 297 b, 306 a, 368 b.]

[The materials for this Note are very imperfect. The text is printed from two unfinished papers of an early date, neither of which appears to have been revised for the present work. The footnotes have been chiefly compiled from jottings and references scattered over various papers, and occasionally filled up from the article on the Philosophy of Perception in the Author's *Discussions*.—Ed.]

The theory of Descartes relative to our perception of external objects,—separating from it what is merely superfluous, and translating his terms, as far as that can be done, without prejudice to his opinions, into language more familiar to us in its application,—is contained in the following positions.

The essential attribute of matter is extension;* the essential attribute of mind is consciousness.†

Extension and Consciousness are qualities not only different, but opposite; consequently the substances to which these attributes essentially belong, are not only necessarily distinct, but even can have no natural intercourse or relation.

Mind and body are, however, united; but as their union cannot originally or subsequently depend on their natural affinity or physical influence on each other, it must be constituted and maintained by some power different from either. The will of God is the immediate cause of this union, and his concourse is the medium of the alliance.*

* Principia, Pars. ii. § 4. Cf. Tennemann, Geschichte der Philosophie, vol. x. p. 252.

† De Methodo, iv.; De Passionibus Animæ, Pars i. art. 4, 17; Principia, P. i. § 8; Epistol, Pars i. Ep. 105; Pars ii. Ep. 6. Cf. Tennemann, Geschichte der Philosophie, vol. x. pp. 230, 258, 260. For *Consciousness*, Descartes says *Thought*; but as he includes under this term thought, properly so called, feeling, and desire, that is, all the energies and affections of which we are conscious, and nothing more, the conversion is both legitimate and convenient. Principia, P. i. § 9. It is needless to say that by Consciousness I mean, here as elsewhere, the fundamental form of all our mental modifications, and not that determination of consciousness, by which, through an act of will, we can attend with greater intensity to the laws under which our mind acts or is affected, than to the external object of the energy or passion. Consciousness properly is conversant equally with the objective and with the subjective. The different faculties and affections are only modified consciousness.

* Cf. De la Forge, Traité de l'Esprit, p. 230 [ed. Amsterdam, chap. xv.] That Descartes was the author of the theory of assistance or occasional causes, and that his explanation of the connection between mind and body rests fundamentally on this hypothesis, it is impossible to doubt. For while he rejected all physical influence in the motion of bodies, which he referred to the general will of the Deity (Principia, P. ii. § 36, &c.), he necessarily *a fortiori* adopted the same supposition in illustrating the influence of mind and body. The fundamental position of the system is not on all occasions explicitly stated by him, though his reasoning always necessarily supposes it; and he has sometimes allowed himself, in conformity to ordinary language, expressions, which, if taken literally, are inconsistent with his general theory. This has frequently led those who had not studied his works in their general relations, into a misrepresentation of his opinions on particular points. Dr Reid does not seem to have been aware of the fundamental principle of the Cartesian philosophy, and has accordingly been unable to reconcile the apparent

This union consists in the harmony and reciprocal action of these two principles: consequently the assistance of God is the hyperphysical and immediate cause of their mutual influence, while the antecedent movement in either is only the occasional and mediate cause of the consequent modification in the other.*

To the body belongs not merely the mass of organised matter potentially capable of life (according to the doctrine of the Aristotelians), but the principle of animal life itself—a subtle and attenuated fluid, which, in connection with the cerebral or nervous system, is the immediate cause of the manifestations of life, and of all corporeal movement.†

To the mind (or soul) belongs all that is within the sphere of consciousness, and as consciousness is necessarily conversant about nothing but what is immaterial, the mind can have no immediate and natural knowledge of body, or of anything beyond its own modifications.

Although the mind (or soul) is exclusively conscious of its own modifications, yet in this state of union it is not solely modified by its intrinsic energy, but in many instances it is affected, in consequence of the antecedent affections of the body, according to the laws under which the two principles are allied. Of the modifications of the mind some, therefore, are affections which owe their origin, and are principally relative to the body; others again, though not altogether independent of corporeal concourse, are more especially to be considered as affections of the mind; while a third class are in themselves purely and absolutely intellectual energies in their origin, continuance, and termination.‡

Although the mind (soul), as unextended, cannot in itself be said to occupy any topical seat, yet in relation to the body as an extended substance, its union must necessarily have reference to place. The mind is not united to the body universally, but its connection is effected at a single point. The point of alliance is the central point of the bodily organisation, which is found somewhere in the brain [the exact spot being probably the] pineal gland.* At this point all organic changes from external causes terminate, and in this corporeal change the mind is, by the nature of its union, hyperphysically determined to a relative modification.† At this point, likewise, all corporeal movements, in obedience to the will, commence; for the animal spirits are here in the same manner determined to produce the bodily movement correspondent to the volition of the mind. To speak only of that modification of the mind which constitutes the perception of an external object, it is evident that the mind perceives at the

---

contradictions be found in his writings in regard to his doctrine of perception. Whether his disciples Geulinx, De la Forge, Bekker, Deurhof, Volder, Malebranche, Spinoza, &c., have not carried this theory farther than their master intended, is a question foreign to the present subject. [See *Discussions*, p. 72.—Ed.]

* De la Forge, pp. 263, 264, [chap. xvi.]

† Descartes, De Methodo, v.; Clerselier, Præf. Cartesii Tractatus De Homine. Cf. Tennemann, vol. x. p. 258; Buhle, p. 16 [Histoire de la Philosophie Moderne, traduite par Jourdan, tome iii. The references to Buhle correspond throughout to the pages of the French translation, from which the quotations in the following notes have been made.—Ed.]

‡ Descartes, De Passionibus Animæ, P. i. art. 17-23; Tennemann, x. p. 251, cf. p. 243. [The distinction may be illustrated by citing the words of Descartes himself. 'Facile est cognoscere nihil in nobis restare quod debeamus tribuere nostræ animæ, exceptis nostris cogitationibus, quæ præcipue duorum generum sunt; quædam enim sunt Actiones animæ, aliæ ejus Passiones sive Affectus. Quas ejus Actiones voco, sunt omnes nostræ voluntates, quia experimur eas directe venire ab anima nostra, et videntur ab illa sola pendere. Sicut è contrario possunt in genere vocari ejus Passiones, omnes species perceptionum sive cognitionum, quæ in nobis reperiuntur; quia sæpe accidit ut anima nostra eas tales non faciat, quales sunt, et semper eas recipiat ex rebus per illas repræsentatis. Rursus nostræ voluntates sunt duplices. Nam quædam sunt actiones animæ, quæ in ipsa anima terminantur; sicuti cum volumus Deum amare, aut in genere applicare nostram cogitationem alicui objecto, quod non est materiale; aliæ sunt actiones, quæ terminantur ad nostrum corpus; ut cum ex eo solo quod habemus ambulandi voluntatem, fit ut nostra crura moveantur et progrediamur.

'Perceptiones nostræ sunt etiam duarum specierum; et quædam animam pro causa habent, aliæ corpus. Eæ quæ animam causam habent, sunt perceptiones nostrarum voluntatum, et omnium imaginationum aut aliarum cogitationum quæ ab ea pendent. Nam certum est nos non posse quicquam velle, quin percipiamus simul nos id velle. Et quamvis respectu nostræ animæ sit Actio aliquid velle, potest etiam dici in illa esse Passionem percipere quod velit. . . . . Inter perceptiones quæ corporis opera producuntur, maxima pars earum pendet a nervis,' &c.

The twofold division of actions is omitted in the text.—Ed.]

* De Passionibus, P. i. art. 31, 32. The principle of life, as well as thought, was placed by Descartes in the pineal gland. See Buhle, t. iii. p. 18. [But see above, p. 234, n. *.—Ed.]

† Principia, P. iv. § 189 sq.

central point of the brain, and not at the point of affection in the organs.*

An external object affects a sense,† that is, determines it as a living organ to certain movements; these are propagated to the central point of the animal system in the brain, where a certain ultimate movement is produced. This is likewise the immediate point of union with the mind; consequently the ultimate organic movement at this point is, in relation to the external object, the proximate cause of its perception. But the ultimate organic motion at the point of union is not in itself an object of consciousness, for the mind is conscious of no affection of matter; that motion likewise does not resemble the original affection of the organ, nor did that original affection of the organ resemble the external object by which that affection was itself excited;‡ consequently there can exist no natural connection between the mental perception of the external object and the organic affections which constitute the conditions of that perception. Neither is it possible that the mind should, on occasion of these corporeal modifications, be determined to the immediate perception of the external object independently of the body; for neither in consequence of its state of union can the mind perceive anything material except indirectly through its hyperphysical alliance with the body, nor independently of this union is it possible that it can have an intuitive perception of the qualities of matter,—that is, it is impossible that an unextended substance can have any consciousness, and consequently any immediate and direct knowledge, of what exists only as extended.§ This ultimate modification of the organic system at the point of union, is, therefore, only the occasion on which, by the Author of our nature, the mind is hyperphysically determined to represent to itself the external object; and this immediate representation and vicarious object is that alone which is known to us in itself, for it is that alone which is within the sphere of consciousness. The mental representation of the external object is properly termed an *idea*.* The organic movement at the point of union in the brain,—though a motion, may metaphorically be termed an *impression*, inasmuch as it is the result of an external impulse,—though bearing no natural resemblance to the external object, it may be

* Dioptrice, c. iv § 1. Principia, P. iv. § 196.

† On the Cartesian theory of Perception, see Buhle, p. 20. [‘Descartes expliquait de la manière suivante la possibilité de connaître les objets qui frappent les sens. Les choses extérieures mettent les esprits vitaux en mouvement par les impressions qu'elles produisent: ces esprits remontent au cerveau, et y forment un canal ou un type, qui correspond aux impressions et à leur nature déterminée. Ce type n'est pas l'idée de l'objet lui-même, mais l'âme en prend connaissance, et alors naît en elle-même l'idée, qui diffère donc totalement du type et de l'objet qui cause l'impression. L'âme combine et élabore ensuite ces idées d'après ses lois intérieures.’—Ed.]

‡ Descartes, Principia, P. iv. § 197. Dioptrice, c. vi. §§ 1, 2.

§ On the relation of mind to body in the Cartesian Philosophy, see Buhle, iii. pp. 328-329.

* Whether the Cartesian *idea* is to be regarded as having an existence independent of the act of consciousness or not, was a point disputed among the followers of Descartes. Arnauld (Des vraies et des fausses idées, c. vi.) holds that Descartes meant by ideas nothing really distinguished from our thought, but our thought itself, in so far as it contains *objectively* what is formally in the object. In support of this view, he quotes the language of Descartes, in the reasonings to prove geometrically the existence of God, which conclude the *Responsio ad Secundas Objectiones*, appended to the *Meditationes*: ‘*Ideæ* nomine intelligo cujuslibet cogitationis formam illam, per cujus immediatam perceptionem ipsius ejusdem cogitationis conscius sum; adeo ut nihil possim verbis exprimere intelligendo id quod dico, quin ex hoc ipso certus sim in me esse ideam ejus quod verbis illis significatur. . . . . . Per *realitatem objectivam ideæ* intelligo entitatem rei repraesentatæ per ideam, quatenus est in idea; eodemque modo dici potest perfectio objectiva, vel artificium objectivum, &c. Nam quæcunque percipimus tanquam in idearum objectis, ea sunt in ipsis ideis objective.’ Malebranche, on the other hand, denies this, and treats the attempt of Arnauld to infer that Descartes denied ideas ‘in the common acceptation,’ as contrary at once to ‘sound sense and justice.’ Réponse de Malebranche, chap. xxiv. § xi. Cf. Arnauld, Lettre à M. le Marquis De Roucy, Œuvres, tome xxxviii. p. 388. [Sir W. Hamilton himself is of opinion that Arnauld's interpretation is right. See above, p. 296 b, n. *—Ed.]

Other Cartesians, while not going so far as Arnauld, in identifying the idea with the act of perception, yet differed from Malebranche, in so far as they considered the ideas of external things to be not distinct entities, but modifications of mind. Thus Regis, Cours de Philosophie, t. p. 190 (Metaph. Liv. ii. P. i. ch. xvi.), expressly says, that the ideas of bodily objects are but modifications of the mind's substance. [In another passage (ch. xx.) he describes these ideas, in their special character as representative of particular objects, as being produced in the mind by God, through the medium of the objects as second causes. See also Röell, Dissertationes, i. § 43, who speaks of ideas as modes or forms of thought, which the mind by attention discovers in itself, as implanted there by God.] Descartes recognised three classes of ideas in the mind. See Buhle, p. 18. [Cf. Descartes, Medit. Tertia, p. 17; Epist. P. i. ep. 99, 115.—Ed.]

called an *image*, as arbitrarily suggesting the representation to the mind,—it may be styled a *corporeal species*, though nothing similar to itself is transmitted from the object,—it may be denominated an *idea*, though it is not the immediate object of the mind,*—and, finally, the mind may be said to contemplate this material motion, impression, image, species, idea, &c., though it has no consciousness of this bodily affection in itself, and only turns or applies itself to this conformation of the brain, in order to find the corporeal antecedent, which, according to the laws and nature of its union, must precede and arbitrarily determine the mental representation of the outward existence which is the immediate object of its perception.†

If it be said, that, on this theory of mediate perception, we retain no evidence of the reality of an external world corresponding to the representations of our own minds, the Cartesian answers, that our assurance for the existence of material architypes of our perceptions rests on our knowledge of the character of God; for to suppose that there existed no external substances, as represented by our minds by the necessity of our nature, would be to suppose the Creator a deceiver of his creatures—an hypothesis inconsistent with the moral and physical perfections of the Deity. And if it further be objected, that we have the same evidence of consciousness for the immediate perception, as for the actual existence, of external objects,—nay, that our belief of the latter is only the necessary consequence of our conviction of the former, and consequently that either God is a deceiver in the one instance, or the hypothesis of a vicarious perception is false in the other,—Descartes is forced to maintain that, notwithstanding the universal belief of mankind, that the immediate object of the mind in perception is the material reality itself, and that, as we perceive that object under its actual conditions, so we are no less conscious of its existence, independently of our minds, than we are conscious of the existence of our own mind, independently of external objects,—notwithstanding this belief, he was bold enough to maintain that we are not precisely conscious that the immediate object of our perception is external and independent of our faculties, although it is difficult, if not impossible, to institute a criticism of the contents of this consciousness, in consequence of the early and deep-rooted prejudice by which we are led to attribute to the immediate objects of our perceptions an external and principal, instead of an internal and vicarious, existence.*

The statement I have here given of the

* Epist. P. ii. ep. 54, 'Alio sensu includo imaginationes in definitione cogitationis; alio sensu excludo; nempe *formas sive species corporeas, quæ debent esse in cerebro, ut quid imaginemur, non sunt cogitationes; sed operatio mentis imaginantis, sive ad istas species se convertentis, est cogitatio.*'

Descartes did not verbally distinguish between the motions in the brain, which are the occasions of perceptions in the mind, and the representations in the mind itself. He called them both *ideas*. The ambiguity is removed by De la Forge, who applies the term '*corporeal species*' to the affection in the brain, and the terms '*idea*,' '*intellectual notion*,' to the spiritual representation in the conscious mind. De l'Esprit, c. 10. The image or modification of the brain in the Cartesian, corresponds to what in the Leibnitio-Wolfian School was called the *material idea*: the idea, properly so called, of Descartes, or the mental representation, answers to what was termed the *sensual idea*, by Wolf.

† [See the Responsiones Quintæ, De iis quæ in Sextam Meditationem objecta sunt. 'Hic quæris, *quomodo existimem in me subjecto inextenso recipi posse speciem, ideamve corporis quod extensum est.* Respondeo nullam speciem corpoream in mente recipi, sed puram intellectionem tam rei corporeæ quam incorporeæ fieri absque ulla specie corporea; ad imaginationem vero, quæ non nisi de rebus corporeis esse potest, opus quidem esse specie quæ sit verum corpus, et ad quam mens se applicet, sed non quæ in mente recipiatur.'—ED.] Compare Le Grand, Institutio Philosophiæ secundum Principia Renati Descartes, P. viii. c. x. (ed. 4, Lond. 1680, p. 537):—'Ita enim a summa Natura comparati, ut occasione quorundam motuum, qui in organis fiunt, quasdam in mente ideas rerum ac figuras nobis repræsentemus.' Ibid., c. xxii. p. 578:—'Phantasia, seu Imaginatio, aliud non est, quam quædam facultatis cognoscitivæ applicatio, ad corpus (scilicet cerebrum) ipsi intime præsens. Imaginationis enim species earum rerum imaginem concipere faciunt, tanquam mentis nostræ oculis præsentem. Nam quando objectum aliquod imaginamur, mens se ad corpus convertit, ut ibi imaginem, aut effigiem, quam apprehendit, veluti suæ cogitationi internæ præsentem, contemplandam.' Cf. Ibid., P. ix. c. iv., p. 598, where the motions from the organs of sense are described as giving *occasion* to the mind to form its ideas, the motions themselves not being conceived.

* Principia, P. i. § 66-69, P. ii. § 1-3; cf. Tennemann, x. pp. 248-51. In Principiis, P. iv. § 196, Descartes maintains that it is a mere self-deceit to suppose that things are perceived in the organ of sensation (e.g. scents in the nose, savours on the tongue, hardness or softness with the fingers), these being really perceived only in that part of the brain which is the root of the soul. Cf. *Schulze*, Kritik der theoretischen Philosophie, vol. ii. p. 35. See also *Le Grand*, Institutio, P. viii. c. xi., p. 540.

Cartesian doctrine of Perception, is the result of an acquaintance with the whole works of Descartes himself, and with the writings both of the most eminent philosophers of his school, and of its most distinguished antagonists. In particular, I may mention the excellent treatise of De la Forge 'De l'Esprit de l'Homme,' the 'Cours de Philosophie' of Silvain Regis, the 'Institutio Philosophiæ' of Le Grand, the Work of Du Hamel, 'De Mente Humana,' the 'Clavis Philosophiæ' of De Raei, to say nothing of the writings of Derodon, Huetius, Gassendi, Chauvin, Vries, Wolf, Malebranche, Arnauld, Purchot, &c., which contribute more or less to illustrate the doctrines of Descartes.

The doctrine of Descartes in regard to the relation of the mind to the organs of sense, proceeds on two principles, of which the one has been boldly postulated as self-evident from the earliest ages of philosophy, and the other has almost universally, though secretly, influenced the doctrines of psychology since the period of Descartes himself.

The former,—which more immediately regards the relation of the mind to the objects of its knowledge,—is contained in the proposition, that the thinking substance can have no immediate knowledge of the qualities of another different from it in the essential properties of its nature. The latter,—which more immediately regards the relation of the mind to the organs of sense,—is the supposition that an immaterial substance cannot be intimately or universally united with the body without arguing its own materiality. The operation of the former principle has either degraded the mind to the nature of the material objects of its sensations, or it has elevated the objects of its sensation to the spiritual nature of the mind: in the former instance it has occasioned the hypothesis of materialism, in the latter all the theories of a vicarious perception, idealism, &c. The latter has likewise produced similar results. Those philosophers who were not disposed to sacrifice the evidence of their consciousness to philosophical hypothesis, held that our perceptions were in fact in the places in which we are conscious of the sensation—an opinion which, from their confidence in the principle, they could not distinguish from materialism; while others sacrificed the evidence of their consciousness, and held that the mind is limited, and only perceives and feels in the region of the brain—a doctrine which they imagined was more easily reconcileable to the immaterial nature of the soul.

As these two [principles] lie at the bottom of almost all philosophical theories, as I believe they have never been fully developed, and as they must necessarily be [examined] in relation to the present discussion, I say a few words in regard to them; and first, of the first.

1. That all knowledge consists in a certain relation of the object known to the subject knowing, is self-evident. What is the nature of this relation, and what are its conditions, is not, and never can be, known to us; because we know only the qualities of our own faculties of knowledge, as relations to their objects, and we only know the qualities of their objects, as relations to our minds. All qualities both of mind and of matter, are therefore only known to us as relations—we know nothing in itself. We know not the cause of this relation, we know nothing of its conditions; the fact is all. The relation is the relation of knowledge. We know nothing consequently of the kind of the relation; we have no consciousness and no possible knowledge whether the relation of knowledge has any analogy to the relations of similarity, contrariety, identity, difference—we have no consciousness that it is like any other, or any modification of any other. These are all relations of a different kind between object and object; this between subject and object: we can institute no point of comparison.

* * * * * * * *

NOTE O.

LOCKE'S OPINION ABOUT IDEAS.

[References.—From I. P. 256 a, 273 a, 296 a, 368 b; compare also I. P. 226 a, 275 b, 279 a.]

[No materials for this Note have been discovered, beyond those which have been already published in the *Discussions*, p. 79 sq., and in the *Lectures on Metaphysics*, vol. ii. p. 53 sq. Some references to Locke, in relation to the history of the term *idea*, have been given above in Note G.—Ed.]

NOTE P.

ON MALEBRANCHE'S THEORY.

[References.—From I. P. 264 b, 358 a, 368 b.]

In so far as the Malebranchian is a modification of the Cartesian doctrine, the genealogy is manifest. But in so far as it differs from the Cartesian, the attempts that have hitherto been made to trace it to anterior sources have not been successful. The passages quoted from ancient authors by Bayle, Dutens, &c.,* have only an apparent,—only a verbal, plausibility, from not distinguishing the different, nay, opposite, meanings in which the term *idea* is used. Malebranche employs it in its Cartesian laxity; the older philosophers in its Platonic rigour. The theory attributed to Plato, and held by St Austin, St Thomas,* and many other philosophers,

* For Bayle, see *Dictionnaire*, art. Amelius, Democrite, Zenon, and *Œuvres Philosophiques*, I. p. 26. For Dutens, see his *Récherche sur l'origine des Découvertes attribuées aux modernes*, Part I. ch. 2. He refers to the Chaldæan Oracles, apud Proclum [in Parmen. Plat. L. iii. p. 23, Cousin]; to Pythagoras, apud Nicom. Arithm. [p. 3, ed. 1538]; to Heraclitus, apud Aristot. Metaph. xii. 4; to Democritus, apud Cicer. De Nat. Deor. i. 43; to Plato, Tim. pp. 28, 52; and to St Augustin, De Divers. Quæst. lxxxiii. qu. 46.—Ed.

* Summa, P. I. Qu. 84, art. 5.—Ed.

and the theory of Malebranche in regard to cognitions in the Divine mind, are precisely the reverse of each other. The former resorted to the Deity, in order to explain the possibility of an intellection by a finite mind of necessary and eternal truths; the latter, to explain the perception by an unextended, spiritual, and immanent subject of extended, material, and external objects. The one, therefore, does not afford the anticipation of the other. For the same and other reasons, the Malebranchian hypothesis cannot be traced to that of Alexander, Themistius, Averroes, and other Mahomedan philosophers, Cajetanus and Zabarella,* in regard to the unity of intellect (active or passive) in the human species, and the identity of that intellect with God. That Malebranche, however, was forestalled in his peculiar hypothesis may, I think, be shown.

A distant approximation to this may be seen in the opinion of Buccaferreus, that the species or immediate object of sensible perception is the product of a celestial agency; and still more in the parallel opinion of Suessanus, that this agency is the Divine. The following, however, is a far more explicit enouncement of the Malebranchian doctrine in regard to our vision of external objects in the Deity. It is from the *Physica Particularis* of Petrus Galtruchius, forming the first part of his *Philosophiæ totius Institutio*, and from the chapter *De Natura Speciei Impressæ*; the edition I quote from is the second, published at Caen in 1665, that is, nine years before the appearance of the *Récherche de la Verité*, but the first remounts to the year 1601. It is curious that this preoccupation of the Malebranchian theory is by a Jesuit—one of that order by whom the philosophy of Malebranche was, with that of Descartes, most zealously opposed, and even proscribed. Speaking of the function of *species impressa*, in regard to sense, he says:—"Notabis 2°. Proprium quidem illud munus debere esse objecti, quantum est de se, ut determinet potentiam ad sui cognitionem, eum ipsa concurrendo ad inferendum cognitionis actum. Eam enim ob causam objectum sufficienter potentiæ unitum, ab ea cognoscitur sine specie impressa: ut quidem fert communis sententia de Angelo seipsum cognoscente, et de Deo fungente vices Speciei impressæ in intellectu beatifico. Quippe Angelus ad cognoscendum alium Angelum, aut aliud creatum objectum, indiget specie impressa ipsius vicaria, cum de se hujusmodi objectum non postulet esse illi semper et necessario intime præsens; et quidem illa præsentia, quæ dicitur *per illapsum*, potentiam cognoscitivam penetrando intimo per jugem influxum ipsius efficienter conservativum. Deus autem sic intime est præsens omni creato intellectui, per suam essentiam: quamobrem potest in eo fungi vices Speciei impressæ, tum ad cognitionem creaturæ cujuscunque; tum ad visionem ipsius Divinæ essentiæ. Neque idcirco hæc Dei actio ad extra erit magis necessaria, quam actio Divinæ omnipotentiæ ad creandum Mundum; siquidem illa omnis est veluti subordinata ejus Libero Arbitrio, unde, *veluti imperative saltem*, ac *denominative*, est libera; ut scribit Suarez *De Deo*, *Lib. ii. c.* 12 *n.* 22. Ne quid etiam dicam de libero ejus concursu universali ad actum visionis beatificæ, a quo præterea multiplex genus determinationis accipit, quemadmodum explicatur *Disp. de Deo*, c. 7, *Ass.* 1. Nec contra hanc doctrinam objicias, Animam rationalem, etsi præsens est intime et per illapsum intellectui suo, indigere tamen specie impressa ad cognitionem sui ipsius, quod a pari dicendum foret de Angelo, &c. Respondeo, Animam quidem separatam non habere opus specie impressa ad sui cognitionem, ob rationem allatam; verum, in corpore adhuc existens, pro hoc statu, siquidem nihil cognoscit, nisi per conversionem ad Phantasmata, ut suo loco exponam, ideo accipit speciem sui impressam, quo, hunc saltem in modum, notitiam sui obtineat."

In the system of Malebranche the existence of a material world is an otiose hypothesis.* This incumbrance to the simplicity of his system was not rejected by Malebranche, and his philosophy modified to an absolute idealism, only, as I have already stated (p. 358 a, n. *), because the negation of the reality of body was apparently inconsistent with the Catholic doctrine of transubstantiation. This likewise seems to have been the reason, as formerly noticed (p. 285 b, n. †), why the Schoolmen were pre-

* For the theory of these philosophers, as for those of Buccaferreus and Suessanus mentioned below, see above, Note M, p. 956.—ED.

* Malebranche, in his Premier Entretien sur la Métaphysique, § 5, supposes that God should annihilate the material world, and should, the world being gone, still produce in our mind the ideas which are now related to it,—all, [he says,] would be as it now is. The supposition is identical with Berkeley's Idealism. The same supposition is often made by the Schoolmen.

vented from fallling over into Idealism, to the verge of which the prevailing doctrine of species carried them, and, they were fully aware, left them no means of philosophical salvation. Since these footnotes were written, I have given some detailed proofs upon this point in the 68th volume of the Edinburgh Review, p. 337, sq.,* and the passages there adduced from the Fathers might be fortified by many others from the Schoolmen of a still more precise application. I may notice that the difference between the Idealism of Malebranche, Berkeley, and Collier, and the Idealism of Fichte, is this, that, on the former hypothesis, God is supposed to represent to us a world unknown, as Malebranche, a world non-existent, as Berkeley and Collier hold, whereas, on the latter hypothesis, the *Mind*, the *Ego*, is supposed to do this in conformity to certain unknown laws to which its agency is astricted. The Theistical and the Egoistical Idealism, considered as philosophical constructions, have each their peculiar merits and defects: on these, however, this is not the place to enter.

* Reprinted in Discussions, p. 198.—Ed.

NOTE Q.

ON HUME'S ASSERTION ABOUT THE IDEAS OF POWER AND CAUSE, AND BROWN'S CRITICISM OF REID.

[References.—From A. P. 522 a; from Supplementary Dissertations, 754 a.]

[Of this Note, nothing appears to have been written beyond two short papers of memoranda, the substance of which is comprised in the following remarks.—Ed.]

Reid not wrong in substance in his criticism of Hume, in saying that Hume denied us the idea (notion) of power or necessary connection. For Hume admitted the notion of necessary connection as an ideal or subjective phænomenon, as a fact; [but,] by tracing its genealogy, he attempted to subvert its real or objective validity. This was the very strongest Scepticism—to shew that belief actual, irresistible—but that belief delusive. (See Ess. II. p. 84.)

The mode he takes to shew that notions of necessary connection—power—cause and effect—are illegitimate, is the following.

Accepting the admitted [hypothesis] of Locke that all our knowledge—all our notions—formed *a posteriori*, or from experience, he shews that the notion in question cannot be derived from that source—from any objective information. But, *as a phænomenon*, it must be admitted to exist subjectively. How, then, is it to be accounted for? On the admitted hypothesis always of Locke's philosophy, he shews, what is true, that we can attempt to explain it only in one other way, viz., by custom or habit. But this basis is insufficient to warrant its universality and necessity, and its objectivation—ergo, notion worthless, delusive.

Now Reid, when he says that Hume subverted the certainty of causation—denied the notion of power or necessary connection — says nothing but what he was entitled to do. Hume subverted the reality, the truth (*i.e.* objective validity) of the notion—ergo, the notion itself.—[For]

1°. Anterior to the formation of the habit out of which the idea comes, the idea could not have existed. It was therefore only after a time that we were trained to it.

2°. When obtained it was wholly illegitimate: —

a.—Because a necessity which we get by being accustomed, we could lose by being unaccustomed. The feeling of necessity is not, therefore, itself necessary.

b.—Because it is, ex hypothesi, a necessity got by a certain limited number of experiences—ergo, we cannot on it logically infer that '*all*' and '*must*.'

c.—A blind principle—only of our animal, not of our intellectual, constitution—we cannot on this hypothesis see that it has any claim.

Reid was therefore warranted in saying that as Hume denied the legitimacy of the phænomenon of the idea (notion) of power, [he virtually denied] the existence of that notion.* Dr Brown seems ignorant of the whole tendency of Hume and Sceptical philosophy. As in Perception he thinks that Hume, in admitting the irresistibility of the belief in an external world, admits that belief to be decisive of its reality, so in regard to the notions of Cause and Effect, Power, &c., he dreams that Hume, in admitting the subjective feeling of necessary connection, admits the objective validity of it.† Brown is wholly wrong in saying that Reid and Hume coincide. (*Cause and Effect*, p. 466, 3d edition.‡)

* * * * * *

* Price also says that Hume holds we have no idea of Cause, &c. (Review of the principal Questions in Morals, p. 41, ed. 1758.)

† See Schulze, Ænesidemus, p. 117, ed. 1792.

‡ Part IV. Sect. vi.—Ed.

NOTE R.

ON THE CARTESIAN DOUBT.

[References.—From Inq. 100 a; from I. P. 269 a, 463 a.]

[On this subject nothing has been discovered except the following references in the Author's Common-Place Book.—Ed.]

Reuchlin, Dubitatio Cartesiana, dissertatione philosophica explicata, vindicata, refutata (1685). *Clauberg*, De Dubitatione Cartesiana, Opera, p. 1131 sq. *Werenfelsius*, Opera, t. ii. p. 18, ed. 1739. *Le Grand*, Apologia pro Cartesio, c. 3. *Garnier*, Précis d'un Cours de Psychologie, p. 213. *Gatien-Arnoult*, Doctrine Philosophique, p. 39. *Cousin*, Cours de l'Histoire de la Philosophie Morale (xviii. Siècle), t. ii. p. 336, ed. Vacherot.

NOTE S.

ON REID'S BORROWING FROM GASSENDI THE OPINION OF ALEXANDER AND THE NOMINALISTS.

[Reference.—From I. P. 301 b.]

The analogy between Reid's doctrine of Perception and that held by the Aphrodisian, and, independently of him, again asserted as true, and the true doctrine of Aristotle, in the latter ages of scholasticism by Occam, Durandus, Gregory of Rimini, Biel, and other of the later Nominalists, had long struck me as remarkable; but I had no suspicion that an opinion which had again so completely fallen into oblivion, could have had any influence on the speculations of an author who was so little excursive in his reading. I am now, however, rather disposed to believe that Reid met with some information at second hand of the rejection of species by these philosophers, and also of their denial of the action—the physical influence—of objects on the percipient mind;—nay, I am even confident, if my surmise be correct, of being able to point out the very passages in which this information was conveyed.

Let the reader consider the tenor of the argument against the agency of the object on the mind, and of the mind on the object, and observe the occurrence of the scholastic expression '*external denomination*.' This being done, I think it will be admitted, as at least a not improbable supposition, (though there are certainly various adverse difficulties), that Reid, in the relative paragraph, had one or both of the following passages in his eye; and this not only by reason of the singular analogy of doctrine and expression, but because they are both taken from a philosopher with whose writings Reid appears to have been acquainted, at least if this can be inferred from his reference on one occasion, if not on more, to certain of that philosopher's opinions. This philosopher is Gassendi.

In one passage, after speaking of the *Intentional Species* of the Schools, and in special reference to the sense of Sight, Gassendi adds:—"Cum Aristoteles porro ipse tale nihil somniârit, sed dixerit solum Colorem rei visibilis movere ipsum actu perspicuum, a quo deinceps oculus moveatur;* cumque Alexander reputârit hunc motum *esse externam solum denominationem*, utpote qui *ne motus quidem alterationis* dici debeat;† fuere nonnulli qui agnoscentes ea, quæ poterant objici, dissensere a cæteris, ut pernegare omnes omnino [species], quam admittere tales sustinuere. Hujusmodi autem fuere maxime, qui Nominales sunt appellati, quique idcirco *nihil aliud ad videndum exigi, quam solam objectorum, verumtamen visibilium coram positorum præsentiam, censuerunt.*" (*Physica*, Sectio I. Lib. vi. c. 13. *Opera*, t. i. p. 443.)

In the other passage treating of the nature of that motion supposed to be determined by the primary object of sight, colour, and having enumerated and rejected several other theories, he proceeds:—"Neque est etiam simplex quædam *denominatio extrinsica*, qualis approbatur ipsi Alexandro, dum perspicuum solum ita pati dicit, ut si quis ad motum alterius, dexter illi ex sinistro evadat; quoniam talis denominatio reale nihil ponit in re;

---

* De Anima, ii. 7.

† De Anima, f. 123 a. b. ed. Ald., (appended to the Aldine edition of Themistius, 1534.—Ed.)

motio autem qua visus percellitur, est quidpiam reale. Tale porro quidpiam deinceps Peripatetici aliqui sensere: cum sicut *visio est in re visa denominatio extrinseca, sic existimarunt nihil esse necesse, ut res visa motionem ullam in ipsum visum exprimat; ac nihil aliud ad visionem esse necessarium voluerunt, quam ut objectum visibile sistatur coram oculo, et in luce sit, debitaque distantia.* Hujusmodi fuere præsertim quos Nominales appellarunt, qui etiam *admissas a cæteris Peripateticis species, seu imagines repudiarunt."* (*Physica* Sectio III. Lib. vii. c. 5. *Opera*, t. ii. p. 373.)

Of the doctrine of Alexander and of the Nominalists I may take another opportunity of treating, (along with the other theories of Perception), in detail. For such a history I am in possession of materials which are not without the greatest difficulty to be obtained. At present I shall only say that Ockam's doctrine on this point may put to shame the pretensions of most modern psychologies.

NOTE T.

ON THE QUALITY OF NECESSITY AS A CRITERION OF THE ORIGINALITY OF A COGNITION.

[References.—From A. P. 521 b, 524 b; from Supplementary Dissertations, 753 b, 755 a.]

[The following Note has been compiled, partly from a MS. Fragment apparently intended for the projected Memoir of Stewart, but cognate in its contents to the matters reserved for discussion in this place; and partly from two papers already printed, the first in the Appendix to the *Lectures on Metaphysics*, vol. ii. p. 526, and the second in the Addenda to the second edition of the *Discussions*, p. 833. —ED.]

Experience, in the philosophy of Matter, is accomplished through External Perception or Sense; in the philosophy of Mind, through Self-consciousness or Internal Perception. By this method we take cognisance simply of Phænomena. There may be Causes and Effects; but (at least out of quantity) they are known merely as phænomena in a relation of proximity in Time or in Time and Space; whilst it is only, objectively, by inference and generalisation, subjectively, by custom or association, and in virtue of the necessity we are under to think a cause for every event, that we regard as causes and effects, phænomena which experience gives us only as closely successive and coadjacent. By experience we learn the *fact that* (ὅτι), not the *reason why* (διότι): for as what we thus know is known merely as existing.

contingently it may be, but not as necessarily existing; so experience informs us only of what *is*, not of what *must be*. This, —that is, what we cannot but think—it consequently behoves us not to refer to mere Experience; for Experience cannot, mediately or immediately, enable us to account for such a phænomenon as a necessary thought. Custom and Association are founded on Experience; and as far as Custom and Association go, Experience avails. But the customary,—the associated, have their commencement, and are not presupposed in thought as united; they may incline to unite in action, they tend to a mutual suggestion in thought. But the problem to be solved is not a strong inclination, but an inevitable compulsion, so to think; and such an original necessity can never be resolved into an acquired propensity.

Philosophers who rely exclusively on the process of Experience in the explanation of psychological phænomena, have erred in two ways. For, on the one hand, they are at fault, either in overlooking the phænomena of mental necessity altogether; or, on the other, in attempting to account for them on the ground of experience alone.

There are *three* degrees or epochs which we must distinguish in philosophical speculation touching the *Necessary*.

In the *first*, which we may call the Aristotelic, or Platonico-Aristotelic, the Necessary was regarded, if not exclusively, principally and primarily, in an *objective* relation;—at least the *objective* and *subjective* were not discriminated; and it was defined *that of which the existence of the contrary is impossible,—what could not but be*.

In the *second*, which we may call the Leibnitian, or Leibnitio-Kantian, the Necessary was regarded primarily in a *subjective* respect; and it was defined *that of which the thought of the contrary is impossible,—what we cannot but think*. It was taken for granted, that what we cannot *think*, cannot *be*, and what we must *think*, must *be*; and from hence there was also inferred, without qualification, that this *subjective* necessity affords the discriminating *criterion of our native or a priori cognitions, notions, and judgments*.

But a *third* discrimination was requisite; for the Necessity of thought behoved to be again distinguished into two kinds, the *Positive* and the *Negative*; the one the necessity of *so* thinking, (the impossibility of *not so* thinking), determined by a mental *Power*; the other the necessity of *not so* thinking, (the impossibility of *so* thinking), determined by a mental *Impotence*. * * * * *

For, 1°, we may not only be able, but be positively determined, to think one alternative, whilst impotent to conceive its counter; and 2°, we may be negatively unable to think one contradictory, and yet find ourselves equally impotent to conceive its opposite. The former, from a Power, is thus primarily inclusive and secondarily exclusive; the latter, from an Impotence, is thus simply and bilaterally exclusive. And while it has always been acknowledged, that of contradictories *the one or the other* must be, and be thought, as *indiscriminately* NECESSARY; we are brought by this novel doctrine to the further confession, that even of contradictories we may, however, not be able to realise in thought the *discriminate* POSSIBILITY of *either*.

This distinction also affords us the all-important contrast of *legitimate* and *illegitimate* thought; thus enabling us to explain some of the most inveterate and pervasive hallucinations in philosophy. For whilst the Positive Necessity of so thinking never illudes, is never even the occasion of illusion; the Negative Necessity of not so thinking is, even naturally, the source of deception. For if, on finding one alternative to be incogitable, we recoil at once to the conclusion,—*that this is false, and the contradictory opposite therefore true*, (and our right—our obligation even, to do this, has been explicitly asserted, especially in the Leibnitian school): the inference, though this be even difficult not pronely to admit, will be logically false,—the consequent containing more than the antecedent; and thus in philosophy (whether of theory or of practice) we shall be precipitated into a variety of errors.*

The development and application of the latter of these Necessities, (in combination however always with the former), constitutes the *Philosophy of the Conditioned;* the Philosophy of the Conditioned is, therefore, the unexclusive complement of a recognised and of an overlooked principle of mind.

[The following references, extracted from the Author's Common-Place Book, relate to the subject of the present Note.]

* See above, p. 377 a, note †.

Origin of our knowledge as discriminated by the character of necessity and contingency.

Aristotle says, that Sense (in actu) not cognisant of aught universal—vide Anal. Post. (Pacii) L. i. c. 31, §§ 1, 7, (et ibi Zabarella, Op. Log. p. 994, ed. 1608); L. ii. c. 19, § 7; Metaph. L. i. c. 1, (et ibi Fonseca, Comm., p. 55.) Conimbricenses, Comm. in Arist. Org. ii. p. 436 sq.

Descartes says, that experience cannot give the universal (a *majori*, not the necessary), Epist., Pars i. ep. cxviii. p. 363, ed. 1668, [ep. xcix. p. 327, ed. 1682.] *Cf.* Gruyer, Essais Philosophiques, t. iv. pp. 88, 115.

Hobbes, Treat. on Hum. Nat., c. iv. § 10. 'Experience concludeth nothing universally,' &c.

Spinoza, De Intell. Emend., § 108. Opera Posth. p. 391 (ed. 1677). 'Ideæ quas claras et distinctas formamus, ita ex sola *necessitate* nostræ naturæ sequi videntur, ut absolute a sola nostra potentia pendere videantur; confusæ autem contra.'

Leibnitz, Nouveaux Essais (ed. Raspe), pp. 5, 30-36, 171, 326-31, 376; [Avant-Propos; L. i. ch. 1, § 1-10; L. ii. ch. 21, § 73; L. iv. ch. 2, § 1; ch. 7, § 7.] Opera (ed. Dutens), t. ii. pars i. p. 233; t. iv. pars i. p. 62; t. v. p. 358; t. vi. pars i. p. 274.

Kant, Kritik der reinen Vernunft, Einleitung, § 2 (p. 3, ed. 1790).*

L'Art de Penser, [Port Royal Logic], Partie iv. ch. vi. p. 481-3 (ed. 1708).

M. Duncan, Institutio Logica, [L. v. c. 2, § 5], p. 232, ed. 1648.

Tetens, Philosophische Versuche, i. p. 466 sq, et alibi.

Ancillon, Ess. Philos. (1817), ii. p. 187.

Maine de Biran, Nouv. Considérations, pp. 198-211, 395.

Cousin, [Concours Général, a. 1819], Frag. Philos. (1826), p. 427; Cours de l'Histoire de la Philosophie (xviiie. Siècle), Leçon xvii. (space); Leçon xviii. (time); Leçon xix. (cause).

Caro, Cours élémentaire de Philosophie, i. p. 176 sq. (resumé of Cousin).

Mazure, Cours de Philosophie (1835), i. p. 41 sq.

Reid, I. P. 323 a, 455 b, 460 a; A. P. 521 b—explicitly enunciates and applies the principle. Stewart neglects it, and accordingly his vacillation and error in regard to the origin of space and time. Dissertation, Part ii. Sect. iii., and Note Y Y,—Coll. Works vol. i. pp. 298, 595; Philos. Essays, Part i. Ess. ii. ch. 2, § 2, —Coll. Works, vol. v. p. 116 sq.

Stewart, Phil. Essays, Part i. Ess. iii. Works, vol. v. p. 135, homologates Leibnitz's doctrine.

* On the analogy between Kant and Leibnitz, see Herder, Metakritik, p. 9 (Carlsruhe edition); Jenisch, Ueber Kant, p. 83-168 (Berlin, 1796).

NOTE U.

ON THE ARGUMENT FROM PRESCIENCE AGAINST LIBERTY.

[References.—From A. P. 629 b, 631 b. Compare 599 a, 602 a b.]

[This Note does not appear to have been written in the form intended for the present work. The substance of the Author's doctrine may, however, be gathered from the remarks published in his *Discussions*, pp 623-633. The portion directly relating to the subject of the present Note will be found in the following extracts. Some footnotes and additional remarks have been supplied from memoranda found among the Author's papers. — ED.]

To suppose a positive and special Principle of Causality, is to suppose that there is expressly revealed to us, through intelligence, an affirmation of the fact, that there exists no free causation; that is, that *there is no cause which is not itself merely an effect*, existence being only a series of determined antecedents and determined consequents. But this is an assertion of Fatalism. Such, however, many of the partisans of that doctrine will not admit. An affirmation of absolute necessity is, they are aware, virtually the negation of a moral universe, consequently, of the moral Governor of a moral universe; in a word, Atheism. Fatalism and Atheism are, indeed, convertible terms. The only valid arguments for the existence of a God, and for the immortality of the human soul, rest on the ground of man's moral nature; consequently, if that moral nature be annihilated, which in any scheme of thoroughgoing necessity it is, every conclusion, established on such a nature, is annihilated likewise. Aware of this, some of those who make the judgment of causality a positive dictate of intelligence, find themselves compelled, in order to escape from the consequences of their doctrine, to deny that this dictate, though universal in its deliverance, should be allowed to hold universally true; and accordingly, they would exempt from it the fact of volition. Will, they hold to be a free cause, a cause which is not an effect; in other words, they attribute to will the power of absolute origination. But here their own doctrine of causality is too strong for them. They say that it is unconditionally promulgated, as an express and positive law of intelligence, that every origination is an apparent only, not a real, commencement. Now, to exempt certain phænomena from this universal law, for the sake of our moral consciousness, cannot validly be done.—For, 1°, this would be, as observed, an admission that the mind is a complement of contradictory revelations. If mendacity be admitted of some of our mental dictates, we cannot vindicate veracity to any. If one be delusive, so may all. "Falsus in uno, falsus in omnibus." Absolute scepticism is here the legitimate conclusion.—But, 2°, waiving this conclusion, what right have we, on this doctrine, to subordinate the unexclusive affirmation of causality to our consciousness of moral liberty, — what right have we, for the interest of the latter, to derogate from the universality of the former? We have none. If both be equally positive, we are not entitled to sacrifice to the other the alternative which our wishes prompt us to abandon.

But the doctrine which I propose is not obnoxious to these objections. It does not maintain that the judgment of causality is dependent on a *power* of the mind, imposing, as necessary in thought, what is necessary in the universe of existence. It does not, at once, universally affirm and specially deny; include without exception and yet except. On the contrary, it resolves this judgment into a mere mental *impotence*, — an impotence to conceive either of two contradictories. And as the *one* or the *other* of contradictories must be true, whilst both cannot; it proves that there is no ground for inferring a certain fact to be impossible, merely from *our inability to conceive its possibility*. At the same time, if the causal judgment be not an express affirmation of mind, but only an incapacity of thinking the opposite; it follows, that such a negative judgment cannot counterbalance the express affirmative, the unconditional testimony, of consciousness,—that we are, though we know not how, the true and responsible authors of our actions, nor merely the worthless links in an adamantine series of effects and causes.* It appears to me, that it is only on such a doctrine that we can philosophically vindicate the liberty of the human will, that we can rationally assert to man—"fatis avolsa voluntas."† *How* the will can possibly be free, must remain to us, under the present limitation of our faculties, wholly incomprehensible. We are unable to conceive an absolute commencement; we cannot, therefore, conceive a free volition.‡ A determination by motives cannot, to our understanding, escape from necessitation. Nay, were we even to admit as true, what we cannot think as possible, still the doctrine of a motiveless volition would be only casualism; and the free acts of an indifferent, are, morally and rationally, as worthless

* That the notion of Causality is not so proximate as that of Liberty, see Ancillon, [Ueber Glauben und Wissen, 1824, p. 109.—ED.]

† Lucretius, ii. 257.—ED.

‡ That a true, a creative Liberty is necessarily incomprehensible, and that the domain of freedom is ignorance, see *Laurentius Valla*, De Libertate Arbitrii, Opera (1540), p. 1009; *Jacobi*, Werke, ii. p. 317. Jacobi defines Liberty, p. 315, 'Ich verstehe unter dem Worte Freiheit dasjenige Vermoegen des Menschen, kraft dessen er selbst ist und alleinthaetig in sich und ausser sich handelt, wirkt, und hervorbringt.'

as the pre-ordered passions of a determined, will. *How*, therefore, I repeat, moral liberty is possible in man or God, we are utterly unable speculatively to understand. But, practically, the *fact*, that we are free, is given to us in the consciousness of an uncompromising law of duty, in the consciousness of our moral accountability;* and this fact of liberty cannot be redargued on the ground that it is incomprehensible, for the philosophy of the Conditioned proves, against the necessitarian, that things there are, which *may*, nay *must* be true, of which the understanding is wholly unable to construe to itself the possibility.

But this philosophy is not only competent to *defend* the fact of our moral liberty, possible though inconceivable, against the assault of the fatalist; it *retorts* against himself the very objection of incomprehensibility by which the fatalist had thought to triumph over the libertarian. It shews, that the scheme of freedom is not more inconceivable than the scheme of necessity. For whilst fatalism is a recoil from the more obtrusive inconceivability of an *absolute* commencement, on the fact of which commencement the doctrine of liberty proceeds; the fatalist is shewn to overlook the equal, but less obtrusive, inconceivability of an *infinite* non-commencement, on the assertion of which non-commencement his own doctrine of necessity must ultimately rest. As equally unthinkable, the two counter, the two one-sided, schemes are thus theoretically balanced. But practically, our consciousness of the moral law, which, without a moral liberty in man, would be a mendacious imperative, gives a decisive preponderance to the doctrine of freedom over the doctrine of fate. We are free in act, if we are accountable for our actions.

Such (φωνᾶντα συνετοῖσιν) are the hints of an undeveloped philosophy, which, I am confident, is founded upon truth. . . . Specially, in its doctrine of Causality, this philosophy brings us back from the aberrations of modern theology, to the truth and simplicity of the more ancient church. It is here shewn to be as irrational as irreligious, on the ground of human understanding, to deny, either, on the one hand, the foreknowledge, predestination, and free grace of God, or, on the other, the free will of man; that we should believe both, and both in unison, though unable to comprehend either, even apart. This philosophy proclaims with *St Augustin*, and Augustin in his maturest writings:—"If there be not free grace in God, how can He save the world; and if there be not free will in man, how can the world by God be judged?"—(Ad Valentinum, Epist. 214.) Or, as the same doctrine is perhaps expressed even better by *St Bernard*:—"Abolish free will, and there is nothing to be saved; abolish free grace, and there is nothing wherewithal to save."—(De Gratia et Libero Arbitrio, c. i.) St Austin repeatedly declares the conciliation of the foreknowledge, predestination, and free grace of God with the free will of man, to be "a most difficult question, intelligible only to a few." Had he denounced it as a fruitless question, and (to understanding) soluble by none, the world might have been spared a large library of acrimonious and resultless disputation. This conciliation is of the things to be believed, not understood.* The futile attempts to harmonise these antilogies, by human reasoning to human understanding, have originated conflictive systems of theology, divided the Church, and, as far as possible, dishonoured religion.

"Vain wisdom all, and false philosophy!"

* The fact of Liberty may be proved:—

1. From the direct consciousness of Liberty. See Crusser, [Skeptische Betrachtungen ueber die Freiheit des Willens, 1793] p. 8 9.

2. Even if we were not immediately conscious, yet from the Moral Law as *ratio cognoscendi*. See Sieffert, [Dissertatio de libera, quam dicunt, hominum voluntate, 1824] p. 12.

* That the conciliation of the liberty of man and prescience of God is to be *believed* but not *understood*, is maintained by *Alexander Aphrodisiensis*, De Fato, [ad calcem Themistii, f 170 b ed. Ald. 1534];—*Cajetanus* in Thomæ Summam, P. i. qu. 22, art. 4 [quoted in Discussions, p. 627];—*Ockam*, [In I. Sent., Dist. xxxviii. qu. 1 L.];—*Biel*, [In I. Sent., Dist. xxxviii. qu. 1 M];—*Ochinus*, Labyrinthi, hoc est, De Libero aut Servo Arbitrio, de divina Prænotione, Destinatione, et Libertate Disputatio (Basileæ, 1561), c. xix. p. 245 sq.;—*Franciscus Stadianus*, (cited by Melanchthon, Resp. ad Artic. Bavar. Opera, Witeb. 1580, i. p. 370: see Copleston, Enquiry into the Doctrines of Necessity and Predestination, p. 188);—*Descartes*, Epist. P. i. Ep. 8, 9, (quoted by Stewart, Dissertation, Note MM, Collected Works, i. p. 575);—*Locke*, Letter to Molyneux, (quoted by Stewart, Coll. Works, i. p. 297);—*Tucker*, Light of Nature pursued, c. 25, quoted by Copleston, Enquiry, p. 85;—*Archbishop King*, Discourse on Predestination, § 29.

Other authors are quoted by Ruiz, [Comm. et Disp. de Scientia, de Ideis, de Veritate, ac de Vita Dei, 1629], pp. 246, 554, 564; and by Genuensis, Elem. Metaph., ii. p. 184, ed. Venet. 1748.

Reid has absurdly argued in favour of Liberty from the analogy of Memory. He says that upon the doctrine of Necessity every thing that is past would be necessary.* And so it is. Whatever has been in past time, is necessary; and so likewise, everything that is, is necessary by the very fact of being. In regard to the past, [Aristotle says] ἔχει τὸ γεγονὸς ἀνάγκην;† in regard to the present, the scholastic brocard [says] *omne quod est, eo quod est, necesse est*. Freedom, contingency, can only regard the *future* — what is not already realised—the difficulty from prescience (divine or other) arises from the fact that what is future is supposed or made past or present. For example, being supposed that it is foreseen that I shall rise on my right side, we get into the insoluble dilemma, 1°, If I cannot rise on my left side, I am *determinatus ad unum*; in which case I have no *liberty* of rising on my left side, but am necessarily determined to my right. On this alternative Liberty is gone. 2°, Supposing that Liberty remain, and accordingly I rise on my left side; in that case the *foreknowledge* is false; that is, there was no foreknowledge. In this way it is absolutely impossible for the human mind to reconcile Liberty and Prescience.

The conviction of this impossibility led men, 1°, to give up the prescience of God in respect of future contingents;‡ or, 2°, to bring down the impossibility to a lower, and this [by one of] two means—either, 1°, to annihilate the futurity in respect of God; or, 2°, to annihilate the contingency. As to the first of these,—the annihilation of time in relation to God—*futura jam facta sunt** — this they endeavoured to explain by various subordinate hypotheses; [but it is] evident that the *contingency of the future* is thus really reduced to the *necessity of the past*.† As to the second, [some] thought that, by shewing that the act of prescience was not the cause or antecedent, but the effect or consequent of the futurition, [it could be shewn] that the certainty—the inevitability it supposed was not an absolute

* See above, p. 631. St Austin makes the same reasoning about memory as Reid in regard to contingents. See Gennensis, ii. p. 184. [The passage of St Austin is from the De Libero Arbitrio, L. iii. c. 4:—'Sicut tu memoria tua non cogis facta esse, quæ præterierunt; sic Deus præscientia sua non cogit facienda, quæ futura sunt. Et sicut tu quædam quæ fecisti meministi, nec tamen quæ meministi omnia fecisti; ita Deus omnia quorum ipse auctor est præscit, nec tamen omnium quæ præscit ipse auctor est.'—Ed.]

† Rhet. iii. 17. ἡ μὲν γὰρ περὶ τὸ μέλλον, ἡ δὲ περὶ ὄντων ἢ μὴ ὄντων, οὐ μᾶλλον ἀπόδειξίς ἐστι καὶ ἀνάγκη· ἔχει γὰρ τὸ γεγονὸς ἀνάγκην. Compare Cicero, De Fato, c. 7. 'Omnia enim vera in præteritis necessaria sunt, ut Chrysippo placet.'—Ed.

‡ A denial of the prescience of God in respect of future contingents has been attributed to:—

Aristotle, who does not expressly deny it, but has been held by some writers implicitly to do so, as by Gregorius Ariminensis and Suarez. [This is an inference from a passage in De Interpretatione, c. 9, where Aristotle denies the determinate truth of one or the other contradictory in the case of future contingent propositions. From this it has been inferred by Gregorius Ariminensis, (In i. Sent., Dist. xxxviii. qu. 1, art. 1) and by Suarez, (Opusc. De Scientia Dei, Lib. i. c. 2; Metaph., Disp. xix. sect. 10) that Aristotle implicitly denies the Divine prescience. Aristotle's doctrine is defended against Gregory by Catharinus, De Veritate Enunciationum, p. 27 sq., ed. 1530.—Ed.]

Cicero, De Divinatione, ii. 7; De Fato, c. 14. [See below, p. 977, n. †.—Ed.]

Aureolus, [In i. Sent., Dist. xxxviii. qu. 1], see Eckius, [De Prædestinatione], iv. 59, Ruiz, [Commentarii ac Disputationes, &c., 1629], p. 189; and other *Parisienses*, mentioned by Vallius, [Logica, 1622], t. i. p. 671.

Socinians [See F. Socinus, Prælect. Theol., c. 8; Crellius, De Deo ejusque Attributis, c. 24; Wolzogen, in Evang. Matth., c. 4, Append. i.—Ed.]

Conrad Vorstius, [De Deo; vide Leibnitii Opera, ed. Dutens, vol. i. p. 44.—Ed.]

Thomas Bonartes, Norditanus, Jesuita Anglus Pseudonymus; v. Leibnitz, Theod. Pref. [Leibnitii Opera, ed. Dutens, vol. i. p. 45. Concerning Thomas Bonart or Bonartes, an anagram of *Barton*, see ibid., p. 115.—Ed.]

The necessity of Divine prescience has also been questioned by:—

Episcopius in some degree, see Waterland, [Importance of the Doctrine of the Trinity, Works, iii. p. 448, ed. 1843.—Ed.]

Hey, [Lectures on Divinity, iv. xvii. 20.—Ed.]

Stewart, Active Powers, [Appendix; Collected Works, vol. vi. p. 398.—Ed.]

For authors who have denied the determinate truth of future contingents, admitting the prescience of God, see Balforeus, [Comm. in Aristotelis Organon], p. 408; Arriaga, [Cursus Philosophicus, p. 204]; Vallius, [Logica], t. i. pp. 671, 672. For those who affirmed the determinate truth of future contingents, see Balforeus [p. 407]; Arriaga [p. 205]; Vallius, t. i. p. 671.

* Augustine, De Trinitate, v. 16. 'Deus . . . . apud quem nec præterita transierunt, et futura jam facta sunt.'—Ed.

† That God sees everything in his eternity as present, though in different ways, see Boethius, De Consol. Phil., Lib. v. Pr. 6; Aquinas, Summa, Pars i. qu. xiv art. 13. Cf. Vallius, Logica, t. i. p. 677.

but a conditional necessity, not a *necessitas consequentis*, but only a *necessitas consequentiæ*.*

[Others] admitted absolute necessity—no contingency,—no liberty.

* * * * * *

For the argument, that prescience, as implying a fixed series of causes, is incompatible with freedom, see St Augustine, De Civ. Dei, L. v. c. 9, § 2, Genuensis, Elem. Metaph., ii. p. 184.—Cicero was so struck with this argument, that he denied the prescience of God, to save the free will of man.† Augustine says elegantly of him, "dum vult facere liberos, fecit sacrilegos."—For Augustine's solution, that our wills are included in the series of causes, see Genuensis, l. c. Augustine also replies, that if all foreseen actions are necessary, God's own future actions are necessary.‡

[Of the opposite argument, which denies the freedom of man to save the prescience of God, there is a] good statement in Pererius, De Principiis, Lib. ix. c. 11:—"Stoici existimantes non posse constare et cohærere *contingentiam* cum Dei *providentia*, ut hanc retinerent, illam e rebus sustulerunt, hac utentes ratione: *Si est providentia, non erit contingentia; sed est providentia; ergo non est contingentia.* Major (nam de minori non est in præsentia certandum) ita probatur. Providentia Dei includit tria, *præscientiam*, *voluntatem*, et *dispositionem* Dei; quæ tria excludunt a rebus contingentiam. Nam quod est provisum a Deo, hoc est, quod Deus *præscivit*, *voluit*, *disposuit*, seu *constituit* ut aliquando eveniat, id non potest non evenire; neque enim potest aut *præscientia Dei falli*, aut *voluntas frustrari*, aut *ordinatio impediri*; sed omnes res sunt a Deo provisæ; ergo omnes necessario et immutabiliter eveniunt, quare nullus contingentiæ locus relinquitur."

See for other arguments in regard to the possibility of contingency in nature, ibid. On the whole opinion of the ancients touching Fate, Contingency, &c., see Scheghius, In Arist. De Ortu et Interitu, p. 237, ed. Basil. 1550.

The Calvinist theologian maintains the predestination and foreknowledge of God in conjunction with the liberty of man, nor ventures to reject either article of his faith, because he is unable to comprehend the mystery of their union. Humbly acknowledging our necessary dependence upon God, he likewise vindicates to man a personal freedom, not wrested from the prerogative, but conceded by the grace, of the Divinity,—not granted for the honour of the creature, but for the glory of the Creator,—and not withdrawn from God's dominion, but affording the noblest subject of his rule.* Asserting the contin-

---

* See F. Bonæ Spei, Logica, p. 173-8. ['Nota necessitatem esse duplicem, unam absolutam, alteram ex suppositione. Absoluta est, quæ habetur nulla facta suppositione, ut necessitas existentiæ Dei. Necessitas ex suppositione est, quæ non habetur nisi facta aliqua suppositione, ut necessitas ambulationis Petri, supposito quod videam Petrum ambulantem. Necessitas ex suppositione est triplex; scilicet, ex suppositione antecedente, ex suppositione concomitante, et ex suppositione consequente. Prima est, ubi aliquid supponitur, quod necessario antecedit, per modum causæ vel conditionis inferens, ut necessitas existentiæ caloris ex prævia suppositione, quod ignis existat, necessitas combustionis stupparum siccarum, ex suppositione, quod sit approximatio ignis ad illas. Secunda, ubi aliquid supponitur concomitans, ut necessitas existentiæ loquelæ meæ, vel ambulationis, ex suppositione, quod loquar, vel ambulem. Tertia, ubi aliquid supponitur consequens, ut necessitas loquelæ, vel ambulationis Petri, ex suppositione, quod audiam ipsum loquentem, vel videam ambulantem. . . . . Adde, necessitatem ortam ex suppositione antecedente, non male aliter vocari *necessitatem consequentis*; quia per illam unum necessario alterum tanquam causam suam necessariam consequitur. Necessitatem vero ortam ex suppositione concomitante vel consequente vocari *necessitatem consequentiæ* tantum, quia per illam unum ex alio per legitimam consequentiam infertur.']

† De Divinatione, ii. 7. 'Nihil est tam contrarium rationi et constantiæ, quam fortuna; ut mihi ne in Deum quidem cadere videatur, ut sciat, quid casu et fortuito futurum sit.' See also De Fato, cc. 10, 14.—ED.

‡ [De Libero Arbitrio, L. iii. c. 3.—ED.] To the argument—human actions cannot be free, for free actions cannot be foreseen even by the Deity—the answer, that this objection abolishes all freedom of action in the Deity himself, is given by *Voltaire*, [Correspondance avec le Roi de Prusse, Lettre 87], and by *Stewart*, Dissertation [Note NN; Coll. Works, vol. i. p. 578.]

* "In the Confession of Faith of the Church of Scotland (the Articles of which are strictly Calvinistic), the freedom of the human will is asserted as strongly as the doctrine of the eternal decrees of God. 'God (it is said, chap. iii.) from all eternity did, by the most wise and holy counsel of his own will, freely and unchangeably ordain whatsoever comes to pass. Yet so as thereby neither is God the author of sin, *nor is violence offered to the will of his creatures*, nor is the liberty or contingency of second causes taken away, but rather established.' And still more explicitly in chap. ix., 'God hath endued the will of man with

gency (not the casualty) of human action, he does not reduce omniscience to the foreknowledge of a necessitated order; and maintaining the universal infallibility of the divine decree, he denies that it imposes an universal *necessity*. Attributing to man in his unfallen state a full and perfect liberty to good and ill, spiritual as well as moral, he still postulates his freedom in actions of natural and civil import; and while he asserts the concourse of the Deity, he still preserves all activity proper to our personality. The loss of man's spontaneous energy, and his subjection to a physical necessity, he declares to be tantamount to the negation of God in the extinction of man as a moral and religious subject. The Calvinist has thus been careful, on the one hand, not to derogate from the perfections of the Deity as the author of our salvation; and on the other, not to destroy the liberty of man as its condition. "*Tolle liberum arbitrium, et non erit quod salvetur; tolle gratiam, non erit unde salvetur.*" *

[The following remarks from the Author's Common-Place Book on the terms connected with this question, were probably intended to be employed in the present Note.—ED.]

1. CONTINGENT (τὸ ἐνδεχόμενον) — its meaning, true and false.

a.—True—'that which when it happens is neither necessary nor impossible.'

Aristotle, An. Pri., L. i. c. 13, § 2.
Plutarch, De Fato, Opera Moralia, p. 570-4.
Alex. Aphrod., [In Arist. Anal. Pri. f. 52, ed. Ald.]
Ammonius, [In Arist. De Interp., ff. 99, 100, ed. Ald. 1546].
Piccolomini, De Rerum Definitionibus, (Francof. 1600), p. 221 sq.
Biel, In Sent., L. i. dist. 38 A.
Nemesius, De Natura Hominis, c. 34, p. 287, ed. Matthæi.
Leibnitz, Opera Philos. (ed. Erdmann), pp. 447, 669.
Budæus, Comm. Ling. Græc. [pp. 565, 566, ed. Paris. 1548.]
Walch, Lexicon, v. Contingens.
Micraelius, Lexicon, v. Contingens.
Goclenius, Lex. Phil., v. Contingens.
'S Gravesande, Introd. ad Phil., p. 18.
Melanchthon, Erotemata Dialectices, L. ii. p. 613, ed. 3, Strigelii, 1579.

b.—False—'that which while we are not sure whether it has happened or will happen, we are not sure of the reverse.'

Copleston, On Necessity and Predestination, pp. 80, 81.
Whately, Elements of Logic, Appendix No. I., vv. Certain, May, Possible.
Monboddo, Anc. Metaph., vol. i. p. 294.
Spinoza, Eth., Pars i. Prop. xxix., xxxiii. Sch. 1; Cogitt. Metaph., Pars i. c. 3, § 8.
Hobbes, Of Liberty and Necessity, Works (folio edition), p. 478. [Vol. iv. p. 259, ed. Molesworth.]

That equivocally *contingent* includes *necessary*, Aristotle, [Anal. Prior. L. i. c. 3, § 5; c. 13, § 2], pp. 131, 177, Pacil.

2. NECESSARY (τὸ ἀναγκαῖον), meanings of. Melanchthon, Erot. Dial., L. ii. p. 604 sq.

3. POSSIBLE and IMPOSSIBLE (τὸ δυνατὸν—τὸ ἀδύνατον), meanings of.

Melanchthon, Erot. Dial., L. ii. p. 612.
Budæus, Comm. Ling. Græc., p. 566.
Wolf, De Differentia Nexus Rerum, &c. (1724), p. 14 sq.
Whately, On King, p. 91; Logic, Appendix, No. I., vv. Possible, Impossibility.

That *possible* includes *necessary*, see Plutarch in Budæus, l. c. [De Fato, c. 6.—ED.]

4. CERTAIN (certus).

Goclenius, Lex. Phil. (Lat.), v. Certitudo.
Conimbricenses, Comm. in Arist. Org., ii. p. 696.
Boethius, De Cons. Phil., L. v. pr. 5.
Copleston, On Necessity, &c., p. 81 sq.
Whately, Logic, Appendix No. I., v. Certain.

5. MECHANICAL.

Defined, Jacobi, Werke, ii. p. 316,

---

that natural liberty, that it is neither forced, nor by any absolute necessity of nature determined to do good or evil.'" Stewart, Dissertation, Note MM.; Collected Works, vol. i. p. 575 (restored in collected edition). Passages to the same effect from the writings of Calvin himself have been collected by Mr Mozley in his work on the Augustinian Doctrine of Predestination, Note xxi.—ED.

* St Bernard, De Gratia et Libero Arbitrio, c. 1. See above, p. 975 b.—ED.

and iv. 2, p. 93. 'Mechanical=concatenation of mere efficient causes, which eo ipso is a necessary concatenation; as also a necessary concatenation is, so far as it is necessary, eo ipso a mechanical.'

[The following extracts from Aquinas and his commentator Cajetanus appear to have been intended for the present Note. A portion of the latter has been translated in *Discussions*, p. 627.—ED.]

AQUINAS. — Summa totius Theologiæ, Pars Prima, Quæstio xxii., Articulus 4. *Utrum providentia rebus provisis necessitatem imponat.*

"1°. Videtur quod divina providentia necessitatem rebus provisis imponat. Omnis enim effectus qui habet aliquam causam per se, quæ jam est vel fuit, ad quam de necessitate sequitur, provenit ex necessitate, ut Philosophus probat in sexto Metaphysicorum.* Sed providentia Dei (cum sit æterna) præexistit, et ad eam sequitur effectus de necessitate: non enim potest divina providentia frustrari. Ergo providentia divina necessitatem rebus provisis imponit."

(Having stated a second and third argument which might be advanced in favour of the affirmative, and one which had been employed in support of the negative, Aquinas proceeds to pronounce his own decision of the question, and to refute the three reasonings opposed to it. The passage to be quoted from his Commentator has exclusive reference to his answer to the first of these.)

"Respondeo, dicendum, quod providentia divina quibusdam rebus necessitatem imponit, non autem omnibus, ut quidam crediderunt. Ad providentiam enim pertinet ordinare res in finem. Post bonitatem autem divinam, quæ est finis a rebus separatus, principale bonum in rebus ipsis existens est perfectio universi: quæ quidem non esset, si non omnes gradus essendi invenirentur in rebus. Unde ad divinam providentiam pertinet omnes gradus entium producere. Et ideo quibusdam effectibus præparavit causas necessarias, ut necessario evenirent; quibusdam vero causas contingentes, ut evenirent contingenter, secundum conditionem proximarum causarum.†

"Ad *primum* ergo dicendum, quod effectus divinæ providentiæ non solum est aliquid evenire quocunque modo, sed aliquid evenire, vel contingenter, vel necessario. Et ideo evenit infallibiliter et necessario, quod divina providentia disponit evenire infallibiliter et necessario: et evenit contingenter, quod divinæ providentiæ ratio habet, ut contingenter eveniat."

CAJETANUS.—"In responsione ad primum, dubitatio occurrit valde ardua, et forte ab humano intellectu insolubilis. Ad cujus evidentiam, ut melius percipiatur in quo consistit dubitatio, advertendum est quod aliud est (1°) 'A *contingenter* evenire,' et aliud est (2°) 'A *necessario* evenire,' et aliud est (3°) 'A *infallibiliter* seu *inevitabiliter* evenire;' tam primum enim quam secundum importat ordinem effectus ad causam in actu positam; illud quidem, quod sua causa habet potentiam ad utrumlibet; hoc vero, quod sua non potest deficere ab ipsius causalitate: sed tertium communius est utroque, quoniam et contingentia et necessaria sequuntur divinam providentiam positam in actu infallibiliter, seu inevitabiliter; et cum hoc illa sequuntur contingenter, et ista necessario. Ex his enim, quamvis quiescat intellectus, attendens ad responsionem in Litera positam circa salvationem contingentiæ, *fluctuat tamen circa connexionem prædictæ infallibilitatis cum libero arbitrio*, —imo, ut rectius loquar, *cum libero eventu ipsarum operationum, quas liberas dicimus*, et similiter cum ambiguo eventu contingentium aliorum.

"Cum enim in operatione libera sit considerare ipsam voluntatem, illius causam, et eventum, seu executionem ipsius nunc, ita quod non opposite;* quamvis difficile non sit salvare naturam talis causæ (scilicet liberæ) cum prædicta infallibilitate, eo quia hujusmodi infallibilitas nihil dat vel aufert causæ ad utrumlibet: sed [tamen] (cum ipsa stat, quod *causa habeat potentiam indifferentem ad illud infallibile et ad ejus oppositum*, et propter hoc, *divina providentia non adimat contingentiam a rebus*) verum *salvare prædictam infalli-*

---

* L. v. c. 3, ed. Bekker.—ED.

† Aquinas is here followed by the authors of the Westminster Confession of Faith, chap. v. *Of Providence*, § 2—"Although in relation to the foreknowledge and decree of God, the first cause, all things come to pass *immutably and infallibly*: yet, by the same providence, he ordereth them to fall out according to the nature of second causes, either *necessarily*, *freely*, or *contingently*." See also chap. iii. § 1.

* "Ita quod non opposite;" "*so that there should be no inconsistency among them.*" There is perhaps, however, some omission.

bilitatem cum indifferentia seu libertate executionis seu eventus—hoc opus, hic labor est. Si enim infallibile est, me diluculo primo futuro scribere; quamvis potentiam habeam ad utrumlibet, (id est, ad scribendum tunc, vel ad non scribendum tunc); attamen potentia ista atque libertas non exbit in actum negationis scribendi, sed affirmationis, sic quod inevitabile est quin affirmatio eveniat. Et si sic est, cum jam ab æterno divina providentia sit in actu determinata respectu omnium, et immutabilis et infallibilis, &c.—sequitur quod, *de facto*, omnia *inevitabiliter* eveniant, quamvis quædam *contingenter*, et quædam *necessario*. Notanter autem dixi, *de facto*, quia de possibili, absolute loquendo, potest Deus non determinare providentiam suam ad hæc, vel illa futura. Sed cum *jam determinata est*, repugnat immutabilitati efficaciæ, universalitati atque certitudini suæ, evitabilitas evenientium. Et si omnia inevitabiliter eveniunt de facto, ut quid consiliamur et conamur ad hæc magis quam illa prosequenda vel vitanda? *Nil enim minus videtur ex hoc destrui pars moralis, omnisque conatus Ecclesiæ atque exhortatio ad bonum, quam ex negatione contingentiæ.* Quamvis enim negatio *evitabilitatis*, et negatio *contingentiæ* non æquivaleant, ut jam patet ex dictis, quoad proposita tamen *inconvenientia* æqualiter videntur. Nullus enim consiliatur de inevitabili, nec aliquis conatur, aut hortatur, aut orat circa inevitabilia.

"Ad hanc dubitationem nihil scriptum reperi in S. Thoma; quoniam nullibi eum movisse hanc recolo, sed semper studuit *ad salvandam contingentiam.* In aliis quoque Doctoribus nihil hactenus comperi ad quæstionem istam, nisi quæ communiter dicuntur *de sensu composito et diviso—de necessitate consequentiæ et consequentis—de libertate electionis divinæ in æternitate—deque natura causarum ad utrumlibet in universo inventarum.* Sed hæc omnia, ut ex dictis patet, intellectum non quietant; quoniam, ut jam dictum est, non de Deo secundum se considerato, sed *secundum quod de facto est*; et similiter non de ipsis naturis causarum aut rerum, nec de necessitate aut contingentia, sed *de compossibilitate inevitabilium eventuum cum contingentia et libertate eorundem*, est quæstio. Non enim satisfit quæsito, dicendo, quod actus eveniens *est evitabilis et inevitabilis*:—evitabilis quidem *secundum se*; inevitabilis vero *secundum quod est provisus.* Licet enim hoc sit verum, non tamen solvit nodum: quoniam actus eveniens de facto est jam provisus ab æterno, et *esse provisum* vincit conditiones ipsius *secundum se*; et consequenter actus eveniens est *simpliciter* (id est, omnibus consideratis) *inevitabilis*, et *secundum quid* (id est, solitarie sumptus) *evitabilis;* sicut projectio mercis tempore naufragii est simpliciter volita, (quia omnibus consideratis est volita,) et secundum quid est nolita, (quia secundum se projectio ipsa displicet.)—Nihil quoque ad propositum facit dicere, *quod esse provisum nihil ponit in actu eveniente;* in hoc enim exemplo manifeste apparet nihil ad rem referre, an ponat vel non ponat. Esse namque volitum, nihil ponit in projecta merce, et tamen, &c.—Nec etiam evaditur dicendo, quod, quia actus eveniens est provisus a Deo, et inevitabilitas ejus sequitur esse provisum, ut res respectiva ad Deum; *actus eveniens est de facto inevitabilis respectu Dei, non autem respectu nostri.* Hoc enim æquivalet nihilo: quoniam si de facto inevitabilis est a Deo, ergo et de facto inevitabilis est, et simpliciter, et a nobis; quoniam impossibile est a quocunque vitari, quod a Deo de facto vitari non potest, propter ipsius summam efficaciam.

"Oportet igitur, si quæstionis hujus veritas quietare debet intellectum nostrum, alterum duorum dicere;—aut *quod esse provisum non sequatur inevitabilitas;* aut *quod inevitabilitas eventus provisi non deroget evitabilitati eorundem eventuum.*—Et hoc *secundum* quidem, propter rationem supra adductam, non capio quomodo possit verificari. Liquet enim, quod non nisi secundum quid evitabilitas salvari apparet. —*Primum*, autem, quamvis communiter a Doctoribus destruatur, dicentibus *quod esse provisum, seu volitum, seu prædestinatum* (pro eodem enim quoad hanc difficultatem omnia accipio) *sequitur inevitabilitas;* ego tamen, non ut opponam me contra torrentem, nec asserendo, sed stante semper captivitate intellectus in obsequium Christi, auspicor, quod, quemadmodum esse provisum, nec contingentiam nec necessitatem ponit in eventu proviso, (ut in Litera dicitur,) eo quia Deus est causa superexcedens, eminenter præhabens necessaria et contingentia (per hoc enim evadit Sanctus Thomas ab illa ratione VI. Metaphysicorum hic allata; intendit enim quod propositiones Aristotelis verificantur in causis particularibus, quarum aliæ sunt necessariæ, aliæ contingentes, aliæ per se, et aliæ per accidens, non autem in causa universalissima excedente necessarias et contingentes per se et per accidens, quoniam ad eam spectat producere, ut effectus electos, non solum res, sed omnes rerum et eventuum modos);—ita elevando altius mentis oculos, ipse Deus, ex sua altiori, quam cogitare possimus, excellentia, *sic rebus eventibusque provideat, ut esse provi-*

sum ab eo sequatur aliquid altius quam evitabilitas vel inevitabilitas, ut sic ex passiva provisione eventus, neutrius combinationis alterum membrum oporteat sequi.

"Et si sic est, *quiescet intellectus, non evidentia veritatis inspectæ, sed altitudine inaccessibili veritatis occultæ.* Et hoc ingeniolo meo satis rationabile videtur;—tum propter rationem prædictam; tum quoniam, ut ait Gregorius, *minus de Deo sentit qui hoc tantum de illo credit, quod suo ingenio metiri potest.* Nec propterea negando aliquid eorum, quæ ad divinam immutabilitatem, actualitatem, certitudinem, atque universalitatem, et similia, spectare scimus, aut ex fide tenemus, suspicor: *sed aliquod occultum latere, vel ex parte ordinis qui est inter Deum et eventum provisum; vel ex glutino inter ipsum eventum et esse provisum, arbitror; et sic intellectum animæ nostræ oculum noctuæ esse considerans,** *in ignorantia sola quietem illius invenio. Melius est enim, tam fidei catholicæ quam philosophiæ, fateri cæcitatem nostram, quam asserere tanquam evidentia, quæ intellectum non quietant; evidentia namque quietativa est.* Nec propterea omnes Doctores præsumptionis accuso, quoniam balbutiendo, ut potuerunt, immobilitatem ac efficaciam summam et æternam divini intellectus, voluntatis, potestatisque insinuare intenderunt omnes, per infallibilitatem ordinis divinæ electionis ad eventus omnes; quorum nihil præfatæ suspicioni obstat, quæ altius quid in eis latere credit. Et vere, si sic prædicaretur, nullus forte circa prædestinationem erraret Christianus, sicut non errat in materia Trinitatis;* quia dicitur et scribitur et ita est, quod occulta est humano intellectui, et sola fides sufficit. Optimum autem atque salubre consilium est in hac re *inchoare ab his, quæ certo scimus et experimur in nobis*—scilicet quod *omnia quæ sub libero arbitrio nostro continentur, evitabilia a nobis sunt, et propterea digni sumus pœna vel præmio.* Quomodo autem, hoc salvo, divina salvetur providentia ac prædestinatio, &c., credere quod sancta mater Ecclesia credit. Scriptum est enim—'*Altiora te ne quæsieris;*' plurima enim sunt tibi supra sensus hominum revelata. Et hoc est unum de illis."

* He refers to Aristotle. [Metaph. A minor, c. 1.] *Note in Discussions*, p. 637.

* This was written before 1507; consequently long before Servetus and Campanus had introduced their unitarian heresies. *Note in Discussions*, p. 628.

NOTE U*.

ON SCIENTIA MEDIA.

[Reference omitted, and to be supplied from A. P. 632 b.]

There is a good account of *Scientia Media* in Fonseca, Comm. in Arist. Metaph., vol. iii. pp. 119, 120. The doctrine was invented by Fonseca, adopted and developed by Molina, Suarez, Vasques, Mendoza, and others. Fonseca does not make the *scientia visionis* and *simplicis intelligentiæ* equivalent to *scientia libera* and *naturalis*, but makes *scientia media* between the two latter, not as given above [p. 632 b, n. *] after Leibnitz.

[The title of this Note is given in the Author's list; but no portion of its contents has been found, except a memorandum, the substance of which is given above. The Note appears to have been intended as a supplement to p. 632 b, n. *, to explain an apparent discrepancy between the account there given, after Leibnitz (Théodicée, Partie i. § 39-42), and that of Fonseca, as regards the origin of the name *scientia media*. Fonseca distinguishes between *scientia naturalis*, or that knowledge which God cannot but have; as of things possible and their possible relations to each other; and *scientia libera*, or that knowledge which God may or may not have, according to his own will; as of things actually existing or destined to exist, which are actual, and therefore known as actual, only in consequence of God's will to bring them into existence. Between these two, there is a knowledge called by Fonseca *scientia conditionata* or *mixta*, and by others *scientia media*, which in one point of view may be regarded as natural, in another as free. This is the knowledge of the future actions of voluntary agents; which is free, inasmuch as it is in the power of the agents to act otherwise, and therefore the actions as foreknown might have been different; but natural, inasmuch as God knows how they will act. This is divided into *scientia conditionata futurorum*, or the knowledge of free acts which will hereafter come to pass, and *scientia pure conditionata*, or the knowledge of acts which would have come to pass under certain conditions never actually realised. As an instance of the latter, Fonseca cites the case of Tyre and Sidon, which would have repented had the works been done in them which were done in Chorazin and Bethsaida. A similar account is given by Molina, Concordia, Disp. lii.; In I. Partem D. Thomæ, Disp. xvii.

This account slightly differs from that given by Leibnitz, inasmuch as Fonseca does not identify the *scientia naturalis* and *libera* with the *scientia simplicis intelligentiæ* and *visionis* respectively. This identification is made, however, by some other exponents of the doctrine, with whom Leibnitz's account agrees. See e.g. Suarez, Opusc. de Scientia Dei futur. conting., Lib. ii. c. 3; Vasquez, In primam Partem S. Thomæ, Disp. lxvii.; Mendoza, Disputationes Philosophicæ, De Anima Disp. ix. Sect. vi. subs. 5; Ruiz, Commentarii ac Disputationes, pp. 799, 802.—ED.]

NOTE V.

ARISTOTLE'S MERITS AS A LOGICIAN: HIS OWN AND KANT'S TESTIMONY.

[Reference.—From P. 708 b.]

ARISTOTLE.—Soph. Elench. c. 34.

'It is thus manifest that we have brought to a satisfactory conclusion what we originally proposed; but the circumstances, under which this doctrine has been evolved, ought not to be passed over in silence.

'Of things invented or discovered,*

* We distinguish in modern English between invention and discovery, which few other languages do; but we want a generic word to express both at once. It is, therefore, necessary so to translate.

all of them [are found in one or other of two stages of progress; for they are] either such, as, received from foreign hands, and in a state of previous cultivation, have obtained a more articulate development from those to whom they have been latterly transmitted; or they are such as are still in the hands of their original authors, and, as is then usually the case, only on the first step of their advancement,—a step, however, of far greater importance than all the progress they can ever accomplish by the aid of any subsequent promoter. For the principle—the commencement—(according to the proverb) is in everything more than half the whole.* But, for that reason, it is also in everything the point of difficulty. For whilst a principle, as in effect the mightiest, is in magnitude the least, nothing is found more difficult than its detection. But this once discovered, all else it is comparatively easy to add and amplify.

'This is what took place in the art of Rhetoric; but nearly the same might be affirmed of every other. Those who first discovered the principles of that art, brought it out but a little way in its development; but by those who are now celebrated as its cultivators, it was only amplified to what it is, as an inheritance gradually accumulated from the acquisitions of a long series of predecessors. Thus Tisias after the founders, Thrasymachus after Tisias, Theodorus after Thrasymachus, and many others, made many partial contributions; so that we need not marvel if the art of Rhetoric be now, in certain respects, not only full, but overflowing.

'But of the doctrine on which we are engaged,† it cannot be said, that, prior to us, one part had been elaborated and another not. There was, in fact, nothing done whatever. For those who made a mercenary profession of teaching the art of disputation, followed a mode of instruction similar to that of Gorgias. For, as he (lege ὁ μὲν) gave ready-made rhetorical, so they gave ready-made questionary, discussions, to be learned off by their disciples, which, as in both cases was intended, should comprise the more usual topics in which an argument on either side could be maintained. With them, indeed, the pupil learned rapidly,—but without principle or method; for the scope of their instruction was to communicate to him, not the art, but certain products of the art. It was as if a man, professing that he would expound the science of protecting the feet, should then, in place of teaching the craft of shoemaking and its subsidiaries, hand you an assortment of every variety of shoe. This, it is true, might satisfy your present need, but not furnish you with the art of always doing so.

'But while on Rhetoric there has been much written, and from an early period, on Syllogism—on the art of Reasoning,* there is absolutely nothing extant previous to our own researches; and these have cost us not a little time and trouble. If, therefore, it may appear to you, upon examination, that this system, in which, from the foundation, everything had to be supplied, may yet worthily stand a comparison with those others which have been built up by the labours of successive generations; it remains for you to accord your indulgence to what in it may be found wanting, and your very grateful acknowledgment for the discoveries which it contains.'

KANT.—Kritik der reinen Vernunft, Vorrede zur zweyten Auflage, p. viii.

'That Logic has, from the earliest times, proceeded in this secure course—that it has never been compelled to fall back in search of another path,—is manifest from this: since left by Aristotle it has not needed to retrace a single step, unless we choose to reckon as improvements—what, however, pertain more to the elegance of the science than to its certainty—the omission of some unessential subtleties, and a more perspicuous exposition of the doctrines. But, moreover, it is remarkable in regard to Logic, that, to the present hour, it has been unable to advance a single step, and thus presents itself, to all appearance, as concluded and complete.'

[The following translations of other testimonies to the same effect have been found among the Author's papers.—ED.]

1.—DEGERANDO.—Des Signes, &c., t. iv. p. 28. 'The philosopher who reflects attentively on the rules of the ancient Logic, is astonished to see how far its authors have carried the analysis of reasoning. With the most severe impartiality, he cannot but confess, that each

---

* See Arist. De Cœlo, L. i. c. 6; Eth. Nic. L. i. c. 6; Probl. x. 15. Cf. Erasmi Adagia, pp. 10, 200, ed. 1670; Magirus, (Polymnemon), v. Principium.

† Alexander leaves it doubtful whether Dialectic or Logic.

* See above, p. 706 b, note 1.

of these rules is of a rigorous exactitude, and that, as a whole, they are so complete that not one of the possible forms of reasoning has escaped them. Aristotle, undoubtedly, was often destitute of the aid which experience supplies,—this was the misfortune of the age in which he saw the light; but he was, perhaps, the profoundest of thinkers, a genius the most eminently didactic, which has arisen on the horizon of philosophy. I question if there have ever subsequently been announced theories so beautiful as those which he has left us for a model. He combined views the most extensive with an eye for details the most acute. He created the art of classification, and then carried it almost to perfection. He executed a work, of all, perhaps, the most astonishing for those who know the march of our intellect; he conceived the method of science, when as yet the sciences did not exist; he pointed out with certainty the way which led to truth as yet unknown; he seemed to reason with prescience of all the future progress of the human mind.'

2.—Pelisson.—a.—Letter to Madame de Brinon, 1690. (Leibnitii Opera, ed. Dutens, t. i. p. 699.) 'He (Leibnitz) very well observes, that the Scholastic philosophy is the product engendered of the Dialectic or Logic of Aristotle, applied to religion; Dialectic or Logic, which, for my own part, I regard as one of the most beautiful discoveries of the human intellect. For who but must marvel, that a single man has, by his own contemplation, been able to reduce and comprehend within certain classes, and under certain forms, the infinite modes in which men reason, and to give us, so to speak, the external marks which may enable us to distinguish the true reason from the false.'

b.—Letter to Leibnitz, 1691. (Leibnitii Opera, ed. Dutens, t. i. p. 726.) 'I was brought up in the philosophy of Aristotle, and with a great veneration for him; but this veneration was greatly increased when, having returned to my Greek in those years of solitude'—(he had just spoken of 'four years and four months of the Bastille, and of leisure perforce'),—'I read him in himself, and found him of an infinite elegance, and beyond comparison clearer than all his commentators. I am aware of no genius more extended or more elevated than his.'

3.—Bilfinger.—a.—De Reductione Philosophiæ ad usus publicos, 1725, Varia, Fasc. ii. p. 62-63. 'To Aristotle we owe the noble design of collecting into the form of a discipline whatever conduces to the exercise of the art of demonstration, and to a security against the arts of deception. And he so accomplished his purpose, that, to the present day, few and small have been the additions made by others; additions made, too, only by following his guidance and method.'

b.—De præcipuis quibusdam Discendi Regulis ex comparatione Corporis et Animi erutis, 1726, Varia, Fasc. ii. p. 247. 'I avail myself of this occasion to state my opinion of the *Organon*, since this has experienced at different times so different a destiny; for what is now neglected, and even despised, had formerly, in all the Universities, a peculiar professor set apart for its interpretation. I do not say this that he may be again recalled into the chair, since the form of the sciences, and of scientific disputations, is at present so different from what it was of old. But this I say confidently, and with a full knowledge of the cause:—That the Organon of Aristotle is a book the first of its class, in order as in excellence, (see Sophist. Elench. c. 34), that it is complete, and demonstrated, and useful, and of consummate execution. If there be any of my readers skilled in the art of invention, let them examine the books of the First and Second Analytics, of the Topics, and of the Sophistics, according to the precepts of that art, and they will admire of it a specimen to which nothing similar is to be found out of Mathematics, nor even within them, if we regard the difficulties which it behoved to conquer in the accomplishment. If any one undervalue this labour of Aristotle, let him go and discover for himself even one of these forms of reasoning. I shall laud the man, if he produce a better; laud him, even if he produce an argument as good. And yet the first inventors are very different from those who follow,' &c.

c.—Præcepta Logica, 1739, p. 2. 'Aristotle has reduced Logic into the form of an art. By him the matter was handled to perfection. The moderns who despise, do not understand him.'

NOTE W.

THE SCIENCES OF OBSERVATION TO BE STUDIED BEFORE THOSE OF REFLECTION.

[Reference—From p. 711 a b. Compare p. 420 a.]

[The following references have been found among the Author's papers. Other testimonies would probably have been added, had the Note been completed.—Ed.]

1.—Plato, in Sauteri Institutiones Logicæ, § 8. [' *Quam maxime*, inquit Plato de Repub. vii.,* *præcipiendum est, ut, qui pulcherrimam hanc habitant civitatem, nullo modo geometriam spernant. Scimus enim, ad disciplinas omnes facilius perdiscendas interesse omnino, attigeritne geometriam aliquis, an non.*'—Ejusdem Platonis ap. Theon. Smyrn. Cap. i. hæc est sententia: *Adolescentibus eorumque ætati conveniunt disciplinæ mathematicæ, quæ animam præparant et defæcant, ut ipsa ad philosophiam capessendam idonea reddatur.* De arctissimo matheseos cum philosophia nexu adeo persuasum erat Platoni, ut neminem geometriæ ignarum in scholas suas recipiendum putavit. Academiæ, ab ipso institutæ, foribus inscriptum legebatur: *Nemo geometriæ expers accedito.*'†]

2.—Aristotle.—a.—Eth. Nic., L. i. c. [3]:—[*Διὸ τῆς πολιτικῆς οὐκ ἔστιν οἰκεῖος ἀκροατὴς ὁ νέος· ἄπειρος γὰρ τῶν κατὰ τὸν βίον πράξεων· οἱ λόγοι δὲ ἐκ τούτων καὶ περὶ τούτων.*]

b.—Ibid., L. vi. c. 8:—[*Σημεῖον δ' ἐστὶ τοῦ εἰρημένου καὶ διότι γεωμετρικοὶ μὲν νέοι καὶ μαθηματικοὶ γίνονται καὶ σοφοὶ τὰ τοιαῦτα· φρόνιμος δ' οὐ δοκεῖ γίνεσθαι. Αἴτιον δ', ὅτι τῶν καθ' ἕκαστά ἐστιν ἡ φρόνησις, ἃ γίνεται γνώριμα ἐξ ἐμπειρίας, νέος δ' ἔμπειρος οὐκ ἔστι· πλῆθος γὰρ χρόνου ποιεῖ τὴν ἐμπειρίαν· ἐπεὶ καὶ τοῦτ' ἄν τις σκέψαιτο, διὰ τί μαθηματικὸς μὲν παῖς γένοιτ' ἄν, σοφὸς δὲ ἢ φυσικὸς οὔ.*]

3.—Milton.—[Of Education], Prose Works (ed. 1835), p. 99.—' And for the usual method of teaching arts, I deem it to be an old errour of universities, not yet well recovered from the scholastic grossness of barbarous ages, that instead of beginning with arts most easy, (and these be such as are most obvious to the sense,) they present their young unmatriculated novices at first coming with the most intellective abstractions of Logic and Metaphysics; so that they having but newly left those grammatic flats and shallows where they stuck unreasonably to learn a few words with lamentable construction, and now on the sudden transported under another climate, to be tossed and turmoiled with their unballasted wits in fathomless and unquiet deeps of controversy, do for the most part grow into hatred and contempt of learning, mocked and deluded all this while with ragged notions and babblements, while they expected worthy and delightful knowledge, &c.']

4.—Leibnitz.—[Schreiben an Wagner], Opera Philosophica (ed. Erdmann), pp. 423 b, 426 a.—[' Ich bin selbst der Meinung, man thaete wohl, dass man die Mathematik, Historie, und anderes vor der ausfuehrlichen Logik lernte; denn wie

* P. 527, Steph.—Ed.

† See *Discussions*, p. 278.—Ed.

will der die Gedanken wohl ordnen, der noch wenig bedacht. . . . .

'Schliesslich bin ich mit meinem gelehrten Herrn einig, dass man ohne allzuviel Wesen von der Logik und der gleichen zu machen, die Jugend sofort auf die thaetlichen Wissenschaften fuehren solle, &c.']

5.—VICO.—Opere Complete, I. p. xxx. —'Hence we may readily understand with how much injury to the cultivation of youth two pernicious practices, in the method of study, must be attended, which some now adopt.—The first is, that to boys, who have scarcely left the school of Grammar, is presented the philosophy of Logic, which, as described by Arnauld, is the depository of the most rigorous judgments, exercised upon materials accumulated by the higher sciences, and altogether removed from the common apprehension of mankind. The effect of this is to stunt and dislocate those faculties in the youthful mind which ought to be regulated and developed each by its appropriate discipline; as the memory by the study of languages; the imagination by the perusal of poets, historians, and orators; the ingenuity by linear Geometry, which in a certain sense is a painting, that invigorates the memory by the great number of its elements—refines the imagination by its delicate figures, like so many designs, defined by the subtlest lines—exercises the ingenuity in the necessity of running rapidly through all, and among all, of selecting what is needed to demonstrate the magnitude required: and all this to produce a harvest, when the time of mature judgment arrives, of a wisdom eloquent, vivid, and acute. But by such logics young men are prematurely hurried on to *critical* philosophy, in other words, made to judge before they are made to apprehend; thus reversing the natural development of thought which first apprehends, then judges, and lastly, reasons. By such a method youth becomes arid and blighted in its evolution; and taught without preliminary knowledge to decide on everything. . . . .

'The other practice is, that of giving to young men the elements of the science of magnitude on the Algebraic method.'*

* For a continuation of this extract, see *Discussions*, p. 318.—ED.

NOTE X.

ON THE DIFFERENCE

BETWEEN

CONCEPTIONS (BEGRIFFE) AND INTUITIONS (ANSCHAUUNGEN).

[References omitted, and to be supplied from I. P. 291 a, 360 a, 305 b, 407 b, 412 b.]

[The title of this Note is given in the Author's MS., with a reference to Bolzano, Wissenschaftslehre, i. p. 344. A translation of this passage is appended.—ED.]

BOLZANO, Wissenschaftslehre, Sulzbach, 1837, § 77, vol. i. p. 343-4.

["Kant is acknowledged to have the merit of having brought the distinction between Intuitions and Conceptions into general recognition. Others indeed, long before him, had observed that some of our representations have only an individual object, others a plurality of objects. Thus Aristotle remarks, (Analyt. Post. i. 31):—*Αἰσθάνεσθαι μὲν γὰρ ἀνάγκη καθ᾽ ἕκαστον· ἡ δὲ ἐπιστήμη τῷ τὸ καθόλου γνωρίζειν ἐστίν . . . . τὸ ὁρᾶν μὲν χωρὶς ἐφ᾽ ἑκάστης, νοῆσαι δὲ ἅμα ὅτι ἐπὶ πάντων οὕτως.* And in Wolf's Logic, (§ 43,) it is said:—'Quidquid sensu percipimus, sive externo, sive interno, aut imaginamur; id singulare quid est, soletque *Individuum* appellari;' and in [Psychologia Empirica] § 49: 'Repræsentatio rerum in universali, seu generum et specierum, *Notio* a nobis appellabitur.' But the clearest distinction is expressed in the words of Baumgarten (Acroas. Log. § 51):—'Objectum conceptus vel est ens singulare seu individuum, vel universale, h. e. pluribus commune. Conceptus singularis seu individui *idea*, (as we now say, *intuition*), conceptus communis, seu ejusdem in pluribus, est *notio* (*conception*).'—Such remarks and divisions might, indeed, have led to the proper distinction, which obtains between Intuitions and Conceptions, as explained above; but as we do not find them further followed up, we cannot say that any one before Kant had a clear apprehension of this distinction; still less, that any made use of it. With regard to the above definitions; in the first place, the expression *individuum* is liable to be misunderstood; for, unless it be more exactly defined, it might be interpreted to mean that the object of an intuition must be simple, which is by no means the case. In the second place, without the addition that the Intuition must be a simple representation, the definition is too wide, inasmuch as there are some complex representations which in like manner represent only a single, (nay, only a simple) real object, and yet are not Intuitions.

"Kant's own statement of the distinction is given in two forms. 1. In his Logik, § 1, he says,—'All Representations relative to an object are either Intuitions or Conceptions. The Intuition is an individual representation (repræsentatio singularis); the Conception is an universal or reflected representation (repræsentatio per notas communes, repræsentatio discursiva). The Conception is opposed to the Intuition, for it is an universal representation, or a representation of that which is common to a plurality of objects; therefore a representation in so far as it can be contained in several things.' 2. In his Kritik der reinen Vernunft, § 11 [p. 377, ed. 1799], we find Intuition defined as a representation 'which is related *immediately* to an object;' whereas Conceptions are related to objects only 'mediately'—that is to say, by means of the Intuitions."

Both Kant's definitions are criticised at considerable length by Bolzano in the continuation of the above passage. The criticisms have not been transcribed, as the purpose of the reference in Sir W. Hamilton's MS. seems to have been historical rather than critical.

To the above anticipations of Kant's doctrine may be added that furnished by the scholastic distinction between *intuitive* and *abstractive cognition*, some account of which has been given by Sir W. Hamilton, above, p. 812, and also in *Discussions*, p. 54, and in *Lectures on Metaphysics*, vol. ii. p. 71. The definition of Durandus (In Prol. Sent. Qu. iii. § 7) nearly resembles one of those above quoted from Kant. "Vocant cognitionem intuitivam, illam quæ immediate tendit ad rem sibi præsentem objective, secundum ejus actualem existentiam: sicut cum video colorem existentem in pariete, vel rosam quam in manu teneo. Abstractivam autem vocant, omnem cognitionem quæ habetur de re non sic realiter præsente in ratione objecti immediate cogniti."—ED.]

NOTE Y.

ON EGOISM.

[Reference omitted, and to be supplied from I. P. 293 b; compare also 269 a.]

[From a reference in the Author's MS. it is probable that he intended in this Note to give some account of the oration of Pfaff, a copy of which he had procured after the printing of the foot-note to p. 293. Pfaff's work is a small pamphlet of 27 pages, entitled "Christoph. Matthæi Pfaffii, Theologi Primarii et Cancellarii Tubingensis Oratio de Egoismo, nova Philosophica Hæresi, Tubingæ d. IV. Nov. MDCCXXII. in Aulâ Novâ publicè recitata, Tubingæ, a. 1722." In the beginning the author speaks of Egoism as a new philosophical heresy, lately sprung up in France, England, and Ireland; and refers to Wolf's "Vernuenftige Gedanken von Gott, der Welt, und der Seele des Menschen," (c. 1, § 2; c. 6, § 944,) as containing mention of a sect of Egoists lately arisen in Paris, and a refutation of their opinions. The greater part of the pamphlet, however, is occupied with a criticism, or rather a denunciation, of Materialism and Idealism; and the only further historical evidence advanced to shew the existence of persons professing Egoism is the following quotation from the Memoires de Trevoux, 1713, p. 922,—"Un de nous connoit dans Paris un Malebranchiste, qui va plus loin que M. Berkeley; il lui a soutenu fort sérieusement, dans une longue dispute, qu'il est très probable qu'il soit le seul être créé qui existe, et que non seulement il n'y ait point de corps, mais qu'il n'y ait point d'autre esprit créé que lui."

Sir W. Hamilton's MS. contains also a reference to Fuelleborn's "Beytraege zur Geschichte der Philosophie," Part V. p. 143, where there is a short notice of a certain Brunet, the author of some philosophical writings, at the beginning of the eighteenth century, one of which was entitled "Projet d'une nouvelle Metaphysique." His philosophy is characterised by Fuelleborn as "der unverholenste und entschlossenste Egoismus der sich nur denken laesst."—Ed.]

END OF SUPPLEMENTARY DISSERTATIONS.

ADDENDA.

P. 12 b, l. 29, add (*), and subjoin the following footnote:—

* The Rhetorician Aquila Romanus. See Stewart's Essays, Prelim. Diss. ch. ii., Collected Works, vol. v. p. 46.—H.

P. 123 b, l. 7, n., insert:—

See, however, below, p. 842 b.

P. 682 b, l. 4, n., add:—

See Scaliger, "De Subtilitate," Exerc. 295. [Aristoteles, ἴσως ἄν, ἔοικεν, δοκεῖ, σκοπεῖν δεῖ, ὡς τύπῳ, ὡς ἐπὶ τὸ πλεῖστον, ὡς λόγῳ, ὡς εἰπεῖν, φαίνεται, et ejusmodi.]

P. 763 a, ult. n.:—

St Augustin's expression "miris modis secretum et publicum lumen" (De Lib. Arb. L. ii. c. 12), is well illustrated by Father André in the fifth discourse of his 'Traité de l'Homme,' Œuvres, Paris, 1766, tom. i. p. 189.

P. 765 b, l. 41, add:—

Under this head the term Axiom has been arbitrarily restricted by individual philosophers to some partial signification. Thus Kant employs it, to denote exclusively what he calls *constructive* (or mathematical) *principles*, those, to wit, which rest on *sensible intuitions* (Anschauungen) *a priori*, that is, the necessary imaginations of Space and Time, in contrast to what he calls *discursive* (or philosophical) *principles*, that is, such as are founded on *notions* or *concepts* (Begriffe) of the understanding. From the Axioms or proper mathematical principles he, however, excludes all those which are merely logical, analytic, or explicative, that is, merely special applications of the principle of contradiction; such are the first seven Common Notions or Axioms of Euclid, and the ninth. (Critik der reinen Vernunft, p. 143, ed. Rosenkranz.) This is more explicitly done by his friend Johann Schultz. On the other hand, Mr Stewart (who was unaware of the Kantian speculations on this subject) would bestow the term Axiom on those very judgments to which Kant refuses it, and would refuse to them the term principle. In either case, the limitation is arbitrary, and contrary to universal usage. [See Stewart's Elements, Part ii. ch. i., Collected Works, vol. iii. pp. 31, 32.]

P. 772 b, l. 57:—

Metaph. L. iv. (Γ.) c. 4,—quoted by Stewart, Elem. vol. ii., Coll. Works, vol. iii. p. 46, footnote. 'But there are some who, through ignorance, make an attempt to prove even this principle—[That it is impossible for the same thing to be and not to be.] For it is a mark of ignorance, not to be able to distinguish those things which ought to be demonstrated, from things of which no demonstration should be attempted. In truth, it is altogether impossible that everything should be susceptible of demonstration; otherwise the process would extend to infinity, and, after all our labour, nothing would be gained.'

P. 773 a, at beginning of l. 46 insert "Cudworth,"* and subjoin the following footnote:—

* For Cudworth see Stewart, Elements, vol. ii., Coll. Works, vol. iii. p. 18, footnote.

P. 776 b, l. 56, add:—

See No. 15, e.

P. 778 b, l. 13, add:—

See Letter (June 29, 1530) to Melanchthon, Luther's Briefe, ed. De Wette, iv. 53, Berlin, 1827, ['Finis et eventus causæ te discrucist, quia non potes eum deprehendere. At si eum comprehendere posses, nollem ego istius causæ me esse participem, multo minus autorem. Deus posuit eam in locum quendam communem, quem in rhetorica tua non habes, nec in philosophia tua; is vocatur fides, in quo loco omnia posita sunt οὐ βλεπόμενα καὶ μὴ φαινόμενα, quæ si quis conetur reddere visibilia, apparentia et comprehensibilia, sicuti facis tu, is referat curas et lachrymas pro mercede laboris.']

P. 778 b, after No. 25:—

25*. CALVIN.—Institutio Christianæ Religionis, L. ii. c. 2, § 12.—'Perpetuæ cæcitatis ita eum damnare, ut nihil intelligentiæ ullo in genere rerum reliquum facias, non modo verbo Dei, sed *sensus* etiam *communis* experimento repugnat.'

P. 779 a, after No. 29:—

29*.—OCHINUS.—[Labyrinthi, hoc est, De libero aut servo Arbitrio, de divina Prænotione, Destinatione, et Libertate Disputatio, c. i. p. 2.—'Dices nos esse liberos, neque necessario ea facere quæ facimus, idque adeo esse perspicuum atque manifestum, ut nihil clarius demonstrari queat. Quinimo primum esse moralis philosophiæ principium: adeo rem esse manifestam, eumque plane stupidum et omnis judicii expertem esse, qui negat liberum arbitrium hominis, cum res sit etiam *communi sensui* nota. Itaque tales homines non esse dignos cum quibus disputetur, quippe qui se rationes expertes esse ostendant; sed esse bestiarum more tractandos, utpote qui sint bestiæ, et fustibus usque adeo contundendos, ut confiteantur eos a quibus vapulent, libertatem habere desinendi verberare.']

P. 780 b, after No. 32:—

32*.—HOOKER.—Eccl. Pol. i. 8. 5.—'The main principles of Reason are in themselves apparent. For to make nothing evident of itself unto man's understanding were to take away all possibility of knowing anything. And herein that of Theophrastus is true, "They that seek a reason of all things do utterly overthrow Reason."'

P. 782 b.

[In reference to Descartes], see 'British Quarterly Review,' vol. v. p. 301; also, 'Edinburgh Review,' vol. xcv. pp. 33, 34, [reprinted in Henry Rogers's 'Essays,' vol. iii. pp. 49, 50.]

P. 783 b, after No. 45:—

45*.—JOSEPH GLANVILL.—Philosophia Pia, 1671, p. 160 sq.—'By the *Principles* of *Reason* we are not to understand the grounds of any man's Philosophy, nor the critical rules of Syllogism; but those *inbred fundamental notices*, that God hath implanted in our souls; such as arise not from external objects, nor particular humours or imaginations, but are immediately lodged in our minds, independent upon other principles or deductions, commanding a sudden assent, and acknowledged by all sober mankind. Of this sort are these: *That God is a being of all perfection; That nothing hath no attributes; That a thing cannot be and not be; That the whole is greater than any of its parts*; and such like others, which are unto us what *instincts* are to other creatures. These I call the *Principles* of *Reason*.'

P. 783 b, after No. 46:—

46*.—SIR MATTHEW HALE.—Primitive Origination of Mankind, 1677, p. 60.—'I come now to consider of those rational instincts, as I call them, the connate principles engraven in the human soul, which, though they are truths acquirable and deducible by rational consequence and argumentation, yet they seem to be inscribed in the very crasis and texture of the soul, antecedent to any acquisition by industry or the exercise of the discursive faculty in man; and therefore they may be well called anticipations, prenotions, or sentiments characterised and engraven in the soul, born with it, and growing up with it, till they receive a check by ill customs or educations, or an improvement and advancement by the due exercise of the faculties.'

P. 784 b, at end of No. 50:—

See Cousin, Des Pensées de Pascal, (Paris 1843,) Avant-propos, p. xxx. note.

P. 786 b, l. 19, add:—

See Cousin, Des Pensées de Pascal, Avant-propos, p. xxvi. note.

P. 789 b, add at the end of the second paragraph:—

In Dr Franklin's Autobiography (a. 1725) the author of this book, Lyons, is said to have been a surgeon; he was a friend of Mandeville, Pemberton, and even of Sir Isaac Newton. See p. 40, Bohn's edition.

P. 790 b, after No. 70:—

70*.—BAXTER.—Enquiry into the Nature of the Human Soul, &c., 2d ed., 1737, vol. i. sect. i. p. 7; et alibi. "*Common Sense*," word and thing.

P. 807 b, l. 47, n., to "Locke" add (*) and subjoin the following Note:—

* Locke, in fact, in The Epistle to the Reader, uses the word *objectively* in a sense exactly counter to the modern meaning, and as equivalent to *subjectively*.

P. 831 a, l. 29, to "it" add (†) and subjoin the following Note:—

† But Rovere, I find, only follows Galluppi.

P. 861 b, l. 50, n., add after reference to *St Gregory of Nyssa*:—

St Augustin, [De Trinitate, vi. 6. 'Ideo simplicior est corpore, quia non mole diffunditur per spatium loci, sed in unoquoque corpore, et in toto tota est, et in qualibet ejus parte tota est.']

P. 894 b, l. 24, n. add :—

But see Stewart's quotation from Brucker in the additions to Note S. of the first volume of his Elements (Collected Works, vol. ii. p. 499.) [' Intelligitur per *associationem idearum* non quævis naturalis et necessaria earundem conjunctio, sed quæ fortuita est, aut per consuetudinem vel affectum producitur, qua ideæ, quæ nullum naturalem inter se habent nexum, ita copulantur, ut recurrente una, tota earum caterva se conspiciendam intellectui præbeat.']

P. 896 a, at beginning of note *, insert the following :—

See Garnier, Traité des Facultés de l'Ame, t. ii. pp. 256, 264, 272.

P. 898 b, l. 6, add :—

But see Hobbes and others as quoted by Stewart, Elements, vol. i., note S.

P. 898 b, l. 35, add :—

Digby and White and Hobbes are all three, in fact, honourably mentioned by Berigard in the second edition of his Circulus Pisanus (1661), pp. 257, 617; and are evidently those, or among those, "viri nobiles Angli, eruditæ philosophiæ percupidi," at whose instances, copies of the first edition being exhausted, the second was published as is noticed in the Dedication. Hobbes is evidently an indebted student of Berigard; has borrowed from him, and without acknowledgment.

P. 898 b, l. 15, n., add the following paragraph :—

The law of Redintegration is clearly expressed by Telesius, De Rerum Natura, L. viii. c. 2. The full work appeared in 1586; the two first books in 1565. 'At et passionum quas patitur, motuumque quibus movetur, nequaquam simul ac pati moverique cessat statim eorum obliviscitur, nihilque eos recolere spiritus potest, sed in summe ipso sentiente summeque mobili (ubi præsertim valide a quibusdam commotus est, et sæpe, et diu) motuum passionumque quibus commotus, et quas passus est, habitus quidam, et quædam cognitio, quæ memoria dicitur, et ipsi pene remanent motus, quibus ubi vult moveri potest, et movetur omnino. Quæcunque igitur sensu percipimus, imaginari ea licet omnia, et navigationis memores, nausea afficimur, et horribile quid imaginantes, nihil interdum minus quam id conspicientes tremore corripimur. Qualis nimirum saltandi canendique et citharam pulsandi, artesque omnino quasvis addiscentibus nobis motuum, quibus in illis movemur, cognitio remanet, talis eorum itidem, quibus a sensibilibus agitamur. Neque enim vel substantia alia in illis, in his vero alia, vel alia movetur ratione, sed idem ubique spiritus, eodemque commovetur modo. Quin et (quod reminisci dicitur) rerum itidem, quarum cujuspiam modo partis, et perexigua interdum cognitio servata est, eas etiam imaginari, et veluti ante oculos ponere potest spiritus, quarum memoria nulla superesse videtur. Motum enim, cujus cognitio servata est, sæpius diligenterque recolens, ad reliquos, quibus cum illo moveri solebat, veluti exciitur et quasi manuducitur. Id vero et in externis, quos didicimus, evenire motibus passim intueri licet: quorum scilicet portionis quantulævis interdum cognitione remanente, ubi ea sæpe intenteque movetur, reliquarum itidem cognitio emergit, quæ scilicet non penitus evanuerat, sed veluti latebat.'

P. 898 b, l. 60, insert the following paragraph :—

Descartes, in a posthumous work, first published in 1662, (*Tractatus de Homine*, Art 73,) has also enounced the law of Redintegration, as observed in the notes to the new edition of Coleridge's Biographia Literaria, 1847, vol. i. p. 91. But that passage is more properly to be considered as only recognising the influence of Custom; and, at any rate, is after the others.

P. 899 a, l. 3, n., insert :—

See André, Traité de l'Homme, 9ème Discourse, t. i. pp. 360-378, ed. 1766.

P. 900 a, l. 36, n.,

See Garnier, Traité des Facultés de l'Ame, ii. p. 273. According to him, Hume's Causality is equivalent to Succession.

P. 909 b, l. 4, n., add :—

Reminiscence and Reasoning have this in common, that they educe one thing or notion out of another; simple apprehension and simple memory (Recollection) agree in being immediate cognitions.

POSTSCRIPT.

The peculiar state in which Sir William Hamilton's edition of Reid was originally published, and in which it has continued to the present time, would make it almost indispensable to attempt to supply a few pages in conclusion of the work; even apart from all consideration of the value of the papers now submitted to the public.

The work, as originally published, ended, as is well known, at p. 914, in the middle of Note D***. It is believed that the remainder of this Note was prepared for publication in a more perfect form than that in which it now appears; but the paper containing this revision cannot be recovered, and it has been found necessary to compile a conclusion to the Note from the fragments of an earlier and very rough copy. The remaining Notes appear in very different states of completeness. One or two of them seem to have been finished, or nearly so, in a form ready for publication. Others have been put together, either from fragments apparently intended for this purpose, or from earlier papers, written on the same subject, but not revised with a view to the present work; to which additions have been sometimes made from the Author's published writings. Others, again, do not appear to have been written at all; and the only materials available in connection with them consist of references to, or extracts from, other writers. A complete list of the titles of the intended Notes has been found among the Author's papers, and the reader is thus furnished with an outline of the entire work as designed.

In putting together the papers intrusted to him, the aim of the Editor has been to publish as much as possible of Sir William Hamilton's, and as little as possible of his own. It would no doubt have been practicable, by making further use of the Author's abundant materials, not indeed to complete the work as he designed it, but to produce a more finished result than he has actually accomplished. But the reason which partly influenced the editors of Pascal (whose practice, however, was by no means faithful to their profession), is decisive in determining the rule to be adopted in all similar cases—"Ce n'eût pas été donner son ouvrage, mais un ouvrage tout différent." A fragment, however imperfect, from the pen of a Pascal or a Hamilton, has a value which would not belong to a more finished production of doubtful authorship.

The few additions which the Editor has found it necessary to make are carefully distinguished from the original matter of the Author's own papers. Those which have been incorporated with the contents of the papers, whether to complete the sense or to supply references or quotations, are included within square brackets. Entire sentences added by the Editor are distinguished by the signature "Ed."*

In those Notes which are compiled from separate fragments, the Editor is responsible for the selection and arrangement. In this, as in the whole of his task, he has received most valuable advice and assistance from the Author's son, Hubert Hamilton, Esq., who has most zealously and efficiently taken part in the endeavour to complete this monument to the memory of his Father.

H. L. M.

Oxford, *August* 23, 1862.

* In reference to this signature, it is necessary to point out an ambiguity which was not discovered till it was too late to correct it. In the portion of the work published by Sir W. Hamilton, he is in the habit of distinguishing Reid as "the Author," and himself as "the Editor." In preparing the subsequent papers for publication, the usual distinction of Author and Editor was adopted, and the discrepancy was not noticed till after some sheets had been stereotyped. In this latter portion of the work, including the Memoranda for a Preface and the Supplementary Dissertations from p. 915, "the Author" is Sir W. Hamilton, and the signature "Ed." denotes the present Editor.

INDICES.

INDEX I.

TO THE

WORKS OF DR THOMAS REID.

[References to Sir W. Hamilton's Foot-Notes are distinguished by the initial H.—Ed.]

INDEX II.

TO THE

SUPPLEMENTARY DISSERTATIONS.

ERRATA.

Page 10 a, l. 17, *for* 1763, *read* 1763 [1764].
„ 11 a, l. 61, *for* 1781, *read* 1781 [1780].
„ 83 b, l. 35, *for* fifteen, *read* sixteen.
„ 803, among the authorities, Omphalius should be entered as *German*, not as *French*.
„ 861 b, l. 51, n, *for* L. ii. c., *read* L. i. c. 8.

www.ingramcontent.com/pod-product-compliance
Lightning Source LLC
Chambersburg PA
CBHW031947290426
44108CB00011B/713